Morality in Practice

EIGHTH EDITION

Edited by

JAMES P. STERBA
University of Notre Dame

PETER BORNSCHEIN
Bowling Green State University

WADSWORTH
CENGAGE Learning·

Australia • Brazil • Japan • Korea • Mexico • Singapore • Spain • United Kingdom • United States

WADSWORTH
CENGAGE Learning·

Morality in Practice, Eighth Edition

Edited by James P. Sterba and Peter Bornschein

Publisher: Clark Baxter

Senior Sponsoring Editor: Joann Kozyrev

Development Editor: Daisuke Yasutake

Assistant Editor: Joshua Duncan

Editorial Assistant: Marri Straton

Associate Media Editor: Kimberly Apfelbaum

Marketing Program Manager: Tami Strang

Art Director: Jennifer Wahi

Content Project Manager: Jessica Rasile

Manufacturing Planner: Mary Beth Hennebury

Rights Acquisition Specialist: Shalice Shah-Caldwell

Production Service/Compositor: PreMediaGlobal

Cover Designer: Kate Scheible

Cover Image: © John Foxx/Getty Images

© 2013, 2011 Wadsworth, Cengage Learning

For product information and technology assistance, contact us at **Cengage Learning Customer & Sales Support, 1-800-354-9706**

For permission to use material from this text or product, submit all requests online at **www.cengage.com/permissions**. Further permissions questions can be emailed to **permissionrequest@cengage.com**.

Library of Congress Control Number: 2003110375

ISBN-13: 978-1-133-04996-8

ISBN-10: 1-133-04996-6

Wadsworth
20 Channel Center Street
Boston, MA 02210
USA

Cengage Learning is a leading provider of customized learning solutions with office locations around the globe, including Singapore, the United Kingdom, Australia, Mexico, Brazil, and Japan. Locate your local office at **international.cengage.com/region**.

Cengage Learning products are represented in Canada by Nelson Education, Ltd.

For your course and learning solutions, visit **www.cengage.com**.

Purchase any of our products at your local college store or at our preferred online store **www.cengagebrain.com**.

Instructors: Please visit login.cengage.com and log in to access instructor-specific resources.

Printed in the United States of America
1 2 3 4 5 6 7 16 15 14 13 12

✴

To Sonya, now a professor herself with an anthology of her own.
——James P. Sterba

To Mom and Dad, thanks for all the help and support.
——Peter Bornschein

Contents

Preface

Moral problems courses tend to teach themselves. It takes a really bad teacher to mess them up. Teachers can mess up a moral problems course in at least three ways:

1. By presenting just one set of views on various topics. Students appreciate the need for fair play here.
2. By encouraging students to hold a crude relativism. Students know that all moral stances are not equally good.
3. By not being relevant to student concerns. Students can reasonably expect that at least an ethics course will be relevant to their lives.

This text enables teachers to avoid the first mistake by presenting radically opposed selections on all topics. It enables teachers to avoid the second mistake by suggesting, through the introductions and through the ordering and selection of topics, how some views turn out to be more defensible than others. It enables teachers to avoid the third mistake by being the only moral problems text to provide in-depth coverage of a broad range of new and standard moral problems. In fact, no other moral problems text combines such breadth and depth. In addition, it has to recommend it the following:

NEW FEATURES

1. Twenty-nine new readings
2. New sections on human enhancement and discrimination against men.
3. A totally revised section on affirmative action.
4. Significantly revised sections on the distribution of income and wealth, distant peoples and future generations, and pornography.

RETAINED FEATURES

1. A general introduction that provides a background discussion of traditional moral approaches to ethics as well as an accessible answer to the question, Why be moral?

2. Section introductions that help to set out the framework for the discussion and criticism of the articles in each section

3. Brief summaries at the beginning of each article that enable students to test and improve their comprehension

4. Concluding each section of the anthology with one or more articles that discuss specific practical applications

5. Suggestions for further reading at the end of each section

CENGAGECOMPOSE

CengageCompose lets you build your own text online to meet specific course learning objectives. Gather what you need from our vast library of market-leading course books and other enrichment content. Build your book the way you want it organized, personalized to your students. Publish the title using easy to use tools, including instant electronic review copies, which guarantee you will get what you have designed.

CengageCompose lets you:

- *Gather* your learning materials online from a vast library of
  - Chapters from leading Cengage Learning texts
  - Case Studies
  - Collections
  - Exercises
  - Lab Materials
  - And more!
- *Build* your text, by
  - Placing content in the order you prefer
  - Selecting and customizing a full-color, vivid cover
  - Keep active projects in your personal online library for future modifications and collaborative review with other educators
- *Publish* with just a few clicks
  - Review an electronic copy that is instantly available to ensure you have created exactly what you want
  - Input basic class information to get timing and pricing estimates
  - Do this all without needing the guidance of a sales representative or custom publisher

In putting together this eighth edition, we have benefited enormously from the advice and help of many different people. Very special thanks go to Clark Power of the University of Notre Dame, John Corvino of Wayne State University, Bill Lawson of the University of Memphis, Kit Wellman of Washington University in St. Louis, Phillip Cole of the University of Wales, Newport, Angelo Corlett of San Diego State University; and Janet Kourany of the University of Notre Dame. We would also like to thank the following reviewers whose suggestions were especially helpful: Alan C. Clune of Sam Houston State University, Janet S. Davis of Marist College, Henry Dmochowski of LaSalle University, Sandor Marai of Sinclair Community College, Robert Muhlnickel of Monroe Community College, Marjorie Nash of Alvin Community College, Loreen Ritter of Premier Education Group, Laurence Thomas of Syracuse University.

General Introduction

Most of us like to think of ourselves as just and moral people. To be truly such, however, we need to know something about the demands of justice and how they apply in our own particular circumstances. We should be able to assess, for example, whether our society's economic and legal systems are just—that is, whether the ways income and wealth are distributed in society as well as the methods of enforcing that distribution give people what they deserve. We should also consider whether other societal institutions, such as the military defense system, the education system, and the foreign aid program, are truly just. Without investigating these systems and coming to an informed opinion, we cannot say with any certainty that we are just and moral persons rather than perpetrators or beneficiaries of injustice.

This anthology has been created to help you acquire some of the knowledge you will need to justify your belief that you are a just and moral person. For this purpose, the anthology contains a wide spectrum of readings on thirteen important, contemporary, practical problems:

1. The problem of the distribution of income and wealth. (Who should control what resources within a society?)

2. The problem of distant peoples and future generations. (What obligations do we have to distant peoples and future generations?)

3. The problem of abortion and euthanasia. (Do fetuses have a right to life, and what should we do for the dying and those requiring life-sustaining medical treatment?)

4. The problem of human enhancement. (Is the use of modern scientific methods to enhance our capabilities morally justified?)

5. The problem of sex equality. (Should the sexes be treated equally, and what constitutes equal treatment?)

6. The problem of power, gender roles, and discrimination against men. (Is sexism and discrimination against men a significant moral problem?)

7. The problem of affirmative action. (What specific policies are required to remedy discrimination and prejudice or justified to achieve diversity?)

8. The problem of pornography. (Should pornography be prohibited because it promotes violence against women?)

9. The problem of sexual harassment. (What is sexual harassment and how can it be avoided?)

10. The problem of gay and lesbian rights. (What rights should gays and lesbians have?)

11. The problem of animal liberation and environmental justice. (What should our policies be for the treatment of animals and the environment?)

12. The problem of punishment and responsibility. (Who should be punished and of what should their punishment consist?)

13. The problem of war, torture, and international terrorism. (What are the moral limits of the international use of force against substantial aggression or acts of terrorism?)

Before you get into these problems, however, you should know what it means to take a moral approach to these issues and how such an approach is justified.

THE ESSENTIAL FEATURES
OF A MORAL APPROACH
TO PRACTICAL PROBLEMS

To begin with, a moral approach to practical problems must be distinguished from various nonmoral approaches. Nonmoral approaches to practical problems include the *legal approach* (what the law requires with respect to this practical problem), the *group* or *self-interest approach* (what the group interest or self-interest is for the parties affected by this problem), and the *scientific approach* (how this practical problem can best be accounted for or understood). To call these approaches nonmoral, of course, does not imply that they are immoral. All that is implied is that the requirements of these approaches may or may not accord with the requirements of morality.

What, then, essentially characterizes a moral approach to practical problems? I suggest that there are two essential features to such an approach:

1. The approach is prescriptive—that is, it issues in prescriptions, such as "do this" and "don't do that."

2. The approach's prescriptions are acceptable to everyone affected by them.

The first feature distinguishes a moral approach from a scientific approach because a scientific approach is not prescriptive. The second feature distinguishes a moral approach from both a legal approach and a group or self-interest approach because the prescriptions that accord best with the law or serve the interest of particular groups or individuals may not be acceptable to everyone affected by them.

Here the notion of *acceptable* means "ought to be accepted" or "is reasonable to accept" and not simply "is capable of being accepted." Understood in this way, certain prescriptions may be acceptable even though they are not actually accepted by everyone affected by them. For example, a particular welfare program may be acceptable even though many people oppose it because it involves an increased tax burden. Likewise, certain prescriptions may be unacceptable even though they have been accepted by everyone affected by them. For example, it may be that most women have been socialized to accept prescriptions requiring them to fill certain social roles even though these prescriptions are unacceptable because they impose second-class status on them.

ALTERNATIVE MORAL
APPROACHES TO PRACTICAL
PROBLEMS

Using the two essential features of a moral approach to practical problems, let us consider three principal alternative moral approaches to practical problems: a *utilitarian approach*, an *Aristotelian approach*, and a *Kantian approach*.[1] The basic principle of a utilitarian approach is:

Do those actions that maximize the net utility or satisfaction of everyone affected by them.

A utilitarian approach qualifies as a moral approach because it is prescriptive and because it can be argued that its prescriptions are acceptable to everyone affected by them since they take the utility or satisfaction of all those individuals equally into account.

To illustrate, let's consider how this approach applies to the question of whether nation A should intervene in the internal affairs of nation B when nation A's choice would have the following consequences:

	Nation A's Choice	
	Intervene	*Don't Intervene*
Net utility to A	4 trillion units	8½ trillion units
Net utility to B	2 trillion units	–2 trillion units
Total utility	6 trillion units	6½ trillion units

Given that these are all the consequences that are relevant to nation A's choice, a utilitarian approach favors not intervening. Note that in this case, the choice favoring a utilitarian approach does not conflict with the group interest of nation A, although it does conflict with the group interest of nation B.

But are such calculations of utility possible? Admittedly, they are difficult to make. At the same time, such calculations seem to serve as a basis for public discussion. Once President Reagan, addressing a group of black business leaders, asked whether blacks were better off because of the Great Society programs, and although many disagreed with the answer he gave, no one found his question unanswerable.[2] Thus, faced with the exigencies of measuring utility, a utilitarian approach simply counsels that we do our best to determine what maximizes net utility and act on the result.

The second approach to consider is an Aristotelian approach. Its basic principle is:

Do those actions that would further one's proper development as a human being.

This approach also qualifies as a moral approach because it is prescriptive and because it can be argued that its prescriptions are acceptable to everyone affected by them.

There are, however, different versions of this approach. According to some versions, each person can determine through the use of reason his or her proper development as a human being. Other versions disagree. For example, many religious traditions rely on revelation to guide people in their proper development as human beings. However, although an Aristotelian approach can take these various forms, I want to focus on what is probably its philosophically most interesting form. That form specifies proper development in terms of virtuous activity and understands virtuous activity to preclude intentionally doing evil that good may come of it. In this form, an Aristotelian approach conflicts most radically with a utilitarian approach, which requires intentionally doing evil whenever a *greater* good would come of it.

The third approach to be considered is a Kantian approach. This approach has its origins in seventeenth- and eighteenth-century social contract theories, which tended to rely on actual contracts to specify moral requirements. However, actual contracts may or may not have been made, and, even if they were made, they may or may not have been moral or fair. This led Immanuel Kant and contemporary Kantian John Rawls to resort to a hypothetical contract to ground moral requirements. A difficulty with this approach is in determining under what conditions a hypothetical contract is fair and moral. Currently, the most favored Kantian approach is specified by the following basic principle.

Do those actions that persons behind an imaginary veil of ignorance would unanimously agree should be done.[3]

This imaginary veil extends to most particular facts about oneself—anything that would bias one's choice or stand in the way of a unanimous agreement. Accordingly, the imaginary veil of ignorance would mask one's knowledge of one's social position, talents, sex, race, and religion, but not one's knowledge of such general information as would be contained in political, social, economic, and psychological theories. A Kantian approach qualifies as a moral approach because it is prescriptive and because it can be argued that its prescriptions would be acceptable to everyone affected by them since they would be agreed to by everyone affected behind an imaginary veil of ignorance.

To illustrate the approach, let's return to the example of nation A and nation B used earlier. The choice facing nation A was the following:

	Nation A's Choice	
	Intervene	Don't Intervene
Net utility to A	4 trillion units	8½ trillion units
Net utility to B	2 trillion units	-2 trillion units
Total utility	6 trillion units	6½ trillion units

Given that these are all the consequences relevant to nation A's choice, a Kantian approach favors intervention because persons behind the imaginary veil of ignorance would have to consider that they might turn out to be in nation B, and in that case, they would not want to be so disadvantaged for the greater benefit of those in nation A. This resolution conflicts with the resolution favored by a utilitarian approach and the group interest of nation A, but not with the group interest of nation B.

ASSESSING ALTERNATIVE MORAL APPROACHES

Needless to say, each moral approach has its strengths and weaknesses. The main strength of a utilitarian approach is that once the relevant utilities are determined, there is an effective decision-making procedure that can be used to resolve all practical problems. After determining the relevant utilities, all that remains is to total the net utilities and choose the alternative with the highest net utility. The basic weakness of this approach, however, is that it does not give sufficient weight to the distribution of utility among the relevant parties. For example, consider a society equally divided between the Privileged Rich and the Alienated Poor, who face the following alternatives:

	Nation A's Choice	
	Alternative A	Alternative B
Net utility to Privileged Rich	5½ trillion units	4 trillion units
Net utility to Alienated Poor	1 trillion units	2 trillion units
Total utility	6½ trillion units	6 trillion units

Given that these are all the relevant utilities, a utilitarian approach favors alternative A even though alternative B provides a higher minimum payoff. And suppose the utility values for two alternatives were:

	Nation A's Choice	
	Alternative A	Alternative B
Net utility to A Privileged Rich	4 trillion units	5 trillion units
Net utility to Alienated Poor	2 trillion units	1 trillion units
Total utility	6 trillion units	6 trillion units

A utilitarian approach would be indifferent between the alternatives, even though alternative A provides a higher minimum payoff. In this way, a utilitarian approach fails to take into account the distribution of utility among the relevant parties. All that matters for this approach is maximizing total utility, and the distribution of utility among the affected parties is taken into account only insofar as it contributes toward the attainment of that goal.

By contrast, the main strength of an Aristotelian approach in the form we are considering is that it limits the means that can be chosen in pursuit of good consequences. In particular, it absolutely prohibits intentionally doing evil that good may come of it. However, although some limit on the means available for the pursuit of good consequences seems desirable, the main weakness of this version of an Aristotelian approach is that the limit it imposes is too strong. Indeed, exceptions to this limit would seem to be justified whenever the evil to be done is:

1. Trivial (e.g., stepping on someone's foot to get out of a crowded subway).
2. Easily reparable (e.g., lying to a temporarily depressed friend to keep her from committing suicide).
3. Sufficiently outweighed by the consequences of the action (e.g., shooting one of 200 civilian hostages to prevent in the only way possible the execution of all 200).

Still another weakness of this approach is that it lacks an effective decision-making procedure for resolving practical problems. Beyond imposing limits on the means that can be employed in the pursuit of good consequences, the advocates of this approach have not agreed on criteria for selecting among the available alternatives.

The main strength of a Kantian approach is that like an Aristotelian approach it seeks to limit the means available for the pursuit of good consequences. However, unlike the version of the Aristotelian approach we considered, a Kantian approach does not impose an absolute limit on intentionally doing evil that good may come of it. Behind the veil of ignorance, persons would surely agree that if the evil were trivial, easily reparable, or sufficiently outweighed by the consequences, there would be an adequate justification for permitting it. On the other hand, the main weakness of a Kantian approach is that although it provides an effective decision-making procedure for resolving some practical problems, such as the problem of how to distribute income and wealth and the problem of near and distant peoples, a Kantian approach cannot be applied to all problems. For example, it will not work for the problems of animals' rights and abortion unless we assume that animals and fetuses should be behind the veil of ignorance.

So far, we have seen that prescriptivity and acceptability of prescriptions by everyone affected by them are the two essential features of a moral approach to practical problems, and we have considered three principal alternative approaches that qualify as moral approaches to these problems. Let's now examine what reasons there are for giving a moral approach to practical problems precedence over any nonmoral approach with which it conflicts.

THE JUSTIFICATION FOR FOLLOWING A MORAL APPROACH TO PRACTICAL PROBLEMS

To begin with, the ethical egoist, by denying the priority of morality over self-interest, presents the most serious challenge to a moral approach to practical problems. Basically, that challenge takes two forms: *individual ethical egoism* and *universal ethical egoism*. The basic principle of individual ethical egoism is:

> Everyone ought to do what is in the overall self-interest of just one particular individual.

The basic principle of universal ethical egoism is:

> Everyone ought to do what is in his or her overall self-interest.

Obviously, the prescriptions deriving from these two forms of egoism would conflict significantly with prescriptions following from a moral approach to practical problems. How then can we show that a moral approach is preferable to an egoist's approach?

In individual ethical egoism, all prescriptions are based on the overall interests of just one particular individual. Let's call that individual Gladys. Because in individual ethical egoism Gladys's interests constitute the sole basis for determining prescriptions, there should be no problem of inconsistent prescriptions, assuming, of course, that Gladys's own particular interests are in harmony. The crucial problem for individual ethical egoism, however, is justifying that only Gladys's interests count in determining prescriptions. Individual ethical egoism must provide at least some reason for accepting that view. Otherwise, it would be irrational to accept the theory. But what reason or reasons could serve this function? Clearly, it will not do to cite as a reason some characteristic Gladys shares with other persons because whatever justification such a characteristic would provide for favoring Gladys's interests, it would also provide for favoring the interests of those other persons. Nor will it do to cite as a reason some unique characteristic of Gladys, such as knowing all of Shakespeare's writings by heart, because such a characteristic involves a comparative element, and consequently others with similar characteristics, like knowing some or most of Shakespeare's corpus by heart, would still have some justification, although a proportionally lesser justification, for having their interests favored. But again the proposed characteristic would not justify favoring only Gladys's interests.

A similar objection could be raised if a unique relational characteristic were proposed as a reason for Gladys's special status—such as that Gladys is Seymour's wife. Because other persons would have similar but not identical relational characteristics, similar but not identical reasons would hold for them. Nor will it do to argue that the reason for Gladys's special status is not the particular unique traits that she possesses, but rather the mere fact that she has unique traits. The same would hold true of everyone else. Every individual has unique traits. If recourse to unique traits is dropped and Gladys claims that she is special simply because she is herself and wants to further her own interests, every other person could claim the same.[4]

For the individual ethical egoist to argue that the same or similar reasons do *not* hold for other people with the same or similar characteristics to those of Gladys, she must explain *why* they do not hold. It must always be possible to understand how a characteristic serves as a reason in one case but not in another. If no explanation can be provided, and in the case of individual ethical egoism none has been forthcoming, the proposed characteristic either serves as a reason in both cases or does not serve as a reason at all.

UNIVERSAL ETHICAL EGOISM

Unfortunately, these objections to individual ethical egoism do not work against universal ethical egoism because universal ethical egoism does provide a reason why the egoist should be concerned simply about maximizing his or her own interests, which is simply that the egoist is herself and wants to further her own interests. The individual ethical egoist could not recognize such a reason without giving up her view, but the universal ethical egoist is willing and able to universalize her claim and recognize that everyone has a similar justification for adopting universal ethical egoism.

Accordingly, the objections that typically have been raised against universal ethical egoism are designed to show that the view is fundamentally inconsistent. For the purpose of evaluating these objections, let's consider the case of Gary Gyges, an otherwise normal human being who, for reasons of personal gain, has embezzled $300,000 while working at People's National Bank and is in the process of escaping to a South Sea island where he will have the good fortune to live a pleasant life protected by the local authorities and untroubled by any qualms of conscience. Suppose that Hedda Hawkeye, a fellow employee, knows that Gyges has been embezzling money from the bank and is about to escape. Suppose, further, that it is in Hawkeye's overall self-interest to prevent Gyges from escaping with the embezzled money because she will be generously rewarded for doing so by being appointed vice president of the bank. Given that it is in Gyges's overall self-interest to escape with the embezzled money, it now appears that we can derive a contradiction from the following:

1. Gyges ought to escape with the embezzled money.

2. Hawkeye ought to prevent Gyges from escaping with the embezzled money.

3. By preventing Gyges from escaping with the embezzled money, Hawkeye is preventing Gyges from doing what he ought to do.

4. One ought never to prevent someone from doing what he or she ought to do.

5. Thus, Hawkeye ought not to prevent Gyges from escaping with the embezzled money.

Because premise 2 and conclusion 5 are contradictory, universal ethical egoism appears to be inconsistent.

The soundness of this argument depends, however, on premise 4, and defenders of universal ethical egoism believe there are grounds for rejecting this premise. For if "preventing an action" means "rendering the action impossible," it would appear that there *are* cases in which a person is justified in preventing someone else from doing what he or she ought to do. Consider, for example, the following case. Suppose Irma and Igor are both actively competing for the same position at a prestigious law firm. If Irma accepts the position, she obviously renders it impossible for Igor to obtain the position. But surely this is *not* what we normally think of as an unacceptable form of prevention. Nor would Hawkeye's prevention of Gyges's escape appear to be unacceptable. Thus, to sustain the argument against universal ethical egoism, one must distinguish between acceptable and unacceptable forms of prevention and then show that the argument succeeds even for forms of prevention that a universal ethical egoist would regard as unacceptable. This requires elucidating the force of "ought" in universal ethical egoism.

To illustrate the sense in which a universal ethical egoist claims that other persons ought to do what is in their overall self-interest, defenders often appeal to an analogy of competitive games. For example, in football a defensive player might think that the opposing team's quarterback ought to pass on third down with five yards to go, while not wanting the quarterback to do so and planning to prevent any such attempt. Or to use Jesse Kalin's example:

I may see how my chess opponent can put my king in check. This is how he ought to move. But believing that he ought to move his bishop and check my king does

not commit me to wanting him to do that, nor to persuading him to do so. What I ought to do is sit there quietly, hoping he does not move as he ought.[5]

The point of these examples is to suggest that a universal ethical egoist may, like a player in a game, judge that others ought to do what is in their overall self-interest while simultaneously attempting to prevent such actions or at least refraining from encouraging them.

The analogy of competitive games also illustrates the sense in which a universal ethical egoist claims that she herself ought to do what is in her overall self-interest. For just as a player's judgment that she ought to make a particular move is followed, other things being equal, by an attempt to perform the appropriate action, so likewise when a universal ethical egoist judges that she ought to do some particular action, other things being equal, an attempt to perform the appropriate action follows. In general, defenders of universal ethical egoism stress that because we have little difficulty understanding the implications of the use of "ought" in competitive games, we should also have little difficulty understanding the analogous use "ought" by the universal ethical egoist.

To claim, however, that the "oughts" in competitive games are analogous to the "oughts" of universal ethical egoism does not mean there are no differences between them. Most important, competitive games are governed by moral constraints such that when everyone plays the game properly, there are acceptable moral limits as to what one can do. For example, in football one cannot poison the opposing quarterback in order to win the game. By contrast, when everyone holds self-interested reasons to be supreme, the only limit to what one can do is the point beyond which one ceases to benefit. But this important difference between the "oughts" of universal ethical egoism and the "oughts" found in publicly recognized activities like competitive games does not defeat the appropriateness of the analogy. That the "oughts" found in publicly recognized activities are always limited by various moral constraints (what else would get publicly recognized?) does not preclude their being a suggestive model for the unlimited action-guiding character of the "oughts" of universal ethical egoism.[6]

FROM RATIONALITY
TO MORALITY

Although the most promising attempts to show that universal ethical egoism is inconsistent have failed, the challenge the view presents to a moral approach to practical problems can still be turned aside. It can be shown that, although consistent, the egoist acts contrary to reason in rejecting a moral approach to practical problems.

To show this, let us begin by imagining that we are members of a society deliberating over what sort of principles governing action we should accept. Let us assume that each of us is capable of entertaining and acting on both self-interested and moral reasons and that the question we are seeking to answer is what sort of principles governing action it would be rational for us to accept.[7] This question is not about what sort of principles we should publicly affirm since people will sometimes publicly affirm principles that are quite different from those they are prepared to act on, but rather it is a question of what principles it would be rational for us to accept at the deepest level—in our hearts of hearts.

Of course, there are people who are incapable of acting on moral reasons. For such people, there is no question about their being required to act morally or altruistically. But the interesting philosophical question is not about such people, but about people, like ourselves, who are capable of acting self-interestedly or morally and are seeking a rational justification for following one course of action over the others.

In trying to determine how we should act, let us assume that we would like to be able to construct a *good* argument favoring morality over egoism, and given that good arguments are non–question-begging, we accordingly would like

to construct an argument that does not beg the question as far as possible. The question at issue here is what reasons each of us should take as supreme, and this question would be begged against egoism if we propose to answer it simply by assuming from the start that moral reasons are the reasons that each of us should take as supreme. But the question would be begged against morality as well if we proposed to answer the question simply by assuming from the start that self-interested reasons are the reasons that each of us should take as supreme. This means, of course, that we cannot answer the question of what reasons we should take as supreme simply by assuming the following principle of universal ethical egoism:

> Each person ought to do what best serves his or her overall self-interest.

We can no more argue for egoism simply by denying the relevance of moral reasons to rational choice than we can argue for pure altruism simply by denying the relevance of self-interested reasons to rational choice and assuming the following general principle of pure altruism:

> Each person ought to do what best serves the overall interest of others.

Consequently, in order not to beg the question, we have no other alternative but to grant the prima facie relevance to both self-interested and moral reasons to rational choice and then try to determine which reasons we would be rationally required to act upon, all things considered. Notice that in order not to beg the question, it is necessary to back off from both the general principle of egoism and the general principle of pure altruism, thus granting the prima facie relevance of both self-interested and moral reasons to rational choice. From this standpoint, it is still an open question whether either egoism or pure altruism will be rationally preferable, all things considered.

In this regard, there are two kinds of cases that must be considered. First, there are cases in which there is a conflict between the relevant self-interested and moral reasons.[8] Second, there are cases in which there is no such conflict.

Now it seems obvious that where there is no conflict, and both reasons are conclusive reasons of their kind, both reasons should be acted on. In such contexts, we should do what is favored both by morality and by self-interest.

Consider the following example. Suppose you accepted a job marketing a baby formula in under-developed countries where the formula was improperly used, leading to increased infant mortality.[9] Imagine that you could just as well have accepted an equally attractive and rewarding job marketing a similar formula in developed countries, where the misuse does not occur, so that a rational weighing of the relevant self-interested reasons alone would not have favored your acceptance of one of these jobs over the other.[10] At the same time, there were obviously moral reasons that condemned your acceptance of the first job—reasons that you presumably are or were able to acquire. Moreover, by assumption in this case, the moral reasons do not clash with the relevant self-interested reasons; they simply made a recommendation where the relevant self-interested reasons are silent. Consequently, a rational weighing of all the relevant reasons in this case could not but favor acting in accord with the relevant moral reasons.[11]

Yet it might be objected that in cases of this sort there would frequently be other reasons significantly opposed to these moral reasons—other reasons that you are or were able to acquire. Such reasons would be *malevolent* reasons seeking to bring about the suffering and death of other human beings, or *benevolent* reasons concerned to promote nonhuman welfare even at the expense of human welfare, or *aesthetic* reasons concerned to produce valuable results irrespective of the effects on human or nonhuman welfare. But assuming that such malevolent reasons are ultimately rooted in some conception of what is good for oneself or others,[12] these reasons would have already been taken into account, and by assumption outweighed by the other relevant reasons in this case. And although neither benevolent reasons (concerned to promote nonhuman welfare) nor aesthetic reasons would have been taken into account, such reasons are not directly relevant to justifying morality over

universal ethical egoism.[13] Consequently, even with the presence of these three kinds of reasons, your acceptance of the first job can still be seen to be contrary to the relevant reasons in this case.

Needless to say, defenders of universal ethical egoism cannot but be disconcerted with this result since it shows that actions that accord with rational egoism are contrary to reason at least when there are two equally good ways of pursuing one's self-interest, only one of which does not conflict with the basic requirements of morality. Notice also that in cases where there are two equally good ways of fulfilling the basic requirements of morality, only one of which does not conflict with what is in a person's overall self-interest, it is not at all disconcerting for defenders of morality to admit that we are rationally required to choose the way that does not conflict with what is in our overall self-interest. Nevertheless, exposing this defect in universal ethical egoism for cases where moral reasons and self-interested reasons do not conflict would be but a small victory for defenders of morality if it were not also possible to show that in cases where such reasons do conflict, moral reasons have priority over self-interested reasons.

Now when we rationally assess the relevant reasons in such conflict cases, it is best to cast the conflict not as a conflict between self-interested reasons and moral reasons but instead as a conflict between self-interested reasons and altruistic reasons.[14] Viewed in this way, three solutions are possible. First, we could say that self-interested reasons always have priority over conflicting altruistic reasons. Second, we could say just the opposite, that altruistic reasons always have priority over conflicting self-interested reasons. Third, we could say that some kind of a compromise is rationally required. In this compromise, sometimes self-interested reasons would have priority over altruistic reasons and sometimes altruistic reasons would have priority over self-interested reasons.

Once the conflict is described in this manner, the third solution can be seen to be the one that is rationally required. This is because the first and second solutions give exclusive priority to one class of relevant reasons over the other, and only a completely question-begging justification can be given for such an exclusive priority. Only the third solution, by sometimes giving priority to self-interested reasons and sometimes giving priority to altruistic reasons, can avoid a completely question-begging resolution.

Consider the following example. Suppose you are in the waste disposal business and you decided to dispose of toxic wastes in a manner that was cost-efficient for you but predictably caused significant harm to future generations. Imagine that there were alternative methods available for disposing of the waste that were only slightly less cost-efficient and which did not cause any significant harm to future generations.[15] In this case, you are to weigh your self-interested reasons favoring the most cost-efficient disposal of the toxic wastes against the relevant altruistic reasons favoring the avoidance of significant harm to future generations. If we suppose that the projected loss of benefit to yourself was ever so slight and the projected harm to future generations was ever so great, then a nonarbitrary compromise between the relevant self-interested and altruistic reasons would have to favor the altruistic reasons in this case. Hence, as judged by a non–question-begging standard of rationality, your method of waste disposal was contrary to the relevant reasons.

Notice also that this standard of rationality would not support just any compromise between the relevant self-interested and altruistic reasons. The compromise must be a nonarbitrary one, for otherwise it would beg the question with respect to the opposing egoistic and altruistic views. Such a compromise would have to respect the rankings of self-interested and altruistic reasons imposed by the egoist and altruistic views, respectively. Since for each individual there is a separate ranking of that individual's relevant self-interested and altruistic reasons, we can represent these rankings from the most important reasons to the least important reasons, as shown in the following diagram.

Accordingly, any nonarbitrary compromise among such reasons in seeking not to beg the question against egoism or altruism will have to give priority to those reasons that rank highest in each category. Failure to give priority to the highest-ranking altruistic or self-interested reasons would, other things being equal, be contrary to reason.

Of course, there will be cases in which the only way to avoid being required to do what is contrary to your highest-ranking reasons is by requiring someone else to do what is contrary to her highest-ranking reasons. Such cases are sometimes called "lifeboat cases." But while such cases are surely difficult to resolve (maybe only a chance mechanism can offer a reasonable resolution), they surely do not reflect the typical conflict between the relevant self-interested and altruistic reasons that we are or were able to acquire. For typically one or the other of the conflicting reasons will rank higher on its respective scale, thus permitting a clear resolution.

Now it is important to see how morality can be viewed as just such a nonarbitrary compromise between self-interested and altruistic reasons. First of all, a certain amount of self-regard is morally required or at least morally acceptable.

Individual A		Individual B	
Self-interested Reasons	*Altruistic Reasons*	*Self-interested*	*Reasons Altruistic Reasons*
1	1	1	1
2	2	2	2
3	3	3	3
•	•	•	•
•	•	•	•
•	•	•	•
N	N	N	N

Where this is the case, high-ranking self-interested reasons have priority over low-ranking altruistic reasons. Second, morality obviously places limits on the extent to which people should pursue their own self-interest. Where this is the case, high-ranking altruistic reasons have priority over low-ranking self-interested reasons. In this way, morality can be seen to be a nonarbirrary compromise between self-interested and altruistic reasons, and the "moral reasons" which constitute that compromise can be seen as having an absolute priority over the self-interested or altruistic reasons that conflict with them.

Of course, exactly how this compromise is to be worked out is a matter of considerable debate. A utilitarian approach favors one sort of resolution, an Aristotelian approach another, and a Kantian approach yet another. However, irrespective of how this debate is best resolved, it is clear that some sort of a compromise view or moral solution is rationally preferable to either ethical egoism or pure altruism when judged from a non–question-begging standpoint.[16]

THE INTERCONNECTEDNESS OF MORAL SOLUTIONS TO PRACTICAL PROBLEMS

Given this justification for following a moral approach to practical problems, we are in a good position to begin examining the thirteen practical problems covered in this anthology. Each section contains readings defending radically opposing solutions to the problem at hand as well as one or more readings discussing specific practical applications. Working through these readings should give you a more informed view about the demands morality places on us with respect to each of these practical problems.

Even if you do not cover all of these practical problems, you should still come to appreciate why a solution to any one of them requires solutions to the others as well. That is to say, the readings on the

distribution of income and wealth (in Section I) may help you to characterize a morally defensible system for distributing income and wealth within a society, but you would still not know fully how to apply such a system in a particular society without also inquiring how just that society is with respect to the other problem areas covered by this anthology.

Or suppose justice requires us to provide for the basic nutritional needs of distant peoples and future generations as well as for people within our own society. (See the readings in Section II.) Such a requirement would at least restrict the use of nonrenewable resources to satisfy the nonbasic or luxury needs of persons *within our society or of those presently existing*—a use that might otherwise be permitted by a morally defensible system for distributing income and wealth within our society.

Further moral restrictions on the satisfaction of nonbasic or luxury needs could arise from a correct determination of who has a right to life. For example, if fetuses have a right to life, many of us may be morally required to sacrifice the satisfaction of certain nonbasic or luxury needs to bring fetuses to term. If, by contrast, euthanasia can be morally justified, scarce resources that are now used to sustain human life could be freed for other purposes. (See the readings in Section III.)

Justice also may demand that we sacrifice some nonbasic or luxury needs to satisfy the requirements of sex equality and remedy past discrimination, correct for harassment, and achieve diversity. For example, at the cost of considerable redistribution, we may be required to provide women with the same opportunities for self-development that are now open to men. (See the readings in Sections V and IX.) We may also be required to turn away qualified candidates for medical schools and law schools in order to achieve the educational benefits of diversity. (See the readings in Section VII.) Obviously, a radical solution to the problem of pornography, prohibiting its distribution, would affect those who derive their income from that $8-billion-a-year industry. (See the readings in Section VIII.)

Moral restrictions on the satisfaction of nonbasic needs and even on the way basic needs are satisfied could arise from a determination of what obligations, if any, we have to animals and the environment. For example, if vegetarianism were morally required, and recognized as such, the impact on our lives would be far reaching. (See the readings in Section XI.)

Similarly, the legitimate costs of legal enforcement must ultimately enter into any calculation of who gets to keep what in society. This will require a solution to the problem of punishment and responsibility. (See the readings in Section XII.)

A solution to the problem of punishment and responsibility, in turn, presupposes solutions to the other practical problems discussed in this anthology. Suppose that in a society with a just distribution of income and wealth, persons who put forth their best efforts receive a yearly income of at least $15,000. (If you think a just distribution of income would provide some other amount, plug that amount in and make the corresponding adjustments in subsequent figures.) Further suppose that the society in which you and I live has an unjust distribution of income and wealth because, although there are enough resources for a just distribution, many persons who put forth their best efforts receive no more than $8,000 a year, whereas others receive as much as $500,000. Let's say that your income is $500,000 and mine is only $8,000, even though I have tried every legal way to increase my income. Assume also that any resort to civil disobedience or armed revolution would be ineffectual and too costly for me personally. If I then rob you of $7,000, thus bringing my yearly income up to the just allotment of $15,000, what would a morally defensible system of punishment and responsibility do to me if I were caught? To require a punishment equal in severity to the $7,000 I took simply reinforces an unjust distribution of income and wealth. So it seems that only a fairly light punishment or no punishment at all should be required.[17] This example shows that the application of a morally defensible solution to the problem of punishment and responsibility depends on a solution to the problem of the distribution of income and wealth in a society. To know, therefore, how to apply a morally defensible system of punishment

and responsibility in a particular society, you must know to what degree that society incorporates a morally defensible distribution of income and wealth.

Finally, as we in the United States are painfully aware at the present time, proposed allocations for distributing income and wealth through social welfare programs can come into conflict with proposed allocations for military expenditures and homeland defense. Many people have argued that when this happens we must sacrifice social welfare programs to meet these requirements, but many other people have disagreed. Obviously, then, to know exactly how your solutions to the other problem areas treated in this anthology should be applied in a particular society, you also need to know the moral limits to the international use of force against substantial aggression or acts of terrorism. (See the readings in Section XIII.)

Many of these practical problems are also interconnected because they deal with the general question of how free people should be. Specifically, the practical problems address the following questions: Should people be free to keep for themselves all they produce? (See the readings in Sections I and II.) Should people be free to enjoy pornography? (See the readings in Section VIII.) Should people be free from legal penalty and from moral condemnation to engage in sodomy? (See the readings in Section X.) Should people be free to enhance their own and their children's capabilities, to whatever extent is possible, using medicine and technology? (See the readings in Section IV).

Put briefly, what is required (or permitted) by a morally defensible solution to the problem of the distribution of income and wealth within a society will depend on what is required (or permitted) by morally defensible solutions to the problems of distant peoples and future generations, abortion and euthanasia, human enhancement, sex equality, power, gender roles, and discrimination against men, affirmative action, pornography, sexual harassment, gay and lesbian rights, animal liberation and environmental justice, punishment and responsibility, and war, torture and terrorism. This means that any solution you might devise to one of these problems is only provisional until you can determine solutions to the others as well. And even if you are unable at the moment to devise solutions to all of these practical problems (because, for example, the course you are now taking is only considering some of them), you must still acknowledge that in the final analysis your solutions to these practical problems will have to be interconnected.

Note, too, that acknowledging the interconnectedness of the solutions to these practical problems does not presuppose a commitment to any particular political or moral ideal. For example, whether you tend to be a libertarian, a welfare liberal, a socialist, or anything else, the interconnectedness of the solutions to the practical problems we are discussing still holds true. Individuals who endorse different political and moral ideals will presumably devise different solutions to these practical problems, but the solutions will still be interconnected.

Working through the readings in this anthology will not always be an easy task. Some articles will be clear on the first reading, whereas others will require closer scrutiny. You should also make sure you give each selection a fair hearing, because although some will accord with your current views, others will not. It is important that you evaluate the latter with an open mind, allowing for the possibility that after sufficient reflection you may come to view them as the most morally defensible. Indeed, to approach the selections of this anthology in any other way would surely undermine the grounds you have for thinking you are a just and moral person.

ENDNOTES

1. Obviously, other moral approaches to practical problems could be distinguished, but I think the three I consider reflect the range of possible approaches that are relevant to the resolution of these problems.

2. In fact, the debate over whether blacks are better off now because of the programs of the Great Society has taken a more scholarly turn. See Charles Murray, *Losing Ground* (New York: Basic Books, 1984), and Christopher Jencks, "How Poor Are the Poor?" *New York Review of Books*, May 9, 1985.

3. See Section II of this text and my book. *The Demands of Justice* (Notre Dame: University of Notre Dame Press, 1980), especially Chapter 2.

4. For further argument on this point, see Marcus Singer, *Generalization in Ethics* (New York: Knopf, 1961), Chapter 2, and Alan Gewirth, "The Non-Trivializability of Universalizability," *Australasian Journal of Philosophy* (1969), pp. 123–131.

5. Jesse Kalin, "In Defense of Egoism," in *Morality and Rational Self-interest*, ed. David Gauthier (Englewood Cliffs, NJ: Prentice-Hall, 1970), pp. 73–74.

6. For additional reasons that ethical egoism is a consistent view, see my article, "Ethical Egoism and Beyond," *Canadian Journal of Philosophy* (1979), pp. 91–108.

7. "Ought" presupposes "can" here. Unless the members of the society have the capacity to entertain and follow both self-interested and moral reasons for acting, it does not make any sense to ask whether they ought or ought not to do so.

8. For an account of what counts as *relevant* self-interested or moral reasons, see my *How to Make People Just* (Totowa, NJ: Rowman & Allenheld, 1988), pp. 165–166.

9. For a discussion of the causal links involved here, see *Marketing and Promotion of Infant Formula in Developing Countries*. Hearing before the Subcommittee of International Economic Policy and Trade of the Committee on Foreign Affairs, U.S. House of Representatives, 1980. See also Maggie McComas et al., *The Dilemma of Third World Nutrition* (Geneva: Nestle S.A., 1983).

10. Assume that both jobs have the same beneficial effects on the interests of others.

11. I am assuming that acting contrary to reason is an important failing with respect to the requirements of reason, and that there are many ways of not acting

in (perfect) accord with reason that do not constitute acting contrary to reason.

12. Otherwise, they would really fall under the classification of aesthetic reasons.

13. Of course, such reasons would have to be taken into account at some point in a complete justification for morality, but the method of integrating such reasons into a complete justification of morality would simply parallel the method already used for integrating self-interested and altruistic reasons.

14. This is because, as I shall argue, morality itself already represents a compromise between egoism and altruism. So to ask that moral reasons be weighed against self-interested reasons is, in effect, to count self-interested reasons twice—once in the compromise between egoism and altruism and then again when moral reasons are weighed against self-interested reasons. But to count self-interested reasons twice is clearly objectionable.

15. Assume that all these methods of waste disposal have roughly the same amount of beneficial effects on the interests of others.

16. For further argument, see my article, "Justifying Morality: The Right and the Wrong Ways" [Kurt Baier Festschift] *Syntheses* (1987), vol. 1, pp. 45–70.

17. For further argument, see my article, "Is There a Rationale for Punishment?" *Philosophical Topics* (1990), pp. 105–125.

✳

The Distribution of Income and Wealth

INTRODUCTION

Basic Concepts

The problem of the distribution of income and wealth within a society has traditionally been referred to as the problem of distributive justice. Less frequently, this problem has included the distribution of other social goods (for example, political freedoms such as speech and press) and sometimes distribution on a worldwide scale. Most philosophers, however, agree that the distribution of income and wealth within a specific society is at the heart of the problem of distributive justice.

Just as traditionally, a variety of solutions have been proposed to the problem of distributive justice. Before examining some solutions, let's observe what they all have in common.

First, even though the solutions may differ as to exactly how much income and wealth people deserve or should rightfully possess, they all purport to tell us what people deserve or have a right to possess. For example, some solutions propose that people deserve to have their needs fulfilled, whereas others state that what people deserve or should rightfully possess is what they can produce by their labor.

Second, all solutions to the problem of distributive justice distinguish between justice and charity. Justice is what we should do as a matter of obligation or duty, whereas charity is what we should do if we want to choose the morally best possible action available. Accordingly, the demands of charity go beyond duty. In addition, failure to fulfill the demands of justice is blameworthy, violates

15

someone's rights, and can legitimately be punished. By contrast, failure to fulfill the demands of charity, although not ideal, is not blameworthy, does not violate anyone's rights, and cannot legitimately be punished. Some solutions to the problem of distributive justice give more scope to justice and less to charity, whereas others do just the opposite.

Turning from common ground to disputed territory, solutions offered to the problem of distributive justice have appealed to many political ideals. In our own time, libertarians have appealed to an ideal of liberty, socialists to an ideal of equality, and welfare liberals to an ideal of contractual fairness.

Libertarianism

Libertarians such as John Hospers (see Selection 1) take liberty as the ultimate political ideal and typically define liberty as "the state of being unconstrained by other persons from doing what one wants." This definition limits the scope of liberty in two ways. First, not all constraints, whatever the source, count as a restriction of liberty; the constraints must come from other persons. For example, people who are constrained by natural forces from getting to the top of Mount Everest do not lack liberty in this regard. Second, the constraints must run counter to people's wants. Thus, people who do not want to hear Beethoven's Fifth Symphony do not feel their liberty is restricted when other people forbid its performance, even though the proscription does in fact constrain what they are able to do.

Of course, libertarians may argue that these constraints do restrict a person's liberty because people normally want to be unconstrained by others. But other philosophers have claimed that such constraints point to a serious defect in the libertarian's definition of liberty, which can only be remedied by defining liberty more broadly as "the state of being unconstrained by other persons from doing what one is able to do." If we apply this revised definition to the previous example, we find that people's liberty to hear Beethoven's Fifth Symphony would be restricted even if they did not want to hear it (and even if, perchance, they did not want to be unconstrained by others), because other people would still be constraining them from doing what they are able to do.

Confident that problems of defining liberty can be overcome in some satisfactory manner, libertarians go on to characterize their political ideal as requiring that each person should have the greatest amount of liberty commensurate with the same liberty for all. From this ideal, libertarians claim that several more specific requirements—in particular, a right to life; a right to freedom of speech, press, and assembly; and a right to property—can be derived.

It is important to note that the libertarian's right to life is not a right to receive from others the goods and resources necessary for preserving one's life; it is simply a right not to be killed. So understood, the right to life is not a right to welfare. In fact, there are no welfare rights in the libertarian view. Accordingly, the libertarian's understanding of the right to property is not a right to receive from others the goods and resources necessary for one's welfare, but rather a right to acquire goods and resources either by initial acquisition or by voluntary agreement.

Obviously, by defending rights such as these, libertarians can only support a limited role for government. That role is simply to prevent and punish initial acts of coercion—the only wrongful actions for libertarians.

Libertarians do not deny that it is a good thing for people to have sufficient goods and resources to meet at least their basic nutritional needs, but libertarians do deny that government has a duty to provide for such needs. Some good things, such as the provision of welfare to the needy, are requirements of charity rather than justice, libertarians claim. Accordingly, failure to make such provisions is neither blameworthy nor punishable.

A basic difficulty with the libertarian solution to the problem of distributive justice as defended by Hospers is the claim that rights to life and property (as the libertarian understands these rights) derive from an ideal of liberty. Why should we think that an ideal of liberty requires a right to life and a right to property that excludes a right to welfare? Surely a right to property might well justify a rich person's depriving a poor person of the liberty to acquire the goods and resources necessary for meeting his or her basic nutritional needs. How then could we appeal to an ideal of liberty to justify such a deprivation? In Selection 2, James P. Sterba argues that we cannot.

Welfare Liberalism

In contrast with libertarians, welfare liberals, such as John Rawls (Selection 3), take contractual fairness to be the ultimate political ideal and contend that the fundamental rights and duties in a society are those that people would agree to under fair conditions.

Note that welfare liberals do not say that the fundamental rights and duties in a society are those to which people actually do agree, because these might not be fair at all. For example, people might agree to a certain system of fundamental rights and duties because they have been forced to do so or because their only alternative is starving to death. Thus, actual agreement is neither sufficient nor necessary for determining an adequate conception of justice. According to welfare liberals, what is necessary and sufficient is that people would agree to such rights and duties under fair conditions.

But what are fair conditions? According to John Rawls, fair conditions can be expressed by an "original position," in which people are concerned to advance their own interests behind a "veil of ignorance." The effect of the veil of ignorance is to deprive people in the original position of the knowledge they would need to advance their own interests in ways that are morally arbitrary.

In Selection 4, Charles W. Mills uses social contract theory both descriptively and prescriptively. Descriptively, he uses the theory to paint a picture of past and present institutional structures based on domination that have characterized most societies. Almost invariably, this domination has been based on race, class, and gender, and, as Mills points out, it has rarely been made central or even recognized in the work of moral and political philosophers, past or present. Employing the theory prescriptively, Mills seeks to develop a social contract theory that makes central the task of undoing the forms of race, class, and gender-based domination that still continue to characterize existing societies. According to Mills, defenders of prescriptive social contract theory of the sort defended and made popular by John Rawls has no real alternative but to follow him in this endeavor.

Practical Applications

The application of the ideals of libertarianism, socialism, or welfare liberalism to a particular society obviously has basic and far-reaching effects. These ideals have implications for constitutional structure, the control of industry, taxing policy, social welfare programs, property law, and much more. The next two readings in this section are from important U.S. Supreme Court decisions to which our three political ideals can be usefully related.

The Supreme Court, of course, does not view itself as directly applying one or the other of these political ideals to the laws of the land. Rather, the Court views itself as deciding whether particular laws accord with the provisions of the U.S. Constitution. However, most people, including Supreme Court justices, do not clearly separate their views about what are the practical applications of the political ideal they take to be the most morally defensible from their views about what sort of laws accord with the U.S. Constitution. Hence, it is frequently possible to see how commitment to a political ideal is decisive in judicial decision making.

Beyond coming to appreciate how political ideals and their presumed applications function in judicial decision making, it is important that you examine Supreme Court decisions to determine to what degree the laws of your society accord with the political ideal you take to be the most morally defensible. To have good reasons to believe that you are a just and moral person, you need to assess to what degree the laws and institutions of your society are just—in this case, to what degree they accord with the requirements of distributive justice. Examining the two U.S. Supreme Court decisions included in this section should serve this purpose well.

In the first decision (*Wyman v. James*), the majority of the Court decided that the rights of welfare recipients are limited in various ways and in particular that recipients are not protected against mandatory visits by caseworkers. Such a decision would surely seem justified if one believed, as libertarians do, that the provision of welfare is, at best, only a requirement of charity. Welfare liberals and socialists, however, would have difficulty accepting this decision, as did the dissenting justices of the Court.

In the second decision (*Plyler v. Doe*), the majority of the Court determined that although public education is not a right, it still cannot be denied to the children of illegal aliens because of the pivotal role of education in sustaining our political and cultural heritage. This decision has some affinity with the way welfare liberals and socialists would understand the practical requirements of their ideals; libertarians would probably find themselves persuaded by the arguments of the dissenting justices.

Notice that you can also work backward from your considered judgments about these Supreme Court cases to the political ideal you should favor. Frequently, we can only clarify our views about a morally defensible position by considering the practical applications of alternative political ideals.

Notice, too, that any fully adequate solution to the problem of distributive justice within a society presupposes a solution to the other moral problems presented in this anthology. In particular, the problem of near and distant peoples, which is discussed in the following section, seems to be clearly connected with the problem of distributive justice. We cannot know for sure what resources particular persons within a society should receive unless we also know what obligations persons within that society have to distant peoples.

1

What Libertarianism Is

JOHN HOSPERS

John Hospers explores various ways of understanding the basic libertarian thesis that every person is the owner of his or her own life. According to Hospers, such ownership entails rights to life, liberty, and property. Since these rights are violated by an initial use of force, the proper role of government is said to be limited to the retaliatory use of force against those who have initiated its use. All other possible roles for government, such as protecting individuals against themselves or requiring people to help one another, are regarded as illegitimate by the libertarian.

The political philosophy that is called libertarianism (from the Latin *libertas*, liberty) is the doctrine that every person is the owner of his own life, and that no one is the owner of anyone else's life—and that consequently every human being has the right to act in accordance with his own choices, unless those actions infringe on the equal liberty of other human beings to act in accordance with their choices.

There are several other ways of stating the same libertarian thesis:

1. *No one is anyone else's master, and no one is anyone else's slave.* Since I am the one to decide how my life is to be conducted just as you decide about yours, I have no right (even if I had the power) to make you my slave and be your master, nor have you the right to become the master by enslaving me. Slavery is *forced* servitude, and since no one owns the life of anyone else, no one has the right to enslave another. Political theories past and present have traditionally been concerned with who should be the master (usually the king, the dictator, or government bureaucracy) and who should be the slaves, and what the extent of the slavery should be. Libertarianism holds that no one has the right to use force to enslave the life of another, or any portion or aspect of that life.

2. *Other men's lives are not yours to dispose of.* I enjoy seeing operas; but operas are expensive to produce. Opera-lovers often say, "The state (or the city, etc.) should subsidize opera, so that we can all see it. Also it would be for the people's betterment, cultural benefit, etc." But what they are advocating is nothing more or less than legalized plunder. They can't pay for the productions themselves, and yet they want to see opera, which involves a large number of people and their labor; so what they are saying in effect is, "Get the money through legalized force. Take a little bit more out of every worker's paycheck every week to pay for the operas we want to see." But I have no right to take by force from the workers' pockets to pay for what I want.

Perhaps it would be better if he *did* go to see opera—then I should try to convince him to

From "What Libertarianism Is," in *The Libertarian Alternative*, edited by Tibor Machan (1974). Reprinted by permission of the author, the editor, and Nelson-Hall, Inc.

go voluntarily. But to take the money from him forcibly, because in my opinion it would be good for *him*, is still seizure of his earnings, which is plunder.

Besides, if I have the right to force him to help pay for my pet projects, hasn't he equally the right to force me to help pay for his? Perhaps he in turn wants the government to subsidize rock-and-roll, or his new car, or a house in the country? If I have the right to milk him, why hasn't he the right to milk me? If I can be a moral cannibal, why can't he too?

We should beware of the inventors of utopias. They would remake the world according to their vision—with the lives and fruits of the labor of *other* human beings. Is it someone's utopian vision that others should build pyramids to beautify the landscape? Very well, then other men should provide the labor; and if he is in a position of political power, and he can't get men to do it voluntarily, then he must *compel* them to "cooperate"—i.e., he must enslave them.

A hundred men might gain great pleasure from beating up or killing just one insignificant human being; but other men's lives are not theirs to dispose of. "In order to achieve the worthy goals of the next five-year plan, we must forcibly collectivize the peasants ..."; but other men's lives are not theirs to dispose of. Do you want to occupy, rent-free, the mansion that another man has worked for twenty years to buy? But other men's lives are not yours to dispose of. Do you want operas so badly that everyone is forced to work harder to pay for their subsidization through taxes? But other men's lives are not yours to dispose of. Do you want to have free medical care at the expense of other people, whether they wish to provide it or not? But this would require them to work longer for you whether they want to or not, and other men's lives are not yours to dispose of....

3. *No human being should be a nonvoluntary mortgage on the life of another.* I cannot claim your life, your work, or the products of your effort as mine. The fruit of one man's labor should not be fair game for every freeloader who comes along and demands it as his own. The orchard that has been carefully grown, nurtured, and harvested by its owner should not be ripe for the plucking for any bypasser who has a yen for the ripe fruit. The wealth that some men have produced should not be fair game for looting by government, to be used for whatever purposes its representatives determine, no matter what their motives in so doing may be. The theft of your money by a robber is not justified by the fact that he used it to help his injured mother.

It will already be evident that libertarian doctrine is embedded in a view of the rights of man. Each human being has the right to live his life as he chooses, compatibly with the equal right of all other human beings to live their lives as they choose.

All men's rights are implicit in the above statement. Each man has the right to life: Any attempt by others to take it away from him, or even to injure him, violates this right, through the use of coercion against him. Each man has the right to liberty: to conduct his life in accordance with the alternatives open to him without coercive actions by others. And every man has the right to property: to work to sustain his life (and the lives of whichever others he chooses to sustain, such as his family) and to retain the fruits of his labor.

People often defend the rights of life and liberty but denigrate property rights, and yet the right to property is as basic as the other two; indeed, without property rights, no other rights are possible. Depriving you of property is depriving you of the means by which you live....

I have no right to decide how *you* should spend your time or your money. I can make that decision for myself, but not for you, my neighbor. I may deplore your choice of life-style, and I may talk with you about it provided you are willing to listen to me. But I have no right to use force to change it. Nor have I the right to decide how you should spend the money you have earned. I may appeal to you to give it to the Red Cross, and you may prefer to go to prizefights. But that is your decision, and however much I may chafe about it I do not have the right to interfere forcibly with it, for example by robbing you in order to use the money in accordance with *my* choices. (If I have the right to rob you, have you also the right to rob me?)

When I claim a right, I carve out a niche, as it were, in my life, saying in effect, "This activity I must be able to perform without interference from others. For you and everyone else, this is off limits." And so I put up a "no trespassing" sign, which marks off the area of my right. Each individual's right is his "no trespassing" sign in relation to me and others. I may not encroach upon his domain any more than he upon mine, without my consent. Every right entails a duty, true—but the duty is only that of *forbearance*—that is, of *refraining* from violating the other person's right. If you have a right to life, I have no right to take your life; if you have a right to the products of your labor (property), I have no right to take it from you without your consent. The nonviolation of these rights will not guarantee you protection against natural catastrophes such as floods and earthquakes, but it will protect you against the aggressive activities *of other men*. And rights, after all, have to do with one's relations to other human beings, not with one's relations to physical nature.

Nor were these rights created by government; governments—some governments, obviously not all—*recognize* and *protect* the rights that individuals already have. Governments regularly forbid homicide and theft; and, at a more advanced stage, protect individuals against such things as libel and breach of contract....

The *right to property* is the most misunderstood and unappreciated of human rights, and it is the one most constantly violated by governments. "Property" of course does not mean only real estate; it includes anything you can call your own—your clothing, your car, your jewelry, your books and papers.

The right of property is not the right to just *take* it from others, for this would interfere with *their* property rights. It is rather the right to work for it, to obtain noncoercively the money or services you can present in voluntary exchange.

The right to property is consistently underplayed by intellectuals today, sometimes even frowned upon, as if we should feel guilty for upholding such a right in view of all the poverty in the world. But the right to property is absolutely basic. It is your hedge against the future. It is your assurance that what you have worked to earn will still be there and be yours, when you wish or need to use it, especially when you are too old to work any longer.

Government has always been the chief enemy of the right to property. The officials of government, wishing to increase their power, and finding an increase of wealth an effective way to bring this about, seize some or all of what a person has earned—and since government has a monopoly of physical force within the geographical area of the nation, it has the power (but not the right) to do this. When this happens, of course, every citizen of that country is insecure: He knows that no matter how hard he works the government can swoop down on him at any time and confiscate his earnings and possessions. A person sees his life savings wiped out in a moment when the tax-collectors descend to deprive him of the fruits of his work; or, an industry which has been fifty years in the making and cost millions of dollars and millions of hours of time and planning, is nationalized overnight. Or the government, via inflation, cheapens the currency, so that hard-won dollars aren't worth anything any more. The effect of such actions, of course, is that people lose hope and incentive: If no matter how hard they work the government agencies can take it all away, why bother to work at all, for more than today's needs? Depriving people of property is *depriving them of the means by which they live*—the freedom of the individual citizen to do what he wishes with his own life and to plan for the future. Indeed only if property rights are respected is there any point to planning for the future and working to achieve one's goals. *Property rights are what makes long-range planning possible*—the kind of planning which is a distinctively human endeavor, as opposed to the day-by-day activity of the lion who hunts, who depends on the supply of game tomorrow but has no real insurance against starvation in a day or a week. Without the right to property, the right to life itself amounts to little: How can you sustain your life if you cannot plan ahead? And how can you plan ahead if the fruits of your labor can at any moment be confiscated by government? ...

Indeed, the right to property may well be considered second only to the right to life. Even the freedom of speech is limited by considerations of property. If a person visiting in your home behaves in a way undesired by you, you have every right to evict him; he can scream or agitate elsewhere if he wishes, but not in your home without your consent. Does a person have a right to shout obscenities in a cathedral? No, for the owners of the cathedral (presumably the Church) have not allowed others on their property for that purpose; one may go there to worship or to visit, but not just for any purpose one wishes. Their property right is prior to your or my wish to scream or expectorate or write graffiti on their building. Or, to take the stock example, does a person have a right to shout "Fire!" falsely in a crowded theater? No, for the theater owner has permitted others to enter and use his property only for a specific purpose, that of seeing a film or watching a stage show. If a person heckles or otherwise disturbs other members of the audience, he can be thrown out. (In fact, he can be removed for any reason the owner chooses, provided his admission money is returned.) And if he shouts "Fire!" when there is no fire, he may be endangering other lives by causing a panic or a stampede. The right to free speech doesn't give one the right to say anything anywhere; it is circumscribed by property rights.

Again, some people seem to assume that the right to free speech (including written speech) means that they can go to a newspaper publisher and demand that he print in his newspaper some propaganda or policy statement for their political party (or other group). But of course they have no right to the use of his newspaper. Ownership of the newspaper is the product of his labor, and he has a right to put into his newspaper whatever he wants, for whatever reason. If he excludes material which many readers would like to have in, perhaps they can find it in another newspaper or persuade him to print it himself (if there are enough of them, they will usually do just that). Perhaps they

can even cause his newspaper to fail. But as long as he owns it, he has the right to put in it what he wishes; what would a property right be if he could not do this? They have no right to place their material in his newspaper without his consent—not for free, nor even for a fee. Perhaps other newspapers will include it, or perhaps they can start their own newspaper (in which case they have a right to put in it what they like). If not, an option open to them would be to mimeograph and distribute some handbills.

In exactly the same way, no one has a right to "free television time" unless the owner of the television station consents to give it; it is his station, he has the property rights over it, and it is for him to decide how to dispose of his time. He may not decide wisely, but it is his right to decide as he wishes. If he makes enough unwise decisions, and courts enough unpopularity with the viewing public or the sponsors, he may have to go out of business; but as he is free to make his own decision, so is he free to face their consequences. (If the government owns the television station, then government officials will make the decisions, and there is no guarantee of *their* superior wisdom. The difference is that when "the government" owns the station, you are forced to help pay for its upkeep through your taxes, whether the bureaucrat in charge decides to give you television time or not.)

"But why have *individual* property rights? Why not have lands and houses owned by everybody together?" Yes, this involves no violation of individual rights, as long as everybody consents to this arrangement and no one is forced to join it. The parties to it may enjoy the communal living enough (at least for a time) to overcome certain inevitable problems: that some will work and some not, that some will achieve more in an hour than others can do in a day, and still they will get the same income. The few who do the most will in the end consider themselves "workhorses" who do the work of two or three or twelve, while the others will be "freeloaders" on the efforts of these few. But as long as they can get out of the arrangement if they no longer like it, no violation of rights is involved. They got in voluntarily, and they can get out voluntarily; no one has used force.

"But why not say that everybody owns every-thing? That we *all* own everything there is?"

To some this may have a pleasant ring—but let us try to analyze what it means. If everybody owns everything, then everyone has an equal right to go everywhere, do what he pleases, take what he likes, destroy if he wishes, grow crops or burn them, trample them under, and so on. Consider what it would be like in practice. Suppose you have saved money to buy a house for yourself and your family. Now suppose that the principle, "everybody owns everything," becomes adopted. Well then, why shouldn't every itinerant hippie just come in and take over, sleeping in your beds and eating in your kitchen and not bothering to replace the food supply or clean up the mess? After all, it belongs to all of us, doesn't it? So we have just as much right to it as you, the buyer, have. What happens if we *all* want to sleep in the bedroom and there's not room for all of us? Is it the strongest who wins?

What would be the result? Since no one would be responsible for anything, the property would soon be destroyed, the food used up, the facilities nonfunctional. Beginning as a house that *one* family could use, it would end up as a house that *no one* could use. And if the principle continued to be adopted, no one would build houses any more—or anything else. What for? They would only be occupied and used by others, without remuneration.

Suppose two men are cast ashore on an island, and they agree that each will cultivate half of it. The first man is industrious and grows crops and builds a shelter, making the most of the situation with which he is confronted. The second man, perhaps thinking that the warm days will last forever, lies in the sun, picks coconuts while they last, and does a minimum of work to sustain himself. At the time of harvest, the second man has nothing to harvest, nor does he assist the first man in his labors. But later when there is a dearth of food on the island, the second man comes to the first man and demands half of the harvest as his right. But of course, he has no right to the product of the first man's labors. The first man may freely choose to give part of his harvest to the second out of charity rather than see him starve; but that is just what it is—charity, not the second man's right.

How can any of man's rights be violated? Ulti-mately, only by the use of force. I can make sugges-tions to you, I can reason with you, entreat you (if you are willing to listen), but I cannot *force* you without violating your rights; only by forcing you do I cut the cord between your free decisions and your actions. Voluntary relations between indi-viduals involve no deprivation of rights, but murder, assault, and rape do, because in doing these things I make you the unwilling victim of my actions. A man's beating his wife involves no violation of rights if she *wanted* to be beaten. *Force is behavior that requires the unwilling involvement of other persons.*

Thus the use of force need not involve the use of physical violence. If I trespass on your property or dump garbage on it, I am violating your property rights, as indeed I am when I steal your watch; although this is not force in the sense of violence, it *is* a case of your being an unwilling victim of my action. Similarly, if you shout at me so that I cannot be heard when I try to speak, or blow a siren in my ear, or start a factory next door which pollutes my land, you are again violating my rights (to free speech, to property); I am, again, an unwilling victim of your actions. Similarly, if you steal a manuscript of mine and publish it as your own, you are confiscat-ing a piece of my property and thus violating my right to keep what is the product of my labor. Of course, if I give you the manuscript with permission to sign your name to it and keep the proceeds, no violation of rights is involved—any more than if I give you permission to dump garbage on my yard.

According to libertarianism, the role of govern-ment should be limited to the retaliatory use of force against those who have initiated its use. It should not enter into any other areas, such as religion, social organization, and economics.

GOVERNMENT

Government is the most dangerous institution known to man. Throughout history it has violated the rights of men more than any individual or group of individuals could do: It has killed people, enslaved them, sent them to forced labor and concentration camps, and regularly robbed and pillaged them of the fruits of their expended labor. Unlike individual criminals, government has the power to arrest and try; unlike individual criminals, it can surround and encompass a person totally, dominating every aspect of one's life, so that one has no recourse from it but to leave the country (and in totalitarian nations even that is prohibited). Government throughout history has a much sorrier record than any individual, even that of a ruthless mass murderer. The signs we see on bumper stickers are chillingly accurate: "Beware: The Government Is Armed and Dangerous."

The only proper role of government, according to libertarians, is that of the protector of the citizen against aggression by other individuals. The government, of course, should never initiate aggression; its proper role is as the embodiment of the *retaliatory* use of force against anyone who initiates its use.

If each individual had constantly to defend himself against possible aggressors, he would have to spend a considerable portion of his life in target practice, karate exercises, and other means of self-defenses, and even so he would probably be helpless against groups of individuals who might try to kill, maim, or rob him. He would have little time for cultivating those qualities which are essential to civilized life, nor would improvements in science, medicine, and the arts be likely to occur. The function of government is to take this responsibility off his shoulders: The government undertakes to defend him against aggressors and to punish them if they attack him. When the government is effective in doing this, it enables the citizen to go about his business unmolested and without constant fear for his life. To do this, of course, government must have physical power—the police, to protect the citizen from aggression within its borders, and the armed forces, to protect him from aggressors outside. Beyond that, the government should not intrude upon his life, either to run his business, or adjust his daily activities, or prescribe his personal moral code.

Government, then, undertakes to be the individual's protector; but historically governments have gone far beyond this function. Since they already have the physical power, they have not hesitated to use it for purposes far beyond that which was entrusted to them in the first place. Undertaking initially to protect its citizens against aggression, it has often itself become an aggressor— a far greater aggressor, indeed, than the criminals against whom it was supposed to protect its citizens. Governments have done what no private citizen can do: arrest and imprison individuals without a trial and send them to slave labor camps. Government must have power in order to be effective—and yet the very means by which alone it can be effective make it vulnerable to the abuse of power, leading to managing the lives of individuals and even inflicting terror upon them.

What then should be the function of government? In a phrase, the *protection of human rights*.

1. *The right to life:* Libertarians support all such legislation as will protect human beings against the use of force by others, for example, laws against killing, attempting killing, maiming, beating, and all kinds of physical violence.

2. *The right to liberty:* There should be no laws compromising in any way freedom of speech, of the press, and peaceable assembly. There should be no censorship of ideas, books, films, or anything else by government.

3. *The right to property:* Libertarians support legislation that protects the property rights of individuals against confiscation, nationalization, eminent domain, robbery, trespass, fraud and misrepresentation, patent and copyright, libel, and slander.

Someone has violently assaulted you. Should he be legally liable? Of course. He has violated one of your rights. He has knowingly injured you, and since he has initiated aggression against you, he should be made to expiate.

Someone has negligently left his bicycle on the sidewalk where you trip over it in the dark and injure yourself. He didn't do it intentionally; he didn't mean you any harm. Should he be legally liable? Of course; he has, however unwittingly, injured you, and since the injury is caused by him and you are the victim, he should pay.

Someone across the street is unemployed. Should you be taxed extra to pay for his expenses? Not at all. You have not injured him, you are not responsible for the fact that he is unemployed (unless you are a senator or bureaucrat who agitated for further curtailing of business, which legislation passed, with the result that your neighbor was laid off by the curtailed business). You may voluntarily wish to help him out, or better still, try to get him a job to put him on his feet again; but since you have initiated no aggressive act against him, and neither purposely nor accidentally injured him in any way, you should not be legally penalized for the fact of his unemployment. (Actually, it is just such penalties that increase unemployment.)

One man, A, works hard for years and finally earns a high salary as a professional man. A second man, B, prefers not to work at all, and to spend wastefully what money he has (through inheritance), so that after a year or two he has nothing left. At the end of this time he has a long siege of illness and lots of medical bills to pay. He demands that the bills be paid by the government—that is, by the taxpayers of the land, including Mr. A.

But of course B has no such right. He chose to lead his life in a certain way—that was his voluntary decision. One consequence of that choice is that he must depend on charity in case of later need. Mr. A chose not to live that way. (And if everyone lived like Mr. B, on whom would he depend in case of later need?) Each has a right to live in the way he pleases, but each must live with the consequences of his own decision (which, as always, fall primarily on himself). He cannot, in time of need, claim A's beneficence as his right.

If a house-guest of yours starts to carve his initials in your walls and break up your furniture, you have a right to evict him and call the police if he makes trouble. If someone starts to destroy the machinery in a factory, the factory-owner is also entitled to evict him and call the police. In both cases, persons other than the owner are permitted on the property only under certain conditions, at the pleasure of the owner. If those conditions are violated, the owner is entitled to use force to set things straight. The case is exactly the same on a college or university campus: If a campus demonstrator starts breaking windows, occupying the president's office, and setting fire to a dean, the college authorities are certainly within their rights to evict him forcibly; one is permitted on the college grounds only under specific conditions, set by the administration: study, peaceful student activity, even political activity if those in charge choose to permit it. If they do not choose to permit peaceful political activity on campus, they may be unwise, since a campus is after all a place where all sides of every issue should get discussed, and the college that doesn't permit this may soon lose its reputation and its students. All the same, the college official who does not permit it is quite within his rights; the students do not own the campus, nor do the hired troublemakers imported from elsewhere. In the case of a privately owned college, the owners, or whoever they have delegated to administer it, have the right to make the decisions as to who shall be permitted on the campus and under what conditions. In the case of a state university or college, the ownership problem is more complex: One could say that the "government" owns the campus or that "the people" do, since they are the taxpayers who support it. But in either case, the university administration has the delegated task of keeping order, and until they are removed by the state administration or the taxpayers, it is theirs to decide who shall be permitted on campus, and what nonacademic activities will be permitted to their students on the premises.

Property rights can be violated by physical trespass, of course, or by anyone entering on your property for any reason without your consent. (If you *do* consent to having your neighbor dump garbage on your yard, there is no violation of your rights.) But the physical trespass of a person is only a special case of violation of property rights. Property rights can be violated by sound-waves, in the form of a loud noise, or the sounds of your neighbor's hi-fi set while you are trying to sleep. Such violations of property rights are of course the subject of action in the courts.

But there is another violation of property rights that has not thus far been honored by the courts; this has to do with the effects of *pollution* of the atmosphere.

From the beginnings of modern air pollution, the courts made a conscious decision not to protect, for example, the orchards of farmers from the smoke of nearby factories or locomotives. They said, in effect, to the farmers: Yes, your private property is being invaded by this smoke, but we hold that "public policy" is more important than private property, and public policy holds factories and locomotives to be good things. These goods were allowed to override the defense of property rights—with our consequent headlong rush into pollution disaster. The remedy is both "radical" and crystal clear, and it has nothing to do with multibillion dollar palliative programs at the expense of the taxpayers, which do not even meet the real issue. The remedy is simply to enjoin anyone from injecting pollutants into the air, and thereby invading the rights of persons and property. Period. The argument that such an injunction prohibition would add to the costs of industrial production is as reprehensible as the pre-Civil War argument that the abolition of slavery would add to the costs of growing cotton, and therefore should not take place. For this means that the polluters are able to impose the high costs of pollution upon those whose property rights they are allowed to invade with impunity.[1]

What about automobiles, the chief polluters of the air? One can hardly sue every automobile owner. But one can sue the manufacturers of automobiles who do not install anti-smog devices on the cars which they distribute—and later (though this is more difficult), owners of individual automobiles if they discard the equipment or do not keep it functional.

The violation of rights does not apply only to air-pollution. If someone with a factory upstream on a river pollutes the river, anyone living downstream from him, finding his water polluted, should be able to sue the owner of the factory. In this way, the price of adding the anti-pollutant devices will be the owner's responsibility, and will probably be added to the cost of the products which the factory produces and thus spread around among all consumers, rather than the entire cost being borne by the users of the river in the form of polluted water, with the consequent impossibility of fishing, swimming, and so on. In each case, pollution would be stopped at the source rather than having its ill effects spread around to numerous members of the population.

What about property which you do not work to earn, but which you *inherit* from someone else? Do you have a right to that? You have no right to it until someone decides to give it to you. Consider the man who willed it to you; it was his, he had the right to use and dispose of it as *he* saw fit; and if he decided to give it to you, this is a windfall for you, but it was only the exercise of *his* right. Had the property been seized by the government at the man's death, or distributed among numerous other people designated by the government, it *would* have been a violation of his rights: for he, who worked to earn and sustain it, would not have been able to dispose of it according to his own judgment. If he doesn't have the right to determine who shall have it, who does?

What about the property status of your intellectual activity, such as inventions you may devise and books you write? These, of course, are your property also; they are the products of your mind; you worked at them, you created them. Prior to that, they did not exist. If you worked five years to write a book, and someone stole it and published it as his own, receiving royalties from its sales, he would have stolen your property just as surely as if he had robbed your home. The same is true if someone used and sold without your permission an invention which was the product of your labor and ingenuity.

The role of government with respect to this issue, at least most governments of the Western world, is a proper one: Government protects the products of your labor from the moment they materialize. Copyright law protects your writings from piracy. In the

United States, one's writings are protected for a period of twenty-seven years, and another twenty-seven if one applies for renewal of the copyright. In most other countries, they are protected for a period of fifty years after the author's death, permitting both himself and his surviving heirs to reap the fruits of his labor. After that they enter the "public domain"— that is, anyone may reprint them without your or your heirs' permission. Patent law protects your inventions for a limited period, which varies according to the type of invention. In no case are you forced to avail yourself of this protection; you need not apply for patent or copyright coverage if you do not wish to do so. But the protection of your intellectual property is there, in case you wish to use it.

What about the property status of the airwaves? Here the government's position is far more questionable. The government now claims ownership of the airways, leasing them to individuals and corporations. The government renews leases or refuses them depending on whether the programs satisfy authorities in the Federal Communications Commission. The official position is that "we all own the airwaves": But since only one party can broadcast on a certain frequency at a certain time without causing chaos, it is simply a fact of reality that "everyone" cannot use it. In fact the government decides who shall use the airwaves and one courts its displeasure only at the price of a revoked license. One can write without government approval, but one cannot use the airwaves without the approval of the government.

What policy should have been observed with regard to the airwaves? Much the same as the policy that was followed in the case of the Homestead Act, when the lands of the American West were opening up for settlement. There was a policy of "first come, first served," with the government parcelling out a certain acreage for each individual who wanted to claim the land as his own. There was no charge for the land, but if a man had not used it and built a dwelling during the first two-year period, it was assumed that he was not homesteading and the land was given to the next man in line. The airwaves too could have been given out on a "first come, first served" basis. The first man who used a given frequency would be its owner, and the government would protect him in the use of it against trespassers. If others wanted to use the same frequency, they would have to buy it from the first man, if he was willing to sell, or try to buy another, just as one now does with the land.

Laws may be classified into three types: (1) laws protecting individuals against themselves, such as laws against fornication and other sexual behavior, alcohol, and drugs; (2) laws protecting individuals against aggressions by other individuals, such as laws against murder, robbery, and fraud; (3) laws requiring people to help one another; for example, all laws which rob Peter to pay Paul, such as welfare.

Libertarians reject the first class of laws totally. Behavior which harms no one else is strictly the individual's own affair. Thus, there should be no laws against becoming intoxicated, since whether or not to become intoxicated is the individual's own decision. But there should be laws against driving while intoxicated, since the drunken driver is a threat to every other motorist on the highway (drunken driving falls into type 2). Similarly, there should be no laws against drugs (except the prohibition of sale of drugs to minors) as long as the taking of these drugs poses no threat to anyone else. Drug addiction is a psychological problem to which no present solution exists. Most of the social harm caused by addicts, other than to themselves, is the result of thefts which they perform in order to continue their habit—and then the *legal* crime is the theft, not the addiction. The actual cost of heroin is about ten cents a shot; if it were legalized, the enormous traffic in illegal sale and purchase of it would stop, as well as the accompanying proselytization to get new addicts (to make more money for the pusher) and the thefts performed by addicts who often require eighty dollars a day just to keep up the habit. Addiction would not stop, but the crimes would: It is estimated that 75 percent of the burglaries in New York City today are performed by addicts, and all these crimes could be wiped out at one stroke through the legalization of drugs. (Only when the taking of drugs could be shown to constitute a threat to *others* should it be prohibited by law. It is only laws protecting people against *themselves* that libertarians oppose.)

Laws should be limited to the second class only: aggression by individuals against other individuals. These are laws whose function is to protect human beings against encroachment by others; and this, as we have seen, is (according to libertarianism) the sole function of government.

Libertarians also reject the third class of laws totally: No one should be forced by law to help others, not even to tell them the time of day if requested, and certainly not to give them a portion of one's weekly paycheck. Governments, in the guise of humanitarianism, have given to some by taking from others (charging a "handling fee" in the process, which, because of the government's waste and inefficiency, sometimes is several hundred percent). And in so doing they have decreased incentive, violated the rights of individuals, and lowered the standard of living of almost everyone.

All such laws constitute what libertarians call *moral cannibalism*. A cannibal in the physical sense is a person who lives off the flesh of other human beings. A *moral* cannibal is one who believes he has a right to live off the "spirit" of other human beings—who believes that he has a moral claim on the productive capacity, time, and effort expended by others.

It has become fashionable to claim virtually everything that one needs or desires as one's *right*. Thus, many people claim that they have a right to a job, the right to free medical care, to free food and clothing, to a decent home, and so on. Now if one asks, apart from any specific context, whether it would be desirable if everyone had these things, one might well say yes. But there is a gimmick attached to each of them: *At whose expense?* Jobs, medical care, education, and so on, don't grow on trees. These are goods and services *produced only by men*. Who then is to provide them, and under what conditions?

If you have a right to a job, who is to supply it? Must an employer supply it even if he doesn't want to hire you? What if you are unemployable, or incurably lazy? (If you say "the government must supply it," does that mean that a job must be created for you which no employer needs done, and that you must be kept in it regardless of how much or little you work?) If the employer is forced to

supply it at his expense even if he doesn't need you, then isn't *he* being enslaved to that extent? What ever happened to *his* right to conduct his life and his affairs in accordance with his choices? If you have a right to free medical care, then, since medical care doesn't exist in nature as wild apples do, some people will have to supply it to you for free: That is, they will have to spend their time and money and energy taking care of you whether they want to or not. What ever happened to *their* right to conduct their lives as they see fit? Or do you have a right to violate theirs? Can there be a right to violate rights?

All those who demand this or that as a "free service" are consciously or unconsciously evading the fact that there is in reality no such thing as free services. All man-made goods and services are the result of human expenditure of time and effort. There is no such thing as "something for nothing" in this world. If you demand something free, you are demanding that other men give their time and effort to you without compensation. If they voluntarily choose to do this, there is no problem; but if you demand that they *be forced* to do it, you are interfering with their right not to do it if they so choose. "Swimming in this pool ought to be free!" says the indignant passerby. What he means is that others should build a pool, others should provide the material, and still others should run it and keep it in functioning order, so that *he* can use it without fee. But what right has he to the expenditure of *their* time and effort? To expect something "for free" is to expect it *to be paid for by others* whether they choose to or not.

Many questions, particularly about economic matters, will be generated by the libertarian account of human rights and the role of government. Should government have a role in assisting the needy, in providing social security, in legislating minimum wages, in fixing prices and putting a ceiling on rents, in curbing monopolies, in erecting tariffs, in guaranteeing jobs, in managing the money supply? To these and all similar questions the libertarian answers with an unequivocal no.

"But then you'd let people go hungry!" comes the rejoinder. This, the libertarian insists, is precisely what would not happen; with the restrictions removed, the economy would flourish as never before. With the controls taken off business, existing enterprises would expand and new ones would spring into existence satisfying more and more consumer needs; millions more people would be gainfully employed instead of subsisting on welfare, and all kinds of research and production, released from the stranglehold of government, would proliferate, fulfilling man's needs and desires as never before. It has always been so whenever government has permitted men to be free traders on a free market. But *why* this is so, and how the free market is the best solution to all problems relating to the material aspect of man's life, is another and far longer story.

ENDNOTE

1. Murray Rothbard, "The Great Ecology Issue," *The Individualist*, 2, no. 2 (February 1970): p. 5.

2

From Liberty to Welfare

JAMES P. STERBA

James P. Sterba argues that when a libertarian ideal of liberty is interpreted in the manner favored by libertarians as the absence of interference by other people, it leads to a right to welfare. He considers a number of objections to this argument and finds them all wanting.

Libertarians like to think of themselves as defenders of liberty. F.A. Hayek, for example, sees his work as restating an ideal of liberty for our times. "We are concerned," says Hayek, "with that condition of men in which coercion of some by others is reduced as much as possible in society."[1] Similarly, John Hospers believes that libertarianism is "a philosophy of personal liberty—the liberty of each person to live according to his own choices, provided that he does not attempt to coerce others and thus prevent them from living according to their choices."[2] And Robert Nozick claims that, if a conception of justice goes beyond libertarian "side-constraints," it cannot avoid the prospect of continually interfering with people's lives.

So let us begin by interpreting the ideal of liberty as a negative ideal in the manner favored by libertarians. So understood, liberty is the absence of interference by other people from doing what one wants or is able to do. Libertarians go on to characterize their political ideal as requiring that each person should have the greatest amount of liberty morally commensurate with the greatest amount of liberty for everyone else.[3] Interpreting their ideal in this way, libertarians claim to derive a number of more specific requirements, in particular, a right to life; a right to freedom of speech, press, and assembly; and a right to property.

Here it is important to observe that the libertarian's right to life is not a right to receive from others the goods and resources necessary for preserving one's life; it is simply a right not to have one's life interfered with or ended unjustly. Correspondingly, the libertarian's right to property is not a right to receive from others the goods and resources necessary for one's welfare, but rather typically a right not to be interfered with in regard to any goods and resources that one has legitimately acquired either by initial acquisition or by voluntary agreement.[4]

Of course, libertarians allow that it would be nice of the rich to share their surplus resources with the poor. Nevertheless, they deny that government has a duty to provide for such needs. Some good things, such as providing welfare to the poor, are requirements of charity rather than justice, libertarians claim. Accordingly, failure to make such provisions is neither blameworthy nor punishable. As a consequence, such acts of charity should not be coercively required. For this reason, libertarians are opposed to coercively supported welfare programs.

CONFLICTING LIBERTIES

Now in order to see why libertarians are mistaken about what their ideal requires, consider a conflict situation between the rich and the poor. In this conflict situation, the rich, of course, have more than enough resources to satisfy their basic needs.[5] In contrast, imagine that the poor lack the resources to meet their most basic needs even though they have tried all the means available to them that libertarians regard as legitimate for acquiring such resources. Under circumstances like these, libertarians maintain that the rich should have the liberty to use their resources to satisfy their luxury needs if they so wish. Libertarians recognize that this liberty might well be enjoyed at the expense of the satisfaction of the most basic needs of the poor; they just think that liberty always has priority over other political ideals, and since they assume that the liberty of the poor is not at stake in such conflict situations, it is easy for them to conclude that the rich should not be required to sacrifice their liberty so that the basic needs of the poor may be met.

Of course, libertarians allow that it would be nice of the rich to share their surplus resources with the poor. Nevertheless, according to libertarians, such acts of charity are not required because the liberty of the poor is not thought to be at stake in such conflict situations.

In fact, however, the liberty of the poor is at stake in such conflict situations. What is at stake is the liberty of the poor not to be interfered with in taking from the surplus possessions of the rich what is necessary to satisfy their basic needs.

Needless to say, libertarians want to deny that the poor have this liberty. But how can they justify such a denial? As this liberty of the poor has been specified, it is not a positive liberty to receive something but a negative liberty of noninterference. Clearly, what libertarians must do is recognize the existence of such a liberty and then claim that it unjustifiably conflicts with other liberties of the rich. But when libertarians see that this is the case, they are often genuinely surprised for they had not previously seen the conflict between the rich and the poor as a conflict of liberties. In responding to my work in recent years, libertarians Tibor Machan, Eric Mack, and Jan Narveson, among others, have come to grudgingly recognize that this liberty of the poor, as I have specified it, is indeed a negative liberty, but then they want to go on to argue that this liberty is illegitimate, or, at least, as Machan sees it, practically illegitimate.[6]

Now when the conflict between the rich and the poor is viewed as a conflict of liberties, we can either say that the rich should have the liberty not to be interfered with in using their surplus resources for luxury purposes, or we can say that the poor should have the liberty not to be interfered with in taking from the rich what they require to meet their basic needs. If we choose one liberty, we must reject the other. What needs to be determined, therefore, is which liberty is morally enforceable: the liberty of the rich or the liberty of the poor.[7]

THE "OUGHT" IMPLIES "CAN" PRINCIPLE

I submit that the liberty of the poor, which is the liberty not to be interfered with in taking from the surplus resources of others what is required to meet one's basic needs, is morally enforceable over the liberty of the rich, which is the liberty not to be interfered with in using one's surplus resources for luxury purposes. To see that this is the case, we need only appeal to one of the most fundamental principles of morality, one that is common to all moral and political perspectives, namely, the "ought" implies "can" principle. According to this principle, people are not morally required to do what they lack the power to do or what would involve so great a sacrifice or restriction that it is unreasonable to ask them, or in cases of severe conflict of interest, unreasonable to require them to abide by.

For example, suppose I promised to attend a departmental meeting on Friday, but on Thursday I am involved in a serious car accident that puts me into a coma. Surely it is no longer the case that I ought to attend the meeting, now that I lack the power to do so. Or suppose instead that on Thursday I develop a severe case of pneumonia for which I am hospitalized. Surely I can legitimately claim that I cannot attend the meeting on the grounds that the risk to my health involved in attending is a sacrifice it is unreasonable to ask me to bear. Or suppose instead the risk to my health from having pneumonia is not so serious, and it is reasonable to ask me to attend the meeting (a supererogatory request). However, it might still be serious enough to be unreasonable to require my attendance at the meeting (a demand that is backed up by blame and coercion).

This "ought" implies "can" principle claims that reason and morality must be linked in an appropriate way, especially if we are going to be able to justifiably use blame or coercion to get people to abide by the requirements of morality. It should be noted, however, that although major figures in the history of philosophy, and most philosophers today, including virtually all libertarian philosophers, accept this linkage between reason and morality, this linkage is not usually conceived to be part of the "ought" implies "can" principle. Nevertheless, I claim that there are good reasons for associating this linkage with the principle, namely, our use of the word "can" as in the example just given, and the natural progression from logical, physical, and psychological possibility found in the traditional "ought" implies "can" principle to the notion of moral possibility found in my formulation of the principle. In any case, the acceptability of my formulation of the "ought" implies "can" principle is determined by the virtually universal, and arguably necessary, acceptance of its components and not by the manner in which I have proposed to join those components together.

Now applying the "ought" implies "can" principle to the case at hand, it seems clear that the poor have it within their power to relinquish such an important liberty as the liberty not to be interfered with in taking from the rich what they require to meet their basic needs. They could do this. Nevertheless, it is unreasonable in this context to require them to accept so great a restriction. In the extreme case, it involves requiring the poor to sit back and starve to death. Of course, the poor may have no real alternative to relinquishing this liberty. To do anything else may involve worse consequences for themselves and their loved ones and may invite a painful death. Accordingly, we may expect that the poor would acquiesce, albeit unwillingly, to a political system that denied them the right to welfare supported by such a liberty, at the same time we recognize that such a system has imposed an unreasonable restriction upon the poor—a restriction that we could not morally blame the poor for trying to evade. Analogously, we might expect that a woman

whose life is threatened would submit to a rapist's demands, at the same time that we recognize the utter unreasonableness of those demands. By contrast, it is not unreasonable to require the rich in this context to sacrifice the liberty to meet some of their luxury needs so that the poor can have the liberty to meet their basic needs. Naturally, we might expect that the rich, for reasons of self-interest or past contribution, might be disinclined to make such a sacrifice. We might even suppose that the past contribution of the rich provides a good reason for not sacrificing their liberty to use their surplus for luxury purposes. Yet, the rich cannot claim that relinquishing such a liberty involves so great a sacrifice that it is unreasonable to require them to make it; unlike the poor, the rich are morally blameworthy and subject to coercion for failing to make such a sacrifice.

Consequently, if we assume that however else we specify the requirements of morality, they cannot violate the "ought" implies "can" principle, it follows that, despite what libertarians claim, the right to liberty endorsed by them actually favors the liberty of the poor over the liberty of the rich.

This means that within the bundle of liberties allotted to each person by the basic principle of libertarianism, there must be the liberty not to be interfered with (when one is poor) in taking from the surplus possessions of the rich what is necessary to satisfy one's basic needs. This must be part of the bundle that constitutes the greatest amount of liberty for each person because this liberty is morally superior to the liberty with which it directly conflicts, that is, the liberty not to be interfered with (when one is rich) in using one's surplus possessions to satisfy one's luxury needs. In this context, the "ought" implies "can" principle establishes the moral superiority and enforceability of the liberty of the poor over the liberty of the rich.[8]

Yet couldn't libertarians object to this conclusion, claiming that it would be unreasonable to require the rich to sacrifice the liberty to meet some of their luxury needs so that the poor can have the liberty to meet their basic needs? As I have pointed out, libertarians don't usually see the situation as a conflict of liberties, but suppose they did. How plausible would such an objection be? Not very plausible at all, I think.

For consider: what are libertarians going to say about the poor? Isn't it clearly unreasonable to require the poor to restrict their liberty to meet their basic needs so that the rich can have the liberty to meet their luxury needs? Isn't it clearly unreasonable to coercively require the poor to sit back and starve to death? If it is, then, there is no resolution of this conflict that is reasonable to coercively require both the rich and the poor to accept. But that would mean that libertarians could not be putting forth a moral resolution because a moral resolution, according to the "ought" implies "can" principle, resolves severe conflicts of interest in ways that it is reasonable to require everyone affected to accept, where it is further understood that a moral resolution can sometimes require us to act in accord with altruistic reasons. Therefore, as long as libertarians think of themselves as putting forth a moral resolution, they cannot allow that it is unreasonable in cases of severe conflict of interest both to require the rich to restrict their liberty to meet some of their luxury needs in order to benefit the poor and to require the poor to restrict their liberty to meet their basic needs in order to benefit the rich. But I submit that if one of these requirements is to be judged reasonable, then, by any neutral assessment, it must be the requirement that the rich restrict their liberty to meet some of their luxury needs so that the poor can have the liberty to meet their basic needs; there is no other plausible resolution, if libertarians intend to put forth a moral resolution.[9]

It should also be noted that this case for restricting the liberty of the rich depends upon the willingness of the poor to take advantage of whatever opportunities are available to them to engage in mutually beneficial work, so that failure of the poor to take advantage of such opportunities would normally cancel the obligation of the rich to restrict their own liberty for the benefit of the poor.[10] In addition, the poor would be required to give back the equivalent of any surplus possessions they have taken from the rich once they are able to do so and still satisfy their basic needs.[11] Nor would the poor be required to keep the liberty to which they are entitled. They could give up part of it, or all of it, provided that they discharge their obligations to themselves and others. Consequently, the case for restricting the liberty of the rich for the benefit of the poor is neither unconditional nor inalienable.[12]

It is sometimes thought that there is a different interpretation of libertarianism where rights, not liberties, are fundamental and where another argument is needed to establish the conclusion I have just established here. Under this presumptively different interpretation, the rights taken as fundamental are a strong right to property and a weak right to life. Yet given that for libertarians such rights are also rights of noninterference, that is, (negative) liberty rights, the question arises of why we should accept these particular rights of noninterference (liberties) and not others—which is just the question that arises when we consider the conflicting liberties to which an ideal of liberty gives rise. What this shows is that the "rights" interpretation of libertarianism is not really distinct from the "liberty" interpretation we have just been discussing,

In brief, I have argued that a libertarian ideal of liberty can be seen to support a right to welfare by applying the "ought" implies "can" principle to conflicts between the rich and the poor. Here the principle supports such rights by favoring the liberty of the poor over the liberty of the rich. Clearly, what is crucial to the derivation of these rights is the claim that it is unreasonable to coercively require the poor to deny their basic needs and accept anything less than these rights as the condition for their willing cooperation.

ENDNOTES

1. F.A. Hayek, *The Constitution of Liberty* (Chicago: University of Chicago Press, 1960), p. 11.

2. John Hospers, *Libertarianism* (Los Angeles: Nash Publishing: 1971).

3. See John Hospers, *Libertarianism* (Los Angeles: Nash, 1971), chapter 7, and Tibor Machan, *Human Rights and Human Liberties* (Chicago: Nelson-Hall, 1975), 231ff. We should think about the libertarian ideal of

liberty as securing for each person the largest morally defensible bundle of liberties possible.

4. Property can also be legitimately acquired on the libertarian view by producing it out of what one already owns or legitimately possesses.

5. Basic needs, if not satisfied, lead to significant lacks or deficiencies with respect to a standard of mental and physical well-being. Thus, a person's needs for food, shelter, medical care, protection, companionship, and self-development are, at least in part, needs of this sort. For a discussion of basic needs, see my *How to Make People Just*, pp. 45–48.

6. Machan, *Libertarianism Defended* (Burlington, VT: Ashgate, 2006), Chapter 20; Eric Mack, "Libertarianism Untamed," *Journal of Social Philosophy* (1991), pp. 64–72; Jan Narveson, "Comments on Sterba's *Ethics* Article," unpublished circulated paper (1994) and Narveson's *Libertarian Idea* (Peterborough, ON: Broadview Press: 2001), p. 35.

7. Libertarians have never rejected the need for enforcement when important liberties are at stake.

8. Here again we should think about the libertarian ideal of liberty as securing for each person the largest morally defensible bundle of liberties possible.

9. By the liberty of the rich to meet their luxury needs, I continue to mean the liberty of the rich not to be interfered with when using their surplus possessions for luxury purposes. Similarly, by the liberty of the poor to meet their basic needs, I continue to mean the liberty of the poor not to be interfered with

when taking what they require to meet their basic needs from the surplus possessions of the rich.

10. The employment opportunities offered to the poor must be honorable and supportive of self-respect. To do otherwise would be to offer the poor the opportunity to meet some of their basic needs at the cost of denying some of their other basic needs.

11. What these "former" poor give back, however, will not likely go to the rich but to others who are still poor.

12. Of course, there will be cases in which the poor fail to satisfy their basic needs, not because of any direct restriction of liberty on the part of the rich, but because the poor are in such dire need that they are unable even to attempt to take from the rich what they require to meet their basic needs. In such cases, the rich would not be performing any act of commission that would prevent the poor from taking what they require. Yet, even in such cases, the rich would normally be performing acts of commission that would prevent other persons from taking part of the rich's own surplus possessions and using it to aid the poor. And when assessed from a moral point of view, restricting the liberty of these allies or agents of the poor would not be morally justified for the very same reason that restricting the liberty of the poor to meet their own basic needs would not be morally justified: It would not be reasonable to require all of those affected to accept such a restriction of liberty.

3

A Social Contract Perspective

JOHN RAWLS

John Rawls believes that principles of justice are those on which free and rational persons would agree if they were in an original position of equality. This original position is characterized as a hypothetical position in which persons are behind an imaginary veil of ignorance with respect to most particular facts about themselves. Rawls claims that persons in this original position would choose principles requiring equal political liberty and opportunity and the highest possible economic minimum because they would be committed to the maximum rule, which requires maximizing the minimum payoff.

My aim is to present a conception of justice which generalizes and carries to a higher level of abstraction the familiar theory of the social contract as found, say, in Locke, Rousseau, and Kant.[1] In order to do this we are not to think of the original contract as one to enter a particular society or to set up a particular form of government. Rather, the guiding idea is that the principles of justice for the basic structure of society are the object of the original agreement. They are the principles that free and rational persons concerned to further their own interests would accept in an initial position of equality as defining the fundamental terms of their association. These principles are to regulate all further agreements; they specify the kinds of social cooperation that can be entered into and the forms of government that can be established. This way of regarding the principles of justice I shall call justice as fairness.

Thus we are to imagine that those who engage in social cooperation choose together, in one joint act, the principles which are to assign basic rights and duties and to determine the division of social benefits. Men are to decide in advance how they are to regulate their claims against one another and what is to be the foundation charter of their society. Just as each person must decide by rational reflection what constitutes his good—that is, the system of ends which it is rational for him to pursue—so a group of persons must decide once and for all what is to count among them as just and unjust. The choice which rational men would make in this hypothetical situation of equal liberty, assuming for the present that this choice problem has a solution, determines the principles of justice.

In justice as fairness the original position of equality corresponds to the state of nature in the traditional theory of the social contract. This original position is not, of course, thought of as an actual historical state of affairs, much less as a primitive condition of culture. It is understood as a purely hypothetical situation characterized so as to lead to a certain conception of justice.[2] Among the essential features of this situation is that no one knows his place in society, his class position or social status, nor does any one know his fortune in the distribution of natural assets and abilities, his intelligence, strength, and the like. I shall even assume that the parties do not know their conceptions of the good or their special psychological propensities. The principles of justice are chosen behind a veil of ignorance. This ensures that no one is advantaged or disadvantaged in the choice of principles by the outcome of natural chance or the contingency of social circumstances. Since all are similarly situated and no one is able to design principles to favor his particular condition, the principles of justice are the result of a fair agreement or bargain. For given the circumstances of the original position, the symmetry of everyone's relations to each other, this initial situation is fair between individuals as moral persons; that is, as rational beings with their own ends and capable, I shall assume, of a sense of justice. The original position is, one might say, the appropriate initial status quo, and thus the fundamental agreements reached in it are fair. This explains the propriety of the name "justice as fairness"; it conveys the idea that the principles of justice are agreed to in an initial situation that is fair. The name does not mean that the concepts of justice and fairness are the same, any more than the phrase "poetry as metaphor" means that the concepts of poetry and metaphor are the same.

Justice as fairness begins, as I have said, with one of the most general of all choices which persons might make together, namely, with the choice of the first principles of a conception of justice which is to regulate all subsequent criticism and reform of institutions. Then, having chosen a conception of justice, we can suppose that they are to choose a constitution and a legislature to enact laws, and so on, all in accordance with the principles of justice initially agreed upon. Our social situation is just if it is such that by this sequence of hypothetical agreements we would have contracted into the general system of rules which defines it. Moreover, assuming that the original position does determine a set of principles (that is, that a particular conception of justice would be chosen), it will then be true that whenever social institutions satisfy these principles those engaged in them can say to one another that they are cooperating on terms to which they would agree if they were free and equal persons whose relations with respect to one another were fair. They could all view their arrangements as meeting

the stipulations which they would acknowledge in an initial situation that embodies widely accepted and reasonable constraints on the choice of principles. The general recognition of this fact would provide the basis for a public acceptance of the corresponding principles of justice. No society can, of course, be a scheme of cooperation which men enter voluntarily in a literal sense; each person finds himself placed at birth in some particular position in some particular society, and the nature of this position materially affects his life prospects. Yet a society satisfying the principles of justice as fairness comes as close as a society can to being a voluntary scheme, for it meets the principles which free and equal persons would assent to under circumstances that are fair. In this sense its members are autonomous and the obligations they recognize self-imposed.

One feature of justice as fairness is to think of the parties in the initial situation as rational and mutually disinterested. This does not mean that the parties are egoists; that is, individuals with only certain kinds of interests, say in wealth, prestige, and domination. But they are conceived as not taking an interest in one another's interests. They are to presume that even their spiritual aims may be opposed, in the way that the aims of those of different religions may be opposed. Moreover, the concept of rationality must be interpreted as far as possible in the narrow sense, standard in economic theory, of taking the most effective means to given ends. I shall modify this concept to some extent ..., but one must try to avoid introducing into it any controversial ethical elements. The initial situation must be characterized by stipulations that are widely accepted.

In working out the conception of justice as fairness one main task clearly is to determine which principles of justice would be chosen in the original position. To do this we must describe this situation in some detail and formulate with care the problem of choice which it presents. It may be observed, however, that once the principles of justice are thought of as arising from an original agreement in a situation of equality, it is an open question whether the principle of utility would be acknowledged. Offhand it hardly seems likely that persons who view themselves as equals, entitled to press their claims upon one another, would agree to a principle which may require lesser life prospects for some simply for the sake of a greater sum of advantages enjoyed by others. Since each desires to protect his interests, his capacity to advance his conception of the good, no one has a reason to acquiesce in an enduring loss for himself in order to bring about a greater net balance of satisfaction. In the absence of strong and lasting benevolent impulses, a rational man would not accept a basic structure merely because it maximized the algebraic sum of advantages irrespective of its permanent effects on his own basic rights and interests. Thus it seems that the principle of utility is incompatible with the conception of social cooperation among equals for mutual advantage. It appears to be inconsistent with the idea of reciprocity implicit in the notion of a well-ordered society. Or, at any rate, so I shall argue.

I shall maintain instead that the persons in the initial situation would choose two rather different principles: The first requires equality in the assignment of basic rights and duties, while the second holds that social and economic inequalities, for example, inequalities of wealth and authority, are just only if they result in compensating benefits for everyone, and in particular for the least advantaged members of society. These principles rule out justifying institutions on the grounds that the hardships of some are offset by a greater good in the aggregate. It may be expedient but it is not just that some should have less in order that others may prosper. But there is no injustice in the greater benefits earned by a few provided that the situation of persons not so fortunate is thereby improved. The intuitive idea is that since everyone's well-being depends upon a scheme of cooperation without which no one could have a satisfactory life, the division of advantages should be such as to draw forth the willing cooperation of everyone taking part in it, including those less well situated. Yet this can be expected only if reasonable terms are proposed. The two principles mentioned seem to be a fair agreement on the basis of which those better endowed, or more fortunate in their social position, neither of which we can be said to deserve, could

expect the willing cooperation of others when some workable scheme is a necessary condition of the welfare of all.[3] Once we decide to look for a conception of justice that nullifies the accidents of natural endowment and the contingencies of social circumstance as counters in quest for political and economic advantage, we are led to these principles. They express the result of leaving aside those aspects of the social world that seem arbitrary from a moral point of view.

The problem of the choice of principles, however, is extremely difficult. I do not expect the answer I shall suggest to be convincing to everyone. It is, therefore, worth noting from the outset that justice as fairness, like other contract views, consists of two parts: (1) an interpretation of the initial situation and of the problem of choice posed there, and (2) a set of principles which, it is argued, would be agreed to. One may accept the first part of the theory (or some variant thereof), but not the other, and conversely. The concept of the initial contractual situation may seem reasonable although the particular principles proposed are rejected. To be sure, I want to maintain that the most appropriate conception of this situation does lead to principles of justice contrary to utilitarianism and perfectionism, and therefore that the contract doctrine provides an alternative to these views. Still, one may dispute this contention even though one grants that the contractarian method is a useful way of studying ethical theories and of setting forth their underlying assumptions.

Justice as fairness is an example of what I have called a contract theory. Now there may be an objection to the term *contract* and related expressions, but I think it will serve reasonably well. Many words have misleading connotations which at first are likely to confuse. The terms *utility* and *utilitarianism* are surely no exception. They too have unfortunate suggestions which hostile critics have been willing to exploit; yet they are clear enough for those prepared to study utilitarian doctrine. The same should be true of the term *contract* applied to moral theories. As I have mentioned, to understand it one has to keep in mind that it implies a certain level of abstraction. In particular, the content of the relevant agreement is not to enter a given society or to adopt a given form of government, but to accept certain moral principles. Moreover, the undertakings referred to are purely hypothetical: A contract view holds that certain principles would be accepted in a well-defined initial situation.

The merit of the contract terminology is that it conveys the idea that principles of justice may be conceived as principles that would be chosen by rational persons, and that in this way conceptions of justice may be explained and justified. The theory of justice is a part, perhaps the most significant part, of the theory of rational choice. Furthermore, principles of justice deal with conflicting claims upon the advantages won by social cooperation; they apply to the relations among several persons or groups. The word *contract* suggests this plurality as well as the condition that the appropriate division of advantages must be in accordance with principles acceptable to all parties. The condition of publicity for principles of justice is also connoted by the contract phraseology. Thus, if these principles are the outcome of an agreement, citizens have a knowledge of the principles that others follow. It is characteristic of contract theories to stress the public nature of political principles. Finally there is the long tradition of the contract doctrine. Expressing the tie with this line of thought helps to define ideas and accords with natural piety. There are then several advantages in the use of the term *contract*. With due precautions taken, it should not be misleading.

A final remark. Justice as fairness is not a complete contract theory. For it is clear that the contractarian idea can be extended to the choice of more or less an entire ethical system; that is, to a system including principles for all the virtues and not only for justice. Now for the most part I shall consider only principles of justice and others closely related to them; I make no attempt to discuss the virtues in a systematic way. Obviously if justice as fairness succeeds reasonably well, a next step would be to study the more general view suggested by the name "rightness as fairness." But even this wider theory fails to embrace all moral relationships, since it would seem to include only our relations with other persons and to leave out of account how we are to conduct ourselves toward animals and the rest of nature. I do not contend that the contract notion offers a way to approach these questions, which are certainly of the first importance; and I shall have to put them aside. We must recognize the limited scope of justice as fairness and of the general type of view that it exemplifies. How far its conclusions must be revised once these other matters are understood cannot be decided in advance.

THE ORIGINAL POSITION AND JUSTIFICATION

I have said that the original position is the appropriate initial status quo which insures that the fundamental agreements reached in it are fair. This fact yields the name "justice as fairness." It is clear, then, that I want to say that one conception of justice is more reasonable than another, or justifiable with respect to it, if rational persons in the initial situation would choose its principles over those of the other for the role of justice. Conceptions of justice are to be ranked by their acceptability to persons so circumstanced. Understood in this way the question of justification is settled by working out a problem of deliberation: We have to ascertain which principles it would be rational to adopt given the contractual situation. This connects the theory of justice with the theory of rational choice.

If this view of the problem of justification is to succeed, we must, of course, describe in some detail the nature of this choice problem. A problem of rational decision has a definite answer only if we know the beliefs and interests of the parties, their relations with respect to one another, the alternatives between which they are to choose, the procedure whereby they make up their minds, and so on. As the circumstances are presented in different ways, correspondingly different principles are accepted. The concept of the original position, as I shall refer to it, is that of the most philosophically favored interpretation of this initial choice situation for the purposes of a theory of justice.

But how are we to decide what is the most favored interpretation? I assume, for one thing, that there is a broad measure of agreement that principles of justice should be chosen under certain conditions. To justify a particular description of the initial situation one shows that it incorporates these commonly shared presumptions. One argues from widely accepted but weak premises to more specific conclusions. Each of the presumptions should by itself be natural and plausible; some of them may seem innocuous or even trivial. The aim of the contract approach is to establish that taken together they impose significant bounds on acceptable principles of justice. The ideal outcome would be that these conditions determine a unique set of principles; but I shall be satisfied if they suffice to rank the main traditional conceptions of social justice.

One should not be misled, then, by the somewhat unusual conditions which characterize the original position. The idea here is simply to make vivid to ourselves the restrictions that it seems reasonable to impose on arguments for principles of justice, and therefore on these principles themselves. Thus it seems reasonable and generally acceptable that no one should be advantaged or disadvantaged by natural fortune or social circumstances in the choice of principles. It also seems widely agreed that it should be impossible to tailor principles to the circumstances of one's own case. We should ensure further that particular inclinations and aspirations, and persons' conceptions of their good, do not affect the principles adopted. The aim is to rule out those principles that it would be rational to propose for acceptance, however little the chance of success, only if one knew certain things that are irrelevant from the standpoint of justice. For example, if a man knew that he was wealthy, he might find it rational to advance the principle that various taxes for welfare measures be counted unjust; if he knew that he was poor, he would most likely propose the contrary principle. To represent the desired restrictions one imagines a situation in which everyone is deprived of this sort of information. One excludes the knowledge of those contingencies which sets men at odds and allows them to be guided by their prejudices. In this manner the veil of ignorance is arrived at in a natural way. This concept should cause no difficulty if we keep in mind the constraints on arguments that it is meant to express. At any time we can enter the original position, so to speak, simply by following a certain procedure; namely, by arguing for principles of justice in accordance with these restrictions.

It seems reasonable to suppose that the parties in the original position are equal. That is, all have the same rights in the procedure for choosing principles; each can make proposals, submit reasons for their acceptance, and so on. Obviously the purpose of these conditions is to represent equality between human beings as moral persons, as creatures having a conception of their good and capable of a sense of justice. The basis of equality is taken to be similarity in these two respects. Systems of ends are not ranked in value; and each man is presumed to have the requisite ability to understand and to act upon whatever principles are adopted. Together with the veil of ignorance, these conditions define the principles of justice as those which rational persons concerned to advance their interests would consent to as equals when none are known to be advantaged or disadvantaged by social and natural contingencies.

There is, however, another side to justifying a particular description of the original position. This is to see if the principles which would be chosen match our considered convictions of justice or extend them in an acceptable way. We can note whether applying these principles would lead us to make the same judgments about the basic structure of society which we now make intuitively and in which we have the greatest confidence; or whether, in cases where our present judgments are in doubt and given with hesitation, these principles offer a resolution which we can affirm on reflection. There are questions which we feel sure must be answered in a certain way. For example, we are confident that religious intolerance and racial discrimination are unjust. We think that we have examined these things with care and have reached what we believe is an impartial judgment not likely to be distorted by an excessive attention to our own interests. These convictions are provisional fixed points which we presume any conception of justice must fit. But we have much less assurance as to what is the correct distribution of wealth and authority. Here we may be looking for a way to remove our doubts. We can check an interpretation of the initial situation, then, by the capacity of its principles to accommodate our firmest convictions and to provide guidance where guidance is needed.

In searching for the most favored description of this situation we work from both ends. We begin by describing it so that it represents generally shared and preferably weak conditions. We then see if these conditions are strong enough to yield a significant set of principles. If not, we look for further premises equally reasonable. But if so, and these principles match our considered convictions of justice, then so far well and good. But presumably there will be discrepancies. In this case we have a choice. We can either modify the account of the initial situation or we can revise our existing judgments, for even the judgments we take provisionally as fixed points are liable to revision. By going back and forth, sometimes altering the conditions of the contractual circumstances, at others withdrawing our judgments and conforming them to principle, I assume that eventually we shall find a description of the initial situation that both expresses reasonable conditions and yields principles which match our considered judgments duly pruned and adjusted. This state of affairs I refer to as reflective equilibrium.[4] It is an equilibrium because at last our principles and judgments coincide; and it is reflective since we know to what principles our judgments conform and the premises of their derivation. At the moment everything is in order. But this equilibrium is not necessarily stable. It is liable to be upset by further examination of the conditions which should be imposed on the contractual situation and by particular cases which may lead us to revise our judgments. Yet for the time being we have done what we can to render coherent and to justify our convictions of social justice. We have reached a conception of the original position.

I shall not, of course, actually work through this process. Still, we may think of the interpretation of the original position that I shall present as the result of such a hypothetical course of reflection. It represents the attempt to accommodate within one scheme both reasonable philosophical conditions on principles as well as our considered judgments of justice. In arriving at the favored interpretation

of the initial situation there is no point at which an appeal is made to self-evidence in the traditional sense either of general conceptions or particular convictions. I do not claim for the principles of justice proposed that they are necessary truths or derivable from such truths. A conception of justice cannot be deduced from self-evident premises or conditions on principles; instead, its justification is a matter of the mutual support of many considerations, of everything fitting together into one coherent view.

A final comment. We shall want to say that certain principles of justice are justified because they would be agreed to in an initial situation of equality. I have emphasized that this original position is purely hypothetical. It is natural to ask why, if this agreement is never actually entered into, we should take any interest in these principles—moral or otherwise. The answer is that the conditions embodied in the description of the original position are ones that we do in fact accept. Or if we do not, then perhaps we can be persuaded to do so by philosophical reflection. Each aspect of the contractual situation can be given supporting grounds. Thus what we shall do is to collect together into one conception a number of conditions on principles that we are ready upon due consideration to recognize as reasonable. These constraints express what we are prepared to regard as limits on fair terms of social cooperation. One way to look at the idea of the original position, therefore, is to see it as an expository device which sums up the meaning of these conditions and helps us to extract their consequences. On the other hand, this conception is also an intuitive notion that suggests its own elaboration, so that led on by it we are drawn to define more clearly the standpoint from which we can best interpret moral relationships. We need a conception that enables us to envision our objective from afar: The intuitive notion of the original position is to do this for us....

TWO PRINCIPLES OF JUSTICE

I shall now state in a provisional form the two principles of justice that I believe would be chosen in the original position. In this section I wish to make only the most general comments, and therefore the first formulation of these principles is tentative. As we go on I shall run through several formulations and approximate step by step the final statement to be given much later. I believe that doing this allows the exposition to proceed in a natural way.

The first statement of the two principles reads as follows:

> First: Each person is to have an equal right to the most extensive basic liberty compatible with a similar liberty for others.

> Second: Social and economic inequalities are to be arranged so that they are both (a) reasonably expected to be to everyone's advantage, and (b) attached to positions and offices open to all.

There are two ambiguous phrases in the second principle, namely "everyone's advantage" and "open to all." Determining their sense more exactly will lead to a second formulation of the principle....

By way of general comment, these principles primarily apply, as I have said, to the basic structure of society. They are to govern the assignment of rights and duties and to regulate the distribution of social and economic advantages. As their formulation suggests, these principles presuppose that the social structure can be divided into two more or less distinct parts, the first principle applying to the one, the second to the other. They distinguish between those aspects of the social system that define and secure the equal liberties of citizenship and those that specify and establish social and economic inequalities. The basic liberties of citizens are, roughly speaking, political liberty (the right to vote and to be eligible for public office) together with freedom of speech and assembly; liberty of conscience and freedom of thought; freedom of the person along with the right to hold personal property; and freedom from arbitrary arrest and seizure as defined by the concept of the rule of law. These liberties are all required to be equal by the first principle, since citizens of a just society are to have the same basic rights.

The second principle applies, in the first approximation, to the distribution of income and wealth and to the design of organizations that make use of differences in authority and responsibility, or chains of command. While the distribution of wealth and income need not be equal, it must be to everyone's advantage, and at the same time, positions of authority and offices of command must be accessible to all. One applies the second principle by holding positions open, and then, subject to this constraint, arranges social and economic inequalities so that everyone benefits.

These principles are to be arranged in a serial order with the first principle prior to the second. This ordering means that a departure from the institutions of equal liberty required by the first principle cannot be justified by, or compensated for, by greater social and economic advantages. The distribution of wealth and income, and the hierarchies of authority, must be consistent with both the liberties of equal citizenship and equality of opportunity.

It is clear that these principles are rather specific in their content, and their acceptance rests on certain assumptions that I must eventually try to explain and justify. A theory of justice depends upon a theory of society in ways that will become evident as we proceed. For the present, it should be observed that the two principles (and this holds for all formulations) are a special case of a more general conception of justice that can be expressed as follows:

> All social values—liberty and opportunity, income and wealth, and the bases of self-respect—are to be distributed equally unless an unequal distribution of any, or all, of these values is to everyone's advantage.

Injustice, then, is simply inequalities that are not to the benefit of all. Of course, this conception is extremely vague and requires interpretation.

As a first step, suppose that the basic structure of society distributes certain primary goods, that is, things that every rational man is presumed to want. These goods normally have a use whatever a person's rational plan of life. For simplicity, assume that the chief primary goods at the disposition of society are rights and liberties, powers and opportunities, income and wealth. (Later on ... the primary good of self-respect has a central place.) These are the social primary goods. Other primary goods such as health and vigor, intelligence and imagination, are natural goods; although their possession is influenced by the basic structure, they are not so directly under its control. Imagine, then, a hypothetical initial arrangement in which all the social primary goods are equally distributed: Everyone has similar rights and duties, and income and wealth are evenly shared. This state of affairs provides a benchmark for judging improvements. If certain inequalities of wealth and organizational powers would make everyone better off than in this hypothetical starting situation, then they accord with the general conception.

Now it is possible, at least theoretically, that by giving up some of their fundamental liberties men are sufficiently compensated by the resulting social and economic gains. The general conception of justice imposes no restrictions on what sort of inequalities are permissible; it only requires that everyone's position be improved. We need not suppose anything so drastic as consenting to a condition of slavery. Imagine instead that men forgo certain political rights when the economic returns are significant and their capacity to influence the course of policy by the exercise of these rights would be marginal in any case. It is this kind of exchange which the two principles as stated rule out; being arranged in serial order they do not permit exchanges between basic liberties and economic and social gains. The serial ordering of principles expresses an underlying preference among primary social goods. When this preference is rational so likewise is the choice of these principles in this order.

In developing justice as fairness I shall, for the most part, leave aside the general conception of justice and examine instead the special case of the two principles in serial order. The advantage of this procedure is that from the first the matter of priorities is recognized and an effort made to find principles to deal with it. One is led to attend throughout to the conditions under which the acknowledgment of the absolute weight of liberty with respect to social and economic advantages, as defined by the lexical order of the two principles, would be reasonable. Offhand, this ranking appears extreme and too special a case to be of much interest; but there is more justification for it than would appear at first sight. Or at any rate,

so I shall maintain…. Furthermore, the distinction between fundamental rights and liberties and economic and social benefits marks a difference among primary social goods that one should try to exploit. It suggests an important division in the social system. Of course, the distinctions drawn and the ordering proposed are bound to be at best only approximations. There are surely circumstances in which they fail. But it is essential to depict clearly the main lines of a reasonable conception of justice; and under many conditions, anyway, the two principles in serial order may serve well enough. When necessary we can fall back on the more general conception.

The fact that the two principles apply to institutions has certain consequences. Several points illustrate this. First of all, the rights and liberties referred to by these principles are those that are defined by the public rules of the basic structure. Whether men are free is determined by the rights and duties established by the major institutions of society. Liberty is a certain pattern of social forms. The first principle simply requires that certain sorts of rules, those defining basic liberties, apply to everyone equally and that they allow the most extensive liberty compatible with a like liberty for all. The only reason for circumscribing the rights defining liberty and making men's freedom less extensive than it might otherwise be is that these equal rights as institutionally defined would interfere with one another.

Another thing to bear in mind is that when principles mention persons, or require that everyone gain from an inequality, the reference is to representative persons holding the various social positions, or offices, or whatever, established by the basic structure. Thus in applying the second principle I assume that it is possible to assign an expectation of well-being to representative individuals holding these positions. This expectation indicates their life prospects as viewed from their social station. In general, the expectations of representative persons depend upon the distribution of rights and duties throughout the basic structure. When this changes, expectations change. I assume, then, that expectations are connected: By raising the prospects of the representative man in one position we presumably increase or decrease the prospects of representative men in other positions. Since it applies to institutional forms, the second principle (or rather the first part of it) refers to the expectations of representative individuals. As I shall discuss below, neither principle applies to distributions of particular goods to particular individuals who may be identified by their proper names. The situation where someone is considering how to allocate certain commodities to needy persons who are known to him is not within the scope of the principles. They are meant to regulate basic institutional arrangements. We must not assume that there is much similarity from the standpoint of justice between an administrative allotment of goods to specific persons and the appropriate design of society. Our common sense intuitions for the former may be a poor guide to the latter.

Now the second principle insists that each person benefit from permissible inequalities in the basic structure. This means that it must be reasonable for each relevant representative man defined by this structure, when he views it as a going concern, to prefer his prospects with the inequality, to his prospects without it. One is not allowed to justify differences in income or organizational powers on the ground that the disadvantages of those in one position are outweighed by the greater advantages of those in another. Much less can infringements of liberty be counterbalanced in this way. Applied to the basic structure, the principle of utility would have us maximize the sum of expectations of representative men (weighted by the number of persons they represent, on the classical view); and this would permit us to compensate for the losses of some by the gains of others. Instead, the two principles require that everyone benefit from economic and social inequalities.

THE REASONING LEADING
TO THE TWO PRINCIPLES
OF JUSTICE

It will be recalled that the general conception of justice as fairness requires that all primary social goods be distributed equally unless an unequal distribution would be to everyone's advantage. No restrictions are placed on exchanges of these goods and therefore a lesser liberty can be compensated for by greater social and economic benefits. Now looking at the situation from the standpoint of one person selected arbitrarily, there is no way for him to win special advantages for himself. Nor, on the other hand, are there grounds for his acquiescing in special disadvantages. Since it is not reasonable for him to expect more than an equal share in the division of social goods, and since it is not rational for him to agree to less, the sensible thing for him to do is to acknowledge as the first principle of justice one requiring an equal distribution. Indeed, this principle is so obvious that we would expect it to occur to anyone immediately.

Thus, the parties start with a principle establishing equal liberty for all, including equality of opportunity, as well as an equal distribution of income and wealth. But there is no reason why this acknowledgment should be final. If there are inequalities in the basic structure that work to make everyone better off in comparison with the benchmark of initial equality, why not permit them? The immediate gain which a greater equality might allow can be regarded as intelligently invested in view of its future return. If, for example, these inequalities set up various incentives which succeed in eliciting more productive efforts, a person in the original position may look upon them as necessary to cover the costs of training and to encourage effective performance. One might think that ideally individuals should want to serve one another. But since the parties are assumed not to take an interest in one another's interests, their acceptance of these inequalities is only the acceptance of the relations in which men stand in the circumstances of justice. They have no grounds for complaining of one another's motives. A person in the original position would, therefore, concede the justice of these inequalities. Indeed, it would be shortsighted of him not to do so. He would hesitate to agree to these regularities only if he would be dejected by the bare knowledge or perception that others were better situated; and I have assumed that the parties decide as if they are not moved by envy. In order to make the principle regulating inequalities determinate, one looks at the system from the standpoint of the least advantaged representative man. Inequalities are permissible when they maximize, or at least all contribute to, the long-term expectations of the least fortunate group in society.

Now this general conception imposes no constraints on what sorts of inequalities are allowed, whereas the special conception, by putting the two principles in serial order (with the necessary adjustments in meaning), forbids exchanges between basic liberties and economic and social benefits. I shall not try to justify this ordering here…. But roughly, the idea underlying this ordering is that if the parties assume that their basic liberties can be effectively exercised, they will not exchange a lesser liberty for an improvement in economic well-being. It is only when social conditions do not allow the effective establishment of these rights that one can concede their limitation; and these restrictions can be granted only to the extent that they are necessary to prepare the way for a free society. The denial of equal liberty can be defended only if it is necessary to raise the level of civilization so that in due course these freedoms can be enjoyed. Thus in adopting a serial order we are in effect making a special assumption in the original position, namely, that the parties know that the conditions of their society, whatever they are, admit the effective realization of the equal liberties. The serial ordering of the two principles of justice eventually comes to be reasonable if the general conception is consistently followed. This lexical ranking is the long-run tendency of the general view. For the most part I shall assume that the requisite circumstances for the serial order obtain.

It seems clear from these remarks that the two principles are at least a plausible conception of justice. The question, though, is how one is to argue for them more systematically. Now there are several things to do. One can work out their consequences for institutions and note their implications for fundamental social policy. In this way they are tested by a comparison with our considered judgments of justice…. But one can also try to find arguments in their favor that are decisive from the standpoint of the original position. In order to see how this might

be done, it is useful as a heuristic device to think of the two principles as the maximin solution to the problem of social justice. There is an analogy between the two principles and the maximin rule for choice under uncertainty.[5] This is evident from the fact that the two principles are those a person would choose for the design of a society in which his enemy is to assign him his place. The maximin rule tells us to rank alternatives by their worst possible outcomes: We are to adopt the alternative the worst outcome of which is superior to the worst outcomes of the others. The persons in the original position do not, of course, assume that their initial place in society is decided by a malevolent opponent. As I note below, they should not reason from false premises. The veil of ignorance does not violate this idea, since an absence of information is not misinformation. But that the two principles of justice would be chosen if the parties were forced to protect themselves against such a contingency explains the sense in which this conception is the maximin solution. And this analogy suggests that if the original position has been described so that it is rational for the parties to adopt the conservative attitude expressed by this rule, a conclusive argument can indeed be constructed for these principles. Clearly the maximin rule is not, in general, a suitable guide for choices under uncertainty. But it is attractive in situations marked by certain special features. My aim, then, is to show that a good case can be made for the two principles based on the fact that the original position manifests these features to the fullest possible degree, carrying them to the limit, so to speak.

Consider the gain-and-loss table in the next column. It represents the gains and losses for a situation which is not a game of strategy. There is no one playing against the person making the decision; instead he is faced with several possible circumstances which may or may not obtain. Which circumstances happen to exist does not depend upon what the person choosing decides or whether he announces his moves in advance. The numbers in the table are monetary values (in hundreds of dollars) in comparison with some initial situation. The gain (g) depends upon the individual's decision (d) and the circumstances (c). Thus $g = f(d,c)$.

Assuming that there are three possible decisions and three possible circumstances, we might have this gain-and-loss table.

Decisions	Circumstances		
	c_1	c_2	c_3
d_1	–7	8	12
d_2	–8	7	14
d_3	5	6	8

The maximin rule requires that we make the third decision. For in this case the worst that can happen is that one gains five hundred dollars, which is better than the worst for the other actions. If we adopt one of these we may lose either eight or seven hundred dollars. Thus, the choice of d_3 maximizes $f(d,c)$ for the value of c which for a given d, minimizes f. The term *maximin* means the maximum minimorum; and the rule directs our attention to the worst that can happen under any proposed course of action, and to decide in the light of that.

Now there appear to be three chief features of situations that give plausibility to this unusual rule.[6] First, since the rule takes no account for the likelihoods of the possible circumstances, there must be some reason for sharply discounting estimates of these probabilities. Offhand, the most natural rule of choice would seem to be to compute the expectation of monetary gain for each decision and then to adopt the course of action with the highest prospect. (This expectation is defined as follows: Let us suppose that g_{ij} represents the numbers in the gain-and-loss table, where i is the row index and j is the column index; and let $p_i, j = 1, 2, 3$, be the likelihoods of the circumstances, with $\Sigma pj = 1$. Then the expectation for the ith decision is equal to $\Sigma p_i g_{ij}$.) Thus it must be, for example, that the situation is one in which a knowledge of likelihoods is impossible, or at best extremely insecure. In this case it is unreasonable not to be skeptical of probabilistic calculations unless there is no other way out, particularly if the decision is a fundamental one that needs to be justified to others.

The second feature that suggests the maximin rule is the following: The person choosing has a conception of the good such that he cares very little, if anything, for what he might gain above the minimum stipend that he can, in fact, be sure of by following the maximin rule. It is not worthwhile for him to take a chance for the sake of a further advantage, especially when it may turn out that he loses much that is important to him. This last provision brings in the third feature; namely, that the rejected alternatives have outcomes that one can hardly accept. The situation involves grave risks. Of course these features work most effectively in combination. The paradigm situation for following the maximin rule is when all three features are realized to the highest degree. This rule does not, then, generally apply, nor of course is it self-evident. Rather, it is a maxim, a rule of thumb, that comes into its own in special circumstances. Its application depends upon the qualitative structure of the possible gains and losses in relation to one's conception of the good, all this against a background in which it is reasonable to discount conjectural estimates of likelihoods.

It should be noted, as the comments on the gain-and-loss table say, that the entries in the table represent monetary values and not utilities. This difference is significant since for one thing computing expectations on the basis of such objective values is not the same thing as computing expected utility and may lead to different results. The essential point, though, is that in justice as fairness the parties do not know their conception of the good and cannot estimate their utility in the ordinary sense. In any case, we want to go behind de facto preferences generated by given conditions. Therefore expectations are based upon an index of primary goods and the parties make their choice accordingly. The entries in the example are in terms of money and not utility to indicate this aspect of the contract doctrine.

Now, as I have suggested, the original position has been defined so that it is a situation in which the maximin rule applies. In order to see this, let us review briefly the nature of this situation with these three special features in mind. To begin with, the veil of ignorance excludes all but the vaguest knowledge of likelihoods. The parties have no basis for determining the probable nature of their society, or their place in it. Thus they have strong reasons for being wary of probability calculations if any other course is open to them. They must also take into account the fact that their choice of principles should seem reasonable to others, in particular their descendants, whose rights will be deeply affected by it. There are further grounds for discounting that I shall mention as we go along. For the present it suffices to note that these considerations are strengthened by the fact that the parties know very little about the gain-and-loss table. Not only are they unable to conjecture the likelihoods of the various possible circumstances, they cannot say much about what the possible circumstances are, much less enumerate them and foresee the outcome of each alternative available. Those deciding are much more in the dark than the illustration by a numerical table suggests. It is for this reason that I have spoken of an analogy with the maximin rule.

Several kinds of arguments for the two principles of justice illustrate the second feature. Thus, if we can maintain that these principles provide a workable theory of social justice, and that they are compatible with reasonable demands of efficiency, then this conception guarantees a satisfactory minimum. There may be, on reflection, little reason for trying to do better. Thus much of the argument … is to show, by their application to the main questions of social justice, that the two principles are a satisfactory conception. These details have a philosophical purpose. Moreover, this line of thought is practically decisive if we can establish the priority of liberty, the lexical ordering of the two principles. For this priority implies that the persons in the original position have no desire to try for greater gains at the expense of the equal liberties. The minimum assured by the two principles in lexical order is not one that the parties wish to jeopardize for the sake of greater economic and social advantages….

Finally, the third feature holds if we can assume that other conceptions of justice may lead to institutions that the parties would find intolerable. For example, it has sometimes been held that under some conditions the utility principle (in either form) justifies, if not slavery or serfdom, at any rate serious infractions of liberty for the sake of greater social benefits. We need not consider here the truth of this claim, or the likelihood that the requisite conditions obtain. For the moment, this contention is only to illustrate the way in which conceptions of justice may allow for outcomes which the parties may not be able to accept. And having the ready alternative of the two principles of justice which secure a satisfactory minimum, it seems unwise, if not irrational, for them to take a chance that these outcomes are not realized.

So much, then, for a brief sketch of the features of situations in which the maximin rule comes into its own and of the way in which the arguments for the two principles of justice can be subsumed under them.…

THE FINAL FORMULATION OF THE PRINCIPLES OF JUSTICE

… I now wish to give the final statement of the two principles of justice for institutions. For the sake of completeness, I shall give a full statement including earlier formulations.

First Principle
Each person is to have an equal right to the most extensive total system of equal basic liberties compatible with a similar system of liberty for all.

Second Principle
Social and economic inequalities are to be arranged so that they are both:
(a) to the greatest benefit of the least advantaged, consistent with the just savings principle, and
(b) attached to offices and positions open to all under conditions of fair equality of opportunity.

The First Priority Rule (The Priority of Liberty)
The principles of justice are to be ranked in lexical order and therefore liberty can be restricted only for the sake of liberty. There are two cases:
(a) a less extensive liberty must strengthen the total system of liberty shared by all;

(b) a less than equal liberty must be acceptable to those with the lesser liberty.

Second Priority Rule (The Priority of Justice over Efficiency and Welfare)

The second principle of justice is lexically prior to the principle of efficiency and to that of maximizing the sum of advantages; and fair opportunity is prior to the difference principle. There are two cases:
(a) an inequality of opportunity must enhance the opportunities of those with the lesser opportunity;
(b) an excessive rate of saving must on balance mitigate the burden of those bearing this hardship.

General Conception

All social primary goods—liberty and opportunity, income and wealth, and the bases of self-respect—are to be distributed equally unless an equal distribution of any or all of these goods is to the advantage of the least favored.

By way of comment, these principles and priority rules are no doubt incomplete. Other modifications will surely have to be made, but I shall not further complicate the statement of the principles. It suffices to observe that when we come to nonideal theory, we do not fall back straightway upon the general conception of justice. The lexical ordering of the two principles, and the valuations that this ordering implies, suggest priority rules which seem to be reasonable enough in many cases. By various examples I have tried to illustrate how these rules can be used and to indicate their plausibility. Thus the ranking of the principles of justice in ideal theory reflects back and guides the application of these principles to nonideal situations. It identifies which limitations need to be dealt with first. The drawback of the general conception of justice is that it lacks the definite structure of the two principles in serial order. In more extreme and tangled instances of nonideal theory there may be no alternative to it. At some point the priority of rules for nonideal cases will fail; and indeed, we may be able to find no satisfactory answer at all. But we must try to postpone the day of reckoning as long as possible, and try to arrange society so that it never comes....

ENDNOTES

1. As the text suggests, I shall regard Locke's *Second Treatise of Government*, Rousseau's *The Social Contract*, and Kant's ethical works beginning with *The Foundations of the Metaphysics of Morals* as definitive of the contract tradition. For all of its greatness, Hobbes's *Leviathan* raises special problems. A general historical survey is provided by J. W. Gough, *The Social Contract*, 2nd ed. (Oxford: The Clarendon Press, 1957), and Otto Gierke, *Natural Law and the Theory of Society*, trans. with an introduction by Ernest Barker (Cambridge: The University Press, 1934). A presentation of the contract view as primarily an ethical theory is to be found in G. R. Grice, *The Grounds of Moral Judgment* (Cambridge: The University Press, 1967).

2. Kant is clear that the original agreement is hypothetical. See *The Metaphysics of Morals*, pt. I (*Rechtslehre*), especially §§ 47, 52; and pt. II of the essay "Concerning the Common Saying: This May Be True in Theory but It Does Not Apply in Practice," in *Kant's Political Writings*, ed. Hans Reiss and trans. by H. B. Nisbet (Cambridge, The University Press, 1970), pp. 73–87. See Georges Vlachos, *Le pensée politique de Kant* (Paris, Presses Universitaires de France, 1962), pp. 326–335; and J. G. Murphy, *Kant: The Philosophy of Right* (London, Macmillan, 1970), pp. 109–112, 133–136, for a further discussion.

3. For the formulation of this intuitive idea I am indebted to Allan Gibbard.

4. The process of mutual adjustment of principles and considered judgments is not peculiar to moral philosophy. See Nelson Goodman, *Fact, Fiction, and Forecast* (Cambridge, Mass., Harvard University Press, 1955), pp. 65–68, for parallel remarks

concerning the justification of the principles of deductive and inductive inference.

5. An accessible discussion of this and other rules of choice under uncertainty can be found in W. J. Baumol, *Economic Theory and Operations Analysis*, 2nd ed. (Englewood Cliffs, N.J., Prentice-Hall, 1965), ch. 24. Baumol gives a geometric interpretation of these rules, including the diagram used ... to illustrate the difference principle. See pp. 558–562. See also R. D. Luce and Howard Raiffa, *Games and Decisions* (New York, John Wiley and Sons, 1957), ch. XIII, for a fuller account.

6. Here I borrow from William Fellner, *Probability and Profit* (Homewood, Ill., Richard D. Irwin, 1965), pp. 140–142, where these features are noted.

4

Race and the Social Contract Tradition

CHARLES MILLS

Charles W. Mills uses social contract theory both descriptively and prescriptively. Descriptively, he uses the theory to paint a picture of past and present institutional structures based on domination that have characterized most societies. Prescriptively, he makes central the task of undoing the forms of race, class, and gender-based domination that still continue to characterize existing societies.

How should political progressives seeking to end class, gender, and racial domination respond to the social contract tradition? Possible criticisms are numerous and obvious. To begin with, the idea of a literal contract is ahistorical, simply untrue to the anthropological facts of human evolution. There is never a "state of nature," but always human beings in social groups of greater or lesser complexity. Correspondingly, the idea of a contract is misleadingly asocial. Its methodological starting-point is "pre-social" individuals, but in fact no such individuals exist. Instead socially created psychological traits and motivations are represented as natural, reversing the actual causal relationship. Moreover, the atomic individualism characteristic of liberalism finds here its clearest statement. Society is represented as being brought into existence by, and composed of, an aggregate of equi-powerful individual decision-makers, which is obviously absurd. Finally, insofar as the contract classically emphasizes the centrality of individual will and consent, it depicts as the result of free and universal consensual agreement relations and structures of domination about which most people have no real choice, and which actually oppress the majority of the population.

A lengthy indictment, then, and no surprise that contract theory is usually seen by the left as ideological mystification. However, the remarkable revival of contractarianism stimulated by John Rawls's *A Theory of Justice* moved some progressives to rethink their aprioristic dismissal, especially since contemporary contractarianism is purely hypothetical in character, thereby seeming to sidestep some of the standard criticisms of the past.[1] No longer a literal representation of the origins of society, the state, or political obligation, the contract is now just a heuristic device, a thought-experiment, for mobilizing our intuitions about justice.

In this chapter, I want to be more explicit than I was in my book, *The Racial Contract*,[2] the strategic and theoretical value of a retention and development of the contract as a heuristic device by political progressives. Moreover, I mean the "contract"—albeit in a scare-quotes sense—not merely in its normative but also in its descriptive role. I will argue for the conceptual usefulness to radical political theory—as both a descriptive model and a normative take-off point—of what I will call the "domination" or "exclusionary" contract that can be seen as common to my own work, Carole Pateman's "sexual contract," and the Rousseauean original (the "class contract" of the *Discourse on Inequality*).[3] I will focus specifically on race, but many of my points will be valid for gender also.

Mills, Charles W. "Race and the Social Contract Tradition," *Social Identities*. Reprinted by permission of Taylor & Francis.

I   THE DOMINATION CONTRACT

Let me begin by quickly running through some of the myriad uses of the idea of the contract. There are contrasts, distinctions, and sub-distinctions of all kinds: modal status, scope, area, purpose. First, there is the familiar (though I will later argue over-simple) contrast between the literal/actual contract and the hypothetical contract, what could be regarded as its modal status. Then there is the contrast between the descriptive/factual contract, as in some sense a representation of actuality, the way things were/are, and the prescriptive/normative contract, as a representation of the way things should be. Fine-grained distinctions within these contracts are also possible, and have been made. Otto Gierke drew a famous demarcation between the contract to establish society, the *Gesellschaftsvertrag* (the social contract proper), and the contract to establish the state, the *Herrschaftsvertrag* (the political contract). Somewhat relatedly, David Boucher and Paul Kelly demarcate the moral, civil, and constitutional contracts.[4]

To this familiar list, I want to add some further contrasts that have been implicit in the literature rather than being explicitly flagged as such. I suggest that the contracts of Rousseau, Pateman, and myself can all usefully be gathered under the heading of the demystificatory *domination* or *exclusionary* contract that must be distinguished from the mainstream consensual or inclusivist contract. There are two main alternative purposes for positing and theorizing a domination contract. The first would be to argue that the apparatus of contractarianism is necessarily flawed, and should be repudiated altogether. The second would be to use the contract as a device for mapping and making vivid the full extent of social subordination, not to argue for the contract's abandonment but to demonstrate how sweeping would be the changes necessary for the reconstruction of the ideal contract.

The descriptive/normative contrast is sometimes taken to be coextensive with the actual/hypothetical contrast, but this is mistaken. The descriptive contract does not have to be the literal contract to be in some sense a representation of the way things actually

happened because the descriptive contract can be sub-divided at least three ways: (i) the literal historical contract; (ii) the hypothetical, idealized reconstruction contract; (iii) the useful model contract.

The first of these is perhaps best represented by Locke, though some theorists have argued that in his work there are actually two sets of explanations, so that in a sense he hedged his bets.[5] But at least one explanation seems to rely on a literal contract, the existence of which can be empirically demonstrated. The hypothetical reconstruction contract is best exemplified by Rousseau in his *Discourse on Inequality*. Here Rousseau gives a detailed account of the human degradation produced by the development of class society, and then concludes: "Such was, *or must have been* [my emphasis], the origin of society and of laws," and later, "I have tried to set out the origin and progress of inequality, the establishment and the abuse of political societies, *to the extent that these things can be deduced from the nature of man by the light of reason alone* [my emphases]."[6] So this is a more cautious formulation than the claim of actuality: the contract as an aprioristic reconstruction of what seems to have happened.

However, it is the third sense that is crucial for us: the contract as a useful model, as a way of thinking about things, with claims neither to literal nor hypothetical (in the sense of possible) representation of the past. It is exemplified by Ernest Barker's judgment that "Even if there had never been a contract, men actually behaved 'as if' there had been such a thing."[7] Similarly, in an *Encyclopedia of Philosophy* entry from 40 years ago, Peter Laslett comments on the "explanatory value" of the contract:

> If the collectivity is understood as embody-ing agreement, it does not necessarily follow that any such agreement between parties ever actually took place in historical time.... A contractarian political theory, therefore, can be entirely hypothetical, analyzing state and society as if agreement must always be presumed.... In this hypothetical form the contract theory is still of importance to political philosophy.[8] (Note that this use of "hypothetical" is different from the second sense.)

Jean Hampton, more recently, has argued that:

> Philosophers hate to admit it, but sometimes they work from pictures rather than ideas.... [T]he contract imagery has struck many as enormously promising.... I will argue that social contract theorists have intended simultaneously to describe the nature of political societies, and to prescribe a new and more defensible form of such societies.... [T]heir invocation of a social contract among the people as the source of the state is, in part, an attempt to make one modest factual statement, namely, that authoritative political societies are human creations.... The contractarian's term of "social contract" is misleading in so far as it suggests that people either tacitly or explicitly exchange promises with one another to create or support certain governmental structures. We do no such thing.... Certain institutions, practices and rules become conventionally entrenched (in a variety of ways) in a social system, and in so far as the people continue to support them, these conventions continue to prevail, and thus comprise the political and legal system in the country.... [S]ocial contract arguments for the state can be interpreted so as to provide plausible descriptions of political societies as conventionally-generated human creations—far more plausible, indeed, than rival divine rights arguments or natural subjugation theories.[9]

Following Hampton, I want to suggest that contract in this sense can still be useful for us, and that—suitably reconceived—it can even be profitably adapted by political progressives. As Hampton emphasizes, the contract provides an iconography, a set of images, that is immensely powerful and appealing, in large measure because it makes most salient, in simplified and abstract form, the modern idea of society and all its various institutions and practices (the state, the legal system) as *human* creations. Thus at the basic level of a conceptual framework, a picture, a story, it provides an overarching optic for thinking about the socio-political that is immediately graspable and that captures some central truths about it.

Now one of the tasks of political philosophy is precisely to provide *competing* abstract pictures of the polity. Political philosophies make general claims about how societies come into existence, how they are typically structured, how the state and the legal system work, how cognition and normative evaluation characteristically function, how the polity should be morally assessed, etc. In Marxism, for example, we have a distinctive analysis in terms of the causal centrality of economic reproduction, the division of society after the hunting and gathering stage into classes, the role of the state as an organ of class power, the pernicious influence of "ideology," and so forth. And these views are obviously radically different from Plato's claims about innate human inequality and the need for a cognitive elite, or Hobbes's claims about the situational logic that generates human conflict between roughly physically and mentally equal self-seeking individuals.

I take it to be uncontroversial that for progressives of the modern period the central fact about society—the fact that they want to be captured in these simple overarching pictures of how the socio-political works—is the reality of group domination. Where mainstream liberal theorists have tended to focus narrowly on the electoral realm, radicals have typically operated with a broader conception of the political. They have recognized and brought to light structures of group domination that are unjust, that arise out of social processes rather than being natural, and that shape the character of society as a whole, both the fundamental institutions and general human interaction and group psychology. If we consider the "big three" of class, gender, and race, this picture is obviously true of Marxism, feminism, and, though the texts may be less familiar here, true also of the black radical political tradition. So whereas mainstream contractarians are operating with a factual picture that makes equality and consent normative, progressives are insistent that actually inequality and domination are the norm. The retention of the contract by progressives can then be seen as an effective strategy for undermining the influence of the (misleading) mainstream theoretical picture by using its own terms and, in an act of conceptual judo, overthrowing it on its own theoretical mat.

The simple central innovation is to posit a group domination contract that is exclusionary rather than genuinely inclusive, and then rethink everything from that perspective. (I do not, of course, mean "excluded" from the polity in the sense of being left in the state of nature, but rather included as an unequal.) In Rousseau, it is a class contract that the rich con the poor into accepting, so that "all ran towards their chains believing that they were securing their liberty."[10] In Pateman and myself, it is a sexual and a racial contract. But the basic idea is to utilize what Hampton sees as central to contractarianism— the shaping role of human causality—and then to show how this is both retained and necessarily transformed in a polity where human causality is group-centered rather than dispersed among equi-powerful individuals. By bringing in groups as the key players rather than individuals, it is then possible to recuperate the insights of radical oppositional theory within a framework still in some sense "contractarian." So if the traditional contract was a valuable polemical tool against Sir Robert Filmer and the patriarchal school, and later conservatives like Edmund Burke and Joseph de Maistre, with their claims about natural obligation and subordination, the radical contract can be a valuable polemical tool against those who, analogously, see gender and racial domination as natural.

The key moves are already laid out, if somewhat schematically, in Rousseau. To begin with, it is, of course, a contract that emerges not from the state of nature, but from an earlier state of society. So it is explicitly historical in outlook, seeking to locate the emergence of class society, or patriarchy, or white supremacy, in specific historical processes. Correspondingly, it is emphatically social, recognizing that the negative traits of the social order, and of human beings themselves, are a product of society rather than projecting them back into the natural, and thus endorsing standard Enlightenment social meliorism as against explanatory recourse to divine will, original sin, biological limitation, etc. Since it is a contract of group domination, it is holistic, anti-atomistic in nature, being explicitly predicated on human collectivities, dominating and dominated. The division and transformation of the human population into certain kinds of entities (for example, "males" and "females," "whites" and "blacks") can now readily be accommodated within the contractarian framework, as can the inculcation of corresponding psychologies. The emphasis of current progressive theory on the "constructed" nature of gender and race thus fits perfectly with the idea of a contract as a set of intersubjective agreements. Finally, while it does see human causality as central, the explanatory emphasis is on coercion, since the "contract" here is an intra-group agreement by which a dominant group imposes its will on a subordinate group.

Nevertheless, the obvious question at this point might be: why bother? If you have to work so hard to qualify and modify the original contract to recuperate these insights, why not just move on to the terrain of some other theory in the first place? And in fact, can it really be said that there is anything left of contractarianism after so many modifications?

The answer to the last question would be, as noted, that there *is* a precedent in the classical tradition itself, in Rousseau. And if Hampton is correct that the central insight of contractarianism is the human-created character of the sociopolitical order, then the concept of a group domination contract does preserve that insight, while developing it against a more sociologically informed and realistic picture of actual modern polities.

As to the point of the exercise: here, of course, individual calculations of costs and benefits will vary, and some may argue that more is lost by moving on to this theoretical terrain than is gained by it. My own feeling, as argued, is that a critique that engages contract in its own terms and shows, given the factual record, how inadequate its prescriptions typically are, is likely to be more polemically effective than one which simply dismisses it altogether. In other words, there are certain strategic benefits to be gained by accepting and working within a very mainstream and highly respectable (what could be more respectable?) framework. Moreover, these texts—Hobbes, Locke, Rousseau, Kant— will be taught as part of the canon, and thus continue to influence students and theorists, as long as political philosophy still exists as a subject. So books like *The Sexual Contract* and *The Racial Contract* can form a natural oppositional section of a standard curriculum on Western political thought. "You want to talk contract? Fine, then let's talk about the *actual* contract ..."

But there are also theoretical advantages on the normative front. Before turning to this, however, I want to say something specifically about race.

II CRITICAL RACE THEORY

What has come to be called "critical race theory" began (under that name) in legal theory, as a response to racial minorities' dissatisfaction with the critical legal studies movement.[11] Their claim was that the latter's analyses of the deficiencies and silences of mainstream legal theory did not pay sufficient attention to race. However, the term has now begun to be used much more widely, referring to theory in a number of different disciplines that operates with race as a central prism of analysis. It is this focus rather than any unified methodology that distinguishes the approach. Just as feminist theory these days is more appropriately referred to in the plural than the singular—*feminisms*—so critical race theory is really a meta-theoretical umbrella covering a wide variety of approaches: deconstructionist, Foucauldian, Marxist, even liberal.

If there is a key point, a common theoretical denominator, it is the simultaneous recognition of the centrality of race and the biological unreality of race, its socio-political rather than natural character. The cliché that has come to express this insight is that race is not natural but "constructed." So race is made, unmade, and remade; race is a product of human activity, both personal and institutional, rather than DNA; race is learned, rehearsed, and performed. People's race is contingent, the result of being socially categorized one way rather than another, and as such people can change race by moving from one country to another or even by having the racial rules change in their own country. But this volatility should not be taken to imply the unqualified unreality of race. Rather, as critical race theorists are quick to emphasize, race is both constructed *and* real, embedded in legal decisions, social mores, networks of belief, folkways, institutions, structures of economic privilege and disadvantage. The reality is a social reality—perhaps better, a socio-political reality—but within this sphere, it is real enough.

Moreover, it is a reality that is structured through and through by relations of domination. The modern world is a world created by European expansionism—settlement, slavery, colonialism—and as such it is fundamentally shaped by the fact of white over nonwhite domination.

Now it is a striking fact about Western political theory that this domination has until recently hardly been theoretically registered and condemned as such. In the preface to his book on European imperialism, Mark Cocker summarizes the account that follows as "the story of how a handful of small, highly advanced and well-populated nation-states at the western extremity of Eurasia embarked on a mission of territorial conquest. And how in little more than 400 years they had brought within their political orbit most of the diverse peoples across five continents."[12] But over the course of these same centuries, Western narratives have *not* generally told this story as a tale of political oppression. Either it has not been represented as political at all, but part of the natural order (a backdrop to the political)—the working out of God's will, or of a European predestinarianism, or the evolutionary process of inevitable racial triumph over the inferior races (or all three)—or it has been represented as political and justifiable, for example the victory of civilization over barbarism. As with male domination of women, the domination of whites over nonwhites has historically been naturalized and/or justified.

These evasions are especially remarkable, and especially culpable, in American political theory, since (non-apologist) historians of race have long pointed out the peculiar centrality of race to the formation of the United States in particular. Thus Pulitzer Prize-winning historian Leon Litwack's exhaustive account of Jim Crow begins with the matter-of-fact statement that "America was founded on white supremacy and the notion of black inferiority and black unfreedom."[13] Similarly, in his pioneering study of a quarter-century ago, George Fredrickson points out that:

> The phrase "white supremacy" applies with
> particular force to the historical experience
> of two nations—South Africa and the
> United States.... More than the other
> multi-racial societies resulting from the

"expansion of Europe" ... South Africa and the United States ... have manifested over long periods of time a tendency to push the principle of differentiation by race to its logical outcome—a kind of *Herrenvolk* society in which people of color ... are treated as permanent aliens or outsiders.[14]

More recently, Matthew Frye Jacobson has tracked the evolution of American "whiteness" over "three great epochs" (1790–1840s, 1840s–1920s, 1920s–present), emphasizing, however, that throughout these changes:

> White privilege in various forms has been a constant in American political culture since colonial times.... [Racism] is a theory of who is who, of who belongs and who does not, of who deserves what and who is capable of what.... [I]t is not just that various white immigrant groups' economic successes came at the expense of non-whites, but that they owe their now stabilized and broadly recognized whiteness *itself* in part to these nonwhite groups.... Racism now appears not anomalous to the working of American democracy, but fundamental to it.[15]

So historians have long recognized the centrality and significance to the American experience of white racism and white supremacy. Yet, as Rogers Smith's major work of a decade ago, *Civic Ideals*, has shown, the obvious political implications of these historical truths have *not* been admitted by the most important theorists of American political culture.[16] Instead, they have been "ignored, minimized, or dismissed." The mainstream conception, as purveyed by such distinguished theorists as Alexis de Tocqueville, Gunnar Myrdal, and Louis Hartz, has been the "anomaly" view of racism, in which racial exclusion and domination have been a marginal feature of the country's political history. Thus in opposition to the mainstream "anomaly" view, Smith puts forward what he calls the "multiple traditions" view, which gives proper weight to the massive historical role of inegalitarian ideologies of racial ascription in American political culture. In a parallel, if not as detailed, treatment of the

state in particular, Desmond King documents how, far from being neutral, the US Federal government has functioned as "a powerful institution upholding arrangements privileging Whites and discriminating against Blacks." Yet, strangely enough, this fact has "been disregarded by most historians of the American Federal government and by students of US politics and government."[17] Taking this claim to a deeper level, Anthony Marx has argued that we need to see the state as not only discriminating by race, but itself contributing to the *making* of race:

> Citizenship is a key institutional mechanism for establishing boundaries of inclusion or exclusion in the nation-state.... But by specifying to whom citizenship applies, states also define those outside the community of citizens, who then live within the state as objects of domination.... Nationhood was institutionalized on the basis of race; the political production of race and the political production of nationhood were linked.

Thus, in contrast to the standard narratives, he suggests that we need to think in terms of an alternative "historical pattern of nation-state building through exclusion."[18]

Finally, in legal theory, as mentioned at the start, critical race theorists have for some time now been mapping the ways in which the law is not merely deeply imbricated in racial discrimination but in the codification and crystallization of race itself—how, for example, one became "white by law."[19]

So there is an emerging body of work which demonstrates in a number of socio-political spheres the pervasiveness of white domination, and which points toward the need for rethinking standard global conceptualizations of the polity. And the silences and evasions in American political science on the question of race certainly have their counterparts in the more rarefied realm of political philosophy. Most white political philosophers, such as John Rawls, have worked with a contractarianism whose factual presuppositions obfuscate or deny the centrality of white racism and white domination to US history. In their exclusion of race, in their denial of the importance of racial group identity and racial group interests, in their ignoring of systemic white privilege, the tacit assumptions of contemporary contractarianism reproduce at a more abstract level and in more exacerbated form the misrepresentations of mainstream political science. And this is manifested most clearly, of course, in the fact that the normative prescriptions of contemporary white contractarians say so little about redressing racial injustice. White supremacy is not seen in the first place (factual picture), so there is no need to prescribe remedies for ending it (normative picture).

The value of formally articulating a group domination contract, then, is to provide a device for making vivid, within the framework of contractarianism, the actual historical record, and thus counteracting the misleading and mystified historical picture most white contractarians have. To begin with, racial domination is made central, as in fact it has been. But this domination is not seen as in any way innate or natural, but explicitly historicized. The idea of a "contract" fits very nicely with what was earlier emphasized to be one of the central points of critical race theory, the "constructed" character of race. So race should be thought of not as biological, but as an intersubjectivist phenomenon, where, however, the parties are not equals, but some have greater power than others. This captures the idea of race—"whiteness" and "non-whiteness"—as a created identity imposed on nonwhites by whites. The *political* character of race is thus highlighted. Just as the orthodox social contract was meant to challenge notions of natural intra-group white male subordination (as in Sir Robert Filmer), so the unorthodox racial contract challenges notions of natural inter-group racial subordination. And correspondingly, rather than any recourse to race as a primordial identity, its social character is conceptually recognized. It is not that whites preexist the contract, but rather that they come into existence *as* white through the contract. Issues of group psychology can then be handled through understanding people's positioning in the racial system. One is not dealing with atomic individuals but people whose identities are significantly constituted by these relations of group domination.

Correspondingly, the group domination contract also obviously does a better job of modeling the real-life workings of the formal juridico-political apparatus of the polity: the legal system and the state. In the idealized mainstream contract, the norm is equal treatment before the law, enforced by an impartial state whose role is to protect the rights of the equal moral individuals whose socially recognized moral personhood triumphantly brings to a close the epoch of ascriptive hierarchy. But this picture obviously bears no correspondence to the actual historical record of the experience of people of color, whose expropriation, enslavement, and colonization have all been facilitated through discriminatory legal systems enforced by a non-neutral state.

Normative questions are also better understood once one realizes that liberal ideology and mainstream morality were also necessarily shaped by this exclusionary contract. By its very structure, the orthodox social contract downplays the theoretical significance of such claims, since it is assuming inclusiveness and egalitarianism as the norm. Everybody who counts is a "person," and there is no inquiry into who *does* count. The domination contract, by contrast, makes exclusion conceptually central, which corresponds to the actual historical record. Instead of taking "person" as gender- and race-neutral, it makes explicit that maleness and whiteness were prerequisites for full personhood. The sexual and racial contracts thus put front and center what is obfuscated and marginalized by the orthodox social contract: that full personhood could only really be taken for granted by white males, and that the classic human rights declarations of the 18th century were really proclaiming equal rights just for them.

Overall, then, it is clear that the domination contract maps the actual sociopolitical reality of recent global history far better than the egalitarian mainstream contract. The domination contract is thus pedagogically useful in providing a more accurate conceptual framework for students (and professors also!) to operate with. To return one last time to Hampton's claim: we work from basic pictures of how things are. When social contract theory is taught, race is ostensibly absent, the polity is represented as basically egalitarian, and structural subordination is nowhere to be found. The domination contract provides in simple and accessible form a competing model, a counter-model that is far truer to the actual historical record. It models racial domination and white supremacy within the same framework that mainstream theory utilizes, thus enabling an effective challenge to be mounted to orthodox conceptions.

III RETHINKING THE NORMATIVE CONTRACT

Finally, I want to turn to the normative contract. Once the superiority of the domination contract as a descriptive model is conceded, two moves are then possible. One may conclude that the contract model itself is necessarily flawed, that contract always produces domination and subordination. So the theoretical point of the exercise would have been to argue for the principled jettisoning of contract itself.

The other approach rejects this conclusion, and insists that the contract is flexible enough to be put to progressive ends once the actual history has been acknowledged. This is Rousseau's move—seven years after the *Discourse on Inequality*, he publishes *The Social Contract*.[20] So from the fact that the actual contract was a bogus contract, it does not follow that an idealized reconstructed contract is not possible. And this is the move I would endorse myself. The actual contract set things up like this—but that was wrong—so we need a new contract that corrects for it.

The debate over the possibility of appropriating contractarianism obviously shades over into the more general controversy about the extent to which liberalism can be turned to progressive ends. As my pro-contractarian argument so far should indicate, I want to endorse liberalism. But this is, so to speak, a hybrid liberalism, detached from what are sometimes taken to be its necessary theoretical presuppositions.

What is "liberalism"? I suggest that if we think of liberalism as a political philosophy, then we need to distinguish different things. First, there is liberalism as a set of value commitments, for example to the individual's freedom, autonomy, self-realization, rights-protection, and so on. Then there is liberalism as predicated on a particular social ontology, classically

portrayed as an ontology of atomic individuals. Finally, it is sometimes thought that liberalism is married to a certain theory of history, for example a Whig progressivism.

Now what I am suggesting is that there are no strong logical entailments between these different components, so that the value commitments can be analytically separated from the social ontology and the theory of history. The liberalism I want to endorse, then, is the normative component. (If this is too minimalist to count as "liberalism," so be it.) I want to link this normative component with an alternative social ontology and an alternative account of recent global history, as summarized in the racial contract, to produce a liberalism informed by the racial facts. The fact that existing liberalism has largely been racial, in its avoidance and denial of the reality of racial domination, or actual accommodation to it, does not mean that a reconstructed non-racial liberalism is impossible. Slavery, segregation, the denial of equal opportunity, racial exploitation in general—these would all be condemned by a non-racial liberalism.

The ideal normative contract, then, would be aimed at undoing the non-ideal racial contract, in all its exploitative manifestations. And the virtue of the preliminary mapping of the racial contract would be to show how far-reaching these manifestations are. Discussions of race in mainstream ethical theory have usually focused narrowly on affirmative action, in keeping with the mainstream anomaly view of racism. The racial contract, as a domination contract, challenges this view and provides a synoptic alternative picture of the polity: not just individual transactions, but the historic functioning of the state and legal system, the workings of the economy, the development of particular moral psychologies and moral codes. If we see the descriptive racial contract as establishing the racial polity, white supremacy, then the task of the rectificatory normative contract should be how to dismantle white supremacy and realize racial justice.

So a much more extensive range of issues can be encompassed than is usually discussed in the mainstream ethics text. Our attention is directed broadly to the functioning of the racial polity as a whole, the structures and mechanisms by which entrenched racial injustice is perpetuated. One would look at white supremacy as a political system of domination in its multiple dimensions. So it is not merely a matter of ending discrimination, but of ending the unfair white advantage that comes from past discrimination and the history of racial exploitation.

In such a discussion, both the "politics of redistribution" and the "politics of recognition" would be involved, insofar as subordinated races have suffered both economic exploitation and systematic social stigmatization.[21] The political figures standardly invoked in these debates are usually in the left and communitarian traditions, Marx and Hegel. But in keeping with the endorsement throughout of a contractarian framework, I want to conclude by showing how much mileage can still be gotten out of those two most respectable and bourgeois theorists of the liberal contractarian tradition, John Locke and Immanuel Kant. This will underline my point that once the actual historical record and the actual social ontology are taken into account, conventional liberal values can themselves do most of the work of rectificatory justice.

Consider, for example, Lockean rights to self-ownership, private property, and the legitimate appropriation of the world, so ideologically foundational to a nation conceived of as a polity of proprietors. The actual normative logic of application of these key terms has been a racial logic, as one would expect of the racial liberalism of the domination contract. Thus Matthew Frye Jacobson points out that "race has been central to American conceptions of property (who can own property and who can *be* property, for example), and property in its turn is central to republican notions of self-possession and the 'stake in society' necessary for democratic participation." Inevitably, then, political liberties are affected also:

> [W]hiteness was tacitly but irretrievably written into republican ideology as well....
> [T]he new democratic order would require of its participants a remarkable degree of
> *self-possession*—a condition already denied literally to Africans in slavery and figuratively to all "nonwhite" or "heathen" peoples in prevailing conceptions of

human capacity.... "Fitness for self-government" [was] a racial attribute whose outer property was whiteness.[22]

So the implications of the original qualified, or non-existent, self-ownership of nonwhites ramify into the broader socio-political sphere. Whiteness is not merely economic but civil advantage. Cheryl Harris has argued that in such an intellectual framework, whiteness *itself* becomes "property," and that once this is understood, the pattern of enduring white privilege over more than a century of post-bellum civil rights legislation ceases to be puzzling and becomes a straightforward outcome of the differential entitlements of the white population.[23]

But this racial liberalism is not inextricably immanent in the concepts themselves. If we theorize from the perspective of a reconstructed, idealized version of Locke's theory, in which "men" or "persons" are genuinely racially inclusive terms, it is obvious that African slavery is wrong, since the captured Africans were clearly not taken in a just war, and in any case nothing is supposed to be able to justify the enslavement of wives and children. Now Locke emphasizes that the victims of crimes against their property have a right to reparations against the perpetrators—"he who hath received any damage, has besides the right of punishment common to him with other Men, a particular Right to seek *Reparation* from him that has done it ... so much as may make satisfaction for the harm he has suffer'd."[24] And presumably this also extends to the heirs of those involved, since otherwise later generations will continue to benefit from the ill-gotten gains of their ancestors, or be unfairly disadvantaged by the property crimes against their ancestors. Moreover, discrimination against blacks did not end with slavery, but continued under Jim Crow, and in more subtle forms is still manifest today.[25]

So whites have benefited massively from a set of differential entitlements predicated on the sub-personhood of the nonwhites population: whiteness has been "property." But inasmuch as nonwhites are *not* sub-persons, this differential entitlement has been illegitimate, a systematic violation of natural law. It follows, then, that a significant proportion at least of this "property" has in effect been stolen, and is an *illegitimate* appropriation of the world. Simply on orthodox Lockean proprietarian grounds, then, blacks have claims to reparations against whites to restore property levels to where they should have been. And note that no distinctive African or African American sets of values are being appealed to here. The radicalness of the conclusion, its dramatic redistributivist challenge to conventional wisdom, comes not from a startling new axiology, but from a demystified look at the actual factual record. Hence the value of the descriptive contract—in its domination version—in condensing and making vivid these facts.[26]

Or consider Kant's (idealized) views on personhood,[27] which might seem by now to be innocuous liberal banalities. Once one takes seriously a social ontology of races rather than colorless (i.e., white) atomic individuals, then the actuality that has to be recognized is that notions of respect for personhood have been systematically racialized. Whites have thought of themselves as the superior race and regarded all other races as inferior, indeed often as barely, or not at all, human. Edward Said describes an imperialist cultural discourse "relegating and confining the non-European to a secondary racial, cultural, ontological status," in which, with only seeming paradox, "this secondariness is … essential to the primariness of the Europeans."[28] Persons and sub-persons are dialectically interrelated, in that white personhood is achieved through maintaining the sub-personhood of non-whites. So respect has been tied to whiteness, while nonwhites have suffered a "disrespect," a "dissin'," that is not a matter of contingent individual bigotry, but part of the moral economy. Now the role of the Kantian *Rechtsstaat* is not to promote happiness, but to secure a moral environment in which citizens can maintain their dignity and autonomy. But if citizenship and personhood have overtly or tacitly been defined as white, the role of the state becomes the maintenance of the official sub-personhood of nonwhites: the *Rechtsstaat* needs to function as the *Rassensstaat*. And this has in fact been the reality, in the United States and elsewhere: official, effectively state-sanctioned moral attitudes have been embedded in social policy, education, national

narratives, technologies of memorialization, etc. The polity has been so structured that nonwhites have been viewed through official lenses as sub-persons rather than persons, unworthy of respect.

Correcting for this history thus requires that we think of "respect" in a framework that recognizes its supra-individual and racial aspects. Michelle Moody-Adams has argued that we need to broaden our usually individualistic conceptions of respect and self-respect to accommodate their actual social dimension: if one is a member of a racially stigmatized group, it will be much harder for one to attain the basic self-respect that whites take for granted.[29] But if nonwhites are full persons, then the existence of this actual moral economy represents a flagrant violation of (idealized) Kantian principles. Justice therefore demands that the situation be redressed to end the inferior caste status of subordinated races, and obviously this will require public policy measures to reconstitute societal structures so that whites no longer get differential recognition. National narratives need to be rethought, educational syllabi revamped, the stories of the racially subordinated officially recognized, and so forth. Again, we see how surprisingly radical conclusions can be extracted from the writings of establishment figures once the actual historical record and the actual social ontology are acknowledged.

In fact, the radicalness of the prerequisites for the full undoing of the racial contract is ultimately manifested in nothing less than the reshaping of ourselves as human beings. Especially in its Rousseauean version, contract is about the constitution and reconstitution of people, their transformation from one kind of entity to another.[30] Since the domination contract involves the creation of an oppressive social ontology, an ontology of persons and sub-persons, undoing it requires a metamorphosis of the *self* as well as social structures. And ultimately the aim would be to eliminate whiteness itself—not through an illusory "color-blindness" that covertly perpetuates white privilege without naming it, but through the actual dismantling of the socio-economic and political supports of illicit white advantage. Whites would have to learn to rethink their whiteness, understanding the basis of oppression on which it has rested, and the ways in which it is tied up with nonwhite inferiority. Thus the end of white supremacy will require not merely material changes in opportunity structures and institutional arrangements, but deep psychological and "metaphysical" changes in whites themselves.

In conclusion, then. The virtue of working within a contractarian framework is its congruence with mainstream intellectual discourse: its centering, normatively, of liberal individualist values and, factually, of claims about the shaping role of human causality and will. Actual societies have been characterized by structures of domination of various kinds, so that the will has not been a mythical general will but the will of powerful groups imposed on others, with most human beings *not* being recognized as fall persons and liberal values realized only for a minority. A group domination contract registers this historical reality, and, while inevitably over-simplifying in various ways, provides a demystified alternative picture. Thus it can help people better grasp the actual historical record of the polity, which has been one of exclusion and oppression. And in this way it can make possible a normative debate on achieving social justice less egregiously uninformed by the social facts.

ENDNOTES

1. John Rawls, *A Theory of Justice*, rev. edn. (Cambridge, Mass.: Harvard University Press, 1999).

2. Charles W. Mills, *The Racial Contract* (Ithaca, NY: Cornell University Press, 1997).

3. Mills, *Racial Contract*; Carole Pateman, *The Sexual Contract* (Stanford: Stanford University Press, 1988); Jean-Jacques Rousseau, *A Discourse on Inequality*, trans. Maurice Cranston (New York: Penguin, 1984).

4. David Boucher and Paul Kelly, "The Social Contract and Its Critics: An Overview," in *The Social Contract from Hobbes to Rawls*, ed. Boucher and Kelly (New York: Routledge, 1994).

5. Jeremy Waldron, "John Locke: Social Contract versus Political Anthropology," in Boucher and Kelly, *Social Contract*.

6. Rousseau, *Discourse on Inequality*, pp. 122, 137.

7. Ernest Barker, Introduction, *Social Contract: Essays by Locke, Hume, and Rousseau* (Oxford: Oxford University Press, 1960), p. vii.

8. Peter Laslett, "Social Contract," in *The Encyclopedia of Philosophy*, ed. Paul Edwards (New York: The Free Press, 1967), vol. 7, p. 466.

9. Jean Hampton, "Contract and Consent," in *A Companion to Contemporary Political Philosophy*, ed. Robert E. Goodin and Philip Pettit (Oxford: Blackwell, 1993), pp. 379–83.

10. Rousseau, *Discourse on Inequality*, p. 122.

11. See, for example, Kimberlé Crenshaw, Neil Gotanda, Gary Peller, and Kendall Thomas, eds., *Critical Race Theory: The Key Writings That Formed the Movement* (New York: New Press, 1995). Of course, it should be pointed out that critical analyses of the social order from a racial perspective long predate such work, if not under that name.

12. Mark Cocker, *Rivers of Blood, Rivers of Gold: Europe's Conflict with Tribal Peoples* (London: Jonathan Cape, 1998), p. xiii.

13. Leon F. Litwack, *Trouble in Mind: Black Southerners in the Age of Jim Crow* (New York: Alfred A. Knopf, 1998), p. xvi.

14. George Fredrickson, *White Supremacy: A Comparative Study in American and South African History* (New York: Oxford University Press, 1981), pp. xi–xii.

15. Matthew Frye Jacobson, *Whiteness of a Different Color: European Immigrants and the Alchemy of Race* (Cambridge, Mass.: Harvard University Press, 1998), pp. 4–12.

16. Rogers M. Smith, *Civic Ideals: Conflicting Visions of Citizenship in US History* (New Haven: Yale University Press, 1997).

17. Desmond King, *Separate and Unequal: Black Americans and the US Federal Government* (Oxford: Clarendon Press, 1995), pp. vii, 17.

18. Anthony W. Marx, *Making Race and Nation: A Comparison of the United States, South Africa, and*

Brazil (New York: Cambridge University Press, 1998), pp. 5, 25.

19. Crenshaw et al., *Critical Race Theory*; A. Leon Higginbotham, Jr., *In the Matter of Color: Race and the American Legal Process: The Colonial Period* (New York: Oxford University Press, 1978) and *Shades of Freedom: Racial Politics and Presumptions of the American Legal Process* (New York: Oxford University Press, 1996); Ian F. Haney López, *White by Law: The Legal Construction of Race* (New York: New York University Press, 1996).

20. Jean-Jacques Rousseau, *The Social Contract*, trans. Maurice Cranston (New York: Penguin, 1968).

21. See Nancy Eraser, *Justice Interruptus: Critical Reflections on the "Postsocialist" Condition* (New York: Routledge, 1997), ch. 1.

22. Jacobson, *Whiteness of a Different Color*, pp. 21, 26, 42.

23. Cheryl Harris, "Whiteness as Property," *Harvard Law Review* 106 (1993): 1709–91.

24. John Locke, *Two Treatises of Government*, ed. Peter Laslett (New York: Cambridge University Press, 1988), p. 273.

25. Litwack, *Trouble in Mind*; Michael K. Brown et al., *Whitewashing Race: The Myth of a Color-Mind Society* (Berkeley and Los Angeles: University of California Press).

26. I make a case via a modified Rawlsian apparatus for reparations for blacks in my "Contract of Breach: Repairing the Racial Contract," ch. 4 of Carole Pateman and Charles Mills, *Contract and Domination* (Malden, Mass.: Polity, 2007).

27. For Kant's racial views and their implications for personhood, see Charles W. Mills, "Kant's *Untermenschen*," in *Race and Racism in Modern Philosophy*, ed. Andrew Valls (Ithaca, NY: Cornell University Press, 2005).

28. Edward Said, *Culture and Imperialism* (New York: Knopf, 1993), p. 59.

29. Michele M. Moody-Adams, "Race, Class, and the Social Construction of Self-Respect," in *African-American Perspectives and Philosophical Traditions*, ed. John Pittman (New York: Routledge, 1996).

30. Rousseau, *Social Contract*, book I, ch. 8.

5

Wyman, Commissioner of New York Department of Social Services v. James
Supreme Court of the United States

The issue before the Supreme Court of the United States was whether the Fourth Amendment prohibition of unreasonable searches applies to visits by welfare caseworkers to recipients of Aid to Families with Dependent Children. The majority of the Court held that the Fourth Amendment does not apply in this case because the visitation is not forced or compelled, and even if it were, the visitation serves the state's overriding interest in the welfare of dependent children. Dissenting justices Douglas and Marshall argued that the Fourth Amendment prohibition does apply because the visitation is forced and compelled (although not normally by a threat of a criminal penalty) and because there are other ways of protecting the state's interest in this case. Justices Douglas and Marshall also argued that the decision of the majority is inconsistent with the Supreme Court's rulings with respect to the allocation of benefits in other cases.

Mr. Justice *Blackmun* delivered the opinion of the Court.

This appeal presents the issue whether a beneficiary of the program for Aid to Families with Dependent Children (AFDC) may refuse a home visit by the caseworker without risking the termination of benefits.

The New York State and City social services commissioners appeal from a judgment and decree of a divided three-judge District Court....

The District Court majority held that a mother receiving AFDC relief may refuse, without forfeiting her right to that relief, the periodic home visit which the cited New York statutes and regulations prescribe as a condition for the continuance of assistance under the program. The beneficiary's thesis, and that of the District Court majority, is that home visitation is a search and, when not consented to or when not supported by a warrant based on probable cause, violates the beneficiary's Fourth and Fourteenth Amendment rights....

Plaintiff Barbara James is the mother of a son, Maurice, who was born in May 1967. They reside in New York City. Mrs. James first applied for AFDC assistance shortly before Maurice's birth. A caseworker made a visit to her apartment at that time without objection. The assistance was authorized.

Two years later, on May 8, 1969, a caseworker wrote Mrs. James that she would visit her home on May 14. Upon receipt of this advice, Mrs. James telephoned the worker that, although she was willing to supply information "reasonable and relevant" to her need for public assistance, any discussion was not to take place at her home. The worker told Mrs. James that she was required by law to visit in her home and that refusal to permit the visit would result in the termination of assistance. Permission was still denied....

A notice of termination [was] issued on June 2.

Thereupon, without seeking a hearing at the state level, Mrs. James, individually and on behalf of Maurice, and purporting to act on behalf of all other persons similarly situated, instituted the present civil rights suit....

When a case involves a home and some type of official intrusion into that home, as this case appears to do, an immediate and natural reaction is one of concern about Fourth Amendment rights and the protection which that Amendment is intended to afford. Its emphasis indeed is upon one of the most precious aspects of personal security in home: "The right of the people to be secure in their persons, houses, papers, and effects...." This Court has characterized that right as "basic to a free society...." And over the years the Court consistently has been most protective of the privacy of the dwelling....

This natural and quite proper protective attitude, however, is not a factor in this case, for the seemingly obvious and simple reason that we are not concerned here with any search by the New York social service agency in the Fourth Amendment meaning of that term. It is true that the governing statute and regulations appear to make mandatory the initial home visit and the subsequent periodic "contacts" (which may include home visits) for the inception and continuance of aid. It is also true that the caseworker's posture in the home visit is perhaps, in a sense, both rehabilitative and investigative. But this latter aspect, we think, is given too broad a character and far more emphasis than it deserves if it is equated with a search in the traditional criminal law context. We note, too, that the visitation in itself is not forced or compelled, and that the beneficiary's denial of permission is not a criminal act. If consent to the visitation is withheld, no visitation takes place. The aid then never begins or merely ceases, as the case may be. There is no entry of the home and there is no search.

If, however, we were to assume that a caseworker's home visit, before or subsequent to the beneficiary's initial qualification for benefits, somehow (perhaps because the average beneficiary might feel she is in no position to refuse consent to the visit), and despite its interview nature, does possess some of the characteristics of a search in the traditional sense, we nevertheless conclude that it does not fall within the Fourth Amendment's proscription. This is because it does not descend to the level

of unreasonableness. It is unreasonableness which is the Fourth Amendment's standard.

There are a number of factors that compel us to conclude that the home visit proposed for Mrs. James is not unreasonable.

The public's interest in this particular segment of the area of assistance to the unfortunate is protection and aid for the dependent child whose family requires such aid for that child.... The dependent child's needs are paramount, and only with hesitancy would we relegate those needs, in the scale of comparative values, to a position secondary to what the mother claims as her rights.

The agency, with tax funds provided from federal as well as from state sources, is fulfilling a public trust. The State, working through its qualified welfare agency, has appropriate and paramount interest and concern in seeing and assuring that the intended and proper objects of that tax-produced assistance are the ones who benefit from the aid it dispenses....

One who dispenses purely private charity naturally has an interest in and expects to know how his charitable funds are utilized and put to work. The public, when it is the provider, rightly expects the same....

We therefore conclude that the home visitation as structured by the New York statutes and regulations is a reasonable administrative tool; that it serves a valid and proper administrative purpose for the dispensation of the AFDC program; that it is not an unwarranted invasion of personal privacy; and that it violates no right guaranteed by the Fourth Amendment.

Reversed and remanded with directions to enter a judgment of dismissal.

It is so ordered....

Mr. Justice *Douglas*, dissenting....

In 1969 roughly 127 billion dollars were spent by the federal, state, and local governments on "social welfare." To farmers alone almost four billion dollars were paid, in part for not growing certain crops....

Yet almost every beneficiary whether rich or poor, rural or urban, has a "house"—one of the places protected by the Fourth Amendment against "unreasonable searches and seizures." The question in this case is whether receipt of largesse from the government makes the *home* of the beneficiary subject to access by an inspector of the agency of oversight, even though the beneficiary objects to the intrusion and even though the Fourth Amendment's procedure for access to one's *house* or *home* is not followed. The penalty here is not, of course, invasion of the privacy of Barbara James, only her loss of federal or state largesse. That, however, is merely rephrasing the problem. Whatever the semantics, the central question is whether the government by force of its largesse has the power to "buy up" rights guaranteed by the Constitution. But for the assertion of her constitutional right, Barbara James in this case would have received the welfare benefit....

The applicable principle, as stated in *Camara* as "justified by history and by current experience" is that "except in certain carefully defined classes of cases, a search of private property without proper consent is 'unreasonable' unless it has been authorized by a valid search warrant."

In *See* we [decided] that the "businessman, like the occupant of a residence, has a constitutional right to go about his business free from unreasonable official entries upon his private commercial property." There is not the slightest hint in *See* that the Government could condition a business license on the "consent" of the licensee to the administrative searches we held violated the Fourth Amendment. It is a strange jurisprudence indeed which safeguards the businessman at his place of work from the warrantless searches but will not do the same for a mother in her *home*.

Is a search of her home without a warrant made "reasonable" merely because she is dependent on government largesse?

Judge Skelly Wright has stated the problem succinctly:

> Welfare has long been considered the equivalent of charity and its recipients have been subjected to all kinds of dehumanizing experiences in the government's effort to police its welfare payments. In fact, over half a billion dollars are expended annually for administration and policing in connection with the Aid to Families with Dependent Children program. Why such large sums are necessary for administration and policing has

never been adequately explained. No such sums are spent policing the government subsidies granted to farmers, airlines, steamship companies, and junk mail dealers, to name but a few. The truth is that in this subsidy area society has simply adopted a double standard, one for aid to business and the farmer and a different one for welfare. (Poverty, Minorities, and Respect for Law, 1970 Duke L. J. 425, 437–438.)

If the welfare recipient was not Barbara James but a prominent, affluent cotton or wheat farmer receiving benefit payments for not growing crops, would not the approach be different? Welfare in aid of dependent children, like social security and unemployment benefits, has an aura of suspicion. There doubtless are frauds in every sector of public welfare whether the recipient be a Barbara James or someone who is prominent or influential. But constitutional rights—here the privacy of the *home*—are obviously not dependent on the poverty or on the affluence of the beneficiary. It is the precincts of the *home* that the Fourth Amendment protects; and their privacy is as important to the lowly as to the mighty.

I would sustain the judgment of the three-judge court in the present case.

Mr. Justice *Marshall*, whom Mr. Justice *Brennan* joins, dissenting.

... The record plainly shows ... that Mrs. James offered to furnish any information that the appellants desired and to be interviewed at any place other than her home. Appellants rejected her offers and terminated her benefits solely on the ground that she refused to permit a home visit. In addition, appellants make no contention that any sort of probable cause exists to suspect appellee of welfare fraud or child abuse.

Simply stated, the issue in this case is whether a state welfare agency can require all recipients of AFDC benefits to submit to warrantless "visitations" of their homes. In answering that question, the majority dodges between constitutional issues to reach a result clearly inconsistent with the decisions of this Court. We are told that there is no such search involved in this case; that even if there were a search, it would not be unreasonable; and that even if this were an unreasonable search, a welfare recipient waives her right to object by accepting benefits. I emphatically disagree with all three conclusions....

... In an era of rapidly burgeoning governmental activities and their concomitant inspectors, caseworkers, and researchers, a restriction of the Fourth Amendment to "the traditional criminal law context" tramples the ancient concept that a man's home is his castle. Only last Term, we reaffirmed that this concept has lost none of its vitality....

... [I]t is argued that the home visit is justified to protect dependent children from "abuse" and "exploitation." These are heinous crimes, but they are not confined to indigent households. Would the majority sanction, in the absence of probable cause, compulsory visits to all American homes for the purpose of discovering child abuse? Or is this Court prepared to hold as a matter of constitutional law that a mother, merely because she is poor, is

substantially more likely to injure or exploit her children? Such a categorical approach to an entire class of citizens would be dangerously at odds with the tenets of our democracy....

Although the Court does not agree with my conclusion that the home visit is an unreasonable search, its opinion suggests that even if the visit were unreasonable, appellee has somehow waived her right to object. Surely the majority cannot believe that valid Fourth Amendment consent can be given under the threat of the loss of one's sole means of support....

In deciding that the homes of AFDC recipients are not entitled to protection from warrantless searches by welfare caseworkers, the Court declines to follow prior case law and employs a rationale that, if applied to the claims of all citizens, would threaten the validity of the Fourth Amendment.... Perhaps the majority has explained why a commercial warehouse deserves more protection than does this poor woman's home. I am not convinced; and, therefore, I must respectfully dissent.

6

Plyler v. Doe

Supreme Court of the United States

The issue before the Supreme Court was whether a Texas statute that withholds from local school districts any state funds for the education of children who were not "legally admitted" into the United States and that authorizes local school districts to deny enrollment to such children violates the Equal Protection Clause of the Fourteenth Amendment. Justice Brennan, delivering the opinion of the Court, argued that the Texas statute did violate the Equal Protection Clause. He contended that although public education is not a right granted to individuals by the Constitution (Marshall dissenting), given the "pivotal role of education in sustaining our political and cultural heritage" and the economic benefits that accrue to Texas from the presence of illegal aliens, petitioners had failed to establish a legitimate state interest in denying an education to illegal aliens. In dissent, Chief Justice Burger with whom Justices White, Rehnquist, and O'Connor joined, argued that although the Texas statute is unwise and unsound, it is not unconstitutional. Burger contended that although illegal aliens are included within the category of persons protected by the Equal Protection Clause, the Texas statute does bear "a relation to a legitimate state purpose," especially in view of the fact that the federal government sees fit to exclude illegal aliens from numerous social welfare programs.

■ ■ ■ In May 1975, the Texas Legislature revised its education laws to withhold from local school districts any state funds for the education of children who were not "legally admitted" into the United States. The 1975 revision also authorized local school districts to deny enrollment in their public schools to children not "legally admitted" to the country.... These cases involve constitutional challenges to those provisions.

[*Plyler v. Doe*] is a class action, filed in the United States District Court for the Eastern District of Texas in September 1977, on behalf of certain school-age children of Mexican origin residing in Smith County, Tex., who could not establish that they had been legally admitted into the United States. The action complained of the exclusion of plaintiff children from the public schools of the Tyler Independent School District. The Superintendent and members of the Board of Trustees of the School District were named as defendants; the State of Texas intervened as a party-defendant. After certifying a class consisting of all undocumented school-age children of Mexican origin residing within the School District, the District Court preliminarily enjoined defendants from denying a free education to members of the plaintiff class. In December 1977, the court conducted an extensive hearing on plaintiffs' motion for permanent injunctive relief....

The District Court held that illegal aliens were entitled to the protection of the Equal Protection Clause of the Fourteenth Amendment, and that [this section] violated that Clause....

The Court of Appeals for the Fifth Circuit upheld the District Court's injunction.

The Fourteenth Amendment provides that "[n]o State shall ... deprive any person of life, liberty, or property, without due process of law; nor deny to *any person within its jurisdiction* the equal protection of the laws." ... [Emphasis added.] Appellants argue at the outset that undocumented aliens, because of their immigration status, are not "persons within the jurisdiction" of the State of Texas, and that they therefore have no right to the equal protection of Texas Law. We reject this argument....

... The Equal Protection Clause was intended to work nothing less than the abolition of all caste-based and invidious class-based legislation. That objective is fundamentally at odds with the power the State asserts here to classify persons subject to its laws as nonetheless excepted from its protection.

Although the congressional debate concerning ... the Fourteenth Amendment was limited, that debate clearly confirms the understanding that the phrase "within its jurisdiction" was intended in a broad sense to offer the guarantee of equal protection to all within a State's boundaries, and to all upon whom the State would impose the obligations of its laws. Indeed, it appears from those debates that Congress, by using the phrase "person within its jurisdiction," sought expressly to ensure that the equal protection of the laws was provided to the alien population. Representative Bingham reported to the House the draft resolution of the Joint Committee of Fifteen on Reconstruction (H.R. 63) that was to become the Fourteenth Amendment.... Two days later, Bingham posed the following question in support of the resolution:

> Is it not essential to the unity of the people that the citizens of each State shall be entitled to all the privileges and immunities of citizens in the several States? Is it not essential to the unity of the Government and the unity of the people that all persons, *whether citizens or strangers, within this land,* shall have equal protection in every State in this Union in the rights of life and liberty and property?

... Our conclusion that the illegal aliens who are plaintiffs in these cases may claim the benefit of the Fourteenth Amendment's guarantee of equal protection only begins the inquiry. The more difficult question is whether the Equal Protection Clause has been violated by the refusal of the State

of Texas to reimburse local school boards for the education of children who cannot demonstrate that their presence within the United States is lawful, or by the imposition by those school boards of the burden of tuition on those children. It is to this question that we now turn....

... In applying the Equal Protection Clause to most forms of state action, we thus seek only the assurance that the classification at issue bears some fair relationship to a legitimate public purpose.

Of course, undocumented status is not irrelevant to any proper legislative goal. Nor is undocumented status an absolutely immutable characteristic since it is the product of conscious, indeed unlawful, action. But [this statute] is directed against children, and imposes its discriminatory burden on the basis of a legal characteristic over which children can have little control. It is thus difficult to conceive of a rational justification for penalizing these children for their presence within the United States. Yet that appears to be precisely the effect of [this statute].

Public education is not a "right" granted to individuals by the Constitution. *San Antonio Independent School Dist. v. Rodriguez* ... (1973). But neither is it merely some governmental "benefit" indistinguishable from other forms of social welfare legislation. Both the importance of education in maintaining our basic institutions, and the lasting impact of its deprivation on the life of the child, mark the distinction. The "American people have always regarded education and [the] acquisition of knowledge as matters of supreme importance." *Meyer v. Nebraska* ... (1923). We have recognized "the public schools as a most vital civic institution for the preservation of a democratic system of government," *Abington School District v. Schempp* ... (1963) ... and as the primary vehicle for transmitting "the values on which our society rests." *Ambach v. Norwick* ... (1979). "[A]s ... pointed out early in our history, ... some degree of education is necessary to prepare citizens to participate effectively and intelligently in our open political system if we are to preserve freedom and independence." *Wisconsin v. Yoder* ... (1972). And these historic "perceptions of the public schools as inculcating fundamental values necessary to the maintenance of a democratic political system have been confirmed by the observations of social scientists." *Ambach v. Norwick* ... In addition, education provides the basic tools by which individuals might lead economically productive lives to the benefit of us all. In sum, education has a fundamental role in maintaining the fabric of our society. We cannot ignore the significant social costs borne by our Nation when select groups are denied the means to absorb the values and skills upon which our social order rests.

In addition to the pivotal role of education in sustaining our political and cultural heritage, denial of education to some isolated group of children poses an affront to one of the goals of the Equal Protection Clause: the abolition of governmental barriers presenting unreasonable obstacles to advancement on the basis of individual merit. Paradoxically, by depriving the children of any disfavored group of an education, we foreclose the means by which that group might raise the level of esteem in which it is held by the majority. But more directly, "education prepares individuals to be self-reliant and self-sufficient participants in society." *Wisconsin v. Yoder....* Illiteracy is an enduring disability. The inability to read and write will handicap the individual deprived of a basic education each and every day of his life. The inestimable toll of that deprivation on the social, economic, intellectual, and psychological well-being of the individual, and the obstacle it poses to individual achievement, make it most difficult to reconcile the cost or the principle of a status-based denial of basic education with the framework of equality embodied in the Equal Protection Clause. What we said 28 years ago in *Brown v. Board of Education*, ... (1954), still holds true:

> Today, education is perhaps the most important function of state and local governments. Compulsory school attendance laws and the great expenditures for education both demonstrate our recognition of the importance of education to our democratic society. It is required in the performance of our most basic public responsibilities, even service in the armed forces. It is the very foundation of good citizenship. Today it is a principal instru-

ment in awakening the child to cultural values, in preparing him for later professional training, and in helping him to adjust normally to his environment. In these days, it is doubtful that any child may reasonably be expected to succeed in life if he is denied the opportunity of an education. Such an opportunity, where the state has undertaken to provide it, is a right which must be made available to all on equal terms....

... [A]ppellants appear to suggest that the State may seek to protect itself from an influx of illegal immigrants. While a State might have an interest in mitigating the potentially harsh economic effects of sudden shifts in population, [this statute] hardly offers an effective method of dealing with an urgent demographic or economic problem. There is no evidence in the record suggesting that illegal entrants impose any significant burden on the State's economy. To the contrary, the available evidence suggests that illegal aliens underutilize public services, while contributing their labor to the local economy and tax money to the state fisc ... The dominant incentive for illegal entry into the State of Texas is the availability of employment; few if any illegal immigrants come to this country, or presumably to the State of Texas, in order to avail themselves of a free education. Thus, even making the doubtful assumption that the net impact of illegal aliens on the economy of the State is negative, we think it clear that "[c]harging tuition to undocumented children constitutes a ludicrously ineffectual attempt to stem the tide of illegal immigration," at least when compared with the alternative of prohibiting the employment of illegal aliens....

Accordingly, the judgment of the Court of Appeals in each of these cases is *Affirmed.*

Justice *Marshall*, concurring.

While I join the Court's opinion, I do so without in any way retreating from my opinion in *San Antonio Independent School District v. Rodriguez....* I continue to believe that an individual's interest in education is fundamental, and that this view is amply supported "by the unique status accorded public education by our society, and by the close relationship between education and some of our most basic constitutional values." ... Furthermore, I believe that the facts of these cases demonstrate the wisdom of rejecting a rigidified approach to equal protection analysis, and of employing an approach that allows for varying levels of scrutiny depending upon "the constitutional and societal importance of the interest adversely affected and the recognized invidiousness of the basis upon which the particular classification is drawn." ... It continues to be my view that a class-based denial of public education is utterly incompatible with the Equal Protection Clause of the Fourteenth Amendment.

Justice *Blackmun*, concurring.

I join the opinion and judgment of the Court.

Like Justice Powell, I believe that the children involved in this litigation "should not be left on the streets uneducated." ... I write separately, however, because in my view the nature of the interest at stake is crucial to the proper resolution of these cases.

The "fundamental rights" aspect of the Court's equal protection analysis—the now-familiar concept that governmental classifications bearing on certain interests must be closely scrutinized—has been the subject of some controversy....

[This controversy], combined with doubts about the judiciary's ability to make fine distinctions in assessing the effects of complex social policies, led the Court in *Rodriguez* to articulate a firm rule: Fundamental rights are those that "explicitly or implicitly [are] guaranteed by the Constitution."... It therefore squarely rejected the notion that "an ad hoc determination as to the social or economic importance" of a given interest is relevant to the level of scrutiny accorded classification involving that interest, ... and made clear that "[i]t is not the province of this Court to create substantive constitutional rights in the name of guaranteeing equal protection of the laws."...

I joined Justice Powell's opinion for the Court in *Rodriguez*, and I continue to believe that it provides the appropriate model for resolving most equal protection disputes. Classifications infringing substantive constitutional rights necessarily will be invalid, if not by force of the Equal Protection Clause, then through operation of other provisions of the Constitution. Conversely, classifications bearing on nonconstitutional interests—even those involving "the most basic economic needs of impoverished human beings" ... —generally are not subject to special treatment under the Equal Protection Clause, because they are not distinguishable in any relevant way from other regulations in "the area of economics and social welfare."

With all this said, however, I believe the Court's experience has demonstrated that the *Rodriguez* formulation does not settle every issue of "fundamental rights" arising under the Equal Protection Clause. Only a pedant would insist that there are *no* meaningful distinctions among the multitude of social and political interests regulated by the States, and *Rodriguez* does not stand for quite so absolute a proposition. To the contrary, *Rodriguez* implicitly acknowledged that certain interests, though not constitutionally guaranteed, must be accorded a special place in equal protection analysis. Thus, the Court's decisions long have accorded strict scrutiny to classifications bearing on the right to vote in state elections, and *Rodriguez* confirmed the "constitutional underpinnings of the right to equal treatment in the voting process." ... Yet "the right to vote, *per se*, is not a constitutionally protected right." ... Instead, regulation of the electoral process receives unusual scrutiny because "the right to exercise the franchise in a free and unimpaired manner is preservative of other basic civil and political rights." ... In other words, the right to vote is accorded extraordinary treatment because it is, in equal protection terms, an extraordinary right: A citizen cannot hope to achieve any meaningful degree of individual political equality if granted an inferior right of participation in the political process. Those denied the vote are relegated, by state fiat, in a most basic way to second-class status....

In my view, when the State provides an education to some and denies it to others, it immediately and inevitably creates class distinctions of a type fundamentally inconsistent with those purposes, mentioned above, of the Equal Protection

Clause. Children denied an education are placed at a permanent and insurmountable competitive disadvantage, for an uneducated child is denied even the opportunity to achieve. And when those children are members of an identifiable group, that group—through the State's action—will have been converted into a discrete underclass. Other benefits provided by the State, such as housing and public assistance, are of course important; to an individual in immediate need, they may be more desirable than the right to be educated. But classifications involving the complete denial of education are in a sense unique, for they strike at the heart of equal protection values by involving the State in the creation of permanent class distinctions.... In a sense, then, denial of an education is the analogue of denial of the right to vote: The former relegates the individual to second-class social status; the latter places him at a permanent political disadvantage.

This conclusion is fully consistent with *Rodriguez*. The Court there reserved judgment on the constitutionality of a state system that "occasioned an absolute denial of educational opportunities to any of its children," noting that "no charge fairly could be made that the system ... fails to provide each child with an opportunity to acquire ... basic minimal skills." ... And it cautioned that in a case "involv[ing] the most persistent and difficult questions of educational policy, ... [the] Court's lack of specialized knowledge and experience counsels against premature interference with the informed judgments made at the state and local levels." ... Thus *Rodriguez* held, and the Court now reaffirms, that "a State need not justify by compelling necessity every variation in the manner in which education is provided to its population." ... Similarly, it is undeniable that education is not a "fundamental right" in the sense that it is constitutionally guaranteed. Here, however, the State has undertaken to provide an education to most of the children residing within its borders. And, in contrast to the situation in *Rodriguez*, it does not take an advanced degree to predict the effects of a complete denial of education upon those children targeted by the

State's classification. In such circumstances, the voting decisions suggest that the State must offer something more than a rational basis for its classification....

Chief Justice *Burger*, with whom Justice *White*, Justice *Rehnquist*, and Justice *O'Connor* join, dissenting.

Were it our business to set the Nation's social policy, I would agree without hesitation that it is senseless for an enlightened society to deprive any children—including illegal aliens—of an elementary education. I fully agree that it would be folly—and wrong—to tolerate creation of a segment of society made of illiterate persons, many having a limited or no command of our language. However, the Constitution does not constitute us as "Platonic Guardians" nor does it vest in this Court the authority to strike down laws because they do not meet our standards of desirable social policy, "wisdom," or "common sense." ... We trespass on the assigned function of the political branches under our structure of limited and separated powers when we assume a policy making role as the Court does today.

The Court makes no attempt to disguise that it is acting to make up for Congress's lack of "effective leadership" in dealing with the serious national problems caused by the influx of uncountable millions of illegal aliens across our borders.... The failure of enforcement of the immigration laws over more than a decade and the inherent difficulty and expense of sealing our vast borders have combined to create a grave socioeconomic dilemma. It is a dilemma that has not yet even been fully assessed, let alone addressed. However, it is not the function of the Judiciary to provide "effective leadership" simply because the political branches of government fail to do so.

The Court's holding today manifests the justly criticized judicial tendency to attempt speedy and wholesale formulation of "remedies" for the failures—or simply the laggard pace—of the political processes of our system of government. The Court employs, and in my view abuses, the Fourteenth Amendment in an effort to become an omnipotent and omniscient problem solver. That the motives for doing so are noble and compassionate does not alter the fact that the Court distorts our constitutional function to make amends for the defaults of others....

The Court acknowledges that, except in those cases when state classifications disadvantage a "suspect class" or impinge upon a "fundamental right," the Equal Protection Clause permits a state "substantial latitude" in distinguishing between different groups of persons.... Moreover, the Court expressly—and correctly—rejects any suggestion that illegal aliens are a suspect class, ... or that education is a fundamental right.... Yet by patching together bits and pieces of what might be termed quasi-suspect-class and quasi-fundamental-rights analysis, the Court spins out a theory custom tailored to the facts of these cases.

In the end, we are told little more than that the level of scrutiny employed to strike down the Texas law applies only when illegal alien children are deprived of a public education.... If ever a court was guilty of an unabashedly result-oriented approach, this case is a prime example....

Once it is conceded—as the Court does—that illegal aliens are not a suspect class, and that education is not a fundamental right, our injury should focus on and be limited to whether the legislative classification at issue bears a rational relationship to a legitimate state purpose....

It is significant that the Federal Government has seen fit to exclude illegal aliens from numerous social welfare programs, such as the food stamp program, ... the old-age assistance, and aid to families with dependent children, aid to the blind, aid to the permanently and totally disabled, and supplemental security income programs, ... the Medicare hospital insurance benefits program, ... and the Medicaid hospital insurance benefits for the aged and disabled program.... Although these exclusions do not conclusively demonstrate the constitutionality of the State's use of the same classification for comparable purposes, at the very least they tend to support the rationality of excluding illegal alien residents of a state from such programs so as to preserve the state's finite revenues for the benefit of lawful residents....

Denying a free education to illegal alien children is not a choice I would make were I a legislator. Apart from compassionate considerations, the long-range costs of excluding any children from the public schools may well outweigh the costs of educating them. But that is not the issue; the fact that there are sound *policy* arguments against the Texas Legislature's choice does not render that choice an unconstitutional one....

The Constitution does not provide a cure for every social ill, nor does it vest judges with a mandate to try to remedy every social problem....

Moreover, when this Court rushes in to remedy what it perceives to be the failings of the political processes, it deprives those processes of an opportunity to function. When the political institutions are not forced to exercise constitutionally allocated powers and responsibilities, those powers, like muscles not used, tend to atrophy. Today's cases, I regret to say, present yet another example of unwarranted judicial action, which in the long run tends to contribute to the weakening of our political processes. Congress, "vested by the Constitution with the responsibility of protecting our borders and legislating with respect to aliens," ... bears primary responsibility for addressing the problems occasioned by the millions of illegal aliens flooding across our southern border. Similarly, it is for Congress, and not this Court, to assess the "social costs borne by our Nation when select groups are denied the means to absorb the values and skills upon which our social order rests."... While the "specter of a permanent caste" of illegal Mexican residents of the United States is indeed a disturbing one, ... it is but one segment of a larger problem, which is for the political branches to solve. I find it difficult to believe that Congress would long tolerate such a self-destructive result—that it would fail to deport these illegal alien families or to provide for the education of their children. Yet instead of allowing the political processes to run their course—albeit with some delay—the Court seeks to do Congress's job for it, compensating for congressional inaction. It is not unreasonable to think that this encourages the political branches to pass their problems to the Judiciary.

The solution to this seemingly intractable problem is to defer to the political processes, unpalatable as that may be to some.

SUGGESTIONS FOR FURTHER READING

Anthologies

Arthur, John, and William Shaw. *Social and Political Philosophy*. Englewood Cliffs: Prentice-Hall, 1992.

Sterba, James P. *Social and Political Philosophy: Classical Western Tests Texts in Feminist and Multicultural Perspectives*. 3rd ed. Belmont, CA: Wadsworth, 2003.

———. *Justice: Alternative Political Perspectives*. 4th ed. Belmont CA: Wadsworth, 2003.

Basic Concepts

Aristotle. *Nicomachean Ethics*. Translated by Martin Ostwald. Indianapolis: Bobbs-Merrill, 1962.

Plato. *The Republic*. Translated by Francis Cornford. New York: Oxford University Press, 1945.

Pieper, Joseph. *Justice*. London: Faber and Faber, 1957.

Libertarianism

Hospers, John. *Libertarianism*. Los Angeles: Nash Publishing, 1971.

Narveson, Jan and Sterba, James P. *Are Liberty and Equality Compatible?* New York: Cambridge University Press, 2010.

Kelly, David. *A Life of One's Own*. Washington, DC: The Cato Institute, 1998.

Machan, Tibor. *Individuals and Their Rights*. LaSalle: Open Court, 1989.

Nozick, Robert. *Anarchy, State and Utopia*. New York: Basic Books, 1974.

Welfare Liberalism

Mill, John Stuart. *On Liberty*. Indianapolis: Bobbs-Merrill, 1956.

Rawls, John. *Political Liberalism*. New York: Columbia University Press, 1993.

———. *A Theory of Justice*. Cambridge: Harvard University Press, 1999.

Singer, Peter. *Practical Ethics*. Cambridge: Cambridge University Press, 1979.

Sterba, James P. *Justice for Here and Now*. New York: Cambridge University Press, 1998.

Socialism

Fisk, Milton. *Ethics and Society: A Marxist Interpretation of Value*. New York: New York University Press, 1980.

Harrington, Michael. *Socialism Past and Future*. New York: Arcade Publishing, 1989.

Howard, Michael. *Self-Management and the Crisis of Socialism*. Lanham, MD: Rowman Littlefield, 2000.

Marx, Karl. *Critique of the Gotha Program*. Edited by C. P. Dutt. New York: International Publishers, 1966.

Schweickart, David. *Against Capitalism*. Cambridge University Press, 1993.

Practical Applications

Friedman, David. *The Machinery of Freedom*. 2nd ed. LaSalle: Open Court, 1989.

Haslett, D. W. *Capitalism with Morality*. Oxford: Clarendon Press, 1994.

Timmons, William. *Public Ethics and Issues*. Belmont, CA: Wadsworth, 1990.

SECTION II

✳

Distant Peoples
and Future Generations

INTRODUCTION

Basic Concepts

The moral problem of distant peoples and future generations has only recently begun to be discussed by professional philosophers. There are many reasons for this neglect, not all of them complimentary to the philosophical profession. Suffice it to say that once it became widely recognized how modern technology could significantly benefit or harm distant peoples and future generations, philosophers could no longer ignore the importance of this moral problem.

With respect to this problem, the key question that must be answered first is: Can we meaningfully speak of distant peoples and future generations as having rights against us or of our having obligations to them? With respect to distant peoples, few philosophers have thought that the mere fact that people are at a distance from us precludes our having any obligations to them or their having any rights against us. Some philosophers, however, have argued that our ignorance of the specific membership of the class of distant peoples does rule out these moral relationships. Yet this cannot be right, given that in other contexts we recognize obligations to indeterminate classes of people, such as a police officer's obligation to help people in distress or the obligation of food processors not to harm those who consume their products.

What does, however, seem to be a necessary requirement before distant peoples can be said to have rights against us is that we are capable of acting across the distance that separates us. (This is simply an implication of the widely accepted philosophical principle that "ought" implies "can.") As long as this

73

condition is met—as it typically is for people living in most technologically advanced societies—there seems to be no conceptual obstacle to claiming that distant peoples have rights against us or that we have obligations to them. Of course, showing that it is conceptually possible does not yet prove that these rights and obligations actually exist. Such proof requires a substantial moral argument.

By contrast, answering the above question with respect to future generations is much more difficult and has been the subject of considerable debate among contemporary philosophers.

One issue concerns the question whether it is logically coherent to speak of future generations as having rights now. Of course, no one who finds talk about rights to be generally meaningful should question whether we can coherently claim that future generations *will* have rights at some point in the future (specifically, when they come into existence and are no longer *future* generations). But what is questioned, since it is of considerable practical significance, is whether we can coherently claim that future generations have rights *now* when they don't yet exist.

Some philosophers, such as Richard T. De George, have argued that such claims are logically incoherent (see Selection 9). According to De George, rights logically require the existence of rights-holders, and obligations logically require the existence of obligation-recipients. There are, however, at least two difficulties with this view.

The first difficulty has to do with the presuppositions said to underlie all talk about rights on the one hand and obligations on the other. The two are treated as if they were similar when they are not. The existence of rights-holders is held to be logically presupposed in any talk about rights, whereas in talk about obligations, it is not the existence of obligation-holders but of obligation-*recipients* that is said to be logically presupposed. So it seems perfectly possible to grant that rights-talk presupposes

the existence of rights-holders and obligation-talk that of obligation-holders, but then deny that obligation-talk also logically presupposes the existence of obligation-recipients. Instead, one might reasonably hold that what obligation-talk presupposes in this regard is only that there either exists or *will exist* obligation-recipients whose interests can be affected by the obligation-holders.

The second difficulty with this view is that even if it were correct about the existence presuppositions we make when talking about rights and obligations, retaining such usage would still be objectionable because it tends to beg important normative questions. For example, since this usage renders rights-talk and obligation-talk inapplicable to future generations, it tends to favor a negative answer to the question of whether we are morally required to begin *now* to provide for the welfare of future generations. On this account, it would be preferable to adopt alternative ways of talking about rights and obligations that are morally neutral and allow the normative and conceptual questions to be addressed more independently.

It used to be argued that the welfare rights of distant peoples and future generations would eventually be met as a by-product of the continued economic growth of the technologically developed societies of the world. It was believed that the transfer of investment and technology to the less developed societies of the world would eventually, if not make everyone well off, at least satisfy everyone's basic needs. Now we are not so sure. Presently more and more evidence points to the conclusion that without some substantial sacrifice on the part of the technologically developed societies of the world, many of the less developed societies will never be able to provide their members with even the basic necessities for survival.

How else are we going to meet the basic needs of the 1.2 billion people who are living today in conditions of absolute poverty without some plausible policy of redistribution? Even those, like Herman Kahn, who argue that an almost utopian world situation will obtain in the distant future, still would have to admit that unless some plausible policy of redistribution is adopted, malnutrition and starvation will continue in the less developed societies for many years to come. Thus, a recognition of the welfare rights of distant peoples and future generations would appear to have significant consequences for developed and underdeveloped societies alike.

Of course, there are various senses in which distant peoples and future generations can be said to have welfare rights and various moral grounds on which those rights can be justified. First of all, the welfare rights of distant peoples and future generations can be understood to be either negative rights or positive rights. A negative right is a right not to be interfered with in some specific manner. For example, a right to liberty is usually understood to be a negative right; it guarantees each person the right not to have her liberty interfered with provided that she does not unjustifiably interfere with the liberty of any other person. On the other hand, a positive right is a right to receive some specific goods or services. Typical positive rights are the right to have a loan repaid and the right to receive one's just earnings. Second, the welfare rights of distant peoples and future generations can be understood to be either *in personam* rights or *in rem* rights. *In personam* rights are rights that hold against some specific nameable person or persons, while *in rem* rights hold against everyone who is in a position to abide by the rights in question. A right to liberty is usually understood to be an *in rem* right while the right to have a loan repaid or the right to receive one's just earnings are typical *in personam* rights. Finally, the rights of distant peoples and future generations can be understood to be either legal rights, that is, rights that *are enforced* by coercive

sanctions, or moral rights, that is, rights that *ought to be enforced* either simply by noncoercive sanctions (for example, verbal condemnations) or by both coercive and noncoercive sanctions. Accordingly, what distinguishes the moral rights of distant peoples and future generations from the requirements of supererogation (the nonfulfillment of which is never blameworthy) is that the former but not the latter can be justifiably enforced either by noncoercive or by coercive and noncoercive sanctions.

Of the various moral grounds for justifying the welfare rights of distant peoples and future generations, quite possibly the most evident are those that appeal either to a right to life or a right to fair treatment. Libertarians interpret a person's right to life as a negative right. Welfare liberals and socialists interpret it as a positive right.

Thus, suppose we interpret a person's right to life as a positive right. So understood, the person's right to life would most plausibly be interpreted as a right to receive those goods and resources that are necessary for satisfying her basic needs. For a person's basic needs are those which must be satisfied in order not to seriously endanger her health or sanity. Thus, receiving the goods and resources that are necessary for satisfying her basic needs would preserve a person's life in the fullest sense. And if a person's positive right to life is to be universal in the sense that it is possessed by every person (as the right to life is generally understood to be), then it must be an *in rem* right. This is because an *in rem* right, unlike an *in personam* right, does not require for its possession the assumption by other persons of any special roles or contractual obligations. Interpreted as a positive *in rem* right, therefore, a person's right to life would clearly justify the welfare rights of distant peoples to have their basic needs satisfied.

Suppose, on the other hand, that we interpret a person's right to life as a negative right. Here again, if the right is to be universal in the sense that it is possessed by all persons, then it must also be an *in rem* right. So understood, the right would require that everyone who is in a position to do so not interfere in certain ways with a person's attempts to meet her basic needs.

But what sort of noninterference would this right to life justify? If one's basic needs have not been met, would a person's right to life require that others not interfere with her taking the goods she needs from the surplus possessions of those who already have satisfied their own basic needs? As it is standardly interpreted, a person's negative right to life would not require such noninterference. Instead, a person's negative right to life is usually understood to be limited in such circumstances by the property rights of those who have more than enough to satisfy their own basic needs. Moreover, those who claim property rights to such surplus goods and resources are usually in a position effectively to prohibit those in need from taking what they require. For surely most underdeveloped nations of the world would be able to sponsor expeditions to the American Midwest or the Australian plains for the purpose of collecting the grain necessary to satisfy the basic needs of their citizens if they were not effectively prohibited from doing so at almost every stage of the enterprise.

But are persons with such surplus goods and resources normally justified in so prohibiting others from satisfying their basic needs? Admittedly, such persons may have contributed greatly to the value of the surplus goods and resources they possess, but why should that give them power over the life and death of those less fortunate? Even though their contribution may well justify favoring their nonbasic needs over the nonbasic needs of others, how could it justify favoring their nonbasic needs over the basic needs of others? After all, a person's negative right to life, being an *in rem* right, does not

depend on the assumption by other persons of any special roles or contractual obligations. By contrast, property rights that are *in personam* rights require the assumption by other persons of the relevant roles and contractual obligations that constitute a particular system of acquisition and exchange, such as the role of a neighbor and the obligations of a merchant. Consequently, with respect to such property rights, it would seem that a person could not justifiably be kept from acquiring the goods and resources necessary to satisfy her basic needs by the property rights of others to surplus possessions, unless the person herself had voluntarily agreed to be so constrained by those property rights. But obviously few people would voluntarily agree to have such constraints placed upon their ability to acquire the goods and resources necessary to satisfy their basic needs. For most people, their right to acquire the goods and resources necessary to satisfy their basic needs would have priority over any other person's property rights to surplus possessions, or alternatively, they would conceive of property rights such that no one could have property rights to any surplus possessions that were required to satisfy their own basic needs.

Even if some property rights could arise, as *in rem* rights by a Lockean process of mixing one's labor with previously unowned goods and resources, there would still be a need for some sort of a restriction on such appropriations. For if these *in rem* property rights are to be *moral rights,* then it must be reasonable for every affected party to accept such rights, since the requirements of morality cannot be contrary to reason. Accordingly, in order to give rise to *in rem* property rights, the appropriation of previously unowned goods and resources cannot justifiably limit anyone's ability to acquire the goods and resources necessary to satisfy her basic needs, unless it would be reasonable for the person voluntarily to agree to be so constrained. But obviously it would not be reasonable for many people, particularly those whose basic needs are not being met, voluntarily to agree to be so constrained by property rights. This means that whether property rights are *in personam* rights and arise by the assumption of the relevant roles and contractual obligations or are *in rem* rights and arise by a Lockean process of mixing one's labor with previously unowned goods and resources, such rights would rarely limit a negative right to life, interpreted as an *in rem* right to noninterference with one's attempts to acquire the goods and resources necessary to satisfy one's basic needs. So interpreted, a negative right to life would clearly justify the welfare rights of distant people.

If we turn to a consideration of a person's right to fair treatment, a similar justification of the welfare rights of distant peoples and future generations emerges. To determine the requirements of fair treatment, suppose we employ a decision procedure analogous to the one John Rawls developed in *A Theory of Justice*. Suppose, that is to say, that in deciding upon the requirements of fair treatment, we were to discount the knowledge of which particular interests happen to be our own. Since we obviously know what our particular interests are, we would just not be taking that knowledge into account when selecting the requirements for fair treatment. Rather, in selecting these requirements, we would be reasoning from our knowledge of all the particular interests of everyone who would be affected by our decision but not from our knowledge of which particular interests happen to be our own. In employing this decision procedure, therefore, we (like judges who discount prejudicial information in order to reach fair decisions) would be able to give a fair hearing to everyone's particular interests. Assuming further that we are well-informed of the particular interests that would be affected by our decision and are fully capable of rationally deliberating with respect to that information, then our deliberations would culminate in a unanimous decision. This is because each of us would be deliberating in a rationally correct manner with respect to the same information and would be using a decision procedure leading to a uniform evaluation of the alternatives. Consequently, each of us would favor the same requirements for fair treatment.

But what requirements would we select by using this decision procedure? Since by using this decision procedure we would not be using our knowledge of which particular interests happen to be our own, we would be quite concerned about the pattern according to which goods and resources would be distributed throughout the world. In addition, since we would not be using our knowledge of what generation we might be a member of, some present or future one, we would be equally concerned about how goods and resources would be distributed across time. By using this decision procedure, we would reason as though our particular interests might be those of persons with the largest share of goods and resources, as those of persons with the smallest share of goods and resources, as those of persons living in the present, as well as those of persons living in the future. Consequently, we would neither exclusively favor the interests of persons with the largest share of goods by endorsing an unlimited right to accumulate goods and resources nor exclusively favor the interests of persons with the smallest share of goods and resources by endorsing the highest possible minimum for those who are least advantaged. Rather, we would compromise by endorsing a right to accumulate goods and resources that was limited by the guarantee of a minimum sufficient to provide each person with the goods and resources necessary to satisfy his or her basic needs. And we would reach the same type of compromise between the interests of present generations and the interests of future generations. We would endorse the right of present generations to accumulate goods and resources that was limited by the welfare rights of future generations to have their basic needs met. It seems clear, therefore, that a right to fair treatment as captured by this Rawlsian decision procedure would also justify the welfare rights of distant peoples and future generations.

So it would seem that the welfare rights of distant peoples and generations can be firmly grounded either in each person's right to life or each person's right to fair treatment. As a result, it would be impossible for one to deny that distant peoples and future generations have welfare rights without also denying that each person has a right to life and a right to fair treatment, unless, that is, one drastically reinterprets the significance of a right to life and a right to fair treatment.

Alternative Views

Not surprisingly, most of the solutions to the problem of distant peoples and future generations that have been proposed are analogous to the solutions we discussed with regard to the problem of the distribution of income and wealth within a society. (See Section I.)

As before, there is a libertarian solution. According to this view, distant peoples and future generations have no right to receive aid from persons living in today's affluent societies, but only a right not to be harmed by them. As before, these requirements are said to be derived from a political ideal of liberty. And, as before, we can question whether such an ideal actually supports these requirements.

Garrett Hardin endorses a "no aid" view in his essay (Selection 7). However, Hardin does not support his view on libertarian grounds. Without denying that there is a general obligation to help those in need, Hardin argues that helping those who live in absolute poverty in today's world would not do any good, and *for that reason* is not required. Hardin justifies this view on empirical grounds, claiming that the giving of aid would be ineffective and even counterproductive for controlling population growth.

In some of his earlier work, Peter Singer has challenged the empirical grounds on which Hardin's view rests. Singer claims that Hardin's view accepts the certain evil of unrelieved poverty in underdeveloped countries—for instance, Bangladesh and Somalia—so as to avoid the future possibility of still greater poverty in underdeveloped countries together with deteriorating conditions in developed and developing countries. Singer argues, however, that with a serious commitment to aid from developed countries, there is a "fair chance" that underdeveloped countries will bring their population growth under control, thus avoiding the greater evil Hardin fears. Given the likelihood of this result, Singer argues that we have no moral justification for embracing, as Hardin does, the certain evil of unrelieved poverty in underdeveloped countries by denying them aid.

In Selection 8, Singer provides his own solution for relieving poverty in underdeveloped countries. He argues that those of us who live in affluent countries ought to stop spending our money on luxuries and instead give that money to help aid the world's poor. To do otherwise, he argues, is hypocritical given many of our own values. As good examples of those who have put their wealth to good use he cites two of today's billionaires, Bill Gates and Warren Buffett. But perhaps the best example Singer provides is Zell Kravinsky, a former real estate millionaire, who, as a middle-aged man, donated almost all his fortune to health-related charities.

In Selection 9, Richard De George supports a "no-aid" view for future generations (but not for distant peoples, who he thinks do have a right to receive aid) on purely conceptual grounds, claiming that future generations cannot logically have rights against us nor we have obligations to them. We have already noted some difficulties with the view De George defends.

In Selection 10, James P. Sterba builds off an argument he made in an earlier selection (Selection 2) where he argued that the libertarian ideal of liberty supports a right to welfare. Here he considers what implications a libertarian right to welfare would have for distant peoples and future generations. He argues that using up no more resources than is necessary for meeting our own basic needs is what is required of us, if we are to take seriously both the welfare rights of distant peoples *and* future generations.

Practical Applications

With respect to distant peoples, one of the hot button issues in U.S. politics today is immigration policy. In Selection 11, Phillip Cole argues against immigration controls. He says that it makes no sense for liberals, who are committed to the moral equality of all persons, to accept immigration controls. Not only are they inconsistent with a set of core values, Cole argues, but in practice they lead to situations of oppression and inequality, since they mainly serve to prevent the movement of people in poverty. We must therefore replace immigration controls, he says, with completely open borders. He also provides a sketch of new ways we could think of citizenship in the near future consistent with seeing all persons as free and equal members of a global community.

In Selection 12, Christopher Heath Wellman defends the right of legitimate states to control their own immigration policies. He argues that just as an individual is free to choose who they will marry or not, the citizens of a legitimate state are free to collectively decide who or who not to allow in their political community.

With respect to the hard case of refugees, Wellman says that states are obligated to help refugees, but states do not *have* to discharge this obligation in the form of accepting them as members in their political community. States have a number of other options they could just as easily turn to in order to discharge their obligations to refugees. But if the only way a state can help is by accepting refugees into its political community, then, Wellman says, it is obligated to do so.

7

Lifeboat Ethics:
The Case against Helping the Poor

GARRETT HARDIN

Garrett Hardin argues that our first obligation is to ourselves and our posterity. For that reason, he contends, it would be foolish for rich nations to share their surplus with poor nations, whether through a World Food Bank, the exporting of technology, or unrestricted immigration. In view of the growing populations and improvident behavior of poor nations, such sharing would do no good—it would only overload the environment and lead to demands for still greater assistance in the future.

Environmentalists use the metaphor of the earth as a "spaceship" in trying to persuade countries, industries, and people to stop wasting and polluting our natural resources. Since we all share life on this planet, they argue, no single person or institution has the right to destroy, waste, or use more than a fair share of its resources.

But does everyone on earth have an equal right to an equal share of its resources? The spaceship metaphor can be dangerous when used by misguided idealists to justify suicidal policies for sharing our resources through uncontrolled immigration and foreign aid. In their enthusiastic but unrealistic generosity, they confuse the ethics of a spaceship with those of a lifeboat.

A true spaceship would have to be under the control of a captain, since no ship could possibly survive if its course were determined by committee. Spaceship Earth certainly has no captain; the United Nations is merely a toothless tiger, with little power to enforce any policy upon its bickering members.

If we divide the world crudely into rich nations and poor nations, two thirds of them are desperately poor, and only one third comparatively rich, with the United States the wealthiest of all. Metaphorically each rich nation can be seen as a lifeboat full of comparatively rich people. In the ocean outside each lifeboat swim the poor of the world, who would like to get in, or at least to share some of the wealth. What should the lifeboat passengers do?

First we must recognize the limited capacity of any lifeboat. For example, a nation's land has a limited capacity to support a population and as the current energy crisis has shown us, in some ways we have already exceeded the carrying capacity of our land.

ADRIFT IN A MORAL SEA

So here we sit, say fifty people in our lifeboat. To be generous, let us assume it has room for ten more, making a total capacity of sixty. Suppose the fifty of us in the lifeboat see one hundred others swimming in the water outside, begging for admission to our boat or for handouts. We have several options: We may be tempted to try to live by the Christian ideal of being "our brother's keeper," or by the Marxist ideal of "to each according to his needs." Since the needs of all in the water are the same, and since they can all be seen as "our brothers," we could take them all into our boat, making a total of 150 in a boat designed for sixty. The boat swamps, everyone drowns. Complete justice, complete catastrophe.

Since the boat has an unused excess capacity of ten more passengers, we could admit just ten more to it. But which ten do we let in? How do we choose? Do we pick the best ten, the neediest ten, "first come, first served"? And what do we say to the ninety we exclude? If we do let an extra ten into our lifeboat, we will have lost our "safety factor," an engineering principle of critical importance. For example, if we don't leave room for excess capacity as a safety factor in our country's agriculture, a new plant disease or a bad change in the weather could have disastrous consequences.

Suppose we decide to preserve our small safety factor and admit no more to the lifeboat. Our survival is then possible, although we shall have to be constantly on guard against boarding parties.

While this last solution clearly offers the only means of our survival, it is morally abhorrent to many people. Some say they feel guilty about their good luck. My reply is simple: "Get out and yield your place to others." This may solve the problem of the guilt-ridden person's conscience, but it does not change the ethics of the lifeboat. The needy person to whom the guilt-ridden person yields his place will not himself feel guilty about his good luck. If he did, he would not climb aboard. The net result of conscience-stricken people giving up their unjustly held seats is the elimination of that sort of conscience from the lifeboat.

This is the basic metaphor within which we must work out our solutions. Let us now enrich the image, step by step, with substantive additions from the real world, a world that must solve real and pressing problems of overpopulation and hunger.

The harsh ethics of the lifeboat become even harsher when we consider the reproductive differences between the rich nations and the poor nations. The people inside the lifeboats are doubling in number every eighty-seven years; those swimming around outside are doubling, on the average, every thirty-five years, more than twice as fast as the rich. And since the world's resources are dwindling, the difference in prosperity between the rich and the poor can only increase.

As of 1973, the United States had a population of 210 million people, who were increasing by 0.8 percent per year. Outside our lifeboat, let us imagine another 210 million people (say the combined populations of Colombia, Ecuador, Venezuela, Morocco, Pakistan, Thailand, and the Philippines), who are increasing at a rate of 3.3 percent per year. Put differently, the doubling time for this aggregate population is twenty-one years, compared to eighty-seven years for the United States.

MULTIPLYING THE RICH AND THE POOR

Now suppose the United States agreed to pool its resources with those seven countries, with everyone receiving an equal share. Initially the ratio of Americans to non-Americans in this model would be one-to-one. But consider what the ratio would be after eighty-seven years, by which time the Americans would have doubled to a population of 420 million. By then, doubling every twenty-one years, the other group would have swollen to 354 billion. Each American would have to share the available resources with more than eight people.

But, one could argue, this discussion assumes that current population trends will continue, and they may not. Quite so. Most likely the rate of population increase will decline much faster in the United States than it will in the other countries, and there does not seem to be much we can do about it. In sharing with "each according to his needs," we must recognize that needs are determined by population size, which is determined by the rate of reproduction, which at present is regarded as a sovereign right of every nation, poor or not. This being so, the philanthropic load created by the sharing ethic of the spaceship can only increase.

THE TRAGEDY
OF THE COMMONS

The fundamental error of spaceship ethics, and the sharing it requires, is that it leads to what I call "the tragedy of the commons." Under a system of private property, the men who own property recognize their responsibility to care for it, for if they don't they will eventually suffer. A farmer, for instance, will allow no more cattle in a pasture than its carrying capacity justifies. If he overloads it, erosion sets in, weeds take over, and he loses the use of the pasture.

If a pasture becomes a commons open to all, the right of each to use it may not be matched by a corresponding responsibility to protect it. Asking everyone to use it with discretion will hardly do, for the considerate herdsman who refrains from overloading the commons suffers more than a selfish one who says his needs are greater. If everyone would restrain himself, all would be well; but it takes only one less than everyone to ruin a system of voluntary restraint. In a crowded world of less than perfect human beings, mutual ruin is inevitable if there are no controls. This is the tragedy of the commons.

One of the major tasks of education today should be the creation of such an acute awareness of the dangers of the commons that people will recognize its many varieties. For example, the air and water have become polluted because they are treated as commons. Further growth in the population or per-capita conversion of natural resources into pollutants will only make the problem worse. The same holds true for the fish of the oceans. Fishing fleets have nearly disappeared in many parts of the world; technological improvements in the art of fishing are hastening the day of complete ruin. Only the replacement of the system of the commons with a responsible system of control will save the land, air, water, and oceanic fisheries.

THE WORLD FOOD BANK

In recent years there has been a push to create a new commons called a World Food Bank, an international depository of food reserves to which nations would contribute according to their abilities and from which they would draw according to their needs. This humanitarian proposal has received support from many liberal international groups, and from such prominent citizens as Margaret Mead, U.N. Secretary General Kurt Waldheim, and Senators Edward Kennedy and George McGovern.

A world food bank appeals powerfully to our humanitarian impulses. But before we rush ahead with such a plan, let us recognize where the greatest political push comes from, lest we be disillusioned later. Our experience with the "Food for Peace program," or Public Law 480, gives us the answer. This program moved billions of dollars worth of U.S. surplus grain to food-short, population-long countries during the past two decades. But when PL. 480 first became law, a headline in the business magazine *Forbes* revealed the real power behind it: "Feeding the World's Hungry Millions; How It Will Mean Billions for U.S. Business."

And indeed it did. In the years 1960 to 1970, U.S. taxpayers spent a total of $7.9 billion on the Food for Peace program. Between 1948 and 1970, they also paid an additional $50 billion for other economic-aid programs, some of which went for food and food-producing machinery and technology. Though all U.S. taxpayers were forced to contribute to the cost of P.L. 480, certain special interest groups gained handsomely under the program. Farmers did not have to contribute the grain; the Government, or rather the taxpayers, bought it from them at full market prices. The increased demand raised prices of farm products generally. The manufacturers of farm machinery, fertilizers, and pesticides benefited by the farmers' extra efforts to grow more food. Grain elevators profited from storing the surplus until it could be shipped. Railroads made money hauling it to ports, and shipping lines profited from carrying it overseas. The implementation of P.L. 480 required the creation of a vast Government bureaucracy, which then acquired its own vested interest in continuing the program regardless of its merits.

EXTRACTING DOLLARS

Those who proposed and defended the Food for Peace program in public rarely mentioned its importance to any of these special interests. The public emphasis was always on its humanitarian effects. The combination of silent selfish interests and highly vocal humanitarian apologists made a powerful and successful lobby for extracting money from taxpayers. We can expect the same lobby to push now for the creation of a World Food Bank.

However great the potential benefit to selfish interests, it should not be a decisive argument against a truly humanitarian program. We must ask if such a program would actually do more good than harm, not only momentarily but also in the long run. Those who propose the food bank usually refer to a current "emergency" or "crisis" in terms of world food supply. But what is an emergency? Although they may be infrequent and sudden, everyone knows that emergencies will occur from time to time. A well-run family, company, organization, or country prepares for the likelihood of accidents and emergencies. It expects them, it budgets for them, it saves for them.

LEARNING THE HARD WAY

What happens if some organizations or countries budget for accidents and others do not? If each country is solely responsible for its own well-being, poorly managed ones will suffer. But they can learn from experience. They may mend their ways and learn to budget for infrequent but certain emergencies. For example, the weather varies from year to year, and periodic crop failures are certain. A wise and competent government saves out of the production of the good years in anticipation of bad years to come. Joseph taught this policy to Pharaoh in Egypt more than 2,000 years ago. Yet the great majority of the governments in the world today do not follow such a policy. They lack either the wisdom or the competence, or both. Should those nations that do manage to put something aside be forced to come to the rescue each time an emergency occurs among the poor nations?

"But it isn't their fault!" some kindhearted liberals argue. "How can we blame the poor people who are caught in an emergency? Why must they suffer for the sins of their governments?" The concept of blame is simply not relevant here. The real question is, what are the operational consequences of establishing a world food bank? If it is open to every country every time a need develops, slovenly rulers will not be motivated to take Joseph's advice. Someone will always come to their aid. Some countries will deposit food in the world food bank, and others will withdraw it. There will be almost no overlap. As a result of such solutions to food shortage emergencies, the poor countries will not learn to mend their ways and will suffer progressively greater emergencies as their populations grow.

POPULATION CONTROL
THE CRUDE WAY

On the average, poor countries undergo a 2.5 percent increase in population each year; rich countries, about 0.8 percent. Only rich countries have anything in the way of food reserves set aside, and even they do not have as much as they should. Poor countries have none. If poor countries received no food from the outside, the rate of their population growth would be periodically checked by crop failures and famines. But if they can always draw on a world food bank in time of need, their population can continue to grow unchecked, and so will their "need" for aid. In the short run, a world food bank may diminish that need, but in the long run it actually increases the need without limit.

Without some system of worldwide food sharing, the proportion of people in the rich and poor nations might eventually stabilize. The overpopulated poor countries would decrease in numbers, while the rich countries that had room for more people would increase. But with a well-meaning system of sharing, such as a world food bank, the growth differential between the rich and the poor countries will not only persist, it will increase. Because of the higher rate of population growth in the poor countries of the world, 88 percent of today's children are born poor, and only 12 percent rich. Year by year the ratio becomes worse, as the fast-reproducing poor outnumber the slow-reproducing rich.

A world food bank is thus a commons in disguise. People will have more motivation to draw from it than to add to any common store. The less provident and less able will multiply at the expense of the abler and more provident, bringing eventual ruin upon all who share in the commons. Besides, any system of "sharing" that amounts to foreign aid from the rich nations to the poor nations will carry the taint of charity, which will contribute little to the world peace so devoutly desired by those who support the idea of a world food bank.

As past U.S. foreign-aid programs have amply and depressingly demonstrated, international charity frequently inspires mistrust and antagonism rather than gratitude on the part of the recipient nation.

CHINESE FISH
AND MIRACLE RICE

The modern approach to foreign aid stresses the export of technology and advice, rather than money and food. As an ancient Chinese proverb goes: "Give a man a fish and he will eat for a day; teach him how to fish and he will eat for the rest of his days." Acting on this advice, the Rockefeller and Ford Foundations have financed a number of programs for improving agriculture in the hungry nations. Known as the "Green Revolution," these programs have led to the development of "miracle rice" and "miracle wheat," new strains that offer bigger harvests and greater resistance to crop damage. Norman Borlaug, the Nobel Prize-winning agronomist who, supported by the Rockefeller Foundation, developed "miracle wheat," is one of the most prominent advocates of a world food bank.

Whether or not the Green Revolution can increase food production as much as its champions claim is a debatable but possibly irrelevant point. Those who support this well-intended humanitarian effort should first consider some of the fundamentals of human ecology. Ironically, one man who did was the late Alan Gregg, a vice-president of the Rockefeller Foundation. Two decades ago he expressed strong doubts about the wisdom of such attempts to increase food production. He likened the growth and spread of humanity over the surface of the earth to the spread of cancer in the human body, remarking that "cancerous growths demand food; but, as far as I know, they have never been cured by getting it."

OVERLOADING
THE ENVIRONMENT

Every human born constitutes a draft on all aspects of the environment: food, air, water, forests, beaches, wildlife, scenery, and solitude. Food can, perhaps, be significantly increased to meet a growing demand. But what about clean beaches, unspoiled forests, and solitude? If we satisfy a growing population's need for food, we necessarily decrease its per capita supply of the other resources needed by men.

India, for example, now has a population of 600 million, which increases by 15 million each year. This population already puts a huge load on a relatively impoverished environment. The country's forests are now only a small fraction of what they were three centuries ago, and floods and erosion continually destroy the insufficient farmland that remains. Every one of the 15 million new lives added to India's population puts an additional burden on the environment and increases the economic and social costs of crowding. However humanitarian our intent, every Indian life saved through medical or nutritional assistance from abroad diminishes the quality of life for those who remain, and for subsequent generations. If rich countries make it possible, through foreign aid, for 600 million Indians to swell to 1.2 billion in a mere twenty-eight years, as their current growth rate threatens, will future generations of Indians thank us for hastening the destruction of their environment? Will our good intentions be sufficient excuse for the consequences of our actions?

My final example of a commons in action is one for which the public has the least desire for rational discussion—immigration. Anyone who publicly questions the wisdom of current U.S. immigration policy is promptly charged with bigotry, prejudice, ethnocentrism, chauvinism, isolationism, or selfishness. Rather than encounter such accusations, one would rather talk about other matters, leaving immigration policy to wallow in the crosscurrents of special interests that take no account of the good of the whole, or the interests of posterity.

Perhaps we still feel guilty about things we said in the past. Two generations ago the popular press frequently referred to Dagos, Wops, Polacks, Chinks, and Krauts, in articles about how America was being "overrun" by foreigners of supposedly inferior genetic stock. But because the implied inferiority of foreigners was used then as justification for keeping them out, people now assume that restrictive policies could only be based on such misguided notions. There are other grounds.

A NATION OF IMMIGRANTS

Just consider the numbers involved. Our Government acknowledges a net inflow of 400,000 immigrants a year. While we have no hard data on the extent of illegal entries, educated guesses put the figure at about 600,000 a year. Since the natural increase (excess of births over deaths) of the resident population now runs about 1.7 million per year, the yearly gain from immigration amounts to at least 19 percent of the total annual increase, and may be as much as 37 percent if we include the estimate for illegal immigrants. Considering the growing use of birth-control devices, the potential effect of educational campaigns by such organizations as Planned Parenthood Federation of America and Zero Population Growth, and the influence of inflation and the housing shortage, the fertility rate

of American women may decline so much that immigration could account for all the yearly increase in population. Should we not at least ask if that is what we want?

For the sake of those who worry about whether the "quality" of the average immigrant compares favorably with the quality of the average resident, let us assume that immigrants and native-born citizens are of exactly equal quality, however one defines that term. We will focus here only on quantity; and since our conclusions will depend on nothing else, all charges of bigotry and chauvinism become irrelevant.

IMMIGRATION VERSUS FOOD SUPPLY

World food banks *move food to the people,* hastening the exhaustion of the environment of the poor countries. Unrestricted immigration, on the other hand, *moves people to the food,* thus speeding up the destruction of the environment of the rich countries. We can easily understand why poor people should want to make this latter transfer, but why should rich hosts encourage it?

As in the case of foreign-aid programs, immigration receives support from selfish interests and humanitarian impulses. The primary selfish interest in unimpeded immigration is the desire of employers for cheap labor, particularly in industries and trades that offer degrading work. In the past, one wave of foreigners after another was brought into the United States to work at wretched jobs for wretched wages. In recent years the Cubans, Puerto Ricans, and Mexicans have had this dubious honor. The interests of the employers of cheap labor mesh well with the guilty silence of the country's liberal intelligentsia. White Anglo-Saxon Protestants are particularly reluctant to call for a closing of the doors to immigration for fear of being called bigots.

But not all countries have such reluctant leadership. Most educated Hawaiians, for example, are keenly aware of the limits of their environment, particularly in terms of population growth. There is only so much room on the islands, and the islanders know it. To Hawaiians, immigrants from the other forty-nine states present as great a threat as those from other nations. At a recent meeting of Hawaiian government officials in Honolulu, I had the ironic delight of hearing a speaker, who like most of his audience was of Japanese ancestry, ask how the country might practically and constitutionally close its doors to further immigration. One member of the audience countered: "How can we shut the doors now? We have many friends and relatives in Japan that we'd like to bring here some day so that they can enjoy Hawaii too." The Japanese-American speaker smiled sympathetically and answered: "Yes, but we have children now, and someday we'll have grandchildren too. We can bring more people here from Japan only by giving away some of the land that we hope to pass on to our grandchildren some day. What right do we have to do that?"

At this point, I can hear U.S. liberals asking: "How can you justify slamming the door once you're inside? You say that immigrants should be kept out. But aren't we all immigrants, or the descendants of immigrants? If we insist on staying, must we not admit all others?" Our craving for intellectual order leads us to seek and prefer symmetrical rules and morals: a single rule for me and everybody else; the same rule yesterday, today, and tomorrow. Justice, we feel, should not change with time and place.

We Americans of non-Indian ancestry can look upon ourselves as the descendants of thieves who are guilty morally, if not legally, of stealing this land from its Indian owners. Should we then give back the land to the now living American descendants of those Indians? However morally or logically sound this proposal may be, I, for one, am unwilling to live by it and I know no one else who is. Besides, the logical consequence would be absurd. Suppose that, intoxicated with a sense of pure justice, we should decide to turn our land over to the Indians. Since all our wealth has also been derived from the land, wouldn't we be morally obliged to give that back to the Indians too?

PURE JUSTICE VERSUS REALITY

Clearly, the concept of pure justice produces an infinite regression to absurdity. Centuries ago, wise men invented statutes of limitations to justify the rejection of such pure justice, in the interest of preventing continual disorder. The law zealously defends property rights, but only relatively recent property rights. Drawing a line after an arbitrary time has elapsed may be unjust, but the alternatives are worse.

We are all the descendants of thieves, and the world's resources are inequitably distributed. But we must begin the journey to tomorrow from the point where we are today. We cannot remake the past. We cannot safely divide the wealth equitably among all peoples so long as people reproduce at different rates. To do so would guarantee that our grandchildren, and everyone else's grandchildren, would have only a ruined world to inhabit.

To be generous with one's own possessions is quite different from being generous with those of posterity. We should call this point to the attention of those who, from a commendable love of justice and equality, would institute a system of the commons, either in the form of a world food bank, or of unrestricted immigration. We must convince them if we wish to save at least some parts of the world from environmental ruin.

Without a true world government to control reproduction and the use of available resources, the sharing ethic of the spaceship is impossible. For the foreseeable future, our survival demands that we govern our actions by the ethics of a lifeboat, harsh though they may be. Posterity will be satisfied with nothing less.

ADDENDUM 1989

Can anyone watch children starve on television without wanting to help? Naturally sympathetic, a normal human being thinks that he can imagine what it is like to be starving. We all want to do unto others as we would have them do unto us.

But wanting is not doing. Forty years of activity by the U.S. Agency for International Development, as well as episodic nongovernmental attempts to feed the world's starving, have produced mixed results. Before we respond to the next appeal we should ask, "Does what we call 'aid' really help?"

Some of the shortcomings of food aid can be dealt with briefly. Waste is unavoidable: Because most poor countries have wretched transportation systems, food may sit on a dock until it rots. Then there are the corrupt politicians who take donated food away from the poor and give it to their political supporters. In Somalia in the 1980s, fully 70 percent of the donated food went to the army.

We can school ourselves to accept such losses. Panicky projects are always inefficient: Waste and corruption are par for the course. But there is another kind of loss that we cannot—in fact, we should not—accept, and that is the loss caused by the boomerang effects of philanthropy. Before we jump onto the next "feed-the-starving" bandwagon we need to understand how well-intentioned efforts can be counter-productive.

Briefly put, it is a mistake to focus only on starving people while ignoring their surroundings. Where there is great starvation there is usually an impoverished environment: poor soil, scarce water, and wildly fluctuating weather. As a result, the "carrying capacity" of the environment is low. The territory simply cannot support the population that is trying to live on it. Yet if the population were much smaller, and if it would stay smaller, the people would not need to starve.

Let us look at a particular example. Nigeria, like all the central African countries, has increased greatly in population in the last quarter-century. Over many generations, Nigerians learned that their farmlands would be most productive if crop-growing alternated with "fallow years"—years in which the land was left untilled to recover its fertility.

When modern medicine reduced the death rate, the population began to grow. More food was demanded from the same land. Responding to that need, Nigerians shortened the fallow periods. The result was counterproductive. In one carefully studied village, the average fallow period was shortened from 5.3 to 1.4 years. As a result, the yearly production (averaged over both fallow and crop years) fell by 30 percent.

Are Nigerian farmers stupid? Not at all! They know perfectly well what they are doing. But a farmer whose family has grown too large for his farm has to take care of next year's need before he can provide for the future. To fallow or not to fallow translates into this choice: zero production in a fallow year or a 30 percent shortfall over the long run. Starvation cannot wait. Long-term policies have to give way to short-term ones. So the farmer plows up his overstressed fields, thus diminishing long-term productivity.

Once the carrying capacity of a territory has been transgressed, its capacity goes down, year after year. Transgression is a one-way road to ruin. Ecologists memorialize this reality with an Eleventh Commandment: "Thou shalt not transgress the carrying capacity."

Transgression takes many forms. Poor people are poor in energy resources. They need energy to cook their food. Where do they get it? Typically, from animal dung or trees and bushes. Burning dung deprives the soil of nitrogen. Cutting down trees and bushes deprives the land of protection against eroding rain. Soil-poor slopes cannot support a crop of fuel-plants. Once the soil is gone, water runs off the slopes faster and floods the valleys below. First poor people deforest their land, and then deforestation makes them poorer.

When Americans send food to a starving population that has already grown beyond the environment's carrying capacity, we become a partner in the devastation of their land. Food from the outside keeps more natives alive; these demand more food and fuel; greater demand causes the community to transgress the carrying capacity more, and transgression results in lowering the carrying capacity. The deficit grows exponentially. Gifts of food to an over-populated country boomerang, increasing starvation over the long run. Our choice is really between letting some die this year and letting more die in the following years.

You may protest, "That's easy enough for a well-fed American to say, but do citizens of poor countries agree?" Well, wisdom is not restricted to the wealthy. The Somali novelist Nuruddin Farrah has courageously condemned foreign gifts as being not truly aid, but a poison, because (if continued) such gifts will make Africans permanently dependent on outside aid.

The ethicist Joseph Fletcher has given a simple directive to would-be philanthropists: "Give if it helps, but not if it hurts." We can grant that giving makes the donor feel good at first—but how will he feel later when he realizes that he has harmed the receiver?

Only one thing can really help a poor country: population control. Having accepted disease control the people must now accept population control.

What the philosopher-economist Kenneth Boulding has called "lovey-dovey charity" is not enough. "It is well to remember," he said, "that the symbol of Christian love is a cross and not a teddy bear." A good Christian should obey the Eleventh Commandment, refusing to send gifts that help poor people destroy the environment that must support the next generation.

8

What Should a Billionaire Give—and What Should You?

PETER SINGER

Peter Singer takes the view that people in affluent countries ought to stop spending their money on luxuries and begin giving that money to aid the world's poor. As examples of those who have put their riches to good use he cites billionaires such as Bill Gates and Warren Buffett.

What is a human life worth? You may not want to put a price tag on a it. But if we really had to, most of us would agree that the value of a human life would be in the millions. Consistent with the foundations of our democracy and our frequently professed belief in the inherent dignity of human beings, we would also agree that all humans are created equal, at least to the extent of denying that differences of sex, ethnicity, nationality and place of residence change the value of a human life.

With Christmas approaching, and Americans writing checks to their favorite charities, it's a good time to ask how these two beliefs—that a human life, if it can be priced at all, is worth millions, and that the factors I have mentioned do not alter the value of a human life—square with our actions. Perhaps this year such questions lurk beneath the surface of more family discussions than usual, for it has been an extraordinary year for philanthropy, especially philanthropy to fight global poverty.

For Bill Gates, the founder of Microsoft, the ideal of valuing all human life equally began to jar against reality some years ago, when he read an article

about diseases in the developing world and came across the statistic that half a million children die every year from rotavirus, the most common cause of severe diarrhea in children. He had never heard of rotavirus. "How could I never have heard of something that kills half a million children every year?" he asked himself. He then learned that in developing countries, millions of children die from diseases that have been eliminated, or virtually eliminated, in the United States. That shocked him because he assumed that, if there are vaccines and treatments that could save lives, governments would be doing everything possible to get them to the people who need them. As Gates told a meeting of the World Health Assembly in Geneva last year, he and his wife, Melinda, "couldn't escape the brutal conclusion that—in our world today—some lives are seen as worth saving and others are not." They said to themselves, "This can't be true." But they knew it was.

Gates's speech to the World Health Assembly concluded on an optimistic note, looking forward to the next decade when "people will finally accept that the death of a child in the developing world is just as tragic as the death of a child in the developed world." That belief in the equal value of all human life is also prominent on the Web site of the Bill and Melinda Gates Foundation, where under Our Values we read: "All lives—no matter where they are being led—have equal value."

We are very far from acting in accordance with that belief. In the same world in which more than a billion people live at a level of affluence never previously known, roughly a billion other people struggle to survive on the purchasing power equivalent of less than one U.S. dollar per day. Most of the world's poorest people are undernourished, lack access to safe drinking water or even the most basic health services and cannot send their children to school. According to Unicef, more than 10 million children die every year—about 30,000 per day—from avoidable, poverty-related causes.

Last June the investor Warren Buffet took a significant step toward reducing those deaths when he pledged $31 billion to the Gates Foundation, and another $6 billion to other charitable foundations. Buffett's pledge, set alongside the nearly $30 billion given by Bill and Melinda Gates to their foundation, has made it clear that the first decade of the 21st century is a new "golden age of philanthropy." On an inflation-adjusted basis, Buffett has pledged to give more than double the lifetime total given away by two of the philanthropic giants of the past, Andrew Carnegie and John D. Rockefeller, put together. Bill and Melinda Gates's gifts are not far behind.

Gates's and Buffett's donations will now be put to work primarily to reduce poverty, disease and premature death in the developing world. According to the Global Forum for Health Research, less than 10 percent of the world's health research budget is spent on combating conditions that account for 90 percent of the global burden of disease. In the past, diseases that affect only the poor have been of no commercial interest to pharmaceutical manufacturers, because the poor cannot afford to buy their products. The Global Alliance for Vaccines and Immunization (GAVI), heavily supported by the Gates Foundation, seeks to change this by guaranteeing to purchase millions of doses of vaccines, when

they are developed, that can prevent diseases like malaria. GAVI has also assisted developing countries to immunize more people with existing vaccines: 99 million additional children have been reached to date. By doing this, GAVI claims to have already averted nearly 1.7 million future deaths.

Philanthropy on this scale raises many ethical questions: Why are the people who are giving doing so? Does it do any good? Should we praise them for giving so much or criticize them for not giving still more? Is it troubling that such momentous decisions are made by a few extremely wealthy individuals? And how do our judgments about them reflect on our own way of living?

Let's start with the question of motives. The rich must—or so some of us with less money like to assume—suffer sleepless nights because of their ruthlessness in squeezing out competitors, firing workers, shutting down plants or whatever else they have to do to acquire their wealth. When wealthy people give away money, we can always say that they are doing it to ease their consciences or generate favorable publicity. It has been suggested—by, for example, David Kirkpatrick, a senior editor at *Fortune* magazine—that Bill Gates's turn to philanthropy was linked to the antitrust problems Microsoft had in the U.S. and the European Union. Was Gates, consciously or subconsciously, trying to improve his own image and that of his company?

This kind of sniping tells us more about the attackers than the attacked. Giving away large sums, rather than spending the money on corporate advertising or developing new products, is not a sensible strategy for increasing personal wealth. When we read that someone has given away a lot of their money, or time, to help others, it challenges us to think about our own behavior. Should we be following their example, in our own modest way? But if the rich just give their money away to improve their image, or to make up for past misdeeds—misdeeds quite unlike any we have committed, of course—then, conveniently, what they are doing has no relevance to what we ought to do.

A famous story is told about Thomas Hobbes, the 17th-century English philosopher, who argued that we all act in our own interests. On seeing him give alms to a beggar, a cleric asked Hobbes if he would have done this if Christ had not commanded us to do so. Yes, Hobbes replied, he was in pain to see the miserable condition of the old man, and his gift, by providing the man with some relief from that misery, also eased Hobbes's pain. That reply reconciles Hobbes's charity with his egoistic theory of human motivation, but at the cost of emptying egoism of much of its bite. If egoists suffer when they see a stranger in distress, they are capable of being as charitable as any altruist.

Followers of the 18th-century German philosopher Immanuel Kant would disagree. They think an act has moral worth only if it is done out of a sense of duty. Doing something merely because you enjoy doing it, or enjoy seeing its consequences, they say, has no moral worth, because if you happened not to enjoy doing it, then you wouldn't do it, and you are not responsible for your likes and dislikes, whereas you are responsible for your obedience to the demands of duty.

Perhaps some philanthropists are motivated by their sense of duty. Apart from the equal value of all human life, the other "simple value" that lies at the core of the work of the Gates Foundation, according to its Web site, is "To whom much has been given, much is expected." That suggests the view that those who have great wealth have a duty to use it for a larger purpose than their own interests. But while such questions of motive may be relevant to our assessment of Gates's or Buffett's character, they pale into insignificance when we consider the effect of what Gates and Buffett are doing. The parents whose children could die from rotavirus care more about getting the help that will save their children's lives than about the motivations of those who make that possible.

Interestingly, neither Gates nor Buffett seems motivated by the possibility of being rewarded in heaven for his good deeds on earth. Gates told a Time interviewer, "There's a lot more I could be doing on a Sunday morning" than going to church. Put them together with Andrew Carnegie, famous for his freethinking, and three of the four greatest American philanthropists have been atheists or agnostics. (The exception is John D. Rockefeller.)

In a country in which 96 percent of the population say they believe in a supreme being, that's a striking fact. It means that in one sense, Gates and Buffett are probably less self-interested in their charity than someone like Mother Teresa, who as a pious Roman Catholic believed in reward and punishment in the afterlife.

More important than questions about motives are questions about whether there is an obligation for the rich to give, and if so, how much they should give. A few years ago, an African-American cabdriver taking me to the Inter-American Development Bank in Washington asked me if I worked at the bank. I told him I did not but was speaking at a conference on development and aid. He then assumed that I was an economist, but when I said no, my training was in philosophy, he asked me if I thought the U.S. should give foreign aid. When I answered affirmatively, he replied that the government shouldn't tax people in order to give their money to others. That, he thought, was robbery. When I asked if he believed that the rich should voluntarily donate some of what they earn to the poor, he said that if someone had worked for his money, he wasn't going to tell him what to do with it.

At that point we reached our destination. Had the journey continued, I might have tried to persuade him that people can earn large amounts only when they live under favorable social circumstances, and that they don't create those circumstances by themselves. I could have quoted Warren Buffett's acknowledgment that society is responsible for much of his wealth. "If you stick me down in the middle of Bangladesh or Peru," he said, "you'll find out how much this talent is going to produce in the wrong kind of soil." The Nobel Prize-winning economist and social scientist Herbert Simon estimated that "social capital" is responsible for at least 90 percent of what people earn in wealthy societies like those of the United States or northwestern Europe. By social capital Simon meant not only natural resources but, more important, the technology and organizational skills in the community, and the presence of good government. These are the foundation on which the rich can begin their work. "On moral grounds," Simon added, "we could argue for a flat income tax of 90 percent." Simon was not, of course, advocating so steep a rate of tax, for he was well aware of disincentive effects. But his estimate does undermine the argument that the rich are entitled to keep their wealth because it is all a result of their hard work. If Simon is right, that is true of at most 10 percent of it.

In any case, even if we were to grant that people deserve every dollar they earn, that doesn't answer the question of what they should do with it. We might say that they have a right to spend it on lavish parties, private jets and luxury yachts, or, for that matter, to flush it down the toilet. But we could still think that for them to do these things while others die from easily preventable diseases is wrong. In an article I wrote more than three decades ago, at the time of a humanitarian emergency in what is now Bangladesh, I used the example of walking by a shallow pond and seeing a small child who has fallen in and appears to be in danger of drowning. Even though we did nothing to cause the child to fall into the pond, almost everyone agrees that if we can save the child at minimal inconvenience or trouble to ourselves, we ought to do so. Anything else would be callous, indecent and, in a word, wrong. The fact that in rescuing the child we may, for example, ruin a new pair of shoes is not a good reason for allowing the child to drown. Similarly if for the cost of a pair of shoes we can contribute to a health program in a developing country that stands a good chance of saving the life of a child, we ought to do so.

Perhaps, though, our obligation to help the poor is even stronger than this example implies, for we are less innocent than the passer-by who did nothing to cause the child to fall into the pond. Thomas Pogge, a philosopher at Columbia University, has argued that at least some of our affluence comes at the expense of the poor. He bases this claim not simply on the usual critique of the barriers that Europe and the United States maintain against agricultural imports from developing countries but also on less familiar aspects of our trade with developing countries. For example, he points out that international corporations are willing to make deals to buy natural resources from any

government, no matter how it has come to power. This provides a huge financial incentive for groups to try to overthrow the existing government. Successful rebels are rewarded by being able to sell off the nation's oil, minerals or timber.

In their dealings with corrupt dictators in developing countries, Pogge asserts, international corporations are morally no better than someone who knowingly buys stolen goods—with the difference that the international legal and political order recognizes the corporations, not as criminals in possession of stolen goods but as the legal owners of the goods they have bought. This situation is, of course, beneficial for the industrial nations, because it enables us to obtain the raw materials we need to maintain our prosperity, but it is a disaster for resource-rich developing countries, turning the wealth that should benefit them into a curse that leads to a cycle of coups, civil wars and corruption and is of little benefit to the people as a whole.

In this light, our obligation to the poor is not just one of providing assistance to strangers but one of compensation for harms that we have caused and are still causing them. It might be argued that we do not owe the poor compensation, because our affluence actually benefits them. Living luxuriously, it is said, provides employment, and so wealth trickles down, helping the poor more effectively than aid does. But the rich in industrialized nations buy virtually nothing that is made by the very poor. During the past 20 years of economic globalization, although expanding trade has helped lift many of the world's poor out of poverty, it has failed to benefit the poorest 10 percent of the world's population. Some of the extremely poor, most of whom live in sub-Saharan Africa, have nothing to sell that rich people want, while others lack the infrastructure to get their goods to market. If they can get their crops to a port, European and U.S. subsidies often mean that they cannot sell them, despite—as for example in the case of West African cotton growers who compete with vastly larger and richer U.S. cotton producers—having a lower production cost than the subsidized producers in the rich nations.

The remedy to these problems, it might reasonably be suggested, should come from the state, not from private philanthropy. When aid comes through the government, everyone who earns above the tax-free threshold contributes something, with more collected from those with greater ability to pay. Much as we may applaud what Gates and Buffett are doing, we can also be troubled by a system that leaves the fate of hundreds of millions of people hanging on the decisions of two or three private citizens. But the amount of foreign development aid given by the U.S. government is, at 22 cents for every $100 the nation earns, about the same, as a percentage of gross national income, as Portugal gives and about half that of the U.K. Worse still, much of it is directed where it best suits U.S. strategic interests—Iraq is now by far the largest recipient of U.S. development aid, and Egypt, Jordan, Pakistan and Afghanistan all rank in the Top 10. Less than a quarter of official U.S. development aid— barely a nickel in every $100 of our G.N.I.—goes to the world's poorest nations.

Adding private philanthropy to U.S. government aid improves this picture, because Americans privately give more per capita to international philanthropic causes than the citizens of almost any other nation. Even when private donations are included, however, countries like Norway, Denmark, Sweden and the Netherlands give three or four times as much foreign aid, in proportion to the size of their economies, as the U.S. gives—with a much larger percentage going to the poorest nations. At least as things now stand, the case for philanthropic efforts to relieve global poverty is not susceptible to the argument that the government has taken care of the problem. And even if official U.S. aid were better-directed and comparable, relative to our gross domestic product, with that of the most generous nations, there would still be a role for private philanthropy. Unconstrained by diplomatic considerations or the desire to swing votes at the United Nations, private donors can more easily avoid dealing with corrupt or wasteful governments. They can go directly into the field, working with local villages and grass-roots organizations.

Nor are philanthropists beholden to lobbyists. As The New York Times reported recently, billions of dollars of U.S. aid is tied to domestic goods. Wheat for Africa must be grown in America, although aid experts say this often depresses local African markets, reducing the incentive for farmers there to produce more. In a decision that surely costs lives, hundreds of millions of condoms intended to stop the spread of AIDS in Africa and around the world must be manufactured in the U.S., although they cost twice as much as similar products made in Asia.

In other ways, too, private philanthropists are free to venture where governments fear to tread.

Through a foundation named for his wife, Susan Thompson Buffett, Warren Buffett has supported reproductive rights, including family planning and pro-choice organizations. In another unusual initiative, he has pledged $50 million for the International Atomic Energy Agency's plan to establish a "fuel bank" to supply nuclear-reactor fuel to countries that meet their nuclear-nonproliferation commitments. The idea, which has been talked about for many years, is widely agreed to be a useful step toward discouraging countries from building their own facilities for producing nuclear fuel, which could then be diverted to weapons production. It is, Buffett said, "an investment in a safer world." Though it is something that governments could and should be doing, no government had taken the first step.

Aid has always had its critics. Carefully planned and intelligently directed private philanthropy may be the best answer to the claim that aid doesn't work. Of course, as in any large-scale human enterprise, some aid can be ineffective. But provided that aid isn't actually counterproductive, even relatively inefficient assistance is likely to do more to advance human wellbeing than luxury spending by the wealthy.

The rich, then, should give. But how much should they give? Gates may have given away nearly $30 billion, but that still leaves him sitting at the top of the Forbes list of the richest Americans, with $53 billion. His 66,000-square-foot high-tech lakeside estate near Seattle is reportedly worth more than $100 million. Property taxes are about $1 million. Among his possessions is the Leicester Codex, the only handwritten book by Leonardo da Vinci still in private hands, for which he paid $30.8 million in 1994. Has Bill Gates done enough? More pointedly, you might ask: if he really believes that all lives have equal value, what is he doing living in such an expensive house and owning a Leonardo Codex? Are there no more lives that could be saved by living more modestly and adding the money thus saved to the amount he has already given?

Yet we should recognize that, if judged by the proportion of his wealth that he has given away, Gates compares very well with most of the other people on the Forbes 400 list, including his former colleague and Microsoft co-founder, Paul Allen. Allen, who left the company in 1983, has given, over his lifetime, more than $800 million to philanthropic causes. That is far more than nearly any of us will ever be able to give. But Forbes lists Allen as the fifth-richest American, with a net worth of $16 billion. He owns the Seattle Seahawks, the Portland Trailblazers, a 413-foot oceangoing yacht that carries two helicopters and a 60-foot submarine. He has given only about 5 percent of his total wealth.

Is there a line of moral adequacy that falls between the 5 percent that Allen has given away and the roughly 35 percent that Gates has donated? Few people have set a personal example that would allow them to tell Gates that he has not given enough, but one who could is Zell Kravinsky. A few years ago, when he was in his mid-40s, Kravinsky gave almost all of his $45 million real estate fortune to health-related charities, retaining only his modest family home in Jenkintown, near Philadelphia, and enough to meet his family's ordinary expenses. After learning that thousands of people with failing kidneys die each year while waiting for a transplant, he contacted a Philadelphia hospital and donated one of his kidneys to a complete stranger.

After reading about Kravinsky in The New Yorker, I invited him to speak to my classes at Princeton. He comes across as anguished by the failure of others to see the simple logic that lies behind his altruism. Kravinsky has a mathematical mind—a talent that obviously helped him in deciding what investments would prove profitable—and he says that the chances of dying as a result of donating a kidney are about 1 in 4,000. For him this implies that to withhold a kidney from someone who would otherwise die means valuing one's own life at 4,000 times that of a stranger, a ratio Kravinsky considers "obscene."

What marks Kravinsky from the rest of us is that he takes the equal value of all human life as a guide to life, not just as a nice piece of rhetoric. He acknowledges that some people think he is crazy, and even his wife says she believes that he goes too far. One of her arguments against the kidney donation was that one of their children may one day need a kidney, and Zell could be the only compatible donor. Kravinsky's love for his children is, as far as I can tell, as strong as that of any normal parent. Such attachments are part of our nature, no doubt the product of our evolution as mammals who give birth to children, who for an unusually long time require our assistance in order to survive. But that does not, in Kravinsky's view, justify our placing a value on the lives of our children that is thousands of times greater than the value we place on the lives of the children of strangers. Asked if he would allow his child to die if it would enable a thousand children to live, Kravinsky said yes. Indeed, he has said he would permit his child to die even if this enabled only two other children to live. Nevertheless, to appease his wife, he recently went back into real estate, made some money and bought the family a larger home. But he still remains committed to giving away as much as possible, subject only to keeping his domestic life reasonably tranquil.

Buffett says he believes in giving his children "enough so they feel they could do anything, but not so much that they could do nothing." That means, in his judgment, "a few hundred thousand" each. In absolute terms, that is far more than most Americans are able to leave their children and, by Kravinsky's standard, certainly too much. (Kravinsky says that the hard part is not giving away the first $45 million but the last $10,000, when you have to live so cheaply that you can't function in the business world.) But even if Buffett left each of his three children a million dollars each, he would still have given away more than 99.99 percent of his wealth. When someone does that much—especially in a society in which the norm is to leave most of your wealth to your children—it is better to praise them than to cavil about the extra few hundred thousand dollars they might have given.

Philosophers like Liam Murphy of New York University and my colleague Kwame Anthony Appiah at Princeton contend that our obligations are limited to carrying our fair share of the burden of relieving global poverty. They would have us calculate how much would be required to ensure that the world's poorest people have a chance at a decent life, and then divide this sum among the affluent. That would give us each an amount to donate, and having given that, we would have fulfilled our obligations to the poor.

What might that fair amount be? One way of calculating it would be to take as our target, at least for the next nine years, the Millennium Development Goals, set by the United Nations Millennium Summit in 2000. On that occasion, the largest gathering of world leaders in history jointly pledged to meet, by 2015, a list of goals that include:

Reducing by half the proportion of the world's people in extreme poverty (defined as living on less than the purchasing-power equivalent of one U.S. dollar per day).

Reducing by half the proportion of people who suffer from hunger.

Ensuring that children everywhere are able to take a full course of primary schooling.

Ending sex disparity in education.

Reducing by two-thirds the mortality rate among children under 5.

Reducing by three-quarters the rate of maternal mortality.

Halting and beginning to reverse the spread of HIV/AIDS and halting and beginning to reduce the incidence of malaria and other major diseases.

Reducing by half the proportion of people without sustainable access to safe drinking water.

Last year a United Nations task force, led by the Columbia University economist Jeffrey Sachs, estimated the annual cost of meeting these goals to be $121 billion in 2006, rising to $189 billion by 2015. When we take account of existing official development aid promises, the additional amount needed each year to meet the goals is only $48 billion for 2006 and $74 billion for 2015.

Now let's look at the incomes of America's rich and superrich, and ask how much they could reasonably give. The task is made easier by statistics recently provided by Thomas Piketty and Emmanuel Saez, economists at the École Normale Supérieure, Paris-Jourdan, and the University of California, Berkeley, respectively, based on U.S. tax data for 2004. Their figures are for pretax income, excluding income from capital gains, which for the very rich are nearly always substantial. For simplicity I have rounded the figures, generally downward. Note too that the numbers refer to "tax units," that is, in many cases, families rather than individuals.

Piketty and Saez's top bracket comprises 0.01 percent of U.S. taxpayers. There are 14,400 of them, earning an average of $12,775,000, with total earnings of $184 billion. The minimum annual income in this group is more than $5 million, so it seems reasonable to suppose that they could, without much hardship, give away a third of their annual income, an average of $4.3 million each, for a total of around $61 billion. That would still leave each of them with an annual income of at least $3.3 million.

Next comes the rest of the top 0.1 percent (excluding the category just described, as I shall do henceforth). There are 129,600 in this group, with an average income of just over $2 million and a minimum income of $1.1 million. If they were each to give a quarter of their income, that would yield about $65 billion, and leave each of them with at least $846,000 annually.

The top 0.5 percent consists of 575,900 taxpayers, with an average income of $623,000 and a minimum of $407,000. If they were to give one-fifth of their income, they would still have at least $325,000 each, and they would be giving a total of $72 billion.

Coming down to the level of those in the top 1 percent, we find 719,900 taxpayers with an average income of $327,000 and a minimum of $276,000. They could comfortably afford to give 15 percent of their income. That would yield $35 billion and leave them with at least $234,000.

Finally, the remainder of the nation's top 10 percent earn at least $92,000 annually, with an average of $132,000. There are nearly 13 million in this group. If they gave the traditional tithe—10 percent of their income, or an average of $13,200 each—this would yield about $171 billion and leave them a minimum of $83,000.

You could spend a long time debating whether the fractions of income I have suggested for donation constitute the fairest possible scheme. Perhaps the sliding scale should be steeper, so that the super-rich give more and the merely comfortable give less. And it could be extended beyond the Top 10 percent of American families, so that everyone able to afford more than the basic necessities of life gives something, even if it is as little as 1 percent. Be that as it may, the remarkable thing about these calculations is that a scale of donations that is unlikely to impose significant hardship on anyone yields a total of $404 billion—from just 10 percent of American families.

Obviously, the rich in other nations should share the burden of relieving global poverty. The U.S. is responsible for 36 percent of the gross domestic product of all Organization for Economic Cooperation and Development nations. Arguably, because the U.S. is richer than all other major nations, and its wealth is more unevenly distributed than wealth in almost any other industrialized country, the rich in the U.S. should contribute more than 36 percent of total global donations. So somewhat more than 36 percent of all aid to relieve global poverty should come from the U.S. For simplicity, let's take half as a fair share for the U.S. On that basis, extending the scheme I have suggested worldwide would provide $808 billion annually for development aid. That's more than six times what the task force chaired by Sachs estimated would be required for 2006 in order to be on track to meet the Millennium Development Goals, and more than 16 times the shortfall between that sum and existing official development aid commitments.

If we are obliged to do no more than our fair share of eliminating global poverty, the burden will not be great. But is that really all we ought to do? Since we all agree that fairness is a good thing, and none of us like doing more because others don't pull their weight, the fair-share view is attractive. In the end, however, I think we should reject it. Let's return to the drowning child in the shallow pond. Imagine it is not 1 small child who has fallen in, but 50 children. We are among 50 adults, unrelated to the children, picnicking on the lawn around the pond. We can easily wade into the pond and rescue the children, and the fact that we would find it cold and unpleasant sloshing around in the knee-deep muddy water is no justification for failing to do so. The "fair share" theorists would say that if we each rescue one child, all the children will be saved, and so none of us have an obligation to save more than one. But what if half the picnickers prefer staying clean and dry to rescuing any children at all? Is it acceptable if the rest of us stop after we have rescued just one child, knowing that we have done our fair share, but that half the children will drown? We might justifiably be furious with those who are not doing their fair share, but our anger with them is not a reason for letting the children die. In terms of praise and blame, we are clearly right to condemn, in the strongest terms, those who do nothing. In contrast, we may withhold such condemnation from those who stop when they have done their fair share. Even so, they have let children drown when they could easily have saved them, and that is wrong.

Similarly, in the real world, it should be seen as a serious moral failure when those with ample income do not do their fair share toward relieving global poverty. It isn't so easy, however, to decide on the proper approach to take to those who limit their contribution to their fair share when they could easily do more and when, because others are not playing their part, a further donation would assist many in desperate need. In the privacy of our own judgment, we should believe that it is wrong not to do more. But whether we should actually criticize people who are doing their fair share, but no more than that, depends on the psychological impact that such criticism will have on them, and on others. This in turn may depend on social practices. If the majority are doing little or nothing, setting a standard higher than the fair-share level may seem so demanding that it discourages people who are willing to make an equitable contribution from doing even that. So it may be best to refrain from criticizing those who achieve the fair-share level. In moving our society's standards forward, we may have to progress one step at a time.

For more than 30 years, I've been reading, writing and teaching about the ethical issue posed by the juxtaposition, on our planet, of great abundance and life-threatening poverty. Yet it was not until, in preparing this article, I calculated how much America's Top 10 percent of income earners actually make that I fully understood how easy it would be for the world's rich to eliminate, or virtually eliminate, global poverty. (It has actually become much easier over the last 30 years, as the rich have grown significantly richer.) I found the result astonishing. I double-checked the figures and asked a research assistant to check them as well. But they were right. Measured against our capacity, the Millennium Development Goals are indecently, shockingly modest. If we fail to achieve them—as on present indications we well might—we have no excuses. The target we should be setting for ourselves is not halving the proportion of people living in extreme poverty, and without enough to eat, but ensuring that no one, or virtually no one, needs to live in such degrading conditions. That is a worthy goal, and it is well within our reach.

9

Do We Owe the Future Anything?

RICHARD T. DE GEORGE

Richard T. De George argues that, because future generations do not exist, they do not have any rights nor do we have any correlative obligations to them. Still, De George thinks we do have an obligation to promote the continuance of the human race—but an obligation based on considerations of value rather than of rights. At the same time, he denies that we have any obligation to produce a continuously increasing standard of living.

The desire to avoid pollution—however defined—involves concern for the duration and quality of human life. Problems dealing with the quality of human life inevitably involve value judgments. And value judgments are notorious candidates for debate and disagreement. Yet in discussions on pollution the desirability of the continuance of the human race is generally taken for granted; most people feel that a continuous rise in the standard of living would be a good thing; and many express a feeling of obligation towards future generations. How well founded are these judgments? The purpose of this paper is to examine the validity and some of the implications of three statements of principles which have a direct bearing on this question and so on the debate concerning pollution and its control. The three principles are the following:

1. Only existing entities have rights.

2. Continuance of the human race is good.

3. Continuous increase in man's standard of living is good.

I

The argument in favor of the principle that only existing entities have rights is straightforward and simple: Non-existent entities by definition do not exist. What does not exist cannot be the subject or bearer of anything. Hence it cannot be the subject or bearer of rights.

Just as non-existent entities have no rights, so it makes no sense to speak about anyone's correlative duty towards non-existent entities. Towards that which does not exist we can have no legal or moral obligation, since there is no subject or term which can be the object of that obligation. Now it is clear that unconceived possible future human beings do not exist, though we can think, e.g., of the class of human beings which will exist two hundred years from now. It follows that since this class does not (yet) exist, we cannot have any obligations to it, nor to any of its possible members. It is a presently empty class.

More generally, then, presently existing human beings have no obligation to any future-and-not-yet

Richard T. De George, Do We Owe the Future Anything? from *Law and the Ecological Challenge*, William S. Hein & Co., Inc., pp. 180–190. Reprinted by permission of Shane Marmion.

existing set or class of human beings. We owe them nothing and they have no legitimate claim on us for the simple reason that they do not exist. No one can legitimately defend their interests or represent their case in court or law or government, because they are not, and so have no interests or rights.

It follows from this that a great deal of contemporary talk about obligations to the future, where this means to some distant future portion of mankind, is simply confused. In dealing with questions of pollution and clean air—as well as with similar issues such as the use of irreplaceable resources—there can be no legitimate question of the rights of unconceived future human beings or of any supposedly correlative obligation of present-day human beings to them.

Some people may find this to be counterintuitive. That it is not so may perhaps become clearer if we consider what I take to be the feelings of many—if not most people with respect to the past.

Consider the general attitude towards the ancient Greeks and Romans. Did they owe us anything? Did they have any duties or obligations to us? It is clear there are no sanctions we can impose on them and no way we can enforce any obligations we may claim they had towards us. But surely even to raise the question of their obligation to us is odd. We may rejoice in what has been saved of the past and handed down to us, and we may regret that some of Plato's dialogues have been lost or that the Library at Alexandria was burned, or that Rome was sacked. But though we may regret such events and though we may judge that they were in some sense ills for mankind or the result of immoral actions, they were not immoral because of any obligation past generations had to us.

The situation is little changed if we come up to more recent—though not too recent—times. The American Founding Fathers had no obligation to us. They could scarcely have envisaged our times or have been expected to calculate the effects of their actions on us. Or consider the unrestrained slaughter of American buffalo for sport. Such action may have been immoral and a waste of a natural resource; but if it was immoral it was not because present-day Americans have any right to have inherited more buffalo than we did.

Since it is not possible to impose sanctions on past generations it makes no sense to speak of legal obligations or even of moral obligations of those generations to us. At best, as some minority groups have been arguing, we might claim that present-day beneficiaries of past injustices are obliged to make restitution to the present descendents of those who in the past suffered injustice. This is a plausible claim, and might serve as a model in the future for some portion of mankind claiming that it has a legal or moral claim against another portion for exploitation or oppression by their forefathers. Whatever the obligation to make restoration for past injustices, however, the injustice was an injustice not primarily against present generations but against those past generations whose rights were violated or whose property or lives were unjustly taken, or who were otherwise oppressed or exploited.

The situation is basically similar today vis-a-vis future generations. Our primary obligation with respect to the control of pollution or to the use of resources is to presently existing human beings rather than to possible future human beings. The best way to protect the interests of future generations—if we choose to use this language—may be to conserve the environment for ourselves. But my present point is that in dealing with questions of public policy or legislation, the primary values to be considered are those of presently existing people, and not the projected or supposed values of future generations. To argue or act as if we could know the wants or needs of generations hundreds or more years hence is to deceive ourselves, perhaps so as to have an excuse to ignore present-day wants and needs. Hence questions about the amount and kind of pollution to be tolerated, the resources to be rationed or preserved, should not be decided in terms of far distant future needs or requirements but in terms of present and near-future needs and requirements.

It is correct that for the first time in the history of mankind presently living human beings have it within their power to annihilate mankind or to use up irreplaceable resources. But these new capacities do not change the status of our responsibilities or obligations, despite the fact that they are increased. If we do annihilate mankind, it will be no injustice to those who never were and never will be. If we were foolishly to use up vital, irreplaceable resources or disrupt the ecosystem, the reason it would be wrong or bad, unjust or immoral—and so the reason why it might now be something requiring legislation to prevent—is not its effects on those who do not yet exist, but its effects on those who do.

The thrust of the principle we are considering is that present generations or individuals must be considered primary in any calculation of value with respect to either pollution control or the distribution and use of the limited resources of the earth. The rights of presently existing people carry with them the obligation to respect their rights, e.g., to enjoy at least minimal levels of food, shelter, and the like. No one and no generation is required to sacrifice itself for imaginary, non-existent generations of the future. What does have to be considered is the future of presently existing persons—infants as well as adults.

We undoubtedly feel closer to our as yet unconceived descendents—those one removed from the present generation of children—than we do to many people living in places far distant from us, with different customs and values; and if we were to choose between raising the standard of living of these to us foreign people and preserving our wealth to be shared by our descendents, we might well opt for the latter. To do so is to aggregate to ourselves the right to conserve present resources for those to whom we choose to pass them on at the expense of those presently existing who do not share them. Since, however, presently existing people have rights to the goods of the earth, there seems to be a prima facie obligation to attempt to raise the level of living and comfort of presently existing people, wherever they may be, rather than ignoring them and worrying only about our own future heirs. Underfed and impoverished areas of the world may require greater attention and impose greater obligations than non-existent future generations.

Insofar as modern technology is world-significant, so too are some aspects of pollution. Mercury poured into streams finds its way into the ocean and into fish caught in international waters and shipped around the world; fall-out from nuclear blasts circles the globe. If present-day legislative principles in the United States are sufficient to handle the problems posed by pollution in our own country, it is certainly not the case that there are effective means of controlling the problem internationally. The cost of pollution control prevents poorer countries from simultaneously developing their technology in order to raise their living standards and spend the money and resources necessary to curb pollution. It is in cases such as these that it becomes especially important to be conscious of the principle discussed here which emphasizes the overbearing rights of existing persons as opposed to the putative rights of nonexistent persons....

Although there is no full fledged obligation to provide, e.g., clean air, for countless future generations, we will have an obligation to provide something for at least those future persons or generations for whom or for which we are rather closely responsible. Generations overlap considerably; but any group in the position to influence and change things, though it cannot be expected to be responsible for generations hundreds, much less thousands of years hence, can be expected to take into account those persons who will be alive within the next fifty or a hundred years. A large number of these people already exist; and if future generations are produced—as barring some global catastrophe they will be—they will have rights and these rights must be considered at least as potential rights. The amount of consideration should be proportional to the probability that they will exist, and should be considered especially by those responsible for bringing them into the world.

Furthermore, if starting from the premise that nonexistent entities can have no rights it follows that presently existing persons have no correlative obligations towards them, and so no such obligations to unborn generations, this does not mean that people may not want to consider future possible generations from some point of view other than one of such obligation and take them into account in other ways and for other reasons.

Obviously men are concerned about their own futures and those of their presently existing children and of the presently acknowledged right of their children to have children; it is a claim which must be weighed. Though we cannot assume that the children of present-day children will have exactly the same desires and values as we, there is good reason to believe they will be sufficiently similar to us so that they will need fresh air, that they will not be able to tolerate excessive amounts of mercury or DDT in their food, and that they will probably share a good many of our desires. To speak of the right of non-existing future persons to have children in their turn is to treat them as actual. It amounts to saying that if conditions remain more or less the same and if the presently possible entities become actual, then, when they do, they will have the rights we presently attribute to actually existing persons. Our present interest in their happiness, however, is already an actual interest which must be considered and it might impel—though not strictly require—us to leave as many options open to those who will come after us as possible, consistent with taking care of our own needs and wants.

Since most people living now would consider it possible to be living twenty years hence, the conditions of life which the next as yet unborn generation will face is a condition of life which we who presently exist will also face. So with respect to at least one, two, three or perhaps four generations hence, or for roughly fifty to a hundred years hence, it can plausibly be argued that we plan not only for unborn generations but also for ourselves. Our concern for them is equally concern for ourselves. And we do have rights. If this is the case, we can legitimately think and plan and act for the future on the basis of our own concerns, which include our hopes and desires for our real or anticipated offspring. But we should be clear about what we are arguing, and not confuse our rights and desires with the supposed rights of non-existent entities.

II

The second principle was: Continuance of the human race is good.

What does this mean and what does it imply?

Can we give any sense to the question: how long should the human race survive? We know that some species have had their span of years on earth and have given way to other species. To ask how long the dinosaur should have survived would be an odd question; for to say that it should have survived for a shorter or longer time than it did would be to speak as if the laws of nature should have been different, or as if the dinosaur's continued existence was a good which it could have done something to prolong beyond the time that it did. It is precisely in this sense—that the survival of the human species is a good in itself and that we should do what we can to keep it going—that we say that the human race should continue to survive. To utter this is to make a value judgment and to express our feelings about the race, despite the fact that we as individuals will die. Some people speak blithely about its being better for the human species to continue for another thousand years than for another five hundred; or for 500,000 rather than 100,000, and so on. But the content which we can give to such statements—other than expressing the judgment that human life is a good in itself, at least under certain circumstances—seems minimal. For we cannot imagine what human life would be like in the far distant future, nor what we can or should do to help make it the case that one of those figures rather than the other is the one that actually becomes the case.

If tomorrow some sort of radiation from the sun were to render all human beings sterile, we could anticipate the demise of the human race as more and more of the present population died off. We could anticipate the difficulties of those who were the relatively last to die. And we could take some solace in the fact that the radiation would have been an act of God and not the result of the acts of men. The demise of the human race would in this case be similar to the extinction of the dinosaur. If a similar occurence was the result of the acts of men, though the result would be the same, it would make more sense in the latter case than in the former to say that man should have continued longer as a species. Just as we consider murder and suicide wrong, so we consider wrong the fouling of the air or water to such an extent that it kills others or ourselves or the whole human race.

Thus, though no injustice is done to those who will never exist because of our actions, and though we do not violate any of their rights—since they have none—we can in some sense say that with the extinction of the human race there would be less value in the world than if it had continued to exist. If we have an obligation to attempt to create and preserve as much value in the world as possible, then we have an obligation to continue the human race, where this does not necessarily mean an obligation to procreate as many people as possible but to achieve as much value as possible, taking into consideration the quality of life of those who will be alive. The basis for the obligation comes not from a consideration of rights, but from a consideration of value.

Such a calculation, obviously, is something which each generation can perform only with respect to the time it is alive and able to act. It can help assure that when it dies those who are still living are in such a condition as to preserve human life and to pass it on at as high a qualitative level as possible. And if that happened consistently each year, each decade, each century, then until there was some act of God presumably man would continue indefinitely—which is a thought we may take some pleasure in contemplating, despite the fact that beyond a rather small number of years we will not be affected by whether the race continues or not.

Thus far, then, though we do not have any obligation to non-existent entities, we can legitimately anticipate the future needs and requirements of ourselves and of those who will probably come soon after us; furthermore, since we can make out the case that it would be good for the human race to continue, we have the obligation to do what we can to forestall its demise. This leads us to the third principle.

III

The last of the three principles I proposed at the start of this paper was: Continuous increase in man's standard of living is good. It is a principle which a large number of people seem to subscribe to, one underlying much of our industrial and technological growth and a good deal of the concern for a constantly expanding GNP. As a principle, however, it is both ambiguous and dubious.

There are at least four basic interpretations which can be given to the principle: 1) it can be taken to refer to advancement up the economic ladder by people on an individual basis; 2) it might be understood as a statement about the hopes and aims of each generation for the succeeding generation; 3) it might mean that the standard of living of at least some men should continue to rise, pushing forward the heights to which men can rise; and 4) it can be interpreted to mean that all men in a given society, or throughout the world, should be brought up to a certain constantly rising level of life.

The differences in interpretation are extremely important and both stem from and give rise to different sets of value judgments concerning production, distribution, development of resources, and expenditure of resources on pollution control.

1. The individualistic interpretation puts its emphasis on an individual's ability through work, savings, ingenuity, or other means to advance himself economically. The Horatio Alger ideal, the rise from poverty to wealth, is the model. Increasing one's standard of living became the goal of workers as expressed in the labor union movements, and its results are clearly visible in the high standard of living enjoyed by many large segments of the population in the United States and other industrialized countries. Together with this rise has come the pollution from automobiles and factories and the birth of a small counterculture which has called into question the necessity, the wisdom, and the value of a constantly rising standard of living.

The hope of a better life expresses an undeniable value when one's life is barely tolerable. It makes less sense as one's needs are more and more taken care of and the principle becomes dubious once one has achieved a certain standard of living somewhere considerably well above the minimal necessary for survival. There is a point of diminishing returns beyond which the price one has to pay in terms of energy, time, money, and resources expended does not produce correspondingly significant benefits. And if enough people reach that state, then the society's energy and efforts become counter-productive. The result we are seeing is that the attempt to achieve a constantly higher standard of living has resulted in a lower quality of life for all, partially through pollution. This fact, admittedly, is little comfort to those who have not yet arrived at a tolerable level of life and for whom the aspiration to raise their standard of living is a real good; the present point, however, is that at least beyond a certain level the principle cannot be achieved and if acted on may serve to produce more harm than good. (The related problem of inequity in a society will be considered further under the fourth interpretation.)

2. The interpretation of the principle which expresses the hope of parents that their children will have a better life than they suffers the same fate as the preceding interpretation. Where the level of life is already good, the desire that their children's be even better may well be questionable for the reasons we have already seen. Children, of course, have no right to be better off than their parents, although those who are badly off might well wish those they love to enjoy more of the goods of life than they themselves have.

If some generation is to enjoy a higher standard of living than others, however, it is not necessary that it always be some future generation. The desire that some future generation of human beings should be better off than present generations may be the desire of some members of present generations. But it is nothing owed to future generations. Some parents sacrifice themselves and deny themselves for the benefit of their children; some carefully save their wealth only to have their children squander it. In some cases such self-sacrifice is noble and evokes our praise; in others, it is foolish. But any such case of self-sacrifice is above the demands of duty, as is obvious when we see children attempting to demand such sacrifice from their parents as if it were their right. Nor does any parent or group have the right through legislation to demand such sacrifice from others for his own or for other people's children.

3. The view that at least some men should live at constantly higher levels so as to push mankind constantly forward seems hardly defensible for a number of reasons. The first is that it is difficult to describe what a constantly higher standard of living

could mean for only a few since their lives are so closely connected to other men and to the energy, pollution, and population problems they all face. Secondly, standard of living is not the same as quality of life. Simple increase in the standard of living, if measured by the goods one has, simply does not make much sense beyond a certain point. For one's needs beyond that point are artificial, and it is not at all clear that satisfying them makes one happier or more comfortable or any of the other things that an increase in the standard of living is supposed to do, and for which reasons it is desired as a good. Thirdly, it can well be argued that it is unlikely that the constantly higher standard advocated for the few—if sense can be made of it—will help do anything but increase the difference between the level of life of the haves and the have-nots. If taken to mean not that a few men in an advanced industrial society should push mankind forward but that the advanced industrial societies should continue to advance at the expense of the non-industrial societies, then this seems to go clearly against the rights of the latter, and so not be a worthy end at all.

4. The fourth interpretation is the most plausible and has the most vocal defenders today. It maintains that all men in a given society (and ideally throughout the world) should be brought up to a certain constantly rising minimal level of life—at least constantly rising for the foreseeable future, given the wide distance between the level of life of the haves and the have-nots. This is the impetus behind minimum income legislation on the American domestic scene. Globally, it affects the relations between have and have-not countries, between the industrially developed and the underdeveloped countries, and is one of the bases for advocating foreign aid programs of various sorts.

The right of all men to a minimal standard of living is one that I would argue in favor of. But my present concern is to note that the right to a constantly rising minimum is contingent upon the ability of the earth and of society to provide it. If world resources are able to adequately sustain only a limited number of people, and if more than that number are born, the distribution of goods cannot extend sufficiently far; and those societies which contributed most to the overpopulation of their land and of the earth in general may well have to bear the brunt of the evil consequences.

A continuously rising standard of living therefore is never a right, not always a good, and most often simply one good to be measured against other goods and available resources.

IV

What then, if anything, do we owe future generations? We do not owe them a better life than we enjoy, nor do we owe them resources which we need for ourselves.

When dealing with renewable resources a sound principle might be that, other things being equal, they should not be used up at a faster rate than that at which they can be replaced. But when they are needed at a greater rate than that at which they can be replaced, rationing is insufficient and they raise a problem similar to that raised by non-renewable resources. One can argue that the latter should be used up sufficiently slowly so that there are always reserves; but this may mean using less and less each year or decade, despite increasing demand. An alternative is simply to use what we need, attempting to keep our needs rational, and to face crucially diminished supplies when we are forced to face them, hoping in the meantime that some substitutes will be discovered or developed.

Frequently problems of this type have been approached from a utilitarian point of view, and such an approach is instructive. Let each man count for one, the argument goes, whether he be a present man or a future man. The happiness of each is on a par as far as importance and intrinsic goodness are concerned. But increasing the sum of total happiness is better than its opposite. If by increased growth or unlimited use now of limited resources we increase our happiness by a small amount, but doom those who come after us to struggling along without some important natural resources; and if by conserving our natural resources now our happiness or at least that part which is made up of comfort is

somewhat less than it could be, but the happiness of many millions or billions who come after us is greater than it would otherwise be, then the moral thing to do is to conserve our resources now and share them with future generations.

This argument presupposes first that there will be the future generations it hypothesizes, that these future generations will want pretty much the same things that we do in order to be happy, that they will not overuse the goods of the earth, and that they will not be able to find any suitable substitutes. If we saved only to have them squander, then no more good might be achieved than if we had spent liberally and they had proportionally less; or if they find, e.g., alternate energy sources; then our penury resulted in less good than there might have been.

In earlier times the ploy of this kind of argument was to trade on the happiness of countless generations in the future as a result of some sacrifice of our happiness now. But there are now a sufficient number of doubts about there being future generations, about their not finding alternative resources, and about our present sacrifices leading to their happiness (since there might be so many of them anyway) as to render the argument less convincing than it might formerly have been.

In any calculus of pleasure or good there is no necessity for future generations to enjoy a higher standard of living at the expense of present generations. If there will be a peak in the standard somewhere along the line, followed by a decline, it might just as well be the present generation which enjoys the peak through the utilization of resources, which, since limited, will be used up sooner or later. There is no greater good served by future generations being the peak since obviously when it comes to their turn, if it is improper for us to enjoy more than our successors, and if this is the proper way to feel, they should feel so also.

Both because of these considerations and because of the large number of unknowables concerning the future, short range considerations are surer and more pertinent than long range considerations. The threshold of pollution has been recently crossed so that it is now obvious that something must be done; legislation consequently is being passed. The amount and kind of pollution to be tolerated, the resources to be rationed or preserved should not be decided in terms of far distant needs or requirements but in terms of present and near-future needs and requirement.

Production involves wastes which have now reached the pollution stage. Its control is costly. The cost must be borne either by the producer (who will pass it on to the consumer) or by society at large through the taxes required, e.g., to purify water. The principle that whoever causes the pollution must pay for cleaning it up, or that no production should be allowed without the mechanism provided to prevent pollution, will make some kinds of production unprofitable. In this case, if such production is considered necessary or desirable, it will have to be subsidized. If society cannot pay for total cleanup it might have to settle for less than it would like; or it might have to give up some of its production or some of the goods to which it had become accustomed; or it might have to forego some of the products it might otherwise produce. Such choices should not be made a priori or by the fiat of government, but by the members of society at large or by as many of them interested and aware and informed enough to help in the decision making process.

There are presently available the means nationally for allocating resources and for controlling use and production through automatic market and natural mechanisms as well as through legislation. Where legislation poses the greatest difficulty is not on the national level but on the international level. For technology has brought us into one closely interdependent world faster than the social and legal mechanisms for solving the world-wide problems of resources, population, and pollution have been able to develop.

The problems posed by the ecological challenge are many and complex. But in dealing with them it should be clear that we owe nothing to those who do not yet and may never exist; that nonetheless we do have an obligation to promote the continuance of the human race, and so have an obligation for those whom we produce; that though at least minimum standards of living for all are desirable, if some generation is to enjoy the peak it need not be other generations; and that the choice of how to use our resources and continue or control our pollution depends on the price all those concerned wish to pay and the values we wish to espouse and promote.

10

The Welfare Rights of Distant Peoples and Future Generations

JAMES P. STERBA

In this selection, James P. Sterba builds on the argument of his earlier selection where he argued that the libertarian ideal of liberty supported a right to welfare. Here he argues that the application of this right to welfare to distant peoples and future generations leads to the equalization of resources over space and time.

For libertarians, fundamental rights are universal rights, that is, rights possessed by all people, not just those who live in certain places or at certain times. Of course, to claim that rights are universal does not mean that they are universally recognized. Rather, to claim that rights are universal, despite their spotty recognition, implies only that they ought to be recognized because people at all times and places have or could have had good reasons to recognize these rights, not that they actually did or do so. Nor need universal rights be unconditional. This is particularly true in the case of the right to welfare, which I have argued in Selection 2, is conditional upon people doing all that they legitimately can to provide for themselves. In addition, this right is conditional upon there being sufficient resources available so that everyone's welfare needs can be met. So where people do not do all that they can to provide for themselves or where there are not sufficient resources available, people do not normally have a right to welfare. Given the universal and conditional character of this libertarian right to welfare, what then are the implications of this right for distant peoples and future generations?

DISTANT PEOPLES
AND FUTURE GENERATIONS

At present, worldwide food production is sufficient to provide everyone in the world with at least 2,720 kilocalories per person per day.[1] To meet the nutritional and other basic needs of each and every person living today, however, would require a significant redistribution of goods and resources. To finance such redistribution, Thomas Pogge has proposed a 1% tax on aggregate global income, netting $312 billion annually.[2] Peter Singer, as an alternative, has proposed a graduated tax on the incomes of the top 10% of U.S. families netting $404 billion annually with an equal sum coming from the family incomes of people living in other industrialized countries.[3] Both Pogge and Singer are confident that their proposals would go a long way toward meeting basic human needs worldwide. In fact, Singer remarks that before coming up with his recent proposal, he never "fully understood how easy it would be for the world's rich to eliminate or virtually eliminate, global poverty."[4]

Yet while Pogge's and Singer's proposals would doubtless do much to secure a right to welfare for existing people, unfortunately, they do not speak very well to the needs of future generations. How then do we best insure that future generations are not deprived of the goods and resources that they will need to meet their basic needs? In the U.S. currently more than one million acres of arable land are lost from cultivation each year due to urbanization, multiplying transport networks and industrial expansion.[5] In addition, another two million acres of farmland are lost each year due to erosion, salinization, and water logging.[6] The state of Iowa alone has lost one-half of its fertile topsoil from farming in the last 100 years. That loss is about 30 times faster than what is sustainable.[7] According to one estimate, only 0.6 of an acre of arable land per person will be available in the U.S. in 2050, whereas more than 1.2 acres per person are needed to provide a diverse diet (currently 1.6 acres of arable land are available).[8] Similar, or even more threatening, estimates of the loss of arable land have been made for other regions of the world.[9] How then are we going to preserve farmland, and other food-related natural resources, so that future generations are not deprived of what they require to meet their basic needs?

And what about other resources as well? It has been estimated that presently a North American uses 75 times more resources than a resident of India. This means that in terms of resource consumption the North American continent's population is the equivalent of 22.5 billion Indians.[10] So unless we assume that basic resources such as arable land, iron, coal, and oil are in unlimited supply, this unequal consumption will have to be radically altered if the basic needs of future generations are to be met.[11] I submit, therefore, that recognizing a universal right to welfare applicable both to existing and future people requires us to use up no more resources than are necessary for meeting our own basic needs, thus, securing for ourselves a decent life but no more.[12] For us to use up more resources than this, we would be guilty of depriving at least some future generations of the resources they would require to meet their own basic needs, thereby violating their libertarian-based right to welfare.[13] Obviously, this would impose a significant sacrifice on existing generations, particularly those in the

developed world, clearly a far greater sacrifice than Pogge and Singer maintain is required for meeting the basic needs of existing generations. Nevertheless, these demands do follow from a libertarian-based right to welfare.[14] In effect, recognizing a right to welfare, applicable to all existing and future people, leads to an equal utilization of resources over place and time.[15]

Now it might be objected that if we fail to respect this welfare requirement for future generations, we would still not really be harming those future generations whom we would deprive of the resources they require for meeting their basic needs. This is because if we acted so as to appropriately reduce our consumption, those same future generations whom we would supposedly harm by our present course of action won't even exist.[16] This is because the changes we would make in our lives in order to live in a resource-conserving manner would so alter our social relations, now and in the future, that the membership of future generations would be radically altered as well. Yet to hold that we only harm those who would still exist if we acted appropriately is too strong a restriction on harming.

Consider an owner of an industrial plant arguing that she really did not harm your daughter who is suffering from leukemia due to the contaminants that leaked into the area surrounding the plant because only by operating the plant so that it leaked these contaminants was it economically feasible in this particular place and time. Hence, the plant would not have opened up, nor would you have moved nearby to work, nor would this daughter of yours even been born, without its operating in this way.[17] In brief, the owner of the plant contends that your daughter was not really harmed at all because, if there had been no contamination, she would not even have been born. Assuming, however, that we reject the plant owner's counterfactual requirement for harming in favor of a direct causal one (the operation of the plant caused your daughter's leukemia), as we should, then, we have to recognize that we too can be held responsible for harming future generations if, by the way we live our lives, we cause the harm from which they will suffer.

Now it might be further objected that if we did limit ourselves to simply meeting our basic needs—a decent life, but no more, we would still be harming future generations at some more distant point of time, leaving those generations without the resources required for meeting their basic needs. While our present non-conserving way of living would begin to harm future generations in, let's say, 200 years, our conserving way of living, should we adopt it, and should it be continued by subsequent generations, would, let's assume, lead to that same result in 2,000 years. So either way, we would be harming future generations.

There is a difference, however. While both courses of action would ultimately harm future generations, if we do limit ourselves to simply meeting our basic needs, a decent life, but no more, and other generations do the same, then, many generations of future people would benefit from this course of action who would not benefit from our alternative, non-conserving course of action. Even more importantly, for us to sacrifice further for the sake of future generations would require us to give up meeting our own basic needs, and this normally we cannot be morally required to do, as the "ought" implies "can" principle makes clear. We can be required to give up the satisfaction of our nonbasic needs so that others can meet their basic needs, but, normally, without our consent, we cannot be required to sacrifice the satisfaction of our own basic needs so that others can meet their basic needs.[18] So while future generations may still be harmed in the distant future as a result of our behavior, no one can justifiably blame us, or take action against us, for using no more resources than we require for meeting our basic needs.

Of course, someone could ask: How do you distinguish basic from nonbasic needs? A person raising this question may not realize how widespread the use of this distinction is. While the distinction is surely important for global ethics, as my use of it attests, it is also used widely in moral, political, and environmental philosophy; it would really be impossible to do much philosophy in these areas, especially at the practical level, without a distinction between basic and nonbasic needs.

Another way that I would respond to the question is by pointing out that the fact that not every need can be clearly classified as either basic or nonbasic, as similarly holds for a whole range of dichotomous concepts like moral/immoral, legal/illegal, living/nonliving, human/nonhuman, should not immobilize us from acting at least with respect to clear cases. This puts our use of the distinction in a still broader context suggesting that if we cannot use the basic/nonbasic distinction in moral, political, and environmental philosophy, the widespread use of other dichotomous concepts is likewise threatened. It also suggests how our inability to clearly classify every conceivable need as basic or nonbasic should not keep us from using such a distinction at least with respect to clear cases.

There is also a further point to be made here. If we begin to respond to clear cases, for example, stop aggressing against the clear basic needs of some humans for the sake of clear luxury needs of others, we will be in an even better position to know what to do in the less clear cases. This is because sincerely attempting to live out one's practical moral commitments helps one to interpret them better, just as failing to live them out makes interpreting them all the more difficult. Consequently, I think we have every reason to act on the moral requirements that I have defended in this paper, at least with respect to clear cases.

ENDNOTES

1. http://www.worldhunger.org/articles/Learn/world%20hunger%20facts%202002

2. Thomas Pogge, *World Poverty and Human Rights* (Cambridge, Polity, 2002), p. 204ff.

3. Peter Singer, "What Should a Billionaire Give—and What Should You?" *New York Times* (2006).

4. *Ibid.*

5. http://www.balance.org/articles/factsheet2001.html

6. *Ibid.*

7. *Ibid.*

8. *Ibid.*

9. Lester Brown, *Plan B 2.0* (New York: W. W. Norton & Co., 2006), pp. 84–91. See also Lester Brown, *Outgrowing the Earth,* (New York: W. W. Norton & Co., 2004), especially Chapter 5.

10. Linda Starke, ed., *State of the World 2004* (New York: W. W. Norton & Co., 2004), 9. For a lower comparative consumption comparison, that still supports the same conclusion, see Jared Diamond, "What's Your Consumption Factor?" International Herald Tribune, January 3, 2008, p. 6.

11. See Starke, *State of the World 2004*. There is no way that the resource consumption of the U.S. can be matched by developing and underdeveloped countries, and even if it could be matched, doing so would clearly lead to ecological disaster. See *Planet Under Stress,* ed. Constance Mungall and Digby McLaren (Oxford: Oxford University Press, 1990) and World Hunger: *Twelve Myths*, Frances Lappe and Joseph Collins (New York: Grove Press, 1986).

12. To say that future generations have right against existing generations, we can simply means that there are enforceable requirements against existing generations that would benefit or prevent harm to future generations.

13. Of course, there is always the problem of others not doing their fair share. Nevertheless, as long as your sacrifice would avoid some basic harm to others, either now or in the future, it would still seem reasonable to claim that you would remain under an obligation to make that sacrifice, regardless of what others are doing.

14. Of course, it could be argued that even if we continue our extravagant consumption of nonrenewable resources, future generations will be able to make up for the loss with some kind of a technological fix. We can even imagine that future generations will be able to make everything they need out of, say, sand and water. While surely this is possible, it would not reasonable for us to risk the basic welfare of future

generations on just such a possibility, any more than it would be reasonable for persons starting out in the lowest paying jobs in the business world to start wildly borrowing and spending on themselves and their families, relying just on the possibility that in 15-20 years their incomes will rise astronomically so they then could easily pay off the large debts they are now amassing. There are also many examples of human civilizations that failed to find an appropriate technological fix. See, for example, Jared Diamond, *Collapse* (New York: Penguin, 2005) and Ronald Wright, *A Short History of Progress* (New York: Carroll & Graf, 2004).

15. What makes this an equal utilization of resources over place and time is that the utilization is limited to fulfilling people's basic needs. Of course, once basic needs are met among existing generations, renewable resources may be used for meeting nonbasic needs in ways that do not jeopardize the meeting of the basic needs of future generations. In addition, existing generations can also justifiably meet their nonbasic needs if this is a byproduct of efficiently meeting just their basic needs. Naturally, this holds equally for each subsequent generation as well.

16. Derek Parfit, *Reasons and Persons* (Oxford: Clarendon Press, 1984).

17. A similar example was used by James Woodward in "The Non-Identity Problem," *Ethics* (1986) 804–31, Woodward also provides the example of Viktor Frankl who suggests that his imprisonment in a Nazi concentration camp enabled him to develop "certain resources of character, insights into the human condition and capacities for appreciation" that he would not otherwise have had. At the same time, we clearly want to say that the Nazis unjustifiably violating Frankl's rights by so imprisoning him. Woodward, p. 809. See also Norman Daniels, "Intergenerational Justice," *Stanford Encyclopedia* (2003).

18. Again, to appeal here to simply libertarian premises, giving up or sacrificing the satisfaction of basic or nonbasic needs can be taken to imply merely noninterference for the sake of the satisfaction of such needs.

11

Immigration Controls and the Failure of Liberal Theory

PHILLIP COLE

Phillip Cole argues that immigration controls are antithetical to the liberal belief in the moral equality of all persons. As such, Cole argues they should be replaced by completely open borders.

1. THE PROBLEM OF MEMBERSHIP

My goal in this essay is to argue that immigration controls have no place in liberal political theory. At present, the movement of people across national borders is seen as "an anomaly to be exceptionally tolerated."[1] This strikes me, intuitively, as itself an extraordinary anomaly, given the ease with which we travel over all other kinds of boundaries, and the extent to which we take this ease for granted. We should remember that the world is crisscrossed with all kinds of "territorial" boundaries, which designate provinces, regions, counties, etc.—national borders are exceptional rather than the rule in how we think about "territorial" boundaries and our right to cross them.

A central assumption of my argument is that a recognisably liberal political theory has at its centre the commitment to the moral equality of persons. National membership restrictions necessarily violate that central ethical commitment. Ethical universalism tells us that moral principles and values apply to all persons equally, in the absence of any morally relevant differences: how can we then prioritise moral commitments to co-nationals over others and still respect the moral equality of those others? The

answer is, I believe, that we cannot, and so immigration controls fail a basic moral test. We—as members of a particular nation—may wish to retain them for pragmatic, self-interested reasons, but we have to accept that we have failed to be ethical.

Liberal theories, in their discussions of social justice and equality, have assumed that these theories are about particular political communities, and so our obligations under the principle of moral equality extend to the boundary of our community but not beyond them; or at least the strength of those obligations weaken once we extend them beyond that boundary. This is an assumption that cosmopolitans and others have questioned. For example, Onora O'Neill points out that liberal theorists have taken it "that the discourse or debate of citizens is fundamental to justice." This is defendable if we assume a bounded society of "insiders who can share a common debate about justice," but such an approach "is strangely silent about the predicaments of outsiders, and about the justice of a world that is segregated into states...."[2] O'Neill eloquently expresses the importance of taking ethical universalism and the scope of the principle of moral equality seriously: "It seems to me that ... an adequate account of justice has to take seriously the often harsh realities of exclusion, whether from citizenship of all states or from citizenship in the more powerful and more prosperous states. Why should the boundaries of states be viewed as presuppositions of justice rather than as institutions whose justice must be assessed?"[3]

This poses a radical challenge for boundaries of exclusion: if persons are morally equal, on what basis can they be excluded? This is especially challenging for liberal theories of social justice, as we cannot show that a particular good has been distributed fairly between members of a particular group unless we also know that membership of that group has been distributed fairly—as Michael Walzer has noted, the most important good that gets distributed is membership itself.[4] If people have been unjustly excluded from membership of the group, then this throws the justness of any distribution between members into doubt. For example, if members of a particular group X are excluded from full membership of a society on the basis of racism, while Y are full members, the fact that members of Y have 'fairly' distributed a particular resource between themselves counts for nothing—there is *no* social justice here at all. And so unless we know that national membership boundaries have been constituted justly, in accordance with the basic moral principles of liberal theory, the fact that members of the nation have distributed a particular resource fairly amongst themselves similarly counts for nothing. That central theories of liberal social justice treat this global question as secondary places them in danger of a fundamental ethical failure.

2. THE LIBERAL DILEMMA

The tension within liberal theory lies between the principle of moral equality and what is perceived as a need for membership in order to achieve sustainable political communities. Walzer and others have argued that the existence of liberal democratic communities depends upon exclusive membership practices: without borders to control immigration and naturalization, political *communities* could not exist. A world without borders would either be a world of economic anarchism or it would be a global

state. Neither option is attractive: the first would be an absence of anything that could be recognized as a political community with all the benefits that brings; the second would be a state bureaucracy on a scale never experienced before, with all the dangers that brings. Therefore in order to sustain political units on a scale that encourages the existence of communities without excessive state bureaucracy, borders are needed. And so while the liberal political project is driven by the principle of equality, the success of that project depends upon organized political communities with a level of cohesiveness and commitment among their members. The achievability of the ideals that lie behind the principle of equality therefore rests upon exclusive practices of membership.

However, those exclusive membership practices must be such that they embody the principle of moral equality, or at the very least do not undermine it, because if we cannot arrive at such a set of practices, the liberal project is not practically achievable at all because it is fundamentally contradictory. Liberal theory recognizes the moral equality of all persons, and yet the practices of citizenship through which it claims to meet the requirements of that principle contradict it. The challenge facing liberal theorists is clear: they must outline practices of membership that do not contradict the principle of equality. This is especially challenging for those who argue that notions of 'nationality' or 'national identity' are essential for the cohesiveness of political communities.[5] Walzer, for example, appeals to the notion of a shared identity as being essential if political communities are going to achieve their purposes. That identity, for Walzer, is based upon a shared understanding of who 'we' are, based upon common meanings, language, history and culture; these "produce a collective consciousness."[6]

Appeals to such notions as nationality and collective consciousness are especially problematic for the liberal theorists, because another characteristic element of liberal philosophy is what could be described as the rationality principle. This is the assumption that all human beings are in principle capable of rational thought, and that all political problems are therefore, in principle, capable of rational solution: appeal to non-rational or arbitrary criteria for 'solving' problems is ruled out. The concern to eliminate arbitrariness from social and political practices leads John Rawls to condemn as unfair any distribution of resources that rests on such factors. He states: "What the theory of justice must regulate is the inequalities of life-prospects between citizens that arise from social starting positions, natural advantages and historical contingencies." These are the "fundamental" inequalities.[7] It seems clear that which side of a border one is born on is such a contingency, such that if it gives rise to inequalities and exclusions these are matters of justice. Julian Le Grand similarly observes: "it seems to be regarded as inequitable if individuals receive less than others because of factors *beyond their control*,"[8] and so: "Distributions that are the outcome of factors beyond individual control are generally considered inequitable; distributions that are the outcome of individual choices are not."[9] As national membership is to a large extent beyond people's control, the distribution of national membership is inequitable. Altogether, the moral arbitrariness of national membership makes it an entirely unsuitable basis for the just distribution of resources and other values, and makes the power of exclusion from membership just that—the exercise of power, not of right.

3. THE LIBERAL OPTIONS

There are four possible positions the liberal theorist could take to solve this problem:

1. The argument above is mistaken. There *are* in fact non-arbitrary criteria for settling the membership question, and therefore there is a rational solution to it: membership restrictions can be rationally justified. However, the notion of a common identity, such as a 'national' identity, is essentially arbitrary and so has no role to play in that solution. The challenge for theorists who take this position is to identify the non-arbitrary criteria that will act as the basis for membership.[10]

2. The membership question cannot be settled without an appeal to some notion of shared identity such as a 'national' identity. However, a notion of

national identity can be arrived at which is non-arbitrary. Therefore the notion of a national identity, or nationality, can play a role in the liberal solution to the problem. The challenge for theorists taking this position is to show how non-arbitrary conceptions of national identity, nationality or nationalism can be constructed.[11]

3. There are no non-arbitrary criteria for settling the membership question, but it must nonetheless be settled: the open-borders option is not acceptable. The need for political community overrides the need for rational criteria for membership, and so the membership question must be settled by appeal to non-rational criteria (criteria which cannot be justified through rational argument). This is what I have called the 'Hobbesian' response,[12] and may strike many as the most 'realistic'. The challenge for theorists who take this position is to show how they can appeal to non-rational notions of membership and yet at the same time keep a moral and political distance from ideologies of nation and nationhood which they themselves would condemn as racist.

4. There are no non-arbitrary criteria for settling the membership question, and there is therefore no rational solution to it. The only liberal solution to the dilemma is therefore to have no membership restrictions—completely open borders. The challenge for theorists taking this position is, of course, to show how political communities can be sustained.

Any theorist working on the membership question within the liberal framework must take one of these positions, and while all the positions face difficult challenges, the main one must be to show how the practices of membership they propose embody the principle of moral equality.

4. THE FAILURE
OF LIBERAL THEORY

I am not going to engage in a negative critique of these arguments here (I have engaged in extensive critiques of the first two positions elsewhere),[13] but will observe that the only two consistent positions, in my view, are the third (Hobbesian) and the fourth (open borders). What this means is that if the open borders option is rejected, the Hobbesian response is inevitable. This position claims that liberal coherence cannot be achieved, and that exclusive membership practices are necessarily non-liberal or even illiberal, but that this should not matter from a liberal point of view. One can remain a liberal, and indeed an egalitarian liberal, and defend even the most severe of immigration constraints. This is because the international situation rules out the need to apply liberal principles at this level: the only ethical obligation that falls upon liberal states is to do whatever is in their interests and the interests of their citizens.

This is a deeply pessimistic road to take, because it means that political philosophy understood as a normative discourse comes to an end at the national border. There can be no ethical principles at the international level, as there is, in effect, a Hobbesian state of nature here. Those liberal theories that implicitly or explicitly outlined systems of distributive justice within the boundaries of a single state are, in the end, absolutely correct: liberal theories of justice are necessarily confined to national borders. Therefore any immigration policy, because it deals with outsiders, need only be informed by whatever the state believes to be in its best interests and the best interests of its citizens, and a liberal democratic state is therefore under no ethical obligation to have anything that can be described as a liberal immigration policy. We have come to the end of political philosophy.

We can, though, resist taking this pessimistic route. The Hobbesian argument makes two assumptions that can be questioned: first, it assumes that the international order *is* a Hobbesian state of nature; and second, it holds a deeply unrealistic theory of sovereignty according to which a nation state has unlimited power over its own affairs (including its ability to control how many people and what kind crosses its borders). These two assumptions lead us to a position that seriously overestimates the powers of the liberal state to control global forces, and equally seriously underestimates the possibilities for international cooperation and global justice. There are grounds, too, for supposing that the Hobbesian

conclusion is too pessimistic about the overall effects of immigration. J. A. Scanlan and O. T. Kent note that immigration policy in the United States has been dominated by this kind of perspective. According to the political and legal authorities: "Immigration from another nation to the United States, at least under some circumstances, should be regarded as the functional equivalent of war, with incoming or intending migrants posing threats to the stability of the state—and hence to the existing government and power structure of the nation—which are similar to those posed by an invading army."[14] If we abandon this Hobbesian perspective, then we can argue that states should be held under an obligation to treat 'outsiders', including potential immigrants, according to moral principles. This means that an immigration policy must be ethical, not just an expression of the self-interest of citizens. We are left, once more, with the question of what an ethical immigration policy would look like.

5. THE OPTIMISM OF OPEN BORDERS

I want to spend the rest of this essay exploring my own particular optimism, that there are positive arguments for open borders and that it makes sense as a practical option for global justice. There are a number of arguments in favour of freedom of international movement. The first rests on the value of freedom itself. Chandran Kukathas bases his defence of open borders on the principle of freedom, stating that "...if freedom is held to be an important value, then there is at least a case for saying that very weighty reasons are necessary to restrict it." In the context of international movement, "such reasons would have to be weighty indeed."[15] This is because border controls interfere with significant freedoms: people's liberty to escape oppression; the freedom to sell or buy labour; and the freedom to associate with others. Kukathas combines this with an argument from a principle of humanity, as border controls can prevent people from achieving their full humanity by keeping them in conditions of poverty.

"To say to ... people that they are forbidden to cross a border in order to improve their condition is to say to them that it is justified that they be denied the opportunity to get out of poverty, or even destitution."[16] Together, these principles make a strong case against border controls: "... if freedom and humanity are important and weighty values, the prima facie case for open borders is a strong one, since very substantial considerations will have to be adduced to warrant ignoring or repudiating them."[17]

But in addition to these approaches, there is an argument based on the equal value of membership of the political community and the importance of freedom of movement to that membership. While freedom of international movement has been posed as a deep problem for the idea of political membership, in fact the two are deeply connected. Freedom of movement *within* a state is so crucial for the equal value of political membership that it is enshrined in international law. Article 13 of the Universal Declaration of Human Rights states: "Everyone has the right to freedom of movement and residence within the borders of each state."[18] The International Covenant on Civil and Political Rights in Article 12 states: "Everyone lawfully within the territory of a State shall, within that territory, have the right to liberty of movement and freedom to choose his residence."[19] This is because the right to national mobility gives members the freedom of movement required to protect their interests as free and equal members of the national political community, and develop their life plans and projects. However, how are they to protect their interests and develop their plans and projects at the international level without the same protection of freedom of movement?

It could be replied that the right to mobility at the international level is not important to protect interests and the capacity to carrying out one's life plans and projects, but the evidence is that international constraints on free movement create conditions of oppression, domination, and inequality, especially when we recognize that border controls, as Chandran Kukathas points out, function mainly to prevent movement of the global poor.[20] There is a hierarchy of power when it comes to

international movement, with the global poor largely immobile at the bottom. Of course, simply declaring a universal right to freedom of international movement may do little to change that, which shows that it has to be embedded in a wider approach to issues of global inequality and injustice in which it could play a valuable role. It also points to the necessity of thinking about the right of migration in the context of questions of power and domination.

I suggest that we should see the right to mobility as an essential component of a holistic view of human agency, and this involves seeing certain rights as conditions of empowerment. Duncan Ivison suggests that we can see rights as conduits, regulating the flow of power along certain dimensions, as "modes for distributing capabilities and forms of power and influence"; and "rights themselves represent a distinctive relation of power."[21] If we are to avoid domination, the key is not the removal of power from the scene, but the redistribution of power and capabilities, and frameworks of rights have a central role in that redistribution. One indication that the right to mobility is an essential component of the freedom and equality of persons is the way in which it goes hand in hand with citizenship in liberal democratic states. That connection is so strong that the creation of the European Union has led to unprecedented levels of freedom of international movement for European citizens. The importance of that connection is not only that the right to mobility is a component of freedom, but that it is also a component of equality, and so is an essential aspect of the agency of European citizens.

6. BEYOND THE NATION-STATE

This argument can only be developed, though, if we are prepared to consider forms of membership that transcend nation-states. This is a radical idea, and as Antoine Pécoud and Paul de Guchteneire note this kind of international mobility is a challenge for democracy: "... one needs to find ways to conciliate freedom of movement with the functioning of democratic institutions." But they do not believe this places an insoluble obstacle in the way of establishing freedom of movement. "A creative solution to these issues is to unpack citizenship and consider that its different components (political, civil, social, family and cultural rights notably) can be distributed in a differentiated way. This approach avoids the binary logic of exclusion, in which people have either all rights or none."[22] Ryan Pevnick also argues that the rights and duties of citizenship are not an all-or-nothing bundle— they can be, and often are, disaggregated.[23]

Harold Kleindschmidt thinks a more radical step would be to unpack the nation-state itself. He cites the work of Yasmin Soysal, who has argued for a deterritorialised 'personhood' as the basis for the allocation of citizenship rights rather than nationality.[24] This is a call for a 'postnational' model of citizenship that "confers upon every person the right and duty of participation in the authority structures and public life of a polity, regardless of their historical or cultural ties to that community."[25] This is a cosmopolitan ideal of citizenship, which captures Robert Fine's principle that "human beings can belong anywhere...".[26]

This is to look towards an idea of membership of a global political community, such that to be a free and equal member of that global community, to be an equally powerful participant within it, is deeply connected with one's freedom of mobility throughout it. This is admittedly a sketchy, if not flimsy, vision. But as Ivison observes: "I take it that one of the great projects of twenty-first-century political thought is to develop new models of transnational and global political order that can provide not only effective security and welfare provision for citizens, but that can also become the object of people's reasoned loyalty; to construct, in other words, new forms of transnational democracy."[27]

At one level, this is of course an enormously ambitious vision, but are good moral reasons to move towards greater freedom of international movement, and few good reasons to resist it. What we should notice is actually how little is involved in changing the nature of borders. As we observed at the start of this essay, the fact is that the vast majority of

political boundaries in the world do not entail a right of exclusion. We tend to think of boundaries around political communities in terms of national borders, but most political boundaries are not like that at all. We are surrounded by an enormous range and number of open but democratic political bodies with boundaries that mark out membership *and* territory. Any liberal democratic state consists of a hierarchy of political bodies with porous boundaries, for which membership is determined by voluntary settlement. The United Kingdom consists of the national regions of England, Scotland, Wales and Northern Ireland, which themselves consist of counties, and there are local authorities below that level. All have political authority determined by democratic voting, and have tax raising and other powers, and so depend on having a political membership with duties and obligations, and all have a territorial boundary. But none of them has the right of exclusion. Why can't national borders be like these? The answer is that they can, and the European Union has demonstrated this possibility.

The reply may be that these open bodies can only work because there is closure at a higher level, and so the regions require closure at the national level, and the European Union open-ness depends on closure at the supranational boundary. But one thing to notice is that the claim that lower bodies can only be open because there is closure at a higher level is hypothetical. It is a 'truism' in political theory, but there is no evidence for or against it. If this is a *theoretical* claim—that the idea of open-ness at the regional level has a logical dependence on closure at the national level—then we need a theoretical argument to demonstrate it. If it is a *practical* claim—that as a matter of fact regional open-ness requires national closure—then we need empirical evidence to test it. We cannot rely on the fact that, as things stand, open regions are embedded within closed ones, to settle the question. I tend to think it is a practical claim and what we need is empirical evidence. One potential source of evidence concerns the impact of opening European Union national borders upon nation-states and their regional and local authorities. Has the free movement of European nationals had an impact on these bodies and their ability to fulfill their functions, or raised insuperable problems for their democratic processes? This evidence, however, is not yet fully gathered, and even if it did show some negative impact, that might arise from a particular way of ordering political authority rather than the fact of open-ness as such.

7. TOWARDS A SYMMETRICAL WORLD

The suggestion here is that immigration should be treated in the same way as emigration. What is often missed is the fact that the right of emigration is not absolute—it is a *prima facie* right which states can limit in times of extreme emergency. Article 4 of the International Covenant on Civil and Political Rights states that in times of public emergency that threaten the life of the nation, states "may take measures derogating from their obligations under the present Covenant to the extent strictly required by the exigencies of the situation, provided that such measures are not inconsistent with their other obligations under international law and do not involve discrimination solely on the ground of race, colour, sex, language, religion or social origin."[28] Some rights cannot be derogated by states under any circumstances, but Article 12 on freedom of movement is not one of these, and therefore it can be limited.

While Article 12 states that everyone is free to leave any country, including their own, it also states that this freedom can be subject to restrictions "which are provided by law, are necessary to protect national security, public order (*ordre publique*), public health or morals or the rights and freedoms of others, and are consistent with other rights recognised by the present Covenant."[29] There has been much debate over precisely what circumstances justify a state in derogating certain rights, and guidance has been given by the Siracusa Principles on the Limitation and Derogation Provisions in the International Covenant on Civil and Political Rights.[30] These Principles were drawn up by a meeting of international legal scholars in order to formulate a set

of interpretations of the limitation clauses in the ICCPR. The Principles take care to spell out what will count as a public emergency which threatens the life of the nation, and in relation to Article 12, what will count as a relevant threat to national security, public order, and public health or morals. Although the Principles are not legally binding, they are considered to offer authoritative legal guidance.

The view that emerges from the Principles and from the ICCPR itself and other international documents is that any restriction must be provided by law, must be necessary to achieve the purpose for which it is put in place, must be proportionate to those purposes, and must be "the least intrusive instrument amongst those that might achieve the desired result."[31] In an interesting discussion of the implications of this for the emigration of health care professionals from developing states, Judith Bueno de Mesquita and Matt Gordon ask whether the Principles would justify the limitation of the right of those professionals to leave their home states. A serious threat to public health is a legitimate ground for restricting freedom of movement, but Mesquita and Gordon conclude that "it is highly unlikely that a policy of restricting freedom of movement of health workers as a response to international health worker migration would meet these threshold requirements. Restriction of freedom of movement is unlikely to be the least intrusive policy that can be adopted to improve the right to health in the context of health worker migration."[32] There are other measures that might be effective which are far less intrusive, and more proportionate to their purpose. An example of a health crisis which would meet the Principles' threshold requirements would be "where it is strictly necessary to contain an outbreak of certain highly infectious diseases."[33]

The point here is just as the right to emigrate is not absolute, we are not insisting that the right to immigrate be absolute. We are faced with an asymmetry where states must meet highly stringent standards to justify any degree of control over emigration, but are not required to justify their control over immigration at all. Not only that, but many of the attempts to justify it in liberal political philosophy are based on hypothetical catastrophes and calamities that have only the most flimsy of evidence offered for them, if any evidence at all. My proposal is that in the absence of any clear case that immigration poses a threat to "the life of the nation" as defined in the Siracusa Principles, it should be brought under the same legal framework as emigration, creating a liberal legal order of universal mobility. Immigration controls would become the exception rather than the rule, and would stand in need of stringent justification in the face of clear and overwhelming evidence of

national or international catastrophe, and so become subject to international standards of fairness, justice and legality. This is far from the picture of borderless, lawless anarchy that many defenders of border controls suggest. Rather, it is a world with a legal and moral symmetry when it comes to migration. In the absence of any clear evidence or argument that this symmetrical world is unachievable or undesirable, we should begin the process of imagining how it can be made reality.

ENDNOTES

1. Antoine Pécoud and Paul de Guchteneire (2005), "Migration without borders: an investigation into the free movement of people," *Global Migration Perspectives*, No 27, Global Commission on International Migration, Geneva, Switzerland; p. 22.

2. Onora O'Neill (2000), *Bounds of Justice* (Cambridge University Press, Cambridge), p. 4.

3. O'Neill (2000), p. 4.

4. Michael Walzer (1983), *Spheres of Justice: A Defense of Pluralism and Equality* (Basic Books, New York), p. 64.

5. The classic statements of this position in contemporary political theory are David Miller (1995), *On Nationality* (Clarendon Press, Oxford) and Yael Tamir (1993), *Liberal Nationalism* (Princeton University Press, Princeton).

6. Walzer (1983), p. 28.

7. John Rawls (1978), "The Basic Structure as Subject," in A. Goldman and J. Kim eds., *Values and Morals* (Reidel, Dordrecht), p. 56.

8. Julian Le Grand (1991), *Equity and Choice: An Essay on Economics and Applied Philosophy*, (HarperCollins, London), p. 86.

9. Le Grand (1991), p. 87.

10. This first kind of approach would appeal to some argument other than nationality, drawing on values central to the liberal tradition such as equality, freedom or welfare. The most recent example is Christopher Heath Wellman's appeal to the idea of freedom of association. See Wellman (2011), "Freedom of Association and the Right to

Exclude," in Christopher Heath Wellman and Phillip Cole, *Debating the Ethics of Immigration: Is There a Right to Exclude?* (Oxford University Press, New York and London).

11. Recent examples of the second approach are those arguments that appeal to the need for a political solidarity to underpin social welfare institutions, and which that some notion of nationality is needed to provide the basis for that political solidarity. See David Miller (2008), "Immigrants, Nations, and Citizenship," *The Journal of Political Philosophy* 16, no. 4, 371–390. For a critique of this approach see Ryan Pevnick (2009), "Social Trust and the Ethics of Immigration Policy," *The Journal of Political Philosophy* 17, no. 2, 146–167.

12. See Phillip Cole (2000) *Philosophies of Exclusion: Liberal Political Theory and Immigration* (Edinburgh University Press, Edinburgh), Chapter 8.

13. See Cole (2000), Chapters 5, 6 and 7. And see Phillip Cole (2011), "Open Borders: An Ethical Defense," in Christopher Heath Wellman and Phillip Cole, *Debating the Ethics of Immigration: Is There a Right to Exclude?* (Oxford University Press, New York and London).

14. John A. Scanlan and O. T. Kent (1998), "The Force of Moral Arguments for a Just ImmigrationPolicy in a Hobbesian Universe: The Contemporary American Example," in M. Gibney (ed.), *Open Borders? Closed Societies? The Ethical and Political Issues* (Greenwood Press, Westport CT, and London), p. 69.

15. Chandran Kukathas (2005), "The Case for Open Immigration," in Andrew I. Cohen and

Christopher Heath Wellman, eds., *Contemporary Debates in Applied Ethics* (Blackwell Publishing, Oxford), p. 210.

16. Kukathas (2005), p. 211.

17. Kukathas (2005), p. 211.

18. www.un.org/en/documents/udhr/index. shtml#a13. Accessed July 14, 2011.

19. www2.ohchr.org/english/law/ccpr.htm#art12. Accessed July 14, 2011.

20. Kukathas (2005), p. 213.

21. Duncan Ivison (2008), *Rights* (Acumen, Stocksfield), p. 180.

22. Pécoud and de Guchteneire (2005), p. 16.

23. Pevnick (2009), p. 155.

24. Harald Kleinschmidt (1996), "Migration and the Making of Transnational Social Spaces," (Public address to Australian Centre, University of Melbourne, June), http://spatialaesthetics.unimelb. edu.au/static/files/assets/55c7d377/Kleinschmidt_ Migration_and_the_Making_of_Transnational_ Social_Spaces.pdf (accessed August 24, 2010), p. 13; Yasmin Soysal (1994), *Limits of Citizenship: Migrants*

and Postnational Membership in Europe (Chicago University Press, Chicago and London).

25. Kleinschmidt (1996), p. 13; Soysal (1994), p. 4.

26. Robert Fine (2007), *Cosmopolitanism* (Routledge, London and New York), p. x.

27. Ivison (2008), p. 212.

28. See the International Covenant on Civil and Political Rights, www.unhchr.ch/html/menu3/b/a_ccpr.htm.

29. Judith Bueno de Mesquita and Matt Gordon (2005), *The International Migration of Health Workers: A Human Rights Analysis* (Medact) www.medact.org/content/ Skills%20drain/Bueno%20de%20Mesquita%20and% 20Gordon.pdf (accessed August 24, 2010), p. 15.

30. See the Siracusa Principles on the Limitation and Derogation Principles in the International Covenant on Civil and Political Rights, UN doc. e/CN.4/1985/4, Annex (1985). Accessible at www1.umn.edu/ humanrts/instree/siracusaprinciples.html.

31. Mesquita and Gordon (2005), p. 15.

32. Mesquita and Gordon (2005), p. 15.

33. Mesquita and Gordon (2005), p. 15.

12

Immigration and Freedom of Association[1]

CHRISTOPHER WELLMAN

Christopher Wellman believes that legitimate states have a right to political self-determination which entitles them to design and enforce their own immigration policies. He admits this right is not absolute, but does not think it is outweighed as easily or as often as most presume. To support these claims, Wellman defends a legitimate state's right to exclude outsiders and then argues that this right is typically not outweighed by the competing claims of refugees.

THE RIGHT TO EXCLUDE

My argument for a legitimate state's right to exclude outsiders is built on three foundational premises: (1) legitimate states are entitled to self-determination, (2) freedom of association is an integral component of self-determination, and (3) freedom of association entitles one to refuse to associate with others as one sees fit. Based on this reasoning, I conclude that, just as an individual's right to self-determination explains why she may choose whether or not to marry any given suitor, the citizens of a legitimate state are free collectively to offer or refuse membership in their political community to any given prospective immigrant.

It is not difficult to establish the truth of the second and third premises. To see that freedom of association is integral to self-determination and that enjoying freedom of association requires that one be free to refuse to associate with others, we need only imagine a setting in which one's father, say, has sole discretion to choose who his children will marry. Whatever one might think of this type of arrangement, it clearly does not respect rights to self-determination. Freedom of association involves more than merely the right to get married, it

includes the right to reject any and all suitors one prefers not to marry. And this explains why those of us who value individual autonomy take such offense at the thought of institutions which bestow upon parents the authority to force spouses on their children.

But while few deny that individuals have a right to freedom of association in the marital realm, some may question whether corporate political entities are the types of things that could have such a right. To see that states are entitled to an analogous sphere of political self-determination, think of a country like Norway and its relations with Sweden and the European Union. Norway is currently an associate member of the EU, and it enjoys close relations with Sweden, the country from which it seceded in 1905. But now imagine that Sweden (inspired, perhaps by the reunification of Germany) wanted to reunite with Norway or that the EU wanted Norway to become a full member. Would Sweden or the EU have the right to unilaterally annex Norway, or would it be impermissible for them to do so without Norway's consent? It seems clear that neither Sweden nor the EU is morally entitled to forcibly annex Norway. If either wants to merge with Norway, then it may invite Norway to join forces, but Norway is free to either accept or decline such an invitation. Indeed, even if it is clear to all that the Norwegians would be better off after the merger, it remains Norway's decision to make, and no other country or international organization may permissibly force itself onto Norway without its consent.

And notice that one cannot insist upon Norway's right to remain independent of Sweden without implicitly affirming its right to self-determination, because the best explanation for the impermissibility of Sweden's unilateral annexation of Norway is that it violates Norway's sovereign right to independence. But if Norway's right to self-determination entitles it to refuse to associate with other corporate political entities like Sweden or the EU, then why is it not similarly within its rights to refuse to associate with any given Swedish or European citizen? It seems to me, then, that just as an individual has a right to determine whom (if anyone) he or she would like to marry, a group of fellow-citizens has a right to determine whom (if anyone) it would like to invite into its political community. And just as an individual's freedom of association entitles one to remain single, a legitimate state's freedom of association entitles it to exclude all foreigners from its political community.

Here two potential objections present themselves. First, it may strike some as misleading to compare having discretion over one's partner in marriage to the selection of potential immigrants, because having control over one's associates is plainly paramount in marital relations but seems of little consequence within the relatively impersonal context of political life. Second, even if we concede that a legitimate state's right to freedom of association applies in its relations to other countries or international institutions, this seems quite different from alleging that large political regimes enjoy freedom of association with respect to individual foreigners.

In response to the first worry, I admit that freedom of association is considerably more important in intimate relations. Acknowledging this is unproblematic, however, since it amounts to conceding only that rights to freedom of association are more valuable in intimate contexts, not that they do not

exist elsewhere. At most, then, this objection merely highlights that it may require more to defeat the presumptive right in intimate contexts. Notice, however, that there are many non-intimate associations where we rightly value freedom of association very highly. Religious associations in which people attend to matters of conscience and political groups through which members express themselves can often be large and impersonal, and yet we are extremely reluctant to restrict their associative rights.

Despite the admitted lack of intimacy, freedom of association is also clearly important for political states. To appreciate this, notice that even members of relatively insignificant associations like golf clubs are often (understandably) concerned about their control over potential members. These members typically care about their club's membership rules for at least two sets of reasons. First and most obviously, the size of the club affects one's experience as a member. In the case of a private golf club, for instance, some may want to expand membership, so that each individual will be required to pay less in dues, while others might well be against adding new members for fear that the increased number of golfers will result in limited access to, and more wear and tear on, the golf course. In short, whereas some might be motivated to cut costs, others will be happy to pay higher fees for a more exclusive golfing experience. Second and perhaps less obviously, members will care about the rules of membership because all new members will subsequently have a say in how the club is organized. In other words, caring about one's experience as a club member gives one reason to care about the rules for admitting new members, because, once admitted, new members will typically have a say in determining the future course of the club.

And if the reasons to concern oneself with the membership rules of one's golf club are straightforward, there is nothing curious about people caring so much about the rules governing who may enter their political communities, even though a citizen will typically never meet, let alone have anything approaching intimate relations with, the vast majority of her compatriots. Indeed, there are a number of obvious reasons why citizens would care deeply about how many and which type of immigrants can enter their country. Even if we put to one side all concerns about the state's culture, economy, and political functioning, for instance, people's lives are obviously affected by substantial changes in population density, so it seems only natural that citizens who like higher population density would welcome huge numbers of immigrants, while those with contrary tastes would prefer a more exclusive policy. And in the real world, of course, a substantial influx of foreigners will also almost invariably affect the host state's cultural make-up, the way its economy functions, and/or how its political system operates. And let me be clear: I am not assuming that all of these changes will necessarily be for the worse. More modestly, I am emphasizing only that citizens will often care deeply about their country's culture, economy and political arrangements, and thus, depending upon their particular preferences, may well seek more or fewer immigrants, or perhaps more or fewer immigrants of a given linguistic, cultural, economic and/or political profile. In the case of Mexican immigrants into the United States, for instance, it is not the least bit surprising that some favor a more open policy, while others lobby for the government to heighten its efforts to stem what they regard as a "flood" of unwelcome newcomers. Without taking a stand on this particular controversy, here I wish to stress only the obvious point that, even with large anonymous groups like contemporary bureaucratic states, the number and types of constituents have an obvious and direct affect upon what it is like to be a member of these groups. Thus, unless one questions why anyone would care about their experience as citizens, there is no reason to doubt that we should be so concerned about our country's immigration policy. What is more, as in the case of golf clubs, the crucial point is that— whether one interacts personally with them or not— one's fellow citizens play roles in charting the course that one's country takes. And since a country's immigration policy determines who has the opportunity to join the current citizens in shaping the country's future, this policy will matter enormously to any citizen who cares what course her political community will take.

This connection between a group's membership and its future direction underscores why freedom of association is such an integral component of self-determination. No collective can be fully self-determining without enjoying freedom of association because, when the members of a group can change, an essential part of group self-determination is exercising control over what the "self" is. To appreciate this point, consider again the controversy over Mexican immigration into the United States. It is not merely that large numbers of these immigrants would almost certainly change the culture of those areas where they tend to relocate *en masse*, it is also that (if legally admitted and given the standard voting rights of citizenship) these new members will help determine future laws in the United States, including its immigration policy toward other potential immigrants from Mexico (and elsewhere). Thus, if I am right that legitimate political states are entitled to political self-determination, there appears to be every reason to conclude that this privileged position of sovereignty includes a weighty presumptive right to freedom of association, a right which entitles these states to include or exclude foreigners as they see fit.

Consider now the worry that, while legitimate states are indeed entitled to freedom of association, this right applies only against other corporate entities, such as foreign countries or international institutions; it does not hold against individual persons who would like to enter a given political community. An objector of this stripe shies away from a blanket denial of political freedom of association in recognition of the unpalatable implications such a position would allow. Think again of contemporary Norway, for instance. If one denied Norway's right to freedom of association, then there seems to be no principled way to explain why Sweden or the European Union would act impermissibly if either were to forcibly annex it. Presumably neither Sweden nor the EU may unilaterally merge with Norway; rather, Norway has the right to either accept or refuse these unions. But affirming Norway's right to reject these mergers is just to say that Norway enjoys a right to freedom of association which holds against foreign countries like Sweden and international organizations like the EU. It does not necessarily follow, this objection continues, that Norway therefore has the right to deny admittance to any given Swede or citizen of an EU country who would like to enter Norway. Indeed, in terms of self-determination, the contrast between merging with Sweden and admitting an individual Swede is striking, in that only the former would appear to seriously impact Norway's control over its internal affairs. Thus, insofar as freedom of association is defended as an important component of self-determination, perhaps sovereign states enjoy freedom of association only with respect to macro institutions and not in their micro dealings with individual persons.

An individual immigrant would admittedly not have anything like the impact upon Norway's political self-determination that a forced merger with Sweden or the EU would. Nonetheless, I am unmoved by this objection for at least two basic reasons. Not only do we routinely (and rightly, I think) ascribe rights of freedom of association against individuals to large, nonpolitical institutions, it seems to me that political states would lose a crucial portion of their self-determination if they were unable to refuse to associate with individuals. Consider these points in turn.

Let us begin by considering two garden-variety large institutions like Microsoft Corporation and Harvard University. Presumably each of these institutions enjoys freedom of association, and thus Microsoft could choose to either accept or reject an offer to merge with Cisco Systems and Harvard would have the discretion as to whether or not to accept an offer to form a cooperative alliance with, say, Stanford University. But notice that we do not restrict their freedom of association exclusively to their dealings with other corporate entities; Microsoft's and Harvard's rights to self-determination also give them discretion over their relations with individuals. No matter how qualified I may be, I may not simply assign myself a paying job at Microsoft, for instance, nor may I unilaterally decide to enroll in Harvard as a student or assume a position on their faculty. And if large bureaucratic organizations like Microsoft and Harvard are perfectly within their rights to refuse to associate with various individuals, why should we think that freedom of association would operate any differently for political states? At the very least, it seems as though anyone who wanted to press this second objection would owe us an explanation as to why the logic of freedom of association does not apply to political states as it plainly does in other contexts.

The best way to make this case would presumably be to point out that (as the Norway case was designed to show), because political states are so enormous, an individual's immigration will have no discernible impact upon any given country's capacity for self-determination. I acknowledge that one person's immigration is typically insignificant, but this fact strikes me as insufficient to vindicate the objection. Notice, for instance, that one unilaterally appointed student at Harvard or a single employee at Microsoft would not make much of a difference at either institution, but we would never conclude from this that Harvard and Microsoft lack discretion over their respective admissions and hiring processes. What is more, as the example of Mexican immigrants into the U.S. illustrates, even if a solitary immigrant would be unlikely to have much of an impact on any given state, a sufficient number of immigrants certainly could make an enormous difference. And unless a state is able to exercise authority over the individuals who might immigrate, it is in no position to control its future self-determination. Thus, the very same principle of political self-determination which entitles Norway to either join or reject an association with other countries like those in the EU also entitles Norway to set its own immigration policy for potential individual immigrants.

To summarize our discussion of these two potential objections: Even though (1) the association among compatriots may be far less important than the intimate relations among family members, and (2) a single immigrant is likely to have no discernible influence upon a political community's capacity to be self-determining, legitimate political states have weighty presumptive rights to freedom of association which entitle them to either accept or reject individual applicants for immigration as they see fit. In short, the principle of political self-determination explains why countries have a right to design and enforce their own immigration policies. Whether any given (legitimate) state wants to have entirely open borders, exclude all outsiders, or enact some intermediate policy, it has a presumptive right to do so.

As mentioned earlier, though, this right is merely presumptive and thus remains liable to being overridden in any given set of circumstances. Below I will consider whether this presumptive right is necessarily outweighed by the competing claims of refugees. First, though, I want to emphasize that I am arguing on behalf of a *deontological* right to limit immigration rather than a *consequential* recommendation as to how any given state should act.

There is a big difference between defending a person's right to X and recommending that a person actually do X. One can defend Norway's right to remain independent of Sweden or the EU, for instance, without taking a stand on the separate question of whether Norway would be wise to join. This combination of positions may at first seem contradictory, but it is not. What Norway ought to do and who is entitled to decide what Norway does are two separate issues. Thus, it is important to bear in mind that, in defending a legitimate state's right to exclude potential immigrants, I am offering no opinion on the separate question as to how countries might best exercise this right.

There are several reasons I am not comfortable making any recommendations as to how jealously states should guard their borders. First and most obviously, determining what immigration policy would be best for a country's citizens and/or humanity as a whole requires a command of a great deal of detailed empirical information that I simply lack. Just as importantly, though, it seems to me that there is unlikely any "one size fits all" prescription which would be appropriate for every country in the world. On the contrary, there is no reason why a certain number and type of immigrants could not be beneficial in one country and yet quite harmful in another; it all depends upon the particular social, cultural, economic and political circumstances of the host country. Consider, for instance, the economic impact of immigration. While some writers warn that opening a country's markets to outsiders will have potentially disastrous effects, others counter that the impact of open

borders will (in the long run, at least) invariably be beneficial, since removing any artificial boundary will allow the market to operate more efficiently. I would guess, however, that the truth lies somewhere between these two polar positions. Even if we restrict our focus exclusively to the economic impact upon those who were initially in the host state (as these debates often implicitly presume we should), how helpful any given influx of newcomers would be seems to me to depend upon a number of factors, such as this country's antecedent level of unemployment and the types of skills and work ethic these immigrants have. In addition to determining what the overall affect of the immigrants would be, it is important to consider how the various costs and benefits are distributed. In many cases the influx of relatively unskilled workers may disproportionately help relatively wealthy business owners (who benefit from the increased supply of labor) and hurt working class people (who now face greater competition for jobs whose wages have been decreased). Thus, if one believes that we should be especially concerned about our worst-off compatriots, then this might provide a reason of justice to limit immigration even in circumstances in which the overall net economic impact of more porous borders would be positive.

In light of these observations, I am reluctant to recommend a specific immigration policy as the ideal solution for any given (let alone every) state to follow. If forced to show my hand, however, I must confess that I would generally favor more open borders than the status quo. I appreciate that countries have a variety of good reasons to refrain from completely opening their borders, but I suspect that many of the world's current policies are more the result of unprincipled politicians' exploiting the xenophobia of their constituents for short-term political gain than of well-reasoned assessments of what will be to the long-term advantage. In saying this, however, I am in no way retreating from my contention that legitimate regimes may set their own immigration policy. In my view, there are deontological reasons to respect a legitimate state's rights of political self-determination, and so those countries which qualify have a deontologically-based moral right to freedom of association. Thus, whether they exercise this right rationally or not, it is their call to make. Just as my friends and family may not forcibly interfere with my imprudent decisions to get married or divorced, for instance, external parties must respect a legitimate state's dominion over its borders, even if the resulting policy seems plainly irrational.

To recapitulate the highlights of what has been a relatively long discussion: One cannot adequately capture why it is in principle wrong for an external body such as Sweden or the EU to forcibly annex a country like Norway without invoking a state's right to political self-determination. But if legitimate political regimes enjoy a sphere of self-determination which allows them to refuse relations with foreign countries and international organizations, it seems only natural to conclude that they are similarly entitled to reject associating with individual foreigners. Thus, any regime which satisfactorily protects and respects human rights is entitled to unilaterally design and enforce its own immigration policy. In sum, just as an individual has the right to determine whom (if anyone) she would like to marry, a group of fellow-citizens has a right to determine whom (if anyone) it would like to invite into its political community. And just as an individual's freedom of association entitles her to remain single, a corporate political entity's freedom of association entitles it to exclude all foreigners.

As striking as this conclusion may sound, it is not ultimately all that controversial once one recalls that the right in question is not absolute, but merely presumptive. Many who insist that morality requires (more) open borders might happily concede all of the conclusions for which I have argued to this point, for instance, because they are confident that whatever presumptive rights legitimate states have to exclude foreigners are often (if not always) overridden by more weighty moral concerns. Space limitations do not allow me to attend to the many powerful arguments that have been offered in defense of open borders, but I will argue below that even refugees do not necessarily have as strong of a claim to immigrate as one might initially suspect. This will not establish that a legitimate state may exclude all prospective immigrants, of course, but hopefully it will lend credence to my claim that a state's presumptive right to exclude outsiders holds up quite well against the competing claims of outsiders.

REFUGEES

Following the 1951 Convention Relating to the Status of Refugees, international law defines a refugee as someone who "owing to a well-founded fear of being persecuted for reasons of race, religion, nationality, membership of a particular social group, or political opinion, is outside the country of his nationality, and is unable to or, owing to such fear, is unwilling to avail himself of the protection of that country."[2] Critics have protested that this definition is too narrow in at least three important ways.[3] First, why focus exclusively on victims of group-based persecution? And even if we do think in terms of groups, why restrict ourselves to these particular groups? What if someone is persecuted *qua* woman or *qua* homosexual, for instance? Second, given the variety of threats to living a minimally decent human life, why insist that only those vulnerable to persecution can qualify as refugees? What about so-called "economic refugees" or those who are fleeing a civil war, for instance? Third, why think that someone must already be "outside the country of his nationality" in order to qualify? What if an individual is being detained at the border or is too frail or impoverished to migrate without assistance, for example?

I share these worries about this restricted definition of refugees. If human rights are best understood as the protections humans need against the standard threats to living a minimally decent life, then it strikes me that anyone whose human rights are in jeopardy should qualify as a refugee. Defined thusly, a refugee would be anyone who has a particularly urgent claim to help because her current state is either unable or unwilling to protect her human rights. I will not press this issue here, however, because our interest in refugees is as a potential exception to my claim that legitimate states have the right to exclude outsiders. Retaining the traditional, narrow definition seems appropriate, then, since this provides the toughest challenge to my account.

It is not difficult to see why refugees are thought to be an especially compelling counterexample to anyone who seeks to defend a state's discretion over immigration. First, unlike someone who merely wants to migrate to improve an already good life (such as an artist who wants to live in New York, for example), the refugee is unable to live a minimally decent human life in her home country. More importantly, insofar as this person specifically needs protection from her state, she cannot be helped from abroad. Unlike a poor Chadian to whom Norwegians might ship resources, for instance, an Iraqi Kurd persecuted by Saddam Hussein's Baathist regime apparently cannot be helped in any other way than by being given refuge in a foreign country. Finally, given that the refugee has fled her home country and is requesting asylum from the new state, the latter is now involved in the situation. As regrettable as it might be for Norway to refuse to send funds to starving Chadians, for instance, Norway is not thought to be implicated in their starvation in the same way it would be if it forcibly returned a Kurdish asylum seeker to Iraq, where she was subsequently tortured. Combining these points, a refugee's plight appears morally tantamount to that of a baby who has been left on one's doorstep in the dead of winter. Only a moral monster would deny the duty to bring this infant into her home, and no theorist who endorses human rights could deny that states must admit refugees.

I agree that the citizens of wealthy states are obligated to help refugees, but I am not convinced that this assistance must come in the form of more open admissions. Just as we might send food and other resources to the world's poor, we can try to help persecuted foreigners in their home state. Imagine that Iraqi Kurds request asylum in Norway, for instance. Assuming that these Kurds are in fact being persecuted, it is natural to conclude that Norway has no choice but to allow them to immigrate. But this conclusion is too hasty. While there would presumably be nothing wrong with welcoming these Iraqis into the Norwegian political community, there are other options if the Norwegians would prefer not to expand their citizenship. If Norway were able to protect these Kurds in their homeland, creating a safe-haven with a no-fly zone in Northern Iraq, for

instance, then there would be nothing wrong with Norway's assisting them in this fashion. (Indeed, in many ways, helping in this manner seems preferable.) The core point, of course, is that if these persecuted Kurds have a right against Norwegians, it is a general right to protection from their persecutors, not the more specific right to refuge *in Norway*. If Norway provides these Kurds refuge in Iraq, then the Kurds cease to qualify as refugees and thus no longer have any special claim to migrate to Norway.

Some will resist my proposal on the grounds that Norway should not meddle in Iraq's domestic affairs, but this objection wrongly presumes a Westphalian orientation in which all *de facto* states occupy a privileged position of moral dominion over all matters on their territory. On my view, only legitimate states are entitled to political self-determination, where legitimacy is understood in terms of satisfactorily protecting the rights of one's constituents and respecting the rights of all others. And any state that persecutes its own citizens (as the Baathist regime did when it targeted Kurds) clearly does not adequately secure the human rights of its citizens and thus is manifestly not entitled to the normal sovereign rights which typically make humanitarian intervention in principle wrong. And note: I am not saying that it will always be easy or advisable to intervene and fix a refugee's problem at its source (on the contrary, I would think that countries would more often prefer to admit refugees than to forcibly intervene on their behalf); I allege only there is nothing in principle which necessarily prohibits foreign states like Norway from providing refuge to persecuted groups like Iraqi Kurds in their native countries.

At this point, one might protest that Norway must admit these Kurdish refugees at least until it has adequately secured a safe-haven in Northern Iraq. This may be right: No matter how jealously the Norwegians might guard their political membership, the Kurds must not be returned until their protection against persecution can be guaranteed. It is important to notice, however, that Norwegians need not extend the benefits of political membership to these temporary visitors any more than it must give citizenship to other guests, like tourists, who are in the country for only a short time. What is more, if I am right that there is nothing wrong with Norway's intervening in Iraq once the Kurdish refugees have already arrived on Norway's doorstep, then presumably it would equally be permissible for Norway to intervene preemptively, so as to avert the mass migration. After all, Norway's intervention is justified by the initial acts of persecution, not by the subsequent migration of masses of refugees.

Before closing, I would like to return to the analogy of the baby on the doorstep, not to insist that it is inapt, but because I think reflecting upon this domestic case actually confirms my analysis of refugees. Suppose, then, that I open my front door in the dead of winter and find a newborn baby wrapped in blankets. Clearly, I must bring the infant in from the cold, but it does not follow that I must then adopt the child and raise her as my own. Perhaps it would be permissible to do so, but it seems clear that I would not be required to incorporate this child into my family if I would prefer not to. This child has a right to a decent future, and its arrival on my doorstep may well obligate me to attend to her needs until I can find her a satisfactory home, but the infant's valid claim not to be left out in the cold does not entail the entirely distinct right to permanent inclusion in my family.

I thus conclude that the analogy between a refugee and a baby left on one's doorstep is both apt and instructive. In both cases, one can nonvoluntarily incur a stringent duty to help the imperiled individual. But just as one can satisfactorily discharge one's duty to the vulnerable child without permanently adopting it, a state can entirely fulfill its responsibility to persecuted refugees without allowing them to immigrate into its political community.

In the end, then, I respond to the challenge posed by the plight of refugees by conceding a stringent duty to help but insisting that this obligation is disjunctive. Just as wealthy states may permissibly respond to global poverty either by opening their borders or by helping to eliminate this poverty at its source, countries that receive refugees on their political doorstep are well within their rights either to invite these refugees into their political communities or to intervene in the refugees' home state to ensure that they are effectively protected from persecution there. I conclude, then, that, as tragic as the cases of many refugees no doubt are, they do not necessarily constitute an exception to my thesis that legitimate states are entitled to exclude all outsiders, even those who desperately seek to gain admission.

ENDNOTES

1. This paper utilizes excerpts from my book (co-authored with Phillip Cole), *Debating the Ethics of Immigration: Is There a Right to Exclude?* (New York: Oxford University Press, 2011), in which these ideas and arguments are developed and defended at greater length.

2. Convention, art. 1A(2).

3. For an excellent discussion of these matters, see Andrew E. Shacknove, "Who Is a Refugee?" *Ethics* 95 (January 1985): 274–284.

SUGGESTIONS FOR FURTHER READING

Anthologies

Brown, Peter, and Henry Shue. *Boundaries.* Totowa, NJ: Rowman & Littlefield, 1981.

Crocker, David, and Toby Linden, *The Ethics of Consumption.* Lanham, MD: Rowman & Littlefield, 1998.

Lucas, George R., Jr., and Thomas W. Ogletree. *Lifeboat Ethics.* New York: Harper & Row, 1976.

Luper-Foy, Steven. *Problems of International Justice.* Boulder, CO: Westview Press, 1988.

Partridge, Ernest. *Responsibilities to Future Generations.* Buffalo, NY: Prometheus, 1981.

Sikora, R. I., and Brian Barry. *Obligation to Future Generations.* Philadelphia: Temple University Press, 1978.

Basic Concepts

Parfit, Derek. *Reasons and Persons.* Oxford: Oxford University Press, 1985.

Alternative Views

Amur, Samir. *Unequal Development.* New York: Monthly Review Press, 1976.

Barbieri, William. *The Ethics of Citizenship.* Durham: Duke University Press, 1998.

Bauer, P. T. *Equality, the Third World and Economic Delusion.* Cambridge: Harvard University Press, 1981.

Bayles, Michael D. *Morality and Population Policy.* Birmingham: University of Alabama Press, 1980.

Beitz, Charles R. *Political Theory and International Relations.* Princeton: Princeton University Press, 1979.

Elfstrom, Gerald. *Ethics for a Shrinking World.* New York: St. Martin's Press, 1990.

Hardin, Garrett. *Promethean Ethics.* Seattle: University of Washington Press, 1980.

Renner, Michael. *Fighting for Survival.* New York: Norton, 1996.

Shue, Henry. *Basic Rights.* Princeton: Princeton University Press, 1980.

Practical Applications

Benhabib, Seyla. *The Rights of Others: Aliens, Residents, and Citizens.* Cambridge: Cambridge University Press, 2004.

Meilaender, Peter C. *Toward a Theory of Immigration.* New York: Palgrave, 2001.

Swain, Carol M. ed. *Debating Immigration.* New York: Cambridge University Press, 2007.

Wellman, Christopher Heath, and Phillip Cole. *Debating the Ethics of Immigration: Is there a Right to Exclude?* New York: Oxford University Press, 2011.

✳

Abortion and Euthanasia

INTRODUCTION

Basic Concepts

The problem of abortion and euthanasia has been as thoroughly discussed as any contemporary moral problem. As a result, the conceptual issues have been fairly well laid out, and there have been some interesting attempts to bridge the troublesome normative and practical disagreements that remain.

First of all, almost everyone agrees that the fundamental issue in justifying abortion is the moral status of the fetus, although considerable disagreement exists as to what that status is.[1] Conservatives on the abortion question, like Pope John Paul II (Selection 13) and Don Marquis (Selection 15), contend that from conception the fetus has full moral status and hence a serious right to life. Liberals like Mary Anne Warren (Selection 16) hold that, at least until birth, the fetus has almost no moral status whatsoever and lacks a serious right to life.[2] Moderates on the question adopt some position in between these two views. And still others, like Judith Jarvis Thomson (Selection 14), adopt for the sake of argument either the conservative or the liberal view on moral status of the fetus and then try to show that such a view does not lead to the consequences its supporters assume.[3]

Second, almost everyone agrees that the position one takes on the moral status of the fetus influences whether one considers either the distinction between killing and letting die or the doctrine of double effect to be relevant to the abortion question. For example, conservatives are quite interested in whether the killing and letting die distinction can be used to show that it is permissible to let the fetus die in certain contexts, even when it would be impermissible to kill it. However, liberals find the use of this distinction in such contexts to be completely unnecessary. They hold that the fetus has almost no moral status, so they do not object to either killing it or letting it die. Similarly, although conservatives are quite interested in whether the doctrine of double effect can be used to permit the death of the fetus as a foreseen but unintended consequence of some legitimate course of action, liberals find no use for the doctrine of double effect in such contexts.

Third, almost everyone agrees that either the killing and letting die distinction or the doctrine of double effect could prove useful in cases of euthanasia. Agreement is possible because most of the subjects of euthanasia are humans who, in everyone's view, have full moral status and hence a serious right to life. Accordingly, despite the disagreement as to where it is useful to apply the killing and letting die distinction and the doctrine of double effect, everyone agrees that both conceptual tools deserve further examination.

The distinction between killing and letting die has its advocates and its critics. Advocates maintain that, other things being equal, killing is morally worse than letting die, with the consequence that letting die is justified in cases where killing is not. The critics of this distinction maintain that, other things being equal, killing is not morally worse than letting die, with the consequence that killing is morally justified whenever letting die is. Both advocates and critics agree that other things would not be equal if the killing were justified or deserved while the letting die unwanted and undeserved. They tend to disagree, however, over whether other things would be equal if the killing were in response to a patient's request to die while the letting die involved a prolonged and excruciatingly painful death, or if the killing resulted in the death of just a few individuals while the letting die resulted in the death of many people.

Yet whatever view one adopts as to when other things are equal, it is hard to defend the moral preferability of letting die over killing when both are taken to be intentional acts. As James Rachels so graphically illustrates (Selection 18), it seems impossible to judge the act of A, who intentionally lets Z die while standing ready to finish Z off if that proves necessary, as being morally preferable to the act of B, who with similar motive and intention kills Y. But it is far from clear whether advocates of the killing and letting die distinction are claiming that the distinction holds when the killing and the letting die are both intentional acts because it is unlikely in such cases that the letting die would be morally justified when the killing is not. Rather, as Bonnie Steinbock argues (Selection 19), advocates of the distinction seem to have in mind a contrast between *intentional* killing and *unintentional* letting die, or more fully stated, a contrast between intentional killing and unintentional letting die when the latter is the foreseen consequence of an otherwise legitimate course of action.

Steinbock maintains that there are at least two types of cases in which letting die, distinguished in this way from killing, seems justified. In the first, a doctor ceases treatment at the patient's request, foreseeing that the patient will die or die sooner than otherwise, yet not intending that result. In the second, a doctor's intention is to avoid employing treatment that is extremely painful and has little hope of benefiting the patient, even though she foresees that this may hasten the patient's death. In addition, conservatives have argued that letting die, distinguished in this way from killing, can be justified in cases of ectopic pregnancy and cancer of the uterus because in such cases the fetus's death is the foreseen but unintended consequence of medical treatment that is necessary to preserve the basic well-being of the pregnant woman.

When the killing and letting die distinction is interpreted in this way, it has much in common with the doctrine of double effect. This doctrine places four restrictions on the permissibility of acting when some of the consequences of one's action are evil. These restrictions are as follows:

1. The act is good in itself or at least indifferent.
2. Only the good consequences of the act are intended.
3. The good consequences are not the effect of the evil.
4. The good consequences are commensurate with the evil consequences.

The basic idea of the killing and letting die distinction, as we have interpreted it, is expressed by restrictions 2 and 3.

When conservatives apply the doctrine of double effect to a case in which a pregnant woman has cancer of the uterus, the doctrine is said to justify an abortion because:

1. The act of removing the cancerous uterus is good in itself.
2. Only the removal of the cancerous uterus is intended.
3. The removal of the cancerous uterus is not a consequence of the abortion.
4. Preserving the life of the mother by removing the cancerous uterus is commensurate with the death of the fetus.

The doctrine is also said to justify unintentionally letting a person die, or "passive euthanasia," at least in the two types of cases described by Steinbock.

In recent moral philosophy, the main objection to the doctrine of double effect has been to question the necessity of its restrictions. Consider the following example. Imagine that a large person who is leading a party of spelunkers gets herself stuck in the mouth of a cave in which flood waters are rising. The trapped

party of spelunkers just happens to have a stick of dynamite with which they can blast the large person out of the mouth of the cave; either they use the dynamite or they all drown, the large person with them. It appears that the doctrine of double effect would *not* permit the use of the dynamite in this case because the evil consequences of the act are intended as a means to securing the good consequences in violation of restrictions 2 and 3. Yet it is plausible to argue in such a case that using dynamite would be justified on the grounds that (a) the evil to be avoided (i.e., the evil of failing to save the party of spelunkers except for the large person) is considerably greater than the evil resulting from the means employed (i.e., the evil of intentionally causing the death of the large person) and/or that (b) the greater part of evil resulting from the means employed (i.e., the death of the large person) would still occur regardless of whether those means were actually employed.

Some people might want to defend the doctrine of double effect against this line of criticism by maintaining that the spelunkers need not intend the death of the large person, but only that "she be blown into little pieces" or that "the mouth of the cave be suitably enlarged." But how is the use of dynamite expected to produce these results except by way of killing the large person? Thus, the death of the large person is part of the means employed by the spelunkers to secure their release from the cause, and thus would be impermissible according to the doctrine of double effect. If, however, we think that bringing about the death of the large person could be morally justified in this case, because, for example, (a) and/or (b) obtain, we are left with a serious objection to the necessity of the restrictions imposed by the doctrine of double effect for acting morally.

Given these objections to the doctrine of double effect, Philippa Foot has suggested that we might more profitably deal with the moral questions at issue by distinguishing between negative and positive duties. *Negative duties* are said to be duties to refrain from doing certain sorts of actions. Typically, these are duties to avoid actions that inflict harm or injury on others. Thus, the duties not to kill or assault others are negative duties. By contrast, *positive duties* are duties to do certain actions, usually those that aid or benefit others. The duties to repay a debt and help others in need are positive duties. This distinction is used to resolve practical disputes by claiming that negative duties have priority over positive duties; accordingly, when negative and positive duties conflict, negative duties always take precedence over positive duties.

Applying this distinction, Foot claims that a doctor is justified in performing an abortion when nothing can be done to save the lives of both child and mother, but the life of the mother can be saved by killing the child. Obviously, this case is quite similar to the example of the large person stuck in the mouth of the cave. But it is not clear how the distinction between positive and negative duties can help us in either situation. Since both the doctor and the group of spelunkers trapped by the large person have a negative duty not to kill that takes precedence over any positive duty to help either themselves or others, it would seem that neither aborting the fetus nor blowing up the large person could be justified on the basis of this distinction. Thus, the distinction between negative and positive duties no more justifies evil consequences in such cases than does the doctrine of double effect. Accordingly, if we want to provide such a justification, we need to find some morally acceptable way of going beyond both of these requirements.

Alternative Views

As we mentioned earlier, conservatives hold that the fetus has full moral status and hence a serious right to life. As a consequence, they oppose abortion in a wide range of cases. Their view is expressed well by Pope John Paul II (Selection 13) who believes abortion to be the intentional killing of an innocent human being at the beginning of its life, from conception until birth. What makes the act of abortion so heinous, he says, is that no human being is so weak, so defenseless, and so innocent, as an unborn child. No doubt, he says, the choice to have an abortion is often a tragic choice, motivated out of unselfish concerns, but regardless they cannot justify intentionally taking the life of an innocent human being.

Finally, Pope John Paul II recognizes that there are many who doubt the Catholic Church's stance on when personhood begins (at conception). His response is that the mere probability that a human person is present at conception is enough, from the standpoint of moral obligation, to prohibit the destruction of the fetus.

Hoping to undercut an antiabortion stance like Pope John Paul II's, Judith Jarvis Thomson adopts, for the sake of argument, the conservative position on the moral status of the fetus (Selection 14). She then tries to show that abortion is still justified in a wide range of cases. She asks us to imagine that we are kidnapped and connected to an unconscious violinist who now shares the use of our kidneys. The situation is such that if we detach ourselves from the violinist before nine months transpire, the violinist will die. Thomson thinks it obvious that we have no obligation to share our kidneys with the violinist in such a case, and hence that, in analogous cases, abortion can be justified. Thomson's view has provoked so much discussion that the authors of the four following selections feel compelled to consider her view in developing their own positions.

First, Don Marquis begins by assuming what Thomson argues against—namely, that if fetuses have the same moral status as adult human beings, then the presumption that any particular abortion is immoral is exceedingly strong (Selection 15). What Marquis wants to defend is the conservative claim that fetuses have the same moral status as adult humans. He argues that what is wrong with killing adults is that it deprives them of "all the experience, activities, projects, and enjoyments that would otherwise have constituted [their] future." Because abortion deprives a typical fetus of a "future like ours," Marquis contends that the moral presumption against abortion is as strong as the moral presumption against killing adult human beings. But there are at least two problems with Marquis's argument. First, his argument would seem to suggest that it would be less wrong to kill an older rather than a younger person and maybe not wrong at all to kill a person who doesn't have much of a future, say only a year or two left to live. Second, Marquis tries to distinguish contraception from abortion on the grounds that only abortion deprives *something* of a "future like ours." But it is not clear why, given that abortion and contraception both prevent a "future like ours," the fact that only abortion deprives something of a "future like ours" suffices to render it morally prohibited while contraception remains morally permissible.

Like Marquis, Mary Anne Warren also distinguishes her view from Thomson's (Selection 16). In particular, she objects to Thomson's violinist example, claiming that, at most, the example justified abortion in cases of rape and hence will not provide the desired support for abortion on demand. Thomson, however, did provide additional examples and arguments in an attempt to show that abortion is justified in cases other than rape.

Like Marquis, Warren wants to build a consensus on the abortion question. To achieve this, she proposes a set of criteria for being a person with full moral status that she thinks pro-abortionists and anti-abortionists alike could accept. The criteria are (1) consciousness; (2) developed reasoning;

(3) self-motivated activity; (4) a capacity to communicate; and (5) the presence of self-concepts and self-awareness. But although most people would certainly agree that these criteria are met in paradigm cases, conservatives would still reject them as necessary requirements for being a person. But it is not clear that the concept of a person is sharp or decisive enough to bear the weight of a solution to the abortion controversy.

Those who find both the conservative and liberal views on abortion unattractive might be inclined toward the moderate view. This view attempts to draw a line—typically at implantation, or at quickening, or at viability—for the purpose of separating those who do not have full moral status from those who do. The U.S. Supreme Court in *Roe v. Wade* (1973) has frequently been understood as supporting a moderate view on abortion. In this decision, the Court, by a majority of seven to two, decided that the constitutional right to privacy, protected by the due process clause of the Fourteenth Amendment to the Constitution, entails that (1) no law may restrict the right of a woman to be aborted by a physician during the first three months (trimester) of her pregnancy; (2) during the second trimester abortion may be regulated by law only to the extent that the regulation is reasonably related to the preservation and protection of maternal health; and (3) when the fetus becomes viable (not before the beginning of the third trimester) a law may prohibit abortion, but only subject to an exception permitting abortion whenever necessary to protect the woman's life or health (including any aspects of her physical or mental health). But regardless of whether the Court's decision was intended to support the moderate view on abortion, some have argued that in the absence of reasonable constraints, the Court's decision has led to abortion on demand.

In Selection 17, Sally Markowitz provides what she regards as a specifically feminist argument for abortion; that is, one that is grounded on awareness of women's oppression and a commitment to a more egalitarian society. She distinguishes her view from other approaches to abortion, which focus either on the moral status of the fetus or on a woman's right to autonomy. Accordingly, Markowitz assumes for the sake of argument that the fetus has a serious right to life. She bases her defense of abortion on two principles: the Impermissible Sacrifice Principle and the Feminist Proviso. According to the Impermissible Sacrifice Principle, when one social group in a society is systematically oppressed by another, it is impermissible to require the oppressed group to make sacrifices that will exacerbate or perpetuate the oppression. According to the Feminist Proviso, women are, as a group, sexually oppressed by men, and this oppression can neither be completely understood in terms of, nor otherwise reduced to, oppressions of other sorts. From these two principles, Markowitz derives the conclusion that, because in the sexist society in which we live women are denied the equality to which they are entitled, a right to abortion is justified. It is interesting to note, however, that Markowitz's stance on abortion might turn out to be reconciled in practice with the conservative stance on abortion, provided that those who support the conservative stance on abortion are willing to first institutionalize the feminist agenda for equality between men and women.

Although most of the contemporary discussion of abortion has focused on the moral status of the fetus, most of the discussion of euthanasia has focused on the killing and letting die distinction and the doctrine of double effect. As we noted before, advocates of the killing and letting die distinction and the doctrine of double effect tend to justify only passive euthanasia (i.e., letting a person die as a foreseen but unintended consequence of an otherwise legitimate course of action). In contrast, critics of the killing and letting die distinction and the doctrine of double effect tend also to justify active euthanasia (i.e., intentional killing) on the basis of its consequences. Rachels (Selection 18) cites the case of a person suffering from cancer of the throat who has three options: (1) with continued treatment she will have a few more days of pain and then die; (2) if treatment is stopped but nothing else is done, it will be a few more hours; or (3) with a lethal injection she will die at once. In such a case, Rachels thinks, the third option—active euthanasia—is justified on the grounds that the person would be better off dying immediately.

But euthanasia is not only passive or active, it is also voluntary or involuntary. Voluntary euthanasia has the (informed) consent of the person involved. Involuntary euthanasia lacks such consent, usually but not always because the person involved is incapable of providing it. This means that at least four different types of euthanasia are possible: voluntary passive euthanasia, involuntary passive euthanasia, voluntary active euthanasia, and involuntary active euthanasia. Of the four types, voluntary passive euthanasia seems easiest to justify, involuntary active euthanasia the most difficult. But voluntary euthanasia, both passive and active, would seem more justifiable if it could be shown that there were a fundamental moral right to be assisted in bringing about one's own death if one so desired. Even if such a right could be supported, however, it would presumably only have force when one could reasonably be judged to be better off dead.

Practical Applications

It is not at all difficult to see how the various proposed solutions to the problem of abortion and euthanasia could be applied in contemporary societies.

In *Planned Parenthood v. Casey* (Selection 20), the U.S. Supreme Court reaffirmed its commitment to what they took to be the essential holding of *Roe v. Wade*, which is a woman's right to terminate her pregnancy before viability, while rejecting *Roe v. Wade*'s trimester analysis in favor of an undue burden standard, which only the spousal notification requirement of Pennsylvania's Abortion Control Act violated.

In Selection 21, Ronald Dworkin, Thomas Nagel, Robert Nozick, John Rawls, Thomas Scanlon, and Judith Jarvis Thomson argue that there is a fundamental liberty protected by the due process clause of the Fourteenth Amendment that guarantees a right of assisted suicide, under certain conditions. They further argue that the risks that would accompany recognizing this right can be minimized through reasonable regulation, the same type of regulation that is now done, for example, in recognizing a patient's right to terminate life-sustaining medical treatment.

In *Washington v. Glucksberg* (Selection 22) the U.S. Supreme Court decided that the Washington state statute which prohibited anyone from knowingly causing or aiding another to attempt suicide does not violate the fundamental liberty that is protected by the due process clause of the Fourteenth Amendment. Hence, all that is required for the state of Washington to justifiably prohibit assisted suicide is some rational grounds to do so. Among other things, the court found that the difficulties of crafting a right of assisted suicide that would sufficiently protect vulnerable people provided just such ground.

But even as you begin to formulate the laws and social institutions, with their demands on social goods and resources, that are needed to enforce what you take to be the most morally defensible solution to the problem of abortion and euthanasia, you will still need to take into account the demands on social goods and resources that derive from solutions to other practical moral problems—such as the problem of sex equality, which is taken up in the next section.

ENDNOTES

1. The term "fetus" is understood to refer to any human organism from conception to birth.

2. Note that liberals on the abortion question need not be welfare liberals, although many of them are. Likewise, conservatives on the abortion question need not be libertarians or political conservatives.

3. Henceforth liberals, conservatives, and moderates on the abortion question are simply referred to as liberals, conservatives, and moderates.

13

The Unspeakable Crime of Abortion

POPE JOHN PAUL II

Pope John Paul II defines abortion as the intentional killing of an innocent human being, at the beginning of its life, from conception to birth. As such, abortion is one of the gravest moral crimes. Even if it is uncertain that personhood begins at conception, the mere probability that a human person is involved is enough to justify the prohibition of abortion.

Among all the crimes which can be committed against life, procured abortion has characteristics making it particularly serious and deplorable. The Second Vatican Council defines abortion, together with infanticide, as an "unspeakable crime."[1]

But today, in many people's consciences, the perception of its gravity has become progressively obscured. The acceptance of abortion in the popular mind, in behaviour and even in law itself, is a telling sign of an extremely dangerous crisis of the moral sense, which is becoming more and more incapable of distinguishing between good and evil, even when the fundamental right to life is at stake. Given such a grave situation, we need now more than ever to have the courage to look the truth in the eye and to *call things by their proper name*, without yielding to convenient compromises or to the temptation of self-deception. In this regard the reproach of the Prophet is extremely straightforward: "Woe to those who call evil good and good evil, who put darkness for light and light for darkness" (*Is* 5:20). Especially in the case of abortion there is a widespread use of ambiguous terminology, such as "interruption of pregnancy," which tends to hide abortion's true nature and to attenuate its seriousness in public opinion. Perhaps this linguistic phenomenon is itself a symptom of an uneasiness of conscience. But no word has the power to change the reality of things: procured abortion is *the deliberate and direct killing, by whatever means it is carried out, of a human being in the initial phase of his or her existence, extending from conception to birth.*

The moral gravity of procured abortion is apparent in all its truth if we recognize that we are dealing with murder and, in particular, when we consider the specific elements involved. The one eliminated is a human being at the very beginning of life. No one more absolutely *innocent* could be imagined. In no way could this human being ever be considered an aggressor, much less an unjust aggressor! He or she is *weak*, defenseless, even to the point of lacking that minimal form of defence consisting in the poignant power of a newborn baby's cries and tears. The unborn child is *totally entrusted* to the protection and care of the woman carrying him or her in the womb. And yet sometimes it is precisely the mother herself who makes the decision and asks for the child to be eliminated, and who then goes about having it done.

It is true that the decision to have an abortion is often tragic and painful for the mother, insofar as the decision to rid herself of the fruit of conception is not made for purely selfish reasons or out of convenience, but out of a desire to protect certain important values such as her own health or a decent standard of living for the other members of the family. Sometimes it is feared that the child to be born would live in such conditions that it would be better if the birth did not take place. Nevertheless, these reasons and others like them, however serious and tragic, *can never justify the deliberate killing of an innocent human being.*

As well as the mother, there are often other people too who decide upon the death of the child in the womb. In the first place, the father of the child may be to blame, not only when he directly pressures the woman to have an abortion, but also when he indirectly encourages such a decision on her part by leaving her alone to face the problems of pregnancy:[2] in this way the family is thus mortally wounded and profaned in its nature as a community of love and in its vocation to be the "sanctuary of life." Nor can one overlook the pressures which sometimes come from the wider family circle and from friends. Sometimes the woman is subjected to such strong pressure that she feels psychologically forced to have an abortion: certainly in this case moral responsibility lies particularly with those who have directly or indirectly obliged her to have an abortion. Doctors and nurses are also responsible, when they place at the service of death skills which were acquired for promoting life.

But responsibility likewise falls on the legislators who have promoted and approved abortion laws, and, to the extent that they have a say in the matter, on the administrators of the health-care centres where abortions are performed. A general and no less serious responsibility lies with those who have encouraged the spread of an attitude of sexual permissiveness and a lack of esteem for motherhood, and with those who should have ensured—but did not—effective family and social policies in support of families, especially larger families and those with particular financial and educational needs. Finally, one cannot overlook the network of complicity which reaches out to include international institutions, foundations and associations which systematically campaign for the legalization and spread of abortion in the world. In this sense abortion goes beyond the responsibility of individuals and beyond the harm done to them, and takes on a distinctly social dimension. It is a most serious *wound* inflicted

on society and its culture by the very people who ought to be society's promoters and defenders. As I wrote in my *Letter to Families*, "we are facing an immense threat to life: not only to the life of individuals but also to that of civilization itself."[3] We are facing what can be called a *"structure of sin"* *which opposes human life not yet born.*

Some people try to justify abortion by claiming that the result of conception, at least up to a certain number of days, cannot yet be considered a personal human life. But in fact, "from the time that the ovum is fertilized, a life is begun which is neither that of the father nor the mother; it is rather the life of a new human being with his own growth. It would never be made human if it were not human already. This has always been clear, and ... modern genetic science offers clear confirmation. It has demonstrated that from the first instant there is established the programme of what this living being will be: a person, this individual person with his characteristic aspects already well determined. Right from fertilization the adventure of a human life begins, and each of its capacities requires time—a rather lengthy time—to find its place and to be in a position to act."[4] Even if the presence of a spiritual soul cannot be ascertained by empirical data, the results themselves of scientific research on the human embryo provide "a valuable indication for discerning by the use of reason a personal presence at the moment of the first appearance of a human life: how could a human individual not be a human person?"[5]

Furthermore, what is at stake is so important that, from the standpoint of moral obligation, the mere probability that a human person is involved would suffice to justify an absolutely clear prohibition of any intervention aimed at killing a human embryo. Precisely for this reason, over and above all scientific debates and those philosophical affirmations to which the Magisterium has not expressly committed itself, the Church has always taught and continues to teach that the result of human procreation, from the first moment of its existence, must be guaranteed that unconditional respect which is morally due to the human being in his or her totality and unity as body and spirit: *"The human being is to be respected and treated as a person from the moment of conception;* and therefore from that same moment his rights as a person must be recognized, among which in the first place is the inviolable right of every innocent human being to life."[6] ...

ENDNOTES

1. Pastoral Constitution on the Church in the Modern World *Gaudium et Spes*, 51: "Abortus necnon infanticidium nefanda sunt crimina."

2. Cf. John Paul II, Apostolic Letter *Mulieris Dignitatem* (15 August 1988), 14: *AAS* 80 (1988), 1686.

3. No. 21: *AAS* 86 (1994), 920.

4. Congregation for the Doctrine of the Faith, *Declaration on Procured Abortion* (18 November 1974), Nos. 12–13: *AAS* 66 (1974), 738.

5. Congregation for the Doctrine of the Faith, Instruction on Respect for Human Life in Its Origin and on the Dignity of Procreation *Donum Vitae* (22 February 1987), I, No. 1: *AAS* 80 (1988), 78–79.

6. *Ibid., loc. cit.,* 79.

14

A Defense of Abortion

JUDITH JARVIS THOMSON

Judith Jarvis Thomson begins by assuming, for the sake of argument, that the fetus is a person. Using a series of examples, she then argues that even granting this assumption, a woman has a right to abortion in cases involving rape, where her life is endangered, and when she has taken reasonable precautions to avoid becoming pregnant. In these cases, Thomson claims, the fetus's assumed right not to be killed unjustly would not be violated by abortion. Thomson further distinguishes between cases in which it would be a good thing for a woman to forego an abortion and cases in which a woman has an obligation to do so.

Most opposition to abortion relies on the premise that the fetus is a human being, a person, from the moment of conception. The premise is argued for, but, as I think, not well. Take, for example, the most common argument. We are asked to notice that the development of a human being from conception through birth into childhood is continuous; then it is said that to draw a line, to choose a point in this development and say "before this point the thing is not a person, after this point it is a person" is to make an arbitrary choice, a choice for which in the nature of things no good reason can be given. It is concluded that the fetus is, or anyway we had better say it is, a person from the moment of conception. But this conclusion does not follow. Similar things might be said about the development of an acorn into an oak tree, and it does not follow that acorns are oak trees or that we had better say they are. Arguments of this form are sometimes called "slippery slope arguments"—the phrase is perhaps self-explanatory—and it is dismaying that opponents of abortion rely on them so heavily and uncritically.

I am inclined to agree, however, that the prospects for "drawing a line" in the development of the fetus look dim. I am inclined to think also that we shall probably have to agree that the fetus has already become a human person well before birth. Indeed, it comes as a surprise when one first learns how early in its life it begins to acquire human characteristics. By the tenth week, for example, it already has a face, arms and legs, fingers and toes; it has internal organs, and brain activity is detectable.[1] On the other hand, I think that the premise is false, that the fetus is not a person from the moment of conception. A newly fertilized ovum, a newly implanted clump of cells, is no more a person than an acorn is an oak tree. But I shall not discuss any of this. For it seems to me to be of great interest to ask what happens if, for the sake of argument, we allow the premise. How, precisely, are we supposed to get from there to the conclusion that abortion is morally impermissible? Opponents of abortion commonly spend most of their time establishing that the fetus is a person, and hardly any time explaining the step from there to the impermissibility of abortion. Perhaps they think the step too simple and obvious to require much comment. Or perhaps instead they are simply being economical in argument. Many of those who defend abortion rely on the premise that the fetus is not a person, but only a bit of tissue that will become a person at birth; and why pay out more arguments than you have to? Whatever the explanation, I suggest that the step they take is neither easy nor obvious, that it calls for closer examination than it is commonly given, and that when we do give it this closer examination we shall feel inclined to reject it.

I propose, then, that we grant that the fetus is a person from the moment of conception. How does the argument go from here? Something like this, I take it. Every person has a right to life. So the fetus has a right to life. No doubt the mother has a right to decide what shall happen in and to her body; everyone would grant that. But surely a person's right to life is stronger and more stringent than the mother's right to decide what happens in and to her body, and so outweighs it. So the fetus may not be killed; an abortion may not be performed.

It sounds plausible. But now let me ask you to imagine this. You wake up in the morning and find yourself back to back in bed with an unconscious violinist. A famous unconscious violinist. He has been found to have a fatal kidney ailment, and the Society of Music Lovers has canvassed all the available medical records and found that you alone have the right blood type to help. They have therefore kidnapped you, and last night the violinist's circulatory system was plugged into yours, so that your kidneys can be used to extract poisons from his blood as well as your own. The director of the hospital now tells you, "Look, we're sorry the Society of Music Lovers did this to you—we would never have permitted it if we had known. But still, they did it, and the violinist now is plugged into you. To unplug you would be to kill him. But never mind, it's only for nine months. By then he will have recovered from his ailment, and can safely be unplugged from you." Is it morally incumbent on you to accede to this situation? No doubt it would be very nice of you if you did, a great kindness. But do you *have* to accede to it? What if it

were not nine months, but nine years? Or longer still? What if the director of the hospital says, "Tough luck, I agree, but you've now got to stay in bed, with the violinist plugged into you, for the rest of your life. Because remember this. All persons have a right to life, and violinists are persons. Granted you have a right to decide what happens in and to your body, but a person's right to life outweighs your right to decide what happens in and to your body. So you cannot ever be unplugged from him." I imagine you would regard this as outrageous, which suggests that something is really wrong with that plausible-sounding argument I mentioned a moment ago.

In this case, of course, you were kidnapped; you didn't volunteer for the operation that plugged the violinist into your kidneys. Can those who oppose abortion on the ground I mentioned make an exception for a pregnancy due to rape? Certainly. They can say that persons have a right to life only if they didn't come into existence because of rape; or they can say that all persons have a right to life, but that some have less of a right to life than others, in particular, that those who came into existence because of rape have less. But these statements have a rather unpleasant sound. Surely the question of whether you have a right to life at all, or how much of it you have, shouldn't turn on the question of whether or not you are the product of a rape. And in fact the people who oppose abortion on the ground I mentioned do not make this distinction, and hence do not make an exception in the case of rape.

Nor do they make an exception for a case in which the mother has to spend the nine months of her pregnancy in bed. They would agree that would be a great pity, and hard on the mother; but all the same, all persons have a right to life, the fetus is a person, and so on. I suspect, in fact, that they would not make an exception for a case in which, miraculously enough, the pregnancy went on for nine years, or even the rest of the mother's life.

Some won't even make an exception for a case in which continuation of the pregnancy is likely to shorten the mother's life; they regard abortion as impermissible even to save the mother's life. Such cases are nowadays very rare, and many opponents of abortion do not accept this extreme view. All the same, it is a good place to begin: A number of points of interest come out in respect to it.

1. Let us call the view that abortion is impermissible even to save the mother's life "the extreme view." I want to suggest first that it does not issue from the argument I mentioned earlier without the addition of some fairly powerful premises. Suppose a woman has become pregnant, and now learns that she has a cardiac condition such that she will die if she carries the baby to term. What may be done for her? The fetus, being a person, has a right to life, but as the mother is a person too, so has she a right to life. Presumably they have an equal right to life. How is it supposed to come out that an abortion may not be performed? If mother and child have an equal right to life, shouldn't we perhaps flip a coin? Or should we add to the mother's right to life her right to decide what happens in and to her body, which everybody seems to be ready to grant—the sum of her rights now outweighing the fetus's right to life?

The most familiar argument here is the following. We are told that performing the abortion would be directly killing[2] the child, whereas doing nothing would not be killing the mother, but only letting her die. Moreover, in killing the child, one would be killing an innocent person, for the child has committed no crime, and is not aiming at his mother's death. And then there are a variety of ways in which this might be continued. (1) But as directly killing an innocent person is always and absolutely impermissible, an abortion may not be performed. Or, (2) as directly killing an innocent person is murder, and murder is always and absolutely impermissible, an abortion may not be performed.[3] Or, (3) as one's duty to refrain from directly killing an innocent person is more stringent than one's duty to keep a person from dying, an abortion may not be performed. Or, (4) if one's only options are directly killing an innocent person or letting a person die, one must prefer letting the person die, and thus an abortion may not be performed.[4]

Some people seem to have thought that these are not further premises which must be added if the conclusion is to be reached, but that they follow from the very fact that an innocent person has a right to life.[5] But this seems to me to be a mistake, and perhaps the simplest way to show this is to bring out that while we must certainly grant that innocent persons have a right to life, the theses in (1) through (4) are all false. Take (2), for example. If directly killing an innocent person is murder, and thus is impermissible, then the mother's directly killing the innocent person inside her is murder, and thus is impermissible. But it cannot seriously be thought to be murder if the mother performs an abortion on herself to save her life. It cannot seriously be said that she *must* refrain, that she *must* sit passively by and wait for her death. Let us look again at the case of you and the violinist. There you are, in bed with the violinist, and the director of the hospital says to you, "It's all most distressing, and I deeply sympathize, but you see this is putting an additional strain on your kidneys, and you'll be dead within the month. But you *have* to stay where you are all the same. Because unplugging you would be directly killing an innocent violinist, and that's murder, and that's impermissible." If anything in the world is true, it is that you do not commit murder, you do not do what is impermissible, if you reach around to your back and unplug yourself from that violinist to save your life.

The main focus of attention in writings on abortion has been on what a third party may or may not do in answer to a request from a woman for an abortion. This is in a way understandable. Things being as they are, there isn't much a woman can safely do to abort herself. So the question asked is what a third party may do, and what the mother may do, if it is mentioned at all, is deduced, almost as an afterthought, from what is concluded that the third parties may do. But it seems to me that to treat the matter in this way is to refuse to grant to the mother that very status of person which is so firmly insisted on for the fetus. For we cannot simply read off what a person may do from what a third party may do. Suppose you find yourself trapped in a tiny house with a growing child. I mean a very tiny house, and a rapidly growing child—you are already up against the wall of the house and in a few minutes you'll be crushed to death. The child on the other hand won't be crushed to death; if nothing is done to stop him from growing he'll be hurt, but in the end he'll simply burst open the house and walk out a free man. Now I could well understand it if a bystander were to say, "There's nothing we can do for you. We cannot chose between your life and his, we cannot be the ones to decide who is to live, we cannot intervene." But it cannot be concluded that you too can do nothing, that you cannot attack it to save your life. However innocent the child may be, you do not have to wait passively while it crushes you to death. Perhaps a pregnant woman is vaguely felt to have the status of a house, to which we don't allow the right of self-defense. But if the woman houses the child, it should be remembered that she is a person who houses it.

I should perhaps stop to say explicitly that I am not claiming that people have a right to do anything whatever to save their lives. I think, rather, that there are drastic limits to the right of self-defense. If someone threatens you with death unless you torture someone else to death, I think you have not the right, even to save your life, to do so. But the case under consideration here is very different. In our case there are only two people involved, one whose life is threatened, and one who threatens it. Both are innocent: The one who is threatened is not threatened because of any fault; the one who threatens does not threaten because of any fault. For this reason we may feel that we bystanders cannot intervene. But the person threatened can.

In sum, a woman surely can defend her life against the threat to it posed by the unborn child, even if doing so involves its death. And this shows not merely that the theses in (1) through (4) are false; it shows also that the extreme view of abortion is false, and so we need not canvass any other possible ways of arriving at it from the argument I mentioned at the outset.

2. The extreme view could of course be weakened to say that while abortion is permissible to save the mother's life, it may not be performed by a third party, but only by the mother herself. But this cannot be right either. For what we have to keep in mind is that the mother and the unborn child are not like two tenants in a small house which has, by

an unfortunate mistake, been rented to both: The mother *owns* the house. The fact that she does adds to the offensiveness of deducing that the mother can do nothing from the supposition that third parties can do nothing. But it does more than this: It casts a bright light on the supposition that third parties can do nothing. Certainly it lets us see that a third party who says "I cannot choose between you" is fooling himself if he thinks this is impartiality. If Jones has found and fastened on a certain coat, which he needs to keep him from freezing, but which Smith also needs to keep him from freezing, then it is not impartiality that says "I cannot choose between you" when Smith owns the coat. Women have said again and again "This body is *my* body!" and they have reason to feel angry, reason to feel that it has been like shouting into the wind. Smith, after all, is hardly likely to bless us if we say to him, "Of course it's your coat, anybody would grant that it is. But no one may choose between you and Jones who is to have it...."

3. Where the mother's life is not at stake, the argument I mentioned at the outset seems to have a much stronger pull. "Everyone has a right to life, so the unborn person has a right to life." And isn't the child's right to life weightier than anything other than the mother's own right to life, which she might put forward as ground for an abortion?

This argument treats the right to life as if it were unproblematic. It is not, and this seems to me to be precisely the source of the mistake.

For we should now, at long last, ask what it comes to, to have a right to life. In some views having a right to life includes having a right to be given at least the bare minimum one needs for continued life. But suppose that what in fact is the bare minimum a man needs for continued life is something he has no right at all to be given? If I am sick unto death, and the only thing that will save my life is the touch of Henry Fonda's cool hand on my fevered brow, then all the same, I have no right to be given the touch of Henry Fonda's cool hand on my fevered brow. It would be frightfully nice of him to fly in from the West Coast to provide it. It would be less nice, though no doubt well meant, if my friends flew out to the West Coast and carried Henry Fonda back with them. But I have no right at all against anybody that he should do this for me. Or again, to return to the story I told earlier, the fact that for continued life that violinist needs the continued use of your kidneys does not establish that he has the right to be given the continued use of your kidneys. He certainly has no right against you that *you* should give him continued use of your kidneys. For nobody has any right to use your kidneys unless you give him such a right; and nobody has the right against you that you shall give him this right—if you do allow him to go on using your kidneys, this is a kindness on your part, and not something he can claim from you as his due. Nor has he any right against anybody else that *they* should give him continued use of your kidneys. Certainly he had no right against the Society of Music Lovers that they should plug him into you in the first place. And if you now start to unplug yourself, having learned that you will otherwise have to spend nine years in bed with him, there is nobody in the world who must try to prevent you, in order to see to it that he is given something he has a right to be given.

Some people are rather stricter about the right to life. In their view, it does not include the right to be given anything, but amounts to, and only to, the right not to be killed by anybody. But here a related difficulty arises. If everybody is to refrain from killing that violinist, then everybody must refrain from doing a great many different sorts of things. Everybody must refrain from slitting his throat, everybody must refrain from shooting him—and everybody must refrain from unplugging you from him. But does he have a right against everybody that they shall refrain from unplugging you from him? To refrain from doing this is to allow him to continue to use your kidneys. It could be argued that he has a right against us that *we* should allow him to continue to use your kidneys. That is, while he had no right against us that we should give him the use of your kidneys, it might be argued that he anyway has a right against us that we shall not now intervene and deprive him of the use of your kidneys. I shall come back to third-party interventions later. But certainly the violinist has no

right against you that *you* shall allow him to continue to use your kidneys. As I said, if you do allow him to use them, it is a kindness on your part, and not something you owe him.

The difficulty I point to here is not peculiar to the right to life. It reappears in connection with all the other natural rights; and it is something which an adequate account of rights must deal with. For present purposes it is enough just to draw attention to it. But I would stress that I am not arguing that people do not have a right to life—quite to the contrary, it seems to me that the primary control we must place on the acceptability of an account of rights is that it should turn out in that account to be a truth that all persons have a right to life. I am arguing only that having a right to life does not guarantee having either a right to be given the use of or a right to be allowed continued use of another person's body—even if one needs it for life itself. So the right to life will not serve the opponents of abortion in the very simple and clear way in which they seem to have thought it would.

4. There is another way to bring out the difficulty. In the most ordinary sort of case, to deprive someone of what he has a right to is to treat him unjustly. Suppose a boy and his small brother are jointly given a box of chocolates for Christmas. If the older boy takes the box and refuses to give his brother any of the chocolates, he is unjust to him, for the brother has been given a right to half of them. But suppose that, having learned that otherwise it means nine years in bed with that violinist, you unplug yourself from him. You surely are not being unjust to him, for you gave him no right to use your kidneys, and no one else can have given him any such right. But we have to notice that in unplugging yourself, you are killing him; and violinists, like everybody else, have a right to life, and thus in the view we were considering just now, the right not to be killed.

So here you do what he supposedly has a right you shall not do, but you do not act unjustly to him in doing it.

The emendation which may be made at this point is this: The right to life consists not in the right not to be killed, but rather in the right not to be killed unjustly. This runs a risk of circularity, but never mind: It would enable us to square the fact that the violinist has a right to life with the fact that you do not act unjustly toward him in unplugging yourself, thereby killing him. For if you do not kill him unjustly, you do not violate his right to life, and so it is no wonder you do him no injustice. But if this emendation is accepted, the gap in the argument against abortion stares us plainly in the face: It is by no means enough to show that the fetus is a person, and to remind us that all persons have a right to life—we need to be shown also that killing the fetus violates its right to life, i.e., that abortion is unjust killing. And is it?

I suppose we may take it as a datum that in a case of pregnancy due to rape the mother has not given the unborn person a right to the use of her body for food and shelter. Indeed, in what pregnancy could it be supposed that the mother has given the unborn person such a right? It is not as if there were unborn persons drifting about the world, to whom a woman who wants a child says "I invite you in."

But it might be argued that there are other ways one can have acquired a right to the use of another person's body than by having been invited to use it by that person. Suppose a woman voluntarily indulges in intercourse, knowing of the chance it will issue in pregnancy, and then she does become pregnant; is she not in part responsible for the presence, in fact the very existence, of the unborn person inside her? No doubt she did not invite it in. But doesn't her partial responsibility for its being there itself give it a right to the use of her body? If so, then her aborting it would be more like the boy's taking away the chocolates, and less like your unplugging yourself from the violinist—doing so would be depriving it of what it does have a right to, and thus would be doing it an injustice.

Then, too, it might be asked whether she can kill it even to save her own life: If she voluntarily called it into existence, how can she now kill it, even in self-defense?

The first thing to be said about this is that it is something new. Opponents of abortion have been so concerned to make out the independence of the fetus, in order to establish that it has a right to life, just as its mother does, that they have tended to overlook the possible support they might gain from making out that the fetus is *dependent* on the mother, in order to establish that she has a special kind of responsibility for it, a responsibility that gives it rights against her which are not possessed by any independent person—such as an ailing violinist who is a stranger to her.

On the other hand, this argument would give the unborn person a right to its mother's body only if her pregnancy resulted from a voluntary act, undertaken in full knowledge of the chance a pregnancy might result from it. It would leave out entirely the unborn person whose existence is due to rape. Pending the availability of some further argument, then, we would be left with the conclusion that unborn persons whose existence is due to rape have no right to the use of their mothers' bodies, and thus that aborting them is not depriving them of anything they have a right to and hence is not unjust killing.

We should also notice that it is not at all plain that this argument really does go as far as it purports to. For there are cases and cases, and the details make a difference. If the room is stuffy, and I therefore open a window to air it, and a burglar climbs in, it would be absurd to say, "Ah, now he can stay, she's given him a right to the use of her house—for she is partially responsible for his presence there, having voluntarily done what enabled him to get in, in full knowledge that there are such things as burglars, and that burglars burgle." It would be still more absurd to say this if I had bars installed outside my windows, precisely to prevent burglars from getting in, and a burglar got in only because of a defect in the bars. It remains equally absurd if we imagine it is not a burglar who climbs in, but an innocent person who blunders or falls in. Again, suppose it were like this: People seeds drift about in the air like pollen, and if you open your windows, one may drift in and take root in your carpets or upholstery. You don't want children, so you fix up your windows with fine mesh screens, the very best you can buy. As can happen, however, and on very, very rare occasions does happen, one of the screens is defective; a seed drifts in and takes root. Does the person-plant who now develops have a right to the use of your house? Surely not—despite the fact that you voluntarily opened your windows, knowingly kept carpets and upholstered furniture, and knew that screens were sometimes defective. Someone may argue that you are responsible for its rooting, that it does have a right to your house, because after all you *could* have lived out your life with bare floors and furniture, or with sealed windows and doors. But this won't do—by the same token anyone can avoid a pregnancy due to rape by having a hysterectomy, or anyway by never leaving home without a (reliable!) army.

It seems to me that the argument we are looking at can establish at most that there are *some* cases in which the unborn person has a right to the use of its mother's body, and therefore *some* cases in which abortion is unjust killing. There is room for much discussion and argument as to precisely which, if any. But I think we should sidestep this issue and leave it open, for at any rate the argument certainly does not establish that all abortion is unjust killing.

5. There is room for yet another argument here, however. We surely must all grant that there may be cases in which it would be morally indecent to detach a person from your body at the cost of his life. Suppose you learn that what the violinist needs is not nine years of your life, but only one hour: All you need do to save his life is to spend one hour in that bed with him. Suppose also that letting him use your kidneys for that one hour would not affect your health in the slightest. Admittedly you were kidnapped. Admittedly you did not give anyone permission to plug him into you. Nevertheless it seems plain to me you *ought* to allow him to use your kidneys for that hour—it would be indecent to refuse.

Again, suppose pregnancy lasted only an hour, and constituted no threat to life or health. And suppose that a woman becomes pregnant as a result of rape. Admittedly she did not voluntarily do anything to bring about the existence of a child. Admittedly she did nothing at all which would give the unborn person a right to the use of her body. All the same it might well be said, as in the newly emended violinist story, that she *ought* to allow it to

remain for that hour—that it would be indecent of her to refuse.

Now some people are inclined to use the term "right" in such a way that it follows from the fact that you ought to allow a person to use your body for the hour he needs, that he has a right to use your body for the hour he needs, even though he has not been given that right by any person or act. They may say that it follows also that if you refuse, you act unjustly toward him. This use of the term is perhaps so common that it cannot be called wrong; nevertheless it seems to me to be an unfortunate loosening of what we would do better to keep a tight rein on. Suppose that box of chocolates I mentioned earlier had not been given to both boys jointly, but was given only to the older boy. There he sits, stolidly eating his way through the box, his small brother watching enviously. Here we are likely to say "You ought not to be so mean. You ought to give your brother some of those chocolates." My own view is that it just does not follow from the truth of this that the brother has any right to any of the chocolates. If the boy refuses to give his brother any, he is greedy, stingy, callous—but not unjust. I suppose that the people I have in mind will say it does follow that the brother has a right to some of the chocolates, and thus that the boy does act unjustly if he refuses to give his brother any. But the effect of saying this is to obscure what we should keep distinct, namely the difference between the boy's refusal in this case and the boy's refusal in the earlier case, in which the box was given to both boys jointly, and in which the small brother thus had what was from any point of view clear title to half.

A further objection to so using the term "right" stems from the fact that if from A ought to do a thing for B, it follows that B has a right against A that A do it for him that it is going to make the question of whether or not a man has a right to a thing turn on how easy it is to provide him with it; and this seems not merely unfortunate, but morally unacceptable. Take the case of Henry Fonda again. I said earlier that I had no right to the touch of his cool hand on my fevered brow, even though I needed it to save my life. I said it would be frightfully nice of him to fly in from the West Coast to provide me with it, but that I had no right against him that he should do so. But suppose he isn't on the West Coast. Suppose he has only to walk across the room, place a hand briefly on my brow—and lo, my life is saved. Then surely he ought to do it, it would be indecent to refuse. Is it to be said "Ah, well, it follows that in this case she has a right to the touch of his hand on her brow, and so it would be an injustice of him to refuse"? So that I have a right to it when it is easy for him to provide it, though no right when it's hard? It's rather a shocking idea that anyone's rights should fade away and disappear as it gets harder and harder to accord them to him.

So my own view is that even though you ought to let the violinist use your kidneys for the one hour he needs, we should not conclude that he has a right to do so—we should say that if you refuse, you are, like the boy who owns all the chocolates and will give none away, self-centered and callous, indecent in fact, but not unjust. And similarly, that even supposing a case in which a woman pregnant due to rape ought to allow the unborn person to use her body for the hour he needs, we should not conclude that he has a right to do so; we should conclude that she is self-centered, callous, indecent, but not unjust, if she refuses. The complaints are no less grave; they are just different. However, there is no need to insist on this point. If anyone does wish to deduce "he has a right" from "you ought," then all the same he must surely grant that there are cases in which it is not morally required of you that you allow that violinist to use your kidneys, and in which he does not have a right to use them, and in which you do not do him injustice if you refuse. And so also for mother and unborn child. Except in such cases as the unborn person has a right to demand it—and we were leaving open the possibility that there may be such cases—nobody is morally *required* to make large sacrifices, of health, of all other interests and concerns, of all other duties and commitments, for nine years, or even for nine months, in order to keep another person alive....

6. My argument will be found unsatisfactory on two counts by many of those who want to regard abortion as morally permissible. First, while I do argue that abortion is not impermissible, I do not argue that it is always permissible. I am inclined to think it a merit of my account precisely that it does *not* give a general yes or a general no. It allows for and supports our sense that, for example, a sick and desperately frightened fourteen-year-old schoolgirl, pregnant due to rape, may *of course* choose abortion, and that any law which rules this out is an insane law. And it also allows for and supports our sense that in other cases resort to abortion is even positively indecent. It would be indecent of the woman to request an abortion, and indecent of a doctor to perform it, if she is in her seventh month, and wants the abortion just to avoid the nuisance of postponing a trip abroad. The very fact that the arguments I have been drawing attention to treat all cases of abortion, or even all cases of abortion in which the mother's life is not at stake, as morally on a par ought to have made them suspect at the outset.

Secondly, while I am arguing for the permissibility of abortion in some cases, I am not arguing for the right to secure the death of the unborn child. It is easy to confuse these two things in that up to a certain point in the life of the fetus it is not able to survive outside the mother's body; hence removing it from her body guarantees its death. But they are importantly different. I have argued that you are not morally required to spend nine months in bed, sustaining the life of that violinist; but to say this is by no means to say that if, when you unplug yourself, there is a miracle and he survives, you then have a right to turn round and slit his throat. You may detach yourself even if this costs him his life; you have no right to be guaranteed his death, by some other means, if unplugging yourself does not kill him. There are some people who will feel dissatisfied by this feature of my argument. A woman may be utterly devastated by the thought of a child, a bit of herself, put out for adoption and never seen or heard of again. She may therefore want not merely that the child be detached from her, but more, that it die. Some opponents of abortion are inclined to regard this as beneath contempt—thereby showing insensitivity to what is surely a powerful source of despair. All the same, I agree that the desire for the child's death is not one which anybody may gratify, should it turn out to be possible to detach the child alive.

At this place, however, it should be remembered that we have only been pretending throughout that the fetus is a human being from the moment of conception. A very early abortion is surely not the killing of a person, and so is not dealt with by anything I have said here.

ENDNOTES

1. Daniel Callahan, *Abortion: Law, Choice and Morality* (New York, 1970), p. 373. This book gives a fascinating survey of the available information on abortion. The Jewish tradition is surveyed in David M. Feldman, *Birth Control in Jewish Law* (New York, 1968), Part 5, the Catholic tradition in John T. Noonan, Jr., "An Almost Absolute Value in History," in *The Morality of Abortion*, ed. John T. Noonan, Jr. (Cambridge, Mass., 1970).

2. The term "direct" in the arguments I refer to is a technical one. Roughly, what is meant by "direct killing" is either killing as an end in itself, or killing as a means to some end, for example, the end of saving someone else's life. See note 5, below, for an example of its use.

3. Cf. *Encyclical Letter of Pope Pius XI on Christian Marriage*, St. Paul Editions (Boston, n.d.), p. 32: "however much we may pity the mother whose health and even life is gravely imperiled in the performance of the duty allotted to her by nature, nevertheless what could ever be a sufficient reason for excusing in any way the direct murder of the innocent? This is precisely what we are dealing with here." Noonan (*The Morality of Abortion*, p. 43) reads this as follows: "What cause can ever avail to excuse in any way the direct killing of the innocent? For it is a question of that."

4. The thesis in (4) is an interesting way weaker than those in (1), (2), and (3): They rule out abortion even in cases in which both mother *and* child will die if the abortion is not performed. By contrast, one who held the view expressed in (4) could consistently say that one needn't prefer letting two persons die to killing one.

5. Cf. the following passage from Pius XII, *Address to the Italian Catholic Society of Midwives:* "The baby in the maternal breast has the right to life immediately from God.— Hence there is no man, no human authority, no science, no medical, eugenic, social, economic, or moral 'indication' which can establish or grant a valid juridical ground for a direct deliberate disposition of an innocent human life, that is a disposition which looks to its destruction either as an end or as a means to another end perhaps in itself not illicit.—The baby, still not born, is a man in the same degree and for the same reason as the mother" (quoted in Noonan, *The Morality of Abortion*, p. 45).

15

Why Abortion Is Immoral

DON MARQUIS

Marquis argues that fetuses have the same moral status as adult human beings on the grounds that what is wrong with killing an adult human being and what is wrong with killing a fetus are the same. Both are deprived of a "future like ours." On this account, Marquis contends that the moral presumption against abortion is as strong as the moral presumption against killing adult human beings.

The view that abortion is, with rare exceptions, seriously immoral has received little support in the recent philosophical literature. No doubt most philosophers affiliated with secular institutions of higher education believe that the anti-abortion position is either a symptom of irrational religious dogma or a conclusion generated by seriously confused philosophical argument. The purpose of this essay is to undermine this general belief. This essay sets out an argument that purports to show, as well as any argument in ethics can show, that abortion is, except possibly in rare cases, seriously immoral, that it is in the same moral category as killing an innocent adult human being.

This argument is based on a major assumption: If fetuses are in the same category as adult human beings with respect to the moral value of their lives, then the *presumption* that any particular abortion is immoral is exceedingly strong. Such a presumption could be overridden only by considerations more compelling than a woman's right to privacy. The defense of this assumption is beyond the scope of this essay.[1]

Furthermore, this essay will neglect a discussion of whether there are any such compelling considerations and what they are. Plainly there are strong candidates: abortion before implantation, abortion when the life of a woman is threatened by a pregnancy, or abortion after rape. The casuistry of these hard cases will not be explored in this essay. The purpose of this essay is to develop a general argument for the claim that, subject to the assumption above, the overwhelming majority of deliberate abortions are seriously immoral....

A necessary condition of resolving the abortion controversy is a ... theoretical account of the wrongness of killing. After all, if we merely believe, but do not understand, why killing adult human beings such as ourselves is wrong, how could we conceivably show that abortion is either immoral or permissible?....

In order to develop such an account, we can start from the following unproblematic assumption concerning our own case: It is wrong to kill *us.* Why is it wrong? Some answers can be easily eliminated. It might be said that what makes killing us wrong is that a killing brutalizes the one who kills. But the brutalization consists of being inured to the performance of an act that is hideously immoral; hence, the brutalization does not explain the immorality. It might be said that what makes killing us wrong is the great loss others would experience

Reprinted, as slightly modified by the author, with permission of the author and the publisher from the *Journal of Philosophy*, vol. 86 (April 1989).

due to our absence. Although such hubris is under-standable, such an explanation does not account for the wrong-ness of killing hermits, or those whose lives are relatively independent and whose friends find it easy to make new friends.

A more obvious answer is better. What primar-ily makes killing wrong is neither its effect on the murderer nor its effect on the victim's friends and relatives, but its effect on the victim. The loss of one's life is one of the greatest losses one can suffer. The loss of one's life deprives one of all the experi-ences, activities, projects, and enjoyments that would otherwise have constituted one's future. Therefore, killing someone is wrong, primarily because the kill-ing inflicts (one of) the greatest possible losses on the victim. To describe this as the loss of life can be mis-leading, however. The change in my biological state does not by itself make killing me wrong. The effect of the loss of my biological life is the loss to me of all those activities, projects, experiences, and enjoyments which would otherwise have constituted my future personal life. These activities, projects, experiences, and enjoyments are either valuable for their own sake or are means to something else that is valuable for its own sake. Some parts of my future are not valued by me now, but will come to be valued by me as I grow older and as my values and capacities change. When I am killed, I am deprived both of what I now value, which would have been part of my future personal life, but also what I would come to value. Therefore, when I die, I am deprived of all of the value of my future. Inflicting this loss on me is ultimately what makes killing me wrong. This being the case, it would seem that what makes killing *any* adult human being prima facie seriously wrong is the loss of his or her future.[2]

How should this rudimentary theory of the wrongness of killing be evaluated? It cannot be faulted for deriving an "ought" from an "is," for it does not. The analysis assumes that killing me (or you, reader) is prima facie seriously wrong. The point of the analysis is to establish which natural property ultimately explains the wrongness of the killing, given that it is wrong. A natural property will ultimately explain the wrongness of killing, only if (1) the explanation fits with our intuitions

about the matter and (2) there is no other natural property that provides the basis for a better explana-tion of the wrongness of killing. This analysis rests on the intuition that what makes killing a particular human or animal wrong is what it does to that par-ticular human or animal. What makes killing wrong is some natural effect or other of the killing. Some would deny this. For instance, a divine-command theorist in ethics would deny it. Surely this denial is, however, one of those features of divine-command theory which renders it so implausible.

The claim that what makes killing wrong is the loss of the victim's future is directly supported by two considerations. In the first place, this theory explains why we regard killing as one of the worst of crimes. Killing is especially wrong, because it deprives the victim of more than perhaps any other crime. In the second place, people with AIDS or cancer who know they are dying believe, of course, that dying is a very bad thing for them. They believe that the loss of a future to them that they would otherwise have experienced is what makes their pre-mature death a very bad thing for them. A better theory of the wrongness of killing would require a different natural property associated with killing which better fits with the attitudes of the dying. What could it be?

The view that what makes killing wrong is the loss to the victim of the value of the victim's future gains additional support when some of its implica-tions are examined. In the first place, it is incom-patible with the view that it is wrong to kill only beings who are biologically human. It is possible that there exists a different species from another planet whose members have a future like ours. Since having a future like that is what makes killing someone wrong, this theory entails that it would be wrong to kill members of such a species. Hence, this theory is opposed to the claim that only life that is biologically human has great moral worth, a claim which many anti-abortionists have seemed to adopt. This opposition, which this theory has in common with personhood theories, seems to be a merit of the theory.

In the second place, the claim that the loss of one's future is the wrong-making feature of one's being killed entails the possibility that the futures of some actual nonhuman mammals on our own planet are sufficiently like ours that it is seriously wrong to kill them also. Whether some animals do have the same right to life as human beings depends on adding to the account of the wrongness of killing some additional account of just what it is about my future or the futures of other adult human beings which makes it wrong to kill us. No such additional account will be offered in this essay. Undoubtedly, the provision of such an account would be a very difficult matter. Undoubtedly, any such account would be quite controversial. Hence, it surely should not reflect badly on this sketch of an elementary theory of the wrongness of killing that it is indeterminate with respect to some very difficult issues regarding animal rights.

In the third place, the claim that the loss of one's future is the wrong-making feature of one's being killed does not entail, as sanctity-of-human-life theories do, that active euthanasia is wrong. Persons who are severely and incurably ill, who face a future of pain and despair, and who wish to die will not have suffered a loss if they are killed. It is, strictly speaking, the value of a human's future which makes killing wrong in this theory. This being so, killing does not necessarily wrong some persons who are sick and dying. Of course, there may be other reasons for a prohibition of active euthanasia, but that is another matter. Sanctity-of-human-life theories seem to hold that active euthanasia is seriously wrong even in an individual case where there seems to be good reason for it independently of public policy considerations. This consequence is most implausible, and it is a plus for the claim that the loss of a future of value is what makes killing wrong that it does not share this consequence.

In the fourth place, the account of the wrongness of killing defended [here] does straightforwardly entail that it is prima facie seriously wrong to kill children and infants, for we do presume that they have futures of value. Since we do believe that it is wrong to kill defenseless little babies, it is important that a theory of the wrongness of killing easily account for this. Personhood theories of the wrongness of killing, on the other hand, cannot

straightforwardly account for the wrongness of killing infants and young children. Hence, such theories must add special ad hoc accounts of the wrongness of killing the young. The plausibility of such ad hoc theories seems to be a function of how desperately one wants such theories to work. The claim that the primary wrong-making feature of killing is the loss to the victim of the value of its future accounts for the wrongness of killing young children and infants directly; it makes the wrongness of such acts as obvious as we actually think it is. This is a further merit of this theory. Accordingly, it seems that this value of a future-like-ours theory of the wrongness of killing shares strengths of both sanctity-of-life and personhood accounts, while avoiding weaknesses of both. In addition, it meshes with a central intuition concerning what makes killing wrong.

The claim that the primary wrong-making feature of killing is the loss to the victim of the value of its future has obvious consequences for the ethics of abortion. The future of a standard fetus includes a set of experiences, projects, activities, and such which are identical with the futures of adult human beings and are identical with the futures of young children. Since the reason that is sufficient to explain why it is wrong to kill human beings after the time of birth is a reason that also applies to fetuses, it follows that abortion is prima facie seriously morally wrong.

This argument does not rely on the invalid inference that, since it is wrong to kill persons, it is wrong to kill potential persons also. The category that is morally central to this analysis is the category of having a valuable future like ours; it is not the category of personhood. The argument to the conclusion that abortion is prima facie seriously morally wrong proceeded independently of the notion of person or potential person or any equivalent. Someone may wish to start with this analysis in terms of the value of a human future, conclude that abortion is, except perhaps in rare circumstances, seriously morally wrong, infer that fetuses have the right to life, and then call fetuses "persons" as a result of their having the right to life. Clearly, in this case, the category of person is being used to state the *conclusion* of the analysis rather than to generate the *argument* of the analysis.

The structure of this anti-abortion argument can be both illuminated and defended by comparing it to what appears to be the best argument for the wrongness of the wanton infliction of pain on animals. This latter argument is based on the assumption that it is prima facie wrong to inflict pain on me (or you, reader). What is the natural property associated with the infliction of pain which makes such infliction wrong? The obvious answer seems to be that the infliction of pain causes suffering, and that suffering is a misfortune. The suffering caused by the infliction of pain is what makes the wanton infliction of pain on me wrong. The wanton infliction of pain on other adult humans causes suffering. The wanton infliction of pain on animals causes suffering. Since causing suffering is what makes the wanton infliction of pain wrong and since the wanton infliction of pain on animals causes suffering, it follows that the wanton infliction of pain on animals is wrong.

This argument for the wrongness of the wanton infliction of pain on animals shares a number of structural features with the argument for the serious prima facie wrongness of abortion. Both arguments start with an obvious assumption concerning what it is wrong to do to me (or you, reader). Both then look for the characteristic or the consequence of the wrong action which makes the action wrong. Both recognize that the wrong-making feature of these immoral actions is a property of actions sometimes directed at individuals other than postnatal human beings. If the structure of the argument for the wrongness of the wanton infliction of pain on animals is sound, then the structure of the argument for the prima facie serious wrongness of abortion is also sound, for the structure of the two arguments is the same. The structure common to both is the key to the explanation of how the wrongness of abortion can be demonstrated without recourse to the category of person. In neither argument, is that category crucial....

Of course, this value of a future-like-ours argument, if sound, shows only that abortion is prima facie wrong, not that it is wrong in any and all circumstances. Since the loss of the future to a standard fetus, if killed, is, however, at least as great a loss as the loss of the future to a standard adult human being who is killed, abortion, like ordinary killing, could be justified only by the most compelling reasons. The loss of one's life is almost the greatest misfortune that can happen to one. Presumably abortion could be justified in some circumstances, only if the loss consequent on failing to abort would be at least as great. Accordingly, morally permissible abortions will be rare indeed unless, perhaps, they occur so early in pregnancy that a fetus is not yet definitely an individual. Hence, this argument should be taken as showing that abortion is presumptively very seriously wrong, where the presumption is very strong—as strong as the presumption that killing another adult human being is wrong....

In this essay, it has been argued that the correct ethic of the wrongness of killing can be extended to fetal life and used to show that there is a strong presumption that any abortion is morally impermissible. If the ethic of killing adopted here entails, however, that contraception is also seriously immoral, then there would appear to be a difficulty with the analysis of this essay.

But this analysis does not entail that contraception is wrong. Of course, contraception prevents the actualization of a possible future of value. Hence, it follows from the claim that futures of value should be maximized that contraception is prima facie immoral. This obligation to maximize does not exist, however; furthermore, nothing in the ethics of killing in this paper entails that it does. The ethics of killing in this essay would entail that contraception is wrong only if something were denied a human future of value by contraception. Nothing at all is denied such a future by contraception, however.

Candidates for a subject of harm by contraception fall into four categories: (1) some sperm or other, (2) some ovum or other, (3) a sperm and an ovum, separately, and (4) a sperm and an ovum together. Assigning the harm to some sperm is utterly arbitrary, for no reason can be given for making a sperm the subject of harm rather than an ovum. Assigning the harm to some ovum is utterly arbitrary, for no reason can be given for making an ovum the subject of harm rather than a sperm. One might attempt to avoid these problems by insisting that contraception deprives both the sperm and the ovum separately of a valuable future like ours. On this alternative, too many futures are lost. Contraception was supposed to be wrong, because it deprived us of one future of value, not two. One might attempt to avoid this problem by holding that contraception deprives the combination of sperm and ovum of a valuable future like ours. But here the definite article misleads. At the time of contraception, there are hundreds of millions of sperm, one (released) ovum, and millions of possible combinations of all of these. There is no actual combination at all. Is the subject of the loss to be a merely possible combination? Which one? This alternative does not yield an actual subject of harm either.

Accordingly, the immorality of contraception is not entailed by the loss of a future-like-ours argument simply because there is no nonarbitrarily identifiable subject of the loss in the case of contraception....

The purpose of this essay has been to set out an argument for the serious presumptive wrongness of abortion subject to the assumption that the moral permissibility of abortion stands or falls on the moral status of the fetus. Since a fetus possesses a property, the possession of which in adult human beings is sufficient to make killing an adult human being wrong, abortion is wrong. This way of dealing with the problem of abortion seems superior to other approaches to the ethics of abortion, because it rests on the ethics of killing which is close to self-evident, because the crucial morally relevant property clearly applies to fetuses, and because the argument avoids the usual equivocations on "human life," "human being," or "person." The argument rests neither on religious claims nor on Papal dogma. It is not subject to the objection of "speciesism." Its soundness is compatible with the moral permissibility of euthanasia and contraception. It deals with our intuitions concerning young children.

Finally, this analysis can be viewed as resolving a standard problem—indeed, *the* standard problem—concerning the ethics of abortion. Clearly, it is wrong to kill adult human beings. Clearly, it is not wrong to end the life of some arbitrarily chosen single human cell. Fetuses seem to be like arbitrarily chosen human cells in some respects and like adult humans in other respects. The problem of the ethics of abortion is the problem of determining the fetal property that settles this moral controversy. The thesis of this essay is that the problem of the ethics of abortion, so understood, is solvable.

ENDNOTES

1. Judith Jarvis Thomson has rejected this assumption in a famous essay, "A Defense of Abortion," *Philosophy and Public Affairs 1*, 1 (1971), 47–66.

2. I have been most influenced on this matter by Jonathan Glover, *Causing Death and Saving Lives* (New York: Penguin, 1977), ch. 3; and Robert Young, "What Is So Wrong with Killing People?" *Philosophy*, LIV, 210 (1979): 515–528.

16

On the Moral and Legal Status of Abortion

MARY ANNE WARREN

Mary Anne Warren argues that if the fetus is assumed to be a person, there is a wide range of cases in which abortion cannot be defended. To provide such a defense, Warren sets out five criteria for being a person she feels should be acceptable to anti-abortionists and pro-abortionists alike. Appealing to these criteria, she contends that fetuses, even when their potentiality is taken into account, do not sufficiently resemble persons to have a significant right to life. In a "Postscript" to her article, Warren defends her view against the objection that it would justify infanticide. Although by her criteria newborn infants would not have a significant right to life, she claims that infanticide would still not be permissible, so long as there are people willing to care and provide for the well-being of such infants.

We will be concerned with both the moral status of abortion, which for our purposes we may define as the act which a woman performs in voluntarily terminating, or allowing another person to terminate, her pregnancy, and the legal status which is appropriate for this act. I will argue that, while it is not possible to produce a satisfactory defense of a woman's right to obtain an abortion without showing that a fetus is not a human being, in the morally relevant sense of that term, we ought not to conclude that the difficulties involved in determining whether or not a fetus is a human make it impossible to produce any satisfactory solution to the problem of the moral status of abortion. For it is possible to show that, on the basis of intuitions which we may expect even the opponents of abortion to share, a fetus is not a person, and hence not the sort of entity to which it is proper to ascribe full moral rights.

Of course, while some philosophers would deny the possibility of any such proof,[1] others will deny that there is any need for it, since the moral permissibility of abortion appears to them to be too obvious to require proof. But the inadequacy of this attitude should be evident from the fact that both the friends and the foes of abortion consider their position to be morally self-evident. Because pro-abortionists have never adequately come to grips with the conceptual issues surrounding abortion, most if not all of the arguments which they advance in opposition to laws restricting access to abortion fail to refute or even weaken the traditional anti-abortion argument, i.e., that a fetus is a human being, and therefore abortion is murder.

These arguments are typically of one of two sorts. Either they point to the terrible side effects of the restrictive laws, e.g., the deaths due to illegal abortions, and the fact that it is poor women who suffer the most as a result of these laws, or else they state that to deny a woman access to abortion is to deprive her of her right to control her own body. Unfortunately, however, the fact that restricting access to abortion has tragic side effects does not,

From "On the Moral and Legal Status of Abortion." Copyright 1973 *The Monist*, LaSalle, Illinois. Reprinted from vol. 57, no. 4, Oct. 1973 by permission; and "Postscript on Infanticide," in *Today's Moral Problems*, edited by Richard Wasserstrom (1979), pp. 135–136. Reprinted by permission of the author and editor.

in itself, show that the restrictions are unjustified, since murder is wrong regardless of the consequences of prohibiting it; and the appeal to the right to control one's body, which is generally construed as a property right, is at best a rather feeble argument for the permissibility of abortion. Mere ownership does not give me the right to kill innocent people whom I find on my property, and indeed I am apt to be held responsible if such people injure themselves while on my property. It is equally unclear that I have any moral right to expel an innocent person from my property when I know that doing so will result in his death.

Furthermore, it is probably inappropriate to describe a woman's body as her property, since it seems natural to hold that a person is something distinct from her property but not from her body. Even those who would object to the identification of a person with his body, or with the conjunction of his body and his mind, must admit that it would be very odd to describe, say, breaking a leg, as damaging one's property, and much more appropriate to describe it as injuring *oneself*. Thus it is probably a mistake to argue that the right to obtain an abortion is in any way derived from the right to own and regulate property.

But however we wish to construe the right to abortion, we cannot hope to convince those who consider abortion a form of murder of the existence of any such right unless we are able to produce a clear and convincing refutation of the traditional anti-abortion argument, and this has not, to my knowledge, been done. With respect to the two most vital issues which that argument involves, i.e., the humanity of the fetus and its implication for the moral status of abortion, confusion has prevailed on both sides of the dispute.

Thus, both pro-abortionists and anti-abortionists have tended to abstract the question of whether abortion is wrong to that of whether it is wrong to destroy a fetus, just as though the rights of another person were not necessarily involved. This mistaken abstraction has led to the almost universal assumption that if a fetus is a human being, with a right to life, then it follows immediately that abortion is wrong (except perhaps when necessary to save the woman's life),

and that it ought to be prohibited. It has also been generally assumed that unless the question about the status of the fetus is answered, the moral status of abortion cannot possibly be determined.... John Noonan is correct in saying that "the fundamental question in the long history of abortion is, How do you determine the humanity of a being?"[2] He summarizes his own anti-abortion argument, which is a version of the official position of the Catholic Church, as follows:

> ... it is wrong to kill humans, however poor, weak, defenseless, and lacking in opportunity to develop their potential they may be. It is therefore morally wrong to kill Biafrans. Similarly, it is morally wrong to kill embryos.[3]

Noonan bases his claim that fetuses are human on what he calls the theologians' criterion of humanity: Whoever is conceived of human beings is human. But although he argues at length for the appropriateness of this criterion, he never questions the assumption that if the fetus is human then abortion is wrong for exactly the same reason that murder is wrong.

Judith Thomson is, in fact, the only writer I am aware of who has seriously questioned this assumption; she has argued that, even if we grant the anti-abortionist his claim that a fetus is a human being, with the same right to life as any other human being, we can still demonstrate that, in at least some and perhaps most cases, a woman is under no moral obligation to complete an unwanted pregnancy.[4] Her argument is worth examining, since if it holds up it may enable us to establish the moral permissibility of abortion without becoming involved in problems about what entitles an entity to be considered human, and accorded full moral rights. To be able to do this would be a great gain in the power and simplicity of the pro-abortion position, since, although I will argue that these problems can be solved at least as decisively as can any other moral problems, we should certainly be pleased to be able to avoid having to solve them as part of the justification of abortion.

On the other hand, even if Thomson's argument does not hold up, her insight—that it requires argument to show that if fetuses are human then abortion is properly classified as murder—is extremely valuable. The assumption she attacks is particularly invidious, for it amounts to the decision that it is appropriate, in deciding the moral status of abortion, to leave the rights of the pregnant woman out of consideration entirely, except possibly when her life is threatened. Obviously, this will not do; determining what moral rights, if any, a fetus possesses is only the first step in determining the moral status of abortion. Step two, which is at least equally essential, is finding a just solution to the conflict between whatever rights the fetus may have, and the rights of the woman who is unwillingly pregnant. While the historical error has been to pay far too little attention to the second step, Ms. Thomson suggests that if we look at the second step first we may find that a woman has a right to obtain an abortion *regardless* of what rights the fetus has.

Our own inquiry will also have two stages. In Section I, we will consider whether or not it is possible to establish that abortion is morally permissible even on the assumption that a fetus is an entity with a full-fledged right to life. I will argue that in fact this cannot be established, at least not with the collusiveness which is essential to our hopes of convincing those who are skeptical about the morality of abortion, and that we therefore cannot avoid dealing with the question of whether or not a fetus really does have the same right to life as a (more fully developed) human being.

In Section II, I will propose an answer to this question, namely, that a fetus cannot be considered a member of the moral community, the set of beings with full and equal moral rights, for the simple reason that it is not a person, and that it is person-hood, and not genetic humanity, i.e., humanity as defined by Noonan, which is the basis for membership in this community. I will argue that a fetus, whatever its stage of development, satisfies none of the basic criteria for personhood, and is not even enough *like* a person to be accorded even some of the same rights on the basis of this resemblance. Nor, as we will see, is a fetus's *potential* personhood a threat to the morality of abortion, since, whatever the rights of potential people may be, they are invariably overridden in any conflict with the moral rights of actual people.

I

We now turn to Professor Thomson's case for the claim that even if a fetus has full moral rights, abortion is still morally permissible, at least sometimes, and for some reasons other than to save the woman's life. Her argument is based upon a clever, but I think faulty, analogy. She asks us to picture ourselves waking up one day, in bed with a famous violinist. Imagine that you have been kidnapped, and your bloodstream hooked up to that of the violinist, who happens to have an ailment which will certainly kill him unless he is permitted to share your kidneys for a period of nine months. No one else can save him, since you alone have the right type of blood. He will be unconscious all that time, and you will have to stay in bed with him, but after the nine months are over he may be unplugged, completely cured; that is, provided that you have cooperated.

Now then, she continues, what are your obligations in this situation? The anti-abortionist, if he is consistent, will have to say that you are obligated to stay in bed with the violinist: for all people have a right to life, and violinists are people, and therefore it would be murder for you to disconnect yourself from him and let him die. But this is outrageous, and so there must be something wrong with the same argument when it is applied to abortion. It would certainly be commendable of you to agree to save the violinist, but it is absurd to suggest that your refusal to do so would be murder. His right to life does not obligate you to do whatever is required to keep him alive, nor does it justify anyone else in forcing you to do so. A law which required you to stay in bed with the violinist would clearly be an unjust law, since it is no proper function of the law to force unwilling people to make huge sacrifices for the sake of other people toward whom they have no such prior obligation.

Thomson concludes that, if this analogy is apt, then we can grant the anti-abortionist claim that a fetus is a human being and still hold that it is at least sometimes the case that a pregnant woman has the right to refuse to be a Good Samaritan towards the fetus, i.e., to obtain an abortion. For there is a great gap between the claim that X has a right to life, and the claim that Y is obligated to do whatever is necessary to keep X alive, let alone that he ought to be forced to do so. It is Y's duty to keep X alive only if he has somehow contracted a *special* obligation to do so; and a woman who is unwillingly pregnant, e.g., who was raped, has nothing which obligates her to make the enormous sacrifice which is necessary to preserve the conceptus.

This argument is initially quite plausible, and in the extreme case of pregnancy due to rape is probably conclusive. Difficulties arise, however, when we try to specify more exactly the range of cases in which abortion is clearly justifiable even on the assumption that the fetus is human. Professor Thomson considers it a virtue of her argument that it does not enable us to conclude that abortion is *always* permissible. It would, she says, be "indecent" for a woman in her seventh month to obtain an abortion just to avoid having to postpone a trip to Europe. On the other hand, her argument enables us to see that "a sick and desperately frightened schoolgirl pregnant due to rape may *of course* choose abortion, and that any law which rules this out is an insane law." So far, so good; but what are we to say about the woman who becomes pregnant not through rape but as a result of her own carelessness, or because of contraceptive failure, or who gets pregnant intentionally and then changes her mind about wanting a child? With respect to such cases, the violinist analogy is of much less use to the defender of the woman's right to obtain an abortion.

Indeed, the choice of a pregnancy due to rape, as an example of a case in which abortion is permissible even if a fetus is considered a human being, is extremely significant; for it is only in the case of pregnancy due to rape that the woman's situation is adequately analogous to the violinist case for our intuitions about the latter to transfer convincingly. The crucial difference between a pregnancy due to rape and the *normal* case of unwanted pregnancy is that in the normal case we cannot claim that the woman is in no way responsible for her predicament;

she could have remained chaste, or taken her pills more faithfully, or abstained on dangerous days, and so on. If, on the other hand, you are kidnapped by strangers, and hooked up to a strange violinist, then you are free of any shred of responsibility for the situation, on the basis of which it could be argued that you are obligated to keep the violinist alive. Only when her pregnancy is due to rape is a woman clearly just as nonresponsible.[5]

Consequently, there is room for the anti-abortionists to argue that in the normal case of unwanted pregnancy, a woman has, by her own actions, assumed responsibility for the fetus. For if X behaves in a way which he could have avoided, and which he knows involves, let us say, a 1 percent chance of bringing into existence a human being, with a right to life, and does so knowing that if this should happen then that human being will perish unless X does certain things to keep him alive, then it is by no means clear that when it does happen X is free of any obligation to what he knew in advance would be required to keep that human being alive.

The plausibility of such an argument is enough to show that the Thomson analogy can provide a clear and persuasive defense of a woman's right to obtain an abortion only with respect to those cases in which the woman is in no way responsible for her pregnancy (e.g., rape). In all other cases, we would almost certainly conclude that it was necessary to look carefully at the particular circumstances in order to determine the extent of the woman's responsibility, and hence the extent of her obligation. This is an extremely unsatisfactory outcome, from the viewpoint of the opponents of restrictive abortion laws, most of whom are convinced that a woman has a right to obtain an abortion regardless of how or why she got pregnant.

Of course, a supporter of the violinist analogy might point out that it is absurd to suggest that forgetting her pill one day might be sufficient to obligate a woman to complete an unwanted pregnancy. And indeed, it *is* absurd to suggest this. As we will see, the moral right to obtain an abortion is not in the least dependent upon the extent to which the woman is responsible for her pregnancy.

But unfortunately, once we allow the assumption that a fetus has full moral rights, we cannot avoid taking this absurd suggestion seriously. Perhaps we can make this point more clear by altering the violinist story just enough to make it more analogous to a normal unwanted pregnancy and less to a pregnancy due to rape, and then seeing whether it is still obvious that you are not obligated to stay in bed with the fellow.

Suppose, then, that violinists are peculiarly prone to the sort of illness the only cure for which is the use of someone else's bloodstream for nine months, and that because of this there has been formed a society of music lovers who agree that whenever a violinist is stricken they will draw lots and the loser will, by some means, be made the one and only person capable of saving him. Now then, would you be obligated to cooperate in curing the violinist if you had voluntarily joined this society, knowing the possible consequences, and then your name had been drawn and you had been kidnapped? Admittedly, you did not promise ahead of time that you would, but you did deliberately place yourself in a position in which it might happen that a human life would be lost if you did not. Surely this is at least a *prima facie* reason for supposing that you have an obligation to stay in bed with the violinist. Suppose you had gotten your name drawn deliberately; surely *that* would be quite a strong reason for thinking that you had such an obligation.

It might be suggested that there is one important disanalogy between the modified violinist case and the case of an unwanted pregnancy, which makes the woman's responsibility significantly less, namely, the fact that the fetus *comes into existence* as the result of the woman's actions. This fact might give her a right to refuse to keep it alive, whereas she would not have had this right had it existed previously, independently, and then as a result of her actions become dependent upon her for its survival.

My own intuition, however, is that X has no more right to bring into existence, either deliberately or as a foreseeable result of actions he could have avoided, a being with full moral rights (Y), and then refuse to do what he knew beforehand would be required to keep that being alive, than

he has to enter into an agreement with an existing person, whereby he may be called upon to save that person's life, and then refuse to do so when so called upon. Thus, X's responsibility for Y's existence does not seem to lessen his obligation to keep Y alive, if he is also responsible for Y's being in a situation in which only he can save him.

Whether this intuition is entirely correct, it brings us back again to the conclusion that once we allow the assumption that a fetus has full moral rights it becomes an extremely complex and difficult question whether and when abortion is justifiable. Thus, the Thomson analogy cannot help us produce a clear and persuasive proof of the moral permissibility of abortion. Nor will the opponents of the restrictive laws thank us for anything less; for their conviction (for the most part) is that abortion is obviously *not* a morally serious and extremely unfortunate, even though sometimes justified, act comparable to killing in self-defense or to letting the violinist die, but rather is closer to being a morally neutral act like cutting one's hair.

The basis of this conviction, I believe, is the realization that a fetus is not a person, and thus does not have a full-fledged right to life. Perhaps the reason why this claim has been so inadequately defended is that it seems self-evident to those who accept it. And so it is, insofar as it follows that what I take to be perfectly obvious claims about the nature of person-hood and about the proper grounds for ascribing moral rights, claims which ought, indeed, to be obvious to both the friends and foes of abortion. Nevertheless, it is worth examining these claims, and showing how they demonstrate the moral innocuousness of abortion, since this apparently has not been adequately done before.

II

The question we must answer in order to produce a satisfactory solution to the problem of the moral status of abortion is this: How are we to define the moral community, the set of beings with full and equal moral rights, such that we can decide whether a human fetus is a member of this community or not? What sort of entity, exactly, has the inalienable rights to life, liberty, and the pursuit of happiness? Jefferson attributed these rights to all *men,* and it may or may not be fair to suggest that he intended to attribute them, *only* to men. Perhaps he ought to have attributed them to all human beings. If so, then we arrive, first, at Noonan's problem of defining what makes a being human, and, second, at the equally vital question which Noonan does not consider, namely: What reason is there for identifying the moral community with the set of all human beings, in whatever way we have chosen to define that term?

1. On the Definition of "Human"

One reason why this vital second question is so frequently overlooked in the debate over the moral status of abortion is that the term *human* has two distinct, but not often distinguished, senses. This fact results in a slide of meaning, which serves to conceal the fallaciousness of the traditional argument that since (1) it is wrong to kill innocent human beings and (2) fetuses are innocent human beings, then (3) it is wrong to kill fetuses. For if *human* is used in the same sense in both (1) and (2) then, whichever of the two senses is meant, one of these premises is question-begging. And if it is used in two different senses then of course the conclusion doesn't follow.

Thus, (1) is a self-evident moral truth[6] and avoids begging the question about abortion, only if "human being" is used to mean something like "a full-fledged member of the moral community." (It may or may not also be meant to refer exclusively to members of the species *Homo sapiens.*) We may call this the *moral* sense of "human." It is not to be confused with what we will call the *genetic* sense, i.e., the sense in which *any* member of the species is a human being, and no member of any other species could be. If (1) is acceptable only if the moral sense is intended, (2) is nonquestion-begging only if what is intended is the genetic sense.

In "Deciding Who Is Human," Noonan argues for the classification of fetuses with human beings by pointing to the presence of the full genetic code, and the potential capacity for rational thought (p. 135). It is clear that what he needs to show, for his version of the traditional argument to be valid, is that fetuses are human in the moral sense, the sense in which it is analytically true that all human beings have full moral rights. But, in the absence of any argument showing that whatever is genetically human is also morally human, and he gives none, nothing more than genetic humanity can be demonstrated by the presence of the human genetic code. And, as we will see, the *potential* capacity for rational thought can at most show that an entity has the potential for *becoming* human in the moral sense.

2. Defining the Moral Community

Can it be established that genetic humanity is sufficient for moral humanity? I think that there are very good reasons for not defining the moral community in this way. I would like to suggest an alternative way of defining the moral community, which I will argue for only to the extent of explaining why it is, or should be, self-evident. The suggestion is simply that the moral community consists of all and only *people,* rather than all and only human beings,[7] and probably the best way of demonstrating its self-evidence is by considering the concept of person-hood, to see what sorts of entity are and are not persons, and what the decision that a being is or is not a person implies about its moral rights.

What characteristics entitle an entity to be considered a person? This is obviously not the place to attempt a complete analysis of the concept of person-hood, but we do not need such a fully adequate analysis just to determine whether and why a fetus is or isn't a person. All we need is a rough and approximate list of the most basic criteria of person-hood, and some idea of which, or how many, of these an entity must satisfy ... to properly be considered a person.

In searching for such criteria, it is useful to look beyond the set of people with whom we are acquainted, and ask how we would decide whether a totally alien being was a person or not. (For we have no right to assume that genetic humanity is necessary for personhood.) Imagine a space traveler who lands on an unknown planet and encounters a race of beings utterly unlike any he has ever seen or heard of. If he wants to be sure of behaving morally toward these beings, he has to somehow decide whether these are people, and hence have full moral rights, or whether they are the sort of thing which he need not feel guilty about treating as, for example, a source of food.

How should he go about making this decision? If he has some anthropological background, he might look for such things as religion, art, and the manufacturing of tools, weapons, or shelters, since these factors have been used to distinguish our human from our prehuman ancestors, in what seems to be closer to the moral than the genetic sense of "human." And no doubt he would be right to consider the presence of such factors as good evidence that the alien beings were people and morally human. It would, however, be overly anthropocentric of him to take the absence of these things as adequate evidence that they were not, since we can imagine people who have progressed beyond, or evolved without ever developing, these cultural characteristics.

I suggest that the traits which are most central to the concept of personhood, or humanity in the moral sense, are, very roughly, the following:

1. consciousness (of objects and events external and/or internal to the being), and in particular the capacity to feel pain;

2. reasoning (the *developed* capacity to solve new and relatively complex problems);

3. self-motivated activity (activity which is relatively independent of either genetic or direct external control);

4. the capacity to communicate, by whatever means, messages of an indefinite variety of types, ... not just with an indefinite number of possible contents, but on indefinitely many possible topics;

5. the presence of self-concepts, and self-awareness, either individual or racial, or both.

Admittedly, there are apt to be a great many problems involved in formulating precise definitions of these criteria, let alone in developing universally valid behavioral criteria for deciding when they apply. But I will assume that both we and our explorer know approximately what (1)–(5) mean, and that he is also able to determine whether or not they apply. How, then, should he use his findings to decide whether ... the alien beings are people? We needn't suppose that an entity must have *all* of these attributes to be properly considered a person; (1) and (2) alone may well be sufficient for personhood, and quite probably (1)–(3) are sufficient. Neither do we need to insist that any one of these criteria is necessary for personhood, although once again (1) and (2) look like fairly good candidates for *necessary* conditions, as does (3), if "activity" is construed to include the activity of reasoning.

All we need to claim, to demonstrate that a fetus is not a person, is that any being which satisfies *none* of (1)–(5) is certainly not a person. I consider this claim to be so obvious that I think anyone who denied it, and claimed that a being which satisfied none of (1)–(5) was a person all the same, would thereby demonstrate that he had no notion at all of what a person is—perhaps because he had confused the concept of a person with that of genetic humanity. If the opponents of abortion were to deny the appropriateness of these five criteria, I do not know what further arguments would convince them. We would probably have to admit that our conceptual schemes were indeed irreconcilably different, and that our dispute could not be settled objectively.

I do not expect this to happen, however, since I think that the concept of a person is one which is very nearly universal (to people), and that it is common to both pro-abortionists and anti-abortionists, even though neither group has fully realized the relevance of this concept to the resolution of their dispute. Furthermore, I think that on reflection even the anti-abortionists ought to agree not only that (1)–(5) are central to the concept of personhood, but also that it is a part of this concept that all and only people have full moral rights. The concept of a person is in part a moral concept; once we have admitted that X is a person, we have recognized, even if we have not agreed to respect, X's right to be treated as a member of the moral community. It is true that the claim that X is a *human being* is more commonly voiced as part of an appeal to treat X decently than is the claim that X is a person, but this is either because "human being" is here used in the sense which implies personhood, or because the genetic and moral senses of "human" have been confused.

Now if (1)–(5) are indeed the primary criteria of personhood, then it is clear that genetic humanity is neither necessary nor sufficient for establishing that an entity is a person. Some human beings are not people, and there may well be people who are not human beings. A man or woman whose consciousness has been permanently obliterated but who remains alive is a human being which is no longer a person; defective human beings, with no appreciable mental capacity, are not and presumably never will be people; and a fetus is a human being which is not yet a person, and which therefore cannot coherently be said to have full moral rights. Citizens of the next century should be prepared to recognize highly advanced, self-aware robots or computers, should such be developed, and intelligent inhabitants of other worlds, should such be found, as people in the fullest sense, and to respect their moral rights. But to ascribe full rights to an entity which is not a person is as absurd as to ascribe moral obligations and responsibilities to such an entity.

3. Fetal Development and the Right to Life

Two problems arise in the application of these suggestions for the definition of the moral community to the determination of the precise moral status of a human fetus. Given that the paradigm example of a person is a normal adult human being, then (1) How like this paradigm, in particular how far advanced since conception, does a human being need to be before it begins to have a right to life by virtue, not of being fully a person as of yet, but of being *like* a person? And (2) To what extent, if any, does the fact that a fetus has the *potential* for becoming a person endow it with some of the same rights? Each of these questions requires some comment.

In answering the first question, we need not attempt a detailed consideration of the moral rights of organisms which are not developed enough, aware enough, intelligent enough, etc., to be considered people, but which resemble people in some respects. It does seem reasonable to suggest that the more like a person, in the relevant aspects, a being is, the stronger is the case for regarding it as having a right to life, and indeed the stronger its right to life is. Thus we ought to take seriously the suggestion that, insofar as "the human individual develops biologically in a continuous fashion ... the rights of a human person might develop in the same way."[8] But we must keep in mind that the attributes which are relevant in determining whether or not an entity is enough like a person to be regarded as having some of the same moral rights are no different from those which are relevant to determining whether or not it is fully a person—i.e., are no different from (1)–(5)— and that being genetically human, or having recognizably human facial and other physical features, or detectable brain activity, or the capacity to survive outside the uterus, is simply not among those relevant attributes.

Thus it is clear that even though a seven or eight-month fetus has features which make it apt to arouse in us almost the same powerful protective instinct as is commonly aroused by a small infant, nevertheless it is not significantly more personlike than a very small embryo. It is *somewhat* more personlike; it can apparently feel and respond to pain, and it may even have a rudimentary form of consciousness, insofar as its brain is quite active. Nevertheless, it seems safe to say that it is not fully conscious, in the way that an infant of a few months is, and that it cannot reason, or communicate messages of indefinitely many sorts, does not engage in self-motivated activity, and has no self-awareness. Thus, in the *relevant* respects, a fetus, even a fully developed one, is considerably less personlike than is the average mature mammal, indeed the average fish. And I think that a rational person must conclude that if the right to life of a fetus is to be based upon its resemblance to a person, then it cannot be said to have any more right to life than, let us say, a newborn guppy (which also seems to be capable of feeling pain), and that a right of that magnitude could never override a woman's right to obtain an abortion, at any stage of her pregnancy.

There may ... be other arguments in favor of placing legal limits on the stage of pregnancy in which abortion may be performed. Given the relative safety of the new techniques of artificially inducing labor during the third trimester, the danger to the woman's life or health is no longer such an argument. Neither is the fact that people tend to respond to the thought of abortion in the later stages of pregnancy with emotional repulsion, since mere emotional responses cannot take the place of moral reasoning in determining what ought to be permitted. Nor, finally, is the ... argument that legalizing abortion, especially late in the pregnancy, may erode the level of respect for human life, leading perhaps, to an increase in unjustified euthanasia and other crimes. For this threat ... can be better met by educating people to the kinds of moral distinctions which we are making here than by limiting access to abortion (which limitation may, in its disregard for the rights of women, be just as damaging to the level of respect for human rights).

Thus, since the fact that even a fully developed fetus is not personlike enough to have any significant right to life on the basis of its personlikeness shows that no legal restrictions upon the stage of pregnancy in which an abortion may be performed can be justified on the grounds that we should protect the rights of the older fetus; and since there is no other apparent justification for such restrictions, we may conclude that they are entirely unjustified. Whether or not it would be *indecent* (whatever that means) for a woman in her seventh month to obtain an abortion just to avoid having to postpone a trip to Europe, it would not, in itself, be *immoral,* and therefore it ought to be permitted.

4. Potential Personhood and the Right to Life

We have seen that a fetus does not resemble a person in any way which can support the claim that it has even some of the same rights. But what about its *potential,* the fact that if nurtured and allowed to

develop naturally it will very probably become a person? Doesn't that alone give it at least some right to life? It is hard to deny that the fact that ... an entity is a potential person is a strong *prima facie* reason for not destroying it; but we need not conclude from this that a potential person has a right to life, by virtue of that potential. It may be that our feeling that it is better, other things being equal, not to destroy a potential person is better explained by the fact that potential people are still (felt to be) an invaluable resource, not to be lightly squandered. Surely, if every speck of dust were a potential person, we would be much less apt to conclude that every potential person has a right to become actual.

Still, we do not need to insist that a potential person has no right to life whatever. There may well be something immoral, and not just imprudent, about wantonly destroying potential people, when doing so isn't necessary to protect anyone's rights. But even if a potential person does have some prima facie right to life, such a right could not possibly outweigh the right of a woman to obtain an abortion, since the rights of any actual person invariably outweigh those of any potential person, whenever the two conflict. Since this may not be immediately obvious in the case of a human fetus, let us look at another case.

Suppose that our space explorer falls into the hands of an alien culture, whose scientists decide to create a few hundred thousand or more human beings by breaking his body into component cells and using these to create fully developed human beings with, of course, his genetic code. We may imagine that each of these newly created men will have all of the original man's abilities, skills, knowledge, and so on, and also have an individual self-concept, in short that each of them will be a bona fide (though hardly unique) person. Imagine that the whole project will take only seconds, and that its chances of success are extremely high, and that our explorer knows all of this, and also knows that these people will be treated fairly. I maintain that in such a situation he would have every right to escape if he could, and thus to deprive all of these potential people of their potential lives; for his right to life outweighs all of theirs together, in spite of the fact that they are all genetically human, all innocent, and all have a very high probability of becoming people very soon, if only he refrains from acting.

Indeed, I think he would have a right to escape even if it were not his life which the alien scientists planned to take, but only a year of his freedom, or, indeed, only a day. Nor would he be obligated to stay if he had gotten captured (thus bringing all of these people potentials into existence) because of his own carelessness, or even if he had done so deliberately, knowing the consequences. Regardless of how he got captured, he is not morally obligated to remain in captivity for *any* period of time for the sake of permitting any number of potential people to come into actuality, so great is the margin by which one actual person's right to liberty outweighs whatever right to life even a hundred thousand potential people have. And it seems reasonable to conclude that the rights of a woman will outweigh by a similar margin whatever right to life a fetus may have by virtue of its potential personhood.

Thus, neither a fetus's resemblance to a person, nor its potential for becoming a person provides any basis whatever for the claim that it has any significant right to life. Consequently, a woman's right to protect her health, happiness, freedom, and even her life[9] by terminating an unwanted pregnancy, will always override whatever right to life it may be appropriate to ascribe to a fetus, even a fully developed one. And thus, in the absence of any overwhelming social need for every possible child, the laws which restrict the right to obtain an abortion, or limit the period of pregnancy during which an abortion may be performed, are a wholly unjustified violation of a woman's most basic moral and constitutional rights.[10] ...

POSTSCRIPT ON
INFANTICIDE

Since the publication of this article, many people have [pointed out] that my argument appears to justify not only abortion, but also infanticide. For a newborn infant is not significantly more personlike than an advanced fetus, and consequently it would seem that if the destruction of the latter is permissible so too must be that of the former. Inasmuch as most people, regardless of how they feel about the morality of abortion, consider infanticide a form of murder, this might appear to represent a serious flaw in my argument.

Now, if I am right in holding that it is only people who have a full-fledged right to life, and who can be murdered, and if the criteria of person-hood are as I have described them, then it obviously follows that killing a newborn infant isn't murder. It does *not* follow, however, that infanticide is permissible, for two reasons. In the first place, it would be wrong, at least in this country and this period of history, and other things being equal, to kill a newborn infant, because even if its parents do not want it and would not suffer from its destruction, there are other people who would like to have it and would, in all probability, be deprived of a great deal of pleasure by its destruction. Thus, infanticide is wrong for reasons analogous to those which make it wrong to wantonly destroy natural resources, or great works of art.

Second, most people, at least in this country, value infants and would much prefer that they be preserved, even if foster parents are not immediately available. Most of us would rather be taxed to support orphanages than allow unwanted infants to be destroyed. So long as there are people who want an infant preserved, and who are willing and able to provide the means of caring for it, under reasonably humane conditions, it is, *ceteris paribus,* wrong to destroy it.

But, it might be replied, if this argument shows that infanticide is wrong, at least at this time and in this country, doesn't it also show that abortion is wrong? After all, many people value fetuses, are disturbed by their destruction, and would much prefer that they be preserved, even at some cost to themselves. Furthermore, as a potential source of pleasure to some foster family, a fetus is just as valuable as an infant. There is, however, a crucial difference between the two cases: So long as the fetus is unborn, its preservation, contrary to the wishes of the pregnant woman, violates her rights to freedom, happiness, and self-determination. Her rights override the rights of those who would like the fetus preserved, just as if someone's life or limb is threatened by a wild animal, his right to protect himself by destroying the animal overrides the rights of those who would prefer that the animal not be harmed.

The minute the infant is born, however, its preservation no longer violates any of its mother's rights, even if she wants it destroyed, because she is free to put it up for adoption. Consequently, while the moment of birth does not mark any sharp discontinuity in the degree to which an infant possesses the right to life, it does mark the end of its mother's right to determine its fate. Indeed, if abortion could be performed without killing the fetus, she would never possess the right to have the fetus destroyed, for the same reasons that she has no right to have an infant destroyed.

On the other hand, it follows from my argument that when an unwanted or defective infant is born into a society which cannot afford and/or is not willing to care for it, then its destruction is permissible. This conclusion will, no doubt, strike many people as heartless and immoral; but remember that the very existence of people who feel this way, and who are willing and able to provide care for unwanted infants, is reason enough to conclude that they should be preserved.

ENDNOTES

1. For example, Roger Wertheimer, who in "Understanding the Abortion Argument" (*Philosophy and Public Affairs 1*. no. 1 [Fall, 1971], 67–95), argues that the problem of the moral status of abortion is insoluble, in that the dispute over the status of the fetus is not a question of fact at all, but only a question of how one responds to the facts.

2. John Noonan, "Abortion and the Catholic Church: A Summary History," *Natural Law Forum, 12* (1967), 125.

3. John Noonan, "Deciding Who Is Human," *Natural Law Forum, 13* (1968), 134.

4. "A Defense of Abortion," *Philosophy and Public Affairs* 11 (Fall, 1971): 173–178.

5. We may safely ignore the fact that she might have avoided getting raped, e.g., by carrying a gun, since by similar means you might likewise have avoided getting kidnapped, and in neither case does the victim's failure to take all possible precautions against a highly unlikely event (as opposed to reasonable precautions against a rather likely event) mean that he is morally responsible for what happens.

6. Of course, the principle that it is (always) wrong to kill innocent human beings is in need of many other modifications, e.g., that it may be permissible to do so to save a greater number of innocent human beings, but we may safely ignore these complications here.

7. From here on, we will use "human" to mean genetically human, since the moral sense seems closely connected to, and perhaps derived from, the assumption that genetic humanity is sufficient for membership in the moral community.

8. Thomas L. Hayes, "A Biological View," *Commonweal, 85* (March 17,1967), 677–678; quoted by Daniel Callahan, in *Abortion: Law, Choice, and Morality* (London: Macmillan & Co., 1970).

9. That is, insofar as the death rate, for the woman, is higher for childbirth than for early abortion.

10. My thanks to the following people, who were kind enough to read and criticize an earlier version of this paper: Herbert Gold, Gene Glass, Anne Lauterbach, Judith Thomson, Mary Mothersill, and Timothy Binkley.

17

A Feminist Defense of Abortion

SALLY MARKOWITZ

Sally Markowitz provides what she regards as a specifically feminist argument for abortion, that is, one that is grounded on awareness of women's oppression and a commitment to a more egalitarian society. She argues that because in the sexist society in which we live women are denied the equality to which they are entitled, a right to abortion is justified until that equality is guaranteed.

In the past few decades, the issue of abortion, long of concern to women, has gained a prominent place in the platforms of politicians and a respectable, if marginal, one in the writings of moral philosophers. It is natural to speculate that the rise of and reactions to the women's liberation movement explain the feverish pitch of the recent debate, and no doubt there is much to this speculation. And yet, philosophical analyses of abortion have had surprisingly little to say directly about either women or feminism. Instead, their primary concern has been to decide whether or not the fetus is a person, with a right to life like yours or mine. That this question deserves philosophical attention becomes especially clear when we consider the frightening (if fanciful) ways it is asked and answered by those in power. Nevertheless, as many feminists and some philosophers have recognized, the way we respond to the problem of personhood will not necessarily settle the dispute over abortion once and for all. On some views, a full account must deal with the rights of pregnant women as well.

In fact, one popular defense of abortion is based on the woman's right to autonomy and avoids the personhood issue altogether. The central claim of the autonomy defense is that anti-abortion policies simply interfere in an impermissible way with the pregnant woman's autonomy. In what has become the classic philosophical statement of this view, Judith Jarvis Thomson ingeniously argues that even if the fetus has a right to life, it need not also have the right to use its mother's body to stay alive. The woman's body is her own property, to dispose of as she wishes.[1] But autonomy theorists need not rest their case on the vaguely disturbing notion of the pregnant woman's property rights to her own body. For example, Jane English, in another version of the view, argues that a woman is justified in aborting if pregnancy and childbearing will prevent her from pursuing the life she wants to live, the expression of her own autonomy.[2]

Philosophers have come to call this strategy the "feminist" or "woman's liberation" approach, and some version of it seems to be favored by many feminists.[3] This is no surprise since such a view may seem to be quite an improvement over accounts that regard personhood as the only essential issue. At least it recognizes women as bearers of rights as well as of babies. In what follows, however, I suggest that this defense may fall short of the feminist mark. Then I shall offer another defense, one derived not from the right to autonomy, but from an awareness of women's oppression and commitment to a more egalitarian society.

Reprinted from *Social Theory and Practice* 16, no. 1 (Spring 1990) by permission.

I will assume throughout that the fetus has a serious right to life. I do so not because I believe this to be true, but rather because a feminist defense of abortion rights should be independent of the status of the fetus. For if, as many feminists believe, the move toward a sexually egalitarian society requires women's control of their reproductive lives, and if the permissibility of this control depends ultimately upon the status of the fetus, then the future of feminism rests upon how we resolve the personhood issue. This is not acceptable to most feminists. No doubt many feminists are comforted by arguments against the fetus's personhood. But regardless of the fetus's status, more must be said.

1.

What, then, from a feminist point of view, is wrong with an autonomy defense? Feminists should be wary on three counts. First, most feminists believe not only that women in our society are oppressed, but also that our failure to face the scope and depth of this oppression does much to maintain it. This makes feminists suspicious of perspectives, often called humanist or liberal, that focus only on the individual and deemphasize the issue of gender by either refusing to acknowledge that women have less power than men or denying that this inequity is worth much attention. While liberals and humanists may try to discuss social issues, including abortion, with as little mention as possible of gender, feminists tend to search for the hidden, unexpected, and perhaps unwelcome ways in which gender is relevant. From this perspective, defenses of abortion that focus only on the personhood of the fetus are not essentially or even especially feminist ones since they completely avoid any mention of gender. Autonomy arguments, though, are not much of an improvement. They may take into account the well-being of individual women, but they manage to skirt the issue of women's status, as a group, in a sexist society.

Second, the autonomy defense incorporates a (supposedly) gender-neutral right, one that belongs to every citizen; there's nothing special about being

a woman—except, of course, for the inescapable fact that only women find themselves pregnant against their wills. Some feminists have become disillusioned with this gender-neutral approach. They reject it both on principle, because it shifts attention away from gender inequality, and for practical reasons, because it often works against women in the courts.[4] Instead, feminists have come to realize that sometimes gender should be relevant in claiming rights. Some of these rights, like adequate gynecological care, may be based on women's special physiology; others may stem from the special needs experienced by female casualties of a sexist society: the impoverished, divorced, or unwed mother, the rape victim, the anorexic teen, the coed who has been convinced that she lacks (or had better lack) mathematical aptitude. A thoroughly feminist analysis, then, will not hesitate, when appropriate, to claim a right on the basis of gender, rather than in spite of it.[5] To do otherwise in the case of abortion may be not only to deny the obvious, but also to obscure the relation of reproductive practices to women's oppression.

The third problem feminists might have with an autonomy defense involves the content of the human ideal on which the right to autonomy rests. Some feminists, influenced by Marxist and socialist traditions, may reject an ideal that seems to be so ultimately connected with the individualistic ideology of capitalism. Others may suspect that this ideology is not just capitalist but male-biased. And if feminists hesitate to justify abortion by appeal to a gender-neutral right derived from a gender-neutral ideal, they are even more suspicious of an ideal that seems to be gender-neutral when really it's not. Increasingly, feminists reject the ideals of older feminists, like Simone de Beauvoir, who, in promoting for women what appeared to be an androgynous human ideal, unwittingly adopted one that was androcentric, or male-centered. Instead, feminists seek to free themselves from the misogynist perspective that sees women as incomplete men and ignores, devalues, or denies the existence of particularly female psychologies, values, and experiences. On this view, to fashion a feminist human ideal we must look to women's values and experiences—or at least we must not look only to men's.[6]

This re-evaluation has important implications for the abortion issue, since many feminists consider an overriding right to autonomy to be a characteristically male ideal, while nurturance and responsibility for others (the paradigmatic case of which is motherhood) to be characteristically female ones. Indeed, in the name of such women's values, some women who call themselves feminists have actually joined the anti-abortionist camp.[7] Most feminists, of course, don't go this far. But, paradoxically, many seem to find the ideal of autonomy less acceptable than the right to abortion it is supposed to justify. Clearly, something is awry.

Feminists, therefore, need another argument. Instead of resting on an ideal many feminists reject, a feminist defense of abortion should somehow reflect an awareness of women's oppression and a commitment to ending it.

2.

Of all the philosophers, feminist and otherwise, who have discussed abortion, Alison Jaggar seems to be the only one to address the problem from this perspective. Jaggar argues that in societies where mothers bear the responsibility for pregnancy, birth, and childrearing, women should control abortion decisions. Women who live in other, more cooperative social communities (wherever they are), where members of both sexes share such responsibilities, cannot claim a right of the same force. The strength of a woman's say about whether or not to abort, then should be relative to the amount of support (financial, emotional, physical, medical, and otherwise) she can expect from those around her.[8]

It is disheartening that the philosophical community has not paid Jaggar's paper the attention it merits in the decade and a half since its publication, but this lapse is hardly surprising. The notion of the individual's right to autonomy is so firmly entrenched that we have difficulty even entertaining other approaches. We find ourselves invoking such rights perhaps without realizing it even when

we neither want nor need to. And Jaggar is no exception; despite the promising intuition with which she starts, Jaggar finally offers us another, albeit more sophisticated, version of the autonomy argument. Quite simply, her argument implies that if abortion ought to be permissible in some societies but not in others, this is only because pregnancy and motherhood create obstacles to personal autonomy in some societies but not in others.

Jaggar bases her argument for abortion rights in our society on two principles. The first, or Right to Life Principle, holds that

> the right to life, when it is claimed for a human being, means the right to a full human life and to whatever means are necessary to achieve this.... To be born, then, is only one of the necessary conditions for a full human life. The others presumably include nutritious food, breathable air, warm human companionship, and so on. If anyone has a right to life, she or he must be entitled to all of these.[9]

According to the second, or Personal Control Principle, "Decisions should be made by those, and only by those, who are importantly affected by them."[10] In our society, then, the state cannot legitimately set itself up as the protector of the fetus's right to life (as Jaggar has characterized it) because the mother and not the state will be expected to provide for this right, both during pregnancy and afterwards. But since, by the Personal Control Principle, only those whose lives will be importantly affected have the right to make a decision, in our society the pregnant woman should determine whether to continue her pregnancy.

Jaggar's argument incorporates both liberal and feminist perspectives, and there is a tension between them. Her argument is feminist rather than merely liberal because it does not rest exclusively on a universal right to autonomy. Instead, it takes seriously the contingent and socially variable features of reproduction and parenting, their relationship to women's position in a society, and the effect of anti-abortion policy on this position. But her argument is also a liberal one. Consider, for example, the Personal Control Principle. While Jaggar doesn't explicitly spell out its motivation, she does state that the principle "provides the fundamental justification for democracy and is accepted by most shades of political opinion."[11] Surely this wide acceptance has something to do with the belief, equally widely held, that citizens should be able to decide for themselves what courses their lives should take, especially when some courses involve sacrifices or burdens. This becomes clear when Jaggar explains that an individual or organization has no moral claim as a protector of the right to life "that would justify its insistence on just one of the many conditions necessary to a full human life, in circumstances where this would place the burden of fulfilling all the other conditions squarely on the shoulders of some other individual or organization." Once again we have an appeal to a universal right to personal autonomy, indeed a right based on an ideal which not only might be unacceptable to many feminists, but may cast the net too widely even for some liberals. For example, one might claim that taxation policies designed to finance social programs interfere with personal choices about how to spend earnings, a matter that will have important consequences for one's life. Such a view also permits a range of private actions which some liberals may believe are immoral: For example, an adult grandchild may decide to stop caring for a burdensome and senile grandparent if such care places a heavy burden on the grandchild.

I shall not attempt to pass judgment here on the desirability of either redistributing income through taxation or passing laws requiring us to be Good Samaritans in our private lives. Nor do I want to beg the question, which I shall discuss later, of whether reproductive autonomy is, in all circumstances, overridingly important in a way other sorts of autonomy may not be. I can leave these matters open because a feminist defense of abortion need not depend on how we settle them. For there is a significant difference between the sacrifices required by restrictive abortion policies and those required by enforcing other sorts of Good Samaritanism: Taxes and laws against letting the aged or handicapped starve to death apply to everyone; those prohibiting abortion apply only to women.

While anyone might end up with a helpless, cantankerous grandparent and most of us end up paying taxes, only women end up pregnant. So anti-abortion laws require sacrifice not of everyone, but only of women.

3.

This brings us to what I regard as the crucial question: When, if ever, can people be required to sacrifice for the sake of others? And how can feminists answer this question in a way that rests not on the individual right to personal autonomy, but on a view of social reality that takes seriously power relations between genders? I suggest the following principle, which I shall call the Impermissible Sacrifice Principle: *When one social group in a society is systematically oppressed by another, it is impermissible to require the oppressed group to make sacrifices that will exacerbate or perpetuate this oppression.* (Note that this principle does not exempt the members of oppressed groups from *all* sorts of sacrifices just because they are oppressed; they may be as morally responsible as anyone for rendering aid in some circumstances. Only sacrifices that will clearly perpetuate their oppression are ruled out.)

The Impermissible Sacrifice Principle focuses on power relationships between groups rather than on the rights of individuals. This approach will suit not only feminists but all who recognize and deplore other sorts of systematic social oppression as well. Indeed, if we take our opposition to oppression seriously, this approach may be necessary. Otherwise, when policy decisions are made, competing goals and commitments may distract us from the conditions we claim to deplore and encourage decisions that allow such conditions to remain. Even worse, these other goals and commitments can be used as excuses for perpetuating oppression. Testing policies against the Impermissible Sacrifice Principle keeps this from happening.

Feminists should welcome the applicability of the Impermissible Sacrifice Principle to groups other than women. Radical feminists are sometimes accused of being blind to any sort of oppression but their own. The Impermissible Sacrifice Principle, however, enables feminists to demonstrate solidarity with other oppressed groups by resting the case for abortion on the same principle that might, for example, block a policy requiring the poor rather than the rich to bear the tax burden, or workers rather than management to take a pay cut. On the other hand, feminists may worry that the Impermissible Sacrifice Principle, taken by itself, may not yield the verdict on abortion feminists seek. For if some radical feminists err by recognizing only women's oppression, some men err by not recognizing it at all. So the Impermissible Sacrifice Principle must be supplemented by what I shall call the Feminist Proviso: *Women are, as a group, sexually oppressed by men; and this oppression can neither be completely understood in terms of, nor otherwise reduced to, oppressions of other sorts.*

Feminists often understand this oppression to involve men's treating women as breeding machines, sexual or aesthetic objects, nurturers who need no nurturance. Women become alienated from their bodies, their sexuality, their work, their intellect, their emotions, their moral agency. Of course, feminists disagree about exactly how to formulate this analysis, especially since women experience oppression differently depending on their class, race, and ethnicity. But however we decide to understand women's oppression, we can be sure an anti-abortion policy will make it worse.

Adding the Feminist Proviso, then, keeps (or makes) sexism visible, ensuring that women are one of the oppressed groups to which the Principle applies. This should hardly need saying. Yet by focusing on other sorts of oppression the Principle might cover, men often trivialize or ignore feminists' demands and women's pain. For example, someone (perhaps a white male) who is more sympathetic to the claims of racial minorities or workers than to those of women might try to trivialize or deny the sexual oppression of a white, affluent woman (perhaps his wife) by reminding her that she's richer than an unemployed black male and so should not complain. The Feminist Proviso also prevents an affluent white woman who rejects the unwelcome sexual advances of a minority or

working class male from being dismissed (or dismissing herself) as a racist or classist. She may well be both. But she also lives in a world where, all things being equal, she is fair sexual game, in one way or another, for any male.[12] Finally, the Impermissible Sacrifice Principle in conjunction with the Feminist Proviso might be used to block the view that a black or Third World woman's first obligation is to bear children to swell the ranks of the revolution, regardless of the consequences of maternity within her culture. Having children for this reason may be a legitimate choice; but she also may have independent grounds to refuse.

I have added the Feminist Proviso so that the Impermissible Sacrifice Principle cannot be used to frustrate a feminist analysis. But I must also emphasize that the point is not to pit one oppressed group against another, but to make sure that the men in otherwise progressive social movements do not ignore women's oppression or, worse, find "politically correct" justifications for it. Women refuse to wait until "after the revolution" not just because they are impatient, but also because they have learned that not all revolutions are feminist ones.

The Impermissible Sacrifice Principle and the Feminist Proviso together, then, justify abortion on demand for women *because they live in a sexist society.* This approach not only gives a more explicitly feminist justification of abortion than the autonomy defense; it also gives a stronger one. For autonomy defenses are open to objections and qualifications that a feminist one avoids. Consider the ways the feminist approach handles these four challenges to the autonomy defense.

First, some philosophers have dismissed autonomy defenses by suggesting blithely that we simply compensate the pregnant woman.[13] Of what, though, will such compensation consist? Maternity leave? Tax breaks? Prenatal healthcare? Twenty points added to her civil-service exam score? Such benefits lighten one's load, no doubt. But what women suffer by being forced to continue unwanted pregnancies is not merely a matter of finances or missed opportunities; in a sexist society, there is reason to expect that an anti-abortion policy will reinforce a specifically *sexual* oppression, whatever sorts of compensation are offered. Indeed, even talk of compensation may be misguided, since it implies a prior state when things were as they should be; compensation seeks to restore the balance after a temporary upset. But in a sexist society, there is no original balance; women's oppression is the status quo. Even if individual women are compensated by money, services, or opportunities, sexual oppression may remain.

Second, an autonomy defense may seem appropriate only in cases where a woman engages in "responsible" sex: It is one thing to be a victim of rape or even contraceptive failure, one might argue; it is quite another voluntarily to have unprotected intercourse. A feminist defense suggests another approach. First, we might question the double standard that requires that women pay for "irresponsible" sex while men don't have to, even though women are oppressed by men. More importantly, if we focus on the *way* women are oppressed, we may understand many unwanted pregnancies to result from fear and paralysis rather than irresponsibility. For in a sexist society, many women simply do not believe they control the conditions under which they have sex. And, sad to say, often they may be right.[14]

Third, what about poor women's access to abortion? The sort of right the autonomy theorists invoke, after all, seems to be a right to noninterference by the state. But this negative right seems to be in tension with a demand for state-funded abortions, especially since not everyone supports abortions. At any rate, we will need another argument to justify the funding of abortion for poor women. The defense I suggest, however, is clearly committed to providing all women with access to abortion, since to allow abortions only for those who can afford them forces poor women, who are doubly oppressed, to make special sacrifices. An egalitarian society must liberate all women, not just the rich ones.

Finally, autonomy defenses allow, indeed invite, the charge that the choice to abort is selfish. Even Thomson finds abortion, while not unjust, often to be "selfish" or "indecent." Although she has deprived nothing of its rights, the woman who aborts has chosen self-interested autonomy over altruism in the same way one might choose to watch while a child starves. Of course, one is tempted to point out that the (largely male) world of commerce and politics thrives on such "morally indecent" but legal actions. But then feminists are reduced to claiming a right to be as selfish as men are. Moreover, once the specter of selfishness is raised, this defense does not allow feminists to make enough of male anti-abortionists' motives. On an autonomy defense, these motives are simply not relevant, let alone damning, and feminists who dwell on them seem to be resorting to *ad hominems*. From a feminist perspective, however, abortion is a political issue, one which essentially concerns the interests of and power relations between men and women. Thus, what women and men can expect to gain or lose from an abortion policy becomes the point rather than the subject of *ad hominem* arguments.[15]

The approach I propose does well on each of these important counts. But its real test comes when we weigh the demands of the Impermissible Sacrifice Principle against fetal rights; for we have required that a feminist analysis be independent of the status of the fetus. Indeed, we may even be tempted to regard fetuses as constituting just the sort of oppressed group to whom the principle applies, and surely a fetus about to be aborted is in worse shape than the woman who carries it.

However, it may not make sense to count fetuses as an oppressed group. A disadvantaged one, perhaps. But the Impermissible Sacrifice Principle does not prescribe that more disadvantaged groups have a right to aid from less disadvantaged ones; it focuses only on the particular disadvantage of social oppression. That the fetus has a serious right to life does not imply that it's the sort of being that can be oppressed, if it cannot yet enter into the sorts of social relationships that constitute oppression. I cannot argue for this here; in any case, I suspect my best argument will not convince everyone. But feminists have another, more pointed response.

Whether or not we can weigh the disadvantage of fetuses against the oppression of women, we must realize what insisting on such a comparison does to the debate. It narrows our focus, turning it back to the conflict between the rights of fetuses and of women (even if now this conflict is between the rights of groups rather than of individuals). This is certainly not to deny that fetal rights should be relevant to an abortion policy. But feminists must insist that the oppression of women should be relevant too. And it is also relevant that unless our society changes in deep and global ways, anti-abortion policies, intentionally or not, will perpetuate women's oppression by men. This, then, is where feminists must stand firm.

Does this mean that instead of overriding the fetus's right to life by women's right to autonomy, I am proposing that feminists override the fetus's right by the right of women to live in a sexually egalitarian society? This is a difficult position for feminists but not an impossible one, especially for feminists with utilitarian leanings. Many feminists, for example, see sexism as responsible for a culture of death: war, violence, child abuse, ecological disaster. Eradicate sexism, it might be argued, and we will save more lives than we will lose. Some feminists might even claim that an oppressed woman's fate can be worse than that of an aborted fetus. Although I will not argue for such claims, they may be less implausible than they seem. But feminists need not rest their case on them. Instead, they must simply insist that society must change so that women are no longer oppressed. Such changes, of course, may require of men sacrifices unwelcome beyond their wildest dreams. But that, according to a feminist analysis, is the point.

So we should not see the choice as between liberating women and saving fetuses, but between two ways of respecting the fetus's right to life. The first requires women to sacrifice while men benefit. The second requires deep social changes that will ensure that men no longer gain and women lose through our practices of sexuality, reproduction, and parenthood. To point out how men gain from women's compulsory pregnancy is to steal the misplaced moral thunder from those male authorities—fathers, husbands, judges, congressmen, priests, philosophers—who, exhorting women to do their duty, present themselves as the benevolent, disinterested protectors of fetuses against women's selfishness. Let feminists insist that the conditions for refraining from having abortions is a sexually egalitarian society. If men do not respond, and quickly, they will have indicated that fetal life isn't so important to them after all, or at least not important enough to give up the privileges of being male in a sexist society. If this makes feminists look bad, it makes men look worse still.

ENDNOTES

1. Judith Jarvis Thomson, "A Defense of Abortion," *Philosophy and Public Affairs 1* (1971): 47–66.

2. Jane English, "Abortion and the Concept of a Person," in *Today's Moral Problems,* ed. by Richard A. Wasserstrom (New York: Macmillan, 1985), pp. 448–57.

3. Peter Singer, *Practical Ethics* (Cambridge: Cambridge University Press, 1979), p. 113.

4. Catherine A. MacKinnon, *Feminism Unmodified: Discourses on Life and Law* (Cambridge: Harvard University Press, 1987), pp. 35–36.

5. See, for example, Alison Jaggar, *Feminist Politics and Human Nature* (Totowa, New Jersey: Rowman & Littlefield, 1983), especially Parts 1 and 2; and Catherine A. MacKinnon, *Feminism Unmodified: Discourses on Life and Law.*

6. See Sara Ruddick, "Maternal Thinking," *Feminist Studies 6* (1980): 345–346; Nancy Chodorow, *The Reproduction of Mothering: Psychoanalysis and the Sociology of Gender* (Berkeley and Los Angeles: University of California Press, 1978); Carol Gilligan, *In a Different Voice: Psychological Theory and Women's Development* (Cambridge: Harvard University Press, 1982).

7. Sidney Callahan, "A Pro-Life Feminist Makes Her Case," *Commonweal* (April 25,1986), quoted in the *Utne Reader 20* (1987); 104–108.

8. Alison Jaggar, "Abortion and a Woman's Right to Decide," in *Philosophy and Sex,* ed. Robert Baker and Frank Elliston (Buffalo: Prometheus Press, 1975), pp. 324–337.

9. "Abortion and a Woman's Right to Decide," p. 328.

10. "Abortion and a Woman's Right to Decide," p. 328.

11. "Abortion and a Woman's Right to Decide," p. 329.

12. For classic discussions of sexism in the civil rights movement, see Susan Brownmiller, *Against Our Will: Men, Women, and Rape* (New York: Simon and Schuster, 1975), especially pp. 210–255; and Michelle Wallace, *Black Macho and the Myth of the Superwoman* (New York: Dial Press, 1978).

13. Michael Tooley "Abortion and Infanticide," in Joel Feinberg, ed., *The Problem of Abortion* (Belmont, California: Wadsworth, 1983).

14. MacKinnon, *Feminism Unmodified*, p. 95.

15. This approach also allows us to understand the deep division between women on this issue. For many women in traditional roles fear the immediate effects on their lives of women's liberation generally and a permissive abortion policy in particular. On this, see Kristen Luker, *Abortion and the Politics of Motherhood* (Berkeley: University of California Press, 1984), especially pp. 158–215.

18

Euthanasia, Killing, and Letting Die

JAMES RACHELS

James Rachels criticizes a policy statement of the American Medical Association on the grounds that it endorses the doctrine that there is an important moral difference between active and passive euthanasia. Rachels denies that there is any moral difference between the two. He argues that once we judge a patient would be better off dead, it should not matter much whether that patient is killed or let die. He points out that both killing and letting die can be intentional and deliberate and can proceed from the same motives; further, that when killing and letting die are similar in these and other relevant respects, our moral assessment of these acts is also similar. Rachels concludes by considering a number of counterarguments to his view and finds them all wanting. In particular, Rachels rejects the idea that the killing and letting die distinction can be supported on the grounds that our duty to refrain from harming people is much stronger than our duty to help people in need. Rather, he contends that when conditions are similar our duty to refrain from harming people and our duty to help people in need have a similar moral force.

Dr. R J. Ingelfinger, former editor of *The New England Journal of Medicine*, observes that this is the heyday of the ethicist in medicine. He delineates the rights of patients, of experimental subjects, of fetuses, of mothers, of animals, and even of doctors. (And what a far cry it is from the days when medical "ethics" consisted of condemning economic improprieties such as fee splitting and advertising!) With impeccable logic—once certain basic assumptions are granted—and with graceful prose, the ethicist develops his arguments....Yet his precepts are essentially the products of armchair exercise and remain abstract and idealistic until they have been tested in the laboratory of experience.[1]

One problem with such armchair exercises, he complains, is that in spite of the impeccable logic and the graceful prose, the result is often an absolutist ethic which is unsatisfactory when applied to particular cases, and which is therefore of little use to the practicing physician. Unlike some absolutist philosophers, "the practitioner appears to prefer the principles of individualism. As there are few atheists in fox holes, there tend to be few absolutists at the bedside."[2]

I must concede at the outset that this chapter is another exercise in "armchair ethics" in the sense that I am not a physician but a philosopher. Yet I am no absolutist; and my purpose is to examine a doctrine that is held in an absolute form by many doctors. The doctrine is that there is an important moral difference between active and passive euthanasia, such that even though the latter is sometimes permissible, the former is always forbidden. This is an absolute which doctors hold "at the bedside" as well as in the seminar room, and the "principles of individualism" make little headway against it.

Ethical Issues Relating to Life and Death, edited by Ladd (1979) Chp. "Euthanasia, Killing, And Letting Die" by Rachels pp. 146–161. Reprinted by permission.

But I will argue that this is an irrational dogma, and that there is no sound moral basis for it.

I will not argue, simply, that active euthanasia is all right. Rather, I will be concerned with the *relation* between active euthanasia and passive euthanasia: I will argue that there is no moral difference between them. By this I mean that there is no reason to prefer one over the other as a matter of principle— the fact that one case of euthanasia is active, while another is passive, is not *itself a* reason to think one morally better than the other. If you already think that passive euthanasia is all right, and you are convinced by my arguments, then you may conclude that active euthanasia must be all right, too. On the other hand, if you believe that active euthanasia is immoral, you may want to conclude that passive euthanasia must be immoral, too. Although I prefer the former alternative, I will not argue for it here. I will only argue that the two forms of euthanasia are morally equivalent—either both are acceptable or both are unacceptable.

I am aware that this will at first seem incredible to many readers, but I hope that this impression will be dispelled as the discussion proceeds. The discussion will be guided by two methodological considerations, both of which are touched on in the editorial quoted above. The first has to do with my "basic assumptions." My arguments are intended to appeal to all reasonable people, and not merely to those who already share my psychological preconceptions. Therefore, I will try not to rely on any assumptions that cannot be accepted by any reasonable person. None of my arguments will depend on morally eccentric premises. Second, Dr. Ingelfinger is surely correct when he says that we must be as concerned with the realities of medical practice as with the more abstract issues of moral theory. As he notes, the philosopher's precepts "remain abstract and idealistic until they are tested in the laboratory of experience." Part of my argument will be precisely that, when "tested in the laboratory of experience," the doctrine in question has terrible results, I believe that if this doctrine were to be recognized as irrational, and rejected by the medical profession, the benefit to both doctors and patients would be enormous. In this sense, my paper is not intended as an "armchair exercise" at all.

THE AMERICAN MEDICAL ASSOCIATION POLICY STATEMENT

"Active euthanasia," as the term is used, means taking some positive action designed to kill the patient; for example, giving him a lethal injection of potassium chloride. "Passive euthanasia," on the other hand, means simply refraining from doing anything to keep the patient alive. In passive euthanasia we withhold medication or other life-sustaining therapy, or we refuse to perform surgery, etc., and let the patient die "naturally" of whatever ills already afflict him.

Many doctors and theologians prefer to use the term *euthanasia* only in connection with active euthanasia, and they use other words to refer to what I am calling "passive euthanasia"—for example, instead of "passive euthanasia" they may speak of "the right to death with dignity." One reason for this choice of terms is the emotional impact of the words: It *sounds* so much better to defend "death with dignity" than to advocate "euthanasia" of any sort. And of course if one believes that there is a great moral difference between active and passive euthanasia—as most doctors and religious writers do—then one may prefer a terminology which puts as much psychological distance as possible between them. However, I do not want to become involved in a pointless dispute about terminology, because nothing of substance depends on which label is used. I will stay with the terms *active euthanasia* and *passive euthanasia* because they are the most convenient; but if the reader prefers a different terminology he may substitute his own throughout, and my arguments will be unaffected.

The belief that there is an important moral difference between active and passive euthanasia obviously has important consequences for medical practice. It makes a difference to what doctors are willing to do. Consider, for example, the following familiar situation. A patient who is dying from incurable cancer of the throat is in terrible pain that we can no longer satisfactorily alleviate. He is certain to die within a few days, but he decides that he does not want to go on living for those days since the pain is unbearable. So he asks the doctor to end his life now; and his family joins in the request. One way that the doctor might comply with this request is simply by killing the patient with a lethal injection. Most doctors would not do that, not only because of the possible legal consequences, but because they think such a course would be immoral. And this is understandable: The idea of killing someone goes against very deep moral feelings; and besides, as we are often reminded, it is the special business of doctors to save and protect life, not to destroy it. Yet, even so, the physician may sympathize with the dying patient's request and feel that it is entirely reasonable for him to prefer death now rather than after a few more days of agony. The doctrine that we are considering tells the doctor what to do: It says that although he may not administer the ethal injection—that would be "active euthanasia," which is forbidden—he *may* withhold treatment and let the patient die sooner than he otherwise would.

It is no wonder that this simple idea is so widely accepted, for it seems to give the doctor a way out of his dilemma without having to kill the patient, and without having to prolong the patient's agony. The idea is not a new one. What *is* new is that the idea is now being incorporated into official documents of medical ethics. What was once unofficially done is now becoming official policy. The idea is expressed, for example, in a 1973 policy statement of the American Medical Association, which says (in its entirety):

> The intentional termination of the life of one human being by another—mercy killing—is contrary to that for which the medical profession stands and is contrary to the policy of the American Medical Association.
>
> The cessation of the employment of extraordinary means to prolong the life of the body when there is irrefutable evidence

that biological death is imminent is the decision of the patient and/or his immediate family. The advice and judgment of the physician should be freely available to the patient and/or his immediate family.[3]

This is a cautiously worded statement, and it is not clear *exactly* what is being affirmed. I take it, however, that at least these three propositions are intended:

1. Killing patients is absolutely forbidden; however, it is sometimes permissible to allow patients to die.

2. It is permissible to allow a patient to die if (a) there is irrefutable evidence that he will die soon anyway; (b) "extraordinary" measures would be required to keep him alive; and (c) the patient and/or his immediate family requests it.

3. Doctors should make their own advice and judgments available to the patient and/or his immediate family when the latter are deciding whether to request that the patient be allowed to die.

The first proposition expresses the doctrine which is the main subject of this paper. As for the third, it seems obvious enough, provided that 1 and 2 are accepted, so I shall say nothing further about it.

I do want to say a few things about 2. Physicians often allow patients to die; however, they do *not* always keep to the guidelines set out in 2. For example, a doctor may leave instructions that if a hopeless, comatose patient suffers cardiac arrest, nothing be done to start his heart beating again. "No-coding" is the name given to this practice, and the consent of the patient and/or his immediate family is not commonly sought. This is thought to be a medical decision (in reality, of course, it is a moral one) which is the doctor's affair. To take a different sort of example, when a Down's syndrome infant is born with an intestinal blockage, the doctor and parents may agree that there will be no operation to remove the blockage, so that the baby will die.[4] (If the same infant were born without the obstruction, it certainly would not be killed. This is a clear application of the idea that "letting die" is all right even though killing is forbidden.) But in such cases it is clear that the baby is *not* going to die soon anyway. If the surgery were performed, the baby would proceed to a "normal" infancy—normal, that is, for a mongoloid. Moreover, the treatment required to save the baby—abdominal surgery—can hardly be called "extraordinary" by today's medical standards.

Therefore, all three conditions which the AMA statement places on the decision to let die are commonly violated. It is beyond the scope of this paper to determine whether doctors are right to violate those conditions. But I firmly believe that the second requirement—2b—is not acceptable. Only a little reflection is needed to show that the distinction between ordinary and extraordinary means is not important. Even a very conservative, religiously oriented writer such as Paul Ramsey stresses this. Ramsey gives these examples:

> Suppose that a diabetic patient long
> accustomed to self-administration of
> insulin falls victim to terminal cancer,
> or suppose that a terminal cancer patient
> suddenly develops diabetes. Is he in the
> first case obliged to continue, and in the
> second case obliged to begin, insulin
> treatment and die painfully of cancer, or in
> either or both cases may the patient choose
> rather to pass into diabetic coma and an
> earlier death? ... Or an old man slowly
> deteriorating who from simply being
> inactive and recumbent gets pneumonia:
> Are we to use antibiotics in a likely
> successful attack upon this disease which
> from time immemorial has been called
> "the old man's friend"?[5]

I agree with Ramsey, and with many other writers, that in such cases treatment may be withheld even though it is not "extraordinary" by any reasonable standard. Contrary to what is implied by the AMA statement, the distinction between heroic and nonheroic means of treatment *cannot* be used to determine when treatment is or is not mandatory.

KILLING AND LETTING DIE

I return now to the distinction between active and passive euthanasia. Of course, not every doctor believes that this distinction is morally important. Over twenty years ago Dr. D. C. S. Cameron of the American Cancer Society said that "Actually the difference between euthanasia (i.e., killing) and letting the patient die by omitting life-sustaining treatment is a moral quibble."[6] I argue that Cameron was right.

The initial thought can be expressed quite simply. In any case in which euthanasia seems desirable, it is because we think that the patient would literally be better off dead—or at least, no worst off dead—than continuing the kind of life available to him. (Without this assumption, even *passive* euthanasia would be unthinkable.) But, as far as the main question of ending the patient's life is concerned, it does not matter whether the euthanasia is active or passive: *In either case,* he ends up dead sooner than he otherwise would. And if the results are the same, why should it matter so much which method is used?

Moreover, we need to remember that, in cases such as that of the terminal cancer patient, the justification for allowing him to die, rather than prolonging his life for a few more hopeless days, is that he is in horrible pain. But if we simply withhold treatment, it may take him *longer* to die, and so he will suffer *more* than he would if we were to administer the lethal injection. This fact provides strong reason for thinking that, once we have made the initial decision not to prolong his agony, active euthanasia is actually preferable to passive euthanasia rather than the reverse. It also shows a kind of incoherence in the conventional view: To say that passive euthanasia is preferable is to endorse the option which leads to more suffering rather than less, and is contrary to the humanitarian impulse which prompts the decision not to prolong his life in the first place.

But many people are convinced that there is an important moral difference between active and passive euthanasia because they think that, in passive euthanasia, the doctor does not really *do* anything. No action whatever is taken; the doctor simply does nothing, and the patient dies of whatever ills already afflict him. In active euthanasia, however, we *do something* to bring about the patient's death. We kill him. Thus, the difference between active and passive euthanasia is thought to be the difference between doing something to bring about someone's death, and not doing anything to bring about anyone's death. And of course if we conceive the matter in *this* way, passive euthanasia seems preferable. Ramsey, who denounces the view I am defending as "extremist" and who regards the active/passive distinction as one of the "flexibly wise categories of traditional medical ethics," takes just this view of the matter. He says that the choice between active and passive euthanasia "is not a choice between directly and indirectly willing and doing something. *It is rather the important choice between doing something and doing nothing,* or (better said) ceasing to do something that was begun in order to do something that is better because now more fitting."[7]

This is a very misleading way of thinking, for it ignores the fact that in passive euthanasia the doctor *does* do one thing which is very important. Namely, he lets the patient die. We may overlook this obvious fact—or at least, we may put it out of our minds—if we concentrate only on a very restricted way of describing what happens: "The doctor does not administer medication or any other therapy; he does not instruct the nurses to administer any such medication; he does not perform any surgery"; and so on. And of course this description of what happens is correct, as far as it goes—these are all things that the doctor does not do. But the point is that the doctor *does* let the patient die when he could save him, and this must be included in the description, too.

There is another reason why we might fall into this error. We might confuse *not saving* someone with *letting him die.* Suppose a patient is dying, and Dr. X could prolong his life. But he decides not to do so and the patient dies. Now it is true of everyone on earth that he did not save the patient. Dr. X did not save him, and neither did you, and neither did I. So we might be tempted to think that all of us are in the same moral position, reasoning that since neither you nor I are responsible for the

patient's death, neither is Dr. X. None of us did anything. This, however, is a mistake, for even though it is true that none of us saved the patient, it is *not* true that we all let him die. In order to let someone die, one must be *in a position* to save him. You and I were not in a position to save the patient, so we did not let him die. Dr. X, on the other hand, was in a position to save him, and did let him die. Thus the doctor is in a special moral position which not just everyone is in.

Here we must remember some elementary points, which are so obvious that they would not be worth mentioning except for the fact that overlooking them is a source of so much confusion in this area. The act of letting someone die may be intentional and deliberate, just as the act of killing someone may be intentional and deliberate. Moreover, the doctor is *responsible* for his decision to let the patient die, just as he would be responsible for giving the patient a lethal injection. The decision to let a patient die is subject to moral appraisal in the same way that a decision to kill is subject to moral appraisal: It may be assessed as wise or unwise, compassionate or sadistic, right or wrong. If a doctor deliberately let a patient die who was suffering from a routinely curable illness, then he would be to blame for what he did, just as he would be to blame if he had needlessly killed the patient. It would be no defense at all for him to insist that, *really,* he didn't "do anything" but just stand there. We would all know that he did do something very serious indeed, for he let the patient die.

These considerations show how misleading it is to characterize the difference between active and passive euthanasia as a difference between doing something (killing), for which the doctor may be morally culpable; and doing nothing (just standing there while the patient dies), for which the doctor is not culpable. The real difference between them is, rather, the difference between *killing* and letting die, both of which are actions for which a doctor, or anyone else, will be morally responsible.

Now we can formulate our problem more precisely. If there is an important moral difference between active and passive euthanasia, it must be because *killing someone is morally worse than letting someone die.* But is it? Is killing, in itself, worse than letting die? In order to investigate this issue, we may consider two cases which are exactly alike except that one involves killing where the other involves letting die. Then we can ask whether this difference makes any difference to our moral assessments. It is important that the cases be *exactly* alike except for this one difference, since otherwise we cannot be confident that it is *this* difference which accounts for any variation in our assessments.

1. Smith stands to gain a large inheritance if anything should happen to his six-year-old cousin. One evening while the child is taking his bath, Smith sneaks into the bathroom and drowns the child, and then arranges things so that it will look like an accident.

2. Jones also stands to gain if anything should happen to his six-year-old cousin. Like Smith, Jones sneaks in planning to drown the child in his bath. However, just as he enters the bathroom Jones sees the child slip, hit his head, and fall face down in the water. Jones is delighted; he stands by, ready to push the child's head back under if it is necessary, but it is not necessary. With only a little thrashing about, the child drowns all by himself, "accidentally," as Jones watches and does nothing.

Now Smith killed the child, while Jones "merely" let the child die. That is the only difference between them. Did either man behave better, from a moral point of view? Is there a moral difference between them? *If the difference between killing and letting die were itself a morally important matter, then we should say that Jones's behavior was less reprehensible than Smith's.* But do we actually want to say that? I think not, for several reasons. In the first place, both men acted from the same motive, personal gain, and both had exactly the same end in view when they acted. We may infer from Smith's conduct that he is a bad man, although we may withdraw or modify that judgment if we learn certain further facts about him; for example, that he is mentally deranged. But would we not also infer the very same thing about Jones from his conduct? And would not the same further considerations also be relevant to any modification of

that judgment? Moreover, suppose Jones pleaded in his defense, "After all, I didn't kill the child. I only stood there and let him die." Again, if letting die were in itself less bad than killing, this defense should have some weight. But—morally, at least—it does not. Such a "defense" can only be regarded as a grotesque perversion of moral reasoning.

Thus, it seems that when we are careful not to smuggle in any further differences which prejudice the issue, the mere difference between killing and letting die does not itself make any difference to the morality of actions concerning life and death.[8]

Now it may be pointed out, quite properly, that the cases of euthanasia with which doctors are concerned are not like this at all. They do not involve personal gain or the destruction of normal, healthy children. Doctors are concerned only with cases in which the patient's life is of no further use to him, or in which the patient's life has become or soon will become a positive burden. However, the point is the same in those cases: The difference between killing or letting die does not, *in itself,* make a difference, from the point of view of morality. If a doctor lets a patient die, for humane reasons, he is in the same moral position as if he had given the patient a lethal injection for humane reasons. If his decision was wrong—if, for example, the patient's illness was in fact curable—then the decision would be equally regrettable no matter which method was used to carry it out. And if the doctor's decision was the right one, then the method he used is not itself important.

The AMA statement isolates the crucial issue very well: "the intentional termination of the life of one human being by another." But then the statement goes on to deny that the cessation of treatment *is* the intentional termination of a life. This is where the mistake comes in, for what is the cessation of treatment, in those circumstances, if it is not "the intentional termination of the life of one human being by another"? Of course it is exactly that; if it were not, there would be no point to it.

COUNTERARGUMENTS

Our argument has now brought us to this point: We cannot draw any moral distinction between active and passive euthanasia on the grounds that one involves killing while the other only involves letting someone die, because that is a difference that does not make a difference, from a moral point of view. Some people will find this hard to accept. One reason, I think, is that they fail to distinguish the question of whether killing is, in itself, worse than letting die, from the very different question of whether most actual cases of killing are more reprehensible than most actual cases of letting die. Most actual cases of killing are clearly terrible—think of the murders reported in the newspapers—and we hear of such cases almost every day. On the other hand, we hardly ever hear of a case of letting die, except for the actions of doctors who are motivated by humanitarian reasons. So we learn to think of killing in a much worse light than letting die; and we conclude, invalidly that there must be something about killing which makes it *in itself* worse than letting die. But this does not follow for it is not the bare difference between killing and letting die that makes the difference in these cases. Rather, it is the other factors—the murderer's motive of personal gain, for example, contrasted with the doctor's humanitarian motivation, or the fact that the murderer kills a healthy person while the doctor lets die a terminal patient racked with disease—that account for our different reactions to the different cases.

There are, however, some substantial arguments that may be advanced to oppose my conclusion. Here are two of them:

The first counterargument focuses specifically on the concept of *being the cause of someone's death*. If we kill someone, then we are the cause of his death. But if we merely let someone die, we are not the cause; rather, he dies of whatever condition he already has. The doctor who gives the cancer patient a lethal injection will have caused his patient's death, and will have this on his conscience; whereas if he merely ceases treatment, the cancer and not the doctor is the cause of death. This is

supposed to make a moral difference. This argument has been advanced many times. Ramsey, for example, urges us to remember that "In omission no human agent causes the patient's death, directly or indirectly."[9] And, writing in the *Vittanova Law Review* for 1968, Dr. J. Russell Elkinton said that what makes the active/passive distinction important is that in passive euthanasia, "the patient does not die from the act [e.g., the act of turning off the respirator] but from the underlying disease or injury."[10]

This argument will not do, for two reasons. First, just as there is a distinction to be drawn between being and not being the cause of someone's death, there is also a distinction to be drawn between letting someone die and not letting anyone die. It is certainly desirable, in general, not to be the cause of anyone's death; but it is also desirable, in general, not to let anyone die when we can save them. (Doctors act on this precept every day.) Therefore, we cannot draw any special conclusion about the relative desirability of passive euthanasia just on these grounds. Second, the reason we think it is bad to be the cause of someone's death is that we think that death is a great evil—and so it is. However, if we have decided that euthanasia, even passive euthanasia, is desirable in a given case, then we have decided that in *this* instance death is no greater an evil than the patient's continued existence. And if this is true, then the usual reason for not wanting to be the cause of someone's death simply does not apply. To put the point just a bit differently: There is nothing wrong with being the cause of someone's death if his death is, all things considered, a good thing. And if his death is *not* a good thing, then *no* form of euthanasia, active or passive, is justified. So once again we see that the two kinds of euthanasia stand or fall together.

The second counterargument appeals to a favorite idea of philosophers, namely that our duty not to harm people is generally more stringent than our duty to help them. The law affirms this when it forbids us to kill people, or steal their goods, but does not require us in general to save people's lives or give them charity. And this is said to be not merely a point about the law, but about morality as well. We do not have a strict moral duty to help some poor man in Ethiopia—although it might be kind and generous of us if we did—but we *do* have a strict moral duty to refrain from doing anything to harm him. Killing someone is a violation of our duty not to harm, whereas letting someone die is merely a failure to give help. Therefore, the former is a more serious breach of morality than the latter; and so, contrary to what was said above, there is a morally significant difference between killing and letting die.

This argument has a certain superficial plausibility, but it cannot be used to show that there is a morally important difference between active and passive euthanasia. For one thing, it only seems that our duty to help people is less stringent than our duty not to harm them when we concentrate on certain sorts of cases: cases in which the people we could help are very far away, and are strangers to us; or cases in which it would be very difficult for us to help them, or in which helping would require a substantial sacrifice on our part. Many people feel that, in *these* types of cases, it may be kind and generous of us to give help, but we are not morally required to do so. Thus it is felt that when we give money for famine relief we are being especially bighearted, and we deserve special praise—even if it would be immodest of us to seek such praise—because we are doing more than, strictly speaking, we are required to do.[11]

However, if we think of cases in which it would be very easy for us to help someone who is close at hand and in which no great personal sacrifice is required, things look very different. Think again of the child drowning in the bathtub: *Of course* a man standing next to the tub would have a strict moral duty to help the child. Here the alleged asymmetry between the duty to help and the duty not to do harm vanishes. Since most of the cases of euthanasia with which we are concerned are of this latter type—the patient is close at hand, it is well within the professional skills of the physician to keep him alive—the alleged asymmetry has little relevance.

It should also be remembered, in considering this argument, that the duty of doctors toward their patients *is* precisely to help them; that is

what doctors are supposed to do. Therefore, even if there were a general asymmetry between the duty to help and the duty not to harm—which I deny—it would not apply in the special case of the relation between doctors and their patients. Finally, it is not clear that killing such a patient *is* harming him, even though in other cases it certainly is a great harm to someone to kill him, for as I said before, we are going under the assumption that the patient would be no worse off dead than he is now; if this is so, then killing him is not harming him. For the same reason we should not classify letting such a patient die as failing to help him. Therefore, even if we grant that our duty to help people is less stringent than our duty not to harm them, nothing follows about our duties with respect to killing and letting die in the special case of euthanasia.

PRACTICAL CONSEQUENCES

This is enough, I think, to show that the doctrine underlying the AMA statement is false. There is no general moral difference between active and passive euthanasia; if one is permissible, so is the other. Now if this were merely an intellectual mistake, having no significant consequences for medical practice, the whole matter would not be very important. But the opposite is true: The doctrine has terrible consequences for, as I have already mentioned—and as doctors know very well—the process of being "allowed to die" can be relatively slow and painful, while being given a lethal injection is relatively quick and painless. Dr. Anthony Shaw describes what happens when the decision has been made not to perform the surgery necessary to "save" a Down's syndrome infant:

> When surgery is denied [the doctor] must try to keep the infant from suffering while natural forces sap the baby's life away. As a surgeon whose natural inclination is to use the scalpel to fight off death, standing by and watching a salvageable baby die is the most emotionally exhausting experience I know. It is easy at a conference, in a

theoretical discussion, to decide that such infants should be allowed to die. It is altogether different to stand by in the nursery and watch as dehydration and infection wither a tiny being over hours and days. This is a terrible ordeal for me and the hospital staff—much more so than for the parents who never set foot in the nursery.[12]

Why must the hospital staff "stand by in the nursery and watch as dehydration and infection wither a tiny being over hours and days"? Why must they merely "try" to reduce the infant's suffering? The doctrine that says the baby may be allowed to dehydrate and wither but not be given an injection that would end its life without suffering is not only irrational but cruel.

The same goes for the case of the man with cancer of the throat. Here there are three options: With continued treatment, he will have a few more days of pain, and then die; if treatment is stopped, but nothing else is done, it will be a few more hours; and with a lethal injection, he will die at once. Those who oppose euthanasia in all its forms say that we must take the first option, and keep the patient alive for as long as possible. This view is so patently inhumane that few defend it; nevertheless, it does have a certain kind of integrity. It is at least consistent. The third option is the one I think best. But the *middle* position—that, although the patient need not suffer for days before dying, he must nevertheless suffer for a few more hours—is a "moderate" view which incorporates the worst, and not the best, features of both extremes.

Let me mention one other practice that we would be well rid of if we stopped thinking that the distinction between active and passive euthanasia is important. About one in six hundred babies born in the United States is mongoloid. Most of these babies are otherwise healthy—that is, with only the usual pediatric care, they will proceed to a "normal" infancy. Some however, are born with other congenital defects such as intestinal obstructions which require surgery if the baby is to live. As I have already mentioned, sometimes the surgery is withheld and the baby dies. But when there is no

defect requiring surgery, the baby lives on.[13] Now surgery to remove an intestinal obstruction is not difficult; the reason it is not performed in such cases is, clearly, that the child [has Down's syndrome] and the parents and doctor judge that because of *this* it is better for the child to die.

But notice that this situation is absurd, no matter what view one takes of the lives and potentials of such babies. If you think that the life of such an infant is worth preserving, then what does it matter if it needs a simple operation? Or, if you think it better that such a baby not live on, then what difference does it make if its intestinal tract is *not* blocked? In either case, the matter of life or death is being decided on irrelevant grounds. It is the mongolism, and not the intestine, that is the issue. The matter should be decided, if at all, on *that* basis, and not be allowed to depend on the essentially irrelevant question of whether the intestinal tract is blocked.

What makes this situation possible, of course, is the idea that when there is an intestinal obstruction we can "let the baby die," but when there is no such defect there is nothing we can do, for we must not "kill" it. The fact that this idea leads to such results as deciding life or death on irrelevant grounds is another good reason it should be rejected.

Doctors may think that all of this is only of academic interest, the sort of thing which philosophers may worry about but which has no practical bearing on their own work. After all, doctors must be concerned about the legal consequences of what they do, and active euthanasia is clearly forbidden by the law. They are right to be concerned about this. There have not been many prosecutions of doctors in the United States for active euthanasia, but there have been some. Prosecutions for passive euthanasia, on the other hand, are virtually nonexistent, even though there are laws under which charges could be brought, and even though this practice is much more widespread. Passive euthanasia, unlike active euthanasia, is by and large tolerated by the law. The law may sometimes compel a doctor to take action which he might not otherwise take to keep a patient alive,[14] but of course this is very different from bringing criminal charges against him after the patient is dead.

Even so, doctors should be concerned with the fact that the law and public opinion are forcing upon them an indefensible moral position, which has a considerable effect on their practices. Of course, most doctors are not now in the position of being coerced in this matter, for they do not regard themselves as merely going along with what the law requires. Rather, in statements such as the AMA statement that I quoted, they are endorsing the doctrine as a central point of medical ethics. In that statement, active euthanasia is condemned not merely as illegal but as "contrary to that for which the medical profession stands," while passive euthanasia is approved. However, if my arguments have been sound, there really is no intrinsic moral difference between them (although there may be morally important differences in their consequences, varying from case to case); so while doctors may have to discriminate between them to satisfy the law, they should not do any *more* than that. In particular, they should not give the distinction any added authority and weight by writing it into official statements of medical ethics.

ENDNOTES

1. F. J. Ingelfinger, "Bedside Ethics for the Hopeless Case," *New England Journal of Medicine 289* (25 October 1973), p. 914.

2. Ibid.

3. This statement was approved by the House of Delegates of the AMA on December 4, 1973. It is worth noting that some state medical societies have advised *patients* to take a similar attitude toward the termination of their lives. In 1973 the Connecticut State Medical Society approved a "background statement" to be signed by terminal patients which includes this sentence: "I value life and the dignity of life, so that I am not asking that my life be directly taken, but that my life not be unreasonably prolonged or the dignity of life be destroyed." Other state medical societies have followed suit.

4. A discussion of this type of case can be found in Anthony Shaw, "'Doctor, Do We Have a Choice?'" *The New York Times Magazine,* 30 January 1972, pp. 44–54. Also see Shaw's "Dilemmas of 'Informed Consent' in Children." *New England Journal of Medicine 289* (25 October 1973), pp. 885–990.

5. Paul Ramsey, *The Patient as Person* (New Haven, Conn.: Yale University Press, 1970), pp. 115–116.

6. D. C. S. Cameron, *The Truth About Cancer* (Englewood Cliffs, N.J.: Prentice-Hall, 1956), p. 116.

7. Ramsey, *The Patient as Person,* p. 151.

8. Judith Jarvis Thomson has argued that this line of reasoning is unsound. Consider, she says, this argument which is parallel to the one involving Smith and Jones:

Alfrieda knows that if she cuts off Alfred's head he will die, and wanting him to die, cuts it off; Bertha knows that if she punches Bert in the nose he will die—Bert is in peculiar physical condition—and, wanting him to die, punches him in the nose. But what Bertha does is surely every bit as bad as what Alfrieda does. So cutting off a man's head isn't worse than punching a man in the nose. ("Killing, Letting Die, and the Trolley Problem," *The Monist 59* [1976], p. 204.)

She concludes that, since this absurd argument doesn't prove anything, the Smith/Jones argument doesn't prove anything either. However, I think that the Alfrieda/Bertha argument is not absurd, as strange as it is. A little analysis shows that it is a sound argument and that its conclusion is true. We need to notice first that the reason it is wrong to chop someone's head off is, obviously, that this causes death. The act is objectionable because of its consequences. Thus, a different act with the same consequences may be equally objectionable. In Thomson's example, punching Bert in the nose has the same consequences as chopping off Alfred's head; and indeed, the two actions are equally bad.

Now the Alfrieda/Bertha argument presupposes a distinction between the act of chopping off someone's head, and the results of this act, the victim's death. (It is stipulated that, except for the fact that Alfrieda chops off someone's head, while Bertha punches someone in the nose, the two acts are "in all other respects alike." The "*other* respects" include the act's consequence, the victim's death.) This is not a distinction we would normally think to make, since we cannot in fact cut off someone's head without killing him. Yet in thought the distinction can be drawn. The question raised in the argument, then, is whether, *considered apart from their consequences,* head-chopping is worse than nose-punching. And the answer to *this* strange question is No, just as the argument says it should be.

The conclusion of the argument should be construed like this: The bare fact that one act is an act of head-chopping, while another act is an act of nose-punching, is not a reason for judging the former to be worse than the latter. At the same time—and this is perfectly compatible with the argument—the fact that one act causes death, while another does not, is a reason for judging the former to be worse. The parallel construal of my conclusion is: The bare fact that one act is an act of killing, while another act is an act of letting die, is not a reason for judging the former to be worse than the latter. At the same time—and this is perfectly compatible with my argument—the fact that an act (of killing, for example) prevents suffering, while another act (of letting die, for example) does not, is a reason for preferring one over the other. So once we see exactly how the Alfrieda/ Bertha argument is parallel to the Smith/Jones argument, we find that Thomson's argument is, surprisingly, quite all right.

9. Ramsey, *The Patient as Person*, p. 151.

10. J. Russell Elkinton, "The Dying Patient, the Doctor, and the Law," *Villanova Law Review 13* (Summer 1968), p. 743.

11. For the purposes of this essay we do not need to consider whether this way of thinking about "charity" is justified. There are, however, strong arguments that it is morally indefensible: see Peter Singer, "Famine, Affluence, and Morality," *Philosophy and Public Affairs 1* (Spring 1972), pp. 229–243. Also see James Rachels, "Killing and Letting People Die of Starvation," *Philosophy 54* (1979), pp. 159–171, for a discussion of the killing/letting die distinction in the context of world hunger, as well as further arguments that the distinction is morally unimportant.

12. Shaw, "'Doctor, Do We Have a Choice?'" p. 54.

13. See the articles by Shaw cited in note 4.

14. For example, in February 1974 a Superior Court judge in Maine ordered a doctor to proceed with an operation to repair a hole in the esophagus of a baby with multiple deformities. Otherwise the operation would not have been performed. The baby died anyway a few days later. "Deformed Baby Dies Amid Controversy," *Miami Herald*, 25 February 1974, p. 4-B.

19

The Intentional Termination of Life

BONNIE STEINBOCK

Bonnie Steinbock defends the policy statement of the American Medical Association on euthanasia against James Rachels's critique. She argues that the statement does not rest on the belief that there is a moral difference between active and passive euthanasia. Rather, she contends that the statement rejects both active and passive euthanasia but permits "the cessation of the employment of extraordinary means," which she claims is not the same as passive euthanasia. She points out that doctors can cease to employ extraordinary means to respect the wishes of the patient or because continued treatment is painful and has little chance of success, without intending to let the patient die. She allows, however, that in some cases, ceasing to employ extraordinary means does amount to intending to let the patient die and also that in other cases, killing may even be morally preferable to letting die.

According to James Rachels[1] a common mistake in medical ethics is the belief that there is a moral difference between active and passive euthanasia. This is a mistake, [he] argues, because the rationale underlying the distinction between active and passive euthanasia is the idea that there is a significant moral difference between intentionally killing and letting die.... Whether the belief that there is a significant moral difference (between intentionally killing and intentionally letting die) is mistaken is not my concern here. For it is far from clear that this distinction is the basis of the doctrine of the American Medical Association which Rachels attacks. And if the killing/letting die distinction is not the basis of the AMA doctrine, then arguments showing that the distinction has no moral force do not, in themselves, reveal in the doctrine's adherents either "confused thinking" or "a moral point of view unrelated to the interests of individuals." Indeed, as we examine the AMA doctrine, I think it will become clear that it appeals to and makes use of a number of overlapping distinctions, which may have moral significance in particular cases, such as the distinction between intending and foreseeing, or between ordinary and extraordinary care. Let us then turn to the statement, from the House of Delegates of the AMA, which Rachels cites:

> The intentional termination of the life of one human being by another—mercy-killing—is contrary to that for which the medical profession stands and is contrary to the policy of the AMA.
>
> The cessation of the employment of extraordinary means to prolong the life of the body when there is irrefutable evidence that biological death is imminent is the decision of the patient and/or his immediate family. The advice and judgment of the physician should be freely available to the patient and/or his immediate family.[2]

Rachels attacks this statement because he believes that it contains a moral distinction between active and passive euthanasia...

I intend to show that the AMA statement does not imply support of the active/passive euthanasia distinction. In forbidding the intentional termination of life, the statement rejects both active and passive euthanasia. It does allow for "... the cessation of the employment of extraordinary means ..." to prolong life. The mistake Rachels makes is in identifying the cessation of life-prolonging treatment with passive euthanasia, or intentionally letting die. If it were right to equate the two, then the AMA statement would be self-contradictory for it would begin by condemning, and end by allowing, the intentional termination of life. But if the cessation of life-prolonging treatment is not always or necessarily passive euthanasia, then there is no confusion and no contradiction.

Why does Rachels think that the cessation of life-prolonging treatment is the intentional termination of life? He says:

> The AMA policy statement isolates the crucial issue very well: The crucial issue is "the intentional termination of the life of one human being by another." But after identifying this issue, and forbidding "mercy-killing," the statement goes on to deny that the cessation of treatment is the intentional termination of a life. This is where the mistake comes in, for what is the cessation of treatment, in these circumstances, if it is not "the intentional termination of the life of one human being by another"? Of course it is exactly that, and if it were not, there would be no point to it.[3]

However, there *can* be a point (to the cessation of life-prolonging treatment) other than an endeavor to bring about the patient's death, and so the blanket identification of cessation of treatment with the intentional termination of a life is inaccurate. There are at least two situations in which the termination of life-prolonging treatment cannot be identified with the intentional termination of the life of one human being by another.

The first situation concerns the patient's right to refuse treatment. Rachels gives the example of a patient dying of an incurable disease, accompanied by unrelievable pain, who wants to end the treatment which cannot cure him but can only prolong his miserable existence. Why, they ask, may a doctor accede to the patient's request to stop treatment, but not provide a patient in a similar situation with a lethal dose? The answer lies in the patient's right to refuse treatment. In general, a competent adult has the right to refuse treatment, even where such treatment is necessary to prolong life. Indeed, the right to refuse treatment has been upheld even when the patient's reason for refusing treatment is generally agreed to be inadequate.[4] This right can be overridden (if, for example, the patient has dependent children) but, in general, no one may legally compel you to undergo treatment to which you have not consented, "Historically, surgical intrusion has always been considered a technical battery upon the person and one to be excused or justified by consent of the patient or justified by necessity created by the circumstances of the moment...."[5]

At this point, it might be objected that if one has the right to refuse life-prolonging treatment, then consistency demands that one have the right to decide to end his life, and to obtain help in doing so. The idea is that the right to refuse treatment somehow implies a right to voluntary euthanasia, and we need to see why someone might think this. The right to refuse treatment has been considered by legal writers as an example of the right to privacy or, better, the right to bodily self-determination. You have the right to decide what happens to your own body, and the right to refuse treatment is an instance of that more general right. But if you have the right to determine what happens to your body, then should you not have the right to choose to end your life, and even a right to get help in doing so?

However, it is important to see that the right to refuse treatment is not the same as, nor does it entail, a right to voluntary euthanasia, even if both can be derived from the right to bodily self-determination. The right to refuse treatment is not itself a "right to die"; that one may choose to exercise this right even at the risk of death, or even *in order to die,* is irrelevant. The purpose of the right to refuse medical treatment is not to give persons a right to decide whether to live or die, but to protect them from the unwanted interferences of others. Perhaps we ought to interpret the right to bodily self-determination more broadly so as to include a right to die: But this would be a substantial extension of our present understanding of the right to bodily self-determination, and not a consequence of it. Should we recognize a right to voluntary euthanasia, we would have to agree that people have the right not merely to be left alone, but also the right to be killed. I leave to one side that substantive moral issue. My claim is simply that there can be a reason for terminating life-prolonging treatment other than "to bring about the patient's death."

The second case in which termination of treatment cannot be identified with intentional, termination of life is where continued treatment has little chance of improving the patient's condition and brings greater discomfort than relief.

The question here is what treatment is appropriate to the particular case. A cancer specialist describes it in this way:

> My general rule is to administer therapy as long as a patient responds well and has the potential for a reasonably good quality of life. But when all feasible therapies have been administered and a patient shows signs of rapid deterioration, the continuation of therapy can cause more discomfort than the cancer. From that time I recommend surgery, radiotherapy, or chemotherapy only as a means of relieving pain. But if a patient's condition should once again stabilize after the withdrawal of active therapy and if it should appear that he could still gain some good time, I would immediately reinstitute active therapy. The decision to cease anticancer treatment is never irrevocable, and often the desire to live will push a patient to try for another remission, or even a few more days of life.[6]

The decision here to cease anticancer treatment cannot be construed as a decision that the patient die, or as the intentional termination of life. It is a decision to provide the most appropriate treatment for that patient at that time. Rachels suggests that the point of the cessation of treatment is the intentional termination of life. But here the point of discontinuing treatment is not to bring about the patient's death but to avoid treatment that will cause more discomfort than the cancer and has little hope of benefiting the patient. Treatment that meets this description is often called "extraordinary."[7] The concept is flexible, and what might be considered "extraordinary" in one situation might be ordinary in another. The use of a respirator to sustain a patient through a severe bout with a respiratory disease would be considered ordinary; its use to sustain the life of a severely brain-damaged person in an irreversible coma would be considered extraordinary.

Contrasted with extraordinary treatment is ordinary treatment, the care a doctor would normally be expected to provide. Failure to provide ordinary care constitutes neglect, and can even be construed as the intentional infliction of harm, where there is a legal obligation to provide care. The importance of the ordinary/extraordinary care distinction lies partly in its connection to the doctor's intention. The withholding of extraordinary care should be seen as a decision not to inflict painful treatment on a patient without reasonable hope of success. The withholding of ordinary care, by contrast, must be seen as neglect. Thus, one doctor says, "We have to draw a distinction between ordinary and extraordinary means. We never withdraw what's needed to make a baby comfortable, we would never withdraw the care a parent would provide. We never kill a baby.... But we may decide certain heroic intervention is not worthwhile."[8]

We should keep in mind the ordinary/extraordinary care distinction when considering an example given by Rachels to show the irrationality of the active/passive distinction with regard to infanticide. The example is this: A child is born with Down's syndrome and also has an intestinal obstruction which requires corrective surgery. If the surgery is not performed, the infant will starve to death, since it cannot take food orally. This may take days or even weeks, as dehydration and infection set in. Commenting on this situation, Rachels says:

> I can understand why some people are opposed to all euthanasia, and insist that such infants must be allowed to live.
> I think I can also understand why other people favor destroying these babies quickly and painlessly. But why should anyone favor letting "dehydration and infection wither a tiny being over hours and days"? The doctrine that says that a baby may be allowed to dehydrate and wither, but may not be given an injection that would end its life without suffering, seems so patently cruel as to require no further refutation.[9]

Such a doctrine perhaps does not need further refutation; but this is not the AMA doctrine. For the AMA statement criticized by Rachels allows only for the cessation of extraordinary means to prolong life when death is imminent. Neither of these conditions is satisfied in this example. Death is not imminent in this situation, any more than it would be if a normal child had an attack of appendicitis. Neither the corrective surgery to remove the intestinal obstruction, nor the intravenous feeding required to keep the infant alive until such surgery is performed, can be regarded as extraordinary means, for neither is particularly expensive, nor does either place an overwhelming burden on the patient or others. (The continued existence of the child might be thought to place an overwhelming burden on its parents, but that has nothing to do with the characterization of the means to prolong its life as extraordinary. If it had, then *feeding* a severely defective child who required a great deal of care could be regarded as extraordinary.) The chances of success if the operation is undertaken are quite good, though there is always a risk in operating on infants. Though the Down's syndrome will not be alleviated, the child will proceed to an otherwise normal infancy.

It cannot be argued that the treatment is withheld for the infant's sake, unless one is prepared to argue that all mentally retarded babies are better off dead. This is particularly implausible in the case of

Down's syndrome babies who generally do not suffer and are capable of giving and receiving love, of learning and playing, to varying degrees.

In a film on this subject entitled, "Who Should Survive?," a doctor defended a decision not to operate, saying that since the parents did not consent to the operation, the doctor's hands were tied. As we have seen, surgical intrusion requires consent, and in the case of infants, consent would normally come from the parents. But, as their legal guardians, parents are required to provide medical care for their children, and failure to do so can constitute criminal neglect or even homicide. In general, courts have been understandably reluctant to recognize a parental right to terminate life-prolonging treatment.[10] Although prosecution is unlikely, physicians who comply with invalid instructions from the parents and permit the infant's death could be liable for aiding and abetting, failure to report child neglect, or even homicide. So it is not true that, in this situation, doctors are legally bound to do as the parents wish.

To sum up, I think that Rachels is right to regard the decision not to operate in the Down's syndrome example as the intentional termination of life. But there is no reason to believe that either the law or the AMA would regard it otherwise. Certainly the decision to withhold treatment is not justified by the AMA statement. That such infants have been allowed to die cannot be denied; but this, I think, is the result of doctors misunderstanding the law and the AMA position.

Withholding treatment in this case is the intentional termination of life because the infant is deliberately allowed to die; that is the point of not operating. But there are other cases in which that is not the point. If the point is to avoid inflicting painful treatment on a patient with little or no reasonable hope of success, this is not the intentional termination of life. The permissibility of such withholding of treatment, then, would have no implications for the permissibility of euthanasia, active or passive.

The decision whether or not to operate, or to institute vigorous treatment, is particularly agonizing in the case of children born with spina bifida, an opening in the base of the spine usually accompanied by hydrocephalus and mental retardation. If left unoperated, these children usually die of meningitis or kidney failure within the first few years of life. Even if they survive, all affected children face a lifetime of illness, operations, and varying degrees of disability. The policy used to be to save as many as possible, but the trend now is toward selective treatment, based on the physician's estimate of the chances of success. If operating is not likely to improve significantly the child's condition, parents and doctors may agree not to operate. This is not the intentional termination of life, for again the purpose is not the termination of the child's life but the avoidance of painful and pointless treatment. Thus, the fact that withholding treatment is justified does not imply that killing the child would be equally justified.

Throughout the discussion, I have claimed that intentionally ceasing life-prolonging treatment is not the intentional termination of life unless the doctor has, as his or her purpose in stopping treatment, the patient's death.

It may be objected that I have incorrectly characterized the conditions for the intentional termination of life. Perhaps it is enough that the doctor intentionally ceases treatment, foreseeing that the patient will die; perhaps the reason for ceasing treatment is irrelevant to its characterization as the intentional termination of life. I find this suggestion implausible, but am willing to consider arguments for it. Rachels has provided no such arguments: Indeed, he apparently shares my view about the intentional termination of life. For when he claims that the cessation of life-prolonging treatment *is* the intentional termination of life, his reason for making the claim is that "if it were not, there would be no point to it," Rachels believes that the point of ceasing treatment, "in these cases," is to bring about the patient's death. If that were not the point, he suggests, why would the doctor cease treatment? I have shown, however, that there can be a point to ceasing treatment which is not the death of the patient. In showing this, I have refuted Rachels's reason for identifying the cessation of life-prolonging treatment with the intentional termination of life, and thus his argument against the AMA doctrine.

Here someone might say: Even if the withholding of treatment is not the intentional termination of life, does that make a difference, morally speaking? If life-prolonging treatment may be withheld, for the sake of the child, may not an easy death be provided, for the sake of the child, as well? The unoperated child with spina bifida may take months or even years to die. Distressed by the spectacle of children "lying around waiting to die," one doctor has written, "It is time that society and medicine stopped perpetuating the fiction that withholding treatment is ethically different from terminating a life. It is time that society began to discuss mechanisms by which we can alleviate the pain and suffering for those individuals whom we cannot help."[11]

I do not deny that there may be cases in which death is in the best interests of the patient. In such cases, a quick and painless death may be the best thing. However, I do not think that, once active or vigorous treatment is stopped, a quick death is always preferable to a lingering one. We must be cautious about attributing to defective children *our* distress at seeing them linger. Waiting for them to die may be tough on parents, doctors, and nurses— it isn't necessarily tough on the child. The decision not to operate need not mean a decision to neglect, and it may be possible to make the remaining months of the child's life comfortable, pleasant, and filled with love. If this alternative is possible, surely it is more decent and humane than killing the child. In such a situation, withholding treatment, foreseeing the child's death, is not ethically equivalent to killing the child, and we cannot move from the permissibility of the former to that of the latter. I am worried that there will be a tendency to do precisely that if active euthanasia is regarded as morally equivalent to the withholding of life-prolonging treatment.

CONCLUSION

The AMA statement does not make the distinction Rachels wishes to attack, i.e., that between active and passive euthanasia. Instead, the statement draws a distinction between the intentional termination of life, on the one hand, and the cessation of the employment of extraordinary means to prolong life, on the other. Nothing said by Rachels shows that this distinction is confused. It may be that doctors have misinterpreted the AMA statement, and that this has led, for example, to decisions to allow defective infants slowly to starve to death. I quite agree with Rachels that the decisions to which they allude were cruel and made on irrelevant grounds. Certainly it is worth pointing out that allowing someone to die can be the intentional termination of life, and that it can be just as bad as, or worse than, killing someone. However, the withholding of life-prolonging treatment is not necessarily the intentional termination of life, so that if it is permissible to withhold life-prolonging treatment, it does not follow that, other things being equal, it is permissible to kill. Furthermore, most of the time, other things are not equal. In many of the cases in which it would be right to cease treatment, I do not think that it would also be right to kill.

ENDNOTES

1. James Rachels, "Active and passive euthanasia." *New England Journal of Medicine, 292,* pp. 78–80, 1975.

2. Rachels, p. 78.

3. Rachels, pp. 79–80.

4. For example, *In re Yetter,* 62 Pa. D. & C. 2d 619, C.P., Northampton County Ct., 1974.

5. David W. Meyers. "Legal aspects of voluntary euthanasia." In *Dilemmas of Euthanasia* (edited by John Behnke and Sissela Bok), p. 56. Anchor Books, New York, 1975.

6. Ernest H. Rosenbaum. *Living with Cancer,* p. 27. Praeger, New York, 1975.

7. Cf. Tristam Engelhardt, Jr. "Ethical issues in aiding the death of young children." In *Beneficent Euthanasia* (edited by Marvin Kohl), Prometheus Books, Buffalo, N.Y, 1975.

8. B. D. Colen, *Karen Ann Ouinlan: Living and Vying in the Age of Eternal Life,* p. 115. Nash, 1976.

9. Rachels, p. 79.

10. Cf. Norman Cantor. "Law and the termination of an incompetent patient's life-preserving care." *Dilemmas of Euthanasia,* op. cit., pp. 69–105.

11. John Freeman, "Is there a right to die—quickly?" *Journal of Pediatrics 80,* p. 905.

20

Planned Parenthood v. Casey

Supreme Court of the United States

The issue before the Supreme Court was whether the Pennsylvania Abortion Control Act as amended in 1988 and 1989 violated the due process clause of the U.S. Constitution by requiring informed consent, a twenty-four-hour waiting period, parental consent in the case of a minor, spousal notification, and certain reporting and record keeping by facilities that provide abortion services. While reaffirming its commitment to the essential holding of Roe v. Wade, the Court allowed that the state had a legitimate interest in imposing all of the above requirements except spousal notification.

Justices *O'Connor, Kennedy,* and *Souter* announcing the judgment of the Court in which Justices *Blackmun* and *Stevens* concurred in part:

Liberty finds no refuge in a jurisprudence of doubt. Yet nineteen years after our holding that the Constitution protects a woman's right to terminate her pregnancy in its early stages, *Roe v. Wade* ... (1973), that definition of liberty, is still questioned ...

At issue in these cases are five provisions of the Pennsylvania Abortion Control Act of 1982 as amended in 1988 and 1989 ... The Act requires that a woman seeking an abortion give her informed consent prior to the abortion procedure, and specifies that she be provided with certain information at least 24 hours before the abortion is performed.... For a minor to obtain an abortion, the Act requires the informed consent of one of her parents, but provides for a judicial bypass option if the minor does not wish to or cannot obtain a parent's consent.... Another provision of the Act requires that, unless certain exceptions apply, a married woman seeking an abortion must sign a statement indicating that she has notified her husband of her intended abortion.... The Act exempts compliance with these three requirements in the event of a "medical emergency"... In addition to the above provisions regulating the performance of abortions, the Act imposes certain reporting requirements on facilities that provide abortion services....

It must be stated at the outset and with clarity that Roe's essential holding, the holding we reaffirm, has three parts. First is a recognition of the right of the woman to choose to have an abortion before viability and to obtain it without undue interference from the State. Before viability, the State's interests are not strong enough to support a prohibition of abortion or the imposition of a substantial obstacle to the woman's effective right to elect the procedure. Second is a confirmation of the State's power to restrict abortions after fetal viability, if the law contains exceptions for pregnancies which endanger a woman's life or health. And third is the principle that the State has legitimate interests from the outset of the pregnancy in protecting the health of the woman and the life of the fetus that may become a child. These principles do not contradict one another; and we adhere to each.

Constitutional protection of the woman's decision to terminate her pregnancy derives from the Due Process Clause of the Fourteenth Amendment. It declares that no State shall "deprive any person of life, liberty, or property, without due process of law." The controlling word in the case before us is "liberty"...

Men and women of good conscience can disagree ... about the profound moral and spiritual implications of terminating a pregnancy, even in its earliest stage. Some of us as individuals find abortion offensive to our most basic principles of morality, but that cannot control our decision. Our obligation is to define the liberty of all, not to mandate our own moral code. The underlying constitutional issue is whether the State can resolve these philosophic questions in such a definitive way that a woman lacks all choice in the matter, except perhaps in those rare circumstances in which the pregnancy is itself a danger to her own life or health, or is the result of rape or incest.

It is conventional constitutional doctrine that where reasonable people disagree, the government can adopt one position or the other.... That theorem, however, assumes a state of affairs in which the choice does not intrude upon a protected liberty. Thus, while some people might disagree about whether or not the flag should be saluted, or disagree about the proposition that it may not be defiled, we have ruled that a State may not compel or enforce one view or the other....

Our law affords constitutional protection to personal decisions relating to marriage, procreation, contraception, family relationships, child rearing, and education.... Our cases recognize "the right of the *individual,* married or single, to be free from unwarranted governmental intrusion into matters so fundamentally affecting a person as the decision whether to bear or beget a child."... Our precedents "have respected the private realm of family life which the state cannot enter."... These matters, involving the most intimate and personal choices a person may make in a lifetime, choices central to personal dignity and autonomy, are central to the liberty protected by the Fourteenth Amendment. At the heart of liberty is the right to define one's own concept of existence, of meaning, of the universe, and of the mystery of human life. Beliefs about these matters could not define the attributes of personhood were they formed under compulsion of the State.

These considerations begin our analysis of the woman's interest in terminating her pregnancy but cannot end it, for this reason: Though the abortion decision may originate within the zone of conscience and belief, it is more than a philosophic exercise. Abortion is a unique act. It is an act fraught with consequences for others: for the woman who must live with the implications of her decision; for the persons who perform and assist in the procedure; for the spouse, family, and society which must confront the knowledge that these procedures exist, procedures some deem nothing short of an act of violence against innocent human life; and, depending on one's beliefs, for the life or potential life that is aborted. Though abortion is conduct, it does not follow that the State is entitled to proscribe it in all instances. That is because the liberty of the woman is at stake in a sense unique to the human condition and so unique to the law. The mother who carries a child to full term is subject to anxieties, to physical constraints, to pain that only she must bear. That these sacrifices have from the beginning of the human race been endured by woman with a pride that ennobles her in the eyes of others and gives to the infant a bond of love cannot alone be grounds for the State to insist she make the sacrifice. Her suffering is too intimate and personal for the State to insist, without more, upon its own vision of the woman's role, however dominant that vision has been in the course of our history and our culture. The destiny of the woman must be shaped to a large extent on her own conception of her spiritual imperatives and her place in society.

It should be recognized, moreover, that in some critical respects the abortion decision is of the same character as the decision to use contraception, to which *Griswold v. Connecticut, Eisenstadt v. Baird,* and *Carey v. Population Services International* afford constitutional protection. We have no doubt as to the correctness of those decisions. They support the reasoning in *Roe* relating to the woman's liberty because they involve personal decisions concerning not only the meaning of procreation but also human responsibility and respect for it. As with abortion, reasonable people will have differences of opinion about these matters. One view is based on such reverence for the wonder of creation that any pregnancy ought to be welcomed and carried to full term no matter how difficult it will be to provide for the child and ensure its well-being. Another is that the inability to provide for the nurture and care of the infant is a cruelty to the child and an anguish to the parent. These are intimate views with infinite variations, and their deep, personal character underlay our decisions in *Griswold, Eisenstadt,* and *Carey.* The same concerns are present when the woman confronts the reality that, perhaps despite her attempts to avoid it, she has become pregnant.

It was this dimension of personal liberty that *Roe* sought to protect, and its holding invoked the reasoning and the tradition of the precedents we have discussed, granting protection to substantive liberties of the person. *Roe* was, of course, an extension of those cases and, as the decision itself indicated, the separate States could act in some degree to further their own legitimate interests in protecting pre-natal life. The extent to which the legislatures of the States might act to outweigh the interests of the woman in choosing to terminate her pregnancy was a subject of debate both in *Roe* itself and in decisions following it.

While we appreciate the weight of the arguments made on behalf of the State in the case before us, arguments which in their ultimate formulation conclude that *Roe* should be overruled, the reservations any of us may have in reaffirming the central holding of *Roe* are outweighed by the explication of individual liberty we have given combined with the force of *stare decisis.* We turn now to that doctrine.

The obligation to follow precedent begins with necessity, and a contrary necessity marks its outer limit. With Cardozo, we recognize that no judicial system could do society's work if it eyed each issue afresh in every case that raised it…. Indeed, the very concept of the rule of law underlying our own Constitution requires such a continuity over time that a respect for precedent is, by definition, indispensable…. At the other extreme, a different necessity would make itself felt if a prior judicial ruling should come to be seen so clearly as error that its enforcement was for that very reason doomed….

So in this case we may inquire whether *Roe*'s central … rule's limitation on state power could be removed without serious inequity to those who have relied upon it or significant damage to the stability of the society governed by the rule in question….

Abortion is customarily chosen as an unplanned response to the consequence of unplanned activity or to the failure of conventional birth control, and except on the assumption that no intercourse would have occurred but for *Roe*'s holding, such behavior may appear to justify no reliance claim. Even if reliance could be claimed on that unrealistic assumption, the argument might run, any reliance interest would be *de minimis.* This argument would be premised on the hypothesis that reproductive planning could take virtually immediate account of any sudden restoration of state authority to ban abortions.

To eliminate the issue of reliance that easily, however, one would need to limit cognizable reliance to specific instances of sexual activity. But to do this would be simply to refuse to face the fact that for two decades of economic and social developments, people have organized intimate relationships and made choices that define their views of themselves and their places in society, in reliance on the availability of abortion in the event that contraception should fail. The ability of women to participate equally in the economic and social life of the nation has been facilitated by their ability to control their reproductive lives….

We have seen how time has overtaken some of *Roe*'s factual assumptions: Advances in maternal health care allow for abortions safe to the mother later in pregnancy than was true in 1973…. But these facts go only to the scheme of time limits on the realization of competing interests, and the divergences from the factual premises of 1973 have no bearing on the validity of *Roe*'s central holding, that viability marks the earliest point at which the State's interest in fetal life is constitutionally adequate to justify a legislative ban on nontherapeutic abortions. The soundness or unsoundness of that constitutional judgment in no sense turns on whether viability occurs at approximately 28 weeks, as was usual at the time of *Roe,* at 23 to 24 weeks, as it sometimes does today, or at some moment even slightly earlier in pregnancy, as it may if fetal respiratory capacity can somehow be enhanced in the future. Whenever it may occur, the attainment of viability may continue to serve as the critical fact, just as it has done since *Roe* was decided; which is to say that no change in *Roe*'s factual underpinning has left its central holding obsolete, and none supports an argument for overruling it.

The sum of the precedential inquiry to this point shows *Roe*'s underpinnings unweakened in any way affecting its central holding. While it has engendered disapproval, it has not been unworkable. An entire generation has come of age free to assume *Roe*'s concept of liberty in defining the capacity of women to act in society, and to make reproductive decisions; no erosion of principle going to liberty or personal autonomy has left *Roe*'s central holding a doctrinal remnant; *Roe* portends no developments at odds with other precedent for the analysis of personal liberty; and no changes of fact have rendered viability more or less appropriate as the point at which the balance of interests tips. Within the bounds of normal *stare decisis* analysis, then, and subject to the considerations on which it customarily turns, the stronger argument is for affirming *Roe*'s central holding, with whatever degree of personal reluctance any of us may have, not for overruling it....

From what we have said so far it follows that it is a constitutional liberty of the woman to have some freedom to terminate her pregnancy. We conclude that the basic decision in *Roe* was based on a constitutional analysis which we cannot now repudiate. The woman's liberty is not so unlimited, however, that from the outset the State cannot show its concern for the life of the unborn, and at a later point in fetal development the State's interest in life has sufficient force so that the right of the woman to terminate the pregnancy can be restricted.

That brings us, of course, to the point where much criticism has been directed at *Roe,* a criticism that always inheres when the Court draws a specific rule from what in the Constitution is but a general standard. We conclude, however, that the urgent claims of the woman to retain the ultimate control over her destiny and her body, claims implicit in the meaning of liberty, require us to perform that function. Liberty must not be extinguished for want of a line that is clear. And it falls to us to give some real substance to the woman's liberty to determine whether to carry her pregnancy to full term.

We conclude the line should be drawn at viability, so that before that time the woman has a right to choose to terminate her pregnancy. Any judicial act of line-drawing may seem somewhat arbitrary, but *Roe* was a reasoned statement, elaborated with great care. We have twice reaffirmed it in the face of great opposition.... The woman's right to terminate her pregnancy before viability is the most central principle of *Roe v. Wade.* It is a rule of law and a component of liberty we cannot renounce.

On the other side of the equation is the interest of the State in the protection of potential life. The *Roe* Court recognized the State's "important and legitimate interest in protecting the potentiality of human life."... The weight to be given this state interest, not the strength of the woman's interest, was the difficult question faced in *Roe.* We do not need to say whether each of us, had we been Members of the Court when the valuation of the State interest came before it as an original matter, would have concluded, as the *Roe* Court did, that its weight is insufficient to justify a ban on abortions prior to viability even when it is subject to certain exceptions. The matter is not before us in the first instance, and coming as it does after nearly 20 years of litigation in *Roe*'s wake we are satisfied that the immediate question is not the soundness of *Roe*'s resolution of the issue, but the precedential force that must be accorded to its holding. And we have concluded that the essential holding of *Roe* should be reaffirmed.

Yet it must be remembered that *Roe v. Wade* speaks with clarity in establishing not only the woman's liberty but also the State's "important and legitimate interest in potential life."... That portion of the decision in *Roe* has been given too little acknowledgement and implementation by the Court in its subsequent cases. Those cases decided that any regulation touching upon the abortion decision must survive strict scrutiny, to be sustained only if drawn in narrow terms to further a compelling state interest…. Not all of the cases decided under that formulation can be reconciled with the holding in *Roe* itself that the State has legitimate interests in the health of the woman and in protecting the potential life within her. In resolving this tension, we choose to rely upon *Roe*, as against the later cases.

Roe established a trimester framework to govern abortion regulations. Under this elaborate but rigid construct, almost no regulation at all is permitted during the first trimester of pregnancy; regulations designed to protect the woman's health, but not to further the State's interest in potential life, are permitted during the second trimester; and during the third trimester, when the fetus is viable, prohibitions are permitted provided the life or health of the mother is not at stake…. Most of our cases since *Roe* have involved the application of rules derived from the trimester framework….

The trimester framework no doubt was erected to ensure that the woman's right to choose not become so subordinate to the State's interest in promoting fetal life that her choice exists in theory but not in fact. We do not agree, however, that the trimester approach is necessary to accomplish this objective. A framework of this rigidity was unnecessary and in its later interpretation sometimes contradicted the State's permissible exercise of its powers.

Though the woman has a right to choose to terminate or continue her pregnancy before viability, it does not at all follow that the State is prohibited from taking steps to ensure that this choice is thoughtful and informed. Even in the earliest stages of pregnancy, the State may enact rules and regulations designed to encourage her to know that there are philosophic and social arguments of great weight that can be brought to bear in favor of continuing the pregnancy to full term and that there are procedures and institutions to allow adoption of unwanted children as well as a certain degree of state assistance if the mother chooses to raise the child herself. "'[T]he Constitution does not forbid a State or city, pursuant to democratic processes, from expressing a preference for normal childbirth'"… It follows that States are free to enact laws to provide

a reasonable framework for a woman to make a decision that has such profound and lasting meaning. This, too, we find consistent with *Roe*'s central premises, and indeed the inevitable consequence of our holding that the State has an interest in protecting the life of the unborn.

We reject the trimester framework, which we do not consider to be part of the essential holding of *Roe*…. Measures aimed at ensuring that a woman's choice contemplates the consequences for the fetus do not necessarily interfere with the right recognized in *Roe*, although those measures have been found to be inconsistent with the rigid trimester framework announced in that case. A logical reading of the central holding in *Roe* itself, and a necessary reconciliation of the liberty of the woman and the interest of the State in promoting prenatal life, require, in our view, that we abandon the trimester framework as a rigid prohibition on all previability regulation aimed at the protection of fetal life. The trimester framework suffers from these basic flaws: In its formulation it misconceives the nature of the pregnant woman's interest; and in practice it undervalues the State's interest in potential life, as recognized in *Roe*….

The very notion that the State has a substantial interest in potential life leads to the conclusion that not all regulations must be deemed unwarranted. Not all burdens on the right to decide whether to terminate a pregnancy will be undue. In our view, the undue burden standard is the appropriate means of reconciling the State's interest with the woman's constitutionally protected liberty….

An undue burden exists, and therefore a provision of law is invalid, if its purpose or effect is to place a substantial obstacle in the path of a woman seeking an abortion before the fetus attains viability. … The Court of Appeals applied what it believed to be the undue burden standard and upheld each of the provisions except for the husband notification requirement. We agree generally with this conclusion….

Studies reveal that family violence occurs in two million families in the United States. This figure, however, is a conservative one that substantially understates (because battering is usually not reported until it reaches life-threatening proportions) the actual number of families affected by domestic violence. In fact, researchers estimate that one of every two women will be battered at some time in their life....

In well-functioning marriages, spouses discuss important intimate decisions such as whether to bear a child. But there are millions of women in this country who are the victims of regular physical and psychological abuse at the hands of their husbands. Should these women become pregnant, they may have very good reasons for not wishing to inform their husbands of their decision to obtain an abortion. Many may have justifiable fears of physical abuse, but may be no less fearful of the consequences of reporting prior abuse to the Commonwealth of Pennsylvania. Many may have a reasonable fear that notifying their husbands will provoke further instances of child abuse.... Many may fear devastating forms of psychological abuse from their husbands, including verbal harassment, threats of future violence, the destruction of possessions, physical confinement to the home, the withdrawal of financial support, or the disclosure of the abortion to family and friends.... And many women who are pregnant as a result of sexual assaults by their husbands will be unable to avail themselves of the exception for spousal sexual assault ... because the exception requires that the woman have notified law enforcement authorities within 90 days of the assault, and her husband will be notified of her report once an investigation begins.... If anything in this field is certain, it is that victims of spousal sexual assault are extremely reluctant to report the abuse to the government; hence, a great many spousal rape victims will not be exempt from the notification requirement....

The spousal notification requirement is thus likely to prevent a significant number of women from obtaining an abortion. It does not merely make abortions a little more difficult or expensive to obtain; for many women, it will impose a substantial obstacle. We must not blind ourselves to the fact that the significant number of women who fear for their safety and the safety of their children are likely to be deterred from procuring an abortion as surely as if the Commonwealth had outlawed abortion in all cases....

We recognize that a husband has a "deep and proper concern and interest ... in his wife's pregnancy and in the growth and development of the fetus she is carrying."... With regard to the children he has fathered and raised, the Court has recognized his "cognizable and substantial" interest in their custody.... If this case concerned a State's ability to require the mother to notify the father before taking some action with respect to a living child raised by both, therefore, it would be reasonable to conclude as a general matter that the father's interest in the welfare of the child and the mother's interest are equal.

Before birth, however, the issue takes on a very different cast. It is an inescapable biological fact that state regulation with respect to the child a woman is carrying will have a far greater impact on the mother's liberty than on the father's. The effect of state regulation on a woman's protected liberty is doubly deserving of scrutiny in such a case, as the State has touched not only upon the private sphere of the family but upon the very bodily integrity of the pregnant woman.... The Court has held that "when the wife and the husband disagree on this decision, the view of only one of the two marriage partners can prevail. Inasmuch as it is the woman who physically bears the child and who is the more directly and immediately affected by the pregnancy, as between the two, the balance weighs in her favor."... This conclusion rests upon the basic nature of marriage and the nature of our Constitution: "[T]he marital couple is not an independent entity with a mind and heart of its own, but an association of two individuals each with a separate intellectual and emotional makeup. If the right of privacy means anything, it is the right of the *individual,* married or single, to be free from unwarranted governmental intrusion into matters so fundamentally affecting a person as the decision whether to bear or beget a child."... The Constitution protects individuals, men and women alike, from unjustified state interference, even when that interference is enacted into law for the benefit of their spouses....

The husband's interest in the life of the child his wife is carrying does not permit the State to empower him with this troubling degree of authority over his wife. The contrary view leads to consequences reminiscent of the common law. A husband has no enforceable right to require a wife to advise him before she exercises her personal choices. If a husband's interest in the potential life of the child outweighs a wife's liberty, the State could require a married woman to notify her husband before she uses a postfertilization contraceptive. Perhaps next in line would be a statute requiring pregnant married women to notify their husbands before engaging in conduct causing risks to the fetus. After all, if the husband's interest in the fetus's safety is a sufficient predicate for state regulation, the State could reasonably conclude that pregnant wives should notify their husbands before drinking alcohol or smoking. Perhaps married women should notify their husbands before using contraceptives or before undergoing any type of surgery that may have complications affecting the husband's interest in his wife's reproductive organs. And if a husband's interest justifies notice in any of these cases, one might reasonably argue that it justifies exactly what the *Danforth* Court held it did not justify—a requirement of the husband's consent as well. A State may not give to a man the kind of dominion over his wife that parents exercise over their children....

Our Constitution is a covenant running from the first generation of Americans to us and then to future generations. It is a coherent succession. Each generation must learn anew that the Constitution's written terms embody ideas and aspirations that must survive more ages than one. We accept our responsibility not to retreat from interpreting the full meaning of the covenant in light of all of our precedents. We invoke it once again to define the freedom guaranteed by the Constitution's own promise, the promise of liberty.

21

Assisted Suicide: The Brief of the Amici Curiae

RONALD DWORKIN, THOMAS NAGEL, ROBERT NOZICK, JOHN RAWLS, THOMAS SCANLON, AND JUDITH JARVIS THOMSON

Ronald Dworkin, Thomas Nagel, Robert Nozick, John Rawls, Thomas Scanlon, and Judith Jarvis Thomson argue that there is a fundamental liberty protected by the due process clause of the Fourteenth Amendment that guarantees a right of assisted suicide, under certain conditions, in the same way that a woman's right to have an abortion is protected under certain conditions. They further argue that the risks that would accompany recognizing this right can be minimized through reasonable regulation, the same type of regulation that is now done, for example, in recognizing a patient's right to terminate life-sustaining medical treatment.

Amici are six moral and political philosophers who differ on many issues of public morality and policy. They are united, however, in their conviction that respect for fundamental principles of liberty and justice, as well as for the American constitutional tradition, requires that the decisions of the Courts of Appeals be affirmed.

INTRODUCTION AND
SUMMARY OF ARGUMENT

These cases do not invite or require the Court to make moral, ethical, or religious judgments about how people should approach or confront their death or about when it is ethically appropriate to hasten one's own death or to ask others for help in doing so. On the contrary, they ask the Court to recognize that individuals have a constitutionally protected interest in making those grave judgments for themselves, free from the imposition of any religious or philosophical orthodoxy by court or legislature. States have a constitutionally legitimate interest in protecting individuals from irrational, ill-informed, pressured, or unstable decisions to hasten their own death. To that end, states may regulate and limit the assistance that doctors may give individuals who express a wish to die. But states may not deny people in the position of the patient-plaintiffs in these cases the opportunity to demonstrate, through whatever reasonable procedures the state might institute—even procedures that err on the side of caution—that their decision to die is indeed informed, stable, and fully free. Denying that opportunity to terminally ill patients who are in agonizing pain or otherwise doomed to an existence they regard as intolerable could only be justified on the basis of a religious or ethical conviction about the value or meaning of life itself. Our Constitution forbids government to impose such convictions on its citizens....

Reprinted from an amicus curiae submitted to the United States Supreme Court in the case of *Washington v. Glucksberg.*

ARGUMENT

I. The Liberty Interest Asserted Here Is Protected by the Due Process Clause

The Due Process Clause of the Fourteenth Amendment protects the liberty interest asserted by the patient-plaintiffs here.

Certain decisions are momentous in their impact on the character of a person's life—decisions about religious faith, political and moral allegiance, marriage, procreation, and death, for example. Such deeply personal decisions pose controversial questions about how and why human life has value. In a free society, individuals must be allowed to make those decisions for themselves, out of their own faith, conscience, and convictions. This Court has insisted, in a variety of contexts and circumstances, that this great freedom is among those protected by the Due Process Clause as essential to a community of "ordered liberty." *Palko v. Connecticut,* 302 U.S. 319, 325 (1937). In its recent decision in *Planned Parenthood v. Casey,* 505 U.S. 833,851 (1992), the Court offered a paradigmatic statement of that principle:

> Matters involving the most intimate and
> personal choices a person may make in
> a lifetime, choices central to a person's
> dignity and autonomy, are central to
> the liberty protected by the Fourteenth
> Amendment.

That declaration reflects an idea underlying many of our basic constitutional protections. As the Court explained in *West Virginia State Board of Education v. Barnett....* (1943):

> If there is any fixed star in our constitu-
> tional constellation, it is that no official ...
> can prescribe what shall be orthodox in
> politics, nationalism, religion, or other
> matters of opinion or force citizens to
> confess by word or act their faith therein.

A person's interest in following his own convictions at the end of life is so central a part of the more general right to make "intimate and personal choices" for himself that a failure to protect that particular interest would undermine the general right altogether. Death is, for each of us, among the most significant events of life. As the Chief Justice said in *Cruzan v. Missouri,* 497 U.S. 261, 281 (1990), "[t]he choice between life and death is a deeply personal decision of obvious and overwhelming finality." Most of us see death—whatever we think will follow it—as the final act of life's drama and we want that last act to reflect our own convictions, those we have tried to live by, not the convictions of others forced on us in our most vulnerable moment.

Different people of different religious and ethical beliefs embrace very different convictions about which way of dying confirms and which contradicts the value of their lives. Some fight against death with every weapon their doctors can devise. Others will do nothing to hasten death even if they pray it will come soon. Still others, including the patient-plaintiffs in these cases, want to end their lives when they think that living on, in the only way they can, would disfigure rather than enhance the lives they had created. Some people make the latter choice not just to escape pain. Even if it were possible to eliminate all pain for a dying patient—and frequently that is not possible—that would not end or even much alleviate the anguish some would feel at remaining alive but intubated, helpless, and often sedated near oblivion.

None of these dramatically different attitudes about the meaning of death can be dismissed as irrational. None should be imposed, either by the pressure of doctors or relatives or by the fiat of government, on people who reject it. Just as it would be intolerable for government to dictate that doctors never be permitted to try to keep someone alive as long as possible, when that is what the patient wishes, so it is intolerable for government to dictate that doctors may never, under any circumstances, help someone to die who believes that further life means only degradation. The Constitution insists that people must be free to make these deeply personal decisions for themselves and must not be forced to end their lives in a way that appalls them, just because that is what some majority thinks proper.

II. This Court's Decisions in *Casey* and *Cruzan* Compel Recognition of a Liberty Interest Here

A. Casey *Supports the Liberty Interest Asserted Here*
In *Casey,* this Court, in holding that a state cannot constitutionally proscribe abortion in all cases, reiterated that the Constitution protects a sphere of autonomy in which individuals must be permitted to make certain decisions for themselves. The Court began its analysis by pointing out that "[a]t the heart of liberty is the right to define one's own concept of existence, of meaning, of the universe, and of the mystery of human life."... Choices flowing out of these conceptions on matters "involving the most intimate and personal choices a person may make in a lifetime, choices central to personal dignity and autonomy, are central to the liberty protected by the Fourteenth Amendment." "Beliefs about these matters," the Court continued, "could not define the attributes of personhood were they formed under compulsion of the State."

In language pertinent to the liberty interest asserted here, the Court explained why decisions about abortion fall within this category of "personal and intimate" decisions. A decision whether or not to have an abortion, "originat[ing] within the zone of conscience and belief," involves conduct in which "the liberty of the woman is at stake in a sense unique to the human condition and so unique to the law."... As such, the decision necessarily involves the very "destiny of the woman" and is inevitably "shaped to a large extent on her own conception of her spiritual imperatives and her place in society." Precisely because of these characteristics of the decision, "the State is [not] entitled to proscribe [abortion] in all instances." Rather, to allow a total prohibition on abortion would be to permit a state to impose one conception of the meaning and value of human existence on all individuals. This the Constitution forbids.

The Solicitor General nevertheless argues that the right to abortion could be supported on grounds other than this autonomy principle, grounds that would not apply here. He argues, for example, that the abortion right might flow from the great burden an unwanted child imposes on its mother's life.... But whether or not abortion rights could be defended on such grounds, they were not the grounds on which this Court in fact relied. To the contrary, the Court explained at length that the right flows from the constitutional protection accorded all individuals to "define one's own concept of existence, of meaning, of the universe, and of the mystery of human life."...

The analysis in *Casey* compels the conclusion that the patient-plaintiffs have a liberty interest in this case that a state cannot burden with a blanket prohibition. Like a woman's decision whether to have an abortion, a decision to die involves one's very "destiny" and inevitably will be "shaped to a large extent on [one's] spiritual imperatives and [one's] place in society"... Just as a blanket prohibition on abortion would involve the improper imposition of one conception of the meaning and value of human existence on all individuals, so too would a blanket prohibition on assisted suicide. The liberty interest asserted here cannot be rejected without undermining the rationale of *Casey.* Indeed, the lower court opinions in the Washington case expressly recognized the parallel between the liberty interest in *Casey* and the interest asserted here....

B. Cruzan *Supports the Liberty Interest Asserted Here*
We agree with the Solicitor General that this Court's decision in *"Cruzan....* supports the conclusion that a liberty interest is at stake in this case." (Brief for the United States at 8.) Petitioners, however, insist that the present cases can be distinguished because the right at issue in *Cruzan* was limited to a right to reject an unwanted invasion of one's body. But this Court repeatedly has held that in appropriate circumstances a state may require individuals to accept unwanted invasions of the body....

The liberty interest at stake in *Cruzan* was a more profound one. If a competent patient has a constitutional right to refuse life-sustaining treatment, then, the Court implied, the state could not override that right. The regulations upheld in *Cruzan* were designed only to ensure that the individual's wishes were ascertained correctly. Thus, if

Cruzan implies a right of competent patients to refuse life-sustaining treatment that implication must be understood as resting not simply on a right to refuse bodily invasions but on the more profound right to refuse medical intervention when what is at stake is a momentous personal decision, such as the timing and manner of one's death. In her concurrence, Justice O'Connor expressly recognized that the right at issue involved a "deeply personal decision" that is "inextricably intertwined" with our notion of "self-determination."...

Cruzan also supports the proposition that a state may not burden a terminally ill patient's liberty interest in determining the time and manner of his death by prohibiting doctors from terminating life support. Seeking to distinguish *Cruzan,* petitioners insist that a state may nevertheless burden that right in a different way by forbidding doctors to assist in the suicide of patients who are not on life-support machinery. They argue that doctors who remove life support are only allowing a natural process to end in death whereas doctors who prescribe lethal drugs are intervening to cause death. So, according to this argument, a state has an independent justification for forbidding doctors to assist in suicide that it does not have for forbidding them to remove life support. In the former case though not the latter, it is said, the state forbids an act of killing that is morally much more problematic than merely letting a patient die.

This argument is based on a misunderstanding of the pertinent moral principles. It is certainly true that when a patient does not wish to die, different acts, each of which foreseeably results in his death, nevertheless have very different moral status. When several patients need organ transplants and organs are scarce, for example, it is morally permissible for a doctor to deny an organ to one patient even though he will die without it, in order to give it to another. But it is certainly not permissible for a doctor to kill one patient in order to use his organs to save another. The morally significant difference between those two acts is not, however, that killing is a positive act and not providing an organ is a mere omission, or that killing someone is worse than merely allowing a "natural" process to result

in death. It would be equally impermissible for a doctor to let an injured patient bleed to death, or to refuse antibiotics to a patient with pneumonia—in each case the doctor would have allowed death to result from a "natural" process—in order to make his organs available for transplant to others. A doctor violates his patient's rights whether the doctor acts or refrains from acting, against the patient's wishes in a way that is designed to cause death.

When a competent patient does want to die, the moral situation is obviously different, because then it makes no sense to appeal to the patient's right not to be killed as a reason why an act designed to cause his death is impermissible. From the patient's point of view, there is no morally pertinent difference between a doctor's terminating treatment that keeps him alive, if that is what he wishes, and a doctor's helping him to end his own life by providing lethal pills he may take himself, when ready, if that is what he wishes—except that the latter may be quicker and more humane. Nor is that a pertinent difference from the doctor's point of view. If and when it is permissible for him to act with death in view, it does not matter which of those two means he and his patient choose. If it is permissible for a doctor deliberately to withdraw medical treatment in order to allow death to result from a natural process, then it is equally permissible for him to help his patient hasten his own death more actively, if that is the patient's express wish.

It is true that some doctors asked to terminate life support are reluctant and do so only in deference to a patient's right to compel them to remove unwanted invasions of his body. But other doctors, who believe that their most fundamental professional duty is to act in the patient's interests and that, in certain circumstances, it is in their patient's best interests to die, participate willingly in such decisions: they terminate life support to cause death because they know that is what their patient wants. *Cruzan* implied that a state may not absolutely prohibit a doctor from deliberately causing death, at the patient's request, in that way and for that reason. If so, then a state may not prohibit doctors from deliberately using more direct and often more humane means to the same end when that is what a patient prefers. The fact that failing to provide life-sustaining treatment may be regarded as "only letting nature take its course" is no more morally significant in this context, when the patient wishes to die, than in the other, when he wishes to live. Whether a doctor turns off a respirator in accordance with the patient's request or prescribes pills that a patient may take when he is ready to kill himself, the doctor acts with the same intention to help the patient die.

The two situations do differ in one important respect. Since patients have a right not to have life-support machinery attached to their bodies, they have in principle a right to compel its removal. But that is not true in the case of assisted suicide: patients in certain circumstances have a right that the state not forbid doctors to assist in their deaths, but they have no right to compel a doctor to assist them. The right in question, that is, *is* only a right to the help of a willing doctor.

III. State Interests Do Not Justify a Categorical Prohibition on all Assisted Suicide

The Solicitor General concedes that "a competent, terminally ill adult has a constitutionally cognizable liberty interest in avoiding the kind of suffering experienced by the plaintiffs in this case." (Brief for the United States at 8.) He agrees that this interest extends not only to avoiding pain, but to avoiding an existence the patient believes to be one of intolerable indignity or incapacity as well.... The Solicitor General argues, however, that states nevertheless have the right to "override" this liberty interest altogether, because a state could reasonably conclude that allowing doctors to assist in suicide, even under the most stringent regulations and procedures that could be devised, would unreasonably endanger the lives of a number of patients who might ask for death in circumstances when it is plainly not in their interests to die or when their consent has been improperly obtained.

This argument is unpersuasive, however, for at least three reasons. *First* in *Cruzan*, this Court noted that its various decisions supported the recognition

of a general liberty interest in refusing medical treatment, even when such refusal could result in death.... The various risks described by the Solicitor General apply equally to those situations. For instance, a patient kept alive only by an elaborate and disabling life-support system might well become depressed, and doctors might be equally uncertain whether the depression is curable: such a patient might decide for death only because he has been advised that he will die soon anyway or that he will never live free of the burdensome apparatus, and either diagnosis might conceivably be mistaken. Relatives or doctors might subtly or crudely influence that decision, and state provision for the decision may (to the same degree in this case as if it allowed assisted suicide) be thought to encourage it.

Yet there has been no suggestion that states are incapable of addressing such dangers through regulation. In fact, quite the opposite is true.... The case law contains no suggestion that such protocols are inevitably insufficient to prevent deaths that should have been prevented.

Indeed, the risks of mistake are overall greater in the case of terminating life support. *Cruzan* implied that a state must allow individuals to make such decisions through an advance directive stipulating either that life support be terminated (or not initiated) in described circumstances when the individual was no longer competent to make such a decision himself, or that a designated proxy be allowed to make that decision. All the risks just described are present when the decision is made through or pursuant to such an advance directive, and a grave further risk is added: that the directive, though still in force, no longer represents the wishes of the patient. The patient might have changed his mind before he became incompetent, though he did not change the directive or his proxy may make a decision that the patient would not have made himself if still competent. In *Cruzan*, this Court held that a state may limit these risks through reasonable regulation. It did not hold—or even suggest—that a state may avoid them through a blanket prohibition that in effect, denies the liberty interest altogether.

Second, nothing in the record supports the [Solicitor General's] conclusion that no system of rules and regulations could adequately reduce the risk of mistake. As discussed above, the experience of states in adjudicating requests to have life-sustaining treatment removed indicates the opposite. The Solicitor General has provided no persuasive reason why the same sort of procedures could not be applied effectively in the case of a competent individual's request for physician-assisted suicide.

Indeed, several very detailed schemes for regulating physician-assisted suicide have been submitted to the voters of some states and one has been enacted. In addition, concerned groups, including a group of distinguished professors of law and other professionals, have drafted and defended such schemes.... Such draft statutes propose a variety of protections and review procedures designed to insure against mistakes, and neither Washington nor New York attempted to show that such schemes would be porous or ineffective. Nor does the Solicitor General's brief: it relies instead mainly on flat and conclusory statements. It cites a New York Task Force report, written before the proposal's just described were drafted, whose findings have been widely disputed and were implicitly rejected in the opinion of the Second Circuit below.... The weakness of the Solicitor General's argument is signaled by his strong reliance on the experience in the Netherlands which, in effect, allows assisted suicide pursuant to published guidelines.... The Dutch guidelines are more permissive than the proposed and model American statutes, however. The Solicitor General deems the Dutch practice of ending the lives of people like neonates who cannot consent particularly noteworthy, for example, but that practice could easily and effectively be made illegal by any state regulatory scheme without violating the Constitution.

The Solicitor General's argument would perhaps have more force if the question before the Court were simply whether a state has any rational basis for an absolute prohibition; if that were the question, then it might be enough to call attention to risks a state might well deem not worth running. But as the Solicitor General concedes the question here is a very different one; whether a state has interests sufficiently compelling to allow it to take the extraordinary step of altogether refusing the exercise of a liberty interest

of constitutional dimension. In those circumstances, the burden is plainly on the state to demonstrate that the risk of mistakes is very high, and that no alternative to complete prohibition would adequately and effectively reduce those risks. Neither of the Petitioners has made such a showing.

Nor could they. The burden of proof on any state attempting to show this would be very high. Consider, for example, the burden a state would have to meet to show that it was entitled altogether to ban public speeches in favor of unpopular causes because it could not guarantee, either by regulations short of an outright ban or by increased police protection, that such speeches would not provoke a riot that would result in serious injury or death to an innocent party. Or that it was entitled to deny those accused of crime the procedural rights that the Constitution guarantees, such as the right to a jury trial, because the security risk those rights would impose on the community would be too great. One can posit extreme circumstances in which some such argument would succeed....

Third, it is doubtful whether the risks the Solicitor General cites are even of the right character to serve as justification for an absolute prohibition on the exercise of an important liberty interest. The risks fall into two groups. The first is the risk of medical mistake, including a misdiagnosis of competence or terminal illness. To be sure, no scheme of regulation, no matter how rigorous, can altogether guarantee that medical mistakes will not be made. But the Constitution does not allow a state to deny patients a great variety of important choices, for which informed consent is properly deemed necessary, just because the information on which the consent is given may, in spite of the most strenuous efforts to avoid mistake, be wrong. Again, these identical risks are present in decisions to terminate life support, yet they do not justify an absolute prohibition on the exercise of the right.

The second group consists of risks that a patient will be unduly influenced by considerations that the state might deem it not in his best interests to be swayed by, for example, the feelings and views of close family members.... But what a patient regards as proper grounds for such a decision normally reflects exactly the judgments of personal ethics—of why his life is important and what affects its value—that patients have a crucial liberty interest in deciding for themselves. Even people who are dying have a right to hear and, if they wish, act on what others might wish to tell or suggest or even hint to them, and it would be dangerous to suppose that a state may prevent this on the ground that it knows better than its citizens when they should be moved by or yield to particular advice or suggestion in the exercise of their right to make fateful personal decisions for themselves. It is not a good reply that some people may not decide as they really wish—as they would decide, for example, if free from the "pressure" of others. That possibility could hardly justify the most serious pressure of all—the criminal law which tells them that they may not decide for death if they need the help of a doctor in dying, no matter how firmly they wish it.

There is a fundamental infirmity in the Solicitor General's argument. He asserts that a state may reasonably judge that the risk of "mistake" to some persons justifies a prohibition that not only risks but insures and even aims at what would undoubtedly be a vastly greater number of "mistakes" of the opposite kind—preventing many thousands of competent people who think that it disfigures their lives to continue living, in the only way left to them, from escaping that—to them—terrible injury. A state grievously and irreversibly harms such people when it prohibits that escape. The Solicitor General's argument may seem plausible to those who do not agree that individuals are harmed by being forced to live on in pain and what they regard as indignity. But many other people plainly do think that such individuals are harmed, and a state may not take one side in that essentially ethical or religious controversy as its justification for denying a crucial liberty.

Of course, a state has important interests that justify regulating physician-assisted suicide. It may be legitimate for a state to deny an opportunity for assisted suicide when it acts in what it reasonably judges to be the best interests of the potential suicide, and when its judgment on that issue does not rest on contested judgments about "matters involving the most intimate and personal choices a person may make in a lifetime, choices central to personal dignity and autonomy." *Casey*, 505 U.S. at 851. A state might assert, for example, that people who are not terminally ill, but who have formed a desire to die, are, as a group, very likely later to be grateful if they are prevented from taking their own lives. It might then claim that it is legitimate, out of concern for such people, to deny any of them a doctor's assistance [in taking their own lives].

This Court need not decide now the extent to which such paternalistic interests might override an individual's liberty interest. No one can plausibly claim, however—and it is noteworthy that neither Petitioners nor the Solicitor General does claim—that any such prohibition could serve the interests of any significant number of terminally ill patients. On the contrary, any paternalistic justification for an absolute prohibition of assistance to such patients would of necessity appeal to a widely contested religious or ethical conviction many of them, including the patient-plaintiffs, reject. Allowing *that* justification to prevail would vitiate the liberty interest.

Even in the case of terminally ill patients, a state has a right to take all reasonable measures to insure that a patient requesting such assistance has made an informed, competent, stable and uncoerced decision. It is plainly legitimate for a state to establish procedures through which professional and administrative judgments can be made about these matters, and to forbid doctors to assist in suicide when its reasonable procedures have not been satisfied. States may be permitted considerable leeway in designing such procedures. They may be permitted, within reason, to err on what they take to be the side of caution. But they may not use the bare possibility of error as justification for refusing to establish any procedures at all and relying instead on a flat prohibition.

CONCLUSION

Each individual has a right to make the "most intimate and personal choices central to personal dignity and autonomy." That right encompasses the right to exercise some control over the time and manner of one's death.

The patient-plaintiffs in these cases were all mentally competent individuals in the final phase of terminal illness and died within months of filing their claims.

Jane Doe described how her advanced cancer made even the most basic bodily functions such as swallowing, coughing, and yawning extremely painful and that it was "not possible for [her] to reduce [her] pain to an acceptable level of comfort and to retain an alert state." Faced with such circumstances, she sought to be able to "discuss freely with [her] treating physician [her] intention of hastening [her] death through the consumption of drugs prescribed for that purpose." *Quill v. Vacco....* (2d Cir. 1996)....

George A. Kingsley in advanced stages of AIDS which included, among other hardships, the attachment of a tube to an artery in his chest which made even routine functions burdensome and the development of lesions on his brain, sought advice from his doctors regarding prescriptions which could hasten his impending death.

Jane Roe, suffering from cancer since 1988, had been almost completely bedridden since 1993 and experienced constant pain which could not be alleviated by medication. After undergoing counseling for herself and her family, she desired to hasten her death by taking prescription drugs. *Compassion in Dying v. Washington,* (1994)....

John Doe, who had experienced numerous AIDS-related ailments since 1991, was "especially cognizant of the suffering imposed by a lingering terminal illness because he was the primary care-giver for his long-term companion who died of AIDS" and sought prescription drugs from his physician to hasten

his own death after entering the terminal phase of AIDS....

James Poe suffered from emphysema which caused him "a constant sensation of suffocating" as well as a cardiac condition which caused severe leg pain. Connected to an oxygen tank at all times but unable to calm the panic reaction associated with his feeling of suffocation even with regular doses of morphine, Mr. Poe sought physician-assisted suicide....

A state may not deny the liberty claimed by the patient-plaintiffs in these cases without providing them an opportunity to demonstrate, in whatever way the state might reasonably think wise and necessary, that the conviction they expressed for an early death is competent, rational, informed, stable, and uncoerced.

Affirming the decisions by the Courts of Appeals would establish nothing more than that there is such a constitutionally protected right in principle. It would establish only that some individuals, whose decisions for suicide plainly cannot be dismissed as irrational or foolish or premature, must be accorded a reasonable opportunity to show that their decision for death is informed and free. It is not necessary to decide precisely which patients are entitled to that opportunity. If, on the other hand, this Court reverses the decisions below, its decision could only be justified by the momentous proposition—a proposition flatly in conflict with the spirit and letter of the Court's past decisions—that an American citizen does not, after all, have the right, even in principle, to live and die in the light of his own religious and ethical beliefs, his own convictions about why his life is valuable and where its value lies.

22

Washington v. Glucksberg

Supreme Court of the United States

The issue before the Supreme Court of the United States was whether the Washington state statute that prohibits anyone from knowingly causing or aiding another to attempt suicide violates the fundamental liberty that is protected by the due process clause of the Fourteenth Amendment. The Court unanimously held that it does not on the grounds that the fundamental liberty protected by the due process clause has not been traditionally understood to entail a right to assisted suicide. Hence, all that is required for the state of Washington to justifiably prohibit assisted suicide is some rational grounds to do so. Among other things, the Court found that the difficulties of crafting a right of assisted suicide that would sufficiently protect vulnerable people provided just such ground.

Chief Justice *Rehnquist* delivered the opinion of the Court.

The question presented in this case is whether Washington's prohibition against "caus[ing]" or "aid[ing]" a suicide offends the Fourteenth Amendment to the United States Constitution. We hold that it does not.

It has always been a crime to assist a suicide in the State of Washington. In 1854, Washington's first Territorial Legislature outlawed "assisting another in the commission of self-murder." Today, Washington law provides: "A person is guilty of promoting a suicide attempt when he knowingly causes or aids another person to attempt suicide." "Promoting a suicide attempt" is a felony, punishable by up to five years' imprisonment and up to a $10,000 fine. At the same time, Washington's Natural Death Act, enacted in 1979, states that the "withholding or withdrawal of life-sustaining treatment" at a patient's direction "shall not, for any purpose, constitute a suicide."...

I

We begin, as we do in all due-process cases, by examining our Nation's history, legal traditions, and practices. In almost every State—indeed, in almost every western democracy—it is a crime to assist a suicide. The States' assisted-suicide bans are not innovations. Rather, they are longstanding expressions of the States' commitment to the protection and preservation of all human life. ("[T]he States—indeed, all civilized nations—demonstrate their commitment to life by treating homicide as a serious crime. Moreover, the majority of States in this country have laws imposing criminal penalties on one who assists another to commit suicide"); ... Indeed, opposition to and condemnation of suicide—and, therefore, of assisting suicide—are consistent and enduring themes of our philosophical, legal, and cultural heritages.

More specifically, for over 700 years, the Anglo-American common-law tradition has punished or otherwise disapproved of both suicide and assisting suicide. *Cruzan* (Scalia, *J.*, concurring). In the 13th century, Henry de Bracton, one of the first legal-treatise writers, observed that "[j]ust as a man may commit felony by slaying another so may he do so by slaying himself." The real and personal property of one who killed himself to avoid conviction and punishment for a crime were forfeit to the king; however, thought Bracton, "if a man slays himself in weariness of life or because he is unwilling to endure further bodily pain ... [only] his movable goods [were] confiscated." Thus, "[t]he principle that suicide of a sane person, for whatever reason, was a punishable felony was ... introduced into English common law." Centuries later, Sir William Blackstone, whose *Commentaries on the Laws of England* not only provided a definitive summary of the common law but was also a primary legal authority for 18th and 19th-century American lawyers, referred to suicide as "self-murder" and "the pretended heroism, but real cowardice, of the Stoic philosophers, who destroyed themselves to avoid those ills which they had not the fortitude to endure...." Blackstone emphasized that "the law has ... ranked [suicide] among the highest crimes," although, anticipating later developments, he conceded that the harsh and shameful punishments imposed for suicide "borde[r] a little upon severity"...

That suicide remained a grievous, though non-felonious, wrong is confirmed by the fact that colonial and early state legislatures and courts did not retreat from prohibiting assisting suicide. The earliest American statute explicitly to outlaw assisting suicide was enacted in New York in 1828, and many of the new States and Territories followed New York's example. Between 1857 and 1865, a New York commission led by Dudley Field drafted a criminal code that prohibited "aiding" a suicide and, specifically, "furnish[ing] another person with any deadly weapon or poisonous drug, knowing that such person intends to use such weapon or drug in taking his own life." By the time the Fourteenth Amendment was ratified, it was a crime in most States to assist a suicide.

Though deeply rooted, the States' assisted-suicide bans have in recent years been reexamined and, generally, reaffirmed. Because of advances in medicine and technology, Americans today are increasingly likely to die in institutions, from chronic illnesses. Public concern and democratic action are therefore sharply focused on how best to protect dignity and independence at the end of life, with the result that there have been many significant changes in state laws and in the attitudes these laws reflect. Many States, for example, now permit "living wills," surrogate health-care decision making, and the withdrawal or refusal of life-sustaining medical treatment. At the same time, however, voters and legislators continue for the most part to reaffirm their States' prohibitions on assisting suicide.

The Washington statute at issue in this case was enacted in 1975 as part of a revision of that State's criminal code. Four years later, Washington passed its Natural Death Act, which specifically stated that the "withholding or withdrawal of life-sustaining treatment ... shall not, for any purpose, constitute a suicide" and that "[n]othing in this chapter shall be construed to condone, authorize, or approve mercy killing...." In 1991, Washington voters rejected a ballot initiative which, had it passed, would have permitted a form of physician-assisted suicide. Washington then added a provision to the Natural Death Act expressly excluding physician-assisted suicide.

California voters rejected an assisted-suicide initiative similar to Washington's in 1993. On the other hand, in 1994, voters in Oregon enacted, also through ballot initiative, that State's "Death with Dignity Act," which legalized physician-assisted suicide for competent, terminally ill adults. Since the Oregon vote, many proposals to legalize assisted suicide have been and continue to be introduced in the States' legislatures, but none has been enacted. And just last year, Iowa and Rhode Island joined the overwhelming majority of States explicitly prohibiting assisted suicide. Also, on April 30, 1997, President Clinton signed the Federal Assisted Suicide Funding Restriction Act of 1997, which prohibits the use of federal funds in support of physician-assisted suicide.

Thus, the States are currently engaged in serious, thoughtful examinations of physician-assisted suicide and other similar issues. For example, New

York State's Task Force on Life and the Law—an ongoing, blue-ribbon commission composed of doctors, ethicists, lawyers, religious leaders, and interested laymen—was convened in 1984 and commissioned with "a broad mandate to recommend public policy on issues raised by medical advances." Over the past decade, the Task Force has recommended laws relating to end-of-life decisions, surrogate pregnancy, and organ donation. After studying physician-assisted suicide, however, the Task Force unanimously concluded that "[legalizing assisted suicide and euthanasia would pose profound risks to many individuals who are ill and vulnerable.... [T]he potential dangers of this dramatic change in public policy would outweigh any benefit that might be achieved."

Attitudes toward suicide itself have changed since Bracton, but our laws have consistently condemned, and continue to prohibit, assisting suicide. Despite changes in medical technology and notwithstanding an increased emphasis on the importance of end-of-life decision-making, we have not retreated from this prohibition. Against this backdrop of history, tradition, and practice, we now turn to respondents' constitutional claim.

II

The Due Process Clause guarantees more than fair process, and the "liberty" it protects includes more than the absence of physical restraint. The Clause also provides heightened protection against government interference with certain fundamental rights and liberty interests. In a long line of cases, we have held that, in addition to the specific freedoms protected by the Bill of Rights, the "liberty" specially protected by the Due Process Clause includes the rights to marry, to have children, to direct the education and upbringing of one's children, to marital privacy, to use contraception, to bodily integrity, and to abortion. We have also assumed, and strongly suggested, that the Due Process Clause protects the traditional right to refuse unwanted lifesaving medical treatment.

But we "ha[ve] always been reluctant to expand the concept of substantive due process because

guideposts for responsible decision-making in this unchartered area are scarce and open-ended." By extending constitutional protection to an asserted right or liberty interest, we, to a great extent, place the matter outside the arena of public debate and legislative action. We must therefore "exercise the utmost care whenever we are asked to break new ground in this field," lest the liberty protected by the Due Process Clause be subtly transformed into the policy preferences of the members of this Court.

Our established method of substantive-due-process analysis has two primary features: First, we have regularly observed that the Due Process Clause specially protects those fundamental rights and liberties which are, objectively, "deeply rooted in this Nation's history and tradition," and "implicit in the concept of ordered liberty," such that "neither liberty nor justice would exist if they were sacrificed," *Palko v. Connecticut* (1937). Second, we have required in substantive-due-process cases a "careful description" of the asserted fundamental liberty interest. Our Nation's history, legal traditions, and practices thus provide the crucial "guideposts for responsible decision-making," that direct and restrain our exposition of the Due Process Clause. As we stated recently in *Flores,* the Fourteenth Amendment "forbids the government to infringe ... 'fundamental' liberty interests at all, no matter what process is provided, unless the infringement is narrowly tailored to serve a compelling state interest."...

Turning to the claim at issue here, the Court of Appeals stated that "[properly analyzed, the first issue to be resolved is whether there is a liberty interest in determining the time and manner of one's death," or, in other words, "[i]s there a right to die?" Similarly, respondents assert a "liberty to choose how to die" and a right to "control of one's final days," and describe the asserted liberty as "the right to choose a humane, dignified death," and "the liberty to shape death." As noted above, we have a tradition of carefully formulating the interest at stake in substantive-due-process cases. For example, although *Cruzan* is often described as a "right to die" case, we were, in fact, more precise: we assumed that the Constitution granted competent persons a "constitutionally protected right to refuse lifesaving hydration and nutrition." *Cruzan* (O'Connor, concurring) ("[A] liberty interest in refusing unwanted medical treatment may be inferred from our prior decisions"). The Washington statute at issue in this case prohibits "aid[ing] another person to attempt suicide," and, thus, the question before us is whether the "liberty" specially protected by the Due Process Clause includes a right to commit suicide which itself includes a right to assistance in doing so.

We now inquire whether this asserted right has any place in our Nation's traditions. Here, as discussed above, we are confronted with a consistent and almost universal tradition that has long rejected the asserted right, and continues explicitly to reject it today, even for terminally ill, mentally competent adults. To hold for respondents, we would have to reverse centuries of legal doctrine and practice, and strike down the considered policy choice of almost every State....

The history of the law's treatment of assisted suicide in this country has been and continues to be one of the rejection of nearly all efforts to permit it. That being the case, our decisions lead us to conclude that the asserted "right" to assistance in committing suicide is not a fundamental liberty interest protected by the Due Process Clause. The Constitution also requires, however, that Washington's assisted-suicide ban be rationally related to legitimate government interests. This requirement is unquestionably met here. As the court below recognized, Washington's assisted-suicide ban implicates a number of state interests.

First, Washington has an "unqualified interest in the preservation of human life."... The State's prohibition on assisted suicide, like all homicide laws, both reflects and advances its commitment to this interest. This interest is symbolic and aspirational as well as practical:

> While suicide is no longer prohibited or penalized, the ban against assisted suicide and euthanasia shores up the notion of limits in human relationships. It reflects the gravity with which we view the decision to take one's own life or the life of another, and our reluctance to encourage

or promote these decisions.—New York Task Force.

Respondents admit that "[t]he State has a real interest in preserving the lives of those who can still contribute to society and enjoy life." The Court of Appeals also recognized Washington's interest in protecting life, but held that, the "weight" of this interest depends on the "medical condition and the wishes of the person whose life is at stake." Washington, however, has rejected this sliding-scale approach and, through its assisted-suicide ban, insists that all persons' lives, from beginning to end, regardless of physical or mental condition, are under the full protection of the law. As we have previously affirmed, the States "may properly decline to make judgments about the 'quality' of life that a particular individual may enjoy"... This remains true, as *Cruzan* makes clear, even for those who are near death.

Relatedly, all admit that suicide is a serious public-health problem, especially among persons in otherwise vulnerable groups. The State has an interest in preventing suicide, and in studying, identifying, and treating its causes.

Those who attempt suicide—terminally ill or not—often suffer from depression or other mental disorders. Research indicates, however, that many people who request physician-assisted suicide withdraw that request if their depression and pain are treated. The New York Task Force, however, expressed its concern that, because depression is difficult to diagnose, physicians and medical professionals often fail to respond adequately to seriously ill patients' needs. Thus, legal physician-assisted suicide could make it more difficult for the State to protect depressed or mentally ill persons, or those who are suffering from untreated pain, from suicidal impulses.

The State also has an interest in protecting the integrity and ethics of the medical profession. In contrast to the Court of Appeals' conclusion that "the integrity of the medical profession would [not] be threatened in any way by [physician-assisted suicide]," the American Medical Association, like many other medical and physicians' groups, has concluded that "[p]hysician-assisted suicide is fundamentally incompatible with the physician's role as healer." And physician-assisted suicide could, it is argued, undermine the trust that is essential to the doctor-patient relationship by blurring the time-honored line between healing and harming.

Next, the State has an interest in protecting vulnerable groups—including the poor, the elderly, and disabled persons—from abuse, neglect, and mistakes. The Court of Appeals dismissed the State's concern that disadvantaged persons might be pressured into physician-assisted suicide as "ludicrous on its face." We have recognized, however, the real risk of subtle coercion and undue influence in end-of-life situations.... Similarly, the New York Task Force warned that "legalizing physician-assisted suicide would pose profound risks to many individuals who are ill and vulnerable.... The risk of harm is greatest for the many individuals in our society whose autonomy and well-being are already compromised by poverty, lack of access to good medical care, advanced age, or membership in a stigmatized social group." If physician-assisted suicide were permitted, many might resort to it to spare their families the substantial financial burden of end-of-life health-care costs.

The State's interest here goes beyond protecting the vulnerable from coercion; it extends to protecting disabled and terminally ill people from prejudice, negative and inaccurate stereotypes, and "societal indifference." The State's assisted-suicide ban reflects and reinforces its policy that the lives of terminally ill, disabled, and elderly people must be no less valued than the lives of the young and healthy, and that a seriously disabled person's suicidal impulses should be interpreted and treated the same way as anyone else's.

Finally, the State may fear that permitting assisted suicide will start it down the path to voluntary and perhaps even involuntary euthanasia. The Court of Appeals struck down Washington's assisted-suicide ban only "as applied to competent, terminally ill adults who wish to hasten their deaths by obtaining medication prescribed by their doctors." Washington insists, however, that the impact of the court's decision will not and cannot be so limited. If suicide is protected as a matter of constitutional right, it is argued, "every man and woman in the United States must enjoy it." The Court of Appeals' decision, and its expansive reasoning, provide ample support for the State's concerns. The court noted, for example, that the "decision of a duly appointed surrogate decision maker is for all legal purposes the decision of the patient himself"; that "in some instances, the patient may be unable to self-administer the drugs and ... administration by the physician ... may be the only way the patient may be able to receive them"; and that not only physicians, but also family members and loved ones, will inevitably participate in assisting suicide. Thus, it turns out that what is couched as a limited right to "physician-assisted suicide" is likely, in effect, a much broader license, which could prove extremely difficult to police and contain. Washington's ban on assisting suicide prevents such erosion.

This concern is further supported by evidence about the practice of euthanasia in the Netherlands. The Dutch government's own study revealed that in 1990, there were 2,300 cases of voluntary euthanasia (defined as "the deliberate termination of another's life at his request"), 400 cases of assisted suicide, and more than 1,000 cases of euthanasia without an explicit request. In addition to these latter 1,000 cases, the study found an additional 4,941 cases where physicians administered lethal morphine overdoses without the patients' explicit consent. This study suggests that, despite the existence of various reporting procedures, euthanasia in the Netherlands has not been limited to competent, terminally ill adults who are enduring physical suffering, and that regulation of the practice may not have prevented abuses in cases involving vulnerable persons, Including severely disabled neonates and elderly persons suffering from dementia. The New York Task Force, citing the Dutch experience, observed that "assisted suicide and euthanasia are closely linked," and concluded that the "risk of ... abuse is neither speculative nor distant." Washington, like most other States, reasonably ensures against this risk by banning, rather than regulating, assisting suicide.

We need not weigh exactly the relative strengths of these various interests. They are unquestionably important and legitimate, and

Washington's ban on assisted suicide is at least reasonably related to their promotion and protection. We therefore hold that Wash. Rev. Code §9A.36.060(1) (1994) does not violate the Fourteenth Amendment, either on its face or "as applied to competent, terminally ill adults who wish to hasten their deaths by obtaining medication prescribed by their doctors."

Throughout the Nation, Americans are engaged in an earnest and profound debate about the morality, legality and practicality of physician-assisted suicide. Our holding permits this debate to continue, as it should in a democratic society. The decision of the … Court of Appeals is reversed, and the case is remanded for further proceedings consistent with this opinion.

SUGGESTIONS FOR FURTHER READING

Anthologies

Brody Baruch, and Tristan Engelhardt. *Bioethics*. Englewood Cliffs, NJ: Prentice-Hall, 1987.

Cohen, Marshall, et al. *The Rights and Wrongs of Abortion*. Princeton: Princeton University Press, 1974.

Feinberg, Joel. *The Problem of Abortion*, 2nd ed. Belmont, CA: Wadsworth, 1984.

Ladd, John. *Ethical Issues Relating to Life and Death*. New York: Oxford University Press, 1979.

Moreno, Jonathan. *Arguing Euthanasia*. New York: Simon and Schuster, 1995.

Munson, Ronald. *Interventions and Reflections*. Belmont, CA: Wadsworth, 1979.

Basic Concepts

Devine, Philip. *The Ethics of Homicide*. Ithaca, NY: Cornell University Press, 1978.

Glover, Jonathan. *Causing Death and Saving Lives*. New York: Penguin Books, 1977.

Steinbock, Bonnie, ed. *Killing and Letting Die*. Englewood Cliffs, NJ: Prentice-Hall, 1980.

Alternative Views

Battin, Margaret Pabst. *The Least Worst Death*. New York: Oxford University Press, 1994.

Bungsjord, Selmer. *Abortion: A Dialogue*. Indianapolis: Hackett, 1997.

Crum, Gary, and Thelma McCormack. *Abortion: Pro-Choice or Pro-Life*. Washington, DC: American University Press, 1992.

Garber, Mark. *Rethinking Abortion*. Princeton: Princeton University Press, 1996.

Luker, Kristin. *Abortion and the Politics of Motherhood*. Berkeley: University of California Press, 1984.

Pojman, Louis P. *Life and Death*. Boston: Jones and Bartlett, 1992.

Rachels, James. *The End of Life*. New York: Oxford University Press, 1986.

Summer, L. W. *Abortion and Moral Theory*. Princeton: Princeton University Press, 1981.

Tooley, Michael, Wolf-Devine, Celia, Jaggar, Alison, Abortion: Three Perspectives. New York: Oxford University Press, 2009.

Tribe, Lawrence. *Abortion: The Clash of Absolutes*. New York: Norton, 1990.

Practical Applications

Denes, Magda. *In Necessity and Sorrow: Life and Death in an Abortion Hospital*. New York: Penguin Books, 1977.

Law Reform Commission of Canada. *Euthanasia, Aiding Suicide and Cessation of Treatment*. Working Paper 28, 1982.

Supreme Court of Michigan, *People v. Kevorkian*, 1994.

✳

Human Enhancement

INTRODUCTION

Basic Concepts

In just the past couple of decades we have seen a convergence of advancements in genetic engineering, cognitive science, pharmacology, and nanotechnology that either are being applied or could be applied to enhance human capabilities. At one end of the spectrum are enhancements that are fairly innocuous; at another end are enhancements that could conceivably change our understanding of what it means to be human.

The types of enhancements made possible by modern science range from those in current use to radical kinds only contemplated, but with science as it is progressing, these are not to be scoffed at. They range from enhancements that can increase our mental performance to those that can increase our physical performance, to some combination of the two. And further, enhancements range from types involving only biological adaptation to those involving only mechanical adaptation, to adaptations that are both the biological and the mechanical. Stimulant prescription drugs taken by students in order to study more effectively before exams are an all too familiar example of the first kind. Another all too familiar example is steroids taken by athletes in order to enhance their physical performance. Enhancements involving mechanical adaptations include exoskeletons that can be "worn" by humans and that amplify the strength of their movements. Models of these exoskeletons include HULC (Human Universal Load Carrier) developed by Lockheed Martin and HAL (Hybrid Assistive Limb) developed by the Japanese corporation Cyberdyne. Other types of human enhancements rely on genetics and include various prenatal selection processes, including sex selection and selection for various birth defects. Methods of genetic engineering now used only for gene therapy may one day be used for enhancement purposes, and may be used at the germ-line level, enabling these enhancements to be passed on to offspring. Nanotechnology has made possible placing nanochips in the brain for brain stimulation, which could be used to enhance our affective states and perhaps similar technology could one day be used to increase our mental capabilities. Some foresee that within only a couple of decades, either through the use of gene therapy, nanomedicine, or some other method available, scientists and doctors will be able to reverse the aging process, meaning that humans could potentially live for 500 to 1,000 years, if not longer.

Much of what is now possible, or soon to be possible, in the field of human enhancement was only found in sci-fi movies and comic books a short while ago. Many enthusiasts look forward to a "posthuman" world; a world where humans have enhanced themselves to such a degree that they are capable of achieving greater experiences and values than the human species is currently capable of even comprehending.

But just as human enhancement has its enthusiasts, so does it have its critics. Its critics have several worries about what the results might be. In the case of genetic engineering, some worry that we will see the return of government sponsored eugenics programs including state-sponsored genetic discrimination favoring the "genetically-enhanced," forced sterilization of the genetically undesirable, and possibly genetically motivated genocides. Another fear is that enhancement technologies will increase the proverbial gap between the haves and have-nots. The rich and their offspring are the most likely to have access to enhancement technologies in the first place. And consider the type of things that can be enhanced: intelligence, looks, physical capabilities,

etc., just the type of things relevant to gaining competitive advantages. And so, these critics argue, enhancement technologies could likely lead to degrees of inequality and social stratification not seen, at least in the West, since the Feudal Age. In addition to worries about any disastrous or unjust consequences that may result from the use of new or radical enhancement technologies there is the concern over what effect these things may have on our characters. Critics worry that that we may become less humble, less grateful for what we have, and that if we develop the means to alter our own nature we will betray the ultimate form of mania: we will come to view ourselves as "god-like."

Plenty of enhancement enthusiasts are not naive about what they advocate. Nor do they advocate approaching human enhancement technology with hubris. And as we shall see, neither do they ignore critics' arguments.

Alternative Views

In Selection 23, Patrick Lin and Fritz Allhoff point out that we are at the beginning of a revolution in human enhancement much like the Industrial Revolution. But not everyone agrees on how to morally assess this revolution, and the aim of Lin and Allhoff's piece is to provide clarity to this ongoing argument.

Lin and Allhoff first provide the reader with a useful understanding of "human enhancement" which they define in terms of what is typical or statistically normal for our species. They also provide several real, possible, and hypothetical examples and scenarios involving human enhancements in order to further clarify the concept. Next they outline and explain in detail what they believe to be the five most important moral issues raised in the human enhancement debate: (1) freedom and autonomy; (2) health and safety; (3) fairness and equity; (4) societal disruption; and (5) human dignity.

Lin and Allhoff conclude their piece by considering different approaches governments might take with respect to restricting human enhancement technologies. One option involves no restrictions. Lin and Allhoff argue this option seems reckless and foolhardy in light of the risks involved. Another option would be an outright ban on any further research or development with respect to enhancement technologies. Lin and Allhoff argue that for such a ban to really work it would need to be world-wide and that such a world-wide ban is unlikely to be achievable. And if it were achievable, it would just drive research and development underground. The most sensible option, Lin and Allhoff conclude, would be a moderate position between the extremes of no restrictions and a full ban, involving some appropriate level of restrictions.

In Selection 24, Michael Sandel objects to genetic engineering on the grounds that it would alter three features of our moral landscape for the worse: humility, responsibility, and solidarity. Genetic engineering would erode our humility. Many of us would not view our talents and abilities as gifts for which to be grateful to God or nature for, but rather as something to be proud of since we may be responsible for them ourselves. This leads Sandel to point out that genetic engineering would lead to the explosion of responsibility. What was once left to chance and nature is now open to control and influence by our choices. The greater control over our genetic endowments entails a greater responsibility for them. Sandel hypothesizes that in the near future basketball coaches won't just be blaming players for messing up on plays, but for being too short! This explosion of responsibility would correspond to a diminishing sense of solidarity amongst one another. The greater sense we have

that each of our lots in life is due to chance the more reason we have to share each other's fate. Hence, insofar as genetic engineering erases that element of chance it erases that reason we feel to share each other's fate.

In Selection 25, John Harris tries to persuade the reader that in the end, objections to human enhancement are irrational. For instance, Harris asks us to consider the difference between wearing reading glasses versus wearing opera glasses. Reading glasses are therapeutic because they are meant to restore a person's vision to some type of normal functioning, whereas opera glasses enhance one's vision beyond normal functioning. But for those who are opposed to human enhancement technologies *per se* they must think there is some significant moral difference between wearing reading glasses and wearing opera glasses, where the former is permissible and the latter is impermissible. But of course, Harris says, that is absurd.

Harris points to work going on by David Baltimore at Caltech who is attempting to engineer resistance or immunity to HIV/AIDS and cancer into cells. One way to do this involves manipulating the immune system by delivering new genes into an individual's cells. If there are truly any objections to genetic enhancements *per se* then those raising such objections, Harris argues, must hope that Baltimore fails in his pursuits at Caltech.

Some concerned about human enhancement technologies argue that such technologies should not be available unless and until they can be made available to all. In response, Harris says that it is unethical to deny anyone a benefit until it is available to all. In addition, Harris points to several examples of procedures or commodities that started out risky, expensive, or rare and then became, often quickly, widely available (e.g., computers, mobile phones, vaccines, transplants, antibiotics). Had such innovations been banned unless or until they were widely available, Harris argues they likely never would have been developed, or at the very least their development would have been delayed. In either case the costs to human well-being would have been considerable.

Finally, insofar as fear of human enhancement technologies relies on the fear of doomsday scenarios, Harris admits that there are risks involved. Where dangers are foreseeable we can avoid them. Where dangers are completely unforeseeable they can be no more guarded against then in any other activity. But, he points out, this is no more of a problem than in any other risky activity, such as eating fatty food.

Practical Applications

Enhancement enthusiasts view as unjustifiably pessimistic, worries over the possibility of genetic enhancement technologies leading to Nazi-style eugenics. After witnessing the atrocities of the Nazis' race-based eugenics, our current values rule out the possibility of repeating them. The future goal to be reached via genetic medicine is the stamping out of genetic diseases and abnormalities which are the cause of so much misery.

This attitude is just naïve argues Daniel Callahan in Selection 26. He points to an implicit, if not explicit, argument made on the side of the enhancement enthusiasts that provides the "back door" to eugenics. The first part of the argument says that parents should not want to have children with defects and should also not run the risk of having them. Given that, so the second part goes, it would be unfair of parents to burden the rest of society with having to help take care of their defective children. And thus we go from a seemingly humane concern to rid the world of genetic diseases and abnormalities to strict control of reproduction in order to have a society full of healthy, better humans.

23

Untangling the Debate: The Ethics of Human Enhancement

PATRICK LIN AND FRITZ ALLHOFF

Patrick Lin and Fritz Allhoff bring to our attention that we are at the beginning of a "Human Enhancement Revolution." However, they point out there is considerable debate on whether this revolution should be a welcome one or not. Lin and Allhoff shed light on this debate by clarifying the meaning of "human enhancement" through several distinctions and examples, as well as by addressing the moral issues that are most relevant to the debate, and possible approaches towards regulating enhancement technologies.

INTRODUCTION

Homo sapiens has been such a prolific species, simply because we are very good at relentlessly adapting to our environment. At the most basic level, we have won control over fire and tools to forge a new world around us, we build shelter and weave clothes to repel the brutal elements, and we raise animals and crops for predictability in our meals. With our intellect and resourcefulness, we are thereby better able to survive this world.

However, it is not just the world around us that we desire to change. Since the beginning of history, we also have wanted to become more than human, to become *Homo superior*. From the godlike command of Gilgamesh, to the lofty ambitions of Icarus, to the preternatural strength of Beowulf, to the mythical skills of Shaolin monks, and to various shamans and shapeshifters throughout the world's cultural history, we have dreamt—and still dream—of transforming ourselves to overcome our all-too-human limitations.

In practice, this means that we improve our minds through education, disciplined thinking, and meditation; we improve our bodies with a sound diet and physical exercise; and we train with weapons and techniques to defend ourselves from those who would conspire to kill. But today, something seems to be different. With ongoing work to unravel the mysteries of our minds and bodies, coupled with the art and science of emerging technologies, we are near the start of the Human Enhancement (or Engineering) Revolution.

Now we are not limited to "natural" methods to enhance ourselves or to merely wield tools such as a hammer or binoculars or a calculator. We are beginning to incorporate technology within our very bodies, which may hold moral significance that we need to consider. These technologies promise great benefits for humanity—such as increased productivity and creativity, longer lives, more serenity, stronger bodies and minds, and more—though, as we will discuss later, there is a

Patrick Lin, "Untangling the Debate: The Ethics of Human Enhancement," *Nanoethics* 2(3) pp. 251–264 (2008). Reprinted with kind permission from Springer Science and Business Media B.V.

question whether these things translate into *happier* lives, which many see as the point of it all [38, 36].

As examples of emerging technologies, in early 2008, a couple imaginative inventions in particular, among many, are closing the gap even more between science fiction and the real world. Scientists have conceptualized an electronic-packed contact lens that may provide the wearer with telescopic and night vision or act as an omnipresent digital monitor to receive and relay information [35]. Another innovation is a touch display designed to be implanted just under the skin that would activate special tattoo ink on one's arm to form images, such as telephone-number keys to punch or even a video to watch [30]. Together with ever-shrinking computing devices, we appear to be moving closer to cybernetic organisms (or "cyborgs"), that is, where machines are integrated with our bodies or at least with our clothing in the nearer-term. Forget about Pocket PCs, mobile phones, GPS devices, and other portable gadgets; we might soon be able to communicate and access those capabilities without having to carry any external device, thus raising our productivity, efficiency, response time, and other desirable measures—in short, enabling us to even better survive our world.

Technology is clearly a game-changing field. The inventions of such things as the printing press, gunpowder, automobiles, computers, vaccines, and so on, have profoundly changed the world, for the better we hope. But at the same time, they have also led to unforeseen consequences, or perhaps consequences that might have been foreseen and addressed had we bothered to investigate them. Least of all, they have disrupted the status quo, which is not necessarily a terrible thing in and of itself; but unnecessary and dramatic disruptions, such as mass displacements of workers or industries, have real human costs to them. As we will discuss, such may be the case as well with human enhancement technologies, enabled by advances in nanotechnology, micro-electro-mechanical systems (MEMS), genetic engineering, robotics, cognitive science, information technology, pharmacology, and other fields [41].[1]

No matter where one is aligned on this issue, it is clear that the human enhancement debate is a deeply passionate and personal one, striking at the heart of what it means to be human. Some see it as a way to fulfill or even transcend our potential; others see it as a darker path towards becoming Frankenstein's monster. But before more fully presenting those issues, it would be helpful to lay out some background and context to better frame the discussion, as follows.

DEFINITIONS

First, we need to draw several important distinctions.[2] Strictly speaking, "human enhancement" includes any activity by which we improve our bodies, minds, or abilities—things we do to enhance our welfare. So reading a book, eating vegetables, doing homework, and exercising may count as enhancing ourselves, though we do not mean the term this way in our discussion here. These so-called "natural" human enhancements are morally uninteresting because they appear to be unproblematic to the extent that it is difficult to see why we should not be permitted to improve ourselves through diet, education, physical training, and so on.

Rather, allow us to stipulate for the moment that "human enhancement" is about boosting our capabilities *beyond the species-typical level or statistically-normal range* of functioning for an individual [6]. Relatedly, "human enhancement" can be understood to be different from "therapy," which is about treatments aimed at pathologies that compromise health or reduce one's level of functioning below this species-typical or statistically-normal level [23]. Another way to think about human enhancement technologies, as opposed to therapy, is that they change the structure and function of the body [16]. Admittedly, none of these definitions is immune to objections, but they are nevertheless useful as a starting point in thinking about the distinction, including whether there really is such a distinction.

Thus, corrective eyeglasses, for instance, would be considered therapeutic rather than enhancement, since they serve to bring your vision back to normal; but strapping on a pair of night-vision binoculars would count as human enhancement, because they give you sight beyond the range of any unassisted human vision. As another example, using steroids to help muscular dystrophy patients regain lost strength is a case of therapy; but steroid use by otherwise-healthy athletes would give them new strength beyond what humans typically have (thereby enabling them to set new performance records in sports). And growing or implanting webbing between one's fingers and toes to enable better swimming changes the structure and function of those body parts, counting then as a case of human enhancement and not therapy.

Likewise, as it concerns the mind, taking Ritalin to treat attention-deficit hyperactivity disorder (ADHD) is aimed at correcting the deficit; but taken by otherwise-normal students to enable them to focus better in studying for exams is a form of human enhancement. And where reading a book may indeed make you more knowledgeable, it does not make you so much smarter than most everyone else or push your intellect past natural limits; on the other hand, a computer chip implanted into your brain that gives you direct access to Google or spreadsheets would provide mental capabilities beyond the species-typical level.

The last example suggests a further distinction we should make. By "human enhancement" we do not mean the mere use of tools; that would render the concept impotent, turning nearly everything we do into cases of human enhancement. But if and when these tools are integrated into our bodies, rather than employed externally, then we will consider them to be instances of human enhancement. Of course, this raises the question: what is so special about incorporating tools as part of our bodies, as opposed to merely using them externally to the body [5]? That is, why should the former count as human enhancement, but not the latter? A neural implant that gives access to Google and the rest of the online world does not seem to be different *in kind* to using a laptop computer or Pocket PC to access the same, so why should it matter that we are imbedding computing power into our heads rather than carrying the same capabilities with us by way of external devices?

We will not attempt to give a full discussion of that point here, though it will be important to explore the issue further, except to suggest that

integrating tools into our bodies (and perhaps with our everyday clothing to the extent that we are rarely without our clothes) appears to give us unprecedented advantages which may be morally significant. These advantages are that we would have easier, immediate, and "always-on" access to those new capabilities as if they were a natural part of our being; we would never be without those devices, as we might forget to bring a laptop computer with us to a meeting. And assimilating tools with our persons creates an intimate or enhanced connection with our tools that evolves our notion of personal identity, more so than simply owning things (as wearing name-brand clothes might boost our sense of self). This may translate into a *substantial* advantage for the enhanced person, more so than gained by purchasing an office computer or reading books or training with the best coaches.

THE THERAPY-ENHANCEMENT DISTINCTION

Returning to an issue previously raised, some scholars have reasonably objected to, or at least raised difficulties with, the distinctions above; that is, they argue that there is no real distinction between therapy and enhancement. For instance, how should we think about vaccinations: are they a form of therapy, or are they an enhancement of our immune system [5, 6, 18]? On one hand, a vaccination seems to be an enhancement in that there is no existing pathology it is attempting to cure, merely a possible or likely pathology we wish to avoid; but we are drawn to declare it as some form of therapy—perhaps preventative therapy—given its close association with medicine? And if enhancements in general are ultimately found to be socially or ethically problematic, then counting vaccinations as enhancement opens the possibility that it should be regulated or restricted, which would create a serious public health disaster as well as a counterexample to the claim that enhancements are problematic. Thus, even critics of human enhancement may be loathe to put vaccinations in the enhancement bucket, though there does not seem to be an obviously superior reason to think otherwise.

Another dilemma: If a genius were to sustain a head injury, thereby reducing her IQ to merely the "average" or "species-normal" range, would raising her intelligence back to its initial "genius" level count as therapy or enhancement [5]? Either one would seem plausible, but is there a non-arbitrary reason for answering the question either way? If an enhancement, then how do we explain the difference between that and a clear (or clearer) case of therapy in which we return an "average" person who sustains a head injury back to the "normal" IQ range?

The therapy-enhancement distinction holds real stakes, beyond athletic and academic competition. Recent news reports show that the US military is increasingly prescribing anti-depressants to soldiers in combat to alleviate post-traumatic stress as well as stimulants to counteract sleep deprivation—actions which could be viewed as either creating a more effective, level-headed soldier or returning the soldier to the initial "normal" state of combat readiness, further blurring the distinction [42, 46].[3]

The above cases notwithstanding, we would agree that there are difficulties in precisely defining "human enhancement" (as there is with making clear definitions of nearly any other concept), but maintaining the enhancement-therapy distinction, at least until it can by more fully explored, is nonetheless important for several reasons:

First, to the extent that pro-enhancement advocates are primarily the ones arguing against the therapy-enhancement distinction, if a goal is to engage the anti-enhancement camp, then it would make for a far stronger case to meet those critics on their own ground (i.e., to grant the assumption that such a distinction exists). If it proves overly charitable to grant this assumption such that the pro-enhancement position is too difficult to defend without it, then perhaps more attention needs to be paid in arguing against the distinction in the first place, given that the debate may hinge on this fundamental issue.

Second, by not making these distinctions, specifically between therapy and enhancement, it may be too easy to argue that all forms of human enhancement are morally permissible given that the things we count as therapy are permissible. That is to say, we risk making a straw man argument that does not make a compelling case either for or against any aspect of human enhancement. Again, if the human enhancement debate turns on this distinction, then much more attention should be paid to defending or criticizing the distinction than has been to date.

Third, at least part of the reason that human enhancement is believed to be the most important issue in the 21st century by both sides of the debate [22] seems to be that it represents a collision between our intuitions and our actions. For instance, critics may believe that human enhancement technologies give an unfair advantage to some persons, fracturing local or global societies (even more) between the haves and have-nots [14, 15, 38, 45], Yet, at the same time, they seem to endorse—to the extent that they have not raised objections to—our use of existing technologies (e.g., mobile phones, computer, Internet) that also seem to countenance the same division to which human enhancement technologies are said to lead us.

As another example, advocates of human enhancement may believe that individual autonomy should trump health and safety concerns, e.g., athletes should be permitted to take steroids or adults should be allowed to take mood-enhancing drugs at will [32, 44]. Yet, at the same time, they do not offer objections to keeping some drugs illegal, such as crystal meth or crack cocaine, which becomes an even more complicated dilemma if they advocate legalizing other contraband such as marijuana.

This is not to say that these tensions with our intuitions are irresolvable, but only that "common sense" is at stake for both sides of the debate. And the initial intuition for the overwhelming majority of us is that there *is* a therapy-enhancement distinction (since we understand "therapy" and "enhancement" as meaningfully discrete terms, even if some cases do not neatly fit into either category). So it would be more interesting for pro-enhancement advocates to reconcile their position with that intuition, if possible, rather than to reject the distinction, which is less satisfying. Or if the therapy-enhancement distinction really is untenable, then more vigorous argument seems to be needed before we are prepared to cast aside our intuition.

Fourth, the famous philosophical puzzle "The Paradox of the Heap" should be recalled here: Given a heap of sand with N number of grains of sand, if we remove one grain of sand, we are still left with a heap of sand (that now only has N-1 grains of sand). If we remove one more grain, we are again left with a heap of sand (that now has N-2 grains). If we extend this line of reasoning and continue to remove grains of sand, we see that there is no clear point P where we can definitely say that a heap of sand exists on one side of P, but less than a heap exists on the other side. In other words, there is no clear distinction between a heap of sand and a less-than-a-heap or even no sand at all. However, the wrong conclusion to draw here is that there is no difference between them or that the distinction between a heap and no-heap should be discarded (or between being bald and having hair, as a variation of the paradox goes). Likewise, it would seem fallacious to conclude that there is no difference between therapy and enhancement or that we should dispense with the distinction. It may still be the case that there is no *moral* difference between the two, but we cannot arrive at it through the argument that there is no clear defining line or that there are some cases (such as vaccinations, etc.) that make the line fuzzy. As with 'heap', the terms 'therapy' and 'enhancement' may simply be vaguely constructed and require more precision to clarify the distinction.

Therefore, at least for the time being and for the purposes of this paper, we will assume that a therapy-enhancement distinction is defensible and illuminative, at least where it aligns with our intuitions.

SCENARIOS

Given the above stipulations about what counts as human enhancement, let us lay out a few more scenarios—real, possible, and hypothetical—to further clarify what we mean by human enhancement. We can loosely group these scenarios into three

categories: mental performance, physical performance, and other applications.

In the area of improving mental performance, individuals are already using pharmaceuticals available today to achieve such goals as increased productivity, creativity, serenity, and happiness. We previously mentioned Ritalin use, intended for ADHD patients, by otherwise-normal students to boost concentration as a way to study more effectively. In sports, drugs such as beta-blockers, intended to treat high blood pressure and other disorders by slowing down the heart rate, have been used to reduce anxiety as a way to boost physical performance, such as in preparing for an important and nerve-racking putt in golf or steadying an archer's hand to better release the arrow in between heartbeats. In warfare, anti-depressants and stimulants have been used to treat post-traumatic stress and sleep deprivation, thereby creating better, more effective soldiers. And, of course, hallucinogenic and other recreational drugs, including alcohol, continue to be used (and used famously by some authors and artists) to achieve greater creativity, relaxation, and even enlightenment.

In the future, as technology becomes more integrated with our bodies, we can expect neural implants of the kind we mentioned above that effectively puts computer chips into our brains or allows devices to be plugging directly into our heads, giving us always-on access to information as well as unprecedented information-processing powers. New and future virtual reality programs are able to much better simulate activities, for instance, to train law enforcement officers and soldiers in dangerous situations so that they can respond better to similar events in the real world.

In the area of physical performance, steroids use by athletes is one of the most obvious examples. Cosmetic surgery has also grown in popularity, not for corrective purposes but to increase (perceived) attractiveness. Prosthetic limbs have improved to such a degree that they are already enabling its wearer greater than normal strength and capabilities, sparking a debate on whether athletes with those artificial limbs may participate in the Olympics [11].

In the future, we can expect continuing advances in robotics and bionanotechnology to give us cybernetic body parts, from bionic arms to artificial noses and ears, that surpass the capabilities of our natural body. Today, research organizations such as MIT's Institute for Soldier Nanotechnologies are working on an exoskeleton to give the wearer super-human strength as well as flexible battlesuits that can, for instance, harden when needed to create a splint or tourniquet to attend to injuries more quickly and effectively [31]. And we previously mentioned inno-vative designs such as for a contact lens that enables us to see in the dark or receive information from a mini-ature digital monitor. Further, designs have already been drawn for even more fantastic innovations such as a respirocyte: an artificial red blood cell that holds a reservoir of oxygen [13]. A respirocyte would come in handy for, say, a heart attack victim to continue breathing for an extra hour until medical treatment is available, despite a lack of blood circulation to the lungs or anywhere else. But in an otherwise-healthy athlete, a respirocyte could boost performance by delivering extra oxygen to the muscles, as if the person were breathing from a pure oxygen tank.

And perhaps as an example of both mental and physical enhancement, we should also consider life extension, whether it comes by curing fatal pathol-ogies (such as cancer) or rejuvenating the body/ mind or developing anti-aging medicine, and whether it enables us to live another 20 years or 100 years or 1,000 years (radical life extension). This is a particularly contentious issue in the human engineering debate, not just for obvious concerns related to the burden of overpopulation on quality of life or loss of meaning in life, but also because it seems that we are already—and pre-sumably unproblematically—extending our lives through better nutrition, medicine, exercise, sanita-tion, and so forth; yet there is something troubling to many about the prospect of radical life extension, even if we can all agree that, in principle, more life is better than less life. We will return to this below.

Other applications include enhancements that may seem gratuitous, such as attempting to physi-cally transform into a lizard by tattooing scales all over one's body and forking one's tongue, or into a cat by implanting whiskers, sharpening teeth and clipping one's ears, or into something other than

human with implanted horns in one's forehead; all of these procedures have been done already. In the future, we can envision the possibility that pros-thetic flippers, designed today for dolphins, might be requested by humans, along with artificial gills, etc., who want to transform into an aquatic animal. This type of enhancements, of course, brings to the forefront the question whether 'enhancement' is the right word to use in the debate in the first place, as opposed to simply 'human engineering' or a more neu-tral term that does not imply improvement. Indeed, even in cases where technology boosts mental and physical capabilities, it seems that we cannot predict with any accuracy whether there will be any negative psychological or physiological side-effects that will off-set the intended benefits of a particular enhancement. For instance, in drinking alcohol as a mood-enhancer of sorts, we already know that it can hold the unin-tended effect of a painful hangover; and steroids taken by athletes can have disastrous health consequences.

Moreover, if human enhancement can be ulti-mately defended, then un-enhancements may seem to be morally permissible as well, if individual auton-omy is the most important value to consider in the debate. There are already medical cases in which: indi-viduals want to amputate some healthy limb from their bodies [10]; parents want to stunt the growth of their bedridden child to keep her portable and easier to care for [12]; and deaf parents who specifically want a deaf baby in selecting embryos for *in vitro* fertilization [9]. Un-enhancements aside, we will continue to use 'enhancement' in this paper for the most part, since there is a presumption that whatever technology is integrated with our bodies will be expected to deliver some net benefit, real or perceived (otherwise, why do it?). Further, we will limit our discussion here primarily to those technologies that enhance human cognitive and physical abilities, rather than seemingly-gratuitous procedures or un-enhancements.

THE ISSUES

Now, given the above understanding of human enhancement, let us tease apart the myriad issues that arise in the debate. These too are loose non-exclusive categories that may overlap with one another, but perhaps are still useful in providing an overview of the debate: (1) freedom & autonomy; (2) health & safety; (3) fairness & equity; (4) societal disruption; (5) human dignity.

Let us make a couple of preliminary notes. First, just as no one could predict with much accuracy how the Internet Revolution would unfold, raising policy issues from privacy to piracy and beyond, the same is likely true with the Human Engineering Revolution; that is, the framework presented below will undoubtedly evolve over time. However, this does not mean that we should not attempt to address the issues we are able to anticipate. Second, the objective of this paper is neither to anticipate nor fully address any given issue, but simply to broadly sketch the major issues, many of which will be expounded upon by the papers in this symposium. Therefore, the following discussion will raise more questions than it answers in constructing that framework.

FREEDOM & AUTONOMY

There is perhaps no greater value, at least in democracies, than the cherished concepts of freedom and autonomy. (The distinction between the two is not critical to this discussion, so we will not take the space to give a precise definition here; but allow us to stipulate that, at minimum, both concepts are about negative liberty, or the absence of constraints.) But because freedom and autonomy are central to the issue of human enhancement, they add much fuel to the impassioned debate.

Pro-enhancement advocates have argued against regulating enhancements on the grounds that it would infringe on our fundamental ability to choose how we want to live our own lives [4, 18, 32]. Or, in other words, if enhancing our bodies does not hurt anyone (other than possibly ourselves; more on this in the next section), then why should we be prevented from doing so? This is a common objection—arguing especially against governmental intervention—to any number of proposals that involve regulation, from hiring practices to home improvements to school clothing and so on.

Though freedom and autonomy may be viewed in democracies as "sacred cows" that ought not be corralled, the reality is that we do not have complete freedom or autonomy is the areas of life that we think we do anyway. As examples, freedom of the press and freedom of speech do not protect the individual from charges of libel, slander, or inciting panic by yelling "Fire!" in a crowded theater; our privacy expectations quietly give way to security measures, such as searches on our property and persons at airports or eavesdropping on our communications; and even ancestral homes built by the hands of one's forefathers could be unilaterally seized (and demolished) by the state under eminent domain laws. This is to say that whatever rights we have also imply responsibilities and exist within some particular political system, therefore it is not unreasonable to expect or define certain limits for those rights, especially where they conflict with other rights and obligations.

Maximal freedom is a hallmark of a laissez-faire or minimal state, but a democratic society is not compelled to endorse such a stance, as some political philosophers have suggested (e.g., [33]). Nor would reasonable people necessarily want unrestricted freedom anyway, e.g., no restrictions or background checks for gun ownership. Even the most liberal democracy today understands the value of regulations as a way to enhance our freedom. For instance, our economic system is not truly a "free market": though we may advocate freedom in general, regulations exist not only to protect our rights, but also to create an orderly process that greases the economic wheel, accelerating both innovations and transactions. As a simpler example, by imposing laws on traffic, we can actually *increase* our freedom: by driving forward on only one side of the road, for instance, we can be (more) assured that we will not be a victim of a head-on collision, which makes driving faster a more sensible proposition.

There is another sense, related to free will, in which cognitive enhancements may be infringing: if an enhancement, such as a mood-altering drug or neural implant, interferes or alters our deliberative process, then it is an open question whether or not we are truly acting freely while under the influence of the enhancement. For instance, a "citizen chip" embedded in the brain might cause us to be unswervingly patriotic and hold different values than we would otherwise have. Further, external pressure by or from peers, employers, competitors, national security, and others also may unduly influence one's decision making. [17].

HEALTH & SAFETY

To justify restrictions on our freedom and autonomy, of course, we would need strong, compelling reasons to offset that *prima facie* harm; specifically, we need to identify conflicting values that ought to be factored into our policymaking. One possible reason is that human enhancement technologies may pose a health risk to the person operated upon, similar to illegal or unprescribed steroids use by athletes: given how precious little we still know about how our brains and other biological systems work, any tinkering with those systems would likely give rise to unintended effects, from mild to most serious [38]. Even drinking pure water—perhaps the safest thing we can do to our own bodies—may have some harms. For example, maybe we become dependent on fluoridated water to prevent tooth decay or drink too much water which dilutes sodium in the body to dangerously-low or fatal levels. Or consider that many of the foods we eat everyday are suspected to have some causal connection to disease or unwanted conditions. It is therefore quite likely that making radical changes to our bodies undoubtedly will have surprising side-effects.

Is this reason enough to restrict human enhancement technologies, for the sake of protecting the would-be patient? The answer is not clear. Even if such technologies prove to be so dangerous or risky that we strongly believe we need to protect individuals from their own decisions to use those technologies (through paternalistic regulations), the well-informed individual

might circumvent this issue by freely and knowingly consenting to those risks, thereby removing this reason for restricted use.

But even this case does not solve the conflict between freedom/autonomy and health/safety. First, it is not always clear whether a person's consent is sufficiently informed or not. For instance, consider a partygoer who may have heard that smoking cigarettes can be addictive and harmful but nonetheless begins to smoke anyway; this seems to be a less-informed decision than one made by a person with a parent whose smoking caused a specific and horrible illness (and associated expenses). Furthermore, the partygoer may be unduly influenced by peers or movies that glamorize smoking. So paternalistic regulations could be justified under some circumstances; *e.g.*, where risks are not adequately communicated or understood, for children, and so on.

Second, the assumption that a procedure to implant some human enhancement technology may affect the health and safety of *only* that patient appears to be much too generous. Indeed, it is rare to find any human activity that has absolutely no impact on other persons, either directly or indirectly, such that our own freedom or autonomy is the only value at stake and clearly should be protected. For instance, opponents to regulating such activities as gambling, recreational drugs (including smoking tobacco), prostitution, segregation, and so forth commonly cite the need to protect their freedom or rights as the primary objection to those regulations. Yet, this objection ignores the opposing argument, which is that such activities may harm *other persons*, either actually or statistically.

To look at just one of many examples, at first glance, unfettered gambling seems to affect only the gambler (it is his money to win or lose, so the argument goes); but a broader analysis would point out that many gamblers have families whose bank accounts are being risked and that desperate gamblers may commit crimes to finance their addiction, never mind harms to the out-of-control gambler himself. Even marijuana use, which in many cases may be justified and allegedly harms no one, might be traced back to dangerous cartels that terrorize or bully the local population. Furthermore, irresponsible use of the drug could cause accidents or the user to neglect his or her obligations, family, etc. Notice here that we are not arguing that activities such as gambling and recreational drug use should be completely banned, but only that some measure of oversight seems to be appropriate for the sake of others, if not also for the welfare of the individual.

Relating back to the human enhancement debate, it seems premature to say that only the would-be enhanced person assumes any risk, even if the procedure does not affect his or her germline (*i.e.*, cannot be passed on to the next generation). The harm or risk to others could also be indirect: Where steroids use by athletes sets the presumably-wrong example for children whose bodies and minds are still developing, we can anticipate a similar temptation to be created with human enhancement technologies among children. Even parents may feel pressure—or even an obligation—to enhance their children, which arises from the natural desire to want the best for our children or, in this case, make them the best they can be.

Third, even if the harm that arises from any given instance of human enhancement is so small to be practically negligible, the individual choices to enhance oneself can lead to aggregate harms that are much larger and substantial. For instance, in today's environmental debate, calls are increasing to limit activities from lawn care or drinking bottled water: on one hand, the amount of extra water needed to keep one's lawn green seems small, as is also the amount of fertilizer or pesticide that might leach into the groundwater, but the cumulative effect of millions of homeowners caring for a pristine patch of grass can be disastrous for a nation's water supply and health.

Likewise, as human enhancement technologies improve and are adopted by more people, the once-negligible harms that arise from individual cases may metastasize into very real harms to large segments of society [34]. Life extension, as one case, may appear to be a great benefit for the individual, but on an aggregate scale, it could put pressure or burdens on families, retirement

programs, overpopulation, and so on; we will return to this below.

FAIRNESS & EQUITY

Even if we can understand why there would be pressure to enhance one's self or children, it is important to note the following: advantages gained by enhanced persons also imply a relative *disadvantage* for the unenhanced, whether in sports, employment opportunities, academic performance, or any other area. That is to say, fairness is another value to consider in the debate. A related worry is that the wealthy would be the first adopters of human enhancement technologies, given that they can best afford such innovations (like LASIK eye surgery), thus creating an even wider gap between the haves and the have-nots [29].

In considering the issue of fairness, we need to be careful to not conflate it with equity. Under most economic theories, fairness does not require that we need to close the gap entirely between economic classes, even when justice is defined as fairness ([39]; for an application of Rawls to enhancement, see [1]). Indeed, there are good reasons to think that we want some gap to exist, for example, to provide incentives for innovations, in order to move up the economic ladder, and to allow flexibility in a workforce to fill vacancies and perform a wide range of tasks. At least some competition seems to be desirable, especially when resources to be allocated are limited or scarce and when compared to the historically-unsuccessful alternative of the state attempting to equalize the welfare of its citizens.

Thus, inequality itself is not so much the point, though any poverty or decline in welfare related to increased inequality may be a serious concern. We do not want people to stop striving to improve their own lives, even if the situation for others is not improved at the same time or ever. And natural advantages and inequities already exist unproblematically anyway; Hobbes recognized that these organic differences did not give any individual or group of individuals so much *net* advantage that they would be invulnerable to the "nasty, brutish, and short" conditions that mark human life [21].

Yet if human enhancement technologies develop as predicted, they can afford us a tremendous advantage in life; *e.g.*, over others in a competition for resources, so much so that it overstretches the natural range of equality to the point where inequality becomes a more salient issue. This is where the gap between enhanced and unenhanced persons may be too wide to bridge, making the latter into dinosaurs in a hypercompetitive world. If we assume that the benefits of being an enhanced person must be largely paid from the welfare of others, *e.g.*, a job-gain by one person is a job-loss by another, since the others are now at a relative disadvantage, this may impoverish the unenhanced, which would limit their access to such things as healthcare, legal representation, political influence, and so on.

Related to the notion of equity is that of fairness. Even if pronounced inequality is morally permissible, there is still a question of *how* an individual accesses or affords a human enhancement technology, which may be unfair or unacceptably magnify the inequality. If the distribution of or access to enhancement technologies is not obviously unfair, *e.g.*, illegally discriminatory, then perhaps we can justify the resulting inequities. But what would count as a fair distribution of those technologies? A scheme based on need or productivity or any other single dimension would be easily defeated by the standard arguments that they overlook other relevant dimensions [40]. Even if a market system is considered to be fair or an acceptable approximation of it—which is highly contestable, especially after a fresh round of job layoffs and mortgage defaults—many still object to the unfairness of our starting points, which may date back to monarchies, aristocracies, "robber barons" (recall the saying that behind every great fortune there is a great crime), bad luck and other arbitrary circumstances [7]. And even if the starting points were fair, the subsequent market processes would need to be fair in order for the results (*e.g.*, that only the wealthy can afford human enhancement technologies,

who then gain significant advantages over the unenhanced) to be declared fair [28].

SOCIETAL DISRUPTION

Fairness and equality are not just theoretical values, but they have practical effects. Gross inequality itself, whether fair or not, can motivate the worse-off masses to revolt against a state or system. But societal disruption need not be so extreme to be taken seriously. Entire institutions today—as well as the lack thereof—are based on a specific range of abilities and rough equality of natural assets. Sports, for instance, would change dramatically, if enhanced persons are permitted to compete to the clear disadvantage to unenhanced athletes, smashing their previous records. (This is not to say that sports should ban enhanced competitors, only that doing so would have a real, significant effect on careers and expend valuable resources to adjust sporting programs and contests; and in the end, it is not clear that sports is better off for its trouble or that which it has caused.)

Other institutions and systems include economic (jobs), privacy, communications, pensions, security, and many other areas of society. For instance, if life-extension technologies can increase our average lifespan by 20 years (let alone the 100+ years predicted by some futurists [8, 24], and assuming that the extra 20 years will be a good life, not one bogged down with illness and unproductivity that afflict many elderly today), then we would need to radically adjust retirement programs: do we move the retirement age to 85, which has negative consequences for job-seekers such as new tenure-track academic faculty, or increase contributions to pension plans, which puts pressure on household budgets and employers? Or both? Also, assuming birth rates do not decline (which causes problems of its own), longer lives will mean more pressure on resources such as energy and food, in addition to jobs, so this could disrupt society in negative ways.

Looking more into the distance, if enhancement technologies enable us to adapt our bodies to, say, underwater living (with implantable gills, flippers, echolocation, new skin, etc.), then we would need to construct new institutions to govern that lifestyle, from underwater real estate to pollution rules to law enforcement to handling electronic devices to currency (replacing paper money of non-waterworlds). Or if this sounds too far-fetched, consider humanity's rush into outer space that will require similar attention to be paid to such issues in the near future [25].

Other nearer-term scenarios that may cause social disruption include: a job candidate with a neural implant that enables better data retention and faster information processing would consistently beat out unenhanced candidates: a person with super-human hearing or sight could circumvent existing privacy protections and expectations by easily and undetectably eavesdropping or spying on others; more students (and professors) using Ritalin may grab admission or tenure at all the best universities, reducing those opportunities for others; and so on.

So societal disruption is a non-trivial concern and seems to be something we want to mitigate where we can, though this does not imply that we should resist change in general. Minimizing disruption might be achieve by transitioning laid-off workers immediately to a new job or job-training program, rather than allowing the layoffs to come unexpectedly which leaves the newly-unemployed with few options but to fend for themselves. Today, without this kind of preparation, we trust that these social and economic disruptions eventually will be handled, but there is still a real cost to those affected by layoff that could have been better mitigated. The typewriter industry, as an example, was blindsided by the fast-growing word-processing industry in the 1980s, leading to the displacement of thousands of workers, both on the manufacturing and the end-users' sides. (Similar situations exist for the spreadsheet industry that displaced countless accountants and book-keepers, the computer-aided design industry that displaced graphic artists, and so on.)

But, unless it will be clearly and seriously harmful, social disruption by itself does not seem enough to count as a strong reason against regulating enhancement technologies. After all, we do not wish that typewriters were never replaced with word-processing programs, though we hope the affected employees readily found gainful jobs elsewhere. Human enhancement technologies, likewise, do not necessarily need to be halted or regulated, but it seems more prudent and responsible to anticipate and prepare for any disruptive effects.

To be clear, there presumably will be benefits to society from enhanced persons. We can expect greater productivity or more creative and intellectual breakthroughs, which is why individuals would want to be enhanced in the first place. But what remains difficult to calculate is whether these gains outweigh the costs or risks, or even the likelihood of either gains or costs—which is needed if we do find it sensible to use a precautionary principle to guide our policymaking.

HUMAN DIGNITY

The fiercest resistance to human enhancement technologies is perhaps a concern about their effect on "human dignity" and what it means to be human [38, 43]. For instance, does the desire for enhancement show ingratitude for what we have and (further) enable an attitude of unquenchable dissatisfaction with one's life? Some researchers suggest that discontent is hardwired into the genetic makeup of humans [20, 48], which is why we constantly innovate, strive to achieve and gain more, etc. However, even if this is true, it does not seem to be so much an argument to promote human enhancement technologies, but more a worry that those technologies are not the panacea or Holy Grail of happiness we might believe them to be; that is, we will still be dissatisfied with ourselves no matter how much we enhance ourselves (unless, of course, we somehow eradicate that part of our DNA that causes discontent).

Would human enhancement technologies hinder moral development? Many believe that "soul-making" is impossible without struggle [19], and achievements ring hollow without sacrifice or effort [38]; so if technology makes life and competitions easier, then we may lose opportunities to feed and grow our moral character. On the other hand, compare our lives today with pre-Internet days: increased connectivity to friends, work, information, etc., is often a double-edged proposition that also increases stress and decreases free time. This, then, raises the related concern of whether enhancement technologies will actually make our lives happier. (If the research mentioned above about discontent in our genes is accurate, then we might have a psychobiological reason to think not.)

Is the frailty of the human condition necessary to best appreciate life? There is something romantic about the notion of being mortal and fallible. But with existing pharmacology, we could eliminate the emotion of sadness today, and work is continuing on drugs that repress memories; but it is not clear that sadness (at least in the normal range, as opposed to clinical depression) is a "pathology" we should want to eliminate, rather than a human experience that we should preserve [38]. Other critics have suggested that life could be too long, leading to boredom after one's life-goals are achieved (e.g., [47]).

Finally, we will mention here the related, persistent concern that we are playing God with world-changing technologies, which is presumably bad [37]. But what exactly counts as "playing God," and why is that morally wrong; *i.e.*, where exactly is the proscription in religious scripture? If we define the concept as manipulating nature, then we all have been guilty of that since the first man picked up a stick. Making life-and-death decisions is a plausible candidate as a definition, but then physicians as well as soldiers (even in holy wars?) could be accused of this charge.

RESTRICTING HUMAN ENHANCEMENT TECHNOLOGIES

Given the preceding discussion, it should be clear that human enhancement is more than just about the individual's freedom or autonomy, but there are plausibly negative consequences on others and society that need to be considered. Or at least an argument needs to be made that freedom/autonomy trumps all other values, but such a position seems

unnecessarily dogmatic. These issues point to the policy dilemma of whether we should have regulations or restrictions on human enhancement technologies, so to prevent or mitigate some of the negative impacts considered. Three answers suggest themselves: (1) no restrictions, (2) some restrictions, or (3) a moratorium or full ban.

A moratorium seems unrealistic to the extent that a worldwide one would be needed to truly stem the use of human enhancement technologies, and that no worldwide moratorium on anything has yet to work, including on (alleged) attempts to clone a human being. A local moratorium would send patients to "back-alley" enhancement clinics or to more liberal regions of the world, as is the case with "cosmetic-surgery vacations" in which those medical procedures are less expensive in other nations. Further, a ban on enhancement research seems to be much too premature—an overreaction to perceived, future risks—as well as a real threat to therapy-related research today.

On the other side of the spectrum, the idea of having no restrictions on human enhancement technologies seems to be reckless or at least unjustifiably optimistic, given that there are plausible risks. As pointed out earlier, complete freedom or autonomy may be a recipe for disaster and chaos in any case; we do not want to grant the right to yell "Fire!" in a crowded venue or the right for dangerous felons to own firearms.[4]

So what about finding middle ground with some non-Draconian regulations? Critics have argued that any regulation would be imperfect and likely ineffectual, much like laws against contraband or prostitution [32]; but it is not clear that eliminating these laws would improve the situation, all things considered. Also, as a society, we still believe we ought to at least try to solve social ills, even if we cannot ultimately fix the entire problem, *e.g.*, we cannot stop any given crime from ever occurring again, yet we still have laws against such acts. And even if there are practical reasons to not pursue regulations, would that send the wrong message; *e.g.*, to children, that we countenance or support enhancement without reservations?

The issue of regulation will surely not be settled here, nor do we intend it to. Yet it is important to keep in mind that the human enhancement debate is not just a theoretical discussion about ethics, but it has bearing on the real world with policy decisions that may affect not just the would-be enhanced, but also researchers, manufacturers, social institutions, as well as our ideals of freedom and human dignity.[5]

ENDNOTES

1. For an overview of ethical and social issues beyond nanotechnology's role in human enhancement, see [1, 26, 28].

2. We recognize that some advocates of human enhancement argue against making such a distinction (e.g., [5]), which seems to serve to more easily justify unrestricted human enhancement; even if this position is tenable, we do not want to take that point for granted here, which we will discuss below.

3. However, if the military were to prescribe such medications *prior* to combat, then one could make the case for counting that as an enhancement; but this may take us full circle back to the vaccination question, particularly as soldiers are routinely vaccinated against bio-threats such as anthrax.

4. Perhaps even the right to be happy may be inappropriately exercised, say, at a funeral?

5. For more about the general debate on regulation in nanotechnology, see [27].

REFERENCES

[1] Allhoff, F. (2005). Germ-line genetic enhancement and Rawlsian primary goods. Kennedy Inst Ethics J 15(1):39–56 doi:10.1353/ken.2005.0007.

[2] Allhoff, F., Lin, P., Moor, J., Weckert, J. (2007). *Nanoethics: the ethical and social dimensions of nanotechnology.* Wiley, Hoboken, NJ.

[3] Allhoff, F., Lin, P. (2008). *Nanotechnology & society: Current and emerging issues.* Springer, Dordecht.

[4] Bailey, R. (2005). *Liberation biology: The scientific and moral case for the biotech revolution.* Prometheus Books, Amherst, NY.

[5] Bostrom, N., Roache, R. (2008). "Ethical issues in human enhancement." In: Ryberg, J., Petersen, T. S., Wolf, C. (eds) *New waves in applied ethics.* Palgrave Macmillan, New York.

[6] Daniels, N. (2000). Normal Functioning and the Treatment-Enhancement Distinction. Camb Q Healthc Ethics 9:309–322 doi:10.1017/S0963180100903037.

[7] de Balzac, H. (1835). *Père Goriot* (Signet Classics edition, 2004), trans. Henry Reed. New York, Signet Classics.

[8] de Grey, A. (2007). *Ending aging: The rejuvenation breakthroughs that could reverse human aging in our lifetime.* St. Martin's Press, New York.

[9] Dennis, C. (2004). Genetics: deaf by design. Nature 431:894–896 doi:10.1038/431894a.

[10] Dyer, C. (2000). Surgeon amputated healthy legs. BMJ 320:332 doi:10.1136/bmj, 320.7231.332.

[11] Edwards, S. D. (2008a). Should Oscar Pistorius be excluded from the 2008 olympic games? Sports Ethics Philos 2:112–125 doi:10.1080/17511320802221802.

[12] Edwards, S. D. (2008b). The Ashley treatment: a step too far, or not far enough? J Med Ethics 34:341–343 doi:10.1136/jme.2007.020743.

[13] Freitas, R. A. Jr. (1998). Exploratory design in medical nanotechnology: a mechanical artificial red cell. Artif Cells Blood Substit Immobil Biotechnol 26:411–430.

[14] Fukuyama, F. (2002). *Our posthuman future: Consequences of the biotechnology revolution.* Picador, New York.

[15] Fukuyama, F. (2006). *Beyond bioethics: A proposal for modernizing the regulation of human biotechnologies.* School of Advanced International Studies, Johns Hopkins University, Washington DC.

[16] Greely, H. (2006) 2005. "Regulating human biological enhancements: questionable justifications and international complications." The Mind, The Body, And The Law: University Of Technology, Sydney,

Law review 7: 87–110 (2005), Santa Clara J Int Law 4:87–110. joint issue.

[17] Guston, D., Parsi, J., Tosi, J., (2007). "Anticipating the ethical and political challenges of human nano-technologies" in Allhoff et al., 2007.

[18] Harris, J. (2007). *Enhancing evolution: The ethical case for making ethical people*. Princeton University Press, Princeton.

[19] Hick, J. (1966). *Evil and the God of love*. Harper and Row, New York.

[20] Hill, S. E. (2006). *Dissatisfied by design: The evolution of discontent (dissertation)*. University of Texas, Austin.

[21] Hobbes, T. (1651). *Leviathan* (Penguin Classics edition, 1982). Penguin Group, New York.

[22] Hurlbut, W. (2006). Opening remarks at "human enhancement technologies and human rights" conference, Stanford University Law School, 26–28 May 2006.

[23] Juengst, E. (1997). Can enhancement be distin-guished from prevention in genetic medicine? J Med Philos 22:125–142.

[24] Kurzweil, R. (2005). *The singularity is near: When humans transcend biology*. Viking Penguin, New York.

[25] Lin, P. (2006). Space ethics: Look before taking another leap for mankind. Astropolitics 4:281–294.

[26] Lin, P., Allhoff, F. (2007). "Nanoscience and Nano-ethics: Defining the Discipline" in Allhoff et al. 2007.

[27] Lin, P. (2007b). "Nanotechnology bound: evaluating the case for more regulation." Nanoethics 2: 105-122.

[28] Lin, P., Allhoff, F. (2008). "Introduction: nanotech-nology, society, and ethics" in Allhoff et al., 2008.

[29] McKibben, B. (2004). *Enough: Staying human in an engineered age*. Henry Holt & Co, New York.

[30] Mielke, J. (2008). "Digital tattoo interface" entry at Greener Gadgets Design Competition 2008. New York, NY, February 2008. Last accessed on 1 August 2008: http://www.core77.com/competitions/GreenerGadgets/projects/4673/.

[31] MIT (2008). Institute for soldier nanotechnologies website. Last accessed on 1 August 2008: http://web.mit.edu/ISN/research/index.html.

[32] Naam, R. (2005). *More than human*. Broadway Books, New York.

[33] Nozick, R. (1974). *Anarchy, state, and utopia*. Basic Books, New York.

[34] Parfit, D. (1986). *Reasons and persons*. Oxford University Press, New York.

[35] Parviz, B. A., et al. (2008). "Contact lens with integrated inorganic semiconductor devices" presentation at 21st IEEE International Conference on Micro Electro Mechanical Systems, Tuscon, AZ, 13–17 January 2008.

[36] Persaud, R. (2006). *"Does smarter mean happier?" in better humans?: The politics of human enhancement and life extension*. Demos, London.

[37] Peters, T. (2007). "Are we playing God with nanoenhancement?" in Allhoff et al. (2007).

[38] President's Council on Bioethics, (2003). *Beyond therapy: Biotechnology and the pursuit of happiness*. Government Printing Office, Washington, DC.

[39] Rawls, J. (1971). *A theory of justice*. Belknap, Cambridge, MA.

[40] Rescher, N. (1980). "The canons of distributive justice." In Sterba J (ed) *Justice: Alternative political perspectives*. Wadsworth, Belmont.

[41] Roco, M., Bainbridge, W. S. (2003). *Converging technologies for improving human performance: Nano-technology, biotechnology, information technology and cognitive science*. Kluwer Academic, Dordrecht.

[42] Saletan, W. (2008). "Night of the living meds: the US Military's sleep-reduction program," Slate, 16 July 2008. Last accessed on 1 August 2008: http://www.slate.com/id/2195466/.

[43] Sandel, M. (2007). *The case against perfection: Ethics in the age of genetic engineering*. Belknap, Cambridge, M.A.

[44] Savulescu, J., Foddy, B. (2007). "Ethics of perfor-mance enhancement in sport: Drugs and gene doping." In: Ashcroft, R. E., Dawson, A., Draper, H., McMillan, J. R. (eds) *Principles of health care ethics*. Wiley, London.

[45] Selgelid, M. (2007). "An argument against arguments for enhancement," studies in ethics, law, and tech-nology 1: Article 12. Last accessed on 1 August 2008: http://www.bepress.com/selt/vol1/iss1/art12/.

[46] Thompson, M. (2008). "America's medicated army," Time, 16 June 2008. Last accessed on 1 August 2008: http://www.time.com/time/nation/article/0,8599,1811858,00.html.

[47] Williams, B. (1973). *Problems of the self*. Cambridge University Press. Cambridge, UK.

[48] Woodall, J. (2007). "Programmed dissatisfaction: does one gene drive all progress in science and the arts?" The Scientist 21(6):63.

24

The Case Against Perfection

MICHAEL SANDEL

Michael Sandel raises several objections to genetic engineering. He argues that if practiced widely, genetic engineering will lead to a loss of humility on our part and, by turning the "self-made man" myth into a reality, will lead to the erosion of social solidarity. Sandel speculates that what motivates us to pursue genetic engineering is our drive to master our world and our own nature. But he judges that this drive threatens to abolish our sense of life, and our world, as a gift.

The problem with eugenics and genetic engineering is that they represent the one-sided triumph of willfulness over giftedness, of dominion over reverence, of molding over beholding. But why, we may wonder, should we worry about this triumph? Why not shake off our unease with enhancement as so much superstition? What would be lost if biotechnology dissolved our sense of giftedness?

HUMILITY, RESPONSIBILITY, AND SOLIDARITY

From the standpoint of religion, the answer is clear: To believe that our talents and powers are wholly our own doing is to misunderstand our place in creation, to confuse our role with God's. But religion is not the only source of reasons to care about giftedness. The moral stakes can also be described in secular terms. If the genetic revolution erodes our appreciation for the gifted character of human powers and achievements, it will transform three key features of our moral landscape—humility, responsibility, and solidarity.

In a social world that prizes mastery and control, parenthood is a school for humility. That we care deeply about our children, and yet cannot choose the kind we want, teaches parents to be open to the unbidden. Such openness is a disposition worth affirming, not only within families but in the wider world as well. It invites us to abide the unexpected, to live with dissonance, to reign in the impulse to control. A *Gattaca*-like world, in which parents became accustomed to specifying the sex and genetic traits of their children, would be a world inhospitable to the unbidden, a gated community writ large.

The social basis of humility would also be diminished if people became accustomed to genetic self-improvement. The awareness that our talents and abilities are not wholly our own doing restrains our tendency toward hubris. If bioengineering made the myth of the "self-made man" come true, it would be difficult to view our talents as gifts for which we are indebted rather than achievements for which we are responsible. (Genetically enhanced children would of course remain indebted rather than responsible for their traits, though their debt would run more to their parents and less to nature, chance, or God.)

It is sometimes thought that genetic enhancement erodes human responsibility by overriding effort and striving. But the real problem is the explosion, not the erosion, of responsibility. As humility gives way, responsibility expands to daunting proportions. We attribute less to chance and more to choice. Parents become responsible for choosing, or failing to choose, the right traits for their children. Athletes become responsible for acquiring, or failing to acquire, the talents that will help their team win.

One of the blessings of seeing ourselves as creatures of nature, God, or fortune is that we are not wholly responsible for the way we are. The more we become masters of our genetic endowments, the greater the burden we bear for the talents we have and the way we perform. Today when a basketball player misses a rebound, his coach can blame him for being out of position. Tomorrow the coach may blame him for being too short.

Even now, the growing use of performance-enhancing drugs in professional sports is subtly transforming the expectations players have for one another. In the past when a starting pitcher's team scored too few runs to win, he could only curse his bad luck and take it in stride. These days, the use of amphetamines and other stimulants is so widespread that players who take the field without them are criticized for "playing naked." A recently retired major league outfielder told *Sports Illustrated* that some pitchers blame teammates who play unenhanced: "If the starting pitcher knows that you're going out there naked, he's upset that you're not giving him [everything] you can. The big-time pitcher wants to make sure you're beaning up before the game."[1]

The explosion of responsibility, and the moral burdens it creates, can also be seen in changing norms that accompany the use of prenatal genetic testing. Once, giving birth to a child with Down syndrome was considered a matter of chance; today many parents of children with Down syndrome or other genetic disabilities feel judged or blamed. A domain once governed by fate has now become an arena of choice. Whatever one believes about which, if any, genetic conditions warrant terminating a pregnancy (or selecting against an embryo, in the case of preimplantation genetic diagnosis), the advent of genetic testing creates a burden of decision that did not exist before. Prospective parents remain free to choose whether to use prenatal testing and whether to act on the results. But they are not free to escape the burden of choice that the new technology creates. Nor can they avoid being implicated in the enlarged frame of moral responsibility that accompanies new habits of control.

The Promethean impulse is contagious. In parenting as in sports, it unsettles and erodes the gifted dimension of human experience. When performance-enhancing drugs become commonplace, unenhanced ballplayers find themselves "playing naked." When genetic screening becomes a routine part of pregnancy, parents who eschew it are regarded as "flying blind" and are held responsible for whatever genetic defect befalls their child.

Paradoxically, the explosion of responsibility for our own fate, and that of our children, may diminish our sense of solidarity with those less fortunate than ourselves. The more alive we are to the chanced nature of our lot, the more reason we have to share our fate with others. Consider the case of insurance. Since people do not know whether or when various ills will befall them, they pool their risk by buying health insurance and life insurance. As life plays itself out, the healthy wind up subsidizing the unhealthy, and those who live to a ripe old age wind up subsidizing the families of those who die before their time. The result is mutuality by inadvertence. Even without a sense of mutual obligation, people pool their risks and resources, and share one another's fate.

But insurance markets mimic the practice of solidarity only insofar as people do not know or control their own risk factors. Suppose genetic testing advanced to the point where it could reliably predict each person's medical history and life expectancy. Those confident of good health and long life would opt out of the pool, causing premiums to skyrocket for those destined for ill health. The solidaristic aspect of insurance would disappear as those with good genes fled the actuarial company of those with bad ones.

The concern that insurance companies would use genetic data to assess risks and set premiums recently led the U.S. Senate to vote to prohibit genetic discrimination in health insurance. But the bigger danger, admittedly more speculative, is that genetic enhancement, if routinely practiced, would make it harder to foster the moral sentiments that social solidarity requires.

Why, after all, do the successful owe anything to the least advantaged members of society? One compelling answer to this question leans heavily on the notion of giftedness. The natural talents that enable the successful to flourish are not their own doing but, rather, their good fortune—a result of the genetic lottery.[2] If our genetic endowments are gifts, rather than achievements for which we can claim credit, it is a mistake and a conceit to assume that we are entitled to the full measure of the bounty they reap in a market economy. We therefore have an obligation to share this bounty with those who, through no fault of their own, lack comparable gifts.

Here, then, is the connection between solidarity and giftedness: A lively sense of the contingency of our gifts—an awareness that none of us is wholly responsible for his or her success—saves a meritocratic society from sliding into the smug assumption that success is the crown of virtue, that the rich are rich because they are more deserving than the poor.

If genetic engineering enabled us to override the results of the genetic lottery, to replace chance with choice, the gifted character of human powers and achievements would recede, and with it, perhaps, our capacity to see ourselves as sharing a common fate. The successful would become even more likely than they are now to view themselves as self-made and self-sufficient, and hence wholly responsible for their success. Those at the bottom of society would be viewed not as disadvantaged, and so worthy of a measure of

compensation, but as simply unfit, and so worthy of eugenic repair. The meritocracy, less chastened by chance, would become harder, less forgiving. As perfect genetic knowledge would end the simulacrum of solidarity in insurance markets, perfect genetic control would erode the actual solidarity that arises when men and women reflect on the contingency of their talents and fortunes.

OBJECTIONS

My argument against enhancement is likely to invite at least two objections: Some may complain that it is overly religious; others may object that it is unpersuasive in consequentialist terms. The first objection asserts that to speak of a gift presupposes a giver. If this is true, then my case against genetic engineering and enhancement is inescapably religious. I argue, to the contrary, that an appreciation for the giftedness of life can arise from either religious or secular sources. While some believe that God is the source of the gift of life, and that reverence for life is a form of gratitude to God, one need not hold this belief in order to appreciate life as a gift or to have reverence for it. We commonly speak of an athlete's gift, or a musician's, without making any assumption about whether or not the gift comes from God. What we mean is simply that the talent in question is not wholly the athlete's or the musician's own doing; whether he has nature, fortune, or God to thank for it, the talent is an endowment that exceeds his control.

In a similar way, people often speak of the sanctity of life, and even of nature, without necessarily embracing the strong metaphysical version of that idea. For example, some hold with the ancients that nature is sacred in the sense of being enchanted, or inscribed with inherent meaning, or animated by divine purpose; others, in the Judeo-Christian tradition, view the sanctity of nature as deriving from God's creation of the universe; and still others believe that nature is sacred simply in the sense that it is not a mere object at our disposal, open to any use we may desire. These various understandings of the sacred all insist that we value nature and the living beings within it as more than mere instruments; to act otherwise displays a lack of reverence, a failure of respect. But this moral mandate need not rest on a single religious or metaphysical background.

It might be replied that nontheological notions of sanctity and gift cannot ultimately stand on their own but must lean on borrowed metaphysical assumptions they fail to acknowledge. This is a deep and difficult question that I cannot attempt to resolve here. It is worth noting, however, that liberal thinkers from Locke to Kant to Habermas accept the idea that freedom depends on an origin or standpoint that exceeds our control. For Locke, our life and liberty, being inalienable rights, are not ours to give away (through suicide or selling ourselves into slavery). For Kant, though we are the authors of the moral law, we are not at liberty to exploit ourselves or to treat ourselves as objects any more than we may do so to other persons. And for Habermas, as we have seen, our freedom as equal moral beings depends on having an origin beyond human manipulation or control. We can make sense of these notions of inalienable and inviolable rights without necessarily embracing religious conceptions of the sanctity of human life. In a similar way, we can make sense of the notion of giftedness, and feel its moral weight, whether or not we trace the source of the gift to God.

The second objection construes my case against enhancement as narrowly consequentialist, and finds it wanting, along the following lines: Pointing to the possible effects of bioengineering on humility, responsibility, and solidarity may be persuasive to those who prize those virtues. But those who care more about gaining a competitive edge for their children or themselves may decide that the benefits to be gained from genetic enhancement outweigh its allegedly adverse effects on social institutions and moral sentiments. Moreover, even assuming that the desire for mastery is bad, an individual who pursues it may achieve some redeeming moral good—a cure for cancer, for example. So why should we assume that the "bad" of mastery necessarily outweighs the good it can bring about?

To this objection I reply that I do not mean to rest the case against enhancement on consequentialist considerations, at least not in the usual sense of the term. My point is not that genetic engineering is objectionable simply because the social costs are likely to outweigh the benefits. Nor do I claim that people who bioengineer their children or themselves are necessarily motivated by a desire for mastery, and that this motive is a sin no good result could possibly outweigh. I am suggesting instead that the moral stakes in the enhancement debate are not fully captured by the familiar categories of autonomy and rights, on the one hand, and the calculation of costs and benefits, on the other. My concern with enhancement is not as individual vice but as habit of mind and way of being.

The bigger stakes are of two kinds. One involves the fate of human goods embodied in important social practices—norms of unconditional love and an openness to the unbidden, in the case of parenting; the celebration of natural talents and gifts in athletic and artistic endeavors; humility in the face of privilege, and a willingness to share the fruits of good fortune through institutions of social solidarity. The other involves our orientation to the world that we inhabit, and the kind of freedom to which we aspire.

It is tempting to think that bioengineering our children and ourselves for success in a competitive society is an exercise of freedom. But changing our nature to fit the world, rather than the other way around, is actually the deepest form of disempowerment. It distracts us from reflecting critically on the world, and deadens the impulse to social and political improvement. Rather than employ our new genetic powers to straighten "the crooked timber of humanity,"[3] we should do what we can to create social and political arrangements more hospitable to the gifts and limitations of imperfect human beings.

THE PROJECT OF MASTERY

In the late 1960s, Robert L. Sinsheimer, a molecular biologist at the California Institute of Technology, glimpsed the shape of things to come. In an article entitled "The Prospect of Designed Genetic Change," he argued that freedom of choice would vindicate the new genetics, and set it apart from the discredited eugenics of old. "To implement the older eugenics of Galton and his successors would have required a massive social program carried out over many generations. Such a program could not have been initiated without the consent and co-operation of a major fraction of the population, and would have been continuously subject to social control. In contrast, the new eugenics could, at least in principle, be implemented on a quite individual basis, in one generation, and subject to no existing restrictions."[4]

According to Sinsheimer, the new eugenics would be voluntary rather than coerced, and also more humane. Rather than segregate and eliminate the unfit, it would improve them. "The old eugenics would have required a continual selection for breeding of the fit, and a culling of the unfit. The new eugenics would permit in principle the conversion of all the unfit to the highest genetic level."[5]

Sinsheimer's paean to genetic engineering caught the heady, Promethean self-image of the age. He wrote hopefully of rescuing "the losers in that chromosomal lottery that so firmly channels our human destinies," including not only those born with genetic defects but also "the 50 million 'normal' Americans with an IQ of less than 90." But he also saw that something bigger was at stake than improving upon nature's "mindless, age-old throw of dice." Implicit in the new technologies of genetic intervention was a new, more exalted place for human beings in the cosmos. "As we enlarge man's freedom, we diminish his constraints and that which he must accept as given." Copernicus and Darwin had "demoted man from his bright glory at the focal point of the universe," but the new biology would restore his pivotal role. In the mirror of our new genetic knowledge, we would see ourselves as more than a link in the chain of evolution: "We can be the agent of transition to a whole new pitch of evolution. This is a cosmic event."[6]

There is something appealing, even intoxicating, about a vision of human freedom unfettered by the given. It may even be the case that the allure of that vision played a part in summoning the genomic age into being. It is often assumed that the powers of enhancement we now possess arose as an inadvertent by-product of biomedical progress—the genetic revolution came, so to speak, to cure disease, but stayed to tempt us with the prospect of enhancing our performance, designing our children, and perfecting our nature. But that may have the story backward. It is also possible to view genetic engineering as the ultimate expression of our resolve to see ourselves astride the world, the masters of our nature. But that vision of freedom is flawed. It threatens to banish our appreciation of life as a gift, and to leave us with nothing to affirm or behold outside our own will.

ENDNOTES

1. Tom Verducci, "Getting Amped: Popping Amphetamines or Other Stimulants Is Part of Many Players' Pregame Routine," *Sports Illustrated*, June 3, 2002, p. 38.

2. See John Rawls, *A Theory of Justice* (Cambridge, MA: Harvard University Press, 1971), pp. 72–75, 102–105.

3. See Isaiah Berlin, "John Stuart Mill and the Ends of Life," in Berlin, *Four Essays on Liberty* (London: Oxford University Press, 1969), p. 193, quoting Kant: "Out of the crooked timber of humanity no straight thing was ever made."

4. Robert L. Sinsheimer, "The Prospect of Designed Genetic Change," *Engineering and Science Magazine*, April 1969 (California Institute of Technology). Reprinted in Ruth F. Chadwick, ed., *Ethics, Reproduction and Genetic Control* (London: Routledge, 1994), pp. 144–145.

5. Ibid., p. 145.

6. Ibid., pp. 145–146.

25

Enhancing Evolution

JOHN HARRIS

John Harris defends human enhancement technologies and claims that objections against pursuing their development are irrational. He provides several examples and scenarios in order to make the case that it is counterintuitive to oppose enhancement. He also responds to several concerns over human enhancement, including concerns about inequality and the possibility of catastrophic risks.

I want now to make a brief but I hope decisive and persuasive case for the ethical imperatives which have placed human enhancement firmly on the agenda of all who care about the future of humankind. In later chapters I will deepen and broaden the arguments needed to defend and elaborate this thesis and consider in more detail the consequences of its acceptance. Here, the discussion is designed to introduce different types of enhancement defined by their modes of operation which give a vivid sense of the various forms the debate about enhancement takes. Different styles of objection to them and possible responses to those objections are "curtain raisers" to the more detailed discussion to come in later chapters.

EXAMPLE 1: MECHANICAL VERSUS CHEMICAL ENHANCEMENTS

I wonder how many readers of this book, like me, use spectacles? All who do are using an enhancement technology. Now you might say "yes, but that restores normal functioning or repairs or corrects disease, damage, or injury." So it does.

Those who say this will probably know of the work of Boorse[1] and Daniels,[2] who have each defined health and, hence, illness in terms of departures from normal functioning or departures from species-typical functioning.

Now consider the use of a telescope or pair of binoculars or a microscope. These tools are not used to restore normalcy or treat disease or injury. They are done to enhance powers and capacities.

Again I wonder how many of those who have ever used binoculars thought they were crossing a moral divide when they did so? How many people thought (or now think) that there is a moral difference between wearing reading glasses and looking through opera glasses? That one is permissible and the other wicked?

Those who think there is something in principle problematic about enhancement will have to show that there is some principled difference between spectacles and binoculars and that in the legendary incident at the battle of Copenhagen, England's great naval hero Horatio Nelson put the telescope to his blind eye to protect himself from moral turpitude!

Some people think that whether the enhancement is mechanical or chemical makes a moral difference. On this view bicycles are permitted but steroids not. Steven Rose, for example, makes this point forcefully. Having used substantially the same contrast as I have made between spectacles and telescopes, he goes on to say:

> It is true that when Galileo developed the telescope there were those among his compatriots who refused to look through it, but few today would share this ethical discomfort. Yet in the context of substances that interact directly with our bodily biochemistry, we feel a considerable unease, reflected in custom and law. It is alright to change our body chemistry by training, but to achieve a similar effect with steroids is illegal for athletes. It is alright to buy educational privilege for one's children by paying for private tuition, but dubious to enhance their skills by feeding them drugs.[3]

If we search in this passage (or elsewhere in Rose's writing) for a rational defense of this difference, we find only an appeal to custom and law or to the "yuck factor." "We feel," he says, "a considerable unease reflected in custom and law," and yet this same unease was felt by Galileo's compatriots with the same degree of justification! I will return to the distinction between mechanical and chemical enhancements in a moment, but first let's consider another example.

EXAMPLE 2: DISEASE AND VACCINATION

Suppose there are some infectious diseases we can eliminate by operating on the environment. We can, we shall suppose, kill airborne infectious agents by introducing into the atmosphere a substance harmless to flora and fauna but lethal only to the target infectious agent, whether a bacterium or a virus. If we could be satisfied that the atmospheric additive was harmless to everything but the target virus, bacteria, or whatever, we would

surely welcome such a discovery. Everything speaks for it and nothing against. Such an intervention would not, however, be an enhancement technology; it would not change human beings in any way. Rather, it would have the effect of rendering them safe from, if not immune to, these infections.

Now suppose we could eliminate the same infectious diseases by the use of effective vaccines in the way we have succeeded in doing with polio and smallpox. Presumably we would welcome this as a wonderful and effective public health measure, which saved lives, saved money, and minimized suffering and distress. Everything speaks for it and nothing against. Vaccination is of course an enhancement technology and one that has been long accepted (since the smallpox vaccine was first used at the end of the eighteenth century). Interestingly, there has been very little resistance to this form of enhancement.

Since vulnerability to smallpox and polio, or to measles, mumps, and rubella, is perfectly normal and natural (for those misguided enough to think that there is any virtue in what's normal or natural), then, if we alter human beings to affect their vulnerability to these things, we are enhancing them. We are interfering with perfectly normal and perfectly healthy human beings (babies or adults) to enhance them. Vaccines then are not "treatments," since the individuals vaccinated are not usually ill. They enhance precisely because they make changes to the normal physiology of humans which improve their resistance to disease and enhance their powers of survival. There may be some people who think this is wrong but you wouldn't want to be their child if you knew what was good for you!

Here again we see Rose's puzzling distinction between the mechanical and the chemical or between direct and indirect interferences with bodily chemistry.

EXAMPLE 3: GENETIC ENHANCEMENT

Is there something qualitatively different about intervening in the natural genetic lottery to improve upon (enhance) a naturally evolved or a naturally created genome? Many people clearly think so.

A number of the world's leading laboratories are currently working on radical therapies which would also constitute enhancements. For example, David Baltimore's lab at Caltech is working on the possibility of engineering resistance or possibly immunity to HIV/AIDS and cancer into cells. The benefits of this and related work around the world are incalculable. Whatever else they are, they would also constitute radical enhancement since, alas, immunity to HIV/AIDS or cancer is not part of "normal species functioning" or "species-typical functioning" for our species.

Baltimore notes that one way in which immunity might be engineered is by manipulating the immune system to resist cancers. "The immune system is genetically controlled," he says, "and it is possible to manipulate its mechanisms using gene therapy methods." Moreover, the way in which this might be done involves bringing "new genes into the cells using a virus as a carrier or vector." This work is a "grand challenge" and success is problematic, but the point for us, for society, is to decide whether we should hope Baltimore and others are successful or hope their work will fail.

It is tempting to speculate as to whether there are any people who think that Baltimore's work is wicked and should be stopped. I don't and I hope you don't, because if it were to succeed and to result in a genetic intervention that was safe and effective, millions of lives would be saved. Since it is difficult to imagine anyone hoping that Baltimore will be unsuccessful, we know that there are no principled objections to genetic enhancements per se nor to enhancements that prevent disease. From this we can conclude, anticipating more detailed arguments to come, that whatever is wrong (if anything) with enhancement, it is not that such modifications operate on genes or even on the germline, nor that they interfere with natural nor normal nor species-typical human functioning, nor that they reject some of the ways in which humans are constituted or find themselves with a "given" nature or set of capacities or vulnerabilities.

Francis Fukuyama is one among many who appeal to a nebulous and ultimately impenetrable notion to show why changes to human nature are absolutely unacceptable. He postulates a "factor X" that "entitles every member of the species to a higher moral status than the rest of the natural world."[4] And, trying to explain what he means by human dignity, he insists that "From a secular perspective, it would have to do with human nature: the species typical characteristics shared by all human beings qua human beings. That is ultimately what is at stake in the biotech revolution."[5] This is impenetrable because Fukuyama insists the factor X is what is left "when we strip all of a person's contingent and accidental characteristics away." He imagines we are left with "some essential human quality underneath."[6] Jonathan Glover[7] has identified the weaknesses of this view with unerring precision and I cannot here do justice to his critique. The essence of the problem with Fukuyama is that he gives no positive account of factor X which might persuade us either that it is worth preserving, or that if we lose it there will be hell to pay. Without this, Fukuyama is simply making a plea for precaution without any indication as to why precaution entails the preservation rather than the sacrifice of factor X. Indeed, if it could be shown that factor X could be enhanced, either to make it resistant to erosion or indeed in ways that boosted its essential X-ness, then presumably Fukuyama would have to endorse human enhancement.

A more radical and even more intemperate objection to genetic enhancement of the sort which might be achieved if Baltimore's work bears fruit comes from George Annas. In a diatribe against cloning and "attempts to cure or prevent genetic diseases and then to 'improve' or 'enhance' genetic characteristics," Annas seems to be against both the cure and the prevention of genetic diseases if it involves any changes to the human genome:

> Cloning, however, is only the beginning of the genetic engineering project. The next steps involve attempts to "cure" or "prevent" genetic diseases, and then to "improve" or "enhance" genetic

characteristics to create the superhuman or posthuman.

It is this project that creates the prospect of genetic genocide as its most likely conclusion. This is because, given the history of humankind, it is extremely unlikely that we will see the posthumans as equal in rights and dignity to us, or that they will see us as equals. Instead, it is most likely either that we will see them as a threat to us, and thus seek to imprison or simply kill them before they kill us. Alternatively, the posthuman will come to see us (the garden variety human) as an inferior subspecies without human rights to be enslaved or slaughtered preemptively.

It is this potential for genocide based on genetic difference, that I have termed "genetic genocide," that makes species-altering genetic engineering a potential weapon of mass destruction, and makes the unaccountable genetic engineer a potential bioterrorist.[8]

Annas is aware that this will seem overblown (and says so in the very next line of his tirade). However, while to say this rhetoric is overblown is something of an understatement, it is problematic not because of all the rather strained huffing and puffing involved, but because, on the basis of mere speculation about future possible effects, Annas seeks to deny millions of people and eventually the entire population of the planet access to possible lifesaving and life-enhancing therapies.[9] To claim that "[i]t is this potential for genocide based on genetic difference, that I have termed 'genetic genocide,' that makes species-altering genetic engineering a potential weapon of mass destruction, and makes the unaccountable genetic engineer a potential bioterrorist" is about as plausible as saying that deliberately reproducing people of Jewish origin made all Jewish parents potential instigators of the Holocaust. Annas claims that the "genetic engineer is a potential bioterrorist" is based on the fact that in the first place the genetic engineer is unaccountable, and secondly she has brought into being an individual or individuals

who are potential victims (or persecutors) because of a genetic difference that has been deliberately or knowingly created. This analogy is telling because all parents are unaccountable. Indeed, parents are more so than scientists, who in most countries have to have their work approved by ethics committees and, unlike parents, undergo lengthy training and education. Moreover, scientists are more extensively subject to national laws and regulations and international conventions. Moreover, where parents create children whom history has shown are likely to be different in a way that promotes hostility, discrimination, and sometimes murder, there is obviously a potential for genocide based on difference. With enhanced groups of people, just as with ethnic or religious or national groups of people, the therapy of choice is surely to operate on the mindless prejudice that creates the hostility rather than to stigmatize as terrorists or potential murderers, and indeed outlaw, those who deliberately create or perpetuate such identifiably "different" groupings.

I have in the past emphasized, contra Annas, that, far from constituting a threat to the preservation of the human genome, human reproductive cloning is the only method of reproduction that preserves the human genome intact (just as it was).[10] This is obvious, since sexual reproduction does not preserve the human genome but constantly varies it through an almost random combination of the genomes of the two parents. Cloning, in that it repeats a given genome, is the technique that can claim priority as method of genomic conservation. Equally, as Sarah Chan has aptly pointed out, only universal cloning (by abolishing genetic difference altogether) can remove any temptation to, or potential for, "genocide" based on genetic difference. If Annas followed his own arguments, he would be the most staunch and fearless advocate for human reproductive cloning.

Annas, Kass, and other critics treat regenerative medicine, and cell-based therapies with enhancing properties, as if the enhancing properties were dispensable and disposable add-ons, as if regenerative medicine could be therapeutic without engaging the mechanisms that do the enhancing. But this is to misunderstand the way the science will work. We are unlikely to be able to separate the enhancing and therapeutic powers of drugs and techniques, as we noticed when considering Baltimore's work. This dual role of new therapies and techniques will be recurring theme of this book, and their probable inseparability is an essential reminder of the complexity of the choices involved.

DOUBLE EFFECT

Of course the notorious doctrine of double effect could be invoked to suggest that it is permissible to use enhancements, as the primary intention "first effect" is therapeutic and the second, enhancing, effect can be condoned because it is the inevitable but unwanted side effect of therapy. However, while such different levels of effect are distinguishable, they do not do the job required, which is to absolve the agent of responsibility for second effects. Anthony Kenny pointed out long ago that if I get drunk tonight knowing full well, foreseeing, that I will have a hangover in the morning, it would be odd to say that I get drunk with the intention of having a hangover in the morning. However, if for some reason having a hangover were morally significant or carried with it criminal responsibility, the fact that the foreseen hangover was unintended would not cut much moral ice. Suppose I am a pilot and if I fly with a hangover I may crash the plane, or I must testify in a crucial trial tomorrow and with a hangover I know I will forget the relevant evidence. While it is true, if you like, that I do not *intend* to have the hangover, it will not be true that I am innocent of the consequences of that hangover, either morally or (probably) criminally.

EXAMPLE 4: CHEMICAL
ENHANCEMENT

There are numerous and varied candidates for chemical cognition enhancers; a recent report listed literally scores of possible candidates from vitamins to amphetamines, from herbs to brain-computer interfaces. Two of the most popular are

- methylphenidate (Ritalin), a cognition enhancer with a good evidence base, which is widely used for improving various aspects of cognition in children and adults,
- modafinil, which enhances wakefulness and alertness and is identified for possible enhancement of the functioning of pilots, long-distance drivers, and military personnel.

Steven Rose, talking of the possible use of so-called "smart" drugs like Ritalin, asks:

Is it cheating to pass a competitive examination under the influence of such a drug? Polls conducted among youngsters make it clear that they do regard it as cheating, in the same way that the use of steroids by athletes is considered to be cheating. However, the military at least has no qualms about such enhancement. U.S pilots in the recent Iraq war were said routinely to be using the attention-enhancing and sleep reducing drug modafinil (Provigil) on bombing missions.[11]

The cocktail of choice for military pilots is apparently amphetamines on the way out to hype them up for combat and modafinil on the way back to keep them awake and alert to get home safe.

The claims Rose is making here are complex and perhaps confused. If we ask why athletes using steroids are considered to be cheats, one obvious answer is that because the use of performance-enhancing drugs in competitive sport is banned their use must be clandestine, and it is cheating because it is contrary to the rules and an attempt to steal an unfair advantage. If, however, the rules permitted such use, then the advantage would not be "unfair" because it would be an advantage available to all.

In the context of education we have noted that Rose and indeed many others think that

[i]t is alright to buy educational privilege for one's children by paying for private tuition, but dubious to enhance their skills by feeding them drugs.

Now, buying educational privilege in a context in which not all can afford to do so is certainly unfair in some sense. But if we defend people's rights to do this it is because we see education as a good and we feel it is right to encourage people to provide goods for their children and wrong to deny them these goods even if not all can obtain them. Indeed, it is somewhat misleading to talk of buying educational privilege or advantage. It is possible that people may be seeking an edge, a relative advantage for their children, but it is more likely (and perhaps more decent) that they are simply seeking excellence, the best for their kids, rather than seeking an unfair advantage over others. Some say "when it comes to examinations, excellence just means being better, more successful" but this is not so. Examinations are not an end in themselves: they are supposed to measure excellence or at least ability in the subjects examined. They are the measure of excellence at, say, philosophy but do not constitute excellence in philosophy. Of course, to seek excellence, to do the best for your kids when others cannot match your efforts, will probably also confer an advantage, but is it doubtful ethics to deny a benefit to any until it can be delivered to all. The same is true of many other goods that cannot be equally provided for all. We will return to this point in a moment. It is not then wrong to attempt to do the best for your kids by providing them with goods that may, because they are unevenly distributed or differentially usable, also confer advantages on them relative to others. Access to performance-enhancing drugs is obviously unlike education in that it is not considered to be an intrinsic good: "education for its own sake." However, it is clearly an instrumental good in the same way that a healthy diet is good, in that it conduces to health and longevity and the only remaining issue is the possible side effects of the drugs—the safety, in other words.

POSITIONAL GOODS

Many people are on long-term drug treatment. I myself, like many men of my age, take daily aspirin and statins. These are widely available, but even if they were not and I could afford them or access them when others could not, I would still take them. I take these drugs not to get the better of my fellow men and women (as a so-called "positional good" to improve my position relative to others) but to give to myself the best chance (in absolute terms) of a long and healthy life. If they are available to all, I lose nothing and indeed I hope that they are or will become available to all. I take them not for advantage but for my own good. Fairness does not require that I should not try to protect myself because others cannot; it does not require that benefits should not be provided to any until they can be made available to all. Fairness might require that we make all reasonable attempts to achieve universal provision. True, taking aspirin is not straightforwardly (or, perhaps one should say, not obviously) a means to a positional good in the same way that taking a performance enhancer before an exam the results of which will mean that some will succeed while others fail would be. But of course if my taking aspirin while others do not means that I live and they do not, I seem to have a positional advantage (despite the fact that my competitors, since many of them will be dead, occupy no position at all). Just as it is not wrong to save some lives when all cannot be saved, it is not wrong to advantage some in ways that also confer a positional advantage when all cannot be bettered in those ways. However, it is of course wrong to save some but not all when all could be saved in order to advantage those who benefit. The discussion of the claim that advantaging more people by using any particular enhancement was or was not possible in any particular set of circumstances is complex and is way beyond the scope of the present discussion.

I favor and defend enhancements as absolute rather than as positional goods. I defend them because they are good for people not because they confer advantages on some but not on others. I am therefore uninterested in any collective action problems that result from their use for positional advantage rather than for the betterment of individuals or of humankind. The morally justifiable enhancements owe their moral justification to the fact that they make lives better, not to the fact that they make some lives better than others. Therefore, the collective action problem that results from the fact that people invest in enhancements—either to get an edge or to protect themselves from being made worse-off by others having them when I do not in a way that leaves everyone poorer and no one better off than anyone else—is a problem for them and not for me or for the enhancing technology. "Serves them right," you might say, and you'd be right! The ethical justification for or defense of enhancements is not that they do or might confer positional advantage but that they make lives better.

Consider a different example. We, in the United Kingdom, are trying (not very seriously in my view) to make kidney transplants available to all who need them, as it is believed the Belgians, the Spanish, and the Austrians have managed to do. Even when that is achieved we know that thousands in the rest of the world cannot obtain the transplants they need. In India, for example, there are about a hundred thousand new cases of end-stage renal failure each year and only about three thousand transplants are performed. We do not (and surely we should not) say that we will perform no more transplants here until the needs of all those in India can be met. And since we currently do not even have enough kidneys available for our own population, we do not think that fairness demands that we suspend our transplant program pending a sufficient supply for U.K. needs. Perhaps this is partially because in seeking to provide enough donor organs for our own population we are not trying to gain an unfair advantage over the people of India; we do this not selfishly but altruistically, knowing that the altruism will fall short of universality. It is not, however, partisan. If and when we have a surplus of donor organs for the United Kingdom, I hope and expect we will donate that surplus abroad, just as other countries that have achieved a surplus do.

Elsewhere[12] I have argued that there are no good moral reasons to prefer to help compatriots rather than strangers; but there are often powerful practical and political reasons why altruism and even obligation must sometimes begin (but not end) at home. We have space for just one obvious example: in the case of transplants the measures required need the backing of law and of a medical and regulatory system that protects donors and recipients. This is not easy to provide internationally, although not of course impossible.

So when enhancements make life or lives better they are justified if they do just that if they also confer positional advantage that is no part of the justification and will in fact always constitute a moral disadvantage of their use, although whether this disadvantage constitutes a decisive argument against either the use or the permissibility of the enhancement will depend upon many other factors, among which are the degree of advantage, the degree of unfairness it creates, and the likelihood of the unfairness being minimized over time or by other factors such as compensation. Some of these factors will occupy us immediately or indeed later in this book. Others may be left unresolved either because they are simply insoluble or because they are beyond me!

PRIORITIES AND DISTRIBUTIVE JUSTICE

It is often suggested that enhancements (and also other high-tech and/or expensive procedures) should never be a priority until more basic treatments and welfare provision can be offered to all. There is much to be said for the sentiment, and for the moral consciousness expressed in this idea, but little for the evidence or argument which might sustain it.

We have already considered that it is doubtful ethics to deny a benefit to some unless and until it can be provided for all. It is also doubtful economics and doubtful policy.

No one can be ignorant of the fact that procedures which start expensive, rare (even elitist), and risky often become widely available, if not universal, cheap, relatively safe (safe enough given the balance of risk and benefit), and widely accessible. In recent times, spectacles, portable timepieces (watches and clocks), radiophonic communications, radar, computers, access to the Internet and to satellite technology, mobile phones, and bicycles, not to mention motor transport, radio and television, and photography, film, and digital technology have followed this path (with mixed benefits to individuals and societies it must be admitted). In medicine, access to a physician, vaccines, antibiotics, transplants, contraception, and many drugs has become commonplace and generally available in industrialized (high-income) societies and widespread even in lower-income countries. There is of course reason to fear the escalating costs of high-tech medicine, but the point for the present argument is that products and procedures need to start somewhere if they are to get anywhere. This means that unless we permit and possibly fund the development, we never benefit from the product or procedure and wide (if not universal) access could never occur. There is no reason to believe that things will be different for human enhancement. If we banned innovations unless and until they could be made available to all, it is probable that they would never be (have been) developed. We cannot know this for sure but it is highly probable. More certain (almost as certain as almost-certainty permits) is that they would be considerably delayed with all the targeted and collateral damage that benefit delayed typically causes.

Of course, if the advantages of particular enhancements were significant or the costs of not receiving them sufficiently substantial, governments or private agencies might (should) step in to fill the gap.

There is no simple answer to the question of justice of access to enhancements any more than there is to justice and access to health care or other technologies. This book is about the ethics of making available and accessing human enhancement, and about the moral and social impact of interventions in the natural lottery of life and in the course of evolution. How these are to be funded is another question entirely. We have examined and will continue to examine some of the constraints on access and funding. Very few new technologies have been given a universal priority. Antibiotics, developed as they were at the outset of World War II, were put into large-scale production by the United States following their success in treating septicemia, to which open war wounds were susceptible. The near universality of smallpox vaccination has eradicated smallpox and the same (it is hoped) will soon be true of polio. These are rare examples of global provision. As indicated above, there is no moral case for delaying access to any treatment or technology with health benefits until we are in a position to provide equitable and universal access. The more beneficial the technology, whether it be therapeutic or enhancing, the greater the moral imperative for wide and equitable access. Some technologies (bicycles, motor transport, and mobile phones) have become widely available because they are highly attractive and useful, and others (vaccines, antibiotics) because national and international programs of access have been initiated. It is far too early to know how access will develop for the more radical and innovative forms of enhancement.

EXAMPLE 5: LIFE EXTENSION

Other groups are working on life-extending therapies using a combination of stem cell research and other research into the ways that cells age to both regenerate aging or diseased tissue and switch off the aging process in cells. Again, to live several hundred years and perhaps eventually to become "immortal" is no part of normal species functioning for our species.

The ethics of trying to do such a thing are complex. For the moment we should reflect that none of them are powerful enough to derogate from an important truth. That truth is that lifesaving is just death-postponing with a positive spin! If it is right and good to postpone death for a short while, it is difficult to see how it would not be better and more moral to postpone death for longer—even indefinitely.

REGENERATIVE MEDICINE

If dramatic increases in life expectancy are ever achieved, it is most probable that they will occur primarily through the use of regenerative medicine, harnessing the regenerative powers of stem cells to repair and replace diseased or damaged tissue. These same powers that can repair and replace diseased or damaged tissue may, in a healthy individual, augment normal functioning. That is why regenerative medicine may never be simply or merely therapeutic, but is likely always to have an enhancing dimension.

Consider the following, as yet imaginary, fragments of a dialogue between doctor and patient:

I can successfully treat your heart disease, but there's a downside. I will be using regenerative medicine so, as a result of my treatment, your cardiovascular system will be healthier, so you will live longer; you will have enhanced life expectancy...

or

I can treat the damage you have sustained to your brain but the problem is that the regenerative therapy I will use will regenerate your brain and the likely outcome is that not only will full function be restored, but in fact your brain will function much better than before, with enhanced memory and intelligence.... I am so sorry!

Who would think this an unacceptable side effect of treatment? Who would think that such people should be left untreated rather than allow these, by hypothesis, unacceptable consequences to occur?

RISK

Of course, once Baltimore (or someone else) is successful, we will want to be sure that we are not tampering with healthy human beings in a way which will harm rather than benefit them or in which the risks are too high. But this insistence on rigorous risk assessment and on only proceeding if in all the circumstances of the case the risks are acceptable is a feature not only of all medical and scientific advance but of all human decision making whatsoever. Some have imagined that enhanced superhumans will be Frankenstein's monsters, powerful, malevolent, and

uncontrollable. We should not of course deliberately create such beings or creatures where there is foreseeable danger of their becoming such beings. Insofar as such possibilities are unforeseeable they can no more be guarded against than the occurrence of any other possible but unforeseeable consequence of any type of intervention whatsoever.

But this is not a general or even a more acute problem with enhancement. It is a problem with any risky procedure, whether it be sex, drugs, or rock-n-roll, eating fatty foods, road transport, or vaccination and gene therapy.

Three further problems merit brief attention.

THE PRECAUTIONARY PRINCIPLE

UNESCO's International Bioethics Committee (IBC), reflecting on the ethics of tinkering with the genes, has maintained that "the human genome must be preserved as common heritage of humanity."[13]

A number of questionable assumptions are involved here. The first is that our present point in evolution is unambiguously good and not susceptible to improvement. Second, it is assumed that the course of evolution, if left alone, will continue to improve things for humankind or at least not make them worse. The incompatibility of these two assumptions is seldom noticed.

However, the common heritage of humanity is a result of evolutionary change. Unless we can compare the future progress of evolution uncontaminated by manipulation of the human genome with its progress influenced by any proposed genetic manipulations, we cannot know which would be best and hence where precaution lies. Put more prosaically, it is unclear why a precautionary approach should apply only to proposed changes rather than to the status quo. In the absence of reliable predictive knowledge as to how dangerous leaving things alone may prove, we have no rational basis for a precautionary approach which prioritizes the status quo.

The fatuousness of the precautionary principle was exposed by the immortal F. M. Cornford in his seminal *Microcosmographia Academica* as "The Principle of the Dangerous Precedent":

> The Principle of the Dangerous Precedent is that you should not now do an admittedly right action for fear you, or your equally timid successors, should not have the courage to do right in some future case.... Every public action which is not customary, either is wrong, or, if it is right, is a dangerous precedent. It follows that nothing should ever be done for the first time.[14]

PLAYING GOD

Another commonly held objection to deliberate interventions in the human genome, or in evolution, is the idea that the human genome and Darwinian evolution are "natural phenomena or processes" and that there is some sort of natural priority of the natural over the artificial. This is often coupled with an argument from superstition: that it is tempting fate or divine wrath to play God and intervene in the natural order.

These suggestions are superstitious, fallacious, or, more usually, both. If it were wrong to interfere with nature we could not, among many other things, practice medicine. People naturally fall ill, are invaded by bacteria, parasites, viruses, or cancers and naturally die prematurely. Medicine can be described as "the comprehensive attempt to frustrate the course of nature."[15]

What is natural is morally inert and progress dependent. It was only natural for people to die of infected wounds before antibiotics were available or of smallpox and polio before effective vaccines.

Thomas Hobbes famously took a more realistic view of nature:

> [A]nd which is worst of all, continual fear, and danger of violent death; and the life of man, solitary, poor, nasty, brutish and short.[16]

Hobbes defended a social and political solution to the problems of the state of nature. If he had had available to him knowledge of the technologies we now have and are developing, he might well have opted for changing not simply the state of nature, but also the natural state of man.

If, as we have suggested, not only are enhancements obviously good for us, but that good can be obtained with safety, then not only should people be entitled to access those goods for themselves and those for whom they care, but they also clearly have moral reasons, perhaps amounting to an obligation, to do so.

ENDNOTES

1. Christopher Boorse, "On the Distinction between Disease and Illness," in *Medicine and Moral Philosophy*, ed. Marshall Cohen, Thomas Nagel, and Thomas Scanlon (Princeton, NJ: Princeton University Press, 1981).

2. Norman Daniels, *Justice and Justification* (Cambridge: Cambridge University Press, 1996), p. 185.

3. Steven Rose, "Brain Gain?," in *Better Humans? The Politics of Human Enhancement and Life Extension*, ed. Paul Miller and James Wilsdon (London: DEMOS, 2006).

4. Francis Fukuyama, *Our Posthuman Future* (New York: Farrar, Straus and Giroux, 2002), p. 160.

5. Ibid., p. 101.

6. Ibid., p. 149.

7. Jonathan Glover, *Choosing Children* (Oxford: Clarendon Press, 2006).

8. George Annas, *Genism, Racism, and the Prospect of Genetic Genocide*, www.thehumanfuture.org/commentaries/annas_genism.html; accessed August 11, 2006; link now discontinued; updated version available at www.thehumanfuture.org/commentaries.

9. Indeed, elsewhere, Annas, along with Lori B. Andrews and Rosario M. Isasi, calls for an

international treaty to ban the use of such technologies. See George Annas, Lori B. Andrews, and Rosario M. Isasi, "Protecting the Endangered Human: Toward an International Treaty Prohibiting Cloning and Inheritable Alterations," *American Journal of Law and Medicine* 28 (2002): 151–78.

10. John Harris, *On Cloning* (London: Routledge, 2004).

11. Rose, *Brain Gain?*

12. John Harris, *Violence and Responsibility* (London: Routledge and Kegan Paul, 1980).

13. UNESCO Press Release no. 97–29; see also UNESCO "Universal Declaration on the Human Genome and Human Rights," December 3, 1997.

14. F. M. Cornford, *Microcosmographia Academica* (London: Bowes and Bowes, 1908). Reprinted 1966.

15. John Harris, *The Value of Life* (London: Routledge, 1985), p. 38.

16. Thomas Hobbes, *Leviathan*, ed. Michael Oakeshott (Oxford: Basil Blackwell, 1960), p. 82.

26

What Price Better Health? Hazards of the Research Imperative

DANIEL CALLAHAN

Daniel Callahan argues that it is naïve not to take seriously the concern that the rise of genetic enhancement technologies may bring about a new eugenics. He argues that from a seemingly humane concern to wipe out genetic diseases and defects, we could end up with eugenics programs whose purpose is to create a society full of healthy, better humans.

It has been common for years now to deride the idea that a new eugenics is on the horizon. The old eugenics, a child of the false biology and genetics of the late nineteenth and early twentieth centuries—and culminating in the Nazi ideology and atrocities—is said to be dead and buried. The times, moreover, are different: because of the Nazis' experience, and particularly their desire for a master race, for genetically superior types of human beings, we have learned the dangers of going down that road. Now our science and our social values are better. It can't happen again and it can't happen here.

This confidence is misplaced. The sociologist Troy Duster over a decade ago came closer to the truth with his book *Back Door to Eugenics.*[1] He noted, as did other observers even then and earlier, that the backdoor route would be through work to improve genetic health in individuals and to rid ourselves of genetically defective fetuses. The intentions of such a move are fine: genetic diseases (and other sources of abnormality) are harmful to human life, the source of premature death and much misery. Is it not perfectly consistent with the traditional goals of medicine to try to cure lethal and harmful conditions, including those with a genetic basis? Does it not make sense, from a societal point of view, to reduce the incidence of genetically damaged babies, who may well live miserable lives and who will, in the process, be a burden on their families and society? The logic of that argument, now well accepted (if not by everyone) seems morally faultless—and hence the popularity of prenatal screening. Research to improve the screening is no less popular. This phenomenon might be termed a subcategory of normalization, a kind of single-minded dedication to health, using not utopian views of human possibilities as the model but instead ordinary, garden-variety models, that of a person or child or fetus without disabling or burdensome flaws.

The hazard here, the backdoor route to eugenics, has been to insinuate over the past few decades a combined individual and economic argument. Parents ought not to want defective children or even to run the risk of such children. If it is wrong for parents to run such risks, particularly risks known to be avoidable, then of course it is unfair for them to impose the burden of the care for such children on society, which is the likely

Callahan, Daniel, "What Price Better Health? Hazards of the Research Imperative," University of California Press Books. Reprinted by permission.

result. There need be no talk of a master race or perfect babies, but simply healthy babies, unproblematic for their parents, for society, or for themselves.

Perhaps we can continue to walk the fine line between an attitude toward genetic disease, especially in the unborn, which has the good of the mother and child only in mind, not infected by fantasies of perfection, and genetic disease reduced to a noxious social and economic burden. But as the historian of science Garland E. Allan has noted in a discussion of eugenics, "We seem to be increasingly unwilling to accept what we view as imperfection in ourselves and others ... if eugenics means making reproductive decisions primarily on the basis of social cost, then we are well on that road."[2]

Here is a fine instance of the way the research imperative, which legitimately pushes us to know more about genetic disease, can turn in a damaging direction. The more we treat genetic disease as a great evil, and genetically defective fetuses and babies as exemplars of that evil, the harder it will be to avoid going down the eugenics road—or going farther down it. There was a slogan that became popular in the 1970s, that of a "right to a healthy life," and it was advanced as a powerful reason to rid ourselves of genetic defects. To go from that kind of right for individuals to the right of society to have healthy individuals in the name of its economic and social well-being requires no long jump. It need not happen, but to argue that never again, and not here, will eugenics stage a comeback seems naive.

ENDNOTES

1. Troy Duster, *Back Door to Eugenics* (New York: Routledge, 1990).

2. Garland E. Allan, "Is a New Eugenics Afoot?" *Science* 294 (2001): 59–61.

SUGGESTIONS FOR FURTHER READING

Anthologies

Allhoff, Fritz, et al. *Nanoethics: The Ethical and Social Implications of Nanotechnology.* Hoboken, NJ: Wiley, 2007.

Savulescu, Julian, and Nick Bostrom. *Human Enhancement.* Oxford: Oxford University Press, 2009.

Alternative Views

Bostrom, Nick. "Human Genetic Enhancements: A Transhumanist Perspective." *Journal of Value Inquiry* 37, no. 4 (2003): 493–506.

Buchanan, Allen. "Human Nature and Enhancement." *Bioethics* 23, no. 3 (2009): 141–150.

Fukuyama, Francis. *Our Posthuman Future: Consequences of the Biotechnology Revolution.* New York: Farrar, Straus and Giroux, 2002.

Harris, John. *Enhancing Evolution: The Ethical Case for Making Better People.* Princeton, NJ: Princeton University Press, 2007.

Sandel, Michael. *The Case Against Perfection: Ethics in the Age of Genetic Engineering.* Cambridge, MA: The Belknap Press of Harvard University Press, 2007.

Practical Applications

President's Council on Bioethics. *Beyond Therapy: Biotechnology and the Pursuit of Happiness.* Washington D.C.: U.S. Government Printing Office, 2003.

SECTION V

Sex Equality

INTRODUCTION

Basic Concepts

The problem of sex equality concerns the question of whether the sexes should be treated equally, and, if so, what constitutes equal treatment. This question was at the heart of the decade-long public debate on the Equal Rights Amendment to the Constitution (the ERA), which began in March 1972, when the Senate passed the amendment with a vote of 84 to 8, and ended in June 1982, when the extended deadline for the ERA expired—three states short of the 38 required for ratification.

The complete text of the ERA was as follows:

1. Equality of rights under the law shall not be denied or abridged by the United States or by any state on account of sex.
2. The Congress shall have the power to enforce by appropriate legislation the provisions of this article.
3. This amendment shall take effect two years after the date of ratification.

Public support for the ERA over this period, judging from opinion polls, hovered between 55 and 60 percent, but in key states anti-ERA forces were able to mount sufficient resistance to prevent its passage. In the end, Alabama, Arizona, Arkansas, Florida, Georgia, Illinois, Louisiana, Mississippi, Missouri, Nevada, North Carolina, Oklahoma, Utah, and Virginia failed to ratify the amendment.

Anti-ERA forces were able to block ratification because they successfully shifted the debate from equal rights to the substantive changes the ERA might bring about. This strategy was effective because support for the amendment generally came from individuals sympathetic to the notion of "equal rights" but not

247

necessarily committed to substantive changes in women's roles.[1] For example, in one national survey, 67 percent of the people who claimed to have heard or read about the ERA favored it, 25 percent were opposed to it, and 8 percent had no opinion. Many people in the sample, however, had quite traditional views about women's roles. Two-thirds of the respondents thought that preschool children would suffer if their mothers worked, 62 percent thought married women should not hold jobs when jobs were scarce and their husbands could support them, and 55 percent thought it was more important for a woman to advance her husband's career than to have one of her own.

But what substantive changes would the ERA have brought about if it had been ratified in 1982? The surprising answer is not many, at least in the short run.[2] In 1970, when the ERA first reached the floor of Congress, a significant number of laws and official practices denied women "equality of rights under the law." For example, in 1970, eight states treated all property that a couple bought with their earnings during marriage as "community property," and these states normally gave the husband managerial control over such property. By 1976, most of these laws had been voluntarily changed or struck down by the Supreme Court's interpretation of the equal protection clause of the Fourteenth Amendment. Of course, supporters of the ERA did attempt to argue for the amendment on the grounds that it would bring about equal pay for equal work. Lobbyists for the ERA in state capitols wore buttons that said "590" to remind legislators that women who worked full-time outside the home still typically earned only 59 cents for every dollar men earned—a ratio that has changed little since the federal government first began publishing such statistics in the 1950s. But the passage of the ERA would have had little immediate impact on that inequality. The ERA would have kept the federal or state governments from legally denying or abridging "equality of rights under the law." However, to help workers, the ERA would have had to do more than just make the law gender blind. It would have had to forbid wage discrimination by private organizations and individuals. And this it did not do.

Moreover, the ERA would have had few of the effects its opponents predicted. For example, Phyllis Schlafly frequently claimed that the ERA would require unisex public toilets and combat duty for women, but the Supreme Court would have found the first requirement an infringement of the right to privacy and the second would have run afoul of the war powers clause of the Constitution, which gives military commanders the freedom to decide how best to use their forces. Yet despite the fact that the immediate impact of the passage of the ERA would have been largely symbolic, neither proponents nor opponents sufficiently recognized this or, if they did, were not willing to surrender their exaggerated claims about the effects the amendment would have. Leaders on both sides of this debate may have feared the difficulty of motivating their followers if these exaggerated claims were abandoned.

Alternative Views

Susan Okin argues (Selection 27) that women have not achieved equality in society. Most of the unpaid labor in the family is done by women. Most jobs assume that workers have wives at home, and traditional gender-structured families make women vulnerable in ways that men are not vulnerable. Okin points out that contemporary political philosophers have ignored all this. They have assumed without argument the justice of traditional gender-structured families. Okin contends that this is a morally unacceptable state of affairs. Families are the first school of justice, and they must be shown to be just if we are to have a just society.

In Selection 28, James P. Sterba argues that if family structures are to be just they must meet the requirements of feminist justice, which he identifies with an ideal of androgyny. This ideal of androgyny requires that traits that are truly desirable and distributable in society be equally available to both women and men, or in the case of virtues, equally expected of both women and men. He considers attempts to derive the ideal of androgyny either from a right to equal opportunity that is a central requirement of a welfare liberal conception of justice or from an equal right of self-development that is a central requirement of a socialist conception of justice. He argues that although the ideal of androgyny is compatible with the requirements of both of these two conceptions of justice, it also transcends them by requiring that all virtues be equally expected of both women and men. Sterba further argues that the ideal of androgyny would require (1) that all children irrespective of their sex must be given the same type of upbringing consistent with their native capabilities, and (2) that mothers and fathers must also have the same opportunities for education and employment consistent with their native capabilities. He then considers how achieving equal opportunity for women and men requires vastly improved day-care facilities and flexible (usually part-time) work schedules for both women and men.

In Selection 29, Christina Hoff Sommers criticizes the attack by feminist philosophers like Okin and Sterba on traditional family structures. She distinguishes liberal feminists from radical feminists and contends that liberal feminists like herself want equal opportunity in the workplace and politics, but would leave marriage and motherhood "untouched and unimpugned." By contrast, Sommers contends that radical feminists are committed to an assimilationist or androgynous ideal that would destroy the (traditional) family and deny most women what they want. Sommers, however, never explains how it is possible to secure for women equal opportunity in the workplace and politics while rejecting androgyny in favor of traditional gender roles. For example, how could women be passive, submissive, dependent, indecisive, and weak and still enjoy the same opportunities in the workplace and politics that are enjoyed by aggressive, dominant, independent, decisive, and strong men?

Marilyn Friedman (Selection 30) does not challenge Sommers's contention that radical feminists are committed to an assimilationist or androgynous ideal. There is, however, an important distinction between these two ideals. According to an assimilationist ideal, "one's sex should be no more noticeable than one's eye color," but according to an androgynous ideal, this need not be the case, as long as all desirable traits are equally open to both women and men, and all virtues equally expected of both women and men.

Friedman does, however, question whether what Sommers supports is really what most women want. She quotes a 1983 survey which indicated that 63 percent of women preferred nontraditional family relationships, and points out that in 1977 only 16 percent of American households were traditional families consisting of a legally married heterosexual couple and their children, in which the man is the sole breadwinner and "head" of the household, and the woman does the domestic work and childcare. In responding to Friedman, Sommers explains that what she means by a traditional family is one that consists of two heterosexual parents and one or more children in which the mother plays a distinctive gender role in caring for the children.[3] This definition obviously broadens the class of families to which Sommers is referring. But in her response, Sommers goes on to renounce any attempt to be promoting even the traditional family—even as she defines it. What she claims to be promoting is simply "the right and liberty to live under the arrangement of one's choice." According to Sommers, if people want to live in non-traditional families, they should be free to do so.

Friedman further disagrees with Sommers, contending that no woman should "swoon at the sight of Rhett Butler carrying Scarlett O'Hara up the stairs to a fate undreamt of in feminist philosophy." According to Friedman, what Rhett Butler is doing in *Gone With the Wind* is raping Scarlett O'Hara. In a subsequent response to Sommers, Friedman, noting that Scarlett O'Hara, although initially unwilling, later appears to be a willing sexual partner, defines "rape" as "any very intimate sexual contact which is *initiated* forcefully or against the will of the recipient."[4] Friedman allows that others might want to define such activity as sexual domination rather than rape, but under either definition, Friedman condemns it, whereas Sommers does

not. In her response, Sommers cites approvingly the following passage from *Scarlett's Women: Gone with the Wind and Its Female Fans*.

> The majority of my correspondents (and I agree) recognize the ambiguous nature of the encounter and interpret it as a scene of mutually pleasurable rough sex.... By far the majority of women who responded to me saw the episode as erotically exciting, emotionally stirring and profoundly memorable. Few of them referred to it as "rape."[5]

Practical Applications

Turning to practical applications, we can see that, at least in the statement of the National Organization for Women (NOW) Bill of Rights (Selection 31), there was never any confusion that the ERA would achieve all the goals of the organization. In this Bill of Rights, the ERA is one of eight goals to be achieved.

ENDNOTES

1. Jane J. Mansbridge, *Why We Lost the ERA* (Chicago: University of Chicago Press, 1986), Chapter 3.

2. Ibid., Chapters 5-7.

3. Christina Hoff Sommers, "Do These Feminists Like Women?" *Journal of Social Philosophy* (1991), pp. 66–74.

4. Marilyn Friedman, "Does Sommers Like Women?" *Journal of Social Philosophy* (1991), pp. 75–90.

5. Ibid., p. 72.

27

Justice, Gender, and the Family

SUSAN OKIN

Susan Okin points out that in the face of the radical inequality that exists between women and men in our society, there is still a widespread failure of political philosophers to address gender issues in their political theories. She claims that this is true even among those philosophers who have seen the need to adopt gender-neutral language. Okin argues that no theory of justice can be adequate until it addresses these issues.

We as a society pride ourselves on our democratic values. We don't believe people should be constrained by innate differences from being able to achieve desired positions of influence to improve their well-being; equality of opportunity is our professed aim. The Preamble to our Constitution stresses the importance of justice, as well as the general welfare and the blessings of liberty. The Pledge of Allegiance asserts that our republic preserves "liberty and justice for all."

Yet substantial inequalities between the sexes still exist in our society. In economic terms, full-time working women (after some very recent improvement) earn on average 71 percent of the earnings of full-time working men. One-half of poor and three-fifths of chronically poor households with dependent children are maintained by a single female parent. The poverty rate for elderly women is nearly twice that for elderly men. On the political front, two out of one hundred U.S. senators are women, one out of nine justices seems to be considered sufficient female representation on the Supreme Court, and the number of men chosen in each congressional election far exceeds the number of women elected in the entire history of the country. Underlying and intertwined with all of these

inequalities is the unequal distribution of the unpaid labor of the family.

An equal sharing between the sexes of family responsibilities, especially child care, is "the great revolution that has not happened." Women, including mothers of young children, are, of course, working outside the household far more than their mothers did. And the small proportion of women who reach high-level positions in politics, business, and the professions command a vastly disproportionate amount of space in the media, compared with the millions of women who work at low-paying, dead-end jobs, the millions who do part-time work with its lack of benefits, and the millions of others who stay home performing for no pay what is frequently not even acknowledged as work. Certainly, the fact that women are doing more paid work does not imply that they are more equal. It is often said that we are living in a postfeminist era. This claim, due in part to the distorted emphasis on women who have "made it," is false, no matter which of its meanings is intended. It is certainly not true that feminism has been vanquished, and equally untrue that it is no longer needed because its aims have been fulfilled. Until there is justice within the family, women will not be able to gain equality in politics, at work, or in any other sphere.

... The typical current practices of family life, structured to a large extent by gender, are not just. Both the expectation and the experience of the division of labor by sex make women vulnerable. As I shall show, a cycle of power relations and decisions pervades both family and workplace, each reinforcing the inequalities between the sexes that already exist within the other. Not only women, but children of both sexes, too, are often made vulnerable by gender-structured marriage. One-quarter of children in the United States now live in families with only one parent—in almost 90 percent of cases, the mother. Contrary to common perceptions—in which the situation of never-married mothers looms largest—65 percent of single-parent families are a result of marital separation or divorce. Recent research in a number of states has shown that, in the average case, the standard of living of divorced women and the children who live with them plummets after divorce, whereas the economic situation of divorced men tends to be better than when they were married.

A central source of injustice for women these days is that the law, most noticeably in the event of divorce, treats more or less as equals those whom custom, workplace discrimination, and the still conventional division of labor within the family have made very unequal. Central to this socially created inequality are two commonly made but inconsistent presumptions: that women are primarily responsible for the rearing of children; and that serious and committed members of the work force (regardless of class) do not have primary responsibility, or even shared responsibility, for the rearing of children. The old assumption of the workplace, still implicit, is that workers have wives at home. It is built not only into the structure and expectations of the workplace but into other crucial social institutions, such as schools, which make no attempt to take account, in their scheduled hours or vacations, of the fact that parents are likely to hold jobs.

Now, of course, many wage workers do not have wives at home. Often, they *are* wives and mothers, or single, separated, or divorced mothers

of small children. But neither the family nor the workplace has taken much account of this fact. Employed wives still do by far the greatest proportion of unpaid family work, such as child care and housework. Women are far more likely to take time out of the workplace or to work part-time because of family responsibilities than are their husbands or male partners. And they are much more likely to move because of their husbands' employment needs or opportunities than their own. All these tendencies, which are due to a number of factors, including the sex segregation and discrimination of the workplace itself, tend to be cyclical in their effects: Wives advance more slowly than their husbands at work and thus gain less seniority, and the discrepancy between their wages increases over time. Then, because both the power structure of the family and what is regarded as consensual "rational" family decision-making reflect the fact that the husband usually earns more, it will become even less likely as time goes on that the unpaid work of the family will be shared between the spouses. Thus the cycle of inequality is perpetuated. Often hidden from view within a marriage, it is in the increasingly likely event of marital breakdown that the socially constructed inequality of married women is at its most visible.

This is what I mean when I say that gender-structured marriage *makes* women vulnerable. These are not matters of natural necessity, as some people would believe. Surely nothing in our natures dictates that men should not be equal participants in the rearing of their children. Nothing in the nature of work makes it impossible to adjust it to the fact that people are parents as well as workers. That these things have not happened is part of the historically, socially constructed differentiation between the sexes that feminists have come to call *gender*. We live in a society that has over the years regarded the innate characteristic of sex as one of the clearest legitimizers of different rights and restrictions, both formal and informal. While the legal sanctions that uphold male dominance have begun to be eroded in the past century, and more rapidly in the last twenty years, the heavy weight of tradition, combined with the effects of socialization, still works powerfully to reinforce sex roles that are commonly regarded as of unequal prestige and worth. The sexual division of labor has not only been a fundamental part of the marriage contract, but so deeply influences us in our formative years that feminists of both sexes who try to reject it can find themselves struggling against it with varying degrees of ambivalence. Based on this linchpin, "gender"—by which I mean *the deeply entrenched institutionalization of sexual difference*—still permeates our society.

THE CONSTRUCTION
OF GENDER

Due to feminism and feminist theory, gender is coming to be recognized as a social factor of major importance. Indeed, the new meaning of the word reflects the fact that so much of what has traditionally been thought of as sexual difference is now considered by many to be largely socially produced. Feminist scholars from many disciplines and with radically different points of view have contributed to the enterprise of making gender fully visible and comprehensible. At one end of the spectrum are those whose explanations of the subordination of women focus primarily on biological difference as causal in the construction of gender, and at the other end are those who argue that biological difference may not even lie at the core of the social construction that is gender; the views of the vast majority of feminists fall between these extremes. The rejection of biological determinism and the corresponding emphasis on gender as a social construction characterize most current feminist scholarship. Of particular relevance is work in psychology, where scholars have investigated the importance of female primary parenting in the formation of our gendered identities, and in history and anthropology, where emphasis has been placed on the historical and cultural variability of gender. Some feminists have been criticized for developing theories of gender that do not take sufficient account of differences *among* women, especially race, class, religion, and ethnicity. While such critiques should always inform our research and

improve our arguments, it would be a mistake to allow them to distract our attention from gender itself as a factor of significance. Many injustices are experienced by women *as women,* whatever the differences among them and whatever other injustices they also suffer from. The past and present gendered nature of the family, and the ideology that surrounds it, affects virtually all women, whether or not they live or ever lived in traditional families. Recognizing this is not to deny or de-emphasize the fact that gender may affect different subgroups of women to a different extent and in different ways.

The potential significance of feminist discoveries and conclusions about gender for issues of social justice cannot be overemphasized. They undermine centuries of argument that started with the notion that not only the distinct differentiation of women and men but the domination of women by men, being natural, was therefore inevitable and not even to be considered in discussions of justice. As I shall make clear ..., despite the fact that such notions cannot stand up to rational scrutiny, they not only still survive but flourish in influential places.

During the same two decades in which feminists have been intensely thinking, researching, analyzing, disagreeing about, and rethinking the subject of gender, our political and legal institutions have been increasingly faced with issues concerning the injustices of gender and their effects. These issues are being decided within a fundamentally patriarchal system, founded in a tradition in which "individuals" were assumed to be male heads of households. Not surprisingly, the system has demonstrated a limited capacity for determining what is just, in many cases involving gender. Sex discrimination, sexual harassment, abortion, pregnancy in the workplace, parental leave, childcare, and surrogate mothering have all become major and well-publicized issues of public policy, engaging both courts and legislatures. Issues of family justice, in particular—from child custody and divorce terms to physical and sexual abuse of wives and children—have become increasingly visible and pressing, and are commanding increasing attention from the police and court systems. There is clearly a major "justice crisis" in contemporary society arising from issues of gender.

THEORIES OF JUSTICE AND
THE NEGLECT OF GENDER

During these same two decades, there has been a great resurgence of theories of social justice. Political theory, which had been sparse for a period before the late 1960s except as an important branch of intellectual history, has become a flourishing field, with social justice as its central concern. Yet, remarkably, major contemporary theorists of justice have almost without exception ignored the situation just described. They have displayed little interest in or knowledge of the findings of feminism. They have largely bypassed the fact that the society to which their theories are supposed to pertain is heavily and deeply affected by gender, and faces difficult issues of justice stemming from its gendered past and present assumptions. Since theories of justice are centrally concerned with whether, how, and why persons should be treated differently from one another, this neglect seems inexplicable. These theories are *about* which initial or acquired characteristics or positions in society legitimize differential treatment of persons by social institutions, laws, and customs. They are *about* how and whether and to what extent beginnings should affect outcomes. The division of humanity into two sexes seems to provide an obvious subject for such inquiries. But, as we shall see, this does not strike most contemporary theorists of justice, and their theories suffer in both coherence and relevance because of it. This piece is ... an attempt to rectify [this neglect], to point the way toward a more fully humanist theory of justice by confronting the question, "How just is gender?"

Why is it that when we turn to contemporary theories of justice, we do not find illuminating and positive contributions to this question? How can theories of justice that are ostensibly about people in general neglect women, gender, and all the inequalities between the sexes? One reason is that most theorists *assume,* though they do not discuss, the traditional, gender-structured family. Another is that they often employ gender-neutral language in a false, hollow way. Let us examine these two points.

The Hidden Gender-Structured Family

In the past, political theorists often used to distinguish clearly between "private" domestic life and the "public" life of politics and the marketplace, claiming explicitly that the two spheres operated in accordance with different principles. They separated out the family from what they deemed the subject matter of politics, and they made closely related, explicit claims about the nature of women and the appropriateness of excluding them from civil and political life. Men, the subjects of the theories, were able to make the transition back and forth from domestic to public life with ease, largely because of the functions performed by women in the family. When we turn to contemporary theories of justice, superficial appearances can easily lead to the impression that they are inclusive of women. In fact, they continue the same "separate spheres" tradition, by ignoring the family, its division of labor, and the related economic dependency and restricted opportunities of most women. The judgment that the family is "nonpolitical" is implicit in the fact that it is simply not discussed in most works of political theory today. In one way or another ... almost all current theorists continue to assume that the "individual" who is the basic subject of their theories is the male head of a fairly traditional household. Thus the application of principles of justice to relations between the sexes, or within the household, is frequently, though tacitly, ruled out from the start. In the most influential of all twentieth-century theories of justice, that of John Rawls, family life is not only assumed, but is assumed to be just—and yet the prevalent gendered division of labor within the family is neglected, along with the associated distribution of power, responsibility, and privilege....

Moreover, this stance is typical of contemporary theories of justice. They persist, despite the wealth of feminist challenges to their assumptions, in their refusal even to discuss the family and its gender structure, much less to recognize the family as a political institution of primary importance. Recent theories that pay even less attention to issues of family justice than Rawls's include Bruce

Ackerman's *Social Justice in the Liberal State,* Ronald Dworkin's *Taking Rights Seriously,* William Galston's *Justice and the Human Good,* Alasdair MacIntyre's *After Virtue* and *Whose Justice? Whose Rationality?,* Robert Nozick's *Anarchy, State, and Utopia,* and Roberto Unger's *Knowledge and Politics and The Critical Legal Studies Movement.* Philip Green's *Retrieving Democracy* is a welcome exception. Michael Walzer's *Spheres of Justice* is exceptional in this regard, but the conclusion that can be inferred from his discussion of the family—that its gender structure is unjust—does not sit at all easily with his emphasis on the shared understandings of a culture as the foundation of justice. For gender is one aspect of social life about which clearly, in the United States in the latter part of the twentieth century, there are no shared understandings.

What is the basis of my claim that the family, while neglected, is *assumed* by theorists of justice? One obvious indication is that they take mature, independent human beings as the subjects of their theories without any mention of how they got to be that way. We know, of course, that human beings develop and mature only as a result of a great deal of attention and hard work, by far the greater part of it done by women. But when theorists of justice talk about "work," they mean paid work performed in the marketplace. They must be assuming that women in the gender-structured family continue to do their unpaid work of nurturing and socializing the young and providing a haven of intimate relations—[or] there would be no moral subjects for them to theorize about. But these activities apparently take place outside the scope of their theories. Typically, the family itself is not examined in the light of whatever standard of justice the theorist arrives at.

The continued neglect of the family by theorists of justice flies in the face of a great deal of persuasive feminist argument.... Scholars have clearly revealed the interconnections between the gender structure inside and outside the family and the extent to which the personal is political. They have shown that the assignment of primary parenting to women is crucial, both in forming the gendered identities of men and women and in influencing their respective choices and opportunities in life. Yet, so far, the simultaneous assumption and neglect of the family has allowed the impact of these arguments to go unnoticed in major theories of justice.

False Gender Neutrality

Many academics ... have become aware of the objectionable nature of using the supposedly generic male forms of nouns and pronouns. As feminist scholars have demonstrated, these words have most often *not* been used, throughout history and the history of philosophy in particular, with the intent to include women. *Man, mankind,* and *he* are going out of style as universal representations, though they have by no means disappeared. But the gender-neutral alternatives that most contemporary theorists employ are often even more misleading than the blatantly sexist use of male terms of reference. They serve to disguise the real and continuing failure of theorists to confront the fact that the human race consists of persons of two sexes. They are by this means able to ignore the fact that there are *some* socially relevant physical differences between women and men, and the even more important fact that the sexes have had very different histories, very different assigned social roles and "natures," and very different degrees of access to power and opportunity in all human societies up to and including the present.

False gender neutrality is not a new phenomenon. Aristotle, for example, used *anthropos*—"human being"—in discussions of "the human good" that turn out not only to exclude women but to depend on their subordination. Kant even wrote of "all rational beings as such" in making arguments that he did not mean to apply to women. But it was more readily apparent that such arguments or conceptions of the good were not about all of us, but only about male heads of families. For their authors usually gave at some point an explanation, no matter how inadequate, of why what they were saying did not apply to women and of the different characteristics and virtues, rights, and responsibilities they thought women ought to have. Nevertheless, their theories have often been read as though they pertain (or can easily be applied) to all of us. Feminist interpretations of the last fifteen years or so have revealed the falsity of this "add women and stir" method of reading the history of political thought.

The falseness of the gender-neutral language of contemporary political theorists is less readily apparent. Most, though not all, contemporary moral and political philosophers use "men and women," "he or she," "persons," or the increasingly ubiquitous "self." Sometimes they even get their computers to distribute masculine and feminine terms of reference randomly. Since they do not explicitly exclude or differentiate women, as most theorists in the past did, we may be tempted to read their theories as inclusive of all of us. But we cannot. Their merely terminological responses to feminist challenges, in spite of giving a superficial impression of tolerance and inclusiveness, often strain credulity and sometimes result in nonsense. They do this in two ways: by ignoring the irreducible biological differences between the sexes, and/or by ignoring their different assigned social roles and consequent power differentials, and the ideologies that have supported them. Thus gender-neutral terms frequently obscure the fact that so much of the real experience of "persons," so long as they live in gender-structured societies, *does* in fact depend on what sex they are.

False gender neutrality is by no means confined to the realm of theory. Its harmful effects can be seen in public policies that have directly affected large numbers of women adversely. It was used, for example, in the Supreme Court's 1976 decision that the exclusion of pregnancy-related disabilities from employers' disability insurance plans was "not a gender-based discrimination at all." In a now infamous phrase of its majority opinion, the Court explained that such plans did not discriminate against women because the distinction drawn by such plans was between pregnant women and "non-pregnant *persons*."

... I will illustrate the concept [of false gender neutrality in contemporary political theory] by citing just two examples. Ackerman's *Social Justice in the Liberal State* is a book containing scrupulously gender-neutral language. He breaks with this neutrality only, it seems, to *defy* existing sex roles; he refers to the "Commander," who plays the lead role in the theory, as "she." However, the argument of the book does not address the existing inequality or role differentiation between the sexes, though it has the potential for doing so. The full impact of Ackerman's gender-neutral language without attention to gender is revealed in his section on abortion: a two-page discussion written, with the exception of a single "she," in the completely gender-neutral language of fetuses and their "parents." The impression given is that there is no relevant respect in which the relationship of the two parents to the fetus differs. Now it is, of course, possible to imagine (and in the view of many feminists, would be desirable to achieve) a society in which differences in the relation of women and men to fetuses would be so slight as to reasonably play only a minor role in the discussion of abortion. But this would have to be a society without gender—one in which sexual difference carried no social significance, the sexes were equal in power and independence, and "mothering" and "fathering" a child meant the same thing, so that parenting and earning responsibilities were equally shared. We certainly do not live in such a society. Neither is there any discussion of one in Ackerman's theory, in which the division of labor between the sexes is not considered a matter of social (in)justice. In such a context, a "gender-neutral" discussion of abortion is almost as misleading as the Supreme Court's "gender-neutral" discussion of pregnancy.

A second illustration of false gender neutrality comes from Derek Phillips's *Toward a Just Social Order*. Largely because of the extent of his concern—rare among theorists of justice—with how we are to *achieve and maintain* a just social order, Phillips pays an unusual amount of attention to the family. He writes about the family as the locus for the development of a sense of justice and self-esteem, of an appreciation of the meaning of reciprocity, of the ability to exercise unforced choice, and of an awareness of alternative ways of life. The problem with this otherwise admirable discussion is that, apart from a couple of brief exceptions, the family itself is presented in gender-neutral terms that bear little resemblance to actual, gender-structured life.[1] It is because of "parental affection," "parental nurturance," and "child rearing" that children in

Phillips's families become the autonomous moral agents that his just society requires its citizens to be. The child's development of a sense of identify very much depends on being raised by "parental figures who themselves have coherent and well-integrated personal identities," and we are told that such a coherent identity is "ideally one built around commitments to work and love." This all sounds very plausible. But it does not take into account the multiple inequalities of gender. In gender-structured societies—in which the child rearers are women, "parental nurturance" is largely mothering, and those who do what society regards as "meaningful work" are assumed *not* to be primary parents—women in even the best of circumstances face considerable conflicts between love (a fulfilling family life) and "meaningful work." Women in less fortunate circumstances face even greater conflicts between love (even basic care of their children) and any kind of paid work at all.

It follows from Philips's own premises that these conflicts are very likely to affect the strength and coherence in women of that sense of identity and self-esteem, coming from love and meaningful work, that he regards as essential for being an autonomous moral agent. In turn, if they are mothers, it is also likely to affect their daughters' and sons' developing senses of their identity. Gender is clearly a major obstacle to the attainment of a social order remotely comparable to the just one Phillips aspires to—but his false gender-neutral language allows him to ignore this fact. Although he is clearly aware of how distant in some other respects his vision of a just social order is from contemporary societies, his falsely gender-neutral language leaves him quite unaware of the distance between the type of family that might be able to socialize just citizens and typical families today.

The combined effect of the omission of the family and the falsely gender-neutral language in recent political thought is that most theorists are continuing to ignore the highly political issue of gender. The language they use makes little difference to what they actually do, which is to write about men and about only those women who manage, in spite of the gendered structures and practices of the society in which they live, to adopt patterns of life that have been developed to suit the needs of men. The fact that human beings are born as helpless infants—not as the purportedly autonomous actors who populate political theories—is obscured by the implicit assumption of gendered families, operating outside the range of theories. To a large extent, contemporary theories of justice, like those of the past, are about men with wives at home.

GENDER AS AN ISSUE OF JUSTICE

For three major reasons, this state of affairs is unacceptable. The first is the obvious point that women must be fully included in any satisfactory theory of justice. The second is that equality of opportunity, not only for women but for children of both sexes, is seriously undermined by the current gender injustices of our society. And the third reason is that, as has already been suggested, the family—currently the linchpin of the gender structure—must be just if we are to have a just society, since it is within the family that we first come to have that sense of ourselves and our relations with others that is at the root of moral development.

Counting Women In

When we turn to the great tradition of Western political thought with questions about the justice of the treatment of the sexes in mind, it is to little avail. Bold feminists like Mary Astell, Mary Wollstonecraft, William Thompson, Harriet Taylor, and George Bernard Shaw have occasionally challenged the tradition, often using its own premises and arguments to overturn its explicit or implicit justification of the inequality of women. But John Stuart Mill is a rare exception to the rule that those who hold central positions in the tradition almost never question the justice of the subordination of women. This phenomenon is undoubtedly due in part to the fact that Aristotle, whose theory of justice has been so influential, relegated women to a sphere of "household justice"—populated by persons who are not fundamentally equal to the free men who partici-pate in political justice, but inferiors whose natural function is to serve those who are more fully human. The liberal tradition, despite its supposed foundation of individual rights and human equality, is more Aristotelian in this respect than is generally acknowledged. In one way or another, almost all liberal theorists have assumed that the "individual" who is the basic subject of the theories is the male head of a patriarchal household. Thus they have not usually considered applying the principles of justice to women or to relations between the sexes.

When we turn to contemporary theories of justice, however, we expect to find more illuminat-ing and positive contributions to the subject of gender and justice. [But as] the omission of the family and the falseness of their gender-neutral language suggest ... mainstream contemporary the-ories of justice do not address the subject any better than those of the past. Theories of justice that apply to only half of us simply won't do; the inclusiveness falsely implied by the current use of gender-neutral terms must become real. Theories of justice must apply to all of us, and to all of human life, instead of *assuming* silently that half of us take care of whole areas of life that are considered outside the scope of social justice. In a just society, the structure and practices of families must afford women the same opportunities as men to develop their capacities, to participate in political power, to influence social choices, and to be economically as well as physically secure.

Unfortunately, much feminist intellectual energy in the 1980s has gone into the claim that "justice" and "rights" are masculinist ways of thinking about morality that feminists should eschew or radically revise, advocating a morality of care. The emphasis is misplaced, I think, for several reasons. First, what is by now a vast literature on the subject shows that the evidence for differences in women's and men's ways of thinking about moral issues is not (at least yet) very clear; neither is the evidence about the source of whatever differences there might be. It may well turn out that any differences can be readily explained in terms of roles, including female primary parenting, that are socially determined and therefore

alterable. There is certainly no evidence—nor could there be, in such a gender-structured society—for concluding that women are somehow naturally more inclined toward contextuality and away from universalism in their moral thinking, a false concept that unfortunately reinforces the old stereotypes that justify separate spheres. The capacity of reactionary forces to capitalize on the "different moralities" strain in feminism is particularly evident in Pope John Paul II's recent Apostolic Letter, "On the Dignity of Women," in which he refers to women's special capacity to care for others in arguing for confining them to motherhood or celibacy.

Second ... I think the distinction between an ethic of justice and an ethic of care has been over-drawn. The best theorizing about justice ... has integral to it the notions of care and empathy, of thinking of the interests and well-being of others who may be very different from ourselves. It is, therefore, misleading to draw a dichotomy as though they were two contrasting ethics. The best theorizing about justice is not some abstract "view from nowhere," but results from the carefully attentive consideration of *everyone's* point of view. This means, of course, that the best theorizing about justice is not good enough if it does not, or cannot readily be adapted to, include women and their points of view as fully as men and their points of view.

Gender and Equality of Opportunity

The family is a crucial determinant of our oppor-tunities in life, of what we "become." It has fre-quently been acknowledged by those concerned with real equality of opportunity that the family presents a problem. But though they have discerned a serious problem, these theorists have underesti-mated it because they have seen only half of it. They have seen that the disparity among families in terms of the physical and emotional environ-ment, motivation, and material advantages they can give their children has a tremendous effect upon children's opportunities in life. We are not born as isolated, equal individuals in our society, but into family situations: some in the social middle, some poor and homeless, and some super-affluent; some to a single or soon-to-be-separated parent, some to parents whose marriage is fraught with conflict, some to parents who will stay together in love and happiness. Any claims that equal opportunity exists are therefore completely unfounded. Decades of neglect of the poor, especially of poor black and Hispanic households, accentuated by the policies of the Reagan years, have brought us farther from the principles of equal opportunity. To come close to them would require, for example, a high and uniform standard of public education and the provision of equal social services—including health care, employment training, job opportunities, drug rehabilitation, and decent housing—for all who need them. In addition to redistributive taxation, only massive reallocations of resources from the military to social services could make these things possible.

But even if all these disparities were somehow eliminated, we would still not attain equal opportunity for all. This is because what has not been recognized as an equal opportunity problem, except in feminist literature and circles, is the disparity *within* the family, the fact that its gender structure is itself a major obstacle to equality of opportunity. This is very important in itself, since one of the factors with most influence on our opportunities in life is the social significance attributed to our sex. The opportunities of girls and women are centrally affected by the structure and practices of family life, particularly by the fact that women are almost invariably primary parents. What nonfeminists who see in the family an obstacle to equal opportunity have *not* seen is that the extent to which a family is gender-structured can make the sex we belong to a relatively insignificant aspect of our identity and our life prospects or an all-pervading one. This is because so much of the social construction of gender takes place in the family, and particularly in the institution of female parenting.

Moreover, ... with the increased rates of single motherhood, separation, and divorce, the inequalities between the sexes have *compounded* the first part of the problem. The disparity among families has grown largely because of the impoverishment of many women and children after separation or divorce. The division of labor in the typical family leaves most women far less capable than men of supporting themselves, and this disparity is accentuated by the fact that children of separated or divorced parents usually live with their mothers. The inadequacy—and frequent nonpayment—of child support has become recognized as a major social problem. Thus the inequalities of gender are now directly harming many children of both sexes as well as women themselves. Enhancing equal opportunity for women, important as it is in itself, is also a crucial way of improving the opportunities of many of the most disadvantaged children.

As ... the parts of this problem [are connected, so are] some of the solutions: Much of what needs to be done to end the inequalities of gender, and to work in the direction of ending gender itself, will also help to equalize opportunity from one family to another. Subsidized, high quality day-care is obviously one such thing; another is the adaptation of the workplace to the needs of parents....

The Family as a School of Justice

One of the things that theorists who have argued that families need not or cannot be just, or who have simply neglected them, have failed to explain is how, within a formative social environment that is *not* founded upon principles of justice, children can learn to develop that sense of justice they will require as citizens of a just society. Rather than being one among many co-equal institutions of a just society, a just family is its essential foundation.

It may seem uncontroversial, even obvious, that families must be just because of the vast influence they have on the moral development of children. But this is clearly not the case. I shall argue that unless the first and most formative example of adult interaction usually experienced by children is one of justice and reciprocity, rather than one of domination and manipulation or of unequal altruism and one-sided self-sacrifice, and unless they themselves are treated with concern and respect, they are likely to be considerably hindered in becoming people who are guided by principles of justice. Moreover, I claim, the sharing of roles by men and women, rather than the division of roles between them, would have a further positive impact because the experience of *being* a physical and psychological nurturer—whether of a child or of another adult—would increase that capacity to identify with and fully comprehend the viewpoints of others that is important to a sense of justice. In a society that minimized gender this would be more likely to be the experience of all of us.

Almost every person in our society starts life in a family of some sort or other. Fewer of these families now fit the usual, although not universal, standard of previous generations, that is, wage-working father, homemaking mother, and children. More families these days are headed by a single parent; lesbian and gay parenting is no longer so rare; many children have two wage-working parents, and receive at least some of their early care outside the home. While its forms are varied, the family in which a child is raised, especially in the earliest years, is clearly a crucial place for early moral development and for the formation of our basic attitudes to others. It is, potentially, a place where we can *learn to be just*. It is especially important for the development of a sense of justice that grows from sharing the experiences of others and becoming aware of the points of view of others who are different in some respects from ourselves, but with whom we clearly have some interests in common.

The importance of the family for the moral development of individuals was far more often recognized by political theorists of the past than it is by those of the present. Hegel, Rousseau, Tocqueville, Mill, and Dewey are obvious examples that come to mind. Rousseau, for example, shocked by Plato's proposal to abolish the family, says that it is

> as though there were no need for a natural base on which to form conventional ties; as though the love of one's nearest were not the principle of the love one owes the state; as though it were not by means of the small fatherland which is the family that the heart attaches itself to the large one.

Defenders of both autocratic and democratic regimes have recognized the political importance of different family forms for the formation of citizens. On the one hand, the nineteenth-century monarchist Louis de Bonald argued against the divorce reforms of the French Revolution, which he claimed weakened the patriarchal family, on the grounds that "in order to keep the state out of the hands of the people, it is necessary to keep the family out of the hands of women and children." Taking this same line of thought in the opposite direction, the U.S. Supreme Court decided in 1879 in *Reynolds v. Nebraska* that familial patriarchy fostered despotism and was therefore intolerable. Denying Mormon men the freedom to practice polygamy, the Court asserted that it was an offense "subversive of good order" that "leads to the patriarchal principle, ... [and] when applied to large communities, fetters the people in stationary despotism, while that principle cannot long exist in connection with monogamy."

However, while de Bonald was consistent in his adherence to a hierarchical family structure as necessary for an undemocratic political system, the Supreme Court was by no means consistent in promoting an egalitarian family as an essential underpinning for political democracy. For in other decisions of the same period—such as *Bradwell v. Illinois,* the famous 1872 case that upheld the exclusion of women from the practice of law—the Court rejected women's claims to legal equality, in the name of a thoroughly patriarchal, though monogamous, family that was held to require the dependence of women and their exclusion from civil and political life. While bigamy was considered patriarchal, and as such a threat to republican, democratic government, the refusal to allow a married woman to employ her talents and to make use of her qualifications to earn an independent living was not considered patriarchal. It was so far from being a threat to the civil order, in fact, that it was deemed necessary for it, and as such was ordained by both God and nature. Clearly in both *Reynolds* and *Bradwell,* "state authorities enforced family forms preferred by those in power and justified as necessary to stability and order." The Court noticed the despotic potential of polygamy, but was blind to the despotic potential of patriarchal monogamy. This was perfectly acceptable to them as a training ground for citizens.

Most theorists of the past who stressed the importance of the family and its practices for the wider world of moral and political life by no means insisted on congruence between the structures or practices of the family and those of the outside world. Though concerned with moral development, they bifurcated public from private life to such an extent that they had no trouble reconciling inegalitarian, sometimes admittedly unjust, relations founded upon sentiment within the family with a more just, even egalitarian, social structure outside the family. Rousseau, Hegel, Tocqueville— all thought the family was centrally important for the development of morality in citizens, but all defended the hierarchy of the marital structure while spurning such a degree of hierarchy in institutions and practices outside the household. Preferring instead to rely on love, altruism, and generosity as the basis for family relations, none of these theorists argued for *just* family structures as necessary for socializing children into citizenship in a just society.

The position that justice within the family is irrelevant to the development of just citizens was not plausible even when only men were citizens. John Stuart Mill, in *The Subjection of Women,* takes an impassioned stand against it. He argues that the inequality of women within the family is deeply subversive of justice in general in the wider social world, because it subverts the moral potential of men. Mill's first answer to the question, "For whose good are all these changes in women's rights to be undertaken?" is: "the advantage of having the most universal and pervading of all human relations regulated by justice instead of injustice." Making marriage a relationship of equals, he argues, would transform this central part of daily life from "a school of despotism" into "a school of moral cultivation." He goes on to discuss, in the strongest of terms, the noxious effect of growing up in a family not regulated by justice. Consider ... "the self-worship, the unjust self-preference," nourished in a boy growing up in a household in which "by the mere fact of

being born a male he is by right the superior of all and every one of an entire half of the human race." Mill concludes that the example set by perpetuating a marital structure "contradictory to the first principles of social justice" must have such "a perverting influence" that it is hard even to imagine the good effects of changing it. All other attempts to educate people to respect and practice justice, Mill claims, will be superficial "as long as the citadel of the enemy is not attacked." Mill felt as much hope for what the family might be as he felt despair at what it was not. "The family, justly constituted, would be the real school of the virtues of freedom," primary among which was "justice, ... grounded as before on equal, but now also on sympathetic association." Mill both saw clearly and had the courage to address what so many other political philosophers either could not see, or saw and turned away from.

Despite the strength and fervor of his advocacy of women's rights, however, Mill's idea of a just family structure falls far short of that of many feminists even of his own time, including his wife, Harriet Taylor. In spite of the fact that Mill recognized both the empowering effect of earnings on one's position in the family and the limiting effect of domestic responsibility on women's opportunities, he balked at questioning the traditional division of labor between the sexes. For him, a woman's choice of marriage was parallel to a man's choice of a profession: Unless and until she had fulfilled her obligations to her husband and children, she should not undertake anything else. But ... however equal the legal rights of husbands and wives, this position largely undermines Mill's own insistence upon the importance of marital equality for a just society. His acceptance of the traditional division of labor, without making any provision for wives who were thereby made economically dependent on their husbands, largely undermines his insistence on family justice as the necessary foundation for social justice.

Thus even those political theorists of the past who have perceived the family as an important school of moral development have rarely acknowledged the need for congruence between the family and the wider social order, which suggests that families themselves need to be just. Even when they have, as with Mill, they have been unwilling to push hard on the traditional division of labor within the family in the name of justice or equality.

Contemporary theorists of justice, with few exceptions, have paid little or no attention to the question of moral development—of how we are to *become* just. Most seem to think, to adapt slightly Hobbes's notable phrase, that just men spring like mushrooms from the earth. Not surprisingly, then, it is far less often acknowledged in recent than in past theories that the family is important for moral development, and especially for instilling a sense of justice. As already noted, many theorists pay no attention at all to either the family or gender. In the rare case that the issue of justice within the family is given any sustained attention, the family is not viewed as a potential school of social justice. In the rare case that a theorist pays any sustained attention to the development of a sense of justice or morality, little if any attention is likely to be paid to the family. Even in the rare event that theorists pay considerable attention to the family *as* the first major locus of moral socialization, they do not refer to the fact that families are almost all still thoroughly gender-structured institutions.

Among major contemporary theorists of justice, John Rawls alone treats the family seriously as the earliest school of moral development. He argues that a just, well-ordered society will be stable only if its members continue to develop a sense of justice. And he argues that families play a fundamental role in the stages by which this sense of justice is acquired. From the parents' love for their child, which comes to be reciprocated, comes the child's "sense of his own value and the desire to become the sort of person that they are." The family, too, is the first of that series of "associations" in which we participate, from which we acquire the capacity, crucial for a sense of justice, to see things from the perspectives of others.... This capacity—the capacity for empathy—is essential for maintaining a sense of justice of the Rawlsian kind. For the perspective [needed to maintain] a sense of justice is not that of the egoistic or disembodied self, or of the dominant few who overdetermine "our" traditions or "shared understandings," or (to use Nagel's term) of "the

view from nowhere," but rather the perspective of every person in the society for whom the principles of justice are being arrived at.... The problem with Rawls's rare and interesting discussion of moral development is that it rests on the unexplained *assumption* that family institutions are just. If gendered family institutions are *not* just, but are ... a relic of caste or feudal societies in which responsibilities, roles, and resources are distributed, not in accordance with the principles of justice he arrives at or with any other commonly respected values, but in accordance with innate differences that are imbued with enormous social significance, then Rawls's theory of moral development would seem to be built on uncertain ground. This problem is exacerbated by suggestions in some of Rawls's most recent work that families are "private institutions," to which it is not appropriate to apply standards of justice. But if families are to help form just individuals and citizens, surely they must *be just families.*

In a just society, the structure and practices of families must give women the same opportunities as men to develop their capacities, to participate in political power and influence social choices, and to be economically secure. But in addition, families must be just because of the vast influence they have on the moral development of children. The family is the primary institution of formative moral development. And the structure and practices of the family must parallel those of the larger society if the sense of justice is to be fostered and maintained. Many theorists of justice, both past and present, appear to have denied the importance of at least one of these factors, [but] my own view is that both are absolutely crucial. A society that is committed to equal respect for all of its members, and to justice in social distributions of benefits and responsibilities, can neither neglect the family nor accept family structures and practices that violate these norms, as do current gender-based structures and practices. Children who are to develop into adults with a strong sense of justice and commitment to just institutions [must] spend their earliest and most formative years in an environment in which they are loved and nurtured, *and* in which principles of justice are abided by and respected. What is a child of either sex to learn about fairness in the average household with two full-time working parents, where the mother does, at the very least, twice as much family work as the father? What is a child to learn about the value of nurturing and domestic work in a home with a traditional division of labor in which the father either subtly or not so subtly uses the fact that he is the wage earner to "pull rank" on or to abuse his wife? What is a child to learn about responsibility for others in a family in which, after many years of arranging her life around the needs of her husband and children, a woman must provide for herself and her children but is totally illequipped for the task by the life she agreed to lead, has led, and is expected to go on leading?

ENDNOTE

1. He points out the shortcomings of the "earlier ethic of sacrifice," especially for women. He also welcomes the recent lessening of women's dependence on their husbands, but at the same time blames it for tending to weaken family stability. The falseness of Phillips's gender neutrality in discussing parenting is clearly confirmed later in the book, where paid work is "men's" and it is "fathers" who bequeath wealth or poverty on their children.

28

Feminist Justice and the Family

JAMES P. STERBA

James P. Sterba sets out and defends an ideal of androgyny that he identifies with feminist justice. This ideal requires that traits that are truly desirable in society be equally available to both women and men, or in the case of virtues, equally expected in both women and men. He considers attempts to derive the ideal of androgyny either from a right to equal opportunity that is a central requirement of a welfare liberal conception of justice or from an equal right of self-development that is a central requirement of a socialist conception of justice. Sterba further argues that the ideal of androgyny would require (1) that all children irrespective of their sex must be given the same type of upbringing consistent with their native capabilities and (2) that mothers and fathers must also have the same opportunities for education and employment consistent with their native capabilities.

Contemporary feminists almost by definition seek to put an end to male domination and to secure women's liberation. To achieve these goals, many feminists support the political ideal of androgyny. According to these feminists, all assignments of rights and duties are ultimately to be justified in terms of the ideal of androgyny. Since a conception of justice is usually thought to provide the ultimate grounds for the assignment of rights and duties in a society, I shall refer to this ideal of androgyny as "feminist justice."

THE IDEAL OF ANDROGYNY

But how is this ideal of androgyny to be interpreted? In a well-known article, Joyce Trebilcot distinguishes two forms of androgyny. The first form postulates the same ideal for everyone. According to this form of androgyny, the ideal person "combines characteristics usually attributed to

men with characteristics usually attributed to women." Thus, we should expect both nurturance and mastery, openness and objectivity, compassion and competitiveness from each and every person who has the capacities for these traits.

By contrast, the second form of androgyny does not advocate the same ideal for everyone but rather a variety of options from "pure" femininity to "pure" masculinity. As Trebilcot points out, this form of androgyny shares with the first the view that biological sex should not be the basis for determining the appropriateness of gender characterization. It differs in that it holds that "all alternatives with respect to gender should be equally available to and equally approved for everyone, regardless of sex."

It would be a mistake, however, to sharply distinguish between these two forms of androgyny. Properly understood, they are simply two different facets of a single ideal. For, as Mary Ann Warren has argued, the second form of androgyny is appropriate *only* "with respect to feminine and masculine

From *Perspectives on the Family* (1990), edited by Robert Moffat, Joseph Grcic, and Michael Bayles. Reprinted with revisions by permission.

traits which are largely matters of personal style and preference and which have little direct moral significance." However, when we consider so-called feminine and masculine *virtues,* it is the first form of androgyny that is required because, then, other things being equal, the same virtues are appropriate for everyone.

We can even formulate the ideal of androgyny more abstractly so that it is no longer specified in terms of so-called feminine and masculine traits. We can, for example, specify the ideal as requiring no more than that the traits that are truly desirable and distributable in society be equally available to both women and men, or in the case of virtues, equally expected of both women and men.

There is a problem, of course, in determining which traits of character are virtues and which traits are largely matters of personal style and preference. To make this determination, Trebilcot has suggested that we seek to bring about the second form of androgyny, where people have the option of acquiring the full range of so-called feminine and masculine traits. But surely when we already have good grounds for thinking that certain traits are virtues, such as courage and compassion, fairness and openness, there is no reason to adopt such a laissez-faire approach to moral education. Although, as Trebilcot rightly points out, proscribing certain options will involve a loss of freedom, nevertheless, we should be able to determine, at least with respect to some character traits, when a gain in virtue is worth the loss of freedom. It may even be the case that the loss of freedom suffered by an individual now will be compensated for by a gain of freedom to that same individual in the future once the relevant virtue or virtues have been acquired.

So understood, the class of virtues will turn out to be those desirable traits that can be reasonably expected of both women and men. Admittedly, this is a restrictive use of the term virtue. In normal usage, "virtue" is almost synonymous with "desirable trait." But there is good reason to focus on those desirable traits that can be justifiably inculcated in both women and men, and, for present purposes, I will refer to this class of desirable traits as virtues.

Unfortunately, many of the challenges to the ideal of androgyny fail to appreciate how the ideal can be interpreted to combine a required set of virtues with equal choice from among other desirable traits. For example, some challenges interpret the ideal as attempting to achieve "a proper balance of moderation" among opposing feminine and masculine traits and then question whether traits like feminine gullibility or masculine brutality could ever be combined with opposing gender traits to achieve such a balance. Other challenges interpret the ideal as permitting unrestricted choice of personal traits and then regard the possibility of Total Women and Hells Angels androgynes as a *reductio ad absurdum* of the ideal. But once it is recognized that the ideal of androgyny can not only be interpreted to expect of everyone a set of virtues (which need not be a mean between opposing extreme traits), but can also be interpreted to limit everyone's choice to desirable traits, then such challenges to the ideal clearly lose their force.

Actually the main challenge raised by feminists to the ideal of androgyny is that [it] is self-defeating in that it seeks to eliminate sexual stereotyping of human beings [while] it is formulated in terms of the very same stereotypical concepts it seeks to eliminate. Or as Warren has put it, "Is it not at least mildly paradoxical to urge people to cultivate both 'feminine' and 'masculine' virtues, while at the same time holding that virtues ought not to be sexually stereotyped?"

But in response to this challenge, it can be argued that to build a better society we must begin where we are now, and where we are now people still speak of feminine and masculine character traits. Consequently, if we want to easily refer to such traits and to formulate an ideal with respect to how they should be distributed in society it is plausible to refer to them in the way that people presently refer to them, that is, as feminine or masculine traits.

Alternatively, to avoid misunderstanding altogether, the ideal could be formulated in the more abstract way I suggested earlier so that it no longer specifically refers to so-called feminine or masculine traits. So formulated, the ideal requires that the traits that are truly desirable and distributable in society be equally available to both women and men or in the case of virtues equally expected of women and men. So formulated, the ideal would, in effect, require that men and women have in the fullest sense an equal right of self-development. The ideal would require this because an equal right to self-development can only be effectively guaranteed by expecting the same virtues of both women and men and by making other desirable traits that are distributable equally available to both women and men.

So characterized, the ideal of androgyny represents neither a revolt against so-called feminine virtues and traits nor their exaltation over so-called masculine virtues and traits. Accordingly, the ideal of androgyny does not view women's liberation as *simply* the freeing of women from the confines of traditional roles thus making it possible for them to develop in ways heretofore reserved for men. Nor does the ideal view women's liberation as *simply* the revaluation and glorification of so-called feminine activities like housekeeping or mothering or so-called feminine modes of thinking as reflected in an ethic of caring. The first perspective ignores or devalues genuine virtues and desirable traits traditionally associated with women while the second ignores or devalues genuine virtues and desirable traits traditionally associated with men. By contrast, the ideal of androgyny seeks a broader-based ideal for both women and men that combines virtues and desirable traits traditionally associated with women with virtues and desirable traits traditionally associated with men. Nevertheless, the ideal of androgyny will clearly reject any so-called virtues or desirable traits traditionally associated with women or men that have been supportive of discrimination or oppression against women or men.

DEFENSES OF ANDROGYNY

Now there are various contemporary defenses of the ideal of androgyny. Some feminists have attempted to derive the ideal from a Welfare Liberal Conception of Justice. Others have attempted to derive the ideal from a Socialist Conception of Justice. Let us briefly consider each of these defenses in turn.

In attempting to derive the ideal of androgyny from a Welfare Liberal Conception of Justice, feminists have tended to focus on the right to equal opportunity, which is a central requirement of a Welfare Liberal Conception of Justice. Of course, equal opportunity could be interpreted minimally as providing people only with the same legal rights of access to all advantaged positions in society for which they are qualified. But this is not the interpretation given to the right by welfare liberals. In a Welfare Liberal Conception of Justice, equal opportunity is interpreted to require in addition the same prospects for success for all those who are relevantly similar, where relevant similarity involves more than simply present qualifications. For example, Rawls claims that persons in his original position would favor a right to "fair equality of opportunity," which means that persons who have the same natural assets and ... willingness to use them would have the necessary resources to achieve similar life prospects. The point feminists have been making is simply that failure to achieve the ideal of androgyny translates into a failure to guarantee equal opportunity to both women and men. The present evidence for this failure to provide equal opportunity is the discrimination that exists against women in education, employment, and personal relations. Discrimination in education begins early in a child's formal educational experience as teachers and school books support different and less desirable roles for girls than for boys. Discrimination in employment has been well documented. Women continue to earn only a fraction of what men earn for the same or comparable jobs and although women make up almost half of the paid labor force in the U.S., 70 percent of them are concentrated in just twenty different job categories, only five more than in 1905. Finally, discrimination in personal relations is the most entrenched of all forms of discrimination against women. It primarily manifests itself in traditional family structures in which the woman is responsible for domestic work and childcare and the man's task is "to protect against the outside world and to show how to meet this world successfully." In none of these areas, therefore, do women have the same prospects for success as compared with men with similar natural talents and similar desires to succeed.

Now the support for the ideal of androgyny provided by a Socialist Conception of Justice appears to be much more direct than that provided by a Welfare Liberal Conception of Justice. This is because the Socialist Conception of Justice and the ideal of androgyny can be interpreted as requiring the very same equal right of self-development. What a Socialist Conception of Justice purports to add to this interpretation of the ideal of androgyny is an understanding of how the ideal is best to be realized in contemporary capitalist societies. For according to advocates of this defense of androgyny, the ideal is best achieved by socializing the means of production and satisfying people's non-basic as well as their basic needs. Thus, the general ideal behind this approach to realizing the ideal of androgyny is that a cure for capitalist exploitation will also be a cure for women's oppression.

Yet despite attempts to identify the feminist ideal of androgyny with a right to equal opportunity endorsed by a Welfare Liberal Conception of Justice or an equal right of self-development endorsed by a Socialist Conception of Justice, the ideal still transcends both of these rights by requiring not only that desirable traits be equally available to both women and men but also that the same virtues be equally expected of both women and men. Of course, part of the rationale for expecting the same virtues in both women and men is to support such rights. And if support for such rights is to be fairly allocated, the virtues needed to support such rights must be equally expected of both women and men. Nevertheless, to hold that the virtues required to support a right to equal opportunity or an equal right to self-development must be equally expected of both women and men is different from claiming, as the ideal of androgyny does, that human virtues, sans phrase, should be equally expected of both women and men. Thus, the ideal of androgyny clearly requires an inculcation of virtues beyond what is necessary to support a right

to equal opportunity or ... self-development. What additional virtues are required by the ideal obviously depends upon what other rights should be recognized. In this regard, the ideal of androgyny is somewhat open-ended. Feminists who endorse the ideal would simply have to go along with the best arguments for additional rights and corresponding virtues. In particular, I would claim that they would have to support a right to welfare that is necessary for meeting the basic needs of all legitimate claimants given the strong case that can be made for such a right from welfare liberal, socialist, and even libertarian perspectives.

Now, in order to provide all legitimate claimants with the resources necessary for meeting their basic needs, there obviously has to be a limit on the resources that will be available for each individual's self-development, and this limit will definitely have an effect upon the implementation of the ideal of androgyny. Of course, some feminists would want to pursue various possible technological transformations of human biology in order to implement their ideal. For example, they would like to make it possible for women to inseminate other women and for men to lactate and even to bring fertilized ova to term. But bringing about such possibilities would be very costly indeed. Consequently, since the means selected for meeting basic needs must be provided to all legitimate claimants including distant peoples and future generations, it is unlikely that such costly means could ever be morally justified. Rather it seems preferable radically to equalize the conventionally provided opportunities to women and men and wait for such changes to have their ultimate effect on human biology as well. Of course, if any "technological fixes" for achieving androgyny should prove to be cost-efficient as a means for meeting people's basic needs, then obviously there would be every reason to utilize them.

Unfortunately, the commitment of a Feminist Conception of Justice to a right of equal opportunity raises still another problem for the view. Some philosophers have contended that equal opportunity is ultimately an incoherent goal. As Lloyd Thomas has put the charge, "We have a problem for those who advocate competitive equality of opportunity: The prizes won in the competitions of the first generation will tend to defeat the requirements of equality of opportunity for the next." The only way to avoid this result, Thomas claims, "is by not permitting persons to be dependent for their self-development on others at all," which obviously is a completely unacceptable solution.

But this is a problem, as Thomas points out, that exists for competitive opportunities. They are opportunities for which, even when each person does her best, there are considerably more losers than winners. With respect to such opportunities, the winners may well be able to place themselves and their children in an advantageous position with respect to subsequent competitions. But under a Welfare Liberal Conception of Justice, and presumably a Feminist Conception of Justice as well, most of the opportunities people have are not competitive opportunities at all, but rather noncompetitive opportunities to acquire the resources necessary for meeting their basic needs. These are opportunities with respect to which virtually everyone who does her best can be a winner. Of course, some people who do not do their best may fail to satisfy their basic needs, and this failure may have negative consequences for their children's prospects. But under a Welfare Liberal Conception of Justice, and presumably a Feminist Conception of Justice as well, every effort is required to insure that each generation has the same opportunities to meet their basic needs, and as long as most of the opportunities that are available are of the non-competitive sort, this goal should not be that difficult to achieve.

Now it might be objected that if all that will be accomplished under the proposed system of equal opportunity is, for the most part, the satisfaction of people's basic needs, then that would not bring about the revolutionary change in the relationship between women and men that feminists are demanding. For don't most women in technologically advanced societies already have their basic needs satisfied, despite the fact that they are not yet fully liberated?

In response, it should be emphasized that the concern of defenders of the ideal of androgyny is not just with women in technologically advanced societies. The ideal of androgyny is also applicable to women in Third World and developing societies, and in such societies it is clear that the basic needs of many women are not being met. Furthermore, it is just not the case that all the basic needs of most women in technologically advanced societies are being met. Most obviously, their basic needs for self-development are still not being met. This is because they are being denied an equal right to education, training, jobs, and a variety of social roles for which they have the native capabilities. In effect, women in technologically advanced societies are still being treated as second-class persons, no matter how well-fed, well-clothed, well-housed they happen to be. This is why there must be a radical restructuring of social institutions even in technologically advanced societies if women's basic needs for self-development are to be met.

ANDROGYNY AND THE FAMILY

Now the primary locus for the radical restructuring required by the ideal of androgyny is the family. Here two fundamental changes are needed. First, all children irrespective of their sex must be given the same type of upbringing consistent with their native capabilities. Second, mothers and fathers must also have the same opportunities for education and employment consistent with their native capabilities.

Surprisingly, however, some welfare liberals have viewed the existence of the family as imposing an acceptable limit on the right to equal opportunity. Rawls, for example, claims the principle of fair opportunity can be only imperfectly carried out, at least as long as the institution of the family exists. The extent to which natural capacities develop and reach fruition is affected by all kinds of social conditions and class attitudes. Even the willingness to make an effort, to try, and so to be deserving in the ordinary sense is itself dependent upon happy family and social circumstances. It is impossible in practice to secure equal chances of achievement and culture for those similarly endowed, and therefore we may want to adopt a principle which recognizes this fact and also mitigates the arbitrary effects of the natural lottery itself.

Thus, according to Rawls, since different families will provide different opportunities for their children, the only way to fully achieve "fair equality of opportunity" would require us to go too far and abolish or radically modify traditional family structures.

Yet others have argued that the full attainment of equal opportunity requires that we go even further and equalize people's native as well as their social assets. For only when everyone's natural and social assets have been equalized would everyone have exactly the same chance as everyone else to attain the desirable social positions in society. Of course, feminists have no difficulty recognizing that there are moral limits to the pursuit of equal opportunity. Accordingly, feminists could grant that other than the possibility of special cases, such as sharing a surplus organ like a second kidney, it would be too much to ask people to sacrifice their native assets to achieve equal opportunity.

Rawls, however, proposes to limit the pursuit of equal opportunity still further by accepting the inequalities generated by families in any given sector of society, provided that there is still equal opportunity between the sectors or that the existing inequality of opportunity can be justified in terms of its benefit to those in the least-advantaged position. Nevertheless, what Rawls is concerned with here is simply the inequality of opportunity that exists between individuals owing to the fact that they come from different families. He fails to consider the inequality of opportunity that exists in traditional family structures, especially between adult members, in virtue of the different roles expected of women and men. When viewed from the original position, this latter inequality of opportunity clearly is sufficient to require a radical modification of traditional family structures, even if the former inequality, for the reasons Rawls suggests, does not require any such modifications.

Yet at least in the United States this need radically to modify traditional family structures to guarantee equal opportunity confronts a serious problem. Given that a significant proportion of the available jobs are at least 9 to 5, families with preschool children require day-care facilities if their adult members are to pursue their careers. Unfortunately, for many families such facilities are simply unavailable. In New York City, for example, more than 144,000 children under the age of six are competing for 46,000 full-time slots in day-care centers. In Seattle, there is licensed day-care space for 8,800 of the 23,000 children who need it. In Miami, two children, 3 and 4 years old, were left unattended at home while their mother worked. They climbed into a clothes dryer while the timer was on, closed the door and burned to death.

Moreover, even the available day-care facilities are frequently inadequate either because their staffs are poorly trained or because the child/adult ratio in such facilities is too high. At best, such facilities provide little more than custodial care; at worst, they actually retard the development of those under their care. What this suggests is that at least under present conditions if preschool children are to be adequately cared for, frequently, one of the adult members of the family will have to remain at home to provide that care. But since most jobs are at least 9 to 5, this will require that the adult members who stay at home temporarily give up pursuing a career. However, such sacrifice appears to conflict with the equal opportunity requirement of Feminist Justice.

Now families might try to meet this equal opportunity requirement by having one parent give up pursuing a career for a certain period of time and the other give up pursuing a career for a subsequent (equal) period of time. But there are problems here too. Some careers are difficult to interrupt for any significant period of time, while others never adequately reward latecomers. In addition, given the high rate of divorce and the inadequacies of most legally mandated child support, those who first sacrifice their careers may find themselves later faced with the impossible task of beginning or reviving their careers while continuing to be the primary caretaker of their children. Furthermore, there is considerable evidence that children will benefit more from equal rearing from both parents. So the option of having just one parent doing the child-rearing for any length of time is, other things being equal, not optimal.

It would seem therefore, that to truly share child-rearing within the family, what is needed is flexible (typically part-time) work schedules that also allow both parents to be together with their children for a significant period every day. Now some flexible job schedules have already been tried by various corporations. But if equal opportunity is to be a reality in our society, the option of flexible job schedules must be guaranteed to all those with preschool children. Of course, to require employers to guarantee flexible job schedules to all those with preschool children would place a significant restriction upon the rights of employers, and it may appear to move the practical requirements of Feminist Justice closer to those of Socialist Justice. But if the case for flexible job schedules is grounded on a right to equal opportunity then at least defenders of Welfare Liberal Justice will have no reason to object. This is clearly one place where Feminist Justice with its focus on equal opportunity within the family tends to drive Welfare Liberal Justice and Socialist Justice closer together in their practical requirements.

Recently, however, Christina Hoff Sommers has criticized feminist philosophers for being "against the family." Her main objection is that feminist philosophers have criticized traditional family structures without adequately justifying what they would put in its place. In this paper, I have tried to avoid any criticism of this sort by first articulating a defensible version of the feminist ideal of androgyny which can draw upon support from both Welfare Liberal and Socialist Conceptions of Justice and then by showing what demands this ideal would impose upon family structures. Since Sommers and other critics of the feminist ideal of androgyny also support a strong requirement of equal opportunity, it is difficult to see how they can consistently do so while denying the radical implications of that requirement (and the ideal of androgyny that underlies it) for traditional family structures.

29

Philosophers Against the Family

CHRISTINA HOFF SOMMERS

Christina Hoff Sommers distinguishes liberal feminists from radical feminists. She contends that liberal feminists, like herself, want equal opportunity in the workplace and politics, but would leave marriage and motherhood "untouched and unimpugned." By contrast, Sommers contends that radical feminists are committed to an assimilationist or androgynous ideal that would destroy the (traditional) family and deny most women what they want.

Much of what commonly counts as personal morality is measured by how well we behave within family relationships. We live our moral lives as son or daughter to this mother and that father, as brother or sister to that sister or brother, as father or mother, grandfather, granddaughter to that boy or girl or that man or woman. These relationships and the moral duties defined by them were once popular topics of moral casuistry; but when we turn to the literature of recent moral philosophy, we find little discussion on what it means to be a good son or daughter, a good mother or father, a good husband or wife, a good brother or sister.

Modern ethical theory concentrates on more general topics. Perhaps the majority of us who do ethics accept some version of Kantianism or utilitarianism, and these mainstream doctrines are better designed for telling us about what we should do as persons in general than about our special duties as parents or children or siblings. We believe, perhaps, that these universal theories can fully account for the morality of special relations. In any case, modern ethics is singularly silent on the bread and butter issues of personal morality in daily life. But silence is only part of it. With the exception of marriage itself, the relationships in the family are

biologically given. The contemporary philosopher is, on the whole, actively unsympathetic to the idea that we have *any* duties defined by relationships that we have not voluntarily entered into. We do not, after all, choose our parents or siblings, and even if we do choose to have children, this is not the same as choosing, say, our friends. Because the special relationships that constitute the family as a social arrangement are, in this sense, not voluntarily assumed, many moralists feel bound in principle to dismiss them altogether. The practical result is that philosophers are to be found among those who are contributing to an ongoing disintegration of the traditional family. In what follows I expose some of the philosophical roots of the current hostility to family morality. My own view that the ethical theses underlying this hostility are bad philosophy is made evident throughout the discussion.

THE MORAL VANTAGE

Social criticism is a heady pastime to which philosophers are professionally addicted. One approach is Aristotelian in method and temperament. It is anti-radical, though it may be liberal, and it approaches

From "Philosophers against the Family," in *Person to Person*, George Graham and Hugh LaFollette, eds. (1989). Reprinted by the permission of the editors.

the task of needed reform with a prima facie respect for the norms of established morality. It is conservationist and cautious in its recommendations for change. It is therefore not given to such proposals as abolishing the family or abolishing private property and, indeed, does not look kindly on such proposals from other philosophers. The antiradicals I am concerned about are not those who would be called Burkean. I call them liberal but this use of the term is somewhat perverse since, in my stipulative use, a liberal is a philosopher who advocates social reform but always in a conservative spirit. My liberals share with Aristotle the conviction that the traditional arrangements have great moral weight and that common opinion is a primary source of moral truth. A good modern example is Henry Sidgwick with his constant appeal to common sense. But philosophers like John Stuart Mill, William James, and Bertrand Russell can also be cited. On the other hand, since no radical can be called a liberal in my sense, many so-called liberals could be perversely excluded. Thus when John Rawls toys with the possibility of abolishing the family because kinship bias is a force inimical to equality of opportunity, he is no liberal.

The more exciting genre of social criticism is not liberal-Aristotelian but radical and Platonist in spirit. Its vantage is external or even supernal to the social institutions it has placed under moral scrutiny. Plato was as aware as anyone could be that what he called the cave was social reality. One reason for calling it a cave was to emphasize the need, as he saw it, for an external, objective perspective on established morality. Another point in so calling it was his conviction that common opinion was benighted, and that reform could not be accomplished except by a great deal of consciousness raising and enlightened social engineering. Plato's supernal vantage made it possible for him to look on social reality in somewhat the way the Army Corps of Engineers looks upon a river that needs to have its course changed and its waywardness tamed. In our own day much social criticism of a Marxist variety has taken this radical approach to social change. And of course much of contemporary feminist philosophy is radical....

FEMINISM AND THE FAMILY

I have said that the morality of the family has been relatively neglected. The glaring exception to this is, of course, the feminist movement. This movement is complex, but I am primarily confined to its moral philosophers, of whom the most influential is Simone de Beauvoir. For de Beauvoir, a social arrangement that does not allow all its participants the scope and liberty of a human subjectivity is to be condemned. De Beauvoir criticizes the family as an unacceptable arrangement since, for women, marriage and childbearing are essentially incompatible with their subjectivity and freedom:

> The tragedy of marriage is not that it fails to assure woman the promised happiness ... but that it mutilates her: It dooms her to repetition and routine.... At twenty or thereabouts mistress of a home, bound permanently to a man, a child in her arms, she stands with her life virtually finished forever (1952, 534).

For de Beauvoir the tragedy goes deeper than marriage. The loss of subjectivity is unavoidable as long as human reproduction requires the woman's womb. De Beauvoir starkly describes the pregnant woman who ought to be a "free individual" as a "stockpile of colloids, an incubator of an egg." And as recently as 1977 she compared childbearing and nurturing to slavery.

It would be a mistake to say that de Beauvoir's criticism of the family is outside the mainstream of Anglo-American philosophy. Her criterion of moral adequacy may be formulated in continental existentialist terms, but its central contention is generally accepted: Who would deny that an arrangement that systematically thwarts the freedom and autonomy of the individual is *eo ipso* defective? What is perhaps a bit odd to Anglo-American ears is that de Beauvoir makes so little appeal to ideals of fairness and equality. For her, it is the loss of autonomy that is decisive.

De Beauvoir is more pessimistic than most feminists she has influenced about the prospects for technological and social solutions. But implicit in her critique is the ideal of a society in which sexual differences are minimal or nonexistent. This ideal is shared by many contemporary feminist philosophers: ... Richard Wasserstrom (1980), Ann Ferguson (1977), and Alison Jaggar (1977; 1983; 1986) are representative.

Wasserstrom's approach to social criticism is Platonist in its use of a hypothetical good society. The ideal society is nonsexist and "assimilationist": "In the assimilationist society in respect to sex, persons would not be socialized so as to see or understand themselves or others as essentially or significantly who they were or what their lives would be like because they were either male or female" (1980, 26). Social reality is scrutinized for its approximation to this ideal, and criticism is directed against all existing norms. Take the custom of having sexually segregated bathrooms: Whether this is right or wrong "depends on what the good society would look like in respect to sexual differentiation." The key question in evaluating any law or arrangement in which sex difference figures is: "What would the good or just society make of [it]?"

Thus the supernal light shines on the cave revealing its moral defects. *There,* in the ideal society, gender in the choice of lover or spouse would be of no more significance than eye color. *There* the family would consist of adults but not necessarily of different sexes and not necessarily in pairs. *There* we find equality ensured by a kind of affirmative action which compensates for disabilities. If women are somewhat weaker than men, or if they are subject to lunar disabilities, then this must be compensated for. (Wasserstrom compares women to persons with congenital defects for whom the good society makes special arrangements.) Male-dominated sports such as wrestling and football will ... be eliminated, and marriage as we know it will not exist.

Other feminist philosophers are equally confident about the need for sweeping change. Ann Ferguson (1977) wants a "radical reorganization of child rearing." She recommends communal living and a de-emphasis on biological parenting. In the ideal society "love relationships would be based on the meshing together of androgynous human beings." Carol Gould (1983) argues for androgyny and for abolishing legal marriage. She favors single

parenting, co-parenting, and communal parenting. The only arrangement she emphatically opposes is the traditional one where the mother provides primary care for the children. Janice Raymond (1975) is an assimilationist who objects to the ideal of androgyny, preferring instead to speak of a genderless ideal free of male or female stereotypes. Alison Jaggar's ideal is described in a science-fiction story depicting a society in which "neither sex bears children, but both sexes, through hormone treatments, suckle them ... thus [the author] envisions a society where every baby has three social 'mothers,' who may be male or female, and at least two of whom agree to breast-feed it" (1983). To those of us who find this bizarre, Jaggar replies that this shows the depth of our prejudice in favor of the natural family.

Though they differ in detail, these feminists hold to a common social ideal that is broadly assimilationist in character and inimical to the traditional family. Sometimes it seems as if the radical feminist simply takes the classical Marxist eschatology of the *Communist Manifesto* and substitutes "gender" for "class." Indeed, the feminist and the old-fashioned Marxist do have much in common. Both see their caves as politically divided into two warring factions: one oppressing, the other oppressed. Both see the need of raising the consciousness of the oppressed group to its predicament and to the possibility of removing its shackles. Both look forward to the day of a classless or genderless society. And both are zealots, paying little attention to the tragic personal costs to be paid for the revolution they wish to bring about. The feminists tell us little about that side of things. To begin with, how can the benighted myriads in the cave who do not wish to mesh together with other androgynous beings be reeducated? And how are children to be brought up in the genderless society? Plato took great pains to explain his methods. Would the new methods be as thoroughgoing? Unless these questions can be given plausible answers, the supernal attack on the family must always be irresponsible. The appeal to the just society justifies nothing until it can be shown that the radical proposals do not have monstrous consequences. That has not been shown.

Indeed, given the perennially dubious state of the social sciences, it is precisely what *cannot* be shown.

Any social arrangement that falls short of the assimilationist ideal is labeled sexist. It should be noted that this characteristically feminist use of the term differs significantly from the popular or literal sense. Literally, and popularly, sexism connotes unfair discrimination. But in its extended philosophical use it connotes discrimination, period. Wasserstrom and many feminists trade on the popular pejorative connotations of sexism when they invite us to be antisexist. Most liberals are antisexist in the popular sense. But to be antisexist in the technical, radical philosophical sense is not merely to be opposed to discrimination against women; it is to be *for* what Wasserstrom calls the assimilationist ideal. The philosopher antisexist opposes any social policy that is nonandrogynous, objecting, for example, to legislation that allows for maternity leave. As Alison Jaggar remarks: "We do not, after all, elevate 'prostate leave' into a special right of men" (1977). From being liberally opposed to sexism, one may in this way insensibly be led to a radical critique of the family whose ideal is assimilationist and androgynous. For it is very clear that the realization of the androgynous ideal is incompatible with the survival of the family as we know it.

The neological extension of labels such as "sexism," "slavery," and "prostitution" is a feature of radical discourse. The liberal too will sometimes call for radical solutions to social problems. Some institutions are essentially unjust. To reform slavery or totalitarian systems of government is to eliminate them. The radical trades on these extreme practices in characterizing other practices—for example, characterizing low wages as "slave" wages and the worker who is paid them as a "slave" laborer. Taking these descriptions seriously may put one on the way to treating a system of a free labor market as a "slave system," which, in simple justice, must be overthrown and replaced by an alternative system of production.

Comparing mothers and wives to slaves is a common radical criticism of the family. Presumably most slaves do not want to be slaves. In fact, the majority of wives and mothers want to be wives and mothers. Calling these women slaves is

therefore a pejorative extension of the term. To be slaves in the literal sense these women would have to be too dispirited and oppressed or too corrupt even to want freedom from slavery. Yet that is how some feminist philosophers look upon women who opt for the traditional family. It does seem fanciful and not a little condescending to see them so, but let us suppose that it is in fact a correct and profound description of the plight of married women and mothers. Would it now follow that the term "slave" literally applies to them? Not quite yet. Before we could call these women slaves, we should have to have made a further assumption. Even timorous slaves too fearful of taking any step to freedom are under no illusion that they are not slaves. Yet it is a fact that most women and mothers do not *think* of themselves as slaves, so we must assume that the majority of women have been systematically deluded into thinking they are free. And that assumption, too, is often explicitly made. Here the radical feminist will typically explain that, existentially, women, being treated by men as sex objects, are especially prone to bad faith and false consciousness. Marxist feminists will see them as part of an unawakened and oppressed economic class. Clearly we cannot call on a deluded woman to cast off her bonds before we have made her *aware* of her bondage. So the first task of freeing the slave woman is dispelling the thrall of a false and deceptive consciousness. One must raise her consciousness to the reality of her situation. (Some feminists acknowledge that it may in fact be too late for many of the women who have fallen too far into the delusions of marriage and motherhood. But the educative process can save many from falling into the marriage and baby trap.)

In this sort of rhetorical climate nothing is what it seems. Prostitution is another term that has been subjected to a radical enlargement. Alison Jaggar believes that a feminist interpretation of the term "prostitution" is badly needed and asks for a "philosophical theory of prostitution" (1986). Observing that the average woman dresses for men, marries a man for protection, and so on, she says, "For contemporary radical feminists, prostitution is the archetypal relationship of women to men" (1986, 115).

Of course, the housewife Jaggar has in mind might be offended at the suggestion that she herself is a prostitute, albeit less well paid and less aware of it than the professional street prostitute. To this the radical feminist reply is, to quote Jaggar:

> Individuals' intentions do not necessarily indicate the true nature of what is going on. Both man and woman might be outraged at the description of their candlelit dinner as prostitution, but the radical feminist argues this outrage is due simply to the participants' failure or refusal to perceive the social context in which the dinner occurs (1986, 117).

Apparently, this failure or refusal to perceive affects most women. Thus we may even suppose that the majority of women who have been treated by a man to a candlelit dinner prefer it to other dining alternatives they have experienced. To say that these preferences are misguided is a hard and condescending doctrine. It would appear that most feminist philosophers are not overly impressed with Mill's principle that there can be no appeal from a majority verdict of those who have experienced two alternatives.

The dismissive feminist attitude to the widespread preferences of women takes its human toll. Most women, for example, prefer to have children, and few of those who have them regret having them. It is no more than sensible, from a utilitarian standpoint, to take note of the widespread preference and to take it seriously in planning one's own life. But a significant number of women discount this general verdict as benighted, taking more seriously the idea that the reported joys of motherhood are exaggerated and fleeting, if not altogether illusory. These women tell themselves and others that having babies is a trap to be avoided. But for many women childlessness has become a trap of its own, somewhat lonelier than the more conventional traps of marriage and babies. Some come to find their childlessness regrettable; this sort of regret is common to those who flout Mill's reasonable maxim by putting the verdict of ideology over the verdict of human experience.

It is a serious defect of American feminism that it concentrates its zeal on impugning femininity and feminine culture at the expense of the grassroot fight against economic and social injustices to which women are subjected. As we have seen, the radical feminist attitude to the woman who enjoys her femininity is condescending or even contemptuous. Indeed, the contempt for femininity reminds one of misogynist biases in philosophers such as Kant, Rousseau, and Schopenhauer, who believed that femininity was charming but incompatible with full personhood and reasonableness. The feminists deny the charm, but they too accept the verdict that femininity is weakness. It goes without saying that an essential connection between femininity and powerlessness has not been established by *either* party.

By denigrating conventional feminine roles and holding to an assimilationist ideal in social policy, the feminist movement has lost its natural constituency. The actual concerns, beliefs, and aspirations of the majority of women are not taken seriously *except* as illustrations of bad faith, false consciousness, and successful brainwashing. What women actually want is discounted and reinterpreted as to what they have been led to *think* they want (a man, children). What most women *enjoy* (male gallantry, candlelit dinners, sexy clothes, makeup) is treated as an obscenity (prostitution).

As the British feminist Jennifer Radcliffe Richards says:

> Most women still dream about beauty, dress, weddings, dashing lovers, domesticity, and babies ... but if feminists seem (as they do) to want to eliminate nearly all of these things—beauty, sex conventions, families, and all—for most people that simply means that removal of everything in life which is worth living for (1980, 341–342).

Radical feminism creates a false dichotomy between sexism and assimilation, as if there were nothing in between. This is to ignore completely the middle ground in which it could be recognized that a woman can be free of oppression and nevertheless feminine in the sense abhorred by many feminists. For women are simply not waiting to be freed from the particular chains the radical feminists are trying to sunder. The average woman enjoys her femininity. She wants a man, not a roommate. She wants fair economic opportunities, and she wants children and the time to care for them. These are the goals that women actually have, and they are not easily attainable. But they will never be furthered by an elitist radical movement that views the actual aspirations of women as the product of a false consciousness. There is room for a liberal feminism that would work for reforms that would give women equal opportunity in the workplace and in politics, but would leave untouched and unimpugned the basic institutions that women want and support: marriage and motherhood. Such a feminism is already in operation in some European countries. But it has been obstructed in the United States by the ideologues who now hold the seat of power in the feminist movement (Hewlett, 1986).

In characterizing and criticizing American feminism, I have not taken into account the latest revisions and qualifications of a lively and variegated movement. There is a kind of feminism-of-the-week that one cannot hope to keep abreast of, short of giving up all other concerns. The best one can do for the present purposes is attend to central theses and arguments that bear on the feminist treatment of the family. Nevertheless, even for this limited purpose, it would be wrong to omit discussion of an important turn taken by feminism in the past few years. I have in mind the recent literature on the idea that there is a specific female ethic that is more concrete, less rule-oriented, more empathetic and caring, and more attentive to the demands of a particular context. The kind of feminism that accepts the idea that women differ from men in approaching ethical dilemmas and social problems from a care perspective is not oriented to androgyny as an ideal. Rather it seeks to develop this special female ethic and give it greater practical scope.

The stress on context might lead one to think these feminists are more sympathetic to the family as the social arrangement that shapes the moral development of women and is the context for many of the moral dilemmas that women actually face. However, one sees as yet no attention being paid to the fact that feminism itself is a force working against the preservation of the family. Psychologists like Carol Gilligan and philosophers like Lawrence Blum concentrate their attention on the moral quality of the caring relationships, but these relationships are themselves not viewed in their concrete embeddedness in any formal social arrangement.

It should also be said that some feminists are moving away from earlier hostility to motherhood (Trebilcot, 1984). Here, too, one sees the weakening of the assimilationist ideal in the acknowledgment of a primary gender role. However, childrearing is not primarily seen within the context of the family but as a special relationship between mother and daughter or—more awkwardly—between mother and son, a relationship that effectively excludes the male parent. And the often cultist celebration of motherhood remains largely hostile to traditional familial arrangements.

It is too early to say whether a new style of nonassimilationist feminism will lead to a mitigation of the assault on the family or even on femininity. In any case, the recognition of a female ethic of care and responsibility is hardly inconsistent with a social ethic that values the family as a vital, perhaps indispensable, institution. And the recognition that women have their own moral style may well be followed by a more accepting attitude to the kind of femininity that the more assimilationist feminists reject.

REFERENCES

De Beauvoir, Simone. 1952. *The Second Sex*. H. M. Parshley, trans. New York: Random House.

___. 1977. "Talking to De Beauvoir." In *Spare Rib*.

Ferguson, Ann. 1977. "Androgyny as an Ideal for Human Development." In M. Vetterling-Braggin, F. Elliston, and J. English, eds. *Feminism and*

Philosophy, pp. 49–69. Totowa, N.J.: Rowman and Littlefield.

Gould, Carol. 1983. "Private Rights and Public Virtues: Woman, the Family and Democracy." In Carol Gould, ed. *Beyond Domination,* pp. 3–18. Totowa, N.J.: Rowman and Allanheld.

Hewlett, Sylvia Ann. 1986. *A Lesser Life: The Myth of Woman's Liberation in America.* New York: Morrow.

Jaggar, Alison. 1977. "On Sex Equality." In Jane English, ed. *Sex Equality.* Englewood Cliffs, N.J.: Prentice-Hall.

___. 1983. "Human Biology in Feminist Theory: Sexual Equality Reconsidered." In Gould, ed. *Beyond Domination.*

___. 1986. "Prostitution." In Marilyn Pearsell, ed.

Women and Valves: Readings in Recent Feminist Philosophy, pp. 108–121. Belmont, Calif.: Wadsworth.

Raymond, Janice. 1975. "The Illusion of Androgyny." *Quest: A Feminist Quarterly, 2.*

Richards, Jennifer Radcliffe. 1980. *The Sceptical Feminist.* Harmondsworth: Penguin.

Sterba, James P. and Farrell, Warren. 2009 *Does Feminism Discriminate Against Men? A Debate.* New York: Oxford University Press.

Trebilcot, Joyce, ed. 1984. *Mothering: Essays in Feminist Theory.* Totowa, N.J.: Rowman and Allanheld.

Wasserstrom, Richard. 1980. *Philosophy and Social Issues.* Notre Dame, Ind.: University of Notre Dame Press.

30

They Lived Happily Ever After:
Sommers on Women and Marriage

MARILYN FRIEDMAN

Marilyn Friedman questions whether what Christina Sommers supports is really what most women want. She quotes a 1983 survey which indicated that 63 percent of women preferred nontraditional family relationships. She points out that in 1977 only 16 percent of American households were traditional families. She argues that femininity as slavishly deferring to men is not good for women and contends that no woman should "swoon at the sight of Rhett Butler carrying Scarlett O'Hara up the stairs to a fate undreamt of in feminist philosophy."

1. In a series of papers which has recently appeared in several philosophical and general academic publications,[1] Christina Sommers mounts a campaign against feminist philosophers (1989a, 85; 1989b, B2) and "American feminism" in general (1989a, 90–91). Sommers blames feminists for contributing to the current divorce rate and the breakdown of the traditional family, and she repudiates feminist critiques of traditional forms of marriage, family, and femininity. In this paper, I explore Sommers's views in some detail. My aim is not primarily to defend her feminist targets, but to ferret out Sommers's own views of traditional marriage, family, and femininity, and to see whether or not they have any philosophical merit.

2. In her writings, Sommers generally defends what she claims that feminists have challenged. Whether or not she is actually discussing the same things is often open to question since she fails to define the key terms behind which she rallies. Sommers, for example, endorses "the family," the "traditional family," and "the family as we know it" (1989a, 87–88). These are not equivalent

expressions. The so-called traditional family—a nuclear family consisting of a legally married heterosexual couple and their children, in which the man is the sole breadwinner and "head" of the household, and the woman does the domestic work and childcare—comprised only 16% of all U.S. households in 1977, according to the U.S. Census Bureau.[2] Hence, the "traditional family" is no longer *"the* family" or *"the* family as we know it" (italics mine) but is only one sort of family that we know.

Sommers also rallies behind "femininity," "feminine culture," "conventional feminine roles," and "a primary gender role" (1989a, 90, 92). These expressions, as well, call for clarification; they do not necessarily refer to the same practices. In recent years, many feminists have defended various aspects of what might also be called "feminine culture." Sommers notes a few of these authors and works (Carol Gilligan, for example), but finds one reason or another for repudiating each one that she cites.[3]

3. To see what Sommers is promoting under the banner of "feminine culture," we should look to Sommers's claims about what women value,

From "They Lived Happily Ever After: Sommers on Women and Marriage," *Journal of Social Philosophy* (1990). Reprinted with permission.

want, and enjoy.[4] First, there are wants, values, and enjoyments pertaining to men.[5] Sommers claims that women want "a man," "marriage," and "to marry good providers."[6] She asserts that "most women" enjoy "male gallantry," that the "majority of women" enjoy being "treated by a man to a candlelit dinner," and that "many women … swoon at the sight of Rhett Butler carrying Scarlett O'Hara up the stairs to a fate undreamt of in feminist philosophy."[7]

Second, there are wants, values, and enjoyments having to do with children. Women, Sommers tells us, want children, motherhood, "*Conventional* motherhood," "family," and "the time to care for children."[8] In a revealing turn of phrase, Sommers also asserts that women are "willing to pay the price" for family and motherhood (1989b, B2). Sommers does not say, however, what she thinks the price is.

Third, there are wants, values, and enjoyments having to do with femininity. Women are said to enjoy their "femininity," makeup, "sexy clothes," and, even more specifically, "clothes that render them 'sex objects.'"[9] On the topic of femininity, Sommers also quotes approvingly (1989a, 90–91) the words of Janet Radcliffe Richards who wrote that, "Most women still dream about beauty, dress, weddings, dashing lovers," and "domesticity," and that, for "most people," "beauty, sex conventions, families, and all" comprise "everything in life which is worth living for."[10]

4. A very few of the wants which Sommers attributes to women do not fit into my three-part classification scheme (men, children, femininity). Sommers claims that women want "fair economic opportunities" (1989a, 91), and that they are "generally receptive to liberal feminist reforms that enhance their political and economic powers" (1989b, B2). Sommers, ironically, does not recognize that the enhanced economic and political power of women makes them less needful of traditional marriage to a "good provider," and when they are married, makes them less afraid to resort to divorce to solve marital and family problems. The economic concerns of liberal feminism directly threaten one colossal support for the "traditional family," namely, the extreme economic vulnerability of the non-income-earning

woman and her concomitant material dependence on a "good provider."

Under traditional arrangements, most women not only *wanted* marriage, they *needed* it. It was by far a woman's most socially legitimate option for economic survival. Take away the need, as liberal feminism seeks to do, and at least some of the want also disappears. One otherwise very traditional aunt of mine became a wealthy widow in her late fifties when my rich uncle died. She never remarried. Now a dynamic woman of 82 who travels widely and lives well, she confesses that no man has interested her enough to make it worthwhile to give up her freedom a second time. "I'm lucky," she confides, "I don't need a meal-ticket." Even a nonfeminist can understand what she is getting at.

5. Before assessing Sommers's overall views, let us rescue Scarlett O'Hara. Sommers's remark that Scarlett O'Hara's rape by Rhett Butler is a fate undreamt of in feminist philosophy is … simply stunning. (Note that Sommers does not use the word *rape* here—one of many omissions in her writings.) Even a passing knowledge of feminist philosophy reveals that rape is hardly undreamt of in it.[11] Rape, of course, is not a dream; it is a nightmare. Any form of sexual aggression can involve coercion, intimidation, degradation, physical abuse, battering, and, in extreme cases, death.

The reality of rape is rendered invisible by the many novels and films, such as *Gone With the Wind,* which romanticize and mystify it. They portray the rapist as a handsome man whose domination is pleasurable in bed, and portray women as happy to have their own sexual choices and refusals crushed by such men. In a culture in which these sorts of portrayals are routine, it is no surprise that this scene arouses the sexual desire of some women. However, the name of Richard Speck,[12] to take one example, can remind us that real rape is not the pleasurable fantasy intimated in *Gone With the Wind.* To put the point graphically: would "many women" still swoon over Butler's rape of O'Hara if they knew that he urinated on her? When you're the victim of rape, you don't have much choice over what goes on.

6. Let us move on to femininity. Sommers never spells out exactly what she means by femininity. For guidance on this topic, we could turn to literature in social psychology which identifies the important traits of femininity and which explores the social devaluation of the feminine (Eagly 1987). However, it might be more revealing to turn to a different sort of "expert." By a lucky coincidence, I recently acquired a gem of a cultural artifact, a 1965 book entitled *Always Ask a Man: Arlene Dahl's Key to Femininity,* written by a rather well-known actress and model of the 1960s, Arlene Dahl. I have learned a great deal from this femininity manifesto.

As you might guess from the title, one guiding theme of the book, and of the femininity it aims to promote, is utter deference to the opinions of men. Dahl instructs the female reader: "Look at Yourself Objectively (try to see yourself through a man's eyes)" (p. 2). In Dahl's view, the "truly feminine" woman works "instinctively" at pleasing men and making men feel important. "When [a man] speaks to her, she listens with rapt attention to every word" (p. 5). Dahl believes that every woman has the capacity to measure up to men's ideals of femininity. This is because "Every woman is an actress. (Admit it!) Her first role is that of a coquette. (If you have any doubts just watch a baby girl with her father)" (p. 6).

Dahl's book is laced with quotations from male celebrities who are treated as incontrovertible authorities on what women should be like. Yul Brynner, for example, wants women to be good listeners who are not particularly logical (p. 3). Richard Burton likes women who are "faintly giggly" (p. 3). Tony Perkins thinks that a "girl should act like a girl and not like the head of a corporation—even if she is" (p. 8). The most revealing observation comes from George Hamilton: "A woman is often like a strip of film— obliterated, insignificant—until a man puts a light behind her" (pp. 5–6).

Surprisingly, some of the traits advocated for women by these male celebrities are actually valuable traits: honesty, straightforwardness, maturity, ingenuity, understanding, dignity, generosity, and humor. These traits are not distinctively feminine, however, and that may be the reason why they quickly disappear from Dahl's discussion. The twin themes that resound throughout this femininity

manual are that of cultivating one's physical attractiveness and slavishly deferring to men. Instead of a chapter on honesty, a chapter on dignity, and so on, the book features chapters on every aspect of bodily grooming and adornment, including a separate chapter on each of the four basic categories of Caucasian hair color: blonde, redhead, "brownette," and brunette.

The slavish deference to men is crucial, since the whole point of the enterprise is to get a man. Thus, Dahl explains in the introduction that this book is written to counteract a tendency for women to dress to please other women, and it is also not for "women who want to be beautiful for beauty's sake. Such beauty serves no purpose, other than self-satisfaction, if that can be considered a purpose" (pp. x–xi).

The quintessential prohibition involved in femininity seems to be this: "NEVER upstage a man. Don't try to top his joke, even if you have to bite your tongue to keep from doing it. Never launch loudly into your own opinion on a subject— whether it's petunias or politics. Instead, draw out his ideas to which you can gracefully add your footnotes from time to time" (p. 12). Dahl is less sanguine than Sommers that the role of motherhood fits comfortably into a feminine life; she advises, "... don't get so involved with your role of MOTHER that you forget to play WIFE" (p. 9). Once married, your own interests should never override your husband's interests, job, and even hobbies, and, "There should be nothing that takes precedence in your day's schedule over making yourself attractive and appealing for the man in your life," not even your 'children's activities" (p. 175)!

Voila, femininity. Such servility shows the dubiousness of Sommers's claim that "a woman can be free of oppression and nevertheless feminine in the sense abhorred by many feminists" (1989a, 91).

7. Let us turn now to Sommers's overall philosophical defense of traditional marriage, family, and femininity. Having asserted that most women value or want all of these traditions, Sommers charges feminist views with a serious defect: They either dismiss or disparage these popular feminine wants and values.[13] Sommers herself defers to these

alleged views of most women as if they were as such authoritative: Because "most women" (as she alleges) want traditional marriage and family, therefore these practices must be better than any alternatives. It is important to note that Sommers does not argue that traditional marriage and so on, on balance, promote important moral values better than any feminist alternatives.[14] No comprehensive moral comparisons appear in her writings. Her argument begins (and ends, as I will argue) with an appeal to popular opinion.

8. Is Sommers right about what "most women" think? She refers to no studies, no representative samples whatsoever to support her generalizations. Whole categories of women are patently excluded from her reference group and are invisible in her writings. This is a fitting moment to mention the "L" word—and I don't mean "liberal." Obviously, no lesbians, unless seriously closeted, are among Sommers's alleged majority of women who want "a man," conventional marriage, or a traditional family.

Even among nonlesbians, [many] women these days do not want a *traditional* marriage or a *traditional* family. Some heterosexual women simply do not want to marry or to have children at all, and many others want *nontraditional* marriages and *nontraditional* families. Surveys show that this attitude, and not the preference for tradition alleged by Sommers, is actually in the majority. In one 1983 study, 63 percent of women surveyed expressed preferences for nontraditional family arrangements (Sapiro, 1990, 355). Sommers's factual claims are, thus, debatable.

Even apart from questions of popularity, the wants, values, and enjoyments which Sommers attributes to "most women" are frankly suspicious as an ensemble. Candlelit dinners do not combine easily with babies. Dashing lovers (extramarital!) can be disastrous for a marriage. This list of wants and values seems to show a failure to separate what is idealized and mythic from what is (to put it very advisedly) authentic and genuinely possible in the daily reality of marital and family relationships over the long haul. To hear Sommers tell it, women are blandly unconcerned about wife-battering, incest, marital rape, or the profound economic vulnerability of the traditional non–income-earning wife.

This is hard to believe. What is more likely is that, for many women, "… they got married and lived happily ever after" is only a fairy tale—especially for those who have been married for awhile. Even the most traditional of women, I am convinced, has some sense of the risks involved in traditional heterosexual relationships. As an old saying goes, "When two hearts beat as one, someone is dead."[15]

Sommers's list of women's wants and values is also woefully short. It suggests that this is *all* that "most women" want, that women's aspirations extend no farther than to being "feminine," getting a man—any man—and having babies. On the contrary, many women want meaningful and fulfilling work apart from childcare and domestic labor. Many women aspire to making a social contribution, or they have artistic impulses seeking expression, spiritual callings, deep friendships with other women, and abiding concerns for moral value and their own integrity.[16] One foundational motivation for feminism has always been the aim to overcome the *constraints* on women's genuinely wide-ranging aspirations posed by traditional marital and family arrangements.

9. What philosophical difference would it make if Sommers were right about women's wants and values in general? The popularity of an opinion is hardly an infallible measure of its empirical or moral credibility. Even popular opinions may be based on misinformation, unfounded rumor, and so on. Sommers ignores these possibilities and recommends that we defer to popular opinion on the basis of "… Mill's principle that there can be no appeal from a majority verdict of those who have experienced two alternatives" (1989a, 89–90). Sommers is evidently suggesting that feminist critiques of traditional family, marriage, and femininity should be judged by whether or not they conform to the "majority verdict of those who have experienced" the relevant alternatives. Now, carefully understood, this is actually not such a bad idea. However, rather than supporting Sommers's deference to popular opinion, this principle repudiates it.

First, there are more than just "two" feminist alternatives to any of the traditions in question. Consider, for example, the traditionally married, heterosexual couple comprised of dominant, bread-winning male and domestic, childrearing female. Feminists have recommended various alternative family arrangements, including egalitarian hetero-sexual marriage, communal living, lesbian rela-tionships, and single parenting when economic circumstances are favorable.[17] To decide the value of traditional marriage and family, one would have to try all the relevant alternatives—or at least *some* of them. And on Mill's view, merely experiencing alternatives is not enough; one must also be capable of "appreciating and enjoying" them (Mill, 1979, 9). If Sommers is right, however, most women want and choose traditional family, traditional marriage, and traditional femininity, and, thus, do not either experience or enjoy living according to any feminist alternatives. Women such as these are not what Mill calls "competent judges" of the value of those tradi-tions since "they know only their own side of the question" (p. 10). And it is only from the verdict of *competent judges* that Mill believes that "there can be no appeal" (p. 11).

Second, of the "competent judges," in Mill's sense, that is, of the women who *have* experienced and enjoyed feminist alternatives to traditional mar-riage and family, most (I would wager) *prefer the feminist alternatives*. I am referring, among others, to women in lesbian relationships, and women in genuinely egalitarian heterosexual relationships. If I am right about this, then by Mill's principle, we must reject "popular opinion" along with tradi-tional marriage and the rest.

10. The truth of the matter is that, in the end, Sommers does not rest her case on Mill's principle. Apparently without realizing that she changes her argument, she ends by appealing to something less vaunted than the majority verdict of those who have experienced and enjoyed *both* traditional fam-ily, etc., and various feminist alternatives. Her final court of appeal is simply to "what most people think," "common sense", and "tradition" itself (1989a, 95, 97). Sommers urges that "A moral phi-losophy that does not give proper weight to the customs and opinions of the community is pre-sumptuous in its attitude and pernicious in its consequences" (1989a, 103). She speaks warmly of

the Aristotelian conviction that "traditional arrange-ments have great moral weight and that common opinion is a primary source of moral truth" (1989a, 83). When it comes to tradition, Sommers would do well to consider Mill again. Mill often deferred to tradition, but it was not a deference from which he thought there was "no appeal," as he amply demon-strated in the important *indictment* of nineteenth century marital traditions on which he collaborated with Harriet Taylor (Mill & Taylor, 1970). (It would be interesting to know what "pernicious … conse-quences," to use Sommers's phrase, flowed from Mill's and Taylor's critique.)

Tradition is a fickle husband. He is constantly changing his mind. On the grounds of tradition, eighty years ago, Sommers would have opposed women's suffrage. One hundred and fifty years ago, she would have opposed women speaking in public (She would have had to do so in private!), opposed the rights of married women to property in their own names, opposed the abolition of slavery, and so on. She would have supported wife-battering since it was permitted by legal tradition—so long as the rod was no bigger around than the size of the husband's thumb.

Not only is tradition ever-changing, it is also plu-ral, both within our own society and globally. Which tradition shall we follow when there is more than one from which to choose? Islam is the world's most widely practiced religion. Shall we non-Islamic women heed the most globally numerous of our sis-ters' voices and don the veil, retire from public life, and allow husbands to marry up to four wives? Within our own society, marital traditions also vary. Shall we follow the traditions of orthodox Jewish and orthodox Catholic women and avoid all contracep-tives? My maternal grandmother did so; she had four-teen births. At nine months per gestation, she spent ten and a half years of her life being pregnant. Although she lingered to the age of eighty-seven, she seemed even older than her age for the final six-teen, worn-out years in which I knew her. Doubtless, that too was part of her tradition.

Why suppose that there is special merit to any of the alternative traditions that we happen to have at this historical moment in this particular geopolitical location? Why suppose that any of our current traditions are better or more deserving of loyalty and support than the traditions toward which we are evolving? And how will we ever evolve if we remain deadlocked in loyalty to all of the traditions we happen to have today?

11. Sommers allows that our traditions may need reform and even recommends "piecemeal social engineering" to deal with "imperfections" in the family (1989a, 97)—although it is noteworthy that she never specifies what these imperfections are, and, in a different passage, she inconsistently calls upon American feminism to leave marriage and motherhood simply "untouched and unimpugned" (1989a, 91).[18] Nevertheless, she insists that her arguments are directed only against those radical feminists who seek the abolition of the family and the "radical reform of preferences, values, aspirations, and prejudices" (1990,151,148).

A serious concern to reform imperfections in the family should lead someone to consider the views of nonradical feminist reformers who also criticize marital and family traditions. Many feminists would be content with piecemeal family reform—so long as it was genuine reform (Thorne & Yalom, 1982; Okin, 1987, 1989). Anyway, this issue is a red herring. A dispute over the pace of reform does not show that radical feminist critiques of family traditions are wrong in substance. Most important, by allowing that change is *needed* in family traditions, Sommers effectively concedes that we should not automatically defer to tradition. To admit that reform of tradition is morally permissible is to reject tradition *per se* as an incontestable moral authority. The controversy can only be decided by directly evaluating the conditions of life established by marital and family traditions—and their alternatives.

12. Sommers has one final twist to her argument which we should consider. She notes briefly—all too briefly—that traditions "have *prima facie* moral force" so long as they are not "essentially unjust" (1989a, 97). Sommers does not explain what she means by "essential injustice." Just how much injustice makes a traditional practice "essentially unjust"?

Despite its vagueness, this concession to injustice is critically important. It makes the merit of

Sommers's own appeal to tradition contingent on the essential noninjustice of the particular traditions in question. Sommers, however, provides no argument to establish that traditional marriage practices and so forth are not essentially unjust. Nor does she respond substantively to those feminist arguments which claim to locate important injustices in these traditional practices. She rejects all feminist criticisms of the traditional family because they do not coincide with "popular opinion," "common sense," or tradition. Traditional marriage and family are not essentially unjust, in Sommers's view, simply because most people allegedly do not *think* they are.

We seem to have come full circle. Sommers rejects feminist critiques of traditional marriage and so on because they are inconsistent with popular opinion, common sense, and tradition. Tradition is to be relied on, in turn, so long as it is not essentially unjust. But Sommers rejects feminist arguments to show injustices in marital and family traditions simply on the grounds that those arguments are inconsistent with popular opinion, common sense, and tradition itself. Sommers's defense of traditional marriage and family is, in the final analysis, circular and amounts to nothing more than simple *deference to tradition*—indeed, to particular traditions which are no longer so pervasive or popular as Sommers thinks.

13. One final concern: Sommers blames feminists for contributing to the growing divorce rate and the "disintegration of the traditional family."[19] However, feminism could only contribute to the divorce rate if married women ended their marriages as a result of adopting feminist ideas. If Sommers is right, however, in thinking that "most women" reject nonliberal feminist values, then nonliberal feminists could not be having a significant impact on the divorce rate. Sommers cannot have it both ways. Either feminism *is* significantly contributing to the growing divorce rate, in which case it must be in virtue of the wide appeal of feminist ideas about marriage and family, or feminist ideas do *not* have wide appeal, in which case they cannot be significantly contributing to the growing divorce rate.

14. To conclude: My overall assessment of Sommers's views on marriage, family, and femininity is grim.[20] Most important, Sommers rejects feminist views of marriage, family, and femininity ultimately on the basis of her own simple deference to (allegedly) popular opinion, common sense, and tradition. This deference is defensible only if feminist views about injustices in those traditions can be shown, on *independent* grounds, to be misguided—and Sommers never provides this independent argument.

ENDNOTES

1. Sommers: 1988, 1989a, 1989b, and 1990.

2. Cited in Thorne & Yalom, 1982, 5.

3. Sommers repudiates the feminist literature which explores the value of mothering (e.g., Trebilcot, 1984) on the grounds that it "remains largely hostile to traditional familial arrangements." She also claims that this literature focuses only on an abstracted mother-child relationship, especially the mother-daughter relationship—a focus that "effectively excludes the male parent" (1989a, 92). Aside from inaccurately summarizing a body of literature, this latter comment, ironically, ignores the fact that under "traditional familial arrangements," the male parent plays a *negligible role* in day-to-day, primary child-care, especially in a child's early years.

   The comment also ignores the work of Dorothy Dinnerstein (1977) and, especially, of Nancy Chodorow (1978), which precisely urges *shared parenting* and a prominent role for the male parent. This work has been extremely influential and widely cited among feminists. I suspect, however, that shared parenting is not the way in which Sommers wants to include the male parent, since this arrangement is not "traditional" and it challenges the idea of a "primary gender role" that Sommers appears to support (1989a, 92). Sommers, herself, thus fails to clarify the role of the male parent in her account.

4. Sommers complains that feminist philosophers have not been entrusted by ordinary women with a mission of speaking on behalf of those ordinary women (1989b, B3). Sommers, however, appears to think that she is thus entrusted, since she does not hesitate to make claims about what "most women ... prefer," what "women actually want," and what "most women *enjoy*" (1989a, 90).

5. The following classification scheme is my own. The categories are not meant to be mutually exclusive.

6. Quotations are, respectively, from: 1989a, 90; 1989a, 91; and 1990, 150.

7. Quotations are, respectively, from: 1989a, 90; 1989a, 89; and 1989b, B3.

8. Quotations are, respectively, from: 1989a, 90; 1989a, 91; 1990, 150, italics mine; 1989b, B2; and 1989a, 91.

9. Quotations are, respectively, from: 1989a, 90; 1989a, 90; 1989a, 90; and 1990, 150.

10. Richards, 1980, 341–342. Quoted in Sommers, 1989a, 90–91.

11. Some important early papers are anthologized in: Vetterling-Braggin et al., 1977, Part VI. Another important, relatively early study is Brownmiller, 1976.

12. In 1966, Richard Speck stunned the city of Chicago and the nation by raping, killing, and, in some cases, mutilating the bodies of eight out of nine nursing students who shared a house together on Chicago's South Side. The nurse who survived did so by hiding under a bed until Speck left the house after having apparently lost count. That woman might well swoon over Scarlett O'Hara's rape, but it would not be a swoon of ecstasy.

13. 1989a, 88–91. Sommers writes: "It is a serious defect of American feminism that it concentrates its zeal on impugning femininity and feminine culture at the expense of the grass root fight against economic and social injustices to which women are subjected" (p. 90). American feminism has hardly neglected the fight against economic or social injustice against women. Apart from that, the *Philosopher's Index* back to 1970 contains no citations of writings by Sommers herself on "the economic and social injustices to which women are subjected." In the essays reviewed here, she does not even identify the injustices she has in mind.

14. Sommers does warn that "many women" who avoid motherhood find themselves lonely (1989a, 90), and she suggests that those who avoid or divorce themselves from the patriarchal family

"often" suffer harm and "might" feel "betrayed by the ideology" which led them to this state (1989b, B3). These faintly threatening suggestions are left unexplained and unsupported.

15. I was reminded of this old saying by an article by Janyce Katz (1990, 88) in which Dagmar Celeste, then the "First Lady of Ohio," is quoted as mentioning it.

16. Raising children involves awesome moral responsibilities, as Sommers herself emphasizes when lamenting the increasing divorce rate. These profound moral responsibilities entail that we should not casually reinforce the cultural ideology which declares that the only hope of women's fulfillment in life depends on their *having* children. Sommers complains about divorce because of the harm it inflicts on children (1989a, 98–102), but she never cautions women to consider these moral obligations before marrying or having children in the first place.

17. Cf. Hunter College Women's Studies Collective, 1983, Ch. 9.

18. My worry is that Sommers's occasional, reasonable call for piecemeal family reform disguises a hidden agenda that aims to deadlock us in certain family traditions as we know them now (or knew them three decades ago). This appearance might be dispelled if she were to identify the imperfections she recognizes in the family.

19. 1989a, 82–83, 99–102. Sommers admits that "no reliable study has yet been made comparing children of divorced parents to children from intact families who [sic] parents do not get on well together." She claims cavalierly that "any such study would be compromised by some arbitrary measures of parental incompatibility and one could probably place little reliance on them" (1989a, 101), However, she ignores her own claims of limited evidence on this issue and argues as if it were fact that children of divorced parents are invariably worse off than if their parents had remained married.

When Sommers discusses the problem of divorce, she tends to assimilate the philosophical culprits onto one model: They are all wrong for disregarding "special duties" to family members, especially to children. This latter accusation is simply irrelevant in regard to feminists; no serious feminist literature suggests that responsibilities toward children should be disregarded.

20. Overall, her presentations are marred by ambiguities, inconsistencies, dubious factual claims, misrepresentations of feminist literature, and faulty arguments.

REFERENCES

Brownmiller, Susan 1976. *Against Our Will: Men, Women and Rape*. New York: Bantam.

Chodorow, Nancy. 1978. *The Reproduction of Mothering*. Berkeley: University of California Press.

Dahl, Arlene. 1965. *Always Ask a Man: Arlene Dahl's Key to Femininity*. Englewood Cliffs, N.J.: Prentice-Hall.

Dinnerstein, Dorothy. 1977. *The Mermaid and the Minotaur: Sexual Arrangements and Human Malaise*. New York: Harper & Row.

Eagly Alice. 1987. *Sex Differences in Social Behavior*. Hillsdale, N.J.: Erlbaum.

Hunter College Women's Studies Collective. 1983. *Women's Realities, Women's Choices*. New York: Oxford University Press.

Katz, Janyce, 1990. "Celestial Reasoning: Ohio's First Lady Talks About Love and Feminism." Ms: *The World of Women, 1, 2* (September/October), p. 88.

Mill, John Stuart. 1979. *Utilitarianism*. George Sher, ed. Indianapolis: Hackett.

Mill, John Stuart, and Harriet Taylor. 1970. *Essays on Sex Equality*. Alice S. Rossi, ed., Chicago: University of Chicago Press.

Okin, Susan Moller. 1987. "Justice and Gender." *Philosophy & Public Affairs*, 16 (Winter), pp. 42–72.

____. 1989. *Justice, Gender, and the Family*. New York: Basic Books.

Richards, Janet Radcliffe. 1980. *The Sceptical Feminist*. Harmondsworth: Penguin.

Sapiro, Virginia. 1990. *Women in American Society*. Mountain View, Calif.: Mayfield Publishing Co.

Sommers, Christina. 1988. "Should the Academy Support Academic Feminism?" *Public Affairs Quarterly*, 2, 3 (July), 99–120.

___. 1989a. "Philosophers Against the Family." In: George Graham and Hugh LaFollette, eds. *Person to Person.* Philadelphia: Temple University Press, 82–105.

___. 1989b. "Feminist Philosophers Are Oddly Unsympathetic to the Women They Claim to Represent." *Chronicle of Higher Education,* October 11, pp. B2.–B3.

___. 1990. "The Feminist Revelation," *Social Philosophy and Policy Center, 8,* 1 (Autumn), 141–158.

Thorne, Barrie, with Marilyn Yalom, eds. 1982. *Rethinking the Family.* New York: Longman.

Trebilcot, Joyce, ed. 1984. *Mothering: Essays in Feminist Theory.* Totowa, N.J.: Rowman and Allanheld.

Vetterling-Braggin, Mary, Frederick A. Elliston, and Jane English, eds. 1977. *Feminism and Philosophy.* Totowa, N.J.: Littlefield, Adams & Co.

31

National Organization for Women (NOW)
Bill of Rights (1995)

I. Equal Rights Constitutional Amendment
II. Enforce Law Banning Sex Discrimination in Employment
III. Maternity Leave Rights in Employment and in Social Security Benefits
IV. Tax Deduction for Home and Childcare Expenses for Working Parents
V. Childcare Centers
VI. Equal and Unsegregated Education
VII. Equal Job Training Opportunities and Allowances for Women in Poverty
VIII. The Right of Women to Control Their Reproductive Lives

WE DEMAND

I That the United States Congress immediately pass the Equal Rights Amendment to the Constitution to provide that "Equality of rights under the law shall not be denied or abridged by the United States or by any State on account of sex," and that such then be immediately ratified by the several States.

II That equal employment opportunity be guaranteed to all women, as well as men, by insisting that the Equal Employment Opportunity Commission enforce the prohibitions against sex discrimination in employment under Title VII of the Civil Rights Act of 1964 with the same vigor as it enforces the prohibitions against racial discrimination.

III That women be protected by law to ensure their rights to return to their jobs within a reasonable time after childbirth without loss of seniority or other accrued benefits, and be paid maternity leave as a form of social security and/or employee benefit.

IV Immediate revision of tax laws to permit the deduction of home and childcare expenses for working parents.

V That childcare facilities be established by law on the same basis as parks, libraries, and public schools, adequate to the needs of children from the preschool years through adolescence, as a community resource to be used by all citizens from all income levels.

VI That the right of women to be educated to their full potential equally with men be secured by Federal and State Legislation, eliminating all discrimination and segregation by sex, written and unwritten, at all levels of education, including colleges, graduate and professional schools, loans and fellowships, and Federal and State training programs such as the Job Corps.

VII The right of women in poverty to secure job training, housing, and family allowances on equal terms with men, but without prejudice to a parent's right to remain at home to care for his or her children; revision of welfare legislation and poverty programs which deny women dignity, privacy, and self-respect.

VIII The right of women to control their own reproductive lives by removing from penal codes laws limiting access to contraceptive information and devices and laws governing abortion.

SUGGESTIONS FOR FURTHER READING

Anthologies

Bishop, Sharon, and Marjorie Weinzweig. *Philosophy and Women*. Belmont, CA: Wadsworth, 1979.

Frazer, Elizabeth, Jennifer Hornsby and Sabina Lovibond. *Ethics: A Feminist Reader*. Oxford: Blackwell, 1992.

Freeman, Jo. *Women: A Feminist Perspective*. 4th ed. Palo Alto, CA: Mayfield, 1989.

Gould, Carol C., and Marx W. Wartofsky. *Women and Philosophy*. New York: Putnam, 1976.

Jaggar, Alison, and W. Iris Young. *A Companion to Feminist Philosophy*. Oxford: Blackwell, 1998.

Kourany Janet, James Sterba, and Rosemarie Tong. *Feminist Philosophies*. 2nd ed. Englewood Cliffs, NJ: Prentice-Hall, 1999.

Pearsall, Marilyn. *Women and Values*. 3rd ed. Belmont, CA: Wadsworth, 1999.

Basic Concepts

Jaggar, Alison M. *Feminist Politics and Human Nature*. Totowa, NJ: Rowman & Allanheld, 1983.

Tong, Rosemarie. *Feminist Thought*. Boulder, CO: Westview Press, 1989.

Tuana, Nancy, and Rosemarie Tong. *Feminism and Philosophy*. Boulder, CO: Westview Press, 1995.

Alternative Views

DeCrow, Karen. *Sexist justice*. New York: Vintage, 1975.

Eisenstein, Zellah. *Feminism and Sexual Equality*. New York: Monthly Review, 1984.

Friedan, Betty. *The Feminine Mystique*. New York: Norton, 1963.

Frye, Marilyn. *The Politics of Reality*. New York: Crossing Press, 1983.

Held, Virginia. *Feminist Morality*. Chicago: University of Chicago Press, 1993.

Okin, Susan. *Justice, Gender and the Family*. New York: Basic Books, 1989.

Pateman, Carole. *The Sexual Contract*. Stanford: Stanford University Press, 1988.

Sommers, Christina Hoff. *Who Stole Feminism?* New York: Simon and Schuster, 1994.

Young, Iris, *Justice and the Politics of Difference*. Princeton: Princeton University Press, 1990.

Practical Applications

Irving, John. *The World According to Garp*. New York: Dutton, 1978.

United States Commission on Civil Rights. *Statement on the Equal Rights Amendment*. Washington, DC: U.S. Government Printing Office, 1978.

※

Power, Gender Roles, and Discrimination Against Men

INTRODUCTION

Basic Concepts

The goal of feminism has long been to secure women's equality with men. Historically, this goal has proven to be very difficult to reach. Not until the mid-1800s did feminism become widespread in Europe and the United States. In 1848, French feminists began publishing a daily newspaper entitled *La Voix des Femmes* ("The Voice of Women"). A year later, Luise Dittmar, a German writer, followed with her journal, *Soziale Reform*. Also in 1848, the first women's rights convention was held in Seneca Falls, New York. The convention passed a Declaration of Sentiments modeled after the U.S. Declaration of Independence that advocated reforms in marriage, divorce, property and child custody law. With black abolitionist Frederick Douglass arguing forcefully on their behalf, all 12 of the Declaration's resolutions drafted by Elizabeth Cady Stanton passed, although the ninth resolution demanding the right to vote for women only passed narrowly upon the insistence of Stanton.

The period from the Seneca Falls Convention until women finally secured the right to vote in 1920 is referred to as the first wave of feminism in the U.S. First wave feminists frequently joined forces with and drew inspiration from the abolition and moral-reform movements of their times. In what is called the second wave of feminism, beginning in the 1960s, feminists frequently joined forces with and drew inspiration from the Black civil rights movement and the anti-Vietnam War movement. As these second wave feminists saw it, suffrage alone had not, and could not, make women equal with men. To be equal, women needed the same educational, occupational, social, and political opportunities that men enjoyed in society.

In 1966, when government agencies refused to take seriously the provision of the Civil Rights Act of 1964 that prohibited discrimination on the basis of sex, a group of feminists led by Betty Friedan founded the National Organization for Women (NOW). NOW then elected Friedan as its first president and launched a broad campaign for legal equality. At the same time, ad hoc groups staged protests, sit-ins, and marches across the country focusing on various issues. One of the most memorable protests was staged at the 1968 Miss America contest, where a "freedom trash can" was set up to dispose of women's oppressive symbols including bras, girdles, wigs, and false eyelashes, and a sheep was crowned Miss America. Although none of the items thrown into the trash can were burned, from that day on, feminists were called "bra burners" thanks to media reports that bra burning was going to be part of the protest.

A third wave of feminism in the U.S. is usually said to have begun around the mid-1980s. According to the standard account, second wave feminism was advanced by white middle-class heterosexual women who presumed that all women were just like them, with the same interests and needs, thus enabling these white middle-class heterosexual women to speak for all women everywhere. But then, in the 1980s, poor, and working-class women, women of color, lesbians, and Third World women entered the picture and challenged the theories held by the second wave feminists. The challengers contended that these theories were biased and had left them out. As a result, third wave feminism was born, and feminists become attentive to differences of race, class, sexual orientation, and national origin.

Of course, feminists must take seriously criticisms that maintain that feminism has gone beyond its goal of equality and is now seeking to unfairly discriminate against men in favor of women. Feminists can no more ignore this challenge than defenders of affirmative action can ignore a similar challenge that affirmative action, a practice that is also said to be grounded in an ideal of equality, in fact, discriminates against white males. Such challenges must be faced head-on if a commitment to the goal of equality is to be legitimately maintained.

Alternative Views

In Selection 32, Warren Farrell argues that people mistakenly think that men have the power. According to Farrell, they make this mistake because they confuse having important roles and responsibilities in society with having power in the most important sense of having control over one's life. When assessed in terms of this appropriate standard of power, for example, Farrell claims that women do not look so powerless because they have more options available to them for combining work and family, and men do not look so powerful given that they tend to have fewer options in this regard. In addition, Farrell thinks that the fact that men, on average, die sooner than women is not a sign of their having greater power.

In Selection 33, James P. Sterba argues against Farrell, that men's having more important roles and responsibilities does frequently translate into their having more power just in the sense that Farrell understands power as having control over one's life. Sterba further argues that the feminist goal of equal power between women and men would require that both women and men have the same options with regard to combining work and family. Currently the expectation to take on household and childcare responsibilities is still placed more on women.

In Selection 34, David Benatar argues that men in society are discriminated against just because they are men in the same way that women in society are discriminated against just because they are women. He calls this discrimination the "second sexism." To show that this discrimination exists and deserves to be condemned, Benatar starts with a number of examples. His main example of discrimination against men is the widespread restriction of combat to men, especially at the present time. Even today when women are either free to join the military or are sometimes conscripted into it, Benatar observes, they are still generally restricted from serving in combat roles. He then seeks to explain and criticize the attitudes that he claims underlie his examples, especially the combat restriction example, and to respond to objections to considering them anything but unjustified discrimination against men.

In Selection 35, James P. Sterba proposes to evaluate David Benatar's claim for a second sexism by focusing on Benatar's main example, the restriction of combat to men, an example to which he returns time and time again throughout his paper. Sterba attempts to show that the restriction of combat to men is a clear example of discrimination against women, not one of discrimination against men. He claims that this is a case where "the wolf" of discrimination against women for the benefit of men is falsely presented in "the sheep's clothing" as really being for the benefit of women. Sterba claims that if Benatar's argument fails with regard to his main example, then it fails for his other examples as well.

In 1952, Simone de Beauvoir published *The Second Sex*, a book that in time became the bible of the second wave of feminism. Nevertheless, Beauvoir's work was initially greeted with a great deal of skepticism, not unlike the skepticism that is likely to greet David Benatar's "second sexism." Regarding sexism against men as the neglected sexism, Benatar claims to look forward to the day when there is at least as much research being directed at uncovering sexism against men as has been devoted in the past to uncovering sexism against women. If Sterba's analysis is correct, however, and Benatar's main example of discrimination against men—the combat exclusion of women—is really a form of discrimination against women with its cost of dominance, then surely Benatar's expectations in this regard are not likely to be fulfilled.

Practical Applications

Turning to practical applications, The Beijing Declaration and Platform for Action (Selection 36), which emerged from the Fourth World Congress on Women sponsored by the United Nations in 1995, expresses in an international context many of the same sentiments found in the NOW statement. Through this declaration, the Congress also reaffirmed a commitment to the equal rights and inherent human dignity of women and men enshrined in the Charter of the United Nations, the Declaration of Human Rights, the Convention on the Elimination of All Forms of Discrimination against Women, and the Declaration on the Elimination of Violence against Women.

32

Does Feminism Discriminate Against Men?

WARREN FARRELL

Warren Farrell argues that people mistakenly think that men have the power because they confuse having important roles and responsibilities in society with having power in the most important sense of having control over one's life.

"The weakness of men is their façade of strength; the strength of women is their façade of weakness."[1]

There are many ways in which a woman experiences a greater sense of powerlessness than her male counterpart does: the fears of aging, rape, and date rape; less physical strength and therefore the fear of being physically overpowered; less socialization to take a career that pays enough to support a husband and children, and therefore the fear of economic dependency or poverty; less exposure to team sports—especially pick-up team sports—and its blend of competitiveness and cooperation that is so helpful to career preparation; greater parental pressure to marry and interrupt career for children without regard for her own wishes; not being part of an "old boys" network; having less freedom to walk into a bar without being bothered; and many more.

Men have a different experience of powerlessness. Men who have seen marriage become alimony payments, their home become their wife's home, and their children become child support payments for children who have been turned against them psychologically feel like they are spending their life working for people who hate them. They feel desperate for someone to love but fear that another marriage might ultimately leave them with another mortgage payment, another set of children turned against them, and a deeper desperation. When they are called "commitment-phobic" they don't feel understood.

When men try to keep up with payments by working overtime and are told they are insensitive or try to handle the stress by drinking and are told they are drunkards, they don't feel powerful, but powerless. When they fear a cry for help will be met with "stop whining" or that a plea to be heard will be met with "yes, buts," they skip past attempting suicide as a cry for help, and just commit suicide. Thus men have remained the silent sex and increasingly become the suicide sex.

Fortunately, almost all industrialized nations have acknowledged female experiences. Unfortunately, they have acknowledged only female experiences—and have concluded that women have problems, and men are the problem.

Industrialization did a better job of creating better homes and gardens for women than it did of creating safer coal mines and construction sites for men. How?

Industrialization pulled men away from the farm and family and into the factory, alienating millions of men from their source of love. Simultaneously, it allowed women to have more conveniences to handle fewer children, and therefore be increasingly connected to their sources of love. For women, industrialization meant more control over whether or not to have children, less likelihood of dying in childbirth, and less likelihood of dying from almost all diseases. It was this combination that led to women living almost 50 percent longer in 1990 than in 1920.[2] And it was this combination that allowed women to go from living only one year longer than men in 1920 to living more than five years longer than men in 2005.

What we have come to call male power, then—men at the helm of industrialization—actually produced female power. It literally gave women a longer life than men.

I am unaware of a single feminist demonstration protesting this inequality—or any other inequality that benefits women at the expense of men.

Almost as important as life is quality of life. Women who were married to men who were at least moderately successful were the first passengers on the bus from the Industrial Revolution to the Fulfillment Revolution. The passengers created an almost all-female club.

While the male role in industrialization expanded women's options, it retained men's obligations. For example, men voted for women to share the option to vote. But when both sexes could vote, they still obligated only men to register for the draft.

We are at a unique moment in history—when a *woman's* body is affected, we say the choice is hers; but when a *boy's* body is affected, we say the choice is *not* his—the law requires only our eighteen-year-old sons to register for the draft, and therefore potential death-if-needed.

"A WOMAN'S BODY, A WOMAN'S CHOICE" VERSUS "A MAN'S GOTTA DO WHAT A MAN'S GOTTA DO"

Even as women were touting equality in the 1980s and 1990s, in post offices throughout the United States, Selective Service posters reminded boys of what is still true today—that only boys must register for the draft—that only "A Man's Gotta Do What A Man's Gotta Do."

If the Post Office had a poster saying, "A Jew's Gotta Do What A Jew's Gotta Do," or if "A Woman's Gotta Do" were written across the body of a pregnant woman. The question is this: How is it that if any other group were singled out to register for the draft based merely on its characteristics at birth—be that group blacks, Jews, women, or gays—we would immediately recognize it as genocide, but when men are singled out based on their sex at birth, men call it power?

The single biggest barrier to getting men to look within is that what any other group would call powerlessness, men have been taught to call power. We don't call "male-killing" sexism; we call it "glory." We don't call the one *million* men who were killed or maimed *in one battle* in World War I (the Battle of the Somme[3]) a holocaust, we call it "serving the country." We don't call those who selected only men to die "murderers." We call them "voters."

Our slogan for women is "A Woman's Body, A Woman's Choice"; our slogan for men is "A Man's Gotta Do What A Man's Gotta Do."

I am unaware of a single feminist demonstration protesting this inequality—or any other inequality that benefits only women at the expense of men.

The Power of Life

We acknowledge that blacks dying six years sooner than whites reflects the powerlessness of blacks in American society.[4] Yet men dying in excess of five years sooner than women is rarely seen as a reflection of the powerlessness of men in American society.

Is the five-year gap biological? If it is, it wouldn't have been just a one-year gap in 1920. (In many preindustrialized countries there is only a small male–female life expectancy gap, and in their more rural areas men sometimes live longer.)

If men lived more than five years *longer* than women, feminists would be helping us understand that life expectancy was the best measure of who has the power. And they would be right. Power is the

TABLE 1.1	Life Expectancy as a Way of Seeing Who Has the Power
Females (white)	80.5
Females (black)	76.1
Males (white)	75.3
Males (black)	69.0

Source: U.S. Department of Health and Human Services, Centers for Disease Control and Prevention, National Center for Health Statistics, *Health, United States, 2005, with Chartbook on Trends in the Health of Americans*, Table 27: "Life Expectancy at Birth, at 65 Years of Age, and at 75 Years of Age, According to Race and Sex: United States, Selected Years 1900–2003," p. 167, http://www.cdc.gov/nchs/data/hus/hus05.pdf#027

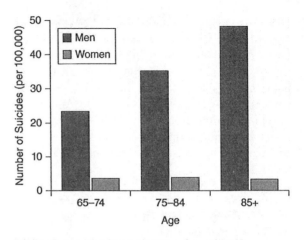

Suicide Rates: Men Versus Women (per 100,000 Population)

Source: U.S Department of Health and Human Services, Centers for Disease Control and Prevention, National Center for Health Statistics, *Health, United States, 2005, with Chartbook on Trends in the Health of Americans*, Table 46 (page 1 of 3): "Death Rates for Suicide, According to Sex, Race, Hispanic Origin, and Age: United States, Selected Years 1900–2003," p. 221, http://www.cdc.gov/nchs/data/hus/hus05.pdf#027

ability to control one's life. Death tends to reduce control. Life expectancy is the bottom line—the ratio of our life's stresses to our life's rewards.

If power means having control over one's own life, then perhaps there is no better ranking of the impact of sex roles and racism on power over our lives than life expectancy. (See Table 1.1.)

The white female outlives the black male by more than eleven years. Imagine the support for affirmative action if a forty-nine-year-old woman was closer to death than a sixty-year-old man.

I am unaware of a single feminist demonstration protesting this inequality.

Suicide as Powerlessness

Just as life expectancy is one of the best indicators of power, suicide is one of the best indicators of powerlessness.

ITEM.   *From ages nine to fourteen, boys' rate of suicide is three times as high as girls'; from fifteen to nineteen, four times as high; and from twenty to twenty-four, almost six times as high.*[5]

ITEM.   *As boys experience the pressures of the male role, their suicide rate increases 25,000 percent.*[6]

ITEM.   *The suicide rate for men over eighty-five is 1,350 percent higher than for women of the same age group.*

The breakdown is shown in the accompanying graph.

Public awareness of this suicide gap could help identify the four most vulnerable moments in the

lives of our sons and fathers: early twenties; after age seventy-five; after divorce, when men are ten times as likely to commit suicide as their exes[7]; and after the death of a spouse, when widowers are also ten times as likely to commit suicide as widows. I am unaware of a single feminist fundraiser to finance hot lines and public service announcements to encourage these men to express their fears to others rather than turn their guns on themselves.

Her Body, Her Choice Versus His Body, Her Choice

If a woman and man make love and she says she is using birth control but is not, she has the right to raise the child without his knowing he even has a child, and then to sue him for retroactive child support even ten to twenty years later (depending on the state). This forces him to take a job with more pay and more stress and therefore earlier death. Although it's his body, he has no choice. He has the option of being a slave (working for another without pay or choice) or being a criminal. *Roe v. Wade* gave women the vote over their bodies. Men still don't have the vote over theirs—whether in love or war.

The Clearest Sign of Powerlessness

Subjection of a group of people to violence based on their membership in that group is a clear indicator of that group's powerlessness, be it Christians to lions or the underclass to war. If a society supports violence against that group by its laws, customs, or socialization, it oppresses that group.

In the United States, women are exposed to greater violence in the form of rape. And therefore rape is punished by law and opposed by religion, custom, socialization, and virtually 100 percent of men and women.

In contrast, men's exposure to violence is required by law (the draft); supported by religion and custom (circumcision); and encouraged by socialization, scholarship incentive, and the education system (telling men who are best at bashing their heads against eleven other men that they have "scholarship potential"); via approval and "love" of beautiful women (cheerleaders cheering for men to "do it again"—to again risk concussions, spinal chord injuries, etc.); via parental approval and love (the parents who attend the Thanksgiving games at which their sons are battering each other); via taxpayer money (high school wrestling and football, ROTC, and the military); and via our entertainment dollar (boxing, football, ice hockey, rodeos, car racing, Westerns, war movies, etc.). After we subject only our sons to this violence (before the age of consent), we blame them for growing into the more violent sex.

But here's the rub. When other groups are subjected to violence, we acknowledge their power*lessness*. Men learn to associate violence against them with love, respect, and power. Instead of helping men who are subjected to violence, we bribe men to accept it by giving them money to entertain us by risking death.

This is deeply ingrained. Virtually every society that has survived has done so via its ability to prepare its men to be disposable—to call it "glory" to be disposable in war, and eligible for marriage to be disposable at work.

ENDNOTES

1. Lawrence Diggs, "Sexual Abuse of Men by Women," *Transitions* (November/December 1990), p. 10.

2. 1920 statistics from the U.S. Department of Health and Human Services, National Center for Health Statistics (hereafter USDHHS, NCHS), *Monthly Vital Statistics Report*, 39, no. 13 (August 28, 1991), p. 17.

3. See John Laffin, *Brassey's Battles: 3500 Years of Conflict, Campaigns, and Wars from A-Z* (London: A. Wheaton & Co., 1986), p. 399.

4. NCHS, *Monthly Vital Statistics Report* 38, no. 5.

5. USDHHS, Centers for Disease Control and Prevention, National Center for Health Statistics, *Health, United States, 2005, with Chartbook on Trends in the Health of Americans*, Table 46 (page 1 of 3): "Death Rates for Suicide, According to Sex, Race, Hispanic Origin, and Age: United States, Selected Years 1900-2003," p. 221, http://www.cdc.gov/nchs/data/hus/hus05.pdf#027.

6. Ibid.

7. Augustine J. Kposowa, "Marital Status and Suicide in the National Longitudinal Mortality Study," *Journal of Epidemiology and Community Health* 54 (April 2000), p. 256.

33

Does Feminism Discriminate Against Men?

JAMES P. STERBA

James P. Sterba argues against Farrell, that men's having more important roles and responsibilities does frequently translate into their having more power just in the sense that Farrell understands power as having control over one's life.

Feminists have long held that men have the power, that is, the dominant power in society. Feminists have never held that women are without power, just that the power *distribution* in society unfairly favors men over women. Actually, one way to understand the feminist ideal of equality is as an ideal of equal power or as an ideal of equal opportunity to acquire power in society.[1] Given that Warren Farrell proposes that we should think about power as having control over one's own life, we could restate the feminist ideal as one of having equal control over one's own life or equal opportunity to acquire control over one's own life.[2]

Farrell goes on to distinguish two stages of human history: Stage I, in which women's and men's roles are simply functional for survival, and Stage II, in which women and men can go beyond survival to seek self-fulfillment. Farrell thinks Stage II is now a possible stage for human history because of effective birth control, increased wealth, and the possibility of divorce. In Stage II relationships, Farrell claims that successful women who are married to successful men face three options when considering whether to have children—option one: work full-time; option two: mother full-time; and option three: some combination of working and mothering. By contrast, the successful men who are married to these successful women have just one option: work full-time, which really means that they have no options at all.[3]

According to Farrell, for thousands of years, in Stage I marriages, neither men nor women had power in the sense of control over their own lives; they simply had roles and responsibilities. Only in Stage II marriages, in which people have options, does Farrell allow that we can properly speak about them as having power in the sense of control over their own lives.[4] So in Farrell's example of the "multi-option woman and the no option man," only the woman would have power in the sense of having control over one's own life. That makes her, Farrell tells us, "more than equal" to her husband.[5]

Yet surely this is an odd way to characterize human history or the options faced by two-career couples today when deciding whether to have children. Why should we think that having roles and responsibilities precludes having power, even power understood as control over one's own life? Even if we think of people's roles and responsibilities as primarily directed at benefiting others, fulfilling those roles and responsibilities usually brings status and privilege to those who fulfill them, as Farrell himself acknowledges.[6] This, in turn, enables them to have control over their own lives.

Consider Bill Clinton. Even with all the adversities of his two terms in office, fulfilling the role and responsibilities of president of the United States surely brought him considerable status and privilege, which, in turn, enabled him to exercise considerable control over his own life, maybe even more so after his terms in office were over. So there is no incompatibility between having roles and responsibilities and having control over one's own life. In fact, the former is frequently a useful way of acquiring the latter.[7]

In addition, while having options usually does increase the power one has over one's own life, Farrell has not fairly characterized the options facing the successful woman and the successful man when they are deciding whether to have children. Consider Jill and Tom, both with equally promising jobs at top law firms.[8] Suppose they both enjoy their work and regard it as important. What options do they have with respect to having children? Jill could choose to continue working full-time. Yet given the long hours her job now requires, this would only permit her to be minimally involved with rearing her child, and she should regard that as undesirable, other things being equal.[9] Of course, that option would look better if Jill knew that Tom was willing to give up his job to care for their child full-time. Yet even if Tom were so willing, Jill should still judge that option not to be in the best interest of Tom or their child. Other things being equal, a better option is for both Jill and Tom to continue with their law careers toward partnerships under reduced workloads so that they can equally share their childcare and housekeeping responsibilities. The option of Jill working part-time and mothering part-time while Tom continues working full-time toward partnership usually requires that Jill move to a lower-paying, nonpartnership track at her firm. Jill should regard that option as undesirable both because of its effects on her career and because it means that Tom would not be as involved in childcare and housekeeping as she would be. Tom should also reject the option of his working part-time and fathering part-time, which usually requires him to move to a lower-paying nonpartnership track at his firm, for the same reasons that Jill should reject that option for herself. Accordingly, other things being equal,

Tom should also prefer the option in which both of them continue with their law careers toward partnerships under reduced workloads so that they can equally share their childcare and housekeeping responsibilities. Thus, if Jill and Tom are equally respectful of each other's interests as well as the best interest of their child, contrary to what Farrell claims, they would each entertain exactly the same options when deciding whether to have a child, even though the circumstances in which they find themselves may preclude them from being able to act upon what they regard as their best option.

It is also a mistake to think that most of human history has been stuck in Stage I, in which people are just struggling to survive. In fact, much of human history, and most of recorded history, is the story of what people and societies have done when motivated by goals that have included but have also gone beyond that of survival. This means that we can criticize such people and societies for not having more equality between women and men. Even among societies that Farrell would surely regard as survival focused, such as American Indian nations, some organized themselves in ways that tended toward equality for women. For example, among the Seneca, women did the farming and controlled what they produced while sharing the childrearing with their men. As a result, Seneca men could not hunt or wage war unless the women agreed to allocate the food they controlled for those purposes. In 1791, Seneca women explained to American Army officers who were attempting to negotiate a peace treaty that "you ought to hear and listen to what we, women shall speak, as well as to the sachems [male chiefs] for we are the owners of this land—and it is ours."[10]

Suppose, then, that we convince men that there was an unfair distribution of power favoring men over women in the past that still persists today—would they be willing to correct for the imbalance? How could men resist this demand for fairness? Of course, many men who seem to gain from discriminating against women suffer themselves from other forms of discrimination directed against them, which may leave them feeling relatively powerless.[11] Feminists have recognized this and have appropriately responded to it by opposing all forms of discrimination, not simply discrimination against women. As

I noted earlier, feminists have taken into account differences of race, class, sexual orientation, national origin, and other relevant differences in formulating their theories. Similarly, at the practical level, feminists have to unite with others in opposing all forms of discrimination. Needless to say, it would help if feminists could show that correcting the imbalance of power between men and women really did serve the interests of men as well. Yet even when this is not obtained, an appeal to fairness should suffice for those who wish to be moral, especially given the willingness of feminists to join forces against all forms of discrimination.

Today, however, there are some special difficulties with shifting power to women in society stemming from the fact that women are not normally associated with a number of the significant forms of power in society. Exemplars of religious power, physical power, economic power, and political power are all normally men. Women who enter these domains of power are perceived as oddities. A number of years ago, there was quite a stir when

Barbara Harris was the first woman to be consecrated a bishop in the Episcopalian church. When Margaret Thatcher was prime minister of Great Britain, journalists referred to her as "the iron maiden" and "Atilla the Hen," thus expressing the incongruity of a woman holding such a high political office. Of course, women do have power or influence on the basis of sexual or personal attractiveness, and mothers are frequently said to have dominant power in the home, although the extent to which mothers have power in the home may be overrated. One study showed that only 16 percent of females and 2 percent of males named their mothers as the most powerful individual they personally knew.[12] The general problem with women acquiring power is that masculinity is traditionally associated with power and femininity is traditionally taken to be its opposite. Hence, the more women are seen as powerful, the more they are seen as unfeminine or unwomanly. Obviously, something has to change here if women are to have equal power or the equal opportunity to acquire power in society.

ENDNOTES

1. For a discussion of these two ways of putting the ideal of equality, see my *How to Make People Just* (Lanham, MD: Rowman & Littlefield, 1988), Chapter 9.

2. Warren Farrell, *The Myth of Male Power* (hereafter *MOMP*) (New York: Simon and Schuster, 1993), pp. 16–17; and Warren Farrell, *The Myth of Male Power*, audiotapes (New York: Simon and Schuster, 1993), Tape 1. Side 1.

3. *MOMP*, p. 52.

4. Ibid., pp. 42–54.

5. Ibid., p. 52.

6. *MOMP*, audiotapes, Tape 1, Side 2. Moreover, some of the roles and responsibilities that people have are not so other-directed, for example, many of the *legal* roles and responsibilities that very wealthy people have. Accordingly, such roles and responsibilities, unless abused, can fairly easily be translated into control over one's own life.

7. Farrell also argues that influence power is not real power. He contends that executives who increase their responsibilities by moving up in their firms and taking on the supervision of more and more people do not thereby have more power any more than mothers would be increasing their power by just having more children for which they are then responsible, where the relevant sense of power is control over one's own life. However, in each case, I think we need to ask what the relevant costs and benefits are to the person involved from taking on the additional responsibilities for others. I think the results of such an assessment will show that frequently in the business context, less frequently in the procreation context, taking on such responsibilities does in fact, contribute to greater control over one's own life. Surely, we cannot claim, as Farrell does, that so increasing one's responsibilities never thereby increases one's control over one's own life. Think again of the Bill Clinton example.

8. For a related real life discussion, see Timothy O'Brien, "Why Do So Few Women Reach the Top of Big Law Firms?" *New York Times*, March 19, 2006.

9. I am assuming here that Jill and Tom are equally capable overall with respect to their careers and family life.

10. Joan Jensen, "Native American Women and Agriculture: A Seneca Case Study," in Ellen DuBois and Vicki Ruiz, *Unequal Sisters* (New York: Routledge, 1990), pp. 51–65.

11. Farrell spends a lot of time talking about what is primarily the class-based oppression of garbage collectors.

12. Hilary Lips, *Women, Men, and Power* (Mountain View, CA: Mayfield, 1991), p. 19. Interestingly, 25 percent of both males and females named their fathers as the most powerful individual they personally knew, and 91 percent of the males and 69 percent of the females named a man as the most powerful individual they personally knew.

34

The Second Sexism

DAVID BENATAR

David Benatar argues that men in society are discriminated against just because they are men in the same way that women in society are discriminated against just because they are women. He calls this discrimination the "second sexism." To show that this discrimination exists and deserves to be condemned, Benatar starts with a number of examples. He then seeks to explain and criticize the attitudes that he claims underlie these examples and to respond to objections to considering them anything but unjustified discrimination against men.

In societies in which sex discrimination has been recognized to be wrong, the assault on this form of discrimination has targeted those attitudes and practices that (directly) disadvantage women and girls. At the most, there has been only scant attention to those manifestations of sex discrimination of which the primary victims are men and boys. What little recognition there has been of discrimination against males has very rarely resulted in amelioration. For these reasons, we might refer to discrimination against males as the "second sexism," to adapt Simone de Beauvoir's famous phrase. The second sexism is the neglected sexism, the sexism that is not taken seriously even by most of those who oppose sex discrimination. This is regrettable not only because of its implications for ongoing unfair male disadvantage, but also, as I shall argue later, because discrimination against *women* cannot fully be addressed without attending to all forms of sexism.

So unrecognized is the second sexism that the mere mention of it will appear laughable to some. For this reason, some examples of male disadvantage need to be provided. Although I think that all the examples I shall provide happen to be, to a considerable extent, either instances or consequences of sex discrimination, there is a conceptual and moral distinction to

be drawn between disadvantage and discrimination. I shall follow the convention of understanding discrimination as the *unfair* disadvantaging of somebody on the basis of some morally irrelevant feature such as a person's sex.

Discrimination need not be intentional. It is the *effect* rather than the intent of a law, policy, convention, or expectation that is relevant to determining whether somebody is unfairly disadvantaged. Discrimination also need not be direct, as it is when one sex is explicitly prohibited from occupying some position. There are powerful social forces that shape the expectations or preferences of men and women so that significantly disproportionate numbers of men and women aspire to particular positions. Here indirect or subtle discrimination is operative. I shall not defend the claims that discrimination can be indirect and need not be intentional. These are accepted by many. Given that many other claims I shall make will be widely disputed, I shall focus on defending those more contentious claims.

Given the distinction between discrimination and disadvantage, outlining the examples of male disadvantage below is, at least for some of the examples, only the first step in the argument. I shall later

Reprinted from *Social Theory and Practice*, Vol. 29, No. 2, (April 2003) by permission.

consider and reject the view that these examples are not instances of discrimination.

MALE DISADVANTAGE

Perhaps the most obvious example of male disadvantage is the long history of social and legal pressures on men, but not on women, to enter the military and to fight in war, thereby risking their lives and bodily and psychological health. Where the pressure to join the military has taken the form of conscription, the costs of avoidance have been either self-imposed exile, imprisonment, or, in the most extreme circumstances, execution. At other times and places, where the pressures have been social rather than legal, the costs of not enlisting have been either shame or ostracism, inflicted not infrequently by women. Even in those few societies where women have been conscripted, they have almost invariably been spared the worst of military life—combat.

Some have noted, quite correctly, that the definition of "combat" often changes, with the result that although women are often formally kept from combat conditions, they are sometimes effectively engaged in risky combat activity.[1] Nevertheless, it remains true that in those relatively few situations in which women are permitted to take combat roles, it is a result of their choice rather than coercion and that even then women are kept insofar as possible from the worst combat situations. Others have noted that the exclusion of women from combat roles has not resulted in universal protection for women in times of war. Where wars are fought on home territory, women are regularly amongst the casualties of the combat. It remains true, however, that such scenarios are viewed by societies as being a deviation from the "ideal" conflict in which (male) combatants fight at a distance from the women and children whom they are supposed to be protecting. A society attempts to protect its own women but not its men from the life-threatening risks of war.

If we shift our attention from combat itself to military training, we find that women are generally not treated in the same demeaning ways reserved for males. Why, for instance, should female recruits not be subject to the same de-individualizing crew-cuts as male recruits? There is nothing outside of traditional gender roles that suggests such allowances. If it is too degrading for a woman, it must be judged also to be too degrading for a man. That the same judgment is not made is testimony to a double standard. Permitting women longer hair as an expression of their "femininity" assumes a particular relationship between hair length and both "femininity" and "masculinity." These special privileges simply reinforce traditional gender roles.

Men are much more likely to be the targets of aggression and violence.[2] Both men and women have been shown, in a majority of experimental studies, to behave more aggressively against men than toward women.[3] Outside the laboratory, men are also more often the victims of violence. Consider some examples. Data from the U.S.A. show that nearly double the number of men than women are the victims of aggravated assault and more than three times more men than women are murdered.[4] In the Kosovo conflict of 1998–99, according to one study, 90% of the war-related deaths were of men, and men constituted 96% of people reported missing.[5] In South Africa, the Truth and Reconciliation Commission found that the overwhelming majority of victims of gross violations of human rights—killing, torture, abduction, and severe ill-treatment—during the Apartheid years (at the hands of both the government and its opponents) were males.[6] Testimony received by the Commission suggests that the number of men who died was six times that of women. Nonfatal gross violations of rights were inflicted on more than twice the number of men than women.[7] Nor can the Commission be accused of having ignored women and their testimony. The majority of the Commission's deponents (55.3%) were female,[8] and so sensitive was the Commission to the relatively small proportion of women amongst the victims of the most severe violations that it held a special hearing on women.[9]

The lives of men are more readily sacrificed in nonmilitary and nonconflict contexts too. Where some lives must be endangered or lost, as a result of a disaster, men are the first to be sacrificed or put at risk. There is a long, but still thriving tradition (at least in western societies) of "women and children first," whereby the preservation of adult female lives is given priority over the preservation of adult male lives.[10]

Although corporal punishment has been inflicted on both males and females, it has been imposed, especially in recent times, on males much more readily than on females.[11] Both mothers and fathers are more likely to hit sons than daughters.[12] Where corporal punishment is permitted in schools, boys are hit much more often than girls are hit.[13] Obvious sex-role stereotypes explain at least some of the difference.[14] These stereotypes also explain why, in some jurisdictions, physical punishment imposed by schools and courts has been restricted by law to male offenders.[15]

Sexual assault on men is also often taken less seriously than such assault on women. For instance, the extent of sexual abuse of males is routinely underestimated.[16] Sexual assaults upon boys are less likely to be reported than are those upon girls.[17] Moreover, while rape by a male of a female is a crime everywhere, there are only a few jurisdictions in which forcing a male to have sex is regarded as rape. In these latter jurisdictions it is only recently that the definition of rape has been broadened to include the possibility of rape of a male. Before that, nonconsensual sex with a man carried less severe penalties than nonconsensual sex with a woman.[18]

In a divorce, men are less likely to gain custody of their children than are women. Mothers gain custody of children in 90% of cases.[19] Some have suggested that this is because very few men want child custody. The evidence does indeed suggest that a smaller percentage of fathers than mothers want custody and that even fewer fathers actually request custody. However, even taking this into account, fathers fare worse than mothers with regard to child custody. In one study, for instance, 90% of cases where there was an uncontested request for maternal physical custody of the children, the mother was awarded this custody.[20] However, in only 75% of cases in which there was an uncontested request for paternal physical custody was the father awarded such custody. In cases of conflicting requests for physical custody, mothers' requests were granted twice as often as fathers' requests.[21] Similarly, when children were residing with the father at the time of the separation the father was more likely to gain custody than when the children were living with the mother at the time of separation, but his chances were not as high as a mother with whom children were living at the time of separation.[22] This study was undertaken in California, which is noted for its progressive legislation and attitudes about both men and women and is thus a state in which men are less likely to be disadvantaged.

Fathers are not the only males to suffer disadvantage from postdivorce and other custodial arrangements. In one important study, divorced mothers showed their sons less affection than their daughters, "treated their sons more harshly and gave them more threatening commands—though they did not systematically enforce them...."[23] "Even after two years ... boys in ... divorced families were ... more aggressive, more impulsive and more disobedient with their mothers than either girls in divorced families or children in intact families."[24] In another study, "a significant proportion of boys who developed serious coping problems in adolescence, had lived in families in which their father was absent temporarily, either because of family discord or work."[25] The same was not true of girls who grew up with an absent father. In short, boys tend to suffer more than girls as a result of divorce and of living with a single parent. This may be because children fare better when placed with the parent of their own sex, at least where that parent is amenable to having custody.[26]

Homosexual men suffer more discrimination than do lesbians. For instance, male homosexual sex has been and continues to be criminalized or otherwise negatively targeted in more jurisdictions than is lesbian sex.[27] Male homosexuals have a harder time adopting children than do lesbians,[28] even in those places where same sex couples are permitted to adopt. Male homosexuals are much more frequently the victims of "gay-bashing" assaults than are lesbians.[29]

In addition to the above examples, for which the evidence is clear, there are also others for which there is only equivocal evidence. For instance, capital punishment is inflicted on men hundreds of times more often than it is inflicted on women. While it is true that men commit more capital crimes than women do, it is not clear that this fully explains the vast disparity in the number of men and women executed.[30] The sex of the criminal may itself influence whether a criminal is executed. Consider also the broader criminal justice system. There is at least some evidence that, controlling for the number and nature of offenses, men are convicted more often and punished more harshly than are women (or, at least, than those women who conform to gender stereotypes).[31] Given that there is conflicting evidence about these latter examples, we cannot be sure that they really are examples of unfair male disadvantage. Nevertheless, they are worth mentioning at least as topics suitable for further investigation.

UNDERLYING ATTITUDES

These are not negligible forms of disadvantage. In seeking to explain how they arise, one can point to at least three related prejudicial attitudes about males. First, male life is often, but not always, valued less than female life. I do not mean by this that every society unequivocally values male lives less than female lives. This cannot be true, because there are some societies in which female infants are killed precisely because they are female. However, even in such societies, the lives of adult males seem to be valued less than those of adult females. The situation is less ambiguous in liberal democracies. It is not my claim that every single person in these societies values male life less, but that these societies generally do. Although, of course, there are countless examples in liberal democracies of fatal violence against women, this tends to be viewed as worse than the killing of men.[32] If violence or tragedy takes the lives of "women and children," that is thought to be worthy of special mention. We are told that X number of people died, including Y number of women and children. That betrays a special concern, the depravity of which would be more widely denounced if newsreaders, politicians, poets, and others commonly saw fit to note the number of "men and children" who had lost their lives in a tragedy.

Sometimes the special concern for female lives is less overt and more sophisticated. Consider, for example, an argument of Amartya Sen and Jean Drèze, who have drawn attention to the number of female lives that have been lost as a result of advantages accorded men. They have spoken about the world's 100 million "missing women."[33] To reach this figure they first observe that everywhere in the world there are around 105 boys born for every 100 girls. However, more males die at every age. For this reason, in Europe, North America, and other places where females enjoy basic nutrition and health care, the proportion of males and females inverts—around 105 females for every 100 males. Thus, the overall female-male ratio in these societies is 1.05. Amartya Sen and Jean Drèze observe, however, that in many countries the ratio falls to 0.94 or even lower. On this basis, they calculate the number of "missing women"—the number of women who have died because they have received less food or less care than their male counterparts. This is indeed an alarming and unacceptable inequity.

It is interesting, however, that no mention is made of "missing men." The implication is that there are only women who are missing. There are, however, millions of missing men, as should be most obvious from the greater number of men than women who die violently. However, there are other less obvious ways in which men become "missing." To highlight these, consider how the figure of 100 million missing women is reached. Amartya Sen says that if we took an equal number of males and females as the baseline, then "the low ratio of 0.94 women to men in South Asia, West Asia and China would indicate a 6 percent deficit in women."[34] However, he thinks it is inappropriate to set the baseline as an equal number of males and females. He says that "since, in countries where men and women receive similar care the ratio is about 1.05, the real shortfall is about 11 percent."[35] This, he says, amounts to 100 million missing women.

Now, I think it is extremely enlightening that the baseline is set as a female to male ratio of 1.05. Why start from that point rather than from the ratio that obtains at birth? The assumption is that the female-male ratio of 1.05 is the one that obtains in societies in which men and women are treated equally in the ways relevant to mortality—and these are taken to be basic nutrition and health care. But clearly males are not faring as well as females in those societies, so why not think that there are relevant inequalities, disadvantageous to males, operative in *those* societies? One answer might be biology—males seem to be not as resilient as females. I cannot see, however, why that would warrant setting the baseline at the female-male ratio of 1.05. Some distributive theories—those that claim that natural inequalities are undeserved—recommend distributing social resources in a way that compensates for natural inequalities. If males are biologically prone to die earlier, perhaps the ideal distribution is the one whereby the mortality imbalance is equalized (by funding research and medical practice that lowers the male mortality level to the female level).[36] This certainly seems to be what feminists would advocate if biology disadvantaged women in the way it does men. If, for instance, 105 girls were born for every 100 boys, but various factors, including parturition, caused more females to die, there would be strong arguments for diverting resources to preventing those deaths. At the very least, the baseline for determining "missing people" would certainly not be thought to be set after the parturition deaths were excluded.

If we accept the male-female sex ratio at birth—105 males for every 100 females—as a baseline, then at birth there is a female-male ratio of 0.95. From that baseline there are millions of missing men, at least in those societies in which the female-male ratio inverts to 1.05, who go unseen in the Sen-Drèze analysis. This analysis fails to take account of the connection between its baseline ratio and how our health resources are currently distributed. That the Sen-Drèze analysis highlights the missing

women of the world, but notes nothing about the missing men, is extremely revealing. It is a sophisticated form of the view that lost female lives are more noteworthy than lost male lives.

It might be suggested that the stronger concern to avoid female deaths rather than male deaths is best explained not by a greater valuing of women's lives but by social and economic considerations. Since the reproduction of a population requires more women than it does men, a society can less afford to lose large numbers of women (in combat, for example). This explanation, however, is not at odds with the claim that female lives are valued more. In fact, it is a possible explanation of *why* female lives are valued more. Note, however, that this explanation does not excuse the differential treatment. If it did, then excluding women from work outside the home, where they might be tempted to delay or abandon procreative activities, could also be excused.

The second prejudicial attitude underlying the examples I have given of male disadvantage is the greater social acceptance of nonfatal violence against males. This is not to deny the obvious truth that women are frequently the victims of such violence. Nor is it to deny that there are *some* ways in which violence against women is accepted. I suggest only that violence against men is much more socially accepted.

At least one author has taken issue with the claim that violence against men is regarded as more acceptable. He has said that those who think it is so regarded "never offer a criterion for determining when a social practice is acceptable."[37] He says that "sometimes they slide from the fact that violence with men as victims is very widespread to the conclusion that it is acceptable."[38] He notes, quite correctly, that a practice can be widespread without its being deemed acceptable. He also thinks that the "penalties for violent acts, social instructions against violent acts, and moral codes prohibiting violent acts" constitute evidence that violence against men is not acceptable.[39]

It is doubtful that a single criterion of the greater acceptability of violence can be provided. However, there can be various kinds of evidence for such a claim. For instance, although violent acts against men do usually carry penalties (as do violent acts against women), the law does reveal bias. When the law prohibits physical punishment of women but permits such punishment of men, it indicates a level of greater societal acceptance of violence against men. Similarly, when the law does not punish male homosexual rape with the same severity as it punishes heterosexual rape of women, it sends a similar message. But the law is not the only evidence of societal bias. There are penalties for wife-batterers and for rape, yet this (appropriately) has not stopped feminists from showing how both legal and extra-legal factors can indicate societal tolerance of such activities.[40] If, for instance, police do not take charges of wife-battery or rape seriously or if there are social impediments to the reporting of such crimes, this can sometimes constitute evidence of a societal complacency and therefore some implicit acceptance of such violence. If that can be true when women are the victims, why can it not be true when men are? There *are* differences in the way people view violence against men and women. For example, a man who strikes a woman is subject to much more disapproval than a man who strikes another man (even if the female victim is bigger and the male victim smaller than he is, which suggests that it is sex not size that counts).

The third prejudicial attitude is the belief that the instances of male disadvantage to which I have pointed are fully explicable by men's being naturally more aggressive, more violent, less caring, and less nurturing than women are. Some—perhaps most—people will take this to be not so much a prejudice as a truism. I shall assess this view shortly and will show that even if there are such natural behavioral differences between the sexes, the magnitude and significance of these differences is exaggerated. At the very least, those exaggerations constitute prejudices.

RESPONDING TO OBJECTIONS

Some will recognize the value of attending to these prejudices and the forms of disadvantage to which they give rise. Among these people will be those feminists who acknowledge that opposition to instances of the second sexism, far from being incompatible with feminism, is an expression of feminism's best impulses. This, for reasons I shall make clear, is the view that I think all those opposed to sex discrimination ought to adopt. Regrettably, however, there will be others who will oppose combating what I have called the second sexism. These will include conservatives who endorse traditional gender roles, but also those feminists who will regard attention to the second sexism as threatening. I shall now consider and respond to four possible objections to concern about the second sexism.

1. The No-Discrimination Argument

What I call the no-discrimination argument suggests that the examples I have provided are not instances of discrimination (against men). The argument denies that there is a second sexism, by suggesting that it is not discrimination that accounts for these phenomena, but rather other factors. On this view, there may indeed be examples of male disadvantage, but these are not instances of *unfair* disadvantage.

I cannot offer a detailed application of this argument to all of the examples of male disadvantage. Therefore, although my discussion will have relevance to a number of them, I shall focus on the unequal pressures on men and women with regard to entering the military and engaging in combat. Many feminists do not question such inequalities. If pressed to explain their silence, some (but not others) might argue that these inequalities are an inevitable consequence of males' greater natural (rather than socially-produced) aggression. We might call this "the biological explanation." Insofar as they do not offer a similar explanation of the disproportionate number of men in the legislature, in specific professions, and in senior academic or management positions, and instead decry these inequalities, they selectively invoke the biological explanation to the advantage of females. Such selectivity is itself a kind of sexism. A similar charge could be laid against those feminists who would attribute both inequalities that disadvantage men and those that disadvantage women to natural differences between the sexes, but who call for an end only to those that adversely affect women.[41]

The biological explanation does have a more consistent application in the hands of evolutionary psychologists and their followers. They argue that natural, evolutionarily explained differences between the sexes account, at least to a considerable extent, for social inequalities between men and women.[42] They are careful to grant that environment also plays a role in psychological differences between the sexes and to acknowledge that no normative implications follow (directly) from the biological explanation. Notwithstanding such disclaimers, however, they regularly use the biological explanation to support conservative views that little if anything can or should be done to address sex inequalities, irrespective of which sex is disadvantaged. I shall now consider the common assumption that males are naturally more aggressive and then consider what implications this assumption, even if true, would really have for the sex inequalities I am considering.

The first point to note is that although males *do* account for more aggression and violence than females, the difference is not as great as it is usually thought to be. This is borne out by some laboratory studies.[43] In real life, we find that there are at least some circumstances, most notably within the family, in which women behave as aggressively and violently as men and sometimes even more so than men. A number of studies have shown that wives use violence against their husbands at least as much as husbands use violence against their wives.[44] Given the counter-intuitive and controversial nature of these findings, at least one well-known author (who shared the prevailing prejudices prior to his quantitative research) examined the data in multiple ways in order to determine whether these could be reconciled with common views. On almost every score, women were as violent as men. It was found that half the violence is mutual, and in the remaining half there were an equal number of female and male aggressors.[45] When a distinction was drawn between "normal violence" (pushing, shoving, slapping, and throwing things) and "severe violence" (kicking, biting, punching, hitting with an object, "beating-up," and attacking the spouse with a knife or gun), the

rate of mutual violence dropped to a third, the rate of violence by only the husband remained the same, but the rate of violence by only the wife *increased*.[46] Wives have been shown to initiate violence as often as husbands do.[47] At least some studies have suggested that there is a *higher* rate of wives[48] assaulting husbands than husbands assaulting wives and most studies of dating violence show higher rates of female-inflicted violence.[49]

Most authors agree that the *effects* of spousal violence are not equivalent for husbands and wives. Husbands, probably because they are generally bigger and stronger, cause more damage than wives.[50] This is an important observation, of course, but in determining whether women are less violent than men are, it would be a mistake to point to the lesser effectiveness of their violence.

Recognizing that the sex differences in aggression and violence are less marked than commonly thought is important for the following reason. Any attempt to explain a phenomenon must be preceded by an accurate understanding of the phenomenon that is to be explained. To the extent that the sex differences in aggression are exaggerated, the posited explanations will be misdirected.

Because there are different possible explanations of the *actual* (that is, unexaggerated) sex differences in aggression, we need to consider next the evidence for the *biological* explanation of these differences. There are considerably divergent readings of the body of evidence on whether males are naturally more aggressive than females. The evolutionary psychologists understand the evidence clearly to support the biological explanation, while many feminists and others take the opposite view. Authoritatively assessing which of these interpretations is correct is too large a task to undertake here. Fortunately, for reasons I shall explain later, it is not necessary to do so. Nevertheless, for those who think that the evidence for the biological explanation is stronger than it really is, I shall first show that at the very least there is considerable room for doubt.

Consider first the alleged connections between aggression and circulating androgens, particularly testosterone. The administering of antiandrogens (and the resultant reduction of circulating testosterone levels) has been successful in curbing compulsive paraphilic sexual thoughts and impulsive and violent sexual behaviors. However, the drugs were not very effective in reducing nonsexual violence.[51] Increasing testosterone levels in women or hypogonadal men to normal or supranormal levels has not been shown to increase aggression consistently. Lowering testosterone levels in men, by castration or antiandrogens, does not consistently decrease aggression.[52]

Some of those reviewing the literature have concluded that the evidence does not support a link between circulating testosterone and human aggression.[53] Some authors claim that the inability to establish this link stands in striking contrast to the ease with which relations have been shown between testosterone and other phenomena, including sexual activity.[54] In those few studies that do suggest connections between circulating testosterone and human aggression, the links are correlational and there is some reason to think that it is the aggressive and dominant behaviors that cause testosterone levels to rise, rather than vice versa.[55]

Now it might be argued that the evidence for androgenic causes of aggression is strongest not in the case of circulating androgens but in the case of prenatal androgen exposure.[56] The suggestion is that exposure to androgens in utero causes the fetal brain to be organized in a way that causes increased aggression in the person that develops. On this view, since males are typically exposed to higher prenatal levels of androgens, they become naturally more aggressive.

There are clearly moral constraints on experimentally altering the androgen levels to which fetuses and infants are exposed. As a result, one of the few ways of testing the above hypothesis is by examining girls with congenital adrenal hyperplasia (CAH), a condition causing them to be exposed to unusually high levels of androgens in utero and until diagnosis soon after birth. Some studies have indeed found CAH girls to be more aggressive than control females,[57] but some found "the difference was not significant."[58] Other studies found no difference in aggression levels between CAH females and control females,[59] even though affected females were, in other ways, found to be behaviorally similar to boys and unlike control females. The latter

studies suggest that even if prenatal androgen exposure has other behavioral effects, an influence on aggression is not demonstrated.

There is, in any event, a significant problem that plagues the CAH studies. Given that the external genitalia of CAH girls tend to become virilized to some degree and parents know of their daughters' condition, one cannot discount social factors as a cause or partial cause of those behavioral differences that are found.[60] One author[61] has suggested that this objection can be rejected because normal children exposed prenatally to higher levels of testosterone have greater brain lateralization.[62] However, unless cerebral lateralization can be shown to affect aggression, we cannot extrapolate from studies about the relationship between testosterone and lateralization to a relationship between testosterone and aggression.

None of this is to deny a biological basis for human aggression. It is possible, for example, that human aggression is rooted in some biological phenomenon other than androgens. There is some evidence that human aggression has many features in common with what is called "defensive aggression" (as distinct from "hormone-dependent aggression") in nonprimate mammals and that this kind of aggression is rooted in the limbic system of the brain.[63] One of the distinctive features of defensive aggression in nonprimate mammals, however, is that it is quantitatively similar in males and females.[64]

It is also possible that there *is* a connection between androgens and aggression even though none has yet been demonstrated. One possible explanation for this is that the posited connection is a complex one. One obvious feature of this complexity is the interaction with environmental factors. Even those who argue that there are (proven) hormone-related differences in aggression between the sexes agree that the environment, including the social environment, plays a significant role. Evolutionary psychologists often ignore the importance of this in drawing normative conclusions. Even if human aggression were shown to be influenced by androgens, current inequalities (in conscription and combat, for example) would still be cause for concern. One reason for this is that at least some of the inequality would be attributable to social factors rather than to natural hormonal differences between the sexes. Any natural differences in aggression that might exist could give rise to, but would also be greatly exaggerated by, sex-role expectations and conventions. This is one reason why conservatism is not a fitting response to current inequalities even if one thinks that natural differences account for some of the inequality. Another reason is that even if men are naturally more aggressive than women, it does not follow that women are not aggressive enough for military purposes or that they cannot be subject to environmental influences that would make them so.

Some feminists make much of how war is carried out by men, implying and sometimes even explicitly claiming that women are above this kind of behavior.[65] But there are obvious social and gender role explanations that can account for why men become soldiers. Where women have had the opportunity to kill, torture, and perpetrate other cruel acts, they have proved very capable of doing so.[66] There is a disingenuity in the arguments of those feminists who will discount the opportunity differentials between men and women for the violence of war, but who rush to explain the greater incidence of (non-sexual) child abuse by women as being a function of sexism. It is women, they correctly note, who have most contact with children and therefore have the greatest opportunity to abuse children. Moreover, we are told that female abusers of children "would probably not have become child abusers had the culture offered them viable alternatives to marriage and motherhood."[67] If this line of argument (contrary to my own view) is acceptable, why can a similar explanation for participation in war not be given for young men "whose culture does not offer them viable alternatives" to machismo and the military?

Some feminists not only refuse to excuse men the violence of war (in the way they excuse women's violence) but, unlike other feminists, they also resist the very changes which would make it a less male affair—namely, parity in enlistment of the sexes. They oppose conscription of women.[68] Feminist defenders of women's absence from combat assume

that women are different and unsuited to war. They maintain that so long as there is (or must be) war, it is men who must wage it. There are a number of problems with this view. First, by seeking to preserve the status quo, they suppress the most effective test of whether men really are better suited to war. Notice how the real test of female competence to perform other tasks has been most unequivocally demonstrated by women actually performing those tasks. Whereas when there were almost no female lawyers people could have appealed to that fact to support claims of female unsuitability to the legal profession, that same line of argument is simply not available when there are vast numbers of successful female lawyers. Second, those who argue that women are ill-suited to war assume that men (unlike women) want to participate in war. Alternatively, male preferences on this score are a matter of indifference to them. The overwhelming majority of men do not wish to be part of the military. Were it otherwise, conscription would never be necessary. Why should these men be forced into the military, while women are not? It simply will not do, as I have explained, to justify this by saying that men are naturally more aggressive than women and thus more suitable to military activity.

Nor will it do, as some have tried, to justify the female exemption-exclusion[69] from combat in other ways. I do not have space here to consider and respond to all the arguments for female exclusion from combat, but I shall examine two by way of illustration.[70] Some have claimed that because women have less strength, stamina, and muscle than men, they are less suited than men to the physical demands of ground combat. There are numerous problems with this argument. For instance, much combat activity, at least in our time, does not require strength. But even if it did, that would not be a reason for excluding all women. Some women are stronger than some men are. If strength were really what counted, that and not sex would be the appropriate criterion.

Others have defended the combat exemption-exclusion as a way of protecting women from the greater risk of being raped which they would bear if captured by the enemy. It might be noted in response to this that it is far from clear that sexual abuse is not experienced by many male prisoners of war. Second, males may well stand a greater chance of being tortured in nonsexual ways than women. Why should there be such rigid (often paternalistic) exclusions of women from combat allegedly to protect them from rape, while men are not only not protected, but often forced into combat situations where they can face harms (including maiming and torture) that are arguably as traumatizing as rape? Finally, the argument that women should be exempted from combat because they need to be protected from rape (or because they are less aggressive or less strong) is one that feminists can advance only at their peril. If some such reason for exempting women were (thought to be) true, it could equally support the exclusion of women from functions they do wish to fulfill. Indeed, such reasons have been used regularly by the conservative defenders of traditional gender roles, including those who have sought to exclude from combat those women who do want such roles.

2. The Distraction Argument

Not all those opposed to highlighting the second sexism will deny that men are sometimes the victims of sex discrimination. However, those who are willing to grant this may argue that attention to the second sexism will distract us from the much greater discrimination against women. On this view, until there is parity between the extent of disadvantage suffered by men and women, we must devote our attention and energies to opposing the greater discrimination—that experienced by females.

This argument presupposes that the position of women is worse than that of men. I do not deny this, if it is a global claim that is being made. In most places, women are generally worse off than men. This is because the traditional gender roles for women are much more restrictive than those for men, and most of the world's human population continues to live in societies that are characterized by traditional gender roles. But what about contemporary liberal democracies, from whose ranks most feminists are drawn and to which substantial

(but not exclusive) feminist attention is devoted? In the light of the substantial inroads against sexism made in such societies, as well as the examples of the second sexism that I have outlined, are women worse off than men in such countries? Many people will confidently offer an affirmative answer. I cannot say that their answer is wrong. Nevertheless, the answer cannot be offered with confidence in a society that has viewed so lightly the serious forms of discrimination against men. The extent of discrimination against men is probably seriously underestimated and this makes fair comparison unlikely. Fortunately, I think that the question of which sex suffers the greater discrimination is simply irrelevant to the question of whether attention should be given to the second sexism. This brings me to my first response to the distraction argument.

Sex discrimination is wrong, irrespective of the victim's sex. It is not only the most severe manifestations of injustice that merit our attention. If it were wrong to focus on lesser forms of discrimination when greater forms were still being practiced, then we would have to attend to racial discrimination rather than sex discrimination, at least in those places in which racial discrimination is worse than sex discrimination.[71] Moreover, where one opposed sex discrimination, one would have to ignore some forms of sex discrimination if one accepted the view that only the most serious injustices deserve our attention. Not all forms of sexism are equally severe. Using the word "man" to refer to people of both sexes, for example, is not as damaging as clitoridectomy or even as unfair as unequal pay. Feminists who think that we should devote our energies only to eliminating the worst forms of sex discrimination would be committed to a very restricted agenda. But if both major and minor forms of discrimination against women deserve attention, why should major forms of discrimination against men not be equally deserving of concern? How can it be acceptable to want an end to sexist speech while males die because of their sex? If one is opposed to injustice, then it is injustice that counts, not the sex of the victim. Even if it is the case that in general women are the greater victims of sex discrimination, it is still the case that some men suffer more from sex discrimination than some women. A young man on the *Titanic* who is denied a place in a lifeboat because of his sex is worse off than the young woman whose life is saved because of her sex. A young man, conscripted and killed in battle, is worse off than his sister who is not. It does not matter here that *had* he survived, the man would have had greater access to higher education or could have earned more. If he is made to lose his life because of his sex and she has her life spared because of her sex, then this man is the greater victim of sex discrimination than this woman. Countering sex discrimination against men will remove some relative advantages that women enjoy, but that is fair in the same way that it is fair that countering sex discrimination against women removes relative advantages that men enjoy.

There is a second important response to the distraction argument. Far from distracting one from those discriminatory practices that disadvantage females, confronting the second sexism can help undo discrimination against women. This is because ending discrimination against one sex is inseparable from ending discrimination against the other sex. One reason for this is that the same sets of stereotypes underlie both kinds of discrimination. For example, the very attitudes that prevent women from being conscripted and from being sent into combat, thereby discriminating against those males and protecting those women who have no wish to be part of the military, also favor those males but disadvantage those females who desire a military career and who do not want to be excluded from combat. Similarly, the stereotypes of men as aggressive and violent and of women as caring and gentle lead to only males' being sent into battle but also entail assumptions that it is women who must bear primary responsibility for childcaring. Or consider the small proportion of women amongst the victims of gross human rights violations in South Africa. This is attributable to gender roles that discouraged women from engaging in political activity, especially dangerous political activity in which men were encouraged or expected to participate.[72] Although these gender roles had beneficial effects for women in protecting them from the violence of adversaries, these same gender roles disadvantaged women in other regards. The "women and children first" mentality is another, related, example. It disadvantages men in life-and-death situations but has obvious disadvantages for women in other circumstances. Women are protected, to be sure, but in the same way and for relics of the same reasons that children are—they are assumed to be weak and to be unable to look after themselves. Similarly, the battered woman syndrome defense, under which the criminal law (at least in the United States) allows evidence of abuse of women, but not of men, to constitute an excuse from criminal responsibility, has the effect of reaffirming prejudices about women as lacking the capacity for rational self-control.[73]

3. The Inversion Argument

By the "inversion argument," I mean the argument that what I have suggested are instances of discrimination against men are instead forms of discrimination against women. On this view, what I have called the second sexism is instead just another form of discrimination against women. Rarely is such an argument explicitly presented. That is to say, those employing this sort of argument do not argue that matters ought to be inverted. Rather they simply invert them. They do not argue that what might be thought to constitute discrimination against men is rather discrimination against women. Instead, they simply present the data as instances of anti-female bias. To this extent, my presentation of the inversion as an argument is a construction of an argument out of a practice. The absence of an explicit argument for inversion is understandable. Were an argument for inversion explicitly presented, its weakness would be much more apparent.

Consider, for example, those authors who present attempts at excluding women from the military as forms of discrimination against women. They say, for instance, that the military, faced with an increase in the number of women soldiers, "seems to have an exaggerated need to pursue more and more refined measures of sexual difference in order to *keep women in their place*,"[74] noting that Western armed forces "search for a difference which can justify women's continued exclusion from the military's ideological core—combat. If they can find this difference, they can also exclude women from the senior command promotions that are open only to officers who have seen combat."[75] As I have argued, excluding women from combat does indeed disadvantage some women. That it is a minority of women whom this exclusion disadvantages—those who seek combat opportunities and the career benefits that come with this in the military—does not alter the fact that *these* women are indeed the victims of sex discrimination. But to present the exclusion exclusively in terms of the negative effects it has on women is to ignore the much greater disadvantage suffered by vast numbers of men who are forced into combat against their wills. It is well and good to note, as I have done, how an instance of sex discrimination can cut both ways. It is quite another to present everything as disadvantaging only women.

Even those with a more balanced approach tend to make much more of the negative impact on women of those discriminatory practices whose primary victims are men. Thus, one author who notes that war is "often awful and meaningless,"[76] observes that there are advantages that combatants enjoy. She cites a prisoner of war graffito "freedom—a feeling the protected will never know" and "the feelings of unity, sacrifice and even ecstasy experienced by the combatant."[77] Moreover, she notes that women "who remain civilians will not receive the post-war benefits of veterans, and those [women] who don uniforms will be a protected, exempt-from-combat subset of the military. Their accomplishments will likely be forgotten."[78] Although true, the significance of these advantages is overdone—even to the point of depravity. Certainly, those who never experience its loss may not have the same acute appreciation of freedom, but that acute appreciation is, at most, a positive side effect of an immensely traumatic and damaging experience. Imagine how we would greet the observation that although paraplegia is "often awful and meaningless" it is only those who have lost the use of some limbs who can truly appreciate the value of having those limbs functional. Next, although veterans do have benefits

denied to others, this is a form of compensation for sacrifice made. It is hardly unfair that compensation is not given to those to whom no compensation is due. People should be free, of course, to decide whether they want to accept the sacrifices of joining the military and the compensation that goes with it, but the absence of that choice is the disadvantage rather than the mere absence of the compensation. Finally, while the tasks of noncombatants are indeed less likely to be remembered, this observation grossly underplays the extent to which the tasks and sacrifices of most *combatants* are unremembered. Many of these who die in battle lie in unmarked graves or are memorialized in monuments to the "Unknown Soldier." In exceptional cases, as with the Vietnam War Memorial, a deceased combatant's memorial consists of an engraving of his name, along with thousands of others—hardly a remembrance proportionate to the sacrifice.

Consider another example of the inversion argument. Males, I noted earlier in my discussion of the Sen-Drèze argument, tend to die earlier than females. Although life expectancy has increased in developed countries over the last century, men have consistently lagged behind women. This suggests that the earlier death of males is (or, at least, was) not attributable to a biologically determined life-expectancy ceiling. As social conditions improved, men lived to be older, but never (on average) as old as women. If it were the case that men tended to live longer than women, we would be told that this inequality would need to be addressed by devoting more attention and resources to women's health. By means of the inversion argument, the call for more attention and resources to women's health is exactly what some people offer even though it is in fact men who die earlier. Such claims do not result from a belief that more is spent on the health care of men than women. A Canadian study on sex differences in the use of health care services showed that the "crude annual per capita use of health care resources (in Canadian dollars) was greater for female subjects ($1,164) than for male subjects ($918)" but that expenditures "for health care are similar for male and female subjects after differences in reproductive biology and higher age-specific mortality rates among men have been accounted for."[79] Accepting that there is indeed an *equal* distribution of health-care dollars between men and women, one practitioner of the inversion argument suggested that such expenditure was not *equitable*.[80] This, we are told, is because the greater longevity (of females) is "associated with a greater lifetime risk of functional disability and chronic illness, including cancer, cardiovascular disease, and dementia, and a greater need for long-term care."[81] I shall assume that that is indeed so. Living longer does carry some costs, but on condition that those costs are not so great as to render the increased longevity a harm rather than a benefit, the infirmities that often accompany advanced age cannot be seen in isolation from the benefit of the longer life-span. An equitable distribution of healthcare resources is not one that both favors a longer life-span for one sex and increases the quality of the additional years of that extra increment of life. Such a distribution would constitute a double favoring of one sex. A genuinely equitable distribution would be one that aimed at parity of life expectancy and the best quality of life for both sexes within that span of life. The proponents of the inversion argument, by contrast, are unsatisfied with any *perceived* trends that lessen the gap between men and the healthier sex. Thus we are told, disapprovingly, that at "a time when there have been improvements in the health status of men, the health status of women does not appear to be improving."[82]

Another example of inversion is the common argument that the educational system disadvantages girls.[83] It is widely thought that girls fare worse than boys in school and university. This is just the message proclaimed by a report from the Wellesley College Center for Research on Women. Sponsored by the American Association of University Women, the report, entitled "How Schools Short-change Girls," has been widely cited. Indeed, there are some ways in which girls fare less well than boys in the educational system. For instance, boys tend to do better in mathematics and science tests and more doctoral degrees are awarded to men than to women. However, there are other ways in which boys are clearly at a disadvantage. In the U.S.A., girls outscore boys on reading and writing by a much greater margin than boys outscore girls in

science and mathematics tests. And although boys do better on science and mathematics tests, girls get better class marks for these subjects. Some have suggested that this differential is to be explained by gender bias in the standardized tests. Christina Hoff Sommers suggests, however, that it could be better explained by a grading bias in schools against boys. Since Taiwanese and Korean girls score much higher than American boys on the same tests, it would seem that the gender-biased explanation of the standardized tests is not entirely satisfactory. Boys are educationally disadvantaged in other ways too. More boys miss classes, fail to do homework, have disciplinary problems, and drop out of school. The higher dropout rate for boys may partially explain the better average performance by boys on standardized tests. The academically weakest boys tend not to write. Boys are also "more likely to be robbed, threatened, and attacked in and out of school."[84] Females now constitute a majority of college graduates and M.A.s in the U.S.A. Only in doctoral degrees are men still in the majority, but now by a much smaller margin than before. Females are worse off in some ways, but these disadvantages are diminishing. The inverters, ignoring the serious ways in which males are disadvantaged, present the educational institutions as disadvantaging only girls and women.

Sometimes the inversion argument or technique applies to a phenomenon that both discriminates against men and against women, but it presents the situation as discriminating only against women. We might call this a *hemi-inversion* argument. It inverts only that aspect that discriminates against men, thus presenting the phenomenon as disadvantaging only women. One example of this is the pair of authors who presented the exclusion of women in the sports media from male locker rooms after matches as an instance of *blatant* discrimination against those women. As they correctly observe, such sportswriters who "cannot get immediate access to athletes after a game … may miss deadlines and will likely be 'scooped' by the competition."[85] They entirely ignore the other side of the issue, however, and quote with disapproval the coach who stated "I will not allow women to walk in on 50 naked men." Had it been a male sports writer seeking access to a locker room of 50 naked female athletes, we can be sure that a different tone would have been evident in feminist commentary on the matter. There are alternative solutions to such equity issues—such as denying all journalists, both male and female, from entering locker rooms. These authors ignore such options just as they ignore the invasion of privacy that would be experienced by the male athletes, who would surely be discriminated against if their female counterparts would not also be subject to such invasions. Instead, the authors view the matter entirely from the perspective of the female sports writers. I am fully aware that for other unfortunate reasons male sports draw more attention, and that female writers thus lose more in not having access to male locker rooms than male writers do in not having access to female locker rooms. However, if this is used to justify female access to male locker rooms but not male access to female locker rooms, then the intensity of the writer's interest rather than the athlete's privacy is taken to be the determining factor. And if that is so, then male journalists should be allowed to corner female politicians, actors, and other public personalities in female-only toilets and locker rooms if that is how they can scoop an important story. If this would not be acceptable, then neither is the intrusion by female sports writers on the privacy of male athletes, irrespective of the writers' interests in getting a story.

The inversion argument is a crass form of partiality. It presents *all* sex inequality as disadvantaging primarily or only women. This is unfair to those males who are the primary victims of some forms of sex discrimination. It also strategically compromises the case against those forms of discrimination that do in fact disadvantage women more than men. Unfairly presenting the relative disadvantages of different practices leads to one's legitimate claims being taken less seriously.[86]

4. The Costs-of-Dominance Argument

A fourth kind of argument suggests that although there may indeed be costs to being a man, these are the costs of dominance—the costs that come with being the privileged sex.[87] Unlike the inversion argument, the costs-of-dominance argument does not suggest that the costs of being a man are *themselves* actually advantages. Instead, this argument recognizes that they are indeed costs, but suggests that they should be seen merely as the by-products of a dominant position and thus not evidence of discrimination against males. In the words of one author, it "is a twist of logic to try to argue … that because there are costs in having power, one does not have power."[88]

Clearly there are some situations in which the costs-of-dominance argument would be sound. Where a cost really is inseparable from one's position of power or (overall) advantage, then it is true that the cost is not a cause for complaint *on behalf of the* power-holder.[89] However, it does not follow from this that all the costs experienced by males really are connected to their having power or privilege. For example, although the exemption-exclusion of women from the military is the result of females' perceived military incapacity, it is hardly obvious that male power would be impossible without this exemption-exclusion. For example, the rich have succeeded in preserving (even enhancing) their privilege while the poor, for various reasons, have endured a disproportionately heavy military burden. Thus, it need not be the case that those with the power in a society must be those who bear arms. Bearing arms is dirty work and there is no shortage of examples of underdogs being forced or enticed to do the dirty work. Similarly, it is far from clear that the higher rates of capital and corporal punishment of males is an inevitable by-product of male power.

It is sometimes alleged that the higher rates of male suicide, the tendency of males to die younger than women, the greater chance that men have of being killed, becoming alcoholic, and so forth, are side-effects of the stresses that come with privilege.[90] It might be argued in response that alleged privileges that have these consequences are not real privileges for those who succumb. Although some men may benefit, many others experience only the costs. However, even if it were true that these were costs of genuine privilege, it would not follow that these costs were *inevitable* results. Those with power can divert resources in order to combat such side-effects of their power, thereby further improving their position.

Moreover, it is curious that as male power has surely (and appropriately) diminished in western democracies, the costs of being male have (inappropriately) increased, not decreased. For example, whereas a century or more ago men were almost guaranteed, following divorce, to gain custody of their children, today they are at a distinct disadvantage. As custody practices were better for men when they really did enjoy more power than they do now, it is clear that the current custody biases are not inevitable by-products of male power.

Thus, although it is true that the powerful cannot complain about having to bear the costs of that power, it does not follow that all disadvantages they suffer are such costs. Even if it is true that men in our society enjoy overall advantage—and I am not convinced that this is true any longer—it can still be true that they suffer genuine discrimination that is not an inevitable consequence of their privilege.

Now some will ask why those who hold most positions of power in a society could be the victims of pervasive discrimination. Why would those with power allow themselves to be treated in this way? Although there are a number of possible answers, the most important one is that insofar as discrimination is indirect and nonintentional, those who hold positions of power may not recognize it for what it is. They might take their disadvantage to be inevitable, perhaps because they share the very prejudices that contribute to their own disadvantage. A captain and officers clearly hold the powerful positions on a ship. Yet when it sinks and they adhere to and enforce a policy of saving "women and children," the social conventions lead them to use their power in a way that advantages women and disadvantages men (including themselves).

TAKING THE SECOND SEXISM SERIOUSLY

The fitting response to the second sexism is to oppose it in the same way that we oppose those sexist attitudes and practices of which women are the primary victims. To date, however, there has been an asymmetrical assault on sexism. Practices that disadvantage women have steadily been uprooted, while very few disadvantages of men have been confronted. Male disadvantage is thought hardly worthy of mention. When it is mentioned it is often excused even by those who purport to oppose sex discrimination. In academic research into gender issues, the trend is to examine ways in which women are disadvantaged. Relatively little research examines the other side of the sexist coin. Because of this, we have every reason to think that the full extent of male disadvantage has not been revealed. If it has taken all the research it has to show the many facets of discrimination against women and girls, it surely will take as much to show the many ways in which men and boys suffer disadvantage.

Recognition of the second sexism sheds some light on the claim that all societies are structured to the exclusive benefit of men and are thus "patriarchal." So powerful is patriarchy, we are told, that women themselves internalize its values and serve its ends. Consider, for instance, female genital excision, which is widespread in some parts of the world. This ritual is almost always performed by women and many women are amongst the most vigorous defenders of the practice. Nevertheless, it is argued, entirely appropriately, that given how damaging the procedure is to the girls on whom it is performed, it cannot reasonably be claimed to serve the interests of women (except, perhaps, those few female performers of the ritual, as they may have a vested interest in it).[91] What is curious, though, is that similar reasoning is not applied to the conscription of only males. Here some feminists are at pains to emphasize that it is men who make wars and men who conscript other men to fight them. This is true, but no less so than the claim that it is females who perform genital excision on little girls. Why is it not the case that the whole system of male-only conscription and combat serves women's interests? Why are the female agents of genital excision serving the interests of men, while the male—and now also female—agents of government, the bureaucracy and the military who send *men* to war, are serving *men's* interests? Why are women not complicit in and partly culpable for the perpetuation of gender role stereotypes that lead to male disadvantage? Once one recognizes the second sexism, claims about universal patriarchy become either absurd or unfalsifiable. The evidence suggests that not *everything* counts against women and in favor of men. Society often favors men, but it also sometimes (perhaps even often) favors women. To the extent that claims about the existence of patriarchy deny this and explain away any conceivable example of male disadvantage, they are unfalsifiable and accordingly unscientific.

Understanding the second sexism also has consequences for the debate about affirmative action for women (qua women, rather than qua some other class of beings). For instance, one objection to strong affirmative action policies is that rather than redressing past disadvantage by making restitution to an identifiably disadvantaged person, such policies make restitution to a person who belongs to a class that has been disadvantaged. This, it is said, sometimes leads to somebody who has not been disadvantaged receiving the benefit of affirmative action. In response to this argument, defenders of affirmative action sometimes argue that given how society works, *all* women have been disadvantaged and thus an affirmative action policy favoring women cannot in practice favor somebody who has not been disadvantaged. What the second sexism shows is that this response will not work. It will sometimes—even often—be the case that a man has been more disadvantaged than a woman. This woman may not have had her career interrupted by childbearing and rearing, but this man may have had his career interrupted by a period of military service. This woman may have had every educational advantage during childhood schooling, while this man may have been one of the many who suffered educational disadvantage.

Moreover, asymmetrical attention has been given to how sexist attitudes lead to lopsiding in social institutions. Feminists regularly tell us that anything less than proportionate representation of the sexes in government, the professions, and other socially desirable positions is an indication of discrimination (whether subtle or otherwise). Although there are relatively few female engineers, for example, despite formal equality of opportunity, we are told that this is due to subtle sexist influences that discourage young girls from aspiring to be engineers. Yet, this sort of reasoning is not used to explain why the vast majority of prisoners or soldiers are male. It is not said that sexist stereotypes dispose (or force) young males to enlist or to behave in ways that make them more susceptible to imprisonment. The proportion of male prisoners and soldiers, for example, is simply taken as natural in a way that the proportion of male engineers or legislators is not.

If the under-representation of women in the academy, for example, must be redressed by affirmative action policies that ensure proportionality, why should similar policies not be used for the purposes of conscription and combat? Affirmative action conscription policies that aimed at enlisting equal numbers of males and females and insisted on sending equal numbers of men and women into battle would not only enforce the desired proportionality, it would also have an immense impact on the prejudicial views about gender roles. Similarly, notice that although women are now heavily represented in what were traditionally male jobs, men have not made comparable inroads into professions such as nursing, which (for about a century and a half) have traditionally been the preserve of women. Part of this is explicable by the lower status of traditionally female jobs, which makes them less attractive to men. But that, it seems to me, is just part of the sexist worldview that feminists are seeking to undo. If the aims of affirmative action include proportional representation of the sexes in each kind of work, and the overcoming of gender-linked jobs, then affirmative action has as much of a role to play in equalizing the nursing profession as it does in equalizing the sexes within the ranks of doctors. In fact, there is reason—including the actual success rates—to think that sexist stereotypes make it easier for women to enter traditionally male professions than for men to enter traditionally female professions.[92] Accordingly, affirmative action policies, if justified, may be more needed in nursing than in medicine. I want to emphasize that I am *not* recommending affirmative action in the military, the nursing profession, and other such areas. My claim is only that the very arguments used to defend affirmative action in other contexts would apply equally here. To apply them selectively is disingenuous.

CONCLUSION

When one considers how much has been written about discrimination against women, it is clear that no one paper can address all aspects of the second sexism. It has not been possible for me to search for and probe all instances of the second sexism, and it has not been possible to consider and respond to all objections to the claim that there is a second sexism. Such constraints on a single paper are innocuous in themselves. Unfortunately, however, the paucity of papers giving attention to discrimination against men leads to those few that there are being taken less seriously. The absence of an extensive academic literature about discrimination against men both results from and further entrenches the neglect of such discrimination. That is to say, it is at least partly because such discrimination is not taken seriously that so little research time and money is devoted to it. But because it is not the vogue to examine such discrimination, much less is known about it and this perpetuates the impression that it is not worthy of detailed consideration. The lopsided information we have about sexism creates a climate in which the research bias is preserved and reinforced. This is dangerous. We have every reason to think that academic neglect of a problem is not an indication of its absence. For example, it was not long ago that sexual abuse of children was thought to be an extremely rare phenomenon. That issue has since become a popular academic and social cause, with the result that we now know much more about it and it is now widely recognized to be more common than was previously thought.

But do (most) men feel as though they are victims of sexism? It has been noted that "women bent on escape from the female sphere do not usually run into hordes of oppressed men swarming in the opposite direction, trying to change places with their wives and secretaries" and that this is evidence for "where the real advantage lies."[93] Notice that one *could* embrace the conclusion that *overall* advantage lies with men, while still acknowledging that men do experience some significant sexist discrimination. In this paper I have sought only to highlight this discrimination and to argue that it should be opposed. I have not sought to claim that men are worse off than women. Nevertheless, the observation that men (generally[94]) do not want to change places with women should not be invested with too much significance. If people's satisfaction or dissatisfaction with their socially mandated roles were determinative (or even suggestive) of whether such roles were advantageous to their bearers, then a few conclusions that are unfortunate for feminists would follow. First, many women forced into traditional female roles could not be viewed as being the victims of sexism, so long as those roles were internalized by those women and found by them to be satisfying. Just such an attitude characterized most women until the dawn of the women's movement, and it is an attitude that is still widespread among women in more traditional societies, if not with respect to every feature of their position then at least to many of its features. Second, the women most dissatisfied with their condition are to be found in disproportionately large numbers amongst women who are subject to the least sexist discrimination and restrictions. For instance, female feminist professors in Western societies are arguably the most liberated women in the world—the women least restricted or disadvantaged by sexism. Yet they are also more concerned about the disadvantages they do face than are many less fortunate women. If the level of one's satisfaction with one's role is what determines the severity of the discrimination to which one is subjected, then the sexism experienced by contemporary Western feminists really is worse than that endured by those women in more traditional societies, past or present, who are satisfied with their position.

Whether one takes that to be absurd will depend, at least in part, on what view one takes about such matters as adaptive preferences and false consciousness. It would be unwise to attempt to settle these issues here. All I wish to observe is that if men's apparent contentment with their position is taken to be evidence that they are not the victims

of discrimination, then from that follow some conclusions that should be unsettling to most feminists. If, by contrast, it is thought that somebody might be the victim of discrimination without realizing it, then the way is opened to recognizing that even if most men are content with their position they might nonetheless be victims of a second sexism.[95]

ENDNOTES

1. Judith Wagner DeCew, "Women, Equality, and the Military," in Dana E. Bushnell (ed.), *Nagging Questions: Feminist Ethics in Everyday Life* (Lanham, Md.: Rowman and Littlefield, 1995), pp. 123–144, at p. 131.

2. Saying that men are more *likely* to be the victims of aggression and violence is not to say that they are *always* over-represented among such victims. Nazi genocide of Jews and others, for example, targeted men and women equally.

3. Ann Frodi, Jacqueline Macaulay and Pauline Ropert Thome, "Are Women Always Less Aggressive than Men? A Review of the Experimental Literature," *Psychological Bulletin* 84 (1977): 634–660, p. 642; Alice H. Eagly and Valerie J. Steffen, "Gender and Aggressive Behavior: A Meta-Analytic Review of the Social Psychological Literature," *Psychological Bulletin* 100 (1986): 309–330, pp. 321–322.

4. Diane Craven, "Sex Differences in Violent Victimization, 1994," Bureau of Justice Statistics Special Report, September 1997.

5. Paul. B. Spiegel and Peter Salama, "War and Mortality in Kosovo, 1988–89: An Epidemiological Testimony," *The Lancet* 355 (24 June 2000): 2204–2209, pp. 2205–2206.

6. *Truth and Reconciliation Commission of South Africa Report,* 1998, vol. 1, p. 171; vol. 4, pp. 259–266.

7. Ibid., vol. 1, p. 171.

8. Ibid. p. 169.

9. Ibid. vol. 4, chap. 10.

10. Two famous examples are those of the ships *Birkenhead* and *Titanic*. When they were wrecked, in 1852 and 1912 respectively, women, and children

were given priority in access to the lifeboats, while adult men were expected to stay on board knowing full well that they would die. See David Bevan, *Drums of the Birkenhead* (Cape Town: Purnell & Sons, 1972); Mark Giroud, *The Return to Camelot: Chivalry and the English Gentleman* (London: Yale University Press, 1981). I am grateful to Ulrik Strandvik for drawing these sources to my attention. Sex and age are not the only relevant variables. Class is another. For statistics on the percentages of surviving men, women and children in each of the three classes on the *Titanic,* see Ian Jack, "Leonardo's Grave," in *Granta* 67 (1999): 7–37, p. 32.

11. For arguments against sex-discrimination in the infliction of corporal punishment, see David Benatar, "The Child, the Rod and the Law," *Ada Juridica* (1996): 197–214; and "Corporal Punishment," *Social Theory and Practice* 24 (1998): 237–260.

12. Hakan Stattin, Harald Janson, Ingrid Klackenberg-Larsson, and David Magnusson, "Corporal Punishment in Everyday Life: An Intergenerational Perspective," in Joan McCord (ed.), *Coercion and Punishment in Long-Term Perspectives* (Cambridge: Cambridge University Press, 1995), pp. 315–347, at pp. 321–323; Murray A. Straus, *Beating the Devil out of Them: Corporal Punishment in American Families* (New York: Lexington Books, 1994), pp. 29–30.

13. Steven R. Shaw and Jeffrey P. Braden, "Race and Gender Bias in the Administration of Corporal Punishment," *School Psychology Review* 19 (1990): 378–383; Irwin A. Hyman, *Reading, Writing and the Hickory Stick* (Lexington, Mass.: Lexington Books, 1990), p. 65; John R. Slate, Emilio Perez, Phillip B. Waldrop, and Joseph E. Justen III, "Corporal

Punishment: Used in Discriminatory Manner?" *The Clearing House,* vol. 64, July/August 1991, pp. 362–364.

14. Straus, *Beating the Devil out of Them,* p. 30.

15. Here are a few examples of jurisdictions where corporal punishment either was or is legally restricted to males. South Africa: J. Sloth-Nielsen, "Legal Violence: Corporal and Capital Punishment," in Brian McKendrick and Wilma Hoffmann, *People and Violence in South Africa* (Cape Town: Oxford University Press, 1990), p. 77. United Kingdom; Section 56 (1) of the (U.K.) Petty Sessions and Summary Jurisdiction Act 1927 (as amended by s. 8 of the Summary Jurisdiction Act 1960), quoted in *Tyrer v. United Kingdom, European Human Rights Reports,* 1978, p. 4. Singapore: Regulation No. 88 under the Schools Regulation Act 1957. Quoted at www.corpun.com/sgscrl.htm *(accessed 18 February 2002).*

16. One of the few works to examine the problem of sexual assault on men is Gillian C. Mezey and Michael B. King's collection, *Male Victims of Sexual Assault,* 2nd ed. (Oxford: Oxford University Press, 2000). A number of authors in this collection demonstrate that the problem is significantly greater than is commonly assumed. Some of them postulate explanations of why sexual assault of males is less well recognized. Some of them also provide evidence that the number of female perpetrators of such assault is considerably greater than most people assume. See also William C. Holmes and Gail B. Slap, "Sexual Abuse of Boys: Definition, Prevalence, Correlates, Sequelae, and Management," *Journal of the American Medical Association* 280, no. 21 (2 December 1998): 1855–1862.

17. Bill Watkins and Arnon Bentovim, "Male Children and Adolescents as Victims: A Review of Current Knowledge," in Mezey and King (eds.), *Male Victims of Sexual Assault,* pp. 35–78, at pp. 40–42.

18. Zsuzsanna Adler, "Male Victims of Sexual Assault— Legal Issues," in Mezey and King (eds.), *Male Victims of Sexual Assault,* pp. 125–140; South African Law Commission, *Sexual Offences,* Discussion Paper 85, 12 August 1999.

19. Ross D. Parke, *Fathers* (Cambridge, Mass.: Harvard University Press, 1981), p. 79; Frank F. Furstenberg, Jr., and Andrew J. Cherlin, *Divided Families: What Happens to Children When Parents Part?* (Cambridge, Mass.: Harvard University Press, 1991), p. 31.

20. Eleanor E. Maccoby and Robert H. Mnookin, *Dividing the Child: Social and Legal Dilemmas of Custody* (Cambridge, Mass.: Harvard University Press, 1992), p. 103.

21. Ibid.

22. Ibid. p. 105.

23. Cited by Ross D. Parke, *Fathers,* pp. 81–82.

24. Ibid.

25. Emmy E. Werner and Ruth S. Smith, *Vulnerable but Invincible: A Longitudinal Study of Resilient Children and Youth* (New York: Adams Bannister Cox, 1982), p. 80.

26. Ibid. pp. 94–95.

27. In 1997–98 there were at least 39 states in which "only male homosexuality [was] targeted in law or practice." Dan Smith, *The State of the World Atlas* (London: Penguin, 1999), pp. 76–77.

28. Kath O'Donnell, "Lesbian and Gay Families," in Gill Jaggar and Caroline Wright (eds.), *Changing Family Values* (London: Routledge, 1999), pp. 77–97, at p. 90.

29. D.J. West, "Homophobia: Covert and Overt," in Mezey and King (eds.), *Male Victims of Sexual Assault,* pp. 17–34, at p. 29.

30. G. Scott, *The History of Capital Punishment* (London: Torchstream Books, 1950); David C. Baldus, George Woodworth, and Charles A. Pulaski Jr., *Equal Justice and the Death Penalty: A Legal and Empirical Analysis* (Boston: Northeastern University Press, 1990), p. 159.

31. Carol Hedderman and Mike Hough, "Does the Criminal Justice System Treat Men and Women Differently?" *Research Findings,* No. 10, Home Office Research and Statistics Department, May 1994; Christy A. Visher, "Gender, Police Arrest Decisions, and Notions of Chivalry," *Criminology* 21 (1983): 5–28; Patricia Godeke Tjaden and Claus D. Tjaden, "Differential Treatment of the Female Felon: Myth or Reality?" in M.Q. Warren (ed.), *Comparing Female and Male Offenders* (London: Sage Publications, 1981), pp. 73–88. There is conflicting evidence, however, because others have found that sex plays no part. See, for example, Imogene L. Moyer, "Demeanor, Sex, and Race in Police Processing," *Journal of Criminal Justice* 9 (1981): 235–246; and Debra A. Curan, "Judicial Discretion and Defendant's Sex," *Criminology* 21 (1983): 41–58. There is

reason to think that authors' agendas often affect the interpretation of data on this topic (as on others). A. Bottomsley and K. Pease point to this problem in their *Crime and Punishment: Interpreting the Data* (Philadelphia: Open University Press, 1986), p. 154.

32. For instance, arguing in favor of a combat exemption-exclusion for women, one representative in the U.S. House of Representatives said, "We do not want our women killed" (quoted by Judith Wagner DeCew, "The Combat Exclusion and the Role of Women in the Military," *Hypatia* 10 [1995]: 56–73, p. 62).

33. Jean Drèze and Amartya Sen, *Hunger and Public Action* (Oxford: Clarendon Press, 1989), pp. 50–59; Amartya Sen, "More Than 100 Million Women Are Missing," *New York Review of Books,* 20 December 1990, pp. 61–66. The idea has been used by, amongst others, Martha Nussbaum and Jonathan Glover in their *Women, Culture and Development* (Oxford: Clarendon Press, 1995), pp. 3, 33.

34. Sen, "More Than 100 Million Women Are Missing," p. 61.

35. Ibid.

36. Consider some research funding disparities that favor women. In 1993, for instance, the National Cancer Institute (in the U.S.A.) "budgeted $273 million for research on cancers specific to women, including breast, cervical, ovarian, and uterine cancers, and $41 million for research on cancers specific to men, including prostate and testicular cancers." Moreover, its research expenditure on breast cancer, which kills 46,000 women a year in the U.S., exceeds the amount spent on research into lung cancer, a disease that kills 93,000 men and 56,000 women annually. See Ace Allen, "Women's Health," *New England Journal of Medicine* vol. 329, 9 December 1993, p. 1816. This is not to suggest that there are no research biases that favor males. See, for example, Marcia Angel, "Caring for Women's Health—What Is the Problem?" *New England Journal of Medicine* 329 (22 July 1993): 271–272. However, the sorts of figures I have cited here show that there are some ways in which current practices might favor women and thereby explain the life-expectancy differentials of males and females.

37. Kenneth Clatterbaugh, "Are Men Oppressed?" in Larry May, Robert Strikwerda, and Patrick D. Hopkins (eds.), *Rethinking Masculinity: Philosophical Explorations in the Light of Feminism,* 2nd ed.

(Lanham, Md.: Rowman and Littlefield, 1996), pp. 289–305, at p. 301.

38. Ibid.

39. Ibid.

40. Susan Estrich, *Real Rape* (Cambridge, Mass.: Harvard University Press, 1987).

41. Because she does not mention male disadvantage, it is hard to tell whether Shulamith Firestone would take there to be any such disadvantage, and, if she does, whether she would attribute it to biology. See *The Dialectic of Sex: The Case for Feminist Revolution* (New York: William Morrow & Co., 1970). She is clearly an example of a feminist who attributes female disadvantage to biological difference between the sexes. She speaks of the "freeing of women from the tyranny of their biology" (p. 270), specifically those features associated with child-bearing and child-rearing. Although she does also speak of the "total integration of women ... into the larger society" (p. 271) and this might be thought to include all aspects of the military, she does not seem sufficiently concerned with the elimination of female advantage to explicitly endorse such an implication.

42. Steven Goldberg, *The Inevitability of Patriarchy* (New York: William Morrow & Co., 1974); Kingsley Browne, *Divided Labours: An Evolutionary View of Women at Work* (London: Weidenfeld and Nicolson, 1998); Kingsley Browne, "Women at War: An Evolutionary Perspective," *Buffalo Law Review* 49 (2001): 51–247.

43. D. J. Albert, M. L Walsh, and R. H. Jonik, "Aggression in Humans: What is its Biological Foundation?" *Neuroscience and Biobehavioral Reviews* 17 (1993): 405–425, p. 417; Ann Frodi et al. say that "[c]ommonly held hypotheses that men are almost always more physically aggressive than women and that women display more indirect or displaced aggression were not supported" ("Are Women Always Less Aggressive than Men?" p. 634).

44. See, for example, Murray Straus, "Victims and Aggressors in Marital Violence," *American Behavioral Scientist* 23 (1980): 681–704; Murray A. Straus and Richard J. Gelles, "Societal Change and Change in Family Violence from 1975 to 1985 as Revealed by Two National Surveys," *Journal of Marriage and the Family* 48 (1986): 465–179. The latter paper notes that a number of other studies have confirmed their

findings about the parity of male and female marital violence (p. 470).

45. Straus, "Victims and Aggressors in Marital Violence," p. 683.

46. Ibid., p. 684.

47. Jan E. Stets and Murray A. Straus, "The Marriage License as a Hitting License: A Comparison of Assaults in Dating, Cohabiting, and Married Couples," *Journal of Family Violence* 4 (1989): 161–180, p. 163. Jean Malone, Andrea Tyree, and K. Daniel O'Leary found that women are more likely to throw an object, slap, kick, bite, hit with a fist, and hit with an object. See "Generalization and Containment: Different Effects of Past Aggression for Wives and Husbands," *Journal of Marriage and the Family* 51 (1989): 687–697, p. 690.

48. K. Daniel O'Leary Julian Barling, Ileana Arias, Alan Rosenbaum, Jean Malone, and Andrea Tyree, "Prevalence and Stability of Physical Aggression Between Spouses: A Longitudinal Analysis," *Journal of Consulting and Clinical Psychology* 57 (1989): 263–268, pp. 264–266.

49. David B. Sugarman and Gerald T. Hotaling, "Dating Violence: A Review of Contextual and Risk Factors," in Barrie Levy (ed.), *Dating Violence: Young Women in Danger* (Seattle: Seal Press, 1991), pp. 100–118, at p. 104.

50. Murray Straus, "Victims and Aggressors in Marital Violence," p. 681; Straus and Gelles, "Societal Change and Change in Family Violence from 1975 to 1985," p. 468; O'Leary et al., "Prevalence and Stability of Physical Aggression Between Spouses," p. 267.

51. Robert T. Rubin, "The Neuroendocrinology and Neurochemistry of Antisocial Behavior," in Sarnoff A. Mednick, Terrie A. Moffit, and Susan A. Stack (eds.). *The Causes of Crime: New Biological Approaches* (Cambridge: Cambridge University Press, 1987), pp. 239–262, at p. 248.

52. Albert et al., "Aggression in Humans," p. 407–410.

53. Robert T. Rubin says "there remains a definite controversy concerning the role of androgenic hormones in human aggressive and violent behaviors ("The Neuroendocrinology and Neurochemistry of Antisocial Behavior," p. 248) and "the data on the neuroendocrine correlates of aggression and violence, with particular reference to the most thoroughly studied relation, that of testosterone in

men, are sparse and conflicting" (ibid., p. 250). D. J. Albert et al. say that "[a]ttempts to demonstrate a correlation between testosterone and aggression in humans have been in progress for almost 30 years ("Aggression in Humans," p. 406). Yet, a clear relation remains to be established," Leslie Brody says "there is very little basis to the widely accepted idea that there is a causal relationship between testosterone levels and human aggression" (*Gender, Emotion and the Family* [Cambridge, Mass.: Harvard University Press, 1999], p. 107).

54. Albert et al., "Aggression in Humans," p. 417.

55. Leslie Brody, *Gender, Emotion and the Family,* p. 111; Ruth Bleier, *Science and Gender: A Critique of Biology and Its Theories on Women* (New York: Pergamon Press, 1984), p. 97.

56. The elevated prenatal androgen levels in boys do not drop immediately at birth, but taper off in the months after birth. Thus the androgens generated in utero may continue to influence development postnatally for a few months.

57. Sheri A. Berenbaum and Susan M. Resnick, "Early Androgen Effects on Aggression in Children and Adults with Congenital Adrenal Hyperplasia," *Psychoneuroendo-chrinology* 22 (1997): 505–515.

58. Anke A. Ehrhardt and Susan W. Baker, "Fetal Androgens, Human Central Nervous System Differentiation, and Behavior Sex Differences," in Richard C Friedman, Ralph M. Richart, and Raymond L. Vande Wiele (eds.), *Sex Differences in Behavior* (Huntington, N.Y.: Robert E. Krieger Publishing Co., 1978), p. 41.

59. John Money and Anke A. Ehrhardt, *Man and Woman, Boy and Girl* (Baltimore: Johns Hopkins University Press, 1972), p. 99; John Money and Mark Schwartz, "Fetal Androgens in Early Treated Adrenogenital Syndrome of 46XX Hemaphroditism: Influence on Assertive and Aggressive Types of Behavior," *Aggressive Behavior* 2 (1976): 19–30, esp. pp. 22–23; Melissa Hines and Francine R. Kaufman, "Androgen and the Development of Human Sextypical Behavior: Rough-and-Tumble Play and Sex of Preferred Playmates in Children with Congenital Adrenal Hyperplasia (CAH)," *Child Development* 65 (1994): 1042–1053.

60. This problem is exacerbated in other studies on which the hypothesis about the prenatal influence of androgens can be tested—those on genetic (that is,

XY) boys with Androgen Insensitivity Syndrome (AIS). These children *look* like normal females.

61. Kingsley R. Browne, "Sex and Temperament in Modern Society; A Darwinian View of the Glass Ceiling and the Gender Gap," *Arizona Law Review* 37 (1995): 971–1106, pp. 1046–1047.

62. Gina M. Grimshaw, M. Philip Bryden, and Jo-Anne K. Finegan, "Relations Between Prenatal Testosterone and Cerebral Lateralization in Children," *Neuropsychology* 9 (1995): pp.68–79.

63. Albert et al., "Aggression in Humans," pp. 405–25.

64. Ibid. p. 414.

65. Jean Bethke Elshtain attributes this sort of view to Virginia Woolf (in *Three Guineas)* and Jane Addams (in *The Long Road to Woman's Memory, Peace and Bread in Time of War* and *Newer Ideals of Peace).* See Jean Bethke Elshtain, *Women and War* (Brighton: Harvester Press, 1987), p. 235.

66. See, for example, Elshtain, *Women and War,* pp. 167–169, 181, 196. See also "Women as Perpetrators," in *Truth and Reconciliation Commission of South Africa Report,* vol. 4, pp. 313–314.

67. Wini Breines and Linda Gordon, "The New Scholarship on Family Violence," *Signs: Journal of Women in Culture and Society* 8 (1983): 490–531, p. 495.

68. Many feminists ignore the question of drafting females. However, feminists were challenged to comment on the matter when the United States Supreme Court considered a sex-discrimination challenge to the males-only draft. The National Organization for Women expressed support for drafting females. Other feminist groups, however, opposed drafting females. See DeCew, "The Combat Exclusion and the Role of Women in the Military," p. 72.

69. Sometimes it is referred to simply as a combat *exclusion.* However, that way of referring to the matter, suggests that it only disadvantages women. I prefer exemption-exclusion because that also incorporates reference to a way in which (most) women are advantaged by not being sent into combat.

70. For a good outline of and response to a number of different arguments see DeCew, "Women, Equality, and the Military," pp. 123–144.

71. Lest it be suggested otherwise, there are at least some places where racial discrimination is worse than sex discrimination. Apartheid South Africa was one particularly obvious example.

72. *Truth and Reconciliation Commission of South Africa Report,* vol. 4, pp. 289–290.

73. See Anne M. Coughlin, "Excusing Women," *California Law Review* 82 (1994): 1–93.

74. Cynthia Enloe, "Some of the Best Soldiers Wear Lipstick," in Alison M. Jaggar (ed.), *Living With Contradictions: Controversies in Feminist Social Ethics* (Boulder: Westview Press, 1994), pp. 599–608, at p. 603 (my emphasis).

75. Ibid.

76. Judith Hicks Stiehm, "The Protected, the Protector, the Defender," in Jaggar (ed.), *Living With Contradictions,* pp. 582–592, at p. 585.

77. Ibid.

78. Ibid. p. 583.

79. Cameron A. Mustard, Patricia Kaufert, Anita Kozyrskyj, and Teresa Mayer, "Sex Differences in the Use of Health Care Services," *New England Journal of Medicine* 338, no. 23 (4 June 1998): 1678–1683, p. 1678.

80. Jennifer Haas, "The Cost of Being a Woman," in ibid., pp. 1694–1695.

81. Ibid. p. 1694.

82. Ibid. p. 1695.

83. See Christina Hoff Sommers' accounts of and rejection of this argument: "The Wellesley Report: A Gender at Risk," in her *Who Stole Feminism?* (New York: Simon & Schuster, 1994), pp. 157–187; "The War Against Boys," *The Atlantic Monthly,* May 2000, pp. 59–74. The details in this paragraph are drawn from these sources.

84. Sommers, *Who Stole Feminism?* p. 161.

85. Nijole V. Benokraitis and Joe R. Feagin, *Modern Sexism: Blatant, Subtle and Covert Discrimination,* 2nd ed. (Englewood Cliffs, N.J.: Prentice-Hall, 1995), p. 40.

86. Paralleling the little boy who cried "wolf," this is a case of what we might call the little girl who cried "wolf-whistle."

87. This view is taken by Kenneth Clatterbaugh, "Are Men Oppressed?"

88. Ibid.

89. An anonymous reviewer has kindly pointed out that this sort of argument might be applied against a view, mentioned earlier, that more health-care resources should be directed to women in order to

improve the quality of the extra years of life they have over men. Since the disadvantage (a lower quality of life in the extra years) is a cost of the advantage (the extra years of life) there is no ground for complaint according to this argument.

90. Some advocates of this view think that the burden of proof lies with those who would deny such connections. (See Clatterbaugh, "Are Men Oppressed?" p. 300.) My own view is that when it comes to unequal and discriminatory treatment, the burden of proof lies with those who seek to defend or condone such treatment.

91. Those who seek to claim that girls are benefited by the procedure, because without it they would be ostracized, fail to notice that that ostracism is just the sort of pressure that reinforces the societal norms.

92. Many feminists seem oblivious to the evidence that women have penetrated traditionally male professions more successfully than men have broken into traditionally female professions. Kenneth Clatterbaugh ("Are Men Oppressed?"), for example, in arguing against the claim that men are oppressed, suggests that the restrictions of a gender role do not constitute oppression unless the restrictions are imposed because of a perceived lack of abilities (which he thinks is not true in the case of restrictions

on males). He says that whereas young women are told they *cannot* be doctors, young men are being told that although they *could* be nurses it would be unworthy of them. But the evidence of men's and women's actual success in entering into professions traditionally reserved for the opposite sex suggests that today in Western societies, women *can* become doctors. Only the paranoid could think otherwise. Even if it is still true that men are not being told that they *cannot* become nurses, and even if they are not thereby being oppressed, it is still true that some individual men are *unfairly disadvantaged* (in ways that women are not) by societal pressures that militate against their becoming nurses.

93. Janet Radcliffe Richards, "Separate Spheres," in Peter Singer (ed.), *Applied Ethics* (Oxford: Oxford University Press, 1986), pp. 185–214, at p. 198.

94. I say "generally" because there are some men who have wanted to change places with women, and not because of a so-called "gender-identity disorder." Men dressing in women's clothing in order to secure places on life-boats is one example.

95. For helpful comments on earlier versions of this paper I am grateful to members of my family, Stephen Nathanson, and anonymous reviewers for *Social Theory and Practice*.

35

The Wolf Again in Sheep's Clothing

JAMES P. STERBA

Regarding sexism against men as the neglected sexism, David Benatar looks forward to the day when there is at least as much research being directed at uncovering sexism against men as has been devoted in the past to uncovering sexism against women. If James P. Sterba's analysis in this article is correct, however, and Benatar's main example of discrimination against men—the combat exclusion of women—is really a form of discrimination against women with its costs of dominance, then surely Benatar's expectations in this regard are not likely to be fulfilled.

David Benatar believes that men in society are discriminated against just because they are men in the same way that women in society are discriminated against just because they are women. He calls this discrimination the "second sexism."[1] To show that this discrimination exists and deserves to be condemned, Benatar starts with a number of examples. He then seeks to explain and criticize the attitudes that he claims underlie these examples and to respond to objections to considering them anything but unjustified discrimination against men.

Benatar's main example of discrimination against men is the widespread restriction of combat to men, especially at the present time. Even today, when women are either free to join the military or are sometimes conscripted into it, Benatar observes, they are still generally restricted from serving in combat roles. In my comments, I will mainly limit myself to evaluating Benatar's claim for a second sexism by focusing on his main example, this restriction of combat to men, an example to which he returns time and time again throughout his paper. What I will show is that the restriction of combat to men is a clear example of discrimination against

women, not one of discrimination against men; I will show that this is a case where "the wolf" of discrimination against women for the benefit of men is falsely presented in "the sheep's clothing" as really being for the benefit of women. The implication of my comments is that if Benatar's argument fails with regard to his main example, then it fails for his other examples as well.

1.

Benatar thinks that three attitudes underlie the widespread restriction of combat to men. The first is that male life is often less valued than female life. The second is a greater social acceptance of nonfatal violence against males. The third is the assumption that men are more (naturally) aggressive.

But at least in the U.S. military, the first two attitudes cannot underlie the U.S. restriction of combat roles to men given what we know about current conflicts. For example, in the 1991 Gulf War, it was predicted that the casualty rate would be higher among the noncombatant troops in the

Reprinted from *Social Theory and Practice*, Vol. 29, No. 2, (April 2003) by permission. For David Benatar's repsonse to this and other criticism, see his "The Second Sexism, a Second Time," in *Social Theory and Practice*, Vol. 29, No. 2, April 2003, pp. 275–296.

rear than in the all-male combat units deployed on the border of Kuwait. Not only was it expected that the concentration of noncombatant troops in the rear would make a more productive target for Iraq's errant Scuds, but these forces would also be the favored target for any missile armed with chemical or nerve agents. This is because given the storms and winds of the desert, it would be too dangerous for the Iraqis to use such agents near their own front-line troops. Though Iraq never used its arsenal of chemical and biological weapons in the Gulf War, this prediction was borne out: more than half of the U.S. deaths in the Gulf War were among noncombatant troops.[2] So at least in the U.S. military, given what we know about current conflicts (and the same would seem to hold for other modern militaries that allow women to serve among noncombatant support troops), it cannot be that restricting combat to men is a recognizable way of limiting either lethal or non-lethal casualties among women serving in the military.

But what about the assumption that men are more (naturally) aggressive than women? Unlike the first two attitudes that Benatar cites, which could not even be believed to underlie the restriction of combat to men under current conditions, this assumption could be regarded as supporting the combat restriction to men. Yet, as Benatar goes on to argue, and here I agree with him completely, the assumption that men are more (naturally) aggressive than women cannot be reasonably maintained. Benatar cites evidence showing that, at least within families, women are just as violent (although they inflict less injury) as men are.[3] He also cites studies that show that there is no consistent link between testosterone and violence, and other studies that show that there is no difference in aggression levels between girls who are exposed to unusually high levels of androgens in utero and those who are not. He further argues that "even if men are naturally more aggressive than women, it does not follow that women are not aggressive enough for military purposes or that they cannot be subject to environmental influences that would make them so" (194). Again, on this point, Benatar and I agree.

Benatar also argues against the exclusion of women from combat on grounds that they have "less strength, stamina, and muscle than men" (195). He points out that much combat activity today does not require strength. Even if it did, he argues that would not be a reason for excluding all women. Surely some women are stronger than some men are. So if strength were really what counted, then strength, and not sex, would be the appropriate criterion.

Here, too, Benatar and I agree. He could have also pointed to numerous examples of male-dominated activities where women have met or exceeded all the physically desirable requirements for those activities, but where they were still excluded from participating. For example, in 1961, NASA invited women pilots to join the race for space against the Russians. Jerrie Cobb, a professional pilot who had logged 7,000 hours in the air, accepted the invitation. She floated for 9 hours and 40 minutes in a pitch-dark isolation tank before hallucinating; male subjects who tested before her had lasted only 4 hours and 30 minutes. Mary Wallace Funk, the holder of several world records in flying, beat John Glenn on the stress tests, bicycle analysis tests, and lung power tests. She also beat Wally Shirra on the vertigo test while setting a record in the bicycle endurance test, and the isolation test, where she lasted 10 hours and 30 minutes before hallucinating. But then without explanation, NASA cancelled the women's tests, with the consequence that male astronauts rocketed into our history books while more qualified women were denied their due.[4]

Moreover, the idea that women cannot withstand the G-forces of combat flying is widely known to be false. Indeed, there is now available a solid body of evidence that women's physiology makes them more tolerant of G-forces than men. According to a U.S. Air Force study done in 1991, because women are smaller on average than men, the shorter distance between their hearts and their brains made it easier for their hearts to counteract the G-forces trying to draw blood out of the brain and keep the brain supplied with blood. So, in this regard, women are, on average, clearly more physically qualified than men to be fighter pilots, which is one of the most prestigious combat positions in the U.S. military.[5]

Yet obviously not all women meet or exceed the physical qualifications of men in all branches of the military. In the U.S. Army, for example, only 32% of women can meet or exceed the minimum male test scores on the Army Physical Fitness Test. Nevertheless, an Army study of forty-one women showed that 78% of the women in the study qualified for "very heavy" military jobs after six months of weight-lifting, jogging with 75-pound backpacks, and performing squats with 100-pound barrels on their shoulders.[6] Given that girls raised in the U.S. are usually two years behind boys in learning the skills needed for physical competence, it is surprising what such catch-up programs are able to accomplish.[7]

Sometimes, Benatar notes, the combat restriction to men is defended as a way of protecting women from a greater risk of being raped if captured by enemy forces. Benatar rejects this justification for the combat restriction, as I do, noting the significant risks men endure in combat and when they are captured. However, what is interesting to note in this regard is that men seem more worried about the risks to women than women are themselves.[8] Nor is their concern about these risks to women all that altruistic. For example, in the final report of the U.S. presidential commission to study the combat restriction to men in 1992, every argument against women in combat focused upon the pain women's capture would cause, not to the women themselves, but rather to their male colleagues. "The mistreatment of women taken as POWs could have a negative impact on male captives," warned one rationale against using women in ground combat. "The presence of women might cause additional morale problems for male prisoners," claimed another argument against employing women in combat.[9] Surely, a restriction that is justified on the basis of its benefits to men cannot be a form of discrimination against men.

2.

Benatar considers four main objections to his case for a second sexism. The first is a "no-discrimination argument," which simply denies that there is sexual

discrimination against men. The second is a "distraction argument," which grants that men are sometimes the victims of sex discrimination, but then argues that attending to these forms of discrimination will *distract* us from the greater discrimination against women. The third is an "inversion argument," which maintains that Benatar's examples of discrimination against men are really examples of discrimination against women. The fourth is a "costs-of-dominance argument," which maintains that although there may indeed be costs of being a man, these costs come from being the privileged sex and thus are costs of dominance.

Since I completely reject Benatar's argument for a second sexism, I must also reject his distraction argument because that argument concedes that there are some forms of sexual discrimination against men. Nevertheless, I will take up the other three objections that Benatar considers. Here I will deny that there is any systematic discrimination against men simply because they are men. I will also contend that what Benatar claims are instances of discrimination against men are really instances of discrimination against women, and I further maintain that the costs of being a man are really the costs of domination.

Benatar thinks that someone who endorses the inversion argument and holds that his examples of discrimination against men are really examples of discrimination against women must also hold that discrimination against women has no costs for men, and so they must reject the costs-of-dominance argument and deny that there are costs to being a man that are the costs of domination. But I see nothing inconsistent in maintaining both arguments and holding that discrimination against women can have its costs.

Let me begin with the inversion argument, the argument that maintains that what Benatar claims are instances of discrimination against men are really instances of discrimination against women, focusing (as I am throughout) on Benatar's main example of the restriction of combat to men. In discussing the inversion argument, Benatar allows that excluding women from combat does disadvantage some women, yet he thinks that to focus on these disadvantages is "to ignore the much greater disadvantage suffered by vast numbers of men who are forced into combat against their wills" (199).

But where today are these vast numbers of men who are forced into combat against their wills, especially in contemporary liberal democracies? If we look to the U.S. and the U.K., countries that both have strong feminist movements promoting women's rights and that have actually recently committed their military forces to combat, we see that they rely on volunteer military forces.[10] In today's world, neither the U.S. nor the U.K. force any men into combat against their will, unless we take the lack of more desirable civilian job opportunities to be a form of coercion.

More significantly, those who seem to be most opposed to eliminating the combatant restriction to men are those men who have voluntarily joined these contemporary militaries. Thus, opposition to women even being in the U.S. military let alone serving in combat remains high among male colleagues. For example, 45% of first-year midshipmen at the U.S. Naval Academy expressed the view that women did not belong in the military, and 38% of fourth-year midshipmen felt the same.[11]

The same view can be found among the highest commanders in the U.S. military. For example, Air Force Chief General Merrill McPeak testified before the Senate Arms Services Committee in 1991 that if he had to choose between a qualified woman and a less qualified man to fill a combat role, he would go with the man. "I admit it does not make much sense but that is the way I feel about it," McPeak responded.[12] A similar view was expressed by another U.S. general:

> War is a man's work. Biological conver-
> gence on the battlefield (women serving
> in combat) would not only be dissatisfying
> in terms of what women could do, but
> it would be an enormous psychological
> distraction for the male, who wants to think
> that he's fighting for that woman some-
> where behind, not up there in the same
> foxhole with him. It tramples the male ego.
> When you get right down to it, you have to
> protect the manhood of war.[13]

Or as retired Army Chief of Staff General William Westmoreland once put it, "No man with gumption wants a woman to fight his nation's battles."[14]

However, Benatar has an explanation for why men in the military, even those men who have voluntarily joined the military, are so opposed to lifting the combat restriction for women, and thus seem so deluded about what is really for their own good. According to Benatar, their support for combat exclusion should be understood as analogous to the support for clitoridectomy found among women who perform these genital excisions on little girls. Since many feminists would maintain that clitoridectomy is a form of sexual discrimination that favors male interests, even though most of the actual genital excisions are performed by women, why then could not the exclusion of women from combat be a form of discrimination against men, even when it is the men in the military who strongly uphold that exclusion?

While there is a surface similarity between the two cases, their underlying reality is quite different. First, where it is practiced, there is strong male support for clitoridectomy that explains why there is female support for it, even among women who actually perform the genital excisions. Where the practice exists, men want the women they marry to have a clitoridectomy because it eliminates or reduces the pleasure women feel from sexual intercourse, and thus is thought to reduce the likelihood that women will be unfaithful in their marriages. Here men's interests are driving the whole practice; women's interest in clitoridectomy is derivative from the interest men have in the practice.

The role of the restriction of combat to men in the U.S. and the U.K. (liberal democratic countries that both have strong feminist movements promoting women's rights and have actually recently committed their military forces to combat) is quite different. Men voluntarily join the militaries in these countries knowing about the restriction of combat to men. If men don't want to engage in combat, they either don't have to join up or they can join up but then request service in the noncombat units of the military. By contrast, women have no comparable option. If they don't want to serve in combat, they can do that by just not joining the military at all. If they do join up, however, they lack the option that men have of serving in combat units if they want to do so. So it is hard to see how the restriction of combat to men that so limits the freedom of women could still serve the interest of women, given that men, like women, have the option of avoiding the risks of combat altogether by simply not joining the military. It is true that serving in combat could lead to one's death or injury, but, as we have noted before, serving in noncombat units in the military can have comparable or even greater risks of such losses.

In addition, many attractive roles and jobs involve risks of injury that many less attractive roles and jobs lack. Consider the injuries associated with professional sports. Surely, we cannot reasonably maintain that those who play such sports and accept the risk of injury involved are really not serving their own interests but the interests of their promoters and spectators— that they are in fact being discriminated against by the way the practice is structured. Of course, it can be argued that the players' long-term interests are not as well served by the practice of professional sports as are the interests of the promoters and spectators, but as long as those who play professional sports can avoid any such risk of injury by not playing professional sports at all, it is hard to see how those who choose to do so are discriminated against by the practice.[15]

An even more exact analogy to the situation of women and the combat restriction to men would be the situation of blacks before they were allowed to participate in the American Baseball Leagues in 1947. If the exclusion of women from combat in today's all-volunteer military forces is to be understood as a benefit to women because of the risks of injury such combat service would involve, then the exclusion of blacks from the American Baseball Leagues before 1947, with all the risks of injury such participation involved, would have to be regarded as a benefit to blacks! But clearly no one thinks this exclusion of blacks from the American Baseball Leagues before 1947 was a benefit to blacks, and so no one should think that the exclusion of women from combat in all-volunteer military forces is a benefit to women.

Accordingly, there is no similarity between support women provide for the practice of clitoridectomy, and the support men provide for the combat exclusion of women in modern volunteer military forces. While men can always avoid the risks of combat by not joining these military forces, or by opting out of combat service if they do join, it is very difficult for women or young girls to opt out of the practice of clitoridectomy in countries where the practice is in place.[16]

Turning to the costs-of-dominance argument, clearly the domination of women has its costs, but it also has its benefits. In modern volunteer militaries, like those of the U.S. and the U.K., serving in combat units is career-enhancing in a way that serving in noncombat units is not. Denying women access to combat roles denies women access to the most prestigious positions in the military, and thus hinders their promotion within it.

In this context, it is important to understand that even the opening up of noncombat roles in the U.S. military to women was not embarked upon as an effort to achieve social equality. Rather, the U.S. Defense Department turned to women into order to save the All-Volunteer Force.[17] The women drawn to military service were smarter and better educated than the men. For example, according to one study, over 90% of women recruited had high school diplomas compared to 63% of the men, and women also scored ten points higher on service exams.[18] In addition, proportionately more female than male cadets have been selected as Rhodes and Marshall Scholars, and proportionately more women entering West Point have been National Honor Society members and high school valedictorians and salutatorians in all but two years since integration in 1976.[19] As one U.S. Defense Department report put it, "The tradeoff in today's recruiting market is between a high quality female and a low quality male."[20]

Of course, women are subject to pregnancy and motherhood, but statistically these have not been much of a problem in the military.[21] In fact, men suffer a higher absentee rate because of disciplinary problems and substance abuse.[22] So when women's strengths and weaknesses are taken into account compared to those of men, women turn out to be highly qualified for many combat and noncombat roles within the military.

A new-found recognition of women's qualifications has led the U.S. Air Force to open up 99% of its positions to women, the U.S. Navy to open up 90% of its positions to women, including all of its combat fighter positions, and the U.S. Army to open up 91% of its positions to women.[23] But there is still resistance to opening up all combat positions in the U.S. military to qualified women. Women are still prohibited from direct combat, and from units that operate behind lines (e.g., all Special Forces units), and from the existing classes of submarines because of the prohibitive cost of ensuring male and female berthing privacy requirements on these vessels.[24] The argument that is often given for retaining most of these restrictions is that of public opinion:

> What we have learned is that the American public is willing to tolerate, indeed supports putting women in combat aircraft; the American public is willing to support putting women in combat vessels; that the American public is very, very reluctant about the idea of women engaging in hand-to-hand combat.[25]

But here the leadership of the U.S. military is clearly reading its own views into public opinion, because as early as 1990, after the U.S. incursion into Panama, a *CBS/New York Times* poll asked: "Do you think women members of the armed forces should be allowed to serve in combat if they want to?" Of those polled, 72% answered "yes." Only 26% answered "no."[26]

To see what allowing women to take on the risks of combat can do, consider the example of Eritrea. In Eritrea's long-drawn-out war with Ethiopia, Eritrean girls learned to use weapons and studied military tactics and survival techniques. When they were old enough, they fought alongside men at the front. As a consequence, young Eritrean women today have powerful role models in their mothers, who fought in this thirty-year-long war of independence from Ethiopia that was won in 1991. After the war, women were able to enter the National Assembly and other political positions for the first time. Today, the ambassador to the European Union and the ministers of justice and labor are all women. It is harder to prevent women from occupying positions of social and political power once they have served their country in combat.[27]

To see the effects of excluding women from combat, consider the case of Israel.[28] In Israel today, both women and men are required to serve in the IDF (Israel Defense Force), but women are generally excluded from combat roles. Thus, 70% of women in the military are assigned to secretarial jobs. Men's willingness to sacrifice their lives for their country confirms their status as good citizens and provides them with "symbolic capital" that they then carry with them into civilian life. The good citizen is the retired soldier or officer who can prove his service to his country by having served in combat. Having served in combat is an important part of one's résumé when applying for almost any job. For example, being a colonel with combat experience is more important than being an educator when applying for a lucrative school principal position. Combat experience, so useful in the general market, is even more useful in the political arena. Accordingly, a retired general (or any high-ranking officer) has almost instant access to high-level political positions. These are the benefits that men reap because of their combat experience in the Israeli military, but that women are denied because they are kept from combat experience in that same military.

Of course, Benatar does not deny that women are discriminated against by being excluded from combat; he just wants to claim that men are discriminated against too, and that this discrimination against men occurs even in the most ardently anti-female sexist societies. In his view, the very stereotypes that underlie sexism against women also support sexism against men. So it looks as if, on his view, it is not possible to discriminate against women without also discriminating against men at the same time. How can this be?

It is clear that there are some costs to men from a system of discrimination against women. No one denies this. This is the starting point for the costs-of-dominance argument. But then Benatar goes on to claim that these costs themselves amount to a form of discrimination against men. Now what is important to recognize here is that the costs of dominance are not borne equally by all men. Some men, to return to Benatar's main example, suffer very little from combat duty, and then go on to become high-ranking officers and later important government officials, while other men are killed. Benatar is focused on the latter—those men who sacrifice their lives in the wars that are fought under patriarchal systems. Surely, such men have not benefited overall from the patriarchy of their societies.[29] Why then cannot we say that such men have been unfairly disadvantaged, and isn't that just the same as saying that they have suffered from discrimination?

Without a doubt some men are disadvantaged overall by a patriarchal system, but it doesn't follow that they have suffered from discrimination. It certainly does not follow that such men have been discriminated against in the same way that women have been discriminated against in a patriarchal society. In a patriarchal society, women are discriminated against on the basis of their sex, but the men who become "cannon fodder"[30] in a patriarchal society are not discriminated against on the basis of their sex. This is because the overall design of a patriarchal society is to benefit men generally, not to discriminate against any of them. The problem with any such patriarchal society, however, is that it is unable to benefit overall *every* male participant. Some men will lose out in a system designed for the overall benefit of men. Yet what is important to recognize is that those who lose out do not lose out simply because they are men. Instead, they lose out, for example, because they lack such and such survival skills or because they are unlucky in a system generally designed for their benefit. The disadvantage they suffer is not part of a system that seeks to disadvantage them simply because they are men. By contrast, women do suffer from a system that seeks to disadvantage them simply because they are women.

Needless to say, if men who become "cannon fodder" were not in a patriarchal society, they may not go on to suffer the disadvantages that are inflicted upon them in such a society. But that does not show that the disadvantages they suffer are the result of a system that seeks to disadvantage them simply because they are men. That is the distinctive nature of the disadvantage that women suffer from in patriarchal societies. It is that disadvantage that sexual discrimination, or discrimination on the basis of one's sex, is all about.

Now it may be the case that both women and men would do better overall if they were in a society premised on equality, as John Stuart Mill and Harriet Taylor seem to have held,[31] or it may even be the case that some women are better off in a patriarchal society than they would be in an egalitarian one. But none of this shows that the disadvantages that some or all men suffer in patriarchal societies—the costs of dominance—can be redescribed as a form of discrimination against men akin to the discrimination women suffer simply because they are women. They are just different sorts of disadvantages. One is the regrettable side-effect of a system designed to generally benefit all men. The other is the foreseeable and/or intended direct effect of a system designed to generally harm or deny benefits to all women.[32]

Having thus defended the inversion argument and the costs-of-dominance argument against Benatar's claim that men have been discriminated against for the benefit of women, I cannot very well go on to defend his no-discrimination argument, which seeks to explain the exclusion of women from combat in some nondiscriminatory way. Now that I have shown that the exclusion of women from combat is due either to discrimination against women or to the costs of that discrimination, I cannot go on to give a nondiscriminatory explanation for that very same exclusion.

3.

Before concluding, however, I would like to briefly consider one nonmilitary example of what Benatar considers to be discrimination against men. It is what he refers to as the "missing men" problem which is supposed to be analogous to Amartya Sen and Jean Drèze's "missing women" problem (184). Sen and Drèze argue that in societies in which men and women are treated equally in ways relevant to mortality, there is a female-male ratio of 1.05 to 1, whereas in South Asia, West Asia, and China the ratio is .94 to 1 or lower. According to Sen and Drèze, the 11% difference between these ratios shows that there are missing women, women whose lives have been ended by discrimination, totaling about 100 million women. Benatar then argues analogously that since the female-male birth ratio is actually .95 to 1, we should also recognize a larger number of missing men in societies where the female-male ratio is transformed to 1.05 to 1.

But if we recognize that there are missing men, does this mean we have to deny that there are missing women? Anyway, how could there be missing women, on Benatar's analysis, given that the female-male birth rate of .95 to 1 is almost identical to the female-male ratio of .94 to 1 found in South Asia, West Asia, and China? Doesn't this show on his analysis that there is no discrimination against women in these countries and, hence, no missing women there? Yet, Benatar does not seem to want to draw this conclusion.

Of course, Benatar could accept Sen and Drèze's estimate of a 100 million missing women on the grounds that we know quite a bit about the widespread practices of discrimination used in South Asia, West Asia, and China directed at limiting the number of female children. It was not until Sen and Drèze did their analysis, however, that we were able to put an overall number on the impact of that discrimination—100 million missing women. So while Benatar could grant that Sen and Drèze have shown that there are 100 million missing women, it is clear that he still wants to hold that there are millions of missing men as well. He thinks that this is the case because in countries where the female-male ratio is 1.05 to 1, it has dropped 10% from the .95 to 1 female-male birth ratio. In such countries, Benatar argues, not enough is being done to maintain the female-male birth ratio, and this constitutes discrimination against men.

But how do we know from a female-male ratio of 1.05 to 1 that not enough is being done to maintain the female-male birth ratio? What if the 1.05 female/male ratio already represents considerable

intervention to maintain the birth ratio, such that without that intervention the female-male ratio would have dropped even further to, say, 1.15 to 1? Actually, there is considerable evidence that until very recently this may have been just what was taking place. Until the U.S. Congress passed the National Institutes of Health Revitalization Act in 1993, which mandated the inclusion of women and minorities in U.S. medical research, women tended to be neglected in both basic and clinical research.[33] Since women were not researched along with the men, it was not discovered for years that women differed from men in symptoms, patterns of disease development, and reactions to treatment. One consequence of this is that adverse reactions to drugs occur twice as often in women as they do in men on whom the drugs were initially tested. Only recently has this long-standing pattern of medical research and treatment favoring men over women begun to be recognized and exposed. The general response, at least in the U.S., to the recognition of this pattern of medical research and treatment has not been to devote even more resources to preserving the female-male birth ratio, but rather has been to broaden research and treatment so that it now more fairly takes into account the interests of women along with men. Benatar needs to show why this is not the right approach to be taken to medical research and treatment today if he wants to establish that there exists discrimination against men in this area, and this he clearly has not done.

The only response that Benatar gives at this point is to claim that "feminists" would not endorse the same sort of view if the data on the female/male birth data were reversed and more females were dying off in societies that clearly were not discriminating against women. But if the data were so reversed, I, for one, would endorse the very same view that I endorsed above on the basis of the existing data. Moreover, most feminists, I think, would agree with me here, which then appears to leave Benatar flailing against an imaginary opponent.

In 1952, Simone de Beauvoir published *The Second Sex,* a book that in time became the bible of the second wave of feminism. Nevertheless, Beauvoir's work was initially greeted with a great deal of skepticism, not unlike the skepticism that is likely to greet the publication of David Benatar's "The Second Sexism." Regarding sexism against men as the neglected sexism, Benatar looks forward to the day when there is at least as much research being directed at uncovering sexism against men as has been devoted in the past to uncovering sexism against women. If my analysis in this essay is correct, however, and Benatar's main example of discrimination against men—the combat exclusion of women—is really a form of discrimination against women with its costs of dominance, then surely Benatar's expectations in this regard are not likely to be fulfilled.[34]

ENDNOTES

1. David Benatar, "The Second Sexism," *Social Theory and Practice* 29 (2003): 177–210. Page numbers in parentheses in the text refer to this paper.

2. See Linda Bird Francke, *Ground Zero: The Gender Wars in the Military* (New York: Simon & Schuster, 1997), p. 74.

3. Yet, although women are just as violent as men within families, some evidence suggests that their violence may be initiated more in self-defense. See Daniel G. Saunders, "Other Truths' about Domestic Violence," *Social Work* 33 (1988): 179–183.

4. Francke, *Ground Zero*, pp. 225–26. Similarly, when Barbara Winters became a finalist at the Acapulco cliff-diving championships, she was promptly disqualified from further jumping—for "her own protection," she was told. The men had complained about having to compete against her. "This is death-defying activity," one male diver protested, "What would be the point if everyone saw that a woman could do the same." Collette Dowling, *The Frailty Myth* (New York: Random House, 2000), p. 194.

5. Francke, *Ground Zero*, p. 236.

6. Francke, *Ground Zero*, p. 248.

7. Dowling, *The Frailty Myth*, p. 54. Interestingly, before puberty boys are neither taller nor heavier than girls (p. 64). Accordingly, one wonders whether if girls were given the same opportunities for physical development as boys, then, as women they would have the same physical accomplishments as men.

8. Francke, *Ground Zero*, pp. 253–254.

9. Ibid., p. 254,

10. There are still many countries today with conscripted military forces, but if we are to imagine that women in particular countries have managed to fashion the military to serve their interests, surely they must have succeeded in doing so in countries that are most strongly committed to enhancing the cause of women and where there is a fairly strong likelihood that members of the military of those countries would engage in combat. That is why Benatar's account of discrimination against men in the military must hold of both the U.S. and the U.K., and why we are not tempted to infer that women have managed to fashion the military to serve in their interest in countries where there are conscripted military forces but no tradition of promoting women's rights.

11. Francke, *Ground Zero*, p. 187.

12. Ibid. p. 232,

13. Marysia Zalewski and Jane Parpart, *The "Man" Question in International Relations* (Boulder: Westview Press, 1998), p. 1.

14. Francke, *Ground Zero*, p. 23.

15. Again, it may be that many would-be players have few viable options but to play professional sports. In that case, the practice would be correctly regarded as discriminating against them.

16. It won't do here for Benatar to respond that all he wanted to show by the analogy is that it is possible for a practice that does not favor a group to be defended by some members of that group. What Benatar needs to establish is a close analogy between the clitoridectomy case and the case of combat exclusion of women, and this I have argued he cannot do.

17. Francke, *Ground Zero*, p. 16.

18. Ibid.

19. Ibid., p. 198.

20. Ibid., p. 16.

21. Ibid., pp. 108–109.

22. Ibid.

23. See http//wwwmanbe.com/news/645542.asp

24. DACOWITS (The Defense Advisory Committee on Women in the Services) has recommended that the U.S. Navy redesign its VIRGINIA class submarines to accommodate mixed male and female crews before this class of submarines comes into full production. See http://dtic.mil/ docowits/Fall-2000_IssueBk_ForceDEv. html

25. Les Aspin, Secretary of Defense, Press Briefing on the New Role of Women in Combat, 13 January 1994.

26. Francke, *Ground Zero*, p. 71.

27. Dowling, *The Frailty Myth*, p. 12.

28. Sigal Benporath, "Feminism Under Fire" (Princeton University, unpublished manuscript).

29. Even in a patriarchical society that was classless and nonracist (which is hard to imagine), there might still be *some* men who would not benefit overall from the patriarchy of such a society.

30. See Kenneth Clatterbaugh, *Contemporary Perspectives on Masculinity, Men, Women, and Politics in Modern Society* (Boulder: Westview Press, 1997), p. 75.

31. See Maria Morales, *Perfect Equality: John Stuart Mill and Well-Constructed Communities* (Lanham, Md.: Rowman & Littlefield, 1996).

32. Of course, in a patriarchical society, the system that disadvantages men as a regrettable side-effect and the system that disadvantages women as a foreseeable and/or intended direct effect are one and the same system.

33. Londa Schiebinger, *Has Feminism Changed Science?* (Cambridge, Mass.: Harvard University Press, 1999).

34. I wish to thank David Benatar and my partner and colleague Janet Kourany for helpful comments and discussion of an earlier draft of this paper.

36

The Beijing Declaration
and Platform for Action

1. We, the Governments participating in the Fourth World Conference on Women,

2. Gathered here in Beijing in September 1995, the year of the fiftieth anniversary of the founding of the United Nations,

3. Determined to advance the goals of equality, development and peace for all women everywhere in the interest of all humanity,

4. Acknowledging the voices of all women every where and taking note of the diversity of women and their roles and circumstances, honouring the women who paved the way and inspired by the hope present in the world's youth,

5. Recognize that the status of women has advanced in some important respects in the past decade but that progress has been uneven, inequalities between women and men have persisted and major obstacles remain, with serious consequences for the well-being of all people,

6. Also recognize that this situation is exacerbated by the increasing poverty that is affecting the lives of the majority of the world's people, in particular women and children, with origins in both the national and international domains,

7. Dedicate ourselves unreservedly to addressing these constraints and obstacles and thus enhancing further the advancement and empowerment of women all over the world, and agree that this requires urgent action in the spirit of determination, hope, cooperation and solidarity, now and to carry us forward into the next century.

We reaffirm our commitment to:

8. The equal rights and inherent human dignity of women and men and other purposes and principles enshrined in the Charter of the United Nations, to the Universal Declaration of Human Rights and other international human rights instruments, in particular the Convention on the Elimination of All Forms of Discrimination against Women and the Convention on the Rights of the Child, as well as the Declaration on the Elimination of Violence against Women and the Declaration on the Right to Development;

9. Ensure the full implementation of the human rights of women and of the girl child as an inalienable, integral and indivisible part of all human rights and fundamental freedoms;

10. Build on consensus and progress made at previous United Nations conferences and summits—on women in Nairobi in 1985, on children in New York in 1990, on environment and development in Rio de Janeiro in 1992, on human rights in Vienna in 1993, on population and development in Cairo in 1994 and on social development in Copenhagen in 1995 with the objective of achieving equality, development and peace;

11. Achieve the full and effective implementation of the Nairobi Forward-looking Strategies for the Advancement of Women;

12. The empowerment and advancement of women, including the right to freedom of thought, conscience, religion and belief, thus contributing to

the moral, ethical, spiritual and intellectual needs of women and men, individually or in community with others and thereby guaranteeing them the possibility of realizing their full potential in society and shaping their lives in accordance with their own aspirations.

We are convinced that:

13. Women's empowerment and their full participation on the basis of equality in all spheres of society, including participation in the decision-making process and access to power, are fundamental for the achievement of equality, development and peace;

14. Women's rights are human rights;

15. Equal rights, opportunities and access to resources, equal sharing of responsibilities for the family by men and women, and a harmonious partnership between them are critical to their well-being and that of their families as well as to the consolidation of democracy;

16. Eradication of poverty based on sustained economic growth, social development, environmental protection and social justice requires the involvement of women in economic and social development, equal opportunities and the full and equal participation of women and men as agents and beneficiaries of people-centered sustainable development;

17. The explicit recognition and reaffirmation of the right of all women to control all aspects of their health, in particular their own fertility, is basic to their empowerment;

18. Local, national, regional and global peace is attainable and is inextricably linked with the advancement of women, who are a fundamental force for leadership, conflict resolution and the promotion of lasting peace at all levels;

19. It is essential to design, implement and monitor, with the full participation of women, effective, efficient and mutually reinforcing gender-sensitive policies and programmes, including development policies and programmes, at all levels that will foster the empowerment and advancement of women;

20. The participation and contribution of all actors of civil society, particularly women's groups and networks and other non-governmental organizations and community-based organizations, with full

respect for their autonomy, in cooperation with Governments, are important to the effective implementation and follow-up of the Platform for Action;

21. The implementation of the Platform for Action requires commitment from Governments and the international community. By making national and international commitments for action, including those made at the Conference, Governments and the international community recognize the need to take priority action for the empowerment and advancement of women.

We are determined to:

22. Intensify efforts and actions to achieve the goals of the Nairobi Forward-looking Strategies for the Advancement of Women by the end of this century;

23. Ensure the full enjoyment by women and the girl child of all human rights and fundamental freedoms and take effective action against violations of these rights and freedoms;

24. Take all necessary measures to eliminate all forms of discrimination against women and the girl child and remove all obstacles to gender equality and the advancement and empowerment of women;

25. Encourage men to participate fully in all actions towards equality;

26. Promote women's economic independence, including employment, and eradicate the persistent and increasing burden of poverty on women by addressing the structural causes of poverty through changes in economic structures, ensuring equal access for all women, including those in rural areas, as vital development agents, to productive resources, opportunities and public services;

27. Promote people-centred sustainable development, including sustained economic growth, through the provision of basic education, lifelong education, literacy and training, and primary health care for girls and women;

28. Take positive steps to ensure peace for the advancement of women and, recognizing the leading role that women have played in the peace movement, work actively towards general and complete disarmament under strict and effective international control, and support negotiations on the conclusion, without delay, of a universal and

multilaterally and effectively verifiable comprehensive nuclear-test-ban treaty which contributes to nuclear disarmament and the prevention of the proliferation of nuclear weapons in all its aspects;

29. Prevent and eliminate all forms of violence against women and girls;

30. Ensure equal access to and equal treatment of women and men in education and health care and enhance women's sexual and reproductive health as well as education;

31. Promote and protect all human rights of women and girls;

32. Intensify efforts to ensure equal enjoyment of all human rights and fundamental freedoms for all women and girls who face multiple barriers to their empowerment and advancement because of such factors as their race, age, language, ethnicity, culture, religion, or disability, or because they are indigenous people;

33. Ensure respect for international law, including humanitarian law, in order to protect women, and girls in particular;

34. Develop the fullest potential of girls and women of all ages, ensure their full and equal participation in building a better world for all and enhance their role in the development process.

We are determined to:

35. Ensure women's equal access to economic resources, including land, credit, science and technology, vocational training, information, communication and markets, as a means to further the advancement and empowerment of women and girls, including through the enhancement of their capacities to enjoy the benefits of equal access to these resources, *inter alia,* by means of international cooperation;

36. Ensure the success of the Platform for Action, which will require a strong commitment on the part of Governments, international organizations and institutions at all levels. We are deeply convinced that economic development, social development and environmental protection are interdependent and mutually reinforcing components of sustainable development, which is the framework for our efforts to achieve a higher quality of life for all people. Equitable social development that recognizes empowering the poor, particularly women living in poverty, to utilize environmental resources sustainably is a necessary foundation for sustainable development. We also recognize that broad-based and sustained economic growth in the context of sustainable development is necessary to sustain social development and social justice. The success of the Platform for Action will also require adequate mobilization of resources at the national and international levels as well as new and additional resources to the developing countries from all available funding mechanisms, including multilateral, bilateral and private sources for the advancement of women; financial resources to strengthen the capacity of national, subregional, regional and international institutions; a commitment to equal rights, equal responsibilities and equal opportunities and to the equal participation of women and men in all national, regional and international bodies and policy-making processes; and the establishment or strengthening of mechanisms at all levels for accountability to the world's women;

37. Ensure also the success of the Platform for Action in countries with economies in transition, which will require continued international cooperation and assistance;

38. We hereby adopt and commit ourselves as Governments to implement the following Platform for Action, ensuring that a gender perspective is reflected in all our policies and programmes. We urge the United Nations system, regional and international financial institutions, other relevant regional and international institutions and all women and men, as well as non-governmental organizations, with full respect for their autonomy, and all sectors of civil society, in cooperation with Governments, to fully commit themselves and contribute to the implementation of this Platform for Action....

CRITICAL AREAS OF CONCERN

41. The advancement of women and the achievement of equality between women and men are a matter of human rights and a condition

for social justice and should not be seen in isolation as a women's issue. They are the only way to build a sustainable, just and developed society. Empowerment of women and equality between women and men are prerequisites for achieving political, social, economic, cultural and environmental security among all peoples.

42. Most of the goals set out in the Nairobi Forward-looking Strategies for the Advancement of Women have not been achieved. Barriers to women's empowerment remain, despite the efforts of Governments, as well as non-governmental organizations and women and men everywhere. Vast political, economic and ecological crises persist in many parts of the world. Among them are wars of aggression, armed conflicts, colonial or other forms of alien domination or foreign occupation, civil wars and terrorism. These situations, combined with systematic or de facto discrimination, violations of and failure to protect all human rights and fundamental freedoms of all women, and their civil, cultural, economic, political and social rights, including the right to development and ingrained prejudicial attitudes towards women and girls are but a few of the impediments encountered since the World Conference to Review and Appraise the Achievements of the United Nations Decade for Women: Equality, Development and Peace, in 1985.

43. A review of progress since the Nairobi Conference highlights special concerns—areas of particular urgency that stand out as priorities for action. All actors should focus action and resources on the strategic objectives relating to the critical areas of concern which are, necessarily, interrelated, interdependent and of high priority. There is a need for these actors to develop and implement mechanisms of accountability for all the areas of concern.

44. To this end, Governments, the international community and civil society, including nongovernmental organizations and the private sector, are called upon to take strategic action in the following critical areas of concern:

- The persistent and increasing burden of poverty on women
- Inequalities and inadequacies in and unequal access to education and training
- Inequalities and inadequacies in and unequal access to health care and related services
- Violence against women
- The effects of armed or other kinds of conflict on women, including those living under foreign occupation
- Inequality in economic structures and policies, in all forms of productive activities and in access to resources
- Inequality between men and women in the sharing of power and decision-making at all levels
- Insufficient mechanisms at all levels to promote the advancement of women
- Lack of respect for and inadequate promotion and protection of the human rights of women
- Stereotyping of women and inequality in women's access to and participation in all communication systems, especially in the media
- Gender inequalities in the management of natural resources and in the safeguarding of the environment
- Persistent discrimination against and violation of the rights of the girl-child

SUGGESTIONS FOR FURTHER READING

Anthologies

Bishop, Sharon, and Marjorie Weinzweig. *Philosophy and Women*. Belmont, CA: Wadsworth, 1979.

Frazer, Elizabeth, Jennifer Hornsby and Sabina Lovibond. *Ethics: A Feminist Reader*. Oxford: Blackwell, 1992.

Freeman, Jo. *Women: A Feminist Perspective*. 4th ed. Palo Alto, CA: Mayfield, 1989.

Gould, Carol C., and Marx W. Wartofsky. *Women and Philosophy*. New York: Putnam, 1976.

Jaggar, Alison, and W. Iris Young. *A Companion to Feminist Philosophy*. Oxford: Blackwell, 1998.

Kourany Janet, James Sterba, and Rosemarie Tong. *Feminist Philosophies*. 2nd ed. Englewood Cliffs, NJ: Prentice-Hall, 1999.

Pearsall, Marilyn. *Women and Values*. 3rd ed. Belmont, CA: Wadsworth, 1999.

Basic Concepts

Jaggar, Alison M. *Feminist Politics and Human Nature*. Totowa, NJ: Rowman & Allanheld, 1983.

Tong, Rosemarie. *Feminist Thought*. Boulder, CO: Westview Press, 1989.

Tuana, Nancy, and Rosemarie Tong. *Feminism and Philosophy*. Boulder, CO: Westview Press, 1995.

Alternative Views

DeCrow, Karen. *Sexist Justice*. New York: Vintage, 1975.

Eisenstein, Zellah. *Feminism and Sexual Equality*. New York: Monthly Review, 1984.

Friedan, Betty. *The Feminine Mystique*. New York: Norton, 1963.

Frye, Marilyn. *The Politics of Reality*. New York: Crossing Press, 1983.

Held, Virginia. *Feminist Morality*. Chicago: University of Chicago Press, 1993.

Okin, Susan. *Justice, Gender and the Family*. New York: Basic Books, 1989.

Pateman, Carole. *The Sexual Contract*. Stanford: Stanford University Press, 1988.

Sommers, Christina Hoff. *Who Stole Feminism?* New York: Simon and Schuster, 1994.

Sterba, James P. and Farrell, Warren. 2009 *Does Feminism Discriminate Against Men? A Debate*. New York: Oxford University Press.

Young, Iris, *Justice and the Politics of Difference*. Princeton: Princeton University Press, 1990.

Practical Applications

Irving, John. *The World According to Garp*. New York: Dutton, 1978.

United States Commission on Civil Rights. *Statement on the Equal Rights Amendment*. Washington, DC: U.S. Government Printing Office, 1978.

Affirmative Action

INTRODUCTION

Basic Concepts

Solutions to the problem of discrimination and prejudice tend to be either backward looking or forward looking. The former seek to rectify and compensate for past injustices caused by discrimination or prejudice. Forward-looking solutions seek to realize an ideal of a society free from discrimination and prejudice. To justify a backward-looking solution to the problem of discrimination and prejudice, it is necessary to determine (1) who has committed or benefited from a wrongful act of discrimination or prejudice, and (2) who deserves compensation for that act. To justify a forward-looking solution to the problem, it is necessary to determine (1) what a society free from discrimination and prejudice would be like, and (2) how such a society might be realized. Solutions of both types have been proposed to deal with racism and sexism, the dominant forms of discrimination and prejudice in our times.

One useful way of approaching the topic of discrimination and prejudice is to note what particular solutions to the problem are favored by the political ideals of libertarianism and welfare liberalism. (See Section I.)

Libertarians, for whom liberty is the ultimate political ideal, are not likely to recognize any need to rectify acts of discrimination and prejudice. Bad as these acts may be, they usually do not—according to libertarians—violate anyone's rights, and hence do not demand rectification. In particular, because no one can demand a right to equal basic educational opportunities (a person's educational opportunities being simply a function of the property he or she controls), no one can justify affirmative action or comparable worth on the basis that such a right was previously denied. By contrast, affirmative action is a central requirement of the political program of welfare liberals, whose ultimate political ideal is contractual fairness.

Proposed solutions to the problem of discrimination and prejudice usually involve favoring or compensating certain qualified individuals when there has been a wrongful denial of opportunities or benefits in the past or to achieve the important goal of diversity. This practice is called affirmative action, preferential treatment, or reverse discrimination when what is provided are jobs or other desirable positions. *Affirmative action* and *preferential treatment* are designations usually employed by proponents of the practice. *Reverse discrimination* is a designation employed by opponents of the practice.

Alternative Views

In Selection 37, James P. Sterba defines affirmative action as a policy of favoring qualified women and minority candidates over qualified men or nonminority candidates with the immediate goals of outreach, remedying discrimination, or achieving diversity, and the ultimate goals of attaining a color-blind (racially just) and gender-free (sexually just) society. Focusing on the defense of diversity affirmative action, Sterba finds the legal basis for this type of affirmative action in *Bollinger v. Grutter* (2003). He then considers and responds to the two main objections that continue to be raised against diversity affirmative action. The first is that diversity is not an important enough state purpose to justify affirmative action. The second is that there are better means for achieving diversity or at least that the use of affirmative action to achieve diversity is not narrowly tailored to the task as the U.S. Supreme Court has required. Sterba finds both these objections wanting. Still, he indicates that he is willing to give up his support for affirmative action in the U.S. for a $25 billion a year education program to

put in place a quality K through 12 education system for every child in the country. Unfortunately, he has yet to find any critics of affirmative action who are also willing to support such a program.

In Selection 38, Terence J. Pell argues that assertions about the value of diversity rely on contradictory and incommensurable claims. As a result, institutions like the Supreme Court find it impossible to articulate an impartial standard for the appropriate use of race in college admissions. Pell further argues that in the absence of such a standard, institutions inevitably fall back on engineering proportional racial outcomes, a method of college admissions that disproportionately harms minority students.

In Selection 39, Bill E. Lawson raises concerns about the ability of arguments for racial diversity to bring together opponents and proponents of affirmative action. He argues that the negative social climate regarding the social and intellectual merits of black Americans works against the acceptance of affirmative action programs. In sum, Lawson argues that Sterba's position continues to put the social onus of changing racial attitudes on blacks with little or no effort on the part of whites other than allowing blacks admittance to formerly segregated educational institutions to interact with white students.

In Selection 40, James P. Sterba considers the premises of Pell's argument against diversity affirmative action. He claims to show how these premises can be either reasonably rejected or reformulated so that what remains is a set of premises that supports, or at least is consistent with, a defense of diversity affirmative action. In responding to Lawson, Sterba claims to have found a way to replace race-based affirmative action with a non-race-based program, which retains all the benefits that a race-based program can provide and secures additional benefits as well.

Practical Applications

In *Grutter v. Bollinger* (Selection 41), the U.S. Supreme Court held that the affirmative action admission program at the University of Michigan Law School did not violate the Fourteenth Amendment and Title VI of the Civil Rights Act of 1964 because it is constitutionally permissible to use racial preferences to achieve the educational benefits of diversity and because the Law School provided the individualized consideration of each and every applicant that is needed if racial preferences are going to be used in admissions.

Conservatives are now talking about using the affirmative action issue as a litmus test for future Supreme Court appointments, hoping thereby to overturn the *Grutter* five to four majority. In addition, there is talk of using referendums, like Proposition 209, where the issue can be framed in terms of racial preferences rather than affirmative action and the benefits of diversity, as yet another way of undercutting the *Grutter* decision.

37

A Defense of Diversity Affirmative Action

JAMES P. STERBA

James P. Sterba endorses the decision of the Supreme Court of the U.S. in Bollinger v. Grutter *(2003). He argues that the educational benefits of diversity are an important enough state interest to justify the use of racial preferences and that, especially due to the absence of race-neutral alternatives, this use of racial preferences is narrowly tailored to that state interest. However, he also indicates that he is willing to give up his support for diversity affirmative action in the U.S. for a $25 billion a year education program to put in place a quality educational system K through 12 for every child in the country. Unfortunately, Sterba has yet to find any critics of affirmative action who are also willing to support such a program.*

I. INTRODUCTION

On June 23, 2003, responding to the Supreme Court decisions in *Grutter v. Bollinger* and *Gratz v. Bollinger* handed down earlier that day, Jeffrey Lehman, the Dean of the University of Michigan Law School, said: "By upholding the University of Michigan's Law School's admissions policy, the Court has approved a model for how to enroll a student body that is both academically excellent and racially integrated. The question is no longer whether affirmative action is legal; it is how to hasten the day when affirmative action is no longer needed." By contrast, that same day, Clint Bolick, Vice President of the Institute for Justice, a private legal advocacy group, claimed that the Supreme Court's failure to answer "no" to the question of whether the government may discriminate on the basis of race in educational opportunities "means that Americans will continue to be racially divided by their government, perpetuating more than two centuries of racial discrimination." Given these quite different reactions to these two U.S. Supreme

Court decisions, the controversy surrounding affirmative action and racial preference in the U.S. is sure to continue for some time to come.

In the Supreme Court's landmark *Grutter* decision, a majority held that it is constitutionally permissible to use racial preferences to achieve the educational benefits of diversity and it also approved the University of Michigan Law School's way of achieving those benefits. In *Gratz*, the majority rejected the University's way of achieving those benefits for its undergraduate program.

Yet without a doubt, the most important finding of the Court was the constitutional permissibility of using racial preferences to achieve the educational benefits of diversity. That, of course, had been the opinion of Justice Powell in *Bakke* (1978). But in recent years there had been considerable debate about whether Powell's opinion represents the holding of the Court in *Bakke*, and whether the Supreme Court's instructions in *Marks* (1977) could be applied to *Bakke* to help determine that holding. In *Grutter*, Justice O'Connor, writing for the majority, cut short that discussion by simply

From James P. Sterba, "The Michigan Cases and Furthering the Justification for Affirmative Action," *International Journal of Applied Philosophy* 18, no. 1 (2004): 1–12.

adopting the opinion of Powell in *Bakke* as the opinion of the majority in *Grutter*. "Today, we hold that the Law School has a compelling interest in attaining a diverse student body." In doing this, the Court also deferred to "the Law School's educational judgment that such diversity is essential to its educational mission." The grounds for this deference is the First Amendment's protection of educational autonomy, which secures the right of a university to select those students who will contribute to the "robust exchange of ideas" (quoting Powell).[1] At the same time, the Court is moved by evidence of the educational benefits of diversity provided by the Law School and by briefs of the *amici curiae* (friends of the court).

> American businesses have made clear that the skills needed in today's increasingly global marketplace can only be developed through exposure to widely diverse people, cultures, ideas, and viewpoints. What is more, high-ranking retired officers and civilian leaders of the United States military assert that "[b]ased on [their] decades of experience," a "highly qualified, racially diverse officer corps ... is essential to the military's ability to fulfill its principle mission to provide national security."

Yet, while affirming the constitutional permissibility of using racial preferences to achieve the educational benefits of diversity, the Supreme Court in *Grutter* accepted the law school's affirmative action admissions program at the same time that the Court in *Gratz* rejected the undergraduate school's program.

The difference between the two programs, according to the majority in *Grutter*, is that the undergraduate program by automatically assigning twenty points on the basis of race or ethnicity operated in a too mechanical, nonindividualized manner. If race or ethnicity is to be a factor in admissions, the majority contends, there needs to be "individualized consideration of each and every applicant." The Law School seeking to admit 350 students from 3,500 applicants had used a more individualized admissions process that the Court

has now endorsed. The College of Literature, Science, and the Arts, facing the task of admitting 5,000 of 25,000 applicants, had chosen a more mechanical admissions process, still believing that it was sufficiently individualized to meet the Court's requirement of strict scrutiny. Now the Court has ruled that its requirement of strict scrutiny, which demands that any use of race or ethnicity in admissions be narrowly tailored to achieve the educational benefits of diversity, cannot be met unless each and every applicant's qualifications are individually considered. Accordingly the University of Michigan will have to significantly increase its undergraduate admissions personnel in order to provide this individualized consideration of each and every applicant that is now required. And I understand that the University of Michigan has now done this, that is, it has increased its admissions personnel to provide more individualized consideration.

Predictably, the Supreme Court's decision in *Grutter* has met with two sorts of objections. Some deny that the educational benefits of diversity are an important enough state purpose to justify the use of racial preferences to achieve them. Others allow that the educational benefits of diversity are an important enough state purpose to justify the use of racial preferences; they just contend that there are race-neutral means for achieving that goal, or, in other ways, that Michigan's use of racial preferences is not narrowly tailored, and so, for that reason, its use of such preferences is not justified. In what follows, I will examine and respond to each of these objections in turn. In so doing, I hope to further support the moral and legal justification for affirmative action.

II. DIVERSITY IS NOT AN IMPORTANT ENOUGH STATE PURPOSE

In their brief before the Supreme Court in the Michigan cases, the Michigan Association of Scholars maintained that "even where diversity in their classrooms is a genuine merit, it is simply not the case that their work, their teaching, their research, cannot go forward successfully in its absence."[2] When making this claim, however, opponents of affirmative action must not be thinking about what happens in classrooms when racial issues are discussed, or analogously, what happens in classrooms when gender issues are discussed.[3] Surely, the teachers among us who have led discussions on racial issues in our classrooms, both with and without minority students being present, know what a significant difference the presence of minorities normally makes in such contexts. And usually there is a similar loss when gender issues are discussed in the absence of women. So when opponents of affirmative action maintain that diversity is unnecessary for successful teaching, they must not be thinking about courses focused on racial (or gender) issues, but rather about courses where the subject matter is logic, math, physics, or something similar. But even in such courses, diversity can have a significant impact. I am reminded of the jarring impact my wife, a fast-talking, chain-smoking New Yorker, had on her Mormon logic students, particularly the men in her class, as the first woman in the philosophy department at the University of Utah in the early 1970s. And more recently, this semester, I noted the impact that the only minority student in my class of thirty had on her classmates when I asked her to read her paper to the rest of the class as an example of what I considered to be an excellent paper on the topic that they were all required to write on. Accordingly, it is really difficult to deny the significant educational benefits that minorities (and women) bring to colleges and universities, especially, but not exclusively, when racial (and gender) issues are being discussed.

Nevertheless, without denying the educational benefits of diversity, it still might be argued that achieving those benefits does not constitute an important enough state purpose to justify the use of racial preferences to secure them. This would seem to be the position of Justice Thomas in his dissent in the *Grutter* case. Thomas argues that the only kind of state purpose that would be important enough to justify the use of racial preferences in a

nonremedial context is national security or, more broadly, "measures the State must take to provide a bulwark against anarchy, or to prevent violence." In the *Grutter* case, no one, except Justice Scalia, joined Thomas in defending such an extreme limitation on the use of racial preferences. Both Thomas and Scalia also argue that the Michigan Law School could secure the educational benefits of diversity without using racial preferences by simply giving up on its goal of being an elite law school. To further show that the Michigan Law School was not serving any compelling state purpose, Thomas noted that while the school accounts for nearly 30 percent of all law students graduating in Michigan, only 6 percent of its graduates take the bar exam in the state, and only 16 percent elect to stay in the state. By contrast, Wayne State University Law School is said to send "88 percent of its graduates on to serve the people of Michigan."

But, of course, percentages do not tell the whole story here, and Thomas neglected to assess how well-placed and influential that 6 percent or 16 percent of Michigan law school graduates who practice law or stay in the state turn out to be. Moreover, the suggestion that Michigan could not have a compelling state interest in doing something that primarily benefits the rest of the country is extremely odd. It is like saying that Michigan could not have a compelling state interest in controlling the sulfur admissions of its power plants that causes, let's suppose, much of the acid rain that negatively affects New England states.

What appeared to particularly bother the majority in *Gratz* was that under Michigan's undergraduate affirmative action program "virtually every qualified underrepresented minority applicant is admitted." By contrast, Michigan's Law School "frequently accepts nonminority applicants with grades and test scores lower than underrepresented minority applicants (and other nonminority applicants) who are rejected." It is probably supposed that the adoption of a more individualized review process in the undergraduate admissions program will tend to eliminate this difference between the two programs. However, it may be that this difference between the two programs is due to the fact that the Law School can be more selective relative to its pool of candidates than the undergraduate school (the Law School admits 10 percent of its applicants, the Undergraduate College 20 percent). On this account, the Law School may have had a comparatively larger pool of qualified minority applicants from which to choose. In any case, what the Supreme Court required in *Grutter* was a more individualized review process, not the guarantee that there will always be some nonminorities who are accepted who have grade and test scores that are lower than some underrepresented minorities who are rejected.

Still, a central issue remains: Whether Michigan should have to choose between having an elite law school and having the educational benefits of diversity? Thomas and Scalia argue that Michigan must make this choice because to do otherwise would involve using racial preferences in a way that is prohibited by the Equal Protection Clause of the Fourteenth Amendment. By contrast, the majority in *Grutter* contends that Michigan is not forced to make this choice—that it can have a law school that is both elite and diverse—because the use of racial preferences to achieve the educational benefits of diversity is permitted by the Equal Protection Clause of the Fourteenth Amendment.

The key question here is: Whose interpretation of the Equal Protection Clause of the Fourteenth Amendment should we accept? The majority, to support their interpretation of the amendment, could have appealed to the original intent of the Congress that formulated and passed the amendment.[4] As it turns out, the same Congress that formulated and passed the Fourteenth Amendment also formulated and passed race-conscious statutes that provided schools and farmland to both free blacks and former slaves. In fact, this same Congress viewed its passing of the Fourteenth Amendment as a necessary means of supporting the legality of its race-conscious statutes. However, rather than appeal to the original intent of the Congress that formulated and passed the Fourteenth Amendment, the majority in Grutter relies upon an interpretation given to the amendment by a number of Supreme Court cases in the last fifty years or so.[5]

The history of this interpretation of the Fourteenth Amendment is usually traced to *Korematsu v.*

United States (1944), although sometimes Justice Harlon Stone's note in *United States v. Caroline Products Co.* (1938) is cited as an earlier source.[6] In *Korematsu*, Justice Hugo Black while upholding the constitutionality of the interment of Japanese Americans during World War II on grounds of national security held that "all legal restrictions which curtail the civil rights of a single racial group are immediately suspect. That is not to say that all such restrictions are unconstitutional. It is to say that courts must subject them to the most rigid scrutiny." Using this interpretation of the Equal Protection Clause of the Fourteenth Amendment, the Supreme Court in a number of decisions prior to *Brown v. Board of Education of Topeka, Kansas* (1954), struck down state laws segregating blacks and whites, but only on the grounds that the segregated facilities were not equal. In *Brown*, the Supreme Court went further ruling that the separation of the races cannot be equal, and demanding the desegregation of public schools on the grounds that the separation of blacks and whites is motivated by and supports attitudes of racial superiority. In so acting, the Court emphasized the invidious nature of this use of racial preferences. In *Regents of the University of California v. Bakke* (1978), however, the Court faced a use of racial preferences that appeared to be motivated, not by invidious intent, but rather by a desire to remedy past wrongs. In a fractured decision, a majority of Powell and the Brennan group held that race can be used as a factor in admissions decisions. But another majority of Powell and the Stevens group held that the appropriate standard for evaluating the use of racial preferences is strict scrutiny. According to this standard, there must be a compelling state interest (which in this case Powell took to be diversity), and the use of racial preferences in pursuit of that interest must be narrowly tailored.

The Brennan group had favored an alternative way of evaluating racial preferences. They wanted to first determine whether a use of racial preferences was benign or invidious, and then, if the use was determined to be benign, intermediate scrutiny rather than strict scrutiny was to be the proper standard of judicial review.

It is widely thought that there is a significant difference between Powell's approach and the approach taken by the Brennan group, but it is not clear that there is. First, both approaches hold similar views about when affirmative action in college or university admissions is no longer justified; they both hold that it is no longer justified when the minorities who are receiving it are no longer underrepresented in the student body. Second, both approaches permit the use of racial classifications that are not invidious.

The real difference between the Powell and the Brennan group's approach is that the latter provides no particular procedure to determine whether racial preferences are invidious or not, while the former regards the standard of strict scrutiny as the appropriate way to make this determination. This does not seem to me to be a significant difference.

What is significant is that Powell's approach has come to be endorsed in a number of subsequent Supreme Court decisions, right up to, and including, the *Grutter* decision. Accordingly, in *Croson* (1989), O'Connor writes:

> the purpose of strict scrutiny is to "smoke out" illegitimate uses of race.... The test also ensures that the means chosen "fit" this compelling goal so closely that there is little or no possibility that the motive for the classification was illegitimate racial prejudice or stereotype.

And again, in *Grutter*, O'Connor writes:

> We have held that all racial classifications imposed by government must be analyzed by the reviewing court under strict scrutiny.

Here, O'Connor also adds, quoting herself in *Adarand* (1995), that strict scrutiny need not be "fatal in fact."

It is just here that the disagreement between the majority in *Grutter* and Thomas and Scalia is joined. In *Adarand*, Thomas had claimed with Scalia in agreement:

> government-sponsored racial discrimination based on benign prejudice is just

as noxious as discrimination inspired by malicious prejudice.

In *Grutter*, Thomas reiterates basically the same claim, making it clear that his grounds for rejecting all racial preferences are the bad consequences that result from their use. This means that, in Thomas's view, it must be the case that the state of Michigan would be better off with a law school that is diverse but not elite than it is with its existing law school which is both diverse and elite. Unfortunately, neither Thomas nor Scalia bother to set out the required consequentialist argument to show that this is the case. And it is surely the failure of Thomas or Scalia to provide the necessary consequentialist argument or counterargument, along with Michigan's Gurin Report and over 100 *amici curiae* briefs attesting to the benefits of affirmative action, that persuaded O'Connor to join with the more liberal side of the Court in this case.[7] In effect, then, without appealing to the original intent of the Congress that formulated and passed the Equal Protection Clause of the Fourteenth Amendment, the Supreme Court in *Grutter* has adopted an interpretation of that amendment that has led to similar constitutional results.[8]

But what if there was a way to oppose the use of racial preferences in the affirmative action program at the University of Michigan that does not require us to weigh the consequences of using racial preferences? Actually I think, my co-symposiast, Terry Pell, believes that he has found such a way.[9] Terry claims that the University of Michigan's way of securing the educational benefits of diversity are opposed to an ideal of formal equality which he claims is embedded in the Equal Protection Clause of the Fourteenth Amendment. According to Terry, this ideal of formal equality is a procedural ideal, something like the due process requirements in the criminal justice system. To reflect this ideal of formal equality, college and university admission systems must have the character of a fair procedure and thus not be governed by end-state-driven requirements like diversity. The problem with Terry's argument here is that although there are some purely procedural requirements that should govern college and university admission systems, e.g., the requirement that application forms be turned in by certain deadlines, most of the standards for admission, even the ones that Terry favors, are really end-state or end-state-driven requirements, not purely procedural ones. Take, for example, the GPA and standardized test scores requirements used by the University of Michigan. These standards are used in the hope of getting students who have sufficient academic ability to benefit from the University of Michigan's educational program. They are used as a means to achieve a certain end-state: a student body whose members have sufficient academic ability to benefit from the University of Michigan's educational program. When athletic preferences are introduced into the standards for admission, the goal that propels their use is to have high-quality sports teams at educational institutions. When geographical preferences are introduced, the goal is to have a significant degree of geographical representation (usually home state representation for state schools). And, of course, when racial preferences are introduced, the goal is to achieve the educational benefits of diversity. So all of these standards governing admission are end-state or end-state driven standards.[10] What this shows is that there is no way to contrast a standard for admission that uses racial preferences with other standards for admission on the grounds that the racial standard aims to achieve an end-state but the others do not. All the standards used in admission decisions, except for a few, like the purely procedural application deadline requirements, are end-state or end-state driven standards; they all aim to achieve certain desirable end-states.

So if we cannot use Terry's procedural/end-state distinction to provide a formal way of showing that the use of racial preferences to achieve the educational benefits of diversity violates the Equal Protection Clause of the Fourteenth Amendment, we are really driven to the consequentialist evaluation required by Powell's strict scrutiny standard in *Bakke* and in subsequent decisions. We are required to assess the impact of using specific racial preferences in various contexts, ultimately trying to determine whether their overall consequences are

not only good and important, but better than the available alternatives, while at the same time ensuring that the use of racial preferences does not impose an invidious burden on anyone.

III. THERE ARE BETTER MEANS AND/OR THE USE IS NOT NARROWLY TAILORED

It is easy to see that the claim that there are better means, typically race-neutral ones, or the claim that in other ways the use of racial preferences is not narrowly tailored is just another way of continuing the consequentialist evaluation required by the strict scrutiny standard.[11] The Texas 10 Percent Plan and the Florida 20 Percent Plan are usually put forward by opponents of affirmative action as race-neutral ways of securing the educational benefits of diversity. Both plans are now successfully admitting minorities into their undergraduate institutions at levels that either match, or, in Florida's case, surpass what they had accomplished with race-based affirmative action programs. This was not accomplished, however, without a substantial increase in scholarship aid for minorities in both states, and without, in the case of Texas, using smaller classes and a variety of remedial programs.[12] Both plans also rely on, at least, de facto segregated high schools in their respective states to produce the diversity they have. If the high schools in both states were in fact more integrated, the plans would not be as effective as they are with respect to undergraduate enrollment.

Even so, the plans as they presently exist still have some serious drawbacks. First, the plans do nothing for law schools, medical schools, and other graduate and professional schools where ending affirmative action has been devastating. African American enrollment at the University of Texas Law School dropped from 5.8 percent (twenty-nine students) in 1996 to 0.9 percent (six students) in 1997. It then rose to 1.8 percent (nine students) in 1998, and fell to 1.7 percent (nine students) in 1999. Second, the Texas Plan has a detrimental effect on the admission of minorities not in the top 10 percent who pre-Hopwood might have been admitted. Minority students who are not in the top 10 percent of their high school graduating classes have little hope of admission under the Texas 10 Percent Plan. Third, such plans restrict universities from doing the individualized assessments that would be required to assemble a student body that is not just racially diversity, but diverse in other desirable ways as well. Fourth, an analysis of data from the Florida Plan showed that students at seventy-five of Florida's high schools could have carried a C+ average and still have ranked in the top 20 percent of their class. Fifth, such plans only work, if at all, for universities that admit primarily from a state-wide population. Colleges and universities that recruit students from a national and international pool cannot apply this model to select their student bodies. For example, at Michigan, one third of the student body comes from outside the state, and most of the Latino students who enroll are not Michigan residents. Over half of the applicants for Michigan's first year class are from out of state, while only 11 percent of the applicants to the University of Texas at Austin are nonresidents. Surely, a race-based affirmative action program can do better.

There is, however, still another reason that may trump all the others as a reason for rejecting these so-called alternatives to a race-based affirmative action. It is that despite their claims to be race-neutral, these alternatives are really all race-based themselves. They are all means that are chosen explicitly because they are thought to produce a desirable degree of racial diversity. In this regard, they are no different from the poll-taxes that were used in the segregated South, which were purportedly race-neutral means, but were clearly designed to produce, in that case, an objectionable racial result—to keep blacks from voting.[13] Accordingly, if we are going to end up using a race-based selection procedure to get the educational benefits of diversity, we might as well use one that most effectively produces that desired result, and that is a selection procedure that explicitly employs race as a factor in admissions.

It is not surprising, therefore, that is exactly what the University of Texas has now proposed

to do under the authority of the *Grutter* decision. Contending that its 10 percent Plan alone has failed to produce a critical mass of minority students at the classroom level, the University of Texas wants to now include race and ethnicity as additional factors in undergraduate, graduate, and law school admissions. A study of undergraduate fall 2002 enrollment at the University of Texas showed that in classes of five or more students:

> 52 percent had no African Americans and
> 79 percent had one or none.
> 12 percent had no Hispanics and 30 percent had one or none.

In smaller classes with 5–24 students:

> 65 percent had no African Americans and
> 90 percent had one or none.
> 18 percent had no Hispanics and 43 percent had one or none.[14]

"We have used race-neutral policies for seven years and still do not have a critical mass of African American or Hispanic students in our classrooms" said Bruce Walker, Director of Admissions at the University of Texas at Austin. So if its proposal is approved by the University of Texas system, which seems likely, then the University of Texas at Austin will again be explicitly using race and ethnicity as a factor in its admissions. What this shows is that the practitioners of the most highly regarded alternative to affirmative action in the country, those very same people who were in the best position to assess its merits and limitations, now want to use affirmative action. That seems to me to be very strong evidence against the viability of the Texas 10 percent Plan and the Florida's 20 percent Plan as alternatives to affirmative action.

There is one important objection to Michigan Law School's affirmative action program, forcefully stated by Chief Justice Rehnquist, that attempts to show that the program is not narrowly tailored. Rehnquist points out that the Law School admitted African American applicants in roughly the same proportion to their number in the applicant pool as Hispanic and American Indian applicants, even though some African American applicants had grade and test scores that were lower than some of the Hispanic applicants who were rejected. Given that the Law School was looking for a critical mass of each underrepresented group, Rehnquist finds the rejection of these Hispanic applicants hard to explain, particularly since the Law School admits twice as many African Americans as Hispanics, and only one-sixth as many American Indians. How could the Law School be admitting a critical mass of each group?

The Law School, however, never claimed to be admitting a critical mass of each group. It was only aiming at that goal, and clearly it was far from reaching it with respect to American Indians. In addition, there surely are other relevant factors, such as the quality of essays, letters of recommendation, and maybe Michigan residency, that could explain why some African Americans with lower grade and test scores were admitted while some Hispanic applicants with higher grade and test scores were rejected. The objection that Rehnquist raises here had not been raised before. Nor was it raised in the oral argument before the Supreme Court. So it is not clear exactly how the Law School would respond. Still, a response of the sort that I have just now sketched surely looks like it would support the Law School's admissions process in this regard.

IV. CONCLUSION

What I have tried to show in this paper is that the Supreme Court in *Grutter* adopted an interpretation of the Equal Protection Clause of the Fourteenth Amendment reaching back over fifty years that requires a strict scrutiny standard of judicial review when racial preferences are involved. In this case, doing the consequentialist evaluation required by the standard of strict scrutiny, shows, I have argued along with the Court, that the educational benefits of diversity are an important enough state interest to justify the use of racial preferences and that, especially due to the absence of race-neutral alternatives, this use of racial preferences is narrowly tailored to that state interest. At some point in the future, rather than continue to challenge affirmative action, or, as I am doing here, to defend it, I propose we join forces and allocate the substantial funds, probably about $25 billion a year, to put in place a quality educational system K through 12 for every child in the country. This is an alternative that I would certainly favor over affirmative action if I were forced to choose between the two.

What this shows is that affirmative action is at best a small part of a fix for a big problem. Many other social programs—a quality educational system K though 12, universal health care, adequate public housing, adequate governmental prosecution against racial and sexual discrimination, guaranteed full employment, and a steeply progressive income/wealth tax system to pay for such programs are much more important.[15] There is also the worry that by focusing our attention on affirmative action, we will be distracted from seeing the need for these other more important programs. Needless to say, defenders of affirmative action, like myself, are not unmindful of this possibility. We just think that a defense of affirmative action is one of the few viable political games in town. We also think that succeeding with respect to this defense can be an important step toward succeeding with respect to these other more important programs as well, and that failing to defend affirmative action will make the achievement of these other more important programs even more unlikely. All of this shows that my defense of affirmative action is, as it should be, both conditional and contextualized to achieve justice for here and now.

ENDNOTES

1. I will not take up this aspect of the majority's defense of affirmative action because I am inclined to agree with Justice Thomas that the First Amendment cannot permit what the Fourteenth Amendment forbids.

2. Brief of *Amicus Curiae* The Michigan Association of Scholars in Support of Petitioners, 5.

3. But not always. Thomas Wood and Malcolm Sherman seem to imagine whites taking ethnic

studies courses in which no blacks or Latinos are present and benefiting just as much as they would have if minorities were present. Unfortunately, they never explain how this is possible. See their *Race and Higher Education* (May, 2001) National Association of Scholars. nas@nas.org 86.

4. See Eric Schnapper, "Affirmative Action and the Legislative History of the Fourteenth Amendment," *Virginia Law Review* vol. 71 (1985), 753–98.

5. Unfortunately, with the end of Reconstruction, the rise of the Ku Klux Klan, and Jim Crow law in the South, appeals to the Fourteenth Amendment ceased, as the U.S. entered a period of almost 100 years of blatant racial segregation that was not all that different from the 200 years of slavery that preceded it.

6. John Hasnas, "Equal Opportunity, Affirmative Action, and the Anti-discrimination Principle: The Philosophical Basis for the Legal Prohibition of Discrimination," *Fordham Law Review*, vol. 71 (2002), 423–542; Helena Silverstein, "Benign Neglect," *Studies in Law, Politics and Society*, vol. 19, (1999), 39–64.

7. The majority in Grutter also granted a certain deference to the Law School with respect to its judgment concerning the educational importance of diversity, which I too would grant although I would not try to ground it in the First Amendment as the Court tries to do.

8. In *Affirmative Action and Racial Preference*, I criticize the Supreme Court for recently adopting too high a standard of proof before racial preferences can be employed. Happily, Grutter represents a relaxing of that standard.

9. Terence J. Pell, "Racial Preferences and Formal Equality" *Journal of Social Philosophy*, vol. 34 (2003), 309–25.

10. Even the due process requirements in the criminal justice system are end-state driven requirements. Their goal is to convict and punish only those who are actually guilty of the crimes with which they are charged.

11. Establishing whether or not there is an important enough state purpose to justify the use of racial preferences/classifications is one part of that consequentialist evaluation.

12. While the Florida Plan seems more generous than the Texas Plan, appearances are a bit deceiving here. The Florida Plan does not guarantee admission to the state's two flagship universities of the University of Florida and Florida State University, whereas the Texas Plan guarantees admission to its two flagship universities of the University of Texas and Texas A&M University.

13. There may be a slight difference here in that these plans may have been adopted both to produce a racial result and a geographical result.

14. The fall 2002 first year class at the University of Texas at Austin included 13.4 percent Hispanics, 3.4 percent African American students. For comparison, the state-wide demographics are 32 percent Hispanics and 11 percent African American.

15. In 1997, the Supreme Court of New Jersey ordered that the State provide increased funding to the twenty-eight districts identified in the Comprehensive Educational Improvement and Financing Act as "Abbott districts" that will assure that each of those districts has the ability to spend an amount per pupil in the school year 1997–1998 that is equivalent to the average per-pupil expenditure in the wealthiest districts for that year. After some initial delay, this decision has been implemented and now these Abbott districts have moved from having 34 percent of their grade school students reading at their grade level to having 51 percent reading at their grade level, which is near the percentage of students reading at their grade level in wealthier districts in New Jersey, such as New Brunswick (56 percent) and Perth Amboy (57 percent). Data provided by Peter Noehrenbert, Department of Education, State of New Jersey.

38

The Nature of Claims about Race
and the Debate over Racial Preferences

TERENCE J. PELL

Terence J. Pell argues that assertions about the value of diversity rely on contradictory and incommensurable claims. As a result, institutions like the Supreme Court find it impossible to articulate an impartial standard for the appropriate use of race in college admissions. He argues that in the absence of such a standard, institutions inevitably fall back on engineering proportional racial outcomes, a method of college admissions that disproportionately harms minority students.

I. INTRODUCTION

The Supreme Court's recent decisions in two cases challenging racial double standards at the University of Michigan, *Grutter v. Bollinger et al.*,[1] and *Gratz v. Bollinger et al.*,[2] occasioned a sustained public debate about whether and when it is appropriate to take race into account in college admissions and employment. The nature of that debate is the concern of this paper.

Both sides advanced serious claims about whether it is just to give someone a seat at a prestigious state university in part because of his or her race. Opponents of racial preferences argued that seldom if ever is it fair to measure an individual's merit on the basis of his or her skin color. They claimed that for many applicants, race is determinative of admissions to schools like the University of Michigan. They pointed out that minority applicants frequently are accepted with credentials that would virtually ensure rejection for non-minority applicants.[3]

Proponents of racial preferences argued that it would be calamitous NOT to take the race of minority applicants into account. A critical mass of minority students adds value to the educational climate of state schools, they said. Moreover, if the schools did not relax the weight given to grades and test scores for minority applicants, no more than 2–3 percent of the entering class would consist of minority students. This result, they contended, would make it impossible for significant numbers of minority students to enter positions of power and prestige later on in life and would deprive the country of the value of racial diversity in such important institutions as major corporations and the military.[4]

While reasonable people understood both points of view, most also understood that there was no logical way to resolve the conflicting claims. The former was expressed in terms of a constitutional right not to be discriminated against on the basis of race no matter how expedient for the state. As such, it was fundamentally opposed to the latter claim, which was

Terence J. Pell, "The Nature of Claims About Race and the Debate Over Racial Preferences," *International Journal of Applied Philosophy* 18, no. 1 (2004): 13–26. Reprinted by permission.

based on a calculation of the costs and benefits of racial preferences to different racial groups.

As the debate dragged on, many sensed that the decision to accept one or the other could be nothing more than a preference, based on one's own outlook or larger political commitments. One writer called discussion about affirmative action "so frozen and ritualistic that debates about [it] are more like Kabuki performances than intellectual exercises." By this he meant that both sides seemed to be rehearsing well-honed positions that did not so much persuade as simply demarcate political and ideological turf.[5]

The Supreme Court's decision to take up the Michigan cases created an historic opportunity to break the impasse. Yet that does not seem to have happened. Whereas the Supreme Court once used such cases to set a just course for the nation as a whole, its Michigan decisions had all the marks of a short-term, temporary accommodation—both to the reality of a splintered court and to sharp political divisions that fracture public debate about race.

Unlike Justice Powell's magisterial effort twenty-five years ago in *Regents of the University of California v. Bakke*[6] to ground racial diversity on a foundation of constitutional principle, Justice O'Connor's opinion in *Grutter* all but conceded that racial preferences are a temporary expedient that must be eliminated by the end of another 25 years.[7] And in contrast to Justice Powell's highly optimistic view that race might not be any more important or significant than dozens of other secondary characteristics,[8] O'Connor's opinion was built on the assumption that race is so important to the perceived legitimacy of our institutions that it must be carefully calibrated at every level of society.[9] Not without reason, Justice Scalia predicted protracted litigation over every element of the Court's decision, particularly given the fact that the Court struck down the University of Michigan's undergraduate admissions system on the very same day.[10]

Lack of confidence in our collective capacity to form an evaluative judgment about racial preferences imposes moral costs on all of us. Often in our private and professional lives we are called upon to make judgments about students, job applicants, and employees. In many cases, these judgments must be made in an institutional context that requires the use of different evaluative standards based on race. The inconclusive nature of public debate about racial preferences does little to satisfy our individual need to know whether we are doing something unjust when we make these decisions partly based on someone's skin color.

I want to argue that the lack of confidence that permeates public debate about race, and consequently limits institutional decisions, is not an accidental or contingent feature of this Court or even politics at this time. Rather, it reflects the deeper conceptual structure that our culture typically uses to think about race. My thesis is that the debate about racial preferences is inconclusive because the categories in which we think about race are in fundamental conflict.

To establish this thesis and persuade you of its significance, I have to do three things. First, I have to describe the specific features of the way our culture thinks about race that explain our difficulty in resolving debates about racial preferences. Second, I have to show how the recent Supreme Court decisions exacerbated the basic problem in the way we think about race. Third, I have to explain why our continued failure to conduct productive debate about race has moral and practical costs that we should not tolerate.

It is to the first task that I now turn.

II. THE CONCEPT OF DIVERSITY

To show conclusively that there is a distinctive way we think about race, I would have to show how that way of thinking is present in a wide variety of our concepts and modes of behavior—not just our explicit legal and moral debates. I will not do that in this short paper. What I propose instead is to describe how important features of the way we think about race are presupposed by one concept central to the current debate—namely the idea of diversity.

The most salient feature of the idea of diversity is the way it blends two claims:

First: those who believe in using racial diversity as a criterion for admission assert that we must go beyond objective criteria of academic ability, as measured by such things as grades and test scores, in order to consider the background and talents of each individual, including "one's own, unique experience of being a racial minority in a society, like our own, in which race unfortunately still matters."[11]

Second: schools that use race as part of their admissions criteria assert that considering the race along with other unique talents and experiences of each individual adds objective value to the quality of the educational experience for all. The University of Michigan, for example, claimed that racial diversity improves the outlook and attitudes of all students.[12]

Together, these two claims lend a somewhat paradoxical quality to the idea of diversity. For the uniqueness of the experiences and talents sought to be considered under the heading of diversity consists precisely in the fact that they do not lend themselves to objective evaluation. Yet if they cannot be measured, it's hard to see how they objectively improve the educational climate.

The paradoxical way we talk about diversity mirrors a deeper paradox in the way we think about race. On the one hand, we believe that attitudes about racial groups are inherently irrational and should play no part in public decision making. On the other, we have a fixed sense that racial minorities ought to be represented in "meaningful numbers" in all areas of endeavor and we expend much public and private effort to make that happen.

But these two claims about race undermine each other. If there is no basis for generalized views about different races, then it is not clear what basis there is for thinking that racial groups will be represented to any particular degree in any area of endeavor, let alone all areas of endeavor.

These paradoxes and others like them undermine our sense of confidence about how to settle contentious issues like the use of racial preferences. If we had an objective basis for knowing what the "right" racial mix would be in the absence of racial discrimination, or if we knew what racial mix produces the best educational climate, we would be able to settle disputes about racial preferences by appeal to objective standards that in principle could be persuasive to all. But even the idea of a "right" racial mix presupposes racial attitudes with which we legitimately are uncomfortable.

The problem, then, is that policies like racial preferences presuppose claims that at bottom may well rest on unsupportable racial attitudes. Yet we continue to treat the policies and the claims on which they rest as if they could be objectively defended, as if there were universal legal, moral, and policy arguments that could settle these disputes.

Because public debate is built upon the possibility of objective claims that we are not confident can be defended by appeal to impartial principles, no one is confident that we can achieve a settled outcome, even in principle. In place of a stable resolution, we accept short-term political accommodations that simply rearrange the legal and moral landscape slightly so that the fight can go on.

III. A MORE AGGRESSIVE CONCEPT OF DIVERSITY

It is important to grasp how and in what ways this situation was made worse by the recent Supreme Court decisions in the two cases challenging racial preferences in admissions at the University of Michigan because of the specific way the university attorneys shaped the diversity interest.

At a deep level, the UM's case challenged the idea that there really is a conflict between claiming, on the one hand, that racial attitudes and preferences are irrational and on the other, that there is an objective basis for concluding that a certain racial mix of students has educational value.

At bottom, the UM conceded that there is no way to reconcile disputed views about the educational contribution made by people of different racial groups. However, the UM contended, that's exactly why there is educational value in admitting significant numbers of all racial groups—because doing so is the only way students ever will question their own assumptions about race.

Underlying this view of diversity is the idea both that racial attitudes pervade society and that they are fundamentally irrational. University of Michigan attorney John Payton expressed this view well in his argument before U.S. District Court Judge Patrick Duggan in November, 2000:

We remain a divided country, certainly separated along racial and ethnic lines in very real and important ways.... We don't go to the same elementary schools. We don't go to the same middle school. We don't play together. We don't have occasion in K through 12 to learn about each other, to learn about differences or to learn about similarities from each other. This is an enormous educational challenge.[13]

According to the UM, the best, perhaps only, way to address this problem is to engineer interaction among college students of different races. Because there is no rational way to change inherently irrational attitudes, it is necessary to influence racial attitudes through non-rational means, by, e.g., having students of different racial groups directly influence each other's racial attitudes during college.

This view easily expands to other areas besides college admissions. On this view, much of institutional life is compromised by the fact that we are an assemblage of racial tribes that "don't go to the same schools, and don't play together and don't learn about each other," to use Payton's description.

There is no objective or impartial basis on which to settle claims about the contribution of race to any area of endeavor because we are all members of separate racial groups with our own set of racial loyalties, perceptions, attitudes, and preferences. While we may be rational in acting consistently with our own loyalties, at bottom, there is no rational way to persuade someone to accept views grounded in the perspectives of other racial groups.

This is both an opportunity and a challenge for the government. It's an opportunity because the government can help the races spend time together and learn about each other. It's a challenge because the legitimacy of all our educational and government institutions would seem to depend on engineering a meaningful presence of every racial group in every institutional context.

This view solves the problem of our lack of confidence in our ability to settle disputed questions about race by affirmatively jettisoning the possibility of impartial claims about race. On this view, there is no way, in principle, to rationally settle disputes about whether or not racial minorities add to the educational climate of an organization. Nor is there any way to settle disputes about the right percentage of minority representation in any other area of endeavor. Nor, finally, is there a neutral basis on which to evaluate the academic potential of applicants from different racial groups.

The only question on the table is what sort of minority representation it takes to confer legitimacy on our institutions given the absence of any agreed upon principle for settling questions of the right racial representation. And, the argument concludes, the only reasonable basis for legitimacy is to assure meaningful numbers—a critical mass of racial minorities in every area of endeavor.

IV. AGGRESSIVE DIVERSITY EXAMINED

But this new more aggressive conception of the diversity interest does not so much solve the fundamental problem as bring it into sharper relief. For, the primary consequence of permitting institutions to use diversity in this way is to obliterate the distinction between treating individuals as ends and using them as a means to an institution's own ends or purposes.

Let's start with college admissions. Treating an applicant as an end is to judge him by public and impersonal criteria, the sufficiency and legitimacy of which he is free to evaluate for himself. It is to offer an applicant good reasons for admitting him, the sufficiency of which he is free to judge for himself. It is to be unwilling to admit someone on the basis of reasons that the school knows in advance could not be good reasons for him to come to the school.

Treating an applicant as a means is to admit him as an instrument to further an extrinsic interest of the institution. It means compromising the institution's impersonal, rational criteria for admission in order to bring in someone useful to the school's reputation, fundraising ability, or political agenda. The most obvious examples of treating an applicant as a means occur when a school admits the son or daughter of a wealthy donor, the child of a politically powerful individual, or any other applicant the school would like to have around in order to further its institutional interests.

Diversity softens but does not change the way schools treat applicants as means instead of as ends in themselves. Instead of relaxing admissions criteria to serve some pecuniary or political interest of the school, diversity allows a school to relax its criteria in order to admit students who are useful to each other. Since the school is relaxing its criteria to serve the interests of students rather than it own interests, it appears as if the school is doing so for objective, impersonal reasons.

But the appearance of a disinterested purpose does not alter the fact that applicants are being selected because their presence serves to promote the education of other students. A candidate who is selected because he or she brings an unusual perspective to the class is being selected because the school thinks he or she will improve the educational climate for the other students. An applicant's value thus depends on her perceived usefulness to the other students. She is being made into an instrument of their purposes. She is not being offered neutral reasons that she could in principle agree were good reasons for her to attend the school.

Under what circumstances is it just for a school to admit students on the basis of their perceived usefulness to other students? One partial answer to this question might be that so long as each student brings something "diverse" to the table, then no student is disadvantaged by being treated as a means rather than an end.

While each is selected in part because of his or her usefulness to the others, each student also is in a position to make use of and benefit from other students. Since everyone uses everyone else, there is reciprocity in treating each student as a means to the ends of other students.

This partial answer is not completely satisfactory. It depends on several idealized assumptions that may or may not be true in practice. It assumes that every student is equally diverse so that when the class arrives, each student both contributes to, and benefits from, the diversity of the class as a whole in proportionate degrees.

The answer is compromised in another way too: it is one thing for adult individuals to freely choose to enter into reciprocally exploitive relationships. It is another to have one's reciprocally exploitive relationships mediated and arranged by third party government officials.

Admissions officers necessarily have only a general sense of what kind of relationships might actually benefit an individual. Their explanations of what they look for in the way of diversity fall into predictable and stereotyped categories. Though a student who plays in a symphony orchestra scores high on the "diversity scale," a student like Barbara Grutter who has raised two children, run her own business, and decides in middle age to go to law school does not, at least at the UM. Given its inherent limits, it is not clear that bureaucratically looking for specific diversity factors increases the opportunities students would enjoy in any event to learn from each other's unique background and histories.

One reason we permit school officials to engage in this sort of social engineering is that diversity considerations are understood to be secondary to the primary basis for admission. We assume that most admissions decisions are made on the basis of an objective judgment about an applicant's academic potential. And at least with reference to judgments about his academic capability, an applicant is not being asked to accept an admissions officer's judgment about how he will add to the chemistry of a class of individuals he's never met.

Because we have worked out ways to rationalize the use of diversity considerations as an adjunct to a school's objective judgment about the academic abilities of individuals, it seems unobjectionable to think about race as another diversity factor. This was the argument put forth by Justice Powell in *Regents of the University of California v. Bakke*, reflecting Harvard College's long use of the diversity rationale.[14]

However, treating applicants as instruments to further the ends of others raises special concerns when it comes to minority admissions. In this case, the school judges that minority race students are useful to the education of other, mostly white students. Not only are the minority students being used instrumentally, they are being used instrumentally because of their race.

In several critical respects, race conscious admissions cannot be rationalized on the basis of the general idea of diversity. To begin with, the use of the diversity rationale to justify race preferences rests on the assumption that there is educational value in students of different racial groups interacting in college. But that is true only if students come to college with a background set of unexamined and faulty racial attitudes that are presumed to exist and fester in the absence of real-life interaction with minority-race individuals.

The premises of this argument are that (i), racial attitudes are both entrenched and irrational and, (ii) the only way to deal with this fact is to force college students into cross-racial interaction. Whether the goal is to educate majority students about the distinctive point of view of minority students, or whether the goal is to educate majority students that minority students do NOT possess a distinctive point of view, the fact remains that minority students are being used instrumentally to repair someone else's presumed irrational attitudes about race.[15]

By its own terms, we have little reason to think such a policy could succeed in its intended purpose of causing students to alter their irrational racial attitudes. If the attitudes are indeed irrational, and thus individuals in their grip are not susceptible to persuasion, it's hard to predict what the actual effect of engineered racial interaction will be. Perhaps greater cross-racial interaction will call faulty attitudes into question, but we have just as much reason to think that it will reinforce precisely the irrational attitudes we seek to address.

But even if it made sense, applying the diversity rationale to race involves little of the reciprocity necessary to rationalize the selection of minority applicants for instrumental reasons. Many minority race students are admitted to improve the educational experience of non-minority applicants, and for no other reason. In contrast, almost no non-minority applicant ever is admitted to improve the "diversity" experience of minority students. While schools say they look at the potential contribution of every applicant to the diversity of the class as a whole,

there is a far greater likelihood that minority applicants are selected because of their race than because of their academic credentials or because of some non-racial contribution to diversity.

Whereas diversity characteristics are a secondary reason for admitting most non-minority applicants, race is the primary reason for admitting many minority applicants. As the evidence in the Michigan cases shows, the presumed value of minority ethnicity offsets far lower academic credentials and is, in fact, the predominant reason many minority students are admitted. One measure of the weight given to the race of minority applicants is reflected in an analysis of the odds ratios of applicants of different racial groups being given offers of admission to the law school. According to the plaintiffs' expert witness, the odds of a minority applicant being accepted to the UM Law School were hundreds of times the odds of a non minority applicant being accepted with the same grades and test scores.[16]

Odds ratios of this magnitude are almost unheard of. By comparison, the odds of a smoker getting lung cancer are about twelve times the odds of a non smoker, and this is considered highly significant. Odd ratios of the magnitude discovered at the UM law school indicate that when race is a factor at all, it is decisive.

But if race is the primary reason minority applicants are accepted and is almost never the reason for accepting nonminority applicants, it undercuts the reciprocity of race as a diversity factor. Many minority race students are admitted to improve the educational experience of non-minority applicants, and for no other reason. Almost no non-minority applicant ever is admitted to improve the educational experience of minority students.

The lack of reciprocity means that the school is using double admissions standards based on race. That is because the school routinely sets aside its normal academic standards in order to admit minority students deemed beneficial to the education of whites, but nearly never sets aside its academic standards in order to admit a white student deemed beneficial to minority students.

The use of double standards based on race creates other forms of unfairness. The lengths to which the school offsets the lower academic credentials of minority applicants means that minority students have a difficult time competing academically once they are admitted. This is reflected in many ways, but particularly in large disparities in drop-out rates.

At the UM undergraduate college, the drop-out rate for African American students is nearly twice the drop-out rate for all other students.[17] This reflects the conscious decision of the admissions department to admit *any* minority student who can do passing level work, while admitting non minority students according to highly competitive measures of cognitive ability.[18] Because students of different races are accepted under different academic standards, predictably they perform at different levels once they are admitted.

Disparities in academic performance at the undergraduate schools like the University of Michigan carry through to graduate and professional schools. In the fall of 2002, there were only 29 self-identified blacks in the whole national law school applicant pool with an undergraduate grade-point average of at least 3.5 and LSAT scores of at least 165—the standard necessary to be competitive at a top-ten law school.[19] Ten years earlier, the situation was about the same. According to a comprehensive study by Linda Wightman, of the 27,000 students who entered law school in the fall of 1991, only 24 black students would have been admitted to the top eighteen law schools based solely on grades and test scores. But as a result of the use of racial preferences by law schools, 420 black students were admitted.[20] This means that only 1 in 17 black law students had credentials comparable to his or her classmates that year.

Predictably, Wightman found racial disparities in graduation rates and bar-passage rates. As Stephan and Abigail Thernstrom point out, Wightman's data shows that more than a fifth of black law students who were admitted on the basis of preferential policies failed to graduate, as compared with less than a tenth of whites.[21] Twenty-seven percent of the portion of this group that got through school were unable to pass the bar within three years of graduation, a failure rate triple that of African American students *not* admitted because of preferences and seven times

the white failure rate.[22] Fully 43 percent of the black students admitted to law school on the basis of race fell by the wayside, either dropping out without a degree or failing to pass a bar examination.[23]

The above considerations suggest that whatever reciprocity is at the bottom of racial preferences, it is not that they provide reciprocal educational benefits. Perhaps racial preferences involve a different kind of reciprocity. One suggestion along these lines has been made by Shelby Steele. He argues that predominantly white institutions have an ongoing need to re-establish their moral legitimacy given the history of racial discrimination against blacks. Correspondingly, after four centuries of repression, blacks have an understandable need to be brought into society not as a matter of merit but as a matter of moral right. Racial preferences serve a mutual moral need of whites and blacks, even if they do not provide mutual educational benefits.[24]

But as Steele points out, racial preferences serve this moral need in a strikingly perverse way. They work because they transfer the stigma of having benefited from racial privilege from whites to blacks. At the end of the day, racial preferences undermine the moral authority of blacks by allowing whites to say, "You, too have benefited from a racial preference." But while racial preferences are a means by which both whites and blacks can come to think of themselves in the same moral boat, so to speak, this still leaves blacks in a genuinely inferior position. That is because the systematic use of racial preferences does little if anything to address persistent inequalities in educational achievement that create the need for preferences in the first place.

V. THE SOCIAL CONTEXT OF DIVERSITY

The model of diversity on which the UM based its case, and which the Supreme Court accepted, erases the distinction between treating applicants as ends and treating them as means. As the Court itself recognized, the breakdown in this distinction in colleges and universities is inextricably linked to a broader social breakdown in the distinction between manipulative and non-manipulative uses of race.

Writing for the Court in *Grutter v. Bollinger*, Justice O'Connor says that diversity doesn't just improve the educational climate at the UM Law School, but that it establishes political legitimacy of other institutions that depend on a supply of UM law graduates—institutions like the U.S. Military, elected representatives of state and federal governments, and the judiciary:

> Individuals with law degrees occupy roughly half the state governorships, more than half the seats in the United States Senate, and more than a third of the seats in the United States House of Representatives.... The pattern is even more striking when it comes to highly selective law schools. A handful of these schools accounts for 25 of the 100 United States Senators, 74 United States Courts of Appeals judges, and nearly 200 of the more than 600 United States District Court judges....
>
> In order to cultivate a set of leaders with legitimacy in the eyes of the citizenry, it is necessary that the path to leadership be visibly open to talented and qualified individuals of every race and ethnicity."[25]

Justice O'Connor's argument is that the political legitimacy of many other institutions depends on engineering a specific racial mix of employees, which in turn depends on the use of race preferences at the UM to assure a ready supply of minority graduates. From this, it is a short step to saying these other institutions have a direct interest in maintaining a preferred racial mix in order to ensure their legitimacy. One court already has taken this step: recently the U.S. Court of Appeals for the Seventh Circuit used Justice O'Connor's suggestion to permit the Chicago Police Department to race-norm examination results used in making promotions.[26]

It is important to understand what it means to institutionalize the idea that there is no impartial basis for judgments about members of other-race groups, that in the end, they must be based on irrational attitudes, preferences, and generalizations that are linked inextricably to someone's particular racial loyalties.

If, as UM lawyers asserted, there is no rational way to adjudicate disputes about the proper racial representation in any area of life, then the only basis for institutions like the UM to resolve such disputes is to confine themselves to the realm of what is verifiable and can be measured, namely the numerical outcome of its admissions system. The racial mix of the entering class assumes significance as a visible measure of the school's effectiveness at promoting diversity and, thus, a measure of its "legitimacy in the eyes of the public."

Once institutions overcome the idea that diversity measures something of objective value they quite reasonably conclude that they have to substitute something they *can* measure objectively, namely the number of minority students and employees they admit or hire year after year. Meeting these arbitrary numerical measures of output assumes heightened importance precisely because of the irrational racial attitudes that are presumed to infect every institutional relation. Achieving acceptable numerical goals insulates the school from both legal and moral challenge that it is insufficiently attentive to its own institutional racial bias.

An institution's need to vindicate its racial bona fides further compromises its ability to treat minority individuals as ends rather than means. To a great extent, minority students and employees serve the institution's interest in establishing its legitimacy by insulating it from charges of racial insensitivity. Since such questions cannot be resolved by appeal to impartial standards, institutions have a great incentive to admit and hire minority applicants in order to make the numbers "come out right."

Moreover, the widespread use of racial preferences by all institutions makes it more difficult for the courts to regulate their use. Indeed, the UM explicitly argued that its use of race was justified in large part because so many other institutions in America use racial preferences. This message was amplified in hundreds of *amicus curiae* ("friend of the court") briefs filed by corporations, government agencies, and even the military.

The extent to which this motivated the Court became clear after the decision in a speech Justice

Stevens gave before the Chicago Bar Association. Justice Stevens revealed that during the weekly "conference" at which the Michigan cases were decided, he told his colleagues that it is improper for "the nine of us sitting in the chambers of the Supreme Court to substitute its judgment for the accumulated wisdom of the country's leaders." Stevens continued, "That wisdom is convincingly shown by the powerful consensus of the dark green [amicus] briefs."[27] In making the diversity rationale available generally to institutions in all parts of society, the Supreme Court has further undermined its ability to scrutinize any single use according to a constitutional standard.

The consequence of institutionalizing the UM's view of race throughout society is to divert attention from real racial inequalities. So long as colleges and universities are permitted to paper over racial disparities in academic preparation, there is little incentive to make needed improvements to the elementary and secondary schools that are the source of the disparities in the first place. The widespread knowledge that minority applicants routinely are accepted with credentials far lower than non-minority applicants makes it difficult for legislatures, school boards, principals, teachers, and parents to do the hard work it takes to reform a complex educational system.

In its recent decisions, the Supreme Court expressed the hope that racial preferences no longer will be necessary in 25 years, because by then racial disparities in academic performance will have disappeared. This seems unlikely if only because the Court has created an incentive structure that makes it extremely difficult for anyone to seriously address those inequalities. More troubling still, the practical effect of the Court's opinion means it may not matter. In twenty-five years, it will be impossible to tell whether racial preferences are or are not necessary, because they likely will have spread throughout society. Racial disparities will have disappeared from social life not because there is genuine equality, but because a majority of American institutions will have come to engineer the appearance of equality.

VI. CONCLUSION

The moral costs of uncertainty about racial justice are high. We pay some of those costs in the form of interminable public debate about such questions as racial preferences. The deeper cost of such uncertainty is that persistent racial inequalities in all areas of society go unanswered. Because public discussion about race presupposes that there can be no impartial principle on which to settle disputed claims about racial representation, the only reasonable strategy for corporations, schools, and other institutions is to engineer acceptable numerical outcomes.

ENDNOTES

1. 123 S.Ct. 2325 (2003).

2. 123 S.Ct. 2411 (2003).

3. In 1995, for example, students from "underrepresented" minority groups who had the same grades and test scores as Jennifer Gratz (GPA of 3.80–3.99 and ACT of 24–26) had an admission rate of 100 percent. In comparison, the admission rate for non-underrepresented students in that category was 32 percent.

   In other cases, the disparity between minority and non-minority admissions was even greater. For example, minority applicants with a GPA of 3.4–3.59 and ACT of 20–21 had a 100 percent admissions rate, whereas non-minority applicants with those same grades and test scores had an admissions rate of 3 percent. See Affidavit and Exhibits in Support of Plaintiff's Motion for Partial Summary Judgment, *Gratz v. Bollinger* (April 7, 1999), Tabs FF and GG, discussed generally in Opening Brief for the Petitioners, *Gratz v. Bollinger*, 123 S.Ct. 2411 (2003), 4–8.

4. See Brief of the Respondents, *Gratz v. Bollinger*, 123 S.Ct. 2411 (February 18, 2003).

5. See Michael Kinsley "Let's Really Get the Government Out of Our Bedrooms," *The Washington Post* (July 3, 2003, A.23).

6. 438 U.S. 265 (1978).

7. 123 S.Ct. at 2347.

8. Justice Powell approvingly cited Harvard College's description of how that school counted race in admissions:

When the Committee on Admissions reviews the large middle group of applicants who are 'admissible' and deemed capable of doing good work in their courses, the race of an applicant may tip the balance in his favor just as geographic origin or a life spent on a farm may tip the balance in other candidates' cases. A farm boy from Idaho can bring something to Harvard College that a Bostonian cannot offer. Similarly, a black student can usually bring something that a white person cannot offer.

438 U.S. at 316.

9. Justice O'Connor wrote:

What is more, high-ranking retired officers and civilian leaders of the United States military assert that, "[b]ased on [their] decades of experience," a "highly qualified, racially diverse officer corps ... is essential to the military's ability to fulfill its principle mission to provide national security." The primary sources for the Nation's officer corps are the service academies and the Reserve Officers Training Corps (ROTC), the latter comprising students already admitted to participating colleges and universities.

Justice O'Connor continued,

[i]n order to cultivate a set of leaders with legitimacy in the eyes of the citizenry, it is necessary that the path to leadership be visibly open to talented and qualified individuals of every race and ethnicity.... Access to legal education (and thus the legal profession) must be inclusive of talented and qualified individuals of every race and ethnicity, so that all members of our heterogeneous society may participate in the educational institutions that provide the training and education necessary to succeed in America.

123 S.Ct. at 2341–42.

10. Justice Scalia wrote, "Unlike a clear constitutional holding that racial preferences in state educational institutions are impermissible, or even a clear anti-constitutional holding that racial preferences in state education institutions are OK, today's *Grutter-Gratz* split double header seems perversely designed to prolong the controversy and the litigation." 123 S.Ct. at 2349–50.

11. 123 S.Ct. 2341.

12. See, e.g., Expert Witness Report of Patricia Y. Gurin, December 15, 1998, available online at http://www.umich.edu/urel/admissions/research/expert/gurintoc.html

13. Transcript of hearing before Hon. Patrick J. Duggan, *Gratz v. Bollinger*, 122 F. Supp.2d 811 (E.D. Mich. Dec. 13, 2000), *aff'd* 123 S.Ct. 2411 (2003) (November 16, 2000 at 34–5).

14. 438 U.S. 265 (1978) at 315–9.

15. The Court itself relied on both the idea that minority students *do* bring a distinctive point of view and that they *don't*. For example, the Court stated that the purpose of the Law School's minority admissions policy was to "include students who may bring to the Law School a perspective different from that of members of groups which have not been the victims of such discrimination." 123 S.Ct. at 2334. Later on, the Court commented that, "The Law School does not premise its need for critical mass on 'any belief that minority students always (or even consistently) express some characteristic minority viewpoint on any issue.'" 123 S.Ct. at 2341.

16. See Petitioners' Opening Brief, *Grutter v. Bollinger*, 123 S.Ct. 2325 (2003) 5–9.

17. See *2002 NCAA Division I Graduation Rates Report*, available on-line at http://www.ncaa.org/grad_rates/2002/d1/Rpt00418.html. The report provides University of Michigan six-year graduation rates for the following racial groups: American Indian—61 percent, Asian—87 percent, Black—61 percent, Hispanic—71 percent, White—87 percent, Non-resident alien—70 percent, "other"—78 percent.

18. It is policy of the University to admit all "qualified" applicants who are members of "underrepresented minority" groups; whereas admission of "qualified" applicants who are not members of underrepresented minority groups is based on competitive considerations due to limited available spaces in the

class. According to a 1995 document authored by the University:

[M]inority guidelines are set to admit all students who qualify and meet the standards set by the unit liaison with each academic unit, while majority guidelines are set to manager [sic] the number of admissions granted to satisfy the various targets set by the colleges and schools....

Thus, the significant difference between our evaluation of underrepresented minority applicants and majority students is the difference between meeting qualifications to predict graduation rather than selecting qualified students one over another due to the large volume of the applicant pool.

Office of Undergraduate Admissions "Admission Policy for Minority Students," 2 (October 4, 1995).

19. See Jonathan Kay, "The Scandal of Diversity," *Commentary* (June, 2003, 44). As Kay notes, detailed information on admission races can be found at the Law School Admission Council web site,

http://officialguide.lsac.organization/docs/cgi-bin/home.asp.

20. See Linda F. Wightman, "The Threat to Diversity in Legal Education: An Empirical Analysis of the Consequences of Abandoning Race as a Factor in Law School Admission Decisions," 72 *N.Y.U. L. Rev.* 1, 30 tbl. 6 (1997).

21. Id., 36, tbl. 7.

22. Id., 38, tbl. 8.

23. Id., 40, tbl. 5. See Thernstrom, Abigail and Stephan, "Reflections on *The Shape of the River*," 46 *UCLA L. Rev.* 1583, 1608–1614 (June, 1999).

24. See, Steele, "A Victory for White Guilt," *Wall Street Journal*, June 26, 2003.

25. 123 S.Ct. 2341–2342 (citations omitted).

26. See, *Petit v. City of Chicago*, 352 F.3d 1111 (7th Cir. 2003), *rehearing den.* 2004 U.S. App. LEXIS 1188 (7th Cir. Ill., Jan. 22, 2004).

27. Charles Lane, "Stevens Gives Rare View Of Court's 'Conference'—Justice Details Thoughts on Affirmative Action Case," *The Washington Post* (Oct 19, 2003, pg. A.01). See also, Mauro, "Courtside: Gearing Up," *Legal Times*, October 6. 2003, 9.

39

Sterba on Affirmative Action,
or It Never Was the Bus, It Was Us!

BILL E. LAWSON

James Sterba argues for two interesting and provocative positions regarding affirmative action. First, affirmative action programs are still needed to ensure diversity in educational institutions of higher learning. Secondly, the proponents and opponents of affirmative action are not as far apart as they seem to think. To this end, he proposes a position that would give weight to race as a category for affirmative action that can withstand the challenges of affirmative action opponents while giving the needed support for affirmative action proponents. It is his contention that both sides can support arguments for diversity affirmative action. His paper raises concerns about the ability of arguments for racial diversity to resolve or bring together opponents and proponents of affirmative action. It is argued that the negative social climate, regarding the social and intellectual merits of black Americans, works against the acceptance of affirmative action programs. In sum, it is argued that Sterba's position continues to put the social onus of changing racial attitudes on blacks with little or no effort on the part of whites other than allowing blacks admittance to formerly segregated educational institutions to interact with white students.

There is much to thank James Sterba for in this exciting and provocative book. He has clearly shown how acts of racism, sexism, and classism have impacted on the life-chances of many citizens of the United States. These acts, which include discriminatory laws, practices, and customs, have a long history. As Sterba aptly notes, given this racist, sexist, and classist history in conjunction with the current racist, sexist, and classist practices, a reasoned program of affirmative actions may be the best we can currently do to ensure that members of those groups subjected to the ills of these "isms" can have some chance of social and economic advancement. Thus, affirmative action programs are needed at this period in history to address and correct practices of social injustice. This is not an uncontroversial claim. There has been and continues to be debate over the merits of affirmative action programs. It is Sterba's contention that those persons who object to affirmative action programs and those who support these programs share some common ideological ground (Sterba 2009, p. ix). He gleaned this view from his debates with affirmative action opponents about the merits of affirmative action. However, in 2006, the character of the affirmative action debate entered a new phase when the Michigan Civil Rights Initiative (MCRI)— a referendum that would rule out any race-and sex-based affirmative action—was being discussed across the state (Sterba 2009, p. x). The proposing of this initiative brought new challenges.

Journal of Ethics, Online First, pp. 1–10 (2011) Lawson. Reprinted with kind permission from Springer Science + Business Media B.V.

Sterba then participated in debates in which affirmative action opponents argued that there would be no negative impact on women and minorities if the initiative were passed. This has not turned out to be the case for black enrollment at the University of Michigan. The number of black students has dropped by 22 percent from 2003 (Sterba 2009, p. x). Given this sort of data, Sterba thinks a new defense of affirmative action is needed. This defense would demand that clarity is brought to the affirmative action debate. Thus, the first order of business is to define "affirmative action." Sterba states:

> I propose to define affirmative action as a policy of favoring qualified women, minorities, or economically disadvantaged candidates over qualified men, nonminority, or economically advantaged candidates respectively with the immediate goals of outreach, remedying discrimination or achieving diversity, and the ultimate goals of attaining a colorblind (racially just), gender-free (sexually just), and equal opportunity (economically just) society (Sterba 2009, p. 32).

This definition takes into account, at least, three important points for Sterba: (1) we have a long way to go to reach a point where there is racial, sexual, and economic justice; (2) past injustices must be addressed; and (3) racial, sexual, and economic diversity are needed to ensure that the country can move to a racially, sexually, and economically just society. A reasoned approach to affirmative action programs is therefore needed. Reaching agreement may not be as difficult as many believe because even those persons opposed to affirmative action in theory understand that given the economic status of members of certain groups, we sometimes have to take race, gender, and class into account to achieve equal opportunity. "The equal protection of the laws does not forbid every racial classification" (Sterba (2009), p. 33). Given what Sterba takes to be the social goals of equal opportunity and redressing past race, sex, and class-based wrongs, along with creating more diverse educational and vocational

workplaces, we must see when these types of affirmative action programs can be justified.

Still, as Sterba rightly notes, and thus the justification for this book, there is opposition to race- or sex-based affirmative action programs. There are those persons who think any form of affirmative action that uses sexual or racial proportionality will be unjust, along with those who think that any form of affirmative action that goes beyond equal opportunity will be unjust. To this end, Sterba wants to defend two types of affirmative action policies: outreach and diversity. The requirements of outreach affirmative action programs could be summed up as: "All reasonable steps must be taken to ensure that qualified minority, women, and economically disadvantaged candidates are made aware of existing jobs and positions that are available to them as are nonminority, males, or economically advantaged candidates" (Sterba 2009, p. 37). While I think there is much that could be said about Sterba's discussion of outreach affirmative action, I want to focus my comments on his discussion of diversity affirmative action. According to Sterba, diversity affirmative action should be regarded as justified by three conditions:

(1) Race is used as a factor to select from the pool of applicants a sufficient number of qualified applications to secure the educational benefits that flow from a racially and ethnically diverse student body.

(2) Preference is given to economically disadvantaged applicants by cutting legacy and other preferences for the rich and relatively rich at elite colleges and universities.

(3) Only candidates are selected whose qualifications are such that when their selection is combined with a suitably designed educational enhancement program, they will normally turn out, within a reasonably short time to be as qualified as, or even more qualified than their peers (Sterba 2009, p. 83).

It is clear that Sterba thinks that racial, gender, and class diversity in the educational and vocational setting is valuable. Like Sterba, I want to discuss diversity in the educational setting, particularly in colleges and universities.

1 DIVERSITY

The lessons we learn in and out of the classroom in our colleges and universities often have a long lasting impact on our lives. The friends we make in college often replace our high school classmates as life long friends. These friends often become part of our social and vocational network. I am sure that many of us have received calls from college classmates about jobs or in the case of professional philosophers about opportunities to publish or otherwise present our research projects. It seems clear that being in this mix is important to one's professional development. People have to know who you are. There are, however, many ways of being known on a college campus. For much of this country's history, black Americans who attended white colleges and universities were often ostracized, shunned, and not allowed to be a part of the mix, an important part of the college experience. They were known, but not in a positive way.

One need not look solely at colleges and universities, the plight of young black children integrating hostile white elementary and high schools is well known. These students were known and not wanted. One explanation for the hostility of whites was their lack of interaction with blacks. But this seems to be a strange response in the south where there were constant daily interactions between blacks and whites. Nevertheless, one response to this antipathy towards blacks was diversity training. It was thought that if white people could get to know blacks, they would come to respect them and treat them like, well, whites. Programs with this aim were often put under the title of multicultural or diversity training.

Jumping ahead to the current day and the presence of black students in major white colleges and universities, we still find arguments for diversity training or, at least, diversity recruitment. Since the mid-nineteen sixties, the number of black students attending white colleges and universities has increased. Apparently the numbers are not enough to claim that there is no longer a need for diversity of views and ideas in pursuit of scholarship to ensure a varied educational experience. To this end, there must be diversity affirmative action programs. These programs, as Sterba notes, are also thought to help ensure that those persons who are members of groups that were historically and currently the victims of discrimination are given an equal opportunity to compete in both business and educational institutions. The ultimate goal is to move the U.S. towards a society that supports institutions that are racially just (colorblind), sexually just (gender-free), and economically just (equal opportunity).

I want to be clear here, I think that diversity is a good thing and something we should work toward in our educational and vocational spaces. I do, however, want to raise some concerns about the proposed benefits. In this case, what does the person bring to the experiential table by being *black*?

There will be persons, both black and white, who will look at me with scorn and contempt just for asking the question. They will say he or she does not have to bring anything to the table. His or her very presence is the important thing, and that it is the contribution that matters. While that answer might satisfy some, Sterba recognizes that the benefits must go beyond the mere black bodily presence. Such a response plays nicely to the claims of the opponents of affirmative action who argue that undeserving blacks are being admitted just because they are black.

In this regard, there are those who think that any move to make diversity affirmative action decisions turn on a person's race is misguided. However, before I discuss this idea, let us think of ways in which being black in and of itself might be of a benefit.

(1) Race troopers: These students or professors have to take the blunt of racist and racism for those blacks who come later. White students have a chance to interact with blacks who may not make it to graduation or professors that may not make it to tenure, but their mere presence was in the pursuit of a good cause, multicultural understanding.

(2) The black person is the experience: In this scenario the black person is the experience.

The student or the professor gives white students and often other white professors a chance to experience being in an academic setting with a black person. It is unclear what the black person gets from this experience.

(3) The black person brings something unique: In this scenario the black student or professor is to be studied for something they bring out of the black experience to the white setting. White professors and students get a chance to experience something outside of their social norms. This again appears to be a benefit for the white students and professors.

(4) Interlocutors in the race discussion: Here the black students are often expected to engage with white students to help them come to grips with black humanity.

(5) Instruments of moral suasion: In this scenario, if black students comport themselves in a positive manner, it can change the perception that white students and white professors have of blacks.

It might be asked how these views differ from each other and I want to contend that it is not their differences but the reinforcing nature of these views that place the weight of social change on the shoulders of the black student or professor. Black students get an education and the professor has a job, but at what cost? Let me repeat, none of this is meant to be an objection to diversity affirmative action, but is only meant to raise the concern as to the nature of the educational benefits.

More importantly and closely related to the point of this discussion, the educational benefits seem to presuppose that the mere interaction between the races could overcome their prior socialization if they are put in the "right" situation. However, when we examine the practices of most universities and colleges with diversity programs, it appears that only in exceptional cases did black students not have black dorms, black student associations, and/or black graduations. Diversity is expressed in a negative manner. Educational administrators realize that they cannot force persons to interact. In fact, they can only promote diversity. For example,

universities can set up situations that encourage like-minded black and white students to share dorms and encourage non-black students to take courses that discuss diversity. This is what Sterba notes when discussing critics of the Michigan's Gurin Report.[1] The report showed that there were educational and social benefits noteworthy to having non-white students in the academic mix. But there is a caveat: "Yet to get a positive correlation … colleges and universities must have in place the diversity courses and informal discussions of race that serve to translate racial and ethnic diversity into positive educational outcomes" (Sterba 2009, p. 96). Thus, consistent and unwavering institutional support is needed to make diversity programs have a strong educational and social component.

What about the other non-black students who desire to have nothing to do with other black students or diversity courses? Sterba contends: "Accordingly, it is difficult to deny the significant educational benefits that minorities and women bring to colleges and universities, especially, but not exclusively, when race and gender issues are being discussed" (Sterba 2009, p. 71). Sterba gives two insightful examples of how the mere presence of a female or black student can change or at least seem to change the views of white students. Again, it appears, it is the mere presence of blacks that is an educational benefit. What is the goal? This is an important question because we know the mere presence of black students and professors may not move many nonblack students to appreciate diversity. This mere presence may do nothing to change the attitudes of those white students who think that the criteria for diversity admissions are contingent on one critical element, namely, that of being black.

Philosopher Laurence Thomas thinks there is a possible solution that draws on the point of diversity affirmative action and then moves beyond mere black body presence. Thomas proposes that we use the concept of "idiosyncratic excellence" (Thomas 2004, p. 939) as a way to foster diversity. This proposal suggest that colleges and universities' admissions committees should look for some special talent that a particular applicant has that would add something different to the academic mix. The special talent should not be race-based because being from a particular race/ethnic group is not a talent in the normal sense of the word, even if the applicants were black. In this manner, if a black student were queried as to why they were admitted, he or she could proudly proclaim what talent or skill they possessed. It would never be race.

While some may think of this as an administrative cheap trick, at least, it has the benefit of praising the black student for something other than being black, and it gives academic institutions a way to admit blacks with diversity affirmative action. When we consider the history of race relations in the U.S., it should be clear that more positive social interaction between the races is needed. Diversity affirmative action is one way to achieve this interaction. While diversity may make for a better educational experience, as Thomas correctly notes:

> One thing is clear: diversity makes for a better learning experience only if from the outset there is mutual respect between the various groups. And it is in no way a part of the logic of diversity that people of different ethnic and racial backgrounds are naturally disposed to respect one another. Diversity, alas, is compatible with utter contempt and disdain, even outright hate, for the other (Thomas 2004, p. 954).

It is important that we take this point into account when we devise diversity affirmative action programs. This means that while the "idiosyncratic excellence" approach may get around some of the oppositions of opponents of race-based affirmative action, these programs may do nothing to enhance the social status of blacks in general. With this in mind, let us consider Sterba's discussion of diversity and affirmative action within the socio-historical context in which these practices are proposed.

2 SOCIAL CLIMATE

Throughout Sterba's book, we find examples of how the objections to affirmative action are not solely about equality of opportunity or diversity or qualifications, these objections seem to turn on the persons who are expected to be the beneficiaries of these programs, namely, black folks. That is, those persons who have ancestry that links them to those persons held as slaves in the U.S. There is a four hundred year history of seeing African Americans as "other." An African American friend of mine who speaks fluent French tells me how white Americans respond to him socially different when he speaks French. He is not seen as one of their "Negroes." It is not necessary to rehearse the history of race and racism in the U.S. to make the point that those persons who are descendants of those persons held as slaves have been viewed negatively. These negative views have included, but are not limited to, being child-like, being wanton, being lazy, and being morally and socially inferior to any white person. These ways of stereotyping blacks have a 400-year legacy in the Americas, particularly in North America. These stereotypes have a profound place in the consciousness of both white and black Americans. If this is true, this seems to raise a very difficult issue for those persons who think that appeals to logical arguments and empirical data will change the opinions of persons who have been raised to think of African Americans as innately inferior to whites. Moreover, because of this perceived natural inferiority, blacks should not get any advantages that should rightfully fall to white persons. This point is made in a striking manner in Derrick Bell's *Faces at the Bottom of the Well* (Bell 1992, pp. 147–157). In the story, "Racism's Secret Bonding," some black scientists are able to broadcast a data storm of statistical data detailing black immiseration. It is clear, according to Bell, becoming cognizant of the data did not affect white racial attitudes; they just wanted the information to stop being broadcast. This led Bell to write about our long-held belief in education, which is held to be the key to the race problem. The old formula states, "Education leads to enlightenment. Enlightenment opens the way to empathy. Empathy foreshadows reform. In other words, that whites–once given a true understanding of the evils of racial discrimination, once able to feel how it harms blacks–would find it easy, or easier, to give up racism" (Bell 1992, p. 150). This turns out not to be the case.

Sterba, in an interesting way, confirms this position. He notes that there is a long and knowable history of the deplorable economic and social conditions of black Americans. Whites want to separate this history from what they take to be the current positive economic condition of blacks. Sterba clearly points out how the current economic condition of many blacks is still deplorable. Citing a survey on white racial attitudes, Sterba writes: "a majority of whites think that educationally the average black American is just as well off as, or better off than, the average white American; 47% think that blacks and whites enjoy the same standards of living. Still another survey found that most in the U.S. believe that "reverse discrimination" is the predominant type of discrimination in the U.S. (Sterba 2009, p. 6).

Sterba notes that surprisingly white racial attitudes have remained consistent for decades. The studies and arguments that highlight the economic and social plight of black American seem to have had minimal impact on white racial attitudes. If whites think that blacks are doing as well as whites, why should they support affirmative action of any type? While the data supports the position that the economic and social status of blacks is not on par with that of whites, many whites do not believe it.[2]

Thus, any attempt to address the historical and current racist, with race-based affirmative action must take into account the attitudes of whites regarding the status of blacks. In this regard, Sterba has to walk the fine line between advocating that not all blacks are unqualified and justifying programs that are meant to enhance the chances of those blacks who may need additional educational or vocational training to compete. The history of race in the U.S. has severely affected the manner in which whites view blacks, and this view is not positive. Affirmative action is thus seen as a way for lazy blacks to get an advantage over whites. It is an advantage blacks do not deserve.

Argumentation and appeals to sociological data that shows how blacks are not fairing well do not seem to move white people. They can, rightly or wrongly, blame the said problems on blacks.

Indeed, the public image of black material success becomes the hallmark for racial progress. That is, black millionaires, a black president, and similar others confirm that blacks could make it if they try. In one way, President Obama's election plays into what I call the "cult of qualifications." If only blacks would get the right and necessary qualifications, then there would be no need for affirmative action.

Unfortunately, there are white persons who think that slavery helped black people and blacks should be happy to be in the U.S. no matter how badly they are treated. Arguments and data will not move these persons to think that the wrongs and injustices suffered by blacks require any sort of redress because the acts are perceived as not, on balance, being genuine wrongs. Given this history, it unclear if an appeal to reason will make, persuade, or convince the white employer, law school, and/or medical school candidate that a black person getting the job or admitted over him or her is just or fair.

3 CONCLUSION

In a provocative way, Sterba's book is a potent reminder of this perhaps sad fact: Racism, sexism, and classism are deeply rooted in the social and moral fibers of the U.S. Affirmative action can help give those members of groups that otherwise would not have equal opportunity to secure employment or educational benefits. It is unknown to what degree affirmative action will change the way many white persons seem to think of blacks as worthy of help in this manner, whether it is affirmative action or remedial affirmative action.

This may speak to the way blacks are perceived as humans in this society. Blacks have not been understood or appreciated as full human beings. This is the psychological change that must take place. This change of white racial attitudes has yet to manifest itself in a major way in U.S. society. Thus, if affirmative action is meant to change the material status of some blacks with the hope that it would change the views that white persons have of blacks, I think it does the former without doing the latter.

I contend that Sterba is correct that racial discrimination has been consistent and persistent for centuries[3]; however, it appears that arguments alone are not going to change white U.S. citizens' attitudes about black people and the need for affirmative action. What this may mean, among other things, is that some sort of institutional change must take place in order to bring about this change in attitudes. Sterba nicely points out how the history of racism has worked against blacks, but he does not seem to want to challenge the impact this racist history has on the mindset of whites and, indeed, some blacks. The racial attitudes regarding black Americans seems to have more impact on how whites view the moral and social status of blacks and what blacks merit. In this case, it is not how we define "affirmative action"; it is how we understand the moral status of the beings that are the objects of any race conscious affirmative action policies; black folks who have the social history of U.S. chattel slavery.

We are all familiar with the saying: "familiarity breeds contempt." I think we should rephrase this saying to what many persons across the racial spectrum believe: Familiarity breeds babies! Ronald Sundstrom notes:

> Contemporary philosophical investigations of the meaning of the significance of racism, unfortunately have largely avoided the topic of interracial intimacy and all that it implies, such as the ethics of interracial romantic relationships, interracial adoption, interracial matters in custody disputes, and so on. This is an immense mistake for those matters make up the content of our most intimate and daily experiences with race and racism (Sundstrom 2008, p. 94).

Likewise, I would contend that this issue extends into the opposition to affirmative action in that blacks are collectively seen as unworthy competition, and black males are viewed as sexual predators. There are still images of black men deflowering young white female virgins and blacks invading white spaces. It is also a history that has not favored black women. The issues concerning black females and affirmative action deserve its own program (Davis 1980).

In sum, affirmative action will only work, as it is now conceived, if blacks convince, make, and/or persuade whites that blacks are human beings who have to be respected as such. But again this places the onus on blacks, when the reality dictates that whites must work to change not only their attitudes but also the policies that that reinforce the notion of blacks inferiority. In a world where this is not the case, we cannot use the model of rationality presupposed by much of western liberal political thought without considering how to make our way in a world that has been deeply impacted by racism, sexism, and classism. Whites must become agents of social change. Without this change in white attitudes emulating from whites, diversity programs will have limited impact.

In sum, we need diversity to ensure that these rational and autonomous individuals have a chance to interact with other members of the society in a civilized manner. However, we also need diversity to ensure that members of historical oppressing groups do not mess over other rational and autonomous individuals (of historically oppressed groups) in their development of public policy. The question is how to get whites to become agents of social change.

I contend that arguments alone are not going to effectively get the job done. I should note that I do not think that Sterba wants to rely solely on argumentation to persuade U.S. whites along these lines. However, he does seem to think that an appeal to reason will make, persuade, and/or convince the white employer, law-makers, and school candidate that a black person getting the job or admitted is just or fair. I have my doubts about this line of reasoning. Arguments aside, I contend that affirmative action programs will be around for a long time. Professor Sterba's book, whether he wanted it to or not, helps us to see why this is the case. In this regard, we can see why it never was the bus!

ENDNOTES

1. http://www.vpcomm.umich.edu/admissions/ research/. Accessed on 12 December 2009.

2. http://www.faireconomy.org/files/SoD_2010_ Drained_Report.pdf. Accessed on 8 June 2010.

3. http://page99test.blogspot.com/2009/11/james-p-sterbas-affirmative-action-for.html. Accessed on 12 December 2009.

REFERENCES

Bell, Derrick, 1992. Faces at the bottom of the well: the permanence of racism (New York: Basic Books, 1992), pp. 147–157.

Davis, Angela Y. 1980. *Woman, race and class*. New York: Random House.

Sterba, James P. 2009. *Affirmative action for the future*. Ithaca: Cornell University Press.

Sundstrom, Ronald. 2008. *The browning of America and the evasion of social justice*. Albany: State University of New York Press.

Thomas, Laurence. 2004. Equality and the mantra of diversity. *University of Cincinnati Law Review* 72 (2004): 931–965.

40

Responses to Pell and Lawson

JAMES P. STERBA

In his comments on Pell's paper, Sterba consider the premises of his argument against diversity affirmative action showing how these premises can be either reasonably rejected or reformulated so that what remains from his argument is a set of premises that supports, or at least is consistent with, a defense of diversity affirmative action.

In responding to Lawson, Sterba claims to have found a way to replace race-based affirmative action with a non-race-based program, which retains all the benefits that a race-based program can provide and secures additional benefits as well.

RESPONSE TO PELL

In his symposium paper, Terry Pell has presented a persuasive and thoughtful argument, or set of arguments, against diversity affirmative action. In my comments, I want to indicate which premises I, as a defender of diversity affirmative action, want to challenge and how I think that challenge ought to go.

Terry begins by claiming that defenders of diversity affirmative action hold that:

1. We must go beyond the objective criteria of academic ability, as measured by such things as grades and test scores, in order to consider the background and talents of each individual, including "one's own, unique experience of being a racial minority in a society, like our own, in which race unfortunately still matters," even though these other factors do not lend themselves to objective assessment.

2. **Considering the backgrounds and talents of each individual adds objective value to the quality of the educational experience for all.**

Terry sees a paradox, if not a contradiction, in (1) and (2). But I think the problem is simply in his formulation. I think that the ability to bring diversity to an educational setting is open to objective assessment in much the same way that the ability to bring analytical skill to an educational setting is open to objective assessment. Currently, first year grades in law school correlate about 14 percent with LSAT scores, not a great correlation, but LSAT scores are still a favored standard of objective analytical assessment. Likewise, the positive effect that the presence of underrepresented minorities in college and university classes have, especially where racial issues are being discussed, is certainly open to objective assessment, as I indicated in my paper.[1] So I would reformulate (1) as:

1'. **We must go beyond relying simply on traditional criteria of grades and standardized test scores and consider as well the contribution that diversity can bring to educational settings.**

This, I think, removes any sense of paradox or contradiction from (1) and (2).

Taken from James P. Sterba, "Comments on Pell's 'The Nature of Claims About Race and the Debate Over Racial Preferences'," *International Journal of Applied Philosophy* 18, no. 1 (2004): 27–33; and James P. Sterba, "Responses to Allen, Appiah, and Lawson," *Journal of Ethics*, Online First (2011): 13–16. The latter is reprinted with kind permission from Springer Science and Business Media B.V.

Terry also thinks that defenders of diversity affirmative action hold:

3. Attitudes (or beliefs) about racial groups are inherently irrational and should play no part in public decision making.

4. Racial minorities ought to be represented in meaningful numbers in all areas of endeavor and we should expend much public and private effort to make that happen.

Again, Terry senses a paradox with (3) and (4). But I think that the sense of paradox here can be removed by radically reformulating both (3) and (4). First of all, not all beliefs about racial groups are inherently irrational. For example, I believe, on the basis of a study conducted by the U.S. Federal Reserve Board, that African Americans in the highest income brackets have the same loan rejection rate as whites in the lowest income brackets. Secondly, I believe that the Federal Reserve Board's study should have an impact on public decision making requiring some type of a corrective. So I would radically reformulate (3) as

3′. **Some attitudes (or beliefs) about racial groups are rationally defensible and should play a part in public decision making, and other attitudes (or beliefs) about racial groups are rationally indefensible and should not play any role in public decision making.**

As for (4), I would simply reject its racial proportionalism, except in specific contexts where it is the appropriate corrective for past discrimination, as in the U.S. Supreme Court decision, Sheetmetal Workers Union vs. EEOC (1986). This would get us:

4′. **Racial proportionalism should be rejected except in specific contexts where it is the appropriate corrective for past discrimination.**

Now Terry's reflection on (3) and (4) appears to lead him to endorse:

5. **If we had an objective basis for knowing what the "right" racial mix would be in the best educational climate, we would be able to settle disputes about racial preferences by appeal to objective standards that in principle could be persuasive to all.**

Now, I like (5) and I am pleased to see that Terry seems to endorse it as well. In line with what I said above, I would go further, as I did in my essay and in our exchange last year, and claim that we know quite a bit about what the right racial mix would be in the best educational climate. For example, I claimed that for a class of 30 students 4 or 5 underrepresented minority students would constitute a critical mass of students "sufficient to enable underrepresented minority students to contribute to classroom dialogue without feeling isolated."[2]

As far as I can tell, the only reason why defenders of diversity affirmative action have not similarly fixed on some such definite number is that they believe that critics of affirmative action are poised to pounce on them for endorsing a quota once they do so. In my judgment, however, an objective standard for a critical mass of underrepresented minority students would not be a quota, provided that it was always weighed against other objective criteria for admissions and was sometimes trumped by them. Nevertheless, I understand the reluctance of other defenders of affirmative action to be more forthcoming on this issue. Presumably, Terry's seeming endorsement of (5) means that he will not play the quota card against me now that I have clearly endorsed the idea that we have objective knowledge about what would be the "right" racial mix in the best educational climate.

Terry goes on to claim that defenders of diversity affirmative action endorse:

6. Racial attitudes (and beliefs) that pervade society and individual thinking are fundamentally irrational.

7. **Engineering close interaction among college students of different races can help in this regard.**

Premise (6) is similar to (3) and so needs to be radically reformulated into a premise that is quite similar or consistent with (3'). In his reflection on (6) and (7), however, Terry wonders how "rational interaction" with students of different races can possibly help if racial attitudes and beliefs are irrationally grounded. But to say that certain racial attitudes and beliefs are irrationally grounded need only mean that they are not grounded in good reasons; this then would not imply that these attitudes and beliefs are impervious to change, especially when challenged by good reasons. In a 1999 survey of 1,800 law students of Harvard University and the University of Michigan, eight out of ten said discussion with students of other races had affected their views of the criminal justice system.[3] Clearly, rational interaction and reflection can change quite a few irrational racial attitudes and beliefs that people hold.

The next part of Terry's argument against diversity affirmative action attempts to show that the practice is harmful for the underrepresented minorities themselves. Accordingly, Terry thinks that defenders of diversity affirmative action are committed to:

8. **Using minorities as a means to an end is permissible, even when non-minorities are not similarly used, unless, of course, they are legacies, or athletes, or come from wealthy families capable of making large donations to the relevant educational institution.**

9. **Lower dropout rates for African Americans than for whites is a permissible consequence of affirmative action.**

10. Transferring the stigma of having benefited from discrimination from whites to blacks is a permissible consequence of affirmative action.

Let me respond to each of these premises. First, I accept (8) and (9). Minorities are used as a means to an end in ways similar to which legacies, athletes, and daughters and sons of wealthy donors are used as a means to an end. At the same time, unlike at least some athletes, they usually serve their own ends as well. In a study of 60,000 students of twenty-eight selective universities from 1970 to 1996, all minority graduates reported high incomes

(averaging $105,000 in 1996 dollars), 75 percent of them reported that the were satisfied with their careers, and 60 percent reported that the engaged in unremunerated service to their communities (compared to a reported 50 percent for white students).[4]

Terry thinks using minorities as a means to provide diversity is only justified if all other students are being similarly used as a means. But this is surely not the case for all those students. It only holds for minorities, legacies, athletes, and sons and daughters of wealthy donors who received preference. So Terry's reason for rejecting minority preferences here is equally a reason for rejecting all preferences. However, he does not reject all preferences.

Nor should he. That one is being used as a means should not be a sufficient condition for rejecting that role. Virtually all of us, in our working lives, are being used as a means by others, and legitimately so. What is crucial is not whether we are being so used but rather whether we thereby serve our own legitimate ends as well. And this is what happens to qualified minorities when a diversity affirmative action program is well designed; they are being used as a means but they are able to serve their own legitimate ends as well.

Nevertheless, Terry still thinks using minorities as a means for diversity is objectionable in yet another way. It is because, unlike most other students who are admitted, most minorities would not have been admitted except for their race. This is surely the case, but it is also the case for other students who receive preference in admission as well. Those legacies, athletes, and sons and daughters of donors who receive preference would not have been admitted except for the preferences they received. And here again, Terry does not take the step of condemning all preferences.

Nor should he. What is relevant is not whether students have received preferences, but whether those preferences are justified, and such preferences are justified when they are sufficiently beneficial both to the educational institution that grants them and to the students who receive them.

Yet, it is only with respect to minorities that Terry questions the justification for such preferences. Specifically, he is concerned that minorities may be harmed at the University of Michigan because they have higher dropout rates than non-minorities have at Michigan. But while blacks do have higher dropout rates at the University of Michigan, it should also be noted that the graduation rate of African Americans is considerably higher at more selective colleges and universities, where there is a greater gap between minority and nonminority students in grade point averages and standardized test scores, than there is at less selective colleges and universities where the gap is sometimes nonexistent. In fact, the graduation rate of African Americans in the University of Michigan undergraduate college is even a few percentage points higher than it is for whites (both athletes and nonathletes) graduating from all 305 large universities that participate in Division I-level NCAA athletics.[5]

Still, Terry is concerned about possible harm to minorities from diversity affirmative action. He notes from Linda Wightman's study that 27 percent of African Americans who received preferences were unable to pass the bar within three years of graduation, a failure rate triple that of African Americans who were not admitted on the basis of preferences.[6] Yet he could have also noted from the same study that the graduation rate from law school for African Americans who received preference was virtually identical with the graduation rate for African Americans who did not receive preference (79 percent to 80 percent) as was the graduation rate of whites who received preference compared to whites who did not receive preference (90 percent to 91 percent). Wrightman's study also showed that the rate at which whites who received preference passed the bar was virtually identical to the rate at which whites who did not receive preference passed (90 percent to 91 percent). So there is no general correlation between receiving preferences and failing to pass the bar. Moreover, given the small number of minorities who would have been admitted under a law school system without preference, it is hard to believe that those who were admitted under the existing system were actually hurt by having only a 78 percent to 88 percent chance of graduating from law school and only a

73 percent to 87 percent chance of passing the bar. In addition, as Wightman points out, financial considerations are among the most common reasons provided by students who drop out of law school. So if one really wants to improve these percentages for minorities, instead of abandoning diversity affirmative action, it would be preferable to provide more scholarships based on need since, as Wightman also points out, minority law schools students are more than twice as likely to come from low-income families.[7] As to (10), while the deserved stigma of having benefited from racial discrimination is rarely *felt* by whites in this country, minorities do sometimes suffer from an undeserved stigma inflicted upon them by whites when the minorities benefit from affirmative action. Fortunately, the benefits are still worth it. So I would just reject (10).

Shifting from claims about the harms of affirmative action to minorities, Terry attempts to showcase the unfairness of diversity affirmative action to whites. He claims that defenders of affirmative action are committed to:

11. The odds of a minority student being accepted is hundreds of times (actually 237 times in an earlier version of this paper) that of a nonminority applicant with the comparable grades and test scores.

But I simply reject (11) as an adequate way of representing the degree to which race is a factor in admissions decisions when grades and LSAT scores are comparable. If we use the Michigan Law School's judgment of when grades and LSAT scores are comparable, the odds of a minority student being accepted is only 2.4 or less times that of a nonminority student being accepted. What this means is that when grades and LSAT scores are comparable, race can be a tiebreaker in admissions decisions. So what is wrong with that?

Here is another way to look at the same data. In 2000, the median college GPA of admitted students at the University of Michigan was 3.68 for white students and 3.4 for African American students, or slightly less than the difference between A and B+. Not a huge difference. Moreover, for Michigan Law School, more than seventy-one white applicants were admitted with grade and test scores the same or worse than minority applicants who were rejected. And if data about "other Hispanic" applicants which were strategically excluded by the plaintiff's statistician are reintegrated into the calculation, the number of white students admitted in preference to rejected minorities with equal or better grades and test scores jumps to 223 of an entering class of 350. So it should be clear that race is not always a decisive factor in admissions, even when grades and test scores are comparable.

Terry concludes by criticizing one final premise of what he takes to be the argument for diversity affirmative action. It is that:

12. Diversity does not just improve the educational climate at our colleges and universities, it also helps to establish the political legitimacy of other institutions in society as well, e.g., the U.S. military.

I accept (12). Justice O'Connor in support of this premise writes:

> In order to cultivate a set of leaders with legitimacy in the eyes of the Citizenry, it is necessary that the path to leadership be visibly open to talented and qualified individuals of every race and ethnicity.

In the U.S., given the widespread racial discrimination and effects of racial discrimination in housing, education, and employment, evidence of which I cite in my book, *Affirmative Action and Racial Preference*, we have anything but the equal opportunity that O'Connor thinks is necessary for legitimacy. The question is what to do about it. We could begin to tackle the problem at its base, as I mentioned at the end of my paper, by allocating substantial funds, probably about $25 billion a year, to put in place a quality education system K through 12 for every child in the country, or we can continue with the bandaid approach of opening up such opportunities to a few minorities using a diversity justification and hoping that this will somehow trickle down through the system to create more equal opportunity overall. I have already expressed my moral preference for something like the $25 billion a year educational plan, and maybe Terry and I can agree on this. Nevertheless, at the present moment, I do endorse diversity affirmative action and the premises of the argument for it, which I have adopted, or reformulated, from Terry's discussion (those given in bold in my text) because at the moment I judge affirmative action to be the only politically feasible option we have.

RESPONSE TO LAWSON

Turning now to Bill Lawson's comments, he too expresses considerable agreement with the arguments of *Affirmative Action for the Future*. However, Lawson wants to focus his comments on my discussion of diversity affirmative action, and he suggests a couple of serious problems for this form of affirmative action and also one way he thinks its institutional practice can be improved.

Who Benefits?

The first problem he notes is how the benefits of diversity affirmative action programs are distributed. He comments:

> The lessons we learn in and out of the classroom in our colleges and universities often have a long lasting impact on our lives. The friends we make in college often replace our high school classmates as life long friends. These friends often become part of our social and vocational network. I am sure that many of us have received calls from college classmates about jobs or in the case of professional philosophers about opportunities to publish or present. It seems clear that being in this mix is important to one's professional development. People have to know who you are. There are, however, many ways of being known on a college campus. For much of this country's history, black Americans that attended white colleges and universities were often ostracized, shunned, and not

allowed to be a part of the mix, an important part of the college experience. They were known, but not in a positive way.

Later he comments: "black students get an education and the professor has a job, but at what cost."

Now I want to agree with Lawson about the costs of affirmative action, particularly for those with identifiable racial and ethnic status who receive it. However, it is not clear to me that other forms of affirmative action, especially remedial affirmative action, would not have the same problem. There would still be the unfair resistance to such affirmative action, at least by those who have failed to appreciate its legal and moral justification. Moreover, we also need to take into account the benefits of affirmative action for those who receive it. In my book, it is noted that without affirmative action at elite law schools, black enrollment would decline from around 8% to 1–2%. I further note that this is particularly significant given that 40% of the lawyers at top law firms and 48% of black law professors come from the top ten law schools. It has also been estimated that without affirmative action, there would be zero, or nearly zero, blacks at Harvard Law School and Yale Law School. Again, this is particularly significant given that 25% of black law professors in the U.S. have graduated from just those two law schools. Furthermore, in a study of 60,000 students of twenty-eight selective universities from 1970 to 1996, all minority graduates reported high incomes (averaging $105,000 in 1996 dollars), 75% of them reported that they were satisfied with their careers, and 60% reported that the engaged in unremunerated service to their communities (compared to a reported 50% for white students) (Bowen and Bok 1998, pp. 355–356).

So there are considerable benefits for affirmative action candidates at elite colleges and universities where it is practiced, despite the various forms of undeserved ill treatment those candidates receive at those same schools while they are being so benefited.

Non-Race-Based Affirmative Action

Lawson, however, borrowing from Laurence Thomas, proposes a modification in how we think about

diversity affirmative action that he thinks will make the practice even better for those who receive it. Lawson proposes that instead of thinking about diversity affirmative action candidates as simply bringing racial or ethnic diversity to elite colleges and universities, we admit them because they have some idiosyncratic excellence that is distinct from their race or ethnicity. Thomas suggests that excellence in Gospel singing might serve as such. Thomas also likes the idea of finding those idiosyncratic excellences that have been "forged by the pain of those who have been wronged." Both Lawson and Thomas are attracted by the idea that ethnic and racial affirmative candidates can point to such excellences as the distinctive reason why they have been admitted, a feature that is distinct from their racial and ethnic status. However, the main problem I see with this approach is that it opens the door to a wide range of idiosyncratic excellences and provides no guarantee that when all such excellences are weighed against each other to determine who will be admitted on the basis of them, anything like the numbers of racial and ethnic affirmative action candidates that are being currently admitted would still continue to be admitted.

Nevertheless, there is another way to proceed here that should produce something like the result that Lawson wants but without the problem that afflicts Thomas's proposal. This approach is implicitly the one I have been following in my book in my discussion of diversity affirmative action. The approach starts with the realization that racial discrimination continues be a very serious problem in the U.S., affecting many different aspects of our society. It goes on to affirm that it is of the utmost importance that we address the problem of racial discrimination effectively in our educational institutions. This is seen to require that we bring to those institutions, students, in particular, who can speak with authority about such racial discrimination. In the U.S., this will typically involve admitting students from disadvantaged racial minorities who have themselves suffered such discrimination. But it can also, as the University of Michigan's undergraduate affirmative action program allowed, admit white students who, say, attended an inner city high school in Detroit and who are otherwise qualified. Put these two elements together such a diversity affirmative action program would be designed to look for students who either have experienced racial discrimination themselves or who understand well, in some other way, how racism harms people in the U.S., and thus are able to authoritatively and effectively speak about it in an educational context. This basis for selecting someone as a diversity affirmative action candidate can then be satisfied by whites who because of their disposition and experience can speak authoritatively and effectively about racial discrimination and it can fail to be met by racial and ethnic minorities who because of their disposition and/or lack of experience cannot speak authoritatively and effectively about racial discrimination. This clearly seems to be a form of non–race-based diversity affirmative action that Lawson, Thomas and I could agree upon.

White Intransigence

Yet Lawson's idea of improving upon diversity affirmative action by finding a non–race-based form of it appears to run counter to the other problem he has with diversity affirmative action that is highlighted by my account. That problem arises because Lawson rejects the view that once whites are given a true understanding of the evils of racial discrimination, "they will find it easy, or easier, to give up racism." He even thinks that my account supports his stance.

Now I do point out that there is a long and knowable history of the deplorable economic and social conditions of African Americans rooted in racial discrimination and the effects thereof. At the same time, I cite studies showing, for example, that a majority of whites think that blacks and whites enjoy the same standard of living and that most whites think that the predominant type of discrimination in the U.S. is reverse discrimination. But I do not conclude from this that argument and empirical data just fail to move people on racial issues. This is because I do not think the history of the continuing discrimination suffered by African Americans is well-known in the U.S. Nor are the strongest arguments for affirmative action well-known either. My experience has been that when this history and these arguments are respectfully presented to those who are generally unaware of them, considerable progress can be made. That is the hope of affirmative action, and, to date at least, I think we can say that its limited practice in the U.S. and elsewhere has achieved some worthwhile results.

ENDNOTES

1. Terry later jumps from the claim that I have just rejected—that a critical mass of minority students cannot be objectively assessed—to the claim that the purpose of minority representation must then be to confer legitimacy on our institutions. I myself would not deny that minority representation can sometimes help confer legitimacy on our institutions. This is especially true in the military, where the question can always be asked: Why can't the military find minority officers capable of leading our soldiers into battle? But the arguments in the Michigan cases did turn prominently on the educational benefits of diversity in educational institutions, and those benefits, I claim, are significant and objectively assessable.

2. This is the University of Michigan's definition of critical mass. To see the exchange between Pell and myself before the U.S. Supreme Court's decisions in Grutter and Gratz last year, which also includes position papers and responses, see the *Journal of Social Philosophy* 34 (Summer, 2003).

3. "Debating the Benefits of Affirmative Action," The Chronicle of Higher Education, 18 May 2001.

4. William Bowen and Derek Bok, *The Shape of the River* (Princeton: Princeton University Press, 1998), 355–6.

5. William Bowen and Derek Bok, "Access to Success," *ABA Journal* (February 1999), 62–3, 67.

6. Linda Wightman, "The Threat to Diversity in Legal Education," *New York University law Review* 72 (April, 1997), 1–51. Being admitted without preference for Wightman means being admitted simply on the basis of one's grades and LSAT scores. Being admitted with preference means that other factors were relevant because one would not have been admitted on the basis of just one's grades and LSAT scores.

7. It should be pointed out that Wightman herself interprets her data, as I do, to support diversity affirmative action.

REFERENCES

Bowen, William, and Derek Bok. 1998. *The shape of the river*. Princeton: Princeton University Press.

Schmidt, Peter. 2001. Debating the benefits of affirmative action. *The Chronicle of Higher Education*, 18 May.

Sterba, J. P. 2009. *Affirmative action for the future*. Ithaca: Cornell University Press.

Sterba, J. P., and Carl Cohen. 2003. *Affirmative action and racial preference*. Oxford: Oxford University Press.

41

Grutter v. Bollinger

Supreme Court of the United States

The issue before the U.S. Supreme Court was whether the affirmative action admission program at the University of Michigan Law School violated the Fourteenth Amendment and Title VI of the Civil Rights Act of 1964. The majority of the Court held that it did not because it is constitutionally permissible to use racial preferences to achieve the educational benefits of diversity and because the law school provided the individualized consideration of each and every applicant that is needed if racial preferences are going to be used in admissions. In his dissent, Justice Clarence Thomas argues that the majority's decision is in conflict with the other Supreme Court decisions.

Justice *O'Connor* delivered the opinion of the Court.

This case requires us to decide whether the use of race as a factor in student admissions by the University of Michigan Law School (Law School) is unlawful.

The Law School ranks among the Nation's top law schools. It receives more than 3,500 applications each year for a class of around 350 students. Seeking to "admit a group of students who individually and collectively are among the most capable," the Law School looks for individuals with "substantial promise for success in law school" and "a strong likelihood of succeeding in the practice of law and contributing in diverse ways to the well-being of others." More broadly, the Law School seeks "a mix of students with varying backgrounds and experiences who will respect and learn from each other." In 1992, the dean of the Law School charged a faculty committee with crafting a written admissions policy to implement these goals. In particular, the Law School sought to ensure that its efforts to achieve student body diversity complied with this Court's most recent ruling on the use of race in university admissions. Upon the unanimous adoption of the committee's report by the Law

School faculty, it became the Law School's official admissions policy.

The hallmark of that policy is its focus on academic ability coupled with a flexible assessment of applicants' talents, experiences, and potential "to contribute to the learning of those around them." The policy requires admissions officials to evaluate each applicant based on all the information available in the file, including a personal statement, letters of recommendation, and an essay describing the ways in which the applicant will contribute to the life and diversity of the Law School. In reviewing an applicant's file, admissions officials must consider the applicant's undergraduate grade point average (GPA) and Law School Admissions Test (LSAT) score because they are important (if imperfect) predictors of academic success in law school. The policy stresses that "no applicant should be admitted unless we expect that applicant to do well enough to graduate with no serious academic problems."

The policy makes clear, however, that even the highest possible score does not guarantee admission to the Law School. Nor does a low score automatically disqualify an applicant. Rather, the policy requires admissions officials to look beyond grades and test scores to other criteria that are important to the Law School's educational objectives. So-called "'soft' variables" such as "the enthusiasm of recommenders, the quality of the undergraduate institution, the quality of the applicant's essay, and the areas and difficulty of undergraduate course selection" are all brought to bear in assessing an "applicant's likely contributions to the intellectual and social life of the institution."

The policy aspires to "achieve that diversity which has the potential to enrich everyone's education and thus make a law school class stronger than the sum of its parts." The policy does not restrict the types of diversity contributions eligible for "substantial weight" in the admissions process, but instead recognizes "many possible bases for diversity admissions." The policy does, however, reaffirm the Law School's long-standing commitment to "one particular type of diversity," that is, "racial and ethnic diversity with special reference to the inclusion of students from groups which have been historically discriminated against, like African-Americans, Hispanics and Native Americans, who without this commitment might not be represented in our student body in meaningful numbers." By enrolling a "'critical mass' of [underrepresented] minority students," the Law School seeks to "ensur[e] their ability to make unique contributions to the character of the Law School."

The policy does not define diversity "solely in terms of racial and ethnic status." Nor is the policy "insensitive to the competition among all students for admission to the [L]aw [[S]chool." Rather, the policy seeks to guide admissions officers in "producing classes both diverse and academically outstanding, classes made up of students who promise to continue the tradition of outstanding contribution by Michigan Graduates to the legal profession."

Petitioner Barbara Grutter is a white Michigan resident who applied to the Law School in 1996 with a 3.8 grade point average and 161 LSAT score. The Law School initially placed petitioner on a waiting list, but subsequently rejected her application. In December 1997, petitioner filed suit in the United States District Court for the Eastern District of Michigan against the Law School, the Regents of the University of Michigan, Lee Bollinger (Dean

of the Law School from 1987 to 1994, and President of the University of Michigan from 1996 to 2002), Jeffrey Lehman (Dean of the Law School), and Dennis Shields (Director of Admissions at the Law School from 1991 until 1998). Petitioner alleged that respondents discriminated against her on the basis of race in violation of the Fourteenth Amendment; Title VI of the Civil Rights Act of 1964.

Petitioner further alleged that her application was rejected because the Law School uses race as a "predominant" factor, giving applicants who belong to certain minority groups "a significantly greater chance of admission than students with similar credentials from disfavored racial groups." Petitioner also alleged that respondents "had no compelling interest to justify their use of race in the admissions process." Petitioner requested compensatory and punitive damages, an order requiring the Law School to offer her admission, and an injunction prohibiting the Law School from continuing to discriminate on the basis of race. Petitioner clearly has standing to bring this lawsuit.

The District Court granted petitioner's motion for class certification and for bifurcation of the trial into liability and damages phases. The class was defined as "all persons who (A) applied for and were not granted admission to the University of Michigan Law School for the academic years since (and including) 1995 until the time that judgment is entered herein; and (B) were members of those racial or ethnic groups, including Caucasian, that Defendants treated less favorably in considering their applications for admission to the Law School."

The District Court heard oral argument on the parties' cross-motions for summary judgment on December 22, 2000. Taking the motions under advisement, the District Court indicated that it would decide as a matter of law whether the Law School's asserted interest in obtaining the educational benefits that flow from a diverse student body was compelling. The District Court also indicated that it would conduct a bench trial on the extent to which race was a factor in the Law School's admissions decisions, and whether the Law School's consideration of race in admissions decisions constituted a race-based double standard.

During the 15-day bench trial, the parties introduced extensive evidence concerning the Law School's use of race in the admissions process. Dennis Shields, Director of Admissions when petitioner applied to the Law School, testified that he did not direct his staff to admit a particular percentage or number of minority students, but rather to consider an applicant's race along with all other factors. Shields testified that at the height of the admissions season, he would frequently consult the so-called "daily reports" that kept track of the racial and ethnic composition of the class (along with other information such as residency status and gender). This was done, Shields testified, to ensure that a critical mass of underrepresented minority students would be reached so as to realize the educational benefits of a diverse student body. Shields stressed, however, that he did not seek to admit any particular number or percentage of underrepresented minority students.

Erica Munzel, who succeeded Shields as Director of Admissions, testified that "critical mass" means "meaningful numbers" or "meaningful representation," which she understood to mean a number that encourages underrepresented minority students to participate in the classroom and not feel isolated. Munzel stated there is no number, percentage, or range of numbers or percentages that constitute critical mass. Munzel also asserted that she must consider the race of applicants because a critical mass of underrepresented minority students could not be enrolled if admissions decisions were based primarily on undergraduate GPAs and LSAT scores.

The current Dean of the Law School, Jeffrey Lehman, also testified. Like the other Law School witnesses, Lehman did not quantify critical mass in terms of numbers or percentages. He indicated that critical mass means numbers such that underrepresented minority students do not feel isolated or like spokespersons for their race. When asked about the extent to which race is considered in admissions, Lehman testified that it varies from one applicant to another. In some cases, according to Lehman's testimony, an applicant's race may play no role, while in others it may be a "determinative" factor.

The District Court heard extensive testimony from Professor Richard Lempert, who chaired the faculty committee that drafted the 1992 policy. Lempert emphasized that the Law School seeks students with diverse interests and backgrounds to enhance classroom discussion and the educational experience both inside and outside the classroom. When asked about the policy's "commitment to racial and ethnic diversity with special reference to the inclusion of students from groups which have been historically discriminated against," Lempert explained that this language did not purport to remedy past discrimination, but rather to include students who may bring to the Law School a perspective different from that of members of groups which have not been the victims of such discrimination. Lempert acknowledged that other groups, such as Asians and Jews, have experienced discrimination, but explained they were not mentioned in the policy because individuals who are members of those groups were already being admitted to the Law School in significant numbers.

Kent Syverud was the final witness to testify about the Law School's use of race in admissions decisions. Syverud was a professor at the Law School when the 1992 admissions policy was adopted and is now Dean of Vanderbilt Law School. In addition to his testimony at trial, Syverud submitted several expert reports on the educational benefits of diversity. Syverud's testimony indicated that when a critical mass of underrepresented minority students is present, racial stereotypes lose their force because nonminority students learn there is no "minority viewpoint" but rather a variety of viewpoints among minority students.

In an attempt to quantify the extent to which the Law School actually considers race in making admissions decisions, the parties introduced voluminous evidence at trial. Relying on data obtained from the Law School, petitioner's expert, Dr. Kinley Larntz, generated and analyzed "admissions grids" for the years in question (1995–2000). These grids show the number of applicants and the number of admittees for all combinations of GPAs and LSAT scores. Dr. Larntz made "cell-by-cell" comparisons between applicants of different races to determine whether a statistically significant relationship existed between race and admission rates. He concluded that membership in certain minority groups "is an extremely strong factor in the decision for acceptance," and that applicants from these minority groups "are given an extremely large allowance for admission" as compared to applicants who are members of nonfavored groups. Dr. Larntz conceded, however, that race is not the predominant factor in the Law School's admissions calculus.

Dr. Stephen Raudenbush, the Law School's expert, focused on the predicted effect of eliminating race as a factor in the Law School's admission process. In Dr. Raudenbush's view, a race-blind admissions system would have a "very dramatic," negative effect on underrepresented minority admissions. He testified that in 2000, 35 percent of underrepresented minority applicants were admitted. Dr. Raudenbush predicted that if race were not considered, only 10 percent of those applicants would have been admitted. Under this scenario, underrepresented minority students would have comprised 4 percent of the entering class in 2000 instead of the actual figure of 14.5 percent.

In the end, the District Court concluded that the Law School's use of race as a factor in admissions decisions was unlawful. Applying strict scrutiny, the District Court determined that the Law School's asserted interest in assembling a diverse student body was not compelling because "the attainment of a racially diverse class ... was not recognized as such by *Bakke* and is not a remedy for past discrimination." The District Court went on to hold that even if diversity were compelling, the Law School had not narrowly tailored its use of race to further that interest. The District Court granted petitioner's request for declaratory relief and enjoined the Law School from using race as a factor in its admissions decisions. The Court of Appeals entered a stay of the injunction pending appeal.

Sitting en banc, the Court of Appeals reversed the District Court's judgment and vacated the injunction. The Court of Appeals first held that Justice Powell's opinion in *Bakke* was binding precedent establishing diversity as a compelling state interest. According to the Court of Appeals, Justice Powell's opinion with respect to diversity comprised the controlling rationale for the judgment

of this Court under the analysis set forth in *Marks v. United States* (1977). The Court of Appeals also held that the Law School's use of race was narrowly tailored because race was merely a "potential 'plus' factor" and because the Law School's program was "virtually identical" to the Harvard admissions program described approvingly by Justice Powell and appended to his *Bakke* opinion.

Four dissenting judges would have held the Law School's use of race unconstitutional. Three of the dissenters, rejecting the majority's *Marks* analysis, examined the Law School's interest in student body diversity on the merits and concluded it was not compelling. The fourth dissenter, writing separately, found it unnecessary to decide whether diversity was a compelling interest because, like the other dissenters, he believed that the Law School's use of race was not narrowly tailored to further that interest.

We granted certiorari, to resolve the disagreement among the Courts of Appeals on a question of national importance: Whether diversity is a compelling interest that can justify the narrowly tailored use of race in selecting applicants for admission to public universities.

We last addressed the use of race in public higher education over 25 years ago. In the landmark *Bakke* case, we reviewed a racial set-aside program that reserved 16 out of 100 seats in a medical school class for members of certain minority groups. The decision produced six separate opinions, none of which commanded a majority of the Court. Four Justices would have upheld the program against all attack on the ground that the government can use race to "remedy disadvantages cast on minorities by past racial prejudice." Four other Justices avoided the constitutional question altogether and struck down the program on statutory grounds. Justice Powell provided a fifth vote not only for invalidating the set-aside program, but also for reversing the state court's injunction against any use of race whatsoever. The only holding for the Court in *Bakke* was that a "State has a substantial interest that legitimately may be served by a properly devised admissions program, involving the competitive consideration of race and ethnic origin." Thus, we reversed that part of the lower court's judgment that enjoined the university "from any consideration of the race of any applicant." ...

Since this Court's splintered decision in *Bakke*, Justice Powell's opinion announcing the judgment of the Court has served as the touchstone for constitutional analysis of race-conscious admissions policies. Public and private universities across the Nation have modeled their own admissions programs on Justice Powell's views on permissible race-conscious policies. We therefore discuss Justice Powell's opinion in some detail.

Justice Powell began by stating that "[t]he guarantee of equal protection cannot mean one thing when applied to one individual and something else when applied to a person of another color. If both are not accorded the same protection, then it is not equal." ... In Justice Powell's view, when governmental decisions "touch upon an individual's race or ethnic background, he is entitled to a judicial determination that the burden he is asked to bear on that basis is precisely tailored to serve a compelling governmental interest." Under this exacting standard, only one of the interests asserted by the university survived Justice Powell's scrutiny.

First, Justice Powell rejected an interest in "'reducing the historic deficit of traditionally disfavored minorities in medical schools and in the medical profession'" as an unlawful interest in racial balancing. Second, Justice Powell rejected an interest in remedying societal discrimination because such measures would risk placing unnecessary burdens on innocent third parties "who bear no responsibility for whatever harm the beneficiaries of the special admissions program are thought to have suffered." Third, Justice Powell rejected an interest in "increasing the number of physicians who will practice in communities currently underserved," concluding that even if such an interest could be compelling in some circumstances the program under review was not "geared to promote that goal."

Justice Powell approved the university's use of race to further only one interest: "the attainment of a diverse student body." With the important proviso that "constitutional limitations protecting individual rights may not be disregarded," Justice Powell grounded his analysis in the academic freedom that "long has been viewed as a special concern of the First Amendment." Justice Powell emphasized that nothing less than the "'nation's future depends upon leaders trained through wide exposure' to the ideas and mores of students as diverse as this Nation of many peoples." In seeking the "right to select those students who will contribute the most to the 'robust exchange of ideas,'" a university seeks "to achieve a goal that is of paramount importance in the fulfillment of its mission." Both "tradition and experience lend support to the view that the contribution of diversity is substantial."

Justice Powell was, however, careful to emphasize that in his view race "is only one element in a range of factors a university properly may consider in attaining the goal of a heterogeneous student body." For Justice Powell, "[i]t is not an interest in simple ethnic diversity, in which a specified percentage of the student body is in effect guaranteed to be members of selected ethnic groups," that can justify the use of race. Rather, "[t]he diversity that furthers a compelling state interest encompasses a far broader array of qualifications and characteristics of which racial or ethnic origin is but a single though important element."

In the wake of our fractured decision in *Bakke*, courts have struggled to discern whether Justice Powell's diversity rationale, set forth in part of the opinion joined by no other Justice, is nonetheless binding precedent under *Marks*. In that case, we explained that "[w]hen a fragmented Court decides a case and no single rationale explaining the result enjoys the assent of five Justices, the holding of the Court may be viewed as that position taken by those Members who concurred in the judgments on the narrowest grounds." As the divergent opinions of the lower courts demonstrate, however, "[t]his test is more easily stated than applied to the various opinions supporting the result in *[Bakke]*."

We do not find it necessary to decide whether Justice Powell's opinion is binding under *Marks*. It does not seem "useful to pursue the *Marks* inquiry to the utmost logical possibility when it has so obviously baffled and divided the lower courts that have considered it." More important, for the reasons set out below, today we endorse Justice Powell's view that student body diversity is a compelling state interest that can justify the use of race in university admissions.

The Equal Protection Clause provides that no State shall "deny to any person within its jurisdiction the equal protection of the laws." Because the Fourteenth Amendment "protect[s] *persons,* not *groups,*" all "governmental action based on race—a *group* classification long recognized as in most circumstances irrelevant and therefore prohibited—should be subjected to detailed judicial inquiry to ensure that the *personal* right to equal protection of the laws has not been infringed." We are a "free people whose institutions are founded upon the doctrine of equality." It follows from that principle that "government may treat people differently because of their race only for the most compelling reasons."

We have held that all racial classifications imposed by government "must be analyzed by a reviewing court under strict scrutiny." This means that such classifications are constitutional only if they are narrowly tailored to further compelling governmental interests. "Absent searching judicial inquiry into the justification for such race-based measures," we have no way to determine what "classifications are 'benign' or 'remedial' and what classifications are in fact motivated by illegitimate notions of racial inferiority or simple racial politics." We apply strict scrutiny to all racial classifications to "'smoke out' illegitimate uses of race by assuring that [government] is pursuing a goal important enough to warrant use of a highly suspect tool."

Strict scrutiny is not "strict in theory, but fatal in fact." Although all governmental uses of race are subject to strict scrutiny, not all are invalidated by it. As we have explained, "whenever the government treats any person unequally because of his or her race, that person has suffered an injury that falls squarely within the language and spirit of the Constitution's guarantee of equal protection." But that observation "says nothing about the ultimate validity of any particular law; that determination is the job of the court applying strict scrutiny." When race-based action is necessary to further a compelling governmental interest, such action does not violate the constitutional guarantee of equal protection so long as the narrow-tailoring requirement is also satisfied.

Context matters when reviewing race-based governmental action under the Equal Protection Clause. In *Adarand Constructors, Inc. v. Peña,* we made clear that strict scrutiny must take "'relevant differences' into account." Indeed, as we explained, that is its "fundamental purpose." Not every decision influenced by race is equally objectionable and strict scrutiny is designed to provide a framework for carefully examining the importance and the sincerity of the reasons advanced by the governmental decision-maker for the use of race in that particular context.

With these principles in mind, we turn to the question whether the Law School's use of race is justified by a compelling state interest. Before this Court, as they have throughout this litigation, respondents assert only one justification for their use of race in the admissions process: obtaining "the educational benefits that flow from a diverse student body." In other words, the Law School asks us to recognize, in the context of higher education, a compelling state interest in student body diversity.

We first wish to dispel the notion that the Law School's argument has been foreclosed, either expressly or implicitly, by our affirmative-action cases decided since *Bakke.* It is true that some language in those opinions might be read to suggest that remedying past discrimination is the only permissible justification for race-based governmental action. But we have never held that the only governmental use of race that can survive strict scrutiny is remedying past discrimination. Nor, since *Bakke,* have we directly addressed the use of race in the context of public higher education. Today, we hold that the Law School has a compelling interest in attaining a diverse student body.

The Law School's educational judgment that such diversity is essential to its educational mission is one to which we defer. The Law School's assessment that diversity will, in fact, yield educational benefits is substantiated by respondents and their *amici.* Our scrutiny of the interest asserted by the

Law School is no less strict for taking into account complex educational judgments in an area that lies primarily within the expertise of the university. Our holding today is in keeping with our tradition of giving a degree of deference to a university's academic decisions, within constitutionally prescribed limits.

We have long recognized that, given the important purpose of public education and the expansive freedoms of speech and thought associated with the university environment, universities occupy a special niche in our constitutional tradition.... In announcing the principle of student body diversity as a compelling state interest, Justice Powell invoked our cases recognizing a constitutional dimension, grounded in the First Amendment, of educational autonomy: "The freedom of a university to make its own judgments as to education includes the selection of its student body." From this premise, Justice Powell reasoned that by claiming "the right to select those students who will contribute the most to the 'robust exchange of ideas,'" a university "seek[s] to achieve a goal that is of paramount importance in the fulfillment of its mission." Our conclusion that the Law School has a compelling interest in a diverse student body is informed by our view that attaining a diverse student body is at the heart of the Law School's proper institutional mission, and that "good faith" on the part of a university is "presumed" absent "a showing to the contrary."

As part of its goal of "assembling a class that is both exceptionally academically qualified and broadly diverse," the Law School seeks to "enroll a 'critical mass' of minority students." The Law School's interest is not simply "to assure within its student body some specified percentage of a particular group merely because of its race or ethnic origin." That would amount to outright racial balancing, which is patently unconstitutional. Rather, the Law School's concept of critical mass is defined by reference to the educational benefits that diversity is designed to produce.

These benefits are substantial. As the District Court emphasized, the Law School's admissions policy promotes "cross-racial understanding," helps to break down racial stereotypes, and "enables [students] to better understand persons of different races." These benefits are "important and laudable," because "classroom discussion is livelier, more spirited, and simply more enlightening and interesting" when the students have "the greatest possible variety of backgrounds."

The Law School's claim of a compelling interest is further bolstered by its *amici,* who point to the educational benefits that flow from student body diversity. In addition to the expert studies and reports entered into evidence at trial, numerous studies show that student body diversity promotes learning outcomes, and "better prepares students for an increasingly diverse workforce and society, and better prepares them as professionals."

These benefits are not theoretical but real, as major American businesses have made clear that the skills needed in today's increasingly global marketplace can only be developed through exposure to widely diverse people, cultures, ideas, and viewpoints. What is more, high-ranking retired officers and civilian leaders of the United States military assert that, "[b]ased on [their] decades of experience," a "highly qualified, racially diverse officer corps ... is essential to the military's ability to fulfill its principle mission to provide national security." The primary sources for the Nation's officer corps are the service academies and the Reserve Officers Training Corps (ROTC), the latter comprising students already admitted to participating colleges and universities. At present, "the military cannot achieve an officer corps that is *both* highly qualified *and* racially diverse unless the service academies and the ROTC used limited race-conscious recruiting and admissions policies." To fulfill its mission, the military "must be selective in admissions for training and education for the officer corps, *and* it must train and educate a highly qualified, racially diverse officer corps in a racially diverse setting." We agree that "[i]t requires only a small step from this analysis to conclude that our country's other most selective institutions must remain both diverse and selective."...

We have repeatedly acknowledged the overriding importance of preparing students for work and citizenship, describing education as pivotal to "sustaining our political and cultural heritage" with a fundamental role in maintaining the fabric of society. This Court has long recognized that "education … is the very foundation of good citizenship." For this reason, the diffusion of knowledge and opportunity through public institutions of higher education must be accessible to all individuals regardless of race or ethnicity. The United States, as *amicus curiae,* affirms that "[e]nsuring that public institutions are open and available to all segments of American society, including people of all races and ethnicities, represents a paramount government objective." And, "[n]owhere is the importance of such openness more acute than in the context of higher education." Effective participation by members of all racial and ethnic groups in the civic life of our Nation is essential if the dream of one Nation, indivisible, is to be realized.

Moreover, universities, and in particular, law schools, represent the training ground for a large number of our Nation's leaders. Individuals with law degrees occupy roughly half the state governorships, more than half the seats in the United States Senate, and more than a third of the seats in the United States House of Representatives. The pattern is even more striking when it comes to highly selective law schools. A handful of these schools accounts for 25 of the 100 United States Senators, 74 United States Courts of Appeals judges, and nearly 200 of the more than 600 United States District Court judges.…

In order to cultivate a set of leaders with legitimacy in the eyes of the citizenry, it is necessary that the path to leadership be visibly open to talented and qualified individuals of every race and ethnicity. All members of our heterogeneous society must have confidence in the openness and integrity of the educational institutions that provide this training. As we have recognized, law schools "cannot be effective in isolation from the individuals and institutions with which the law interacts." Access to legal education (and thus the legal profession) must be inclusive of talented and qualified individuals of every race and ethnicity, so that all members of our heterogeneous society may participate in the educational institutions that provide the

training and education necessary to succeed in America.

The Law School does not premise its need for critical mass on "any belief that minority students always (or even consistently) express some characteristic minority viewpoint on any issue." To the contrary, diminishing the force of such stereotypes is both a crucial part of the Law School's mission, and one that it cannot accomplish with only token numbers of minority students. Just as growing up in a particular region or having particular professional experiences is likely to affect an individual's views, so too is one's own, unique experience of being a racial minority in a society, like our own, in which race unfortunately still matters. The Law School has determined, based on its experience and expertise, that a "critical mass" of underrepresented minorities is necessary to further its compelling interest in securing the educational benefits of a diverse student body.

Even in the limited circumstance when drawing racial distinctions is permissible to further a compelling state interest, government is still "constrained in how it may pursue that end: [T]he means chosen to accomplish the [government's] asserted purpose must be specifically and narrowly framed to accomplish that purpose." The purpose of the narrow tailoring requirement is to ensure that "the means chosen 'fit'… th[e] compelling goal so closely that there is little or no possibility that the motive for the classification was illegitimate racial prejudice or stereotype."

Since *Bakke,* we have had no occasion to define the contours of the narrow-tailoring inquiry with respect to race-conscious university admissions programs. That inquiry must be calibrated to fit the distinct issues raised by the use of race to achieve student body diversity in public higher education. Contrary to Justice Kennedy's assertions, we do not "abandon strict scrutiny." Rather, as we have already explained, we adhere to *Adarand's* teaching that the very purpose of strict scrutiny is to take such "relevant differences into account."

To be narrowly tailored, a race-conscious admissions program, cannot use a quota system— it cannot "insulat[e] each category of applicants with certain desired qualifications from competition with all other applicants." Instead, a university may consider race or ethnicity only as a "'plus' in a particular applicant's file," without "insulat[ing] the individual from, comparison with all other candidates for the available seats." In other words, an admissions program must be "flexible enough to consider all pertinent elements of diversity in light of the particular qualifications of each applicant, and to place them on the same footing for consideration, although not necessarily according them the same weight."

We find that the Law School's admissions program bears the hallmarks of a narrowly tailored plan. As Justice Powell made clear in *Bakke,* truly individualized consideration demands that race be used in a flexible, nonmechanical way. It follows from this mandate that universities cannot establish quotas for members of certain racial groups or put members of those groups on separate admissions tracks. Nor can universities insulate applicants who belong to certain racial or ethnic groups from the competition for admission. Universities can, however, consider race or ethnicity more flexibly as a "plus" factor in the context of individualized consideration of each and every applicant.

We are satisfied that the Law School's admissions program, like the Harvard plan described by Justice Powell, does not operate as a quota. Properly understood, a "quota" is a program in which a certain fixed number or proportion of opportunities are "reserved exclusively for certain minority groups." Quotas "'impose a fixed number or percentage which must be attained, or which cannot be exceeded,'" and "insulate the individual from comparison with all other candidates for the available seats." In contrast, "a permissible goal ... require[s] only a good-faith effort ... to come within a range demarcated by the goal itself," and permits consideration of race as a "plus" factor in any given case while still ensuring that each candidate "compete[s] with all other qualified applicants."

Justice Powell's distinction between the medical school's rigid 16-seat quota and Harvard's flexible use of race as a "plus" factor is instructive. Harvard certainly had minimum *goals* for minority

enrollment, even if it had no specific number firmly in mind. ("10 or 20 black students could not begin to bring to their classmates and to each other the variety of points of view, backgrounds and experiences of blacks in the United States"). What is more, Justice Powell flatly rejected the argument that Harvard's program was "the functional equivalent of a quota" merely because it had some "'plus'" for race, or gave greater "weight" to race than to some other factors, in order to achieve student body diversity.

The Law School's goal of attaining a critical mass of underrepresented minority students does not transform its program into a quota. As the Harvard plan described by Justice Powell recognized, there is of course "some relationship between numbers and achieving the benefits to be derived from a diverse student body, and between numbers and providing a reasonable environment for those students admitted." ... "[S]ome attention to numbers," without more, does not transform a flexible admissions system into a rigid quota.

That a race-conscious admissions program does not operate as a quota does not, by itself, satisfy the requirement of individualized consideration. When using race as a "plus" factor in university admissions, a university's admissions program must remain flexible enough to ensure that each applicant is evaluated as an individual and not in a way that makes an applicant's race or ethnicity the defining feature of his or her application. The importance of this individualized consideration in the context of a race-conscious admissions program is paramount.

Here, the Law School engages in a highly individualized, holistic review of each applicant's file, giving serious consideration to all the ways an applicant might contribute to a diverse educational environment. The Law School affords this individualized consideration to applicants of all races. There is no policy, either *de jure* or *de facto,* of automatic acceptance or rejection based on any single "soft" variable. Unlike the program at issue in *Gratz v. Bollinger,* the Law School awards no mechanical, predetermined diversity "bonuses" based on race or ethnicity (distinguishing a race-conscious admissions program that automatically awards 20 points based on race from the Harvard plan, which considered race but "did not contemplate that any single characteristic automatically ensured a specific and identifiable contribution to a university's diversity"). Like the Harvard plan, the Law School's admissions policy "is flexible enough to consider all pertinent elements of diversity in light of the particular qualifications of each applicant, and to place them on the same footing for consideration, although not necessarily according them the same weight."

We also find that, like the Harvard plan Justice Powell referenced in *Bakke,* the Law School's race-conscious admissions program adequately ensures that all factors that may contribute to student body diversity are meaningfully considered alongside race in admissions decisions. With respect to the use of race itself, all underrepresented minority students admitted by the Law School have been deemed qualified. By virtue of our Nation's struggle with racial inequality, such students are both likely to have experiences of particular importance to the Law School's mission, and less likely to be admitted in meaningful numbers on criteria that ignore those experiences.

The Law School does not, however, limit in any way the broad range of qualities and experiences that may be considered valuable contributions to student body diversity. To the contrary, the 1992 policy makes clear "[t]here are many possible bases for diversity admissions," and provides examples of admittees who have lived or traveled widely abroad, are fluent in several languages, have overcome personal adversity and family hardship, have exceptional records of extensive community service, and have had successful careers in other fields. The Law School seriously considers each "applicant's promise of making a notable contribution to the class by way of a particular strength, attainment, or characteristic—*e.g.,* an unusual intellectual achievement, employment experience, nonacademic performance, or personal background." All applicants have the opportunity to highlight their own potential diversity contributions through the submission of a personal statement, letters of recommendation, and an essay describing the ways in which the applicant

will contribute to the life and diversity of the Law School.

What is more, the Law School actually gives substantial weight to diversity factors besides race. The Law School frequently accepts nonminority applicants with grades and test scores lower than underrepresented minority applicants (and other nonminority applicants) who are rejected. This shows that the Law School seriously weighs many other diversity factors besides race that can make a real and dispositive difference for nonminority applicants as well. By this flexible approach, the Law School sufficiently takes into account, in practice as well as in theory, a wide variety of characteristics besides race and ethnicity that contribute to a diverse student body. Justice Kennedy speculates that "race is likely outcome determinative for many members of minority groups" who do not fall within the upper range of LSAT scores and grades. But the same could be said of the Harvard plan discussed approvingly by Justice Powell in *Bakke,* and indeed of any plan that uses race as one of many factors. ("'When the Committee on Admissions reviews the large middle group of applicants who are "admissible" and deemed capable of doing good work in their courses, the race of an applicant may tip the balance in his favor'").

Petitioner and the United States argue that the Law School's plan is not narrowly tailored because race-neutral means exist to obtain the educational benefits of student body diversity that the Law School seeks. We disagree. Narrow tailoring does not require exhaustion of every conceivable race-neutral alternative. Nor does it require a university to choose between maintaining a reputation for excellence or fulfilling a commitment to provide educational opportunities to members of all racial groups. See *Wygant v. Jackson Bd. of Ed.* (1986) (alternatives must serve the interest "'about as well'"). Narrow tailoring does, however, require serious, good faith consideration of workable race-neutral alternatives that will achieve the diversity the university seeks.

We agree with the Court of Appeals that the Law School sufficiently considered workable race-neutral alternatives. The District Court took the Law School to task for failing to consider race-neutral alternatives such as "using a lottery system" or "decreasing the emphasis for all applicants on undergraduate GPA and LSAT scores." But these alternatives would require a dramatic sacrifice of diversity, the academic quality of all admitted students, or both.

The Law School's current admissions program considers race as one factor among many, in an effort to assemble a student body that is diverse in ways broader than race. Because a lottery would make that kind of nuanced judgment impossible, it would effectively sacrifice all other educational values, not to mention every other kind of diversity. So too with the suggestion that the Law School simply lower admissions standards for all students, a drastic remedy that would require the Law School to become a much different institution and sacrifice a vital component of its educational mission. The United States advocates "percentage plans," recently adopted by public undergraduate institutions in Texas, Florida, and California to guarantee admission to all students above a certain class-rank threshold in every high school in the State. The United States does not, however, explain how such plans could work for graduate and professional schools. Moreover, even assuming such plans are race-neutral, they may preclude the university from conducting the individualized assessments necessary to assemble a student body that is not just racially diverse, but diverse along all the qualities valued by the university. We are satisfied that the Law School adequately considered race-neutral alternatives currently capable of producing a critical mass without forcing the Law School to abandon the academic selectivity that is the cornerstone of its educational mission.

We acknowledge that "there are serious problems of justice connected with the idea of preference itself." Narrow tailoring, therefore, requires that a race-conscious admissions program not unduly harm members of any racial group. Even remedial race-based governmental action generally "remains subject to continuing oversight to assure that it will work the least harm possible to other innocent persons competing for the benefit." To be narrowly tailored, a race-conscious admissions program must not "unduly burden individuals who are not members of the favored racial and ethnic groups."

We are satisfied that the Law School's admissions program does not. Because the Law School considers "all pertinent elements of diversity," it can (and does) select nonminority applicants who have greater potential to enhance student body diversity over underrepresented minority applicants. As Justice Powell recognized in *Bakke,* so long as a race-conscious admissions program uses race as a "plus" factor in the contest of individualized consideration, a rejected applicant

> "will not have been foreclosed from all consideration for that seat simply because he was not the right color or had the wrong surname…. His qualifications would have been weighed fairly and competitively, and he would have no basis to complain of unequal treatment under the Fourteenth Amendment."

We agree that, in the context of its individualized inquiry into the possible diversity contributions of all applicants, the Law School's race-conscious admissions program does not unduly harm nonminority applicants.

We are mindful, however, that "[a] core purpose of the Fourteenth Amendment was to do away with all governmentally imposed discrimination based on race." Accordingly, race-conscious admissions policies must be limited in time. This requirement reflects that racial classifications, however compelling their goals, are potentially so dangerous that they may be employed no more broadly than the interest demands. Enshrining a permanent justification for racial preferences would offend this fundamental equal protection principle. We see no reason to exempt race-conscious admissions programs from the requirement that all governmental use of race must have a logical end point. The Law School, too, concedes that all "race-conscious programs must have reasonable durational limits."

In the context of higher education, the durational requirement can be met by sunset provisions in race-conscious admissions policies and periodic reviews to determine whether racial preferences are still necessary to achieve student body diversity. Universities in California, Florida, and Washington State, where racial preferences in admissions are prohibited by state law, are currently engaged in experimenting with a wide variety of alternative approaches. Universities in other States can and should draw on the most promising aspects of these race-neutral alternatives as they develop. ("[T]he States may perform their role as laboratories for experimentation to devise various solutions where the best solution is far from clear").

The requirement that all race-conscious admissions programs have a termination point "assure[s] all citizens that the deviation from the norm of equal treatment of all racial and ethnic groups is a temporary matter, a measure taken in the service of the goal of equality itself."

We take the Law School at its word that it would "like nothing better than to find a race-neutral admissions formula" and will terminate its race-conscious admissions program as soon as practicable. It has been 25 years since Justice Powell first approved the use of race to further an interest in student body diversity in the context of public higher education. Since that time, the number of minority applicants with high grades and test scores has indeed increased. We expect that 25 years from now, the use of racial preferences will no longer be necessary to further the interest approved today.

In summary, the Equal Protection Clause does not prohibit the Law School's narrowly tailored use of race in admissions decisions to further a compelling interest in obtaining the educational benefits that flow from a diverse student body. Consequently, petitioner's statutory claims based on Title VI also fail. The judgment of the Court of Appeals for the Sixth Circuit, accordingly, is affirmed.

It is so ordered.

Justice *Thomas* in dissent. I believe blacks can achieve in every avenue of American life without the meddling of university administrators. Because I wish to see all students succeed whatever their color, I share, in some respect, the sympathies of those who sponsor the type of discrimination advanced by the University of Michigan Law

School (Law School). The Constitution does not, however, tolerate institutional devotion to the status quo in admissions policies when such devotion ripens into racial discrimination. Nor does the Constitution countenance the unprecedented deference the Court gives to the Law School, an approach inconsistent with the very concept of "strict scrutiny."

No one would argue that a university could set up a lower general admission standard and then impose heightened requirements only on black applicants. Similarly, a university may not maintain a high admission standard and grant exemptions to favored races. The Law School, of its own choosing, and for its own purposes, maintains an exclusionary admissions system that it knows produces racially disproportionate results. Racial discrimination is not a permissible solution to the self-inflicted wounds of this elitist admissions policy.

The Constitution abhors classifications based on race, not only because those classifications can harm favored races or are based on illegitimate motives, but also because every time the government places citizens on racial registers and makes race relevant to the provision of burdens or benefits, it demeans us all. "Purchased at the price of immeasurable human suffering, the equal protection principle reflects our Nation's understanding that such classifications ultimately have a destructive impact on the individual and our society."

Unlike the majority, I seek to define with precision the interest being asserted by the Law School before determining whether that interest is so compelling as to justify racial discrimination. The Law School maintains that it wishes to obtain "educational benefits that flow from student body diversity." This statement must be evaluated carefully, because it implies that both "diversity" and "educational benefits" are components of the Law School's compelling state interest. Additionally, the Law School's refusal to entertain certain changes in its admissions process and status indicates that the compelling state interest it seeks to validate is actually broader than might appear at first glance.

Undoubtedly there are other ways to "better" the education of law students aside from ensuring that the student body contains a "critical mass" of underrepresented minority students. Attaining "diversity," whatever it means,[1] is the mechanism by which the Law School obtains educational benefits, not an end of itself. The Law School, however, apparently believes that only a racially mixed student body can lead to the educational benefits it seeks. How, then, is the Law School's interest in these allegedly unique educational "benefits" *not* simply the forbidden interest in "racial balancing," that the majority expressly rejects?

A distinction between these two ideas (unique educational benefits based on racial aesthetics and race for its own sake) is purely sophistic—so much so that the majority uses them interchangeably.... ("[T]he Law School has a compelling interest in attaining a diverse student body"), (referring to the "compelling interest in securing the *educational benefits* of a diverse student body"). The Law School's argument, as facile as it is, can only be understood in one way: Classroom aesthetics yields educational benefits, racially discriminatory admissions policies are required to achieve the right racial mix, and therefore the policies are required to achieve the educational benefits. It is the *educational benefits* that are the end, or allegedly compelling state interest, not "diversity."

One must also consider the Law School's refusal to entertain changes to its current admissions system that might produce the same educational benefits. The Law School adamantly disclaims any race-neutral alternative that would reduce "academic selectivity," which would in turn "require the Law School to become a very different institution, and to sacrifice a core part of its educational mission." In other words, the Law School seeks to improve marginally the education it offers without sacrificing too much of its exclusivity and elite status.

The proffered interest that the majority vindicates today, then, is not simply "diversity." Instead the Court upholds the use of racial discrimination as a tool to advance the Law School's interest in offering a marginally superior education while maintaining an elite institution. Unless each constituent part of this state interest is of pressing public necessity, the Law School's use of race is unconstitutional.

Under the proper standard, there is no pressing public necessity in maintaining a public law school at all and, it follows, certainly not an elite law school. Likewise, marginal improvements in legal education do not qualify as a compelling state interest.

While legal education at a public university may be good policy or otherwise laudable, it is obviously not a pressing public necessity when the correct legal standard is applied. Additionally, circumstantial evidence as to whether a state activity is of pressing public necessity can be obtained by asking whether all States feel compelled to engage in that activity. Evidence that States, in general, engage in a certain activity by no means demonstrates that the activity constitutes a pressing public necessity, given the expansive role of government in today's society. The fact that some fraction of the States reject a particular enterprise, however, creates a presumption that the enterprise itself is not a compelling state interest. In this sense, the absence of a public, American Bar Association (ABA) accredited, law school in Alaska, Delaware, Massachusetts, New Hampshire, and Rhode Island, provides further evidence that Michigan's maintenance of the Law School does not constitute a compelling state interest.

As the foregoing makes clear, Michigan has no compelling interest in having a law school at all, much less an *elite* one. Still, even assuming that a State may, under appropriate circumstances, demonstrate a cognizable interest in having an elite law school, Michigan has failed to do so here.

The Court's deference to the Law School's conclusion that its racial experimentation leads to educational benefits will, if adhered to, have serious collateral consequences. The Court relies heavily on social science evidence to justify its deference. The Court never acknowledges, however, the growing evidence that racial (and other sorts) of heterogeneity actually impairs learning among black students. See, *e.g.,* "Flowers & Pascarella, Cognitive Effects of College Racial Composition on African American Students After 3 Years of College," *Journal of College Student Development* (1999) (concluding that black students experience superior cognitive development at Historically Black Colleges (HBCs) and that, even among blacks, "a substantial diversity moderates the cognitive effects of attending an HBC"); Allen, The Color of Success: African-American College Student

Outcomes at Predominantly White and Historically Black Public Colleges and Universities, Harv. Educ. Rev. 26, (1992) (finding that black students attending HBCs report higher academic achievement than those attending predominantly white colleges).

The majority grants deference to the Law School's "assessment that diversity will, in fact, yield educational benefits." It follows, therefore, that an HBCs assessment that racial homogeneity will yield educational benefits would similarly be given deference.[2] An HBCs rejection of white applicants in order to maintain racial homogeneity seems permissible, therefore, under the majority's view of the Equal Protection Clause. But see *United States v. Fordice* (1992) ("Obviously, a State cannot maintain … traditions by closing particular institutions, historically white or historically black, to particular racial groups"). Contained within today's majority opinion is the seed of a new constitutional justification for a concept I thought long and rightly rejected—racial segregation.

Moreover one would think, in light of the Court's decision in *United States v. Virginia* (1996), that before

being given license to use racial discrimination, the Law School would be required to radically reshape its admissions process, even to the point of sacrificing some elements of its character. In *Virginia*, a majority of the Court, without a word about academic freedom, accepted the all-male Virginia Military Institute's (VMI) representation that some changes in its "adversative" method of education would be required with the admission of women, but did not defer to VMI's judgment that these changes would be too great. Instead, the Court concluded that they were "manageable." That case involved sex discrimination, which is subjected to intermediate, not strict, scrutiny. So in *Virginia*, where the standard of review dictated that greater flexibility be granted to VMI's educational policies than the Law School deserves here, this Court gave no deference. Apparently where the status quo being defended is that of the elite establishment— here the Law School—rather than a less fashionable Southern military institution, the Court will defer without serious inquiry and without regard to the applicable legal standard.…

ENDNOTES

1. "[D]iversity," for all of its devotees, is more a fashionable catchphrase than it is a useful term, especially when something as serious as racial discrimination is at issue. Because the Equal Protection Clause renders the color of one's skin constitutionally irrelevant to the Law School's mission, I refer to the Law School's interest as an "aesthetic." That is, the Law School wants to have a certain

appearance, from the shape of the desks and tables in its classrooms to the color of the students sitting at them.…

2. For example, North Carolina A&T State University, which is currently 5.4% white, College Admissions Data Handbook 643, could seek to reduce the representation of whites in order to gain additional educational benefits.

SUGGESTIONS FOR FURTHER READING

Anthologies

Cahn, Steven. *The Affirmative Action Debate.* New York: Routledge, 1995.

Cohen, Marshall, Thomas Nagel, and Thomas Scanlon. *Equality and Preferential Treatment.* Princeton, NJ: Princeton University Press, 1977.

Gould, Carol C., and Marx W. Wartofsky. *Women and Philosophy.* New York: Putnam, 1976.

Gross, Barry R. *Reverse Discrimination.* Buffalo, NY: Prometheus, 1976.

Alternative Views

Appiah, Anthony. *Color Consciousness*. Princeton: Princeton University Press, 1996.

Bergman, Barbara. *The Economic Emergence of Women*. New York: Basic Books, 1986.

Bower, William, and Derek Bok. *The Shape of the River*. Princeton: Princeton University Press, 1998.

Capaldi, Nicholas. *Out of Order: Affirmative Action and the Crisis of Doctrinaire Liberalism*. Buffalo, NY: Prometheus Press, 1985.

Cohen, Carl, and James P. Sterba. *Affirmative Action and Racial Preference* New York: Oxford University Press, 2000.

Ezorsky Gertrude. *Racism and Justice: The Case for Affirmative Action*. Ithaca, NY: Cornell University Press, 1991.

Sterba, James P. *Affirmative Action for the Future*. Ithaca: Cornell University Press, 2009.

Fullinwider, Robert K. *The Reverse Discrimination Controversy*. Totowa, NJ: Rowman & Littlefield, 1980.

Nieli, Russell. *Racial Preference and Racial Justice*. Washington, DC: Ethics and Public Policy Center, 1991.

Rosenfeld, Michel. *Affirmative Action and Justice*. New Haven, CT: Yale University Press, 1991.

Sowell, Thomas. *Markets and Minorities*. New York: Basic Books, 1981.

Practical Applications

United States Commission on Civil Rights. *Toward an Understanding of Bakke*. Washington, DC: U.S. Government Printing Office, 1979.

SECTION VIII

Pornography

INTRODUCTION

Basic Concepts

The problem of pornography, as Catharine MacKinnon formulates it in Selection 43, is whether pornography should be prohibited for promoting discrimination and violence against women. But this has not been how the problem has been traditionally understood. In the Anglo-American legal tradition, pornography has always been identified with obscenity.[1] The test for obscenity set forth by the U.S. Supreme Court in *Roth v. United States* (1957) is "whether to the average person, applying contemporary community standards, the dominant theme of the material taken as a whole appeals to prurient interest." This test itself was an attempt to improve upon an 1868 test of obscenity that was taken over from English law. According to this earlier test, obscene materials are such that they have the tendency "to deprave and corrupt those whose minds are open to such immoral influences, and into whose hands a publication of this sort may fall." In *Roth v. United States*, the U.S. Supreme Court sought to remedy three defects in this 1868 test. First, the 1868 test permitted books to be judged obscene on the basis of isolated passages read out of context. In contrast, the Roth test requires that material be judged as obscene only if "the dominant theme of the material taken as a whole" is so judged. Second, the 1868 test allowed the obscenity of a work to be determined by its likely effects on unusually susceptible persons. By contrast, the Roth test judges material to be obscene on the basis of its likely effect on the "average person." Third, the 1868 test posited standards of obscenity fixed for all time. By contrast, the Roth test only appeals to "contemporary community standards."

Yet despite these advantages of the Roth test, problems remained. First, who was the average person to whose prurience the obscene materials have to appeal? In *Miskin v. New York* (1966), the Supreme Court needed to apply its Roth test to books that described sadomasochistic sexual acts, fetishism, lesbianism, and male homosexuality. Since these works did not appeal to the prurient interest of the average person in the population at large, the Supreme Court reformulated its Roth test so that when "material is designed for and primarily disseminated to a clearly defined deviant sexual group, ... the prurient-appeal requirement of the Roth test is satisfied if the dominant theme of the material taken as a whole appeals to the prurient interest in sex of the members of that group." Second, how was the Supreme Court to avoid the task of having to determine what are community standards for an endless number of obscenity cases? In *Miller v. California* (1973), the Supreme Court dealt with the problem by delegating and relativizing the task of determining contemporary community standards to local communities. Henceforth, the application of local community standards determines whether material appeals to prurient interest. Obviously, this puts a severe burden on national publishers who now have to take into account local community standards for any work they distribute. For example, when Larry C. Flynt routinely mailed a copy of his publication *Hustler* to a person who had ordered it by mail from a town in Ohio, he was subsequently tried for a violation of the Ohio obscenity statutes and sentenced to seven to twenty-five years in prison. So even with these improvements in the Supreme Court's test for obscenity, problems still remain.

Alternative Views

In Selection 42, Andrew Altman argues that liberals have too often appealed to freedom of speech in their arguments against laws against pornography,

whereas according to Altman, the central liberty relevant to the issue is *sexual autonomy*. The right to sexual autonomy, according to Altman, is the expression of a liberal sexual morality, a viewpoint which understands adults as having broad rights to determine for themselves their own sexual identities and activities, insofar as they respect the same right of others. Liberal sexual morality contrasts with traditional sexual morality where a person had very little control over his or her own sexual life and the rules concerning sex were extremely rigid.

Altman writes that liberal sexual morality places the right to sexual autonomy at the center of the pornography debate and in doing so places a heavy burden on those who argue for legal restrictions on adults' access to pornography. Altman examines attempts to meet this burden by those who claim that pornography leads to sexual violence, reinforces gender inequality, and involves unconsenting women in the industry. In each case, argues Altman, the burden has not been met.

In Selection 43, Catharine MacKinnon takes an entirely new approach to pornography and obscenity. She sees pornography as a practice of sex discrimination, a violation of women's civil rights. She defines pornography "as the graphic sexually explicit subordination of women through pictures or words that also includes women dehumanized as sexual objects, things or commodities; enjoying pain or humiliation or rape; being tied up, cut up, mutilated, bruised, or physically hurt; in postures of sexual submission or servility or display; reduced to body parts, penetrated by objects or animals, or presented in scenarios of degradation, injury, torture; shown as filthy or inferior; bleeding, bruised or hurt in a context that makes these conditions sexual." By contrast, she defines erotica "as sexually explicit materials premised on equality." She argues that pornography is a harmful form of gender inequality that outweighs any social interest in its protection by recognized First Amendment standards. She points to recent experimental research that shows that pornography causes harm to women through increasing men's attitudes and behavior of discrimination in both violent and nonviolent forms.

In Selection 44, Pamela Paul worries about the corrosive effects pornography has had on a culture that seems obsessed with its consumption, a "pornified" culture as she puts it. Exploring ways to combat that culture is the aim of her piece.

Paul points out that it was only very recently that anyone even considered that pornography would be protected by the First Amendment. Images of porn stretch the definition of "speech," says Paul. She compares them to someone making a threatening or vulgar racial epithet against someone else, which courts have ruled as unprotected by the First Amendment.

Paul suggests a different approach than conservatives and feminists in dealing with pornography. Whereas conservatives and feminists wish to focus on the supply of pornography, Paul insists that the best solution involves focusing on the demand for it. She believes various public institutions and private institutions, the media and popular culture, and individuals can all work together to discourage use of pornography through disseminating information and through regulation, much in the same way the use of tobacco is discouraged and regulated, although not outright banned.

As Catherine Mackinnon does, Paul delves into the negative effects pornography has on women. But, additionally, Paul delves into the negative effects pornography has on men. Paul cites the negative impact excessive pornography consumption has on men's relationships with women and their sexual performance. She also points to the sense of shame and humiliation many men feel when their pornography consumption is exposed. And, she adds, pornography, by presenting as arousing, scenarios where women are degraded and sex is trivialized, assumes the very worst in men.

Practical Applications

In *American Booksellers v. Hudnutt* (Selection 45), the federal judiciary ruled against an Indianapolis ordinance, contending that pornography which qualified as constitutionally protected speech could not be prohibited on the grounds that it caused harm to women. At the same time, the Court seemed to regard the issue of harm to women to be relevant when it argued that pornography did not harm those who cooperated in the production of pornography because they "generally have the capacity to protect themselves from participating in and being personally victimized by pornography." By contrast, the Supreme Court of Canada (Selection 46) judged that preventing harm to women is an acceptable grounds for restricting pornography, and that, moreover, restricting pornography would in fact prevent harm to women.

One explanation for the difference between the rules of the U.S. and Canadian courts is that, as MacKinnon points out, in sexist societies, it is difficult to recognize the harm that pornography causes women. Yet if MacKinnon is right, treating women equally in this regard will require a radical transformation of our society that will also affect the solutions to the other moral problems discussed in this anthology. Moreover, this radical transformation would be the kind that libertarians would be expected to champion since they are so concerned with preventing harm to others.

ENDNOTE

1. In ordinary usage, to call something obscene is to condemn that thing as blatantly disgusting, whereas to call something pornographic is simply to characterize it as sexually explicit. So in ordinary usage, unlike the law, it is an open question whether the pornographic is also obscene.

42

The Right to Get Turned On: Pornography, Autonomy, and Equality

ANDREW ALTMAN

Andrew Altman objects to laws restricting adults' access to pornography on the grounds that they are a violation of the right to sexual autonomy. Understood this way, such laws are in a sense no different than laws that prohibit the use of contraceptives or homosexual activity. Because of the immense importance of sexual autonomy, Altman argues there is quite a challenge for those who argue in defense of restricting adults' access to pornography. Altman considers several attempts to meet the challenge, but in each case, he judges that the attempts have failed.

I INTRODUCTION

Debates over whether adults have a right to produce, distribute, and view pornographic materials have typically proceeded on the premise that freedom of speech is the central liberty at stake. Those who argue that there is a moral "right to pornography" contend that it is part of a person's freedom of speech. Those who argue that there is no such right contend that pornographic material is "low value" speech or more like conduct than speech. They proceed to claim that some other value such as sexual equality between men and women overrides an individual's claim to have access to pornography.

I believe that the premise behind this debate is mistaken. While there are certain respects in which freedom of speech is at stake in the matter of pornography, such freedom is not the central liberty relevant to the issue. Rather, the right to pornography should be understood primarily as an element of another form of freedom: sexual autonomy. Individuals ought to have a broad liberty to define and enact their own sexuality. Persons who view pornography are exercising their sexual autonomy, and the debate over pornography should be seen from the standpoint of that liberty.

When seen from such a standpoint, the claim that there is a right to pornography is analogous to claims that there is a right to use contraceptives, to engage in sexual relations outside of marriage, and to engage in homosexual activity. Freedoms that protect sexuality-defining decisions get closer to the heart of the pornography issue than freedoms that protect speech and other activities whose primary intent is to communicate ideas or attitudes.

The principle of sexual autonomy has its limits. The moral right to have sex without being married does not include the moral right to have sex with children or with an unconsenting adult. A moral right to pornography does not include the moral right to buy or possess photographs of children having sex, or of people who are actually being raped or sexually assaulted. However, I will argue that sexual autonomy does entail a moral right to buy and possess a wide range of pornographic materials, including those that depict sexual violence.

II WHAT IS PORNOGRAPHY?

It is not realistic to think that there is a succinct definition of pornography that would prove acceptable to the different sides in the debate and capture all of the material that might reasonably be thought pornographic. This does not mean that we should remain content with Justice Potter Stewart's attitude: "I know it when I see it" (*Jacobellis v. Ohio*, 1964, p. 197). Rather, we can formulate a concise description of a class of materials that includes much, if not all, of the materials which the different sides in the debate could agree are reasonably described as pornographic. The description would be a kind of starting point that could be qualified and expanded in various ways as the debate proceeded. The point is that we need some reasonable starting point that can be accepted without unfairly tilting the debate over the existence of a moral right to pornography.

My suggestion for such a starting point is this: pornography is sexually explicit material, in words or images, which is intended by its creators to excite sexually those who are willing viewers of the material. By a "willing viewer," I mean a person who voluntarily pays something—in time, effort, or money—to view the material and who is willing to pay because he expects to become sexually aroused by viewing it. Thus, pornography is a commodity which represents a kind of sexual meeting of the minds between producer and consumer: the producer intends that the consumer be sexually aroused by the product and the consumer pays for the product in the expectation of becoming aroused by it.

The intention to cause sexual arousal is clearly not the only one for which a producer of pornography may be acting. Commercial producers intend to make money. However, the intent to cause sexual arousal is central, even in the commercial case. The producers intend to make money by creating a product which causes sexual arousal and the buyer expects to be aroused by viewing the product.

In contrast, consider the authors or publishers of a medical textbook which contains photographs of sexual organs and their various diseases. Such persons intend to make money. However, it is not their intention to make it by causing sexual arousal but rather by communicating medical information. Moreover, buyers of medical textbooks do not generally purchase them in order to stimulate themselves sexually: there is no sexual meeting of the minds between the authors or publishers and the consumers.

It is an important fact about human sexuality that different people are sexually excited by very different kinds of sexually explicit material. The makers of pornography know this fact well. Much hardcore pornography is explicitly addressed to the viewer's preference for particular types of sexual content: oral, anal, sadomasochist, gay, lesbian, and so on.

It seems clear that the vast majority of pornography in contemporary society is directed at males. Among all of the hours spent watching pornography, the vast majority of those hours belong to men. However, even within the group of heterosexual men, there are differences in the pornographic content which they willingly seek out. In addition, empirical studies show that a significant percentage of willing viewers of pornography are women (Slade, 2001, p. 967).

III SEXUAL AUTONOMY

Individuals have a right to a substantial degree of control over their own lives. This right does not mean that any individual has the liberty to do whatever she or he chooses: one person's liberty is limited by the duties that she has toward others. Moreover, individual control is invariably exercised within a social context created by the choices and actions of other people who are exercising control over their own lives. Yet, it would be mistaken to think that individual control is rendered factually impossible by the unchosen character of our social context or morally meaningless by the existence of duties we owe to others. Persons are not puppets of their social circumstances, nor are they smothered by moral duties owed to others. Rather, they are agents who have the broad right to decide for themselves how to live their lives. Other individuals and the government have a duty to respect those decisions.

Under the rules of traditional sexual morality, a person's sexual life was, to a large extent, not his or her own: the rules imposed a highly confining set of duties on sexual choices and actions. In particular, sexual activity was condemned as "unnatural" if it was outside of heterosexual marriage or if the activities were undertaken for purposes of other than procreation. Traditional sexual morality looked askance on pornography because such materials excite passions which do not stay neatly confined within the narrow channels of sexual activity that traditional morality deemed the only natural and acceptable way of expressing human sexuality. Accordingly, pornography was seen as corrupting individual character and subverting the proper order of society.

The sexual revolution of the 1960s replaced the traditional sexual morality with a liberal one. This liberal morality located a person's sexual life much more within his or her own dominion than did traditional morality. One way of characterizing the liberal rules is to say that they left adults morally free to engage in the sexual activities of their choice, so long as the activities had no direct unwilling victims. This characterization will require some qualification, but it does help to highlight the difference between traditional and liberal sexual morality.

From the liberal viewpoint, traditional sexual morality violated the rights of the individual by treating a person's sexual choices as if they belonged to society. Where the traditional morality reigned, sexuality was conscripted by society to promote its interest in procreation and in preserving a certain model of the family. Individuals were expected to follow the "appropriate" social scripts, which were defined by gender and restricted a person to marital (heterosexual) intercourse without the use of contraceptives. Liberal morality does not deny the importance of procreation or family, but it does assert that adult individuals have the right to decide for themselves when and whether to have children and when and whether to engage in sexual activity

for purposes other than procreation. And the liberal view is that this right of sexual autonomy is possessed equally by each adult. David Richards, a leading proponent of a liberal sexual morality, puts the central point plainly: "Legal enforcement of a particular sexual ideal fails ... to accord due respect to individual autonomy" (Richards, 1982, p. 99).

The new liberal principles cast a very different light on pornography than did the traditional morality. There is nothing inherent to the activities of producing or consuming pornography which raises a presumption that there is some direct unwilling victim of the activities. Pornography does not necessarily involve children or any unwilling adult. The sole participants in the production and use of pornographic materials may be consenting adults, and, in such a situation, the strong liberal presumption is that those adults have a moral right to do what they are doing. The basis of this presumption is the idea that the sexuality-defining decisions of adults are up to them, and those decisions include ones that involve voluntary association for purposes of sexual pleasure or for profit from the manufacture of materials that help produce sexual arousal.

Accordingly, on the liberal sexual morality, a right to pornography is akin to the right to use contraceptives: adults must be free to manufacture and use pornographic materials, just as they must be free to make and use contraceptive devices, and others must not interfere with those choices. Other sexuality-defining activities, such as the right to engage in homosexual activity, are also central to the liberal sexual morality.[1] Some people may be revolted by homosexuality and regard it as depraved, just as some are revolted by pornography and regard it as depraved. But such attitudes are not adequate grounds, on the liberal view, for restricting a person's sexual activities.

At the same time, it is important to understand that any reasonable version of liberal sexual morality must go beyond the idea that there is an absolute right to choose one's sexual activities as long as there is no direct unwilling victim. Some room must be left for the possibility that, in some circumstances, such choices are outside the boundaries of the person's right to sexual autonomy. In the next two sections, we will examine some possible circumstances which mark the limits of an individual's right. For the present, the key point is that, for a reasonable version of liberal morality, any restriction on the right of sexual autonomy must rest on considerations which possess considerable weight and are supported by clear and convincing evidence.

It is also important to note that the liberal claim that individuals have a broad right to define their own sexual identity is compatible with the idea that some of the activities which individuals have a right to engage in are, nonetheless, morally deficient. For example, one may agree that an adult has the right to view violent pornography but still contend that any adult who does seek sexual arousal by viewing violent sexual images has a morally deficient character. Put another way, it is consistent for a liberal to assert that a person who has an impeccable character would refrain from certain activities, even though people have a right to do those activities.[2]

Liberal sexual morality has become the dominant morality of contemporary society, although the traditional morality still survives and exerts some influence. Defenders of traditional morality claim that liberal "permissiveness" leads to social disintegration. Thus, Robert George, a contemporary proponent of the traditional view, asserts that "it is plain that moral decay has profoundly damaged the morally valuable institutions of marriage and the family" (George, 1993, p. 36).

It is true that divorce rates are much higher than in past generations, and family life has taken on a much different shape. However, one cannot infer that profound moral damage has been done without making many unproven assumptions about how good family was in "the good old days," when marriages often were forcibly held together by the economic dependence of the wife and the powerful social stigma of divorce. While it would be wrong for liberals to presume that liberal society is, in every aspect, better than traditional society was, there are two important respects in which liberals should insist that people are better off under the liberal morality: (1) men and women are freer to define a central aspect of their existence, their sexuality, in ways that fit their individual character, and (2) women are freer and more equal participants in society. Without attempting any full-scale assessment of the traditional morality, in sections V and VII, I will elaborate on these two considerations in favor of liberal sexual morality. However, the principal task of the remainder of this essay is to examine critically several feminist arguments that, if sound, would show that any liberal right to pornography must be far more limited than I have suggested.

IV SEXUAL VIOLENCE

Suppose that the viewing of certain types of pornography has very harmful indirect effects on unwilling victims. For example, consider pornographic movies which depict the gang rape of a woman. Even assuming that all of the participants in such movies are consenting adults—so that the rapes are staged and not real—it is possible that the movies could lead some male viewers to "imitate" what they see and commit real rapes. Similar possibilities could obtain for other kinds of violent pornography.

Moreover, in contemporary society, there are many willing viewers of violent pornography: the material is commercially produced and widely distributed. Even if most viewers do not directly violate anyone's rights, some of them may be prompted to commit sexual violence as a result of their exposure to violent pornography. Accordingly, Helen Longino expresses the view of many feminist thinkers when she claims, "Pornography, especially violent pornography, is implicated in the committing of crimes of violence against women" (Longino, 1995, p. 41). Longino proceeds to argue on the basis of her claim that the access of adults to pornography made by adults should be legally restricted. In the light of such an argument, it is important to address the question of whether the right to view pornography reaches its limit when sexual violence is depicted.[3]

It is true that a willing viewer of violent pornography who becomes sexually aroused does not necessarily harm any unwilling victim. Under liberal principles, this means that there is a presumption that the viewer is simply exercising his right of sexual autonomy. But we should not ignore the societal consequences of the availability of violent pornography in deciding whether that presumption is overridden by countervailing considerations.

If the availability of violent pornography led to substantial increases in sexual violence, then the victims of this increased violence would be paying the price for the availability of violent pornography to all adults. And it seems wrong to make those victims pay such a steep price so that some can have ready access to violent sexual materials for purposes of sexually arousing themselves. In such a situation, it would appear that any presumptive right to violent pornography would be overridden by countervailing considerations.

Notice that the considerations here consist precisely of rights-based concerns to which a liberal sexual morality must give considerable weight. The victims of the criminals who commit pornography-inspired sex crimes have their basic liberal right to sexual autonomy violated egregiously by the perpetrators. However, there are obstacles which need to be surmounted before one can reasonably conclude that, in contemporary society, any right to pornography must stop short of including a right to pornographic materials depicting sexual violence.

First, there must be clear evidence of a causal connection between the production of violent pornography and sexual violence. In the absence of such evidence, there are insufficient grounds for limiting the right of sexual autonomy so as to leave out a right to make and view violent pornography. Yet, the evidence for the existence of a causal connection is, at best, mixed.

Experimental studies suggest that when males repeatedly view violence against women in films, they tend to undergo attitudinal changes making them desensitized to such violence and more accepting of it.[4] However, the films used in the studies were R-rated "slasher movies," such as

Texas Chain Saw Massacre, lacking the sort of graphic depictions of sexual activity characteristic of paradigm cases of pornography. Moreover, the extrapolation from the experimental studies to conclusions about sexual crimes is rather tenuous: no one knows how long the attitudinal changes measured by the studies persist or whether they produce behavioral changes leading to the perpetration of sex crimes.

Since the 1960s, violent pornography has become much more readily accessible in many countries, including the United States. The incidence of sexual crime has also increased in those countries. However, data collected over many decades in the US show that the number of rapes rises in virtual lock-step with the rate of non-sexual assaults (Kutchinsky, 1991, p. 55). It is not plausible to think that violent pornography causes a rise in non-sexual violence.[5] Indeed, much more reasonable is the hypothesis that sociological variables such as poverty rates and the extent of alcohol consumption explain the equal increases in both sexual and non-sexual violence.

On the other hand, there are studies that provide some evidence for the conclusion that sexual crimes increase as a result of an increase in the availability of pornography. One such study found that the rise in rape rates around the world was traceable to pornography. However, other studies have found no correlation and some have even concluded that rape drops as a result of the availability of pornography (Slade, 2001, pp. 997–8).

The existing state of the evidence, then, is quite far from clearly establishing any causal connection between violent pornography and sexual violence, and appears to weigh against any such connection. Yet, even if a causal connection between violent pornography and sexual violence were clearly established, it would still be insufficient to conclude that, in contemporary society, the production, distribution, and viewing of violent pornography lay beyond the limits of an adult's right of sexual autonomy. Additionally, one would need to justify selecting out such pornography and distinguishing it from the myriad of other forms of media violence that have the potential to cause violence.

Consider the slasher films mentioned earlier. It is reasonable to suspect that such films and much else in the mass media cause at least some amount of violence against women, sexual and otherwise. However, it is not reasonable to deny that adults have a right to produce, distribute, and view such movies, even if we were to assume the existence of an established causal relation between the films and sexual violence. Adults who find the films entertaining are subject to criticism for getting enjoyment from watching depictions of terrified women inhumanely attacked. However, these adults do not violate anyone's rights by getting their enjoyment in that way. The situation with respect to viewing violent pornography is different only in the respect that watching such pornography is typically an exercise of sexual autonomy. To the extent that viewing slasher films is seen as non-sexual entertainment, the right to see them would actually be *less* strong than the right to view violent pornography.

Accordingly, it is unclear how one could justify selecting out violent pornography as setting a limit to the individual's right of sexual autonomy, while at the same time conceding that there is a right to view forms of media which, as far as we know, could contribute just as much to sexual violence as does violent pornography. It might be argued that violent pornography is a more powerful stimulus to sexual violence. However, we have seen that the evidence of any causal connection between pornography and violence is mixed. And there is simply no evidence indicating the relative contribution which different factors make to the overall level of sexual violence in society.

It may seem that liberal sexual morality is indifferent to the actual violence that may be caused by the production and viewing of the depictions of sexual violence found in films and other media. However, we must be careful in our understanding of what the liberal right of sexual autonomy involves. I have argued that it does include the right to produce and view violent pornography. However, liberal sexual morality also holds that each adult has an equal right to sexual autonomy. If sexual violence is widespread in society, as it is in

ours, then liberal morality cannot simply brush off that fact. Widespread sexual violence means widespread violation of the equal right of sexual autonomy. Liberal morality demands that something be done about it. But there are ways of reducing levels of sexual violence without placing the production and viewing of violent pornography—or any other media depictions of violence against women—beyond the bounds of the right of autonomy.

The most straightforward ways involve more vigorous prosecution of, and more serious punishments for, crimes of sexual violence. In a similar vein, laws regarding rape and sexual assault can and should be changed, so that the women who are the victims of such crimes are treated in a respectful manner by the criminal justice system. Additionally, efforts at educating individuals—especially young men—about sexual violence should be more seriously pursued.[6] In sum, then, subscribing to a liberal sexual morality does not require that one ignore or exhibit indifference to the level of sexual violence in society and its harmful impact on women.

V SEXUAL INEQUALITY

Even if we set aside the issue of whether violent pornography causes sexual violence, the question remains as to whether pornography in general helps to maintain many of the important social and economic inequalities that disadvantage females. Many feminists assert that pornography plays a pivotal role in maintaining such sexual inequalities, and they cast the issue of pornography as one that is "not a moral issue," but rather is a matter of the civil rights of women (MacKinnon, 1988, pp. 146–62).

For example, Catherine Itzin claims that "women are oppressed in every aspect of their public and private lives," and she sees pornography as playing a central role in maintaining the system of oppression. Itzin proceeds to defend "civil sex discrimination legislation against pornography [that] would enable women to take action on grounds of harm done to them by pornography" (Itzin, 1992, p. 424). The legislation is seen as a kind of civil rights law for women.[7]

There is little doubt that the vast bulk of pornography willingly viewed by heterosexual men—whether violent or not—involves women in positions of sexual servility or subordination: the women are there to serve the sexual pleasure of the men. And serve it they do, not only to the men who are their "co-stars" in the movie or photograph, but also to the men who masturbate to the scene or who have sex with their partners while using the scene to help arouse them. These facts are what lead some feminists to argue that pornography is unique in its power to create a psychological nexus between the social subordination of women and the sexual pleasure of men, and so is unique in its power to create and sustain patterns of sex inequality that severely disadvantage females. Catharine MacKinnon puts the matter plainly: "Pornography is masturbation material.... With pornography, men masturbate to women being exposed, humiliated, violated, degraded, mutilated, dismembered, bound, gagged, tortured and killed.... Men come doing this" (MacKinnon, 1993, p. 17).

MacKinnon is right to take the focus off of pornography as a form of speech and instead look at its role in sexual behavior. However, there is a crucial consideration which renders her line of thinking problematic as a viable basis for rejecting a right to pornography. The evidence does not support the idea of any robust correlation, much less a causal relation, between the level of sex inequality in a society and the availability of pornography in it. Quite the opposite; the most repressive countries in the world for women are ones where pornography is least available. Compared to Saudi Arabia, the United States is awash in pornography. Indeed, MacKinnon herself insists that the United States is "a society saturated with pornography" (MacKinnon, 1993, p. 7)—a description which might be arguably applied to the US but clearly does not apply to Saudi Arabia. Nonetheless, on the indices of sex inequality developed by the United Nations Development Programme, the United States and

other Western countries where pornography circulates widely are the nations with the highest levels of *equality*, while Saudi Arabia and other sexually repressive regimes have among the highest levels of inequality (United Nations Development Programme, 2002, pp. 222–42). Thus, it is hard to credit the notion that pornography is a kind of causal linchpin in the creation and maintenance of large inequalities between males and females.

There is certainly an analogy between the ways in which much pornography depicts women in relation to men and the ways in which social practices actually treat women in relation to men. In much pornography, there is a sexual hierarchy dominated by men; in much of society, there is a social hierarchy dominated by men. Moreover, it is plausible to think that pornography plays some causal role in the perpetuation of sexual hierarchy. But, as with the matter of sexual violence, any limitation of the right of adults to sexual autonomy requires more than a plausible belief that some indeterminate degree of connection exists between pornography and sexual hierarchy.

VI MAKING PORNOGRAPHY

Much pornography depicts the subordination of women. Even though the symbolic representation of inequality is not the same as the inequality that is represented, it may be argued that in making pornography, women humiliate and subordinate themselves. They get on their knees and suck on men's cocks. They let men ejaculate into their mouth and on their face and breasts. They have several men simultaneously penetrating their anus, vagina, and mouth. They are tied up and gagged. The humiliation seems all the more acute because it is done before cameras that will circulate the images to untold numbers of men to view. One might claim that this means that making pornography is making female inequality and not simply depicting it.

However, context counts in deciding whether a person's sexual conduct is a form of humiliation and subordination. It is difficult to see why fellatio is any more inherently degrading than cunnilingus, or why either form of oral sex has that feature. If the parties are adults and consent, the assessment of the activity as humiliating is highly contestable. Multiple penetration also seems inherently innocuous.

Nonetheless, the key point is this: even if we grant that much pornography does involve women performing humiliating or degrading sexual acts, it does not follow that the actors have no right to participate in making such material or that viewers have no right to see it. A willingness to sexually degrade oneself before a camera for commercial purposes may constitute a serious deficiency in one's character. A willingness to view such pornography may also reflect a character flaw. But the men and women who perform in such pornography have a right to make their choices, and consumers have a right to view the commercial product.

If women are intimidated by violent threats into performing in pornography, then their rights have been violated and their victimizers ought to be prosecuted and punished. But it is simply an ideological prejudice to assume a priori that any woman who performs humiliating or degrading sexual acts in pornography has been threatened or coerced in some way. Especially in matters of sex, the line between humiliation, on one side, and breaking the procrustean bed of traditional morality, on the other, is a very tricky one to draw.

Some feminist advocates of laws against pornography claim that physical threats, violence, and economic coercion against women pervade the actual operation of the pornography industry (Dworkin, 2000, pp. 27–9). It may be said that the only way to stop such threats is by closing down the industry. But even if that were true, it would not justify closing down the industry. It does not make sense to think that the only industries that should be allowed are those that can operate without anyone abusing them by threatening violence. Such abuse can be found in any industry. Criminal prosecution of the perpetrators should be the main remedy for physical abuse and coercion in the pornography industry.

Moreover, there are less draconian ways of diminishing violence in the industry than shutting the industry down. For example, some feminists have argued for the unionization of women who work in pornography and other sex-related industries (Cornell, 2000, p. 552). While unionization efforts may not have good prospects at present, especially in the US, the prospects for banning pornography under a civil rights approach are no better. And the unionization strategy has the decided advantage of treating women in the pornography industry as agents who are capable of exercising their own right of sexual autonomy.

Some of the females who get caught up in the pornography industry are legal minors. The industry executives who intentionally, or negligently, hire minors ought to be prosecuted and punished. Legal minors may have some aspects of the right of sexual autonomy (for example, a 17-year-old girl has the right to purchase and use contraceptives), but the law should rest on the premise that minors are too easily manipulated by industry executives and other adults with vested interests to have a right to decide for themselves to perform in commercial pornographic films or pose for pornographic pictures.

Some feminists contend that women accede to make pornography only because they have no other economic options (except perhaps prostitution, a close cousin of pornography). This contention may have some truth in countries of the underdeveloped world, where educational opportunities for women are highly restricted, rampant sexism operates in all quarters of life, and economic opportunities even for many men are bleak at best. However, in the economically advanced liberal democracies, the situation of almost all women is drastically better, and claims of economic coercion are considerably less plausible as a result.

The clear conclusion seems to be that uncoerced adults have a right to be legally free to make, market, and view pornography. However, it might be objected that if some women voluntarily choose to make pornography in which they are engaged in humiliating or degrading conduct, then their actions affect all women in a detrimental way. The idea here is that the manufacture and circulation of such pornography shapes the sex-role expectations of men and women in society at large, and it does so by showing women as the sexual servants of men. The result is that individuals are not free to control their sexual identities: just as much as in a society ruled by traditional sexual morality, sexual identities are controlled by social forces which are beyond their control and which are hostile to their basic interests.

VII SEXUAL IDENTITY

It must be admitted that, even in a society governed by a liberal sexual morality, the sexual autonomy of a person is significantly circumscribed. There is a built-in tension between living in a society and possessing the autonomy to define oneself sexually or in any other way. Without connections to other people in an organized and ongoing system of relations, the life-options of the individual would be radically limited. But those connections also mean that a person's life-defining choices are not entirely her own. The patterns of behavior and attitude that other people adopt not only establish pathways through life which would not otherwise exist but also create barriers and limits on the individual's exercise of her autonomy. The ability of the individual to shape her own identity is both enabled by, and held hostage to, the actions and attitudes of other people.

There is no solution to this problem. The conditions of meaningful autonomy are also conditions that can inhibit the exercise of such autonomy. Nonetheless, even though this conflict cannot be eliminated, it can be mitigated. And some kinds of society do a much better job of mitigating it than others. Societies with a liberal sexual morality are much better in this respect than those with a traditional sexual morality, and that is the decisive consideration in favor of the liberal morality. Individuals have many more meaningful options in living out the sexual aspects of their lives: their sexuality is not held hostage to what other people do and think to nearly the extent that is found traditional societies. The grip of pre-existing social scripts that define a sexual identity for each person is dramatically weaker in liberal societies and the power of individuals to shape a centrally important aspect of their lives is correspondingly greater.

However, even in a liberal society, there is no escaping the fact that how other women act and think affects the opportunities and obstacles for any given woman's efforts to define her own sexual identity. The same is true, of course, for men, but the problem of concern here is the willingness of some women to participate in the creation of pornography in which they engage in conduct that is humiliating and servile. Such conduct may be voluntary on the part of the woman, but—the claim goes—it also makes it more difficult for other women to define their own sexual identities as the equals of men.

I think that it is reasonable to hold that the existence of such pornography makes it more difficult for women to live their lives as the sexual equals of men, i.e., more difficult relative to a society which was ruled by a liberal sexual morality and had fewer women, or none at all, who were willing to engage in humiliating conduct as part of the production of pornographic materials. However, women are far better off in societies where a liberal sexual morality dominates than in traditional societies, even when the liberal ones contain much pornography degrading to women. Although the freedom of women to humiliate or degrade themselves in making pornography creates costs that all women in a liberal society bear, the gains for women that have resulted from society moving to a liberal sexual morality from a traditional morality far outweighs the costs.

It might be argued that the costs are still too great, and I would not dissent. However, there are ways to lessen those costs without incursions on the right to sexual autonomy. Those ways are likely to be far more effective in promoting sexual equality than restricting the freedom of willing adults to view pornography made by willing adults.

VIII CONCLUSION

The recognition of a right to sexual autonomy is critical in adequately addressing the issue of pornography. There are other important dimensions of the issue, including the levels of sexual violence perpetrated against women and the social inequalities that systematically disadvantage women. Also relevant is the question of whether there is some character defect in those who make and enjoy pornographic materials.

However, liberal sexual morality correctly places the right of sexual autonomy at the center of the pornography issue. In doing so, the liberal morality places a substantial burden on those who argue for legal restrictions on the access of adults to pornography made by consenting adults. Those who argue for such restrictions tacitly concede that the burden is theirs, as they make claims aimed at meeting it, for example, that pornography causes sexual violence, reinforces sexual hierarchy, and involves unconsenting women who are forced to perform.

When examined carefully, though, we find that the burden has not been met. The empirical claims are insufficiently verified, and some of the empirical assertions, even if substantiated, would be inadequate to justify restricting an adult's right of sexual autonomy. We are left, then, with the claim that the producers and viewers of pornography exhibit a defect of moral character. Such a claim is consistent with a liberal sexual morality. However, it is also inadequate to justify restrictions on adults who willingly create and view pornography.

ENDNOTES

1. Cf. Richards (1982, pp. 29, 39).

2. Cf. Waldron (1993, chap. 3), and Driver (1992).

3. Longino also contends that pornography defames women by communicating falsehoods about them and reinforces the societal oppression of women. The oppression argument is considered in section V below. The defamation argument would license sweeping restrictions on communication, including political expression.

4. See, for example, Linz et al. (1984).

5. Kutchinsky (1991) also found that in West Germany, Denmark, and Sweden rape increased less than nonsexual assault, despite the greatly increased availability of violent pornography in those countries as well.

6. Many thinkers assert that pornography fosters the myth that women enjoy being forced to have sex (the rape myth) and some studies support the assertion. However, other studies show that better educating young men can counteract their acceptance of the rape myth. Moreover, mainstream movies in which rapes take place also appear to foster the rape myth. See Slade (2001, pp. 992–3).

7. Catharine MacKinnon and Andrea Dworkin helped draft anti-pornography, civil rights laws in the United States, but the courts have found them to be unconstitutional on free-speech grounds. See *American Booksellers v. Hudnut* 771 F.2d 323 (7th Cir. 1985).

REFERENCES

American Booksellers v. Hudnut (1985) 771 F.2d 323 (7th Cir. 1985).

Cornell, Drucilla (2000) "Pornography's Temptation." In Drucilla Cornell (ed.), *Feminism and Pornography*. New York: Oxford University Press, pp. 552–68.

Driver, Julia (1992) "The Suberogatory," *Australasian Journal of Philosophy* 70: 286–95.

Dworkin, Andrea (2000) "Against the Male Flood." In Drucilla Cornell (ed.), *Feminism and Pornography*. New York: Oxford University Press, pp. 19–44.

George, Robert P. (1993) *Making Men Moral*. Oxford: Oxford University Press.

Itzin, Catherine (1992) "Legislating against Pornography without Censorship." In Catherine Itzin (ed.),

Pornography; Women, Violence, and Civil Liberties.
New York: Oxford University Press, pp. 401–34.

Jacobellis v. Ohio (1964) 378 US 184 (1964).

Kutchinsky, Bert (1991) "Pornography and Rape:
Theory and Practice," *International Journal of Law and
Psychiatry* 14: 47–64.

Linz, Daniel, Donnerstein, Edward, and Penrod,
Stephen (1984) "The Effects of Multiple Exposures
to Filmed Violence against Women," *Journal of
Communication* 34: 130–47.

Longino, Helen (1995) "Pornography, Oppression, and
Freedom: a Closer Look." In Susan Dwyer (ed.),
The Problem of Pornography. Belmont, CA:
Wadsworth Publishing, pp. 34–47.

MacKinnon, Catharine (1988) *Feminism Unmodified.*
Cambridge, MA: Harvard University Press.

——— (1993) *Only Words.* Cambridge, MA: Harvard
University Press.

Richards, David A. J. (1982) *Sex, Drugs, Death and the
Law.* Totowa, NJ: Rowman and Littlefield.

Slade, Joseph W. (2001) *Pornography and Sexual
Representation,* vol. III. Westport, CT:
Greenwood Press.

United Nations Development Programme (2002) *Human
Development Report 2002.* New York: Oxford
University Press.

Waldron, Jeremy (1993) *Liberal Rights.* New York:
Cambridge University Press.

43

Pornography, Civil Rights, and Speech

CATHARINE MACKINNON

Catharine MacKinnon argues that pornography is a practice of sex discrimination and hence a violation of women's civil rights. According to MacKinnon, pornography celebrates and legitimizes rape, battery, sexual harassment, and the sexual abuse of children. More generally, it eroticizes the dominance and submission that is the dynamic common to them all. She argues for the constitutionality of city ordinances, which she has helped design, that prohibit pornography.

■ ■ ■ There is a belief that this is a society in which women and men are basically equals. Room for marginal corrections is conceded, flaws are known to exist, attempts are made to correct what are conceived as occasional lapses from the basic condition of sex equality. Sex discrimination law has concentrated most of its focus on these occasional lapses. It is difficult to overestimate the extent to which this belief in equality is an article of faith for most people, including most women, who wish to live in self-respect in an internal universe, even (perhaps especially) if not in the world. It is also partly an expression of natural law thinking: If we are inalienably equal, we can't "really" be degraded.

This is a world in which it is worth trying. In this world of presumptive equality, people make money based on their training or abilities or diligence or qualifications. They are employed and advanced on the basis of merit. In this world of just deserts, if someone is abused, it is thought to violate the basic rules of the community. If it doesn't, victims are seen to have done something they could have chosen to do differently, by exercise of will or better judgment. Maybe such people

have placed themselves in a situation of vulnerability to physical abuse. Maybe they have done something provocative. Or maybe they were just unusually unlucky. In such a world, if such a person has an experience, there are words for it. When they speak and say it, they are listened to. If they write about it, they will be published. If certain experiences are never spoken about, if certain people or issues are seldom heard from, it is supposed that silence has been chosen. The law, including much of the law of sex discrimination and the First Amendment, operates largely within the realm of these beliefs.

Feminism is the discovery that women do not live in this world, that the person occupying this realm is a man, so much more a man if he is white and wealthy. This world of potential credibility, authority, security, and just rewards, recognition of one's identity and capacity, is a world that some people do inhabit as a condition of birth, with variations among them. It is not a basic condition accorded humanity in this society, but a prerogative of status, a privilege, among other things, of gender.

I call this a discovery because it has not been an assumption. Feminism is the first theory, the first practice, the first movement, to take seriously the situation of all women from the point of view of all women, both on our situation and on social life as a whole. The discovery has therefore been made that the implicit social content of humanism, as well as the standpoint from which legal method has been designed and injuries have been defined, has not been women's standpoint. Defining feminism in a way that connects epistemology with power as the politics of women's point of view, this discovery can be summed up by saying that women live in another world: specifically, a world of *not* equality, a world of inequality.

Looking at the world from this point of view, a whole shadow world of previously invisible silent abuse has been discerned. Rape, battery, sexual harassment, forced prostitution, and the sexual abuse of children emerge as common and systematic. We find that rape happens to women in all contexts, from the family, including rape of girls and babies, to students and women in the workplace, on the streets, at home, in their own bedrooms by men they do not know and by men they do know, by men they are married to, men they have had a social conversation with, and, least often, men they have never seen before. Overwhelmingly, rape is something that men do or attempt to do to women (44 percent of American women according to a recent study) at some point in our lives. Sexual harassment of women by men is common in workplaces and educational institutions. Based on reports in one study of the federal workforce, up to 85 percent of women will experience it, many in physical forms. Between a quarter and a third of women are battered in their homes by men. Thirty-eight percent of little girls are sexually molested inside or outside the family. Until women listened to women, this world of sexual abuse was *not spoken* of. It was the unspeakable. What I am saying is, if you *are* the tree falling in the epistemological forest, your demise doesn't make a sound if no one is listening. Women did not "report" these events, and overwhelmingly do not today, because no one is listening, because no one believes us. This silence does not mean nothing happened, and it does not mean consent.

It is the silence of women of which Adrienne Rich has written, "Do not confuse it with any kind of absence."

Believing women who say we are sexually violated has been a radical departure, both methodologically and legally. The extent and nature of rape, marital rape, and sexual harassment itself were discovered in this way. Domestic battery as a syndrome, almost a habit, was discovered through refusing to believe that when a woman is assaulted by a man to whom she is connected, it is not an assault. The sexual abuse of children was uncovered, Freud notwithstanding, by believing that children were not making up all this sexual abuse. Now what is striking is that when each discovery is made, and somehow made real in the world, the response has been: It happens to men too. If women are hurt, men are hurt. If women are raped, men are raped. If women are sexually harassed, men are sexually harassed. If women are battered, men are battered. Symmetry must be reasserted. Neutrality must be reclaimed. Equality must be reestablished.

The only areas where the available evidence supports this, where anything like what happens to women also happens to men, involve children— little boys are sexually abused—and prison. The liberty of prisoners is restricted, their freedom restrained, their humanity systematically diminished, their bodies and emotions confined, defined, and regulated. If paid at all, they are paid starvation wages. They can be tortured at will, and it is passed off as discipline or as means to a just end. They become compliant. They can be raped at will, at any moment, and nothing will be done about it. When they scream, nobody hears. To be a prisoner means to be defined as a member of a group for whom the rules of what can be done to you, of what is seen as abuse of you, are reduced as part of the definition of your status. To be a woman is that kind of definition and has that kind of meaning.

Men *are* damaged by sexism. (By men I mean the status of masculinity that is accorded to males on the basis of their biology but is not itself biological.) But whatever the damage of sexism to men, the condition of being a man is not defined as subordinate to women by force. Looking at the facts of the abuses of women all at once, you see that a woman is socially defined as a person who, whether or not she is or has been, can be treated in these ways by men at any time, and little, if anything, will be done about it. This is what it means when feminists say that maleness is a form of power and femaleness is a form of powerlessness.

In this context, all of this "men too" stuff means that people don't really believe the things I have just said are true, though there really is little question about their empirical accuracy. The data are extremely simple, like women's pay figure of fifty-nine cents on the dollar. People don't really seem to believe that either. Yet there is no question of its empirical validity. This is the workplace story: What women do is seen as not worth much, or what is not worth much is seen as something for women to do. *Women* are seen as not worth much.... Now why are these basic realities of the subordination of women to men, for example, that only 7.8 percent of women have never been sexually assaulted, not effectively believed, not perceived as real in the face of all this evidence? Why don't *women* believe our own experiences? In the face of all this evidence, especially of systematic sexual abuse—subjection to violence with impunity is one extreme expression, although not the only one, of a degraded status—the view that basically the sexes are equal in this society remains unchallenged and unchanged. The day I got this was the day I understood its real message, its real coherence: *This is equality for us.*

I could describe this, but I couldn't explain it until I started studying a lot of pornography. In pornography, there it is, in one place, all of the abuses that women had to struggle so long even to begin to articulate, all the *unspeakable* abuse: the rape, the battery, the sexual harassment, the prostitution, and the sexual abuse of children. Only in pornography it is called something else: sex, sex, sex, and sex, respectively. Pornography sexualizes rape, battery, sexual harassment, prostitution, and child sexual abuse; it thereby celebrates, promotes, authorizes, and legitimizes them. More generally, it eroticizes the dominance and submission

that is the [common] dynamic. It makes hierarchy sexy and calls that "the truth about sex" or just a mirror of reality. Through this process pornography constructs what a woman is as what men want from sex. This is what pornography means.

Pornography constructs what a woman is in terms of its view of what men want sexually, such that acts of rape, battery, sexual harassment, prostitution, and sexual abuse of children become acts of sexual equality. Pornography's world of equality is a harmonious and balanced place. Men and women are perfectly complementary and perfectly bipolar. Women's desire to be fucked by men is equal to men's desire to fuck women. All the ways men love to take and violate women, women love to be taken and violated. The women who most love this are most men's equals, the most liberated; the most participatory child is the most grown-up, the most equal to an adult. Their consent merely expresses or ratifies these preexisting facts.

The content of pornography is one thing. There, women substantively desire dispossession and cruelty. We desperately want to be bound, battered, tortured, humiliated, and killed. Or, to be fair to the soft core, merely taken and used. This is erotic to the male point of view. Subjection itself, with self-determination ecstatically relinquished, is the content of women's sexual desire and desirability. Women are there to be violated and possessed, men to violate and possess us, either on screen or by camera or pen on behalf of the consumer. On a simple descriptive level, the inequality of hierarchy, of which gender is the primary one, seems necessary for sexual arousal to work. Other added inequalities identify various pornographic genres or subthemes, although they are always added through gender: age, disability, homosexuality, animals, objects, race (including anti-Semitism), and so on. Gender is never irrelevant.

What pornography *does* goes beyond its content: It eroticizes hierarchy, it sexualizes inequality. It makes dominance and submission into sex. Inequality is its central dynamic; the illusion of freedom coming together with the reality of force is central to its working. Perhaps because this is a bourgeois culture, the victim must look free, appear to be freely acting. Choice is how she got there. Willing is what she is when she is being equal. It seems equally important that then and there she actually be forced and that forcing be communicated on some level, even if only through still photos of her in postures of receptivity and access, available for penetration. Pornography in this view is a form of forced sex, a practice of sexual politics, an institution of gender inequality.

From this perspective, pornography is neither harmless fantasy nor a corrupt and confused misrepresentation of an otherwise natural and healthy sexual situation. It institutionalizes the sexuality of male supremacy, fusing the erotization of dominance and submission with the social construction of male and female. To the extent that gender is sexual, pornography is part of constituting the meaning of that sexuality. Men treat women as who they see women as being. Pornography constructs who that is. Men's power over women means that the way men see women defines who women can be. Pornography is that way. Pornography is not imagery in some relation to a reality elsewhere constructed. It is not a distortion, reflection, projection, expression, fantasy, representation, or symbol either. It is a sexual reality.

In Andrea Dworkin's definitive work, *Pornography: Men Possessing Women*, sexuality itself is a social construct gendered to the ground. Male dominance here is not an artificial overlay upon an underlying inalterable substratum of uncorrupted essential sexual being. Dworkin presents a sexual theory of gender inequality of which pornography is a constitutive practice. The way pornography produces its meaning constructs and defines men and women as such. Gender has no basis in anything other than the social reality its hegemony constructs. Gender is what gender means. The process that gives sexuality its male supremacist meaning is the same process through which gender inequality becomes socially real.

In this approach, the experience of the (overwhelmingly) male audiences who consume pornography is therefore not fantasy or simulation or catharsis but sexual reality, the level of reality on which sex itself largely operates. Understanding this dimension of the problem does not require noticing that pornography models are real women to whom, in most cases, something real is being done; nor does it even require inquiring into the systematic infliction of pornography and its sexuality upon women, although it helps. What matters is the way in which the pornography itself provides what those who consume it want. Pornography *participates* in its audience's eroticism by creating an accessible sexual object, the possession and consumption of which *is* male sexuality, as socially constructed; to be consumed and possessed as which, *is* female sexuality, as socially constructed; pornography is a process that constructs it that way.

The object world is constructed according to how it looks with respect to its possible uses. Pornography defines women by how we look according to how we can be sexually used. Pornography codes how to look at women, so you know what you can do with one when you see one. Gender is an assignment made visually, both originally and in everyday life. A sex object is defined on the basis of its looks, in terms of its usability for sexual pleasure, such that both the looking—the quality of the gaze, including its point of view—and the definition according to use become eroticized as part of the sex itself. This is what the feminist concept "sex object" means. In this sense, sex in life is no less mediated than in art. Men have sex with their image of a woman. It is not that life and art imitate each other; in this sexuality, they *are* each other.

To give a set of rough epistemological translations, to defend pornography as consistent with the equality of the sexes is to defend the subordination of women to men as sexual equality. What in the pornographic view is love and romance looks a great deal like hatred and torture to the feminist. Pleasure and eroticism become violation. Desire appears as lust for dominance and submission. The vulnerability of women's projected sexual availability, that acting we are allowed (that is, asking to be acted upon), is victimization. Play conforms to scripted roles. Fantasy expresses ideology, is not exempt from it. Admiration of natural physical beauty becomes objectification. Harmlessness becomes harm. Pornography is a harm of male supremacy made difficult to see because of its pervasiveness, potency, and, principally, because of its success in making the world a pornographic place. Specifically, its harm cannot be discerned, and will not be addressed, if viewed and approached neutrally, because it *is* so much of "what is." In other words, to the extent pornography succeeds in constructing social reality, it becomes invisible as harm. If we live in a world that pornography creates through the power of men in a male-dominated situation, the issue is not what the harm of pornography is, but how that harm is to become visible.

Obscenity law provides a very different analysis and conception of the problem of pornography. In 1973 the legal definition of obscenity became that which the average person, applying contemporary community standards, would find that, taken as a whole, appeals to the prurient interest; that which depicts or describes in a patently offensive way— you feel like you're a cop reading someone's *Miranda rights*—sexual conduct specifically defined by the applicable state law; and that which, taken as a whole, lacks serious literary, artistic, political, or scientific value. Feminism doubts whether the average person gender-neutral exists; has more questions about the content and process of defining what community standards are than it does about deviations from them; wonders why prurience counts but powerlessness does not and why sensibilities are better protected from offense than women are from exploitation; defines sexuality, and thus its violation and expropriation, more broadly than does state law; and questions why a body of law that has not in practice been able to tell rape from intercourse should, without further guidance, be entrusted with telling pornography from anything less. Taking the work "as a whole" ignores that which the victims of pornography have long known: Legitimate settings diminish the perception of injury done to those whose trivialization and objectification they contextualize. Besides, and this is a heavy one, if a woman is subjected, why should it matter that the work has other value? Maybe what redeems the work's value is what enhances its injury to women, not to mention

that existing standards of literature, art, science, and politics, examined in a feminist light, are remarkably consonant with pornography's mode, meaning, and message. And finally—first and foremost, actually— although the subject of these materials is overwhelmingly women, their contents almost entirely made up of women's bodies, our invisibility has been such, our equation as a sex *with* sex has been such, that the law of obscenity has never even considered pornography a women's issue.

Obscenity, in this light, is a moral idea, an idea about judgments of good and bad. Pornography, by contrast, is a political practice, a practice of power and powerlessness. Obscenity is ideational and abstract; pornography is concrete and substantive. The two concepts represent two-entirely different things. Nudity, excess of candor, arousal or excitement, prurient appeal, illegality of the acts depicted, and unnaturalness or perversion are all qualities that bother obscenity law when sex is depicted or portrayed. Sex forced on real women so that it can be sold at a profit and forced on other real women; women's bodies trussed and maimed and raped and made into things to be hurt and obtained and accessed, and this presented as the nature of women in a way that is acted on and acted out, over and over; the coercion that is visible and the coercion that has become invisible—this and more bothers feminists about pornography. Obscenity as such probably does little harm. Pornography is integral to attitudes and behaviors of violence and discrimination that define the treatment and status of half the population.

At the request of the city of Minneapolis, Andrea Dworkin and I conceived and designed a local human rights ordinance in accordance with our approach to the pornography issue. We define pornography as a practice of sex discrimination, a violation of women's civil rights, the opposite of sexual equality. Its point is to hold those who profit from and benefit from that injury accountable to those who are injured. It means that women's injury—our damage, our pain, our enforced inferiority—should outweigh their pleasure and their profits, or sex equality is meaningless.

We define pornography as the graphic sexually explicit subordination of women through pictures or words that also includes women dehumanized as sexual objects, things, or commodities; enjoying pain or humiliation or rape; being tied up, cut up, mutilated, bruised, or physically hurt; in postures of sexual submission or servility or display; reduced to body parts, penetrated by objects or animals, or presented in scenarios of degradation, injury, torture; shown as filthy or inferior; bleeding, bruised, or hurt in a context that makes these conditions sexual. Erotica, defined by distinction as not this, might be sexually explicit materials premised on equality. We also provide that the use of men, children, or transsexuals in the place of women is pornography. The definition is substantive in that it is sex-specific, but it covers everyone in a sex-specific way, so is gender neutral in overall design....

This law aspires to guarantee women's rights consistent with the First Amendment by making visible a conflict of rights between the equality guaranteed to all women and what, in some legal sense, is now the freedom of the pornographers to make and sell, and their consumers to have access to, the materials this ordinance defines. Judicial resolution of this conflict, if the judges do for women what they have done for others, is likely to entail a balancing of the rights of women arguing that our lives and opportunities, including our freedom of speech and action, are constrained by—and in many cases flatly precluded by, in, and through—pornography, against those who argue that the pornography is harmless, or harmful only in part but not in the whole of the definition; or that it is more important to preserve the pornography than it is to prevent or remedy whatever harm it does.

In predicting how a court would balance these interests, it is important to understand that this ordinance cannot now be said to be either conclusively legal or illegal under existing law or precedent, although I think the weight of authority is on our side. This ordinance enunciates a new form of the previously recognized governmental interest in sex equality. Many laws make sex equality a governmental interest. Our law is designed to further the equality of the sexes, to help make sex equality real. Pornography is a practice of discrimination on the basis of sex, on one level because of its role in creating and maintaining sex as a basis for discrimination. It harms many women one at a time and helps keep all women in an inferior status by defining our subordination as our sexuality and equating that with our gender. It is also sex discrimination because its victims, including men, are selected for victimization on the basis of their gender. But for their sex, they would not be so treated.

The harm of pornography, broadly speaking, is the harm of the civil inequality of the sexes made invisible as harm because it has become accepted as the sex difference. Consider this analogy with race: If you see Black people as different, there is no harm to segregation; it is merely a recognition of that difference. To neutral principles, separate but equal was equal. The injury of racial separation to Blacks arises "solely because [they] choose to put that construction upon it." Epistemologically translated: How you see it is not the way it is. Similarly, if you see women as just different, even or especially if you don't know that you do, subordination will not look like subordination at all, much less like harm. It will merely look like an appropriate recognition of the sex difference.

Pornography does treat the sexes differently, so the case for sex differentiation can be made here. But men as a group do not tend to be (although some individuals may be) treated the way women are treated in pornography. As a social group, men are not hurt by pornography the way women as a social group are. Their social status is not defined as *less* by it. So the major argument does not turn on mistaken differentiation, particularly since the treatment of women according to pornography's dictates makes it all too often accurate. The salient quality of a distinction between the top and the bottom in a hierarchy is not difference, although top is certainly different from bottom; it is power. So the major argument is: Subordinate but equal is not equal.

Particularly since this is a new legal theory, a new law, and "new" facts, perhaps the situation of women it newly exposes deserves to be considered on its own terms. Why do the problems of 53 percent of the population have to look like somebody else's problems before they can be recognized as existing? Then, too, they can't be addressed if they do look like other people's problems, about which something might have to be done if something is done about these. This construction of the situation truly deserves inquiry. Limiting the justification for this law to the situation of the sexes would serve to limit the precedential value of a favorable ruling.

Its particularity aside, the *approach* to the injury is supported by a whole array of prior decisions that have justified exceptions to First Amendment guarantees when something that matters is seen to be directly at stake. What unites many cases in which speech interests are raised and implicated but not, on balance, protected, is harm, harm that counts. In some existing exceptions, the definitions are much more open-ended than ours. In some the sanctions are more severe, or potentially more so. For instance, ours is a civil law; most others, although not all, are criminal. Almost no other exceptions show as many people directly affected. Evidence of harm in other cases tends to be vastly less concrete and more conjectural, which is not to say that there is necessarily less of it. None of the previous cases addresses a problem of this scope or magnitude—for instance, an eight-billion-dollar-a-year industry. Nor do other cases address an abuse that has such widespread legitimacy. Courts have seen harm in other cases. The question is, will they see it here, especially given that the pornographers got there first. I will confine myself here to arguing from cases on harm to people, on the supposition that, pornographers notwithstanding, women are not flags....

To reach the magnitude of this problem on the scale it exists, our law makes trafficking in pornography—production, sale, exhibition, or distribution—actionable. Under the obscenity rubric, much legal and psychological scholarship has centered on a search for the elusive link between harm and pornography defined as obscenity. Although they were not very clear on what obscenity was, it was its harm they truly could not find. They looked high and low—in the mind of the male consumer, in society or in its "moral fabric," in correlations between variations in levels of antisocial acts and liberalization

of obscenity laws. The only harm they have found has been harm to "the social interest in order and morality." Until recently, no one looked very persistently for harm to women, particularly harm to women through men. The rather obvious fact that the sexes *relate* has been overlooked in the inquiry into the male consumer and his mind. The pornography doesn't just drop out of the sky, go into his head, and stop there. Specifically, men rape, batter, prostitute, molest, and sexually harass women. Under conditions of inequality, they also hire, fire, promote, and grade women, decide how much or whether we are worth paying and for what, define and approve and disapprove of women in ways that count, that determine our lives.

If women are not just born to be sexually used, the fact that we are seen and treated as though that is what we are born for becomes something in need of explanation. If we see that men relate to women in a pattern of who they see women as being, and that forms a pattern of inequality, it becomes important to ask where that view came from or, minimally, how it is perpetuated or escalated. Asking this requires asking different questions about pornography than the ones obscenity law made salient.

Now I'm going to talk about causality in its narrowest sense. Recent experimental research on pornography shows that the materials covered by our definition cause measurable harm to women through increasing men's attitudes and behaviors of discrimination in both violent and nonviolent forms. Exposure to some of the pornography in our definition increases the immediately subsequent willingness of normal men to aggress against women under laboratory conditions. It makes normal men more closely resemble convicted rapists attitudinally, although as a group they don't look all that different from them to start with. Exposure to pornography also significantly increases attitudinal measures known to correlate with rape and self-reports of aggressive acts, measures such as hostility toward women, propensity to rape, condoning rape, and predicting that one would rape or force sex on a woman if one knew one would not get caught. On this latter measure, by the way, about a third of all men predict that they would rape, and half would force sex on a woman.

As to that pornography covered by our definition in which normal research subjects seldom perceive violence, long-term exposure still makes them see women as more worthless, trivial, non-human, and object like, that is, the way those who are discriminated against are seen by those who discriminate against them. Crucially, all pornography by our definition acts dynamically over time to diminish the consumer's ability to distinguish sex from violence. The materials work behaviorally to diminish the capacity of men (but not women) to perceive that an account of a rape is an account of a rape. The so-called sex-only materials, those in which subjects perceive no force, also increase perceptions that a rape victim is worthless and decrease the perception that she was harmed. The overall direction of current research suggests that the more expressly violent materials accomplish with less exposure what the less overtly violent—that is, the so-called sex-only materials—accomplish over the longer term. Women are rendered fit for use and targeted for abuse. The only thing that the research cannot document is which individual women will be next on the list. (This cannot be documented experimentally because of ethics constraints on the researchers—constraints that do not operate in life.) Although the targeting is systematic on the basis of sex, for individuals it is random. They are selected on a roulette basis. Pornography can no longer be said to be just a mirror. It does not just reflect the world or some people's perceptions. It *moves* them. It increases attitudes that are lived out, circumscribing the status of half the population.

What the experimental data predict will happen actually does happen in women's real lives. It's fairly frustrating that women have known for some time that these things do happen. As Ed Donnerstein, an experimental researcher in this area, often puts it, "We just quantify the obvious." It is women, primarily, to whom the research results have been the obvious, because we live them. But not until a laboratory study predicts that these things *will* happen do people begin to believe you

when you say they *did* happen to you. There is no—*not any*—inconsistency between the patterns the laboratory studies predict and the data on what actually happens to real women. Show me an abuse of women in society, I'll show it to you made sex in the pornography. If you want to know who is being hurt in this society, go see what is being done and to whom in pornography and then go look for them in other places in the world. You will find them being hurt in just that way. We did in our hearings.

In our hearings women spoke, to my knowledge for the first time in history in public, about the damage pornography does to them. We learned that pornography is used to break women, to train women to sexual submission, to season women, to terrorize women, and to silence their dissent. It is this that has previously been termed "having no effect." The way men inflict on women the sex they experience through the pornography gives women no choice about seeing the pornography or doing the sex. Asked if anyone ever tried to inflict unwanted sex acts on them that they knew came from pornography, 10 percent of women in a recent random study said yes. Among married women, 24 percent said yes. That is a lot of women. A lot more don't know. Some [who do know] testified in Minneapolis. One wife said of her ex-husband, "He would read from the pornography like a textbook, like a journal. In fact when he asked me to be bound, when he finally convinced me to do it, he read in the magazine how to tie the knots." Another woman said of her boyfriend, "[H]e went to this party, saw pornography, got an erection, got me … to inflict his erection on…. There is a direct causal relationship there." One woman, who said her husband had rape and bondage magazines all over the house, discovered two suitcases full of Barbie dolls with rope tied on their arms and legs and with tape across their mouths. Now think about the silence of women. She said, "He used to tie me up and he tried those things on me." A therapist in private practice reported:

> Presently or recently I have worked with clients who have been sodomized by

broom handles, forced to have sex with over 20 dogs in the back seat of their car, tied up and then electrocuted on their genitals. These are children, [all] in the ages of 14 to 18, all of whom [have been directly affected by pornography,] [e]ither where the perpetrator has read the manuals and manuscripts at night and used these as recipe books by day or had the pornography present at the time of the sexual violence.

One woman, testifying that all the women in a group of ex-prostitutes were brought into prostitution as children through pornography, characterized their collective experience: "[I]n my experience there was not one situation where a client was not using pornography while he was using me or that he had not just watched pornography or that it was verbally referred to and directed me to pornography." "Men," she continued, "witness the abuse of women in pornography constantly and if they can't engage in that behavior with their wives, girlfriends or children, they force a whore to do it."

Men also testified about how pornography hurts them. One young gay man who had seen *Playboy* and *Penthouse* as a child said of such heterosexual pornography: "It was one of the places I learned about sex and it showed me that sex was violence. What I saw there was a specific relationship between men and women.... [T]he woman was to be used, objectified, humiliated, and hurt; the man was in a superior position, a position to be violent. In pornography I learned that what it meant to be sexual with a man or to be loved by a man was to accept his violence." For this reason, when he was battered by his first lover, which he described as "one of the most profoundly destructive experiences of my life," he accepted it.

Pornography also hurts men's capacity to relate to women. One young man spoke about this in a way that connects pornography—not the prohibition on pornography—with fascism. He spoke of his struggle to repudiate the thrill of dominance, of his difficulty finding connection with a woman

to whom he is close. He said: "My point is that if women in a society filled by pornography must be wary for their physical selves, a man, even a man of good intentions, must be wary for his mind.... I do not want to be a mechanical, goose-stepping follower of the Playboy bunny, because that is what I think it is.... [T]hese are the experiments a master race perpetuates on those slated for extinction." The woman he lives with is Jewish. There was a very brutal rape near their house. She was afraid; she tried to joke. It didn't work. "She was still afraid. And just as a well-meaning German was afraid in 1933, I am also very much afraid."

Pornography stimulates and reinforces, it does not mirror the connection between one-sided freely available sexual access to women and masculine sexual excitement and sexual satisfaction. The catharsis hypothesis is fantasy. The fantasy theory is fantasy. Reality is: Pornography conditions male orgasm to female subordination. It tells men what sex means, what a real woman is, and codes them together in a way that is behaviorally reinforcing. This is a real five-dollar sentence, but I'm going to say it anyway: Pornography is a set of hermeneutical equivalences that work on the epistemological level. Substantively, pornography defines the meaning of what a woman is seen to be by connecting access to her sexuality with masculinity through orgasm. What pornography means *is* what it does.

So far, opposition to our ordinance centers on the trafficking provision. This means not only that it is difficult to comprehend a group injury in a liberal culture—that what it *means* to be a woman is defined by this and that it is an injury for all women, even if not for all women equally. It is not only that the pornography has got to be accessible, which is the bottom line of virtually every objection to this law. It is also that power, as I said, is when you say something, it is taken for reality. If you talk about rape, it will be agreed that rape is awful. But rape is a conclusion. If a victim describes the facts of a rape, maybe she was asking for it or enjoyed it or at least consented to it, or the man might have thought she did, or maybe she had had sex before. It is now agreed that there is something wrong with sexual harassment. But describe what happened to you, and it may be trivial or personal or paranoid, or maybe you should have worn a bra that day. People are against discrimination. But describe the situation of a real woman, and they are not so sure she wasn't just unqualified. In law, all these disjunctions between women's perspective on our injuries and the standards we have to meet go under dignified legal rubrics like burden of proof, credibility, defenses, elements of the crime, and so on. These standards all contain a definition of what a woman is in terms of what sex is and the low value placed on us through it. They reduce injuries done to us to authentic expressions of who we are. Our silence is written all over them. So is the pornography.

We have as yet encountered comparatively little objection to the coercion, force, or assault provisions of our ordinance. I think that's partly because the people who make and approve laws may not yet see what they do as that. They *know* they use the pornography as we have described it in this law, and our law defines that, the reality of pornography, as a harm to women. If they suspect that they might on occasion engage in or benefit from coercion or force or assault, they may think that the victims won't be able to prove it—and they're right. Women who charge men with sexual abuse are not believed. The pornographic view of them is: They want it; they all want it. When women bring charges of sexual assault, motives such as veniality or sexual repression must be invented, because we cannot really have been hurt. Under the trafficking provision, women's lack of credibility cannot be relied on to negate the harm. There's no woman's story to destroy, no credibility-based decision on what happened. The hearings establish the harm. The definition sets the standard. The grounds of reality definition are authoritatively shifted. Pornography is bigotry, *period*. We are now—in the world pornography has decisively defined—having to meet the burden of proving, once and for all, for all of the rape and torture and battery, all of the sexual harassment, all of the child sexual abuse, all of the forced prostitution, *all* of it that the pornography is part of and that is part of the pornography, that the harm *does*

happen and that when it happens it looks like this. Which may be why all this evidence never seems to be enough.

It is worth considering what evidence has been enough when other harms involving other purported speech interests have been allowed to be legislated against. By comparison to our trafficking provision, analytically similar restrictions have been allowed under the First Amendment, with a legislative basis far less massive, detailed, concrete, and conclusive. Our statutory language is more ordinary, objective, and precise and covers a harm far narrower than the legislative record substantiates. Under *Miller*, obscenity was allowed to be made criminal in the name of the "danger of offending the sensibilities of unwilling recipients, or exposure to juveniles." Under our law, we have direct evidence of harm, not just a conjectural danger, that unwilling women in considerable numbers are not simply offended in their sensibilities, but are violated in their persons and restricted in their options. Obscenity law also suggests that the applicable standard for legal adequacy in measuring such connections may not be statistical certainty. The Supreme Court has said that it is not their job to resolve empirical uncertainties that underlie state obscenity legislation. Rather, it is for them to determine whether a legislature could reasonably have determined that a connection might exist between the prohibited material and harm of a kind in which the state has legitimate interest. Equality should be such an area. The Supreme Court recently recognized that prevention of sexual exploitation and abuse of children is, in its words, "a governmental objective of surpassing importance." This might also be the case for sexual exploitation and abuse of women, although I think a civil remedy is initially more appropriate to the goal of empowering adult women than a criminal prohibition would be.

Other rubrics provide further support for the argument that this law is narrowly tailored to further a legitimate governmental interest consistent with the goals underlying the First Amendment. Exceptions to the First Amendment—you may have gathered from this—exist. The reason they exist is that the harm done by some speech out-weighs its expressive value, if any. In our law a legislature recognizes that pornography, as defined and made actionable, undermines sex equality. One can say—and I have—that pornography is a causal factor in violations of women; one can also say that women will be violated so long as pornography exists; but one can also say simply that pornography violates women. Perhaps this is what the woman had in mind who testified at our hearings that for her the question is not just whether pornography causes violent acts to be perpetrated against some women. "Porn is already a violent act against women. It is our mothers, our daughters, our sisters, and our wives that are for sale for pocket change at the newsstands in this country." *Chaplinsky v. New Hampshire* recognized the ability to restrict as "fighting words" speech which "by [its] very utterance inflicts injury." Perhaps the only reason that pornography has not been "fighting words"—in the sense of words that by their utterance tend to incite immediate breach of the peace—is that women have seldom fought back, yet.

Some concerns that are close to those of this ordinance underlie group libel laws, although the differences are equally important. In group libel law, as Justice Frankfurter's opinion in *Beauharnais* illustrates, it has been understood that an individual's treatment and alternatives in life may depend as much on the reputation of the group to which that person belongs as on their own merit. Not even a partial analogy can be made to group libel doctrine without examining the point made by Justice Brandeis and recently underlined by Larry Tribe: Would more speech, rather than less, remedy the harm? In the end, the answer may be yes, but not under the abstract system of free speech, which only enhances the power of the pornographers while doing nothing substantively to guarantee the free speech of women, for which we need civil equality. The situation in which women presently find ourselves with respect to the pornography is one in which more *pornography* is inconsistent with rectifying or even counterbalancing its damage through speech, because so long as the pornography exists in the way it does there *will not be more speech by women*. Pornography strips and devastates women of credibility, from our accounts of sexual assault to our everyday reality of sexual subordination. We are stripped of authority and reduced and devalidated and silenced. Silenced here means that the purposes of the First Amendment, premised upon conditions presumed and promoted by protecting free speech, do not pertain to women because they are not our conditions. Consider them: Individual self-fulfillment—how does pornography promote our individual self-fulfillment? How does sexual inequality even permit it? Even if she can form words, who listens to a woman with a penis in her mouth? Facilitating consensus—to the extent pornography does so, it does so one-sidedly by silencing protest over the injustice of sexual subordination. Participation in civic life—central to Professor Meiklejohn's theory—how does pornography enhance women's participation in civic life? Anyone who cannot walk down the street or even lie down in her own bed without keeping her eyes cast down and her body clenched against assault is unlikely to have much to say about the issues of the day, still less will she become Tolstoy. Facilitating change—*this law* facilitates the change that existing First Amendment theory had been used to throttle. Any system of freedom of expression that does not address a problem where the free speech of men silences the free speech of women, a real conflict between speech interests as well as between people, is not serious about securing freedom of expression in this country.

For those of you who still think pornography is only an idea, consider the possibility that obscenity law got one thing right. Pornography is more act-like than thoughtlike. That pornography, in a feminist view, furthers the idea of the sexual inferiority of women, which is a political idea, doesn't make the pornography itself a political idea. One can express the idea a practice embodies. That does not make that practice an idea. Segregation expresses the idea of the inferiority of one group to another on the basis of race. That does not make segregation an idea. A sign that says "Whites Only" is only words. Is it therefore protected by the First Amendment? Is it not an act, a practice, of segregation because what it means is inseparable from what it does? *Law* is only words.

The issue here is whether the fact that words and pictures are the central link in the cycle of abuse will immunize that entire cycle, about which we cannot do anything without doing something about the pornography. As Justice Stewart said in *Ginsburg*, "When expression occurs in a setting where the capacity to make a choice is absent, government regulation of that expression may coexist with and *even implement* First Amendment guarantees." I would even go so far as to say that the pattern of evidence we have closely approaches Justice Douglas's requirement that "freedom of expression can be suppressed if, and to the extent that, it is so closely brigaded with illegal action as to be an inseparable part of it." Those who have been trying to separate the acts from the speech—that's an act, that's an act, there's a law against that act, regulate that act, don't touch the speech—notice here that the illegality of the acts involved doesn't mean that the speech that is "brigaded with" it *cannot* be regulated. This is when it *can* be.

I take one of two penultimate points from Andrea Dworkin, who has often said that pornography is not speech for women, it is the silence of women. Remember the mouth taped, the woman gagged, "Smile, I can get a lot of money for that." The smile is not her expression, it is her silence. It is not her expression not because it didn't happen, but because it *did* happen. The screams of the women in pornography are silence, like the screams of Kitty Genovese, whose plight was misinterpreted by some onlookers as a lovers' quarrel. The flat expressionless voice of the woman in the New Bedford gang rape, testifying, is silence. She was raped as men cheered and watched, as they do in and with the pornography. When women resist and men say, "Like this, you stupid bitch, here is how to do it" and shove their faces into the pornography, this "truth of sex" is the silence of women. When they say, "If you love me, you'll try," the enjoyment we fake, the enjoyment we learn is silence. Women who submit because there is more dignity in it than in losing the fight over and over live in silence. Having to sleep with your publisher or director to

get access to what men call speech is silence. Being humiliated on the basis of your appearance, whether by approval or disapproval, because you have to look a certain way for a certain job, whether you get the job or not, is silence. The absence of a woman's voice, everywhere that it cannot be heard, is silence. And anyone who thinks that what women say in pornography is women's speech—the "Fuck me, do it to me, harder," all of that—has never heard the sound of a woman's voice.

The most basic assumption underlying First Amendment adjudication is that, socially, speech is free. The First Amendment says Congress shall not abridge the freedom of speech. Free speech, get it, *exists*. Those who wrote the First Amendment *had* speech—they wrote the Constitution. *Their* problem was to keep it free from the only power that realistically threatened it: the federal government. They designed the First Amendment to prevent government from constraining that which, if unconstrained by government, was free, meaning *accessible to them*. At the same time, we can't tell much about the intent of the framers with regard to the question of women's speech, because I don't think we crossed their minds. It is consistent with this analysis that their posture toward freedom of speech tends to presuppose that whole segments of the population are not systematically silenced socially, prior to government action. If everyone's power were equal to theirs, it this were a nonhierarchical society, that might make sense. But the place of pornography in the inequality of the sexes makes the assumption of equal power untrue.

This is a hard question. It involves risks. Classically, opposition to censorship has involved keeping government off the backs of people. Our law is about getting some people off the backs of other people. The risks that it will be misused have to be measured against the risks of the status quo. Women will never have that dignity, security, compensation that is the promise of equality so long as the pornography exists as it does now. The situation of women suggests that the urgent issue of our freedom of speech is not primarily the avoidance of state intervention as such, but getting affirmative access to speech for those to whom it has been denied.

44

Pornified

PAMELA PAUL

Pamela Paul discusses some of the many negative effects of a culture obsessed with pornography and suggests ways to deal with them. She thinks that one way to deal with them is to focus on the demand for pornography rather than find ways to prohibit its supply. She also discusses the negative impact pornography has on some men, which is a topic that is often ignored.

THE TRUTH ABOUT PORNOGRAPHY

Please read and comply with the following conditions before you continue:

I am at least 21 years of age.

The sexually explicit material I am viewing is for my own personal use and I will not expose minors to the material.

I desire to view sexually explicit material.

I believe that as an adult it is my inalienable right to receive/view sexually explicit material....

All images and videos within this website are nonviolent. All performers on this site are over the age of 18, have consented to being photographed and/or filmed, have signed model release and provided proof of age, believe it is their right to engage in consensual sexual acts for the entertainment and education of other adults and believe it is your right as an adult to watch them doing what adults do.

The videos and images in this site are intended to be used by responsible adults as sexual aids, to provide sexual education and to provide sexual entertainment.

—*Welcome page on a pornography Web site*

Once those "21 or older" who choose to comply get inside this Web site, which bills itself as "The Home of the Asshole Milkshake," it blares, "The most extreme shit you'll ever see. See why the U.S. government is after us!"[1] Viewers are "educated" as to how multiple men can anally penetrate a woman and then force her to drink the ejaculated semen extracted from her own anus. Others can be "entertained" by viewing *Forced Entry*, a video simulating vivid rape and murder scenes of women. Despite the site's self-professed renegade status, it does not differ substantially in content or tone from vast numbers of pornographic Web sites, and it's only a click away from "softer" sites. Moreover, nothing prevents minors from making the transition. In a study by the Pew Internet Research Center, 15 percent of boys twelve to seventeen (and 25 percent of boys fifteen to seventeen) have lied about their age to access a Web site—surely a lowball figure. The Internet and other technologies have changed the rules of the game, obscuring the boundaries between softcore and hardcore, upgrading customers to harder, faster—more quickly than ever before.

Incidents that muster outrage in the "real world" elicit little response when supposedly relegated to the realm of pornography. In a coffee-table book of photos of porn stars and related essays, Salman Rushdie claimed that, though pornography is particularly popular in Muslim countries due to the segregation of the sexes, a free and civilized society should be judged by its willingness to accept pornography. Given the popularity of porn in America, what does this say about our country? Are we sexually repressed or are we free? Moreover, such seemingly liberal observations ignore the similarities between the sexual repression outside pornography and the repression within it. As a prisoner tortured and photographed pornographically at the Abu Ghraib prison in Iraq explained, "We are men. It's okay if they beat me…. But no one would want their manhood to be shattered. They wanted us to feel as though we were women, the way women feel, and this is the worst insult, to feel like a woman."[2] For the prisoner, to be made into pornography—to be pornified—was to be dehumanized; yet when presented in the context of pornography proper, it's acceptable, even entertaining, for people to be treated as such. In the United States, the outrage over the actions at Abu Ghraib was accompanied by a strange hush regarding the inspiration of those acts and images, which are perpetrated in pornography, in this country as elsewhere in the world, every day. Few people think to question, let alone fulminate over, the messages sent by "legitimate" porn.

We have entered the twenty-first century immersed in a new pornified culture with little language to describe or decry it. Instead, there is silence, nervous laughter, ignorance, and outdated arguments. We shrug or nod when told that pornography is natural. Masculine. Empowering to women. Harmless. Progressive. Necessary. It's time to start questioning these assumptions.

Pornography: A Right or Wrong?

But rather than fight for people's right to speak out against pornography, Americans have instead fought for the right of pornographers to distribute their product without regulation and for consumers to lap it up unhindered. "Isn't it our right to look at and read and masturbate to whatever we want?" has become a rallying cry. "What right does the government have in our bedrooms?" Businesses have made a fortune by linking pornography with civil liberties, arguing that to use pornography is to turn one's nose up at the Ed Meeses and the hypocritical reactionaries. They've managed to equate the use of pornography with a defense of the Bill of Rights, convincing an entire generation that pornography is not only okay, it's the American citizen's right. Today, according to the *Pornified*/Harris poll, 23 percent of Americans believe that whether one likes it or not, people should have full access to pornography under the U.S. Constitution's First Amendment. Democrats were only slightly more likely (24 percent) than Republicans (20 percent) to take this position. Not surprisingly, those of the baby-boomer generation and younger are nearly twice as likely to believe pornography is protected speech than Americans age fifty-nine and older, and men are more than twice as likely as women to consider pornography a political right.

The major pornography lobbying group calls itself the Free Speech Coalition, much in the spirit of anti-environmentalist groups that adorn themselves in leafy labels like the Blue Skies Society to obscure their true agendas. The rhetoric of the pro-pornography movement also bears a striking resemblance to the gun rights movement. Each popularizes the idea of a Big Brother federal government tyranny out to strip Main Street citizens of their fundamental rights. Just as the Second Amendment was never intended to encourage the sale of semiautomatic military weapons to ex-cons, the First Amendment was never meant to sanction the dissemination of speech that is free of social merit, artistic quality, or political purpose. In a country obsessed with the Founding Fathers and their vision, little thought is given to what they would make of the current application of the Constitution's free political speech.

By defending pornography as free speech, so-called advocates could actually be seen as threatening its foundations, as the Supreme Court noted in the 1973 *Miller v. California* obscenity case, the federal court's last major ruling defining pornography: "In our view, to equate the free and robust exchange of ideas and political debate with commercial exploitation of obscene material demeans the grand conception of the First Amendment and its high purposes in the historic struggle for freedom." According to the decision, obscenity—which is not protected by the Constitution's First Amendment—is material that a judge or jury finds is, as a whole, appealing to a prurient interest in sex, depicts sexual conduct in a patently offensive manner, and lacks serious literary, artistic, political, and scientific value. Using that definition, would *Gag Factor 15* pass muster? How about the online how-to guide to creating an Asshole Milkshake? Until very recently, no one even conceived that the First Amendment would apply to pornography, which was considered by common consent and by law to be unworthy of protection. Not only do pornographic images stretch the definition of "speech" but, as disseminated in the marketplace, they have a similar demonstrable effect on women as a white person making a threatening and vulgar racial epithet toward a black man or woman, which courts have already ruled to be unprotected by the First Amendment.

Certainly, to get the government involved in people's private sex lives is a scary proposition. What's deemed dangerous by one person may be normal, even pleasurable to another. Reasonable people might assume that it's "obvious" what we mean by obscenity—a definition that would likely include violent pornography, scatological porn, bukkake—but it takes just one government administration to decree that all homosexual acts are obscene to understand why obscenity is an uneasy standard to enforce. Most Americans are probably like Justice Potter Stewart when they say that while they cannot define pornography they know it when they see it. To pretend that the line between an R-rated film with depictions of sexuality and a XXX movie with hardcore double penetration and "money shots" is anywhere close to being blurred is willfully obtuse and plays into the worst fears of those who might otherwise naturally oppose pornography.

Nonetheless, we have to be able to draw a line somewhere; throwing up our hands, or defending the indefensible because the dilemma poses difficulty, is not the answer. The vast majority of Americans support the First Amendment, but pornography is not solely or even primarily an issue of free speech. Nor should one interpretation of the First Amendment be the only guideline, the only right, the only moral that matters. Just as pro-choice Americans can advocate fewer abortions while defending the right to have abortions, surely Americans can find practical ways to limit and regulate the pornified culture without challenging our constitutional foundations and rights. We shouldn't just worry about the consequences of banning pornography; we also need to worry about the consequences of letting porn proliferate unfettered. Pornography should move beyond a discussion of censorship and into one of standards.

Out with the Old

Just as there are problems with the arguments in favor of pornography so are there with existing arguments in opposition. To date, the outcry against pornography has predominantly come from otherwise distant corners of the political spectrum. Religious opponents deem pornography a sin, a moral offense against God, and a desecration of the holy bonds of matrimony. Right-wing political opponents cite the frequent abuse of pornography among pedophiles or noted serial killers like Ted Bundy and Jeffrey Dahmer. And many feminist and legal opponents argue that pornography leads to rape and that all sex is violence.

To date, the federal government's response to pornography has made it easy to ignore or oppose. John Ashcroft's efforts in the first Bush administration could be easily lumped with his Patriot Act tinkerings with civil liberties or with his intolerance for a nude sculpture of Justice in a government building. Asked about Ashcroft's efforts to clamp down on pornography, Hugh Hefner blamed the religious Right, telling CNN, "We're dealing with religious fanaticism overseas ... and at the same time, we're allowing a certain amount of religious fanaticism to do the same kind of foolish things at home."[3] Proponents of pornography, not surprisingly, find it easy to defang these brands of opposition through mockery and exaggeration.

One of the main problems with the conservative and religious opponents to pornography is they tend to oppose the very thing that would help alleviate the problem: sex education. For example, Patrick Fagan, formerly of the Child and Family Protection Institute and currently a Heritage Foundation fellow, has said, "Pornography can lead to sexual deviancy for disturbed and normal people alike. They become desensitized to pornography. Sexual fulfillment in marriage can decrease. Marriages can be weakened. Users of pornography frequently lose faith in the viability of marriage. They do not believe that it has any effect on them. Furthermore, pornography is addictive. 'Hardcore' and 'softcore' pornography, *as well as sex-education materials*, have similar effects."[4] Sex education is a far cry from pornography; only such pornography opponents—and, ironically, pornographers—fail to see a distinction. Yet sex education could help clarify the differences between pornography and other forms of sexual expression. The solution to pornography's insidious message to men, women, and children is not isolating the information available, but ensuring that people have context. For children to understand why pornography is wrong, they need sex education programs that explain healthy sexuality and demonstrate why pornography is fundamentally opposed to the exercise of positive sexual pleasures. By perpetuating the idea that all sexuality is "taboo," conservative opponents only encourage and legitimize pornographic rebellion.

Many conservative opponents lump pornography with what they deem to be other forms of sexual deviancy, such as homosexuality and extramarital sex. Opponents use pornography as an easy opportunity—who wants to come out in favor of smut?—to legislate other forms of sexual behavior, such as homosexuality and birth control education.

Such arguments against pornography create a problem for all of pornography's opponents by giving substance to fears of a slippery slope. Similarly, on the civil libertarian side, where many liberals dislike or disapprove of pornography, advocates bundle the issue with sex education and classic erotic novels, deliberately blurring the lines to win liberals to their side. On both sides, deliberate obfuscation is the way the game is played.

As for what would seem to be an expected female opposition to pornography, women have largely silenced themselves on the issue, not having made much of a peep since Gloria Steinem donned her bunny ears more than thirty years ago.* Many women seem to have bought into the idea that they should either accept men's involvement with pornography or get in on it themselves. The only arguments against pornography from women come from conservative hothouses like the Eagle Forum and Concerned Women of America and from feminist hardliners Andrea Dworkin and Catherine MacKinnon, making for strange bedfellows. Cultural conservatives argue that pornography subverts the biblical view of womanhood, while legally oriented feminists argue that pornography endangers real-life walking and talking women. Cultural conservatives argue that pornography is one of several threatening sexual perversions, while feminists typically defend and support homosexuality. Cultural conservatives oppose the dissemination of sexual information, while feminists are the authors of *Our Bodies, Ourselves*.

The result is that both sides have lost what may otherwise be a natural, broad-based following among women. Those on the Right moralize about sex and erotica and the state of the family in general, thereby alienating women who want to celebrate their sexuality while rejecting pornography. Meanwhile, women on the Left focus their sights on a legal battle against pornography, and in gathering their arguments and their statistics ignore anyone who rejects the idea that all women are victims and that all sex is rape. While pornography does exacerbate discrimination, the legalistic attack

---

*Steinem worked undercover as a Playboy Bunny and then wrote about her experience in *New York* magazine.

on pornography has been forced into an untenable position. "Harm" legally must be proved, thus opponents spend their time trying to show that pornography *inevitably* leads to violence, that pornography *causes* men to rape. The backflips of logic and evidence required to make that point strike most people, and most courtrooms, as unpersuasive. Meanwhile, all other feminist, liberal, and moderate arguments against pornography have gotten lost.

When pressed or questioned, most people—even those who dislike pornography—bleat out defenses of pornography like recordings, falling back on legalistic jargon and irrelevant abstractions. But the bottom line is that none of the old arguments about pornography reflect how it affects people's lives and infiltrates their relationships today. Nor are there proposals to contend with the new reality of our pornified culture. In fact, most people don't talk about whether they're "for" or "against" pornography anymore; the cultural consensus seems to consider the matter beyond debate. Through complacency and carelessness, the majority of Americans shrug or laugh off the issue as inconsequential and irrelevant to their lives. But as we have seen, the costs to our relationships, our families, and our culture are great, and will continue to mount. Clearly, we need to find new ways to approach the problem.

In some instances, it's just a matter of limiting personal consumption, in others of enforcing existing restrictions. Magazines could once again get brown-paper wrappers and back-of-the-store or behind-the-counter placement. Better technology could provide effective filtering systems that would make it harder to access pornography online. Thus far, the pornography lobby has made regulating the supply difficult. As industry analyst Dennis McAlpine explained on the PBS show *Frontline*, when it comes to enforcing obscenity laws on cable operators, "It's a lot easier to get somebody when they first go over that line than when they have been over that line for five years and nobody said anything, because that line has then been moved. As you keep moving the line and it becomes accepted, it's a lot tougher to go get them.... Going back is a lot tougher to do. They can keep moving it forward. And the longer that

nobody tries this in court, the more likely they've got a case that it is acceptable."[5]

Still, once enough people are awakened to the reality of life in a pornified culture, once they realize that the consequences are much more dear than an embarrassed chuckle over seeing Janet Jackson's breast, the difficulties of regulating pornography will not seem so insurmountable. People might bring enough pressure for politicians to buck lobbyists and take action. They might even get the court system to uphold regulatory decisions made long ago but subsequently ignored or overwhelmed by spurious challenges from the pornography industry. Indeed, a number of new regulatory measures have been floated in recent years. One suggestion put forth on the *New York Times* op-ed page by Jonathan A. Knee, director of the media program at Columbia Business School, is to criminalize the giving and receiving of payment to perform sexual acts, which would make the laws against pornography consistent with those of prostitution. Such a proposal, he suggests, would skirt the First Amendment issue while not requiring new leaps in the law. After all, he points out, "society objects on principal to the commodification and commercialization of sexual relations, even between consenting adults."[6] Other efforts aim to regulate the distribution of pornography, particularly in countries such as Australia and Britain. In the United Kingdom, one mobile company, Vodafone, recently blocked handset access to sex, dating, and gambling Web sites unless users could prove their eighteen-or-over age status and opt in to receive such services.[7] In Israel, cell-phone pornography has been banned.

But while much of the blame for pornified culture lies with an unfettered and out-of-control supply, it is in the demand for pornography that the most practical and effective solution lies. Consider a taping of *Girls Gone Wild*. A bunch of drunken college women on spring break decide it's cool and funny to lift up their shirts for the ogling crowds. They're encouraged by the hooting cries of college guys surrounding them on the beach, yelling at them to just "go for it." They're urged on by the cameramen and producers from the *Girls Gone Wild* team, who need the footage to justify their paychecks. Who started this and who is to blame? Is it the women's fault for not having enough self-respect and courage to mock the jeering crowds and walk away? Is it the men's fault for encouraging the women to behave like fools? Or are the cameramen and producers to blame, cynically exploiting young men and women in order to make a buck? Perhaps some reasonable blame could be assigned to all three. But none of these people would be doing any of this if there weren't a considerable demand for *Girls Gone Wild* videos among viewers at home. If demand didn't exist, the product wouldn't sell—and would disappear. There may be fault distributed across the board in the production of pornography, but the most consequential players are the men eager and willing to pay for it.

While the supply of pornography can be effectively limited, the greatest potential for change lies with the demand, and it's the demand that may well prove to be the easiest, most efficient target for effecting change. The government and the private sector, the media and the popular culture, private citizens and public institutions could all work to quell consumer demand. Just as cigarette smoking was glamorized and encouraged in popular culture throughout most of the twentieth century, and then discouraged and regulated once its harm became clear, Americans need to be informed about pornography's negative impact—about how its unabashed acceptance is not a step forward for women, nor a harmless diversion for men, nor a step toward a more open and liberalized sexuality.

What we need is a mind-set shift, one that moves us from viewing porn as hip and fun and sexy to one that recognizes pornography as harmful, pathetic, and decidedly unsexy. Once pornography becomes discredited and derided by both men and women, consumption will become less brazen, and will eventually decline. Imagine a public service TV spot: "Think porn's sexy? Ask former porn star Lara about the director who sexually harassed her. About the fact that she can't get any other jobs that pay nearly as much. How bruised and sore she is, how fearful that she can't have more children. Growing up, Lara wanted to

be a lawyer, then an actress. Instead, she's trying to support her three-year-old son while hiding where she gets her money. Sure, porn's sexy—if you like your women desperate, depressed, and defeated." Once people learn how a girl like Nora Kuzma grew up to become exploited pornography star Traci Lords, once they realize that the pornography trade isn't all about seedy-cool *Boogie Nights*, people will choose not to buy into the porn world's conception of sexuality. In her memoir, *Underneath It All*, Lords complains, "Today porn is everywhere I look. I find it in the junk mail folder on my computer … porn stars play themselves on television shows, appear on billboards, and give interviews about how 'liberating' porn is for women. Well, I believe it's anything but."

The difference individuals can make via their own behavior and standards should not be underestimated. Imagine if one man, a good friend of the groom, were to say to the departing bachelor, "Actually, I don't think going to a strip club for your bachelor party celebrates your impending marriage. It's not respectful to your wife or to women in general, and I don't think it reflects well on you or on any of us. And while I support your marriage and am excited to celebrate with you, this isn't the way to do it." Imagine if women were to speak out about their discomfort and dislike of pornography, about how their partners become distant, disconnected, and lonely, rather than pretend to be game and go along. Imagine if women who pursued pornography themselves because it was deemed hip or sexy or fun decided instead that it was hipper and sexier and more fun to actually have sex with another live, completely engaged individual.

Men and the Reality of Pornography

Men have been sold on the idea that pornography is a harmless amusement and a natural pursuit, both a right of passage and a man's right. Not surprisingly, this message has come courtesy of the industry itself, put forward in the earliest pornographic magazines and pounded home through the years. When objections to pornography were made, men were to understand that those cries came only from women, and that, naturally, women couldn't understand. When questioned, most men readily concede that pornography probably isn't the greatest thing for women. But few men have stopped to consider what pornography does to men.

It's time they took notice. Pornography has a corrosive effect on men's relationships with women and a negative impact on male sexual performance and satisfaction. It plays a rising role in intimacy disorders. More than ever, it aids and abets sexually compulsive behavior in ways that can become seriously disruptive and psychologically damaging. Men who become addicted to pornography feel helpless and degraded, often losing themselves and their loved ones to the habit. Even men who use pornography regularly, but not compulsively, question the effect it has on their lives. For married or otherwise monogamous men, pornography often signals discomfort or uneasiness in a relationship. They hide their porn from their girlfriends and wives, make light of it with other men, and even lie about it to themselves—underestimating their consumption, writing off the impact, telling themselves they only ended up looking for two hours because they were stressed, tired, bored, or annoyed. Men caught with pornography by their bosses or their wives often feel humiliated and pathetic. They get defensive and angry, alienating the people who matter most to them. They can lose their jobs and jeopardize their careers. They can weaken or destroy their marriages and isolate their children. What titillates in the short term hardly merits the long-term costs.

Pornography is degrading in its own way to men. In interviews, porn stars and strippers typically say they view their male patrons with revulsion and disrespect. They see men who frequent strip clubs as pathetic, egotistical, women-hating, superficial, stupid, out of control, predatory, or just plain rude. Yet men who use pornography have been stamped by the pornified culture as manly, virile, powerful, suave, and confident. They have been told that they're "getting" women through the pages of magazines, the purchase of lap dances, the downloading of images. In reality, they are most certainly *not* getting any women while engaged in such pursuits. So why should men allow themselves to be manipulated in this way? And why shouldn't men be allowed to speak out? If a man chooses not to go to a strip club for a bachelor party, not only out of respect for women but out of self-respect, he should be commended rather than mocked for his actions. If enough men did so decisively, pornography would no longer be fated for mass acceptance.

One of the greatest myths spread by the pornified culture is that all men look at pornography. Yet the *only* men who believed this to be true in interviews happen to be the men who looked at pornography themselves. According to the *Pornified*/Harris poll, only 27 percent of Americans agreed with the statement "All men look at pornography." The truth is, despite what fans tell themselves about the ubiquity and necessity of porn, many men do not look at it, and their disinterest isn't necessarily about religion or politics. Many men who do not look are neither asexual nor repressed, neither afraid nor unaware of pornography's "appeal." Yet expressing distaste or disinterest is considered shameful or foolish in a pornified culture. Those who oppose pornography are branded as pussies or wimps, cowed by women or afraid of their own sexuality. This is startling when you consider that, given most men's preference for actual sex to pornography, to use pornography is to declare oneself amorously inept or impotent, unable to relate to women, socially and emotionally immature, unwanted, or lonely. If men truly prefer sex to porn, they should be allowed and encouraged to act that way.

The humiliation of using pornography back when it was a lot less anonymous and accessible wasn't exclusively about religious guilt. It was about the embarrassing reality that using pornography denotes a lack of confidence in one's manhood and insecurity in one's sexuality. Women in pornography exist to tell men, "We want you"—we women of the Ivy League, we Hollywood starlets, we girls next door, we the blonde you could never get. A man's sense of manhood is affirmed only by his acquiescence to the idea that he cannot get this woman in the real world, but needs to feel as though he can. Why should men be considered so pathetic as to need these forms of self-esteem trickery? Pornography is sold as something manly and adult, even though pornographic fantasy often stems from sorry episodes of adolescent rejection. It's not just for their nubile beauty that men use pornography to get off on women who look like teenagers. It also serves an emotional need to prove themselves, to be able to say, "Look at me now, I can have you if I want." Many men use pornography as a way to get back at the girls who rebuffed them during their adolescence—they still want to "get" the high school prom queen. Pornography allows men to feel better and stronger and more powerful than those women/girls, mirroring and mining their adolescent fear of emotions and vulnerability. Pornography allows men to fall backward into an arena in which sex is devoid of emotions and fear and risk. It coddles the grown man, then tells him to feel "manly" about his own regression.

In asking men to buy into its myths, pornography underestimates and assumes the worst in men. Most men are intelligent enough to distinguish material that celebrates women from material that denigrates women; they can recognize images that depict healthy sexuality and humanity and images that ridicule and cheapen sexuality and deprive participants of their humanity. It's disrespectful of men's capabilities to expect them to condone viewing pornography that quite clearly shows women in a negative light, doing things that men presume most women would not want to do—gag on semen, get doubly penetrated to the point of pain, be ejaculated on in derogatory ways—treated in so many ways like something less than human.

The pornography user might ask himself how comfortable he would be viewing such material with his teenage daughter or his mother, his sister, or his wife. There's a reason for uneasiness that extends beyond the fact that for most men, as for women, sexuality and masturbation in particular are private matters. The material itself adds an unendurable aspect to public sharing. Few men want their wives to know precisely what they've become accustomed to getting off to. It's usually a far cry

from shared fantasies over pillow talk. Most men would not want their female boss at the office to know they spend evenings at home fantasizing over the humiliation of countless interchangeable female bodies. Most men take great pains to deny or rationalize it themselves. What if the lonely, isolated individual clicking away on his Internet browser were to log off not because he was forced to nor because he felt a sense of religious or puritanical guilt, but because he knows to stay online is self-defeating?

Women and the Reality of Pornography

Men are not the only ones who have been taught to seek a false sense of empowerment through pornography. Liberal female college students, third-wave feminists, and even female conservative realists of the "boys will be boys" school now argue that women deserve pornography, too. They claim that to "own" pornography is to make it theirs and that women empower themselves by harnessing their sexual wiles and using it to their advantage. In the same way that certain women's groups have rallied behind prostitutes, demanding they be called "sex workers" and accorded labor rights, the pornography-as-empowerment movement sees no problem with women being bought for their bodies—as long as *they* are making the profit.

Indeed, pro-porn women are most definitely in favor of women raking in money for sex, and they angrily denounce those women who would have it otherwise. Pro-porn women such as Melinda Gallagher, founder of CAKE, accuse feminists of squelching women's sexuality: "The imperialistic mentality of the anti-porn feminists, who came into women's lives and said, 'You shouldn't like this and that's bad and we're gonna draw that line,' created a lot of damage. CAKE is not going to buy into that mentality."[8] Tristan Taormino, a writer and director who bills herself as a "feminist pornographer," travels to college campuses to speak out about women's right to "pornify themselves." At the first international conference on pornography in 1998, advocates on a panel called "Women and Pornography: Victims or Visionaries?" theorized that anti-porn women were more responsible for driving men and women apart than were their pro-porn counterparts. One went so far as to lay derogatory hardcore pornography at the feet of women who oppose pornography. "You've got them so scared sexually that they're mad!" said Nina Hartley, a porn star who was featured in the film *Boogie Nights*. "They can't get laid! They can't get blow jobs! They can't cum! That's why you're seeing more of these women getting dragged on their faces, and spit on, and having their heads dunked in the toilet. Men are mad!"[9]

When they're not accusing anti-porn women of generating hardcore male pornography, many of the new feminist pornography purveyors claim to be subverting "patriarchal porn" with their own version of "alterna-porn." Missy Suicide, the founder of the female-operated pornography Web site Suicide Girls, explains, "Sex and sexuality is [*sic*] nothing for a woman to be ashamed of, but for a long time it felt that way, even in feminism. It's that old attitude that any time you take your clothes off you're being objectified or exploited. I think the women on Suicide Girls are brave in saying, 'I'm confident, I'm intelligent, and I don't have a problem sharing my sexuality with the world. This is what a real body looks like, and it's beautiful.' This is what should be celebrated."[10] Of course, it is unclear where amid the naked poses women can be heard expressing intelligence or confidence. Nor is it clear that their message is getting through amid the barrage of male-oriented pornography out there. There is something almost futile about the new alterna-porn sites, which, in featuring women who are less attractive to the mainstream man, are also vastly less popular than more stereotypical pornography Web sites. This lesson was learned the hard way when the Suicide Girls site was linked to Playboy.com for several months. Playboy.com members greeted the Suicide Girls' untraditional bodies, piercings, and hipster hairstyles with anger and disgust.

Is it even desirable for women to become producers and consumers of pornography? Certainly there is no advantage to women's sexuality becoming more visually cued so that women judge potential partners by their physical appearance to the same extent men do. Equality should come from elevating women to where men hold an advantage, not lowering them to share the costs of pornography with men. Even men who enjoy pornography recognize its degrading nature. One thirty-five-year-old who works in the used-car business and looks at pornography weekly said almost impatiently, "*Of course* pornography is degrading to women. They're being used and that's why I don't like seeing porn where you can tell that they're not enjoying it. If it seems like they're enjoying it you can rationalize in your head while you're looking at it that they're enjoying it as much as the guy is…. I guess it's *possible* she's enjoying it, but I highly doubt it. Still, when you're looking at porn, you just try not to pay too much attention to what the woman is thinking and what's going beyond the scenes. Otherwise, you just won't enjoy it at all." By co-opting pornography, women will sink into the same pattern of denial and rationalization.

So why are women so eager to embrace porn? The women's movement during the sixties, seventies, and eighties was accused of being elitist and of not understanding the needs, pressures, and desires of average American women and, in particular, poor, uneducated women. Part of the female pro-porn movement stems from an attempt to correct this alleged attitude. In their effort to be "nonjudgmental," many younger feminists have become uncomfortable condemning pornography when its participants and stars are largely women who choose their work out of financial desperation. Embracing pornography has become almost a new form of political correctness—heaven forbid that someone might appear to "denounce" another person's sexuality or "chosen" profession. Commenting on the university administration's acceptance of Harvard's pornographic magazine *H Bomb*, one of its female founders explained, "I guess they got past their fear of porn." Such phrasing is carefully chosen. Rather than be opposed to pornography for ethical, feminist, or humanist reasons, the only opposition one could have to pornography is fear—that is, phobia as in homophobia.

Pornography proponents have even taken to calling their opponents "pornophobic." In other words, to disapprove of pornography is to be intolerant of other lifestyles, and people who disapprove of pornography are just as bigoted as homophobes. And naturally, this accusation of intolerance applies only to those who oppose pornography, not those who perpetuate it.

In other ways, the pro-pornography movement among women is more reactive than proactive. For years, women who fight for women's rights—and especially women who oppose pornography—have been accused of having no sense of humor. If they could just laugh it off, they would realize pornography is fine, their opponents argued. Many women have bought into this absurd proposition, accepting the idea that if you don't find porn funny or amusing or ironic, you just don't get it. Anti-pornography feminists have also been accused of perpetuating a culture of victimization: by pointing out that many women who participate in the production of pornography suffer sexual and emotional abuse, pornography opponents supposedly turn these women into victims. Shouldn't the real target of such accusations be the pornographers themselves?

Perhaps women who choose to participate in or consume pornography *are* making their own "choices." But rather than make choices based on a regressive male ideal of sexuality and limited options, they could make choices based on something beyond body parts and financial desperation. Indeed, hypocrisy reigns in the pro-porn feminist movement. Why insist that it is okay for women to exploit other women, but when men do so, it is harm, harassment, or sexual crime? Some pro-porn feminists remain opposed to prostitution, failing to see the thin line that separates the two forms of sex for sale. Others advocate prostitution as well as pornography, yet are opposed to other forms of human sale, arguing against the sex slavery trade and championing labor rights. In all likelihood, many of those who suggest that pornography is about sexual liberation have probably not seen the kind of pornography that many, perhaps most, men find alluring: the glorification of male promiscuity and adultery, the subordination of women, the sexualization of pain, and even hardcore depictions of female torture. In this context, pornography is not about desire and fantasy; it's about hostility and shame.

The pioneering feminists of the seventies anti-pornography movement were denounced as "radical" in their time; today, pro-porn feminists sometimes refer to their anti-porn counterparts as "conservative feminists." Have women really progressed so far as to make the changes advocated in the seventies somehow retrograde?

Today, the next generation seems all too ready to mock or reject arguments against pornography without giving them serious thought. The truth is, we have not moved forward or beyond those supposedly out-dated ideas—we've merely resigned ourselves to them or rationalized them away. Women need to ask themselves, Is this progress or is it prurience? It's sad that ours is a culture where the inclusion of Olympic athletes in *Playboy* magazine is considered a leap forward. That female athletic achievement is reduced to a tool for male masturbatory pleasure is a sentiment scoffed at or ignored. The idea that women will do anything for a buck and a fleeting moment of fame not only still exists, women willingly propagate it. While pornography purports to value the female body above all, it devalues it substantially. Selling one's image online for paying customers doesn't exactly reflect a strong sense of self-respect.

One of the more insidious attacks against women who oppose pornography accuses them of being prudish and uncomfortable with their own sexuality, "insecure," and "jealous." Terrified of being labeled "anti-sex," "humorless," or "feminist," many women have neglected to stand up to pornography. Yet to be opposed to porn in no way means a person is opposed to sexuality in all of its healthy and positive forms. Women who are the most secure and confident, who have the temerity to stand up to such fallacious claims, are surely stronger than the women held in sway by the pornified culture's myths. Moreover, the idea that a woman can't "own" or "explore" her own sexuality without incorporating pornography into her life (as "sex-positive" pro-porn feminists would have it) is insulting, and an extraordinarily narrow and limiting view of sexuality.

The idea persists that people who dislike pornography are somehow repressed or wrestling under religious dogma or stymied by a conservative upbringing doesn't hold true. Interviewing women for this book, I repeatedly heard things like, "I don't mean to sound like a prude but ..." bookending comments criticizing pornography, and sometimes chased down with the disclaimer, "And I'm liberal!" Sadly, women seem to have absorbed the message that to criticize pornography is to be uncool, unsexy, and reactionary. The reality is that women who are opposed to pornography or troubled by its effects on our society come from all walks of life and espouse a wide range of political ideologies. Many are attractive, happily single, sexually active, married, or fulfilled. They are strong, smart, opinionated women who, when it comes to articulating their feelings about pornography, feel silenced or fearful. They are reluctant to complain about pornography or to speak out about the subject. They are afraid to confront their boyfriends and husbands about it, nervous talking to their teenaged sons, cowed into accepting what they know in their hearts to be unacceptable.

Their reticence is understandable. It is tempting to acquiesce to the defensive cries of, "But it's just naked women! It's just sex!" For there is nothing wrong with naked women or sex. But pornography is not just naked women, and it is not sex. The sexual acts depicted in pornography are more about shame, humiliation, solitude, coldness, and degradation than they are about pleasure, intimacy, and love. The word *pornography* comes from the Greek *porne*, which means prostitute or whore, and *graphos*, which means depiction or writing. Pornography is, at its core, the commercialization of women, turning men into consumers and women into a product to be used and discarded. If pornography were truly just about sex and naked bodies, there would be nothing to get upset over, but those who know better, those who bother to think while they gaze or who stop averting their eyes for a moment and address what's on-screen

in the cubicle behind them, should—and can—no longer be ignored.

The longer we ignore the problem of pornography, the worse it becomes. The dissemination and availability of pornography inevitably bring about increased individual and societal acceptance. Research shows that the more pornography one is exposed to, the more tolerant of pornography and indeed in favor of pornography one becomes. What was once softcore pornography has become mainstream; magazines that were once considered pornographic are now filed under "men's lifestyle"; men's lifestyle magazines have in turn aspired toward the pornographic. As porn creeps into the mainstream press and into popular culture, it crowds out other, more positive forms of sexual expression. It also keeps raising the bar higher for "real" pornography, which stretches to surpass every imaginable ethical, humanistic, and societal limit. Pregnant women become pornified, their naked torsos wrested from personal Web sites onto "pregnant porn" Web sites, incest becomes fetishized, child pornography blends with adult pornography into an ageless "teen porn" middle ground. Any sense of taboo dissipates in a free-for-all porn world.

Not only does pornography viewing indulge and abet the pornographic culture, it also has policy implications. Studies have shown that those who view heavy doses of pornography are less likely to believe there's a need for restrictions on pornography for minors and are less likely to favor restrictions in broadcasting. Passively accepting life in a pornified culture is helping pornography flourish, a fact of which the industry is well aware. Our eyes become blinded by porn.

Pornography is a moving target and it's time we catch up with it. For years, the pornography industry and the pornified culture have told both men and women who oppose pornography to shut up or turn a blind eye. They have accused anti-pornography activists, or even those who have dared question their profit equation, of being anti-sex and anti-freedom. They have done so while creating a forcefully anti-sex product that limits the freedom of men, women, and children. They have sold America on the idea of fantasy while inciting us to ignore reality. Those who have been silenced have only served to further legitimize pornography with their lack of censure. Those who are now quiet must speak out.

ENDNOTES

1. www.extremeassociates.com

2. Anne Kingston, "Porn of Another Kind: To Sexually Humiliate Someone Is to Destroy His Sense of Self," *National Post* (Ontario), May 11, 2004.

3. Anderson Cooper, *360 Degrees*, CNN, April 13, 2004.

4. Michael S. Kimmel, *Men Confront Pornography* (New York: Crown Publishers, 1990), p. 13. Author's emphasis.

5. Dennis McAlpine, interview, "Porn America," *Frontline*, PBS, August 2001.

6. Jonathan A. Knee, "Is That Really Legal?" *New York Times*, May 2, 2004.

7. Jonathan Prynn, "Vodafone Restricts Sex Sites," *Evening Standard* (London), July 2, 2004.

8. Virginia Vitzthum, "Stripped of Our Senses," *Elle*, December 2003, p. 188.

9. Carina Chocano, "Scholars of Smut," Salon.com, October 5, 1998.

10. Neva Chonin, "Pretty in Porn: Alterna-Porn Is Challenging the Playboy Body Ideal," *San Francisco Chronicle*, July 25, 2004.

45

American Booksellers v. Hudnutt

United States District Court and Court of Appeals

The issue before the federal judiciary was whether the Indianapolis ordinance that sought to prohibit pornography as a practice that discriminated against women was restricting speech rather than conduct—and, if it was restricting speech, whether it was restricting speech that was protected by the First Amendment to the U.S. Constitution. The federal judiciary ruled that the ordinance was indeed restricting speech protected by the First Amendment rather than conduct.

Indianapolis enacted an ordinance defining "pornography" as a practice that discriminates against women. "Pornography" is to be redressed through the administrative and judicial methods used for other discrimination....

"Pornography" under the ordinance is "the graphic sexually explicit subordination of women, whether in pictures or in words, that also includes one or more of the following:

1. Women are presented as sexual objects who enjoy pain or humiliation; or

2. Women are presented as sexual objects who experience sexual pleasure in being raped; or

3. Women are presented as sexual objects tied up or cut up or mutilated or bruised or physically hurt, or as dismembered or truncated or fragmented or severed into body parts; or

4. Women are presented as being penetrated by objects or animals; or

5. Women are presented in scenarios of degradation, injury, abasement, torture, shown as filthy or inferior, bleeding, bruised, or hurt in a context that makes these conditions sexual; or

6. Women are presented as sexual objects for domination, conquest, violation, exploitation, possession, or use, or through postures or positions of servility or submission or display."...

FIRST AMENDMENT
REQUIREMENTS

This Ordinance cannot be analyzed adequately without first recognizing this: The drafters of the Ordinance have used what appears to be a legal term of art, "pornography," but have in fact given the term a specialized meaning which differs from the meanings ordinarily assigned to that word in both legal and common parlance. In Section 16–3(v) (page 6), the Ordinance states:

Pornography shall mean the sexually explicit subordination of women, graphically depicted, whether in pictures or in words, that includes one or more of the following:

There follows ... a listing of five specific presentations of women in various settings which serve as examples of "pornography" and as such further define and describe that term under the Ordinance.

As is generally recognized, the word "pornography" is usually associated, and sometimes synonymous, with the word, "obscenity." "Obscenity" not only has its own separate and specialized meaning in the law, but in laymen's use also, and it is a much broader meaning than the definition given the word "pornography" in the Ordinance which is at issue in this action. There is thus a considerable risk of confusion in analyzing this Ordinance unless care and precision are used in that process.

The Constitutional analysis of this Ordinance requires a determination of several underlying issues: First, the Court must determine whether the Ordinance imposes restraints on speech or behavior (content versus conduct); if the Ordinance is found to regulate speech, the Court must next determine whether the subject speech is protected or not protected under the First Amendment; if the speech ... regulated by this Ordinance is protected speech under the Constitution, the Court must then decide whether the regulation is constitutionally permissible ... based on a compelling state interest justifying the removal of such speech from First Amendment protections.

Do the Ordinances Regulate Speech or Behavior (Content or Conduct)?

It appears to be central to the defense of the Ordinance by defendants that the Court accept their premise that the City-County Council has not attempted to regulate speech, let alone protected speech. Defendants repeat throughout their briefs the incantation that their Ordinance regulates conduct, not speech. They contend (one senses with a certain sleight of hand) that the production, dissemination, and use of sexually explicit words and pictures is the actual subordination of women and not an expression of ideas deserving of First Amendment protection....

Defendants claim support for their theory by analogy, arguing that it is an accepted and established legal distinction that has allowed other courts to find that advocacy of a racially "separate but equal" doctrine in a civil rights context is protected speech under the First Amendment though "segregation"

is not constitutionally protected behavior. Accordingly, defendants characterize their Ordinance here as a civil rights measure, through which they seek to prevent the distribution, sale, and exhibition of "pornography," as defined in the Ordinance, in order to regulate and control the underlying unacceptable conduct.

The content-versus-conduct approach espoused by defendants is not persuasive, however, and is contrary to accepted First Amendment principles. Accepting as true the City-County Council's finding that pornography conditions society to subordinate women, the means by which the Ordinance attempts to combat this sex discrimination is nonetheless through the regulation of speech.

For instance, the definition of pornography, the control of which is the whole thrust ..., states that it is "the sexually explicit subordination of women, graphically *depicted*, whether in *pictures* or in *words*, that includes one or more of the following: (emphasis supplied) and the following five descriptive subparagraphs begin with ..., *Women are presented* ..."

The unlawful acts and discriminatory practices regulated by this Ordinance are set out in Section 16–3(g):

> (4) Trafficking in pornography: the production, sale, exhibition, or distribution of pornography, ...
> (5) Coercion into pornographic performance: coercing, intimidating or fraudulently inducing any person ... into performing for pornography ...
> (6) Forcing pornography on a person: ....
> (7) Assault or physical attack due to pornography: the assault, physical attack, or injury of any woman, man, child or transsexual in a way that is directly caused by specific pornography ...

Section (7), *supra*, goes on to provide a cause of action in damages against the perpetrators, makers, distributors, sellers, and exhibitors of pornography and injunctive relief against the further exhibition, distribution or sale of pornography.

In summary, therefore, the Ordinance establishes through the legislative findings that pornography causes a tendency to commit these various harmful acts, and outlaws the pornography (that is, the "depictions"), the activities involved in the production of pornography, and the behavior caused by or resulting from pornography.

Thus, though the purpose of the Ordinance is cast in civil rights terminology—"to prevent and prohibit all discriminatory practices of sexual subordination or inequality through pornography" ...—it is clearly aimed at controlling the content of the speech and ideas that the City-Country Council has found harmful and offensive. Those words and pictures which depict women in sexually subordinate roles are banned by the Ordinance. Despite defendants' attempt to redefine offensive speech as harmful action, the clear wording of the Ordinance discloses that they seek to control speech, and those restrictions must be analyzed in light of applicable constitutional requirements and standards.

Is the Speech Regulated by the Ordinance Protected or Unprotected Speech under the First Amendment?

The First Amendment provides that government shall make no law abridging the freedom of speech. However, "the First and Fourteenth Amendments have never been thought to give absolute protection to every individual to speak whenever or wherever he pleases or to use any form of address in any circumstances that he chooses." *Cohen v. California* (1971). Courts have recognized only a "relatively few categories of instances," ... where the government may regulate certain forms of individual expression. The traditional categories of speech subject to permissible government regulation include "the lewd and obscene, the profane, the libelous, and the insulting or 'fighting' words— those which by their very utterance inflict injury or tend to incite an immediate breach of the peace." *Chaplinsky v. State of New Hampshire* (1942). In addition, the Supreme Court has recently upheld legislation prohibiting the dissemination of material depicting children engaged in sexual conduct. *New York v. Ferber* (1982).

Having found that the Ordinance at issue here seeks to regulate speech (and not conduct), the next question before the Court is whether the Ordinance, which seeks to restrict the distribution, sale, and exhibition of "pornography" as a form of sex discrimination against women, falls within one of the established categories of speech subject to permissible government regulation, that is, speech deemed to be unprotected by the First Amendment.

It is clear that this case does not present issues relating to profanity, libel, or "fighting words." In searching for an analytical "peg," the plaintiffs argue that the Ordinance most closely resembles obscenity, and is, therefore, subject to the requirements set forth in *Miller v. California* (1973).... But the defendants admit that the scope of the Ordinance is not limited to the regulation of legally obscene material as defined in *Miller*.... In fact, defendants concede that the "pornography" they seek to control goes beyond obscenity, as defined by the Supreme Court and excepted from First Amendment protections. Accordingly, the parties agree that the materials ... in the restrictions set out in the Ordinance include to some extent what have traditionally been protected materials.

The test under *Miller* for determining whether material is legal obscenity is:

> (a) whether "the average person, applying contemporary community standards" would find that the work, taken as a whole, appeals to the prurient interest....; (b) whether the work depicts or describes, in a patently offensive way, sexual conduct specifically defined by the applicable state law; and (c) whether the work, taken as a whole, lacks serious literary, artistic, political, or scientific value....

It is obvious that this three-step test is not directly applicable to the present case, because, as has been noted, the Ordinance goes beyond legally obscene material in imposing its controls. The restrictions in the Indianapolis ordinance reach what has otherwise traditionally been regarded as protected speech under the *Miller* test. Beyond that, the Ordinance does not speak in terms of a "community standard" or attempt to restrict the dissemination of material that appeals to the "prurient interest." Nor has the Ordinance been drafted in a way to limit only distributions of "patently offensive" materials. Neither does it provide for the dissemination of works which, though "pornographic," may have "serious literary, artistic, political or scientific value." Finally, the Ordinance does not limit its reach to "hard-core sexual conduct," though conceivably "hard-core" materials may be included in its proscriptions.

Because the Ordinance spans so much more ... in its regulatory scope than merely "hard-core" obscenity by limiting the distribution of "pornography," the proscriptions in the Ordinance intrude with defendants' explicit approval into areas of otherwise protected speech. Under ordinary constitutional analysis, that would be sufficient grounds to overturn the Ordinance, but defendants argue that this case is not governed by any direct precedent, that it raises a new issue for the Court and even though the Ordinance regulates protected speech, it does so in a constitutionally permissible fashion.

Does Established First Amendment Law Permit the Regulation Provided for in the Ordinance of Otherwise Protected Speech?

In conceding that the scope of this Ordinance extends beyond constitutional limits, it becomes clear that what defendants actually seek by enacting this legislation is a newly defined class of constitutionally unprotected speech, labeled "pornography" and characterized as sexually discriminatory.

Defendants vigorously argue that *Miller* is not the "'constitutional divide' separating protected from unprotected expression in this area." ... Defendants point to three cases which allegedly support their proposition that *Miller* is not the exclusive guideline for disposing of pornography/obscenity cases, and that the traditional obscenity test should not be applied in the present case....

Defendants first argue that the Court must use the same reasoning applied by the Supreme Court

in *New York v. Ferber* ... which upheld a New York statute prohibiting persons from promoting child pornography by distributing material which depicted such activity, and carve out another similar exception to protected speech under the First Amendment.

Defendants can properly claim some support for their position in *Ferber*. There the Supreme Court allowed the states "greater leeway" in their regulation of pornographic depictions of children in light of the State's compelling interest in protecting children who, without such protections, are extraordinarily vulnerable to exploitation and harm. The court stated in upholding the New York statute:

> The prevention of sexual exploitation and abuse of children constitutes a government objective of surpassing importance. The legislative findings accompanying passage of the New York laws reflect this concern:....

The Supreme Court continued in *Ferber* by noting that the *Miller* standard for legal obscenity does not satisfy the unique concerns and issues posed by child pornography where children are involved; it is irrelevant, for instance, that the materials sought to be regulated contain serious literary, artistic, political, or scientific value. In finding that some speech, such as that represented in depictions of child pornography, is outside First Amendment protections, the *Ferber* court stated:

> When a definable class of material ... bears so heavily and pervasively on the welfare of children engaged in its production, we think the balance of competing interests is clearly struck and that it is permissible to consider these materials as without the protection of the First Amendment.

Defendants, in the case at bar, argue that the interests of protecting women from sex-based discrimination are analogous to and every bit as compelling and fundamental as those which the Supreme Court upheld in *Ferber* for the benefit of children. But *Ferber* appears clearly distinguishable from the instant case on both the facts and law.

As has already been shown, the rationale applied by the Supreme Court in *Ferber* appears intended to apply solely to child pornography cases. In *Ferber*, the court recognized "that a state's interest in 'safeguarding the physical and psychological well-being of a minor' is 'compelling.'"... Also, the obscenity standard in *Miller* is appropriately abandoned in child pornography cases because it "[does] not reflect the State's particular and more compelling interest in prosecuting those who promote the sexual exploitations of children." ... Since a state's compelling interest in preventing child pornography outweighs an individual's First Amendment rights, the Supreme Court held that "the states are entitled to greater leeway in the regulation of pornographic depictions of children." ...

In contrast, the case at bar presents issues more far reaching than those in *Ferber*. Here, the City-County Council found that the distribution, sale, and exhibition of words and pictures depicting the subordination of women is a form of sex discrimination and as such is appropriate for governmental regulation. The state has a well-recognized interest in preventing sex discrimination, and, defendants argue, it can regulate speech to accomplish that end.

But the First Amendment gives primacy to free speech and any other state interest (such as the interest of sex-based equality under law) must be so compelling as to be fundamental; only then can it be deemed to outweigh the interest of free speech. This Court finds no legal authority or public policy argument which justifies so broad an incursion into First Amendment freedoms as to allow that which defendants attempt to advance here. *Ferber* does not open the door to allow the regulation contained in the Ordinance for the reason that adult women as a group do not, as a matter of public policy or applicable law, stand in need of the same type of protection which has long been afforded children. This is true even of women who are subject to the sort of inhuman treatment defendants have described and documented to the Court in support of this Ordinance. The Supreme Court's finding in *Ferber* of the uncontroverted state interest in "safeguarding the physical and psychological well-being of a minor" and its resultant characterization of that interest as "compelling," ... is an interest that inheres to children and is not an interest which is readily transferable to adult women as a class. Adult women generally have the capacity to protect themselves from participating in and being personally victimized by pornography, which makes the State's interest in safeguarding the physical and psychological well-being of women by prohibiting "the sexually explicit subordination of women, graphically depicted, whether in pictures or in words" not so compelling as to sacrifice the guarantees of the First Amendment. In any case, whether a state interest is so compelling as to be a fundamental interest sufficient to warrant an exception from constitutional protections, therefore, surely must turn on something other than mere legislative dictate, which issue is discussed more fully further on in this Opinion....

The second case relied upon by defendants to support their contention that *Miller* is not controlling in the present case is *FCC v. Pacifica Foundation* ... (1978). According to defendants, *Pacifica* exemplifies the Supreme Court's refusal to make obscenity the sole legal basis for regulating sexually explicit conduct.

In *Pacifica*, the Supreme Court was faced with the question of whether a broadcast of patently offensive words dealing with sex and excretion may be regulated on the basis of their content.... The Court held that this type of speech was not entitled to absolute constitutional protection in every context.... Since the context of the speech in *Pacifica* was broadcasting, it was determined only to be due "the most limited First Amendment protection." The reason for such treatment was two-fold:

> First, the broadcast media have established a uniquely pervasive presence in all the lives of all Americans. Patently offensive, indecent material presented over the airwaves confronts the citizen, not only in public, but also in the privacy of the home, where the individual's right to be left alone plainly outweighs the First Amendment rights of an intruder.
>
> Second, broadcasting is uniquely accessible to children, even those too young to read....

Although the defendants correctly point out that the Supreme Court did not use the traditional obscenity test in *Pacifica*, this Court is not persuaded that the rule enunciated there is applicable to the facts of the present case. The Ordinance does not attempt to regulate the airwaves; in terms of its restrictions, it is not even remotely concerned with the broadcast media. The reasons for the rule in *Pacifica*, that speech in certain contexts should be afforded minimal First Amendment protection, are not present here, since we are not dealing with a medium that "invades" the privacy of the home. In contrast, if an individual is offended by "pornography," as defined in the Ordinance, the logical thing to do is avoid it, an option frequently not available to the public with material disseminated through broadcasting.

In addition, the Ordinance is not written to protect children from the distribution of pornography, in contrast to the challenged FCC regulation in *Pacifica*. Therefore, the peculiar state interest in protecting the "well-being of its youth," ... does not underlie this Ordinance and cannot be called upon to justify a decision by this Court to uphold the Ordinance.

The third case cited by defendants in support of their proposition that the traditional obscenity standard in *Miller* should not be used to overrule the Ordinance is *Young v. American Mini Theatres, Inc* ... (1976). In *Young* the Supreme Court upheld a city ordinance that restricted the location of movie theatres featuring erotic films. The Court, in a plurality opinion, stated that "[e]ven though the First Amendment protects communication in this area from total suppression, we hold that the State may legitimately use the content of these materials as the basis for placing them in a different classification from other motion pictures." ... The Court concluded that the city's interest in preserving the character of its neighborhoods justified the ordinance which required that adult theaters be separated, rather than concentrated, in the same areas as it is permissible for other theaters to do without limitation....

Young is distinguishable from the present case because we are not here dealing with an attempt by the City-County Council to restrict the time, place, and manner in which "pornography" may be distributed. Instead, the Ordinance prohibits completely the sale, distribution, or exhibition of material depicting women in a sexually subordinate role, at all times, in all places and in every manner.

The Ordinance's attempt to regulate speech beyond one of the well-defined exceptions to protected, speech under the First Amendment is not supported by other Supreme Court precedents. The Court must, therefore, examine the underlying premise of the Ordinance: That the State has so compelling an interest in regulating the sort of sex discrimination imposed and perpetuated through "pornography" that it warrants an exception to free speech.

Is Sex Discrimination a Compelling State Interest Justifying an Exception to First Amendment Protections?

It is significant to note that the premise of the Ordinance is the sociological harm, *i.e.*, the discrimination, which results from "pornography" to degrade women as a class. The Ordinance does not presume or require specifically defined, identifiable victims for most of its proscriptions. The Ordinance seeks to protect adult women, as a group, from the diminution of their legal and sociological status as women, that is, from the discriminatory stigma which befalls women *as women* as a result of "pornography." On page one of the introduction to defendants' *Amicus Brief*, counsel explicitly argues that the harm which underlies this legislation is the "harm to the treatment and *status* of women ... on the basis of sex."...

This is a novel theory advanced by the defendants, an issue of first impression in the courts. If this Court were to accept defendants' argument— that the State's interest in protecting women from the humiliation and degradation which comes from being depicted in a sexually subordinate context is so compelling as to warrant the regulation of otherwise free speech to accomplish that end—one wonders what would prevent the City-County

Council (or any other legislative body) from enacting protections for other equally compelling claims against exploitation and discrimination as are presented here. Legislative bodies, finding support here, could also enact legislation prohibiting other unfair expression—the publication and distribution of racist material, for instance, on the grounds that it causes racial discrimination,[1] or legislation prohibiting ethnic or religious slurs on the grounds that they cause discrimination against particular ethnic or religious groups, or legislation barring literary depictions which are uncomplimentary or oppressive to handicapped persons on the grounds that they cause discrimination against that group of people, and so on. If this Court were to extend to this case the rationale in *Ferber* to uphold the Amendment, it would signal so great a potential encroachment upon First Amendment freedoms that the precious liberties reposed within those guarantees would not survive. The compelling state interest, which defendants claim gives constitutional life to their Ordinance, though important and valid as that interest may be in other contexts, is not so fundamental an interest as to warrant a broad intrusion into otherwise free expression.

Defendants contend that pornography is not deserving of constitutional protection because its harms victimize all women. It is argued that "pornography" not only negatively affects women who risk and suffer the direct abuse of its production, but also, those on whom violent pornography is forced through such acts as compelled performances of "dangerous acts such as being hoisted upside down by ropes, bound by ropes and chains, hung from trees and scaffolds or having sex with animals...." It is also alleged that exposure to pornography produces a negative impact on its viewers, causing in them an increased willingness to aggress toward women, *ibid.*...., and experience self-generated rape fantasies, increases in sexual arousal and a rise in the self-reported possibility of raping.... In addition, it causes discriminatory attitudes and behavior toward all women.... The City-County Council, after considering testimony and social research studies, enacted the Ordinance in order to "combat" pornography's "concrete and tangible harms to women."...

Defendants rely on *Paris Adult Theatre I v. Slaton* ... (1973) to justify their regulation of "pornography." In that case the Supreme Court held "there are legitimate state interests at stake in stemming the tide of commercialized obscenity ... [that] include the interest of the public in the quality of life and the total community environment, the tone of commerce in the great city centers, and, possibly, ... public safety itself."...

The Georgia Legislature had determined that in that case exposure to obscene material adversely affected men and women, that is to say, society as a whole. Although the petitioners argued in that case that there was no scientific data to conclusively prove that proposition, the Court said, "[i]t is not for us to resolve empirical uncertainties underlying state legislation, save in the exceptional case where that legislation plainly impinges upon rights protected by the constitution itself." ...

Based on this reasoning, defendants argue that there is more than enough "empirical" evidence in the case at bar to support the City-County Council's conclusion that "pornography" harms women in the same way obscenity harms people, and, therefore, this Court should not question the legislative finding. As has already been acknowledged, it is not the Court's function to question the City-County Council's legislative finding. The Court's solitary duty is to ensure that the Ordinance accomplishes its purpose without violating constitutional standards or impinging upon constitutionally protected rights. In applying those tests, the Court finds that the Ordinance cannot withstand constitutional scrutiny.

It has already been noted that the Ordinance does not purport to regulate legal obscenity, as defined in *Miller*. Thus, although the City-County Council determined that "pornography" harms women, this Court must and does declare the Ordinance invalid without being bound by the legislative findings because "pornography," as defined and regulated in the Ordinance, is constitutionally protected speech under the First Amendment and such an exception to [its] protections is constitutionally unwarranted. This Court cannot legitimately embark on judicial policy making, carving out a new exception to the First Amendment simply to uphold the Ordinance, even when there may be many good reasons to support legislative action. To permit every interest group, especially those who claim to be victimized by unfair expression, their own legislative exceptions to the First Amendment so long as they succeed in obtaining a majority of legislative votes in their favor demonstrates the potentially predatory nature of what defendants seek through this Ordinance and defend in this lawsuit.

It ought to be remembered by defendants and all others who would support such a legislative initiative that, in terms of altering sociological patterns, much as alteration may be necessary and desirable, free speech, rather than being the enemy, is a long-tested and worthy ally. To deny free speech in order to engineer social change in the name of accomplishing a greater good for one sector of our society erodes the freedoms of all and, as such, threatens tyranny and injustice for those subjected to the rule of such laws. The First Amendment protections presuppose the evil of such tyranny and prevent a finding by this Court upholding the Ordinance....

ENDNOTE

1. In *Beauharnais v. Illinois* ... the Supreme Court upheld an Illinois libel statute prohibiting the dissemination of materials promoting racial or religious hatred and which tended to produce a breach of the peace and riots. It has been recognized that "the rationale of that decision turns quite plainly on the strong tendency of the prohibited utterances to cause violence and disorder." *Collin v. Smith* (7th Cir. 1978). The Supreme Court has recognized breach of the peace as the traditional justification for upholding a criminal libel statute, *Beauharnais* ... Therefore, a law preventing the distribution of material that causes racial discrimination, an attitude, would be upheld under this analysis. Further, the underlying reasoning of the *Beauharnais* opinion, that the punishment of libel raises no constitutional problems, has been questioned in many recent cases....

46

Donald Victor Butler v. Her Majesty the Queen
The Supreme Court of Canada

The issue before the Supreme Court of Canada was that of determining whether and to what extent Parliament may legitimately criminalize obscenity. The Court ruled that the criminalization of obscenity accorded with the Canadian Charter of Rights and Freedom. In particular, the material to be suppressed depicted women "as sexual playthings, hysterically and instantly responsive to male sexual demands" and was produced simply for economic profit. The Court ruled that just as in the case of hate propaganda, it need not require conclusive social science evidence of harm to women before justifying prohibition. The Court judged that "a reasonable apprehension of harm" sufficed. The Court further judged that less intrusive legislation would not be as effective in preventing harm to women.

This appeal [challenges] the constitutionality of the obscenity provisions of the *Criminal Code,*... s. 163. They are attacked on the ground that they contravene ... the *Canadian Charter of Rights and Freedoms*. The case requires the Court to address one of the most difficult and controversial of contemporary issues, ... determining whether, and to what extent, Parliament may legitimately criminalize obscenity. [We] begin with a review of the facts that gave rise to this appeal, as well as of the proceedings in the lower courts.

FACTS AND PROCEEDINGS

In August 1987, the appellant, Donald Victor Butler, opened the Avenue Video Boutique located in Winnipeg, Manitoba. The shop sells and rents "hard-core" videotapes and magazines as well as sexual paraphernalia. Outside the store is a sign that reads:

Avenue Video Boutique; a private members only adult video/visual club. Notice: If sex-oriented material offends you, please do not enter. No admittance to persons under 18 years.

On August 21, 1987, the City of Winnipeg Police entered the appellant's store with a search warrant and seized [its] inventory. The appellant was charged with 173 counts in the first indictment: 3 counts of selling obscene material ... 41 counts of possessing obscene material for the purpose of distribution ... 128 counts of possessing obscene material for the purpose of sale ... and 1 count of exposing obscene material to public view....

On October 19, 1987, the appellant reopened the store at the same location. As a result of a police operation a search warrant was executed on October 29, 1987, resulting in the arrest of an employee, Norma McCord. The appellant was arrested at a later date.

A joint indictment was laid against the appellant doing business as Avenue Video Boutique and Norma McCord. The joint indictment contains 77 counts: ... 2 counts of selling obscene material, ... 73 counts of possessing obscene material for the purpose of distribution ... 1 count of possessing obscene material for the purpose of sale ... and 1 count of exposing obscene material to public view....

The trial judge convicted the appellant on eight counts relating to eight films. Convictions were entered against the co-accused McCord with respect to two counts relating to two of the films. Fines of $1,000 per offence were imposed on the appellant. Acquittals were entered on the remaining charges.

The Crown appealed the 242 acquittals with respect to the appellant and the appellant cross-appealed the convictions. The majority of the Manitoba Court of Appeal allowed the appeal of the Crown and entered convictions for the appellant with respect to all of the counts, Twaddle and Helper J. J. A. dissenting....

In reaching the conclusion that legislation proscribing obscenity is a valid objective that justifies some encroachment of the right to freedom of expression, I am persuaded in part that such legislation may be found in most free and democratic societies. As Nemetz C. J. B. C. aptly pointed out in *R. v. Red Hot Video,* ... for centuries democratic societies have set certain limits to freedom of expression. He cited ... the following passage of Dickson J. A.... in *R. v. Great West News Ltd.:*

> All organized societies have sought in one manner or another to suppress obscenity. The right of the state to legislate to protect its moral fibre and well-being has long been recognized, with roots deep in history. It is within this frame that the Courts and Judges must work.

The advent of the *Charter* did not have the effect of dramatically depriving Parliament of a power that it has historically enjoyed. It is also noteworthy that the criminalization of obscenity was considered to be compatible with the *Canadian Bill of Rights*. As Dickson J. A. stated in *R. v. Prairie Schooner News Ltd.....:*

> Freedom of speech is not unfettered either in criminal law or civil law. The *Canadian Bill of Rights* was intended to protect, and does protect, basic freedoms of vital importance to all Canadians. It does not serve as a shield behind which obscene matter may be disseminated without

concern for criminal consequences. The interdiction of the publications which are the subject of the present charges in no way trenches upon the freedom of expression which the *Canadian Bill of Rights* assures.

... Finally ... the burgeoning pornography industry renders the concern even more pressing and substantial than when the impugned provisions were first enacted. [Therefore,] the objective of avoiding the harm associated with the dissemination of pornography in this case is sufficiently pressing and substantial to warrant some restriction on full exercise of the right to freedom of expression. The analysis of whether the measure is proportional to the objective must ... be undertaken in light of the conclusion that the objective of the impugned section is valid only insofar as it relates to the harm to society associated with obscene materials. Indeed, the section as interpreted in previous decisions and in these reasons is fully consistent with that objective. The objective of maintaining conventional standards of propriety, independently of any harm to society, is no longer justified in light of the values of individual liberty that underlie the *Charter*. This, then, being the objective of s. 163, which [is] pressing and substantial, I must now determine whether the section is rationally connected and proportional to this objective. As outlined above, s. 163 criminalizes the exploitation of sex, and sex and violence, when, on the basis of the community test, it is undue. The determination of when such exploitation is undue is directly related to the immediacy of a risk of harm to society that is reasonably perceived as arising from its dissemination....

The proportionality requirement has three aspects:

1. the existence of a rational connection between the impugned measures and the objective;

2. minimal impairment of the right or freedom; and

3. a proper balance between the effects of the limiting measures and the legislative objective.

In assessing whether the proportionality test is met ... keep in mind the nature of expression that has been infringed. In the *Prostitution Reference* ... Dickson C. J. wrote:

> When a *Charter* freedom has been infringed by state action that takes the form of criminalization, the Crown bears the heavy burden of justifying that infringement. Yet the expressive activity, as with any infringed *Charter* right, should also be analysed in the particular context of the case. Here, the activity to which the impugned legislation is directed is expression with an economic purpose. It can hardly be said that communications regarding an economic transaction of sex for money lie at, or even near, the core of the guarantee of freedom of expression.

The values that underlie the protection of freedom of expression relate to the search for truth, participation in the political process, and individual self-fulfillment. The Attorney General for Ontario argues that, of these, only "individual self-fulfillment," and only in its most base aspect, that of physical arousal, is engaged by pornography.... [C]ivil liberties groups argue that pornography forces us to question conventional notions of sexuality and thus launches us into an inherently political discourse. In their factum, the B. C. Civil Liberties Association adopts a passage from R. West, "The Feminist-Conservative Anti-Pornography Alliance and the 1986 Attorney General's Commission on Pornography Report."...:

> Good pornography has value because it validates women's will to pleasure. It celebrates female nature. It validates a range of female sexuality that is wider and truer than that legitimated by the non-pornographic culture. Pornography when it is good celebrates both female pleasure and male rationality.

A proper application of the test should not suppress what West refers to as "good pornography." The objective of the impugned provision is not to inhibit the celebration of human sexuality. However, it cannot be ignored that the realities of the pornography industry are far from the picture which the B.C. Civil Liberties Association would have us paint. Shannon J., in *R. v. Wagner* ..., describes the materials more accurately when he observed:

> Women, particularly, are deprived of unique human character or identity and are depicted as sexual playthings, hysterically and instantly responsive to male sexual demands. They worship male genitals and their own value depends upon the quality of their genitals and breasts.

In my view, the kind of expression that is sought to be advanced does not stand on equal footing with other kinds of expression that directly engage the "core" of the freedom of expression values. This conclusion is further buttressed by the fact that the targeted material is expression that is motivated, in the overwhelming majority of cases, by economic profit. This Court held in *Rocket v. Royal College of Dental Surgeons of Ontario* ... that an economic motive for expression means that restrictions on the expression might "be easier to justify than other infringements."

I will now turn to an examination of the three basic aspects of the proportionality test.

RATIONAL CONNECTION

The message of obscenity that degrades and dehumanizes is analogous to that of hate propaganda. As the Attorney General of Ontario has argued.... obscenity wields the power to wreak social damage in that a significant portion of the population is humiliated by its gross misrepresentations.

Accordingly, the rational link between s. 163 and the objective of Parliament relates to the actual causal relationship between obscenity and the risk of harm to society at large. On this point, it is clear that the literature of the social sciences remains subject to controversy. In *Fringe Product Inc.*.... Charron Dist. Ct. J. considered numerous written reports and works and heard six days of testimony from experts who endeavoured to describe the status of the social sciences with respect to the study of the effects of pornography. Charron Dist. Ct. J. reached the conclusion that the relationship between pornography and harm was sufficient to justify Parliament's intervention. This conclusion is not supported unanimously.

The recent conclusions of the Fraser Report ... could not postulate any causal relationship between pornography and the commission of violent crimes, the sexual abuse of children, or the disintegration of communities and society....

While a direct link between obscenity and harm to society may be difficult, if not impossible, to establish, it is reasonable to presume that exposure to images bears a causal relationship to changes in attitudes and beliefs. The Meese Commission Report ... concluded in respect of sexual violent material:

> The available evidence strongly supports the hypothesis that substantial exposure to sexually violent materials ... bears a causal relationship to antisocial acts of sexual violence and, for some subgroups, possibly to unlawful acts of sexual violence.
>
> Although we rely for this conclusion on significant scientific empirical evidence, we feel it worthwhile to note the underlying logic of the conclusion. The evidence says simply that the images that people are exposed to bear a causal relationship to their behavior. This is hardly surprising. What would be surprising would be to find otherwise, and we have not so found. We have not, of course, found that the images people are exposed to are a greater cause of sexual violence than all or even many other possible causes.... Nevertheless, it would be strange indeed if graphic representations of a form of behavior, especially in a form that almost exclusively portrays such behavior as desirable, did not have at least some effect on patterns of behavior.

In the face of inconclusive social science evidence, the approach adopted ... in *Irivin Toy* is instructive. In that case, the basis for the legislation was that television advertising directed at young children is *per se* manipulative. The Court made it clear that in choosing its mode of intervention, it is sufficient that Parliament had a *reasonable basis:*

> In the instant case, the Court is called on to assess competing social science evidence respecting the appropriate means for addressing the problem of children's advertising. The question is whether the government had a reasonable basis, on the evidence tendered, for concluding that the ban on all advertising directed at children impaired freedom of expression as little as possible given the government's pressing and substantial objective.
>
> ... The Court also recognized that the government was afforded a margin of appreciation to form legitimate objectives based on somewhat inconclusive social science evidence.

Similarly, ... the absence of proof of a causative link between hate propaganda and hatred of an identifiable group was discounted as a determinative factor in assessing the constitutionality of the hate literature provisions of the *Criminal Code*. Dickson C. J. stated:

> First, to predicate the limitation of free expression upon proof of actual hatred gives insufficient attention to the severe psychological trauma suffered by members of those identifiable groups targeted by hate propaganda. Second, it is clearly difficult to prove a causative link between a specific statement and hatred of an identifiable group.

McLachlin J. (dissenting) expressed it as follows:

> To view hate propaganda as "victimless" in the absence of any proof that it moved its listeners to hatred is to discount the wrenching impact it may have on members of the target group.... Moreover, it is simply not possible to assess [precisely] the

effects that expression of a particular message will have on all those who are ultimately exposed to it.

The American approach on the necessity of a causal link between obscenity and harm to society was set out by Burger C. J. *in Paris Adult Theatre* ... :

Although there is no conclusive proof of a connection between antisocial behavior and obscene material, the legislature ... could quite reasonably determine that such a connection does or might exist....

I am in agreement with Twaddle J. A. who expressed the view that Parliament was entitled to have a "reasoned apprehension of harm" resulting from the desensitization of individuals exposed to materials that depict violence, cruelty, and dehumanization in sexual relations.

Accordingly ... there is a sufficiently rational link between the criminal sanction, which demonstrates our community's disapproval of the dissemination of materials that potentially victimize women and restricts the negative influence that such materials have on changes in attitudes and behaviour,...

MINIMAL IMPAIRMENT

In determining whether less intrusive legislation may be imagined, this Court stressed in the *Prostitution Reference* ... that it is not necessary that the legislative scheme be the "perfect" scheme, but that it be appropriately tailored *in the context of the infringed right*.... Furthermore, in *Irwin Toy*, Dickson C.J., Lamer and Wilson J. J. stated:

While evidence exists that other less intrusive options reflecting more modest objectives were available to the government, there is evidence establishing the necessity of a ban to meet the objectives the government had reasonably set. This Court will not, in the name of minimal impairment, take a restrictive approach to social science evidence and require

legislatures to choose the least ambitious means to protect vulnerable groups....

There are several factors that contribute to the finding that the provision minimally impairs the freedom which is infringed.

First, the impugned provision does not proscribe sexually explicit erotica without violence that is not degrading or dehumanizing. It is designed to catch material that creates a risk of harm to society. It might be suggested that proof of actual harm should be required. It is apparent from [that] above that it is sufficient ... for Parliament to have a reasonable basis for concluding that harm will result and this requirement does not demand actual proof of harm.

Second, materials [with] scientific, artistic or literary merit are not captured by the provision. As discussed above, the Court must be generous in [applying] the "artistic defence." For example, in certain cases, materials such as photographs, prints, books and films that may undoubtedly be produced with some motive for economic profit may nonetheless claim the protection of the *Charter* insofar as their defining characteristic is ... aesthetic expression and thus represent the artist's attempt at individual fulfillment. The existence of an accompanying economic motive does not of itself deprive a work of significance as an example of individual artistic or self-fulfillment.

Third, in considering whether the provision minimally impairs the freedom in question, it is legitimate for the Court to take into account Parliament's past abortive attempts to replace the definition with one that is more explicit. In *Irwin Toy*, our Court recognized that it is legitimate to [consider] the fact that earlier laws and proposed alternatives were thought to be less effective than the legislation [now] being challenged. The attempt to provide exhaustive instances of obscenity has been shown to be destined to fail.... [The] only practicable alternative is to strive toward a more abstract definition of obscenity that is contextually sensitive and responsive to progress in the knowledge and understanding of the phenomenon to which the legislation is directed.... [The] standard of "undue exploitation" is therefore appropriate. The intractable nature of the problem and the impossibility of precisely defining a notion that is inherently elusive makes the possibility of a more explicit provision remote. In this light, it is appropriate to question whether, and at what cost, greater legislative precision can be demanded.

Fourth, while the discussion in this appeal has been limited to the definition portion of s. 163, I would note that the impugned section … has been held by this Court not to extend its reach to the private use or viewing of obscene materials. *R. v. Rioux* … unanimously upheld the finding of the Quebec Court of Appeal that s. 163 … does not include the private viewing of obscene materials. Hall J. affirmed the finding of Pratte J.:

> … I would therefore say that showing obscene pictures to a friend or projecting an obscene film in one's own home is not in itself a crime nor is it enough to establish intention of circulating them nor help to prove such an intention.…

This Court also cited with approval the words of Hyde J.:

> Before I am prepared to hold that private use of written matter or pictures within an individual's residence may constitute a criminal offence, I require a much more specific text of law than we are now dealing with. It would have been very simple for Parliament to have included the word "exhibit" in this section if it had wished to cover this situation.…

Accordingly, it is only the public distribution and exhibition of obscene materials which is in issue here.

Finally, I wish to address the arguments of the interveners, Canadian Civil Liberties Association and Manitoba Association for Rights and Liberties, that the objectives of this kind of legislation may be met by alternative, less intrusive measures. First, it is submitted that reasonable time, manner and place restrictions would be preferable to outright prohibition. I am of the view that this argument should

be rejected. Once it has been established that the objective is the avoidance of harm caused by the degradation which many women feel as "victims" of the message of obscenity, and of the negative impact exposure to such material has on perceptions and attitudes towards women, it is untenable to argue that these harms could be avoided by placing restrictions on access to such material. Making the materials more difficult to obtain by increasing their cost and reducing their availability does not achieve the same objective. Once Parliament has reasonably concluded that certain acts are harmful to certain groups in society and to society in general, it would be inconsistent, if not hypocritical, to argue that such acts could be committed in more restrictive conditions. The harm sought to be avoided would remain the same in either case.

It is also submitted that there are more effective techniques to promote the objectives of Parliament. For example, if pornography is seen as encouraging violence against women, there are certain activities which discourage it—counselling rape victims to charge their assailants, provision of shelter and assistance for battered women, campaigns for laws against discrimination on the grounds of sex, education to increase the sensitivity of law enforcement agencies and other governmental authorities. In addition, it is submitted that education is an underused response.

It is noteworthy that many of the above suggested alternatives are in the form of *responses* to the harm engendered by negative attitudes against women. The role of the impugned provision is to control the dissemination of the very images that contribute to such attitudes. Moreover, it is true that there are additional measures which could alleviate the problem of violence against women. However, given the gravity of the harm, and the threat to the values at stake, I do not believe that the measure chosen by Parliament is equalled by the alternatives which have been suggested. Education, too, may offer a means of combating negative attitudes to women, just as it is currently used as a means of addressing other problems dealt with in the *Code*. However, there is no reason to rely on education alone. It should be emphasized that this is in no way intended to deny the value of other educational and counselling measures to deal with the roots and effects of negative attitudes. Rather, it is only to stress the arbitrariness and unacceptability of the claim that such measures represent the sole legitimate means of addressing the phenomenon. Serious social problems such as violence against women require multipronged approaches by government. Education and legislation are not alternatives but complements in addressing such problems. There is nothing in the *Charter* which requires Parliament to choose between such complementary measures.

BALANCE BETWEEN EFFECTS OF LIMITING MEASURES AND LEGISLATIVE OBJECTIVE

The final question to be answered in the proportionality test is whether the [law's] effects so severely trench on a protected right that the legislative

objective is outweighed by the infringement. The infringement on freedom of expression is confined to a measure designed to prohibit the distribution of sexually explicit materials accompanied by violence and those without violence that are degrading or dehumanizing. As ... already concluded, this kind of expression lies far from the core of the guarantee of freedom of expression. It appeals only to the most base aspect of individual fulfillment and is primarily economically motivated.

The objective of the legislation, on the other hand, is of fundamental importance in a free and democratic society. It is aimed at avoiding harm, which Parliament has reasonably concluded will be caused directly or indirectly, to individuals, groups such as women and children, and ... to society as a whole, by the distribution of these materials. It thus seeks to enhance respect for all members of society, and nonviolence and equality in their relations with each other.

I therefore conclude that the restriction on freedom of expression does not outweigh the importance of the legislative objective.

SUGGESTIONS FOR FURTHER READING

Anthologies

Copp, David, and Susan Wendell. *Pornography and Censorship*. Buffalo: Prometheus, 1983.

Donnerstein, Edward, Daniel Linz, and Steven Penrod. *The Question of Pornography*. New York: Free Press, 1987.

Dwyer, Susan. *The Problem of Pornography*. Belmont, CA: Wadsworth, 1995.

Wekesser, Carol. *Pornography: Opposing Viewpoints*. San Diego: Greenhaven Press, 1997.

Alternative Views

Dworkin, Andrea. *Pornography: Men Possessing Women*. New York: Perigee, 1981.

Griffin, Susan. *Pornography and Silence*. New York: Harper & Row, 1981.

Juffer, Jane. *At Home with Pornography*. New York: New York University Press, 1998.

Lovelace, Linda, with Mike McGrady. *Ordeal*. New York: Berkeley Books, 1980.

MacKinnon, Catharine. *Only Words*. Cambridge: Harvard University Press, 1993.

————. *Women's Lives, Men's Laws*. Harvard University Press, 2007.

Soble, Alan. *Pornography*. New Haven: Yale University Press, 1986.

Practical Applications

Report of the Attorney General's Commission on Pornography. Washington, DC: Government Printing Office, 1986.

MacKinnon, Catharine, and Andrea Dworkin. *In Harm's Way: The Pornography Civil Rights Hearings*. Cambridge: Harvard University Press, 1998.

Sexual Harassment

INTRODUCTION

Basic Concepts

The moral problem of sexual harassment is the problem of determining the nature of sexual harassment and how to avoid it. Actually, sexual harassment was not recognized by U.S. trial courts as an offense until the late 1970s, and it was only affirmed by the U.S. Supreme Court as an offense in the 1980s. The term *sexual harassment* itself was not even coined until the 1970s. So the moral problem of sexual harassment is one that many people have only recently come to recognize. Obviously, the Senate Judiciary Committee hearings on Anita Hill's charge that Clarence Thomas had sexually harassed her heightened people's awareness of this problem.

In 1980, the Equal Employment Opportunity Commission issued guidelines finding harassment on the basis of sex to be a violation of Title VII of the Civil Rights Act of 1964, labeling sexual harassment "unwelcome sexual advances, requests for sexual favors, and other verbal or physical conduct of a sexual nature" when such behavior occurred in any of three circumstances:

1. Where submission to such conduct is made either explicitly or implicitly a term or condition of an individual's employment.
2. Where submission to or rejection of such conduct by an individual is used as the basis for employment decisions affecting such an individual.
3. Where such conduct has the purpose or effect of unreasonably interfering with an individual's work performance or creating an intimidating, hostile, or offensive working environment.

In 1986, the U.S. Supreme Court in *Meritor Savings Bank v. Vinson* agreed with the EEOC ruling that there could be two types of sexual harassment: harassment that conditions concrete employment benefits on granting sexual favors (often called the *quid pro quo* type) and harassment that creates a hostile or offensive work environment without affecting economic benefits (the hostile environment type). Nevertheless, the court made it quite difficult for a plaintiff to establish that either of these types of sexual harassment had occurred. For example, a polite verbal "no" does not suffice to show that sexual advances are unwelcome; a woman's entire conduct both in and outside the workplace is subject to appraisal determining whether or not she welcomed the advances. But isn't it odd that a woman should have to prove that an offer "if you don't sleep with me you will be fired" is unwelcomed? Moreover, if a woman rejects such an offer and is fired, unless she is a perfect employee, she will have difficulty proving that she was fired because she rejected the offer. Actually, in such a case, what the Supreme Court should have required is that the employer be able to show that a woman who rejects a sexual advance would still have been fired even if she had said yes.

U.S. courts have also made it difficult to classify work environments as hostile to women. In *Christoforou v. Ryder Truck Rental, Inc.*, a supervisor's actions of fondling a plaintiff's rear end and breasts, propositioning her, and trying to force a kiss at a Christmas party were considered "too sporadic and innocuous" to support a finding of a hostile work environment. In *Rabidue v. Osceola Refining Co.*, a workplace where pictures of nude and scantily clad women abounded, including one, which hung on a wall for eight years, of a woman with a golf ball on her breasts and a man with his golf club, standing over her and yelling "fore," and where a co-worker, never disciplined despite repeated complaints, routinely referred to women as "whores," "cunts," and "pussy" was judged not sufficiently hostile an environment to constitute sexual harassment. At times,

the courts seem to be appealing to the pervasiveness of certain forms of harassment as grounds for tolerating them, as though we should only prohibit wrongful acts if most people aren't doing them. At other times, the courts appear to be judging sexual harassment to be what men, but not women, say it is. What this shows is that the problem of avoiding sexual harassment is intimately tied to its definition, and women and men seem to disagree radically about what constitutes sexual harassment.

Alternative Views

In Selection 47, Barbara A. Gutek surveys the research that has been done on defining sexual harassment and determining how frequently it occurs. Gutek notes that a number of factors influence whether some behavior is classified as sexual harassment:

1. How intrusive and persistent the behavior is. (The more physically intrusive and persistent the behavior is, the more likely that it will be defined as sexual harassment.)
2. The nature of the relationship between the actors. (The better the actors know each other, the less likely the behavior will be labeled sexual harassment.)
3. The characteristics of the observer. (Men and people in authority are less likely to label behavior as sexual harassment.)
4. The inequality in the relationship. (The greater the inequality, the more likely the behavior will be labeled sexual harassment.)

Gutek contends that the frequency of sexual harassment in the workplace is relatively high. For example, the U.S. Merit System Protection Board found that 42 percent of the women responding to its study reported experiencing sexual harassment on the job within the previous two years. She seeks to explain this frequency as due to the fact that women are stereotypically identified as sexual objects in ways that men are not. She notes that women are stereotypically characterized as sexy, affectionate, and attractive, whereas men are stereotypically characterized as competent and active. These stereotypes, Gutek claims, spill over into the workplace, making it difficult for women to be perceived as fellow workers rather than sex objects, and these perceptions foster sexual harassment. It would seem, therefore, that eliminating the problem of sexual harassment from our society will require breaking down these stereotypes.

Unlike Gutek, Ellen Frankel Paul (Selection 48) argues that the problem of sexual harassment is overblown. She thinks sexual harassment has been exaggerated to include everything from rape to "looks." Paul argues that the extortion of sexual favors by a supervisor from a subordinate by threatening to penalize, fire, or fail to reward is sexual harassment, but she argues that a hostile working environment should be regarded as sexual harassment only when the "reasonable man" of tort law would find the working environment offensive. However, as one of Gutek's studies shows, reasonable men and reasonable women can disagree over what constitutes sexual harassment in the workplace. In this study, 67.2 percent of men as compared to 16.8 percent of women would be flattered if asked to have sex, while 15 percent of the men and 62.8 percent of the women said they would be insulted by such an offer. So the crucial question is: Whose perspective should be determinative?

In Selection 49, Nancy Davis notes that between 25 and 40 percent of female college students report they have been subjected to some sort of harassment from their instructors. She maintains that the frequency and seriousness of sexual harassment in the university are widely underestimated because of such factors as the unequal power between students and professors, traditional gender roles and

expectations, popular academic fiction that portrays "co-eds" as lusty seducers of respectable male professors, and the reluctance of educators to "break ranks" with their colleagues. She also claims that when many women are faced with sexual harassment at the university, they tend to deal with the problem by dropping the course, not coming to office hours, changing their major, or even dropping out of school altogether—all with unfortunate consequences.

In Selection 50, James P. Sterba reviews the developments in sexual harassment law and proposes a definition of what is—or better, what should be—sexual harassment. He then offers a partial explanation of why sexual harassment happens in both civilian and military life. Finally, he sets out two positive norms, a principle of androgyny and a principle of desert, in addition to the negative norm that prohibits sexual harassment. We need to focus on these positive principles, he claims, in order to make progress toward reducing the frequency of sexual harassment.

Practical Application

In *Harris v. Forklift Systems Inc.* (Selection 51), the Supreme Court took an important step toward a more reasonable stance on sexual harassment. In this case, Teresa Harris worked as a rental manager at Forklift Systems. Charles Hardy, Forklift's president, told Harris on several occasions, in the presence of other employees, "You're a woman, what do you know?" and "We need a man as the rental manager." Again in front of others, he suggested that the two of them "go to the Holiday Inn to negotiate (Harris's) raise." Hardy occasionally asked Harris and other female employees to get coins from his front pants pockets. On other occasions, he threw objects on the ground in front of Harris and other women, and asked them to pick the objects up. He made sexual innuendos about Harris's and other women's clothing. On one occasion, while Harris was arranging a deal with one of Forklift's customers, Hardy asked Harris in front of other employees, "What did you do, promise some (sex) Saturday night?" Soon after, Harris quit her job at Forklift.

In this case, the Supreme Court struck down the district court's requirement that in order for sexual harassment to be established, Harris needed to show that Hardy's conduct had "seriously affected her psychological well-being." This was an important decision, but obviously it does not go far enough in specifying a reasonable standard for sexual harassment.

47

Understanding Sexual Harassment at Work

BARBARA A. GUTEK

Barbara A. Gutek surveys the research that has been done on defining sexual harassment and determining how frequently it occurs. She notes that several factors influence whether a behavior is classified as sexual harassment: (1) how intrusive and persistent the behavior is; (2) the nature of the relationship between the actors; (3) the characteristics of the observer; and (4) the inequality in the relationship. Gutek contends that the frequency of sexual harassment in the workplace is relatively high. For example, the U.S. Merit System Protection Board found that 42 percent of the women responding to its study reported experiencing sexual harassment on the job within the previous two years. Gutek seeks to explain this frequency as due to the fact that women are stereotypically identified as sexual objects in ways that men are not.

I. INTRODUCTION

The topic of sexual harassment at work was virtually unstudied until the concern of feminists brought the issue to the attention of the public and researchers. Much of the research on sexual harassment addresses two complementary questions. (1) How do people define sexual harassment? (2) How common is it? Research on these issues provides useful background information for lawyers and policy makers interested in seeking legal redress for harassment victims, and ultimately in eradicating sexual harassment....

The first issue, people's definitions of sexual harassment, shows the extent to which laws and regulations reflect broad public consensus. Knowing the frequency of sexual harassment—a workplace problem that had no name until the mid-1970s—is important for those seeking to establish laws and procedures to remedy the problem. Further, frequency or prevalence deserves study because

sexual harassment has negative consequences for women workers and organizations. These two areas—definition and prevalence—are often studied independently, using different research subjects, research designs, and methods of data collection.

This article traces the development of research on sexual behavior in the workplace from its early emphasis on defining and documenting sexual harassment through other findings on sexual non-harassment. To understand sex at work, several frameworks or theories are discussed, with special emphasis on the concept of sex-role spillover.

The term *sexual behavior* will be used throughout this article to encompass the range of sexual behaviors, such as nonwork-related behavior with sexual content or overtones, found within the workplace and included in many research studies. Few studies attempt to limit themselves to legally liable sexual harassment. Thus, the term "sexual behavior" consists of behavior that is legally considered sexual harassment as well as nonharassing sexual behavior.

From "Understanding Sexual Harassment at Work," *Notre Dame Journal of Law, Ethics and Public Policy* (1992). Reprinted by permission.

Finally, it should be noted that this article is not a review of the status of sexual harassment laws or legal practices. It is limited to the social science research which addresses issues relevant to sexual harassment policy and lawsuits.

II. THE DISCOVERY OF SEXUAL HARASSMENT

In the mid-1970s, sexuality in the workplace suddenly received considerable attention through the discovery of sexual harassment, which appeared to be relatively widespread and to have long-lasting, harmful effects on a significant number of working women. This "discovery" was somewhat counterintuitive, since some women were believed to benefit from seductive behavior and sexual behaviors at work, gaining unfair advantage and acquiring perks and privileges from their flirtatious and seductive behavior. The first accounts of sexual harassment were journalistic reports and case studies. Soon the topic was catapulted into public awareness through the publication of two important books. Lin Farley's book, *Sexual Shakedown: The Sexual Harassment of Women on the Job*, aimed to bring sexual harassment to public attention, create a household word, and make people aware of harassment as a social problem. Catharine MacKinnon's book, *Sexual Harassment of Working Women*, sought a legal mechanism for handling sexual harassment and compensating its victims. In a strong and compelling argument, MacKinnon contended that sexual harassment was primarily a problem for women, that it rarely happened to men, and therefore that it should be viewed as a form of sex discrimination. Viewing sexual harassment as a form of sex discrimination would make available to victims the same legal protection available to victims of sex discrimination. In 1980, the Equal Employment Opportunity Commission (EEOC) established guidelines consistent with MacKinnon's position and defined sexual harassment under Title VII of the 1964 Civil Rights Act as a form of unlawful sex-based discrimination. Several states have passed their own increasingly

strong laws aimed at eliminating sexual harassment and legal scholars have sought additional avenues to recover damages incurred from sexual harassment. Various public and private agencies as well as the courts have seen a steady if uneven increase in sexual harassment complaints since the early 1980s.

The various guidelines and regulations define sexual harassment broadly. For example, the updated EEOC guidelines state that:

> [u]nwelcome sexual advances, requests for sexual favors, and other verbal or physical conduct of a sexual nature constitute sexual harassment when (1) submission to such conduct is made either explicitly or implicitly a term or condition of an individual's employment or academic advancement, (2) submission to or rejection of such conduct by an individual is used as the basis for employment decisions, or academic decisions affecting such individual, or (3) such conduct has the purpose or effect of reasonably interfering with an individual's work or academic performance or creating an intimidating, hostile, or offensive working or academic environment.

Researchers began serious study of sex at work only after Farley's and MacKinnon's books and two compendia of information on sexual harassment were in progress and generally after the EEOC had established guidelines in 1980. Not surprisingly, researchers were heavily influenced by these important developments in policy and law. These developments focused the concerns of researchers on the two specific issues mentioned above: definition of harassment and frequency of occurrence.

III. DEFINING SEXUAL HARASSMENT

The first issue can be succinctly stated: "What constitutes sexual harassment?" For lawyers, the courts, personnel managers, ombudspersons, and others, this is perhaps the most important issue that they must face. If "it" is harassment, it is illegal; otherwise it is not. Researchers, aware of the problems in defining harassment and perhaps eager to contribute to the developments in law and policy, began to supply a spate of studies.

Studies concerned with the definition of sexual harassment come in two types. First are surveys of various populations of people who are asked to tell whether various acts constitute sexual harassment. Second are experimental studies in which students, employees, or managers are asked to rate one or more hypothetical situations in which aspects of the situation are varied along important dimensions. These experimental studies using a hypothetical situation, also known as the "paper people paradigm," come in two variants. In the first variant, subjects are asked to determine whether a particular scenario depicts an instance of sexual harassment. In the second variant, researchers examine the attributions of subjects to understand how subjects' interpretations of a scenario affect their use of the label, sexual harassment.

The strengths of the experimental research design—random assignment to conditions and manipulation of causal variables—allow researchers to make causal statements about what affects how people define sexual harassment. The weakness of the design is that the situation is invariably insufficiently "real": Subjects who have limited information and little appreciation of, or experience with, the subject matter may not respond the way people would in a real (rather than hypothetical) situation.

The survey studies show that sexual activity as a requirement of the job is defined as sexual harassment by about 81 percent to 98 percent of working adults, and similar results have been reported with students as subjects. Lesser forms of harassment such as sexual touching are not as consistently viewed as sexual harassment. For example, I found that 59 percent of men but 84 percent of women asserted that sexual touching at work is sexual harassment. A sizable minority (22 percent of men and 33 percent of women) considered sexual comments at work meant to be complimentary to be sexual harassment.

In contrast to the survey studies which often ask respondents to specify which of a set of actions constitutes harassment, in experimental studies, subjects are usually asked to rate how harassing some incident is, on a five-point or seven-point scale. Such a method makes it impossible to say what percentage of people consider any particular act or event harassment and results are usually reported as mean scores (on, say, a three-, five-, or seven-point scale). It should be noted that experimental studies are generally not concerned with the percentage of their subjects, usually students, who consider behavior X to be harassment, but instead address the factors or variables which affect whether or not some specified incident or act is labeled harassment.

The experimental studies show that except for the most outrageous and clearly inappropriate behavior, whether or not an incident is labeled harassment varies with several characteristics of the incident and the people involved. In these studies, the following variables make a difference: (1) the behavior in question, (2) the relationship between harasser and victim, (3) the sex of the harasser, (4) the sex and age of the victim, (5) the sex of the rater, and (6) the occupation of the person doing the rating. Another way of categorizing these factors is shown below: Characteristics of the behavior, nature of the relationship between the actors, characteristics of the observer/rater, and context factors all affect whether or not a particular act or event is considered sexual harassment.

Factors Affecting the Definition of Sexual Harassment

1. *Characteristics of the behavior.* The more physically intrusive and persistent the behavior, the more likely it is to be defined as sexual harassment by an observer.

2. *The nature of the relationship between actors.* The better the two actors know each other (friends, spouses, long-time co-workers) the less likely the behavior will be labeled sexual harassment by an observer.

3. *Characteristics of the observer.* Men and people in authority (e.g., senior faculty, senior

managers) are less likely than others to label a behavior sexual harassment.

4. ***Context factors.*** The greater the inequality (in position, occupation, age), the more likely the behavior will be labeled sexual harassment by an observer. When the "recipient" of the behavior is low status or relatively powerless (female, young, poor), the behavior is more likely to be judged harassment than when the "recipient" is high status or relatively powerful.

The most important factor determining judgment of sexual harassment is the behavior involved. The experimental studies and survey studies yield the same pattern of findings: Explicitly sexual behavior and behavior involving implied or explicit threats are more likely to be perceived as harassment than other, less threatening or potentially complimentary behavior. Touching is also more likely to be rated as sexual harassment than comments, looks, or gestures. In addition, Weber-Burdin and Rossi concluded that the initiator's behavior is much more important than the recipient's behavior, although if a female recipient behaved seductively, college student raters may reduce the ratings of harassment.

The relationship between the two people is also important. The situation is considered more serious harassment when the initiator is a supervisor of the recipient rather than an equal or a subordinate or more serious if the person previously declined to date the harasser than if the two people had a prior dating relationship. The incident is more likely to be viewed as sexual harassment when a man is the harasser, a woman is the victim and when the female victim is young.

The person doing the rating makes a difference. The most important characteristic … is gender. When women are doing the rating, they define a wide variety of sexual behavior at work as sexual harassment, while men tend to rate only the more extreme behavior as harassment. Similarly, on a scale of Tolerance for Sexual Harassment (TSHI), college men reported more tolerance than women, that is, men objected less than women to sexual harassing behavior. In short, the finding that women apply a broader definition of sexual harassment than men is

pervasive and widely replicated although not universally found. It is worth noting that at least one factor strongly associated with gender, sex-role identity, did not make much of a difference in people's judgments of sexual harassment. Powell, using a student sample, found that sex-role identity generally did not affect definition of sexual harassment although highly feminine subjects were somewhat more likely than others to label some behaviors sexual harassment and highly masculine male students were somewhat less likely than others to label insulting sexual remarks sexual harassment. In addition, organizational status seems to have an effect. Higher-level managers rating an incident are less likely to see it as serious harassment than middle-level or lower-level managers. In one study, faculty tended to view an incident as less serious than students whereas in another, there were no substantial differences in the ratings of faculty and students.

The experimental studies using attribution analysis probe an evaluator's thought processes as he or she makes a determination whether or not a particular scenario constitutes harassment. Pryor suggested that people are more likely to judge a man's behavior [to be] sexual harassment if his behavior is attributed to his enduring negative intentions toward the target woman. Such negative intentions can either reflect hostility or insensitivity to women. Pryor and Day found that the perspective people take in interpreting a social-sexual encounter affects their judgments of sexual harassment. This may help explain why men and women tend to differ in their judgments of sexual harassment, that is, men may take the man's (usually the initiator's) point of view whereas women are more likely to take the woman's (the victim in many experimental studies) point of view. In support of this view, Konrad and Gutek found that women's greater experience with sexual harassment helps to explain the sex differences in defining sexual harassment. In a similar vein, Kenig and Ryan came to the conclusion that men's and women's perceptions of sexual harassment reflect their self-interest. It is in men's self-interest to see relatively little sexual harassment because men are most often the offenders whereas it is in women's self-interest to see relatively more sexual harassment because women tend to be the victims in sexual harassment encounters.

Cohen and Gutek's analyses suggest that people may make different attributions depending on whether they view the initiator and recipient as friends. More specifically, they found that when student subjects were asked to evaluate an ambiguous, potentially mildly sexually harassing encounter, they tended to assume that the two participants were friends, perhaps dating partners, and that the behavior was welcome and complimentary rather than harassing. Similarly, student subjects were less likely to rate a behavior harassment if they knew that the parties [had] dated and were more likely to rate a behavior harassment if the woman recipient had ... refused to date the male initiator. In the latter case, subjects may attribute the man's overture to his "enduring negative intentions" toward the woman since her prior refusal of a date presumably eliminates the explanation that he was unsure how she felt about him.

IV. FREQUENCY OF SEXUAL HARASSMENT AT WORK

The other area of research that developed in response to legal and policy development was a documentation of the forms and prevalence of harassment experienced. In 1979, MacKinnon wrote: "The unnamed should not be taken for the nonexistent." Thus, providing a label and then a definition for sexual harassment was an important step in developing ways to measure the prevalence of sexual harassment.

The research on frequency of harassment focuses heavily but not exclusively on heterosexual encounters. It is often studied separate from the research on definition and employs a different research design, and different subjects. Research aiming to establish rates of harassment in a population must be concerned with drawing a representative sample from a known population in order to generalize results in that population.

The research on prevalence shows a broad range of rates, depending in part on the time frame used. The U.S. Merit System Protection Board's study found that 42 percent of the women respondents reported experiencing sexual harassment on the job within the previous two years. When the study was repeated several years later, the figure remained the same. In a Seattle, Washington, study of city employees, more than one-third of all respondents reported sexual harassment in the previous twenty-four months of employment. Dunwoody-Miller and Gutek found that 20 percent of California state civil service employees reported being sexually harassed at work in the previous five years. Reviewing the results from several different measures of prevalence ..., Gutek suggested that up to 53 percent of women had been harassed sometime in their working life. The figures are higher in the military; two-thirds of women surveyed in a 1990 study said they had been sexually harassed.

Other studies using purposive or convenience samples generally show higher rates of harassment. In a study by the Working Women's Institute, 70 percent of the employed women respondents said they had experienced sexual harassment.... An early study of the readers of *Redbook* magazine found that 88 percent of those mailing in questionnaires had experienced sexual harassment. Schneider reported that more than two-thirds of her matched sample of lesbian and heterosexual working women had experienced unwelcome sexual advances within the previous year.

Because respondents in purposive or convenience samples can choose whether or not to respond, and participating in the study may require some expenditure of effort, researchers assume that people who have been harassed may be more motivated to participate. Thus, the incidence rates are likely to be somewhat inflated.

Although women of all ages, races, occupations, income levels, and marital statuses experience harassment, research suggests that young and unmarried women are especially vulnerable. Not surprisingly, most women are harassed by men, not by women. In addition, women in nontraditional jobs (e.g., truck driver, neurosurgeon, engineer, roofer) and in nontraditional industries such as the military and mining are more likely to experience harassment than other women. These higher rates are over and above what is expected by their high amount of work contact with men. On the basis of the set of studies done so far, it seems likely that overall, from one-third to one-half of all women have been sexually harassed at some time in their working lives, although frequency rates in some types of work may be higher.

Sexual harassment at work has also been reported by men in several studies. The U.S. Merit System Protection Board's study found 15 percent of the men to be harassed by males or females at work. On the basis of men's reports of specific behavior, Gutek suggested that up to 9 percent of men could have been harassed by women sometime in their working lives. After a careful analysis of men's accounts of harassment, however, Gutek concluded that few of the reported incidents were sexual harassment as legally defined, and some of the incidents may not have even been considered sexual if the same behavior had been initiated by a man or by another woman who was considered a less desirable sexual partner by the man.

V. FREQUENCY OF SEXUAL NONHARASSMENT

Several studies have also examined other kinds of sexual behavior at work, behavior that most people do not consider harassment, including comments or whistles intended to be compliments, quasi-sexual touching such as hugging or an arm around the shoulder, requests for a date or sexual activity often in a joking manner, and sexual jokes or comments that are not directed to a particular person. These other "nonharassing," less serious, and presumably nonproblematic behaviors are considerably more common than harassment. For example, Gutek found that 61 percent of men and 68 percent of women said that they had received at least one sexual comment that was meant to be complimentary

sometime in their working lives. In addition, 56 percent of men and 67 percent of women reported that they had been the recipient of at least one sexual look or gesture that was intended to be complimentary. About eight out of every ten workers have been recipients of some kind of sexual overture that was intended [as] a compliment. Schneider found that 55 percent of a sample of heterosexual working women and 67 percent of a sample of lesbian working women reported that within the last year at work, someone had joked with them about their body or appearance. Other studies show similar findings. Dunwoody-Miller and Gutek reported that 76 percent of women and 55 percent of men indicated that as California state civil service employees, they had received complimentary comments of a sexual nature. Looks and gestures of a sexual nature that were meant as compliments were also common (reported by 67 percent of women and 47 percent of men).

Although men [are rarely] harassed, the amount of sexual behavior reported by them at work remains substantial. For example, Gutek found that men were more likely than women to say that they were sexually touched by an opposite-sex person on their job. According to Abbey, Davies, and Gottfried and Fasenfest, men are more likely than women to perceive the world in sexual terms. Also, men are more likely than women to mistake friendliness for seduction and find the office ... a little too exciting with women around. This seems consistent with the common stimulus-response view that women's presence elicits sexual behavior from men. Reports from men, however, suggest that sex is present in male-dominated workplaces, whether or not women are actually present. This "floating sex" takes the form of posters, jokes, sexual metaphors for work, comments, obscene language, and the like. The relationship seems to be quite straightforward: the more men, the more sexualized the workplace. [That much] of this sexualization ... is degrading ... as well as sexual is what creates the "hostile" environment that government regulations aim to eliminate.

[Altogether,] the research on harassment and "nonharassment" shows that sexual behavior is so common at work that one might say that sex permeates work. An equally important conclusion ... is that the legal behavior is considerably more common than the illegal sexual harassment. This finding is not surprising, but it is important; when some people first hear about sexual harassment, they may confuse it with the more common legal behavior at work which they, themselves, have seen and experienced. This confusion of nonthreatening legal behavior with sexual harassment can lead some to incorrectly denigrate women's complaints as prudish or overly sensitive.

VI. IMPACTS OF SEXUAL BEHAVIOR AT WORK

Any behavior as common as sexual harassment and nonharassment at work is likely to have a wide variety of ramifications for the individuals involved. So far researchers have concentrated on identifying negative effects of sexual harassment to call attention to harassment as a social and workplace problem. But only scattered attempts have been made [to study] the impacts of other types of sexual behavior at work.

Sexual harassment has a variety of negative consequences for women.... In addition to the discomfort associated with the sexually harassing experiences and violation of physical privacy, women often find that their careers are interrupted. Up to 10 percent of women have quit a job because of sexual harassment. Others fear becoming victims of retaliation if they complain about the harassment, and some are asked to leave. For example, Coles found that among eighty-one cases filed with the California Department of Fair Employment and Housing between 1979 and 1983, almost half of the complainants were fired and another quarter quit out of fear or frustration.

Women may also experience lower productivity, less job satisfaction, reduced self-confidence, and a loss of motivation and commitment to their work and their employer. They may avoid men who are known harassers, even though contact with those men is important for their work. Thus,

harassment constrains the potential for forming friendships or work alliances with male workers. Furthermore, women are likely to feel anger and resentment and even exhibit self-blame, which leads to additional stress. Crull and Cohen also stated that, while the implicit/overt types of harassment may not have the same direct repercussions as those of the explicit/overt types, all types of sexual harassment at work create high stress levels and serve as a hidden occupational hazard. Finally, sexual harassment helps to maintain the sex segregation of work when it is used to coerce women out of nontraditional jobs.

Besides affecting their work, sexual harassment affects women's personal lives in the form of physical and emotional illness and disruption of marriage or other relationships.... For example, Tangri, Burt, and Johnson reported that 33 percent of women said their emotional or physical condition became worse, and Gutek found that 15 percent of women victims ... said their health was affected and another 15 percent said it damaged their relationships with men.

[Even] more intriguing ... nonharassing sexual behavior also has negative work-related consequences for women workers, although even they are not always aware of them. For example, Gutek found that the experience of all kinds of sexual behavior, including remarks intended to be complimentary, was associated with lower job satisfaction among women.... In addition, women reported that they are not flattered, and in fact are insulted, by sexual overtures of all kinds from men. In one study, 62 percent of women said they would be insulted by a sexual proposition from a man at work. Another example, the office "affair," can have serious detrimental effects on a woman's credibility as well as her career, especially if the relationship is with a supervisor.

Men seem to suffer virtually no work-related consequences of sexual behavior at work. Less than 1 percent of men reported that they quit a job because of sexual harassment, and, in the course of discussing sexual incidents, not one man said he lost a job as a consequence of a sexual overture or request from a woman at work. In the same study,

67 percent of men said they would be flattered by sexual overtures from women. In addition, many men view a certain amount of sexual behavior as appropriate to the work setting, and, as noted above, are less likely to consider any given behavior as sexual harassment. In one study, 51 percent of the men who received overtures from women said they themselves were at least somewhat responsible for the incident. That men experience so few work-related consequences of sex at work is especially odd, since they report so much sexual behavior both that is directed at them by women and that seems to float throughout the workplace.

When men do report "consequences," they are personal rather than work-related, and again, they are viewed in a positive manner. Most often, they report dating relationships or affairs that they find enjoyable; for instance, "There was this little blonde who had the hots for me" or "I think she liked me. I was young and she was married. She wasn't very happy with her husband."

VII. UNDERSTANDING SEXUAL BEHAVIOR AT WORK

[M]ost studies of sexual behavior at work have been in response to the discovery of sexual harassment and policies developed to address harassment. Much of the research is descriptive and diverse, providing interesting information about sexual behavior at work, and useful information for policy makers and lawyers. Some researchers have begun to develop frameworks for studying sexual behavior at work.

One framework sometimes used to study harassment is the power perspective: that is, sexual harassment is an expression of power relationships, and women constitute a threat to men's economic and social standing. With that perspective, Lipman-Blumen viewed the women's "seductive" behavior as micro-manipulation, as a response to male control of social institutions—including the workplace and the academy—which she labeled macro-manipulation. Other researchers explicitly borrowed

from the literature on rape. They contend that sexual harassment is analogous to rape: Power, not sexual drive, is the dominant motivation. They further contend that victims of rape and harassment experience similar effects.

In an attempt to explain their own findings on sexual harassment, Tangri, Burt, and Johnson developed three models: the natural/biological model, the organizational model, and the sociocultural model. The natural/biological model assumes that sexual harassment and other forms of sexual expression at work are simply manifestations of natural attraction between two people. According to Tangri, Burt, and Johnson, one version of this model suggests that because men have a stronger sex drive, they more often initiate sexual overtures at work [and] in other settings. The organizational model assumes that sexual harassment is the result of certain opportunity structures within ... hierarchies. People in higher positions can use their authority (their legitimate power) and their status to coerce lower-status people into accepting a role of sex object or engaging in sexual interactions. The third model, the sociocultural model, "argues that sexual harassment reflects the larger society's differential distribution of power and status between the sexes." Harassment is viewed as a mechanism for maintaining male dominance over women.... Male dominance is maintained by patterns of male-female interaction as well as by male domination of economic and political matters. Tangri, Burt, and Johnson's analysis revealed that none of the three models could by itself offer an adequate explanation of their data on sexual harassment. Another model, emphasizing the effects of sex-role expectations in an organizational context, is called sex-role spillover.

The following analysis builds on earlier research on this concept.

VIII. SEX-ROLE SPILLOVER

Sex-role spillover denotes the carryover of gender-based expectations into the workplace. Among the characteristics assumed by many to be associated with femaleness (such as passivity, loyalty, emotionality, nurturance) is being a sex object. Women are assumed to be sexual and to elicit sexual overtures from men rather naturally. In a thirty-nation study of sex stereotypes, the characteristics of sexy, affectionate, and attractive were associated with femaleness. This aspect of sex-role spillover, the sex-object aspect, is most relevant to the study of sex at work.

Sex-role spillover occurs when women, more than men in the same work roles, are expected to be sex objects or are expected to project sexuality through their behavior, appearance, or dress. What is equally important is the fact that there is no strongly held comparable belief about men. For example, of the forty-nine items that were associated with maleness in at least nineteen of the twenty-five countries studied by Williams and Best, none was directly or indirectly related to sexuality. While it is generally assumed that men are more sexually active than women and men are the initiators in sexual encounters, the cluster of characteristics that are usually associated with the male personality do not include a sexual component. Rather the stereotype of men revolves around the dimension of competence and activity. It includes the belief that men are rational, analytic, assertive, tough, good at math and science, competitive, and make good leaders. The stereotype of men—the common view of the male personality—is the perfect picture of asexuality. Sex-role spillover thus introduces the view of women as sexual beings in the workplace, but it simply reinforces the view of men as organizational beings—"active, work-oriented." [Note also] these stereotypes of female characteristics and male characteristics have remained quite stable through the 1970s and into the 1980s.

The spillover of the female sex-role, including the sexual aspect, occurs at work for at least four reasons. First, gender is the most noticeable social characteristic: People immediately notice whether a person is a man or a woman. Second, men may feel more comfortable reacting to women at work in the same manner that they react to other women in their lives, and unless a woman is too young, old, or unattractive, that includes viewing her as a potential sexual partner. Third, women may feel comfortable reacting to men in a manner expected by the men—that is, conforming to the men's stereotype. Fourth, characteristics of work and sex roles may facilitate the carryover of sex role into work role. Sex roles remain relatively stable throughout our lives and permeate all domains of life. On the other hand, the work role may change many times and is specific to only one domain of life. Sex roles are also learned much earlier than are work roles, and they entail a wide variety of diffuse skills and abilities. Work roles, on the other hand, call for more specific skills and abilities.

The important point here is that being sexual and being a sex object are aspects of the female sex role that frequently are carried over to the workplace by both men and women. A variety of subtle pressures may encourage women to behave in a sexual manner at work, and this then confirms their supposedly essential sexual nature. Because it is expected, people notice female sexuality, and they believe it is normal, natural, an outgrowth of being female.

Unfortunately, women do not seem to be able to be sex objects and analytical, rational, competitive, and assertive at the same time because femaleness is viewed as "not-maleness," and it is the men who are viewed as analytic, logical, and assertive. [Even though] the model of male and female as polar opposites has been severely criticized on several grounds, a dichotomy is used by researchers and laypersons alike (for example, we speak of the "opposite" sex). This is an important part of sex-role spillover. [The] sexual aspects the female role [not only are] carried over to work, but also swamp or overwhelm a view of women as capable, committed workers. This is especially true in an environment where sexual jokes, innuendos, posters, and small talk are common. A recent study by Mohr and Zanna showed that sex-role traditional men exposed to sexually explicit material behaved in a significantly more sexual and obtrusive manner toward women than men who did not see sexually explicit material. As Kanter noted, a woman's perceived sexuality can "blot out" all other characteristics, particularly in a sexualized work environment.

Thus, sex role interferes with and takes precedence over work role.

What is doubly troublesome about this inability to be sexual and a worker at the same time is that women are not the ones who usually choose between the two. A female employee might decide to be a sex object at work, especially if her career or job is not very important to her. More often, however, the working woman chooses not to be a sex object but may be so defined by male colleagues or supervisors anyway, regardless other own actions. A woman's sexual behavior is noticed and labeled sexual even if it is not intended as such. To avoid being cast into the role of sex object, a woman may have to act completely asexual. Then she is subject to the charge of being a "prude," an "old maid," or "frigid," and in her attempt to avoid being a sex object, she is still stereotyped by her sexuality, or more accurately, by her perceived lack of sexuality. The situation for men is entirely different. Benefiting from the stereotype of men as natural inhabitants of organizations—goal-oriented, rational, analytic, competitive, assertive, strong, or,..."active, work-oriented"—men may be able to behave in a blatantly sexual manner, seemingly with impunity. Even when a man goes so far as to say that he encourages overtures from women by unzipping his pants at work, he may escape being viewed as sexual or more interested in sex than work by supervisors and colleagues. While the image of women acting in a seductive manner and distracting men from work is viewed as a detriment to the organization, many executives know of men who are "playboys" and harassers, yet they may not see them as detriments to the organization. These men may hire the wrong women for the wrong reasons, make poor use of female human resources in the organization, squander the organization's resources in their quests for new sexual partners, and make elaborate attempts to impress potential sexual partners—all of this may escape the notice of employers. In short, men's sexual behavior at work often goes unnoticed [for at least two reasons]. First, ... there is no strongly recognized sexual component of the male sex role. Thus, men's sexual behavior is neither salient nor noticed. Second,

perhaps sexual pursuits and conquests, jokes, and innuendos can be subsumed under the stereotype of the organizational man—goal-oriented, rational, competitive, and assertive—which are expected and recognized as male traits. Men may make sexual overtures in an assertive, competitive manner. Likewise, sexual jokes, metaphors, and innuendos may be seen as part of competitive male horseplay. Thus the traits of competitiveness, assertiveness, and goal orientation are noticed, while the sexual component is not....

IX. THE SPILLOVER PERSPECTIVE: BEHAVIORS, IMPACTS, AND BELIEFS CONCERNING SEX AT WORK

How does the sex-role spillover perspective enrich our understanding of sex at work or integrate the diverse findings about sexual harassment? This perspective leads to an examination of both men's and women's behavior at work and stereotypes or beliefs about how men and women behave.... It helps to explain the apparent paradox that women are perceived as using sex to their advantage, while, in practice, they are hurt by sex at work. On the other hand, while men are not perceived as sexual at work, they may display [and benefit from] more sexual behavior.

Sex-role spillover is also useful in explaining why sexual harassment remained invisible for so long. In the absence of data on the subject, women were labeled as sexy, men as asexual. Sexual overtures including harassment were elicited by the sexy women; men who are normally active and work-oriented, "all-business," could be distracted by seductively behaving women, but these distractions were considered a trivial part of men's overall work behavior. If the woman felt uncomfortable with the situation, it was her problem. If she could not handle [it] and complained..., it was at least partially her fault. Men and women, including women victims, shared this belief. Thus a woman who complained might be labeled a troublemaker and be asked to leave....

[Although] the spillover perspective is not incompatible with a power perspective, it falls short in accounting for hostile sexual coercion at work. To take an extreme (but not unknown) case, rape in the office [could hardly be considered] a spillover from externally imposed sex roles. Rather, it is best construed as aggression or power, and a power perspective of sexual harassment may be a better explanatory model.

X. CLOSING REMARKS

Much of the research on sexual harassment was inspired by innovations and developments in law and policy, and ... so far has focused primarily on two issues, definition and prevalence, although topics such as consequences to victims and conditions under which harassment occurs have also been studied.

Recently, Terpstra and his colleagues have engaged in ... research in a new area: the factors that affect the outcome of decisions in sexual harassment cases. Terpstra and Baker studied Illinois state EEOC cases and examined the factors associated with the outcomes of sexual harassment charges; only 31 percent of formal charges (twenty of sixty-five cases) resulted in a settlement favorable to the complainant. Using the same set of EEOC cases, Terpstra and Cook found that employment-related consequences experienced by the complainant were the most critical factor in filing a charge. Other research, for example, on men who harass and the way men respond to women when sexually explicit material is or is not available, represent other new and important areas of research.

Overall, the research on sexual harassment and sex at work has provided data showing that many of the common beliefs about sexual behavior at work are false. The contribution of research toward understanding and explaining sex at work has been valuable. A domain of human behavior that was largely invisible a decade ago is now visible, numerous misconceptions have been uncovered, and some facts have been exposed as myths by researchers.

48

Bared Buttocks and Federal Cases

ELLEN FRANKEL PAUL

Ellen Frankel Paul argues that sexual harassment has been exaggerated to include every-thing from rape to "looks." She argues that the extortion of sexual favors by a supervisor from a subordinate by threatening to penalize, fire, or fail to reward is sexual harassment. But she argues that a hostile working environment should be regarded as sexual harassment only when the "reasonable man" of tort law would find the working environment offensive. She contends that given this understanding of sexual harassment, scatological jokes, leers, unwanted offers of dates, and other sexual annoyances would no longer have their day in court.

Women in American society are victims of sexual harassment in alarming proportions. Sexual harassment is an inevitable corollary to class exploitation; as capitalists exploit workers, so do males in positions of authority exploit their female subordinates. Male professors, supervisors, and apartment managers in ever increasing numbers take advantage of the financial dependence and vulnerability of women to extract sexual concessions.

VALID ASSERTIONS?

These are the assertions that commonly begin discussions of sexual harassment. For reasons that will be adumbrated below, dissent from the prevailing view is long overdue. Three recent episodes will serve to frame this disagreement.

Valerie Craig, an employee of Y & Y Snacks, Inc., joined several co-workers and her supervisor for drinks after work one day in July 1978. Her supervisor drove her home and proposed that they become more intimately acquainted. She refused

his invitation for sexual relations, whereupon he said that he would "get even" with her. Ten days [later] she was fired from her job. She soon filed a complaint of sexual harassment with the Equal Employment Opportunity Commission (EEOC), and the case wound its way through the courts. Craig prevailed, the company was held liable for damages, and she received back pay, reinstatement, and an order prohibiting Y & Y from taking reprisals against her in the future.

Carol Zabowicz, one of only two female fork-lift operators in a West Bend Co. warehouse, charged that her co-workers ... from 1978 to 1982 sexually harassed her by such acts as: asking her whether she was wearing a bra; two of the men exposing their buttocks between ten and twenty times; a male co-worker grabbing his crotch and making obscene suggestions or growling; subjecting her to offensive and abusive language; and exhibiting obscene drawings with her initials on them. Zabowicz began to show symptoms of physical and psychological stress, necessitating several medical leaves, and she filed a sexual harassment complaint with the EEOC. The district court judge remarked that "the sustained, malicious, and brutal harassment meted out ... was more than merely unreasonable; it was malevolent and outrageous." The company knew of the harassment and took corrective action only after the employee filed an EEOC complaint. The company was thus held liable, and Zabowicz was awarded back pay for the period of her medical absence, and a judgment that her rights were violated under the Civil Rights Act of 1964.

On September 17, 1990, Lisa Olson, a sports reporter for the *Boston Herald*, charged five football players of the just-defeated New England Patriots with sexual harassment for making sexually suggestive and offensive remarks to her when she entered their locker room to conduct a post-game interview. The incident amounted to nothing short of "mind rape," according to Olson. After vociferous lamentations in the media, the National Football League fined the team and its players $25,000 each. The National Organization for Women called for a boycott of Remington electric shavers because the owner of the company, Victor Kiam, also owns the Patriots and ... allegedly displayed insufficient sensitivity at the time ... the episode occurred.

UTOPIAN TREATMENT
FOR WOMEN

All these incidents are indisputably disturbing. In an ideal world—one far different from the one that we inhabit or are ever likely to inhabit—women would not be subjected to such treatment in the course of their work. Women (and men) would be accorded respect by co-workers and supervisors, their feelings would be taken into account, and their dignity would be left intact. For women to expect reverential treatment in the workplace is utopian, yet they should not have to tolerate outrageous, offensive sexual overtures and threats as they go about earning a living.

One question that needs to be pondered is: What kinds of undesired sexual behavior should

women be protected against by law? That is, what kind of actions are deemed so outrageous and violate a woman's rights to such extent that the law should intervene, and what actions should be considered inconveniences of life, to be morally condemned but not adjudicated? A subsidiary question concerns the type of legal remedy appropriate for the wrongs that do require redress. Before directly addressing these questions, it might be useful to diffuse some of the hyperbole adhering to the sexual harassment issue.

HARASSMENT SURVEYS

Surveys are one source of this hyperbole. If their results are accepted at face value, they lead to the conclusion that women are disproportionately victims of legions of sexual harassers. A poll by the Albuquerque *Tribune* found that nearly 80 percent of the respondents reported that they or someone they knew had been victims of sexual harassment. The Merit System Protection Board determined that 42 percent of the women (and 14 percent of men) working for the federal government had experienced some form of unwanted sexual attention between 1985 and 1987, with unwanted "sexual teasing" identified as the most prevalent form. A Defense Department survey found that 64 percent of women in the military (and 17 percent of the men) suffered "uninvited and unwanted sexual attention" within the previous year. The United Methodist Church established that 77 percent of its clergy-women experienced incidents of sexual harassment, with 41 percent of these naming a pastor or colleague as the perpetrator, and 31 percent mentioning church social functions as the setting.

A few caveats about polls in general, and these in particular ... Pollsters looking for a particular social ill tend to find it, usually in gargantuan proportions. (What fate would lie in store for a pollster who concluded that child abuse, or wife beating, or mistreatment of the elderly had dwindled to the point of negligibility!) Sexual harassment is a notoriously ill-defined and almost infinitely expandable concept, including everything from rape to unwelcome neck massage, discomfiture on witnessing sexual overtures directed at others, yelling at and blowing smoke in the ears of female subordinates, and displaying pornographic pictures in the workplace. Defining sexual harassment, as the United Methodists did, as "any sexually related behavior that is unwelcome, offensive, or ... fails to respect the rights of others," [makes] the concept broad enough to include everything from "unsolicited suggestive looks or leers [or] pressures for dates" to "actual sexual assaults or rapes." Categorizing everything from rape to "looks" as sexual harassment makes us all victims, a state of affairs satisfying to radical feminists, but not very useful for distinguishing serious injuries from the merely trivial.

Yet even if the surveys exaggerate the extent of sexual harassment, however defined, what they do reflect is a great deal of tension between the sexes. As women in ever-increasing numbers entered the workplace in the last two decades, as the women's movement challenged alleged male hegemony and exploitation with ever greater intemperance, and as women entered previously all-male preserves from the board rooms to the coal pits, it is lamentable, but should not be surprising, that this tension sometimes takes sexual form. Not that sexual harassment on the job, in the university, and in other settings is a trivial or insignificant matter, but a sense of proportion needs to be restored and, even more important, distinctions need to be made. In other words, sexual harassment must be de-ideologized. Statements that paint nearly all women as victims and all men and their patriarchal, capitalist system as perpetrators, are ideological fantasy. Ideology blurs the distinction between being injured—being a genuine victim—and merely being offended. An example is this statement by Catharine A. MacKinnon, a law professor and feminist activist:

> Sexual harassment perpetuates the interlocked structure by which women have been kept sexually in thrall to men and at the bottom of the labor market. Two forces of American society converge: men's control over women's sexuality and capital's control over employees' work lives. Women

historically have been required to exchange sexual services for material survival, in one form or another. Prostitution and marriage as well as sexual harassment in different ways institutionalize this arrangement.

Such hyperbole needs to be diffused, and distinctions need to be drawn. Rape, a nonconsensual invasion of a person's body, is a crime clear and simple, a violation of the right to the physical integrity of the body (the right to life, as John Locke or Thomas Jefferson would have put it). Criminal law should and does prohibit rape. Whether it is useful to call rape "sexual harassment" is doubtful, for it makes the latter concept overly broad while trivializing the former.

EXTORTION OF SEXUAL FAVORS

Intimidation in the workplace of the kind that befell Valerie Craig—that is, extortion of sexual favors by a supervisor from a subordinate by threatening to penalize, fire, or fail to reward—is what the courts term *quid pro quo* sexual harassment. Since the mid-1970s, the federal courts have treated this type of sexual harassment as a form of sex discrimination in employment proscribed under Title VII of the Civil Rights Act of 1964. A plaintiff who prevails against an employer may receive such equitable remedies as reinstatement and back pay, and the court can order the company to prepare and disseminate a policy against sexual harassment. Current law places principal liability on the company, not the harassing supervisor, even when higher management is unaware of the harassment and thus cannot take any steps to prevent it.

Quid pro quo sexual harassment is morally objectionable and analogous to extortion: The harasser extorts property (use of the woman's body) through the leverage of fear for her job. The victim of such behavior should have legal recourse, but serious reservations can be held about rectifying these injustices through the blunt instrument of Title VII. In egregious cases the victim is left less than whole (back pay will not compensate her for ancillary losses), and no prospect for punitive damages are offered to deter would-be harassers. Even more distressing about Title VII is that the primary target of litigation is not the actual harasser, but the employer. This places a double burden on a company. The employer is swindled by the supervisor because he spent his time pursuing sexual gratification and thereby impairing the efficiency of the workplace by mismanaging his subordinates, and the employer must endure lengthy and expensive litigation, pay damages, and suffer loss to its reputation. It would be fairer to both the company and the victim to treat sexual harassment as a tort—that is, as a private wrong or injury for which the court can assess damages. Employers should be held vicariously liable only when they know of an employee's behavior and do not try to redress it.

DEFINING HARASSMENT
IS DIFFICULT

As for the workplace harassment endured by Carol Zabowicz—bared buttocks, obscene portraits, etc.—that too should be legally redressable. Presently, such incidents also fall under the umbrella of Title VII and are termed hostile environment sexual harassment, a category accepted later than *quid pro quo* and with some judicial reluctance. The main problem with this category is that it has proven too elastic: Cases have reached the courts based on everything from off-color jokes to unwanted, persistent sexual advances by co-workers. A new tort of sexual harassment would handle these cases better. Only instances above a certain threshold of egregiousness or outrageousness would be actionable. In other words, the behavior that the plaintiff found offensive would also have to be offensive to the proverbial "reasonable man" of the tort law. That is, the behavior would have to be objectively injurious rather than merely subjectively offensive. The defendant would be the actual harasser, not the

company, unless it knew about the problem and failed to act. Victims of scatological jokes, leers, unwanted offers of dates, and other sexual annoyances would no longer have their day in court.

A distinction must be restored between morally offensive behavior and behavior that causes serious harm. Only the latter should fall under the jurisdiction of criminal or tort law. Do we really want legislators and judges delving into our most intimate private lives, deciding when a look is a leer, and when a leer is a Civil Rights Act offense? Do we really want courts deciding, as one recently did, whether a school principal's disparaging remarks about a female school district administrator was sexual harassment and, hence, a breach of Title VII, or merely the act of a spurned and vengeful lover? Do we want judges settling disputes such as the one that arose at a car dealership after a female employee turned down a male co-worker's offer of a date and his colleagues retaliated by calling her offensive names and embarrassing her in front of customers? Or another case in which a female shipyard worker complained of an "offensive working environment" because of the prevalence of pornographic material on the docks? Do we want the state to prevent or compensate us for any behavior that someone might find offensive? Should people have a legally enforceable right not to be offended by others? At some point, the price for such protection is the loss of both liberty and privacy rights.

NO PERFECT WORKING
ENVIRONMENT EXISTS

Workplaces are breeding grounds of envy, personal grudges, infatuation, and jilted loves, and beneath a fairly high threshold of outrageousness, these travails should be either suffered in silence, complained of to higher management, or left behind as one seeks other employment. No one, female or male, can expect to enjoy a working environment that is perfectly stress-free, or to be treated always and by everyone with kindness and respect. To the extent that sympathetic judges have encouraged women to seek monetary compensation for slights and annoyances, they have not done them a great service. Women need to develop a thick skin in order to survive and prosper in the work force. It is patronizing to think that they need to be recompensed by male judges for seeing a few pornographic pictures on a wall. By their efforts to extend sexual harassment charges to even the most trivial behavior, the radical feminists send a message that women are not resilient enough to ignore the run-of-the-mill, churlish provocation from male co-workers. It is difficult to imagine a suit by a longshoreman complaining of mental stress due to the display of nude male centerfolds by female co-workers. Women cannot expect to have it both ways: equality where convenient, but special dispensations when the going gets rough. Equality has its price and that price may include unwelcome sexual advances, irritating and even intimidating sexual jests, and lewd and obnoxious colleagues.

Egregious acts—sexual harassment per se—must be legally redressable. Lesser but not trivial offenses, whether at the workplace or in other more social settings, should be considered moral lapses for which the offending party receives opprobrium, disciplinary warnings, or penalties, depending on the setting and the severity. Trivial offenses, dirty jokes, sexual overtures, and sexual innuendoes do make many women feel intensely discomfited, but, unless they become outrageous through persistence or content, these too should be taken as part of life's annoyances. The perpetrators should be either endured, ignored, rebuked, or avoided, as circumstances and personal inclination dictate. Whether Lisa Olson's experience in the locker room of the Boston Patriots falls into the second or third category is debatable. The media circus triggered by the incident was certainly out of proportion to the event.

As the presence of women on road gangs, construction crews, and oil rigs becomes a fact of life, the animosities and tensions of this transition period are likely to abate gradually. Meanwhile, women should "lighten up," and even dispense a few risqué barbs of their own, a sure way of taking the fun out of it for offensive male bores.

49

Sexual Harassment in the University

NANCY ("ANN") DAVIS

Nancy Davis notes that between 25 and 40 percent of female college students report they have been subjected to some sort of harassment from their instructors. She maintains that the frequency and seriousness of sexual harassment in the university are widely underestimated. She also claims that when many women are faced with sexual harassment at the university, they tend to deal with the problem in ways that have unfortunate consequences for themselves.

The notion of sexual harassment entered public consciousness in the United States with the publication of a survey on sexual harassment in the workplace conducted by *Redbook* in 1976. More than 9,000 women responded to the survey, and almost nine out of ten reported experiencing some sort of sexual harassment on the job.[1] Unsurprisingly, these revelations stimulated a lot of discussion in the news media, the popular press, and academic journals.[2] At about the same time, sexual harassment was found by the courts to constitute a form of sex discrimination and thus to be illegal under the terms of Title VII of the 1964 Civil Rights Act, which prohibits discrimination on the basis of race, sex, religion, or national origin.[3] Shortly thereafter, the same sorts of protections were held to extend to the educational sphere.[4] Title IX of the Education Amendments Act of 1972 forbids sex discrimination in all public and private institutions that receive federal money from grants, loans, or contracts.

Though sexual harassment in the university began to receive attention in the media in the late 1970s, not until 1986 did educational institutions themselves really begin to sit up and take notice. In that year, in *Meritor Savings Bank FSB v. Vinson*, the courts held that it was possible for an employer

to be found guilty under Title VII if an employee's harassing conduct created a "hostile environment" for the harassed employee, and it allowed individuals who were the victims of sexual harassment to sue employers that did not have a policy that clearly prohibited sexual harassment.[5] These findings have been held to be applicable to educational institutions, and though many institutions had initially been slow to react, most were not slow to draw the obvious moral, namely, that it was not just an individual harassing instructor who might be liable to prosecution but the university that employed that instructor as well.[6]

Most educational institutions have formulated or are in the process of formulating policies concerning sexual harassment.

In addition to being illegal and in opposition to expressed policies of many (if not most) educational institutions, sexual harassment is condemned as unethical by the American Association of University Professors, and by many of the myriad professional organizations that most faculty members are associated with.[7] It is difficult to produce a comprehensive, uncontroversial definition of sexual harassment,[8] or a philosophically watertight account that explains just what it is about the different kinds of behavior that have been described as sexual harassment that makes them all of a piece unethical. Although, as we shall see, these difficulties pose problems for attempts to formulate fair and effective policies about sexual harassment, they pose no serious impediment to the achievement of consensus about the more blatant forms of sexual harassment. In the classic *quid pro quo* case in which an instructor puts unwelcome sexual pressure on a student and makes it clear that ... academic evaluation or professional advancement [depends] on her yielding to that pressure, what the instructor does is obviously coercive, unjust, disrespectful, and discriminatory.[9] It is an abuse of power, a betrayal of trust, and inimical to the existence of a healthy educational environment in several ways.

Yet surveys conducted at college campuses around the nation reveal that a sizable proportion of female college students—somewhere between 25 percent and 40 percent—report they have been subjected to some sort of sexual harassment on the part of their instructors,[10] and anecdotal evidence provided by female students, faculty members, and administrators corroborates those findings. Surveys may be difficult to interpret and compare, for they do not all employ the same definition of sexual harassment, and anecdotal evidence must always be treated with caution, but it is clear that sexual harassment and other forms of sexually inappropriate behavior are no rarity in the university.[11] Any serious participant in higher education must be puzzled and distressed by this fact.

Commentators have identified many different ... factors contributing to the prevalence of sexual harassment in the university. Some have emphasized that the university was and remains a male-dominated institution whose ground rules and procedures were fashioned by men. Traditionally, the influential teaching and administrative jobs in the university have been occupied by men, and it is men who have made the policies and interpreted the rules of university governance. Though things have changed considerably in the past decade or so, most of the senior faculty and administrative positions are still occupied by men. And women remain significantly in the minority in most, if not all,

academic fields. This situation is thought, in itself, to be a problem. It is women, not men, who are almost always the victims of sexual harassment and men, not women, who are almost always the harassers.[12] And men are likely to both operate with a narrower notion of sexual harassment and have lower estimates of the incidence of sexual harassment on campus than women. They are also likelier to view the incidents of sexual harassment they acknowledge do occur as isolated personal incidents rather than as expressions of an institutional (or broader) problem. Commentators thus often cite the dearth of senior women and the associated inexperience and insensitivity of academic men as among the principal factors contributing to sexual harassment on campus. If women were less of a minority on campus or if they occupied positions of power that enabled them to have greater influence on rules, practices, and policies, then (it is thought) the incidence of sexual harassment on campus would decrease.

The women's movement and other associated movements have led many women—and many men—to question received gender stereotypes. But it is clear, nevertheless, that those stereotypes continue to exert a powerful influence on people's views about the relations between male professors and female students. Although it is a truism that social attitudes about status, gender, and sexuality frame people's expectations about "proper" relations between the sexes, most of us are blind to many of the effects of those attitudes, and implications of those expectations often go unnoticed.[13] Though fewer people may now regard liaisons between experienced and influential older men and inexperienced, comparatively powerless younger women as the ideal sort of relationship, such liaisons are still widely thought to be acceptable (if not simply normal). And the persistence of romanticized Pygmalionesque views of the educational process appears to legitimate such relations between male professors and female students. It is clear that gender stereotypes and associated differential social expectations contribute in a number of ways to the incidence of sexual harassment on campus.

Until we have a better understanding of why there has been so much sexual harassment in the university, we are not likely to be able to arrive at a solid understanding of what can or should be done to curtail it: The formulation of a cogent and successful sexual harassment policy thus requires more reflection on the factors that have contributed to the existence—or persistence—of sexual harassment in the university. Commentators are correct, I believe, in citing both the dearth of senior women in the university and the persistence of conventional gender expectations as significant contributing factors....

It is clear that both the frequency and the seriousness of sexual harassment in the university are widely underestimated (even when sexual harassment is given its narrow interpretation and taken to refer only to such things as *quid pro quo* threats and actual sexual assault). There are a number of reasons why this is so. Personal, institutional, ideological, and societal factors all conspire to deter students from reporting incidents of sexual harassment and from taking concerted action to follow through with the reports of sexual harassment that they do make. If the data on sexual harassment are correct, it is clear that very few of the victims of sexual harassment in the workplace or in the university report it at all.[14] It is worth making clear what in the university context specifically discourages students from reporting sexual harassment.

Students and professors possess unequal power, influence, confidence, experience, and social standing.[15] And this inequality contributes to students' fears of being ridiculed, disbelieved, punished, or thought incompetent if they come forward with reports of sexually inappropriate conduct on the part of their instructors. Fear of the humiliations that befall many of the women who report rape and other forms of sexual assault evidently makes many women wary of reporting sexual offenses, especially when—as is evidently true in cases of sexual harassment—the attacker is someone who is known to the accuser. The student who has been sexually harassed by her professor is in a particularly vulnerable position, especially if she is known to have had an ongoing personal association with him or has previously submitted to his coercion. The stereotype of the professor as brilliant, principled,

and passionately dedicated to his work and to the educational growth of his students leads students to doubt that their allegations would be believed. After all, professors are widely regarded as respectable members of the community.

Often enough, students lose confidence in their perceptions of their own actions: If they hadn't done something wrong, then why would this respectable citizen behave so bizarrely?[16] "Blame the victim" sensibilities pervade our society, and so it is not too hard to understand why a confused and distressed victim of sexual harassment would shoulder the blame herself, rather than attribute it to the distinguished, respectable, and (formerly) much-admired professor who was (or appeared to be) so generous with his time and concern.

There are also other factors that erode a woman's confidence, and make her fear that the instructor's harassing behavior must somehow be her fault.[17] Late adolescence and early adulthood are vulnerable and psychologically chaotic times. Among the many difficulties that college-age students face is the struggle to come to terms with their sexuality, and it is easy for them to be insecure in the midst of that process, unclear about their own desires and unsure about how to interpret (and deal with) the many conflicting and ambivalent desires that they have. Though both men and women undoubtedly undergo personal upheaval, their behavior does not meet with the same social interpretation or response, nor are men and women supposed to handle their ambivalences the same way. Men are expected to become more confident and hence more persistent in their pursuit of sexual relationships as they mature. The myth endures that women enjoy being the object of persistent male attentions and invitations but like to play "hard to get" and thus refuse invitations they really wish to accept: When a woman says "no," what she really means is "maybe" or "ask me again later." Since, moreover, women are taught to be polite and nonconfrontational, the woman who tries to act "decently" when confronted with an unwelcome sexual invitation/offer/threat may be seen as thereby expressing ambivalence, which, according to the foregoing myth, may be construed as an expression of interest. If the woman actually does feel ambivalent—she wants to refuse the invitation, but she feels some attraction to the man who has issued it—then she may guiltily believe that she "led him on" even when she said no. And so she may regard the instructor's sexually inappropriate behavior as her fault.[18]

Gender roles and social expectations affect perceptions in other ways as well. Traditionally, women have been judged by their appearance, and they have thus been obliged to devote considerable energy to the attempt to look "attractive," for except among the most wealthy, it was a woman's appearance and good (compliant) manners that were the principal determinant of whether or not she would attract a man and marry, which was essential for her economic security. Though economics have changed, the traditional view continues to exert an influence on people's thinking, and women still feel pressure to dress attractively and act politely. Yet a woman who is attractive is seen as open to, and perhaps as actually inviting, sexual responses from men. This perception, plus the myth that men's sexual self-control is so fragile that it can be overwhelmed by the presence of an attractive woman, contributes to the view that the women who are sexually harassed are those who "asked for it" (by being physically attractive, or attractively dressed).

Surveys make it clear that there is no correlation between a woman's being attractive (or "sexily" dressed) and her being sexually harassed. Sexual harassment, like rape, is primarily an issue of power, not sex. But the myth persists that it is a female student's appearance that is the cause of her instructor's sexually inappropriate behavior toward her. This myth influences female students' perceptions of both their own and their professors' conduct. And if, as she may well suppose, she bears responsibility for the instructor's behaving as he does, she is likely not to think of his conduct as being sexual harassment.[19]

Popular academic fiction has done a lot to perpetuate these myths, and a lot to reinforce unfortunate gender stereotypes. "Co-eds" are portrayed as lusty seducers of respectable male professors, who are often, portrayed as hapless victims of those feminine wiles. One can conjecture that most college-age women have read a few of the standard academic novels and that those novels provide some of the background for their interpretation of their professors' conduct.[20]

Believing that her experience of sexual harassment is rare, believing, perhaps, the various myths surrounding the mechanics of male and female attraction, and being influenced by the myth-supporting academic fiction she reads in English courses, the sexually harassed student may believe that the whole thing is her fault. It is not something that she should report but something she should be ashamed of. And so her energies are likely to be spent trying to cope with or "manage" the incident, not reporting it or attempting to bring the sexual harasser to justice.[21]

The asymmetrical power and influence of students and professors not only affect the student's perception of whether or not her claims of sexual harassment would be believed, they also affect her perception of the risks involved in making such a report (even when she does not fear being disbelieved). The professor holds the power of evaluation, and often enough, the student sees him as gatekeeper to her desired career. If she displeases him, then—whether it is through the mechanism of letters of reference or the more informal workings of the "old boy network"—he may, she fears, ruin her career prospects.[22]

The structural organization of the university also serves to deter victims from reporting sexually inappropriate behavior. The myriad of departments, programs, divisions, and colleges may be quite daunting to an undergraduate, who may not understand the relations between them or be able easily to determine who has authority with respect to what.[23] Nor does it help that some of those people to whom a student might turn appear as confused and powerless as the student herself—or altogether uninterested. A student may summon up her courage to report an incident of sexual misconduct to a professor whom she feels she can trust, only to be told to report it to the department chair, whom she may not know at all. If the department chair has not been through this before or if the chair is over-worked or less than sympathetic to her plight, then the student may be met with (what she inter-prets as) annoyance and indifference ("Well, what do you want me to do about it?") or referred to a dean, who may seem to the student a distant, busy, and daunting individual. The organization of the university, with its convoluted procedures and divi-sions of responsibility, is quotidian to experienced faculty members who understand the hierarchy and the system. But they may be intimidating to some-one who does not understand them and who is already traumatized and alienated.

The attitudes of academics toward their col-leagues and students and their views about their own intellectual mission and personal responsibilities may also serve to discourage students from report-ing sexual harassment. What is perhaps more important, however, is that those attitudes clearly serve to deter faculty members who learn of a colleague's sexually inappropriate behavior from taking action on it. "Educators see themselves as a community of scholars bound together by common interests and goals."[24]

They are reluctant to "break ranks," to do things that they perceive as disloyal or damaging to a colleague. In some cases this reluctance may be an expression of a long-standing liberal commit-ment to tolerance of difference or a manifestation of the desire to uphold academic freedom or respect the autonomy of one's colleagues.[25] In other cases, and less (ostensibly) nobly, it may be thought to stem from academics' desire to be left alone to get on with their own work, protect their own inter-ests, or stay out of academic politics. But whatever the precise blend of factors (what might be called) the ideology of the faculty tends to support the stance of uninvolvement.

Untenured and nontenure-track faculty are in an especially precarious position. The accused senior colleague may wield a good deal of power in the university and in his particular academic field. If displeased or moved to seek retaliation, he may do things that place the untenured faculty mem-ber's job at risk. Female faculty members—who are statistically more likely to be untenured or not

tenure-track and very much in the minority in their profession—may be particularly vulnerable. Both their professional success thus far and their profes-sional future may well depend upon their being perceived as "good colleagues," people who happen to be female in a largely male context and profession and "don't make a fuss about it." Becoming involved with a sexual harassment case may call attention to a female instructor's gender in ways that make her uncomfortable and may place her in double jeopardy, for she may feel that she is being obliged to risk her own credibility, her good relations with her colleagues, and her own profes-sional connections. And oddly enough, though there is no shortage of good motivations for helping a student who reports an incident of sexual misconduct—a desire to help and protect a student who is hurt and frightened and feels she has nowhere else to turn, the desire to uphold the express and tacit values of the institution, the perception of the need to show students that female faculty members can act with strength and integrity—the female instructor who is willing to assist a student who complains of sexual harassment may find her own motives impugned by resentful male colleagues. As an older woman (and therefore, as convention has it, a less-attractive woman) she may be accused of projecting her unfulfilled desires for male sexual attention onto the student, of being a harridan, or a lesbian who wants to get even with men, of being bitter about her own lack of academic success (which she wrongly and wrongfully attributes to being a woman), and so on.[26]

It is clear that both students' reluctance to come forward with complaints of sexual harassment and faculty members' disinclination to get involved when students do come forward contribute to an underestimation of the scope of the problem of sexual harassment in academia. It is not only the frequency with which sexually inappropriate behavior occurs that is underestimated, however, but the extent of the damage it causes as well. The explanation of why this is so is both complex and multifaceted.

Part of the explanation lies in the invisibility of much of the damage in question. It is easy to see the harm in an instructor's following through on a threat to take reprisals against a student who rejects his demands or in an instructor's tendering an unduly (though perhaps not deliberately or even consciously) harsh evaluation of the student who does not respond favorably to his sexual overtures. Those students are the victims of unfair academic evaluations, and both the professor's integrity and the integrity of the institution's grading practices are severely compromised by such behavior. But other harms—to the individual student, to other students, to the educational institution and to the society at large—are less obvious.

Many of the students who find themselves the recipients of unwelcome sexual overtures, remarks, or questions deal with the problem by "managing" it, and the most common form of management is avoidance: The student drops the course, ceases to attend the class, withdraws the application to be a lab assistant, quits coming to office hours, changes her major, or, in the most extreme cases, drops out of school altogether.[27] Though these avoidance tactics may effectively remove the opportunity for an instructor to engage in harassing behavior, they do so at a cost. The student who thinks she can avoid being sexually harassed by simply avoiding the professor in question may thereby be deprived of valuable academic and professional opportunities, and the pool of motivated and intelligent aspirants to the relevant profession is thus reduced. Though, on such a scenario, both the damage to the individual and the loss to society are real, they are largely undetectable. If the number of women in the profession is already low, then the temptation may be to suppose, for example, that "women just aren't interested in engineering" or that "most women just aren't able to do the sort of abstract thinking required for graduate-level physics," adding the insult of misdiagnosis to the injury of sexual harassment. Women who were in fact driven out of the profession by being robbed of the opportunity to pursue their studies in peace are deemed uninterested or incapable. And viewing these women as uninterested or incapable obviously has implications for how other female aspirants to such careers are likely to be viewed, and to view themselves.

Nor does the damage stop there. When a student is given grounds for wondering whether her instructor's academic interest and encouragement were motivated by his sexual interest in her, she may well come to doubt the legitimacy of her previous accomplishments: Perhaps her success thus far has owed more to sexual attributes that instructors found attractive than to her own hard work and ability. A good, serious, hardworking student may thus lose the sort of self-confidence that anyone needs to succeed in a competitive field, and that women especially need if they are to succeed in traditionally male professions that remain statistically (if not ideologically) male dominated. If, in addition, other students and instructors attribute the harassed student's academic success to sexual involvement with, or manipulation of, her instructors, then relationships with her peers and her other instructors (and with her own students, if she is a teaching assistant) may well be harmed, and suspicion may be cast on the success of other women. More subtly, both students and instructors may be drawn into a familiar form of overgeneralization and thus may come to harbor the suspicion that women's successes in the academic and professional fields in which they are a significant minority owe more to the women's skills at sexually manipulating those in power than to their hard work and ability. Generalized resentment of women or the unspoken background belief that women do not play fair or cannot "pull their own weight" may result, and this consequence may silently lead instructors to interact differently with male and female students and to approach them with different expectations. Given the insidious working of socialization, neither the students nor the instructors may be aware of the existence of such differential treatment; yet it may well be prejudicial and, ultimately, extremely detrimental. Again, both the existence of the harm and its causation are difficult to pin down in such cases and difficult to distinguish from the apparently statistically supported view that "women just aren't good at (or interested in) physics."

It should be clear from this discussion that sexual harassment (or, more broadly, sexually inappropriate behavior) can cause significant damage to the individuals who are its direct victims, to other women, and to the society at large. But it is hard to make the estimation of that damage more precise, for attempts to arrive at a more precise measure of the damage are complicated by the many other factors that make academic and professional success more difficult for women. It is not likely, after all, that a woman's first or only experience of sex discrimination will occur in a college lecture hall or in a professor's office, and it is plausible to suppose that a woman's prior experiences will influence how much damage will be done to her by an instructor's sexual harassment or other sexually inappropriate behavior. Prior experiences may both magnify the harm that is done to her by sexual harassment and, at the same time, diminish the possibility of perceiving that behavior as the cause of the harm. If women have routinely been victims of sex discrimination or societal sexist attitudes, then how can one say that it is the experience of sexual harassment in the university that is the cause of a woman's subsequent distress or the explanation of her decision to enter a "traditionally female" job or profession?[28]

Reflection on this problem suggests a connection between widespread ignorance about the extent of sexually inappropriate behavior in the university and the seriousness of the damage it may cause, and the difficulties involved in attempting to come up with a widely acceptable definition of sexual harassment. In a society that many people would characterize as pervaded by sexist attitudes (if not actual sex discrimination) and in one in which there is disagreement about what constitutes (objectionable) sexism and what is merely a response to differences between men and women, it may be difficult, if not impossible, to reach a consensus about what constitutes sexual harassment. Any university policy that hopes to do any good must take note of this fact.

ENDNOTES

Acknowledgment: I wish to thank Susan Hobson-Panico, Thomas A. Stermitz, and S. Mickie Grover for their helpful discussion of some of the issues addressed in this essay.

1. Claire Saffran, "What Men Do to Women on the Job," *Redbook* (November 1976), pp. 149, 217–223; see p. 217: "In fact, nearly 9 out of 10 report that they have experienced one or more forms of unwanted attentions on the job. This can be visual (leering and ogling) or verbal (sexual remarks and teasing). It can escalate to pinching, grabbing and touching, to subtle hints and pressures, to overt requests for dates and sexual favors—with the implied threat that it will go against the woman if she refuses."

2. See, e.g., Karen Lindsay, "Sexual Harassment on the Job and How to Stop It," *Ms.* (November 1977), pp. 47–48, 50–51, 74–75, 78; Margaret Mead, "A Proposal: We Need Taboos on Sex at Work," *Redbook* (April 1978). pp. 31, 33, 38; Caryl Rivers, "Sexual Harassment: The Executive's Alternative to Rape," *Mother Jones* (June 1978), pp. 21–24, 28; Claire Saffran, "Sexual Harassment: The View From the Top," *Redbook* (March 1981), pp. 45–51. See

also Constance Backhouse and Leah Cohen, *Sexual Harassment on the Job* (Englewood Cliffs, N.J.: Prentice-Hall, 1981), originally published in 1978 as *The Secret Oppression;* and Catherine A. MacKinnon, *Sexual Harassment of Working Women* (New Haven: Yale University Press, 1979).

   Popular discussions of sexual harassment in academia include Adrienne Munich, "Seduction in Academe," *Psychology Today* (February 1978), pp. 82–84. 108; Anne Nelson, "Sexual Harassment at Yale," *Nation,* January 14, 1978, pp. 7–10; Lorenz Middleton, "Sexual Harassment by Professors: An 'Increasingly Visible' Problem." *Chronicle of Higher Education,* September 15, 1980, pp. 1, 4–5; Noel Epstein, "When Professors Swap Good Grades for Sex," *Washington Post,* September 6, 1981, pp. C1, C4; Anne Field, "Harassment on Campus: Sex in a Tenured Position?" *Ms.* (September 1981), pp. 68, 70, 73, 100–102; Suzanne Perry, "Sexual Harassment on the Campuses: Deciding Where to Draw the Line," *Chronicle of Higher Education,* March 23, 1983, pp. 21–22.

3. In *Barnes v. Castle.* 561 F2d 983 (D.C. Cir. 1977), which held that sexual harassment is actionable as

sex-based discrimination under Title VII and also extended some liability to an employer for the discriminatory acts of its supervisors.

4. *Alexander v. Yale University*, 549 F. Supp. 1 (D. Conn 1977), established sexual harassment as sex discrimination under Title IX.

5. *Meritor Savings Bank FSB v. Vinson*, 1206 S. Ct. 2399 (1986).

6. Thus both Title VII and Title IX apply when a student is sexually harassed by an instructor. Under Title IX, a student may have a cause of action against the individual instructor who sexually harassed her, and under Title VII, a cause of action against the university that employed that instructor. For relevant discussion, see Annette Gibbs and Robin B. Balthorpe. "Sexual Harassment in the Workplace and Its Ramifications for Academia," *Journal of College Student Personnel* 23 (1982), 158–162.

7. See, for example, "Statement on Professional Ethics," adopted in 1966 (pp. 133–134 of the *AAUP Policy Documents and Reports*, Washington, D.C: AAUP, 1984), which condemns "any exploitation for [a teacher's] private advantage" (p. 133); "A Statement of the Association's Council: Freedom and Responsibility" (pp. 135–136), adopted in 1970, which declares that "students are entitled to an atmosphere conducive to learning and to even handed treatment in all aspects of the teacher-student relationship" (p. 135); and "Sexual Harassment Suggested Policy and Procedures for Handling Complaints." (pp. 98–100), adopted in 1984, which states, "It is the policy of this institution that no member of the academic community may sexually harass another" (p. 99).

8. See, e.g., Eliza G. C. Collins and Timothy B. Blodgett, "Sexual Harassment … Some See It … Some Won't," *Harvard Business Review* 59 (1981), 76–95; Phyllis L. Crocker, "An Analysis of University Definitions of Sexual Harassment," *Signs* 8 (1983), 696–707; John Hughes and Larry May, "Sexual Harassment," *Social Theory and Practice* 6 (1980), 249–280; Catherine A. MacKinnon, "Sexual Harassment: Its First Decade in Court," in her *Feminism Unmodified* (Cambridge: Harvard University Press, 1987), pp. 103–116, 251–256; Rosemary Tong, "Sexual Harassment," in her *Women, Sex, and the Law* (Totowa, N.J.: Rowman and Littlefield, 1983).

9. There is some disagreement as to whether it is sex discrimination, but there can be no serious doubt that it is wrongful discrimination. Whether he

follows through on the threat and whether or not she submits to it are irrelevant. See, e.g., Crocker, "Analysis of University Definitions," p. 704: "Once a student is propositioned, all her future interactions with, and evaluations by, the professor are tainted and suspect, whether a promise or threat was ever made or carried out."

10. See Phyllis L. Crocker, "Annotated Bibliography on Sexual Harassment in Education," *Women's Rights Law Reporter* 7 (1982), 91–106. And see *Symposium on Sexual Harassment* in *Thought & Action* 5 (1989): 17–52, especially the essay by Anne Traux, "Sexual Harassment in Higher Education: What We've Learned," pp. 25–38, for an overview of surveys and results. Though a good deal of the sexual harassment on campus involves faculty members and administrators as victims, and some involves students as harassers, considerations of space and focus require that I confine this essay to the discussion of sexual harassment that involves students as victims and instructors as harassers. Discussion will also be confined to cases in which it is male instructors who are the harassers and female students who are the victims. As many commentators have observed, the cases in which a female instructor harasses a male student or a male instructor harasses a male student are few and far between. According to Traux, p. 25: "Nationally, about 95 percent of all sexual harassment reports involve men harassing females." See also Gibbs and Balthorpe, "Sexual Harassment in the Workplace"; MacKinnon, "Sexual Harassment: Its First Decade"; Tong, "Sexual Harassment"; Donna J. Benson and Gregg E. Thomson. "Sexual Harassment on a University Campus: The Confluence of Authority Relations, Sexual Interest, and Gender Stratification," *Social Problems* 29 (1982), 236–251; Bernice Lott, Mary Ellen Reilly, and Dale R. Howard, "Sexual Assault and Harassment: A Campus Community Case Study," *Signs* 8 (1982), 296–319.

11. Because … there is so much disagreement about what sorts of conduct constitute actual sexual harassment, and because *sexual harassment* is a legal term that is used to describe certain forms of legally proscribed sex discrimination, I prefer to use the broader (and vaguer) terms *sexually inappropriate behavior* and *sexual misconduct* whenever context and expression permit. If, as I shall argue, there are different kinds of sexually inappropriate behavior that may be wrong but are not (for various reasons)

happily classified with the sorts of wrongful behavior that constitute blatant sexual harassment, then it may be misleading to use *sexual harassment* as omnivorously as many commentators—and the Equal Opportunity Commission—have done.

12. It is, of course, possible for a female professor to harass a male student or for a professor of one sex to harass a student of the same sex. But it is clear that the vast majority of harassers are men, and the vast majority of victims are women, and surveys suggest that the incidence of sexual harassment of male students by female instructors is indeed very small. It is of course possible for a female instructor to make a *quid pro quo* offer/threat to a male student. But the fact that women are a minority, both in the upper echelons of the teaching and administrative staff and in most departments, together with the familiar facts about gender expectations and status, suggests that such harassment will be rare. And subtler forms of sexually inappropriate behavior, which the perpetrator does not perceive as unwelcome or coercive, will probably be even rarer. Involvements between older, established men and young women are accepted as normal, while those between older, established women and young, unestablished men clearly are not. Women who are involved in relationships with young, less-established men are generally the object of criticism, not admiration or even tolerance. In addition, since the determination of a woman's social status is held to depend heavily on the status of the male she is associated with, the attractions of such a relationship are likely not to be great: Whereas a female student may gain status by involvement with a male professor, a female professor forfeits status by involvement with a male student. If, as most commentators point out, sexual harassment is primarily an issue of power, not sex, there is considerably less incentive for a female faculty member to seek involvement with a male student, and considerably more disincentive. Finally, one can reasonably suppose that because women have long been in the minority in academia and have long been subject to various forms of sex discrimination and disparagement, they are likely to be more sensitive to the risks and problems that even well-intentioned relationships between persons of unequal power create. Whether it is accurate to say that gender is itself a form of hierarchy in a society that has been and continues to be so male-dominated (see MacKinnon, "Sexual Harassment:

Its First Decade"), there are good reasons to recognize that, as things now stand, the problem of sexual harassment is almost always one of men harassing women. Though, in the abstract, the issue of sexual harassment—the exploitative use of power—is sex-neutral, if not sex-blind, in circumstances in which it is men who (by and large) possess the power, it is women who will (by and large) be the victims.

That both males and females can be the victims of sexually inappropriate behavior has sometimes—mistakenly—been thought to undercut the claim that sexual harassment is a form of sex discrimination. But the existence of cases in which a male student is victimized by a female instructor does nothing to undercut such a claim, for the effects of being so victimized may be different for men and women, and the background of long-standing and ongoing discrimination against women makes it plausible to suppose that the effects would indeed be different. People suppose that because wrongs are committed both in the case in which a male professor harasses a female student and in the case in which a female professor harasses a male student, they must be the same wrong. But this is not obviously a correct assumption. In both cases there is a wrongful abuse of power and authority, but in one case ... there is also—because of the longstanding and ongoing discrimination against women—another wrong, namely, that of sex discrimination.

Nor does the existence of cases of single-sex harassment undercut the claim that sexual harassment is sex discrimination, unless one regards the obvious and widespread discrimination against homosexuals as some form of discrimination other than sex discrimination or construes sex discrimination so narrowly that conventional gender identity is seen as defining one's sex. Neither of these assumptions is plausible.

There are reasons for being uneasy at the characterization of sexual harassment as a form of sex discrimination. In some cases of sexually inappropriate behavior (which the Equal Opportunity Commission Guidelines would classify as sexual harassment), it is primarily an instructor's obvious disrespect, rather than the sexual cast of that disrespect, that seems more perspicuously identified as the thing that makes his actions wrong.

But the best reasons for uneasiness are probably pragmatic ones. Recent Supreme Court decisions have significantly weakened the scope of protections against racial discrimination (from Title VII and elsewhere); there is reason to suspect that sex discrimination protections will fare no better. They may even fare worse, for there is good reason to insist that there are no important ineliminable differences between persons of different races, but there are obviously differences between the sexes.

13. One has only to look at advertising or television sitcoms, or—as Billie Wright Dziech and Linda Weiner point out in *The Lecherous Professor* (Boston: Beacon Press, 1984)—watch teenagers interact in a shopping mall to be reminded how powerful and pervasive gender expectations are. See Benson and Thomson, "Sexual Harassment on a University Campus"; MacKinnon, *Sexual Harassment of Working Women;* MacKinnon, "Sexual Harassment: Its First Decade."

14. According to Traux, "Sexual Harassment in Higher Education," p. 26, "Of those harassed, not more than one in 10 actually report the harassment."

15. And as many would point out, women and men are not peers in these areas either.

16. To some degree, what medical ethicists have called "the fallacy of the generalization of expertise" is at work here. People who are thought to be successful or expert in one area are frequently—and unreasonably—thought to be successful or expert in others. Thus some people wrongly suppose that physicians are knowledgeable in matters of medical ethics (simply) because they are knowledgeable in medical matters, and others suppose that the good scholar of history (e.g.) must also be a good and decent person.

17. See Robert Shrank, "Two Women, Three Men on a Raft," *Harvard Business Review* 55 (1977), 100–109 for an interesting discussion of how men may unreflectively work to undermine women's self-confidence.

18. Or she may think that she should "be complimented, not incensed, if confronted with male sexual interest" (see Benson and Thomson, "Sexual Harassment on a Campus," p. 237) and thus feel that she has no right to complain.

19. One woman interviewed by Collins and Blodgett ("Sexual Harassment," p. 93) said: "A lot of women hesitate to report sexual harassment because women: (1) don't think they'll be believed; (2) will be punished by smaller raises or cruddy jobs [the analogue in the university context: will be punished by lower grades or undeservedly harsh evaluations]; (3) will be ostracized by male and female employees [students and other instructors]; (4) will be accused of inviting the advance; (5) have guilt feelings that perhaps it was invited subconsciously; (6) fear publicity; (7) are unsure exactly what is harassment and what is just interaction of people."

20. Some of the novels that come to mind here are Joyce Carol Oates, *Them;* John Barth, *The End of the Read;* and Bernard Malamud, *Dubin's Lives.* See Dziech and Weiner, *The Lecherous Professor,* pp. 62–63, 68, 118.

21. See especially Benson and Thomson, "Sexual Harassment on Campus"; and Dziech and Weiner, *The Lecherous Professor,* chap. 4. Also relevant is Judith Berman Brandenburg, "Sexual Harassment in the University: Guidelines for Establishing a Grievance Procedure" *Signs* 8 (1982), 321–336. See Mary P. Rowe, "Dealing with Sexual Harassment," *Harvard Business Review* 59 (1981), 42–7, for a detailed set of proposed procedures for harassed employees that places more emphasis on "management" of sexual harassment in the workplace than on prevention or redress.

22. A quotation from Dziech and Weiner. *The Lecherous Professor,* p. 83, drives this point home. One premed student said: It's easy for someone else to say that I should do something about Dr. —, but how can I? He was the first person at—to take my work seriously. At least I think it's my work that made him notice me. He's the one who's pushing for me to get into med school. If I refuse him, then I ruin my whole life.

23. Material in this and the succeeding paragraph benefited from the discussion in chap. 2 of Dziech and Weiner, *The Lecherous Professor.*

24. Ibid., p. 49.

25. I do not mean to suggest that respect for academic freedom or one's colleagues' autonomy requires (or even permits) a faculty member who learns of an incident of sexual harassment to ignore the student who reports it or otherwise discourage her from pressing her complaint. Neither academic freedom nor professional autonomy is absolute, and it is difficult to see what intellectually respectable academic purpose is served by the tolerance of sexual harassment. Of course, a faculty member who believes that some respectable academic purpose is served by

tolerating a colleague's sexually inappropriate behavior should be given the opportunity to explain his or her views. But such an opportunity can arise only if students are listened to and encouraged, not dissuaded from bringing their sexual harassment complaints forward in the first place.

26. See Dziech and Weiner, *The Lecherous Professor,* chap. 6.

27. See note 21.

28. The old adage that "defendants must take plaintiffs as they find them" is of some help here, but not much.

50

Understanding, Explaining, and Eliminating Sexual Harassment

JAMES P. STERBA

James P. Sterba reviews the developments in sexual harassment law, hoping to increase our understanding of what is, or better, what should be, sexual harassment. He then offers a partial explanation of why sexual harassment happens in both civilian and military life. He goes on to propose two positive norms, a Principle of Androgyny and a Principle of Desert, in addition to the negative one that prohibits sexual harassment. He claims we need to focus on these positive norms in order to make progress toward reducing the frequency of sexual harassment.

In 1998, the U.S. Supreme Court made four attempts to clarify sexual harassment law (Oncale v. Sundowner Offshore Services, Inc., Burlington Industries, Inc. v. Ellerth, Faragher v. City of Boca Raton, and Gebseret al. v. Lago Vista Independent School District). In 1998 as well, Judge Susan Webber Wright of the U.S. Court of Appeals for the Eighth Circuit dismissed the sexual harassment case of Paula Corbin Jones against President Clinton on the somewhat controversial grounds that even if Clinton as governor of Arkansas had done all Jones claimed he had done (i.e., summoned her from her convention post to his hotel suite, dropped his pants in front of Jones, asked her to "kiss it," touched her thigh and tried to kiss her on the neck, and despite apparently accepting her "no" for an answer, partially and momentarily blocked her exit for enough time to tell her that he knew her boss and that it would be best if the incident were kept between the two of them), Clinton would not have sexually harassed Jones because she could not demonstrate any tangible job detriment or adverse employment action for her refusal to submit to Clinton's alleged advances. Thus, while the flurry of judicial activity in 1998 did increase the scope of sexual harassment law— sitting U.S. presidents are now liable for sexual harassment suits, as are grade school and high school teachers—unfortunately our understanding of the nature of sexual harassment has yet to achieve a comparable advance. Nor as yet do we have a very good explanation of why sexual harassment occurs as frequently as it does in our society.

Accordingly, in Part I of this chapter, I will review the developments in sexual harassment law, hoping to increase our understanding of what is—or better, what should be—sexual harassment. In Part II, I will offer a partial explanation of why sexual harassment happens in both civilian and military life. In Part III, I will determine what positive norms, in addition to the negative one that prohibits sexual harassment, we need to focus on in order to make progress toward reducing its frequency.

Reprinted from *Justice for Here and Now* (Cambridge, 1998), pp. 93–99, by permission with substantial additions.

PART I: UNDERSTANDING SEXUAL HARASSMENT

Sexual harassment was not recognized by U.S. trial courts as an offense until the late 1970s, and it was only affirmed by the U.S. Supreme Court as an offense in the 1980s. The term *sexual harassment* itself was not even coined until the 1970s. So the problem of sexual harassment is one that many people have only recently come to recognize. Obviously, the Senate Judiciary Committee hearings in 1991 on Anita Hill's charge that Clarence Thomas had sexually harassed her,[1] the U.S. Navy's Tailhook scandal in 1992, the Bob Packwood scandal in 1995, and more recently in 1997, Paula Jones's amended sexual harassment suit against President Clinton have all helped heighten people's awareness of this problem.

In 1976, a federal district judge, in the first legal case using the term "sexual harassment," ruled that Diane Williams, a public information specialist at the U.S. Department of Justice who was dismissed after turning down her supervisor's sexual advances, had been harassed "based on sex" within the meaning of Title VII of the Civil Rights Act of 1964. Four years later, the Equal Employment Opportunity Commission issued guidelines finding harassment on the basis of sex to be a violation of Title VII of the Civil Rights Act of 1964, labeling sexual harassment as "unwelcome sexual advances, requests for sexual favors, and other verbal or physical conduct of a sexual nature when such behavior occurred in any of three circumstances:

1. Where submission to such conduct is made either explicitly or implicitly a term or condition of an individual's employment,

2. Where submission to or rejection of such conduct by an individual is used as the basis for employment decisions affecting such individual, or

3. Where such conduct has the purpose or effect of unreasonably interfering with an individual's work performance or creating an intimidating, hostile, or offensive working environment."

In 1986, the U.S. Supreme Court in *Meritor Savings Bank v. Vinson* unanimously agreed with the EEOC, ruling that there could be two types of sexual harassment: harassment that conditions concrete employment benefits on granting sexual favors (called the *quid pro quo* type) and harassment that creates a hostile or offensive work environment without affecting economic benefits (the *hostile environment* type). Nevertheless, the court made it quite difficult for a plaintiff to establish that either of these types of sexual harassment had occurred. For example, a polite verbal "no" does not suffice to show that sexual advances are unwelcome, and a woman's entire conduct both in and outside the workplace is subject to appraisal determining whether or not she welcomed the advances. For example, in the *Vinson* case, there was "voluminous testimony regarding Vinson's dress and personal fantasies," and in the Senate Judiciary Committee hearings, Anita Hill was not able to prevent intensive examination of her private life, although Clarence Thomas was able to declare key areas of his private life off limits, such as his practice of viewing and discussing pornographic films.

The Supreme Court also made it difficult to classify work environments as hostile to women unless the harassment is sufficiently severe or pervasive. Applying the Supreme Court's standard, a lower court, in *Christoforou v. Ryder Truck Rental*, judged a supervisor's actions of fondling a plaintiff's rear end and breasts, propositioning her, and trying to force a kiss at a Christmas party to be "too sporadic and innocuous" to support a finding of a hostile work environment.[2] Similarly, in *Rabidue v. Osceola Refining Co.*, a workplace where pictures of nude and scantily clad women abounded (including one, which hung on a wall for eight years, of a woman with a golf ball on her breasts and a man with his golf club standing over her and yelling "Fore!") and where a co-worker, never disciplined despite repeated complaints, routinely referred to women as "whores," "cunts," "pussies," and "tits," was judged by a lower court not to be a sufficiently hostile environment to constitute sexual harassment.[3] Notice, by contrast, that the U.S. Senate Arms Services Committee, in its hearings on homosexuals in the military, regarded an environment in which known homosexuals are simply doing their duty in the military to be too hostile an environment in which to ask male heterosexuals to serve.

Yet why should we accept the Supreme Court's characterization of sexual harassment, especially given its requirements of unwelcomeness and pervasiveness?[4] As the Supreme Court interprets sexual harassment, a person's behavior must be unwelcome in a fairly strong sense before it constitutes sexual harassment. But why should a woman have to prove that the offer "If you don't sleep with me, you will be fired" is unwelcome before it constitutes sexual harassment?[5] Isn't such an offer objectively unwelcome? Isn't it just the kind of offer that those in positions of power should not be making to their subordinates, an offer that purports to make their continuing employment conditional upon providing sexual favors? Surely, unless we are dealing with some form of legalized prostitution, and maybe not even then, such offers are objectively unwelcome.[6] Given, then, that such offers are objectively unwelcome, why is there any need to show that they are also subjectively unwelcome before regarding them as violations of Title VII of the Civil Rights Act? The requirement of subjective unwelcomeness is simply a gratuitous obstacle that makes the plaintiff's case far more difficult to prove than it should be.[7]

In addition, if the plaintiff is fired after refusing such an offer, the Supreme Court requires her to prove that the firing occurred because the offer was refused, which is very difficult to do unless one is a perfect employee. Wouldn't it be fairer to require the employer to prove that the plaintiff would have been fired even if she had said "yes" to the offer?[8] Of course, employers could avoid this burden of proof simply by not making any such offers in the first place.[9] But when they do make objectively unwelcome offers, why shouldn't the burden of proof be on them to show that any subsequent firing was clearly unrelated to the plaintiff's refusal of the offer? Fairness is particularly relevant in this context because we are committed to equal opportunity in the workplace, which requires employing women and men on equal terms. Accordingly, we must guard against imposing special burdens on women in the workplace when there are no comparable burdens imposed on men.[10]

The demand for equal opportunity in the workplace also appears to conflict with the Supreme Court's pervasiveness requirement for establishing a hostile environment. Citing a lower court, the Supreme Court contends that, to be actionable, sexual harassment "must be sufficiently severe or pervasive 'to alter the conditions of the [victim's] employment and create an abusive working environment.'"[11] But as this standard has been interpreted by lower courts, the pervasiveness of certain forms of harassment in the workplace has become grounds for tolerating them. In *Rabidue*, the majority argued that

> It cannot seriously be disputed that in some work environments, humor and language are rough hewn and vulgar. Sexual jokes, sexual conversations and girlie magazines abound. Title VII was not meant to or can change this. Title VIII is the federal court mainstay in the struggle for equal employment opportunity for the female workers of America. But it is quite different to claim that Title VII was designed to bring about a magical transformation in the social mores of American workers.[12]

The Supreme Court itself seems to sound a similar theme by emphasizing the application of Title VII to only extreme cases of sexual harassment as found in *Vinson*.

However, as the EEOC interprets Title VII, the law has a broader scope. It affords employees the right to work in an environment free from discriminatory intimidation, ridicule, and insult. According to the EEOC, sexual harassment violates Title VII where conduct creates an intimidating, hostile, or offensive environment or where it unreasonably interferes with work performance.

But how are we to determine what unreasonably interferes with work performance? In *Rabidue*, the majority looked to prevailing standards in the workplace to determine what was reasonable or unreasonable. Yet Justice Keith, in dissent, questioned this endorsement of the status quo, arguing that just as a Jewish employee can rightfully demand a change in her working environment if her employer maintains an anti-Semitic workforce and tolerates a workplace in which "kike" jokes, displays of Nazi literature, and anti-Jewish conversation "may abound," surely women can rightfully demand a change in the sexist practices that prevail in their working environments.[13] In *Henson v. Dundee*, the majority also drew an analogy between sexual harassment and racial harassment:

> Sexual harassment which creates a hostile or offensive environment for members of one sex is every bit the arbitrary barrier to sexual equality at the workplace that racial harassment is to racial equality. Surely, a requirement that a man or woman run a gauntlet of sexual abuse in return for the privilege of being allowed to work and make a living can be as demeaning and disconcerting as the harshest of racial epithets.[14]

And this passage is also quoted approvingly by the Supreme Court in *Vinson*.

Moved by such arguments, the majority in *Ellison v. Brady* proposed that rather than looking to prevailing standards to determine what is reasonable, we should look to the standard of a reasonable victim, or given that most victims of sexual harassment are women—the standard of a reasonable woman.[15] They contend that this standard may be different from the standard of a "reasonable man." For example, what male superiors may think is "harmless social interaction" may be experienced by female subordinates as offensive and threatening.[16]

Nevertheless, if we are concerned to establish equal opportunity in the workplace, there should be no question about what standard of reasonableness to use here. It is not that of a reasonable woman, nor that of a reasonable man for that matter, but the standard of what is reasonable for everyone affected to accept. For equal opportunity is a moral requirement, and moral requirements are those which are reasonable for everyone affected to accept. This assumes that apparent conflicts over what is reasonable to accept—for example,

conflicts between the standard of a reasonable woman and that of a reasonable man—are conflicts that can and should be resolved by showing that one of these perspectives is more reasonable than the other, or that some still other perspective is more reasonable still. However, at least in the context of sexual harassment, this standard of what is reasonable for everyone affected to accept will accord closely with the standard of a reasonable woman, given that once women's perspectives are adequately taken into account, the contrasting perspective of a reasonable man will be seen as not so reasonable after all.[17]

In its decision in *Harris v. Forklift Systems, Inc.* (1993), the Supreme Court took an important step toward a more reasonable stance on sexual harassment. In this case, Teresa Harris worked as a rental manager at Forklift Systems. Charles Hardy, Forklift's president, said to Harris on several occasions, in the presence of other employees, "You're a woman, what do you know?" and "We need a man as the rental manager." Again in front of others, he suggested that the two of them "go to the Holiday Inn to negotiate [Harris's] raise." Hardy occasionally asked Harris and other female employees to get coins from his front pants pockets. On other occasions, he threw objects on the ground in front of Harris and other women and asked them to pick the objects up. He made sexual innuendoes about Harris's and other women's clothing. On one occasion, while Harris was arranging a deal with one of Forklift's customers, Hardy asked her in front of other employees, "What did you do, promise some [sex] Saturday night?" Soon after, Harris quit her job at Forklift.

In this case, the Supreme Court struck down the district court's requirement that in order for sexual harassment to be established Harris needed to show that Hardy's conduct had "seriously affected her psychological well-being." This was an important decision, but obviously it does not go far enough in specifying a reasonable standard for sexual harassment.

It is also important to recognize here that achieving equal opportunity in the workplace will conflict, to some degree, with freedom of speech.

Consider the case of *Robinson v. Jacksonville Shipyards*, in which a U.S. District Court upheld claims of sexual harassment on hostile work environment grounds and issued extensive remedial orders.[18] Plaintiff Lois Robinson was one of a very small number of female skilled craftworkers employed at the Shipyards—one of six women out of 832 craftworkers. Her allegations of sexual harassment centered around "the presence in the workplace of pictures of women in various stages of undress and in sexually suggestive or submissive poses, as well as remarks by male employees and supervisors which demean women." Although there was some evidence of several incidents in which the sexually suggestive pictures and comments were directed explicitly at Robinson, most were not.

In analyzing this case, Nadine Strossen, past president of the ACLU, argues that even sexually offensive speech should be protected unless it is explicitly directed at a particular individual or group of individuals.[19] Accordingly, Strossen endorses the ACLU's amicus brief in the *Robinson v. Jacksonville Shipyards* case, which considered the court's ban on the public display of sexually suggestive material without regard to whether the expressive activity was explicitly directed toward any employee as too broad. However, in light of the fact that Jacksonville Shipyards had itself banned all public displays of expressive activity except sexual materials, the amicus brief went on to favor the imposition of a workplace rule that would right the balance and permit the posting of other materials as well—materials critical of such sexual expression, as well as other political and religious or social messages that are currently banned. Such a rule would implement a "more speech" approach in an effort to counter offensive speech.

But would such a rule work? Would it succeed in protecting the basic interests of women, especially their right to equal opportunity in the workplace? It is not clear that it would be effective in male-dominated workplaces like Jacksonville Shipyards, where women are a tiny minority of the workforce, and so are likely to have their voices drowned out in the free market of expression that this rule would permit.

Nor does Strossen's distinction between offensive speech explicitly directed at a particular person or group and offensive speech that is not so directed seem all that useful, given that most sexual harassment is directed at women not because they are Jane Doe or Lois Robinson, but because they are women.

So why should we distinguish between sexual harassment that is explicitly directed at a particular woman because she is a woman, and sexual harassment that is only directed at a particular woman because it is explicitly directed at all women? Of course, sexually harassing speech can be more or less offensive, and maybe its offensiveness does correlate, to some degree, with the manner in which that harassment is directed at women. Nevertheless, what is crucial here is that the offensiveness of sexually harassing speech becomes unacceptable when it undermines the equal opportunity of women in the workplace—that is, when it imposes special burdens on women in the workplace where there are no comparable burdens on men. It is at this point that justice demands that we impose whatever limitations on sexually harassing speech are needed to secure equal opportunity in the workplace.

Most recently, in *Oncale v. Sundowner Offshore Services, Inc.* (1998) the Supreme Court expanded the scope of sexual harassment to include same-sex sexual harassment even when the harasser is not homosexual. In this case, Joseph Oncale was working for Sundowner Offshore Services on a Chevron U.S.A. oil platform in the Gulf of Mexico. He was employed as a roustabout on an eight-man crew which included John Lyons, Danny Pippen, and Brandon Johnson. Lyons, the crane operator, and Pippen, the driller, had supervisory authority. On several occasions, Oncale was forcibly subjected to sex-related, humiliating actions against him by Lyons, Pippen, and Johnson in the presence of the rest of the crew. On one occasion, the men grabbed him in the company shower and forced a bar of soap between his buttocks and threatened to rape him. When he complained to the company's safety compliance clerk, Valent Hohen, about Lyons and Pippen's behavior, Hohen told Oncale that he was also being harassed by the two men himself. So Oncale quit, asking that his pink slip reflect that he "voluntarily left due to sexual harassment and verbal abuse."

The Supreme Court, seeking to end conflicting stances taken by lower courts in same-sex sexual harassment cases (some of which found sexual harassment in cases like Oncale's, while others held that same-sex sexual harassment could not be supported by Title VII of the Civil Rights Act, and still others held that same-sex sexual harassment is only actionable when the harasser is homosexual) held in a unanimous decision that nothing in Title VII necessarily bars a claim of discrimination "because of ... sex" merely because the plaintiff and the defendant (or the person charged with acting on behalf of the defendant) are of the same sex. In these same-sex cases of sexual harassment, as in the more standard different-sex cases, special burdens are imposed on the victims of sexual harassment where there are no comparable burdens imposed on others similarly situated. In Oncale's case, sexual taunts, threats, and abuse were directed at him because his appearance and behavior was judged not to be "masculine" enough by his harassers.

It is also important to see that while sexual harassers are usually either the same-sex or different-sex harassers, they can also be what has been called "equal opportunity sexual harassers," that is, harassers who target both men and women. Moreover, some lower courts have argued that equal opportunity sexual harassment falls outside the scope of the protection of Title VII of the Civil Rights Act because such harassers do not limit their harassment to the members of one sex, and so their victims could not claim that they would not have been harassed "but for their sex." Fortunately, in the light of the Oncale decision, it should be possible to reinterpret the "because of ... sex" restriction of Title VII in such a way that all three forms of sexual harassment are prohibited. This is because what is objectionable about all three forms of sexual harassers is that they engage in degrading and abusive sexual conduct that is chosen on the basis of or "because of" the sex of their victims.

Moreover, sexual harassers, whether they be same-sex, different-sex, or equal opportunity sexual harassers, typically impose special burdens on some when there are no comparable burdens imposed on others who are similarly situated, and this frequently is part of what is wrong with sexual harassment. Yet sexual harassment, understood as engaging in degrading and abusive sexual conduct that is chosen on the basis of the victim's sex, would still be wrong even if it were inflicted on everyone within the harasser's reach. Thus, the comparative harm that frequently results from sexual harassment does not exhaust its offensiveness.

Accordingly, drawing on the foregoing discussion, I offer the following definition of sexual harassment:

> **Sexual harassment** is objectively unwelcome sexual advances, requests for sexual favors and other verbal or physical conduct of a sexual nature, which are determined to be both objectionable and actionable by the standard of what is reasonable for everyone affected to accept, and which usually, but not always, imposes a special burden on some individuals when there are no comparable burdens imposed on others who are similarly situated.

Sexual harassment so defined can clearly be of the quid pro quo or the hostile environment type, but given that these two types of sexual harassment share this common definition, their features will tend to overlap in particular cases, such as in the *Burlington Industries* case recently taken up by the Supreme Court.[20] Moreover, assuming that neither Kimberly Ellerth suffered any economic detriment from the vice president of Burlington Industries who harassed her nor Paula Jones from then-Governor Clinton, they still could have suffered from sexual harassment, according to my definition. It all depends on whether the sexual behavior to which they were allegedly exposed is both objectionable and actionable as determined by the standard of what is reasonable for everyone affected to accept. Of course, when the burdens imposed by sexual harassment are slight, they will presumably not be reasonably judged as legally actionable by everyone affected and so will not properly fall within the scope of the law.

PART II: SEXUAL HARASSMENT IN CIVILIAN AND MILITARY LIFE

As is well known, there is a high incidence of sexual harassment in both civilian and military life. In research conducted by psychologists, 50 percent of women questioned in the civilian workplace said they had been sexually harassed. According to the U.S. Merit Systems Protection Board, within the federal government, 56 percent of 8,500 female civilian workers surveyed claimed to have experienced sexual harassment. According to the *National Law Journal*, 64 percent of women in "pink-collar" jobs reported being sexually harassed and 60 percent of 3,000 women lawyers at 250 top law firms said that they had been harassed at some point in their careers. In a survey by *Working Women* magazine, 60 percent of high-ranking corporate women said they have been harassed; 33 percent more knew of others who had been.[21] Similarly, in a 1995 survey of 90,000 female soldiers, sailors, and fliers, 60 percent of the women said they had been sexually harassed. Only 47 percent of the Army women surveyed said that they believed their leaders were serious about putting a stop to sexual harassment.[22] According to another study, 66 percent of women in the military experienced at least one form of sexual harassment in the past year.[23] Another study found that 50 percent of women at the Naval Academy, 59 percent of women at the Air Force Academy, and 76 percent of women at the Military Academy experienced some form of sexual harassment at least twice a month.[24]

Yet despite the high incidence of sexual harassment in both civilian and military life, at least in the United States, there are some important differences that suggest somewhat different explanations of why sexual harassment is taking place in these contexts. The most important difference of this sort is the still widely expressed belief that women do not belong in the military. For example, 45 percent of first-year midshipmen expressed the view that women did not belong in the military and 38 percent of fourth-year midshipmen felt the same.[25] The same view can be found among the highest commanders in the U.S. military. For example, Air Force Chief General Merrill McPeak testified before the Senate Arms Services Committee in 1991 that if he had to choose between a qualified woman and a less qualified man to fill a combat role, he would go with the man. "I admit it does not make much sense, but that is the way I feel about it," McPeak responded.[26] Surely, it would be difficult to find a male CEO of a Fortune 500 company who would be willing to publicly express the same feelings as General McPeak about the suitability of employing qualified women.

There are, of course, some parallels in civilian life to this attitude toward women found in the military. For example, probably a significant number of the 863 craftworkers who worked along with the six women craftworkers at Jacksonville Shipyards in the case previously cited thought that the women did not belong there, either. But what is distinctive about the U.S. military is the degree to which the belief that women do not belong there is still widely and openly held. As another general put it,

> War is a man's work. Biological convergence on the battlefield (women serving in combat) would not only be dissatisfying in terms of what women could do, but it would be an enormous psychological distraction for the male, who wants to think that he's fighting for that woman somewhere behind, not up there in the same foxhole with him. It tramples the male ego. When you get right down to it, you have to protect the manhood of war.[27]

What I am suggesting is that this widely and openly held belief that women do not belong is distinctive of military life and helps explain the prevalence of sexual harassment there.

But what then explains the prevalence of sexual harassment in civilian life? Since at present there is no comparable widely and openly held belief that women don't belong in civilian life, or even in the civilian workplace, where women now occupy 50 percent of the labor force,[28] there must be another belief that supports the sexual harassment that occurs there. I suggest that is the belief that while women do belong in civilian life, it is still appropriate to treat them as sexual objects in ways that men are not to be treated, with the consequence that they are sexually subordinate to men. It is this belief, I think, which primarily fuels sexual harassment in civilian life. According to this belief, women are classified as having a lesser status than men and so are open to sexual harassment in ways that men are not. Of course, the belief that it is appropriate to treat women as sexual objects in ways that men are not, such that they are sexually subordinate to men, also functions in the military, but there, I think, sexual harassment is more strongly supported by the belief that women just don't belong in the military.

Obviously, so far I have been seeking to explain the sexual harassment of ostensibly heterosexual women by ostensibly heterosexual men, which is the dominant form of different-sex sexual harassment. But what about same-sex and equal opportunity sexual harassment? Same-sex and equal opportunity sexual harassment are, I believe, best explained in a way analogous to the way I have sought to explain different-sex sexual harassment. In same-sex sexual harassment, either the harassers believe that their victims do not belong in some social setting, as was true in the *Oncale* case, or they believe their victims do belong but that it is still appropriate to treat them as sexual objects in ways that others (including the harasser) are not to be treated, as is standardly the case when the same-sex harasser is homosexual.

Similarly, the same holds true of equal opportunity sexual harassers. Either equal opportunity sexual harassers believe that their particular victims do not belong in some social setting, or they believe that they do belong but that it is still appropriate to treat them as sexual objects in ways that others (including the harasser) are not to be treated.

PART III: THE NEED FOR POSITIVE AS WELL AS NEGATIVE NORMS

Suppose, then, that I am right that the high incidence of different-sex sexual harassment in civilian life is explained by the belief, held by many men and also women, that it is appropriate to treat women as sexual objects, and hence as sexually subordinate to men, and that the high incidence of different-sex sexual harassment in military life is explained by the fact that many men and women hold this same belief, but even more so by the fact that they also hold the belief that women just don't belong in the military. And suppose further that I am right that same-sex and equal opportunity sexual harassment can be similarly explained. What, then, can be done to rid society of the problem of sexual harassment? Obviously, sexual harassment law and the moral and legal theory that supports it are an attempt to rid society of this problem. This approach primarily tells men not to harass women and then tries to explain what constitutes sexual harassment. However, this approach is essentially negative. It tells men what not to do, not what to do. Of course, in most moral contexts, it is far easier to come up with negative norms than positive ones—easier to tell people what they should not be doing than what they should be doing. Nevertheless, when we can come up with appropriate positive norms, they can be helpful in ways that merely negative ones cannot. So what I am suggesting is that specifying some appropriate positive norms can help us to better rid ourselves of this social problem. Accordingly, I want to propose two positive norms for dealing with the problem of sexual harassment. The first is:

The Principle of Androgyny (or Equal Opportunity), which requires that the traits desirable and distributable in society be equally open to both women and men or, in the case of virtues, equally expected of both women and men, other things being equal.

Why this principle? We all know that when we think stereotypically about men and women in our society, we come up with different lists of desirable traits and undesirable traits, such as the following:

Men	Women
Men	**Women**
Independent	**Dependent**
Competitive	Cooperative
Aggressive, assertive	Nurturant, caring
Unemotional, stoic, detached	Emotional
Active, **violent**	**Passive**, nonviolent
Unconcerned with appearances	**Concerned with appearances (vain)**
Dominant	**Submissive**
Decisive	self-effacing
Seen as subject	**Indecisive**
Sloppy	Seen as object (of beauty or sexual attraction)
Sexually active	Neat
Reasonable, rational, logical	**Slut** or **nun**
Protective	Intuitive, **illogical**
Insensitive	In need of protection
	Sensitive

And if we assume that the traits in bold are obviously undesirable ones, then in addition to having quite different stereotypical traits associated with men and women in our society, we will also have more undesirable traits on the women's list than on the men's list. Such lists clearly reflect the gender roles and traits with which boys and girls, men and women are socialized into in society. In the past, the desirable gender traits stereotypically associated with men were thought to characterize mental health.[29] More recently, these same traits have been used to describe the successful corporate executive.[30]

Accordingly, distinctive gender roles and traits have been used in these ways to favor men over women and heterosexuals over homosexuals.

Nevertheless, there is good reason to think that the only morally defensible attitude we could take toward these gender roles and traits is expressed by the principle of androgyny (or equal opportunity). This is because for any stereotypical masculine role or trait that is desirable and distributable in society, we can always ask: Why shouldn't women who have the capability be able to fulfill that role or acquire that trait as well? And similarly, for any stereotypical feminine role or trait that is desirable and distributable in society, we can ask: Why shouldn't men who have the capability be able to fulfill that role or acquire that trait as well? And surely the answer to both of these questions is that there is no reason at all why both women and men shouldn't be able to fulfill those roles and acquire those traits. This means that the principle of androgyny (or equal opportunity) is the only norm that is morally defensible in this regard. It opposes enforced gender roles and traits in favor of requiring that the traits that are truly desirable and distributable in society be equally open to both women and men or, in the case of virtues, equally expected of both women and men, other things being equal.[31]

So characterized, the principle of androgyny (or equal opportunity) represents neither a revolt against so-called feminine virtues and traits nor their exaltation over so-called masculine virtues and traits.[32] This is because it does not view women's liberation as simply the freeing of women from the confines of traditional roles, which makes it possible for them to develop in ways heretofore reserved for men. Nor does it view women's liberation as simply the reevaluation and glorification of so-called feminine activities like housekeeping or mothering or so-called feminine modes of thinking as reflected in an ethic of caring. The first perspective ignores or devalues genuine virtues and desirable traits traditionally associated with women while the second ignores or devalues genuine virtues and desirable traits traditionally associated with men. In contrast, the principle of androgyny (or equal opportunity) seeks a broader-based norm for both women and men that combines virtues and desirable traits traditionally associated with women with virtues and desirable trails tradition-ally associated with men. For this reason, the prin-ciple of androgyny (or equal opportunity) is a common norm for both men *(andro-)* and women *(-gym)*.

So the principle of androgyny (or equal oppor-tunity), by undermining enforced gender roles and traits, will also be undermining those very social structures that give rise to the problem of sexual harassment. Discrimination "because of ... sex" will be much rarer when there is very little, possibly nothing at all, that is desirable and distributable that stereotypically characterizes men over women or homosexuals over heterosexuals. When people will have the chance to develop themselves in accord with their natural abilities and their free choices rather than socially imposed gender roles and traits, there will arise too many in-group differ-ences and too many between-group similarities either with respect to women and men or with respect to homosexuals and heterosexuals to sup-port anything like the existing practice of sexual harassment. The success of androgyny (or equal opportunity) will thus undercut the very possibility of sexual harassment.

The second positive norm I wish to propose is:

The **Principle of Desert**, which requires that we treat and evaluate people on the basis of their proper role- or job-related qualifications and excellences when this is appropriate or required.

Ideally, this principle would pick up where the principle of androgyny (or equal opportunity) left off. If we have been successful in following the principle of androgyny (or equal opportunity), then we would have been successful in developing ourselves on the basis of our natural abilities and free choices, and thus we would have had the chance to acquire the proper role- and job-related qualifications and excellences that accord with our natural abilities and free choices. Yet whether or not the principle of androgyny (or equal opportu-nity) has been followed, the principle of desert still requires that we treat and evaluate people on the basis of their proper role- or job-related

qualifications and excellences when this is appropri-ate or required.

Now if women in the military were treated and evaluated according to this norm, it would surely undermine the belief that they do not belong there and thus drastically reduce the sexual harass-ment to which that belief gives rise. What most people do not realize is that the opening up of the military to women was not embarked upon as an effort to achieve social equality. Rather, the U.S. Defense Department turned to women into order to save the All-Volunteer Force.[33] The women drawn to military service were smarter and better educated than the men. For example, according to one study, over 90 percent of women recruited had high school diplomas, compared to 63 percent of the men, and women also scored ten points higher on service exams.[34] In addition, proportionately more female than male cadets have been selected as Rhodes and Marshall scholars, and proportion-ately more women entering West Point have been National Honor Society members and high school valedictorians and salutatorians in all but two years since integration in 1976.[35] As one Defense Depart-ment report put it, "The trade-off in today's recruiting market is between a high quality female and a low quality male."[36]

Of course, women have less upper body strength, but 32 percent of women have met or exceeded the minimum male test scores and 78 percent of women have qualified for "very heavy" military jobs after six months of weight lifting, jogging with 75-pound backpacks, and performing squats with 100-pound barrels on their shoulders.[37] Women's physiology also makes them more tolerant of G-forces than men and so more suitable as fighter pilots, one of the most prestigious jobs in the military[38] Interest-ingly, in 1961 NASA invited women civilian pilots to join the race for space against the Russians, and the women began testing out extraordinarily well. One woman, Mary Wallace Funk, who held several world records in flying, had beaten John Glenn on the stress tests, bicycle analysis tests, lung power tests, and Wally Schirra on vertigo while setting a record in the bicycle endurance and isolation tests; she lasted 10 hours and 30 minutes before hallucinating. But then, without explanation, NASA canceled any further women's tests, and later in 1961, as Linda Bird Francke puts it, "Male astronauts rocketed into our history books."[39]

Of course, women are subject to pregnancy and motherhood, but statistically these have not been much of a problem in the military.[40] In fact, men suffer a higher absentee rate because of disciplinary problems and substance abuse.[41] So when women's strengths and weaknesses are taken into account compared to those of men, women turn out to be highly qualified for many combat and noncombat roles within the military and, in fact, qualified for many more combat roles than those in which they are allowed to serve. Accordingly, attending to women's proper role- or job-related qualifications should undermine the belief that they do not belong in the military and significantly reduce the sexual harassment to which that belief gives rise.

Similarly, attending to women's proper role- or job-related qualifications in civilian life should undermine the belief that it is appropriate to treat women as sexual objects in ways that men are not treated, such that they are sexually subordinate to men, as well as significantly reducing the sexual harassment to which that belief gives rise. In fact, it will simply not be possible for men to treat and evaluate women on the basis of their proper role- or job-related qualifications and excellences when this is appropriate or required and at the same time treat women as sexual objects, and hence as sexually subordinate to men. Nevertheless, treating and evaluating women on the basis of their proper role- or job-related qualifications and excellences when this is appropriate or required will sometimes require a certain degree of creative imagination. For example, Lani Guinier points out that New York City once used a height requirement favoring tall men to select for police officers. When standards changed and more women became police officers, it became apparent that often they were actually better at keeping the peace than their male counterparts in some situations. For example, in New York City housing projects, black and Puerto Rican women police officers chose to mentor rather than confront teenage boys, thereby offering

them respect, and the young men, grateful for the attention from adults, reciprocated by checking their own behavior. And women of all colors have been found to be better at defusing domestic violence situations.[42] Furthermore, when the Los Angeles Police Department wanted to do something about the problem of police abuse, the Christopher Commission Report told the city to hire more women. The commission found that women were not reluctant to use force, but that they were not nearly as likely to be involved in the use of excessive force. The women were also more communicative and more skillful at deescalating potentially violent situations. The report concluded that current approaches to policing underemphasize communication skills, sensitivity to cultural differences, and courteousness.[43] What this shows is that it is not always easy to determine what are the proper role- or job-related qualifications. Assuming that these can be determined, however, treating and evaluating women on the basis of them when this is appropriate or required should help to undermine the belief that it is appropriate to treat women as sexual objects and hence as sexually subordinate to men, and should also significantly reduce the sexual harassment to which that belief gives rise.

In the case of homosexuals, because of the ability of many to hide their status as homosexuals, they have already been able to demonstrate their ability to perform well in all sorts of social roles and jobs from which they would be excluded if they were openly homosexual. With respect to homosexuals, therefore, the principle of desert demands that they be given what they deserve—that is, that they be treated and evaluated according to their proper role- or job-related qualifications and excellences.

Now it is sometimes argued that discrimination can be justified against homosexuals because they engage in forms of sexual intercourse that are not open to procreation. But heterosexuals also engage in those same forms of sexual intercourse, and they are not similarly discriminated against. In the United States, in fact, heterosexuals who can reproduce are allowed to marry other heterosexuals who are sterile with the blessings of both church and state, even though the relationships they form are no different from homosexual relationships with respect to their openness to procreation.[44] Correctly applying the principle of desert, therefore, should put an end to this discrimination against homosexuals.

Of course, more can and should be said about how we should apply the principle of desert to treat and evaluate people on the basis of their proper role- or job-related qualifications and excellences when this is appropriate or required, but hopefully I have said enough to indicate how endorsing both this principle and the principle of androgyny (or equal opportunity) will, in fact, help to undermine the existing practice of sexual harassment.

In sum, what I have tried to do in this paper is, first, provide a definition of sexual harassment:

> **Sexual harassment** is objectively unwelcome sexual advances, requests for sexual favors, and other verbal or physical conduct of a sexual nature, which are determined to be both objectionable and actionable by the standard of what is reasonable for everyone affected to accept, and which usually, but not always, imposes a special burden on some individuals when there are no comparable burdens imposed on others who are similarly situated.

Second, I have tried to show how two fundamental beliefs help explain the high incidence of sexual harassment in military and civilian life respectively: the belief that women do not belong in the military and the belief that while women do belong in civilian life, it is still appropriate to treat them as sexual objects, and, hence, as such sexually subordinate to men. Third, I have suggested two positive norms we need to attend to, in addition to the negative one prohibiting sexual harassment, if we want to better rid society of this practice. Those norms are:

> The **Principle of Androgyny** (or **Equal Opportunity)**, which requires that the traits that are truly desirable and distributable in society be equally open to both women and men or, in the case of virtues, equally expected of both women and men, other things being equal.
>
> The **Principle of Desert**, which requires that we treat and evaluate people on the basis of their proper role- or job-related qualifications and excellences when this is appropriate or required.[45]

Clearly, sexual harassment is a very difficult and troubling problem in our society, but dealing with it also provides us with an opportunity to rethink individually and collectively the roles of men and women in our society, which is one of the most important moral tasks we face.

ENDNOTES

1. In 1991, in response to these hearings of the Senate Judicial Committee, Congress amended the Civil Rights Act to allow victims to claim monetary damages in cases involving all kinds of international discrimination, including sexual harassment. As a result, the financial stakes in harassment cases rose dramatically. (*South Bend Tribune*, April 6, 1998)
2. *Christoforou v. Ryder Truck Rental.* 668 F. Supp. 294 (S.D.N.Y. 1987).
3. *Rabidue v. Osceola Refining Co.* 805 F.2d 611, 620 (6th Cir. 1986).
4. In a recent study, Barbara A. Gutek determined that a number of factors influence whether people tend to classify certain behavior as sexual harassment. They are:

   (1) How intrusive and persistent the behavior (the more physically intrusive and persistent the behavior is, the more likely that it will be defined as sexual harassment); (2) the nature of relationship between the actors (the better the actors know each other, the less likely the behavior will be labeled sexual harassment); (3) the characteristics of the observer (men and people in authority are less likely to label behavior as sexual harassment); and (4) the inequality in the relationship (the greater the

inequality, the more likely the behavior will be labeled sexual harassment).

5. Obviously, most offers of this sort will be more subtle. If they are going to serve their purpose, however, their message must still be relatively easy to discern.

6. Even where there is legalized prostitution, such offers may still be objectively unwelcome because women would have wanted and could have reasonably expected a fairer, and thus better array of occupations open to them.

7. There is an analogous requirement of subjective consent in the law concerning rape that is similarly indefensible. See Susan Estrich, "Sex at Work," *Stanford Law Review* 43(1991), pp. 813–861.

8. Nor should one be concerned that this suggestion would undercut an appropriate presumption of innocence. This is because the presumption of innocence is weaker for civil cases than for criminal cases. Thus, in a civil law sexual harassment case, the making of an objectively unwanted sexual offer and then firing the person who refused that offer should be sufficient grounds for removing that presumption.

9. Or they could simply not fire those to whom they make the offers.

10. Barbara Gutek contends that sexual harassment is caused by the fact that women are stereotypically identified as sexual objects in ways that men are not. She notes that women are stereotypically characterized as sexy, affectionate, and attractive, whereas men are stereotypically characterized as competent and active. These stereotypes, Gutek claims, spill over into the workplace, making it difficult for women to be perceived as fellow workers rather than sex objects, and it is these perceptions that foster sexual harassment. (See Selection 3.) It would seem, therefore, that eliminating the problem of sexual harassment from our society will require breaking down these stereotypes. See my *Justice for Here and Now* (Cambridge, 1998), Chapter 4.

11. *Meritor Savings Bank v. Vinson.*

12. *Rabidue v. Osceola Refining Co.* 805 F.2d 611, 620 (6th Cir. 1986).

13. *Rabidue v. Osceola Refining Co.* 805 F.2d 611, 620 (6th Cir. 1986).

14. *Henson v. Dundee,* 682 F.2d 897, 904 (11th Cir. 1982).

15. *Ellison v. Brady,* 924 F.2d 872 (9th Cir. 1991).

16. As one of Gutek's studies shows, reasonable men and reasonable women can disagree over what constitutes sexual harassment in the workplace. In this study, 67.2 percent of men as compared to 16.8 percent of women would be flattered if asked to have sex, while 15 percent of the men and 62.8 percent of the women said they would be insulted by such an offer. (See Selection 3.)

17. Of course, men in particular will have to make a considerable effort to arrive at this most reasonable perspective, and it certainly will not be easy for them to attain it.

18. *Robinson v. Jacksonville Shipyards,* 760 F. Supp. 1486 (M. D. Fla. 1991).

19. Nadine Strossen, "Regulating Workplace Sexual Harassment and Upholding the First Amendment—Avoiding a Collision," *Villanova Law Review* 37 (1992), pp. 211–228.

20. It does seem reasonable to grant, however, that there is a stronger presumption of employee liability with respect to *quid pro quo* sexual harassment than hostile environment sexual harassment, if only because a company is normally presumed to be more responsible for those who occupy positions of power within it.

21. Cherly Gomez-Preston, *When No Means No* (New York: Carol Publishing Co., 1993), pp. 35–36. Ellen Bravo and Ellen Cassedy, *The 9 to 5 Guide to Combating Sexual Harassment* (New York: John Wiley and Sons, 1992), pp. 4–5: The problem is international as well as national. A three-year study of women in Estonia, Finland, Sweden, and the Soviet Union showed that nearly 50 percent of all working women experience sexual harassment. A survey released in 1991 by the Santama Group to Consider Sexual Harassment at Work showed that about 70 percent of Japanese women say they have experienced some type of sexual harassment on the job. See Susan Webb, *Step Forward* (New York: Master Media, 1991), pp. xiv, xvii.

22. *New York Times,* November 11, 1996, February 4, 1997.

23. Linda Bird Francke, *Ground Zero* (New York: Simon and Schuster, 1997), p. 157.

24. Ibid., p. 191.

25. Ibid., p. 187.

26. Ibid., p. 232.

27. Marysia Zalewski and Jane Parpart, *The "Man" Question in International Relations* (Boulder: Westview, 1998), p. 1.

28. Time, March 23, 1998, p. 49.

29. Beverly Walker, "Psychology and Feminism—If You Can't Beat Them, Join Them," in Dale Spender, ed., *Men's Studies Modified* (Oxford: Pergamon Press, 1981), pp. 112–114.

30. Debra Renee Kaufman, "Professional Women: How Real Are the Recent Gains?" in Janet A. Kourany, James P. Sterba and Rosemarie Tong, eds., *Feminist Philosophies*, 2nd ed. (Upper Saddle River: Prentice-Hall, 1999), pp. 189–202.

31. To distinguish traits of character that are virtues from those that are just desirable traits, we could define the class of virtues as those desirable and distributable traits that can be reasonably expected of both women and men. Admittedly, this is a restrictive use of the term *virtue*. In normal usage, the term *virtue* is almost synonymous with the term *desirable trait*. But there is good reason to focus on those desirable traits that can be justifiably inculcated in both women and men, and so for our purposes let us refer to this class of desirable traits as virtues.

32. For a valuable discussion and critique of these two viewpoints, see Iris Young, "Humanism, Gynocentrism, and Feminist Politics," *Women's Studies International Forum* 8 (1985), pp. 173–183.

33. Francke, *Ground Zero*, p. 16.

34. Ibid.

35. Ibid., p. 198.

36. Ibid., p. 16.

37. Ibid., p. 248.

38. Ibid., p. 236.

39. Ibid., p. 226.

40. Ibid., p. 18.

41. Ibid., p. 16.

42. Lani Guinier, *Becoming (Zentlemen)* (Boston: Beacon, 1997), pp. 18–19.

43. *Report of the Independent Commission of the Los Angeles Police Department* (Christopher Commission, 1991).

44. John Corvino, *Same Sex* (Lanham: Rowman & Littlefield, 1997), p. 6.

45. These two norms, of course, are not the only positive norms that are relevant to sexual harassment cases, although they are probably the most important ones. Other norms would provide guidance as to how romantic overtures should be made so as to avoid sexual harassment.

51

Harris v. Forklift Systems, Inc.

Supreme Court of the United States

The issue before the Supreme Court was whether a hostile work environment under Title VII of the Civil Rights Act of 1964 must cause serious harm to a reasonable person's psychological well-being. The Court unanimously ruled that behavior that fell short of seriously harming a reasonable person's psychological well-being could still be sexual harassment if in other ways it unreasonably interfered with a person's work environment.

■ ■ ■ In this case we consider the definition of a discriminatorily "abusive work environment" (also known as a "hostile work environment") under Title VII of the Civil Rights Act of 1964.

Teresa Harris worked as a manager at Forklift Systems, Inc., an equipment rental company, from April 1985 until October 1987. Charles Hardy was Forklift's president.

The magistrate found that, throughout Harris's time at Forklift, Hardy often insulted her because of her gender and often made her the target of unwanted sexual innuendos. Hardy told Harris on several occasions, in the presence of other employees, "You're a woman, what do you know" and "We need a man as the rental manager"; at least once, he told her she was "a dumb ass woman." Again in front of others, he suggested that the two of them "go to the Holiday Inn to negotiate [Harris's] raise." Hardy occasionally asked Harris and other female employees to get coins from his front pants pocket. He threw objects on the ground in front of Harris and other women, and asked them to pick the objects up. He made sexual innuendos about Harris's and other women's clothing.

In mid–August 1987, Harris complained to Hardy about his conduct. Hardy said he was surprised that Harris was offended, claimed he was only joking, and apologized. He also promised he would stop, and based on this assurance Harris stayed on the job. But in early September, Hardy began anew: While Harris was arranging a deal with one of Forklift's customers, he asked her, again in front of other employees, "What did you do, promise the guy ... some [sex] Saturday night?" On October 1, Harris collected her paycheck and quit.

Harris then sued Forklift, claiming that Hardy's conduct had created an abusive work environment for her because of her gender. The United States District Court for the Middle District of Tennessee, adopting the report and recommendation of the Magistrate, found this to be "a close case," but held that Hardy's conduct did not create an abusive environment. The court found that some of Hardy's comments "offended [Harris], and would offend the reasonable woman," but that they were not

> so severe as to be expected to seriously affect [Harris's] psychological well-being. A reasonable woman manager under like circumstances would have been offended by Hardy, but his conduct would not have risen to the level of interfering with that person's work performance.
>
> Neither do I believe that [Harris] was subjectively so offended that she suffered injury.... Although Hardy may at times have genuinely offended [Harris], I do not

believe that he created a working environment so poisoned as to be intimidating or abusive to [Harris].

In focusing on the employee's psychological well-being, the District Court was following Circuit precedent.

We granted certiorari to resolve a conflict among the Circuits on whether conduct, to be actionable as "abusive work environment" harassment (no *quid pro quo* harassment issue is present here), must "seriously affect [an employee's] psychological well-being" or lead the plaintiff to "suffe[r] injury."

Title VII of the Civil Rights Act of 1964 makes it "an unlawful employment practice for an employer ... to discriminate against any individual with respect to his compensation, terms, conditions, or privileges of employment, because of such individual's race, color, religion, sex, or national origin." As we made clear in *Meritor Savings Bank v. Vinson* (1986), this language "is not limited to 'economic' or 'tangible' discrimination. The phrase 'terms, conditions, or privileges of employment' evinces a congressional intent 'to strike at the entire spectrum of disparate treatment of men and women' in employment" which includes requiring people to work in a discriminatorily hostile or abusive environment. When the workplace is permeated with "discriminatory intimidation, ridicule, and insult," that is "sufficiently severe or pervasive to alter the conditions of the victim's employment and create an abusive working environment," Title VII is violated.

This standard, which we reaffirm today, takes a middle path between making actionable any conduct that is merely offensive and requiring the conduct to cause a tangible psychological injury. As we pointed out in *Meritor*, "mere utterance of an ... epithet which engenders offensive feelings in an employee" does not sufficiently affect the conditions of employment to implicate Title VII. Conduct that is not severe or pervasive enough to create an objectively hostile or abusive work environment—an environment that a reasonable person would find hostile or abusive—is beyond Title VII's purview. Likewise, if the victim does not subjectively perceive the environment to be abusive, the conduct has not actually altered the conditions of the victim's employment, and there is no Title VII violation.

But Title VII comes into play before the harassing conduct leads to a nervous breakdown. A discriminatorily abusive work environment, even one that does not seriously affect employees' psychological well-being, can and often will detract from employees' job performance, discourage employees from remaining on the job, or keep them from advancing in their careers. Moreover, even without regard to these tangible effects, the very fact that the discriminatory conduct was so severe or pervasive that it created a work environment abusive to employees because of their race, gender, religion, or national origin offends Title VII's broad rule of workplace equality. The appalling conduct alleged in *Meritor*, and the reference in that case to environments "'so heavily polluted with discrimination as to destroy completely the emotional and psychological stability of minority group workers,'" merely present some especially egregious examples of harassment. They do not mark the boundary of what is actionable.

We therefore believe the District Court erred in relying on whether the conduct "seriously affect[ed] plaintiff's psychological well-being" or led her to "suffe[r] injury." Such an inquiry may needlessly focus the fact finder's attention on concrete psychological harm, an element Title VII does not require. Certainly Title VII bars conduct that would seriously affect a reasonable person's psychological well-being, but the statute is not limited to such conduct. So long as the environment would reasonably be perceived, and is perceived, as hostile or abusive, there is no need for it also to be psychologically injurious.

This is not, and by its nature cannot be, a mathematically precise test. We need not answer today all the potential questions it raises, nor specifically address the EEOC's new regulations on this subject. But we can say that whether an environment is "hostile" or "abusive" can be determined only by looking at all the circumstances. These may include the frequency of the discriminatory conduct; its severity; whether it is physically threatening or humiliating, or a mere offensive utterance; and whether it unreasonably interferes with an employee's work performance. The effect on the employee's psychological well-being is, of course, relevant to determining whether the plaintiff actually found the environment abusive. But while psychological harm, like any other relevant factor, may be taken into account, no single factor is required.

Forklift, while conceding that a requirement that the conduct seriously affect psychological well-being is unfounded, argues that the District Court nonetheless correctly applied the *Meritor* standard. We disagree. Though the District Court did conclude that the work environment was not "intimidating or abusive to [Harris]," it did so only after finding that the conduct was not "so severe as to be expected to seriously affect plaintiff's psychological well-being," and that Harris was not "subjectively so offended that she suffered injury." The District Court's application of these incorrect standards may well have influenced its ultimate conclusion, especially given that the court found this to be a "close case."

We therefore reverse the judgment of the Court of Appeals, and remand the case for further proceedings consistent with this opinion.

SUGGESTIONS FOR FURTHER READING

Bouchard, Elizabeth. *Everything You Need to Know about Sexual Harassment.* New York: Rosen, 1997.

Bravo, Ellen, and Ellen Cassedy. *The 9 to 5 Guide to Combating Sexual Harassment.* New York: Wiley, 1992.

Copeland, Lois, and Leslie R. Wolfe. *Violence against Women as Bias Motivated Hate Crime: Defining the Issues.* Washington, DC: Center for Women Policy Studies, 1991.

Dooling, Richard. *Blue Streak: Swearing, Free Speech, and Sexual Harassment.* New York: Random House, 1996.

Dziech, Billie Wright, and Linda Weiner. *The Lecherous Professor: Sexual Harassment on Campus.* Champaign: University of Illinois Press, 1992.

Gerdes, Louise I., ed. *Sexual Harassment: Current Controversies.* San Diego, CA: Greenhaven Press, 1999.

Hill, Anita. *Speaking Truth to Power.* New York: Doubleday, 1997.

Larkin, June. *Sexual Harassment: High School Girls Speak Out.* Toronto: Second Story Press, 1994.

McKenzie, Richard B. "The Thomas/Hill Hearings: A New Legal Harassment." *The Freeman,* January 1992. Available from the Foundation for Economic Education, Irvington-on-Hudson, NY 10533.

MacKinnon, Catharine A. *Sexual Harassment of Working Women: A Case of Sex Discrimination.* New Haven: Yale University Press, 1979.

Morris, Celia. *Bearing Witness: Sexual Harassment, Citizenship, Government.* New York: Little, Brown, 1994.

Paludi, Michele A., ed. *Sexual Harassment on College Campuses: Abusing the Ivory Power.* Albany: State University of New York Press, 1996.

Patai, Daphne, *Heterophobia: Sexual Harassment and the Future of Feminism.* Lanham, MD: Rowman & Littlefield, 1999.

Phelps, Timothy M., and Helen Winternitz. *Capital Games: Clarence Thomas, Anita Hill, and the Story of a Supreme Court Nomination.* Westport, CT: Hyperion, 1992.

Repa, Barbara Kate, and William Petrocelli. *Sexual Harassment on the Job.* Berkeley, CA: Nolo Press, 1992.

Riggs, Robert, Patricia Murrell, and JoAnn Cutting. *Sexual Harassment in Higher Education.* Washington, DC: George Washington University Press, 1993.

Saguy, Abigail, What is Sexual Harassment?: From Capitol Hill to the Sorbonne. Berkeley: University of California Press, 2003.

Stein, Laura W. *Sexual Harassment in America.* Westport, CT: Greenwood Publishing Group, 1999.

Sterba, James P., and Le Moncheck, Linda. *Sexual Harassment: Issues and Answers.* New York: Oxford University Press, 2001.

Sunrall, Amber Coverdale. *Sexual Harassment: Women Speak Out.* Freedom, CA: Crossing Press, 1992.

Webb, Susan L. *Step Forward: Sexual Harassment in the Workplace: What You Need to Know!* 2d. ed. New York: MasterMedia, 1997.

✳

Gay and Lesbian Rights

INTRODUCTION

Basic Concepts

The prohibition of homosexuality has ancient roots, but its enforcement has usually been haphazard at best because acts between consenting adults make it hard to find a complainant. Even so, 24 states and the District of Columbia still have statutes prohibiting homosexual acts. Penalties range from three months in prison or one year's probation to life imprisonment.

Moreover, these statutes prohibit *sodomy*, which involves more than just homosexuals. For example, the Georgia statute whose constitutionality was upheld by the Supreme Court in *Bowers v. Hardwick* holds that "a person commits the offense of sodomy when he performs or submits to any sexual act involving the sex organs of one person and the mouth or anus of another." Sodomy is defined broadly here because the main complaint against homosexual acts—that they are unnatural—also applies to a range of other acts. More specifically, the complaint applies to oral and anal intercourse between heterosexuals, masturbation, and bestiality, as well as homosexual acts.

Now we must understand what is considered unnatural about these acts. One sense of *natural* refers to what is found in nature as contrasted with what is artificial or the product of human artifice. In this sense, homosexuality would seem natural: It is found in virtually every human society. But even if homosexuality is understood to be a product of a certain type of upbringing or socialization and hence artificial, that would hardly seem grounds for condemning it: Much human behavior has a similar origin.

Another sense of natural refers to what is common or statistically normal as contrasted with what is uncommon or statistically abnormal. In this sense, homosexuality would not be natural: Most people are not homosexuals, even though one study found that about half of all American males have engaged in homosexual acts at some time in their lives. But being unnatural in this sense could not be grounds for condemning homosexuality because many traits we most value in people are also statistically abnormal and, hence, unnatural in this sense.

Still another sense of natural refers to a thing's proper function; it is this sense of natural that is frequently used to condemn homosexuality. If we maintain that the proper function of human sexual organs is simply procreation, then any use of those organs for any other purpose would be unnatural. Thus, homosexuality, contraception, masturbation, and bestiality would all be unnatural. But clearly the proper function of human sexual organs is not limited to procreation. These organs are also used to express love and provide pleasure for oneself and others. Given that our sexual organs can be properly used for these other purposes, we would need to argue that every use of these organs must serve their procreative function if we are to be able to condemn homosexuality. No nontheologically based argument has succeeded in establishing this conclusion.[1] Moreover, once we grant that, for example, contraception and masturbation can be morally permissible, no ground seems to be left, based on the proper functioning of our sexual organs, for denying that homosexuality can be morally permissible as well.

Alternative Views

In Selection 52, John Finnis sets out the following argument against homosexuality:

1. In masturbating as in being masturbated or sodomized, one disintegrates oneself in two ways: (a) by treating one's body as an instrument for one's own gratification and (b) by making one's choosing self the quasi-slave of one's experiencing self.

2. By so doing one is not actualizing or experiencing a common good.

3. Marriage with its twofold goals of procreation and friendship is a common good.

4. Marriage is a common good that can be experienced in the orgasmic union of the reproductive organs of a man and a woman united in commitment to that good.

5. This common good makes husband and wife a biological and a personal unit.

6. The common good of friends who are not and cannot be married has nothing to do with procreation and hence their procreative organs cannot make them a biological and a personal unit.

7. Hence, homosexual acts cannot actualize the common good of friendship.

8. Nor is such conduct the participation in some intelligible good because it is not focused on the exercise of a skill but rather on the satisfaction of a desire for one's own pleasure.

9. Such conduct is also deeply hostile to the self-understanding of those members of the community who are committed to real marriage with its shared responsibilities.

10. For this reason, a political community is justified in denying the validity of such conduct, and in taking appropriate steps to discourage it.

The thrust of Finnis's argument is directed not only at homosexual acts, but also at heterosexual masturbation and sodomy, bestiality, and contraception. For Finnis, all of these acts are wrong for the same reason. So, if we accept Finnis's argument, we cannot consistently allow for the moral permissibility of some of these acts but not of others; the moral permissibility of all of these acts must stand or fall together.

In Selection 53, Martha Nussbaum criticizes Finnis for assuming without argument that the purpose of homosexual acts is always the instrumental use of another person's body for one's own gratification. She contends that both the past and the present provide ample evidence against this assumption. Nussbaum also criticizes Finnis for assuming without argument that the only type of community that a sexual relationship can create is a procreative community. Again, she contends that both, the past and the present provide ample evidence against this assumption.

In Selection 54, Maggie Gallagher argues that children are helped best when they grow up in families headed by two biological parents in a low-conflict marriage. Hence, she argues societies should limit marriage to a man and a woman as a means of promoting this best outcome for children. She argues that marriage between a man and a women is a natural family, not something we can make or unmake by legislation. In this, she thinks it resembles private property, which is not something governments can make either. But private property institutions can take many forms only some of which are morally justified. And the same would seem to hold about marriage. We still need to know what form or forms are morally justified.

In Selection 55, John Corvino points out that there have to be missing steps in Gallagher's argument against same-sex marriages, because there are a lot of marriages we currently legally sanction that do not result in children living with their two biological parents in low-conflict.

Practical Applications

An important Supreme Court case dealing with homosexuality is *Bowers v. Hardwick* (1986). In this case, the issue before the Court was whether the Georgia sodomy statute violates the federal Constitution. In delivering the opinion of the court, Justice White argues that the statute does

not because the Constitution does not confer a fundamental right on homosexuals to engage in sodomy. While in previous cases, the Constitution was interpreted to confer a right to decide whether or not to beget or bear a child and a right not to be convicted for possessing and reading obscene material in the privacy of one's home, White argues that the Constitution cannot analogously be interpreted to confer a fundamental right on homosexuals to engage in sodomy. Justice Burger concurs, stressing the ancient roots of sodomy statutes. Justice Blackmun, joined by Justices Brennan and Marshall, argues that notwithstanding the ancient roots of prohibitions against homosexuality, a right to be let alone that is the underpinning of previous court decisions justifies in this case a right to engage in sodomy at least in the privacy of one's home.

In this case, the majority of the Supreme Court seemed to reach its conclusion by interpreting previous decisions in an excessively literal manner in much the same way that the majority of the court ruled in *Olmstead v. United States* (1928) that warrantless wiretapping did not violate Fourth Amendment prohibitions against search and seizure because the framers of the amendment were not explicitly prohibiting this method of obtaining incriminating evidence. Just as it later repudiated its ruling in *Olmstead*, the Supreme Court in *Romer v. Evans* (1996), recently struck down Colorado's Amendment 2 for imposing a disability on homosexuals—a decision that appears to be at least a partial repudiation of *Bowers v. Hardwick*.

In one of the most important court decisions on gay and lesbian rights to date, the New York State legislature adopted the Marriage Equality Act (Selection 56) and Governor Andrew Cuomo signed it into law in 2011.

The Marriage Equality Act amends New York's Domestic Relations Law to state:

A marriage that is otherwise valid shall be valid regardless of whether the parties to the marriage are of the same or different sex

No government treatment or legal status, effect, right, benefit, privilege, protection or responsibility relating to marriage shall differ based on the parties to the marriage being the same sex or a different sex

All relevant gender-specific language set forth in or referenced by New York law shall be construed in a gender-neutral manner

No application for a marriage license shall be denied on the ground that the parties are of the same or a different sex.

In the summer of 2003, the U.S. Supreme Court in *Lawrence v. Texas* (Selection 57) overturned *Bower v. Harwick*, ruling that the right to liberty under the due process clause gives consenting adults the right to engage in private conduct without government intervention. This is an extraordinary victory for gay and lesbian rights. Conservatives claim, however, that the decision will open the door to the legalization of bigamy, adult incest, polygamy, and prostitution.

It is also important to note that adherents of both of our political ideals generally tend to favor granting homosexuals the same rights as heterosexuals. Libertarians favor this view because to do otherwise would deny homosexuals important basic liberties. Welfare liberals favor this view because to do otherwise would deny homosexuals fundamental fairness.

ENDNOTE

1. Clearly if there is to be freedom of religion, a nontheologically based argument is needed here.

52

Homosexual Conduct Is Wrong

JOHN FINNIS

John Finnis argues against homosexuality on the grounds that it involves treating one's body as an instrument for one's own gratification rather than actualizing or experiencing a common good. He also argues that because homosexual conduct is deeply hostile to the self-understanding of those members of the community who are committed to real marriage with its shared responsibilities, a political community is justified in taking appropriate steps to discourage it.

The underlying thought is on the following lines. In masturbating, as in being masturbated or sodomized, one's body is treated as instrumental for the securing of the experiential satisfaction of the conscious self. Thus one disintegrates oneself in two ways, (1) by treating one's body as a mere instrument of the consciously operating self, and (2) by making one's choosing self the quasi-slave of the experiencing self which is demanding gratification. The worthlessness of the gratification, and the disintegration of oneself, are both the result of the fact that, in these sorts of behavior, one's conduct is not the actualizing and experiencing of a real common good. Marriage, with its double blessing—procreation and friendship—is a real common good. Moreover, it is a common good that can be both actualized and experienced in the orgasmic union of the reproductive organs of a man and a woman united in commitment to that good. Conjugal sexual activity, and—as Plato and Aristotle and Plutarch and Kant all argue—*only* conjugal activity is free from the shamefulness of instrumentalization that is found in masturbating and in being masturbated or sodomized.

It is also important to note that adherents of all three of our political ideals generally tend to favor granting homosexuals the same rights as heterosexuals. Libertarians favor this view because to do otherwise would deny homosexuals important basic liberties. Welfare liberals favor this view because to do otherwise would deny homosexuals fundamental fairness. Socialists favor this view because to do otherwise would deny homosexuals basic equality.

At the very heart of the reflections of Plato, Xenophon, Aristotle, Musonius Rufus, and Plutarch on the homoerotic culture around them is the very deliberate and careful judgment that homosexual *conduct* (and indeed all extramarital sexual gratification) is radically incapable of participating in, or actualizing, the common good of friendship. Friends who engage in such conduct are following a natural impulse and doubtless often wish their genital conduct to be an intimate expression of their mutual affection. But they are deceiving themselves. The attempt to express affection by orgasmic nonmarital sex is the pursuit of an illusion. The orgasmic union of the reproductive organs of husband and wife really unites them biologically (and their biological reality is part of, not merely an instrument of, their *personal* reality); that orgasmic union therefore can actualize and allow

Reprinted from the legal deposition from the trial in Colorado on the constitutionality of Amendment 2.

them to experience their real common good—their marriage with the two goods, children and friendship, which are the parts of its wholeness as an intelligible common good. But the common good of friends who are not and cannot be married (man and man, man and boy, woman and woman) has nothing to do with their having children by each other, and their reproductive organs cannot make them a biological (and therefore a personal) unit. So their genital acts together cannot do what they may hope and imagine.

In giving their considered judgment that homosexual conduct cannot actualize the good of friendship, Plato and the many philosophers who followed him intimate an answer to the questions why it should be considered shameful to use, or allow another to use, one's body to give pleasure, and why this use of one's body differs from one's bodily participation in countless other activities (e.g., games) in which one takes and/or gets pleasure. Their response is that pleasure is indeed a good, when it is the experienced aspect of one's participation in some intelligible good, such as a task going well, or a game or a dance or a meal or a reunion. Of course, the activation of sexual organs with a view to the pleasures of orgasm is sometimes spoken of as if it were a game. But it differs from real games in that its point is not the exercise of skill; rather, this activation of reproductive organs is focused upon the body precisely as a source of pleasure for one's consciousness. So this is a "use of the body" in a strongly different sense of "use." The body now is functioning not in the way one, as a bodily person, acts to instantiate some other intelligible good, but precisely as providing a service to one's consciousness, to satisfy one's desire for satisfaction.

This disintegrity is much more obvious when masturbation is solitary. Friends are tempted to think that pleasuring each other by some forms of mutual masturbation could be an instantiation or actualization or promotion of their friendship. But that line of thought overlooks the fact that if their friendship is not marital ... activation of their reproductive organs cannot be, in reality, an instantiation or actualization of their friendship's common good.

In reality, whatever the generous hopes and dreams with which the loving partners surround their use of their genitals, *that use* cannot express more than is expressed if two strangers engage in genital activity to give each other orgasm, or a prostitute pleasures a client, or a man pleasures himself. Hence, Plato's judgment, at the decisive moment of the *Gorgias*, that there is no important distinction in essential moral worthlessness between solitary masturbation, being sodomized as a prostitute and being sodomized for the pleasure of it....

Societies such as classical Athens and contemporary England (and virtually every other) draw a distinction between behavior found merely (perhaps extremely) offensive (such as eating excrement) and behavior to be repudiated as destructive of human character and relationships. Copulation of humans with animals is repudiated because it treats human sexual activity and satisfaction as something appropriately sought in a manner that, like the coupling of animals, is divorced from the expressing of an intelligible common good—and so treats human bodily life, in one of its most intense activities, as merely animal. The deliberate genital coupling of persons of the same sex is repudiated for a very similar reason. It is not simply that it is sterile and disposes the participants to an abdication of responsibility for the future of humankind. Nor is it simply that it cannot *really* actualize the mutual devotion that some homosexual persons hope to manifest and experience by it; nor merely that it harms the personalities of its participants by its disintegrative manipulation of different parts of their one personal reality. It is also that it treats human sexual capacities in a way that is deeply hostile to the self-understanding of those members of the community who are willing to commit themselves to real marriage (even one that happens to be sterile) in the understanding that its sexual joys are not mere instruments or accompaniments to, or mere compensation for the accomplishments of marriage's responsibilities, but rather are the *actualizing and experiencing* of the intelligent commitment to share in those responsibilities....

This pattern of judgment, both widespread and sound, concludes as follows. Homosexual orientation—the deliberate willingness to promote and engage in homosexual acts—is a standing denial of the intrinsic aptness of sexual intercourse to actualize and give expression to the exclusiveness and open-ended commitment of marriage as something good in itself. All who accept that homosexual acts can be a humanly appropriate use of sexual capacities must, if consistent, regard sexual capacities, organs, and acts as instruments to be put to whatever suits the purposes of the individual "self" who has them. Such an acceptance is commonly (and in my opinion rightly) judged to be an active threat to the stability of existing and future marriages; it makes nonsense, for example, of the view that adultery is per se (and not merely because it may involve deception), and in an important way, inconsistent with conjugal love. A political community that judges that the stability and educative generosity of family life is of fundamental importance to the community's present and future can rightly judge that it has a compelling interest in denying that homosexual conduct is a valid, humanly acceptable choice and form of life, and in doing whatever it properly can, as a community with uniquely wide but still subsidiary functions, to discourage such conduct.

53

Homosexual Conduct Is Not Wrong

MARTHA NUSSBAUM

Martha Nussbaum criticizes John Finnis for assuming without argument that the purpose of homosexual acts is always the instrumental use of another person's body for one's own gratification. Nussbaum also criticizes Finnis for assuming without argument that the only type of community that a sexual relationship can create is a procreative community.

Finnis's arguments against homosexuality set themselves in a tradition of "natural law" argumentation that derives from ancient Greek traditions. The term "law of nature" was first used by Plato in his *Gorgias*. The approach is further developed by Aristotle, and, above all, by the Greek and Roman Stoics, who are usually considered to be the founders of natural law argumentation in the modern legal tradition, through their influence on Roman law. This being so, it is worth looking to see whether those traditions did in fact use "natural law" arguments to rule homosexual conduct morally or legally substandard.

Plato's dialogues contain several extremely moving celebrations of male–male love, and judge this form of love to be, on the whole, superior to male–female love because of its potential for spirituality and friendship. The *Symposium* contains a series of speeches, each expressing conventional views about this subject that Plato depicts in an appealing light. The speech by Phaedrus points to the military advantages derived by including homosexual couples in a fighting force: Because of their intense love, each will fight better, wishing to show himself in the best light before his lover. The speech of Pausanias criticizes males who seek physical pleasure alone in their homosexual relationships, and praises those who seek in sex deeper

spiritual communication. Pausanias mentions that tyrants will sometimes promulgate the view that same-sex relations are shameful in order to discourage the kind of community of dedication to political liberty that such relations foster. The speech of Aristophanes holds that all human beings are divided halves of formerly whole beings, and that sexual desire is the pursuit of one's lost other half; he points out that the superior people in any society are those whose lost "other half" is of the same sex—especially the male–male pairs—since these are likely to be the strongest and most warlike and civically minded people. Finally, Socrates's speech recounts a process of religious-mystical education in which male–male love plays a central guiding role and is a primary source of insight and inspiration into the nature of the good and beautiful.

Plato's *Phaedrus* contains a closely related praise of the intellectual, political, and spiritual benefits of a life centered around male–male love. Plato says that the highest form of human life is one in which a male pursues "the love of a young man along with philosophy," and is transported by passionate desire. He describes the experience of falling in love with another male in moving terms, and defends relationships that are mutual and reciprocal over relationships that are one-sided. He depicts his pairs of lovers as spending their life together in the

Reprinted from the legal deposition from the trial in Colorado on the constitutionality of Amendment 2.

pursuit of intellectual and spiritual activities, combined with political participation. (Although no marriages for these lovers are mentioned, it was the view of the time that this form of life does not prevent its participants from having a wife at home, whom they saw only rarely and for procreative purposes.)

Aristotle speaks far less about sexual love than does Plato, but it is evident that he too finds in male-male relationships the potential for the highest form of friendship, a friendship based on mutual well-wishing and mutual awareness of good character and good aims. He does not find this potential in male-female relationships, since he holds that females are incapable of good character. Like Pausanias in Plato's *Symposium*, Aristotle is critical of relationships that are superficial and concerned only with bodily pleasure; but he finds in male-male relationships—including many that begin in this way—the potential for much richer developments.

The ideal city of the Greek Stoics was built around the idea of pairs of male lovers whose bonds gave the city rich sources of motivation for virtue. Although the Stoics wished their "wise man" to eliminate most passions from his life, they encouraged him to foster a type of erotic love that they defined as "the attempt to form a friendship inspired by the perceived beauty of young men in their prime." They held that this love, unlike other passions, was supportive of virtue and philosophical activity.

Furthermore, Finnis's argument ... against homosexuality is a bad moral argument by any standard, secular or theological. First of all, it assumes that the purpose of a homosexual act is always or usually casual bodily pleasure and the instrumental use of another person for one's own gratification. But this is a false premise, easily disproved by the long historical tradition I have described and by the contemporary lives of real men and women. Finnis offers no evidence for this premise, or for the equally false idea that procreative relations cannot be selfish and manipulative. Second, having argued that a relationship is better if it seeks not casual pleasure but the creation of a community, he then assumes without argument that the only sort of community a sexual relationship can create is a "procreative community." This is, of course, plainly false. A sexual relationship may create, quite apart from the possibility of procreation, a community of love and friendship, which no religious tradition would deny to be important human goods. Indeed, in many moral traditions, including those of Plato and Aristotle, the procreative community is ranked beneath other communities created by sex, since it is thought that the procreative community will probably not be based on the best sort of friendship and the deepest spiritual concerns. That may not be true in a culture that values women more highly than ancient Greek culture did; but the possibility of love and friendship between individuals of the same sex has not been removed by these historical changes.

54

What Marriage Is For

MAGGIE GALLAGHER

Maggie Gallagher argues that children are helped best when they grow up in families headed by two biological parents within a low-conflict marriage. Hence, she argues societies should limit marriage to a man and a woman as a means of promoting this best outcome for children.

The timing could not be worse for a large national fight about the core meaning of marriage.

Marriage is in crisis, as everyone knows: High rates of divorce and illegitimacy have eroded marriage norms and created millions of fatherless children, whole neighborhoods where lifelong marriage is no longer customary, driving up poverty, crime, teen pregnancy, welfare dependency, drug abuse, and mental and physical health problems. And yet, until just before the advent of the U.S. gay marriage debate, amid the broader negative trends, at least some signs pointed to a modest but significant recovery.

Around 2000, divorce rates appeared to have declined a little from historic highs; illegitimacy rates, after doubling every decade from 1960 to 1990, appeared to be beginning to leveled off, albeit at a high level (33 percent of American births are to unmarried women); teen pregnancy and sexual activity are down; the proportion of homemaking mothers is up; marital fertility appears to be on the rise. Research suggests that married adults are more committed to marital permanence than they were twenty years ago. A new generation of children of divorce appears on the brink of making a commitment to lifelong marriage. In 1977, 55 percent of American teenagers thought a divorce should be harder to get; in 2001, 75 percent did.

In the waning days of the last century, a new marriage movement—a distinctively American phenomenon—was born. The scholarly consensus on the importance of marriage has broadened and deepened; it is now the conventional wisdom among child welfare organizations. As a Child Trends research brief summed up: "Research clearly demonstrates that family structure matters for children, and the family structure that helps children the most is a family headed by two biological parents in a low-conflict marriage. Children in single-parent families, children born to unmarried mothers, and children in stepfamilies or cohabiting relationships face higher risks of poor outcomes.... There is thus value for children in promoting strong, stable marriages between biological parents."

What has gay marriage done and what will it likely continue to do to this incipient recovery of marriage as a public idea? Will same-sex marriage help or hurt marriage as a social institution?

Why should it do either, some may ask? How can Bill and Bob's marriage hurt Mary and Joe? In an exchange with me in the book "Marriage and Same Sex Unions: A Debate," Evan Wolfson, chief legal strategist for same-sex marriage in the Hawaii case, Baer v. Lewin, argues there is "enough marriage to share." What counts, he says, "is not family structure, but the quality of dedication, commitment, self-sacrifice, and love in the household."

Family structure does not count and anyway marriage has little or nothing to do with children. That is an assumption widely shared and repeatedly expressed both by gay marriage advocates and by courts who have accepted arguments that "marriage equality" requires gay marriage.[1]

Do children need mothers and fathers, or will any sort of family do equally well? When the sexual desires of adults clash with the interests of children, which carries more weight, socially and legally?

These are the questions that same-sex marriage raises. The debate over gay marriage is taking place in the context of a broader debate over marriage, its public purpose, meaning and relevance. The answers we give will affect not only gay and lesbian families, but marriage as a whole.

In ordering gay marriage on June 10, 2003, the highest court in Ontario, Canada, explicitly endorsed a brand new vision of marriage along the lines Wolfson suggests: "Marriage is, without dispute, one of the most significant forms of personal relationships.... Through the institution of marriage, individuals can publicly express their love and commitment to each other. Through this institution, society publicly recognizes expressions of love and commitment between individuals, granting them respect and legitimacy as a couple."

The Ontario court views marriage as a kind of Good Housekeeping Seal of Approval that government stamps on certain registered intimacies because, well, for no particular reason the court can articulate except that society likes to recognize expressions of love and commitment. In this view, endorsement of gay marriage is a no-brainer, for nothing really important rides on whether anyone gets married or stays married. Marriage is merely individual expressive conduct, and there is no obvious reason why some individual's expression of gay love should hurt other individual's expressions of non-gay love.

Why only two people? Why sexual exclusivity? Why a sexual union at all? The court articulates no clear reason for the longstanding boundaries of marriage in our law, our culture and our society, because it is bowing to the urgent imperative: whatever the rationale, gay couples must be included.

There is, however, a different view—indeed, a view that is radically opposed to this idea that marriage is a form of speech involving primarily the expression of individual commitment. In this, call it the cross-cultural or historic view, marriage is the fundamental, cross-cultural institution for bridging the male-female divide so that children have identified and committed fathers, as well as mothers. Marriage is inherently normative: It is about holding out a certain kind of relationship as a social ideal, one which is critical to the common good of all, whether or not we individually choose to marry—especially because the well-being of children is involved. Marriage is not simply an artifact of law; neither is it a mere delivery mechanism for a set of legal benefits that might as well be shared more broadly. The laws of marriage do not create marriage, but in societies ruled by law they help trace the boundaries and sustain the public meanings of marriage, which are grounded in persistent facts of human nature, in the realities of the natural family and its limitations.

In other words, while individuals freely choose to enter marriage for many private and personal reasons, society upholds the marriage option, formalizes its definition, and surrounds it with norms and reinforcements, so we can raise boys and girls who aspire to become the kind of men and women who can make successful marriages. Without this shared, public aspect, perpetuated generation after generation, marriage becomes what its critics say it is: an individual decision to create a loving relationship of primary importance to the couple, whose job it is to define what they want and need from marriage, indeed what marriage is.

In this other, cross-cultural view, marriage is a public institution not because love is grand (although it is) but because marriage is necessary to the whole society: that children need mothers and fathers, that societies need babies, and that adults have an obligation to shape their sexual behavior so as to give their children stable families in which to grow up. Marriage is rooted in the natural family; it was not invented by legislatures but merely recognized and supported by them.

Which view of marriage is true? We have seen what has happened in our communities where marriage norms have failed. What has happened is not a flowering of libertarian freedom, but a breakdown of social and civic order that can reach frightening proportions. When law and culture retreat from sustaining the marriage idea, individuals cannot create marriage on their own.

In a complex society governed by positive law, social institutions require both social and legal support. To use an analogy, the government does not create private property. But to make a market system a reality requires the assistance of law as well as culture. People have to be raised to respect the property of others, and to value the traits of entrepreneurship, and to be law abiding generally. The law cannot allow individuals to define for themselves what private property (or law-abiding conduct) means. The boundaries of certain institutions (such as the corporation) also need to be defined legally, and the definitions become socially shared knowledge. We need a shared system of meaning, publicly enforced, if market-based economies are to do their magic and individuals are to maximize their opportunities.

Successful social institutions generally function without people's having to think very much about how they work. But when a social institution is contested—as marriage is today—it becomes critically important to think and speak clearly about its public meanings.

Again, what is marriage, as a government-backed public and legal institution, for?

There is a great cross-cultural answer that human beings have arrived at through trial and error, in diverse cultures. Marriage is a virtually universal human institution. In all the wildly rich and various cultures flung throughout the ecosphere, in society after society, whether tribal or complex, and however bizarre, human beings have created systems of publicly approved sexual union between men and women that entail well-defined responsibilities of mothers and fathers.

Not all these marriage systems look like our own, which is rooted in a fusion of Greek, Roman, Jewish, and Christian culture. Many contain element we consider quite properly bad or evil. (Polygamy is very a common human variant, for

example). Yet everywhere, in isolated mountain valleys, parched deserts, jungle thickets, and broad plains, people have come up with some version of this thing called marriage.

I am not raising this question to prove marriage cannot be changed. I am raising it to ask a different question: Why? What purpose does it serve? It must serve some urgent and necessary purpose or it would not recur time and time again in diverse human cultures.

Here's the answer, I believe, to the puzzle of marriage's universality as a male-female sexual union.

Because sex between men and women makes babies, that's why. Even today, in our technologically advanced contraceptive culture, half of all pregnancies are unintended: Sex between men and women still makes babies. Most men and women are powerfully drawn to perform a sexual act that can and does generate life. Marriage is our attempt to reconcile and harmonize the erotic, social, sexual, and financial needs of men and women with the needs of their partner and their children.

How to reconcile the needs of children with the sexual desires of adults? Every society has to face that question, and some resolve it in ways that inflict horrendous cruelty on children born outside marriage. Some cultures decide these children don't matter: Men can have all the sex they want, and any children they create outside of marriage will be throwaway kids; marriage is for citizens—slaves and peasants need not apply. You can see a version of this elitist vision of marriage emerging in America under cover of acceptance of family diversity. Marriage will continue to exist as the social advantage of elite communities. The poor and the working class? Who cares whether their kids have dads? We can always import people from abroad to fill our need for disciplined, educated workers.

Our better tradition, and the only one consistent with democratic principles, is to hold up a single ideal for all parents, which is ultimately based on our deep cultural commitment to the equal dignity and social worth of all children. All kids need and deserve a married mom and dad. All parents are supposed to at least try to behave in ways that will give their own children this important protection. Privately, religiously, emotionally, individually, marriage may have many meanings. But this is the core of its public, shared meaning: Marriage is the place where having children is not only tolerated but welcomed and encouraged, because it gives children a father as well as a mother.

Of course, many couples fail to live up to this ideal. Many of the things men and women have to do to sustain their own marriages, and a culture of marriage, are hard. Few people will do them consistently if the larger culture does not affirm the critical importance of marriage as a social institution. Why stick out a frustrating relationship, turn down a tempting new love, abstain from sex outside marriage, or even take pains not to conceive children out of wedlock if family structure does not matter?

If marriage is not a shared norm, and if successful marriage is not socially valued, do not expect it to survive as the generally accepted context for raising children. If marriage is just a way of publicly celebrating private love, then there is no need to encourage couples to stick it out for the sake of the children. If family structure does not matter, why have marriage laws at all? Do adults, or do they not, have a basic obligation to control their desires so that children can have mothers and fathers?

The problem with endorsing gay marriage is not that it would allow a handful of people to choose alternative family forms, but that it would require society at large to gut marriage of its central presumptions about family in order to accommodate a few adults' desires.

The core of the gay marriage argument is not a benefit-distribution mechanism, but a proposed new moral narrative, backed by the government's inflexible commitment to equality. The moral of gay marriage is: there are no differences between gay and straight unions, and if you see a difference, if you prioritize as different, unique and socially important unions of husband and wife that can give children mothers and fathers—there is something wrong with you. Government may literally tolerate you, but it will increasingly seek, within the limits of liberal society, to marginalize and suppress you, your views, and especially any public influence of your views.

This new moral narrative is already producing consequences: rulings by courts that those committed to traditional understanding of marriage can be deemed unfit to foster children; is remaking school curriculum; it is producing public calls and legal complaints in Illinois that adoption agencies that refuse to do gay adoptions should be excluded in the public square. It has led to calls to end the tax exempt status of churches that promote bigotry, taking a cue from the 1983 court case.[2]

A legal environment where litigation like this is already taking place indicates a cultural environment in which sustaining the idea that children need mothers and fathers is going to become increasingly difficult for private actors, including religious communities.

The recent translation of the gay marriage debate into a "marriage equality" debate only serves to underscore that after gay marriage, both same-sex and opposite unions will have to be considered equal and equally important; preferences for mothers and fathers for children represent outmoded bigotry.

Both types of unions, since they are quite different, can be viewed as equally valuable, only if the capacity to create new life and connect children to mothers and fathers is viewed as either unimportant in itself, or only marginally if at all related to marriage.

The features that point to these unique and irreplaceable contributions will have to be downgraded and marginalized (or excluded) from our public idea of marriage if the promise of marriage equality is to be fulfilled.

The debate over same-sex marriage, then, is not some sideline discussion. It is the marriage debate. The great problem "marriage equality" poses to marriage as a social institution is not some distant or nearby slippery slope, it is a present question: If we cannot explain why unisex marriage is, in itself, a disaster, we have already lost the marriage ideal.

Same-sex marriage would enshrine in law a public judgment that the desire of adults for families of choice to be treated with equal dignity in all respects outweighs the need of children for mothers and fathers. It would give sanction and approval to the creation of a motherless or fatherless family as a deliberately chosen "good." It would mean the law was neutral as to whether children had mothers and fathers.

Same-sex marriage advocates are startlingly clear on this point. Marriage law, they repeatedly claim, has nothing to do with babies or procreation or getting mothers and fathers for children. In forcing the state legislature to create civil unions for gay couples, the high court of Vermont explicitly ruled that marriage in the state of Vermont has nothing to do with procreation. Evan Wolfson made the same point in "Marriage and Same Sex Unions": "[I]sn't having the law pretend that there is only one family model that works (let alone exists) a lie?" He goes on to say that in law, "marriage is not just about procreation— indeed is not necessarily about procreation at all."

Wolfson is right that in the course of the sexual revolution the Supreme Court struck down many legal features designed to reinforce the connection of marriage to babies. The animus of elites (including legal elites) against the marriage idea is not brand new. It stretches back at least thirty years. That is part of the problem we face, part of the reason 40 percent of our children are growing up without their fathers.

It is also true, as gay-marriage advocates note, that we impose no fertility tests for marriage: Infertile and older couples marry, and not every fertile couple chooses procreation. But every marriage between a man and a woman is capable of giving any child they create or adopt a mother and a father. Every marriage between a man and a woman discourages either from creating fatherless children outside the marriage vow. In this sense, neither older married couples nor childless husbands and wives publicly challenge or dilute the core meaning of marriage. Even when a man marries an older woman and they do not adopt, his marriage helps protect children. How? His marriage means, if he keeps his vows, that he will not produce out-of-wedlock children.

Does marriage discriminate against gays and lesbians? Formally speaking, no. There are no sexual-orientation tests for marriage; many gays

and lesbians do choose to marry members of the opposite sex, and some of these unions succeed. Our laws do not require a person to marry the individual to whom he or she is most erotically attracted, so long as he or she is willing to promise sexual fidelity, mutual caretaking, and shared parenting of any children of the marriage.

But marriage is unsuited to the wants and desires of many gays and lesbians, precisely because it is designed to bridge the male-female divide and sustain the idea that children need mothers and fathers. To make a marriage, what you need is a husband and a wife. Redefining marriage so that it suits gay and lesbian couple would require fundamentally changing our legal, public, and social conception of what marriage is in ways that change its core public purposes. For millions of Americans this is obvious.

For others, who have already changed their concept of marriage, it is literally invisible.

Some who criticize the refusal to embrace gay marriage liken it to the outlawing of interracial marriage, but the analogy is woefully false. The Supreme Court overturned anti-miscegenation laws because they frustrated the core purpose of marriage in order to sustain a racist legal order.

Marriage laws, by contrast, were not invented to express animus toward homosexuals or anyone else. Their purpose is not negative, but positive: They uphold an institution that developed, over thousands of years, in thousands of cultures, to help direct the erotic desires of men and women into a relatively narrow but indispensably fruitful channel. We need men and women to marry and make babies for our society to survive. We have no similar public stake in any other family form—in the union of same-sex couples or in the singleness of single moms.

Meanwhile, cui bono? To meet the desires of whom would we put our most basic social institution at risk?

Netherlands has had gay marriage for the longest time. In the last 10 years, there were 14,813 same sex marriages. Dutch survey data suggest that 2.8% of Dutch men and 1.4% of Dutch women are gay or lesbian.[3] If every person who contracted a same-sex marriage in the Netherlands was a resident and was gay or lesbian, 29,626 of these 349,755 have chosen to marry. This means about eight per-cent of gay and lesbian people have chosen to marry.

Meanwhile Nordic research indicates that same-sex couples have not only lower rates of entry but significantly higher rates of divorce than opposite sex couples (not an easy feat) as well as much lower commitment to sexual fidelity.[4]

It is fairly clear that lasting marriage is and will remain a minority taste in the gay community, not a dominant social institution. It is a right, not a communal necessity for same-sex couples, and it is being supported and promoted in that way—as a taste or preference not as a social institution. What is urgent for the gay community is the new moral narrative of equality.

But, say some advocates, gay people have chil-dren. True. Many children live in loving families that are not marital families. How many children might benefit if we change our public understand-ing to incorporate same-sex couples on an equal basis with conjugal unions?

Very, very few. According to Census data about one half of one percent of all children live in a household headed by a same-sex couple. Let's assume that half of these enter marriage, if it is available (a much higher proportion than other gay people): one-quarter of one percent of chil-dren. Let's further assume the dissolution rate is no higher than that of opposite sex couples: around 50 percent. One-eighth of one percent of children might experience a stable marriage as a result of gay marriage. Now let's add in the information provided by Gary Gates, the nation's leading demographer of gay people, that likely 80 percent of these children are products of previous hetero-sexual relationships[5], meaning the marriage is a re-marriage which has no known social science benefit to the children—children in blended fam-ilies do no better on average than children raised by solo mothers.

One-fifth of one-eighth of one percent of chil-dren in America might experience a benefit from gay marriage, assuming it stabilized their parents union, and that provided benefits for children: one-fortieth of one percent of all U.S. children

might experience a benefit from gay marriage, if gay marriage adds value to gay unions with children.

Meanwhile 98 percent of the population is at risk of creating fatherless children across multiple households, unless we restore and renew our his-toric understanding of marriage.

If children were our first or primary concern in the public institution of marriage, we would not do this. Gay marriage is a decision that marriage as a public institution is committed primarily and at its core to other needs than the needs of children.

It would take very little interference by gay marriage with the social message that children ought to have a mom and dad and marriage is how we get that for children, to swamp any poten-tial benefit.

Do we care?

People who argue for creating gay marriage do so in the name of high ideals: justice, compassion, fairness. Their sincerity is not in question. Never-theless, to take the already troubled institution most responsible for the protection of children and throw out its most basic presumption in order to further adult interests in sexual freedom would not be high-minded. It would be morally callous and socially irresponsible.

Some have come to me and argued we should make another case against gay marriage. But this is the case I care about. If we cannot stand and defend this ground, then marriage as a public idea is no longer important to defend.

"Institutional messages" may not be sexy and in fact may be hard for Americans with our individu-alistic mindset to grasp. But they are real.

Those of us who engaged in the last century's fight against fatherless America have seen the strong early warning signs that gay marriage is not a conservative cornerstone of the revival of a mar-riage culture, but part of an embrace of the idea of family diversity that will be and is being used to marginalize, silence and repress the traditional understanding of marriage.

This will happen not because gay marriage advocates want to be mean, but because that is what marriage equality *means*.

ENDNOTES

1. For some examples see Maggie Gallagher, "(How) Will Gay Marriage Weaken Marriage as a Social Institution," 2 *University of St. Thomas Law Review* 33 (2004); David Blankenhorn, *The Future of Marriage* (Encounter Books 2007).

2. Manya A. Brachear, "State Probes Religious Foster Care Agencies Over Discrimination" *Chicago Tribune*, March 2, 2011 at http://articles.chicagotribune.com/2011-03-02/news/ct-met-gay-foster-care-20110301_1_care-andadoption-catholic-charities-parents; Joseph Erbentraut, "Foster-Care Agencies that Deny Gay Parents Under Review" *Windy City Times*, March 9, 2011 at http://www.windycitymediagroup.com/gay/lesbian/news/ARTICLE.php?AID=30852; "Illinois Catholic Charities Warns It May Halt Adoptions, Foster Care Over New Civil Unions Law" *Chicago Tribune*, May 4, 2011 at http://www.chicagotribune.com/news/local/sns-ap-il-xgr--civilunions-adoption,0,439697.story; Manya A. Brachearm "Rockford Catholic Charities Ending Foster Care" *Chicago Tribune*, May 26, 2011 at http://www.chicagotribune.com/news/local/breaking/chibrknews-rockfordcatholic-charities-ending-foster-care-adoptions-20110526,0,4532788.story?track=rss; Maggie Gallagher, *Banned in Boston* WEEKLY STANDARD 20 (May 15, 2006); *Same-Sex Marriage and Religious Liberty: Emerging Conflicts*, Robin Fretwell Wilson, Douglas Laycock, & Anthony Picarello, editors (Rowman & Littlefield 2008); Robin Fretwell Wilson, "Insubstantial Burdens: The Case for Government Employee Exemptions to Same-Sex Marriage Laws" 5 *Northwestern University Journal of Law & Social Policy* 318 (2010).

3. Theo G. Sandfort, Ron de Graaf, Rob V. Bijl, & Paul Schnabel, "Same-sex sexual behavior and psychiatric disorders: Findings from the Netherlands Mental Health Survey and Incidence Study (NEMESIS)," 58 *Archives of General Psychiatry* 85 (2001).

4. Maggie Gallagher & Joshua K. Baker, "Same-Sex Unions and Divorce Risk: Data from Sweden" *iMAPP Policy Brief*, May 3, 2004 at http://www.marriagedebate.com/pdf/SSdivorcerisk.pdf.

5. Katie Worth, "SF same-sex couples increasingly going without kids, census shows" *San Francisco Examiner*, June 29, 2011 at http://www.sfexaminer.com/local/2011/06/sf-same-sex-couples-increasingly-going-without-kids-censusshows?utm_source=feedburner+sfexaminer%2FLocal&utm_medium=feed+Local+News&utm_campaign=Feed%3A+sfexaminer%2FLocal+%28Local+News%29feed&utm_content=feed&utm_term=feed#ixzz1Qa4YiujT ("That research showed that about 80 percent of the children raised in same-sex households come from prior heterosexual relationships, while less than 20 percent come from adoption, fostering or surrogacy.").

55

Is Same-Sex Marriage Bad for Children?

JOHN CORVINO

John Corvino points out that there have to be missing steps in Gallagher's argument against same-sex marriages, because there are a lot of marriages we currently legally sanction that do not result in children living with their two biological parents in low-conflict.

The debate over whether same-sex couples should have the freedom to marry tends to get complicated. In making the case for such marriages, it may be helpful to start simple.

A simple case in favor of same-sex marriage goes like this. There are gay and lesbian people in the world. Such people tend to fall in love with, and settle down with, persons of the same sex.[1] When they do, they appreciate having the same rights and responsibilities as their heterosexual counterparts. Giving them those rights and responsibilities doesn't involve taking them away from heterosexuals: marriage licenses are not a limited resource. And same-sex marriage doesn't just benefit same-sex couples. When people commit "to have and to hold; from this day forward; for better, for worse; for richer, for poorer; in sickness and in health; to love and to cherish; until death do us part," that's not just good for them, it's good for those around them, since happy, stable couples make happy, stable neighbors.

Of course, the simple case is too simple. There is much more to be said, and indeed, entire books have been written elaborating on this simple case.[2] But it is worth remembering it during what follows. The widespread human desire to find a "special someone" is powerful, regardless of sexual orientation, and long-term relationships can be an important path to happiness. If society can help gays sustain that path without taking anything away from straights, there is strong prima facie case for doing so.

NARROWING THE FOCUS

What I want to do here is to rebut one of the main objections to that case, namely, that same-sex marriage is somehow bad for children. There are countless versions of this objection, and for reasons of space I will ignore many. For example, I will not consider the argument that same-sex marriage will cause more children to grow up gay, a claim for which there is absolutely no evidence. I will also set aside the contention that children with gay or lesbian parents will be teased by their peers. That contention is almost certainly true—as it is for those whose parents are too short or too tall, too fat or too thin, too poor or too rich; have funny accents, wear outdated clothing, or give their children names like "Seattle." Children get teased about all kinds of things, and while this fact should affect childrearing, it should seldom affect whether people should have children in the first place—much less whether they should have the freedom to marry.

MARRIAGE'S MULTIPLE ROLES

Let me be clear: one of the most important things marriage does is to protect children. There is no serious debate about this. But protecting children is hardly the *sole* function of marriage, and besides, it is entirely unclear how same-sex marriages would threaten that function.

Walter is a neighbor of mine, a widower in his 70's. Recently, he announced that he was getting married, to a similarly-aged woman. What did we all say to Walter? We said "Congratulations," of course. Were we just being polite, secretly thinking "Why bother"? At their age, Walter and his new wife won't have children. And yet his marriage makes sense—indeed, it seems like a very positive thing. Why?

Maggie Gallagher, a prominent same-sex-marriage opponent, writes,

It is also true, as gay-marriage advocates note, that we impose no fertility tests for marriage: Infertile and older couples marry, and not every fertile couple chooses pro-creation. But every marriage between a man and a woman is capable of giving any child they create or adopt a mother and a father. Every marriage between a man and a woman discourages either from creating fatherless children outside the marriage vow. In this sense, neither older married couples nor childless husbands and wives publicly challenge or dilute the core meaning of marriage. Even when a man marries an older woman and they do not adopt, his marriage helps protect children. How? His marriage means, if he keeps his vows, that he will not produce out-of-wedlock children.[3]

Congratulations, Walter. If you keep your vows, you won't produce any out-of-wedlock children. Let's have a toast!

Obviously, that is *not* what we meant when we congratulated Walter. We congratulated Walter—and regard his marriage as a good thing—because Walter now (again) has someone special to take care of him and vice-versa. Contra Gallagher, marriage has important social functions even when children are not on the horizon.

It is also worth noting that there are hundreds of thousands of children being raised in the U.S. by gay (single and partnered) parents.[4] Some of these parents have children from prior heterosexual relationships, others have them by adoption, still others by insemination. All else being equal, these children would surely be better off if their parents—the people actually raising them—had the prospect of marriage.

But perhaps all else is not equal. Let us now turn more directly to the "bad for children" claim.

BAD FOR CHILDREN?

Most of the more plausible "bad for children" arguments share the premise that the best setting for childrearing involves a mother and a father, and more specifically, *the child's own biological mother and father*. (Even more specifically, the child's own married biological mother and father in a low-conflict relationship.[5]) This claim is based upon extensive empirical research regarding child welfare in different family forms. Let me note two important things from the start.

First, the claim that children do better with their own biological mother and father involves a generalization that obscures a number of confounding variables. Take, for example, economic class. Because they lack many basic material necessities, poor children tend to fare less well than other children. And because of complex cultural factors, poor children are also far less likely to grow up with both biological parents than others. These facts affect the overall statistic about children's doing better on average with their own biological parents—take away the poor kids, and the differences between biological-parent families and other family forms are no longer so sharp.

Second, the specific issue of same-sex families has not been studied nearly as much as other family forms: children raised by single parents, children of divorced parents, children in (heterosexual) step-families and so on. But to the extent that researchers have made direct comparisons between children raised by same-sex parents and children raised by opposite-sex parents (biological and otherwise), the children seem to fare just as well in either group. According to the American Academy of Pediatrics, the nation's premier child-welfare orga-nization, there is "a considerable body of profes-sional literature that suggests children with parents who are homosexual have the same advantages and the same expectations for health, adjustment, and development as children whose parents are heterosexual."[6] And here's the American Psycho-logical Association:

> There is no scientific basis for concluding that lesbian mothers or gay fathers are unfit parents on the basis of their sexual orien-tation. On the contrary, results of research suggest that lesbian and gay parents are as likely as heterosexual parents to provide supportive and healthy environments for their children.... Overall, results of research suggest that the development, adjustment, and well-being of children with lesbian and gay parents do not differ markedly from that of children with het-erosexual parents.[7]

So too says the Child Welfare League of America, the National Association of Social Workers, the American Academy of Family Physicians—indeed, every major health and welfare organization that has examined the data. Mainstream professional opinion is in resounding agreement on this point.

That doesn't change the truth of the generali-zation about *biological* two-parent households: on average, children in that family form appear to do better than children in other family forms. But what follows?

What follows is that same-sex couples should stop kidnapping children from their own biological parents.

Back on Planet Earth, where same-sex couples are not involved in a mass-kidnapping scheme, it is less clear what follows. Same-sex marriage never—and I mean *never*—takes children away from com-petent biological parents who want them. I don't wish to be glib, but from the premise

On average, children do better with their own biological parents

to the conclusion

We should not allow same-sex couples to marry

there are a lot of missing steps. Indeed, more like entire missing staircases. I have yet to see any marriage-equality opponents fill in those missing staircases. Most do not even bother to try.

One immediate problem is that allowing peo-ple to marry is different from declaring that it would be ideal for them to raise children. Most gay and lesbian couples don't have children. Those who do generally put a great deal of thought into it: they do not wake up one day and say "Oops, we're pregnant." In that sense, they are not like the "average" parent, who may or may not have planned for the child and may or may not be prepared for its arrival.

What's more, we allow many couples to marry who fall short of the purported parenting ideal—as we should. Notably, we allow stepfamilies to form, even though the *very same research* that opponents cite against same-sex marriage applies to them: chil-dren in such families on average do less well than children raised by their own biological parents. We allow poor people to marry, people without college degrees to marry, people in rural areas to marry, and so on, even though there is *substantial* research—far more extensive than that concerning same-sex parents—suggesting that children in these environ-ments do less well than in the alternatives.

We even allow convicted felons serving prison sentences to marry—in fact, we allow it as a matter of constitutional right. The U.S. Supreme Court in

Turner v. Safley unanimously affirmed that right, noting that "inmate marriages, like others, are expressions of emotional support and public commitment," even given the obvious limitations of prison life.[8] In reaching this decision the Court drew on *Zablocki v. Redhail*, which held that persons delinquent on child support retain the fundamental right to marry.[9]

So a convicted murderer serving a life sentence may marry, but loving, law-abiding same-sex couples may not, because "On average, children do better with their own biological parents." Do you see what I mean about missing staircases?

Is there any logical way for marriage-equality opponents to get from the premise "On average, children do better with their own biological parents," to the conclusion "We should not allow gays and lesbians to marry"? Let us consider two, which I'll call the Emboldening Argument and the Message Argument.

THE EMBOLDENING
ARGUMENT

The Emboldening Argument asserts that extending marriage to gay and lesbian couples would encourage (or "embolden") more of them to have children. The problem with the Emboldening Argument—aside from the fact that it's speculative—is that it runs up against the "no kidnapping" point: remember, gays and lesbians who have children never take them away from competent biological parents who want them. When we consider whether a same-sex household would be a good environment for a child, we must always ask "Compared to what?"

Putting aside the cases where gay and lesbian individuals have children from prior heterosexual relationships, there are two ways in which same-sex couples usually acquire children. The first (and more common) is adoption. In most of these cases, the couple is taking the child, not from its biological parents, but from the state, and almost no one—including Gallagher—argues that it would be better

for children to languish in foster care than to be raised by loving same-sex couples. There are over 100,000 foster children in the U.S. alone waiting to be adopted.[10] If marriage would "embolden" some same-sex couples to provide homes for such children, then that is a reason *for* letting them marry, not against it.

The other way in which same-sex couples acquire children is by insemination, such as when lesbians use sperm banks. Is this bad for the children? Again we must ask, "Compared to what?" In such cases, the realistic alternative is not for the child to live with both biological parents, but for the child not to exist at all. Public-policy decisions must be evaluated by real-world results, and in the real world, lesbians who visit sperm banks are generally not contemplating marrying the father.

Would it be better for such children *not to exist*? It's a difficult question to answer. Better for whom? Not for the individual children themselves, obviously. The best one could argue that it would be better for the world at large, somehow, if such children didn't exist, though I'm not sure what such an argument would look like.

My point is this: whether or not it would be better for such children to be raised by both biological parents, *that's not an option on the table*—at least not one that marriage policy will affect. At the risk of repeating the obvious: banning same-sex marriage does not cause lesbians to marry their sperm donors and form traditional heterosexual families.

More generally, we should not conflate the donor-conception debate with the marriage debate. By substantial margins, most people who use sperm banks are heterosexual, most same-sex couples never use sperm banks, and most sperm banks don't restrict usage to married persons. Activists concerned about the proliferation of donor conception should fight to regulate donor conception, not to deny the personal and social benefits of marriage to gays and lesbians.

One last point: while I would welcome a thoughtful conversation about the moral dimensions of having children via various technologies, I don't think that conversation should proceed independently of a conversation about the moral dimensions of having children, period—including heterosexual people's doing it the old-fashioned way. Just because heterosexual couples have the right-shaped body parts for having children, it doesn't automatically follow that they *should*. I would love to see this debate transformed into a more general discussion about whether, when, and why to bring children into the world, rather than just another opportunity for scapegoating gays.

THE MESSAGE ARGUMENT

Thus far I've argued that the Emboldening Argument won't connect the dots between the premise "On average, children do better with their own biological parents," and the conclusion "We should not allow gays and lesbians to marry." I want to turn to a second, related argument, one that captures Maggie Gallagher's main concerns. Let's call it the Message Argument.

The idea is as follows. Children do better with their own biological parents, but parents—and specifically, fathers—are not always naturally inclined to stick around for their children. (As my 95-year-old Sicilian grandfather recently put it, expressing concern about an unwed mother in our family, "A man pulls up his pants and walks away.") So one of society's important functions is to pressure people to take responsibility for their offspring. We do this mainly through the social institution of marriage, with all its complex and interrelated elements. We discourage sex outside of marriage because it might create babies for parents who are not bound together for the long haul. We nudge people to get married and stay married. We stigmatize divorce and illegitimacy (though far more mildly than we once did). All of these elements work toward promoting a message. In Gallagher's words:

> The marriage idea is that children need mothers and fathers, that societies need babies, and that adults have an obligation to shape their sexual behavior so as to give their children stable families in which to grow up.[11]

Great, you might say, but what's the problem with same-sex marriage? How would it make mothers and fathers any less connected to their children?

The problem, in Gallagher's view, is that endorsing same-sex marriage means endorsing same-sex families, and you cannot do that while simultaneously insisting that children need their own mothers and fathers:

> Same-sex marriage would enshrine in law a public judgment that the desire of adults for families of choice outweighs the need of children for mothers and fathers. It would give sanction and approval to the creation of a motherless or fatherless family as a deliberately chosen "good." It would mean the law was neutral as to whether children had mothers and fathers. Motherless and fatherless families would be deemed just fine.[12]

The central premise of the marriage-equality movement is that John and Jim's marriage is just as legitimate, qua marriage, as Jack and Jill's. But if we make that equivalence, we cannot also insist that children—some of whom John and Jim may be raising—need their mothers and fathers. That insistence would now seem insensitive, even insulting. So Gallagher's argument poses a dilemma: either maintain the message that children need their mothers and fathers, and thus oppose marriage equality; or else embrace marriage equality, and thus relinquish the message. You can't have both.

The Message Argument has several noteworthy strengths. It's based on a premise that seems well motivated, at least on the surface: children need their mothers and fathers. (Not in the same sense in which they "need" oxygen, but in the sense that, on average, that's the environment in which they're likely to do best.) This premise has personal resonance for Gallagher, who has spoken candidly of her own past struggles as a young single mother. Moreover, the Message Argument appears impervious to some standard rebuttals. Two of these are worth noting.

First, it's not vulnerable to the "infertile couples" rebuttal, at least not at first glance. (There will be a second glance a few paragraphs down, so stay tuned.) Yes, we extend marriage to my elderly neighbor Walter, but doing so doesn't the dilute the message that children need mothers and fathers in the way that treating same-sex couples as married does. Walter and his wife won't have children, but *if somehow they did*, those children would have a mother and a father. Not so for the same-sex couple.

Second, it's not vulnerable to the "Compared to what?" rebuttal, the idea that it's unfair to compare same-sex parents to heterosexual biological parents since gays aren't snatching children away from straights. Of course they're not, but that's beside the point. Gallagher would likely concede that it's better for children to be adopted by a loving same-sex couple than to languish in foster care. But if we call that couple "married;" if the law sanctions and approves them as "just fine," then it becomes harder to maintain the message that children need their own biological mothers and fathers. In a sense, same-sex couples are "collateral damage" in Gallagher's culture war: her express aim is not to attack gays, but to maintain a message about children's needs—and she can't do that while also endorsing same-sex couples.

The Message Argument is probably the best argument that same-sex marriage opponents have. It is still pretty weak.

Return for a moment to Walter and his (postmenopausal) bride. If they were to have children, it would be by the same means a gay male couple could have children: adoption or surrogacy. Then they would provide those children with a mother and father. But they would not provide them with *their own biological* mother and father. The problem is that research doesn't show that on average, children do better with mothers and fathers; it shows that, on average, they do better with *their own biological* mothers and fathers. Take away the two-parent biological link, and Gallagher's argument implodes: there is *no data whatsoever* showing that children do better in heterosexual stepfamilies and adoptive families than they do in same-sex households.

This problem points to a second, and related, flaw in the Message Argument. Earlier I noted that children don't "need" their own biological parents in the same sense that they need, say, oxygen. But how strong is the need? What do the studies show, and how does the "biological parent" factor compare to other relevant factors?

The honest answer is that it's a factor, but not nearly as strong a factor as certain others that Gallagher and other marriage-equality opponents routinely overlook. Take economic class. Compared to their more affluent counterparts, poor children show significantly worse outcomes in terms of physical health, cognitive development, academic achievement, behavioral adjustment, crime, graduation rates, mortality and eventual adult income. And yet we allow poor couples to marry—as long as they're different-sex. How do we do this, without undermining the message that children "need" economic security and declaring that its absence "just fine"? Marriage-equality opponents are strikingly inconsistent in their willingness to make the ideal the enemy of the good.

Which brings me to a third problem. Suppose you were interested in promoting marriage, and in particular, in addressing the problem of fatherlessness. What could you do? You could work on comprehensive sex education programs, including accurate information about both abstinence and contraception. You could aim at some of the purported root causes, including poverty, lack of educational and employment opportunities, and incarceration policy. You could tighten up divorce laws, or promote relationship counseling. You could do all of these things, and a hundred more.

Or you could do what the National Organization for Marriage does. The National Organization for Marriage (NOM), of which Maggie Gallagher is the founding president, styles itself as America's premier organization to protect marriage. Of the various ways just mentioned to address the problem of fatherlessness, how many do you think that NOM pursues? If you guessed "zero," you are correct. *Not a single one.* The National Organization for Marriage focuses on fighting gays, and gays alone. Which makes it very hard to believe that gays are just collateral damage in their effort to promote children's welfare.

There is a fourth problem with the Message Argument. Gallagher claims that marriage's message is that children need mothers and fathers. That's certainly *a* message of marriage, but it's scarcely the only one. Marriage also sends the message that it's good for people to have a special someone to care for them and vice-versa—to have and to hold, for better or worse, 'til death do they part. It sends a message about the importance of forming family, even when those families don't include children; about making the transition from being a child in one's family of origin to being an adult in one's family of choice. All of these messages matter, and all are important to gay and lesbian citizens.

Meanwhile, to *deny* marriage to a group of people also sends a message. When we consider other groups that historically were excluded from marriage—notably, slaves and prisoners—that mes-sage is pretty clear: you are less than a full citizen. Your relationships aren't "real;" your families don't matter. Gallagher claims that she loves and respects gay people, and I'd like to believe her. But how can she sustain that message while also opposing marriage equality? How is she not telling same-sex couples, including thousands of same-sex couples *with children*, that they are unworthy of equal respect? Gallagher's dilemma has a flip side: either gays are full-fledged members of our society, in which case they too deserve marriage; or else they are second-class citizens, people whose relationships and families aren't "real." You can't have both.

Every decent citizen should be concerned about protecting children. But excluding same-sex couples from marriage doesn't protect children: it just scapegoats gays.[13]

ENDNOTES

1. So do bisexual people, who—though they don't appear in my "simple" case—certainly belong in the case more generally. With respect to the marriage debate, the main difference between gay men and lesbians, on the one hand, and bisexuals, on the other, is that a prohibition against same-sex marriage generally means that gay men and lesbians are pro-hibited from marrying *any* people they might fall in love with whereas bisexuals are prohibited from marrying *some* people they might fall in love with. But both groups experience the prohibition as a deprivation.

2. See for example Jonathan Rauch, *Gay Marriage: Why It Is Good for Gays, Good for Straights, and Good for America.* New York: Henry Holt and Co., 2004.

3. Maggie Gallagher, "What Marriage is For," *The Weekly Standard* Vol. 8 No. 5 Aug. 4, 2003, p. 25.

4. Some estimates are considerably higher. For some statistics on gay and lesbian parenting, see Gary J. Gates, M.V. Lee Badgett, Jennifer Ehrle Macomber, and Kate Chambers, "Adoption and foster care by gay and lesbian parents in the United States," Joint Report of the Williams Institute and the Urban Institute (March 2007). Available here:

http://www3.law.ucla.edu/williamsinstitute/publications/FinalAdoptionReport.pdf

5. For a useful summary of the research on the effects of family structure on children's well-being, see the Center for Law and Social Policy (CLASP) brief, "Are Married Parents Really Better for Children? What Research Says About the Effects of Family Structure on Child Well-Being," by Mary Parke (May 2003).

6. *Pediatrics* Vol. 109 No. 2 February 2002, pp. 339–340.

7. http://www.apa.org/about/governance/council/policy/parenting.aspx

8. *Turner v. Safley*, 482 U.S. 78 (1987).

9. *Zablocki v. Redhail*, 434 U.S. 374 (1978).

10. According to a 2002 study. See http://statistics.adoption.com/information/foster-care-statistics.html

11. Gallagher, p. 23.

12. Gallagher, p. 24.

13. I am indebted to Loren Cannon, Hayley Goren-berg, Lawrence Lombard, Katherine Paesani, Jona-than Rauch, Sean Stidd, and Susan Vineberg for helpful comments on earlier drafts of this paper.

56

The Marriage Equality Act of New York State

THE PEOPLE OF THE STATE OF NEW YORK, REPRESENTED IN SENATE AND ASSEMBLY, DO ENACT AS FOLLOWS:

Section 1. This act shall be known and may be cited as the "Marriage Equality Act."

S 2. Legislative intent. Marriage is a fundamental human right. Same-sex couples should have the same access as others to the protections, responsibilities, rights, obligations, and benefits of civil marriage. Stable family relationships help build a stronger society. For the welfare of the community and in fairness to all New Yorkers, this act formally recognizes otherwise-valid marriages without regard to whether the parties are of the same or different sex.

It is the intent of the legislature that the marriages of same-sex and different-sex couples be treated equally in all respects under the law. The omission from this act of changes to other provisions of law shall not be construed as a legislative intent to preserve any legal distinction between same-sex couples and different-sex couples with respect to marriage. The legislature intends that all provisions of law which utilize gender-specific terms in reference to the parties to a marriage, or which in any other way may be inconsistent with this act, be construed in a gender-neutral manner or in any way necessary to effectuate the intent of this act.

S 3. The domestic relations law is amended by adding two new sections 10-a and 10-b to read as follows:

S 10-a. Parties to a marriage. 1. A marriage that is otherwise valid shall be valid regardless of whether the parties to the marriage are of the same or different sex.

2. No government treatment or legal status, effect, right, benefit, privilege, protection or responsibility relating to marriage, whether deriving from statute, administrative or court rule, public policy, common law or any other source of law, shall differ based on the parties to the marriage being or having been of the same sex rather than a different sex. When necessary to implement the rights and responsibilities of spouses under the law, all gender-specific language or terms shall be construed in a gender-neutral manner in all such sources of law.

S 10-b. Application. 1. Notwithstanding any other provision of law, pursuant to subdivision nine of section two hundred ninety-two of the executive law, a corporation incorporated under the benevolent orders law or described in the benevolent orders law but formed under any other law of this state or a religious corporation incorporated under the education law or the religious corporations laws shall be deemed to be in its nature distinctly private and therefore, shall not be required to provide accommodations, advantages, facilities or privileges related to the solemnization or celebration of a marriage.

2. A refusal by a benevolent organization or a religious corporation, incorporated under the education law or the religious corporations law, to provide accommodations, advantages, facilities or privileges in connection with section ten-a of this article shall not create a civil claim or cause of action.

New York State Legislature.

3. Pursuant to subdivision eleven of section two hundred ninety-six of the executive law, nothing in this article shall be deemed or construed to prohibit any religious or denominational institution or organization, or any organization operated for charitable or educational purposes, which is operated, supervised or controlled by or in connection with a religious organization from limiting employment or sales or rental of housing accommodations or admission to or giving preference to persons of the same religion or denomination or from taking such action as is calculated by such organization to promote the religious principles for which it is established or maintained.

S 4. Section 13 of the domestic relations law, as amended by chapter 720 of the laws of 1957, is amended to read as follows:

S 13. Marriage licenses. It shall be necessary for all persons intended to be married in New York state to obtain a marriage license from a town or city clerk in New York state and to deliver said license, within sixty days, to the clergyman or magistrate who is to officiate before the marriage ceremony may be performed. In case of a marriage contracted pursuant to subdivision four of section eleven of this chapter, such license shall be delivered to the judge of the court of record before whom the acknowledgment is to be taken. If either party to the marriage resides upon an island located not less than twenty-five miles from the office or residence of the town clerk of the town of which such island is a part, and if such office or residence is not on such island such license may be obtained from any justice of the peace residing on such island, and such justice, in respect to powers and duties relating to marriage licenses, shall be subject to the provisions of this article governing town

clerks and shall file all statements or affidavits received by him while acting under the provisions of this section with the town clerk of such town. No application for a marriage license shall be denied on the ground that the parties are of the same, or a different, sex.

S 5. Subdivision 1 of section 11 of the domestic relations law, as amended by chapter 319 of the laws of 1959, is amended and a new subdivision 1-a is added to read as follows:

1. A clergyman or minister of any religion, or by the senior leader, or any of the other leaders, of The Society for Ethical Culture in the city of New York, having its principal office in the borough of Manhattan, or by the leader of The Brooklyn Society for Ethical Culture, having its principal office in the borough of Brooklyn of the city of New York, or of the Westchester Ethical Society, having its principal office in Westchester county, or of the Ethical Culture Society of Long Island, having its principal office in Nassau county, or of the River-dale-Yonkers Ethical Society having its principal office in Bronx county, or by the leader of any other Ethical Culture Society affiliated with the American Ethical Union; provided that no clergyman or minister as defined in section two of the religious corporations law, or society for ethical culture leader shall be required to solemnize any marriage when acting in his or her capacity under this subdivision.

1-a. A refusal by a clergyman or minister as defined in section two of the religious corporations law, or society for ethical culture leader to solemnize any marriage under this subdivision shall not create a civil claim or cause of action.

S 6. This act shall take effect on the thirtieth day after it shall have become a law.

57

Lawrence v. Texas
Supreme Court of the United States

The issue before the U.S. Supreme Court was whether a Texas statute forbidding two persons of the same sex to engage in certain intimate sexual conduct is unconstitutional under the due process clause of the Fourteenth Amendment. The majority of the Court, overturning an earlier Supreme Court decision in Bowers v. Hardwick *(1986), held that the right to liberty under the due process clause does give consenting adults the right to engage in private conduct without government intervention.*

Justice Kennedy delivered the opinion of the Court

Liberty protects the person from unwarranted government intrusions into a dwelling or other private places. In our tradition the state is not omnipresent in the home. And there are other spheres of our lives and existence, outside the home, where the state should not be a dominant presence. Freedom extends beyond spatial bounds. Liberty presumes an autonomy of self that includes freedom of thought, belief, expression, and certain intimate conduct. The instant case involves liberty of the person both in its spatial and more transcendent dimensions.

The question before the Court is the validity of a Texas statute making it a crime for two persons of the same sex to engage in certain intimate sexual conduct.

In Houston, Texas, officers of the Harris County Police Department were dispatched to a private residence in response to a reported weapons disturbance. They entered an apartment where one of the petitioners, John Geddes Lawrence, resided. The right of the police to enter does not seem to have been questioned. The officers observed Lawrence and another man, Tyron Garner, engaging in a sexual act. The two petitioners were arrested, held in custody over night, and charged and convicted before a Justice of the Peace.

The complaints described their crime as deviate sexual intercourse, namely anal sex, with a member of the same sex (man).... The petitioners exercised their right to a trial de novo in Harris County Criminal Court. They challenged the statute as a violation of the Equal Protection Clause of the Fourteenth Amendment and of a like provision of the Texas Constitution. Those contentions were rejected. The petitioners, having entered a plea of nolo contendere, were each fined $200 and assessed court costs of $141.25.

The Court of Appeals for the Texas Fourteenth District considered the petitioners' federal constitutional arguments under both the Equal Protection and Due Process Clauses of the Fourteenth Amendment. After hearing the case en banc the court, in a divided opinion, rejected the constitutional arguments and affirmed the convictions. The majority opinion indicates that the Court of Appeals considered our decision in *Bowers v. Hardwick* to be controlling on the federal due process aspect of the case. Bowers then being authoritative, this was proper.

We granted certiorari to consider three questions:

1. Whether petitioners' criminal convictions under the Texas Homosexual Conduct law which criminalizes sexual intimacy by same-sex couples, but not identical behavior by

different-sex couples violate the Fourteenth Amendment guarantee of equal protection of laws?

2. Whether petitioners' criminal convictions for adult consensual sexual intimacy in the home violate their vital interests in liberty and privacy protected by the Due Process Clause of the Fourteenth Amendment?

3. Whether *Bowers v. Hardwick* should be overruled?

The petitioners were adults at the time of the alleged offense. Their conduct was in private and consensual.

We conclude the case should be resolved by determining whether the petitioners were free as adults to engage in the private conduct in the exercise of their liberty under the Due Process Clause of the Fourteenth Amendment to the Constitution. For this inquiry we deem it necessary to reconsider the Court's holding in *Bowers*.

There are broad statements of the substantive reach of liberty under the Due Process Clause in earlier cases, including *Pierce v. Society of Sisters*, and *Meyer v. Nebraska*, but the most pertinent beginning point is our decision in *Griswold v. Connecticut*.

In *Griswold* the Court invalidated a state law prohibiting the use of drugs or devices of contraception and counseling or aiding and abetting the use of contraceptives. The Court described the protected interest as a right to privacy and placed emphasis on the marriage relation and the protected space of the marital bedroom.

After *Griswold* it was established that the right to make certain decisions regarding sexual conduct extends beyond the marital relationship. In *Eisenstadt v. Baird*, the Court invalidated a law prohibiting the distribution of contraceptives to unmarried persons. The case was decided under the Equal Protection Clause, but with respect to unmarried persons, the Court went on to state the fundamental proposition that the law impaired the exercise of their personal rights....

The opinions in *Griswold* and *Eisenstadt* were part of the background for the decision in *Roe v.*

Wade. As is well known, the case involved a challenge to the Texas law prohibiting abortions, but the laws of other states were affected as well. Although the Court held the woman's rights were not absolute, her right to elect an abortion did have real and substantial protection as an exercise of her liberty under the Due Process Clause. The Court cited cases that protect spatial freedom and cases that go well beyond it. *Roe* recognized the right of a woman to make certain fundamental decisions affecting her destiny and confirmed once more that the protection of liberty under the Due Process Clause has a substantive dimension of fundamental significance in defining the rights of the person ...

The facts in *Bowers* had some similarities to the instant case. A police officer, whose right to enter seems not to have been in question, observed Hardwick, in his own bedroom, engaging in intimate sexual conduct with another adult male. The conduct was in violation of a Georgia statute making it a criminal offense to engage in sodomy. One difference between the two cases is that the Georgia statute prohibited the conduct whether or not the participants were of the same sex, while the Texas statute, as we have seen, applies only to participants of the same sex. Hardwick was not prosecuted, but he brought an action in federal court to declare the state statute invalid. He alleged he was a practicing homosexual and that the criminal prohibition violated rights guaranteed to him by the Constitution. The Court, in an opinion by Justice White, sustained the Georgia law. Chief Justice Burger and Justice Powell joined the opinion of the Court and filed separate, concurring opinions. Four Justices dissented.

The Court began its substantive discussion in *Bowers* as follows: "The issue presented is whether the federal Constitution confers a fundamental right upon homosexuals to engage in sodomy and hence invalidates the laws of the many states that still make such conduct illegal and have done so for a very long time." That statement, we now conclude, discloses the Court's own failure to appreciate the extent of the liberty at stake. To say that the issue in *Bowers* was simply the right to engage in certain sexual conduct demeans the claim the individual put forward, just as it would demean a married couple were it to be said marriage is simply about the right to have sexual intercourse. The laws involved in *Bowers* and here are, to be sure, statutes that purport to do no more than prohibit a particular sexual act. Their penalties and purposes, though, have more far-reaching consequences, touching upon the most private human conduct, sexual behavior, and in the most private of places, the home. The statutes do seek to control a personal relationship that, whether or not entitled to formal recognition in the law, is within the liberty of persons to choose without being punished as criminals.

This, as a general rule, should counsel against attempts by the state, or a court, to define the meaning of the relationship or to set its boundaries absent injury to a person or abuse of an institution the law protects. It suffices for us to acknowledge that adults may choose to enter upon this relationship in the confines of their homes and their own private lives and still retain their dignity as free persons. When sexuality finds overt expression in intimate conduct with another person, the conduct can be but one element in a personal bond that is more enduring. The liberty protected by the Constitution allows homosexual persons the right to make this choice.

Having misapprehended the claim of liberty there presented to it, and thus stating the claim to be whether there is a fundamental right to engage in consensual sodomy, the *Bowers* Court said: "Proscriptions against that conduct have ancient roots." In academic writings, and in many of the scholarly amicus briefs filed to assist the Court in this case, there are fundamental criticisms of the historical premises relied upon by the majority and concurring opinions in *Bowers*. We need not enter this debate in the attempt to reach a definitive historical judgment, but the following considerations counsel against adopting the definitive conclusions upon which *Bowers* placed such reliance.

At the outset it should be noted that there is no longstanding history in this country of laws directed at homosexual conduct as a distinct matter. Beginning in colonial times there were prohibitions of sodomy derived from the English criminal laws passed in the first instance by the Reformation Parliament of 1533. The English prohibition was understood to include relations between men and women as well as relations between men and men....The historical grounds relied upon in *Bowers* are more complex than the majority opinion and the concurring opinion by Chief Justice Burger indicate. Their historical premises are not without doubt and, at the very least, are overstated.

It must be acknowledged, of course, that the Court in *Bowers* was making the broader point that for centuries there have been powerful voices to condemn homosexual conduct as immoral. The condemnation has been shaped by religious beliefs, conceptions of right and acceptable behavior, and respect for the traditional family. For many persons these are not trivial concerns but profound and deep convictions accepted as ethical and moral principles to which they aspire and which thus determine the course of their lives. These considerations do not answer the question before us, however. The issue is whether the majority may use the power of the state to enforce these views on the whole society through operation of the criminal law. "Our obligation is to define the liberty of all, not to mandate our own moral code."

Chief Justice Burger joined the opinion for the Court in *Bowers* and further explained his views as follows: "Decisions of individuals relating to homosexual conduct have been subject to state intervention throughout the history of Western civilization. Condemnation of those practices is firmly rooted in Judeao-Christian moral and ethical standards." As with Justice White's assumptions about history, scholarship casts some doubt on the sweeping nature of the statement by Chief Justice Burger as it pertains to private homosexual conduct between consenting adults. In all events we think that our laws and traditions in the past half century are of most relevance here. These references show an emerging awareness that liberty gives substantial protection to adult persons in deciding how to conduct their private lives in matters pertaining to sex. "[H]istory and tradition are the starting point but not in all cases the ending point of the substantive due process inquiry."

This emerging recognition should have been apparent when *Bowers* was decided. In 1955 the American Law Institute promulgated the Model Penal Code and made clear that it did not recommend or provide for criminal penalties for consensual sexual relations conducted in private. It justified its decision on three grounds: (1) The prohibitions undermined respect for the law by penalizing conduct many people engaged in; (2) the statutes regulated private conduct not harmful to others; and (3) the laws were arbitrarily enforced and thus invited the danger of blackmail. In 1961 Illinois changed its laws to conform to the Model Penal Code. Other states soon followed.

In *Bowers* the Court referred to the fact that before 1961 all 50 states had outlawed sodomy, and that at the time of the Court's decision 24 states and the District of Columbia had sodomy laws. Justice Powell pointed out that these prohibitions often were being ignored, however. Georgia, for instance, had not sought to enforce its law for decades.

The sweeping references by Chief Justice Burger to the history of Western civilization and to Judeo-Christian moral and ethical standards did not take account of other authorities pointing in an opposite direction. A committee advising the British Parliament recommended in 1957 repeal of laws punishing homosexual conduct. Parliament enacted the substance of those recommendations 10 years later....

In our own constitutional system the deficiencies in *Bowers* became even more apparent in the years following its announcement. The 25 states with laws prohibiting the relevant conduct referenced in the *Bowers* decision are reduced now to 13, of which 4 enforce their laws only against homosexual conduct. In those states where sodomy is still proscribed, whether for same-sex or heterosexual conduct, there is a pattern of nonenforcement with respect to consenting adults acting in private. The State of Texas admitted in 1994 that as of that date it had not prosecuted anyone under those circumstances.

Two principal cases decided after *Bowers* cast its holding into even more doubt. In *Planned Parenthood of Southeastern Pa. v. Casey*, the Court reaffirmed the substantive force of the liberty protected by the Due Process Clause. The *Casey* decision again confirmed that our laws and tradition afford constitutional protection to personal decisions relating to marriage, procreation, contraception, family relationships, child rearing, and education. In explaining the respect the Constitution demands for the autonomy of the person in making these choices, we stated as follows:

"These matters, involving the most intimate and personal choices a person may make in a lifetime, choices central to personal dignity and autonomy, are central to the liberty protected by the Fourteenth Amendment. At the heart of liberty is the right to define one's own concept of existence, of meaning, of the universe, and of the mystery of human life. Beliefs about these matters could not define the attributes of personhood were they formed under compulsion of the State."

Persons in a homosexual relationship may seek autonomy for these purposes, just as heterosexual persons do. The decision in Bowers would deny them this right.

The second *post-Bowers* case of principal relevance is *Romer v. Evans*. There the Court struck down class-based legislation directed at homosexuals as a violation of the Equal Protection Clause. *Romer* invalidated an amendment to Colorado's constitution which named as a solitary class persons who were homosexuals, lesbians, or bisexual either by "orientation, conduct, practices or relationships," and deprived them of protection under state antidiscrimination laws. We concluded that the provision was born of animosity toward the class of persons affected and further that it had no rational relation to a legitimate governmental purpose.

As an alternative argument in this case, counsel for the petitioners and some amici contend that *Romer* provides the basis for declaring the Texas statute invalid under the Equal Protection Clause. That is a tenable argument, but we conclude the instant case requires us to address whether *Bowers* itself has continuing validity. Were we to hold the statute invalid under the Equal Protection Clause some might question whether a prohibition would be valid if drawn differently, say, to prohibit the conduct both between same-sex and different-sex participants.

Equality of treatment and the due process right to demand respect for conduct protected by the substantive guarantee of liberty are linked in important respects, and a decision on the latter point advances both interests. If protected conduct is made criminal and the law which does so remains unexamined for its substantive validity, its stigma might remain even if it were not enforceable as drawn for equal protection reasons. When homosexual conduct is made criminal by the law of the state, that declaration in and of itself is an invitation to subject homosexual persons to discrimination both in the public and in the private spheres. The central holding of *Bowers* has been brought in question by this case, and it should be addressed. Its continuance as precedent demeans the lives of homosexual persons.

The stigma this criminal statute imposes, moreover, is not trivial. The offense, to be sure, is but a class C misdemeanor, a minor offense in the Texas legal system. Still, it remains a criminal offense with all that imports for the dignity of the persons charged. The petitioners will bear on their record the history of their criminal convictions. Just this term we rejected various challenges to state laws requiring the registration of sex offenders. We are advised that if Texas convicted an adult for private, consensual homosexual conduct under the statute here in question the convicted person would come within the registration laws of a least four states were he or she to be subject to their jurisdiction. This underscores the consequential nature of the punishment and the state-sponsored condemnation attendant to the criminal prohibition. Furthermore, the Texas criminal conviction carries with it the other collateral consequences always following a conviction, such as notations on job application forms, to mention but one example....

The rationale of *Bowers* does not withstand careful analysis. In his dissenting opinion in *Bowers* Justice Stevens came to these conclusions:

"Our prior cases make two propositions abundantly clear. First, the fact that the governing majority in a state has traditionally viewed a particular practice as immoral is not a sufficient reason for upholding a law prohibiting the practice; neither history nor tradition could save a law prohibiting miscegenation from constitutional attack. Second, individual decisions by married persons, concerning the intimacies of their physical relationship, even when not intended to produce offspring, are a form of liberty protected by the Due Process Clause of the Fourteenth Amendment. Moreover, this protection extends to intimate choices by unmarried as well as married persons."

Justice Stevens' analysis, in our view, should have been controlling in *Bowers* and should control here.

Bowers was not correct when it was decided, and it is not correct today. It ought not to remain binding precedent. *Bowers v. Hardwick* should be and now is overruled.

The present case does not involve minors. It does not involve persons who might be injured or coerced or who are situated in relationships where consent might not easily be refused. It does not involve public conduct or prostitution. It does not involve whether the government must give formal recognition to any relationship that homosexual persons seek to enter. The case does involve two adults who, with full and mutual consent from each other, engaged in sexual practices common to a homosexual lifestyle. The petitioners are entitled to respect for their private lives. The state cannot demean their existence or control their destiny by making their private sexual conduct a crime. Their right to liberty under the Due Process Clause gives them the full right to engage in their conduct without intervention of the government. "It is a promise of the Constitution that there is a realm of personal liberty which the government may not enter." The Texas statute furthers no legitimate state interest which can justify its intrusion into the personal and private life of the individual.

Had those who drew and ratified the Due Process Clauses of the Fifth Amendment or the Fourteenth Amendment known the components of liberty in its manifold possibilities, they might have been more specific. They did not presume to have this insight. They knew times can blind us to certain truths and later generations can see that laws once thought necessary and proper in fact serve only to oppress. As the Constitution endures, persons in every generation can invoke its principles in their own search for greater freedom.

SUGGESTIONS FOR FURTHER READING

Anthologies

Baird, Robert, and Katherine Baird. *Homosexuality: Debating the Issues*. Amherst: Prometheus Books, 1995.

Batchelor, Edward, Jr. *Homosexuality and Ethics*. New York: Pilgrim Press, 1980.

Dudley, William. *Homosexuality—Opposing Viewpoints*. San Diego: Greenhaven Press, 1993.

Rolefl, Tamara. *Gay Rights*. San Diego: Greenhaven Press, 1997.

Basic Concepts

"Survey on the Constitutional Right to Privacy in the Context of Homosexual Activity." *Miami Law Review*, 1986, pp. 521–657.

Alternative Views

du Mas, Frank M. *Gay Is Not Good*. Nashville, TN: Thomas Nelson, 1979.

Finnis, John. "Law, Morality, and 'Sexual Orientation,'" *Notre Dame Law Review*, 1994.

Friedman, Richard. *Male Homosexuality*. New Haven, CT: Yale University Press, 1988.

Harrigan, J. *Homosexuality: The Test Case for Christian Ethics*. Mahwah, NJ: Paulist Press, 1988.

Hoagland, Sarah. *Lesbian Ethics*. Palo Alto: Institute of Lesbian Studies, 1988.

Kaplan, Morris. *Sexual Justice*. New York: Routledge, 1997.

Malloy, Edward A. *Homosexuality and the Christian Way of Life*. Lanham, MD: University Press of America, 1981.

Mohr, Richard D. *Gays/Justice*. New York: Columbia University Press, 1988.

Nussbaum, Martha. "Platonic Love and Colorado Law: The Relevance of Ancient Greek Norms to Modern Sexual Controversies," *Virginia Law Review*, 1994.

Ruse, Michael. *Homosexuality*. Oxford: Basil Blackwell, 1988.

Thomas, Laurence, and Michael Levin. *Sexual Orientation*. Lanham, MD: Rowman & Littlefield, 1999.

❋

Animal Liberation and Environmental Justice

INTRODUCTION

Basic Concepts

The problem of animal liberation and environmental concern has begun to attract widespread public attention. Beginning with the 1973 publication of Peter Singer's article, "Animal Liberation," in the *New York Review of Books*, followed by the publication two years later of his book of the same title, people have become increasingly concerned with two of the most serious forms of exploitation: animal experimentation and factory farming.

Animal experimentation is a big business, involving 60 to 100 million animals a year. Two experiments alone—the rabbit-blinding Draize eye test and the LD50 toxicity test designed to find the lethal dose for 50 percent of a sample of animals—cause the deaths of more than 5 million animals per year in the United States alone. In factory farming, millions of animals are raised in such a way that their short lives are dominated by pain and suffering. Veal calves are put in narrow stalls and tethered with a chain so that they cannot turn around, lie down comfortably, or groom themselves. They are fed a totally liquid diet to promote rapid weight gain, and they are given no water because thirsty animals eat more than those who drink water.

In recent years, environmental concern has focused on a myriad of problems from acid rain to the destruction of rainforests and the ozone layer. For example, the acidity of rainfall over the northeastern United States has quadrupled since 1900. Moreover, in 1995, some 12,350 square miles of Brazilian rainforest—an area larger than Belgium—was reduced to ashes, and over the past decade, ozone levels over Antarctica have diminished by 50 percent. In many cases, resolving these problems will require extensive programs and international cooperation. For example, in the Montreal protocol of 1987, dozens of nations agreed to cut their chlorofluorocarbon emissions (which are thought to be the major cause of ozone depletion) in half by the end of the century, and several countries and the major chlorofluorocarbon manufacturers have more recently announced their intentions to eliminate the chemicals by that deadline.

At the most general level, the problem of animal liberation and environmental concern raises the question of what should be our policies for treating animals and preserving the environment, or alternatively, what is the moral status of nonhuman living things. One possible answer is that nonhuman living things have no independent moral status at all; their moral status depends completely on the impact they have on human welfare. Another possible answer is that nonhuman living things have an independent moral status such that their welfare has to be weighed against, and at least sometimes outweigh, considerations of human welfare.

Obviously, supporters of animal liberation favor the view that animals have independent moral status, but they disagree as to the grounds for this independent moral status. Some claim that animals have independent moral status because taking their welfare into account would maximize overall utility. Others claim that the independent moral status of animals rests on a nonutilitarian foundation.

This conflict among supporters of animal liberation reflects a general conflict among utilitarians and nonutilitarians on a wide range of practical problems (see the General Introduction to this anthology). With respect to this problem, however, supporters of animal liberation cannot rely on some form of a Kantian theory to reach an acceptable resolution because most animals are incapable of forming either an actual or hypothetical contract with human beings for the purpose of securing their common welfare. Kantian theory, however, is only a means to a goal, which is to achieve a fair resolution of morally relevant interests. Consequently, if nonhuman living things do have morally relevant interests, then to achieve that goal, some means other than Kantian theory will have to be employed.

This is not to say that Kantian theory is not useful for achieving a fair resolution of conflicts when only human interests pertain. In fact, it would seem that a fair resolution of conflicts among human and nonhuman interests would mirror a fair resolution of conflicts among purely human interests. For example, if a utilitarian (or a nonutilitarian) resolution were fair when only human interests are taken into account, a utilitarian (or a nonutilitarian) resolution would seem to be fair when both human and nonhuman interests are considered.

With respect to environmental concern, supporters do not agree that all nonhuman living things have independent moral status. Those who maintain that only sentient beings have independent moral status attempt to ground human concern for other living things on the impact they have on the welfare of sentient beings. Accordingly, to resolve the problem of animal liberation and environmental concern, we must determine which living beings have independent moral status and what sort of justification best accounts for that status.

Alternative Views

In Selection 58, Peter Singer argues for the independent moral status of animals by comparing the bias against animals, which he calls "speciesism," with biases against blacks and women. According to Singer, the grounds we have for opposing racism and sexism are also grounds for opposing speciesism because all forms of discrimination run counter to the principle of equal consideration. Racists violate this principle by giving greater weight to the interests of members of their own race in cases of conflict; sexists violate this principle by favoring the interests of their own specific sex; and speciesists violate this principle by allowing the interests of their own species to override the greater interests of other species.

Animals have interests, Singer maintains, because they have a capacity for suffering and enjoyment. According to the principle of equal consideration, there is no justification for regarding the pain animals feel as less important than the same amount of pain (or pleasure) humans feel. As for the practical requirements of this view, Singer contends that we cannot go astray if we give the same respect to the lives of animals that we give to the lives of humans at a similar mental level. In the end, Singer thinks, this requires a utilitarian weighing of both human and animal interests.

Singer's view has been challenged on grounds that utilitarianism does not ultimately support a strong case for animal rights for several reasons. First of all, by Singer's own admission, it is permissible to eat farm animals, typically cattle and sheep, that are reared and killed without suffering. Second, Singer's objection to the suffering inflicted on animals in factory farms can be overcome by reforming the practices used on such farms rather than by requiring that we become vegetarians. Third, a radical turn to vegetarianism would probably result in the elimination of most farm animals as we know them because they certainly cannot survive in the wild. This would seriously disrupt and/or eliminate many industries and social practices, resulting in significant disutility.

Responding to these criticisms in an article in the *New York Review of Books*, Singer makes two points. He first claims that adopting vegetarianism would improve people's general health, eliminate Third World poverty, and create new and beneficial industries and social practices. Second, Singer claims that in political campaigning, opposition to the current techniques of factory farming is not taken seriously unless one is also a committed vegetarian. According to Singer, only vegetarians can silence that invariable objection to reforming our treatment of animals: But don't you eat them?

Nevertheless, Singer's response turns on the political effectiveness of being a vegetarian and the effects vegetarianism would have on human welfare rather than its effects on animal welfare. However, it is in terms of animal welfare that the case for animal rights must ultimately be made.

In Selection 59, Michael Pollan reviews Peter Singer's arguments for animal liberation or animal rights and concludes that we should be working for animal welfare rather than animal rights. Rather than endorsing a complete vegetarianism, Pollan thinks we should try to ensure that farm animals do not suffer and that their deaths are swift and painless. He recognizes, however, that this way of raising farm animals would mean that we would have fewer farm animals to eat. He also recognizes that Peter Singer would have little reason to object to this radical reform of factory farming except to wonder whether it was sustainable in the face of market forces.

In Selection 60, Paul W. Taylor argues that all living beings have independent moral status. He grounds his view on two central claims: (1) that each individual organism is a teleological center of life, pursuing its own good in its own way, and (2) that whether we are concerned with standards of merit or with the concept of inherent worth, there is no ground for believing that humans by their very nature are superior to other species. Taylor's argument for his second claim is similar to the argument used in the General Introduction to support morality against rational egoism. Both claim that their view represents a non-question-begging solution.

The main difficulty with Taylor's view is how we are to weigh human welfare against the good of other living beings if we were to grant that human beings are not superior to other species. In a later book that develops the argument of this essay, Taylor distinguishes between basic and nonbasic interests of living beings, but because he doesn't hold that the basic interests always have priority over nonbasic interests, it is difficult to know how decisions should be made when there is conflict between human and nonhuman interests.

In Selection 61, David Schmidtz critiques biocentrists who are known for their commitment to the equality of species. In particular, Schmidt critiques Paul Taylor's argument for species egalitarianism. He argues that while other species do command respect, they do not command equal respect. He closes by questioning whether the biocentrist's commitment to species egalitarianism is even compatible with respect for nature.

In Selection 62, James P. Sterba defends the biocentrism that Schmidtz critiques. He argues that the biocentrist's commitment to species egalitarianism needs to be understood by analogy with the equality of humans. Accordingly, just as we claim that humans are equal, yet justifiably treat them differently, so too we think that we should be able to claim that all species are equal, yet justifiably treat them differently. He then argues for a set of conflict resolution principles, which, he claims, are not biased in favor of the human species, and thus provide a defensible interpretation of the biocentrist's commitment to the equality of species.

In Selection 63, Karen Warren raises an important challenge to mainstream environmental ethics. The challenge is that such mainstream ethics have failed to recognize that the domination of nature is rooted in the domination of women, or at least has failed to recognize that both forms of domination are interconnected. To elucidate this connection, Warren claims that at least within the dominant Western culture, the following argument is sanctioned:

1. Women are identified with nature and the realm of the physical; men are identified with the "human" and the realm of the mental. (For example, naturist language describes women as cows, foxes, chicks, serpents, bitches, beavers, old bats, pussy-cats, cats, bird-brains, hare-brains. Sexist language feminizes and sexualizes Nature: Nature is raped, mastered, conquered, controlled, mined. Her "secrets" are "penetrated" and her "womb" is put into the services of the "man of science." "Virgin timber" is felled, cut down. "Fertile soil" is tilled and land that lies "fallow" is "barren," useless.)

2. Whatever is identified with nature and the realm of the physical is inferior to whatever is identified with the "human" and the realm of the mental; or, conversely, the latter is superior to the former.

3. Thus, women are inferior to men; or, conversely, men are superior to women.

4. For any X and Y, if X is superior to Y, then X is justified in subordinating Y.

5. Thus, men are justified in subordinating women.

Warren points out that there is a "logic of domination" to this argument. It begins with a *claim of difference*. It then moves from a claim of difference to a *claim of superiority* and then from a claim of superiority to a *claim of subordination* or domination. Warren contends that this same logic of domination is common to all forms of domination and so is used to support, for example, racism, classism, and ageism, as well as sexism and naturism (Warren's term for the domination of nature). If Warren is correct, it follows that if one is against any one of these forms of domination, one should be against them all.

Practical Applications

The next two selections come from the only federal law in the United States pertaining to the treatment of animals. The provisions of the Animal Welfare Act (Selection 64) pertain only to the transportation of animals and the treatment of animals for research and experimentation. The Act does not mention the treatment of animals in factory farms. The amendments to the Animal Welfare Act (Selection 65) passed in 1985 represent a considerable strengthening of the original Act. Specifically, the amendments call for a national data bank that will list the results of all animal experiments and thus prevent needless repetition. All laboratories using live animals are also required, under the amendments, to set up animal-care committees and submit to annual inspections. Facilities that house dogs must let them exercise, and those that house primates must provide for their "psychological well-being." Unfortunately, the implementation of these amendments is currently held up by the federal budget office.

In *Tennessee Valley Authority v. Hill* (Selection 66), the issue before the Supreme Court was whether the Endangered Species Act of 1973 prohibited the completion of a dam whose operation would destroy the habitat of the snail darter, an endangered species; the dam was virtually complete and Congress continued to appropriate large sums of money to the project even after the congressional appropriations committees were apprised of the project's apparent impact on the snail darter's survival. The Court held that the act did prohibit the dam's completion because its language and the debate that led to its passage required that its provisions be applied without exceptions. Immediately after this court decision, however, Congress amended the act to provide a "review" process that would relax the protection accorded endangered species in some circumstances. In the case of the snail darter, protection was relaxed because it was possible to transport snail darters to another river. Additional populations of snail darters were found in other rivers. An interesting sidelight to this case, however, was that an interim economic study found that the dam was a pork barrel construction project. Its benefits to the Tennessee economy could have been achieved in less costly ways while the natural state of the river was preserved.

Although there is no denying that existing federal laws that protect animals and the environment are quite limited in scope, it seems clear that any solution to the problem of animal liberation and environmental concern that gives independent moral status to all living beings, or even just to all sentient beings will, if implemented, have a significant impact on the way we live and work and, accordingly, on how we are able to solve the other practical problems discussed in this anthology.

58

Animal Liberation

PETER SINGER

Peter Singer begins his defense of animal liberation by comparing the bias against animals with biases against blacks and women, arguing that all of these forms of discrimination violate the principle of equal consideration. According to this principle, there is no justification for regarding the pain that animals feel as less important than the same amount of pain (or pleasure) felt by humans.

"Animal Liberation" may sound more like a parody of other liberation movements than a serious objective. The idea of "The Rights of Animals" actually was once used to parody the case for women's rights. When Mary Wollstonecraft, a forerunner of today's feminists, published her *Vindication of the Rights of Women* in 1792, her views were widely regarded as absurd, and before long an anonymous publication appeared entitled *A Vindication of the Rights of Brutes*. The author of this satirical work (now known to have been Thomas Taylor, a distinguished Cambridge philosopher) tried to refute Mary Wollstonecraft's arguments by showing that they could be carried one stage further. If the argument for equality was sound when applied to women, why should it not be applied to dogs, cats, and horses? The reasoning seemed to hold for these "brutes" too; yet to hold that brutes had rights was manifestly absurd; therefore the reasoning by which this conclusion had been reached must be unsound, and if unsound when applied to brutes, it must also be unsound when applied to women, since the very same arguments had been used in each case.

In order to explain the basis of the case for the equality of animals, it will be helpful to start with an examination of the case for the equality of women.

Let us assume that we wish to defend the case for women's rights against the attack by Thomas Taylor. How should we reply?

One way in which we might reply is by saying that the case for equality between men and women cannot validly be extended to nonhuman animals. Women have a right to vote, for instance, because they are just as capable of making rational decisions about the future as men are; dogs, on the other hand, are incapable of understanding the significance of voting, so they cannot have the right to vote. There are many other obvious ways in which men and women resemble each other closely, while humans and animals differ greatly. So, it might be said, men and women are similar beings and should have similar rights, while humans and nonhumans are different and should not have equal rights.

The reasoning behind this reply to Taylor's analogy is correct up to a point, but it does not go far enough. There *are* important differences between humans and other animals, and these differences must give rise to *some* differences in the rights that each have. Recognizing this obvious fact, however, is no barrier to the case for extending the basic principle of equality to nonhuman animals. The differences that exist between men and

From *Animal Liberation* (New York: New York Review, 1975), pp. 1–22. Reprinted by permission of Peter Singer.

women are equally undeniable, and the supporters of Women's Liberation are aware that these differences may give rise to different rights. Many feminists hold that women have the right to an abortion on request. It does not follow that since these same feminists are campaigning for equality between men and women they must support the right of men to have abortions too. Since a man cannot have an abortion, it is meaningless to talk of his right to have one. Since a dog can't vote, it is meaningless to talk of its right to vote. There is no reason why either Women's Liberation or Animal Liberation should get involved in such nonsense.

The extension of the basic principle of equality from one group to another does not imply that we must treat both groups in exactly the same way, or grant exactly the same rights to both groups. Whether we should do so will depend on the nature of the members of the two groups. The basic principle of equality does not require equal or identical *treatment*; it requires equal *consideration*. Equal consideration for different beings may lead to different treatment and different rights.

So there is a different way of replying to Taylor's attempt to parody the case for women's rights, a way that does not deny the obvious differences between humans and nonhumans but goes more deeply into the question of equality and concludes by finding nothing absurd in the idea that the basic principle of equality applies to so-called "brutes." At this point such a conclusion may appear odd; but if we examine more deeply the basis [for] our opposition to discrimination on grounds of race or sex ultimately, we will see that we would be on shaky ground if we were to demand equality for Blacks, women, and other groups of oppressed humans while denying equal consideration to nonhumans. To make this clear we need to see first exactly why racism and sexism are wrong.

When we say that all human beings, whatever their race, creed, or sex, are equal, what is it that we are asserting? Those who wish to defend hierarchical, inegalitarian societies have often pointed out that by whatever test we choose it simply is not true that all humans are equal. Like it or not we

must face the fact that humans come in different shapes and sizes; they come with different moral capacities, different intellectual abilities, different amounts of benevolent feeling and sensitivity to the needs of others, different abilities to communicate effectively, and different capacities to experience pleasure and pain. In short, if the demand for equality were based on the actual equality of all human beings, we would have to stop demanding equality.

Still, one might cling to the view that the demand for equality among human beings is based on the actual equality of the different races and sexes. Although, it may be said, humans differ as individuals there are no differences between the races and sexes *as such*. From the mere fact that a person is Black or a woman we cannot infer anything about that person's intellectual or moral capacities. This, it may be said, is why racism and sexism are wrong. The white racist claims that whites are superior to Blacks, but this is false—although there are differences among individuals, some Blacks are superior to some whites in all of the capacities and abilities that could conceivably be relevant. The opponent of sexism would say the same: A person's sex is no guide to his or her abilities, and this is why it is unjustifiable to discriminate on the basis of sex.

The existence of individual variations that cut across the lines of race or sex, however, provides us with no defense at all against a more sophisticated opponent of equality, one who proposes that, say, the interests of all those with IQ scores below 100 be given less consideration than the interests of those with ratings over 100. Perhaps those scoring below the mark would, in this society, be made the slaves of those scoring higher. Would a hierarchical society of this sort really be so much better than one based on race or sex? I think not. But if we tie the moral principle of equality to the factual equality of the different races or sexes, taken as a whole, our opposition to racism and sexism does not provide us with any basis for objecting to this kind of inegalitarianism.

There is a second important reason why we ought not to base our opposition to racism and sexism on any kind of actual equality, even the limited kind that asserts that variations in capacities and abilities are spread evenly between the different races and sexes: We can have no absolute guarantee that these capacities and abilities really are distributed evenly, without regard to race or sex, among human beings. So far as actual abilities are concerned there do seem to be certain measurable differences between both races and sexes. These differences do not, of course, appear in each case, but only when averages are taken. More important still, we do not yet know how much of these differences is really due to the different genetic endowments of the different races and sexes, and how much is due to poor schools, poor housing, and other factors that are the result of past and continuing discrimination. Perhaps all of the important differences will eventually prove to be environmental rather than genetic. Anyone opposed to racism and sexism will certainly hope that this will be so, for it will make the task of ending discrimination a lot easier; nevertheless it would be dangerous to rest the case against racism and sexism on the belief that all significant differences are environmental in origin. The opponent of, say, racism who takes this line will be unable to avoid conceding that *if* differences in ability do after all prove to have some genetic connection with race, racism would in some way be defensible.

Fortunately there is no need to pin the case for equality to one particular outcome of a scientific investigation. The appropriate response to those who claim to have found evidence of genetically based differences in ability between the races or sexes is not to stick to the belief that the genetic explanation must be wrong, whatever evidence to the contrary may turn up: Instead we should make it quite clear that the claim to equality does not depend on intelligence, moral capacity, physical strength, or similar matters of fact. Equality is a moral idea, not an assertion of fact. There is no logically compelling reason for assuming that a factual difference in ability between two people justifies any difference in the amount of consideration we give to their needs and interests. *The principle of the equality of human beings is not a description of an alleged actual equality among humans: It is a prescription of how we should treat humans.*

Jeremy Bentham, the founder of the reforming utilitarian school of moral philosophy, incorporated the essential basis of moral equality into his system of ethics by means of the formula: "Each to count for one and none for more than one." In other words, the interests of every being affected by an action are to be taken into account and given the same weight as the like interests of any other being. A later utilitarian, Henry Sidgwick, put the point in this way: "The good of any one individual is of no more importance, from the point of view (if I may say so) of the Universe, than the good of any other." More recently leading figures in contemporary moral philosophy have shown a great deal of agreement in specifying as a fundamental presupposition of their moral theories some similar requirement which operates so as to give everyone's interests equal consideration—although these writers generally cannot agree on how this requirement is best formulated.[1]

It is an implication of this principle of equality that our concern for others and our readiness to consider their interests ought not depend on what they are like or on what abilities they may possess. Precisely what this concern or consideration requires us to do may vary according to the characteristics of those affected by what we do: Concern for the well-being of a child growing up in America would require that we teach him to read; concern for the well-being of a pig may require no more than that we leave him alone with other pigs in a place where there is adequate food and room to run freely. But the basic element—the taking into account of the interests of the being, whatever those interests may be—must, according to the principle of equality, be extended to all beings, Black or white, masculine or feminine, human or nonhuman.

Thomas Jefferson, who was responsible for writing the principle of the equality of men into the American Declaration of Independence, saw this point. It led him to oppose slavery even though he was unable to free himself fully from his slaveholding background. He wrote in a letter to the author of a book that emphasized the notable intellectual achievements of Negroes in order to refute the then common view that they had limited intellectual capacities:

> Be assured that no person living wishes more sincerely than I do, to see a complete refutation of the doubts I have myself entertained and expressed on the grade of understanding allotted to them by nature, and to find that they are on a par with ourselves ... but whatever be their degree of talent it is no measure of their rights. Because Sir Isaac Newton was superior to others in understanding, he was not therefore lord of the property or person of others.[2]

Similarly when in the 1850s the call for women's rights was raised in the United States a remarkable Black feminist named Sojourner Truth made the same point in more robust terms at a feminist convention:

> ... they talk about this thing in the head; what do they call it? ["Intellect," whispered someone near by.] That's it. What's that got to do with women's rights or Negroes' rights? If my cup won't hold but a pint and yours holds a quart, wouldn't you be mean not to let me have my little half-measure full?[3]

It is on this basis that the case against racism and the case against sexism must both ultimately rest; and it is in accordance with this principle that the attitude that we may call "speciesism," by analogy with racism, must also be condemned. Speciesism—the word is not an attractive one, but I can think of no better term—is a prejudice or attitude of bias toward the interests of members of one's own species and against those of members of other species. It should be obvious that the fundamental objections to racism and sexism made by Thomas Jefferson and Sojourner Truth apply equally to speciesism. If possessing a higher degree of intelligence does not entitle one human to use another for his own ends, how can it entitle humans to exploit nonhumans for the same purpose?[4]

Many philosophers and other writers have proposed the principle of equal consideration of interests, in some form or other, as a basic moral principle; but not many of them have recognized that this principle applies to members of other species as well as to our own. Jeremy Bentham was one of the few who did realize this. In a forward-looking passage written at a time when Black slaves had been freed by the French but in the British dominions were still being treated in the way we now treat animals, Bentham wrote:

> The day *may* come when the rest of the animal creation may acquire those rights which never could have been withholden from them but by the hand of tyranny. The French have already discovered that the blackness of the skin is no reason why a human being should be abandoned without redress to the caprice of a tormentor. It may one day come to be recognized that the number of the legs, the villosity of the skin, or the termination of the *os sacrum* are reasons equally insufficient for abandoning a sensitive being to the same fate. What else is it that should trace the insuperable line? Is it the faculty of reason, or perhaps the faculty of discourse? But a full-grown horse or dog is beyond comparison a more rational, as well as a more conversable animal, than an infant of a day or a week or even a month, old. But suppose they were otherwise, what would it avail? The question is not, Can they *reason?* nor Can they *talk?* but, *Can they suffer?*[5]

In this passage Bentham points to the capacity for suffering as the vital characteristic that gives a being the right to equal consideration. The capacity for suffering—or more strictly, for suffering and/or enjoyment or happiness—is not just another characteristic like the capacity for language or higher mathematics. Bentham is not saying that those who try to mark "the insuperable line" that determines whether the interests of a being should be considered happen to have chosen the wrong characteristic. By saying that we must consider the interests of all beings with the capacity for suffering or enjoyment Bentham does not arbitrarily exclude from consideration any interests at all—as those who draw the line with reference to the possession of reason or language do. The capacity for suffering and enjoyment is *a prerequisite for having interests at all,* a condition that must be satisfied before we can speak of interests in a meaningful way. It would be nonsense to say that it was not in the interests of a stone to be kicked along the road by a schoolboy. A stone does not have interests because it cannot suffer. Nothing that we can do to it could possibly make any difference to its welfare. A mouse, on the other hand, does have an interest in not being kicked along the road, because it will suffer if it is.

If a being suffers there can be no moral justification for refusing to take that suffering into consideration. No matter what the nature of the being, the principle of equality requires that its suffering be counted equally with the like suffering—in so far as rough comparisons can be made—of any other being. If a being is not capable of suffering, or of experiencing enjoyment or happiness, there is nothing to be taken into account. So the limit of sentience (using the term as a convenient if not strictly accurate shorthand for the capacity to suffer and/or experience enjoyment) is the only defensible boundary of concern for the interests of others. To mark this boundary by some other characteristic like intelligence or rationality would be to mark it in an arbitrary manner. Why not choose some other characteristic, like skin color?

The racist violates the principle of equality by giving greater weight to the interests of members of his own race when there is a clash between their interests and the interests of those of another race. The sexist violates the principle of equality by favoring the interests of his own sex. Similarly the speciesist allows the interests of his own species to override the greater interests of members of other species. The pattern is identical in each case.

Most human beings are speciesists.... Ordinary human beings—not a few exceptionally cruel or heartless humans, but the overwhelming majority of humans—take an active part in, acquiesce in, and allow their taxes to pay for practices that require the sacrifice of the most important interests of members of other species in order to promote the most trivial interests of our own species.

There is, however, one general defense of these practices ... that needs to be disposed of.... It is a defense which, if true, would allow us to do anything at all to nonhumans for the slightest reason, or for no reason at all, without incurring any justifiable reproach. This defense claims that we are never guilty of neglecting the interests of other animals for one breathtakingly simple reason: They have no interests. Nonhuman animals have no interests, according to this view, because they are not capable of suffering. By this is not meant merely that they are not capable of suffering in all the ways that humans are—for instance, that a calf is not capable of suffering from the knowledge that it will be killed in six months time. That modest claim is, no doubt, true; but it does not clear humans of the charge of speciesism, since it allows that animals may suffer in other ways—for instance, by being given electric shocks, or being kept in small, cramped cages. The defense I am about to discuss is the much more sweeping, although correspondingly less plausible, claim that animals are incapable of suffering in any way at all; that they are ... unconscious automata, possessing neither thoughts nor feelings nor a mental life of any kind.

Although ... the view that animals are automata was proposed by the seventeenth-century French philosopher René Descartes, to most people, then and now, it is obvious that if, for example, we stick a sharp knife into the stomach of an unanesthetized dog, the dog will feel pain. That this is so is assumed by the laws in most civilized countries which prohibit wanton cruelty to animals. Readers whose common sense tells them that animals do suffer may prefer to skip the next few paragraphs ... since they do nothing but refute a position which they do not hold. Implausible as it is, though, for the sake of completeness this skeptical position must be discussed.

Do animals other than humans feel pain? How do we know? Well, how do we know if anyone, human or nonhuman, feels pain? We know that we ourselves can feel pain. We know this from the direct experiences of pain that we have when, for instance, somebody presses a lighted cigarette against the back of our hand. But how do we know that anyone else feels pain? We cannot directly experience anyone else's pain, whether that "anyone" is our best friend or a stray dog. Pain is a state of consciousness, a "mental event," and as such it can never be observed. Behavior like writhing, screaming, or drawing one's hand away from the lighted cigarette is not pain itself; nor are the recordings a neurologist might make of activity within the brain observations of pain itself. Pain is something that we feel, and we can only infer that others are feeling it from various external indications.

In theory, we *could* always be mistaken when we assume that other human beings feel pain. It is conceivable that our best friend is really a very cleverly constructed robot, controlled by a brilliant scientist so as to give all the signs of feeling pain, but really no more sensitive than any other machine. We can never know, with absolute certainty, that this is not the case. But while this might present a puzzle for philosophers, none of us has the slightest real doubt that our best friends feel pain just as we do. This is an inference, but a perfectly reasonable one, based on observations of their behavior in situations in which we would feel pain, and on the fact that we have every reason to assume that our friends are beings like us, with nervous systems like ours that can be assumed to function as ours do, and to produce similar feelings in similar circumstances.

If it is justifiable to assume that other humans feel pain as we do, is there any reason why a similar inference should be unjustifiable in the case of other animals?

Nearly all the external signs that lead us to infer pain in other humans can be seen in other species, especially [those] most closely related to us—other species of mammals, and birds. Behavioral signs—writhing, facial contortions, moaning, yelping, or other forms of calling, attempts to avoid the source of pain, appearance of fear at the prospect of its repetition, and so on—are present. In addition, we know that these animals have nervous systems very like ours, which respond physiologically as ours do when the animal is in circumstances in which we would feel pain: an initial rise of blood pressure, dilated pupils, perspiration, an increased pulse rate, and, if the stimulus continues, a fall in blood pressure. Although humans have a more developed cerebral cortex than other animals, this part of the brain is concerned with thinking functions rather than with basic impulses, emotions, and feelings. These impulses, emotions, and feelings are located in the diencephalon, which is well developed in many other species of animals, especially mammals and birds.[6]

We also know that the nervous systems of other animals were not artificially constructed to mimic the pain behavior of humans, as a robot might be artificially constructed. The nervous systems of animals evolved as our own did, and in fact the evolutionary history of humans and other animals, especially mammals, did not diverge until the central features of our nervous systems were already in existence. A capacity to feel pain obviously enhances a species' prospects of survival, since it causes members of the species to avoid sources of injury. It is surely unreasonable to suppose that nervous systems which are virtually identical physiologically, have a common origin and a common evolutionary function, and result in similar forms of behavior in similar circumstances should actually operate in an entirely different manner on the level of subjective feelings.

It has long been accepted as sound policy in science to search for the simplest possible explanation of whatever it is we are trying to explain. Occasionally it has been claimed that it is for this reason "unscientific" to explain the behavior of animals by theories that refer to the animal's conscious feelings, desires, and so on—the idea being that if the behavior in question can be explained without invoking consciousness or feelings, that will be the simpler theory. Yet we can now see that such explanations, when placed in the overall context of the behavior of both human and nonhuman animals, are far more complex than their rivals. We know from our own experience that explanations of our own behavior that did not refer to consciousness and the feeling of pain would be incomplete; it is simpler to assume that the similar behavior of animals with similar nervous systems is to be explained in the same way than to try to invent some other explanation for the behavior of nonhuman animals as well as an explanation for the divergence between humans and nonhumans in this respect.

The overwhelming majority of scientists who have addressed themselves to this question agree. Lord Brain, one of the most eminent neurologists of our time, has said:

> I personally can see no reason for conceding mind to my fellow men and denying it to animals.... I at least cannot doubt that the interests and activities of animals are correlated with awareness and feeling in the same way as my own, and which may be, for aught I know, just as vivid.[7]

While the author of a recent book on pain writes:

> Every particle of factual evidence supports the contention that the higher mammalian vertebrates experience pain sensations at least as acute as our own. To say that they feel less because they are lower animals is an absurdity; it can easily be shown that many of their senses are far more acute than ours—visual acuity in certain birds, hearing in most wild animals, and touch in others; these animals depend more than we do today on the sharpest possible awareness of a hostile environment. Apart from the complexity of the cerebral cortex (which does not directly perceive pain) their nervous systems are almost identical to ours and their reactions to pain remarkably similar, though lacking (so far as we know) the philosophical and moral overtones. The emotional element is all too evident, mainly in the form of fear and anger.[8]

In Britain, three separate expert government committees on matters relating to animals have accepted the conclusion that animals feel pain. After noting the obvious behavioral evidence for this view, the Committee on Cruelty to Wild Animals said:

> ... we believe that the physiological, and more particularly the anatomical, evidence fully justifies and reinforces the common-sense belief that animals feel pain.

And after discussing the evolutionary value of pain they concluded that pain is "of clear-cut biological usefulness" and this is "a third type of evidence that animals feel pain." They then went on to consider forms of suffering other than mere physical pain, and added that they were "satisfied that animals do suffer from acute fear and terror." In 1965, British government [reports] on experiments on animals, and on the welfare of animals under intensive farming methods, agreed with this view, concluding that animals are capable of suffering both from straightforward physical injuries and from fear, anxiety, stress, and so on.[9]

That might well be thought enough to settle the matter; but there is one more objection that needs to be considered. There is, after all, one behavioral sign that humans have when in pain which nonhumans do not have. This is a developed language. Other animals may communicate with each other, but not, it seems, in the complicated way we do. Some philosophers, including Descartes, have thought it important that while humans can tell each other about their experience of pain in great detail, other animals cannot. (Interestingly, this once neat dividing line between humans and other species has now been threatened by the discovery that chimpanzees can be taught a language.)[10] But as Bentham pointed out long ago, the ability to use language is not relevant to the question of how a being ought to be treated—unless that ability can be linked to the capacity to suffer, so that the absence of a language casts doubt on the existence of this capacity.

This link may be attempted in two ways. First, there is a hazy line of philosophical thought, stemming perhaps from some doctrines associated with influential philosopher Ludwig Wittgenstein, that maintains we cannot meaningfully attribute states of consciousness to beings without language. This position seems to me very implausible. Language may be necessary for abstract thought, at some level anyway; but states like pain are more primitive, and have nothing to do with language.

The second and more easily understood way of linking language and the existence of pain is to say that the best evidence that we can have that another creature is in pain is when he tells us that he is. This is a distinct line of argument, for it is not being denied that a non–language-user conceivably *could* suffer, but only that we could ever have sufficient reason to *believe* that he is suffering. Still, this line of argument fails too. As Jane Goodall has pointed out in her study of chimpanzees, *In the Shadow of Man*, when it comes to the expressions of feelings and emotions language is less important than in other areas. We tend to fall back on nonlinguistic modes of communication such as a cheering pat on the back, an exuberant embrace, a clasp of the hands, and so on. The basic signals we use to convey pain, fear, anger, love, joy, surprise, sexual arousal, and many other emotional states are not specific to our own species.[11]

Charles Darwin made an extensive study of this subject, and the book he wrote about it, *The Expression of the Emotions in Man and Animals*, notes countless nonlinguistic modes of expression. The statement "I am in pain" may be one piece of evidence for the conclusion that the speaker is in pain, but it is not the only possible evidence, and since people sometimes tell lies, not even the best possible evidence.

Even if there were stronger grounds for refusing to attribute pain to those who do not have a language, the consequences of this refusal might lead us to reject the conclusion. Human infants and young children are unable to use language. Are we to deny that a year-old child can suffer? If not, language cannot be crucial. Of course, most parents understand the responses of their children better than they understand the responses of other animals; but this is just a fact about the relatively greater knowledge that we have of our own species, and the greater contact we have with infants, as compared to animals. Those who have studied the behavior of other animals, and those who have pet animals, soon learn to understand their responses as well as we understand those of an infant, and sometimes better. Jane Goodall's account of the chimpanzees she watched is one [example], but the same can be said of those who have observed species less closely related to our own. Two among many possible examples are Konrad Lorenz's observations of geese and jackdaws, and N. Tinbergen's extensive studies of herring gulls.[12] Just as we can understand infant human behavior in the light of adult human behavior, so we can understand the behavior of other species in the light of our own behavior—and sometimes we can understand our own behavior better in the light of the behavior of other species.

So to conclude: There are no good reasons, scientific or philosophical, for denying that animals feel pain. If we do not doubt that other humans feel pain we should not doubt that other animals do so too.

Animals can feel pain. As we saw earlier, there can be no moral justification for regarding the pain (or pleasure) that animals feel as less important than the same amount of pain (or pleasure) felt by humans. But what exactly does this mean, in practical terms? To prevent misunderstanding I shall spell out what I mean a little more fully.

If I give a horse a hard slap across its rump with my open hand, the horse may start, but it presumably feels little pain. Its skin is thick enough to protect it against a mere slap. If I slap a baby in the same way, however, the baby will cry and presumably does feel pain, for its skin is more sensitive. So it is worse to slap a baby than a horse, if both slaps are administered with equal force. But there must be some kind of blow … perhaps a blow with a heavy stick … that would cause the horse as much pain as we cause a baby by slapping it with our hand. That is what I mean by "the same amount of pain" and if we consider it wrong to inflict that much pain on a baby for no good reason then we must, unless we are speciesists, consider it equally wrong to inflict the same amount of pain on a horse for no good reason.

There are other differences between humans and animals that cause other complications. Normal adult human beings have mental capacities which will, in certain circumstances, lead them to suffer more than animals would in the same circumstances. If, for instance, we decided to perform extremely painful or lethal scientific experiments on normal adult humans, kidnapped at random from public parks for this purpose, every adult who entered a park would become fearful that he would be kidnapped. The resultant terror would be a form of suffering additional to the pain of the experiment. The same experiments performed on nonhuman animals would cause less suffering since the animals would not have the anticipatory dread of being kidnapped and experimented upon. This does not mean, of course, that it would be right to perform the experiment on animals, but only that there is a reason, which is *not* speciesist, for preferring to use animals rather than normal adult humans, if the experiment is to be done at all. Note, however, that this same argument gives us a reason for preferring to use human infants—orphans perhaps—or retarded humans for experiments, rather than adults, since infants and retarded humans would also have no idea of what was going to happen to them. So far as this argument is concerned nonhuman animals and infants and retarded humans are in the same category; and if we use this argument to justify experiments on nonhuman animals we have to ask ourselves whether we are also prepared to allow experiments on human infants and retarded adults; and if we make a distinction between animals and these humans, on what basis can we do it, other than a barefaced—and morally indefensible—preference for members of our own species?

There are many areas in which the superior mental powers of normal adult humans make a difference: anticipation, more detailed memory, greater knowledge of what is happening, and so on. Yet these differences do not all point to greater suffering on the part of the normal human being. Sometimes an animal may suffer more because of his more limited understanding. If, for instance, we are taking prisoners in wartime we can explain to them that while they must submit to capture, search, and confinement they will not otherwise be harmed and will be set free at the conclusion of hostilities. If we capture a wild animal, however, we cannot explain that we are not threatening its life. A wild animal cannot distinguish an attempt to overpower and confine from an attempt to kill; the one causes as much terror as the other.

It may be objected that comparisons of the sufferings of different species are impossible to make, and that for this reason when the interests of animals and humans clash the principle of equality gives no guidance. It is probably true that comparisons of suffering between members of different species cannot be made precisely, but precision is not essential. Even if we were to prevent the infliction of suffering on animals only when it is quite certain that the interests of humans will not be affected to anything like the extent that animals are affected, we would be forced to make radical changes in our treatment of animals that would involve our diet, the farming methods we use, experimental procedures in many fields of science, our approach to wildlife and to hunting, trapping, and the wearing of furs, and areas of entertainment like circuses, rodeos, and zoos. As a result, a vast amount of suffering would be avoided.

So far I have said a lot about the infliction of suffering on animals, but nothing about killing them. This omission has been deliberate. The application of the principle of equality to the infliction of suffering is, in theory at least, fairly straightforward. Pain and suffering are bad and should be prevented or minimized, irrespective of the race, sex, or species of the being that suffers. How bad a pain is depends on how intense it is and how long it lasts, but pains of the same intensity and duration are equally bad, whether felt by humans or animals.

The wrongness of killing a being is more complicated. I have kept, and shall continue to keep, the question of killing in the background because in the present state of human tyranny over other species the more simple, straightforward principle of equal consideration of pain or pleasure is a sufficient basis for identifying and protesting all the major abuses of animals that humans practice. Nevertheless, it is necessary to say something about killing.

Just as most humans are speciesists in their readiness to cause pain to animals when they would not cause a similar pain to humans for the same reason, so most humans are speciesists in their readiness to kill other animals when they would not kill humans. We need to proceed more cautiously here, however, because people hold widely differing views about when it is legitimate to kill humans, as the continuing debates over abortion and euthanasia attest. Nor have moral philosophers been able to agree on exactly what it is that makes it wrong to kill humans, and under what circumstances killing a human being may be justifiable.

Let us consider first the view that it is always wrong to take an innocent human life. We may call this the "sanctity of life" view. People who take this view oppose abortion and euthanasia. They do not usually, however, oppose the killing of nonhumans—so perhaps it would be more accurate to describe this view as the "sanctity of *human* life" view.

The belief that human life, and only human life, is sacrosanct is a form of speciesism. To see this, consider the following example.

Assume that, as sometimes happens, an infant has been born with massive and irreparable brain damage. The damage is so severe that the infant can never be any more than a "human vegetable," unable to talk, recognize other people, act independently of others, or develop a sense of self-awareness. The parents of the infant, realizing that they cannot hope for any improvement in their child's condition and being in any case unwilling to spend, or ask the state to spend, the thousands of dollars that would be needed annually for proper care of the infant, ask the doctor to kill the infant painlessly.

Should the doctor do what the parents ask? Legally, he should not, and in this respect the law reflects the sanctity of life view. The life of every human being is sacred. Yet people who would say this about the infant do not object to the killing of nonhuman animals. How can they justify their different judgments? Adult chimpanzees, dogs, pigs, and many other species far surpass the brain-damaged infant in their ability to relate to others,

act independently, be self-aware, and any other capacity that could reasonably be said to give value to life. With the most intensive care possible, there are retarded infants who can never achieve the intelligence level of a dog. Nor can we appeal to the concern of the infant's parents, since they themselves, in this imaginary example (and in some actual cases), do not want the infant kept alive.

The only thing that distinguishes the infant from the animal, in the eyes of those who claim it has a "right to life," is that it is, biologically, a member of the species *Homo sapiens*, whereas chimpanzees, dogs, and pigs are not. But to use *this* difference as the basis for granting a right to life to the infant and not to the other animals is, of course, pure speciesism.[13] It is exactly the kind of arbitrary difference that the most crude and overt kind of racist uses in attempting to justify racial discrimination.

This does not mean that to avoid speciesism we must hold that it is as wrong to kill a dog as it is to kill a normal human being. The only position that is irredeemably speciesist is the one that tries to make the boundary of the right to life run exactly parallel to the boundary of our own species. Those who hold the sanctity of life view do this because while distinguishing sharply between humans and other animals they allow no distinctions to be made within our own species, objecting to the killing of the severely retarded and the hopelessly senile as strongly as they object to the killing of normal adults.

To avoid speciesism we must allow that beings which are similar in all relevant respects have a similar right to life—and mere membership in our own biological species cannot be a morally relevant criterion for this right. Within these limits we could still hold that, for instance, it is worse to kill a normal adult human, with a capacity for self-awareness, and the ability to plan for the future and have meaningful relations with others, than it is to kill a mouse, which presumably does not share all of these characteristics; or we might appeal to the close family and other personal ties which humans have but mice do not have to the same degree; or we might think that it is the consequences for other humans, who will be put in fear of their own lives, that make the crucial difference; or we might think it is some combination of these factors, or other factors altogether.

Whatever criteria we choose, however, we will have to admit that they do not follow precisely the boundary of our own species. We may legitimately hold that there are some features of certain beings which make their lives more valuable than those of other beings; but there will surely be some nonhuman animals whose lives, by any standards, are more valuable than the lives of some humans. A chimpanzee, dog, or pig, for instance, will have a higher degree of self-awareness and a greater capacity for meaningful relations with others than a severely retarded infant or someone in a state of advanced senility. So if we base the right to life on these characteristics we must grant these animals a right to life as good as, or better than, such retarded, or senile humans.

Now this argument cuts both ways. It could be taken as showing that chimpanzees, dogs, and pigs, along with some other species, have a right to life and we commit a grave moral offense whenever we kill them, even when they are old and suffering and our intention is to put them out of their misery. Alternatively one could take the argument as showing that the severely retarded and hopelessly senile have no right to life and may be killed for quite trivial reasons, as we now kill animals.

Since the focus of this [reading] is on ethical questions concerning animals and not on the morality of euthanasia I shall not attempt to settle this issue finally. I think it is reasonably clear, though, that while both of the positions just described avoid speciesism, neither is entirely satisfactory. What we need is some middle position which would avoid speciesism but would not make the lives of the retarded and senile as cheap as the lives of pigs and dogs now are, nor make the lives of pigs and dogs so sacrosanct that we think it wrong to put them out of hopeless misery. What we must do is bring nonhuman animals within our sphere of moral concern and cease to treat their lives as expendable for whatever trivial

purposes we may have. At the same time, once we realize that the fact that a being is a member of our own species is not in itself enough to make it always wrong to kill that being, we may come to reconsider our policy of preserving human lives at all costs, even when there is no prospect of a meaningful life or of existence without terrible pain.

I conclude, then, that a rejection of speciesism does not imply that all lives are of equal worth. While self-awareness, intelligence, the capacity for meaningful relations with others, and so on are not relevant to the question of inflicting pain—since pain is pain, whatever other capacities, beyond the capacity to feel pain, the being may have—these capacities may be relevant to the question of taking life. It is not arbitrary to hold that the life of a self-aware being, capable of abstract thought, of planning for the future, of complex acts of communication, and so on, is more valuable than the life of a being without these capacities. To see the difference between the issues of inflicting pain and taking life, consider how we would choose within our own species. If we had to choose to save the life of a normal human or a mentally defective human, we would probably choose to save the life of the normal human; but if we had to choose between preventing pain in the normal human or the mental defective—imagine that both have received painful but superficial injuries, and we only have enough painkiller for one of them—it is not nearly so clear how we ought to choose. The same is true when we consider other species. The evil of pain is, in itself, unaffected by the other characteristics of the being that feels the pain; the value of life is affected by these other characteristics.

Normally this will mean that if we have to choose between the life of a human being and the life of another animal we should choose to save the life of the human; but there may be special cases in which the reverse holds true, because the human being in question does not have the capacities of a normal human being. So this view is not speciesist, although it may appear to be at first glance. The preference, in normal cases, for saving a human life over the life of an animal when a choice *has* to be made is a preference based on the characteristics that normal humans have, and not on the mere fact that they are members of our own species. This is why when we consider members of our own species who lack the characteristics of normal humans we can no longer say their lives are always to be preferred to those of other animals.... In general, though, the question of when it is wrong to kill (painlessly) an animal is one to which we need give no precise answer. As long as we remember that we should give the same respect to the lives of animals as we give to the lives of those humans at a similar mental level, we shall not go far wrong.

ENDNOTES

1. For Bentham's moral philosophy, see his *Introduction to the Principles of Morals and Legislation*, and for Sidgwick's see *The Methods of Ethics* (the passage quoted is from the seventh edition, p. 382). As examples of leading contemporary moral philosophers who incorporate a requirement of equal consideration of interests, see R. M. Hare, *Freedom and Reason* (New York: Oxford University Press, 1963) and John Rawls, *A Theory of Justice* (Cambridge: Harvard University Press, Belknap Press, 1972). For a brief account of the essential agreement on this issue between these and other positions, see R. M. Hare, "Rules of War and Moral Reasoning," *Philosophy and Public Affairs*, vol. 1, no. 2 (1972).

2. Letter to Henri Gregoire, February 25, 1809.

3. Reminiscences by Francis D. Gage, from Susan B. Anthony, *The History of Woman Suffrage*, vol. 1; the passage is to be found in the extract in Leslie Tanner, ed., *Voices from Women's Liberation* (New York: Signet, 1970).

4. I owe the term "speciesism" to Richard Ryder.

5. *Introduction to the Principles of Morals and Legislation*, chapter 17.

6. Lord Brian, "Presidential Address," in C. A. Keele and R. Smith, eds., *The Assessment of Pain in Men and Animals* (London: Universities Federation for Animal Welfare, 1962).

7. Ibid., p. 11.

8. Richard Serjeant, *The Spectrum of Pain* (London: Hart-Davis, 1969), p. 72.

9. See the reports of the Committee on Cruelty to Wild Animals (Command Paper 8268, 1951), paragraphs 36–42; the Departmental Committee on Experiments on Animals (Command Paper 2641, 1965), paragraphs 179-182; and the Technical Committee to Enquire into the Welfare of Animals Kept under Intensive Livestock Husbandry Systems (Command Paper 2836, 1965), paragraphs 26–28 (London: Her Majesty's Stationery Office).

10. One chimpanzee, Washoe, has been taught the sign language used by deaf people, and acquired a vocabulary of 350 signs. Another, Lana, communicates in structured sentences by pushing buttons on a special machine. For a brief account of Washoe's abilities, see Jane van Lawick-Goodall, *In the Shadow of Man* (Boston: Houghton Mifflin, 1971), pp. 252–254; and for Lana, see *Newsweek*, 7 January, 1974, and *New York Times*, 4 December 1974.

11. *In the Shadow of Man*, p. 225; Michael Peters makes a similar point in "Nature and Culture," in Stanley and Roslind Godlovitch and John Harris, eds., *Animals, Men and Morals* (New York: Taplinger Publishing Co., 1972).

12. Konrad Lorenz, *King Solomon's Ring* (New York: T. Y. Crowell, 1952); N. Tinbergen, *The Herring Gull's World*, rev. ed. (New York: Basic Books, 1974).

13. I am here putting aside religious views, for example the doctrine that all and only humans have immortal souls, or are made in the image of God. Historically these views have been very important, and no doubt are partly responsible for the idea that human life has a special sanctity. Logically, however, these religious views are unsatisfactory, since a reasoned explanation of why it should be that all humans and no nonhumans have immortal souls is not offered. This belief too, therefore, comes under suspicion as a form of speciesism. In any case, defenders of the "sanctity of life" view are generally reluctant to base their position on purely religious doctrines, since these doctrines are no longer as widely accepted as they once were.

59

An Animal's Place

MICHAEL POLLAN

Michael Pollan reviews Peter Singer's arguments for animal liberation or animal rights and concludes that we should be working for animal welfare rather than animal rights. Rather than endorsing a complete vegetarianism, Pollan thinks that we should try to ensure that farm animals do not suffer and that their deaths are swift and painless. He recognizes, however, that this way of raising farm animals would mean that we would have fewer farm animals to eat.

The first time I opened Peter Singer's "Animal Liberation," I was dining alone at the Palm, trying to enjoy a rib-eye steak cooked medium-rare. If this sounds like a good recipe for cognitive dissonance (if not indigestion), that was sort of the idea. Preposterous as it might seem, to supporters of animal rights, what I was doing was tantamount to reading "Uncle Tom's Cabin" on a plantation in the Deep South in 1852.

Singer and the swelling ranks of his followers ask us to imagine a future in which people will look back on my meal, and this steakhouse, as relics of an equally backward age. Eating animals, wearing animals, experimenting on animals, killing animals for sport: all these practices, so resolutely normal to us, will be seen as the barbarities they are, and we will come to view "speciesism"—a neologism I had encountered before only in jokes—as a form of discrimination as indefensible as racism or anti-Semitism.

Even in 1975, when "Animal Liberation" was first published, Singer, an Australian philosopher now teaching at Princeton, was confident that he had the wind of history at his back. The recent civil rights past was prologue, as one liberation movement followed on the heels of another. Slowly but surely, the white man's circle of moral consideration was expanded to admit first blacks, then women, then homosexuals. In each case, a group once thought to be so different from the prevailing "we" as to be undeserving of civil rights was, after a struggle, admitted to the club. Now it was animals' turn.

That animal liberation is the logical next step in the forward march of moral progress is no longer the fringe idea it was back in 1975. A growing and increasingly influential movement of philosophers, ethicists, law professors and activists are convinced that the great moral struggle of our time will be for the rights of animals.

So far the movement has scored some of its biggest victories in Europe. Earlier this year, Germany became the first nation to grant animals a constitutional right: the words "and animals" were added to a provision obliging the state to respect and protect the dignity of human beings. The farming of animals for fur was recently banned in England. In several European nations, sows may no longer be confined to crates nor laying hens to "battery cages"—stacked wired cages so small the birds cannot stretch their wings. The Swiss are amending their laws to change the status of animals from "things" to "beings."

Though animals are still very much "things" in the eyes of American law, change is in the air. Thirty-seven states have recently passed laws making some forms of animal cruelty a crime, 21 of them by ballot initiative. Following protests by activists, McDonald's and Burger King forced significant improvements in the way the U.S. meat industry slaughters animals. Agribusiness and the cosmetics and apparel industries are all struggling to defuse mounting public concerns over animal welfare.

Once thought of as a left-wing concern, the movement now cuts across ideological lines. Perhaps the most eloquent recent plea on behalf of animals, a new book called "Dominion," was written by a former speechwriter for President Bush. And once outlandish ideas are finding their way into mainstream opinion. A recent Zogby poll found that 51 percent of Americans believe that primates are entitled to the same rights as human children.

What is going on here? A certain amount of cultural confusion, for one thing. For at the same time many people seem eager to extend the circle of our moral consideration to animals, in our factory farms and laboratories we are inflicting more suffering on more animals than at any time in history. One by one, science is dismantling our claims to uniqueness as a species, discovering that such things as culture, tool making, language and even possibly self-consciousness are not the exclusive domain of *Homo sapiens*. Yet most of the animals we kill lead lives organized very much in the spirit of Descartes, who famously claimed that animals were mere machines, incapable of thought or feeling. There's a schizoid quality to our relationship with animals, in which sentiment and brutality exist side by side. Half the dogs in America will receive Christmas presents this year, yet few of us pause to consider the miserable life of the pig—an animal easily as intelligent as a dog—that becomes the Christmas ham.

We tolerate this disconnect because the life of the pig has moved out of view. When's the last time you saw a pig? (Babe doesn't count.) Except for our pets, real animals—animals living and dying—no longer figure in our everyday lives. Meat comes from the grocery store, where it is cut and packaged to look as little like parts of animals as possible. The disappearance of animals from our lives has opened a space in which there's no reality check, either on the sentiment or the brutality. This is pretty much where we live now, with respect to animals, and it is a space in which the Peter Singers and Frank Perdues of the world can evidently thrive equally well.

Several years ago, the English critic John Berger wrote an essay, "Why Look at Animals?" in which he suggested that the loss of everyday contact between ourselves and animals—and specifically the loss of eye contact—has left us deeply confused about the terms of our relationship to other species. That eye contact, always slightly uncanny, had provided a vivid daily reminder that animals were at once crucially like and unlike us; in their eyes we glimpsed something unmistakably familiar (pain, fear, tenderness) and something irretrievably alien. Upon this paradox people built a relationship in which they felt they could both honor and eat animals without looking away. But that accommodation has pretty much broken down; nowadays, it seems, we either look away or become vegetarians. For my own part, neither option seemed especially appetizing. Which might explain how I found myself reading "Animal Liberation" in a steakhouse.

This is not something I'd recommend if you're determined to continue eating meat. Combining rigorous philosophical argument with journalistic description, "Animal Liberation" is one of those rare books that demand that you either defend the way you live or change it. Because Singer is so skilled in argument, for many readers it is easier to change. His book has converted countless thousands to vegetarianism, and it didn't take long for me to see why: within a few pages, he had succeeded in throwing me on the defensive.

Singer's argument is disarmingly simple and, if you accept its premise, difficult to refute. Take the premise of equality, which most people readily accept. Yet what do we really mean by it? People are not, as a matter of fact, equal at all—some are smarter than others, better looking, more gifted. "Equality is a moral idea," Singer points out, "not an assertion of fact." The moral idea is that everyone's interests ought to receive equal consideration, regardless of "what abilities they may possess." Fair enough; many philosophers have gone this far. But fewer have taken the next logical step. "If possessing a higher degree of intelligence does not entitle one human to use another for his or her own ends, how can it entitle humans to exploit nonhumans for the same purpose?"

This is the nub of Singer's argument, and right around here I began scribbling objections in the margin. But humans differ from animals in morally significant ways. Yes they do, Singer acknowledges, which is why we shouldn't treat pigs and children alike. Equal consideration of interests is not the same as equal treatment, he points out: children have an interest in being educated; pigs, in rooting around in the dirt. But where their interests are the same, the principle of equality demands they receive the same consideration. And the one all-important interest that we share with pigs, as with all sentient creatures, is an interest in avoiding pain.

Here Singer quotes a famous passage from Jeremy Bentham, the 18th-century utilitarian philosopher, that is the wellspring of the animal rights movement. Bentham was writing in 1789, soon after the French colonies freed black slaves, granting them fundamental rights. "The day may come," he speculates, "when the rest of the animal creation may acquire those rights." Bentham then asks what characteristic entitles any being to moral consideration. "Is it the faculty of reason or perhaps the faculty of discourse?" Obviously not, since "a full-grown horse or dog is beyond comparison a more rational, as well as a more conversable animal, than an infant." He concludes: "The question is not, Can they reason? nor, Can they talk? but, Can they suffer?"

Bentham here is playing a powerful card philosophers call the "argument from marginal cases," or A.M.C. for short. It goes like this: there are humans—infants, the severely retarded, the demented—whose mental function cannot match that of a chimpanzee. Even though these people cannot reciprocate our moral attentions, we nevertheless include them in the circle of our moral consideration. So on what basis do we exclude the chimpanzee?

Because he's a chimp, I furiously scribbled in the margin, and they're human! For Singer that's not good enough. To exclude the chimp from moral consideration simply because he's not human is no different from excluding the slave simply because he's not white. In the same way we'd call that exclusion racist, the animal rightist contends that it is speciesist to discriminate against the chimpanzee solely because he's not human.

But the differences between blacks and whites are trivial compared with the differences between my son and a chimp. Singer counters by asking us to imagine a hypothetical society that discriminates against people on the basis of something nontrivial—say, intelligence. If that scheme offends our sense of equality, then why is the fact that animals lack certain human characteristics any more just as a basis for discrimination? Either we do not owe any justice to the severely retarded, he concludes, or we do owe it to animals with higher capabilities.

This is where I put down my fork. If I believe in equality, and equality is based on interests rather than characteristics, then either I have to take the interests of the steer I'm eating into account or concede that I am a speciesist. For the time being, I decided to plead guilty as charged. I finished my steak.

But Singer had planted a troubling notion, and in the days afterward, it grew and grew, watered by the other animal rights thinkers I began reading: the philosophers Tom Regan and James Rachels; the legal theorist Steven M. Wise; the writers Joy Williams and Matthew Scully. I didn't think I minded being a speciesist, but could it be, as several of these writers suggest, that we will someday come to regard speciesism as an evil comparable to racism? Will history someday judge us as harshly as it judges the Germans who went about their ordinary lives in the shadow of Treblinka? Precisely that question was recently posed by J.M. Coetzee, the South African novelist, in a lecture delivered at Princeton; he answered it in the affirmative. If animal rightists are right, "a crime of stupefying proportions" (in Coetzee's words) is going on all around us every day, just beneath our notice.

It's an idea almost impossible to entertain seriously, much less to accept, and in the weeks following my restaurant face-off between Singer and the steak, I found myself marshaling whatever mental power I could muster to try to refute it. Yet Singer and his allies managed to trump almost all my objections.

My first line of defense was obvious. Animals kill one another all the time. Why treat animals more ethically than they treat one another? (Ben Franklin tried this one long before me: during a fishing trip, he wondered, "If you eat one another, I don't see why we may not eat you." He admits, however, that the rationale didn't occur to him until the fish were in the frying pan, smelling "admirably well." The advantage of being a "reasonable creature," Franklin remarks, is that you can find a reason for whatever you want to do.) To the "they do it, too" defense, the animal rightist has a devastating reply: do you really want to base your morality on the natural order? Murder and rape are natural, too. Besides, humans don't need to kill other creatures in order to survive; animals do. (Though if my cat, Otis, is any guide, animals sometimes kill for sheer pleasure.)

This suggests another defense. Wouldn't life in the wild be worse for these farm animals? "Defenders of slavery imposed on black Africans often made a similar point," Singer retorts. "The life of freedom is to be preferred."

But domesticated animals can't survive in the wild; in fact, without us they wouldn't exist at all. Or as one 19th-century political philosopher put it, "The pig has a stronger interest than anyone in the demand for bacon. If all the world were Jewish, there would be no pigs at all." But it turns out that this would be fine by the animal rightists: for if pigs don't exist, they can't be wronged.

Animals on factory farms have never known any other life. Singer replies that "animals feel a need to exercise, stretch their limbs or wings, groom themselves and turn around, whether or not they have ever lived in conditions that permit this." The measure of their suffering is not their prior experiences but the unremitting daily frustration of their instincts.

O.K., the suffering of animals is a legitimate problem, but the world is full of problems, and surely human problems must come first! Sounds good, and yet all the animal people are asking me to do is to stop eating meat and wearing animal furs and hides. There's no reason I can't devote myself to solving humankind's problems while being a vegetarian who wears synthetics.

But doesn't the fact that we could choose to forgo meat for moral reasons point to a crucial moral difference between animals and humans? As Kant pointed out, the human being is the only moral animal, the only one even capable of entertaining a concept of "rights." What's wrong with reserving moral consideration for those able to reciprocate it? Right here is where you run smack into the A.M.C.: the moral status of the retarded, the insane, the infant and the Alzheimer's patient. Such "marginal cases," in the detestable argot of modern moral philosophy, cannot participate in moral decision making any more than a monkey can, yet we nevertheless grant them rights.

That's right, I respond, for the simple reason that they're one of us. And all of us have been, and will probably once again be, marginal cases ourselves. What's more, these people have fathers and mothers, daughters and sons, which makes our interest in their welfare deeper than our interest in the welfare of even the most brilliant ape.

Alas, none of these arguments evade the charge of speciesism; the racist, too, claims that it's natural to give special consideration to one's own kind. A utilitarian like Singer would agree, however, that the feelings of relatives do count for something. Yet the principle of equal consideration of interests demands that, given the choice between performing a painful medical experiment on a severely retarded orphan and on a normal ape, we must sacrifice the child. Why? Because the ape has a greater capacity for pain.

Here in a nutshell is the problem with the A.M.C.: it can be used to help the animals, but just as often it winds up hurting the marginal cases. Giving up our speciesism will bring us to a moral cliff from which we may not be prepared to jump, even when logic is pushing us.

And yet this isn't the moral choice I am being asked to make. (Too bad; it would be so much easier!) In everyday life, the choice is not between babies and chimps but between the pork and the tofu. Even if we reject the "hard utilitarianism" of a Peter Singer, there remains the question of whether we owe animals that can feel pain any moral consideration, and this seems impossible to deny. And if we do owe them moral consideration, how can we justify eating them?

This is why killing animals for meat (and clothing) poses the most difficult animal rights challenge. In the case of animal testing, all but the most radical animal rightists are willing to balance the human benefit against the cost to the animals. That's because the unique qualities of human consciousness carry weight in the utilitarian calculus: human pain counts for more than that of a mouse, since our pain is amplified by emotions like dread; similarly, our deaths are worse than an animal's because we understand what death is in a way they don't. So the argument over animal testing is really in the details: is this particular procedure or test really necessary to save human lives? (Very often it's not, in which case we probably shouldn't do it.) But if humans no longer need to eat meat or wear skins, then what exactly are we putting on the human side of the scale to outweigh the interests of the animal?

I suspect that this is finally why the animal people managed to throw me on the defensive. It's one thing to choose between the chimp and the retarded child or to accept the sacrifice of all those pigs surgeons practiced on to develop heart-bypass surgery. But what happens when the choice is between "a lifetime of suffering for a nonhuman animal and the gastronomic preference of a human being?" You look away—or you stop eating animals. And if you don't want to do either? Then you have to try to determine if the animals you're eating have really endured "a lifetime of suffering."

Whether our interest in eating animals outweighs their interest in not being eaten (assuming for the moment that is their interest) turns on the vexed question of animal suffering. Vexed, because it is impossible to know what really goes on in the mind of a cow or a pig or even an ape. Strictly speaking, this is true of other humans, too, but since humans are all basically wired the same way, we have excellent reason to assume that other people's experience of pain feels much like our own. Can we say that about animals? Yes and no.

I have yet to find anyone who still subscribes to Descartes's belief that animals cannot feel pain because they lack a soul. The general consensus among scientists and philosophers is that when it comes to pain, the higher animals are wired much like we are for the same evolutionary reasons, so we should take the writhings of the kicked dog at face value. Indeed, the very premise of a great deal of animal testing—the reason it has value—is that animals' experience of physical and even some psychological pain closely resembles our own. Otherwise, why would cosmetics testers drip chemicals into the eyes of rabbits to see if they sting? Why would researchers study head trauma by traumatizing chimpanzee heads? Why would psychologists attempt to induce depression and "learned helplessness" in dogs by exposing them to ceaseless random patterns of electrical shock?

That said, it can be argued that human pain differs from animal pain by an order of magnitude. This qualitative difference is largely the result of our possession of language and, by virtue of language, an ability to have thoughts about thoughts and to imagine alternatives to our current reality. The philosopher Daniel C. Dennett suggests that we would do well to draw a distinction between pain, which a great many animals experience, and suffering, which depends on a degree of self-consciousness only a few animals appear to command. Suffering in this view is not just lots of pain but pain intensified by human emotions like loss, sadness, worry, regret, self-pity, shame, humiliation and dread.

Consider castration. No one would deny the procedure is painful to animals, yet animals appear to get over it in a way humans do not. (Some rhesus monkeys competing for mates will bite off a rival's testicle; the very next day the victim may be observed mating, seemingly little the worse for wear.) Surely the suffering of a man able to comprehend the full implications of castration, to anticipate the event and contemplate its aftermath, represents an agony of another order.

By the same token, however, language and all that comes with it can also make certain kinds of pain more bearable. A trip to the dentist would be a torment for an ape that couldn't be made to understand the purpose and duration of the procedure.

As humans contemplating the pain and suffering of animals, we do need to guard against projecting on to them what the same experience would feel like to us. Watching a steer force-marched up the ramp to the kill-floor door, as I have done, I need to remind myself that this is not Sean Penn in "Dead Man Walking," that in a bovine brain the concept of nonexistence is blissfully absent. "If we fail to find suffering in the animal lives we can see," Dennett writes in "Kinds of Minds," "we can rest assured there is no invisible suffering somewhere in their brains. If we find suffering, we will recognize it without difficulty."

Which brings us—reluctantly, necessarily—to the American factory farm, the place where all such distinctions turn to dust. It's not easy to draw lines between pain and suffering in a modern egg or confinement hog operation. These are places where the subtleties of moral philosophy and animal cognition mean less than nothing, where everything we've learned about animals at least since Darwin has been simply ... set aside. To visit a modern CAFO (Confined Animal Feeding Operation) is to enter a world that, for all its technological sophistication, is still designed according to Cartesian principles: animals are machines incapable of feeling pain. Since no thinking person can possibly believe this any more, industrial animal agriculture depends on a suspension of disbelief on the part of the people who operate it and a willingness to avert your eyes on the part of everyone else.

From everything, I've read, egg and hog operations are the worst. Beef cattle in America at least still live outdoors, albeit standing ankle deep in their own waste eating a diet that makes them sick. And broiler chickens, although they do get their beaks snipped off with a hot knife to keep them from cannibalizing one another under the stress of their confinement, at least don't spend their eight-week lives in cages too small to ever stretch a wing. That fate is reserved for the American laying hen, who passes her brief span piled together with a half-dozen other hens in a wire cage whose floor a single page of this magazine could carpet. Every natural instinct of this animal is thwarted, leading to a range of behavioral ".vices" that can include cannibalizing her cagemates and rubbing her body against the wire mesh until it is featherless and bleeding. Pain? Suffering? Madness? The operative suspension of disbelief depends on more neutral descriptors, like "vices" and "stress." Whatever you want to call what's going on in those cages, the 10 percent or so of hens that can't bear it and simply die is built into the cost of production. And when the output of the others begins to ebb, the hens will be "force-molted"—starved of food and water and light for several days in order to stimulate a final bout of egg laying before their life's work is done.

Simply reciting these facts, most of which are drawn from poultry-trade magazines, makes me sound like one of those animal people, doesn't it? I don't mean to, but this is what can happen when ... you look. It certainly wasn't my intention to ruin anyone's breakfast. But now that I probably have spoiled the eggs, I do want to say one thing about the bacon, mention a single practice (by no means the worst) in modern hog production that points to the compound madness of an impeccable industrial logic.

Piglets in confinement operations are weaned from their mothers 10 days after birth (compared with 13 weeks in nature) because they gain weight faster on their hormone- and antibiotic-fortified feed. This premature weaning leaves the pigs with a lifelong craving to suck and chew, a desire they gratify in confinement by biting the tail of the animal in front of them. A normal pig would fight off his molester, but a demoralized pig has stopped caring. "Learned helplessness" is the psychological term, and it's not uncommon in confinement operations, where tens of thousands of hogs spend their entire lives ignorant of sunshine or earth or straw, crowded together beneath a metal roof upon metal slats suspended over a manure pit. So it's not surprising that an animal as sensitive and intelligent as a pig would get depressed, and a depressed pig will allow his tail to be chewed on to the point of infection. Sick pigs, being underperforming "production units," are clubbed to death on the spot. The U.S.D.A.'s recommended solution to the problem is called "tail docking." Using a pair of pliers (and no anesthetic), most but not all of the tail is snipped off. Why the little stump? Because the whole point of the exercise is not to remove the object of tail-biting so much as to render it more sensitive. Now, a bite on the tail is so painful that even the most demoralized pig will mount a struggle to avoid it.

Much of this description is drawn from "Dominion," Matthew Scully's recent book in which he offers a harrowing description of a North Carolina hog operation. Scully, a Christian conservative, has no patience for lefty rights talk, arguing instead that while God did give man "dominion" over animals ("Every moving thing that liveth shall be meat for you"), he also admonished us to show them mercy. "We are called to treat them with kindness, not because they have rights or power or some claim to equality but … because they stand unequal and powerless before us."

Scully calls the contemporary factory farm "our own worst nightmare" and, to his credit, doesn't shrink from naming the root cause of this evil: unfettered capitalism. (Perhaps this explains why he resigned from the Bush administration just before his book's publication.) A tension has always existed between the capitalist imperative to maximize efficiency and the moral imperatives of religion or community, which have historically served as a counterweight to the moral blindness of the market. This is one of "the cultural contradictions of capitalism"—the tendency of the economic impulse to erode the moral underpinnings of society. Mercy toward animals is one such casualty.

More than any other institution, the American industrial animal farm offers a nightmarish glimpse of what capitalism can look like in the absence of

moral or regulatory constraint. Here in these places life itself is redefined—as protein production—and with it suffering. That venerable word becomes "stress," an economic problem in search of a cost-effective solution, like tail-docking or beak-clipping or, in the industry's latest plan, by simply engineering the "stress gene" out of pigs and chickens. "Our own worst nightmare" such a place may well be; it is also real life for the billions of animals unlucky enough to have been born beneath these grim steel roofs, into the brief, pitiless life of a "production unit" in the days before the suffering gene was found.

Vegetarianism doesn't seem an unreasonable response to such an evil. Who would want to be made complicit in the agony of these animals by eating them? You want to throw something against the walls of those infernal sheds, whether it's the Bible, a new constitutional right or a whole platoon of animal rightists bent on breaking in and liberating the inmates. In the shadow of these factory farms, Coetzee's notion of a "stupefying crime" doesn't seem far-fetched at all.

But before you swear off meat entirely, let me describe a very different sort of animal farm. It is typical of nothing, and yet its very existence puts the whole moral question of animal agriculture in a different light. Polyface Farm occupies 550 acres of rolling grassland and forest in the Shenandoah Valley of Virginia. Here, Joel Salatin and his family raise six different food animals—cattle, pigs, chickens, rabbits, turkeys and sheep—in an intricate dance of symbiosis designed to allow each species, in Salatin's words, "to fully express its physiological distinctiveness."

What this means in practice is that Salatin's chickens live like chickens; his cows, like cows; pigs, pigs. As in nature, where birds tend to follow herbivores, once Salatin's cows have finished grazing a pasture, he moves them out and tows in his "eggmobile," a portable chicken coop that houses several hundred laying hens—roughly the natural size of a flock. The hens fan out over the pasture, eating the short grass and picking insect larvae out of the cowpats—all the while spreading the cow manure and eliminating the farm's parasite problem. A diet of grubs and grass makes for exceptionally tasty eggs and contented chickens, and their nitrogenous manure feeds the pasture. A few weeks later, the chickens move out, and the sheep come in, dining on the lush new growth, as well as on the weed species (nettles, nightshade) that the cattle and chickens won't touch.

Meanwhile, the pigs are in the barn turning the compost. All winter long, while the cattle were indoors, Salatin layered their manure with straw, wood chips—and corn. By March, this steaming compost layer cake stands three feet high, and the pigs, whose powerful snouts can sniff out and retrieve the fermented corn at the bottom, get to spend a few happy weeks rooting through the pile, aerating it as they work. All you can see of these pigs, intently nosing out the tasty alcoholic morsels, are their upturned pink hams and corkscrew tails churning the air. The finished compost will go to feed the grass; the grass, the cattle; the cattle, the chickens; and eventually all of these animals will feed us.

I thought a lot about vegetarianism and animal rights during the day I spent on Joel Salatin's extraordinary farm. So much of what I'd read, so much of what I'd accepted, looked very different from here. To many animal rightists, even Polyface Farm is a death camp. But to look at these animals is to see this for the sentimental conceit it is. In the same way that we can probably recognize animal suffering when we see it, animal happiness is unmistakable, too, and here I was seeing it in abundance.

For any animal, happiness seems to consist in the opportunity to express its creaturely character—its essential pigness or wolfness or chickenness. Aristotle speaks of each creature's "characteristic form of life." For domesticated species, the good life, if we can call it that, cannot be achieved apart from humans—apart from our farms and, therefore, our meat eating. This, it seems to me, is where animal rightists betray a profound ignorance about the workings of nature. To think of domestication as a form of enslavement or even exploitation is to misconstrue the whole relationship, to project a human idea of power onto what is, in fact, an instance of mutualism between species.

Domestication is an evolutionary, rather than a political, development. It is certainly not a regime humans imposed on animals some 10,000 years ago.

Rather, domestication happened when a small handful of especially opportunistic species discovered through Darwinian trial and error that they were more likely to survive and prosper in an alliance with humans than on their own. Humans provided the animals with food and protection, in exchange for which the animals provided the humans their milk and eggs and—yes—their flesh. Both parties were transformed by the relationship: animals grew tame and lost their ability to fend for themselves (evolution tends to edit out unneeded traits), and the humans gave up their hunter-gatherer ways for the settled life of agriculturists. (Humans changed biologically, too, evolving such new traits as a tolerance for lactose as adults.)

From the animals' point of view, the bargain with humanity has been a great success, at least until our own time. Cows, pigs, dogs, cats and chickens have thrived, while their wild ancestors have languished. (There are 10,000 wolves in North America, 50,000,000 dogs.) Nor does their loss of autonomy seem to trouble these creatures. It is wrong, the rightists say, to treat animals as "means" rather than "ends," yet the happiness of a working animal like the dog consists precisely in serving as a "means." Liberation is the last thing such a creature wants. To say of one of Joel Salatin's caged chickens that "the life of freedom is to be preferred" betrays an ignorance about chicken preferences—which on this farm are heavily focused on not getting their heads bitten off by weasels.

But haven't these chickens simply traded one predator for another—weasels for humans? True enough, and for the chickens this is probably not a bad deal. For brief as it is, the life expectancy of a farm animal would be considerably briefer in the world beyond the pasture fence or chicken coop. A sheep farmer told me that a bear will eat a lactating ewe alive, starting with her udders. "As a rule," he explained, "animals don't get 'good deaths' surrounded by their loved ones."

The very existence of predation—animals eating animals—is the cause of much anguished hand-wringing in animal rights circles. "It must be admitted," Singer writes, "that the existence of carnivorous animals does pose one problem for the ethics of Animal Liberation, and that is whether we should do anything about it." Some animal rightists train their dogs and cats to become vegetarians. (Note: cats will require nutritional supplements to stay healthy.) Matthew Scully calls predation "the intrinsic evil in nature's design ... among the hardest of all things to fathom." Really? A deep Puritan streak pervades animal rights activists, an abiding discomfort not only with our animality but with the animals' animality too.

However it may appear to us, predation is not a matter of morality or politics; it, also, is a matter of symbiosis. Hard as the wolf may be on the deer he eats, the herd depends on him for its well-being; without predators to cull the herd, deer overrun their habitat and starve. In many places, human hunters have taken over the predator's ecological role. Chickens also depend for their continued well-being on their human predators—not individual chickens, but chickens as a species. The surest way to achieve the extinction of the chicken would be to grant chickens a "right to life."

Yet here's the rub: the animal rightist is not concerned with species, only individuals. Tom Regan, author of "The Case for Animal Rights," bluntly asserts that because "species are not individuals ... the rights view does not recognize the moral rights of species to anything, including survival." Singer concurs, insisting that only sentient individuals have interests. But surely a species can have interests—in its survival, say—just as a nation or community or a corporation can. The animal rights movement's exclusive concern with individual animals makes perfect sense given its roots in a culture of liberal individualism, but does it make any sense in nature?

In 1611 Juan da Goma (aka Juan the Disoriented) made accidental landfall on Wrightson Island, a six-square-mile rock in the Indian Ocean. The island's sole distinction is as the only known home of the Arcania tree and the bird that nests in it, the Wrightson giant sea sparrow. Da Goma and his crew stayed a week, much of that time spent in a failed bid to recapture the ship's escaped goat—who happened to be pregnant. Nearly four centuries later, Wrightson Island is home to 380 goats that have consumed virtually every scrap of vegetation in their reach. The youngest Arcania tree on the island is more than 300 years old, and only 52 sea sparrows remain. In the animal rights view, any one of those goats have at least as much right to life as the last Wrightson sparrow on earth, and the trees, because they are not sentient, warrant no moral consideration whatsoever. (In the mid-80's a British environmental group set out to shoot the goats, but was forced to cancel the expedition after the Mammal Liberation Front bombed its offices.)

The story of Wrightson Island (recounted by the biologist David Ehrenfeld in "Beginning Again") suggests at the very least that a human morality based on individual rights makes for an awkward fit when applied to the natural world. This should come as no surprise: morality is an artifact of human culture, devised to help us negotiate social relations. It's very good for that. But just as we recognize that nature doesn't provide an adequate guide for human social conduct, isn't it anthropocentric to assume that our moral system offers an adequate guide for nature? We may require a different set of ethics to guide our dealings with the natural world, one as well suited to the particular needs of plants and animals and habitats (where sentience counts for little) as rights suit us humans today.

To contemplate such questions from the vantage of a farm is to appreciate just how parochial and urban an ideology animals rights really is. It could thrive only in a world where people have lost contact with the natural world, where animals no longer pose a threat to us and human mastery of nature seems absolute. "In our normal life," Singer writes, "there is no serious clash of interests between human and nonhuman animals." Such a statement assumes a decidedly urbanized "normal life," one that certainly no farmer would recognize.

The farmer would point out that even vegans have a "serious clash of interests" with other animals. The grain that the vegan eats is harvested with a combine that shreds field mice, while the farmer's tractor crushes woodchucks in their burrows, and his pesticides drop songbirds from the sky. Steve Davis, an animal scientist at Oregon State University, has estimated that if America were to adopt a strictly vegetarian diet, the total number of animals killed every year would actually increase, as animal pasture gave way to row crops. Davis contends that if our goal is to kill as few animals as possible, then people should eat the largest possible animal that can live on the least intensively cultivated land: grass-fed beef for everybody. It would appear that killing animals is unavoidable no matter what we choose to eat.

When I talked to Joel Salatin about the vegetarian utopia, he pointed out that it would also condemn him and his neighbors to importing their food from distant places, since the Shenandoah Valley receives too little rainfall to grow many row crops. Much the same would hold true where I live, in New England. We get plenty of rain, but the hilliness of the land has dictated an agriculture based on animals since the time of the Pilgrims. The world is full of places where the best, if not the only, way to obtain food from the land is by grazing animals on it—especially ruminants, which alone can transform grass into protein and whose presence can actually improve the health of the land.

The vegetarian utopia would make us even more dependent than we already are on an industrialized national food chain. That food chain would in turn be even more dependent than it already is on fossil fuels and chemical fertilizer, since food would need to travel farther and manure would be in short supply. Indeed, it is doubtful that you can build a more sustainable agriculture without animals to cycle nutrients and support local food production. If our concern is for the health of nature—rather than, say, the internal consistency of our moral code or the condition of our souls—then eating animals may sometimes be the most ethical thing to do.

There is, too, the fact that we humans have been eating animals as long as we have lived on this earth. Humans may not need to eat meat in order to survive, yet doing so is part of our evolutionary heritage, reflected in the design of our teeth and the structure of our digestion. Eating meat helped make us what we are, in a social and biological sense. Under the pressure of the hunt, the human brain grew in size and complexity, and around the fire where the meat was cooked, human culture first flourished. Granting rights to animals may lift us up from the brutal world of predation, but it will entail the sacrifice of part of our identity—our own animality.

Surely this is one of the odder paradoxes of animal rights doctrine. It asks us to recognize all that we share with animals and then demands that we act toward them in a most unanimalistic way. Whether or not this is a good idea, we should at least acknowledge that our desire to eat meat is not a trivial matter, no mere "gastronomic preference." We might as well call sex—also now technically unnecessary—a mere "recreational preference." Whatever else it is, our meat eating is something very deep indeed.

Are any of these good enough reasons to eat animals? I'm mindful of Ben Franklin's definition of the reasonable creature as one who can come up with reasons for whatever he wants to do. So I decided I would track down Peter Singer and ask him what he thought. In an e-mail message, I described Polyface and asked him about the implications for his position of the Good Farm—one where animals got to live according to their nature and to all appearances did not suffer.

"I agree with you that it is better for these animals to have lived and died than not to have lived at all," Singer wrote back. Since the utilitarian is concerned exclusively with the sum of happiness and suffering and the slaughter of an animal that doesn't comprehend that death need not involve suffering, the Good Farm adds to the total of animal happiness, provided you replace the slaughtered animal with a new one. However, he added, this line of thinking doesn't obviate the wrongness of killing an animal that "has a sense of its own existence over time and can have preferences for its own future." In other words, it's O.K. to eat the chicken, but he's not so sure about the pig. Yet, he wrote, "I would not be sufficiently confident of my arguments to condemn someone who purchased meat from one of these farms."

Singer went on to express serious doubts that such farms could be practical on a large scale, since the pressures of the marketplace will lead their owners to cut costs and corners at the expense of the animals. He suggested, too, that killing animals is not conducive to treating them with respect. Also, since humanely raised food will be more expensive, only the well-to-do can afford morally defensible animal protein. These are important considerations, but they don't alter my essential point: what's wrong with animal agriculture—with eating animals—is the practice, not the principle.

What this suggests to me is that people who care should be working not for animal rights but animal welfare—to ensure that farm animals don't suffer and that their deaths are swift and painless. In fact, the decent-life merciful-death line is how Jeremy Bentham justified his own meat eating. Yes, the philosophical father of animal rights was himself a carnivore. In a passage rather less frequently quoted by animal rightists, Bentham defended eating animals on the grounds that "we are the better for it, and they are never the worse…. The death they suffer in our hands commonly is, and always may be, a speedier and, by that means, a less painful one than that which would await them in the inevitable course of nature."

My guess is that Bentham never looked too closely at what happens in a slaughterhouse, but the argument suggests that, in theory at least, a utilitarian can justify the killing of humanely treated animals—for meat or, presumably, for clothing. (Though leather and fur pose distinct moral problems. Leather is a byproduct of raising domestic animals for food, which can be done humanely. However, furs are usually made from wild animals that die brutal deaths—usually in leg-hold traps—and since most fur species aren't domesticated, raising them on farms isn't necessarily more humane.) But whether the issue is food or fur or hunting, what should concern us is the suffering, not the killing. All of which I was feeling pretty good about—until I remembered that utilitarians can also justify killing retarded orphans. Killing just isn't the problem for them that it is for other people, including me.

During my visit to Polyface Farm, I asked Salatin where his animals were slaughtered. He does the chickens and rabbits right on the farm, and would do the cattle, pigs and sheep there too if only the U.S.D.A. would let him. Salatin showed me the open-air abattoir he built behind the farmhouse—a sort of outdoor kitchen on a concrete slab, with stainless-steel sinks, scalding tanks, a feather-plucking machine and metal cones to hold the birds upside down while they're being bled. Processing chickens is not a pleasant job, but Salatin insists on doing it himself because he's convinced he can do it more humanely and cleanly than any processing plant. He slaughters every other Saturday through the summer. Anyone's welcome to watch.

I asked Salatin how he could bring himself to kill a chicken.

"People have a soul; animals don't" he said. "It's a bedrock belief of mine." Salatin is a devout Christian. "Unlike us, animals are not created in God's image, so when they die, they just die."

The notion that only in modern times have people grown uneasy about killing animals is a flattering conceit. Taking a life is momentous, and people have been working to justify the slaughter of animals for thousands of years. Religion and especially ritual has played a crucial part in helping us reckon the moral costs. Native Americans and other hunter-gathers would give thanks to their prey for giving up its life so the eater might live (sort of like saying grace). Many cultures have offered sacrificial animals to the gods, perhaps as a way to convince themselves that it was the gods' desires that demanded the slaughter, not their own. In ancient Greece, the priests responsible for the slaughter (priests!—now we entrust the job to minimum-wage workers) would sprinkle holy water on the sacrificial animal's brow. The beast would promptly shake its head, and this was taken as a sign of assent. Slaughter doesn't necessarily preclude respect. For all these people, it was the ceremony that allowed them to look, then to eat.

Apart from a few surviving religious practices, we no longer have any rituals governing the slaughter or eating of animals, which perhaps helps to explain why we find ourselves where we do, feeling that our only choice is to either look away or give up meat. Frank Perdue is happy to serve the first customer; Peter Singer, the second.

Until my visit to Polyface Farm, I had assumed these were the only two options. But on Salatin's farm, the eye contact between people and animals whose loss John Berger mourned is still a fact of life—and of death, for neither the lives nor the deaths of these animals have been secreted behind steel walls. "Food with a face," Salatin likes to call what he's selling, a slogan that probably scares off some customers. People see very different things when they look into the eyes of a pig or a chicken or a steer—a being without a soul, a "subject of a life" entitled to rights, a link in a food chain, a vessel for pain and pleasure, a tasty lunch. But figuring out what we do think, and what we can eat, might begin with the looking.

We certainly won't philosophize our way to an answer. Salatin told me the story of a man who showed up at the farm one Saturday morning. When Salatin noticed a PETA bumper sticker on the man's car, he figured he was in for it. But the man had a different agenda. He explained that after 16 years as a vegetarian, he had decided that the only way he could ever eat meat again was if he killed the animal himself. He had come to look.

"Ten minutes later we were in the processing shed with a chicken," Salatin recalled. "He slit the bird's throat and watched it die. He saw that the animal did not look at him accusingly, didn't do a Disney double take. The animal had been treated with respect when it was alive, and he saw that it could also have a respectful death—that it wasn't being treated as a pile of protoplasm."

Salatin's open-air abattoir is a morally powerful idea. Someone slaughtering a chicken in a place where he can be watched is apt to do it scrupulously, with consideration for the animal as well as for the eater. This is going to sound quixotic, but maybe all we need to do to redeem industrial animal agriculture in this country is to pass a law requiring that the steel and concrete walls of the CAFO's and slaughterhouses be replaced with ... glass. If there's any new "right" we need to establish, maybe it's this one: the right to look.

No doubt the sight of some of these places would turn many people into vegetarians. Many others would look elsewhere for their meat, to farmers like Salatin. There are more of them than I would have imagined. Despite the relentless consolidation of the American meat industry, there has been a revival of small farms where animals still live their "characteristic form of life." I'm thinking of the ranches where cattle still spend their lives on grass, the poultry farms where chickens still go outside and the hog farms where pigs live as they did 50 years ago—in contact with the sun, the earth and the gaze of a farmer.

For my own part, I've discovered that if you're willing to make the effort, it's entirely possible to limit the meat you eat to nonindustrial animals. I'm tempted to think that we need a new dietary category, to go with the vegan and lactovegetarian and piscatorian. I don't have a catchy name for it yet (humanocarnivore?), but this is the only sort of meat eating I feel comfortable with these days. I've become the sort of shopper who looks for labels indicating that his meat and eggs have been humanely grown (the American Humane Association's new "Free Farmed" label seems to be catching on), who visits the farms where his chicken and pork come from and who asks kinky-sounding questions about touring slaughterhouses. I've actually found a couple of small processing plants willing to let a customer onto the kill floor, including one, in Cannon Falls, Minn., with a glass abattoir.

The industrialization—and dehumanization—of American animal farming is a relatively new, evitable and local phenomenon: no other country raises and slaughters its food animals quite as intensively or as brutally as we do. Were the walls of our meat industry to become transparent, literally or even figuratively, we would not long continue to do it this way. Tail-docking and sow crates and beak-clipping would disappear overnight, and the days of slaughtering 400 head of cattle an hour would come to an end. For who could stand the sight? Yes, meat would get more expensive. We'd probably eat less of it, too, but maybe when we did eat animals, we'd eat them with the consciousness, ceremony and respect they deserve.

60

The Ethics of Respect for Nature

PAUL W. TAYLOR

According to Paul W. Taylor, the ethics of respect for nature is made up of three elements: a belief system, an ultimate moral attitude, and a set of rules of duty and standards of character. The belief system is said to justify the adoption of the attitude of respect for nature, which in turn requires a set of rules and standards of character. Two central elements of the belief system are (1) that each individual organism is a teleological center of life, pursuing its own good in its own way, and (2) that whether we are concerned with standards of merit or with the concept of inherent worth, the claim that humans by their very nature are superior to other species is groundless.

HUMAN-CENTERED AND LIFE-CENTERED SYSTEMS OF ENVIRONMENTAL ETHICS

In this paper I show how the taking of a certain ultimate moral attitude toward nature, which I call "respect for nature," has a central place in the foundations of a life-centered system of environmental ethics. I hold that a set of moral norms (both standards of character and rules of conduct) governing human treatment of the natural world is a rationally grounded set if and only if, first, commitment to those norms is a practical entailment of adopting the attitude of respect for nature as an ultimate moral attitude, and second, the adopting of that attitude on the part of all rational agents can itself be justified. When the basic characteristics of the attitude of respect for nature are made clear, it will be seen that a life-centered system of environmental ethics need not be holistic or organicist in its conception of the kinds of entities that are deemed the appropriate objects of moral concern and consideration. Nor does such a system require that the concepts of ecological homeostasis, equilibrium, and integrity provide us with normative principles from which could be derived (with the addition of factual knowledge) our obligations with regard to natural ecosystems. The "balance of nature" is not itself a moral norm, however important may be the role it plays in our general outlook on the natural world that underlies the attitude of respect for nature. I argue that finally it is the good (well-being, welfare) of individual organisms, considered as entities having inherent worth, that determines our moral relations with the Earth's wild communities of life.

In designating the theory ... as life-centered, I intend to contrast it with all anthropocentric views. According to the latter, human actions that affect the natural environment and its nonhuman inhabitants are right (or wrong) by either of two criteria: They have consequences that are favorable (or unfavorable) to human well-being, or they are consistent (or inconsistent) with the system of norms that protect and implement human rights. From

From "The Ethics of Respect for Nature," *Environmental Ethics* (1986), pp. 197–218. Reprinted with permission of the publisher. Notes renumbered.

this human-centered standpoint it is to humans and only to humans that all duties are ultimately owed. We may have responsibilities *with regard to* the natural ecosystems and biotic communities of our planet, but these responsibilities are in every case based on the contingent fact that our treatment of those ecosystems and communities of life can further the realization of human values and/or human rights. We have no obligation to promote or protect the good of nonhuman living things, independently of this contingent fact.

A life-centered system of environmental ethics is opposed to human-centered ones precisely on this point. From the perspective of a life-centered theory, we have prima facie moral obligations that are owed to wild plants and animals themselves as members of the Earth's biotic community. We are morally bound (other things being equal) to protect or promote their good for *their* sake. Our duties to respect the integrity of natural ecosystems, to preserve endangered species, and to avoid environmental pollution stem from the fact that these are ways in which we can help make it possible for wild species populations to achieve and maintain a healthy existence in a natural state. Such obligations are due those living things out of recognition of their inherent worth. They are entirely additional to and independent of the obligations we owe to our fellow humans. Although many of the actions that fulfill one set of obligations also fulfill the other, two different grounds of obligation are involved. Their well-being, as well as human well-being, is something to be realized *as an end in itself.*

If we were to accept a life-centered theory of environmental ethics, a profound reordering of our moral universe would take place. We would begin to look at the whole of the Earth's biosphere in a new light. Our duties with respect to the "world" of nature would be seen as making prima facie claims on us to be balanced against our duties with respect to the "world" of human civilization. We could no longer simply take the human point of view and consider the effects of our actions exclusively from the perspective of our own good.

THE GOOD OF A BEING AND THE CONCEPT OF INHERENT WORTH

What would justify acceptance of a life-centered system of ethical principles? In order to answer this it is first necessary to make clear the fundamental moral attitude that underlies and makes intelligible the commitment to live by such a system. It is then necessary to examine the considerations that would justify any rational agent's adopting that moral attitude.

Two concepts are essential to the taking of a moral attitude of the sort in question. A being which does not "have" these concepts, that is, which is unable to grasp their meaning and conditions of applicability, cannot be said to have the attitude as part of its moral outlook. These concepts are, first, that of the good (well-being, welfare) of a living thing, and second, the idea of an entity possessing inherent worth. I examine each concept in turn.

(1) Every organism, species population, and community of life has a good of its own which moral agents can intentionally further or damage by their actions. To say that an entity has a good of its own is simply to say that, without reference to any *other* entity, it can be benefited or harmed. One can act in its overall interest or contrary to its overall interest, and environmental conditions can be good for it (advantageous to it) or bad for it (disadvantageous to it). What is good for an entity is what "does it good" in the sense of enhancing or preserving its life and well-being. What is bad for an entity is something that is detrimental to its life and well-being.[1]

We can think of the good of an individual nonhuman organism as consisting in the full development of its biological powers. Its good is realized to the extent that it is strong and healthy. It possesses whatever capacities it needs to successfully cope with its environment and so preserve its existence throughout the various stages of the normal life cycle of its species. The good of a population or community of such individuals consists in the population or community maintaining itself from generation to generation as a coherent system of genetically and ecologically related organisms whose average good is at an optimum level for the given environment. (Here *average good* means that the degree of realization of the good of *individual organisms* in the population or community is, on average, greater than would be the case under any other ecologically functioning order of interrelations among those species populations in the given ecosystem.)

The idea of a being having a good of its own ... does not entail that the being must have interests or take an interest in what affects its life for better or for worse. We can act in a being's interest or contrary to its interest without its being interested in what we are doing to it in the sense of wanting or not wanting us to do it. It may, indeed, be wholly unaware that favorable and unfavorable events are taking place in its life. [Trees], for example, have no knowledge or desires or feelings. Yet it is undoubtedly the case that trees can be harmed or benefited by our actions. We can crash their roots by running a bulldozer too close to them. We can see to it that they get adequate nourishment and moisture by fertilizing and watering the soil around them. Thus we can help or hinder them in the realization of their good. It is the good of trees themselves that is thereby affected. We can similarly act so as to further the good of an entire tree population of a certain species (say, all the redwood trees in a California valley) or the good of a whole community of plant life in a given wilderness area, just as we can do harm to such a population or community.

When construed in this way, the concept of a being's good is not coextensive with sentience or the capacity for feeling pain. William Frankena has argued for a general theory of environmental ethics in which the ground of a creature's being worthy of moral consideration is its sentience. I have offered some criticisms of this view elsewhere, but the full refutation of such a position ... finally depends on the positive reasons for accepting a life-centered theory of the kind I am defending in this essay.[2]

It should be noted further that I am leaving open the question of whether machines—in particular, those which are not only goal-directed, but also self-regulating—can properly be said to have a good of their own.[3] Since I am concerned only with human treatment of wild organisms, species populations, and communities of life as they occur in our planet's natural ecosystems, it is to those entities alone that the concept "having a good of its own" will here be applied. I am not denying that other living things, whose genetic origin and environmental conditions have been produced, controlled, and manipulated by humans for human ends, do have a good of their own in the same sense as do wild plants and animals. It is not my purpose in this essay, however, to set out or defend the principles that should guide our conduct with regard to their good. It is only insofar as their production and use by humans have good or ill effects upon natural ecosystems and their wild inhabitants that the ethics of respect for nature comes into play.

(2) The second concept essential to the moral attitude of respect for nature is the idea of inherent worth. We take that attitude toward wild living things (individuals, species populations, or whole biotic communities) when and only when we regard them as entities possessing inherent worth. Indeed, it is only because they are conceived in this way that moral agents can think of themselves as having validly binding duties, obligations, and responsibilities that are *owed* to them as their *due*. I am not at this juncture arguing why they *should* be so regarded; I consider it at length below. But so regarding them is a presupposition of our taking the attitude of respect toward them and accordingly understanding ourselves as bearing certain moral relations to them. This can be shown as follows:

What does it mean to regard an entity that has a good of its own as possessing inherent worth? Two general principles are involved: the principle of moral consideration and the principle of intrinsic value.

According to the principle of moral consideration, wild living things are deserving of the concern and consideration of all moral agents simply in virtue of their being members of the Earth's community of life. From the moral point of view their good must be taken into account whenever it is affected for better or worse by the conduct of rational agents. This holds no matter what species the creature belongs to. The good of each is to be accorded some value and so acknowledged as having some weight in the deliberations of all rational agents. Of course, it may be necessary for such agents to act in ways contrary to the good of this or that particular organism or group of organisms in order to further the good of others, including the good of humans. But the principle of moral consideration prescribes that, with respect to each being an entity having its own good, every individual is deserving of consideration.

The principle of intrinsic value states that, regardless of what kind of entity it is in other respects, if it is a member of the Earth's community of life, the realization of its good is something *intrinsically* valuable. This means that its good is prima facie worthy of being preserved or promoted as an end in itself and for the sake of the entity whose good it is. Insofar as we regard any organism, species population, or life community as an entity with inherent worth, we believe that it must never be treated as if it were a mere object or thing whose entire value lies in being instrumental to the good of some other entity. The well-being of each is judged to have value in and of itself.

Combining these two principles, we can now define what it means for a living thing or group of living things to possess inherent worth. To say that it possesses inherent worth is to say that its good is deserving of the concern and consideration of all moral agents, and that the realization of its good has intrinsic value, to be pursued as an end in itself and for the sake of the entity whose good it is.

The duties owed to wild organisms, species populations, and communities of life in the Earth's natural ecosystems are grounded on their inherent worth. When rational, autonomous agents regard such entities as possessing inherent worth, they place intrinsic value on the realization of their good and so hold themselves responsible for performing actions that will have this effect and for refraining from actions having the contrary effect.

THE ATTITUDE OF RESPECT FOR NATURE

Why should moral agents regard wild living things in the natural world as possessing inherent worth? To answer this question we must first take into account the fact that, when rational, autonomous agents subscribe to the principles of moral consideration and intrinsic value and so conceive of wild living things as having that kind of worth, such agents are *adopting a certain ultimate moral attitude toward the natural world*. This is the attitude I call "respect for nature." It parallels the attitude of respect for persons in human ethics. When we adopt the attitude of respect for persons as the proper (fitting, appropriate) attitude to take toward all persons as persons, we consider the fulfillment of the basic interests of each individual to have intrinsic value. We thereby make a moral commitment to live a certain kind of life in relation to other persons. We place ourselves under the direction of a system of standards and rules that we consider validly binding on all moral agents as such.[4]

Similarly, when we adopt the attitude of respect for nature as an ultimate moral attitude we make a commitment to live by certain normative principles. These principles constitute the rules of conduct and standards of character that are to govern our treatment of the natural world. This is, first, an *ultimate* commitment because it is not derived from any higher norm. The attitude of respect for nature is not grounded on some other, more general, or more fundamental attitude. It sets the total framework for our responsibilities toward the natural world. It can be justified, as I show below, but its justification cannot consist in referring to a more general attitude or a more basic normative principle.

Second, the commitment is a *moral* one because it is understood to be a disinterested matter of principle. It is this feature that distinguishes the attitude of respect for nature from the set of feelings and dispositions that comprise the love of nature. The latter stems from one's personal interest in and response to the natural world. Like the affectionate feelings we have toward certain individual human beings, one's love of nature is nothing more than the particular way one feels about the natural environment and its wild inhabitants. And just as our love for an individual person differs from our respect for all persons as such (whether we happen to love them or not), so love of nature differs from respect for nature.

Respect for nature is an attitude we believe all moral agents ought to have simply as moral agents, regardless of whether or not they also love nature. Indeed, we have not truly taken the attitude of respect for nature ourselves unless we believe this. To put it in a Kantian way, to adopt the attitude of respect for nature is to take a stance that one wills it to be a universal law for all rational beings. It is to hold that stance categorically, as being validly applicable to every moral agent without exception, irrespective of whatever personal feelings toward nature such an agent might have or might lack.

Although the attitude of respect for nature is, in this sense, a disinterested and universalizable attitude, anyone who does adopt it has certain steady, more or less permanent dispositions. These dispositions, which are themselves to be considered disinterested and universalizable, comprise three interlocking sets: dispositions to seek certain ends, dispositions to carry on one's practical reasoning and deliberation in a certain way, and dispositions to have certain feelings. We may accordingly analyze the attitude of respect for nature into the following components. (a) The disposition to aim at, and to take steps to bring about, as final and disinterested ends, the promoting and protecting of the good of organisms, species populations, and life communities in natural ecosystems. (These ends are "final" in not being pursued as means to further ends. They are "disinterested" in being independent of the self-interest of the agent.) (b) The disposition to consider actions that tend to realize those ends to be prima facie obligatory *because* they have that tendency. (c) The disposition to experience positive and negative feelings toward states of affairs in the world *because* they are favorable or unfavorable to the good of organisms, species populations, and life communities in natural ecosystems.

The logical connection between the attitude of respect for nature and the duties of a life-centered system of environmental ethics can now be made clear. Insofar as one sincerely takes that attitude and so has the three sets of dispositions, one will at the same time be disposed to comply with certain rules of duty (such as nonmaleficence and noninterference) and with standards of character (such as fairness and benevolence) that determine the obligations and virtues of moral agents with regard to the Earth's wild living things. We can say that the actions one performs and the character traits one develops in fulfilling these moral requirements are the way one *expresses* or *embodies* the attitude in one's conduct and character. In his famous essay, "Justice as Fairness," John Rawls describes the rules of the duties of human morality (such as fidelity, gratitude, honesty, and justice) as "forms of conduct in which recognition of others as persons is manifested."[5] I hold that the rules of duty governing our treatment of the natural world and its inhabitants are forms of conduct in which the attitude of respect for nature is manifested.

THE JUSTIFIABILITY OF THE ATTITUDE OF RESPECT FOR NATURE

I return to the question posed earlier, which has not yet been answered: Why *should* moral agents regard wild living things as possessing inherent worth? I now argue that the only way we can answer this question is by showing how adopting the attitude of respect for nature is justified for all moral agents. Let us suppose that we were able to establish that there are good reasons for adopting the attitude, reasons which are intersubjectively valid for every rational agent. If there are such reasons, they would justify anyone's having the three sets of dispositions mentioned above as constituting what it means to have the attitude. Since these include the disposition to promote or protect the good of wild living things as a disinterested and ultimate end, as well as the disposition to perform actions for the reason that they tend to realize that end, we see that such dispositions commit a person to the principles of moral consideration and intrinsic value. To be disposed to further, as an end in itself, the good of any entity in nature just because it is that kind of entity, is to be disposed to give consideration to *every* such entity and to place intrinsic value on the realization of its good. Insofar as we subscribe to these two principles we regard living things as possessing inherent worth. Subscribing to the principles is what it *means* to so regard them. To justify the attitude of respect for nature, then, is to justify commitment to these principles and thereby to justify regarding wild creatures as possessing inherent worth.

We must keep in mind that inherent worth is not some mysterious sort of objective property belonging to living things that can be discovered by empirical observation or scientific investigation. To ascribe inherent worth to an entity is not to describe it by citing some feature discernible by sense perception or inferable by inductive reasoning. Nor is there a logically necessary connection between the concept of a being having a good of its own and the concept of inherent worth. We do not contradict ourselves by asserting that an entity that has a good of its own lacks inherent worth. In order to show that such an entity "has" inherent worth we must give good reasons for ascribing that kind of value to it (placing that kind of value upon it, conceiving of it to be valuable in that way). Although it is humans (persons, valuers) who must do the valuing, for the ethics of respect for nature, the value so ascribed is not a human value. That is to say, it is not a value derived from considerations regarding human well-being or human rights. It is a value that is ascribed to nonhuman animals and plants themselves, independently of their relationship to what humans judge to be conducive to their own good.

Whatever reasons, then, justify our taking the attitude of respect for nature as defined above are also reasons that show why we *should* regard the living things of the natural world as possessing inherent worth. We saw earlier that, since the

attitude is an ultimate one, it cannot be derived from a more fundamental attitude nor shown to be a special case of a more general one. On what sort of grounds, then, can it be established?

The attitude we take toward living things in the natural world depends on the way we look at them, on what kind of beings we conceive them to be, and on how we understand the relations we bear to them. Underlying and supporting our attitude is a certain *belief system* that constitutes a particular world view or outlook on nature and the place of human life in it. To give good reasons for adopting the attitude of respect for nature, then, we must first articulate the belief system which underlies and supports that attitude. If it appears that the belief system is internally coherent and well ordered, and if, as far as we can now tell, it is consistent with all known scientific truths relevant to our knowledge of the object of the attitude (which in this case includes the whole set of the Earth's natural ecosystems and their communities of life), then there remains the task of indicating why scientifically informed and rational thinkers with a developed capacity of reality awareness can find it acceptable as a way of conceiving of the natural world and our place in it. To the extent we can do this we provide at least a reasonable argument for accepting the belief system and the ultimate moral attitude it supports.

I do not hold that such a belief system can be *proven* to be true, either inductively or deductively. As we shall see, not all of its components can be stated in the form of empirically verifiable propositions. Nor is its internal order governed by purely logical relationships. But the system as a whole, I contend, constitutes a coherent, unified, and rationally acceptable "picture" or "map" of a total world. By examining each of its main components and seeing how they fit together, we obtain a scientifically informed and well-ordered conception of nature and the place of humans in it.

This belief system underlying the attitude of respect for nature I call (for want of a better name) "the biocentric outlook on nature." Since it is not wholly analyzable into empirically conformable assertions, it should not be thought of as simply a compendium of the biological sciences concerning our planet's ecosystems. It might best be described as a philosophical world view, to distinguish it from a scientific theory or explanatory system. However, one of its major tenets is the great lesson we have learned from the science of ecology: the interdependence of all living things in an organically unified order whose balance and stability are necessary conditions for the realization of the good of its constituent biotic communities.

Before turning to an account of the main components of the biocentric outlook, it is convenient here to set forth the overall structure of my theory of environmental ethics as it has now emerged. The ethics of respect for nature is made up of three basic elements: a belief system, an ultimate moral attitude, and a set of rules of duty and standards of character. These elements are connected with each other in the following manner. The belief system provides a certain outlook on nature which supports and makes intelligible an autonomous agent's adopting, as an ultimate moral attitude, the attitude of respect for nature. It supports and makes intelligible the attitude in the sense that, when an autonomous agent understands its moral relations to the natural world in terms of this outlook, it recognizes the attitude of respect to be the only *suitable* or *fitting* attitude to take toward all wild forms of life in the Earth's biosphere. Living things are now viewed as *the appropriate objects of the attitude of respect* and are accordingly regarded as entities possessing inherent worth. One then places intrinsic value on the promotion and protection of their good. As a consequence of this, one makes a moral commitment to abide by a set of rules of duty and to fulfill (as far as one can by one's own efforts) certain standards of good character. Given one's adoption of the attitude of respect, one makes that moral commitment because one considers those rules and standards to be validly binding on all moral agents. They are seen as embodying forms of conduct and character structures in which the attitude of respect for nature is manifested.

This three-part complex which internally orders the ethics of respect for nature is symmetrical with a theory of human ethics grounded on respect

for persons. Such a theory includes, first, a conception of oneself and others as persons, that is, as centers of autonomous choice. Second, there is the attitude of respect for persons as persons. When this is adopted as an ultimate moral attitude it involves the disposition to treat every person as having inherent worth or "human dignity." Every human being, just in virtue of her or his humanity, is understood to be worthy of moral consideration, and intrinsic value is placed on the autonomy and well-being of each. This is what Kant meant by conceiving of persons as ends in themselves. Third, there is an ethical system of duties which are acknowledged to be owed by everyone to everyone. These duties are forms of conduct in which public recognition is given to each individual's inherent worth as a person.

This structural framework for a theory of human ethics is meant to leave open the issue of consequentialism (utilitarianism) versus nonconsequentialism (deontology). That issue concerns the particular kind of system of rules defining the duties of moral agents toward persons. Similarly, I am leaving open [here] the question of what particular kind of system of rules defines our duties with respect to the natural world.

THE BIOCENTRIC OUTLOOK
ON NATURE

The biocentric outlook on nature has four main components. (1) Humans are thought of as members of the Earth's community of life, holding that membership on the same terms as apply to all the nonhuman members. (2) The Earth's natural ecosystems as a totality are seen as a complex web of interconnected elements, with the sound biological functioning of each being dependent on the sound biological functioning of the others. (This is the component referred to above as the great lesson that the science of ecology has taught us.) (3) Each individual organism is conceived of as a teleological center of life, pursuing its own good in its own way. (4) Whether we are concerned with standards of merit or with the concept of inherent worth, the claim that humans by their very nature are superior to other species is a groundless claim and, in the light of elements (1), (2), and (3) above, must be rejected as nothing more than an irrational bias in our own favor....

THE DENIAL OF HUMAN SUPERIORITY

This fourth component of the biocentric outlook on nature is the single most important idea in establishing the justifiability of the attitude of respect for nature. Its central role is due to the special relationship it bears to the first three components of the outlook. This relationship will be brought out after the concept of human superiority is examined and analyzed.[6]

In what sense are humans alleged to be superior to other animals? We are different from them in having certain capacities that they lack. But why should these capacities be a mark of superiority? From what point of view are they judged to be signs of superiority and what sense of superiority is meant? After all, various nonhuman species have capacities that humans lack. There is the speed of a cheetah, the vision of an eagle, the agility of a monkey. Why should not these be taken as signs of *their* superiority over humans?

One answer ... is that these capacities are not as *valuable* as the human capacities that are claimed to make us superior. Such uniquely human characteristics as rational thought, aesthetic creativity, autonomy and self-determination, and moral freedom, it might be held, have a higher value than the capacities found in other species. Yet we must ask: valuable to whom, and on what grounds?

The human characteristics mentioned are all valuable to humans. They are essential to the preservation and enrichment of our civilization and culture. Clearly it is from the human standpoint that they are being judged to be desirable and good. It is not difficult here to recognize a begging of the question. Humans are claiming human superiority

from a strictly human point of view, that is, from a point of view in which the good of humans is taken as the standard of judgment. All we need to do is to look at the capacities of nonhuman animals (or plants, for that matter) from the standpoint of *their* good to find a contrary judgment of superiority. The speed of the cheetah, for example, is a sign of its superiority to humans when considered from the standpoint of the good of its species. If it were as slow a runner as a human, it would not be able to survive. And so for all the other abilities of nonhumans which further their good but which are lacking in humans. In each case the claim to human superiority would be rejected from a nonhuman standpoint.

When superiority assertions are interpreted in this way, they are based on judgments of *merit*. To judge the merits of a person or an organism one must apply grading or ranking standards to it. (As I show below, this distinguishes judgments of merit from judgments of inherent worth.) Empirical investigation then determines whether it has the "good-making properties" (merits) in virtue of which it fulfills the standards being applied. In the case of humans, merits may be either moral or nonmoral. We can judge one person to be better than (superior to) another from the moral point of view by applying certain standards to their character and conduct. Similarly, we can appeal to nonmoral criteria in judging someone to be an excellent piano player, a fair cook, a poor tennis player, and so on. Different social purposes and roles are implicit in the making of such judgments, providing the frame of reference for the choice of standards by which the nonmoral merits of people are determined. Ultimately such purposes and roles stem from a society's way of life as a whole. Now a society's way of life may be thought of as the cultural form given to the realization of human values. Whether moral or nonmoral standards are being applied, then, all judgments of people's merits finally depend on human values. All are made from an exclusively human standpoint.

The question that naturally arises at this juncture is: Why should standards that are based on human values be assumed to be the only valid criteria of merit and hence the only true signs of superiority? This question is especially pressing when humans are being judged superior in merit to nonhumans. [A] human being may be a better mathematician than a monkey, but the monkey may be a better tree climber than a human being. If we humans value mathematics more than tree climbing, that is because our conception of civilized life makes the development of mathematical ability more desirable than the ability to climb trees. But is it not unreasonable to judge nonhumans by the values of human civilization, rather than by values connected with what it is for a member of *that* species to live a good life? If all living things have a good of their own, it makes sense to judge the merits of nonhumans by standards derived from *their* good. To use only standards based on human values is already to commit oneself to holding that humans are superior to nonhumans, which is the point in question.

A further logical flaw arises in connection with the widely held conviction that humans are *morally* superior beings because they possess, while others lack, the capacities of a moral agent (free will, accountability, deliberation, judgment, practical reason). This view rests on a conceptual confusion. As far as moral standards are concerned, only beings that have the capacities of a moral agent can properly be judged to be *either* moral (morally good) or immoral (morally deficient). Moral standards are simply not applicable to beings that lack such capacities. Animals and plants cannot therefore be said to be morally inferior in merit to humans. Since the only beings that can have moral merits *or be deficient in such merits* are moral agents, it is conceptually incoherent to judge humans as superior to nonhumans on the ground that humans have moral capacities while nonhumans don't.

Up to this point I have been interpreting the claim that humans are superior to other living things as a grading or ranking judgment regarding their comparative merits. There is, however, another way of understanding the idea of human superiority. According to this interpretation, humans are superior to nonhumans not as regards their merits but as regards their inherent worth.

Thus the claim of human superiority is to be understood as asserting that all humans, simply in virtue of their humanity, have *a greater inherent worth* than other living things.

The inherent worth of an entity does not depend on its merits.[7] To consider something as possessing inherent worth, we have seen, is to place intrinsic value on the realization of its good. This is done regardless of whatever particular merits it might have or might lack, as judged by a set of grading or ranking standards. In human affairs, we are all familiar with the principle that one's worth as a person does not vary with one's merits or lack of merits. The same can hold true of animals and plants. To regard such entities as possessing inherent worth entails disregarding their merits and deficiencies, whether they are being judged from a human standpoint or from the standpoint of their own species.

The idea of one entity having more merit than another, and so being superior to it in merit, makes perfectly good sense. Merit is a grading or ranking concept, and judgments of comparative merit are based on the different degrees to which things satisfy a given standard. But what can it mean to talk about one thing being superior to another in inherent worth? In order to get at what is being asserted in such a claim it is helpful first to look at the social origin of the concept of degrees of inherent worth.

The idea that humans can possess different degrees of inherent worth originated in societies having rigid class structures. Before the rise of modern democracies with their egalitarian outlook, one's membership in a hereditary class determined one's social status. People in the upper classes were looked up to, while those in the lower classes were looked down upon. In such a society one's social superiors and social inferiors were clearly defined and easily recognized.

Two aspects of these class-structured societies are especially relevant to the idea of degrees of inherent worth. First, those born into the upper classes were deemed more worthy of respect than those born into the lower orders. Second, the superior worth of upper class people had nothing to do with their merits nor did the inferior worth of those in the lower classes rest on their lack of merits. One's superiority or inferiority entirely derived from a social position one was born into. The modern concept of a meritocracy simply did not apply. One could not advance into a higher class by any sort of moral or nonmoral achievement. Similarly, an aristocrat held his title and all the privileges that went with it just because he was the eldest son of a titled nobleman. Unlike the bestowing of knighthood in contemporary Great Britain, one did not earn membership in the nobility by meritorious conduct.

We who live in modern democracies no longer believe in such hereditary social distinctions. Indeed, we would wholeheartedly condemn them on moral grounds as fundamentally unjust. We have come to think of class systems as a paradigm of social injustice, it being a central principle of the democratic way of life that among humans there are no superiors and no inferiors. Thus we have rejected the whole conceptual framework in which people are judged to have different degrees of inherent worth. That idea is incompatible with our notion of human equality based on the doctrine that all humans, simply in virtue of their humanity, have the same inherent worth. (The belief in universal human rights is one form that this egalitarianism takes.)

The vast majority of people in modern democracies, however, do not maintain an egalitarian outlook when it comes to comparing human beings with other living things. Most people consider our own species to be superior to all other species and this superiority is understood to be a matter of inherent worth, not merit. There may exist thoroughly vicious and depraved humans who lack all merit. Yet because they are human they are thought to belong to a higher class of entities than any plant or animal. That one is born into the species *Homo sapiens* entitles one to have lordship over those who are one's inferiors, namely, those born into other species. The parallel with hereditary social classes is very close. Implicit in this view is a hierarchical conception of nature according to which an organism has a position of superiority or inferiority in the Earth's community of life simply on the basis of its genetic background. The "lower" orders of life are looked down upon and it is considered perfectly proper that they serve the interests of those belonging to the highest order, namely humans. The intrinsic value we place on the well-being of our fellow humans reflects our recognition of their rightful position as our equals. No such intrinsic value is to be placed on the good of other animals, unless we choose to do so out of fondness or affection for them. But their well-being imposes no moral requirement on us. In this respect there is an absolute difference in moral status between ourselves and them.

This is the structure of concepts and beliefs that people are committed to insofar as they regard humans to be superior in inherent worth to all other species. I now wish to argue that this structure of concepts and beliefs is completely groundless. If we accept the first three components of the biocentric outlook and from that perspective look at the major philosophical traditions which have supported that structure, we find it to be at bottom nothing more than the expression of an irrational bias in our own favor. The philosophical traditions themselves rest on very questionable assumptions or else simply beg the question. I briefly consider three of the main traditions to substantiate the point. These are classical Greek humanism, Cartesian dualism, and the Judeo-Christian concept of the Great Chain of Being.

The inherent superiority of humans over other species was implicit in the Greek definition of man as a rational animal. Our animal nature was identified with "brute" desires that need the order and restraint of reason to rule them (just as reason is the special virtue of those who rule in the ideal state). Rationality was then seen to be the key to our superiority over animals. It enables us to live on a higher plane and endows us with a nobility and worth that other creatures lack. This familiar way of comparing humans with other species is deeply ingrained in our Western philosophical outlook. The point to consider here is that this view does not actually provide an argument *for* human superiority but rather makes explicit the framework of thought, that is implicitly used by those who think of humans as inherently superior to nonhumans. The Greeks who held that humans, in virtue of their rational capacities, have a kind of worth greater than any nonrational being, never looked at rationality as but one capacity of living things among many others. But when we consider rationality from the standpoint of the first three elements of the ecological outlook, we see that its value lies in its importance for *human* life. Other creatures achieve their species-specific good without the need of rationality, although they often make use of capacities that humans lack. So the humanistic outlook of classical Greek thought does not give us a neutral (non–question-begging) ground on which to construct a scale of degrees of inherent worth possessed by different species of living things.

The second tradition, centering on the Cartesian dualism of soul and body, also fails to justify the claim to human superiority. That superiority is supposed to derive from the fact that we have souls while animals do not. Animals are mere automata and lack the divine element that makes us spiritual beings. I will not go into the now familiar criticisms of this two-substance view. I only add the point that, even if humans are composed of an immaterial, unextended soul and a material, extended body, this in itself is not a reason to deem them of greater worth than entities that are only bodies. Why is a soul substance a thing that adds value to its possessor? Unless theological reasoning is offered here (which many, including, myself, would find unacceptable on epistemological grounds), no logical connection is evident. An immaterial something that thinks is better than a material something that doesn't think only if thinking itself has value, either intrinsically or instrumentally. Now it is intrinsically valuable to humans alone, who value it as an end in itself, and it is instrumentally valuable to those who benefit from it, namely humans.

For animals that neither enjoy thinking for its own sake nor need it for living the kind of life for which they are best adapted, it has no value. Even if "thinking" is broadened to include all forms of consciousness, there are still many living things that can do without it and yet live what is, for their species,

a good life. The anthropocentricity underlying the claim to human superiority runs throughout Cartesian dualism.

A third major source of the idea of human superiority is the Judeo-Christian concept of the Great Chain of Being. Humans are superior to animals and plants because their Creator has given them a higher place on the chain. It begins with God at the top, and then moves to the angels, who are lower than God but higher than humans, then to humans, positioned between the angels and the beasts (partaking of the nature of both), and then on down to the lower levels occupied by nonhuman animals, plants, and finally inanimate objects. Humans, being "made in God's image," are inherently superior to animals and plants by virtue of their being closer (in their essential nature) to God.

The metaphysical and epistemological difficulties with this conception of a hierarchy of entities are, in my mind, insuperable. Without entering into this matter here, I point out that if we are unwilling to accept the metaphysics of traditional Judaism and Christianity, we are again left without good reasons for holding to the claim of inherent human superiority.

The foregoing considerations (and others like them) leave us with but one ground for the assertion that a human being, regardless of merit, is a higher kind of entity than any other living thing. This is the mere fact of the genetic makeup of the species *Homo sapiens*. But this is surely irrational and arbitrary. Why should the arrangement of genes of a certain type be a mark of superior value, especially when this fact about an organism is taken by itself, unrelated to any other aspect of its life? We might just as well refer to any other genetic makeup as a ground of superior value. Clearly we are confronted here with a wholly arbitrary claim that can only be explained as an irrational bias in our own favor.

That the claim is nothing more than a deep-seated prejudice is brought home to us when we look at our relation to other species in the light of the first three elements of the biocentric outlook. Those elements taken conjointly give us a certain overall view of the natural world and of the place of humans in it. When we take this view we come to understand other living things, their environmental conditions, and their ecological relationships in such a way as to awake in us a deep sense of our kinship with them as fellow members of the Earth's community of life. Humans and nonhumans alike are viewed together as integral parts of one unified whole in which all living things are functionally interrelated. Finally, when our awareness focuses on the individual lives of plants and animals, each is seen to share with us the characteristic of being a theological center of life striving to realize its own good in its own unique way.

As this entire belief system becomes part of the conceptual framework by which we understand and perceive the world, we come to see ourselves as bearing a certain moral relation to nonhuman forms of life. Our ethical role in nature takes on a new significance. We begin to look at other species as we look at ourselves, seeing them as beings which have a good they are striving to realize just as we have a good we are striving to realize. We accordingly develop the disposition to view the world from the standpoint of their good as well as from the standpoint of our own good. Now if the groundlessness of the claim that humans are inherently superior to other species were brought clearly before our minds, we would not remain intellectually neutral toward that claim but would reject it as fundamentally at variance with our total world outlook. In the absence of any good reasons for holding it, the assertion of human superiority would then appear simply as the expression of an irrational and self-serving prejudice that favors one particular species over several million others.

Rejecting the notion of human superiority entails its positive counterpart: the doctrine of species impartiality. One who accepts that doctrine regards all living things as possessing inherent worth—the *same* inherent worth, since no one species has been shown to be either "higher" or "lower" than any other. Now we saw earlier that, insofar as one thinks of a living thing as possessing inherent worth, one considers it to be the appropriate object of the attitude of respect and believes that attitude to be the only fitting or suitable one for all moral agents to take toward it.

Here, then, is the key to understanding how the attitude of respect is rooted in the biocentric outlook on nature. The basic connection is made through the denial of human superiority. Once we reject the claim that humans are superior either in merit or in worth to other living things, we are ready to adopt the attitude of respect. The denial of human superiority is itself the result of taking the perspective on nature built into the first three elements of the biocentric outlook.

Now the first three elements of the biocentric outlook, it seems clear, would be found acceptable to any rational and scientifically informed thinker who is fully "open" to the reality of the lives of nonhuman organisms. Without denying our distinctively human characteristics, such a thinker can acknowledge the fundamental respects in which we are members of the Earth's community of life and in which the biological conditions necessary for the realization of our human values are inextricably linked with the whole system of nature. In addition, the conception of individual living things as teleological centers of life simply articulates how a scientifically informed thinker comes to understand them as the result of increasingly careful and detailed observations. Thus, the biocentric outlook recommends itself as an acceptable system of concepts and beliefs to anyone who is clear-minded, unbiased, and factually enlightened, and who has a developed capacity of reality awareness with regard to the lives of individual organisms. This is as good a reason for making the moral commitment involved in adopting the attitude of respect for nature as any theory of environmental ethics could possibly have.

MORAL RIGHTS AND THE MATTER OF COMPETING CLAIMS

I have not asserted anywhere in the foregoing account that animals or plants have moral rights. This omission was deliberate. I do not think that the reference class of the concept, bearer of moral rights, should be extended to include nonhuman living things. My reasons for taking this position, however, go beyond the scope of this paper. I believe I have been able to accomplish many of the same ends which those who ascribe rights to animals or plants wish to accomplish. There is no reason, moreover, why plants and animals, including whole species populations and life communities, cannot be accorded *legal* rights under my theory. To grant them legal protection could be interpreted as giving them legal entitlement to be protected, and this would be a means by which a society that subscribed to the ethics of respect for nature could give public recognition to their inherent worth.

There remains the problem of competing claims, even when wild plants and animals are not thought of as bearers of moral rights. If we accept the biocentric outlook and accordingly adopt the attitude of respect for nature as our ultimate moral attitude, how do we resolve conflicts that arise from our respect for persons in the domain of human ethics and our respect for nature in the domain of environmental ethics? This is a question that cannot adequately be dealt with here. My main purpose in this paper has been to try to establish a base point from which we can start working toward a solution to the problem. I have shown why we cannot just begin with an initial presumption in favor of the interests of our own species. It is after all within our power as moral beings to place limits on human population and technology with the deliberate intention of sharing the Earth's bounty with other species. That such sharing is an ideal difficult to realize even in an approximate way does not take away its claim to our deepest moral commitment.

ENDNOTES

1. The conceptual links between an entity *having* a good, something being good *for* it, and events doing good *to* it are examined by G. H. Von Wright in *The Varieties of Goodness* (New York: Humanities Press, 1963), chaps. 3 and 5.

2. See W. K. Frankena, "Ethics and the Environment," in K. E. Goodpaster and K. M. Sayre, eds., *Ethics and Problems of the 21st Century* (Notre Dame: University of Notre Dame Press, 1979), pp. 3–20. I critically examine Frankena's views in "Frankena on Environmental Ethics," *Monist* (1981): 237–243.

3. In the light of considerations set forth in Daniel Dennett's *Brainstorms: Philosophical Essays on Mind and Psychology* (Montgomery, Vt.: Bradford Books, 1978), it is advisable to leave this question unsettled at this time. When machines are developed that function in the way our brains do, we may well come to deem them proper subjects of moral consideration.

4. I have analyzed the nature of this commitment of human ethics in "On Taking the Moral Point of View," *Midwest Studies in Philosophy*, vol. 3, *Studies in Ethical Theory* (1978), pp. 35–61.

5. John Rawls, "Justice as Fairness," *Philosophical Review* 67 (1958): 183.

6. My criticisms of the dogma of human superiority gain independent support from a carefully reasoned essay by R. and V. Routley showing the many logical weaknesses in arguments for human-centered theories of environmental ethics. R. and V. Routley, "Against the Inevitability of Human Chauvinism," in K. E. Goodpaster and K. M. Sayre, eds., *Ethics and Problems of the 21st Century* (Notre Dame: University of Notre Dame Press, 1979), pp. 36–59.

7. For this way of distinguishing between merit and inherent worth, I am indebted to Gregory Vlastos, "Justice and Equality," in R. Brandt, ed., *Social Justice* (Englewood Cliffs, N.J.: Prentice-Hall, 1962), pp. 31–72.

61

Are All Species Equal?

DAVID SCHMIDTZ

David Schmidtz critiques biocentrists who are known for their commitment to the equality of species. In particular, Schmidtz critiques Paul Taylor's argument for species egalitarianism. He argues that while other species do command respect, they do not command equal respect.

I. RESPECT FOR NATURE

Species egalitarianism is the view that all species have equal moral standing.[1] To have moral standing is, at a minimum, to command respect, to be something more than a mere thing. Is there any reason to believe that all species have moral standing in even this most minimal sense? If so—that is, if all species command respect—is there any reason to believe they all command *equal* respect?

The following sections summarise critical responses to the most famous philosophical argument for species egalitarianism. I then try to explain why other species command our respect but also why they do not command equal respect. The intuition that we should have respect for nature is part of what motivates people to embrace species egalitarianism, but one need not be a species egalitarian to have respect for nature. I close by questioning whether species egalitarianism is even compatible with respect for nature.

II. THE GROUNDING OF SPECIES EGALITARIANISM

According to Paul Taylor, anthropocentrism 'gives either exclusive or primary consideration to human interests above the good of other species'.[2] The alternative to anthropocentrism is biocentrism, and it is biocentrism that, in Taylor's view, grounds species egalitarianism:

The beliefs that form the core of the biocentric outlook are four in number:

(a) The belief that humans are members of the Earth's Community of life in the same sense and on the same terms in which other living things are members of that community.

(b) The belief that the human species, along with all other species, are integral elements in a system of interdependence.

(c) The belief that all organisms are teleological centres of life in the sense that each is a unique individual pursuing its own good in its own way.

(d) The belief that humans are not inherently superior to other living beings.[3]

Taylor concludes, 'Rejecting the notion of human superiority entails its positive counterpart: the doctrine of species impartiality. One who accepts that doctrine regards all living things as possessing inherent worth—the *same* inherent worth, since no one species has been shown to be either higher or lower than any other.'[4]

Taylor does not claim that this is a valid argument, but he thinks that if we concede (a), (b), and (c), it would be unreasonable not to move to (d), and then to his egalitarian conclusion. Is he right? For those who accept Taylor's three premises (and who thus interpret those premises in terms innocuous enough to render them acceptable), there are two responses. First, we may go on to accept (d), following Taylor, but then still deny that there is any warrant for moving from there to Taylor's egalitarian conclusion. Having accepted that our form of life is not superior, we might choose instead to regard it as inferior. More plausibly, we might view our form of life as noncomparable. We simply do not have the same kind of value as nonhumans. The question of how we compare to nonhumans has a simple answer: we do not compare to them.

Alternatively, we may reject (d) and say humans are indeed inherently superior but our superiority is a moot point. Whether we are inherently superior (that is, superior as a form of life) does not matter much. Even if we are superior, the fact remains that within the web of ecological interdependence mentioned in premises (a) and (b), it would be a mistake to ignore the needs and the telos of the other species referred to in premise (c). Thus, there are two ways of rejecting Taylor's argument for species egalitarianism. Each, on its face, is compatible with the respect for nature that motivates Taylor's egalitarianism in the first place.

Taylor's critics, such as James Anderson and William French, have taken the second route. They reject (d). After discussing their arguments, and building on some while rejecting others, I explore some of our reasons to have respect for nature and ask whether they translate into reasons to be species egalitarians.

III. IS SPECIES EGALITARIANISM HYPOCRITICAL?

Paul Taylor and Arne Naess[5] are among the most intransigent of species egalitarians, yet they allow that human needs override the needs of nonhumans.

William C. French argues that they cannot have it both ways.[6] French perceives a contradiction between the egalitarian principles that Taylor and Naess officially endorse and the unofficial principles they offer as the real principles by which we should live. Having proclaimed that we are all equal, French asks, what licenses Taylor and Naess to say that, in cases of conflict, nonhuman interests can legitimately be sacrificed to vital human interests?

French has a point. James C. Anderson[7] makes a similar point. Yet, somehow the inconsistency of Taylor and Naess is too obvious. Perhaps their position is not as blatantly inconsistent as it appears. Let me suggest how Taylor and Naess could respond to French. Suppose I find myself in a situation of mortal combat with an enemy soldier. If I kill my enemy to save my life, that does not entail that I regard my enemy as inherently inferior (i.e., as an inferior form of life). Likewise, if I kill a bear to save my life, that does not entail that I regard the bear as inherently inferior. Therefore, Taylor and Naess can, without hypocrisy, deny that species egalitarianism requires a radically self-effacing pacifism.

What, then, does species egalitarianism require? It requires us to avoid mortal combat whenever we can, not just with other humans but with living things in general. On this view, we ought to regret finding ourselves in kill-or-be-killed situations that we could have avoided. There is no point in regretting the fact that we must kill in order to eat, though, for there is no avoiding that. Species egalitarianism is compatible with our having a limited license to kill.

What seems far more problematic for species egalitarianism is that it seems to suggest that it makes no difference *what* we kill. Vegetarians typically think it is worse to kill a cow than to kill a potato. Are they wrong?[8] Yes they are, according to species egalitarianism. In this respect, species egalitarianism cannot be right. I do believe we have reason to respect nature. But we fail to give nature due respect if we say we should have no more respect for a cow than for a potato.

IV. IS SPECIES EGALITARIANISM ARBITRARY?

Suppose interspecies comparisons are possible. Suppose the capacities of different species, and whatever else gives species moral standing, are commensurable. In that case, it could turn out that all species are equal, but that would be quite a fluke.

Taylor says a being has intrinsic worth if and only if it has a good of its own. Anderson does not disagree, but he points out that if we accept Taylor's idea of a thing having a good of its own, then that licenses us to notice differences among the various kinds of 'good of its own.' (We can notice differences without being committed to ranking them.) For example, we can distinguish, along Aristotelian lines, vegetative, animal, and cognitive goods of one's own. To have a vegetative nature is to be what Taylor, in premise (c), calls a teleological centre of life. A being with an animal nature is a teleological centre of life, and more. A being with a cognitive as well as animal nature is a teleological centre of life, and more still. Cognitive nature may be something we share with whales, dolphins, and higher primates. It is an empirical question. Anderson's view is that so long as we do not assume away this possibility, valuing cognitive capacity is not anthropocentric. The question is what would make *any* species superior to another (p. 348).

As mentioned earlier, Taylor defines anthropocentrism as giving exclusive or primary consideration to human interests above the good of other species. So, when we acknowledge that cognitive capacity is one valuable capacity among others, are we giving exclusive or primary considerations to human interests? Anderson thinks not, and surely he is right. Put it this way: if biocentrism involves resolving to ignore the fact that cognitive capacity is something we value—if biocentrism amounts to a resolution to value only those capacities that all living things share—then biocentrism is at least as arbitrary and question-begging as anthropocentrism.

It will not do to defend species egalitarianism by singling out a property that all species possess, arguing that this property is morally important, and then concluding that all species are therefore of equal moral importance. The problem with this sort of argument is that, where there is one property that provides a basis for moral standing, there might be others. Other properties might be possessed by some but not all species, and might provide bases for different kinds or degrees of moral standing.

V. THE MULTIPLE BASES OF MORAL STANDING

Taylor is aware of the Aristotelian classification scheme, but considers its hierarchy of capacities to be question-begging. Taylor himself assumes that human rationality is on a par with a cheetah's foot-speed.[9] In this case, though, perhaps it is Taylor who begs the question. It hardly seems unreasonable to see the difference between the foot-speed of chimpanzees and cheetahs as a difference of degree, while seeing the difference between the sentience of a chimpanzee and the nonsentience of a tree as a difference in kind.

Anthropocentrists might argue that the good associated with cognitive capacity is superior to the good associated with vegetative capacity. Could they be wrong? Let us suppose they are wrong. For argument's sake, let us suppose *vegetative* capacity is the superior good. Even so, the exact nature of the good associated with an organism's vegetative capacity will depend upon the organism's other capacities. For example, Anderson (p. 358) points out that even if health in a human and health in a tree are instances of the same thing, they need not have the same moral standing. Why not? Because health in a human has an instrumental value that health in a tree lacks. John Stuart Mill's swine can take pleasure in its health but trees cannot. Animals have a plant's capacities plus more. In turn, humans (and possibly dolphins, apes, and so on) have an animal's capacities plus more. The comparison between Socrates and swine therefore is less a matter of comparing swine to non-swine and more a matter of comparing swine to 'swine-plus' (Anderson, p. 361). Crucially, Anderson's argument for the superiority of Socrates over swine does not presume that one capacity is higher than another. We do not need to make any assumptions about the respective merits of animal or vegetative versus cognitive capacities in order to conclude that the capacities of 'swine-plus' are superior to those of swine.

We may of course conclude that *one* of the grounds of our moral standing (i.e., our vegetative natures) is something we share with all living things. Beyond that, nothing about equality even suggests itself. In particular, it begs no questions to notice that there are grounds for moral standing that we do not share with all living things.

VI. IN PRAISE OF SPECIESISM

William French invites us to see species rankings not 'as an assessment of some inherent superiority, but rather as a considered moral recognition of the fact that greater ranges of vulnerability are generated by broader ranges of complexity and capacities' (p. 56). One species outranks another not because it is a superior form of life but rather because it is a more vulnerable form of life. French, if I understand correctly, interprets vulnerability as a matter of having *more* to lose. This interpretation is problematic. It implies that a millionaire, having more to lose than a pauper, is by that fact more vulnerable than the pauper. Perhaps this interpretation is forced upon French, though. If French had instead chosen a more natural interpretation—if he had chosen to interpret vulnerability as a matter of *probability* of loss—then a ranking by vulnerability would not be correlated to complex capacities in the way he wants. Ranking by probability of loss would change on a daily basis, and the top-ranked species often would be an amphibian.

If we set aside questions about how to interpret vulnerability, there remains a problem with French's

proposal. If having complex capacities is not itself morally important, then being in danger of losing them is not morally important either. Vulnerability, on any interpretation, is essentially of derivative importance; any role it could play in ranking species must already be played by the capacities themselves.

Yet, although I reject French's argument, I do not reject his inegalitarian conclusion. The conclusion that mice are the moral equals of chimpanzees is about as insupportable as a conclusion can be. Suppose that, for some reason, we take an interest in how chimpanzees rank compared to mice. Perhaps we wonder what we would do in an emergency where we could save a drowning chimpanzee or a drowning mouse but not both. More realistically, we might wonder whether, other things equal, we have any reason to use mice in our medical experiments rather than chimpanzees. Species egalitarianism seems to say not.

Suppose we decide upon reflection that, from our human perspective, chimpanzees are superior to mice and humans are superior to chimpanzees. Would the perceived superiority of our form of life give us reason to think we have no obligations whatsoever to mice, or to chimpanzees? Those who believe we have fewer obligations to inferior species might be pressed to say whether they also would allow that we have fewer obligations to inferior human beings. Lawrence Johnson, for example, rhetorically asks whether it is worse to cause a person pain if the person is a Nobel Prize winner.[10] Well, why not? Echoing Peter Singer,[11] Johnson argues that if medical researchers had to choose between harvesting the organs of a chimpanzee or a brain-damaged human baby, 'one thing we cannot justify is trying to have it both ways. If rationality is what makes the basic moral difference, then we cannot maintain that the brain-damaged infant ought to be exempt from utilisation just because it is human while at the same time allowing that the animal can be used if utility warrants' (p. 52).

Does this seem obvious? It should not. Johnson presumes that rationality is relevant to justification at the *token* level when speciesists (i.e., those who believe some species, the human species in particular, are superior to others) presumably would invoke rationality as a justification at the *type* level. One can say rationality makes a moral difference at the type level without thereby taking any position on whether rationality makes a moral difference at the token level. A speciesist could say humanity's characteristic rationality mandates respect for humanity, not merely for particular humans who exemplify human rationality. Similarly, once we note that chimpanzees have characteristic cognitive capacities that mice lack, we do not need to compare individual chimpanzees and mice on a case by case basis in order to have a moral justification for planning to use a mouse rather than a chimpanzee in an experiment.

Of course, some chimpanzees lack the characteristic features in virtue of which chimpanzees command respect as a species, just as some humans lack the characteristic features in virtue of which humans command respect as a species. It is equally obvious that some chimpanzees have cognitive capacities (for example) that are superior to the cognitive capacities of some humans. But whether every human being is superior to every chimpanzee is beside the point. The point is that we can, we do, and we should make decisions on the basis of our recognition that mice, chimpanzees, and humans are relevantly different types. We can have it both ways after all. Or so a speciesist could argue.

VII. EQUALITY AND TRANSCENDENCE

Even if speciesists are right to see a nonarbitary distinction between humans and other species, though, the fact remains that, as Anderson (p. 362) points out, claims of superiority do not easily translate into justifications of domination.[12] We can have reasons to treat nonhuman species with respect, regardless of whether we consider them to be on a moral par with *homo sapiens*.

What kind of reasons do we have for treating other species with respect? We might have respect for chimpanzees or even mice on the grounds that they are sentient. Even mice have a rudimentary point of view and rudimentary hopes and dreams, and we might well respect them for that. But what about plants? Plants, unlike mice and chimpanzees, do not care what happens to them. It is literally true that they could not care less. So, why should we care? Is it even possible for us to have any good reason, other than a purely instrumental reason, to care what happens to plants?

When we are alone in a forest wondering whether it would be fine to chop down a tree for fun, our perspective on what happens to the tree is, so far as we know, the only perspective there is. The tree does not have its own. Thus, explaining why we have reason to care about trees requires us to explain caring from our point of view, since that (we are supposing) is all there is. In that case, we do not have to satisfy *trees* that we are treating them properly; rather, we have to satisfy *ourselves*. So, again, can we have noninstrumental reasons for caring about trees—for treating them with respect?

One reason to care (not the only one) is that gratuitous destruction is a failure of self-respect. It is a repudiation of the kind of self-awareness and self-respect that we can achieve by repudiating wantonness. So far as I know, no one finds anything puzzling in the idea that we have reason to treat our lawns or living rooms with respect. Lawns and living rooms have instrumental value, but there is more to it than that. Most of us have the sense that taking reasonable care of our lawns and living rooms is somehow a matter of self-respect, not merely a matter of preserving their instrumental value. Do we have similar reasons to treat forests with respect? I think we do. There is an aesthetic involved, the repudiation of which would be a failure of self-respect. (Obviously, not everyone feels the same way about forests. Not everyone feels the same way about lawns and living rooms, either. But the point here is to make sense of respect for nature, not to argue that respect for nature is in fact universal or that failing to respect nature is irrational.[13]) If and when we identify with a Redwood, in the sense of being inspired by it, having respect for its size and age and so on, then as a psychological fact, we really do face moral questions about how we ought to treat it. If and when we come to see a Redwood in that light, subsequently turning our backs on it becomes a kind of self-effacement. The values that we thereby fail to take seriously are *our* values, not the tree's.

A related way of grounding respect for nature is suggested by Jim Cheney's remark that 'moral regard is appropriate wherever we are *able* to manage it—in light of our sensibilities, knowledge, and cultural/personal histories ... The limits of moral regard are set only by the limitations of one's own (or one's species' or one's community's) ability to respond in a caring manner.'[14] Should we believe Cheney's rather startling proposal that moral regard is appropriate whenever we can manage it? One reason to take it very seriously is that exercising our capacity for moral regard is a way of expressing respect for that capacity. Developing that capacity is a form of self-realization.

Put it this way. I am arguing that the attitude we take toward gazelles (for example) raises issues of self-respect insofar as we see ourselves as relevantly like gazelles. My reading of Cheney suggests a different and complementary way of looking at the issue. Consider that lions owe nothing to gazelles. Therefore, if we owe it to gazelles not to hunt them, it must be because we are *unlike* lions, not (or not only) because we are *like* gazelles.

Unlike lions, we have a choice about whether to hunt gazelles, and we are capable of deliberating about that choice in a reflective way. We are capable of caring about the gazelle's pain, the gazelle's beauty, the gazelle's hopes and dreams (such as they are), and so forth. And if we do care, then in a more or less literal way, something is wrong with us—we are less than fully human—if we cannot adjust our behaviour in the light of what we care about. If we do not care, then we are missing something. For a human being, to lack a broad respect for living things and beautiful things and well-functioning things is to be stunted in a way.

Our coming to see other species as commanding respect is itself a way of transcending our animal natures. It is ennobling. It is part of our animal natures unthinkingly to see ourselves as superior, and to try to dominate accordingly; our capacity to see ourselves as equal is one of the things that

makes us different. Thus, our capacity to see ourselves as equal may be one of the things that makes us superior. Coming to see all species as equal may not be the best way of transcending our animal natures—it does not work for me—but it is one way. Another way of transcending our animal natures and expressing due respect for nature is simply to not worry so much about ranking species. This latter way is, I think, better. It is more respectful of our own reflective natures. It does not dwell on rankings. It does not insist on seeing equality where a more reflective being simply would see what is there to be seen and would not shy away from respecting the differences as well as the commonalities. The whole idea of ranking species, even as equals, sometimes seems like a child's game. It seems beneath us.

VII. RESPECT FOR EVERYTHING

Thus, a broad respect for living or beautiful or well-functioning things need not translate into equal respect. It need not translate into universal respect, either. I can appreciate mosquitoes to a degree. My wife (a biochemist who studies mosquito immune systems) even finds them beautiful, or so she says. My own appreciation, by contrast, is thin and grudging and purely intellectual. In neither degree nor kind is it anything like the appreciation I have for my wife, or for human beings in general, or even for the rabbits I sometimes find eating my flowers in the morning. Part of our responsibility as moral agents is to be somewhat choosy about what we respect and how we respect it. I can see why people shy away from openly accepting that responsibility, but they still have it.

Johnson says speciesism is as arbitrary as racism unless we can show that the differences are morally relevant (p. 51). This is, to be sure, a popular sentiment among radical environmentalists and animal liberationists.[15] But are we really like racists when we think it is worse to kill a dolphin than to kill a tuna? The person who says there is a relevant similarity between speciesism and racism has the burden of proof: go ahead and identify the similarity. Is seeing moral significance in biological differences between chimpanzees and potatoes anything like seeing moral significance in biological differences between races? I think not.

Is it true that we need good reason to *exclude* plants and animals from the realm of things we regard as commanding respect? Or do we need reason to include them? Should we be trying to identify properties in virtue of which a thing forfeits presumptive moral standing? Or does it make more sense to be trying to identify properties in virtue of which a thing commands respect? The latter seems more natural to me, which suggests the burden of proof lies with those who claim we should have respect for other species.

I would not say, though, that this burden is unbearable. One reason to have regard for other species has to do with self-respect. (As I said earlier, when we mistreat a tree that we admire, the values we fail to respect are our values, not the tree's.) A second reason has to do with self-realisation. (As I said, exercising our capacity for moral regard is a form of self-realisation.) Finally, at least some species seem to share with human beings precisely those cognitive and affective characteristics that lead us to see human life as especially worthy of esteem. Johnson describes experiments in which rhesus monkeys show extreme reluctance to obtain food by means that would subject monkeys in neighbouring cages to electric shock (p. 64n). He describes the case of Washoe, a chimpanzee who learned sign language. Anyone who has tried to learn a foreign language ought to be able to appreciate how astonishing an intellectual feat it is that an essentially nonlinguistic creature could learn a language—a language that is not merely foreign but the language of another species.

Johnson believes Washoe has moral standing (pp. 27–31), but he does not believe that the moral standing of chimpanzees, and indeed of all living creatures, implies that we must resolve never to kill (p. 136). Thus, Johnson supports killing introduced animal species (feral dogs, rabbits, and so forth) to prevent the extermination of

Australia's native species, including native plant species (p. 174).

Is Johnson guilty of advocating the speciesist equivalent of ethnic cleansing? Has he shown himself to be no better than a racist? I think not. Johnson is right to want to take drastic measures to protect Australia's native flora, and the idea of respecting trees is intelligible. Certainly one thing I feel in the presence of Redwoods is something like a feeling of respect. But I doubt that what underlies Johnson's willingness to kill feral dogs is mere respect for Australia's native plants. I suspect that his approval of such killings turns on the needs and aesthetic sensibilities of human beings, not just the interests of plants.[16] For example, if the endangered native species happened to be a malaria-carrying mosquito, I doubt that Johnson would advocate wiping out an exotic but minimally intrusive species of amphibian in order to save the mosquitoes.

Aldo Leopold[17] urged us to see ourselves as plain citizens of, rather than conquerors of, the biotic community, but there are some species with whom we can never be fellow citizens. The rabbits eating my flowers in the back yard are neighbours, and I cherish their company, minor frictions notwithstanding. I feel no sense of community with mosquitoes, though, and not merely because they are not warm and furry. Some mosquito species are so adapted to making human beings miserable that mortal combat is not accidental; rather, combat is a natural state. It is how such creatures live. Recall Cheney's remark that the limits of moral regard are set by the limits of our ability to respond in a caring manner. I think it is fair to say human beings are not able to respond to malaria-carrying mosquitoes in a caring manner. At very least, most of us would think less of a person who did respond to them in a caring manner. We would regard the person's caring as a parody of respect for nature.

The conclusion that *all* species have moral standing is unmotivated. For human beings, viewing apes as having moral standing is a form of self-respect. Viewing viruses as having moral standing is not. It is good to have a sense of how amazing living things are, but being able to marvel at living things is not the same as thinking all species have moral standing. Life as such commands respect only in the limited but nonetheless important sense that for self-aware and reflective creatures who want to act in ways that make sense, deliberately killing something is an act that does not make sense unless we have good reason to do it. Destroying something for no good reason is (at best) the moral equivalent of vandalism.

IX. THE HISTORY
OF THE DEBATE

There is an odd project in the history of philosophy that equates what seem to be three distinct projects:

1. determining our essence;
2. specifying how we are different from all other species;
3. specifying what makes us morally important.

Equating these three projects has important ramifications. Suppose for the sake of argument that what makes us morally important is that we are capable of suffering. If what makes us morally important is necessarily the same property that constitutes our essence, then our essence is that we are capable of suffering. And if our essence necessarily is what makes us different from all other species, then we can deduce that dogs are not capable of suffering.

Likewise with rationality. If rationality is our essence, then rationality is what makes us morally important and also what makes us unique. Therefore, we can deduce that chimpanzees are not rational. Alternatively, if some other animal becomes rational, does that mean our essence will change? Is that why some people find Washoe, the talking chimpanzee, threatening?

The three projects, needless to say, should not be conflated in the way philosophy seems historically to have conflated them, but we can reject species equality without conflating them.[18] If we like, we can select a property with respect to which all species are the same, then argue that that property confers moral standing, then say all species have moral standing. To infer that all species have the same standing, though, would be to ignore the possibility that there are other morally important properties with respect to which not all species are equal.

There is room to wonder whether species egalitarianism is even compatible with respect for nature. Is it true that we should have no more regard for dolphins than for tuna? Is it true that the moral standing of chimpanzees is no higher than that of mosquitoes? I worry that these things are not only untrue, but also disrespectful. Dolphins and chimpanzees command more respect than species egalitarianism allows.

There is no denying that it demeans us to destroy species we find beautiful or otherwise beneficial. What about species in which we find neither beauty nor benefit? It is, upon reflection, obviously in our interest to enrich our lives by finding them beautiful or beneficial, if we can. By and large, we must agree with Leopold that it is too late for conquering the biotic community. Our most pressing task now is to find ways of fitting in. Species egalitarianism is one way of trying to understand how we fit in. In the end, it is not an acceptable way. Having respect for nature and being a species egalitarian are two different things.

ENDNOTES

1. A species egalitarian may or may not believe that individual living things all have equal moral standing. A species egalitarian may think a given whooping crane matters more than a given bald eagle because the cranes are endangered, despite believing that the differences between the two species qua species are not morally important. I thank Stephen Clark for this observation.

2. Paul W. Taylor (1983) In defense of biocentrism, *Environmental Ethics*, 5: 237–43, here p. 240. Taylor takes pains to distinguish anthropocentrism from the trivial and unobjectionable position that human beings make judgments from a human point of view.

3. Paul Taylor (1986) *Respect for Nature* (Princeton: Princeton University Press) p. 99ff. See also Taylor (1994) The ethics of respect for nature, *Planet in Peril*, edited by Dale & Fred Westphal (Orlando, Harcourt Brace) 15–37.

4. Taylor (1994), op. cit., p. 35.

5. Arne Naess (1973) The shallow and the deep, long-range ecology movement: a summary, *Inquiry*, 16: 95–100.

6. William C. French (1995) Against biospherical egalitarianism, *Environmental Ethics*, 17: 39–57, here pp. 44ff.

7. James C. Anderson (1993) Species equality and the foundations of moral theory, *Environmental Values*, 2: 347–65, here p. 350.

8. I thank Austin Dacey for raising this question.

9. Taylor (1994), op. cit., p. 33.

10. Lawrence Johnson (1991) *A Morally Deep World* (New York: Cambridge University Press), p. 52.

11. Peter Singer (1990) *Animal Liberation*, 2nd edition (New York: Random House), pp. 1–23.

12. James Sterba evidently thinks otherwise, for he considers it true by *definition* that 'To treat humans as superior overall to other living beings is to aggress against them by sacrificing their basic needs to meet the nonbasic needs of humans (definition).' James P. Sterba (1995) From biocentric individualism to biocentric pluralism, *Environmental Ethics*, 17: 191–207, here p. 194.

   Sterba does not say whether regarding chimpanzees as superior to mice is, by definition, a way of aggressing against mice.

13. Thus, the objective is to explain how a rational agent could have respect for trees, not to argue that a rational agent could not fail to have respect. In utilitarian terms, a person whose utility function leaves no room to derive pleasure from respecting trees is not irrational for failing to respect trees, but people whose utility functions include a potential for deriving pleasure from respecting trees have reason (other things equal) to enrich their lives by realising that potential.

14. Jim Cheney (1987) Eco-feminism and deep ecology, *Environmental Ethics* 9: 115–45, here p. 144.

15. See Peter Singer (1994) All animals are equal, in Dale & Fred Westphal, eds, *Planet in Peril* (Orlando: Harcourt Brace), 175–94, here p. 189.

16. Johnson believes ecosystems as such have moral standing and that, consequently, 'we should always stop short of entirely destroying or irreparably degrading any ecosystem' (p. 276). 'Chopping some trees is one thing, then, but destroying a forest is something else' (p. 276). But this is impossible to square with his remark that there 'is an ecosystem in a tiny puddle of water in a rotting stump' (p. 265). Thus, when Johnson says ecosystems should never be destroyed, he does not mean ecosystems per se. Rather he means forests, deserts, marshes, and so on—ecosystems that are recognisable as habitat either for humans or for species that humans care about.

17. Leopold Aldo (1966, first published in 1949) *Sand County Almanac* (New York: Oxford University Press) p. 240.

18. Will Kymlicka notes that Mary Midgley makes a similar point in a critique of Karl Marx. *Contra* Marx, Midgley says, what constitutes a good life for a human being is not a question 'about biological classification. It is a question in moral philosophy. And we do not help ourselves at all in answering it if we decide in advance that the answer ought to be a single, simple characteristic, unshared by other species, such as the differentia is meant to be. Mary Midgley (1978) *Beast and Man: The roots of human nature* (New York: New American Library) p. 204.

62

Biocentrism Defended

JAMES P. STERBA

James P. Sterba defends the biocentrism that Schmidtz critiques. He argues that the bio-centrist's commitment to species egalitarianism needs to be understood by analogy with the equality of humans. Accordingly, just as we claim that humans are equal, yet justifiably treat them differently, so too we think that we should be able to claim that all species are equal, yet justifiably treat them differently.

Biocentrists are well known for their commitment to species egalitarianism, that is, to the equality of species. In "A Critique of Biocentrism," David Schmidtz seems unsure whether all, or only just some, species deserve respect, but what he is definitely sure about is that species are not equal. So what do biocentrists, like Paul Taylor and myself, understand by our commitment to the equality of species.

To begin with, our commitment needs to be understood by analogy with the equality of humans. Accordingly, just as we claim that humans are equal, yet justifiably treat them differently, so too we think that we should be able to claim that all species are equal, yet justifiably treat them differently. Now in human ethics, there are various interpretations that we give to human equality that allow for different treatment of humans. In libertarianism, everyone has an equal right to liberty, but although this imposes some limits on the pursuit of self-interest, it is said to allow us to refrain from helping others in severe need. In welfare liberalism, everyone has an equal right to welfare and to opportunity, but this need not commit us to providing everyone with exactly the same resources. So just as there are these various ways to interpret human equality that still allow us to treat humans differently, Taylor and I think that there are various ways that we can interpret

species equality that still allow species to be treated differently.

Suppose then we interpret species equality as akin to the equality found in welfare liberalism or in libertarianism with respect to the degree of preference it allows for oneself and the members of one's own species. That preference can be maintained, in part, on grounds of preservation. Accordingly, we have:

> *A Principle of Human Preservation:* Actions that are necessary for meeting one's basic needs or the basic needs of other human beings are permissible even when they require aggressing against the basic needs of individual animals and plants, or even of whole species or ecosystems.

Now needs, in general, if not satisfied, lead to lacks or deficiencies with respect to various standards. The basic needs of humans, if not satisfied, lead to lacks or deficiencies with respect to a standard of a decent life. The basic needs of animals and plants, if not satisfied, lead to lacks or deficiencies with respect to a standard of a healthy life. The basic needs of species and ecosystems, if not satisfied, lead to lacks or deficiencies with respect to a standard of a healthy living system. The means necessary for meeting the basic needs of humans can vary widely from society to society. By contrast, the means necessary for meeting the basic needs of particular species of animals and plants tend to be invariant.[1] Of course, while only some needs can be clearly classified as basic, and others clearly classified as nonbasic, there still are other needs that are more or less difficult to classify. Yet the fact that not every need can be clearly classified as either basic or nonbasic, as similarly holds for a whole range of dichotomous concepts like moral/immoral, legal/illegal, living/nonliving, human/nonhuman, should not immobilize us from acting at least with respect to clear cases.

In human ethics, there is no principle that is strictly analogous to this Principle of Human Preservation. There is a principle of self-preservation in human ethics that permits actions that are necessary for meeting one's own basic needs or the basic needs of other people, even if this requires failing to meet (through an act of omission) the basic needs of still other people. For example, we can use our resources to feed ourselves and our families, even if this necessitates failing to meet the basic needs of people in underdeveloped countries. But, in general, we don't have a principle that allows us to aggress against (through an act of commission) the basic needs of some people in order to meet our own basic needs or the basic needs of other people to whom we are committed or happen to care about. One place where we do permit aggressing against the basic needs of other people in order to meet our own basic needs or the basic needs of people to whom we are committed or happen to care about is our acceptance of the outcome of life and death struggles in lifeboat cases, where no one has an antecedent right to the available resources. For example, if you had to fight off others in order to secure the last place in a lifeboat for yourself or for a member of your family, we might say that you justifiably aggressed against the basic needs of those whom you fought to meet your own basic needs or the basic needs of the member of your family.

Now the Principle of Human Preservation does not permit aggressing against the basic needs of humans even if it is the only way to meet our own basic needs or the basic needs of other human beings. Rather this principle is directed at a different range of cases with respect to which we can meet our own basic needs and the basic needs of other humans simply by aggressing against the basic needs of nonhuman living beings. With respect to those cases, the Principle of Human Preservation permits actions that are necessary for meeting one's own basic needs or the basic needs of other human beings, even when they require aggressing against the basic needs of individual animals and plants, or even of whole species or ecosystems.

Of course, we could envision an even more permissive principle of human preservation, one that would permit us to aggress against the basic needs of both humans and nonhumans to meet our own basic needs or the basic needs of other human beings. But while adopting such a principle, by permitting cannibalism, would clearly reduce the degree of predation of humans on other species, and so would be of some benefit to other species, it would clearly be counterproductive with respect to meeting basic human needs. This is because implicit nonaggression pacts based on a reasonable expectation of a comparable degree of altruistic forbearance from fellow humans have been enormously beneficial and probably were necessary for the survival of the human species. So it is difficult to see how humans could be justifiably required to forgo such benefits.

Moreover, beyond the prudential value of such implicit nonaggression pacts against fellow humans, there appears to be no morally defensible way to exclude some humans from their protection. This is because any exclusion would fail to satisfy an expanded "Ought" implies "Can" principle, given that it would impose a sacrifice on at least some humans that would be unreasonable to ask and/or require them to accept.[2]

But are there no exceptions to the Principle of Human Preservation? Consider, for example, the following real-life case.[3] Thousands of Nepalese have cleared forests, cultivated crops, and raised cattle and buffalo on land surrounding the Royal Chitwan National Park in Nepal, but they have also made incursions into the park to meet their own basic needs. In so doing, they have threatened the rhino, the Bengal tiger, and other endangered species in the park. Assume that the basic needs of no other humans are at stake. For this case, then, would would-be human guardians of these nonhuman endangered species be justified in preventing the Nepalese from meeting their basic needs in order to preserve these endangered species? It seems to me that before the basic needs of disadvantaged Nepalese could be sacrificed, the would-be human guardians of these endangered species first would be required to use whatever surplus was available to them and to other humans to meet the basic needs of the Nepalese whom they propose to restrict. Yet clearly it would be very difficult to have first used all the surplus available to the whole human population for meeting basic human needs. Under present conditions, this requirement has certainly not been met. Moreover, insofar as rich people are unwilling to make the necessary transfers of resources so that poor people would not be led to prey on endangered species in order to survive, then, the appropriate means of preserving endangered species should be to use force against such rich people rather than against poor people, like the Nepalese near Royal Chitwan National Park. So for all present purposes, the moral permissibility in the Principle of Human Preservation remains that of strong permissibility, which means that other humans are prohibited from interfering with the aggression against nonhumans that is permitted by the principle.[4]

Nevertheless, preference for humans can still go beyond bounds, and the bounds that are required are captured by the following:

> *A Principle of Disproportionality:* Actions that meet nonbasic or luxury needs of humans are prohibited when they aggress against the basic needs of individual animals and plants or even of whole species or ecosystems.

This principle is strictly analogous to the principle in human ethics that similarly prohibits meeting some people's nonbasic or luxury needs by aggressing against the basic needs of other people. Without a doubt, the adoption of such a principle with respect to nonhumans would significantly change the way we live our lives. Such a principle is required, however, if there is to be any substance

to the claim that the members of all species have moral status. We can no more consistently claim that the members of all species count morally and yet aggress against the basic needs of animals or plants whenever this serves our own nonbasic or luxury needs than we can consistently claim that all humans have moral status and then aggress against the basic needs of other human beings whenever this serves our nonbasic or luxury needs. Consequently, if saying that species have moral status is to mean anything, it must be the case that the basic needs of the members of nonhuman species are protected against aggressive actions that only serve to meet the nonbasic needs of humans, as required by the Principle of Disproportionality. Another way to put the central claim here is to hold that having moral status rules out domination, where domination means aggressing against the basic needs of some for the sake of satisfying the nonbasic needs of others.

Nevertheless, in order to avoid imposing an unacceptable sacrifice on the members of our own species, we can also justify a preference for humans on grounds of defense. Thus, we have

> *A Principle of Human Defense:* Actions that defend oneself and other human beings against harmful aggression are permissible even when they necessitate killing or harming individual animals or plants, or even destroying whole species or ecosystems.

This Principle of Human Defense allows us to defend ourselves and other human beings from harmful aggression first against our persons and the persons of other humans beings that we are committed to or happen to care about and second against our justifiably held property and the justifiably held property of other humans beings that we are committed to or happen to care about.

This principle is analogous to the principle of self-defense that applies in human ethics and permits actions in defense of oneself or other human beings against harmful human aggression. In the case of human aggression, however, it will sometimes be possible to effectively defend oneself and other human beings by first suffering the aggression and then securing adequate compensation later. Since in the case of nonhuman aggression by the members of other species with which we are familiar, this is unlikely to obtain, more harmful preventive actions such as killing a rabid dog or swatting a mosquito will be justified. There are simply more ways to effectively stop aggressive humans than there are to effectively stop the aggressive nonhumans with which we are familiar.

Lastly, we need one more principle to deal with violations of the above three principles. Accordingly, we have

> *A Principle of Rectification*: Compensation and reparation are required when the other principles have been violated.

Obviously, this principle is somewhat vague, but for those who are willing to abide by the other three principles, it should be possible to remedy that vagueness in practice. Here too would-be human guardians of the interests of nonhumans could have a useful role figuring out what is appropriate compensation or reparation for violations of the Principle of Disproportionality, and, even more importantly, designing ways to get that compensation or reparation enacted.

Taken altogether, these three principles constitute a set of environmental principles that are clearly not biased in favor of the human species, and thus provide a defensible interpretation of the biocentrist's commitment to the equality of species.

Now it does not seem that the Schmidtz's argument against the equality of species works when a commitment to species equality is understood to simply rule out domination as specified by the above principles. As it turns out, I have been defending this interpretation of biocentrism in print since 1994. Taylor has publicly endorsed my development of his view in the preface to the Chinese translation of *Respect for Nature* published in 2003. So I don't think it makes sense, at this point in time, to distinguish between Taylor's biocentrism and my own.

Now Schmidtz does raise an important worry concerning how a biocentric commitment to the equality of species can make sense of the vegetarian's opposition to meat eating. I would make sense of this preference as a way to preventing suffering to animals, a problem that does not present itself when we dine on vegetables. By dining on vegetables, we thereby prevent additional harm from being done. As I see it, there really is no problem with biocentists being committed both to avoiding unnecessary harm and to avoiding domination, and hence, to the equality of species, provided that the first commitment is made subordinate to the second.

So while I have only been able to briefly sketch a defense of biocentrism here, I hope that I have said enough to indicate how the version of biocentrism that I, and now Paul Taylor, endorse is, for the most part, not directly challenged by Schmidtz's critique.

ENDNOTES

1. For further discussion of basic needs, see my *How to Make People Just* (Totowa, N.J.: Rowman & Littlefield, 1988), 45ff.

2. For a discussion of the "ought" implies "can" principle, see chapter 3.

3. See Holmes Rolston III, "Enforcing Environmental Ethics: Civil Law and Natural Value," in *Social and Political Philosophy: Contemporary Perspectives*, ed. James P. Sterba (London: Routledge, 2001).

4. In the nonideal world in which we live, the Nepalese and their human allies should press rich people to acquire the available surplus to meet the basic needs of the Nepalese until their own lives are threatened. At that point, regrettably, the Nepalese would be justified in preying on endangered species as the only way for them to survive.

63

The Power and the Promise
of Ecological Feminism

KAREN J. WARREN

Karen Warren challenges mainstream environmental ethics to recognize that the domination of nature is rooted in the domination of women or at least to recognize that both these forms of domination are interconnected. According to Warren, women are identified with nature and the realm of the physical, while men are identified with the "human" and the realm of the mental. On the basis of this identification, Warren argues that women are judged inferior to men and their subordination to men is taken to be thereby justified. She calls the argumentative move from a claim of difference to a claim of superiority to a claim of domination the "logic of domination."

Ecological feminism (ecofeminism) has begun to receive a fair amount of attention lately as an alternative feminism and environmental ethic. Since Francoise d'Eaubonne introduced the term *eco-feminisme* in 1974 to bring attention to women's potential for bringing about an ecological revolution, the term has been used in a variety of ways. As I use the term here, ecological feminism is the position that there are important connections—historical, experiential, symbolic, and theoretical—between the domination of women and the domination of nature, an understanding of which is crucial to both feminism and environmental ethics. I argue that the promise and power of ecological feminism is that *it provides a distinctive framework both for reconceiving feminism and for developing an environmental ethic which takes seriously connections between the domination of women and the domination of nature.* I do so by discussing the nature of a feminist ethic and the ways in which ecofeminism provides a feminist and environmental ethic. I conclude that any feminist theory *and*

any environmental ethic which fails to take seriously the twin and interconnected dominations of women and nature is at best incomplete and at worst simply inadequate.

FEMINISM, ECOLOGICAL FEMINISM, AND CONCEPTUAL FRAMEWORKS

Whatever else it is, feminism is at least the movement to end sexist oppression. It involves the elimination of any and all factors that contribute to the continued and systematic domination or subordination of women. While feminists disagree about the nature of and solutions to the subordination of women, all feminists agree that sexist oppression exists, is wrong, and must be abolished.

A "feminist issue" is any issue that contributes in some way to understanding the oppression of

Reprinted from *Environmental Ethics* (1990) by permission of the author.

women. Equal rights, comparable pay for comparable work, and food production are feminist issues whenever an understanding of them contributes to an understanding of the continued exploitation or subjugation of women. Carrying water and searching for firewood are feminist issues wherever and whenever women's primary responsibility for these tasks contributes to their lack of full participation in decision making, income producing, or high status positions engaged in by men. What counts as a feminist issue, then, depends largely on context, particularly the historical and material conditions of women's lives.

Environmental degradation and exploitation are feminist issues because an understanding of them contributes to an understanding of the oppression of women. In India, for example, both deforestation and reforestation through the introduction of a monoculture species tree (e.g., eucalyptus) intended for commercial production are feminist issues because the loss of indigenous forests and multiple species of trees has drastically affected rural Indian women's ability to maintain a subsistence household. Indigenous forests provide a variety of trees for food, fuel, fodder, household utensils, dyes, medicines, and income-generating uses, while monoculture species forests do not. Although I do not argue for this claim here, a look at the global impact of environmental degradation on women's lives suggests important respects in which environmental degradation is a feminist issue.

Feminist philosophers claim that some of the most important feminist issues are *conceptual* ones: These issues concern how one conceptualizes such mainstay philosophical notions as reason and rationality, ethics, and what it is to be human. Ecofeminists extend this feminist philosophical concern to nature. They argue that, ultimately, some of the most important connections between the domination of women and the domination of nature are conceptual. To see this, consider the nature of conceptual frameworks.

A *conceptual framework* is a set of *basic* beliefs, values, attitudes, and assumptions which shape and reflect how one views oneself and one's world. It is a socially constructed lens through which we perceive ourselves and others. It is affected by such factors as gender, race, class, age, affectional orientation, nationality, and religious background.

Some conceptual frameworks are oppressive. An *oppressive conceptual framework* is one that explains, justifies, and maintains relationships of domination and subordination. When an oppressive conceptual framework is *patriarchal*, it explains, justifies, and maintains the subordination of women by men.

I have argued elsewhere that there are three significant features of oppressive conceptual frameworks: (1) value-hierarchical thinking, i.e., "up-down" thinking which places higher value, status, or prestige on what is "up" rather than on what is "down"; (2) value dualisms, i.e., disjunctive pairs in which the disjuncts are seen as oppositional (rather than as complementary) and exclusive (rather than as inclusive), and which place higher value (status, prestige) on one disjunct rather than the other (e.g., dualisms which give higher value or status to that which has historically been identified as "mind," "reason," and "male" than to that which has historically been identified as "body," "emotion," and "female"); and (3) logic of domination, i.e., a structure of argumentation which leads to a justification of subordination.

The third feature of oppressive conceptual frameworks is the most significant. A logic of domination is *not just* a logical structure. It also involves a substantive value system, since an ethical premise is needed to permit or sanction the "just" subordination of that which is subordinate. This justification typically is given on grounds of some alleged characteristic (e.g., rationality) which the dominant (e.g., men) have and the subordinate (e.g., women) lack.

Contrary to what many feminists and ecofeminists have said or suggested, there may be nothing *inherently* problematic about "hierarchical thinking" or even "value-hierarchical thinking" in contexts other than contexts of oppression. Hierarchical thinking is important in daily living for classifying data, comparing information, and organizing material. Taxonomies (e.g., plant taxonomies) and biological nomenclature seem to require *some* form of "hierarchical thinking." Even "value-hierarchical thinking" may be quite acceptable in certain contexts. (The same may be said of "value dualisms" in nonoppressive contexts.) For example, suppose it is true that what is unique about humans is our conscious capacity to radically reshape our social environments (or "societies"), as Murray Bookchin suggests. Then one could truthfully say that humans are better equipped to radically reshape their environments than are rocks or plants—a "value-hierarchical" 'way of speaking.

The problem is not simply *that* value-hierarchical thinking and value dualisms are used, but *the way* in which each has been used *in oppressive conceptual frameworks* to establish inferiority and to justify subordination.[1] It is the logic of domination, *coupled* with value-hierarchical thinking and value dualisms, which "justifies" subordination. What is explanatorily basic, then, about the nature of oppressive conceptual frameworks is the logic of domination.

For ecofeminism, that a logic of domination is explanatorily basic is important for at least three reasons. First, without a logic of domination, a description of similarities and differences would be just that: a description of similarities and differences. Consider the claim, "Humans are different from plants and rocks in that humans can (and plants and rocks cannot) consciously and radically reshape the communities in which they live; humans are similar to plants and rocks in that they are both members of an ecological community." Even if humans are "better" than plants and rocks with respect to the conscious ability of humans to radically transform communities, one does not *thereby* get any *morally* relevant distinction between humans and nonhumans, or an argument for the domination of plants and rocks by humans. To get *those* conclusions one needs to add at least two powerful assumptions, viz., (A2) and (A4) in argument A below:

A1. Humans do, and plants and rocks do not, have the capacity to consciously and radically change the community in which they live.

A2. Whatever has the capacity to consciously and radically change the community in which it lives is morally superior to whatever lacks this capacity.

A3. Thus, humans are morally superior to plants and rocks.

A4. For any X and Y, if X is morally superior to Y, then X is morally justified in subordinating Y.

A5. Thus, humans are morally justified in subordinating plants and rocks.

Without the two assumptions that *humans are morally superior* to (at least some) nonhumans, (A2), and that *superiority justifies subordination*, (A4), all one has is some difference between humans and some nonhumans. This is true *even if* that difference is given in terms of superiority. Thus, it is the logic of domination, (A4), which is the bottom line in ecofeminist discussions of oppression.

Second, ecofeminists argue that, at least in Western societies, the oppressive conceptual framework which sanctions the twin dominations of women and nature is a patriarchal one characterized by all three features of an oppressive conceptual framework. Many ecofeminists claim that, historically, within at least the dominant Western culture, a patriarchal conceptual framework has sanctioned the following argument B:

B1. Women are identified with nature and the realm of the physical; men are identified with the "human" and the realm of the mental.

B2. Whatever is identified with nature and the realm of the physical is inferior to ("below") whatever is identified with the "human" and the realm of the mental; or, conversely, the latter is superior to ("above") the former.

B3. Thus, women are inferior to ("below") men; or, conversely, men are superior to ("above") women.

B4. For any X and Y, if X is superior to Y, then X is justified in subordinating Y.

B5. Thus, men are justified in subordinating women.

If sound, argument B establishes *patriarchy*, i.e., the conclusion given at (B5) that the systematic domination of women by men is justified. But according to ecofeminists, (B5) is justified by just those three features of an oppressive conceptual framework identified earlier: value-hierarchical thinking, the assumption at (B2); value dualisms, the assumed dualism of the mental and the physical at (B1) and the assumed inferiority of the physical vis-à-vis the mental at (B2); and a logic of domination, the assumption at (B4), the same as the previous premise (A4). Hence, according to ecofeminists, insofar as an oppressive patriarchal conceptual framework has functioned historically (within at least dominant Western culture) to sanction the twin dominations of women and nature (argument B), both argument B and the patriarchal conceptual framework, from when it comes, ought to be rejected.

Of course, the preceding does not identify which premises of B are false. What is the status of premises (B1) and (B2)? Most, if not all, feminists claim that (B1), and many ecofeminists claim that (B2), have been assumed or asserted within the dominant Western philosophical and intellectual tradition.[2] As such, these feminists assert, as a matter of historical fact, that the dominant Western philosophical tradition has assumed the truth of (B1) and (B2). Ecofeminists, however, either deny (B2) or do not affirm (B2). Furthermore, because some ecofeminists are anxious to deny any historical identification of women with nature, some ecofeminists deny (B1) when (B1) is used to support anything other than a strictly historical claim about what has been asserted or assumed to be true within patriarchal culture—e.g., when (B1) is used to assert that women properly are identified with the realm of nature and the physical.[3] Thus, from an ecofeminist perspective, (B1) and (B2) are properly viewed as problematic though historically sanctioned claims: They are problematic precisely because of the way they have functioned historically in a patriarchal conceptual framework and culture to sanction the dominations of women and nature.

What all ecofeminists agree about, then, is the way in which the *logic of domination* has functioned historically within patriarchy to sustain and justify the twin dominations of women and nature.[4] Since all feminists (and not just ecofeminists) oppose patriarchy, the conclusion given at (B5), all feminists (including ecofeminists) must oppose at least the logic of domination, premise (B4), on which

argument B rests—whatever the truth-value status of (B1) and (B2) *outside* of a patriarchal context.

That *all* feminists must oppose the logic of domination shows the breadth and depth of the ecofeminist critique of B; It is a critique not only of the three assumptions on which this argument for the domination of women and nature rests, viz., the assumptions at (B1), (B2), and (B4); it is also a critique of patriarchal conceptual frameworks generally, i.e., of those oppressive conceptual frameworks which put men "up" and women "down," allege some way in which women are morally inferior to men, and use that alleged difference to justify the subordination of women by men. Therefore, ecofeminism is necessary to *any* feminist critique of patriarchy, and, hence, necessary to feminism (a point I discuss again later).

Third, ecofeminism clarifies why the logic of domination, and any conceptual framework which gives rise to it, must be abolished in order both to make possible a meaningful notion of difference which does not breed domination and to prevent feminism from becoming a "support" movement based primarily on shared experiences. In contemporary society, there is no one "woman's voice," no *woman* (or *human*) *simpliciter*: Every woman (or human) is a woman (or human) of some race, class, age, affectional orientation, marital status, regional or national background, and so forth. Because there are no "monolithic experiences" that all women share, feminism must be a "solidarity movement" based on shared beliefs and interests rather than a "unity in sameness" movement based on shared experiences and shared victimization. In the words of Maria Lugones, "Unity—not to be confused with solidarity—is understood as conceptually tied to domination."

Ecofeminists insist that the sort of logic of domination used to justify the domination of humans by gender, racial or ethnic, or class status is also used to justify the domination of nature. Because eliminating a logic of domination is part of a feminist critique—whether a critique of patriarchy, white supremacist culture, or imperialism— ecofeminists insist that *naturism* is properly viewed as an integral part of any feminist solidarity movement to end sexist oppression and the logic of domination which conceptually grounds it.

ECOFEMINISM RECONCEIVES FEMINISM

The discussion so far has focused on some of the oppressive conceptual features of patriarchy. As I use the phrase, the "logic of traditional feminism" refers to the location of the conceptual roots of sexist oppression, at least in Western societies, in an oppressive patriarchal conceptual framework characterized by a logic of domination. Insofar as other systems of oppression (e.g., racism, classism, ageism, heterosexism) are also conceptually maintained by a logic of domination, appeal to the logic of traditional feminism ultimately locates the basic conceptual interconnections among *all* systems of oppression in the logic of domination. It thereby explains at a *conceptual* level why the eradication of sexist oppression requires the eradication of the other forms of oppression. It is by clarifying this conceptual connection between systems of oppression that a movement to end sexist oppression—traditionally the special turf of feminist theory and practice—leads to a reconceiving of feminism as *a movement to end all forms of oppression.*

Suppose one agrees that the logic of traditional feminism requires the expansion of feminism to include other social systems of domination (e.g., racism and classism). What warrants the inclusion of nature in these "social systems of domination"? Why must the logic of traditional feminism include the abolition of "naturism" (i.e., the domination or oppression of nonhuman nature) among the "isms" feminism must confront? The conceptual justification for expanding feminism to include ecofeminism is twofold. One basis has already been suggested: By showing that the conceptual connections between the dual dominations of women and nature are located in an oppressive and, at least in Western societies, patriarchal conceptual framework characterized by a logic of domination, ecofeminism explains how and why feminism,

conceived as a movement to end sexist oppression, must be expanded and reconceived as also a movement to end naturism. This is made explicit by the following argument C:

C1. Feminism is a movement to end sexism.

C2. But sexism is conceptually linked with naturism (through an oppressive conceptual framework characterized by a logic of domination).

C3. Thus, feminism is (also) a movement to end naturism.

Because, ultimately, these connections between sexism and naturism are conceptual—embedded in an oppressive conceptual framework—the logic of traditional feminism lends to the embracement of ecological feminism.

The other justification for reconceiving feminism to include ecofeminism has to do with the concepts of gender and nature. Just as conceptions of gender are socially constructed, so are conceptions of nature. Of course, the claim that women and nature are social constructions does not require anyone to deny that there are actual humans and actual trees, rivers, and plants. It simply implies that *how* women and nature are conceived is a matter of historical and social reality. These conceptions vary cross-culturally and by historical time period. As a result, any discussion of the "oppression or domination of nature" involves reference to historically specific forms of social domination of nonhuman nature by humans, just as discussion of the "domination of women" refers to historically specific forms of social domination of women by men. Although I do not argue for it here, an ecofeminist defense of the historical connections between the dominations of women and of nature, claims (B1) and (B2) in argument B, involves showing that within patriarchy the feminization of nature and the naturalization of women have been crucial to the historically successful subordinations of both.

If ecofeminism promises to reconceive traditional feminism in ways which include naturism as a legitimate feminist issue, does ecofeminism also promise to reconceive environmental ethics in ways which are feminist? I think so. This is the subject of the remainder of the paper.

CLIMBING FROM ECOFEMINISM TO ENVIRONMENTAL ETHICS

Many feminists and some environmental ethicists have begun to explore the use of first-person narrative as a way of raising philosophically germane issues in ethics often lost or underplayed in mainstream philosophical ethics. Why is this so? What is it about narrative which makes it a significant resource for theory and practice in feminism and environmental ethics? Even if appeal to first-person narrative is a helpful literary device for describing ineffable experience or a legitimate social science methodology for documenting personal and social history, how is first-person narrative a valuable vehicle of argumentation for ethical decision making and theory building? One fruitful way to begin answering these questions is to ask them of a particular first-person narrative.

Consider the following first-person narrative about rock climbing:

> For my very first rock climbing experience, I chose a somewhat private spot, away from other climbers and onlookers. After studying "the chimney," I focused all my energy on making it to the top. I climbed with intense determination, using whatever strength and skills I had to accomplish this challenging feat. By midway I was exhausted and anxious. I couldn't see what to do next—where to put my hands or feet. Growing increasingly more weary as I clung somewhat desperately to the rock, I made a move. It didn't work. I fell. There I was, dangling midair above the rocky ground below, frightened but terribly relieved that the belay rope had held me. I knew I was safe. I took a look up at the climb that remained. I was determined to make it to the top. With renewed confidence and concentration, I finished the climb to the top.

On my second day of climbing, I rappelled down about 200 feet from the top of the Palisades at Lake Superior to just a few feet above the water level. I could see no one—not my belayer, not the other climbers, no one. I unhooked slowly from the rappel rope and took a deep cleansing breath. I looked all around me—really looked—and listened. I heard a cacophony of voices—birds, trickles of water on the rock before me, waves lapping against the rocks below. I closed my eyes and began to feel the rock with my hands—the cracks and crannies, the raised lichen and mosses, the almost imperceptible nubs that might provide a resting place for my fingers and toes when I began to climb. At that moment I was bathed in serenity. I began to talk to the rock in an almost inaudible, childlike way, as if the rock were my friend. I felt an overwhelming sense of gratitude for what it offered me—a chance to know myself and the rock differently, to appreciate unforeseen miracles like the tiny flowers growing in the even tinier cracks in the rock's surface, and to come to know a sense of *being in relationship* with the natural environment. It felt as if the rock and I were silent conversational partners in a longstanding friendship. I realized then that I had come to care about this cliff which was so different from me, so unmovable and invincible, independent and seemingly indifferent to my presence. I wanted to be with the rock as I climbed. Gone was the determination to conquer the rock, to forcefully impose my will on it; I wanted simply to work respectfully with the rock as I climbed. And as I climbed, that is what I felt. I felt myself *caring* for this rock and feeling thankful that climbing provided the opportunity for me to know it and myself in this new way.

There are at least four reasons why use of such a first-person narrative is important to feminism and environmental ethics. First, such a narrative gives voice to a felt sensitivity often lacking in traditional analytical ethical discourse, viz., a sensitivity to conceiving of oneself as fundamentally "in relationship with" others, including the nonhuman environment. It is a modality which *takes relationships themselves seriously*. It thereby stands in contrast to a strictly reductionist modality that takes relationships seriously only or primarily because of the nature of the *relators* or parties to those relationships (e.g., relators conceived as moral agents, right holders, interest carriers, or sentient beings). In the rock-climbing narrative above, it is the climber's relationship with the rock she climbs which takes on special significance—which is itself a locus of value—in addition to whatever moral status or moral considerability she or the rock or any other parties to the relationship may also have.[5]

Second, such a first-person narrative gives expression to a variety of ethical attitudes and behaviors often overlooked or underplayed in mainstream Western ethics, e.g., the difference in attitudes and behaviors toward a rock when one is "making it to the top" and when one thinks of oneself as "friends with" or "caring about" the rock one climbs.[6] These different attitudes and behaviors suggest an ethically germane contrast between two different types of relationship humans or climbers may have toward a rock: an imposed conqueror-type relationship, and an emergent caring-type relationship. This contrast grows out of, and is faithful to, felt, lived experience.

The difference between conquering and caring attitudes and behaviors in relation to the natural environment provides a third reason why the use of first-person narrative is important to feminism and environmental ethics: It provides a way of conceiving of ethics and ethical meaning as *emerging out of* particular situations moral agents find themselves in, rather than as being *imposed on* those situations (e.g., as a derivation or instantiation of some predetermined abstract principle or rule). This emergent feature of narrative centralizes the importance of *voice*. When a multiplicity of cross-cultural *voices* are centralized, narrative is able to give expression to a range of attitudes, values, beliefs, and behaviors which may be overlooked or silenced by imposed

ethical meaning and theory. As a reflection of and on felt, lived experiences, the use of narrative in ethics provides a stance from which ethical discourse can be held accountable to the historical, material, and social realities in which moral subjects find themselves.

Lastly, and for our purposes perhaps most importantly, the use of narrative has argumentative significance. Jim Cheney calls attention to this feature of narrative when he claims, "To contextualize ethical deliberation is, in some sense, to provide a narrative or story, from which the solution to the ethical dilemma emerges as the fitting conclusion." Narrative has argumentative force by suggesting *what counts* as an appropriate conclusion to an ethical situation. One ethical conclusion suggested by the climbing narrative is that what counts as a proper ethical attitude toward mountains and rocks is an attitude of respect and care (whatever that turns out to be or involve), not one of domination and conquest.

In an essay entitled "In and Out of Harm's Way: Arrogance and Love," feminist philosopher Marilyn Frye distinguishes between "arrogant" and "loving" perception as one way of getting at this difference in the ethical attitudes of care and conquest. Frye writes:

> The loving eye is a contrary of the arrogant eye.
>
> The loving eye knows the independence of the other. It is the eye of a seer who knows that nature is indifferent. It is the eye of one who knows that to know the seen, one must consult something other than one's own will and interests and fears and imagination. One must look at the thing. One must look and listen and check and question.
>
> The loving eye is one that pays a certain sort of attention. This attention can require a discipline but not a self-denial. The discipline is one of self-knowledge, knowledge of the scope and boundary of the self.... In particular, it is a matter of being able to tell one's own interests from

those of others and of knowing where one's self leaves off and another begins....

The loving eye does not make the object of perception into something edible, does not try to assimilate it, does not reduce it to the size of the seer's desire, fear, and imagination, and hence does not have to simplify. It knows the complexity of the other as something which will forever present new things to be known. The science of the loving eye would favor The Complexity Theory of Truth [in contrast to The Simplicity Theory of Truth] and presuppose The Endless Interestingness of the Universe.

According to Frye, the loving eye is not an invasive, coercive eye which annexes others to itself, but one which "knows the complexity of the other as something which will forever present new things to be known."

When one climbs a rock as a conqueror, one climbs with an arrogant eye. When one climbs with a loving eye, one constantly "must look and listen and check and question." One recognizes the rock as something very different, something perhaps totally indifferent to one's own presence, and finds in that difference joyous occasion for celebration. One knows "the boundary of the self," where the self— the "I," the climber—leaves off and the rock begins. There is no fusion of two into one, but a complement of two entities *acknowledged* as separate, different, independent, yet *in relationship;* they are in relationship *if only* because the loving eye is perceiving it, responding to it, noticing it, attending to it.

An ecofeminist perspective about both women and nature involves this shift in attitude from "arrogant perception" to "loving perception" of the nonhuman world. Arrogant perception of nonhumans by humans presupposes and maintains *sameness* in such a way that it expands the moral community to those beings who are thought to resemble (be like, similar to, or the same as) humans in some morally significant way. Any environmental movement or ethic based on arrogant perception builds a moral hierarchy of beings and assumes

some common, denominator of moral considerability in virtue of which like beings deserve similar treatment or moral consideration and unlike beings do not. Such environmental ethics are or generate a "unity in sameness." In contrast, "loving perception" presupposes and maintains *difference*—a distinction between the self and other, between human and at least some nonhumans—in such a way that perception of the other as other is an expression of love for one who/which is recognized at the outset as independent, dissimilar, different. As Maria Lugones says, in loving perception, "Love is seen not as fusion and erasure of difference but as incompatible with them." "Unity in sameness" alone is an *erasure of difference.*

"Loving perception" of the nonhuman natural world is an attempt to understand what it *means for humans* to care about the nonhuman world, a world *acknowledged* as being independent, different, perhaps even indifferent to humans. Humans are different from rocks in important ways, even if they are also both members of some ecological community. A moral community based on loving perception of oneself *in relationship with* a rock, or with the natural environment as a whole, is one which acknowledges and respects difference, whatever "sameness" also exists. The limits of loving perception are determined only by the limits of one's (e.g., a person's, a community's) ability to respond lovingly (or with appropriate care, trust, or friendship)—whether it is to other humans or to the nonhuman world and elements of it.

If what I have said so far is correct, then there are very different ways to climb a mountain, and *how* one climbs it and *how* one narrates the experience of climbing it matter ethically. If one climbs with "arrogant perception," with an attitude of "conquer and control," one keeps intact the very sorts of thinking that characterize a logic of domination and an oppressive conceptual framework. Since the oppressive conceptual framework which sanctions the domination of nature is a patriarchal one, one also thereby keeps intact, even if unwittingly, a patriarchal conceptual framework. Because the dismantling of patriarchal conceptual frameworks is a feminist issue, *how* one climbs a mountain and *how* one narrates—or tells the story—about the experience of climbing also are *feminist issues*. In this way, ecofeminism makes visible why, at a conceptual level, environmental ethics is a feminist issue.

CONCLUSION

I have argued in this paper that ecofeminism provides a framework for a distinctively feminist and environmental ethic. Ecofeminism grows out of the felt and theorized about connections between the domination of women and the domination of nature. As a contextualist ethic, ecofeminism refocuses environmental ethics on what nature might mean, morally speaking, *for* humans, and on how the relational attitudes of humans to others—humans as well as nonhumans—sculpt both what it is to be human, and the nature and ground of human responsibilities to the nonhuman environment. Part of what this refocusing does is to take seriously the voices of women and other oppressed persons in the construction of that ethic.

A Sioux elder once told me a story about his son. He sent his seven-year-old son to live with the child's grandparents on a Sioux reservation so that he could "learn the Indian ways." Part of what the grandparents taught him was how to hunt the four-leggeds of the forest. As I heard the story, the boy was taught, "to shoot your four-legged brother in his hind area, slowing it down but not killing it. Then, take the four-legged's head in your hands, and look into his eyes. The eyes are where all the suffering is. Look into your brother's eyes and feel his pain. Then, take your knife and cut the four-legged under his chin, here, on his neck, so that he dies quickly. And as you do, ask your brother, the four-legged, for forgiveness for what you do. Offer also a prayer of thanks to your four-legged kin for offering his body to you just now, when you need food to eat and clothing to wear. And promise the four-legged that you will put yourself back into the earth when you die, to become nourishment for the earth, and for the sister flowers, and for the brother deer. It is appropriate that you should offer this blessing for the four-legged and, in due time, reciprocate in turn with your body in this way, as the four-legged gives life to you for your survival." As I reflect on that story, I am struck by the power of the environmental ethic that grows out of and takes seriously narrative, context, and such values and relational attitudes as care, loving perception, and appropriate reciprocity, and doing what is appropriate in a given situation—however that notion of appropriateness eventually gets filled out. I am also struck by what one is able to see, once one begins to explore some of the historical and conceptual connections between the dominations of women and of nature. A *re-conceiving* and *re-visioning* of both feminism and environmental ethics, is, I think, the power and promise of ecofeminism.

ENDNOTES

1. It may be that in contemporary Western society, which is so thoroughly structured by categories of gender, race, class, age, and affectional orientation, that there simply is no meaningful notion of "value-hierarchical thinking" which does not function in an oppressive context. For the purposes of this paper, I leave that question open.

2. Many feminists who argue for the historical point that claims (B1) and (B2) have been asserted or assumed to be true within the dominant Western philosophical tradition do so by discussion of that tradition's conceptions of reason, rationality, and science. For a sampling of the sorts of claims made within that context, see "Reason, Rationality, and Gender," ed. Nancy Tuana and Karen J. Warren, a special issue of the American Philosophical Association's *Newsletter on Feminism and Philosophy* 88, no. 2 (March 1989): 17–71. Ecofeminists who claim that (B2) has been assumed to be true within the dominant Western philosophical tradition include: Gray,

Green Paradise Lost; Griffin, *Woman and Nature: The Roaring Inside Her;* Merchant, *The Death of Nature;* Ruether, *New Woman/New Earth.* For a discussion of some of these ecofeminist historical accounts, see Plumwood, "Eco-feminism." While I agree that the historical connections between the domination of women and the domination of nature is a crucial one, I do not argue for that claim here.

3. Ecofeminists who deny (B1) when (B1) is offered as anything other than a true, descriptive, historical claim about patriarchal culture often do so on grounds that an objectionable sort of biological determinism, or at least harmful female sex-gender stereotypes, underlie (B1). For a discussion of this "split" among those ecofeminists ("nature feminists") who assert and those ecofeminists ("social feminists") who deny (B1) as anything other than a true historical claim about how women are described in patriarchal culture, see Griscom, "On Healing the Nature/History Split."

4. I make no attempt here to defend the historically sanctioned truth of these promises.

5. Suppose ... that a necessary condition for the existence of a moral relationship is that at least one party to the relationship is a moral being (leaving open for our purposes what counts as a "moral being"). If this is so, then the Mona Lisa cannot properly be said to have or stand in a moral relationship with the wall on which she hangs, and a wolf cannot have or properly be said to have or stand in a moral relationship with a moose. Such a necessary-condition account leaves open the question whether *both* parties to the relationship must be moral beings. The point here is simply that however one resolves *that* question, recognition of the relationships themselves as a locus of value is a recognition of a source of value that is different from and not reducible to the values of the "moral beings" in those relationships.

6. It is interesting to note that the image of being friends with the Earth is one which cytogeneticist Barbara McClintock uses when she describes the importance of having "a feeling for the organism," "listening to the material [in this case the corn plant]," in one's work as a scientist. See Evelyn Fox Keller, "Women, Science, and Popular Mythology," in *Machina Ex Dea: Feminist Perspectives on Technology,* ed. Joan Rothschild (New York: Pergamon Press, 1983), and Evelyn Fox Keller, *A Feeling For the Organism: The Life and Work of Barbara McClintock* (San Francisco: W. H. Freeman, 1983).

64

From the Animal Welfare Act
Congress of the United States

Sec. 13. The Secretary shall promulgate standards to govern the humane handling, care, treatment, and transportation of animals by dealers, research facilities, and exhibitors. Such standards shall include minimum requirements with respect to handling, housing, feeding, watering, sanitation, ventilation, shelter from extremes of weather and temperatures, adequate veterinary care, including the appropriate use of anesthetic, analgesic, or tranquilizing drugs, when such use would be proper in the opinion of the attending veterinarian of such research facilities, and separation by species when the Secretary finds such separation necessary for the humane handling, care, or treatment of animals. In promulgating and enforcing standards established pursuant to this section, the Secretary is authorized and directed to consult experts, including outside consultants where indicated ... Nothing in this Act shall be construed as authorizing the Secretary to promulgate rules, regulations, or orders with regard to design, outlines, guidelines, or performance of actual research or experimentation by a research facility as determined by such research facility: Provided That the Secretary shall require, at least annually, every research facility to show that professionally acceptable standards governing the care, treatment, and use of animals, including appropriate use of anesthetic, analgesic, and tranquilizing drugs, during experimentation are being followed by the research facility during actual research or experimentation.

From the *Animal Welfare Act*.

65

Amendments to the Animal Welfare Act
Congress of the United States

The bill amends the Animal Welfare Act as follows:

1. Expands the definition of the term *research facility* to include each department, agency or instrumentality of the United States which uses animals for research or experimentation; defines the term *Federal agency* to mean any Executive agency from which a research facility has received or may receive Federal funds to support the conduct of research, experimentation, or testing involving the use of animals; and, makes it clear that the definition of "animal" is the same as that provided under the current Act.

2. Deletes the language stating that minimum requirements be applied to the standards promulgated by the Secretary of Agriculture to govern the humane handling, care, treatment, and transportation of animals by dealers, research facilities and exhibitors; adds exercise for dogs as a standard; and, allows the Secretary to make exceptions to the standards, but only when such exceptions are specified by the research protocol.

3. Requires the Secretary to promulgate standards for research facilities, including requirements for animal care, treatment, and practices in experimental procedures, to ensure that animal pain and distress are minimized. Requires each research facility, in its annual statement of compliance, to provide the Secretary of Agriculture with assurances that such standards are being followed. Also requires the research

facility to provide annual training sessions for personnel involved with animal care and treatment.

4. Provides that any State (or political subdivision of that State) may promulgate standards in addition to those promulgated, by the Secretary.

5. Mandates the establishment and makeup of an animal research committee of three or more members within each research facility. Makes it unlawful for any member of the committee to release trade secrets or confidential information. The committee must make inspections at least semiannually of all animal study areas of the research facility and file an inspection report which must remain on file at the research facility for three years. The committee must notify, in writing, the Animal and Plant Health Inspection Service (APHIS) of the Department of Agriculture and the funding Federal agency of any unacceptable conditions that are not corrected despite notification. Federal support for a particular project can be suspended or revoked for continued failure by a research facility to comply with the standards of animal care, treatment, or practices; such suspension or revocation may be appealed.

6. The inspection results of the animal research committee must be available to the Department of Agriculture's inspectors for review during inspection. These inspectors must forward to APHIS and the funding Federal agency any inspection records of the

committee which include reports of any deficient conditions of animal care or treatment and any deviations of research practices from the originally approved proposal that adversely affect animal welfare.

7. Prohibits the Secretary from promulgating rules, regulations, or orders that may require a research facility to disclose trade secrets or commercial or financial information which is privileged, or confidential.

8. Mandates the establishment of an information service on improved methods of animal experimentation at the National Agricultural Library....

66

Tennessee Valley Authority v. Hill

Supreme Court of the United States

The issue before the Supreme Court was whether the Endangered Species Act of 1973 prohibited the completion of a dam whose operation would destroy the habitat of the snail darter, an endangered species. The dam was virtually completed, and Congress had continued to appropriate large sums of money to the project even after congressional appropriations committees were apprised of the apparent impact on the snail darter's survival. Chief Justice Burger, delivering the opinion of the Court, held that the Endangered Species Act did prohibit the completion of the dam because the language of the act and the history that led to its passage required that its provisions be applied without exceptions.

We begin with the premise that operation of the Tellico Dam will either eradicate the known population of snail darters or destroy their critical habitat. Petitioner does not now seriously dispute this fact.... The Secretary of the Interior is vested with exclusive authority to determine whether a species such as the snail darter is "endangered" or "threatened" and to ascertain the factors which have led to such a precarious existence.... Congress has authorized—indeed commanded— the Secretary to "issue such regulations as he deems necessary and advisable to provide for the conservation of such species."... As we have seen, the Secretary promulgated regulations which declared the snail darter an endangered species whose critical habitat would be destroyed by creation of the Tellico Dam. Doubtless petitioner would prefer not to have these regulations on the books, but there is no suggestion that the Secretary exceeded his authority or abused his discretion in issuing the regulations. Indeed, no judicial review of the Secretary's determinations has ever been sought and hence the validity of his actions are not open to review in this Court....

[It is] curious ... that the survival of a relatively small number of three-inch fish among all the countless millions of species extant would require the permanent halting of a virtually completed dam for which Congress has expended more than $100 million. The paradox is not minimized by the fact that Congress continued to appropriate large sums of public money for the project, even after congressional Appropriations Committees were apprised of its apparent impact on the survival of the snail darter. We conclude, however, that the explicit provisions of the Endangered Species Act require precisely that result....

... By 1973, when Congress held hearings on what would later become the Endangered Species Act of 1973, it was informed that species were still being lost at the rate of about one per year, ... and "the pace of disappearance of species" appeared to be "accelerating." Moreover, Congress was also told that the primary cause of this trend was something other than the normal process of natural selection:

> [M]an and his technology has [*sic*] continued at an ever-increasing rate to disrupt the natural ecosystem. This has resulted in a dramatic rise in the number and severity of the threats faced by the world's wildlife.

The truth in this is apparent when one realizes that half of the recorded extinctions of mammals over the past 2,000 years have occurred in the most recent 50-year period....

That Congress did not view these developments lightly was stressed by one commentator:

The dominant theme pervading all Congressional discussion of the proposed [Endangered Species Act of 1973] was the overriding need *to devote whatever effort and resources were necessary* to avoid further diminution of national and worldwide wildlife resources. Much of the testimony at the hearings and much debate was devoted to the biological problem of extinction. Senators and Congressmen uniformly deplored the irreplaceable loss to aesthetics, science, ecology, and the national heritage should more species disappear....

The legislative proceedings in 1973 are ... replete with expressions of concern over the risk that might lie in the loss of *any* endangered species. Typifying these sentiments is the Report of the House Committee on Merchant Marine and Fisheries on ... a bill that contained the essential features of the subsequently enacted Act of 1973; in explaining the need for the legislation, the Report stated:

As we homogenize the habitats in which these plants and animals evolved, and as we increase the pressure for products that they are in a position to supply (usually unwillingly) we threaten their—and our own—genetic heritage.

The value of this genetic heritage is, quite literally, incalculable.

From the most narrow possible point of view, *it is in the best interest of mankind to minimize the losses of genetic variations.* The reason is simple: They are potential resources. They are keys to puzzles which we cannot solve, and may provide answers to questions which we have not yet learned to ask.

To take a homely, but apt, example: One of the critical chemicals in the regulation of ovulations in humans was found in a common plant. Once discovered, and analyzed, humans could duplicate it synthetically, but had it never existed—or had it been driven out of existence before we knew its potentialities—we would never have tried to synthesize it in the first place.

Who knows, or can say, what potential cures for cancer or other scourges, present or future, may lie locked up in the structures of plants which may yet be undiscovered, much less analyzed.... Sheer self-interest impels us to be cautious....

As the examples cited here demonstrate, Congress was concerned about the *unknown* uses that endangered species might have and about the *unforeseeable* place such creatures may have in the chain of life on this planet....

... Representative Dingell provided an interpretation of what the Conference bill would require, making it clear that the mandatory provisions ... were not casually or inadvertently included:

... A recent article ... illustrates the problem which might occur absent this new language in the bill. It appears that the whooping cranes of this country, perhaps the best known of our endangered species, are being threatened by Air Force bombing activities along the gulf coast of Texas. Under existing law, the Secretary of Defense has some discretion as to whether or not he will take the necessary action to see that this threat disappears.... [O]nce the bill is enacted, [the Secretary of Defense] *would be required to take the proper steps....*

Another example ... [has] to do with the continental population of grizzly bears which may or may not be endangered, but which is surely threatened.... Once this bill is enacted, the appropriate Secretary, whether of Interior, Agriculture or whatever, *will have to take action* to see that this situation is not permitted to worsen, and that these bears are not driven to extinction. The purposes of the bill included the conservation of the species and of the ecosystems upon which they depend, and *every agency of government is committed* to see that those purposes are carried out.... [T]he agencies of Government can no longer plead that they can do nothing about it. *They can, and they must. The law is clear....*

Notwithstanding Congress's expression of intent in 1973, we are urged to find that the continuing appropriations for Tellico Dam constitute an implied repeal of the 1973 Act, at least insofar as it applies to the Tellico Project. In support of this view, TVA points to the statements found in various House and Senate Appropriations Committees' Reports.... Since we are unwilling to assume that these latter Committee statements constituted advice to ignore the provisions of a duly enacted law, we assume that these Committees believed that the Act simply was not applicable in this situation. But even under this interpretation of the Committees' actions, we are unable to conclude that the Act has been in any respect amended or repealed....

...The starting point in this analysis must be the legislative proceedings leading to the 1977 appropriations since the earlier funding of the dam occurred prior to the listing of the snail darter as an endangered species. In all successive years, TVA confidently reported to the Appropriations Committees that efforts to transplant the snail darter appeared to be successful; this surely gave those Committees some basis for the impression that there was no direct conflict between the Tellico Project and the Endangered Species Act. Indeed, the special appropriation for 1978 of $2 million for transplantation of endangered species supports the view that the Committees saw such relocation as the means whereby collision between Tellico and the Endangered Species Act could be avoided....

... Here we are urged to view the Endangered Species Act "reasonably," and hence shape a remedy "that accords with some modicum of common sense and the public weal." ... But is that our function?

We have no expert knowledge on the subject of endangered species, much less do we have a mandate from the people to strike a balance of equities on the side of the Tellico Dam. Congress has spoken in the plainest of words, making it abundantly clear that the balance has been struck in favor of affording endangered species the highest of priorities, thereby adopting a policy which it described as "institutionalized caution."

Our individual appraisal of the wisdom or unwisdom of a particular course consciously selected by the Congress is to be put aside in the process of interpreting a statute. Once the meaning of an enactment is discerned and its constitutionality determined, the judicial process comes to an end. We do not sit as a committee of review, nor are we vested with the power of veto. The lines ascribed to Sir Thomas More by Robert Bolt are not without relevance here:

> The law, Roper, the law. I know what's legal, not what's right. And I'll stick to what's legal.... I'm *not* God. The currents and eddies of right and wrong, which you find such plain-sailing, I can't navigate, I'm no voyager. But in the thickets of the law, oh there I'm a forester.... What would you do? Cut a great road through the law to get after the Devil? ... And when the last law was down, and the Devil turned round on you—where would you hide, Roper, the laws all being flat? This country's planted thick with laws from coast to coast—Man's laws, not God's—and if you cut them down ... d'you really think you could stand upright in the winds that would blow then? ... Yes, I'd give the Devil benefit of law, for my own safety's sake.
>
> —R. Bolt, *A Man for All Seasons*

We agree with the Court of Appeals that ... the commitment to the separation of powers is too fundamental for us to pre-empt congressional action by judicially decreeing what accords with "common sense and the public weal." Our Constitution vests such responsibilities in the political branches.

SUGGESTIONS FOR FURTHER READING

Anthologies

Armstrong, Susan, and Richard Botzler. *Environmental Ethics*. 2nd ed. New York: McGraw-Hill, 1998.

Beauchamp, Tom L. and Frey, R. G. *The Oxford Handbook of Animal Ethics*, New York: Oxford University Press, 2011.

Sterba, James P. *Earth Ethics*. 2nd ed. Upper Saddle River, NJ: Prentice-Hall, 2000.

Alternative Views

Attfield, Robin. *Environmental Philosophy*. Aldershot: Avebury, 1994.

Carruthers, Peter. *The Animals Issue*. Cambridge: Cambridge University Press, 1992.

DesJardins, Joseph. *Environmental Ethics*. 2nd ed. Belmont, CA: Wadsworth, 1997.

Dombrowski, Daniel A. *The Philosophy of Vegetarianism*. Amherst: University of Massachusetts Press, 1984.

Frey, R. G. *Rights, Killing and Suffering*. Oxford, England: Basil Blackwell, 1983.

Hargrove, Eugene. *The Foundations of Environmental Ethics*. Englewood Cliffs, NJ: Prentice-Hall, 1988.

Marrietta, Don. *For People and the Planet*. Philadelphia: Temple University Press, 1995.

Plumwood, Val. *Feminism and the Mastery of Nature*. London: Routledge, 1993.

Rachels, James. *Created from Animals*. Oxford: Oxford University Press, 1990.

Regan, Tom. *The Case for Animal Rights*. Berkeley: University of California Press, 1984.

Singer, Peter. *Animal Liberation*. rev. ed. New York: New York Review, 1990.

Stone, Christopher D. *Earth and Other Ethics*. New York: Harper & Row, 1987.

Taylor, Paul W. *Respect for Nature*. Princeton: Princeton University Press, 1986.

Practical Applications

Akers, Keith. *A Vegetarian Sourcebook*. New York: Putnam, 1983.

Boas, Max, and Steve Chain, *Big Mac: The Unauthorized Story of McDonald's*. New York: New American Library, 1976.

Gore, Al. *Earth in the Balance*. New York: Houghton Mifflin, 1992.

Singer, Peter. *Ethics into Actions*. Lanham, MD: Rowman & Littlefield, 1998.

Swanson, Wayne, and George Schultz. *Prime Rip*. Englewood Cliffs, NJ: Prentice-Hall, 1982.

Punishment and Responsibility

INTRODUCTION

Basic Concepts

The problem of punishment and responsibility is the problem of who should be punished and of what their punishment should consist. It is a problem of punishment *and* responsibility because determining who should be punished and what their punishment should consist of involves an assessment of responsibility. However, before discussing alternative justifications for assigning punishment, it is important to first clarify the concepts of punishment and responsibility.

Let us begin with the concept of punishment. Consider the following definition:

a.   Punishment is hardship inflicted on an offender by someone entitled to do so.

This definition certainly seems adequate for many standard cases of punishment. For example, suppose you pursue and capture a young man who has just robbed a drugstore. The police then arrive and arrest the fellow. He is tried, convicted, and sentenced to two years in prison. Surely it would seem that a sentence of two years in prison in this case would constitute punishment, and obviously the sentence meets the conditions of (a).

But suppose we vary the example a bit. Suppose that, as before, you pursue the robber, but this time he gets away and in the process drops the money he took from the drugstore which you then retrieve. Suppose further that two eyewitnesses identify you as the robber, and you are arrested by the police, tried, and sentenced to two years in prison. Surely we would like to say that in this example it is you who is being punished, albeit unjustly; however, according to (a), this is not the case. For according to this definition, punishment can only be inflicted on offenders, and you are not an offender. But this simply shows that (a) is too narrow a definition of punishment. There clearly are cases, like our modified example, in which we can truly say that nonoffenders, that is, innocent people, are being punished. Accordingly, an acceptable definition of punishment should allow for such cases.

Let us consider, then, the following definition of punishment, which does allow for the possibility that nonoffenders can be punished:

b. Punishment is hardship inflicted on a person by someone entitled to do so.

Although (b) clearly represents an advance over (a) in that it allows for the possibility that innocent people can be punished, serious difficulties remain. For according to (b), paying taxes is punishment, as is civil commitment of mentally ill persons who have not committed any offense. And even though we may have good reasons for opposing taxation and even good reasons for opposing civil commitment, it is usually not because we regard such impositions as punishments. Clearly, then, a definition of punishment that includes paying taxes and civil commitment as punishments is simply too broad; what is needed is a definition that is narrower than (b) but broader than (a).

Consider the following possibility:

c. Punishment is hardship inflicted on a person who is found guilty of an offense by someone entitled to do so.

This definition, like (b), allows that innocent people can be punished, because it is possible that a person can be found guilty by some procedure or other without really being guilty. Yet (c), unlike (b), does not allow that just any hardship imposed by someone entitled to do so is punishment. Rather, only a hardship imposed *for an offense* can be a punishment.

But is this definition adequate? It would seem not. According to (c), paying a $5 parking ticket or suffering a 15-yard penalty in a football game are both punishments. Yet in both cases the hardship imposed lacks the moral condemnation and denunciation that is characteristic of punishment. This suggests the following definition:

d. Punishment is hardship involving moral condemnation and denunciation inflicted on a person who is found guilty of an offense by someone entitled to do so.

Examples like the $5 parking ticket and the 15-yard penalty indicate that we need to distinguish between punishments proper, which satisfy the conditions of (d), and mere penalties, which only satisfy the conditions of (c). When we impose mere penalties, we are claiming that a person has done something wrong, perhaps even something morally wrong, but, because of the insignificant nature of the offense, we don't attempt to determine whether the person is morally blameworthy for so acting. Because we do not make this determination, we do not go on to morally condemn and denounce those we penalize. By contrast, when we impose punishments proper, we do make such a determination and, as a consequence, we do condemn and denounce those we penalize.

Turning to the concept of responsibility, we find that this concept is employed in a variety of different but related ways. For example, in everyday usage, we say that people are responsible for their actions if they could have acted otherwise than they did. In making this claim, we usually assume that people could have acted otherwise than they did in two respects. First, we assume that they could have acted otherwise if they had the ability to do so; for example, as presumably most varsity athletes have even when they play badly. Second, we assume that people could have acted otherwise if they had the opportunity to do so; for example, as you or I might have, even if we lacked the relevant ability, when, by chance, we were substituted in some varsity game and performed miserably. Thus, we can say that people are responsible for their actions if they had the ability and opportunity to act otherwise than they did.

Lawyers, however, usually approach the concept of responsibility differently. They are typically concerned with determining whether people have *mens rea*, which translated means "a guilty mind." When people are said to have *mens rea*, they are held responsible for their actions.

Mens rea is said to involve three conditions:

1. Knowledge of circumstances
2. Foresight of consequences
3. Voluntariness

The first condition of *mens rea* is said to be absent when, for example, you didn't know the gun was loaded, or you didn't know the person you shot breaking into your home was a plainclothes police officer operating on a false lead. In such a case, lawyers would say you lacked *mens rea* because you lacked the knowledge of the relevant circumstances. The second condition of *mens rea* is said to be absent when, for example, you had no reason to suspect the person you shot would be wandering behind your target in a fenced-off range. In such a case, lawyers would say you lacked *mens rea* because you lacked foresight of the relevant consequences. The third condition of *mens rea* is said to be absent when, for example, you are having an epileptic fit or being attacked by a swarm of bees. This third condition is the least understood of the three conditions of *mens rea*.

But actually this weakness of the lawyer's *mens rea* notion of responsibility with respect to its third condition seems to be the strength of the everyday notion. This is because the everyday notion of responsibility is an unpacking of what it is for an action to be voluntary. Consequently, if we put the two notions together, we arrive at the following more adequate analysis.

People are responsible for their action if they have:

1. Knowledge of circumstances
2. Foresight of consequences
3. The ability and opportunity to act otherwise than they did

Armed with a clearer understanding of the notions of punishment and responsibility, we should be in a better position to examine alternative justifications for assigning punishment in a society.

Forward-Looking and Backward-Looking Views

There are basically two kinds of justification for punishment: forward-looking and backward-looking. Forward-looking justifications maintain that punishment is justified because of its relationship to what *will occur*. Backward-looking justifications maintain that punishment is justified because of its relationship to what *has occurred*. An example of a forward-looking justification would be the claim that punishment is justified because it deters or reforms persons from crime. An example of a backward-looking justification would be the claim that punishment is justified because it fits or is proportionate to a crime or is applied to a person who is responsible for a crime. Those who adopt forward-looking justifications for punishment view punishment from the point of view of a social engineer seeking to produce certain good consequences in society. By contrast, those who adopt backward-looking justifications view punishment from the point of view of a stern balancer seeking to achieve a moral balance between punishment and the crime.

Karl Menninger provides us with a forceful example of a forward-looking justification for punishment—one that is directed at the reform of the offender (Selection 67). Menninger criticizes the existing criminal justice system as ineffective at preventing crime, grounded as it is on a theory of human motivation that fails to recognize the similarities between the motives of offenders and non-offenders. In its place, Menninger advocates a therapeutic treatment program that would detain offenders, and possibly potential offenders, until they are reformed. Thus, Menninger would replace vengeful punishment—which he regards as itself a crime—with humanitarian reform.

One prerequisite for the justification of Menninger's system of humanitarian reform that is not generally recognized is that the opportunities open to offenders for leading a good life must be reasonably adequate, or at least arguably just and fair. If this is not the case, there would be little justification for asking criminal offenders to live their lives within the bounds of the legal system. Nor for that matter could we expect any attempt at implementing a system of reform like Menninger's to be generally effective in a society characterized by basic social and economic injustices. In such a society, criminal offenders who perceive these injustices will have a strong moral reason to resist any attempt to turn them into law-abiding citizens.

C. S Lewis (Selection 68) claims that the goals of both reform and deterrence are opposed to a fundamental requirement of justice: giving people what they deserve. Obviously, if Lewis's critique is sound, it presents a serious difficulty for both Menninger's and Brandt's views, as well as for any other forward-looking view.

Obviously, raising difficulties for forward-looking justifications for punishment is not the same as directly defending backward-looking justifications, thus the importance of the attempt by Edmund L. Pincoffs (Selection 69) to provide us

with such a defense. Pincoffs begins by setting out the following three principles that he claims are characteristic of the traditional backward-looking justification for punishment:

1. The only acceptable reason for punishing a person is that he or she has committed a crime.

2. The only acceptable reason for punishing a person in a given manner and degree is that the punishment is equal to the crime.

3. Whoever commits a crime must be punished in accordance with his or her desert.

Pincoffs claims that the underlying rationale for these principles can be expressed as follows:

a. A proper justification for punishment is one that justifies it to the criminal.

b. Punishment is justified because the criminal has willed the punishment he or she now suffers.

But how can criminals be said to will their own punishment if they do not like or want to be punished? One possible answer, which seems consistent with Pincoffs's analysis, is that criminals, by deliberately violating the rights of others (e.g., by harming others in some way), imply that they think it is reasonable for them to do so. But if this were the case, it would be reasonable for anyone else in similar circumstances to do the same. As a result, criminals would be implicitly conceding that it is all right for others to violate their rights by punishing them, and in this sense they could be said to will their own punishment.

In response to such a defense of a backward-looking justification for punishment, supporters of the forward-looking view might claim that the above principles and their underlying rationale are only proximate answers to the question of why punishment is justified, the ultimate answer to which is still given by the forward-looking view. Since Pincoffs's principles and their underlying rationale do not seem to be compatible with

Menninger's system of humanitarian reform, such a response does imply that the ultimate forward-looking justification for punishment is to be found more in general deterrence, as in Brandt's system, than in humanitarian reform. But even if this were the case, the ultimate justification for punishment would still be forward-looking.

To meet this response, supporters of a backward-looking view need to show why Pincoffs's principles and their underlying rationale cannot be subsumed under a forward-looking justification. This might be done by showing that Pincoffs's principles and their underlying rationale can be grounded in a social contract theory of corrective justice analogous to the social contract theory of distributive justice discussed in Section I. Because many philosophers believe that a social contract theory of distributive justice conflicts with forward-looking goals, it should be possible to argue that a social contact theory of corrective justice does the same.[1]

In Selection 70, James P. Sterba attempts to provide a rational choice justification of punishment. He argues that a non-question-begging standard of rationality would lead to Morality as Rational Compromise. He further argues that Morality as Rational Compromise would lead to the principle for Restoring Fairness and the Principle for Fair Procedure for meting out punishment in a basically just society and to these two principles combined with the Principle for Withholding Punishment for meting out punishment in a basically just society.

Practical Applications

Obviously, a crucial area for the application of forward-looking and backward-looking views is capital punishment. Ernest van den Haag (Selection 71) argues that although we don't know for sure whether capital punishment deters would-be offenders, the greater severity of capital punishment

still gives us reason to expect more deterrence from it. Accordingly, van den Haag maintains that the burden of proof is on opponents of capital punishment to show why the greater severity of capital punishment does not lead to more deterrence. In Selection 72, Jeffrey Reiman attempts to meet van den Haag's challenge. He maintains that greater severity in and of itself does not mean more deterrence; a less severe punishment might suffice to deter a particular crime. Moreover, Reiman argues if greater severity were always justified on grounds of producing more deterrence, then torturing criminals to death would be justified because torturing criminals to death is clearly a more severe punishment than simply executing them. Since van den Haag presumably does not want to endorse torturing criminals to death, he must reject one or more of the premises on which his argument for capital punishment is based.

In 1976 the U.S. Supreme Court (Selection 73) examined the question of whether capital punishment violates the Eighth Amendment prohibition of cruel and unusual punishment. The majority of the Court held that it does not violate that prohibition. In support of its ruling, the majority maintained that capital punishment does not offend contemporary standards of decency as shown by recent legislation in this area. But on the harder question of whether capital punishment is contrary to human dignity and so lacks either a forward-looking or a backward-looking justification, the Court simply deferred to state legislatures. That left the Court with the easier task of deciding whether the procedures for imposing capital punishment, as provided by the Georgia statute that was under review, were capricious and arbitrary. On this score the Court found no reason to fault the Georgia statute.

In more recent cases, however, the Court has gone beyond this purely procedural issue and ruled that the imposition of capital punishment for rape (*Coker v. Georgia*) and on anyone who did not fire a fatal shot or intend the death of a victim (*Locket v. Ohio*) would be unconstitutional. Given that the Court has not seen fit to defer to the judgment of state legislatures in these matters, it is not clear why the Court should continue to defer to their judgment with regard to the question of whether capital punishment can be supported by an adequate forward-looking or backward-looking justification.

In any case, once you have faced that question yourself and worked out a theory of corrective justice, you will still not know exactly how to apply that theory unless you also know how just the distribution of goods and resources is in your society. This is because, regardless of whether you adopt an essentially forward- or backward-looking theory of corrective justice, you will need to know what economic crimes—that is, crimes against property—should be punished according to your theory; and in order to know that, you will need to know what demands are placed on the available goods and resources by solutions to the other problems discussed in this anthology. Of course, some crimes (e.g., many cases of murder and rape) are crimes against people rather than property. And presumably these crimes would be proscribed by your theory of corrective justice independent of the solutions to other contemporary moral problems. Nevertheless, because most crimes are crimes against property, the primary application of your theory will still depend on solutions to the other moral problems discussed in this anthology. In particular, you will need to know to what extent goods and resources can legitimately be expended for military purposes—which just happens to be the moral problem taken up in the next section of this anthology.

ENDNOTE

1. James P. Sterba, "Retributive Justice," *Political Theory* (1977); "Social Contract Theory and Ordinary Justice," *Political Theory* (1981); "Is There a Rationale for Punishment?" *American Journal of Jurisprudence* (1984); "A Rational Choice Justification for Punishment," *Philosophical Topics* (1990).

67

The Crime of Punishment

KARL MENNINGER

Karl Menninger argues that the reason crime is so difficult to eradicate is that it serves the needs of offenders and nonoffenders alike. In fact, according to Menninger, the motives of offenders and nonoffenders are quite similar; what distinguishes serious offenders is simply a greater sense of helplessness and hopelessness in the pursuit of their goals. Menninger concludes that we must find better ways to enable people to realize their goals. Menninger also argues that punishment as a vengeful response to crime does not work because crime is an illness requiring treatment by psychiatrists and psychologists. Thus, Menninger finds vengeful punishment itself to be a crime.

Few words in our language arrest our attention as do "crime," "violence," "revenge," and "injustice." We abhor crime; we adore justice; we boast that we live by the rule of law. Violence and vengefulness we repudiate as unworthy of our civilization, and we assume this sentiment to be unanimous among all human beings.

Yet crime continues to be a national disgrace and a worldwide problem. It is threatening, alarming, wasteful, expensive, abundant, and apparently increasing! In actuality it is decreasing in frequency of occurrence, but it is certainly increasing in visibility and the reactions of the public to it.

Our system for controlling crime is ineffective, unjust, expensive. Prisons seem to operate with revolving doors—the same people going in and out and in and out. *Who cares?*

Our city jails and inhuman reformatories and wretched prisons are jammed. They are known to be unhealthy, dangerous, immoral, indecent, crime-breeding dens of iniquity. Not everyone has smelled them, as some of us have. Not many have heard the groans and the curses. Not everyone has seen the hate and despair in a thousand blank, hollow faces. But, in a way, we all know how miserable prisons are. *We want them to be that way.* And they are. *Who cares?*

Professional, big-time criminals prosper as never before. Gambling syndicates flourish. White-collar crime may even exceed all others but goes undetected in [most] cases. We are all being robbed and we know who the robbers are. They live nearby. *Who cares?*

The public filches millions of dollars worth of food and clothing from stores, towels and sheets from hotels, jewelry and knick-knacks from shops. The public steals, and the same public pays it back in higher prices. *Who cares?*

Time and time again somebody shouts about this state of affairs, just as I am shouting now. The magazines shout. The newspapers shout. The television and radio commentators shout (or at least they "deplore"). Psychologists, sociologists, leading jurists, wardens, and intelligent police chiefs join the chorus. Governors and mayors and Congressmen are sometimes heard. They shout that the situation is bad, bad,

bad, and getting worse. Some suggest that we immediately replace obsolete procedures with scientific methods. A few shout contrary sentiments. Do the clear indications derived from scientific discovery for appropriate changes continue to fall on deaf ears? Why is the public so long-suffering, so apathetic and thereby so continuingly self-destructive? How many Presidents (and other citizens) do we have to lose before we do something?

The public behaves as a sick patient does when a dreaded treatment is proposed for his ailment. We all know how the aching tooth may suddenly quiet down in the dentist's office, or the abdominal pain disappear in the surgeon's examining room. Why should a sufferer seek relief and shun it? Is it merely the fear of pain of the treatment? Is it the fear of unknown complications? Is it distrust of the doctor's ability? All of these, no doubt.

But, as Freud made so incontestably clear, the sufferer is always somewhat deterred by a kind of subversive, internal opposition to the work of cure. He suffers on the one hand from the pains of his affliction and yearns to get well. But he suffers at the same time from traitorous impulses that fight against the accomplishment of any change in himself, even recovery! Like Hamlet, he wonders whether it may be better after all to suffer the familiar pains and aches associated with the old method than to face the complications of a new and strange, even though possibly better way of handling things.

The inescapable conclusion is that society secretly *wants* crime, *needs* crime, and gains definite satisfactions from the present mishandling of it! We condemn crime; we punish offenders for it; but we need it. The crime and punishment ritual is a part of our lives. We need crimes to wonder at, to enjoy vicariously, to discuss and speculate about, and to publicly deplore. We need criminals to identify ourselves with, to envy secretly, and to punish stoutly. They do for us the forbidden, illegal things we *wish* to do and, like scapegoats of old, they bear the burdens of our displaced guilt and punishment—"the iniquities of us all."

We have to confess that there is something fascinating for us all about violence. That most

crime is not violent we know but we forget, because crime is not a breaking, a rupturing, a tearing—even when it is quietly done. To all of us crime seems like violence.

The very word "violence" has a disturbing, menacing quality.... In meaning it implies something dreaded, powerful, destructive, or eruptive. It is something we abhor—or do we? Its first effect is to startle, frighten—even to horrify us. But we do not always run away from it. For violence also intrigues us. It is exciting. It is dramatic. Observing it and sometimes even participating in it gives us acute pleasure.

The newspapers constantly supply us with tidbits of violence going on in the world. They exploit its dramatic essence often to the neglect of conservative reporting of more extensive but less violent damage—the flood disaster in Florence, Italy, for example. Such words as crash, explosion, wreck, assault, raid, murder, avalanche, rape, and seizure evoke pictures of eruptive devastation from which we cannot turn away. The headlines often impute violence metaphorically even to peaceful activities. Relations are "ruptured," a tie is "broken," arbitration "collapses," a proposal is "killed."

Meanwhile on the television and movie screens there constantly appear for our amusement scenes of fighting, slugging, beating, torturing, clubbing, shooting, and the like which surpass in effect anything that the newspapers can describe. Much of this violence is portrayed dishonestly; the scenes are only semirealistic; they are "faked" and romanticized.

Pain cannot be photographed; grimaces indicate but do not convey its intensity. And wounds—unlike violence—are rarely shown. This phony quality of television violence in its mentally unhealthy aspect encourages irrationality by giving the impression to the observer that being beaten, kicked, cut, and stomped, while very unpleasant, are not very painful or serious. For after being slugged and beaten the hero rolls over, opens his eyes, hops up, rubs his cheek, grins, and staggers on. The *suffering* of violence is a part both the TV and movie producers *and* their audience tend to repress.

Although most of us *say* we deplore cruelty and destructiveness, we are partially deceiving ourselves. We disown violence, ascribing the love of it to other people. But the facts speak for themselves. We do love violence, all of us, and we all feel secretly guilty for it, which is another clue to public resistance to crime-control reform.

The great sin by which we all are tempted is the wish to hurt others, and this sin must be avoided if we are to live and let live. If our destructive energies can be mastered, directed, and sublimated, we can survive. If we can love, we can live. Our destructive energies, if they cannot be controlled, may destroy our best friends, as in the case of Alexander the Great, or they may destroy supposed "enemies" or innocent strangers. Worst of all—from the standpoint of the individual—they may destroy us.

Over the centuries of man's existence, many devices have been employed in the effort to control these innate suicidal and criminal propensities. The earliest of these undoubtedly depended upon fear—fear of the unknown, fear of magical retribution, fear of social retaliation. These external devices were replaced gradually with the law and all its machinery, religion and its rituals, and the conventions of the social order.

The routine of life formerly required every individual to direct much of his aggressive energy against the environment. There were trees to cut down, wild animals to fend off, heavy obstacles to remove, great burdens to lift. But the machine has gradually changed all of this. Today, the routine of life, for most people, requires no violence, no fighting, no killing, no life-risking, no sudden supreme exertion: occasionally, perhaps, a hard pull or a strong push, but no tearing, crushing, breaking, forcing.

And because violence no longer has legitimate and useful vents or purposes, it must *all* be controlled today. In earlier times, its expression was often a virtue; today, its control *is* the virtue. The control involves symbolic, vicarious expressions of violence—violence modified; "sublimated," as Freud called it, "neutralized," as Hartmann described it. Civilized substitutes for direct violence

are the objects of daily search by all of us. The common law and the Ten Commandments, traffic signals and property deeds, fences and front doors, sermons and concerts, Christmas trees and jazz bands—these and a thousand other things exist today to help in the control of violence.

My colleague Bruno Bettelheim thinks we do not properly educate our youth to deal with their violent urges. He reminds us that nothing fascinated our forefathers more. The *Iliad* is a poem of violence. Much of the Bible is a record of violence. Our penal system and many methods of child-rearing express violence—"violence to suppress violence." And, he concludes [in the article "Violence: A Neglected Mode of Behavior"]: "We shall not be able to deal intelligently with violence unless we are first ready to see it as a part of human nature, and then we shall come to realize the chances of discharging violent tendencies are now so severely curtailed that their regular and safe draining-off is not possible anymore."

Why aren't we all criminals? We all have the impulses; we all have the provocations. But becoming civilized, which is repeated ontologically in the process of social education, teaches us what we may do with impunity. What then evokes or permits the breakthrough? Why is it necessary for some to bribe their consciences and do what they do not approve of doing? Why does all sublimation sometimes fail and overt breakdown occur in the controlling and managing machinery of the personality? Why do we sometimes lose self-control? Why do we "go to pieces"? Why do we explode?

These questions point up a central problem in psychiatry. Why do some people do things they do not want to do? Or things we do not want them to do? Sometimes crimes are motivated by a desperate need to act, to do *something* to break out of a state of passivity, frustration, and helplessness too long endured, like a child who shoots a parent or a teacher after some apparently reasonable act. Granting the universal presence of violence within us all, controlled by will power, conscience, fear of punishment, and other devices, granting the tensions and the temptations that are also common to us all, why do the mechanisms of self-control fail so completely in some individuals? Is there not some pre-existing defect, some moral or cerebral weakness, some gross deficiency of common sense that lets some people tumble or kick or strike or explode, while the rest of us just stagger or sway?

When a psychiatrist examines many prisoners, writes [Seymour] Halleck [in *Psychiatry and the Dilemmas of Crime*], he soon discovers how important in the genesis of the criminal outbreak is the offender's previous *sense of helplessness or hopelessness*. All of us suffer more or less from infringement of our personal freedom. We fuss about it all the time; we strive to correct it, extend it, and free ourselves from various oppressive or retentive forces. We do not want others to push us around, to control us, to dominate us. We realize this is bound to happen to some extent in an interlocking, interrelated society such as ours. No one truly has complete freedom. But restriction irks us.

The offender feels this way, too. He does not want to be pushed around, controlled, or dominated. And because he often feels that he is thus oppressed (and actually is) and because he does lack facility in improving his situation without violence, he suffers more intensely from feelings of helplessness.

Violence and crime are often attempts to escape from madness; and there can be no doubt that some mental illness is a flight from the wish to do the violence or commit the act. Is it hard for the reader to believe that suicides are sometimes committed to forestall the committing of murder? There is no doubt of it. Nor is there any doubt that murder is sometimes committed to avert suicide.

Strange as it may sound, many murderers do not realize whom they are killing, or, to put it another way, that they are killing the wrong people. To be sure, killing anybody is reprehensible enough, but the worst of it is that the person who the killer thinks should die (and he has reasons) is not the person he attacks. Sometimes the victim himself is partly responsible for the crime committed against him. It is this unconscious (perhaps sometimes conscious) participation in the crime by the victim that has long held up the very humanitarian and progressive-sounding program of giving compensation to victims. The public often judges the victim as well as the attacker.

Rape and other sexual offenses are acts of violence so repulsive to our sense of decency and order that it is easy to think of rapists in general as raging, oversexed, ruthless brutes (unless they are conquering heroes). Some rapists are. But most sex crimes are committed by undersexed rather than oversexed individuals, often undersized rather than oversized, and impelled less by lust than by a need for reassurance regarding an impaired masculinity. The unconscious fear of women goads some men with a compulsive urge to conquer, humiliate, hurt, or render powerless some available sample of womanhood. Men who are violently afraid of their repressed but nearly emergent homosexual desires, and men who are afraid of the humiliation of impotence, often try to overcome these fears by violent demonstrations.

The need to deny something in oneself is frequently an underlying motive for certain odd behavior—even up to and including crime. Bravado crimes, often done with particular brutality and ruthlessness, seem to prove *to the doer* that "I am no weakling! I am no sissy! I am no coward! I am no homosexual! I am a tough man who fears nothing." The Nazi storm troopers, many of them mere boys, were systematically trained to stifle all tender emotions and force themselves to be heartlessly brutal.

Man perennially seeks to recover the magic of his childhood days—the control of the mighty by the meek. The flick of an electric light switch, the response of an automobile throttle, the click of a camera, the touch of a match to a skyrocket—these are keys to a sudden and magical display of great power induced by the merest gesture. Is anyone already so blasé that he is no longer thrilled at the opening of a door specially for him by a magic-eye signal? Yet for a few pennies one can purchase a far more deadly piece of magic—a stored explosive and missile encased within a shell which can be ejected from a machine at the touch of a finger so swiftly that no eye can follow. A thousand yards away something falls dead—a rabbit, a deer, a beautiful mountain sheep, a sleeping child, or the President of the United States. Magic! Magnified, projected power. "Look what I can do. I am the greatest!"

It must have come to every thoughtful person, at one time or another, in looking at the revolvers on the policemen's hips, or the guns soldiers and hunters carry so proudly, that these are instruments made for the express purpose of delivering death to someone. The easy availability of these engines of destruction, even to children, mentally disturbed people, professional criminals, gangsters, and even high school girls is something to give one pause. The National Rifle Association and its allies have been able to kill scores of bills that have been introduced into Congress and state legislatures for corrective gun control since the death of President Kennedy. Americans still spend about $2 billion on guns each year.

Fifty years ago, Winston Churchill declared that the mood and temper of the public in regard to crime and criminals is one of the unfailing tests of the civilization of any country. Judged by this standard, how civilized are we?

The chairman of the President's National Crime Commission, Nicholas Katzenbach, declared … that organized crime flourishes in the United States because enough of the public wants its services, and most citizens are apathetic about its impact. It will continue uncurbed as long as Americans accept it as inevitable and, in some instances, desirable.

Are there steps that we can take which will reduce the aggressive stabs and self-destructive lurches of our less well-managing fellow men? Are there ways to prevent and control the grosser violations, other than the clumsy traditional maneuvers which we have inherited? These depend basically upon intimidation and slow-motion torture. We call it punishment, and justify it with our "feeling." We know it doesn't work.

Yes, there *are* better ways. There are steps that could be taken; some *are* taken. But we move too slowly. Much better use … could be made of the members of my profession and other behavioral

scientists than having them deliver courtroom pronunciamentos. The consistent use of a diagnostic clinic would enable trained workers to lay what they can learn about an offender before the judge who would know best how to implement the recommendation.

This would no doubt lead to a transformation of prisons, if not to their total disappearance in their present form and function. Temporary and permanent detention will perhaps always be necessary for a few, especially the professionals, but this could be more effectively and economically performed with new types of "facility" (that strange, awkward word for institution).

I assume it to be a matter of common and general agreement that our object in all this is to protect the community from a repetition of the offense by the most economical method consonant with our other purposes. Our "other purposes" include the desire to prevent these offenses from occurring, to reclaim offenders for social usefulness, if possible, and to detain them in protective custody, if reclamation is *not* possible. But how?

The treatment of human failure or dereliction by the infliction of pain is still used and believed in by many nonmedical people. "Spare the rod and spoil the child" is still considered wise counsel by many.

Whipping is still used by many secondary schoolmasters in England, I am informed, to stimulate study, attention, and the love of learning. Whipping was long a traditional treatment for the "crime" of disobedience on the part of children, pupils, servants, apprentices, employees. And slaves were treated for centuries by flogging for such offenses as weariness, confusion, stupidity, exhaustion, fear, grief, and even overcheerfulness. It was assumed and stoutly defended that these "treatments" cured conditions for which they were administered.

Meanwhile, scientific medicine was acquiring many new healing methods and devices. Doctors can now transplant organs and limbs; they can remove brain tumors and cure incipient cancers; they can halt pneumonia, meningitis, and other infections; they can correct deformities and repair breaks and tears and scars. But these wonderful achievements are accomplished on *willing* subjects, people who voluntarily ask for help by even heroic measures. And the reader will be wondering, no doubt, whether doctors can do anything with or for people who *do not want* to be treated at all, in any way! Can doctors cure willful aberrant behavior? Are we to believe that crime is a *disease* that can be reached by scientific measures? Isn't it merely "natural meanness" that makes all of us do wrong things at times even when we "know better"? And are not self-control, moral stamina, and will power the things needed? Surely there is no medical treatment for the lack of those!

Let me answer this carefully, for much misunderstanding accumulates here. [With] the prevalent understanding of the words, crime is *not* a disease. Neither is it an illness, although I think it *should* be! It *should* be treated, and it could be; but it mostly isn't.

These enigmatic statements are simply explained. Diseases are undesired states of being which have been described and defined by doctors, usually given Greek or Latin appellations, and treated by long-established physical and pharmacological formulae. Illness, on the other hand, is best defined as a state of impaired functioning of such a nature that the public expects the sufferer to repair to the physician for help. The illness may prove to be a disease; more often it is only vague and nameless misery; but something which doctors, not lawyers, teachers, or preachers, are supposed to be able and willing to help.

When the community begins to look upon the expression of aggressive violence as the symptom of an illness or as indicative of illness, it will be because it believes doctors can do something to correct such a condition. At present, some better-informed individuals do believe and expect this. However angry at or sorry for the offender, they want him "treated" in an effective way so that he will cease to be a danger to them. And they know that the traditional punishment, "treatment-punishment," will not effect this.

What *will*? What effective treatment is there for such violence? It will surely have to begin with motivating or stimulating or arousing in a cornered individual the wish and hope and intention to change his methods of dealing with the realities of life. Can this be done by education, medication, counseling, training? I would answer *yes*. It can be done successfully, in a majority of cases, if undertaken in time.

The present penal system and the existing legal philosophy do not stimulate or even expect such a change to take place in the criminal. Yet change is what medical science always aims for. The prisoner, like the doctor's other patients, should emerge from his treatment experience a different person, differently equipped, differently functioning, and headed in a different direction than when he began treatment.

It is natural for the public to doubt that this can be accomplished with criminals. But remember that the public *used* to doubt that change could be effected in the mentally ill. No one a hundred years ago believed mental illness to be curable. Today *all* people know (or should know) that *mental illness is curable* in the great majority of instances and that the prospects and rapidity of cure are directly related to the availability and intensity of proper treatment.

The forms and techniques of psychiatric treatment used today number in the hundreds. No one patient requires or receives all forms, but each patient is studied with respect to his particular needs, basic assets, interests, and special difficulties. A therapeutic team may embrace a dozen workers—as in a hospital setting—or it may narrow down to the doctor and the spouse. Clergymen, teachers, relatives, friends, and even fellow patients often participate informally but helpfully in the process of readaptation.

All of the participants in this effort to bring about a favorable change in the patient—i.e., in his vital balance and life program—are imbued with what we may call a *therapeutic attitude*. This is one in direct antithesis to attitudes of avoidance, ridicule, scorn, or punitiveness. Hostile feelings toward the subject, however justified by his unpleasant and even destructive behavior, are not in the curriculum of therapy or in the therapist.

This does not mean that therapists approve of the offensive and obnoxious behavior of the patient; they distinctly disapprove of it. But they recognize it as symptomatic of continued imbalance and disorganization, which is what they are seeking to change. They distinguish between disapproval, penalty, price, and punishment.

Doctors charge fees; they impose certain "penalties" or prices, but they have long since put aside primitive attitudes of retaliation toward offensive patients. A patient may cough in the doctor's face or vomit on the office rug; a patient may curse or scream or even struggle in the extremity of his pain. But these acts are not "punished." Doctors and nurses have no time or thought for inflicting unnecessary pain even on patients who may be difficult, disagreeable, provocative, and even dangerous. It is their duty to care for them, to try to make them well, and to prevent them from doing themselves or others harm. This requires love, not hate. This is the deepest meaning of the therapeutic attitude. Every doctor knows it; every worker in a hospital or clinic knows it (or should).

There is another element in the therapeutic attitude. It is the quality of hopefulness. If no one believes that the patient can get well, if no one—not even the doctor—has any hope, there probably won't be any recovery. Hope is just as important as love in the therapeutic attitude.

"But you were talking about the mentally ill," readers may interject, "those poor, confused, bereft, frightened individuals who yearn for help from you doctors and nurses. Do you mean to imply that willfully perverse individuals, our criminals, can be similarly reached and rehabilitated? Do you really believe that effective treatment of the sort you visualize can be applied to people *who do not want any help,* who are so willfully vicious, so well aware of the wrongs they are doing, so lacking in penitence or even common decency that punishment seems the only thing left?"

Do I believe there is effective treatment for offenders, and that they *can* be changed? *Most certainly and definitely I do*. Not all cases, to be sure; there are also some physical afflictions which we cannot cure at the moment. Some provision has to be made for incurables—pending new knowledge—and these will include some offenders. But I believe the majority of them would prove to be curable. The willfulness and the viciousness of offenders are part of the thing for which they have to be treated. These must not thwart the therapeutic attitude.

It is simply not true that most of them are "fully aware" of what they are doing, nor is it true that they want no help from anyone, although some of them say so. Prisoners are individuals: Some want treatment, some do not. Some don't know what treatment is. Many are utterly despairing and hopeless. Where treatment is made available in institutions, many prisoners seek it even with the full knowledge that doing so will not lessen their sentences. In some prisons, seeking treatment by prisoners is frowned upon by the officials.

Various forms of treatment are even now being tried in some progressive courts and prisons over the country—educational, social, industrial, religious, recreational, and psychological treatments. Socially acceptable behavior, new work-play opportunities, new identity and companion patterns all help toward community reacceptance. Some parole officers and some wardens have been extremely ingenious in developing these modalities of rehabilitation and reconstruction—more than I could list here even if I knew them all. But some are trying. The secret of success in all programs, however, is the replacement of the punitive attitude with a therapeutic attitude.

Offenders with propensities for impulsive and predatory aggression should not be permitted to live among us unrestrained by some kind of social control. *But the great majority of offenders, even "criminals," should never become prisoners if we want to "cure" them.*

There are now throughout the country many citizens' action groups and programs for the prevention and control of crime and delinquency. With such attitudes of inquiry and concern, the public could acquire information (and incentive) leading to a change of feeling about crime and criminals. It will discover how unjust is much so-called "justice," how baffled and frustrated many judges are by the ossified rigidity of old-fashioned, obsolete laws and state constitutions which effectively prevent the introduction of sensible procedures to replace useless, harmful ones.

I want to proclaim to the public that things are not what it wishes them to be, and will only become so if it will take an interest in the matter and assume some responsibility for its own self-protection.

Will the public listen?

If the public does become interested, it will realize that we must have more facts, more trial projects, more checked results. It will share the dismay of the President's Commission in finding that no one knows much about even the incidence of crime with any definiteness or statistical accuracy.

The average citizen finds it difficult to see how any research would in any way change his mind about a man who brutally murders his children. But just such inconceivably awful acts most dramatically point up the need for research. Why should—how can—a man become so dreadful as that in our culture? How is such a man made? Is it comprehensible that he can be born to become so depraved?

There are thousands of questions regarding crime and public protection which deserve scientific study. What makes some individuals maintain their interior equilibrium by one kind of disturbance of the social structure rather than by another kind, one that would have landed him in a hospital? Why do some individuals specialize in certain types of crime? Why do so many young people reared in areas of delinquency and poverty and bad example never become habitual delinquents? (Perhaps this is a more important question than why some of them do.)

The public has a fascination for violence, and clings tenaciously to its yen for vengeance, blind and deaf to the expense, futility, and dangerousness of the resulting penal system. But we are bound to hope that this will yield in time to the persistent, penetrating light of intelligence and accumulating scientific knowledge. The public will grow increasingly ashamed of its cry for retaliation, its persistent demand to punish. This is its crime, *our* crime against criminals—and, incidentally, our crime against ourselves. For before we can diminish our sufferings from the ill-controlled aggressive assaults of fellow citizens, we must renounce the philosophy of punishment, the obsolete, vengeful penal attitude. In its place we would seek a comprehensive constructive social attitude—therapeutic in some instances, restraining in some instances, but preventive in its total social impact.

In the last analysis this becomes a question of personal morals and values. No matter how glorified or how piously disguised, vengeance as a human motive must be personally repudiated by each and every one of us. This is the message of old religions and new psychiatries. Unless this message is heard, unless we, the people—the man on the street, the housewife in the home—can give up our delicious satisfactions in opportunities for vengeful retaliation on scapegoats, we cannot expect to preserve our peace, our public safety, or our mental health.

68

A Critique of the Humanitarian Theory of Punishment

C. S. LEWIS

C. S. Lewis argues that the humanitarian theory of punishment is not in the interests of the criminal. According to Lewis, this is because the theory is concerned with the goals of reform and deterrence and not the requirements of justice. Hence, it permits the violation of the criminal's rights as a way of promoting these goals. Moreover, Lewis claims, deciding what promotes reform and deterrence, unlike deciding what is required by justice, seems best left to experts. Yet these experts, Lewis argues, even with the best of intentions, may act "as cruelly and unjustly as the greatest tyrants."

In England we have lately had a controversy about Capital Punishment. I do not know whether a murderer is more likely to repent and make a good end on the gallows a few weeks after his trial or in the prison infirmary thirty years later. I do not know whether the fear of death is an indispensable deterrent. I need not [here] decide whether it is a morally permissible deterrent. Those are questions which I propose to leave untouched. My subject is not Capital Punishment in particular, but that theory of punishment in general which the controversy showed to be almost universal among my fellow countrymen. It may be called the Humanitarian theory. Those who hold it think that it is mild and merciful. In this I believe that they are seriously mistaken. I believe that the "Humanity" which it claims is a dangerous illusion and disguises the possibility of cruelty and injustice without end. I urge a return to the traditional or Retributive theory not solely, not even primarily, in the interests of society, but in the interests of the criminal.

According to the Humanitarian theory, to punish a man because he deserves it, and as much as he deserves, is mere revenge, and, therefore, barbarous and immoral. It is maintained that the only legitimate motives for punishing are the desire to deter others by example or to mend the criminal. When this theory is combined, as frequently happens, with the belief that all crime is more or less pathological, the idea of mending tails off into that of healing or curing and punishment becomes therapeutic. Thus it appears at first sight that we have passed from the harsh and self-righteous notion of giving the wicked their deserts to the charitable and enlightened one of tending the psychologically sick. What could be more amiable? One little point which is taken for granted in this theory needs, however, to be made explicit. The things done to the criminal, even if they are called cures, will be just as compulsory as they were in the old days when we called them punishments. If a tendency to steal can be cured by psychotherapy, the thief

Abridged from *Ethical Theory* (Prentice-Hall, 1959), pp. 480, 489–495, 503–505. Reprinted by permission of Richard B. Brandt. Notes renumbered.

will no doubt be forced to undergo the treatment. Otherwise, society cannot continue.

[T]his doctrine, merciful though it appears, really means that each one of us, from the moment he breaks the law, is deprived of the rights of a human being.

The reason is this: The Humanitarian theory removes from Punishment the concept of Desert. But the concept of Desert is the only connecting link between punishment and justice. It is only as deserved or undeserved that a sentence can be just or unjust. I do not here contend that the question "Is it deserved?" is the only one we can reasonably ask about a punishment. We may very properly ask whether it is likely to deter others and to reform the criminal. But neither of these two last questions is a question about justice. There is no sense in talking about a "just deterrent" or a "just cure." We demand of a deterrent not whether it is just but whether it will deter. We demand of a cure not whether it is just but whether it succeeds. Thus when we cease to consider what the criminal deserves and consider only what will cure him or deter others, we have tacitly removed him from the sphere of justice altogether; instead of a person, a subject of rights, we now have a mere object, a patient, a "case."

The distinction will become clearer if we ask who will be qualified to determine sentences when sentences are no longer held to derive their propriety from the criminal's deservings. On the old view the problem of fixing the right sentence was a moral problem. Accordingly, the judge who did it was a person trained in jurisprudence: trained, that is, in a science which deals with rights and duties, and which, in origin at least, was consciously accepting guidance from the Law of Nature, and from Scripture. We must admit that in the actual penal code of most countries at most times these high originals were so much modified by local custom, class interests, and utilitarian concessions, as to be very imperfectly recognizable. But the code was never in principle, and not always in fact, beyond the control of the conscience of the society. And when (say, in eighteenth-century England) actual punishments conflicted too violently with the moral sense of the community, juries refused to

convict and reform was finally brought about. This was possible because, so long as we are thinking in terms of Desert, the propriety of the penal code, being a moral question, is a question on which every man has the right to an opinion, not because he follows this or that profession, but because he is simply a man, a rational animal enjoying the Natural Light. But all this is changed when we drop the concept of Desert. The only two questions we may now ask about a punishment are whether it deters and whether it cures. But these are not questions on which anyone is entitled to have an opinion simply because he is a man. He is not entitled to an opinion even if, in addition to being a man, he should happen also to be a jurist, a Christian, and a moral theologian. For they are not questions about principle but about matter of fact; and for such *cui-quam in sua arte credendum*. Only the expert "penologist" (let barbarous things have barbarous names), in the light of previous experiment, can tell us what is likely to deter: Only the psychotherapist can tell us what is likely to cure. It will be in vain for the rest of us, speaking simply as men, to say, "but this punishment is hideously unjust, hideously disproportionate to the criminal's deserts." The experts with perfect logic will reply, "but nobody was talking about deserts. No one was talking about *punishment* in your archaic vindictive sense of the word. Here are the statistics proving that this treatment deters. Here are the statistics proving that this other treatment cures. What is your trouble?"

The Humanitarian theory, then, removes sentences from the hands of jurists whom the public ... is entitled to criticize and places them in the hands of technical experts whose special sciences do not even [use] such categories as rights or justice.... [S]ince this transference results from an abandonment of the old idea of punishment, and, therefore, of all vindictive motives, it will be safe to leave our criminals in such hands. I will not ... comment on the simple-minded view of fallen human nature which such a belief implies. Let us rather remember that the "cure" of criminals is to be compulsory; and let us then watch how the theory actually works in the mind of the Humanitarian. The immediate starting point of this article was a letter I read in [a leftist weekly]. The author [pleaded] that a certain sin, now treated by our laws as a crime, should henceforward be treated as a disease. And he complained that under the present system the offender, after a term in gaol, was simply let out to return to his original environment where he would probably relapse. What he complained of was not the shutting up but the letting out. On his remedial view of punishment the offender should ... be detained until he was cured. And of course the official straighteners are the only people who can say when that is. The first result of the Humanitarian theory is, therefore, to substitute for a definite sentence (reflecting to some extent the community's moral judgment on the degree of ill-desert involved) an indefinite sentence terminable only by the word of those experts—and they are not experts in moral theology or ... the Law of Nature—who inflict it. Which of us, if he stood in the dock, would not prefer to be tried by the old system?

It may be said that by the continued use of the word *punishment* and the use of the verb "inflict" I am misrepresenting Humanitarians. They are not punishing, not inflicting, only healing. But do not ... be deceived by a name. To be taken without consent from my home and friends; to lose my liberty; to undergo all those assaults on my personality that modern psychotherapy knows how to deliver; to be remade after some pattern of "normality" hatched in a Viennese laboratory to which I never professed allegiance; to know that this process will never end until either my captors have succeeded or I have grown wise enough to cheat them with apparent success—who cares whether this is called Punishment or not? That it includes most of the elements for which any punishment is feared—shame, exile, bondage, and years eaten by the locust—is obvious. Only enormous ill-desert could justify it; but ill-desert is the very conception which the Humanitarian theory has thrown overboard.

If we turn from the curative to the deterrent justification of punishment we shall find the new theory even more alarming. When you punish a man *in terrorem*, make of him an "example" to others, you are admittedly using him as a means to an end; someone else's end. This, in itself, would be a very wicked thing to do. On the classical theory of Punishment it was of course justified on the ground that the man deserved it. That was assumed to be established before any question of "making him an example" arose. You then, as the saying is, killed two birds with one stone; in the process of giving him what he deserved you set an example to others. But take away desert and the whole morality of the punishment disappears. Why, in Heaven's name, am I to be sacrificed to the good of society in this way?—unless, of course, I deserve it.

But that is not the worst. If the justification of exemplary punishment is not to be based on desert but solely on its efficacy as a deterrent, it is not absolutely necessary that the man we punish should even have committed the crime. The deterrent effect demands that the public should draw the moral, "If we do such an act we shall suffer like that man." The punishment of a man actually guilty whom the public think innocent will not have the desired effect; the punishment of a man actually innocent will, provided the public think him guilty. But every modern State has powers which make it easy to fake a trial. When a victim is urgently needed for exemplary purposes and a guilty victim cannot be found, all the purposes of deterrence will be equally served by the punishment (call it "cure" if you prefer) of an innocent victim, provided that the public can be cheated into thinking him guilty. It is no use to ask me why I assume that our rulers will be so wicked. The punishment of an innocent, that is, an undeserving, man is wicked only if we grant the traditional view that righteous punishment means deserved punishment. Once we have abandoned that criterion, all punishments have to be justified, if at all, on other grounds that have nothing to do with desert. Where the punishment of the innocent can be justified on those grounds (and it could in some cases be justified as a deterrent) it will be no less moral than any other punishment. Any distaste for it on the part of a Humanitarian will be merely a hangover from the Retributive theory.

It is, indeed, important to notice that my argument so far supposes no evil intentions on the part of the Humanitarian and considers only what is involved in the logic of his position. My contention is that good men (not bad men) consistently acting upon that position would act as cruelly and unjustly as the greatest tyrants. They might in some respects act even worse. Of all tyrannies a tyranny sincerely exercised for the good of its victims may be the most oppressive. It may be better to live under robber barons than under omnipotent moral busybodies. The robber baron's cruelty may sometimes sleep, his cupidity may at some point be satiated; but those who torment us for our own good will torment us without end for they do so with the approval of their own conscience. They may be more likely to go to Heaven yet at the same time likelier to make a Hell of earth. Their very kindness stings with intolerable insult. To be "cured" against one's will and cured of states which we may not regard as disease is to be put on a level with those who have not yet reached the age of reason or those who never will; to be classed with infants, imbeciles, and domestic animals. But to be punished, however severely, because we have deserved it, because we "ought to have known better," is to be treated as a human person made in God's image.

In reality, however, we must face the possibility of bad rulers armed with a Humanitarian theory of punishment. A great many popular blueprints for a Christian society are merely what the Elizabethans called "eggs in moonshine" because they assume that the whole society is Christian or that the Christians are in control. This is not so in most contemporary States. Even if it were, our rulers would still be fallen men, and, therefore, neither very wise nor very good. As it is, they will usually be unbelievers. And since wisdom and virtue are not the only or the commonest qualifications for a place in the government, they will not often be even the best unbelievers. The practical problem of Christian politics is not that of drawing up schemes for a Christian society, but that of living as innocently as we can with unbelieving fellow-subjects under unbelieving rulers who will never be perfectly wise and good and who will sometimes be very wicked and very foolish. And when they are wicked the Humanitarian theory of punishment will put in their hands a finer instrument of tyranny than wickedness ever had before. For if crime and disease are regarded as the same thing, it follows that any state of mind which our masters choose to call "disease" can be treated as crime and compulsorily cured. It will be vain to plead that states of mind which displease government need not always involve moral turpitude and do not therefore always deserve forfeiture of liberty. For our masters will not be using the concepts of Desert and Punishment but those of disease and cure. We know that one school of psychology already regards religion as a neurosis. When this particular neurosis becomes inconvenient to government, what is to hinder government from proceeding to "cure" it? Such "cure" will, of course, be compulsory; but under the Humanitarian theory it will not be called by the shocking name of Persecution. No one will blame us for being Christian, no one will hate us, no one will revile us. The new Nero will approach us with the silky manners of a doctor, and though all will be in fact as compulsory as the *tunica molesta* or Smithfield or Tyburn, all will go on within the unemotional therapeutic sphere where words like *right* and *wrong* or *freedom* and *slavery* are never heard. And thus when the command is given, every prominent Christian in the land may vanish overnight into Institutions for the Treatment of the Ideologically Unsound, and it will rest with the expert gaolers to say when (if ever) they are to reemerge. But it will not be persecution. Even if the treatment is painful, even if it is life-long, even if it is fatal, that will be only a regrettable accident; the intention was purely therapeutic. Even in ordinary medicine there were painful operations and fatal operations; so in this. But because they are "treatment," not punishment, they can be criticized only by fellow experts and on technical grounds, never by men as men and on grounds of justice.

That is why I think it essential to oppose the Humanitarian theory of punishment, root and branch, wherever we encounter it. It carries on its front a semblance of mercy which is wholly false.

That is how it can deceive men of good will. The error began, perhaps, with Shelley's statement that the distinction between mercy and justice was invented in the courts of tyrants. It sounds noble, and was indeed the error of a noble mind. But the distinction is essential. The older view was that mercy "tempered" justice, or (on the highest level of all) that mercy and justice had met and kissed. The essential act of mercy was to pardon; and pardon in its very essence involves the recognition of guilt, and ill-desert in the recipient. If crime is only a disease which needs cure, not sin which deserves punishment, it cannot be pardoned. How can you pardon a man for having a gumboil or a club foot? But the Humanitarian theory wants simply to abolish Justice and substitute Mercy for it. This means that you start being "kind" to people before you have considered their rights, and then force upon them supposed kindnesses which they in fact had a right to refuse, and finally kindnesses which no one but you will recognize as kindnesses and which the recipient will feel as abominable cruelties. You have overshot the mark. Mercy, detached from justice, grows unmerciful. That is the important paradox.

As there are plants which will flourish only in mountain soil, so it appears that Mercy will flower only when it grows in the crannies of the rock of Justice: Transplanted to the marshlands of mere Humanitarianism, it becomes a man-eating weed, all the more dangerous because it is still called by the same name as the mountain variety. But we ought long ago to have learned our lesson. We should be too old now to be deceived by those humane pretensions that have served to usher in every cruelty of the revolutionary period in which we live. These are the "precious balms" that will "break our heads."

There is a fine sentence in Bunyan: "It came burning hot into my mind, whatever he said, and however he flattered, when he got me home to his house, he would sell me for a slave." There is a fine couplet, too, in John Ball:

> *Beware ere ye be woe*
> *Know your friend from your foe.*

One last word. You may ask why I sent this to an Australian periodical. The reason is simple ...: I can get no hearing for it in England.

69

The Humanitarian Theory of Punishment?

EDMUND L. PINCOFFS

Edmund L. Pincoffs begins by setting out three principles that, he holds, express the essence of a Kantian retributive theory of punishment. He then claims that the underlying rationale for these principles is to provide a justification of the punishment to the criminal on the grounds that she has willed the punishment she now suffers. Pincoffs concludes by noting two difficulties for the retributive theory of punishment that he has not addressed: how to make punishment equal to the crime and how to distinguish punishment from revenge.

I

The classification of Kant as a retributivist[1] is usually accompanied by a reference to some part of the following passage from the *Rechtslehre,* which is worth quoting at length.

> Juridical punishment can never be administered merely as a means for promoting another good either with regard to the criminal himself or to civil society, but must in all cases be imposed only because the individual on whom it is inflicted *has committed a crime.* For one man ought never to be dealt with merely as a means subservient to the purpose of another, nor be mixed up with the subjects of real right. Against such treatment his inborn personality has a right to protect him, even though he may be condemned to lose his civil personality. He must first be found guilty and *punishable* before there can be any thought of drawing from his punishment any benefit for himself or his fellow-citizens. The penal law is a categorical imperative; and woe to him who creeps through the serpent-windings of utilitarianism to discover some advantage that may discharge him from the justice of punishment, or even from the due measure of it, according to the Pharisaic maxim: "It is better that *one* man should die than the whole people should perish," For if justice and righteousness perish, human life would no longer have any value in the world....

But what is the mode and measure of punishment which public justice takes as its principle and standard? It is just the principle of equality, by which the pointer of the scale of justice is made to incline no more to the one side than the other. It may be rendered by saying that the undeserved evil which any one commits on another, is to be regarded as perpetrated on himself. Hence it may be said: "If you slander another, you slander yourself; if you steal from another, you steal from yourself; if you strike another, you strike yourself; if you kill another, you kill yourself." This is the Right of RETALIATION *(jus talionis);* and properly understood, it is the only principle which in regulating a

From "The Humanitarian Theory of Punishment?" *Res Judicatae* (1953), pp. 224–230. Reprinted by permission of the Melbourne University Law Review and the Trustee for the C. S. Lewis Estate.

public court, as distinguished from mere private judgment, can definitely assign both the quality and the quantity of a just penalty. All other standards are wavering and uncertain; and on account of other considerations involved in them, they contain no principle conformable to the sentence of pure and strict justice.[2]

Obviously we could mull over this passage for a long time. What, exactly, is the distinction between the Inborn and the Civil Personality? How is the Penal Law a Categorical Imperative: by derivation from one of the five formulations in the *Grundlegung,* or as a separate formulation? But we are on the trail of the traditional retributive theory of punishment and do not want to lose ourselves in niceties.

There are two main points in this passage to which we should give particular attention:

i. The only acceptable reason for punishing a man is that he has committed a crime.

ii. The only acceptable reason for punishing a man in a given manner and degree is that the punishment is "equal" to the crime for which he is punished.

These propositions, I think it will be agreed, express the main points of the first and second paragraphs respectively. Before stopping over these points, let us go on to a third. It is brought out in the following passage from the *Rechtslehre,* which is also often referred to by writers on retributivism.

> Even if a civil society resolved to dissolve itself with the consent of all its members—as might be supposed in the case of a people inhabiting an island resolving to separate and scatter themselves throughout the whole world—the last murderer lying in prison ought to be executed before the resolution was carried out. This ought to be done [so] that everyone may realize the desert of his deeds, and that bloodguiltiness may not remain upon the people; for otherwise they will all be regarded as participators in the murder as a public violation of justice.[3]

It is apparent from this passage that, [as far] as the punishment of death for murder is concerned, the punishment awarded not only may but must be carried out. If it must be carried out "so that everyone may realize the desert of his deeds," then punishment for deeds other than murder must be carried out too. We will take it, then, that Kant holds that:

iii. Whoever commits a crime must be punished in accordance with his desert.

Whereas (i) tells us what kind of reason we must have *if we* punish, (iii) now tells us that we must punish *whenever* there is desert of punishment. Punishment, Kant tells us elsewhere, is "The *juridical* effect or consequence of a culpable act of Demerit."[4] Any crime is a culpable act of demerit, in that it is an *"intentional* transgression—that is, an act accompanied with the consciousness that it is a transgression."[5] This is an unusually narrow definition of crime, since crime is not ordinarily limited to intentional acts of transgression but may also include unintentional ones, such as acts done in ignorance of the law, and criminally negligent acts. However, Kant apparently leaves room for "culpable acts of demerit" outside of the category of crime. These he calls "faults," which are unintentional transgressions of duty; but "are nevertheless imputable to a person."[6] I can only suppose, though it is a difficulty in the interpretation of the *Rechtslehre,* that when Kant says that punishment must be inflicted "only because he has committed a crime," he is not including in "crime" what he would call a fault. Crime would, then, refer to any *intentional* imputable transgressions of duty and these are what must be punished as involving ill desert. The difficulties involved in the definition of crime as the transgression of duty, as opposed to the mere violation of a legal prohibition, will be taken up later.

Taking the three propositions we have isolated as expressing the essence of the Kantian retributivistic position, we must now ask a direct and obvious question. What makes Kant hold this position? Why does he think it apparent that consequences should have *nothing to do* with the decision whether, and how, and how much to punish? There are two directions any answer to this question might follow. One would lead us into an extensive excursus on the philosophical position of Kant, the relation of this to his ethical theory, and the relation of his general theory of ethics to his philosophy of law. It would, in short, take our question as one about the consistency of Kant's position concerning the justification of punishment with the whole of Kantian philosophy. This would involve discussion of Kant's reasons for believing that moral laws must be universal and categorical in virtue of their form alone, and divorced from any empirical content; of his attempt to make out a moral decision-procedure based on an "empty" categorical imperative; and, above all, of the concept of freedom as a postulate of practical reason, and as the central concept of the philosophy of law. This kind of answer, however, we must forego here; for while it would have considerable interest in its own right, it would lead us astray from our purpose, which is to understand as well as we can the retributivist position, not as a part of this or that philosophical system but for its own sake. It is a position taken by philosophers with diverse philosophical systems; we want to take another direction, then, in our answer. Is there any *general* (nonspecial, non-systematic) reason why Kant rejects consequences in the justification of punishment?

Kant believes that consequences have nothing to do with the justification of punishment partly because of his assumptions about the *direction* of justification; and these assumptions are ... also to be found underlying the thought of Hegel and Bradley. Justification is not only *of* something, it is also *to* someone: It has an addressee. Now there are important confusions in Kant's and other traditional justifications of punishment turning on the question what the "punishment" *is* which is being justified.... But if we are to feel the force of the retributivist position, we can no longer put off the question of the addressee of justification.

To whom is the Kantian justification of punishment directed? The question may seem a difficult one to answer, since Kant does not consider it

himself as a separate issue. Indeed, it is not the kind of question likely to occur to a philosopher of Kant's formalistic leanings. A Kantian justification or rationale stands, so to speak, on its own. It is a structure which can be examined, tested, probed by any rational being. Even to speak of the addressee of justification has an uncomfortably relativistic sound, as if only persuasion of A or B or C is possible, and proof impossible. Yet, in practice, Kant does not address his proffered justification of punishment so much to any rational being (which, to put it otherwise, is to address it not at all), as to the being most affected: the criminal himself.

It is the criminal who is cautioned not to creep through the serpent-windings of utilitarianism. It is the criminal's rights which are in question in the debate with Beccaria over capital punishment. It is the criminal we are warned not to mix up with property or things: the "subjects of Real Right." In the *Kritik der Praktischen Vernunft,* the intended direction of justification becomes especially clear.

> Now the notion of punishment, as such, cannot be united with that of becoming a partaker of happiness; for although he who inflicts the punishment may at the same time have the benevolent purpose of directing this punishment to this end, yet it must be justified in itself as punishment, that is, as mere harm, so that if it stopped there, and the person punished could get no glimpse of kindness hidden behind this harshness, he must yet admit that justice was done him, and that his reward was perfectly suitable to his conduct. In every punishment, as such, there must first be justice, and this constitutes the essence of the notion. Benevolence may, indeed, be united with it, but the man who has deserved punishment has not the least reason to reckon upon this.[7]

Since this matter of the direction of justification is central in our understanding of traditional retributivism, and not generally appreciated, it will be worth our while to pause over this paragraph. Kant holds here, as he later holds in the *Rechtslehre,* that once it has been decided that a given "mode and measure" of punishment is justified, then "he who inflicts punishment" may do so in such a way as to increase the long-term happiness of the criminal. This could be accomplished, for example, by using a prison term as an opportunity for reforming the criminal. But Kant's point is that reforming the criminal has nothing to do with justifying the infliction of punishment. It is not inflicted because it will give an opportunity for reform, but because it is merited. The passage does not need my gloss; it is transparently clear. Kant wants the justification of punishment to be such that the criminal "who could get no glimpse of kindness behind this harshness" would have to admit that punishment is warranted.

Suppose we tell the criminal, "We are punishing you for your own good." This is wrong because it is then open to him to raise the question whether he deserves punishment, and what you consider good to be. If he does not deserve punishment, we have no right to inflict it, especially in the name of some good of which the criminal may not approve. So long as we are to treat him as rational—a being with dignity—we cannot force our judgements of good upon him. This is what makes the appeal to supposedly good consequences "wavering and uncertain." They waver because the criminal has as much right as anyone to question them. They concern ends which he may reject, and means which he might rightly regard as unsuited to the ends.

In the "Supplementary Explanations of the Principles of Right" of the *Rechtslehre,* Kant distinguishes between "punitive justice *(jutstitia punitiva),* in which the ground of the penalty is moral *(quia peccatum est),*" and "punitive *expediency,* the foundation of which is merely pragmatic *(ne peccetur)* as being grounded on the experience of what operates most effectively to prevent crime." Punitive justice, says Kant, has an "entirely distinct place *(locus justi)* in the topical arrangement of the juridical conceptions."

It does not seem reasonable to suppose that Kant makes this distinction merely to discard punitive expediency entirely, that he has no concern at all for the *ne peccetur.* But he does hold that there is no place for it in the justification of punishment proper: For this can only be to show the criminal that the punishment is just.

How is this to be done? The difficulty is that on the one hand the criminal must be treated as a rational being, an end in himself; but on the other hand the justification we offer him cannot be allowed to appear as the opening move in a rational discussion. It cannot turn on the criminal's acceptance of some premise which, as a rational being, he has a perfect right to question. If the end in question is the well-being of society, we are assuming that the criminal will not have a different view of what that well-being consists in, and we are telling him that he should sacrifice himself *to* that end. As a rational being, he can question whether any end we propose is a good end. And we have no right to demand that he sacrifice himself to the public well-being, even supposing he agrees with us on what that consists in. No man has a duty, in Kant's view, to be benevolent.[8]

The way out of the quandary is to show the criminal that we are not inflicting the punishment on him for some questionable purpose of our own choice, but that he, as a free agent, has exercised *his* choice in such a way as to make the punishment a necessary consequence. "His own evil deed draws the punishment upon himself."[9] The undeserved evil which anyone commits on another, is to be regarded as perpetuated on himself."[10] But may not the criminal rationally question this asserted connection between crime and punishment? Suppose he wishes to regard the punishment *not* as "drawn upon himself" by his own "evil deed?" Suppose he argues that no good purpose will be served by punishing him? But this line of thought leads into the "serpent-windings of utilitarianism," for if it is good consequences that govern, then justice goes by the board. What may not be done to him in the name of good consequences? What proportion would remain between what he has done and what he suffers?[11]

But punishment is *inflicted.* To tell the criminal that he "draws it upon himself" is all very well, only how do we justify *to ourselves* the infliction of it? Kant's answer is found early in the *Rechtslehre.*[12] There he relates punishment to crime *via* freedom. Crime consists in compulsion or constraint of some kind: a hindrance of freedom.[13] If it is wrong that freedom should be hindered, it is right to block this hindrance. But to block the constraint of freedom it is necessary to apply constraint. Punishment is a "hindering of a hindrance of freedom." Compulsion of the criminal is, then, justified only to the extent that it hinders his compulsion of another.

But how are we to understand Kant here? Punishment comes after the crime. How can it hinder [it]? The reference cannot be to the hindrance of future crime, or Kant's doctrine reduces to a variety of utilitarianism. The picture of compulsion versus compulsion is clear enough, but how are we to apply it? Our answer must be somewhat speculative, since there is no direct answer to be found in the *Rechtslehre*. The answer must begin from yet another extension of the concept of a crime. For the crime cannot consist merely in an act. What is criminal is acting in accordance with a wrong maxim—a maxim which would, if made universal, destroy freedom. The adoption of the maxim is criminal. Should we regard punishment, then, as the hindrance of a wrong maxim? But how do we hinder a maxim? We show, exhibit, its wrongness by taking it at face value. If the criminal has adopted it, he is claiming that it can be universalized. But if it is universalized it warrants the same treatment of the criminal as he has accorded to his victim. So if he murders he must be executed; if he steals we must "steal from" him.[14] What we do to him he willed, in willing, to adopt his maxim as universalizable. To justify the punishment to the criminal is to show him that the compulsion we use on him proceeds according to the same rule by which he acts. This is how he "draws the punishment upon himself." In punishing, we are not adopting his maxim but demonstrating its logical consequences if universalized: We show the criminal *what* he has willed. This is the positive side of the Kantian rationale of punishment.

II

Hegel's version of this rationale has attracted more attention, and disagreement, in recent literature. It is the Hegelian metaphysical terminology that is partly responsible for the disagreement and that has stood in the way of an understanding of the retributivist position. The difficulty turns around the notions of "annulment of crime" and punishment as the "right" of the criminal. Let us consider "annulment" first.

In the *Philosophic des Rechts*[15] Hegel tells us that

> Abstract right is a right to coerce, because the wrong which transgresses it is an exercise of force against the existence of my freedom in an external thing. The maintenance of this existent against the exercise of force therefore itself takes the form of an external act and an exercise of force annulling the force originally brought against it.[16]

Holmes complains that by the use of his logical apparatus, involving the negation of negations (or annulment), Hegel professes to establish what is only a mystic (though generally felt) bond between wrong and punishment.[17] Hastings Rashdall asks how any rational connection can be shown between the evil of the pain of punishment, and the twin evils of the suffering of the victim and the moral evil which "pollutes the offender's soul," unless appeal is made to the probable good consequences of punishment. The notion that the "guilt" of the offense must be, in some mysterious way, wiped out by the suffering of the offender does not seem to provide it.[18] Crime, which is an evil, is apparently to be "annulled" by the addition to it of punishment, which is another evil. How can two evils yield a good?[19]

But in fact Hegel is following the *Rechtslehre* quite closely here, and his doctrine is very near to Kant's. In the notes taken at Hegel's lectures,[20] we find Hegel quoted as follows:

> If crime and its annulment ... are treated as if they were unqualified evils, it must, of course, seem quite unreasonable to will an evil merely because "another evil is there already"... But it is not merely a question of an evil or of this, that, or the other good; the precise point at issue is wrong,

and the righting of it.... The various considerations which are relevant to punishment as a phenomenon and to the bearing it has on the particular consciousness, and which concern its effects (deterrent, reformative, etcetera) on the imagination, are an essential topic for examination in their place, especially in connection with modes of punishment, but all these considerations presuppose as their foundation the fact that punishment is inherently and actually just. In discussing this matter the only important things are, first, that crime is to be annulled, not because it is the producing of an evil, but because it is the infringing of the right as right, and secondly, the question of what that positive existence is which crime possesses and which must be annulled; it is this existence which is the real evil to be removed, and the essential point is the question of where it lies. So long as the concepts here at issue are not clearly apprehended, confusion must continue to reign in the theory of punishment.[21]

While this passage is not likely to dethrone confusion, it does bring us closer to the basically Kantian heart of Hegel's theory. To "annul crime" should be read "right wrong." Crime is a wrong which consists in an "infringement of the right as right."[22] It would be unjust, says Hegel, to allow crime, which is the invasion of a right, to go unrequited. For to allow this is to admit that the crime is "valid": that is, that it is not in conflict with justice. But this is what we do not want to admit, and the only way of showing this is to pay back the deed to the agent: Coerce the coercer. For by intentionally violating his victim's rights, the criminal in effect claims that the rights of others are not binding on him; and this is to attack *das Recht* itself: the system of justice in which there are rights which, must be respected. Punishment not only keeps the system in balance, it vindicates the system itself. Besides talking about punishment's "annulment" of crime, Hegel has argued that it is the "right of the criminal." The obvious reaction to this is that it

is a strange justification of punishment which makes it someone's right, for it is at best a strange kind of right which no one would ever want to claim! McTaggatt's explanation of this facet of Hegel's theory is epitomized in the following quotation:

> What, then, is Hegel's theory? It is, I think, briefly this: In sin, man rejects and defies the moral law. Punishment is pain inflicted on him because he has done this, and in order that he may, by the fact of his punishment, be forced into recognizing as valid the law which he rejected in sinning, and so repent of his sin—really repent, and not merely be frightened out of doing it again.[23]

If McTaggart is right, then we are obviously not going to find in Hegel anything relevant to the justification of legal punishment, where the notions of sin and repentance are out of place. And this is the conclusion McTaggart of course reaches. "Hegel's view of punishment," he insists, "cannot properly be applied in jurisprudence, and ... his chief mistake regarding it lay in supposing that it could."[24]

But though McTaggart may be right in emphasizing the theological aspect of Hegel's doctrine of punishment, he is wrong in denying it a jurisprudential aspect. In fact, Hegel is only saying what Kant emphasized: That to justify punishment to the criminal is to show him that *he* has chosen to be treated as he is being treated.

> The injury (the penalty) which falls on the criminal is not merely *implicitly* just—as just, it is *eo ipso* his implicit will, an embodiment of his freedom, his right; on the contrary, it is also a right *established* within the criminal himself, that is, in his objectively embodied will, in his action. The reason for this is that his action is the action of a rational being and this implies that it is something universal and that by doing it the criminal has laid down a law which he has explicitly recognized in his action and under which in consequence he should be brought as under his right.[25]

To accept the retributivist position, then, is to accept a thesis about the burden of proof in the justification of punishment. Provided we make the punishment "equal" to the crime it is not up to us to justify it to the criminal, beyond pointing out to him that it is what he willed. It is not that he initiated a chain of events likely to result in his punishment, but that in willing the crime he willed that he himself should suffer in the same degree as his victim. But what if the criminal simply wanted to commit his crime and get away with it (break the window and run, take the funds and retire to Brazil, kill but live)? Suppose we explain to the criminal that *really* in willing to kill he willed to lose his life; and, unimpressed, he replies that *really* he wished to kill and save his skin. The retributivist answer is that to the extent that the criminal understands freedom and justice he will understand that his punishment was made inevitable by his own choice. No moral theory can hope to provide a justification of punishment which will seem such to the criminal merely as a nexus of passions and desires. The retributivist addresses him as a rational being, aware of the significance of his action. The burden of proof, the retributivist would argue, is on the theorist who would not start from this assumption. For to assume from the beginning that the criminal is not rational is to treat him, from the beginning, as merely a "harmful animal."

> What is involved in the action of the criminal is not only the concept of crime, the rational aspect present in crime as such whether the individual wills it or not, the aspect which the state has to vindicate, but also the abstract rationality of the individual's *volition*. Since that is so, punishment is regarded as containing the criminal's right and hence by being punished he is honored as a rational being. He does not receive this due of honor unless the concept and measure of his punishment are derived from his own act. Still less does he receive it if he is treated as a harmful animal who has to be made harmless, or with a view to deterring and reforming him.[26]

To address the criminal as a rational being aware of the significance of his action is to address him as a person who knows that he has not committed a "bare" act; to commit an act is to commit oneself to the universalization of the rule by which one acted. For a man to complain about the death sentence for murder is as absurd as for a man to complain that when he pushed down one tray of the scales, the other tray goes up; whereas the action, rightly considered, is of pushing down *and* up. "The criminal gives his consent already by his very act."[27] "The Eumenides sleep, but crime awakens them, and hence it is the very act of crime which vindicates itself."[28]

F. H. Bradley's contribution to the retributive theory of punishment adds heat but not much light. The central, and best-known, passage is the following:

> If there is any opinion to which the man of uncultivated morals is attached, it is the belief in the necessary connection of punishment and guilt. Punishment is punishment, only where it is deserved. We pay the penalty because we owe it, and for no other reason; and if punishment is inflicted for any other reason whatever than because it is merited by wrong, it is a gross immorality, a crying injustice, an abominable crime, and not what it pretends to be. We may have regard for whatever considerations we please—our own convenience, the good of society, the benefit of the offender; we are fools, and worse, if we fail to do so. Having once the right to punish, we may modify the punishment according to the useful and the pleasant; but these are external to the matter, they cannot give us a right to punish, and nothing can do that but criminal desert. This is not a subject to waste words over; if the fact of the vulgar view is not palpable to the reader, we have no hope, and no wish, to make it so.[29]

Bradley's sympathy with the "vulgar view" should be apparent. And there is at least a seeming variation between the position he expresses here and that we have attributed to Kant and Hegel. For Bradley can be read here as leaving an open field for utilitarian reasoning, when the question is how and how much to punish. Ewing interprets Bradley this way, and argues at some length that Bradley is involved in an inconsistency[30] However, it is quite possible that Bradley did not mean to allow kind and quantity of punishment to be determined by utilitarian considerations. He could mean, as Kant meant, that once punishment is awarded, then "it" (what the criminal must suffer: time in jail, for example) may be made use of for utilitarian purposes. But, it should by this time go without saying, the retributivist would then wish to insist that we not argue backward from the likelihood of attaining these good purposes to the rightness of inflicting the punishment.

Bradley's language is beyond question loose when he speaks, in the passage quoted, of our "modifying" the punishment, "having once the right to punish." But when he says that "we pay the penalty because we owe it, and for no other reason," Bradley must surely be credited with the insight that we may owe more or less according to the gravity of the crime. The popular view, he says, is "that punishment is justice; that justice implies the giving what is due."[31] And "punishment is the complement of criminal desert; is justifiable only so far as deserved."[32] If Bradley accepts this popular view, then Ewing must be wrong in attributing to him the position that kind and degree of punishment may be determined by utilitarian considerations.[33]

III

Let us sum up traditional retributivism, as we have found it expressed in the paradigmatic passage we have examined. We have found no reason in Hegel or Bradley to take back or qualify importantly the *three propositions* we found central in Kant's retributivism:

i. The only acceptable reason for punishing a man is that he has committed a crime.

ii. The only acceptable reason for punishing a man in a given manner and degree is that the punishment is "equal" to the crime.

iii. Whoever commits a crime must be punished in accordance with his desert.

To these propositions should be added *two underlying assumptions:*

i. An assumption about the direction of justification: to the criminal.

ii. An assumption about the nature of justification: To show the criminal that it is he who has willed what he now suffers.

Though it may have been stated in forbidding metaphysical terms, traditional retributivism cannot be dismissed as unintelligible, or absurd, or implausible.[34] There is no obvious contradiction in it; and there are no important disagreements among the philosophers we have studied over what it contends. Yet in spite of the importance of the theory, no one has yet done much more than sketch it in broad strokes. If, as I have surmised, it turns mainly on an assumption concerning the direction of justification, then this assumption should be explained and defended.

And the key concept of "desert" is intolerably vague. What does it mean to say that punishment must be proportionate to what a man *deserves*? This seems to imply, in the theory of the traditional retributivists, that there is some way of measuring desert, or at least of balancing punishment against it. How this measuring or balancing is supposed to be done, we will discuss later. What we must recognize here is that there are alternative criteria of "desert," and that it is not always clear which of these the traditional retributivist means to imply.

When we say of a man that he "deserves severe punishment" how, if at all, may we support our position by arguments? What kind of considerations tend to show what a man does or does not deserve? There are at least two general sorts: those which tend to show that what he has done is a member of a class of action which is especially heinous; and those which tend to show that his doing of this action was, in (or because of) the circumstances, particularly wicked. The argument that a man deserves punishment may rest on the first kind of appeal alone, or on both kinds. Retributivists who rely on the first sort of consideration alone would say that anyone who would do a certain sort of thing, no matter what the circumstances may have been, deserves punishment. Whether there are such retributivists I do not know. Kant, because of his insistence on *intention* as a necessary condition of committing a crime, clearly wishes to bring in considerations of the second sort as well. It is not, on his view, merely *what* was done, but the intention of the agent which must be taken into account. No matter what the intention, a man cannot commit a crime deserving punishment if his deed is not a transgression. But if he does commit a transgression, he must do so intentionally to commit a crime; and all crime is deserving of punishment. The desert of the crime is a factor both of the seriousness of the transgression, considered by itself, and the degree to which the intention to transgress was present. If, for Kant, the essence of morality consists in knowingly acting from duty, the essence of immorality consists in knowingly acting against duty.

The retributivist can perhaps avoid the question of how we decide that one crime is morally more heinous than another by hewing to his position that no such decision is necessary so long as we make the punishment "equal" to the crime. To accomplish this, he might argue, it is not necessary to argue to the *relative* wickedness of crimes. But at best this leaves us with the problem how we *do* make punishments equal to crimes, a problem which will not stop plaguing retributivists. And there is the problem *which* transgressions, intentionally committed, the retributivist is to regard as crimes. Surely not every morally wrong action!

And how is the retributivist to fit in appeals to punitive expediency? None of our authors denies that such appeals may be made, but where and how do they tie into punitive justice? It will not do simply to say that justifying punishment to the criminal is one thing, and justifying it to society is another. Suppose we must justify in both directions at once? And who are "we" anyway—the players of which roles, at what stage of the game? And has the retributivist cleared himself of the charge, sure to arise, that the theory is but a cover for a much less commendable motive than respect for justice: elegant draping for naked revenge?

ENDNOTES

1. ... [S]ince in our own time there are few defenders of retributivism, the position is most often referred to by writers who are opposed to it. This does not make for clarity. In the past few years, however, there has been an upsurge of interest, and some good articles have been written. Cf. esp. J. D. Mabbott, "Punishment," *Mind,* XLVIII (1939), pp. 152–167; C. S. Lewis, "The Humanitarian Theory of Punishment," *20th Century* (Australian), March, 1949; C. W. K. Mundle, "Punishment and Desert," *The Philosophical Quarterly.* IV (1954), pp. 216–228; A. S. Kaufman, "Anthony Quinton on Punishment," *Analysis,* October, 1959; and K. G. Armstrong, "The Retributivist Hits Back," *Mind,* LXX (1961), pp. 471–90.

2. *Rechtslehre.* Part Second, 49, E. Hastie translation, Edinburgh, 1887, pp. 195–197.

3. Ibid., p. 198. Cf. also the passage on p. 196 beginning "What, then, is to be said of such a proposal as to keep a Criminal alive who has been condemned to death...."

4. Ibid., Prolegomena, General Divisions of the Metaphysic of Morals. IV (Hastie, p. 38).

5. Ibid., p. 32.

6. Ibid., p. 32.

7. Book 1, Ch. 1, Sec. VIII, Theorem IV, Remark 11 (T. K. Abbott translation, 5th ed., revised, London, 1898, p. 127).

8. *Rechtslehre.*

9. "Supplementary Explanation of The Principles of Right," V.

10. Cf. long quote from the *Rechtslehre* above.

11. How can the retributivist allow utilitarian considerations even in the administration of the sentence? Are we not then opportunistically imposing our conception of good on the convicted man? How did we come by this right, which we did not have when he stood before the bar awaiting sentence? Kant would refer to the loss of his "Civil Personality"; but what rights remain with the "Inborn Personality," which is not lost? How is human dignity modified by conviction of crime?

12. Introduction to The Science of Right, General Definitions and Divisions, D. Right is Joined with the Title to Compel (Hastie, p. 47).

13. This extends the definition of crime Kant has given earlier by specifying the nature of an imputable transgression of duty.

14. There are serious difficulties in the application of the "Principle of Equality" to the "mode and measure" of punishment. This will be considered....

15. I shall use this short title for the work with the formidable double title of *Naturrecht und Stattswissenschaft in Grundrisse; Grundlinien der Philosophie des Rechts (Natural Law and Political Science in Outline: Elements of the Philosophy of Right)*. References will be to the T. M. Knox translation (*Hegel's Philosophy of Right*, Oxford, 1942).

16. *Philosophie des Rechts*, Sect. 93 (Knox, p. 67).

17. O. W. Holmes, Jr., *The Common Law*, Boston, 1881, p. 42.

18. Hastings Rashdall, *The Theory of Good and Evil*, 2nd. Edn., Oxford, 1924, vol. 1, pp. 285–286.

19. G. E. Moore holds that, consistently with his doctrine of organic wholes, they might; or at least they might yield that which is less evil than the sum of the constituent evils. This indicates for him a possible vindication of the Retributive theory of punishment. (*Principia Ethica*, Cambridge, 1903, pp. 213–214).

20. Included in the Knox translation.

21. Knox translation, pp. 69–70.

22. There is an unfortunate ambiguity in the German word *Recht*, here translated as "right." The word can mean either that which is a right or that which is in accordance with the law. So when Hegel speaks of "infringing the right as right" it is not certain whether he means a right as such or the law as such, or whether, in fact, he is aware of the ambiguity. But to say that the crime infringes the law is analytic, so we will take it that Hegel uses *Recht* here to refer to that which is right. But what the criminal does is not merely to infringe a right, but "the right *(das recht)* as right," that is, to challenge by his action the whole system of rights. (On "*Recht*," Cf. J. Austin, *The Province of Jurisprudence Determined* [London, Library of Ideas Edition, 1954], Note 26, pp. 285–288 esp. pp. 287–288.)

23. J. M. E. McTaggart, *Studies in The Hegelian Cosmology*, Cambridge, 1901, Ch. V, p. 133.

24. Ibid., p. 145.

25. Op. Cit., Sect. 100 (Hastie, p. 70).

26. Ibid., Lecture-notes on Sect. 100, Hastie, p. 71.

27. Ibid., Addition to Sect. 100, Hastie, p. 246.

28. Ibid., Addition to Sect. 101, Hastie, p. 247. There is something ineradicably *curious* about retributivism. We keep coming back to the metaphor of the balance scale. Why is the metaphor powerful and at the same time strange? Why do we agree so readily that "the assassination" cannot "trammel up the consequence," that "even-handed justice commends the ingredients of our poisoned chalice to our own lips?"

29. F. H. Bradley, *Ethical Studies*, Oxford, 1952, pp. 26–27.

30. A. C. Ewing, *The Morality of Punishment*, London, 1929, pp. 41–42.

31. Op. Cit., p. 29.

32. Ibid., p. 30.

33. Op. Cit., p. 41.

34. Or, more ingeniously, "merely logical," the "elucidation of the use of a word"; answering the question, "When (logically) *can* we punish?" as opposed to the question answered by the utilitarians, "When (morally) *may* or *ought* we to punish?" (Cf. A. M. Quinton, "On Punishment," *Analysis*, June, 1954, pp. 133–142.)

70

A Rational Choice Theory of Punishment

JAMES P. STERBA

James P. Sterba attempts to provide a rational choice justification of punishment. He argues that a non-question-begging standard of rationality would lead to Morality as Rational Compromise. He further argues that Morality as Rational Compromise would lead to the principle for Restoring Fairness and the Principle for Fair Procedure for meting out punishment in a basically just society.

All the normative theories of punishment with which I am familiar begin with some particular moral perspective, utilitarian or nonutilitarian, retributivist or nonretributivist, as the case may be, and then proceed to derive specific principles of punishment. The basic problem with this approach is self-evident: Only those who accept the particular moral perspective with which the theories begin will be inclined to accept the specific principles of punishment that are derived therefrom. Those who are committed to other moral perspectives, or to no moral perspective at all, will tend to favor different principles of punishment. In this paper, I propose to remedy this problem by deriving principles of punishment not from some moral perspective or other but from a nonquestion-begging conception of rational choice.

I

Let us begin by imagining the members of a society deliberating over what sort of principles of punishment they should accept. Let us assume that each member is capable of entertaining and acting upon both self-interested and moral reasons and that the question they are seeking to answer is what sort of principles of punishment it would be rational for them to accept.[1] This question is not about what sort of principles of punishment they should publicly affirm since people will sometimes publicly affirm principles that are quite different from those they are prepared to act upon, but rather it is a question of what principles of punishment it would be rational for these individuals to accept at the deepest level—in their heart of hearts.

Obviously, the egoists in the society, assuming that there are some, would think that the only principles of punishment they should accept in this fashion are those that can be derived from the following general principle of egoism:

> Each person ought to do what best serves his or her overall self-interest.

But egoists can no more defend this view by simply denying the relevance of moral reasons to rational choice than can pure altruists by simply denying the relevance of self-interested reasons to rational choice defend the view that the principles of punishment they should accept are those that can be derived from the following general principle of altruism:

> Each person ought to do what best serves the overall interest of others.

Consequently, egoists seem to have no other alternative but to grant the prima facie relevance of moral reasons to rational choice and then try to show that they would never be rationally required to act upon such reasons, all things considered. Likewise, pure altruists seem to have no other alternative by to grant the prima facie relevance of self-interested reasons to rational choice and then try to show that they would never be rationally required to act upon such reasons, all things considered.

In this regard, there are two kinds of cases that must be considered. First, there are cases in which there is a conflict between the relevant self-interested and moral reasons.[2] Second, there are cases in which there is no such conflict.

Now it seems obvious that, where there is no conflict and both reasons are conclusive reasons of their kind, both reasons should be acted upon. In such contexts, we should do what is favored both by morality and by self-interest. Consider the following example: Suppose you accepted a job marketing a baby formula in underdeveloped countries, where the formula was improperly used, leading to increased infant mortality.[3] You could just as well have accepted an equally attractive and rewarding job marketing a similar formula in developed countries, where the misuse does not occur, so that a rational weighing of the relevant self-interested reasons alone would not have favored your acceptance of one of these jobs over the other.[4] At the same time, there were obviously moral reasons that condemned your acceptance of the first job— reasons that you presumably are or were able to acquire. Moreover, by assumption in this case, the moral reasons do not clash with the relevant self-interested reasons; they simply made a recommendation where the relevant self-interested reasons are silent. Consequently, a rational weighing of all the relevant reasons in this case could not but favor acting in accord with the relevant moral reasons.[5]

Obviously egoists can only be disconcerted with this result, since it shows that actions in accord with egoism are contrary to reason, at least when there are two equally good ways of pursuing one's self-interest, only one of which does not conflict with the basic requirements of morality. Nevertheless, exposing this defect in egoism for cases where moral reasons and self-interested reasons do not conflict would be but a small victory if it were not also possible to show that in cases where such reasons do conflict, moral reasons would have priority over self-interested reasons.

Now when one rationally assesses the relevant reasons in such conflict cases, it is best to view the conflict not as a conflict between self-interested reasons and moral reasons, but as a conflict between self-interested reasons and altruistic reasons. Viewed in this way, three solutions are possible. First, one could say that self-interested reasons always have priority over conflicting altruistic reasons. Second, one could say just the opposite: altruistic reasons always have priority over conflicting self-interested reasons. Third, one could say that some kind of compromise is rationally required. In this compromise, sometimes self-interested reasons would have priority over altruistic reasons, and sometimes altruistic reasons would have priority over self-interested reasons.

Once the conflict is described in this manner, the third solution can be seen to be the one that is rationally required. This is because the first and second solutions give exclusive priority to one class of relevant reasons over the other, and no non-question-begging justification can be given for such an exclusive priority. Only the third solution, by sometimes giving priority to self-interested reasons and sometimes giving priority to altruistic reasons, can provide a non-question-begging resolution.[6]

Consider the following example. Suppose you are in the waste disposal business and you decided to dispose of toxic wastes in a manner that was cost-efficient for you but predictably caused significant harm to future generations. Imagine that alternative waste-disposal methods are available to you that were only slightly less cost efficient and did not cause any significant harm to future generations.[7] In this case, you are required to weigh your self-interested reasons favoring the most cost-efficient disposal of the toxic wastes against the relevant altruistic reasons favoring the avoidance of significant harm to future generations.

If we suppose that the projected loss of benefit to your self was ever so slight and the projected harm to future generations was ever so great, a non-arbitrary compromise between the relevant self-interested and altruistic reasons would have to favor the altruistic reasons. Hence, as judged by a non-question-begging standard of rationality, your choice of method of waste disposal was contrary to the relevant reasons.

Notice also that this standard of rationality would not support just any compromise between the relevant self-interested and altruistic reasons. The compromise must be a nonarbitrary one, for otherwise it would beg the question with respect to the opposing egoist and altruist views. Such a compromise would have to respect the rankings of self-interested and altruistic reasons imposed by the egoist and altruist views, respectively. Since for each individual there is a separate ranking of the individual's relevant self-interested and altruistic reasons, we can represent these rankings from the most important to the least important as follows:

Individual A

Self-interested reasons	Altruistic reasons
1	1
2	2
3	3
•	•
•	•
•	•
N	N

Individual B

Self-interested reasons	Altruistic reasons
1	1
2	2
3	3
•	•
•	•
•	•
N	N

Accordingly, any nonarbitrary compromise among such reasons would have to give priority to those reasons that rank highest in each category. Failure to give priority to the highest-ranking altruistic or self-interested reasons would, other things being equal, be contrary to reason.

Of course, there will always be cases in which the only way to avoid being required to do what is contrary to one's highest-ranking reasons is by requiring someone else to do what is contrary to their highest-ranking reasons. Such cases are sometimes called "lifeboat cases." But while such cases are difficult to resolve (maybe only a chance mechanism can offer a reasonable resolution), they surely do not reflect the typical conflict between the relevant self-interested and altruistic reasons that people are capable of acting upon. For typically one or the other of the conflicting reasons will rank higher on its respective scale, thus permitting a clear resolution.

Now it is important to see how morality can be viewed as just such a nonarbitrary compromise between self-interested and altruistic reasons. First, a certain amount of self-regard is morally required or at least morally acceptable. When this is the case, high-ranking self-interested reasons have priority over low-ranking altruistic reasons. Second, morality obviously places limits on the extent to which people should pursue their own self-interest. Where this is the case, high-ranking altruistic reasons have priority over low-ranking self-interested reasons. In this way morality can be seen to be a nonarbitrary compromise between self-interested and altruistic reasons, and the "moral reasons" that constitute that compromise can be seen as having an absolute priority over the self-interested or altruistic reasons that conflict with them.

Unfortunately, this approach to defending morality has been generally neglected by moral theorists. The reason it has been neglected is that moral theorists have tended to view the basic conflict with egoism as a conflict between morality and self-interest. For example, according to Kurt Baier, "The very *raison d'être* of a morality is to yield reasons which overrule the reasons of self-interest in those cases when everyone's following self-interest would be harmful to everyone."[8]

Viewed in this light, it does not seem possible for the defender of morality to support a compromise view, for how can such a defender say that when morality and self-interest conflict, morality should sometimes be sacrificed for the sake of self-interest? But while previous theorists understood correctly that moral reasons could not be compromised in favor of self-interested reasons, they failed to recognize that this is because moral reasons are already the result of a nonarbitrary compromise between self-interested and altruistic reasons. Thus, unable to see how morality could be represented as a rational compromise, previous theorists have generally failed to recognize this approach to defending morality.

II

But what specific principles of punishment would be required by "Morality as Rational Compromise"? Obviously, if we assume that the members of the society will all act in accord with the best reasons, there will be no need for them to worry about principles of punishment. In a society where everyone always act morally, principles of punishment would be superfluous. However, if we assume that at least some members of the society do not always act morally, it does make sense to ask what specific principles of punishment would be required by Morality as Rational Compromise.

Here we need to consider two cases. First, there is the case where immoral actions by some are not so severe as to render the society basically unjust. Second, there is the case where the immoral actions of some are severe enough to render the society basically unjust.

In the first case, those who make themselves criminals by violating the basic requirements of morality would have acted as they did simply to unfairly benefit themselves at the expense of others. They would have had ample legal means of pursuing their own interest. Unlike their victims, they would have had sufficient opportunity to avoid their fate. Accordingly, it would be reasonable to impose a burden on them sufficient to restore as much as possible the fair distribution of benefits and burdens that was disrupted by their criminal activity.

Now criminals, by disrupting the fair distribution of benefits and burdens in a society benefit in two ways. Firstly, when others have assumed the burden of self-restraint required by the criminal law, criminals benefit by renouncing that burden.[9] Secondly, criminals also benefit in a more crime-specific manner, either by illegally depriving others of goods they possess, as in cases of burglary or fraud, or by illegally using force against others to satisfy their desires, as in cases of murder, rape, or assault. More importantly still, criminals sometimes benefit from their crimes more than their victims are harmed by them, e.g., when a wealthy person is robbed of a small sum of money. At other times criminals harm their victims more than they benefit themselves, e.g., when someone is killed for her meager possessions. Taking into account these various ways in which criminals can disrupt a fair distribution of benefits and burdens, the members of the society would be led by Morality as Rational Compromise to the following principle for fixing the amount of punishment:

PRINCIPLE FOR RESTORING FAIRNESS

Punishment is to be restricted to a burden that either prevents criminals from gaining any benefit from crimes or approximates the burden the criminals inflicted on their victims in the first place, whichever is greater.[10]

This punishment would be meted out by depriving criminals of the goods they possess (which are needed to meet compensation, enforcement, and other social welfare costs), and/or by forcing criminals to benefit others (e.g., by providing deterrence, reform or products of their labor). In this way, the burdens to be imposed on criminals would serve to benefit the victims of crime, the legal enforcement systems, and the general public.

Of course this principle of punishment assumes a certain commensurability between benefits and burdens, and some philosophers would surely reject the possibility of such commensurability.[11] Yet the commensability that is presupposed is actually less demanding than might initially appear, for it is not assumed we can make any cardinal interpersonal comparisons of benefits and burden—as, for example, would be required by the claim that the benefit to criminal from her crime was twice as great as the harm to her victim. Rather it is only assumed we can make ordinal interpersonal comparisons—which simply allow us to claim that the benefit a criminal derives from her crime is either greater than, equal to, or less than the harm to her victim, without claiming anything more precise. In other contexts, we do seem to be able to make such comparisons. For instance, in deciding how to allocate family resources, we might judge that Johnny is better off having a new pair of shoes than Suzy is hurt by not having a new catcher's mitt. Or in assessing university policies on leaves and sabbaticals, we might judge that students would benefit more from a policy of limiting leaves and sabbaticals than professors would be harmed by such a policy. Consequently, there seems to be no reason to think that the member of a society cannot make the same sort of ordinal interpersonal comparisons implementing this principle of punishment.

Moreover, it would surely suffice for fixing the amount of punishment to simply compare the benefit that criminals *standardly* derive from particular crimes with the harm their victims *standardly* suffer from such crimes. In fact, it may be the case that all that can be done in making this assessment is to group crimes into four or five different categories.[12] Of course, more precise information about particular criminals and the particular victims would certainly be relevant when available, but it would not be necessary for implementing the Principle for Restoring Fairness.

Nevertheless this principle of punishment would apply straightforwardly only in cases in which a person has been fairly determined to be fully culpable for committing a crime. It is not enough that a fair distribution of benefits and burdens be achieved as much as possible. The means of achieving that distribution must also be fair. Accordingly,

the society's legal enforcement system would have to have certain safeguards against punishing behavior that was excusable for reasons of accident, mistake, provocation, duress, or insanity. This means that punishment would only be morally justified when it is inflicted on a person who has committed an offense with the cognitive and volitional conditions of *mens rea*. On the same account, the society would need procedural safeguards against punishing the innocent, safeguards such as the requirement of conduct, the presumption of innocence, and the evidentiary restrictions of due process. In short, the society would require the following principle:

PRINCIPLE FOR FAIR PROCEDURE

Punishment is to be applied only when
1) there are excusing conditions based on a general requirement of *mens rea*, and
2) there are safeguards to protect the innocent, safeguards such as the requirement of conduct, the presumption of innocence, and the evidentiary restrictions of due process.

So in a basically just society, punishment must be meted out in accord with both the Principle for Restoring Fairness and the Principle for Fair Procedure. Futhermore, there is no reason not to apply these principles strictly because in a basically just society the comparative opportunity judgment that the criminal, unlike the victim of crime, could have been reasonably expected to act otherwise would generally hold true for the broadest range of criminal activity.

Unfortunately, in a basically unjust society, the situation would be radically different. In a basically unjust society, there would be widespread violations of people's basic rights with the consequence that many people would be deprived of a reasonable opportunity to lead a good life. Frequently, this deprivation would be reflected in an unjust distribution of property since the opportunities people have are frequently a function of the property they control or the property that is controlled by the family or friends. (For example, the lack of opportunity many people experience in the United States is not unrelated to the fact that 10% of families own 57% of the total net wealth and 86% of total financial assets).[13] Of course, in order to know when people have been deprived of a reasonable opportunity to lead a good life we need to know what are morally defensible principles of distributive justice.

Elsewhere I have attempted to establish what are morally defensible principles of distributive justice in the same way that I have sought to establish the foregoing principles of punishment by ultimately basing their defense on the same nonquestion-begging standard of rationality.[14] Here I will simply assume the main result of that defense which is that every member of society has a basic right to welfare and equal opportunity. Accordingly, in a basically unjust society, basic rights of welfare and equal opportunity would be widely rejected with the consequence that many people would lack the resources and opportunities necessary for leading a decent life.

Now suppose that one of these individuals who has been unfairly deprived commits a crime in order to secure for herself the opportunities essential for her basic welfare. Should she be punished? As we have seen, the grounds for applying the foregoing principles of punishment in a basically just society is the comparative opportunity judgment that the criminal, unlike the victim of crime, could have been reasonably expected to act otherwise. Yet while this comparative opportunity judgment generally holds in a basically just society, it does not generally hold in a basically unjust society. And in cases where it fails to hold, there would be no grounds for punishing criminal activity.

But what specifically would characterize cases in which punishing criminal activity would not be justified? First, in these cases, other options (e.g., legal protest, civil disobedience, or revolutionary action) would have to be either ineffective for achieving reasonable progress toward a just society or too costly for those persons they would be intended to benefit. Secondly, in these cases, there would only be minimal violations of the moral rights of others as determined by defensible principles of distributive justice. This means that in these cases the criminal activity would be directed at appropriating surplus goods from people who have more than a fair share of opportunities to lead a good life, and appropriating

such goods with a minimum of physical force. Hence, criminal activity that harms the less advantaged in society would not be justified. Nor would it be justified to kill or seriously injure the more advantaged, except in self-defense, when attempting to dispossess them of their unjust holdings. Accordingly, the members of the society would favor the following principle:

PRINCIPLE FOR WITHHOLDING PUNISHMENT

Punishment should be withheld from persons who engage in criminal activity that 1) is undertaken after other options for achieving reasonable progress toward a just society have proven ineffective or too costly for those whom they are intended to benefit and that 2) involves only minimal violations of the moral rights of others.

Thus, in a basically unjust society, the Principle for Withholding Punishment combines with the Principle for Restoring Fairness and the Principle for Fair Procedure to determine when punishment should be meted out and when it should be withheld. In general, in a basically unjust society, punishment will still be justified for most crimes against persons but for only *some* crimes against property. Happily, for those who dislike the limited justification for punishment in a basically unjust society there is an appropriate remedy: Provide a fairer distribution of benefits and burdens in the society and more punishment for crimes will then be justified.

In sum, I have attempted to provide a rational choice justification for punishment. I have argued that a non-question-begging standard of rationality would lead to Morality as Rational Compromise. I further argued that Morality as Rational Compromise would lead to the principle for Restoring Fairness and the Principle for Fair Procedure for meting out punishment in a basically just society and to these two principles combined with the Principle for Withholding Punishment for meting out punishment in a basically unjust society. The next step is to suggest specific radical reforms that are required for our own system of punishment.

ENDNOTES

1. "Ought" presupposes "can" here. Unless the members of the society have the capacity to entertain and follow both self-interested and moral reasons for acting, it does not make any sense asking whether they ought or ought not to do so.

2. For an account of what counts as *relevant* self-interested or moral reasons, see my *How to Make People Just* (Totowa, NJ: Rowman & Littlefield, 1988), 165–66.

3. For a discussion of the causal links involved here, see *Marketing and Promotion of Infant Formula in Developing Countries*, hearing before the Subcommittee of International Economic Policy and Trade of the Committee on Foreign Affairs, U.S. House of Representatives, 1980. See also Maggie McComas et al., *The Dilemma of Third World Nutrition* (Washington, DC: GPO, 1983).

4. Assume that both jobs have the same beneficial effects on the interests of others.

5. I am assuming that acting contrary to reason is an important failing with respect to the requirements of reason, and that there are many ways of not acting in (perfect) accord with reason that do no constitute acting contrary to reason.

6. For a slight qualification, see "How To Make People Moral" (forthcoming).

7. Assume that all these methods of waste disposal have roughly the same amount of beneficial effects on the interests of others.

8. Kurt Baier, *The Moral Point of View* (Ithaca: Cornell UP, 1958), 150.

9. Herbert Morris and Andrew Von Hirsch appear to restrict the role of the fair distribution rationale to correcting for just this type of benefit to the criminal. See Herbert Morris, "Persons and Punishment," *The Monist* (1968) 475–501; and Andrew von Hirsh, *Doing Justice* (New York: 1976), 160–61, 40.

10. Of course, if there were some noncoercive way of restoring a fair distribution of benefits and burdens, such an alternative would clearly be morally preferable to the use of punishment. However, it is hard to imagine how this would ever be the case. I owe this point to Hugo Bedau.

11. See George Sher, "An Unsolved Problem about Punishment," *Social Theory and Practice* (1977): 156–57; Hugo Bedau, "Retributivism and the Concept of Punishment," *The Journal of Philosophy* (1978), 612–13; Richard Wasserstrom, *Philosophy and Social Issues* (South Bend, IN: U of Notre Dame P, 1980), 143–46. For a more general challenge to the possibility of such comensurability, see Kenneth Arrow, *Social Choice and Individual Values*, 2nd ed. (New Haven, CT: Yale UP, 1963) and my response, "A Rawlsian Solution to Arrow's Paradox," *Pacific Philosophical Quarterly* (1981): 282–92.

12. For a similar view, see Von Hirsch, 82–83.

13. Federal Reserve Board, "Survey of Consumer Finances, 1983: A Second Report," reprinted from the *Federal Reserve Bulletin* (Washington, DC, Dec. 1984) 857–68. Richard Parker, *The Myth of the Middle Class* (New York: Harper & Row, 1972), 212.

14. *How To Make People Just*. I have also tried to show how contemporary conceptions of justice can be practically reconciled.

71

Deterrence and Uncertainty

ERNEST VAN DEN HAAG

Ernest van den Haag argues that although we don't know for sure whether capital punishment deters would-be offenders, the greater severity of capital punishment still gives us reason to expect more deterrence from it. Accordingly, van den Haag maintains that the burden of proof is on opponents of capital punishment to show why the greater severity of capital punishment does not lead to more deterrence.

If we do not know whether the death penalty will deter others [in a uniquely effective way], we are confronted with two uncertainties. If we impose the death penalty, and achieve no deterrent effect thereby, the life of a convicted murderer has been expended in vain (from a deterrent viewpoint). There is a net loss. If we impose the death sentence and thereby deter some future murderers, we spared the lives of some future victims (the prospective murderers gain too; they are spared punishment because they were deterred). In this case, the death penalty has led to a net gain, unless the life of a convicted murderer is valued more highly than that of the unknown victim, or victims (and the nonimprisonment of the deterred nonmurderer).

The calculation can be turned around, of course. The absence of the death penalty may harm no one and therefore produce a gain—the life of the convicted murderer. Or it may kill future victims of murderers who could have been deterred, and thus produce a loss—their life.

To be sure, we must risk something certain—the death (or life) of the convicted man, for something uncertain—the death (or life) of the victims of murderers who may be deterred. This is in the nature of uncertainty—when we invest, or gamble, we risk the money we have for an uncertain gain. Many human actions, most commitments—including marriage and crime—share this characteristic with the deterrent purpose of any penalization, and with its rehabilitative purpose (and even with the protective).

More proof is demanded for the deterrent effect of the death penalty than is demanded for the deterrent effect of other penalties. This is not justified by the absence of other utilitarian purposes such as protection and rehabilitation; they involve no less uncertainty than deterrence.[1]

Irrevocability may support a demand for some reason to expect more deterrence than revocable penalties might produce, but not a demand for more proof of deterrence.... The reason for expecting more deterrence lies in the greater severity, the terrifying effect inherent in finality. Since it seems more important to spare victims than ... murderers, the burden of proving that the greater severity inherent in irrevocability adds nothing to deterrence lies on those who oppose capital punishment. Proponents of the death penalty need show only that there is no more uncertainty about it than about greater severity in general.

The demand that the death penalty be proved more deterrent than alternatives cannot be satisfied

Reprinted with permission of the publisher from the *Journal of Criminal Law, Criminology and Political Science,* vol. 60, no. 2 (1969).

any more than the demand that six years in prison be proved to be more deterrent than three. But the uncertainty that confronts us favors the death penalty as long as [it] might save future victims of murder. This effect is as plausible as the general idea that penalties have deterrent effects which increase with their severity. Though we have no proof of the positive deterrence of the penalty, we also have no proof of zero, or negative effectiveness. I believe we have no right to risk additional future victims of murder for the sake of sparing convicted murderers; on the contrary, our moral obligation is to risk the possible ineffectiveness of executions. However rationalized, the opposite view appears to be motivated by the simple fact that executions are more subjected to social control than murder. However, this applies to all penalties and does not argue for the abolition of any.

ENDNOTE

1. Rehabilitation or protection are of minor importance in our actual penal system (though not in our theory). We confine many people who do not need rehabilitation and against whom we do not need protection (e.g., the exasperated husband who killed his wife); we release many unrehabilitated offenders against whom protection is needed. Certainly rehabilitation and protection are not, and deterrence is, the main actual function of legal punishment, if we disregard nonutilitarian purposes.

72

Justice, Civilization, and the Death Penalty: Answering van den Haag

JEFFREY H. REIMAN

Jeffrey Reiman maintains that greater severity in and of itself does not mean more deterrence. Moreover, Reiman argues if greater severity were always justified on grounds of producing more deterrence, then torturing criminals to death would be justified because torturing criminals to death is clearly a more severe punishment than simply executing them.

... By placing execution alongside torture in the category of things we will not do to our fellow human beings even when they deserve them, we broadcast the message that totally subjugating a person to the power of others *and* confronting him with the advent of his own humanly administered demise is too horrible to be done by civilized human beings to their fellows even when they have earned it: too horrible to do, and too horrible to be capable of doing. And I contend that broadcasting this message loud and clear would in the long run contribute to the general detestation of murder and be, to the extent to which it worked itself into the hearts and minds of the populace, a deterrent. In short, refusing to execute murderers though they deserve it both reflects and continues the taming of the human species that we call civilization. Thus, I take it that the abolition of the death penalty, though it is a just punishment for murder, is part of the civilizing mission of modern states....

... I said that judging a practice too horrible to do even to those who deserve it does not exclude the possibility that it could be justified if necessary to avoid even worse consequences. Thus, were the death penalty clearly proven a better deterrent to the murder of innocent people than life in prison, we might have to admit that we had not yet reached a level of civilization at which we could protect ourselves without imposing this horrible fate on murderers, and thus we might have to grant the necessity of instituting the death penalty. But this is far from proven. The available research by no means clearly indicates that the death penalty reduces the incidence of homicide more than life imprisonment does....

Conceding that it has not been proven that the death penalty deters more murders than life imprisonment, van den Haag has argued that neither has it been proven that the death penalty does *not* deter more murders, and thus we must follow common sense which teaches that the higher the cost of something, the fewer people will choose it, and therefore at least some potential murderers who would not be deterred by life imprisonment will be deterred by the death penalty. Van den Haag writes:

... our experience shows that the greater the threatened penalty, the more it deters.

... Life in prison is still life, however unpleasant. In contrast, the death penalty

From Jeffrey H. Reiman, "Justice, Civilization, and the Death Penalty: Answering van den Haag." *Philosophy and Public Affairs*, vol. 14 (Spring 1985). Excerpt, pp. 141–147. © 1985 John Wiley & Sons. Reprinted with permission of Blackwell Publishing Ltd.

does not just threaten to make life unpleasant—it threatens to take life altogether. This difference is perceived by those affected. We find that when they have the choice between life in prison and execution, 99 percent of all prisoners under sentence of death prefer life in prison....

From this unquestioned fact a reasonable conclusion can be drawn in favor of the superior deterrent effect of the death penalty. Those who have the choice in practice ... fear death more than they fear life in prison.... If they do, it follows that the threat of the death penalty, all other things equal, is likely to deter more than the threat of life in prison. One is most deterred by what one fears most. From which it follows that whatever statistics fail, or do not fail, to show, the death penalty is likely to be more deterrent than any other.[1]

Those of us who recognize how common sensical it was, and still is, to believe that the sun moves around the earth, will be less willing than Professor van den Haag to follow common sense here, especially when it comes to doing something awful to our fellows. Moreover, there are good reasons for doubting common sense on this matter. Here are four:

1. From the fact that one penalty is more feared than another, it does not follow that the more feared penalty will deter more than the less feared, unless we know that the less feared penalty is not fearful enough to deter everyone who can be deterred— and this is just what we don't know with regard to the death penalty. Though I fear the death penalty more than life in prison, I can't think of any act that the death penalty would deter me from that an equal likelihood of spending my life in prison wouldn't deter me from as well. Since it seems to me that whoever would be deterred by a given likelihood of death would be deterred by an *equal* likelihood of life behind bars, I suspect that the

commonsense argument only seems plausible because we evaluate it unconsciously assuming that potential criminals will face larger likelihoods of death sentences than of life sentences. If the likelihoods were equal, ... where life imprisonment was improbable enough to make it too distant a possibility to worry much about, a similar low probability of death would have the same effect. After all, we are undeterred by small likelihoods of death every time we walk the streets. And if life imprisonment were sufficiently probable to pose a real deterrent threat, it would pose as much of a deterrent threat as death. And this is just what most of the research we have on the comparative deterrent impact of execution versus life imprisonment suggests.

2. In light of the fact that roughly 500 to 700 suspected felons are killed by the police in the line of duty every year, and the fact that the number of privately owned guns in [the United States] is substantially larger than the number of households ..., it must be granted that anyone contemplating committing a crime *already* faces a substantial risk of ending up dead.... It's hard to see why anyone *who is not already deterred by this* would be deterred by the addition of the more distant risk of death after apprehension, conviction, and appeal. Indeed, this suggests that people consider risks in a much cruder way than van den Haag's appeal to common sense suggests— which should be evident to anyone who contemplates how few people use seatbelts (14 percent of drivers, on some estimates), when it is widely known that wearing them can spell the difference between life (outside prison) and death.

3. Van den Haag has maintained that deterrence does not work only by means of cost-benefit calculations made by potential criminals. It works also by the lesson about the wrongfulness of murder that is slowly

learned in a society that subjects murderers to the ultimate punishment.[2] But if I am correct in claiming that the refusal to execute even those who deserve it has a civilizing effect, then the refusal to execute also teaches a lesson about the wrongfulness of murder. My claim here is admittedly speculative, but no more so than van den Haag's to the contrary. [My] view has the added virtue of accounting for the failure of research to show an increased deterrent effect from executions *without having to deny the plausibility of van den Haag's commonsense argument that at least some additional potential murders will be deterred by the prospect of the death penalty.* If there is a deterrent effect from *not executing,* then ... while executions will deter some murderers, this effect will be balanced by the weakening of the deterrent effect of not executing, such that no net reduction in murders will result. And this ... also disposes of van den Haag's argument that, in the absence of knowledge one way or the other on the deterrent effect of executions, we should execute murderers rather than risk the lives of innocent people whose murders might have been deterred.... If there is a deterrent effect of not executing, it follows that we risk innocent lives either way. And if this is so, it seems that the only reasonable course of action is to refrain from imposing what we know is a horrible fate.

4. Those who still think that van den Haag's commonsense argument for executing murderers is valid will find that the argument proves more than they bargained for.

Van den Haag maintains that, in the absence of conclusive evidence on the relative deterrent impact of the death penalty versus life imprisonment, we must follow common sense and assume that if one punishment is more fearful than another, it will deter some potential criminals not deterred by the less fearful punishment. Since people sentenced to death will almost universally try to get their sentences changed to life in prison, it follows that death is more fearful than life imprisonment, and thus ... will deter some additional murderers. Consequently, we should institute the death penalty to save the lives these additional murderers would have taken. But, since people sentenced to be tortured to death would surely try to get their sentences changed to simple execution, the same argument proves that death-by-torture will deter still more potential murderers. Consequently, we should institute death-by-torture to save the lives these additional murderers would have taken. Anyone who accepts van den Haag's argument is then confronted with a dilemma: Until we have conclusive evidence that capital punishment is a greater deterrent to murder than life imprisonment, he must grant *either* that we should not follow common sense and not impose the death penalty; *or* we should follow common sense and torture murderers to death. In short, either we must abolish the electric chair or reinstitute the rack. Surely, this is the *reductio ad absurdum* of van den Haag's commonsense argument.

ENDNOTES

1. Ernest van don Haag and John P. Conrad, *The Death Penalty: A Debate* (New York: Plenum Press, 1983), pp. 68–69.

2. Ibid., 63.

73

Gregg v. Georgia

Supreme Court of the United States

The issue before the Supreme Court of the United States was whether capital punishment violates the Eighth Amendment's prohibition of cruel and unusual punishment. The majority of the Court held that it does not violate this prohibition because capital punishment (1) accords with contemporary standards of decency, (2) may serve some deterrent or retributive purpose that is not degrading to human dignity, and (3) is no longer arbitrarily applied in the case of the Georgia law under review. Dissenting Justice Brennan argued that (1) through (3) do not suffice to show that capital punishment is constitutional; it would further have to be shown that capital punishment is not degrading to human dignity. Dissenting Justice Marshall objected to the majority's decision on the grounds that capital punishment is not necessary for deterrence and that a retributive purpose for it is not consistent with human dignity. He also contended that contemporary standards of decency with respect to capital punishment are not based on informed opinion.

We address initially the basic contention that the punishment of death for the crime of murder is, under all circumstances, "cruel and unusual" in violation of the Eighth and Fourteenth Amendments of the Constitution....

The Court on a number of occasions has both assumed and asserted the constitutionality of capital punishment. In several cases that assumption provided a necessary foundation for the decision, as the Court was asked to decide whether a particular method of carrying out a capital sentence would be allowed to stand under the Eighth Amendment. But until *Furman v. Georgia* (1972), the Court never confronted squarely the fundamental claim that the punishment of death always, regardless of the enormity of the offense or the procedure followed in imposing the sentence, is cruel and unusual punishment in violation of the Constitution. Although this issue was presented and addressed in *Furman,* it was not resolved.... Four Justices would have held that capital punishment is not unconstitutional *per se;* two Justices would have reached the opposite

conclusion; and three Justices, while agreeing that the statutes then before the Court were invalid as applied, left open the question whether such punishment may ever be imposed. We now hold that the punishment of death does not invariably violate the Constitution....

It is clear from the foregoing precedents that the Eighth Amendment has not been regarded as a static concept. As Mr. Chief Justice Warren said, in an oft-quoted phrase, "[T]he Amendment must draw its meaning from the evolving standards of decency that mark the progress of a maturing society." ... Thus, an assessment of contemporary values concerning the infliction of a challenged sanction is relevant to the application of the Eighth Amendment. As we develop below more fully, this assessment does not call for a subjective judgment. It requires, rather, that we look to objective indicia that reflect the public attitude toward a given sanction.

But our cases also make clear that public perceptions of standards of decency with respect to criminal sanctions are not conclusive. A penalty also must accord with "the dignity of man," which is the "basic concept underlying the Eighth Amendment" This means, at least, that the punishment not be "excessive." When a form of punishment in the abstract (in this case, whether capital punishment may ever be imposed as a sanction for murder) rather than in the particular (the propriety of death as a penalty to be applied to a specific defendant for a specific crime) is under consideration, the inquiry into "excessiveness" has two aspects. First, the punishment must not involve the unnecessary and wanton infliction of pain. Second, the punishment must not be grossly out of proportion to the severity of the crime.

Of course, the requirements of the Eighth Amendment must be applied with an awareness of the limited role to be played by the courts. This does not mean that judges have no role to play, for the Eighth Amendment is a restraint upon the exercise of legislative power....

But, while we have an obligation to insure that constitutional bounds are not overreached, we may not act as judges as we might as legislators.

> Courts are not representative bodies. They are not designed to be a good reflex of a democratic society. Their judgment is best informed, and therefore most dependable, within narrow limits. Their essential quality is detachment, founded on independence. History teaches that the independence of the judiciary is jeopardized when courts become embroiled in the passions of the day and assume primary responsibility in choosing between competing political, economic and social pressures. *Dennis v. United States* (1951)

Therefore, in assessing a punishment selected by a democratically elected legislature against the constitutional measure, we presume its validity. We may not require the legislature to select the least severe penalty possible so long as the penalty selected is not cruelly inhumane or disproportionate to the crime involved. And a heavy burden rests on those who would attack the judgment of the representatives of the people.

This is true in part because the constitutional test is intertwined with an assessment of contemporary standards and the legislative judgment weighs heavily in ascertaining such standards. "[I]n a democratic society legislatures, not courts, are constituted to respond to the will and consequently the moral values of the people." *Furman v. Georgia.* The deference we owe to the decisions of the state legislatures under our federal system, is enhanced where the specification of punishments is concerned, for "these are peculiarly questions of legislative policy." *Gore v. United States....* A decision that a given punishment is impermissible under the Eighth Amendment cannot be reversed short of a constitutional amendment. The ability of the people to express their preference through the normal democratic processes, as well as through ballot referenda, is shut off. Revisions cannot be made in the light of further experience.

... We now consider specifically whether ... death for the crime of murder is a *per se* violation of the Eighth and Fourteenth Amendments to the Constitution. We note first that history and precedent strongly support a negative answer to this question.

The imposition of the death penalty for the crime of murder has a long history of acceptance both in the United States and in England. The common-law rule imposed a mandatory death sentence on all convicted murderers. And the penalty continued to be used into the twentieth century by most American States, although the breadth of the common-law rule was diminished, initially by narrowing the class of murders to be punished by death and subsequently by widespread adoption of laws expressly granting juries the discretion to recommend mercy.

It is apparent from the text of the Constitution itself that the existence of capital punishment was accepted by the Framers. At the time the Eighth Amendment was ratified, capital punishment was a common sanction in every State. Indeed, the First Congress of the United States enacted legislation providing death as the penalty for specific crimes....

For nearly two centuries, this Court, repeatedly and often expressly, has recognized that capital punishment is not invalid *per se....*

Four years ago, the petitioners in *Furman* and its companion cases predicated their argument primarily on the asserted proposition that standards of decency had evolved to the point where capital punishment no longer could be tolerated. The petitioners in those cases said, in effect, that the evolutionary process had come to an end, and that standards of decency required that the Eighth Amendment be construed finally as prohibiting capital punishment for any crime regardless of its depravity and impact on society. This view was accepted by two Justices. Three others were unwilling to go so far; focusing on the procedures by which convicted defendants were selected for the death penalty rather than on the actual punishment inflicted, they joined in the conclusion that the statutes before the Court were constitutionally invalid.

The petitioners ... before the Court today renew the "standards of decency" argument, but developments ... since *Furman* have undercut substantially the assumptions on which their argument rested. Despite the continuing debate, dating back to the nineteenth century, over the morality and utility of capital punishment, it is now evident that a large proportion of American society continues to regard it as an appropriate and necessary criminal sanction.

The most marked indication of society's endorsement of the death penalty for murder is the legislative response to *Furman*. The legislatures of at least thirty-five States have enacted new statutes that provide for the death penalty for at least some crimes that result in the death of another person. And the Congress of the United States, in 1974, enacted a statute providing the death penalty for aircraft piracy that results in death. These recently adopted statutes have attempted to address the concerns expressed by the Court in *Furman* primarily (i) by specifying the factors to be weighed and the procedures to be followed in deciding when to impose a capital sentence, or (ii) by making the death penalty mandatory for specified crimes. But all of the *post-Furman* statutes make clear that capital punishment itself has not been rejected by the elected representatives of the people....

As we have seen, however, the Eighth Amendment demands more than that a challenged punishment be acceptable to contemporary society. The Court also must ask whether it comports with the basic concept of human dignity at the core of the Amendment. Although we cannot "invalidate a category of penalties because we deem less severe penalties adequate to serve the ends of penology," the sanction imposed cannot be so totally without penological justification that it results in the gratuitous infliction of suffering.

The death penalty is said to serve two principal social purposes: retribution and deterrence of capital crimes by prospective offenders.

In part, capital punishment is an expression of society's moral outrage at particularly offensive conduct. This function may be unappealing to many, but it is essential in an ordered society that asks its citizens to rely on legal processes rather than self-help to vindicate their wrongs.

> The instinct for retribution is part of the nature of man, and channeling that instinct in the administration of criminal justice serves an important purpose in promoting the stability of a society governed by law. When people begin to believe that organized society is unwilling or unable to impose upon criminal offenders the punishment they "deserve," then there are sown the seeds of anarchy—of self-help, vigilante justice, and lynch law. *Furman v. Georgia.*

"Retribution is no longer the dominant objective of the criminal law," but neither is it a forbidden objective nor one inconsistent with our respect for the dignity of men. Indeed, the decision that capital punishment may be the appropriate sanction in extreme cases is an expression of the community's belief that certain crimes are themselves so grievous an affront to humanity that the only adequate response may be the penalty of death.

Statistical attempts to evaluate the worth of the death penalty as a deterrent to crimes by potential offenders have occasioned a great deal of debate.

The results simply have been inconclusive. As one opponent of capital punishment has said:

> [A]fter all possible inquiry, including the probing of all possible methods of inquiry, we do not know; and for systematic and easily visible reasons cannot know; what the truth about this "deterrent" effect may be....
>
> The inescapable flaw is ... that social conditions in any state are not constant through time, and that social conditions are not the same in any two states. If an effect were observed (and the observed effects, one way or another, are not large) then one could not at all tell whether any of this effect is attributable to the presence or absence of capital punishment. A "scientific"—that is to say, a soundly based—conclusion is simply impossible, and no methodological path out of this tangle suggests itself. C. Black, *Capital Punishment: The Inevitability of Caprice and Mistake* 25–26 (1974).

Although some of the studies suggest that the death penalty may not function as a significantly greater deterrent than lesser penalties, there is no convincing empirical evidence either supporting or refuting this view. We may nevertheless assume safely that there are murderers, such as those who act in passion, for whom the threat of death has little or no deterrent effect. But for many others, the death penalty undoubtedly is a significant deterrent. There are carefully contemplated murders, such as murder for hire, where the possible penalty of death may well enter into the cold calculus that precedes the decision to act. And there are some categories of murder, such as murder by a life prisoner, where other sanctions may not be adequate.

The value of capital punishment as a deterrent of crime is a complex factual issue the resolution of which properly rests with the legislatures, which can evaluate the results of statistical studies in terms of their own local conditions and with a flexibility of approach that is not available to the courts....

In sum, we cannot say that the judgment of the Georgia Legislature that capital punishment may be necessary in some cases is clearly wrong. Considerations of federalism, as well as respect for the ability of a legislature to evaluate, in terms of its particular State, the moral consensus concerning the death penalty and its social utility as a sanction, require us to conclude, in the absence of more convincing evidence, that the infliction of death as a punishment for murder is not without justification and thus is not unconstitutionally severe.

Finally, we must consider whether the punishment of death is disproportionate in relation to the crime for which it is imposed. There is no question that death as a punishment is unique in its severity and irrevocability. When a defendant's life is at stake, the Court has been particularly sensitive to insure that every safeguard is observed. But we are concerned here only with the imposition of capital punishment for the crime of murder, and when a life has been taken deliberately by the offender, we cannot say that the punishment is invariably disproportionate to the crime. It is an extreme sanction, suitable to the most extreme of crimes.

We hold that the death penalty is not a form of punishment that may never be imposed, regardless of the circumstances of the offense, regardless of the character of the offender, and regardless of the procedure followed in reaching the decision to impose it.

We now consider whether Georgia may impose the death penalty on the petitioner in this case....

The basic concern of *Furman* centered on those defendants who were being condemned to death capriciously and arbitrarily. Under the procedures before the Court in that case, sentencing authorities were not directed to give attention to the nature or circumstances of the crime committed or the [defendant's] character or record.... Left unguided, juries imposed the death sentence in a way that could only be called freakish. The new Georgia sentencing procedures, by contrast, focus the jury's attention on the particularized nature of the crime and the particularized characteristics of the individual defendant. While the jury is permitted to consider any aggravating or mitigating circumstances, it must find and identify at least one statutory aggravating factor before it may impose a penalty of death. In this way the jury's discretion is channeled. No longer can a jury wantonly and freakishly impose the death sentence; it is always circumscribed by legislative guidelines. In addition, the review function of the Supreme Court of Georgia affords additional assurance that the concerns that prompted our decision in *Furman* are not present to any significant degree in the Georgia procedure applied here.

For the reasons expressed in this opinion, we hold that the statutory system under which Gregg was sentenced to death does not violate the Constitution. Accordingly, the judgment of the Georgia Supreme Court is affirmed....

Mr. Justice *Brennan*, dissenting.[1]

The Cruel and Unusual Punishments Clause "must draw its meaning from the evolving standards of decency that mark the progress of a maturing society." The opinions of Mr. Justice Stewart, Mr. Justice Powell, and Mr. Justice Stevens today hold that "evolving standards of decency" require focus not on the essence of the death penalty itself but primarily upon the procedures employed by the State to single out persons to suffer the penalty of death. Those opinions hold further that, so viewed, the Clause invalidates the mandatory infliction of the death penalty but not its infliction under sentencing procedures that Mr. Justice Stewart, Mr. Justice Powell, and Mr. Justice Stevens conclude adequately safeguard against the risk that the death penalty was imposed in an arbitrary and capricious manner.

In *Furman v. Georgia,* I read "evolving standards of decency" as requiring focus on the essence of the death penalty itself and not primarily or solely on the procedures under which the determination to inflict the penalty upon a particular person was made....

This Court inescapably has the duty, as the ultimate arbiter of the meaning of our Constitution, to say whether, when individuals condemned to death stand before our Bar, "moral concepts" require us to hold that the law has progressed to the point where we should declare that the punishment of death, like punishments on the rack, the screw, and the wheel, is no longer morally tolerable in our civilized society. My opinion in *Furman v. Georgia* concluded that our civilization and the law had progressed to this point and that therefore the punishment of death, for whatever crime and under all circumstances, is "cruel and unusual" in violation of the Eighth and Fourteenth Amendments of the Constitution. I shall not again canvass the reasons that led to that conclusion. I emphasize only that foremost among the "moral concepts" recognized in our cases and inherent in the Clause is the primary moral principle that the State, even as it punishes, must treat its citizens in a manner consistent with their intrinsic worth as human beings—a punishment must not be so severe as to be degrading to human dignity. A judicial determination whether the punishment of death comports with human dignity is therefore not only permitted but compelled by the Clause.

... Death for whatever crime and under all circumstances "is truly an awesome punishment. The calculated killing of a human being by the State involves, by its very nature, a denial of the executed person's humanity.... An executed person has indeed 'lost the right to have rights.'" Death is not only an unusually severe punishment, unusual in its pain in its finality, and in its enormity, but it serves no penal purpose more effectively than a less severe punishment; therefore the principle inherent in the Clause that prohibits pointless infliction of excessive punishment when less severe punishment can adequately achieve the same purposes invalidates the punishment....

Mr. Justice *Marshall,* dissenting.

... My sole purposes here are to consider the suggestion that my conclusion in *Furman* has been undercut by developments since then, and briefly to evaluate the basis for my Brethren's holding that the extinction of life is a permissible form of punishment under the Cruel and Unusual Punishments Clause.

In *Furman* I concluded that the death penalty is constitutionally invalid for two reasons. First, the death penalty is excessive. And second, the American people, fully informed as to the purposes of the death penalty and its liabilities, would in my view reject it as morally unacceptable.

Since the decision in *Furman,* the legislatures of thirty-five States have enacted new statutes authorizing the imposition of the death sentence for certain crimes, and Congress has enacted a law providing the death penalty for air piracy resulting in death. I would be less than candid if I did not acknowledge that these developments have a significant bearing on a realistic assessment of the moral acceptability of the death penalty to the American people. But if the constitutionality of the death penalty turns, as I have urged, on the opinion of an *informed* citizenry, then even the enactment of new death statutes cannot be viewed as conclusive. In *Furman,* I observed that the American people are largely unaware of the information critical to a judgment on the morality of the death penalty, and concluded that if they were better informed they would consider it shocking, unjust, and unacceptable. A recent study, conducted after the enactment of the *post-Furman* statutes, has confirmed that the American people know little about the death penalty, and that the opinions of an informed public would differ significantly from those of a public unaware of the consequences and effects of the death penalty.

Even assuming, however, that the *post-Furman* enactment of statutes authorizing the death penalty renders the prediction of the views of an informed citizenry an uncertain basis for a constitutional decision, the enactment of those statutes has no bearing whatsoever on the conclusion that the death penalty is unconstitutional because it is excessive. An excessive penalty is invalid under the Cruel and Unusual Punishments Clause "even though popular sentiment may favor" it. The inquiry here, then, is simply whether the death penalty is necessary to accomplish the legitimate legislative purposes in punishment, or whether a less severe penalty—life imprisonment—would do as well.

The two purposes that sustain the death penalty as nonexcessive in the Court's view are general deterrence and retribution. In *Furman,* I canvassed the relevant data on the deterrent effect of capital punishment. The state of knowledge at that point, after literally centuries of debate, was summarized as follows by a United Nations Committee:

It is generally agreed between the retentionists and abolitionists, whatever their opinions about the validity of comparative studies of deterrence, that the data which now exist show no correlation between the existence of capital punishment and lower rates of capital crime.

The available evidence, I concluded in *Furman,* was convincing that "capital punishment is not necessary as a deterrent to crime in our society."

The Solicitor General in his *amicus* brief in these cases relies heavily on a study by Isaac Ehrlich, reported a year after *Furman,* to support the contention that the death penalty does deter murder....

... Ehrlich found a negative correlation between changes in the homicide rate and changes in execution risk. His tentative conclusion was that for the period from 1933 to 1967 each additional execution in the United States might have saved eight lives.

The methods and conclusions of the Ehrlich study have been severely criticized on a number of grounds....

... Analysis of Ehrlich's data reveals that all empirical support for the deterrent effect of capital punishment disappears when the five most recent years are removed from his time series—that is to say, whether a decrease in the execution risk corresponds to an increase or a decrease in the murder rate depends on the ending point of the sample period. This finding has cast severe doubts on the reliability of Ehrlich's tentative conclusions....

The Ehrlich study, in short, is of little, if any, assistance in assessing the deterrent impact of the death penalty. The evidence I reviewed in *Furman* remains convincing, in my view, that "capital punishment is not necessary as a deterrent to crime in our society." The justification for the death penalty must be found elsewhere.

The other principal purpose said to be served by the death penalty is retribution. The notion that retribution can serve as a moral justification for the sanction of death finds credence in the opinion of my Brothers Stewart, Powell, and Stevens, and that of my Brother White in *Roberts v. Louisiana.* It is this notion that I find to be the most disturbing aspect of today's unfortunate decisions.

The concept of retribution is a multifaceted one, and any discussion of its role in the criminal law must be undertaken with caution. On one level, it can be said that the notion of retribution or reprobation is the basis of our insistence that only those who have broken the law be punished, and in this sense the notion is quite obviously central to a just system of criminal sanctions. But our recognition that retribution plays a crucial role in determining who may be punished by no means requires approval of retribution as a general justification for punishment. It is the question whether retribution can provide a moral justification for punishment—in particular, capital punishment—that we must consider....

The ... contentions—that society's expression of moral outrage through the imposition of the death penalty pre-empts the citizenry from taking the law into its own hands and reinforces moral values—are not retributive in the purest sense. They are essentially utilitarian in that they portray the death penalty as valuable because of its beneficial results. These justifications for the death penalty are inadequate because the penalty is, quite clearly I think, not necessary to the accomplishment of those results.

There remains for consideration, however, what might be termed the purely retributive justification for the death penalty—that the death penalty is appropriate, not because of its beneficial effect on society, but because the taking of the murderer's life is itself morally good....

The mere fact that the community demands the murderer's life in return for the evil he has done cannot sustain the death penalty for ... "The Eighth Amendment demands more than that a challenged punishment be acceptable to contemporary society." To be sustained under the Eighth Amendment, the death penalty must "compor[t] with the basic concept of human dignity at the core of the Amendment"; the objective in imposing it must be "[consistent] with our respect for the dignity of [other] men." Under these standards, the taking of life "because the wrongdoer deserves it" surely must fall, for such a punishment has at its very basis the total denial of the wrongdoer's dignity and worth.

The death penalty, unnecessary to promote the goal of deterrence or to further any legitimate notion of retribution, is an excessive penalty forbidden by the Eighth and Fourteenth Amendments. I respectfully dissent from the Court's judgment upholding the sentences of death imposed upon the petitioners in these cases.

ENDNOTE

1. [This opinion applies also to No. 75–5706, *Proffitt v. Florida, post,* p. 242, and No. 75–5394, *Jurek v. Texas, post,* p. 262.]

SUGGESTIONS FOR FURTHER READING

Anthologies

Action, H. B. *The Philosophy of Punishment.* London: Macmillan, 1969.

Adams, David. *Philosophical Problems in the Law.* Belmont, CA: Wadsworth, 1996.

Altman, Andrew. *Arguing About Law.* Belmont, CA: Wadsworth, 1996.

Ezorsky, Gertrude. *Philosophical Perspectives on Punishment.* Albany: State University of New York Press, 1972.

Feinberg, Joel, and Hyman Gross. *Philosophy of Law.* Belmont, CA: Wadsworth, 1980.

Gorr, Michael, and Sterling Harwood. *Crime and Punishment.* Boston: Jones & Bartlett, 1995.

Murphy, Jeffrie G. *Punishment and Rehabilitation.* Belmont, CA: Wadsworth, 1984.

Basic Concepts

Golding, Martin P. *Philosophy of Law.* Englewood Cliffs: Prentice-Hall, 1975.

Richards, David A. J. *The Moral Criticism of Law.* Belmont, CA: Dickenson, 1977.

The Forward-Looking and Backward-Looking Views

Adams, Robert. *The Abuses of Punishment.* New York: St. Martin's Press, 1998.

Andenaes, Johannes. *Punishment and Deterrence.* Ann Arbor: University of Michigan Press, 1974.

Gross, Hyman. *A Theory of Criminal Justice.* New York: Oxford University Press, 1979.

Menninger, Karl. *The Crime of Punishment.* New York: Viking Press, 1968.

Montague, Philip. *Punishment as Societal Defense.* Lanham, MD: Rowman & Littlefield, 1995.

Murphy, Jeffrie G. *Retribution, Justice and Therapy.* Boston: Reidel, 1979.

Packer, Herbert. *The Limits of the Criminal Sanction.* Stanford: Stanford University Press, 1968.

Von Hirsh, Andrew. *Doing Justice.* New York: Hill & Wang, 1976.

Practical Application

Bedau, Hugo. *The Death Penalty in America.* New York: Oxford University Press, 1996.

Black, Charles L., Jr. *Capital Punishment.* New York: Norton, 1974.

————. "Reflections on Opposing the Penalty of Death." *St. Mary's Law Journal,* 1978, pp. 1–12.

Prejean, Helen. *Dead Man Walking.* New York: Random House, 1993.

van den Haag, Ernest. *Punishing Criminals.* Lanham, MD: University Press of America, 1991.

✳

War and International Terrorism

INTRODUCTION

Basic Concepts

The problem of war and international terrorism is basically the problem of determining what would be the moral limits of the international use of force against substantial aggression or acts of terrorism. *Just war theories* attempt to specify what these moral limits are. Such theories have two components: a set of criteria that establishes a right to go to war *(jus ad bellum)*, and a set of criteria that determines legitimate conduct in war *(jus in bello)*. The first set of criteria can be grouped under the label "just cause," the second under "just means."

Consider the following specification of just cause:

1. There must be substantial aggression.
2. Nonbelligerent correctives must be either hopeless or too costly.
3. Belligerent correctives must be neither hopeless nor too costly.

This specification of just cause excludes the criterion of legitimate authority, which has had a prominent place in just war theories. This criterion is excluded because it has the character of a second-order requirement; it is a requirement that must be satisfied whenever there is a question of group action with respect to any moral problem whatsoever. For example, with respect to the problem of the distribution of goods and resources in a society, we can certainly ask who has the (morally legitimate) authority to distribute or redistribute goods and resources in a society. But before we ask such questions with respect to particular moral problems, it is important to understand first what are the morally defensible solutions to these problems because a standard way of identifying morally legitimate authorities is by their endorsement of such solutions. With respect to the problem of war and humanitarian intervention, we first need to determine the nature and existence of just causes before we try to identify morally legitimate authorities by their endorsement of such causes.

Assuming that there are just causes, just war theorists go on to specify just means. Consider the following specification of just means:

1. The harm inflicted on the aggressor must not be disproportionate to the aggression.

2. Harm to innocents should not be directly intended as an end or a means.

The first criterion is a widely accepted requirement of just means. The second criterion is also widely accepted and contains the main requirement of the doctrine of double effect (see the introduction to Section III). Many philosophers seem willing to endorse the application of the doctrine in this context given that those to whom the doctrine applies are generally recognized to be persons with full moral status.

To evaluate these requirements of just war theory, we need to determine to what degree they can be supported by the moral approaches to practical problems presented in the General Introduction. Of course, one or more of these approaches may ultimately favor the pacifist position, but assuming that these approaches favored some version of a just war theory, which version would that be?

Obviously, a utilitarian approach would have little difficulty accepting the requirement of just cause and requirement (1) on just means because these requirements can be interpreted as having a utilitarian backing. However, this approach would only accept requirement (2) on just means conditionally, because occasions would surely arise when violations of this requirement would maximize net utility.

Unlike a utilitarian approach, an Aristotelian approach is relatively indeterminate in its requirements. All that is certain, as I have interpreted the approach, is that it would be absolutely committed to requirement (2) on just means.[1] Of course, the other requirements on just cause and just means would be required by particular versions of this approach.

A Kantian approach is distinctive in that it seeks to combine and compromise both the concern of a utilitarian approach for maximal net utility and the concern of an Aristotelian approach for the proper development of each individual.[2] In its hypothetical choice situation, persons would clearly favor the requirement of just cause and requirement (1) on just means, although they would not interpret them in a strictly utilitarian fashion.

Yet what about the requirement (2) on just means? Because persons behind a veil of ignorance would not be committed simply to whatever maximizes net utility, they would want to put a stricter limit on the harm that could be inflicted on innocents in defense of a just cause than could be justified on utilitarian grounds alone. This is because persons behind a veil of ignorance would be concerned not only with what maximizes net utility, but also with the distribution of utility to particular individuals. Persons imagining themselves to be ignorant of what position they are in would be particularly concerned that they might turn out to be in the position of those who are innocent, and, consequently, they would want strong safeguards against harming those who are innocent, such as requirement (2) on just means.

Yet even though persons behind a veil of ignorance would favor differential restriction on harm to innocents, they would not favor an absolute restriction on intentional harm to innocents. They would recognize as exceptions to such a restriction cases where intentional harm to innocents is either:

1. Trivial (e.g., stepping on someone's foot to get out of a crowded subway).

2. Easily reparable (e.g., lying to a temporarily depressed friend to keep her from committing suicide).

3. Sufficiently outweighed by the consequences of the action (e.g., shooting one of two hundred civilian hostages to prevent in the only way possible the execution of all two hundred).

Accordingly, while persons behind a veil of ignorance would favor requirement (2) on just means, their commitment to this requirement would also have to incorporate the above exceptions. Even so, these exceptions are far more limited than those that would be tolerated by a utilitarian approach.

In sum, a Kantian approach would strongly endorse the requirement of just cause and requirements (1) and (2) on just means. Yet its commitment to requirement (2) on just means would fall short of the absolute commitment that is characteristic of an Aristotelian approach to practical problems.

It is clear, therefore, that our three moral approaches to practical problems differ significantly with respect to their requirements for a just war theory. A utilitarian approach strongly endorses the requirement of just cause and requirement (1) on just means, but only conditionally endorses requirement (2) on just means. An Aristotelian approach endorses requirement (2) on just means as an absolute requirement, but is indeterminate with respect to the other requirements of just war theory. Only a Kantian approach strongly endorses all of the basic requirements of a traditional just war theory, although it does not regard requirement (2) on just means as an absolute requirement. Fortunately for traditional just war theory, there are good reasons for favoring a Kantian approach over the other two moral approaches to practical problems.

One reason for favoring a Kantian over a utilitarian approach is that its requirements are derived from a veil of ignorance decision procedure that utilitarians and Kantians alike recognize to be fair. It is not surprising, therefore, to find such utilitarians as John Harsanyi and R. M. Hare simply endorsing this decision procedure and then trying to show that the resulting requirements would maximize utility.[3] Yet we have just seen how the concern of persons behind a veil of ignorance with the distribution of utility would lead them to impose a stricter limit on the harm that could be inflicted on innocents in defense of a just cause than could be justified on grounds of maximizing utility alone. At least with respect to just war theory, therefore, a utilitarian approach and a Kantian approach differ significantly in their practical requirements.

Utilitarians who endorse this decision procedure are faced with a difficult choice: give up their commitment to this decision procedure or modify their commitment to utilitarian goals. Utilitarians cannot easily choose to give up their commitment to this decision procedure because the acceptability of utilitarianism as traditionally conceived has always depended on showing that fairness and utility rarely conflict, and that when they do, it is always plausible to think that the requirements of utility are morally overriding. Consequently, when a fair decision procedure significantly conflicts with utility—which it is not plausible to think can always be morally overridden by the requirements of utility—that procedure exposes the inadequacy of a utilitarian approach to practical problems.

These reasons for favoring a Kantian over a utilitarian approach to practical problems are also reasons for favoring an Aristotelian approach, because an Aristotelian approach is also concerned with fairness and the distribution of utility to particular individuals. Nevertheless, there are other reasons for favoring a Kantian approach over an Aristotelian approach.

One reason is that a Kantian approach does not endorse any absolute requirements. In particular, a Kantian approach does not endorse an absolute requirement not to intentionally harm innocents. A Kantian approach recognizes that if the harm is trivial, easily reparable, or sufficiently outweighed by the consequences, such harm can be morally justified.

Another reason for favoring a Kantian approach over an Aristotelian is that a Kantian approach is determinate in its requirements; it actually leads to a wide range of practical recommendations. By contrast, an Aristotelian approach lacks a deliberative procedure that can produce agreement with respect to practical requirements. This is evident because supporters of this approach tend to endorse radically different practical requirements. In this regard, the veil of ignorance decision procedure employed by a Kantian approach appears to be just the sort of morally defensible device needed to achieve determinate requirements.

Finally, the particular requirements of just war theory endorsed by a Kantian approach are further supported by the presence of analogous requirements for related areas of conduct. Thus, the strong legal prohibitions that exist against punishing the innocent provide support for the strong prohibition against harming innocents expressed by requirement (2) on just means. This is the type of correspondence we would expect from an adequate moral theory; requirements in one area of conduct would be analogous to those in related areas of conduct.

Alternative Views

In the first selection (Selection 74), James P. Sterba argues that when pacifism and just war theory are given their most morally defensible interpretations, they can be reconciled both in theory and practice. He argues that the most morally defensible form of pacifism is antiwar pacifism (which prohibits participation in all wars) rather than nonviolent pacifism (which prohibits any use of violence against other human beings) or nonlethal pacifism (which prohibits any use of lethal force against other human beings). He also argues that when just war theory is given its most morally defensible interpretation, it favors a strong just means prohibition against intentionally harming innocents and favors the use of

belligerent means only when such means (1) minimize the loss and injury to innocent lives overall; (2) threaten innocent lives only to prevent the loss of innocent lives; and (3) threaten or take the lives of unjust aggressors when it is the only way to prevent serious injury to innocents. He contends that the few wars and large-scale conflicts that meet these stringent requirements of just war theory (e.g., India's military action against Pakistan in Bangladesh and the Tanzanian incursion into Uganda during the rule of Idi Amin) are the only wars and large-scale conflicts to which antiwar pacifists cannot justifiably object. He calls the view that emerges from this reconciliation "just war pacifism."

In Selection 75, Sam Harris comes out in favor of using torture as a method of extracting information from suspected terrorists in order to save the lives of innocents. He starts out by having the reader imagine a familiar ticking-bomb scenario and a similar set of scenarios. Harris suggests that few of us would object to torture in such cases. But the classic ticking-bomb scenario involves the assumption that one is as certain as one can be that the person they are torturing is a terrorist. What if, much more realistically, one is far less certain?

Harris argues that it is strange that so many of us are bothered by the prospect of torturing, say, one innocent person in order to potentially save thousands of innocent lives, when so many of us are also willing to accept the death of innocents in waging war. After all, Harris asks, what is "collateral damage" other than the torture of innocents? If, he concludes, we are willing to wage modern warfare in the fight against terrorism, we should be willing to accept the use of torture in certain cases.

In Selection 76, David Luban criticizes what he calls the "liberal ideology of torture" which accepts torture, but only as an anomaly; when it is necessary to prevent catastrophe. A type of circumstance in which it would be necessary is best captured by the ticking-bomb scenario. But Luban argues that the recurrent ticking-bomb example is a "picture that bewitches us" The conditions it describes are unlikely to ever be met. In addition, Luban maintains, if we become only slightly permissive of torture, given certain facts about the nature of bureaucracy and social psychology, we will eventually become *too* permissive of torture and incidents like those at Abu Grahib prison will become the new norm.

In Selection 77, Stephen Nathanson raises the question: Can people who believe that war is sometimes morally permissible consistently condemn terrorism? He thinks they can. He begins with a definition of terrorism, the most important feature of which is that terrorism involves killing or injuring innocent people or the threat thereof. He then considers attempts by Michael Walzer and Gerry Wallace to condemn terrorist acts, but then permit such acts as the allied bombing of civilian targets in the early stages of World War II. He finds them wanting. He also criticizes Igor Primoratz's attempt to distinguish between terrorist acts and legitimate acts of warfare by distinguishing between what is intended and what is merely foreseen. Nathanson claims that attackers, like those who flew planes into the World Trade Center, could have claimed that they did not intend to kill the innocent people who died in their attack but that they only intended to destroy the buildings they hit, and so they would turn out not to be terrorists on Primoratz's account. But merely saying that our intentions are such and such does not make them so. According to Sterba's account of the foreseen/intended distinction given in the previous selection, one's intentions are part of the best explanation for one's action, and at least part of the best explanation for why the 9/11 attackers did what they did is that they wanted to kill the civilians in the World Trade Center. If the

attackers had wanted to just destroy the buildings, then, at the very least, they would have attacked the buildings at night when fewer people would have been in them.

More likely, if destroying just the buildings was their real intent, they would have attacked other symbolic structures that would be virtually empty of people at night, like the Washington Monument or the Statue of Liberty.

Nathanson goes on to offer a "bend over backwards" rule for when foreseen harm to innocents can be justified. However, most of those who have defended the foreseen/intended distinction would agree with Nathanson about the need for something like his "bend over backwards" rule as either implied by the intended/ foreseen distinction itself, or as an important supplement to it. "I really didn't mean to do it" is not a sufficient excuse for causing serious harm on anyone's account. Finally, Nathanson suggests that his "bend over backwards" rule might be further justified, on grounds of fairness, behind Rawls's veil of ignorance. However, if Rawlsian fairness is the ultimate standard that Nathanson wants to appeal to here, it turns out that he will also be committed to accepting the moral permissibility of terrorist acts of intentionally killing the innocent, at least in certain circumstances.

Consider the case of an explorer, let us call her Sonya, who arrives in a South American village just as Pedro, an army officer, is able to kill a random group of twenty Indians in retaliation for protests against the local government. In honor of Sonya's arrival, Pedro offers to spare nineteen of the twenty Indians if Sonya will shoot one of the Indians herself.[4] Can't we easily imagine all of these innocent Indians, either in their imagined circumstances or behind a veil of ignorance, pleading with Sonya to kill one of them, knowing that is the only way that any of them have any chance of surviving? So Nathanson has not succeeded in finding grounds for rejecting terrorist acts in all circumstances. Rather, the grounds he provides actually permit terrorist acts of killing the innocent in certain circumstances.

In Selection 78, James P. Sterba approaches the question of how we should think about terrorism from the perspective of *just war pacifism*. Just war pacifism, as Sterba defends it, does not impose an absolute prohibition on intentionally harming innocents. Specifically, it allows that harm to innocents can be justified if it is greatly outweighed by the consequences. Using both hypothetical and historical examples as analogies, Sterba argues that suicide bombing can be morally justified under certain conditions. He also argues that neither the actions taken by the Israeli government with respect to the Palestinians nor the actions taken by the U.S. government with respect to Al Qaeda are morally justified because neither government exhausted its nonbelligerent correctives before engaging in a military response. He further argues that the United States itself has arguably engaged in terrorist acts and supported the terrorist acts of others and so needs to correct its own wrongdoing if it is to respond justly to the wrongdoing of others. Lastly, he argues that the United States has to do more to be a good world citizen. It must stop being a conspicuous holdout with respect to international treaties, and it must do its fair share to redistribute resources from the rich to the poor as international justice requires.

Practical Application

We get some insight into what international law says about torture with the Geneva Convention of 1949 (Selection 79). As you shall see, signatory states to the convention agreed that torture and degrading treatment of prisoners of war was unacceptable.

In Selection 80 we have the U.S. Supreme Court's majority and dissenting opinions in *Boumedience v. Bush* et al. (2008). In this case, petitioners designated as enemy combatants, who were being detained at the United States Naval Station in Guantanamo Bay, Cuba claimed that they had the constitutional privilege of habeas corpus. The Supreme Court's opinion, which was delivered by Justice Anthony Kennedy, was that the petitioners did have the habeas corpus privilege. The dissenting opinion was delivered by Justice Antonin Scalia.

What is profound about the court's decision, which Justice Kennedy recognizes, is that for the first time, the U.S. Supreme Court recognizes rights under the U.S. Constitution that belong to noncitizens of the U.S. detained by the government, in territory over which the United States does not have *de jure* sovereignty.[5]

ENDNOTES

1. See General Introduction.
2. See General Introduction.
3. See John Harsanyi, *Rational Behavior and Bargaining Equilibrium in Games and Social Situations* (Cambridge: Cambridge University Press, 1977), and R. M. Hare, "Justice and Equality," *in Justice: Alternative Political Perspectives,* ed. James P. Sterba (Belmont, CA: Wadsworth, 1991).

4. See Bernard Williams and J. J. G. Smart. *Utilitarianism: For and Against* (Cambridge: Cambridge University Press, 1973).

5. *De jure* sovereignty means the recognized *legal* right to rule over or control a territory. This is understood in contrast to *de facto* sovereignty, which means *in fact* having control over a territory.

74

Reconciling Pacifists and Just War Theorists

JAMES P. STERBA

James P. Sterba argues that when pacifism and just war theory are given their most morally defensible interpretations, they can be reconciled both in theory and practice. He argues that the most morally defensible form of pacifism is antiwar pacifism rather than nonviolent pacifism or nonlethal pacifism. He also argues that when just war theory is given its most morally defensible interpretation, it favors a strong just means prohibition against intentionally harming innocents and favors the use of belligerent means only when such means (1) minimize the loss and injury to innocent lives overall, (2) threaten innocent lives only to prevent the loss of innocent lives, and (3) threaten or take the lives of unjust aggressors when it is the only way to prevent serious injury to innocents. Sterba contends that the few wars and large-scale conflicts that meet these stringent requirements of just war theory are the only wars and large-scale conflicts to which antiwar pacifists cannot justifiably object.

Traditionally, pacifism and just war theory have represented radically opposed responses to aggression. Pacifism has been interpreted to rule out any use of violence in response to aggression. Just war theory has been interpreted to permit a measured use of violence in response to aggression.[1] It has been thought that the two views might sometimes agree in particular cases—for example, that pacifists and just war theorists might unconditionally oppose nuclear war, but beyond that it has been generally held that the two views lead to radically opposed recommendations. In this paper, I hope to show that this is not the case. I will argue that pacifism and just war theory, in their most morally defensible interpretations, can be substantially reconciled both in theory and practice.

In traditional just war theory there are two basic elements: an account of just cause and an account of just means. Just cause is usually specified as follows:

1. There must be substantial aggression;
2. Nonbelligerent correctives must be either hopeless or too costly; and
3. Belligerent correctives must be neither hopeless nor too costly.

Needless to say, the notion of substantial aggression is a bit fuzzy, but it is generally understood to be the type of aggression that violates people's most fundamental rights. To suggest some specific examples of what is and is not substantial aggression, usually the taking of hostages is regarded as substantial aggression while the nationalization of particular firms owned by foreigners is not so regarded. But even when substantial aggression occurs, frequently nonbelligerent correctives are neither hopeless nor too costly. And even when nonbelligerent correctives are either hopeless or too costly, in order for there to be a just cause, belligerent correctives must be neither hopeless nor too costly.

Reprinted from *Social Theory and Practice*, vol. 18, no. 1 (Spring 1992) by permission.

Traditional just war theory assumes, however, that there are just causes and goes on to specify just means as imposing two requirements:

1. Harm to innocents should not be directly intended as an end or a means.
2. The harm resulting from the belligerent means should not be disproportionate to the particular defensive objective to be attained.

While the just means conditions apply to each defensive action, the just cause conditions must be met by the conflict as a whole.

It is important to note that these requirements of just cause and just means are not essentially about war at all. Essentially, they constitute a theory of just defense that can apply to war but can also apply to a wide range of defensive actions short of war. Of course, what needs to be determined is whether these requirements can be justified. Since just war theory is usually opposed to pacifism, to secure a non–question-begging justification for the theory and its requirements we need to proceed as much as possible from premises that are common to pacifists and just war theorists alike. The difficulty here is that there is not just one form of pacifism but many. So we need to determine which form of pacifism is most morally defensible.

Now when most people think of pacifism they tend to identify it with a theory of nonviolence. We can call this view "nonviolent pacifism." It maintains that:

Any use of violence against other human beings is morally prohibited.

It has been plausibly argued, however, that this form of pacifism is incoherent. In a well-known article, Jan Narveson rejects nonviolent pacifism as incoherent because it recognizes a right to life yet rules out any use of force in defense of that right.[2] The view is incoherent, Narveson claims, because having a right entails the legitimacy of using force in defense of that right at least on some occasions.

Given the cogency of objections of this sort, some have opted for a form of pacifism that does not rule out all violence but only lethal violence.

We can call this view "nonlethal pacifism." It maintains that:

Any lethal use of force against other human beings is morally prohibited.

In defense of nonlethal pacifism, Cheyney Ryan has argued that there is a substantial issue between the pacifist and the nonpacifist concerning whether we can or should create the necessary distance between ourselves and other human beings in order to make the act of killing possible.[3] To illustrate, Ryan cites George Orwell's reluctance to shoot at an enemy soldier who jumped out of a trench and ran along the top of a parapet half-dressed and holding up his trousers with both hands. Ryan contends that what kept Orwell from shooting was that he couldn't think of the soldier as a thing rather than a fellow human being.

However, it is not clear that Orwell's encounter supports nonlethal pacifism. For it may be that what kept Orwell from shooting the enemy soldier was not his inability to think of the soldier as a thing rather than a fellow human being but rather his inability to think of the soldier who was holding up his trousers with both hands as a threat or a combatant. Under this interpretation, Orwell's decision not to shoot would accord well with the requirements of just war theory.

Let us suppose, however, that someone is attempting to take your life. Why does that permit you, the defender of nonlethal pacifism might ask, to kill the person making the attempt? The most cogent response, it seems to me, is that killing in such a case is not evil, or at least not morally evil, because anyone who is wrongfully engaged in an attempt upon your life has already forfeited his or her right to life by engaging in such aggression.[4] So, provided that you are reasonably certain that the aggressor is wrongfully engaged in an attempt upon your life, you would be morally justified in killing, assuming that it is the only way of saving your own life.

There is, however, a form of pacifism that remains untouched by the criticisms I have raised against both nonviolent pacifism and nonlethal pacifism. This form of pacifism neither prohibits all violence nor even all uses of lethal force. We can call the view "antiwar pacifism" because it holds that:

> Any participation in the massive use of lethal force in warfare is morally prohibited.[5]

In defense of antiwar pacifism, it is undeniable that wars have brought enormous amounts of death and destruction in their wake and that many of those who have perished in them are noncombatants or innocents. In fact, the tendency of modern wars has been to produce higher and higher proportions of noncombatant casualties, making it more and more difficult to justify participation in such wars. At the same time, strategies for nonbelligerent conflict resolution are rarely intensively developed and explored before nations choose to go to war, making it all but impossible to justify participation in such wars.[6]

To determine whether the requirements of just war theory can be reconciled with those of antiwar pacifism, however, we need to consider whether we should distinguish between harm intentionally inflicted upon innocents and harm whose infliction on innocents is merely foreseen. On the one hand, we could favor a uniform restriction against the infliction of harm upon innocents that ignores the intended/foreseen distinction. On the other hand, we could favor a differential restriction which is more severe against the intentional infliction of harm upon innocents but is less severe against the infliction of harm that is merely foreseen. What needs to be determined, therefore, is whether there is any rationale for favoring this differential restriction on harm over a uniform restriction. But this presupposes that we can, in practice, distinguish between what is foreseen and what is intended, and some have challenged whether this can be done. So first we need to address this challenge.

Now the practical test that is frequently appealed to in order to distinguish between foreseen and intended elements of an action is the Counterfactual Test. According to this test, two questions are relevant:

1. Would you have performed the action if only the good consequences would have resulted and not the evil consequences?

2. Would you have performed the action if only the evil consequences resulted and not the good consequences?

If an agent answers "Yes" to the first question and "No" to the second, some would conclude that (1) the action is an intended means to the good consequences; (2) the good consequences are an intended end; and (3) the evil consequences are merely foreseen.

But how well does this Counterfactual Test work? Douglas Lackey has argued that the test gives the wrong result in any case where the "act that produces an evil effect produces a larger good effect."[7] Lackey cites the bombing of Hiroshima as an example. That bombing is generally thought to have had two effects: the killing of Japanese civilians and the shortening of the war. Now suppose we were to ask:

1. Would Truman have dropped the bomb if only the shortening of the war would have resulted but not the killing of the Japanese civilians?

2. Would Truman have dropped the bomb if only the Japanese civilians would have been killed and the war not shortened?

And suppose that the answer to the first question is that Truman would have dropped the bomb if only the shortening of the war would have resulted but not the killing of the Japanese civilians, and that the answer to the second question is that Truman would not have dropped the bomb if only the Japanese civilians would have been killed and the war not shortened. Lackey concludes from this that the killing of civilians at Hiroshima, self-evidently a means for shortening the war, is by the Counterfactual Test classified not as a means but as a mere foreseen consequence. On these grounds, Lackey rejects the Counterfactual Test as an effective device for distinguishing between the foreseen and the intended consequences of an action.

Unfortunately, this is to reject the Counterfactual Test only because one expects too much from it. It is to expect the test to determine all of the following:

1. Whether the action is an intended means to the good consequences;

2. Whether the good consequences are an intended end of the action; and

3. Whether the evil consequences are simply foreseen consequences.

In fact, this test is only capable of meeting the first two of these expectations. And the test clearly succeeds in doing this for Lackey's own example, where the test shows the bombing of Hiroshima to be an intended means to shortening the war, and shortening the war an intended consequence of the action. To determine whether the evil consequences are simply foreseen consequences, however, an additional test is needed, which I shall call the Non-explanation Test. According to this test, the relevant question is:

> Does the bringing about of the evil consequences help explain why the agent undertook the action as a means to the good consequences?

If the answer is "No," that is, if the bringing about of the evil consequences does not help explain why the agent undertook the action as a means to the good consequences, the evil consequences are merely foreseen. But if the answer is "Yes," the evil consequences are an intended means to the good consequences.

Of course, there is no guaranteed procedure for arriving at an answer to the Nonexplanation Test. Nevertheless, when we are in doubt concerning whether the evil consequences of an act are simply foreseen, seeking an answer to the Nonexplanation Test will tend to be the best way of reasonably resolving that doubt. For example, applied to Lackey's example, the Nonexplanation Test comes up with a "Yes," since the evil consequences in this example do help explain why the bombing was undertaken to shorten the war. For according to the usual account, Truman ordered the bombing to bring about the civilian deaths which by their impact upon Japanese morale were expected to shorten the war. So, by the Nonexplanation Test, the civilian deaths were an intended means to the good consequences of shortening the war.[8]

Assuming then that we can distinguish in practice between harm intentionally inflicted upon innocents and harm whose infliction on innocents is merely foreseen, we need to determine whether there is any rationale for favoring a differential restriction that is more severe against the intentional infliction of harm upon innocents but is less severe against the infliction of harm that is merely foreseen over a uniform restriction against the infliction of harm upon innocents that ignores the intended/foreseen distinction.

Let us first examine the question from the perspective of those suffering the harm. Initially, it might appear to matter little whether the harm would be intended or just foreseen by those who cause it. From the perspective of those suffering harm, it might appear that what matters is simply that the overall amount of harm be restricted irrespective of whether it is foreseen or intended. But consider—don't those who suffer harm have more reason to protest when the harm is done to them by agents who are directly engaged in causing harm to them than when the harm is done incidentally by agents whose ends and means are good? Don't we have more reason to protest when we are being used by others than when we are affected by them only incidentally?

Moreover, if we examine the question from the perspective of those causing harm, additional support for this line of reasoning can be found. For it would seem that we have more reason to protest a restriction against foreseen harm than we have reason to protest a comparable restriction against intended harm. This is because a restriction against foreseen harm limits our actions when our ends and means are good whereas a restriction against intended harm only limits our actions when our ends or means are evil or harmful, and it would seem that we have greater grounds for acting when both our ends and means are good than when they are not. Consequently, because we have more reason to protest when we are being used by others than when we are being affected by them only incidentally, and because we have more reason to act when both our ends and means are good than when they are not, we should favor the foreseen/intended distinction that is incorporated into just means.

It might be objected, however, that at least sometimes we could produce greater good overall by violating the foreseen/intended distinction of just means and acting with the evil means of intentionally harming innocents. On this account, it might be argued that it should be permissible at least sometimes to intentionally harm innocents in order to achieve greater good overall.

Now it seems to me that this objection is well-taken insofar as it is directed against an absolute restriction upon intentional harm to innocents. It seems clear that there are exceptions to such a restriction when intentional harm to innocents is:

1. Trivial (for example, as in the case of stepping on someone's foot to get out of a crowded subway);

2. Easily repairable (for example, as in the case of lying to a temporarily depressed friend to keep him from committing suicide); or

3. Greatly outweighed by the consequences of the action, especially to innocent people (for example, as in the case of shooting one of two hundred civilian hostages to prevent in the only way possible the execution of all two hundred).

Yet while we need to recognize these exceptions to an absolute restriction upon intentional harm to innocents, there is good reason not to permit simply maximizing good consequences overall because that would place unacceptable burdens upon particular individuals. More specifically, it would be an unacceptable burden on innocents to allow them to be intentionally harmed in cases other than the exceptions we have just enumerated. And, allowing for these exceptions, we would still have reason to favor a differential restriction against harming innocents that is more severe against the intentional infliction of harm upon innocents but is less severe against the infliction of harm upon innocents that is merely foreseen. Again, the main grounds for this preference is that we would have more reason to protest when we are being used by others than when we are being affected by them only incidentally, and more reason to act when

both our ends and means are good than when they are not.

So far, I have argued that there are grounds for favoring a differential restriction on harm to innocents that is more severe against intended harm and less severe against foreseen harm. I have further argued that this restriction is not absolute so that when the evil intended is trivial, easily reparable or greatly outweighed by the consequences, intentional harm to innocents can be justified. Moreover, there is no reason to think that antiwar pacifists would reject either of these conclusions. Antiwar pacifists are opposed to any participation in the massive use of lethal force in warfare, yet this need not conflict with the commitment of just war theorists to a differential but nonabsolute restriction on harm to innocents as a requirement of just means.[9] Where just war theory goes wrong, according to antiwar pacifists, is not in its restriction on harming innocents but rather in its failure to adequately determine when belligerent correctives are too costly to constitute a just cause or lacking in the proportionality required by just means. According to antiwar pacifists, just war theory provides insufficient restraint in both of these areas. Now to evaluate this criticism, we need to consider a wide range of cases where killing or inflicting serious harm on others in defense of oneself or others might be thought to be justified, beginning with the easiest cases to assess from the perspectives of antiwar pacifism and the just war theory and then moving on to cases that are more difficult to assess from those perspectives.

Case 1. Only the intentional or foreseen killing of an unjust aggressor would prevent one's own death.[10] This case clearly presents no problems. In the first place, antiwar pacifists adopted their view because they were convinced that there were instances of justified killing. And, in this case, the only person killed is an unjust aggressor. So surely antiwar pacifists would have to agree with just war theorists that one can justifiably kill an unjust aggressor if it is the only way to save one's life.

Case 2. Only the intentional or foreseen killing of an unjust aggressor and the foreseen killing of one innocent bystander would prevent one's own death and that of five other innocent people.[11] In this case, we have the foreseen killing of an innocent person as well as the killing of the unjust aggressor, but since it is the only way to save one's own life and the lives of five other innocent people, antiwar pacifists and just war theorists alike would have reason to judge it morally permissible. In this case, the intended life-saving benefits to six innocent people are judged to outweigh the foreseen death of one innocent person and the intended or foreseen death of the unjust aggressor.

Case 3. Only the intentional or foreseen killing of an unjust aggressor and the foreseen killing of one innocent bystander would prevent the death of five other innocent people. In this case, despite the fact that we lack the justification of self-defense, saving the lives of five innocent people in the only way possible should still provide antiwar pacifists and just war theorists with sufficient grounds for granting the moral permissibility of killing an unjust aggressor, even when the killing of an innocent bystander is a foreseen consequence. In this case, the intended lifesaving benefits to five innocent people would still outweigh the foreseen death of one innocent person and the intended or foreseen death of the unjust aggressor.

Case 4. Only the intentional or foreseen killing of an unjust aggressor and the foreseen killing of five innocent people would prevent the death of two innocent people. In this case, neither antiwar pacifists nor just war theorists would find the cost and proportionality requirements of just war theory to be met. Too many innocent people would have to be killed to save too few. Here the fact that the deaths of the innocents would be merely foreseen does not outweigh the fact that we would have to accept the deaths of five innocents and the death of the unjust aggressor in order to be able to save two innocents.

Notice that up to this point in interpreting these cases, we have simply been counting the number of innocent deaths involved in each case and opting for whichever solution minimized the loss of innocent lives that would result. Suppose, however, that an unjust aggressor is not threatening the lives of innocents but only their welfare or property. Would the taking of the unjust aggressor's

life in defense of the welfare and property of innocents be judged proportionate? Consider the following case.

Case 5. Only the intentional or foreseen killing of an unjust aggressor would prevent serious injury to oneself and five other innocent people. Since in this case the intentional or foreseen killing of the unjust aggressor is the only way of preventing serious injury to oneself and five other innocent people, then, by analogy with Cases 1–3, both antiwar pacifists and just war theorists alike would have reason to affirm its moral permissibility. Of course, if there were any other way of stopping unjust aggressors in such cases short of killing them, that course of action would clearly be required. Yet if there is no alternative, the intentional or foreseen killing of the unjust aggressor to prevent serious injury to oneself and/ or five other innocent people would be justified.

In such cases, the serious injury could be bodily injury, as when an aggressor threatens to break one's limbs, or it could be serious psychological injury, as when an aggressor threatens to inject mind-altering drugs, or it could be a serious threat to property. Of course, in most cases where serious injury is threatened, there will be ways of stopping aggressors short of killing them. Unfortunately, this is not always possible.

In still other kinds of cases, stopping an unjust aggressor would require indirectly inflicting serious harm, but not death, upon innocent bystanders. Consider the following cases.

Case 6. Only the intentional or foreseen infliction of serious harm upon an unjust aggressor and the foreseen infliction of serious harm upon one innocent bystander would prevent serious harm to oneself and five other innocent people.

Case 7. Only the intentional or foreseen infliction of serious harm upon an unjust aggressor and the foreseen infliction of serious harm upon one innocent bystander would prevent serious harm to five other innocent people.

In both of these cases, serious harm is indirectly inflicted upon one innocent bystander in order to prevent greater harm from being inflicted by an unjust aggressor upon other innocent people. In Case 6, we also have the justification of self-defense, which is lacking in Case 7. Nevertheless, with regard to both cases, antiwar pacifists and just war theorists should agree that preventing serious injury to five or six innocent people in the only way possible renders it morally permissible to inflict serious injury upon an unjust aggressor, even when the serious injury of one innocent person is a foreseen consequence. In these cases, by analogy with Cases 2 and 3, the foreseen serious injury of one innocent person and the intended or foreseen injury of the unjust aggressor should be judged proportionate given the intended injury-preventing benefits to five or six other innocent people.

Up to this point there has been the basis for general agreement among antiwar pacifists and just war theorists as to how to interpret the proportionality requirement of just means, but in the following case this no longer obtains.

Case 8. Only the intentional or foreseen killing of an unjust aggressor and the foreseen killing of one innocent bystander would prevent serious injuries to the members of a much larger group of people.

The interpretation of this case is crucial. In this case, we are asked to sanction the loss of an innocent life in order to prevent serious injuries to the members of a much larger group of people. Unfortunately, neither antiwar pacifists nor just war theorists have explicitly considered this case. Both antiwar pacifists and just war theorists agree that we can inflict serious injury upon an unjust aggressor and an innocent bystander to prevent greater injury to other innocent people, as in Cases 6 and 7, and that one can even intentionally or indirectly kill an unjust aggressor to prevent serious injury to oneself or other innocent people as in Case 5. Yet neither antiwar pacifists nor just war theorists have explicitly addressed the question of whether we can indirectly kill an innocent bystander in order to prevent serious injuries to the members of a much larger group of innocent people. Rather they have tended to confuse Case 8 with Case 5 where it is agreed that one can justifiably kill an unjust aggressor in order to prevent serious injury to oneself and five other innocent people. In Case 8, however, one is doing something quite different: One is killing an innocent bystander in order to prevent serious injury to oneself and five other innocent people.

Now this kind of trade-off is not accepted in standard police practice. Police officers are regularly instructed not to risk innocent lives simply to prevent serious injury to other innocents. Nor is there any reason to think that a trade-off that is unacceptable in standard police practice would be acceptable in larger-scale conflicts. Thus, for example, even if the Baltic republics could have effectively freed themselves from the Soviet Union by infiltrating into Moscow several bands of saboteurs who would then attack several military and government installations in Moscow, causing an enormous loss of innocent lives, such trade-offs would not have been justified. Accordingly, it follows that if the proportionality requirement of just war theory is to be met, we must save more innocent lives than we cause to be lost, we must prevent more injuries than we bring about, and we must not kill innocents, even indirectly, simply to prevent serious injuries to ourselves and others.

Of course, sometimes our lives and well-being are threatened together. Or better, if we are unwilling to sacrifice our well-being then our lives are threatened as well. Nevertheless, if we are justified in our use of lethal force to defend ourselves in cases where we will indirectly kill innocents, it is because our lives are also threatened, not simply our well-being. And the same holds for when we are defending others.

What this shows is that the constraints imposed by just war theory on the use of belligerent correctives are actually much more severe than antiwar pacifists have tended to recognize.[12] In determining when belligerent correctives are too costly to constitute a just cause or lacking in the proportionality required by just means, just war theory under its most morally defensible interpretation:

1. Allows the use of belligerent means against unjust aggressors only when such means minimize the loss and injury to innocent lives overall;

2. Allows the use of belligerent means against unjust aggressors to indirectly threaten innocent lives only to prevent the loss of innocent lives, not simply to prevent injury to innocents; and

3. Allows the use of belligerent means to directly or indirectly threaten or even take the lives of unjust aggressors when it is the only way to prevent serious injury to innocents.

Now it might be objected that all that I have shown through the analysis of the above eight cases is that killing in defense of oneself or others is morally permissible, not that it is morally required or morally obligatory. That is true. I have not established any obligation to respond to aggression with lethal force in these cases, but only that it is morally permissible to do so. For one thing, it is difficult to ground an obligation to use lethal force on self-defense alone, as would be required in Case 1 or in one version of Case 5. Obligations to oneself appear to have an optional quality that is absent from obligations to others. In Cases 2, 3, and 5–7, however, the use of force would prevent serious harm or death to innocents, and here I contend it would be morally obligatory if either the proposed use of force required only a relatively small personal sacrifice from us or if we were fairly bound by convention or a mutual defense agreement to come to the aid of others. In such cases, I think we can justifiably speak of a moral obligation to kill or seriously harm in defense of others.

Another aspect of Cases 1–3 and 5–7 to which someone might object is that it is the wrongful actions of others that put us into situations where I am claiming that we are morally justified in seriously harming or killing others.[13] But for the actions of unjust aggressors, we would not be in situations where I am claiming that we are morally permitted or required to seriously harm or kill.

Yet doesn't something like this happen in a wide range of cases when wrongful actions are performed? Suppose I am on the way to the bank to deposit money from a fundraiser, and someone accosts me and threatens to shoot if I don't hand over the money. If I do hand over the money, I would be forced to do something I don't want to do, something that involves a loss to myself and others. But surely it is morally permissible for me to hand over the money in this case. And it may even be morally required for me to do so if resistance

would lead to the shooting of others in addition to myself. So it does seem that bad people, by altering the consequences of our actions, can alter our obligations as well. What our obligations are under non-ideal conditions are different from what they would be under ideal conditions. If a group of thugs comes into this room and makes it very clear that they intend to shoot me if each of you doesn't give them one dollar, I think, and I would hope that you would also think, that each of you now has an obligation to give the thugs one dollar when before you had no such obligation. Likewise, I think that the actions of unjust aggressors can put us into situations where it is morally permissible or even morally required for us to seriously harm or kill when before it was not.

Now it might be contended that antiwar pacifists would concede the moral permissibility of Cases 1–3 and 5–7 but still maintain that any participation in the massive use of lethal force in warfare is morally prohibited. The scale of the conflict, antiwar pacifists might contend, makes all the difference. Of course, if this simply means that many large-scale conflicts will have effects that bear no resemblance to Cases 1–3 or 5–7, this can hardly be denied. Still, it is possible for some large-scale conflicts to bear a proportionate resemblance to the above cases. For example, it can be argued plausibly that India's military action against Pakistan in Bangladesh and the Tanzanian incursion into Uganda during the rule of Idi Amin resemble Cases 3, 5, or 7 in their effects upon innocents.[14] What this shows is that antiwar pacifists are not justified in regarding every participation in the massive use of lethal force in warfare as morally prohibited. Instead, antiwar pacifists must allow that at least in some real-life cases, wars and other large-scale military operations both have been and will be morally permissible.

This concession from antiwar pacifists, however, needs to be matched by a comparable concession from just war theorists themselves, because too frequently they have interpreted their theory in morally indefensible ways.[15] When just war theory is given a morally defensible interpretation, I have argued that the theory favors a strong just means prohibition against intentionally harming innocents. I have also argued that the theory favors the use of belligerent means only when such means (1) minimize the loss and injury to innocent lives overall; (2) threaten innocent lives only to prevent the loss of innocent lives, not simply to prevent injury to innocents; and (3) threaten or even take the lives of unjust aggressors when it is the only way to prevent serious injury to innocents.

Obviously, just war theory, so understood, is going to place severe restrictions on the use of belligerent means in warfare. In fact, most of the actual uses of belligerent means in warfare that have occurred turn out to be unjustified. For example, the U.S. involvement in Nicaragua, El Salvador, and Panama; Soviet involvement in Afghanistan; and Israeli involvement in the West Bank and the Gaza Strip all violate the just cause and just means provisions of just war theory as I have defended them. Even the recent U.S.-led war against Iraq violated both the just cause and just means provisions of just war theory[16] In fact, one strains to find examples of justified applications of just war theory in recent history. Two examples I have already referred to are India's military action against Pakistan in Bangladesh and the Tanzanian incursion into Uganda during the rule of Idi Amin. But after mentioning these two examples it is difficult to go on. What this shows is that when just war theory and antiwar pacifism are given their most morally defensible interpretations, both views can be reconciled. In this reconciliation, the few wars and large-scale conflicts that meet the stringent requirements of just war theory are the only wars and large-scale conflicts to which antiwar pacifists cannot justifiably object.[17] We can call the view that emerges from this reconciliation "just war pacifism."[18] It is the view which claims that due to the stringent requirements of just war theory, only very rarely will participation in a massive use of lethal force in warfare be morally justified. It is the view on which I rest my case for the reconciliation of pacifism and just war theory.[19]

ENDNOTES

An earlier version of this paper was presented as the presidential address for the 1990 National Meeting of Concerned Philosophers for Peace. For their comments on various versions of this paper, I would like to thank Timo Airaksinen, Joseph Boyle, Laurence Bove, Duane Cady, Sheldon Cohen, Peter Dalton, Barry Gan, Robert Holmes, Robert Johansen, Janet Kourany, Douglas Lackey, Robert Phillips, Ronald Santoni, Jonathan Schonsheck, Paula Smithka, Richard Werner, and the anonymous reviewers for this journal.

1. Some would say with too generous a measure.

2. Jan Narveson, "Pacifism: A Philosophical Analysis," *Ethics* 75 (1965): 259–271.

3. Cheyney Ryan, "Self-Defense, Pacifism and the Possibility of Killing," *Ethics* 93 (1983): 514–524. Also reprinted in James P. Sterba, *The Ethics of War and Nuclear Deterrence* (Belmont, CA: Wadsworth, 1985).

4. Alternatively, one might concede that even in this case killing is morally evil, but still contend that it is morally justified because it is the lesser of two evils.

5. For two challenging defenses of this view, see Duane L. Cady, *From Warism to Pacifism* (Philadelphia: Temple University Press, 1989), and Robert L. Holmes, *On War and Morality* (Princeton: Princeton University Press, 1989). In Concerned Philosophers for Peace, antiwar pacifism seems to be the most widely endorsed pacifist view.

6. See *From Warism to Pacifism*, pp. 51, 89 ff, and *On War and Morality*, p. 278.

7. Douglas P. Lackey, "The Moral Irrelevance of the Counterforce/Counter-value Distinction," *The Monist* 70 (1987): 255–276. For a similar view, see Susan Levine, "Does the 'Counterfactual Test' Work for Distinguishing a Means from a Foreseen Concomitant," *Journal of Value Inquiry* 18 (1984): 155–157.

8. This Nonexplanation Test also solves a related problem of distinguishing foreseen from intended consequences noted by Charles Fried. (Charles Fried, *Right and Wrong* [Cambridge, MA: Harvard University Press 1978], 23–24). Fried was

concerned with the following example, first discussed by Philippa Foot (Philippa Foot, "The Problem of Abortion and the Doctrine of Double Effect," *Oxford Review* 5 [1967]: 5–15): "Imagine that a large person who is leading a party of spelunkers gets herself stuck in the mouth of a cave in which flood waters are rising. The trapped party of spelunkers just happens to have a stick of dynamite with which they can blast the large person out of the mouth of the cave; either they use the dynamite or they all drown, the large person with them." Now suppose someone would claim that using the dynamite was simply a means of freeing the party of spelunkers and that the death of the large person was just a foreseen side effect. Fried's problem was that while she rejected this account of the action, she could find no way of successfully challenging it. What she clearly needed was the Nonexplanation Test. For suppose we employ the test and ask whether the death of the large person helps explain why the dynamite was used to free the spelunkers from the cave; the answer we get is clearly "Yes." For how else could the use of the dynamite free the party of spelunkers from the cave except by removing the large person from the mouth of the cave in such a way as to cause her death? It follows, according to the Non-explanation Test, that the death of the large person was a means intended for freeing the party of spelunkers and not merely a foreseen consequence of the use of the dynamite.

9. This is because the just means restrictions protect innocents quite well against the infliction of intentional harm.

10. By an "unjust aggressor" I mean someone who the defender is reasonably certain is wrongfully engaged in an attempt upon her life or the lives of other innocent people.

11. What is relevant in this case is that the foreseen deaths are a relatively small number (one in this case) compared to the number of innocents whose lives are saved (six in this case). The primary reason for using particular numbers in this case and those that follow is to make it clear that at this stage of the argument no attempt is being made to justify the large-scale killing that occurs in warfare.

12. And more severe than some just war theorists have tended to recognize. See, for example, William V. O'Brien, *The Conduct of Just and Limited War* (Praeger, 1981), and John Courtney Murray,

Morality and Modern War, Council on Religion and International Affairs, New York, 1959.

13. See *On War and Morality*, pp. 208–211.

14. Although there is a strong case for India's military action against Pakistan in Bangladesh and the Tanzanian incursion into Uganda during the rule of Idi Amin, there are questions that can be raised about the behavior of Indian troops in Bangladesh following the defeat of the Pakistani forces and about the regime Tanzania put in power in Uganda.

15. See, for example, William V. O'Brien and John Courtney Murray, works previously cited.

16. The just cause provision was violated because the extremely effective economic sanctions were not given enough time to work. It was estimated that when compared to past economic blockades, the blockade against Iraq had a near 100% chance of success if given about a year to work. (See the *New York Times,* Jan. 14, 1991.) The just means provision was violated because the number of combatant and noncombatant deaths was disproportionate. As many as 120,000 Iraqi soldiers were killed, according to U.S. intelligence sources.

17. Of course, antiwar pacifists are right to point out that virtually all wars that have been fought have led to unforeseen harms and have been fought with less and less discrimination as the wars progressed. Obviously, these are considerations that in just war theory must weigh heavily against going to war.

18. For another use of this term, see Kenneth H. Wenker, "Just War Pacifism," Proceedings of the American Catholic Philosophical Association (1983): 135–141. For a defense of a similar view to my own, which is considered by the author to be a defense of pacifism, see Richard Norman, "The Case for Pacifism," *Journal of Applied Philosophy* (1988): 197–210.

19. Of course, more needs to be done to specify the requirements of just war pacifism. One fruitful way to further specify these requirements is to appeal to a hypothetical social contract decision procedure as has been done with respect to other practical problems. Here I have simply tried to establish the defensibility of just war pacifism without appealing to any such procedure. Yet once the defensibility of just war pacifism has been established, such a decision procedure will prove quite useful in working out its particular requirements.

75

In Defense of Torture

SAM HARRIS

Sam Harris argues that torture is justified if there is the probability it will help save innocent lives. In cases where we are 100% certain the person we are about to torture is guilty, Harris says we should have no squeamishness. In realistic scenarios, where we are not 100% certain the person about to be tortured is guilty, we are likely to be squeamish. But Harris argues this squeamishness is unjustified insofar as we are willing to accept the means of modern warfare, which involves "collateral damage", which in itself, he argues, is the torturing and killing of innocents on a much grander scale than the kind he is defending here.

Imagine that a known terrorist has planted a large bomb in the heart of a nearby city. This man now sits in your custody. As to the bomb's location, he will say nothing except that the site was chosen to produce the maximum loss of life. Given this state of affairs—in particular, given that there is still time to prevent an imminent atrocity—it seems there would be no harm in dusting off the *strappado* and exposing this unpleasant fellow to a suasion of bygone times.

If a ticking bomb doesn't move you, picture your seven-year-old daughter being slowly asphyxiated in a warehouse just five minutes away, while the man in your custody holds the keys to her release. If your daughter won't tip the scales, then add the daughters of every couple for a thousand miles—millions of little girls have, by some perverse negligence on the part of our government, come under the control of an evil genius who now sits before you in shackles. Clearly, the consequences of one man's uncooperativeness can be made so grave, and his malevolence and culpability so transparent, as to stir even the most self-hating moral relativist from his dogmatic slumbers.

It is generally thought that the gravest ethical problem we face in resorting to torture is that we would be bound to torture some number of innocent men and women. Most of us who were eager to don the Inquisitor's cap in the case above begin to falter in more realistic scenarios, as a person's guilt becomes a matter of some uncertainty. And this is long before other concerns even attract our notice. What, for instance, is the *reliability* of testimony elicited under torture? We need not even pose questions of this sort yet, since we have already balked at the knowledge that, in the real world, we will not be able to tell the guilty from the innocent just by looking.

So it seems that we have two situations that will strike most sane and decent people as ethically distinct: in the first case, as envisioned by Dershowitz, it seems perverse to worry about the rights of an admitted terrorist when so many innocent lives are at stake; while under more realistic conditions, uncertainty about a person's guilt will generally preclude the use of torture. Is this how the matter really sits with us? Probably not.

It appears that such restraint in the use of torture cannot be reconciled with our willingness to wage war in the first place. What, after all is "collateral damage" but the inadvertent torture of innocent men, women, and children? Whenever we consent to drop bombs, we do so with the knowledge that some number of children will be blinded, disemboweled, paralyzed, orphaned, and killed by them. It is curious that while the torture of Osama bin Laden himself could be expected to provoke convulsions of conscience among our leaders, the unintended (though perfectly foreseeable, and therefore accepted) slaughter of children does not.

So we can now ask, if we are willing to act in a way that guarantees the misery and death of some considerable number of innocent children, why spare the rod with suspected terrorists? What is the difference between pursuing a course of action where we run the risk of inadvertently subjecting some innocent men to torture, and pursuing one in which we will inadvertently kill far greater numbers of innocent men, women, and children? Rather, it seems obvious that the misapplication of torture should be far *less* troubling to us than collateral damage: there are, after all, no *infants* interned at Guantanamo Bay, just rather scrofulous young men, many of whom were caught in the very act of trying to kill our soldiers.[1] Torture need not even impose a significant risk of death or permanent injury on its victims; while the collaterally damaged are, almost by definition, crippled or killed. The ethical divide that seems to be opening up here suggests that those who are willing to drop bombs might want to abduct the nearest and dearest of suspected terrorists—their wives, mothers, and daughters—and torture *them* as well, assuming anything profitable to our side might come of it. Admittedly, this would be a ghastly result to have reached by logical argument, and we will want to find some way of escaping it.

In this context, we should note that many variables influence our feelings about an act of physical violence, as well as our intuitions about its ethical status. As Glover points out, "in modern war, what is most shocking is a poor guide to what is most harmful." To learn that one's grandfather flew a bombing mission over Dresden in the Second World War is one thing; to hear that he killed five little girls and their mother with a shovel is another.

We can be sure that he would have killed more women and girls by dropping bombs from pristine heights, and they are likely to have died equally horrible deaths, but his culpability would not appear the same. Indeed, we seem to know, intuitively, that it would take a different kind of person to perpetrate violence of the latter sort. And, as we might expect, the psychological effects of participating in these types of violence are generally distinct. Consider the following account of a Soviet soldier in Afghanistan: "It's frightening and unpleasant to have to kill, you think, but you soon realize that what you really find objectionable is shooting someone point-blank. Killing *en masse*, in a group, is exciting, even—and I've seen this myself—fun."[2] This is not to say that no one has ever enjoyed killing people up close; it is just that we all recognize that such enjoyment requires an unusual degree of callousness to the suffering of others.

It is possible that we are simply unequipped to rectify this disparity—to be, in Glover's terms, most shocked by what is most harmful. A biological rationale is not hard to find, as millions of years on the African veldt could not possibly have selected for an ability to make emotional sense of twenty-first-century horror. That our Paleolithic genes now have chemical, biological, and nuclear weapons at their disposal is, from the point of view of our evolution, little different from our having delivered this technology into the hands of chimps. The difference between killing one man and killing a thousand just doesn't seem as salient to us as it should. And, as Glover observes, in many cases we will find the former far more disturbing. Three million souls can be starved and murdered in the Congo, and our Argus-eyed media scarcely blink. When a princess dies in a car accident, however, a quarter of the earth's population falls prostrate with grief. Perhaps we are unable to feel what we must feel in order to change our world.

What does it feel like to see three thousand men, women, and children incinerated and crushed to ash in the span of a few seconds? Anyone who owned a television on September 11, 2001, now knows. But most of us know nothing of the sort. To have watched the World Trade Center absorbing two jet planes, along with the lives of thousands, and to have felt, above all things, *disbelief*, suggests some form of neurological impairment. Clearly, there are limits to what the human mind can make of the deliverances of its senses—of the mere sight of an office building, known to be full of people, dissolving into rubble. Perhaps this will change.

In any case, if you think the equivalence between torture and collateral damage does not hold, because torture is up close and personal while stray bombs aren't, you stand convicted of a failure of imagination on at least two counts: first, a moment's reflection on the horrors that must have been visited upon innocent Afghanis and Iraqis by our bombs will reveal that they are on par with those of any dungeon. That such an exercise of the imagination is required to bring torture and collateral damage to parity accounts for the dissociation between what is most shocking and what is most harmful that Glover notes. It also demonstrates the degree to which we have been bewitched by our own euphemisms. Killing people at a distance is easier, but perhaps it should not be *that* much easier.

Second, if our intuition about the wrongness of torture is born of an aversion to how people generally behave while being tortured, we should note that this particular infelicity could be circumvented pharmacologically, because paralytic drugs make it unnecessary for screaming ever to be heard or writhing seen. We could easily devise methods of torture that would render a torturer as blind to the plight of his victims as a bomber pilot is at thirty thousand feet. Consequently, our natural aversion to the sights and sounds of the dungeon provide no foothold for those who would argue against the use of torture. To demonstrate just how abstract the torments of the tortured can be made to seem, we need only imagine an ideal "torture pill"—a drug that would deliver both the instruments of torture and the instrument of their utter concealment. The action of the pill would be to produce transitory paralysis and transitory misery of a kind that no human being would willingly submit to a second time. Imagine how we torturers would feel if, after giving this pill to captive terrorists, each lay down for what appeared to be an hour's nap only to arise

and immediately confess everything he knows about the workings of his organization. Might we not be tempted to call it a "truth pill" in the end?

No, there is no ethical difference to be found in how the suffering of the tortured or the collaterally damaged *appears*.

Which way should the balance swing? Assuming that we want to maintain a coherent ethical position on these matters, this appears to be a circumstance of forced choice: if we are willing to drop bombs, or even risk that pistol rounds might go astray, we should be willing to torture a certain class of criminal suspects and military prisoners; if we are unwilling to torture, we should be unwilling to wage modern war.

Opponents of torture will be quick to argue that confessions elicited by torture are notoriously unreliable. Given the foregoing, however, this objection seems to lack its usual force. Make these confessions as unreliable as you like—the chance that our interests will be advanced in any instance of torture need only equal the chance of such occasioned by the dropping of a single bomb. What was the chance that the dropping of bomb number 117 on Kandahar would effect the demise of Al Qaeda? It had to be pretty slim. Enter Khalid Sheikh Mohammed: our most valuable capture in our war on terror. Here is a character who actually seems cut from Dershowitzian cloth. U.S. officials now believe that his was the hand that decapitated the *Wall Street Journal* reporter Daniel Pearl. Whether or not this is true, his membership in Al Qaeda more or less rules out his "innocence" in any important sense, and his rank in the organization suggests that his knowledge of planned atrocities must be extensive. The bomb is ticking. Given the damage we were willing to cause to the bodies and minds of innocent children in Afghanistan and Iraq, our disavowal of torture in the case of Khalid Sheikh Mohammed seems perverse. If there is even one chance in a million that he will tell us something under torture that will lead to the further dismantling of Al Qaeda, it seems that we should use every means at our disposal to get him talking.

In all likelihood you began reading this chapter, much as I began writing it, convinced that torture is a very bad thing and that we are wise not to practice it—indeed that we are civilized, in large measure, *because* we do not practice it. Most of us feel, intuitively at least, that if we can't quite muster a retort to Dershowitz and his ticking bomb, we can take refuge in the fact that the paradigmatic case will almost never arise. From this perspective, adorning the machinery of our justice system with a torture provision seems both unnecessary and dangerous, as the law of unintended consequences may one day find it throwing the whole works into disarray. Because I believe the account offered above is basically sound, I believe that I have successfully argued for the use of torture in any circumstance in which we would be willing to cause collateral damage.[3] Paradoxically, this equivalence has not made the practice of torture seem any more acceptable to me; nor has it, I trust, for most readers. I believe that here we come upon an ethical illusion of sorts—analogous to the perceptual illusions that are of such abiding interest to scientists who study the visual pathways in the brain. The full moon appearing on the horizon is no bigger than the full moon when it appears overhead, but it *looks* bigger, for reasons that are still obscure to neuroscientists. A ruler held up to the sky reveals something that we are otherwise incapable of seeing, even when we understand that our eyes are deceiving us. Given a choice between acting on the basis of the way things seem in this instance, or on the deliverances of our ruler, most of us will be willing to dispense with appearances—particularly if our lives or the lives of others depended on it. I believe that most readers who have followed me this far will find themselves in substantially the same position with respect to the ethics of torture. Given what many of us believe about the exigencies of our war on terrorism, the practice of torture, in certain circumstances, would seem to be not only permissible but necessary. Still, it does not seem any more acceptable, in ethical terms, than it did before. The reasons for this are, I trust, every bit as neurological as those that give rise to the moon illusion. In fact, there is already some scientific evidence that our ethical intuitions are driven by considerations of proximity and emotional salience.[4] Clearly, these intuitions are fallible. In the present case, many innocent lives could well be lost as a result of our inability to feel a moral equivalence where a moral equivalence seems to exist. It may be time to take out our rulers and hold them up to the sky.

ENDNOTES

1. That these men are being held indefinitely, without access to legal counsel, should be genuinely troubling to us, however.

2. Jonathan Glover, *Humanity: A Moral History of The Twentieth Century* (New Haven: Yale University Press, 1999), 55.

3. I suspect that if our media did not censor the more disturbing images of war, our moral sentiments would receive a correction on two fronts: first, we would be more motivated by the horrors visited upon us by our enemies: seeing Daniel Pearl decapitated, for instance, would have surely provoked a level of national outrage that did not arise in the absence of such imagery. Second, if we did not conceal the horrible reality of collateral damage from ourselves, we would be far less likely to support the dropping of "dumb" bombs, or even "smart" ones. While our newspapers and newscasts would be horrible to look at, I believe we would feel both greater urgency and greater restraint in our war on terrorism.

4. See Joshua D. Greene et al., "An fMRI Investigation of Emotional Engagement in Moral Judgment," *Science* 293 (Sept. 14, 2001): 2105-8; and Joshua D. Greene, "From Neural 'Is' to Moral 'Ought': What Are the Moral Implications of Neuroscientific Moral Psychology?" *Nature Reviews Neuroscience* 4 (2003): 846–49.

76

Liberalism, Torture, and the Ticking Bomb

DAVID LUBAN

David Luban takes on the "ticking-bomb" scenario made familiar to us from countless action films and TV episodes. He argues the imagined scenario seduces those who would otherwise outright condemn torture because it grossly distorts reality. The reality, Luban argues, is that if we become too permissive of torture, scenes like those at Abu Grahib prison will become all too common place.

Liberals, I have said, rank cruelty first among vices—not because liberals are more compassionate than anyone else, but because of the close connection between cruelty and tyranny. Torture is the living manifestation of cruelty, and the peculiar horror of torture within liberalism arises from the fact that torture is tyranny in microcosm, at its highest level of intensity. The history of torture reinforces this horror because torture has always been bound up with military conquest, regal punishment, dictatorial terror, forced confessions, and the repression of dissident belief—a veritable catalogue of the evils of absolutist government that liberalism abhors. For all these reasons, it should hardly surprise us that liberals wish to ban torture absolutely—a wish that became legislative reality in the Torture Convention's insistence that nothing can justify torture.[1]

But what about torture as intelligence gathering, torture to forestall greater evils? I suspect that throughout history this has been the least common motivation for torture, and thus the one most readily overlooked. And yet it alone bears no essential connection with tyranny. This is not to say that the torture victim experiences it as any less terrifying, humiliating, or tyrannical. The victim, after all, undergoes abject domination by the torturer. But it will dawn on reluctant liberals that the torturer's goal of forestalling greater evils is one that liberals share. It seems like a rational motivation, far removed from cruelty and power-lust. In fact, the liberal may for the first time find it possible to view torture from the torturer's point of view rather than the victim's.

Thus, even though absolute prohibition remains liberalism's primary teaching about torture, and the basic liberal stance is empathy for the torture victim, a more permissive stance remains an unspoken possibility, the Achilles' heel of absolute prohibitions. As long as the intelligence needs of a liberal society are slight, this possibility within liberalism remains dormant, perhaps even unnoticed. But when a catastrophe like 9/11 happens, liberals may cautiously conclude that, in the words of a well-known *Newsweek* article, it is "Time to Think About Torture."[2]

But the pressure of liberalism will compel them to think about it in a highly stylized and artificial way, what I will call the "liberal ideology of torture." The liberal ideology insists that the sole purpose of torture must be intelligence gathering to prevent a catastrophe; that torture is necessary to prevent the catastrophe; that torturing is the

David Luban, "Liberalism, Torture, and the Ticking Bomb," *Virginia Law Review*. Reprinted by permission.

exception, not the rule, so that it has nothing to do with state tyranny; that those who inflict the torture are motivated solely by the looming catastrophe, with no tincture of cruelty; that torture in such circumstances is, in fact, little more than self-defense; and that, because of the associations of torture with the horrors of yesteryear, perhaps one should not even call harsh interrogation "torture."

And the liberal ideology will crystallize all of these ideas in a single, mesmerizing example: the ticking time bomb.

THE TICKING BOMB

Suppose the bomb is planted somewhere in the crowded heart of an American city, and you have custody of the man who planted it. He won't talk. Surely, the hypothetical suggests, we shouldn't be too squeamish to torture the information out of him and save hundreds of lives. Consequences count, and abstract moral prohibitions must yield to the calculus of consequences.

Everyone argues the pros and cons of torture through the ticking time bomb. Senator Schumer and Professor Dershowitz, the Israeli Supreme Court and indeed every journalist devoting a think-piece to the unpleasant question of torture, begins with the ticking time bomb and ends there as well. The Schlesinger Report on Abu Ghraib notes that "[f]or the U.S., most cases for permitting harsh treatment of detainees on moral grounds begin with variants of the 'ticking time-bomb' scenario."[3] At this point in my argument, I mean to disarm the ticking time bomb and argue that it is the wrong thing to think about. If so, then the liberal ideology of torture begins to unravel.

But before beginning these arguments, I want to pause and ask why this jejune example has become the alpha and omega of our thinking about torture. I believe the answer is this: The ticking time bomb is proffered against liberals who believe in an absolute prohibition against torture. The idea is to force the liberal prohibitionist to admit that yes, even he or even she would agree to torture in at least this one situation. Once the prohibitionist admits that, then

she has conceded that her opposition to torture is not based on principle. Now that the prohibitionist has admitted that her moral principles can be breached, all that is left is haggling about the price. No longer can the prohibitionist claim the moral high ground; no longer can she put the burden of proof on her opponent. She is down in the mud with them, and the only question left is how much further down she will go. Dialectically, getting the prohibitionist to address the ticking time bomb is like getting the vegetarian to eat just one little oyster because it has no nervous system. Once she does that—*gotcha!*

The ticking time-bomb scenario serves a second rhetorical goal, one that is equally important to the proponent of torture. It makes us see the torturer in a different light—one of the essential points in the liberal ideology of torture because it is the way that liberals can reconcile themselves to torture even while continuing to "put cruelty first." Now, he is not a cruel man or a sadistic man or a coarse, insensitive brutish man. The torturer is instead a conscientious public servant, heroic the way that New York firefighters were heroic, willing to do desperate things only because the plight is so desperate and so many innocent lives are weighing on the public servant's conscience. The time bomb clinches the great divorce between torture and cruelty; it placates liberals, who put cruelty first.

Wittgenstein once wrote that confusion arises when we become bewitched by a picture.[4] He meant that it's easy to get seduced by simplistic examples that look compelling but actually misrepresent the world in which we live. If the subject is the morality of torture, philosophical confusions can have life-or-death consequences. I believe the ticking time bomb is the picture that bewitches us.

I don't mean that the time-bomb scenario is completely unreal. To take a real-life counterpart: in 1995, an al Qaeda plot to bomb eleven U.S. airliners and assassinate the Pope was thwarted by information tortured out of a Pakistani bomb-maker by the Philippine police.[5] According to journalists Marites Dañguilan Vitug and Glenda M. Gloria, the police had received word of possible threats against the Pope. They went to work. "For weeks, agents hit him with a chair and a long piece of wood, forced water into his mouth, and crushed lighted cigarettes into his private parts.... His ribs were almost totally broken that his captors were surprised that he survived...."[6] Grisly, to be sure—but if they hadn't done it, thousands of innocent travelers might have died horrible deaths.

But look at the example one more time. The Philippine agents were surprised he survived—in other words, they came close to torturing him to death *before* he talked. And they tortured him *for weeks*, during which time they didn't know about any specific al Qaeda plot. What if he too didn't know? Or what if there had been no al Qaeda plot? Then they would have tortured him for weeks, possibly tortured him to death, for nothing. For all they knew at the time, that is exactly what they were doing. You cannot use the argument that preventing the al Qaeda attack justified the decision to torture, because *at the moment the decision was made* no one knew about the al Qaeda attack.

The ticking-bomb scenario cheats its way around these difficulties by stipulating that the bomb is there, ticking away, and that officials know it and know they have the man who planted it. Those conditions will seldom be met.[7] Let us try some more realistic hypothetical and the questions they raise:

1. The authorities know there may be a bomb plot in the offing, and they have captured a man who may know something about it, but may not. Torture him? How much? For weeks? For months? The chances are considerable that you are torturing a man with nothing to tell you. If he doesn't talk, does that mean it's time to stop, or time to ramp up the level of torture? How likely does it have to be that he knows something important? Fifty-fifty? Thirty-seventy? Will one out of a hundred suffice to land him on the waterboard?

2. Do you really want to make the torture decision by running the numbers? A one-percent chance of saving a thousand lives yields ten statistical lives. Does that mean that you can torture up to nine people on a one-percent chance of finding crucial information?

3. The authorities think that one out of a group of fifty captives in Guantanamo might know where Osama bin Laden is hiding, but they do not know which captive. Torture them all? That is: Do you torture forty-nine captives with nothing to tell you on the uncertain chance of capturing bin Laden?

4. For that matter, would capturing Osama bin Laden demonstrably save a single human life? The Bush administration has downplayed the importance of capturing bin Laden because American strategy has succeeded in marginalizing him. Maybe capturing him would save lives, but how certain do you have to be? Or does it not matter whether torture is intended to save human lives from a specific threat, as long as it furthers some goal in the War on Terror? This last question is especially important once we realize that the interrogation of al Qaeda suspects will almost never be employed to find out where the ticking bomb is hidden. Instead, interrogation is a more general fishing expedition for any intelligence that might be used to help "unwind" the terrorist organization. Now one might reply that al Qaeda is itself the ticking time bomb, so that unwinding the organization meets the formal conditions of the ticking-bomb hypothetical. This is equivalent to asserting that any intelligence that promotes victory in the War on Terror justifies torture, precisely because we understand that the enemy in the War on Terror aims to kill American civilians. Presumably, on this argument, Japan would have been justified in torturing American captives in World War II on the chance of finding intelligence that would help them shoot down the Enola Gay; I assume that a ticking-bomb hard-liner will not flinch from this conclusion. But at this point, we verge on declaring all military threats and adversaries that menace American civilians to be ticking bombs whose defeat justifies torture. The limitation of torture to emergency exceptions, implicit in the ticking-bomb story, now threatens to unravel, making torture a legitimate instrument of military policy. And then the question becomes inevitable: Why not torture in pursuit of any worthwhile goal?

5. Indeed, if you are willing to torture forty-nine innocent people to get information from the one who has it, why stop there? If suspects will not break under torture, why not torture their loved ones in front of them? They are no more innocent than the forty-nine you have already shown you are

prepared to torture. In fact, if only the numbers matter, torturing loved ones is almost a no-brainer if you think it will work. Of course, you won't know until you try whether torturing his child will break the suspect. But that just changes the odds; it does not alter the argument.

The point of the examples is that in a world of uncertainty and imperfect knowledge, the ticking-bomb scenario should not form the point of reference. The ticking bomb is the picture that be-witches us. The real debate is not between one guilty man's pain and hundreds of innocent lives. It is the debate between the certainty of anguish and the mere possibility of learning something vital and saving lives. And, above all, it is the question about whether a responsible citizen must unblinkingly think the unthinkable and accept that the morality of torture should be decided purely by totaling up costs and benefits.[8] Once you accept that only the numbers count, then anything, no matter how gruesome, becomes possible. "Consequentialist rationality," as Bernard Williams notes sardonically, "will have something to say even on the difference between massacring seven million, and massacring seven million and one."[9]

I am inclined to think that the path of wisdom instead lies in Holocaust survivor David Rousset's famous caution that normal human beings do *not* know that everything is possible.[10] As Williams says, "there are certain situations so monstrous that the idea that the processes of moral rationality could yield an answer in them is insane" and "to spend time thinking what one would decide if one were in such a situation is also insane, if not merely frivolous."[11]

TORTURE AS A PRACTICE

There is a second, insidious, error built into the ticking-bomb hypothetical. It assumes a single, ad hoc decision about whether to torture, by officials who ordinarily would do no such thing except in a desperate emergency. But in the real world of inter-rogations, decisions are not made one-off. The real world is a world of policies, guidelines, and directives. It is a world of *practices*, not of ad hoc emergency

measures. Therefore, any responsible discussion of torture must address the practice of torture, not the ticking-bomb hypothetical. I am not saying anything original here; other writers have made exactly this point.[12] But somehow, we always manage to forget this and circle back to the ticking time bomb. Its rhe-torical power has made it indispensable to the sensi-tive liberal soul, and we would much rather talk about the ticking bomb than about torture as an organized social practice.

Treating torture as a practice rather than as a desperate improvisation in an emergency means changing the subject from the ticking bomb to other issues like these: Should we create a profes-sional cadre of trained torturers? That means a group of interrogators who know the techniques, who learn to overcome their instinctive revulsion against causing physical pain, and who acquire the legendary surgeon's arrogance about their own infallibility. It has happened before. Medieval executioners were schooled in the arts of agony as part of the trade: how to break men on the wheel, how to rack them, and even how to surreptitiously strangle them as an act of mercy without the blood-thirsty crowd catching on.[13] In Louis XVI's Paris, torture was a hereditary family trade whose tricks were passed on from father to son.[14] Who will teach torture techniques now? Should universities create an undergraduate course in torture? Or should the subject be offered only in police and military academies?[15] Do we want federal grants for research to devise new and better techniques? Patents issued on high-tech torture devices? Com-panies competing to manufacture them? Trade conventions in Las Vegas? Should there be a medi-cal sub-specialty of torture doctors, who ensure that captives do not die before they talk?[16] The ques-tions amount to this: Do we really want to create a torture culture and the kind of people who inhabit it? The ticking time bomb distracts us from the real issue, which is not about emergencies, but about the normalization of torture.

Perhaps the solution is to keep the practice of torture secret in order to avoid the moral corrup-tion that comes from creating a public culture of torture. But this so-called "solution" does not reject the normalization of torture. It accepts it, but layers on top of it the normalization of state secrecy. The result would be a shadow culture of torturers and those who train and support them, operating outside the public eye and accountable only to other insiders of the torture culture.

Just as importantly: Who guarantees that case-hardened torturers, inured to levels of violence and pain that would make ordinary people vomit at the sight, will know where to draw the line on when torture should be used? They rarely have in the past. They didn't in Algeria.[17] They didn't in Israel, where in 1999, the Israeli Supreme Court backpedaled from an earlier consent to torture lite because the interrogators were running amok and torturing two-thirds of their Palestinian captives.[18] In the Argentinian Dirty War, the tortures began because terrorist cells had a policy of fleeing when one of their members had disappeared for forty-eight hours, leaving authorities two days to wring the information out of the captive.[19] Mark Osiel, who has studied the Argentinean military in the Dirty War, reports that many of the torturers initially had qualms about what they were doing, until their priests reassured them that they were fighting God's fight.[20] By the end of the Dirty War, the qualms were gone, and, as John Simpson and Jana Bennett report, hardened young officers were placing bets on who could kidnap the prettiest girl to rape and torture.[21] Escalation is the rule, not the aberration.[22]

There are two fundamental reasons for this: one rooted in the nature of bureaucracy and the other in social psychology. The liberal ideology of torture presupposes a torturer impelled by the desire to stop a looming catastrophe, not by cruelty. Implicitly, this image presumes that the interrogator and the decisionmaker are the same person. But the defining fact about real organizations is the division of labor. The person who decides whether this prisoner presents a genuine ticking-bomb case is not the interrogator. The decision about what counts as a ticking-bomb case—one where torture is the lesser evil—depends on complex value judgments, and these are made further up the chain of command. The interrogator simply executes decisions made elsewhere.

Interrogators do not inhabit a world of loving kindness, or of equal concern and respect for all human beings. Interrogating resistant prisoners non-violently and non-abusively still requires a relationship that in any other context would be morally abhorrent. It requires tricking information out of the subject, and the interrogator does this by setting up elaborate scenarios to disorient the subject and propel him into an alternative reality. The subject must be deceived into thinking that his high-value intelligence has already been revealed by someone else, so that it is no longer of any value. He must be fooled into thinking that his friends have betrayed him or that the interrogator is his friend. The interrogator disrupts his sense of time and place, disorients him with sessions that never take place at predictable times or intervals, and manipulates his emotions. The very names of interrogation techniques show this: "Emotional Love," "Emotional Hate," "Fear Up Harsh," "Fear Up Mild," "Reduced Fear," "Pride and Ego Up," "Pride and Ego Down," "Futility."[23] The interrogator may set up a scenario to make the subject think he is in the clutches of a much-feared secret police organization from a different country ("False Flag"). Every bit of the subject's environment is fair game for manipulation and deception, as the interrogator aims to create the total lie that gets the subject talking.[24]

Let me be clear that I am not objecting to these deceptions. None of these practices rises to the level of abuse or torture lite, let alone torture heavy, and surely tricking the subject into talking is legitimate if the goals of the interrogation are legitimate. But what I have described is a relationship of totalitarian mind-control more profound than the world of Orwell's *1984*. The interrogator is like Descartes' Evil Deceiver, and the subject lives in a false reality reminiscent of *The Matrix*. The liberal fiction that interrogation can be done by people who are neither cruel nor tyrannical runs aground on the fact that regardless of the interrogator's character off the job, on the job, every fiber of his concentration is devoted to dominating the mind of the subject.

Only one thing prevents this from turning into abuse and torture, and that is a clear set of bright-line rules, drummed into the interrogator with the intensity of a religious indoctrination, complete with warnings of fire and brimstone. American interrogator Chris Mackey reports that warnings about the dire consequences of violating the Geneva Conventions "were repeated so often that by the end of our time at [training school] the three syllables 'Leaven-worth' were ringing in our ears."[25]

But what happens when the line is breached? When, as in Afghanistan, the interrogator gets mixed messages about whether Geneva applies, or hears rumors of ghost detainees, of high-value captives held for years of interrogation in the top-secret facility known as "Hotel California," located in some nation somewhere?[26] Or when the interrogator observes around him the move from deception to abuse, from abuse to torture lite, from torture lite to beatings and waterboarding? Without clear lines, the tyranny innate in the interrogator's job has nothing to hold it in check.[27] Perhaps someone, somewhere in the chain of command, is wringing hands over whether this interrogation qualifies as a ticking-bomb case; but the interrogator knows only that the rules of the road have changed and the posted speed limits no longer apply. The liberal fiction of the conscientious interrogator overlooks a division of moral labor in which the person with the fastidious conscience and the person doing the interrogation are not the same.

The fiction must presume, therefore, that the interrogator operates only under the strictest supervision, in a chain of command where his every move gets vetted and controlled by the superiors who are actually doing the deliberating. The trouble is that this assumption flies in the face of everything that we know about how organizations work. The basic rule in every bureaucratic organization is that operational details and the guilty knowledge that goes with them get pushed down the chain of command as far as possible. As sociologist Robert Jackall explains,

[i]t is characteristic ... that details are pushed down and credit is pulled up. Superiors do not like to give detailed instructions to subordinates.... [O]ne of the privileges of authority is the divestment of humdrum intricacies.... Perhaps more important, pushing details down protects the privilege of authority to declare that a mistake has been made.... Moreover, pushing down details relieves superiors of the burden of too much knowledge, particularly guilty knowledge.[28]

We saw this phenomenon at Abu Ghraib, where military intelligence officers gave military police vague orders like: "'Loosen this guy up for us;' 'Make sure he has a bad night.' 'Make sure he gets the treatment.'"[29] Suppose that the eighteen-year-old guard interprets "[m]ake sure he has a bad night" to mean, simply, "keep him awake all night." How do you do that without physical abuse?[30] Furthermore, personnel at Abu Ghraib witnessed far harsher treatment of prisoners by "other governmental agencies" (OGA),[31] a euphemism for the Central Intelligence Agency. They saw OGA spirit away the dead body of an interrogation subject, and allegedly witnessed a contract employee rape a youthful prisoner.[32] When that is what you see, abuses like those in the Abu Ghraib photos will not look outrageous. Outrageous compared with what?

This brings me to the point of social psychology. Simply stated, it is this: we judge right and wrong against the baseline of whatever we have come to consider "normal" behavior, and if the norm shifts in the direction of violence, we will come to tolerate and accept violence as a normal response. The psychological mechanisms for this renormalization have been studied for more than half a century, and by now they are reasonably well understood.[33] Rather than detour into psychological theory, however, I will illustrate the point with the most salient example—one that seems so obviously applicable to Abu Ghraib that the Schlesinger Commission discussed it at length in an appendix to its report.[34] This is the famous Stanford Prison Experiment. Male volunteers were divided randomly into two groups who would simulate the guards and inmates in a mock prison. Within a matter of days, the inmates began acting like actual prison inmates – depressed, enraged, and anxious. And the guards began to abuse the inmates to such an alarming degree that the researchers had to halt the two-week experiment after just seven days. In the words of the experimenters:

> The use of power was self-aggrandising and self-perpetuating. The guard power, derived initially from an arbitrary label, was intensified whenever there was any perceived threat by the prisoners and this new level subsequently became the baseline from which further hostility and harassment would begin…. [T]he absolute level of aggression as well as the more subtle and "creative" forms of aggression manifested, increased in a spiralling function.[35]

It took only five days before a guard, who prior to the experiment described himself as a pacifist, was forcing greasy sausages down the throat of a prisoner who refused to eat; and in less than a week, the guards were placing bags over prisoners' heads, making them strip, and sexually humiliating them in ways reminiscent of Abu Ghraib.[36]

My conclusion is very simple. Abu Ghraib is the fully predictable image of what a torture culture looks like. Abu Ghraib is not a few bad apples—it is

the apple tree. And you cannot reasonably expect that interrogators in a torture culture will be the fastidious and well-meaning torturers that the liberal ideology fantasizes.

This is why Alan Dershowitz has argued that judges, not torturers, should oversee the permission to torture, which in his view must be regulated by warrants. The irony is that Jay S. Bybee, who signed the Justice Department's highly permissive torture memo, is now a federal judge. Politicians pick judges, and if the politicians accept torture, the judges will as well. Once we create a torture culture, only the naive would suppose that judges will provide a safeguard. Judges do not fight their culture—they reflect it.

For all these reasons, the ticking-bomb scenario is an intellectual fraud. In its place, we must address the real questions about torture—questions about uncertainty, questions about the morality of consequences, and questions about what it does to a culture and the torturers themselves to introduce the practice. Once we do so, I suspect that few Americans will be willing to accept that everything is possible.

ENDNOTES

1. "No exceptional circumstances whatsoever, whether a state of war or a threat of war, internal political instability or any other public emergency, may be invoked as a justification of torture." Convention Against Torture and Other Cruel, Inhuman or Degrading Treatment or Punishment, art. 2, Mar. 4, 1984, S. Treaty Doc. No. 100-20, 1465 U.N.T.S. 85, 114 [hereinafter Convention Against Torture].

2. Jonathan Alter, Time to Think About Torture, Newsweek, Nov. 5, 2001, at 45, 45.

3. Schlesinger Report, supra note 39, at 908, 974.

4. Ludwig Wittgenstein, Philosophical Investigations 47e–48e (G.E.M. Anscombe trans., 3d ed. 1958).

5. Doug Struck et al., Borderless Network Of Terror: Bin Laden Followers Reach Across Globe, Wash. Post, Sept. 23, 2001, at A1.

6. Marites Dañguilan Vitug & Glenda M. Gloria, Under the Crescent Moon: Rebellion in Mindanao 223 (2000).

7. See Oren Gross, Are Torture Warrants Warranted? Pragmatic Absolutism and Official Disobedience, 88 Minn. L. Rev. 1481, 1501–03 (2004). Gross reminds us, however, that the catastrophic case can actually occur. Id. at 1503–04. The ticking-bomb case might occur if a government has extremely good intelligence about a terrorist group—good enough to know that it has dispatched operatives to carry out an operation, and good enough to identify and capture someone in the group who knows the details—but not good enough to know the details without getting them from the captive. Israel seems like a setting in which cases like this might arise, and indeed, Mark Bowden reports on just such a case. Mark Bowden, The Dark Art of Interrogation, Atlantic Monthly, Oct. 2003, at 51, 65–68. Importantly, however, the Israeli interrogator obtained the information through trickery, not torture.

8. For a powerful version of the consequentialist argument, which acknowledges these consequences and accepts them (at least for dialectical purposes), see Louis Michael Seidman, Torture's Truth, 72 U. Chi. L. Rev. 881 (2005).

9. Bernard Williams, A critique of utilitarianism, *in* J.J.C. Smart & Bernard Williams, Utilitarianism: for and against 75, 93 (1973).

10. David Rousset, The Other Kingdom 168 (Ramon Guthrie trans., Howard Fertig, Inc. 1982).

11. Williams, supra note 48, at 92. Williams suggests "that the *unthinkable* was itself a moral category." Id.

12. See, e.g., Bowden, supra note 46, at 74, 76; Michael Ignatieff, The Torture Wars, New Republic, Apr. 22, 2002, at 40, 40; Marcy Strauss, Torture, 48 N.Y.L. Sch. L. Rev. 201, 270–71 (2003).

13. Arthur Isak Applbaum, Professional Detachment: The Executioner of Paris, 109 Harv. L. Rev. 458, 459–60, 475 (1995).

14. Id. at 459.

15. We should recall that for years American instructors taught torture to Latin American military officers at the School of the Americas in Fort Benning, Georgia. See Dana Priest, U.S. Instructed Latins On Executions, Torture, Wash. Post, Sept. 21, 1996, at A1.

16. Summarizing extensive studies by researchers, Jean Maria Arrigo notes medical participation in 20% to 40% of torture cases. One study, a random survey of 4,000 members of the Indian Medical Association (of whom 743 responded), revealed that "58% believed torture interrogation permissible; 71% had come across a case of probable torture; 18% knew of health professionals who had participated in torture; 16% had witnessed torture themselves; and 10% agreed that false medical and autopsy reports were sometimes justified." Jean Maria Arrigo, A Consequentialist Argument against Torture Interrogation of Terrorists (Jan. 30–31, 2003), at http://www.atlas.usafa.af.mil/jscope/JSCOPE03/Arrigo03.html.

17. This is the conclusion Michael Ignatieff draws from the memoirs of French torturer Paul Aussaresses, who remains completely unapologetic for torturing and killing numerous Algerian terrorists. Ignatieff, supra note 51, at 42.

18. Bowden, supra note 46, at 74–76.

19. Mark J. Osiel, Mass Atrocity, Ordinary Evil, and Hannah Arendt: Criminal Consciousness in Argentina's Dirty War 40 (2002).

20. Id. at 120–21.

21. John Simpson & Jana Bennett, The Disappeared and the Mothers of the Plaza: The Story of the 11,000 Argentinians Who Vanished 109 (1985).

22. Ignatieff, supra note 51, at 42.

23. Schlesinger Report, supra note 39, at 908, 966–67; see also Chris Mackey & Greg Miller, The Interrogator's War: Inside the Secret War Against Al Qaeda 479–83 (2004).

24. See Bowden, supra note 46, at 64–65.

25. Mackey & Miller, supra note 62, at 31.

26. Toby Harnden, Welcome to the CIA's Hotel California, Daily Telegraph (London), Mar. 4, 2003, at 11 (describing a secret interrogation center named for an Eagles song because "you can check in any time, but you can never leave").

27. This point is made in the Fay-Jones Report on Abu Ghraib. After noting that conflicting directives about stripping prisoners and using dogs were floating around simultaneously, the Report adds:

> Furthermore, some military intelligence personnel executing their interrogation duties at Abu Ghraib had previously served as interrogators in other theaters of operation, primarily Afghanistan and GTMO. These prior interrogation experiences complicated understanding at the interrogator level. The extent of "word of mouth" techniques that were passed to the interrogators in Abu Ghraib by assistance teams from Guantanamo, Fort Huachuca, or amongst themselves due to prior assignments is unclear and likely impossible to definitively determine. The clear thread in the CJTF-7 policy memos and published doctrine is the humane treatment of detainees and the applicability of the Geneva Conventions. Experienced interrogators will confirm that interrogation is an art, not a science, and knowing the limits of authority is crucial. Therefore, the existence of confusing and inconsistent interrogation technique policies contributed to the belief that additional interrogation techniques were condoned in order to gain intelligence.

Fay-Jones Report, supra note 22, at 987, 1004.

28. Robert Jackall, Moral Mazes: The World of Corporate Managers 20 (1988).

29. Seymour M. Hersh, Chain of Command: The Road from 9/11 to Abu Ghraib 30 (2004).

30. As a military police captain told Hersh, "when you ask an eighteen-year-old kid to keep someone awake, and he doesn't know how to do it, he's going to get creative." Id. at 34.

31. See Fay-Jones Report, supra note 22, at 987, 990 ("Working alongside non-DOD organizations/agencies in detention facilities proved complex and demanding. The perception that non-DOD agencies had different rules regarding interrogation and detention operations was evident.... The appointing authority and investigating officers made a specific finding regarding the issue of 'ghost detainees' within Abu Ghraib. It is clear that the interrogation practices of other government agencies led to a loss of accountability at Abu Ghraib.").

32. Hersh, supra note 68, at 44–45.

33. For details, see David Luban, The Ethics of Wrongful Obedience, in Ethics in Practice: Lawyers' Roles, Responsibilities, and Regulation 94, 101–03 (Deborah L. Rhode ed., 2000); David Luban, Integrity: Its Causes and Cures, 72 Fordham L. Rev. 279, 293–98 (2003).

34. Schlesinger Report, supra note 39, at 908, 970–71.

35. Craig Haney et al., Interpersonal Dynamics of a Simulated Prison, 1 Int'l. J. Criminology & Penology 69, 94 (1973); see also Philip G. Zimbardo et al., The Mind is a Formidable Jailer: A Pirandellian Prison, N.Y. Times Mag., Apr. 8, 1973, at 40–42 and the remarkable internet slide-show of the experiment, Philip G. Zimbardo, Stanford Prison Experiment: A Simulation Study of the Psychology of Imprisonment Conducted at Stanford University (1999), at http://www.prisonexp.org.

36. John Schwartz, Simulated Prison in '71 Showed a Fine Line Between 'Normal' and 'Monster,' N.Y. Times, May 6, 2004, at A20; Zimbardo, supra note 74, at slides 8, 18, 21, 28, 33. The sausage incident is described in Craig Haney & Philip G. Zimbardo, The Socialization into Criminality: *On Becoming a Prisoner and a Guard,* in Law, Justice, and the Individual in Society: Psychological and Legal Issues 198, 209 (June Louin Tapp & Felice J. Levine eds., 1977).

77

Can Terrorism Be Morally Justified?

STEPHEN NATHANSON

Stephen Nathanson begins with a definition of terrorism, the most important feature of which is that terrorism involves killing or injuring innocent people or the threat thereof. He rejects various attempts to distinguish terrorism from legitimate acts of warfare. He offers his own "bend over backwards" rule as the most appropriate way of distinguishing legitimate acts of warfare from terrorist acts. He further claims that something like Rawls's veil of ignorance decision procedure can be used to justify his "bend over backwards" rule.

Can terrorism be morally justified? Even asking this question can seem like an insult—both to victims of terrorist actions and to moral common sense. One wants to say: if the murder of innocent people by terrorists is not clearly wrong, what is?

But the question is more complicated than it looks. We can see this by broadening our focus and considering some of the other beliefs held by people who condemn terrorism. Very few of us accept the pacifist view that all violence is wrong. Most of us believe that some acts of killing and injuring people are morally justified. Indeed, most of us think that war is sometimes justified, even though it involves organized, large-scale killing, injuring, and destruction and even though innocent civilians are usually among the victims of war. So, most of us believe that even the killing of innocent people is sometimes morally justified. It is this fact that makes the condemnation of terrorism morally problematic. We pick out terrorism for special condemnation because its victims are civilian, noncombatants rather than military or governmental officials, but we also believe that such killings are sometimes morally permissible. Seen in this broader context, judgments about terrorism often seem hypocritical.

Seen in a broader context, moral judgments of terrorism often seem hypocritical. They often presuppose self-serving definitions of "terrorism" that allow people to avoid labeling actions that they approve as instances of terrorism, even though these actions are indistinguishable from other acts that are branded with this negative label. On other occasions, moral judgments of terrorism rest on biased, uneven applications of moral principles to the actions of friends and foes. Principles that are cited to condemn the actions of foes are ignored when similar actions are committed by friends.

We need to ask then: Can people who believe that war is sometimes morally permissible consistently condemn terrorist violence? Or are such condemnations necessarily hypocritical and self-serving?

If we are to avoid hypocrisy, then we need both (a) a definition of terrorism that is neutral with respect to who commits the actions, and (b) moral judgments of terrorism that derive from the consistent, even-handed applications of moral criteria.

This paper aims to achieve both of these things. First, I begin with a definition of terrorism and then discuss why terrorism is always wrong. In addition, I want to show that the condemnation of terrorism does not come without other costs. A consistent approach to terrorism requires us to revise some common judgments about historical events and forces us to reconsider actions in which civilians are killed as "collateral damage" (i.e., side effects) of military attacks.

My aim, then, is to criticize both terrorist actions and a cluster of widespread moral views about violence and war. This cluster includes the following beliefs:

1. Terrorism is always immoral.
2. The allied bombing of cities in World War II was morally justified because of the importance of defeating Nazi Germany and Japan.
3. It is morally permissible to kill civilians in war if these killings are not intended.

The trouble with this cluster is that the first belief expresses an absolute prohibition of acts that kill innocent people while the last two are rather permissive. If we are to avoid inconsistency and hypocrisy, we must revise our views either (a) by accepting that terrorism is sometimes morally permissible, or (b) by judging that city bombings and many collateral damage killings are morally wrong. I will defend the second of these options.

DEFINING TERRORISM

I offer the following definition of terrorism to launch my discussion of the moral issues.[1] Terrorist acts have the following features:

1. They are acts of serious, deliberate violence or destruction.
2. They are generally committed by groups as part of a campaign to promote a political or social agenda.
3. They generally target limited numbers of people but aim to influence a larger group and/or the leaders who make decisions for the group.
4. They either kill or injure innocent people or pose a serious threat of such harms to them.

This definition helps in a number of ways. First, it helps us to distinguish acts of terrorism from other acts of violence. Nonviolent acts are not terrorist acts; nor are violent actions that are unrelated to a political or social agenda. Ironically, some terrible kinds of actions are not terrorist because they are too destructive. As condition 3 tells us, terrorism generally targets limited numbers of people in order to influence a larger group. Acts of genocide that aim to destroy a whole group are not acts of terrorism, but the reason why makes them only worse, not better.

Second, the definition helps us to identify the moral crux of the problem with terrorism. Condition 1 is not the problem because most of us believe that some acts of violence are morally justified. Condition 2 can't be the problem because anyone who believes in just causes of war must accept that some causes are so important that violence may be a legitimate way to promote them. Condition 3 is frequently met by permissible actions, as when we punish some criminals to deter other people from committing crimes. Condition 4 seems closer to what is essentially wrong with terrorism. If terrorism is always immoral, it is because it kills and injures innocent people.

As I have already noted, however, morally conscientious people sometimes want to justify acts that kill innocent people. If a blanket condemnation of terrorism is to be sustained, then we must either condemn all killings of innocent people, or we must find morally relevant differences between the killing of innocents by terrorists and the killing of innocents by others whose actions we find morally acceptable.

TERRORISM AND CITY BOMBING: THE SAME OR DIFFERENT?

Many people who condemn terrorism believe that city bombing in the war against Nazism was justified, even though the World War II bombing campaigns intentionally targeted cities and their inhabitants. This view is defended by some philosophical theorists, including Michael Walzer, in his book *Just and Unjust Wars,* and G. Wallace in "Terrorism and the Argument from Analogy."[2] By considering these theorists, we can see if there are relevant differences that allow us to say that terrorism is always wrong but that the World War II bombings were morally justified.

One of the central aims of Michael Walzer's *Just and Unjust Wars* is to defend what he calls the "war convention," the principles that prohibit attacks on civilians in wartime. Walzer strongly affirms the principle of noncombatant immunity, calling it a "fundamental principle [that] underlies and shapes the judgments we make of wartime conduct." He writes:

> A legitimate act of war is one that does not violate the rights of the people against whom it is directed.... [N]o one can be threatened with war or warred against, unless through some act of his own he has surrendered or lost his rights.[3]

Unlike members of the military, civilians have not surrendered their rights in any way, and therefore, Walzer says, they may not be attacked.

Given Walzer's strong support for noncombatant immunity and his definition of terrorism as the "method of random murder of innocent people," it is no surprise that he condemns terrorism.[4] At one point, after describing a terrorist attack on an Algerian milk bar frequented by teenagers, he writes:

> Certainly, there are historical moments when armed struggle is necessary for the sake of human freedom. But if dignity and self-respect are to be the outcomes of that struggle, it cannot consist of terrorist attacks against children.[5]

Here and elsewhere, Walzer denounces terrorism because it targets innocent people.

Nonetheless, he claims that the aerial attacks on civilians by the British early in World War II were justified. In order to show why, he develops the concept of a "supreme emergency." Nazi Germany, he tells us, was no ordinary enemy; it was an "ultimate threat to everything decent in our lives."[6] Moreover, in 1940, the Nazi threat to Britain

was imminent. German armies dominated Europe and sought to control the seas. Britain feared an imminent invasion by a country that threatened the basic values of civilization.

According to Walzer, the combination of the enormity and the imminence of the threat posed by Nazi Germany produced a supreme emergency, a situation in which the rules prohibiting attacks on civilians no longer held. If killing innocents was the only way to ward off this dreadful threat, then it was permissible. Since air attacks on German cities were the only means Britain had for inflicting harm on Germany, it was morally permissible for them to launch these attacks.

Walzer does not approve all of the city bombing that occurred in World War II. The emergency lasted, he thinks, only through 1942. After that, the threat diminished, and the constraints of the war convention should once again have been honored. In fact, the bombing of cities continued throughout the war, climaxing in massive attacks that killed hundreds of thousands of civilians: the bombing of Dresden, the fire bombings of Japanese cities by the United States, and the atomic bombings of Hiroshima and Nagasaki. According to Walzer, none of these later attacks were justified because the supreme emergency had passed.[7]

While Walzer's discussion begins with the special threat posed by Nazism, he believes that supreme emergencies can exist in more ordinary situations. In the end, he supports the view that if a single nation is faced by "a threat of enslavement or extermination[,]" then its "soldiers and statesmen [may] override the rights of innocent people for the sake of their own political community...."[8] While he expresses this view with "hesitation and worry," he nevertheless broadens the reach of the concept of "supreme emergency" to include circumstances that arise in many wars.

The problem for Walzer is that his acceptance of the broad "supreme emergency" exception threatens to completely undermine the principle of noncombatant immunity that lies at the heart of his own view of the ethics of warfare. How can the principle of noncombatant immunity be fundamental if it can be overridden in some cases? Moreover, his condemnation of terrorism is weakened because it seems to be possible that people might resort to terrorism in cases that qualify as supreme emergencies, as when their own people are threatened by extermination or enslavement. Walzer's defense of the bombing of cities, then, seems to be inconsistent with his sweeping denunciation of terrorism.

WALLACE'S ARGUMENT FROM ANALOGY

While Walzer does not directly address the tension between the two parts of his view, G. Wallace explicitly tries to defend the view that terrorism is wrong and that the bombing of cities was justified. According to Wallace, the bombing campaign was justified because it satisfied all four of the following criteria:[9]

1. It was a measure of last resort.
2. It was an act of collective self-defense.
3. It was a reply in kind against a genocidal, racist aggressor.
4. It had some chance of success.

He then asks whether acts of terrorism might be justified by appeal to these very same criteria.

Wallace's answer is that the terrorism cannot meet these criteria. Or, more specifically, he says that while any one of the criteria might be met by a terrorist act, all four of them cannot be satisfied. Why not? The problem is not with criteria 2 and 3; a community might well be oppressed by a brutal regime and might well be acting in its own defense. In these respects, its situation would be like that of Britain in 1940.

But, Wallace claims, conditions 1 and 4 cannot both be satisfied in this case. If the community has a good chance of success through the use of terrorism (thus satisfying condition 4), then other means of opposition might work as well, and terrorism will fail to be a last resort. Hence it will not meet condition 1. At the same time, if terrorist tactics are a last resort because all other means of opposition will fail, then the terrorist tactics are also likely to fail, in which case condition 4 is not met.

What Wallace has tried to show is that there are morally relevant differences between terrorism and the city bombings by Britain. Even if some of the criteria for justified attacks on civilians can be met by would-be terrorists, all of them cannot be. He concludes that "[E]ven if we allow that conditions (1) and (4) can be met separately, their joint satisfaction is impossible."[10]

Unfortunately, this comforting conclusion—that the British city bombing was justified but that terrorism cannot be—is extremely implausible. Both terrorism and city bombing involve the intentional killing of innocent human beings in order to promote an important political goal. Wallace acknowledges this but claims that the set of circumstances that justified city bombing could not possibly occur again so as to justify terrorism.

There is no basis for this claim, however. Wallace accepts that the right circumstances occurred in the past, and so he should acknowledge that it is at least possible for them to occur in the future. His conclusion ought to be that if city bombing was justifiable, then terrorism is in principle justifiable as well. For these reasons, I believe that Wallace, like Walzer, is logically committed to acknowledging the possibility of morally justified terrorism.

This is not a problem simply for these two authors. Since the historical memory of city bombing in the United States and Britain sees these as justifiable means of war, the dilemma facing these authors faces our own society. We condemn terrorists for intentionally killing innocent people while we think it was right to use tactics in our own wars that did the same. Either we must accept the view that terrorism can sometimes be justified, or we must come to see our own bombings of cities as violations of the prohibitions on killing civilians in wartime.[11]

TERRORISM, COLLATERAL DAMAGE, AND THE PRINCIPLE OF DOUBLE EFFECT

Many of us believe that wars are sometimes justified, but we also know that even if civilians are not intentionally killed, the deaths of civilians is a common feature of warfare. Indeed, during the twentieth century, civilian deaths became a larger and larger proportion of the total deaths caused by war. A person who believes that wars may be justified but that terrorism cannot be must explain how this can be.

One common approach focuses on the difference between intentionally killing civilians, as terrorists do, and unintentionally killing civilians, as sometimes happens in what we regard as legitimate acts of war. According to this approach, terrorism is wrong because it is intentional while so-called "collateral damage" killings and injuries are morally permissible because they are not intended.

This type of view is developed by Igor Primoratz in "The Morality of Terrorism."[12] Primoratz attempts to show why terrorism is morally wrong and how it differs from other acts of wartime killing that are morally permissible.

First, he makes it clear that, by definition, terrorism always involves the intentional killing of innocent people. He then offers a number of arguments to show why such killings are wrong. The first two have to do with the idea that persons are moral agents who are due a high level of respect and concern. He writes:

> [E]very human being is an individual, a person separate from other persons, with a unique, irreproducible thread of life and a value that is not commensurable with anything else.[13]

Given the incommensurable value of individual persons, it is wrong to try to calculate the worth of some hoped-for goal by comparison with the lives and deaths of individual people. This kind of calculation violates the ideal of giving individual lives our utmost respect and concern. Terrorists ignore this central moral ideal. They treat innocent people as political pawns, ignoring their individual worth and seeing their deaths simply as means toward achieving their goals.

In addition, Primoratz argues, terrorists ignore the moral relevance of guilt and innocence in their treatment of individuals. They attack people who have no responsibility for the alleged evils that the terrorists oppose and thus violate the principle that people should be treated in accord with what they deserve.

Terrorists, Primoratz tells us, also forsake the ideal of moral dialogue amongst equals. They not only decide who will live and who will die, but they feel no burden to justify their actions in ways that the victims might understand and accept. People who take moral ideals seriously engage in open discussion in order to justify their actions. They engage others in moral debate. Ideally, according to Primoratz, a moral person who harms others should try to act on reasons that are so compelling that they could be acknowledged by the victims. Terrorist acts cannot be justified to their victims, and terrorists are not even interested in trying to do so.[14]

Though these ideas are sketched out rather than fully developed, Primoratz successfully expresses some important moral values. Drawing on these values, he concludes that terrorism is incompatible with "some of the most basic moral beliefs many of us hold."[15]

Primoratz vs. Trotsky

Having tried to show why terrorism is wrong, Primoratz considers an objection put forward by Leon Trotsky, who defended terrorism as a revolutionary tactic. Trotsky claims that people who approve traditional war but condemn revolutionary violence are in a weak position because the differences between these are morally arbitrary. If wars that kill innocent people can be justified, Trotsky claims, then so can revolutions that kill innocent people.

Primoratz replies by arguing that there is an important moral difference between terrorism and some acts of war that kill innocent people. While he acknowledges that the "suffering of civilians … is surely inevitable not only in modern, but in almost all wars," Primoratz stresses that the moral evaluation of acts of killing requires that we "attend not only to the suffering inflicted, but also to the way it is inflicted."[16] By this, he means that we need, among other things, to see what the person who did the act intended.

To illustrate his point, he contrasts two cases of artillery attacks on a village. In the first case, the artillery attack is launched with the explicit goal of killing the civilian inhabitants of the village. The civilians are the target of the attack. This attack is the equivalent of terrorism since both intentionally target innocent people, and just like terrorism, it is immoral.

In a second case, the artillery attack is aimed at "soldiers stationed in the village." While the soldiers know that innocent people will be killed, that is not their aim.

> Had it been possible to attack the enemy unit without endangering the civilians in any way, they would certainly have done so. This was not possible, so they attacked although they knew that the attack would cause civilian casualties too; but they did their best to reduce those inevitable, but undesired consequences as much as possible.[17]

In this second case, the civilian deaths and injuries are collateral damage produced by an attack on a legitimate military target. That is the key difference between terrorism and legitimate acts of war. Terrorism is intentionally directed at civilians, while legitimate acts of war do not aim to kill or injure civilians, even when this is their effect.

Primoratz concludes that Trotsky and other defenders of terrorism are wrong when they equate war and terrorism. No doubt, the intentional killing of civilians does occur in war, and when it does, Primoratz would condemn it for the same reason he condemns terrorism. But if soldiers avoid the intentional killing of civilians, then their actions can be morally justified, even when civilians die as a result of what they do. As long as soldiers and revolutionaries avoid the intentional killing of innocent people, they will not be guilty of terrorist acts.

Problems with Primoratz's View

Primoratz's view has several attractive features. Nonetheless, it has serious weaknesses.

In stressing the role of intentions, Primoratz appeals to the same ideas expressed by what is called the "principle of double effect." According to this principle, we should evaluate actions by their intended goals rather than their actual consequences. An act that produces collateral damage deaths is an unintentional killing and hence is not wrong in the way that the same act would be if the civilians' deaths were intended.

While the principle of double effect is plausible in some cases, it is actually severely defective. To see this, suppose that the September 11 attackers had only intended to destroy the Pentagon and the World Trade Center and had no desire to kill anyone. Suppose that they knew, however, that thousands would die in the attack on the buildings. And suppose, following the attack, they said "We are not murderers. We did not mean to kill these people."

What would be our reaction? I very much doubt that we would think them less culpable. They could not successfully justify or excuse their actions by saying that although they foresaw the deaths of many people, these deaths were not part of their aim. We would certainly reject this defense. But if we would reject the appeal to double effect in this case, then we should do so in others.

In Primoratz's example, the artillery gunners attack the village with full knowledge of the high probability of civilian deaths. The artillery gunners know they will kill innocent people, perhaps even in large numbers, and they go ahead with the attack anyway. If it would not be enough for my imagined September 11 attackers to say that they did not intend to kill people, then it is not enough for Primoratz's imagined soldiers to say that they did not mean to kill the villagers when they knew full well that this would result from their actions.

If we accept Primoratz's defense of collateral damage killings, his argument against terrorism is in danger of collapsing because terrorists can use Primoratz's language to show that their actions, too, may be justifiable. If Primoratz succeeds in justifying the collateral damage killings and if the distinction between these killings and terrorism cannot rest solely on whether the killings are intentional, then the criteria that he uses may justify at least some terrorist acts. Like the soldiers in his example, the terrorists may believe that the need for a particular attack is "so strong and urgent that it prevailed over the prohibition of killing or maiming a comparatively small number of civilians." Consistency would require Primoratz to agree that the terrorist act was justified in this case.

Recall, too, Primoratz's claim that actions need to be capable of being justified to the victims themselves. Would the victims of the artillery attack accept the claim that the military urgency justified the "killing or maiming a comparatively small number of civilians."?[18] Why should they accept the sacrifice of their own lives on the basis of this reasoning?

In the end, then, Primoratz does not succeed in showing why terrorism is immoral while collateral damage killing can be morally justified. Like Wallace and Walzer, he has trouble squaring the principles that he uses to condemn terrorism with his own approval of attacks that produce foreseeable collateral damage deaths.

The problem revealed here is not merely a problem for a particular author. The view that collateral damage killings are permissible because they are unintended is a very widespread view. It is the view that United States officials appealed to when our bombings in Afghanistan produced thousands of civilian casualties.[19] Our government asserted that we did not intend these deaths to occur, that we were aiming at legitimate targets, and that the civilian deaths were merely collateral damage. Similar excuses are offered when civilians are killed by cluster bombs and land mines, weapons whose delayed detonations injure and kill people indiscriminately, often long after a particular attack is over.[20]

There are many cases in which people are morally responsible for harms that they do not intend to bring about, but if these harms can be foreseen, their claims that they "did not mean to do it" are not taken seriously. We use labels like "reckless disregard" for human life or "gross negligence" to signify that wrongs have been done, even though they were not deliberate. When such actions lead to

serious injury and death, we condemn such actions from a moral point of view, just as we condemn terrorism. The principle of double effect does not show that these condemnations are mistaken. If we want to differentiate collateral damage killings from terrorism so as to be consistent in our moral judgments, we will need something better than the principle of double effect and the distinction between intended and unintended effects.

A SKETCH OF A DEFENSE

I want to conclude by sketching a better rationale for the view that terrorist attacks on civilians are always wrong but that some attacks that cause civilian deaths and injuries as unintended consequences are morally justified.

I have argued that a central problem with standard defenses of collateral damage killings is that they lean too heavily on the distinction between what is intended and what is foreseen. This distinction, when used with the doctrine of double effect, is too slippery and too permissive. As I noted above, it might provide an excuse for the September 11 attacks if (contrary to fact) the attackers were only targeting the World Trade Center *building* and the Pentagon *building* and did not actually aim to kill innocent civilians.

Michael Walzer makes a similar criticism of the double effect principle. "Simply not to intend the death of civilians is too easy," he writes. "What we look for in such cases is some sign of a positive commitment to save civilian lives."[21] Walzer calls his revised version the principle of "double intention." It requires military planners and soldiers to take positive steps to avoid or minimize these evils, even if these precautions increase the danger to military forces.

Walzer's rule is a step in the right direction, but we need to emphasize that the positive steps must be significant. They cannot be *pro forma* or minimal efforts. In order to show a proper respect for the victims of these attacks, serious efforts must be made to avoid death and injury to them. I suggest the following set of requirements for just, discriminate fighting, offering them as a sketch rather than a full account. The specifics might have to be amended, but the key point is that serious efforts must be made to avoid harm to civilians. Not intending harm is not enough. In addition, military planners must really exert themselves. They must, as we say, *bend over backwards* to avoid harm to civilians. For example, they must:

1. Target attacks as narrowly as possible on military resources;

2. Avoid targets where civilian deaths are extremely likely;

3. Avoid the use of inherently indiscriminate weapons (such as land mines and cluster bombs) and inherently indiscriminate strategies (such as high-altitude bombing of areas containing both civilian enclaves and military targets); and

4. Accept that when there are choices between damage to civilian lives and damage to military personnel, priority should be given to saving civilian lives.

If a group has a just cause for being at war and adheres to principles like these, then it could be said to be acknowledging the humanity and value of those who are harmed by its actions. While its attacks might expose innocent people to danger, its adherence to these principles would show that it was not indifferent to their well-being. In this way, it would show that its actions lack the features that make terrorism morally objectionable.

Why is this? Because the group is combining its legitimate effort to defend itself or others with serious efforts to avoid civilian casualties. The spirit of their effort is captured in the phrase I have already used: "bending over backwards." The "bend over backwards" ideal is superior to the principle of double effect in many ways. First, it goes beyond the weak rule of merely requiring that one not intend to kill civilians. Second, while the double effect rule's distinction between intended and unintended results permits all sorts of fudges and verbal tricks, the "bend over backwards" rule can be applied in a more objective and realistic way. It would be less likely to approve sham compliance than is the doctrine of double effect.

The "bend over backwards" rule might even satisfy Primoratz's requirement that acts of violence be justifiable to their victims. Of course, no actual victim is likely to look favorably on attacks by others that will result in the victim's death or serious injury. But suppose we could present the following situation to people who might be victims of an attack (a condition that most of us inhabit) and have them consider it from something like Rawls's veil of ignorance. We would ask them to consider the following situation:

■ Group A is facing an attack by group B; if successful, the attack will lead to death or the severest oppression of group A.

■ The only way that group A can defend itself is by using means that will cause death and injury to innocent members of group B.

■ You are a member of one of the groups, but you do not know which one.

Would you approve of means of self-defense that will kill and injure innocent members of B in order to defend group A?

In this situation, people would not know whether they would be victims or beneficiaries of whatever policy is adopted. In this circumstance, I believe that they would reject a rule permitting either intentional or indiscriminate attacks on civilians. Thus, they would reject terrorism as a legitimate tactic, just as they would reject indiscriminate attacks that kill and injure civilians.

At the same time, I believe that they would approve a rule that combined a right of countries to defend themselves against aggression with the restrictions on means of fighting contained in the "bend over backwards" rule. This would have the following benefits. If one were a member of a group that had been attacked, one's group would have a right of self-defense. At the same time, if one were an innocent citizen in the aggressor country, the defenders would be required to take serious steps to avoid injury or death to you and other civilians.

If people generally could accept such a rule, then actions that adhere to that rule would be justifiable to potential victims as well as potential attackers. This would include actions that cause civilian causalities but that adhere to the "bend over backwards" principle.

I believe that this sort of approach achieves what nonpacifist critics of terrorism want to achieve. It provides a principled basis for condemning terrorism, no matter who it is carried out by, and a principled justification of warfare that is genuinely defensive. Moreover, the perspective is unified in a desirable way. Terrorist actions cannot be morally justified because the *intentional* targeting of civilians is the most obvious kind of violation of the "bend over backwards" rule.

At the same time that these principles allow for the condemnation of terrorism, they are immune to charges of hypocrisy because they provide a basis for criticizing not only terrorist acts but also the acts of any group that violates the "bend over backwards" rule, either by attacking civilians directly or by failing to take steps to avoid civilian deaths.

CONCLUSION

Can terrorism be morally justified? Of course not. But if condemnations of terrorism are to have moral credibility, they must rest on principles that constrain our own actions and determine our judgments of what we ourselves do and have done. To have moral credibility, opponents of terrorism must stand by the principles underlying their condemnations, apply their principles in an evenhanded way, and bend over backwards to avoid unintended harms to civilians. Only in this way can we begin inching back to a world in which those at war honor the moral rules that prohibit the taking of innocent human lives. As long as condemnations of terrorism are tainted by hypocrisy, moral judgments will only serve to inflame people's hostilities rather than reminding them to limit and avoid serious harms to one another.

ENDNOTES

1. For development and defense of this definition, see my "Prerequisites for Morally Credible Condemnations of Terrorism," in William Crotty, ed., *The Politics of Terrorism: Consequences for an Open Society* (Boston: Northeastern University Press, 2003).

2. Michael Walzer, *Just and Unjust Wars* (New York: Basic Books, 1977); Gerry Wallace, "Terrorism and the Argument from Analogy," *Journal of Moral and Social Studies*, vol. 6 (1991), 149–160.

3. Walzer, 135.

4. Walzer, 197.

5. Walzer, 205.

6. Walzer, 253.

7. Kenneth Brown, "'Supreme Emergency': A Critique of Michael Walzer's Moral Justification for Allied Obliteration Bombing in World War II," *Manchester College Bulletin of the Peace Studies Institute*, 1983 (13, nos. 1–2), 6–15.

8. Walzer, 254.

9. Wallace, 155.

10. Wallace, 155–156.

11. See Rawls on city bombing and the atomic bombings in *The Law of Peoples* and *Collected Papers*.

12. Igor Primoratz, "The Morality of Terrorism?" *Journal of Applied Philosophy*, vol. 14 (1997), 222. Primoratz defends his definition of terrorism in "What Is Terrorism?" *Journal of Applied Philosophy*, vol. 7 (1990), 129–138. These subjects are also helpfully discussed in Haig Khatchadourian, "Terrorism and Morality," *Journal of Applied Philosophy*, vol. 5 (1988), 131–145.

13. Primoratz, 224.

14. For a similar idea, see Thomas Nagel, *Equality and Partiality* (New York: Oxford, 1991), 23. "[W]e are looking for principles to deal with conflict that can at some level be endorsed by everyone...."

15. Primoratz, "The Morality of Terrorism," 225.

16. Primoratz, 227.

17. Primoratz, 227.

18. Primoratz, 228.

19. Marc Herold, an economist at the University of New Hampshire, studied foreign press reports and has concluded that over 3,500 Afghan civilians were killed in the first 2 months of U.S. attacks in Afghanistan (http://www.media-alliance.org/ mediafile/20-5/dossier/ heroldl2-6.htm). For later reports by Herold, see http:// pubpages.unh.edu/ ~mwherold/. The *Boston Globe* estimated 1,000 civilian deaths, but their estimate is based on investigations at 14 sites, which they admit "represent only a small fraction of the total sites targeted by the 18,000 bombs, missiles, and ordnance fired by U.S. forces since October...." See John Donnelly and Anthony Shadid, "Civilian toll in US raids put at 1,000," *Boston Globe,* Feb. 17,2002,1. For further information on attacks on civilian targets, see John Donnelly, "U.S. targeting of vehicles is detailed," *Boston Globe,* Feb. 19, 2002, 1.

20. According to Human Rights Watch, cluster bombs "have proven to be a serious and long-lasting threat to civilians, soldiers, peacekeepers, and even clearance experts." Human Rights Watch, "Cluster Bombs in Afghanistan," www.hrw.org/backgrounder/arms/ cluster-bck 1031.htm.

21. Walzer, 155–156.

78

Terrorism and International Justice

JAMES P. STERBA

James P. Sterba approaches the question of how we should think about terrorism from the perspective of just war pacifism. Just war pacifism, as Sterba defends it, does not impose an absolute prohibition on intentionally harming innocents. In fact, using both hypothetical and historical examples as analogies, Sterba argues that suicide bombing can be morally justified under certain conditions. He also argues that neither the actions taken by the Israeli government with respect to the Palestinians nor the actions taken by the U.S. government with respect to Al Qaeda were morally justified because neither government exhausted its nonbelligerent correctives before engaging in a military response. He further argues that the United States itself has arguably engaged in terrorist acts and supported the terrorist acts of others and so needs to correct its own wrongdoing if it is to respond justly to the wrongdoing of others.

INTRODUCTION

How should we think about terrorism within a context of international justice? To answer this question it is helpful to start with a definition of terrorism.

Since 1983, the U.S. State Department has defined terrorism as follows:

> Terrorism is premeditated, politically motivated violence perpetrated against noncombatant targets by subnational groups or clandestine agents, usually intended to influence an audience.[1]

In a recent State Department document in which this definition is endorsed, there is also a section that discusses state-sponsored terrorism.[2] It is clear then that the State Department does not hold that only subnational groups or individuals can commit terrorist acts; it further recognizes that states can commit terrorist acts as well. So let me offer the following definition of terrorism, which is essentially the same as the U.S. State Department's definition once it is allowed that states too can commit terrorist acts.

> Terrorism is the use or threat of violence against innocent people to further some political objective.

Using this definition, there is no problem seeing the attacks on New York City and Washington, D.C., particularly the attacks on the World Trade Center, as terrorist acts.[3] Likewise, the bombing of the U.S. embassies in Kenya and Tanzania in 1998 as well as the suicide bombings directed at Israeli civilians are terrorist acts.[4]

But what about the U.S. bombing of a pharmaceutical plant in Sudan with respect to which we blocked a UN inquiry and later compensated the owner, but not the thousands of victims who were deprived of drugs,[5] or what about the U.S.-sponsored sanctions against Iraq, which kill an estimated three to five thousand children in Iraq each month,[6] or what about the United States' four-billion-dollar-a-year support for Israel's occupation of Palestinian lands now in its thirty-fifth year, which is illegal, that is, in violation of UN resolutions that specifically forbid "the acquisition of territory by force," and which has resulted in many thousands of deaths? Or if we want to go back further, what about the U.S. support for the Contras in Nicaragua, and of death squads in El Salvador, especially during the Reagan years, our use of terrorist counter-*city* threats of nuclear retaliation during the Cold War, and our actual use of nuclear weapons against Hiroshima and Nagasaki at the end of World War II, resulting in over 100,000 deaths?[7] Surely, all of these U.S. actions also turn out to be either terrorist acts or support for terrorist acts, according to our definition. How can we tell then, which, if any, of these terrorist acts, or support for terrorist acts, are morally justified?

THE PERSPECTIVE OF JUST WAR THEORY AND PACIFISM

My preferred approach to addressing this question is provided by pacifism and just war theory, combined in a view I have called "just war pacifism." Now one might think that from the perspective of just war pacifism, acts of terrorism could never be morally justified. But this would require an absolute prohibition on intentionally harming innocents, and such a prohibition would not seem to be justified, even from the perspective of just war pacifism.[8] Specifically, it would seem that harm to innocents can be justified for the sake of achieving a greater good when the harm is:

1. Trivial (e.g., stepping on someone's foot to get out of a crowded subway);

2. Easily reparable (e.g., lying to a temporarily depressed friend to keep her from committing suicide); or

3. Nonreparable but greatly outweighed by the consequences of the action. Obviously, it is this third category of harm that is relevant to the possible justification of terrorism. But when is intentional harm to innocents nonreparable yet greatly outweighed by the consequences?

Consider the following example often discussed by moral philosophers.[9] A large person who is leading a party of spelunkers gets himself stuck in the mouth of a cave in which flood waters are rising. The trapped party of spelunkers just happens to have a stick of dynamite with which they can blast the large person out of the mouth of the cave; either they use the dynamite or they all drown, the large person with them. Now it is usually assumed in this case that it is morally permissible to dynamite the large person out of the mouth of the cave. After all, if that is not done, the whole party of spelunkers will die, the large person with them. So the sacrifice imposed on the large person in this case would not be that great.

But what if the large person's head is outside rather than inside the cave as it must have been in the previous interpretation of the case. Under those circumstances, the large person would not die when the other spelunkers drown. Presumably after slimming down a bit, he would eventually just squeeze his way out of the mouth of the cave. In this case, could the party of spelunkers trapped in the cave still legitimately use the stick of dynamite they have to save themselves rather than the large person?

Suppose there were ten, twenty, one hundred, or whatever number you want of spelunkers trapped in the cave. At some point, won't the number be sufficiently great that it would be morally acceptable for those in the cave to use the stick of dynamite to save themselves rather than the large person, even if this meant that the large person would be morally required to sacrifice his life? The answer has to be yes, even if you think it has to be a very unusual case when we can reasonably demand that people sacrifice their lives in this way.

Is it possible that some acts of terrorism are morally justified in this way? It is often argued that our dropping of atomic bombs on Hiroshima and Nagasaki was so justified. President Truman, who ordered the bombing, justified it on the grounds that it was used to shorten the war. In 1945, the United States demanded the unconditional surrender of Japan. The Japanese had by that time lost the war, but the leaders of their armed forces were by no means ready to accept unconditional surrender.[10] While the Japanese leaders expected an invasion of their mainland islands, they believed they could make that invasion so costly that the United States would accept a conditional surrender. Truman's military advisors also believed the costs would be high. The capture of Okinawa had cost almost 80,000 American casualties, while almost the entire Japanese garrison of 120,000 men died in battle. If the mainland islands were defended in a similar manner, hundreds of thousands of Japanese would surely die. During that time, the bombing of Japan would continue, and perhaps intensify, resulting in casualty rates that were no different from those that were expected from the atomic attack. A massive incendiary raid on Tokyo early in March 1945 had set off a firestorm and killed an estimated 100,000 people. Accordingly, Truman's secretary of state James Byrnes admitted that the two atomic bombs did cause "many casualties, but not nearly so many as there would have been had our air force continued to drop incendiary bombs on Japan's cities."[11] Similarly, Winston Churchill wrote in support of Truman's decision: "To avert a vast, indefinite butchery ... at the cost of a few explosions seemed, after all our toils and perils, a miracle of deliverance."[12]

Yet the "vast, indefinite butchery" that the United States sought to avert by dropping atomic bombs on Hiroshima and Nagasaki was one that the United States itself was threatening, and had already started to carry out with its incendiary attack on Tokyo. And the United States itself could have easily avoided this butchery by dropping its demand for unconditional Japanese surrender. Moreover, a demand of unconditional surrender can almost never be morally justified since defeated aggressors almost always have certain rights that they never are required to surrender.[13] Hence, the United States' terrorist acts of dropping atomic bombs on Hiroshima and Nagasaki cannot be justified on the grounds of shortening the war and avoiding a vast, indefinite butchery because the United States could have secured those results simply by giving up its unreasonable demand for unconditional surrender.

A more promising case for justified terrorism is the counter-city bombing of the British during the early stages of World War II. Early in the war, it became clear that British bombers could fly effectively only at night because too many of them were being shot down during day raids by German anti-aircraft fire. In addition, a study done in 1941 showed that of those planes flying at night recorded as having actually succeeded in attacking their targets, only one-third managed to drop their bombs within five miles of what they were aiming at.[14] This meant that British bombers flying at night could reasonably aim at no target smaller than a fairly large city.[15]

Michael Walzer argues that under these conditions, the British terror bombing was morally justified because at this early stage of the war, it was the only way the British had left to them to try to avert a Nazi victory.[16] Walzer further argues that the time period when such terror bombing was justified was relatively brief. Once the Russians began to inflict enormous casualties on the German army and the United States made available its manpower and resources, other alternatives opened up. Unfortunately, the British continued to rely heavily on terror bombing right up until the end of the war, culminating in the firebombing of Dresden in which something like 100,000 people were killed. However, for that relatively brief period of time when Britain had no other way to try to avert a Nazi victory, Walzer argues, its reliance on terror bombing was morally justified.

Suppose then we accept this moral justification for British terror bombing during World War II. Doesn't this suggest a comparable moral justification for Palestinian suicide bombings against Israeli civilians? Israel has been illegally occupying Palestinian land for thirty-five years now in violation of

UN resolutions following the 1967 Arab-Israeli War. Even a return to those 1967 borders, which the UN resolutions require, still permits a considerable expansion of Israel's original borders as specified in the mandate of 1947.[17] Moreover, since the Oslo Peace Accords in 1993, Israeli settlements have doubled in the occupied territories. In the year that Sharon has been prime minister, some thirty-five new settlements have been established in the occupied territories.[18] In Gaza, there are 1.2 million Palestinians and 4,000 Israelis, but the Israelis control 40 percent of the land and 70 percent of the water.[19] In the West Bank, there are 1.9 million Palestinians and 280,000 Israelis, but the Israelis control 37 percent of the water. In addition, Israel failed to abide by its commitments under the Oslo Peace Accords to release prisoners, to complete a third redeployment of its military forces, and to transfer three Jerusalem villages to Palestinian control.[20] Moreover, at the recent Camp David meeting, Israel's proposals did not provide for Palestinian control over East Jerusalem upon which 40 percent of the Palestinian economy depends.[21] Nor did Israel's proposals provide for a right of return or compensation for the half of the Palestinian population that lives in exile (President Clinton proposed that Arafat should just forget about them), most of them having been driven off their land by Israeli expansion. So the Palestinian cause is clearly a just one, but just as clearly the Palestinians lack the military resources to effectively resist Israeli occupation and aggression by directly attacking Israeli military forces. The Israelis have access to the most advanced U.S. weapons and $4 billion a year from the United States to buy whatever weapons they want. The Palestinians have no comparable support from anyone. It is under these conditions that a moral justification for Palestinian suicide bombers against Israeli civilians emerges.[22] Given that the Palestinians lack any effective means to try to end the Israeli occupation or to stop Israel's further expansion into Palestinian territories other than by using suicide bombers against Israeli civilians, why would this use of suicide bombers not be justified in much the same way that Walzer justifies the British terror bombing in

the early stages of World War II?[23] If the Israelis have the ultimate goal of confining most Palestinians to a number of economically nonviable and disconnected reservations, similar to those on which the United States confines American Indian nations, then surely the Palestinians have a right to resist that conquest as best they can.[24]

Beginning with just war pacifism, I have argued that there are morally defensible exceptions to the just means prohibition against directly killing innocents. The cave-analogy argument aims to establish that conclusion. British terror bombing at the beginning of World War II, but not the American dropping of atomic bombs on Hiroshima and Nagasaki at the end of that war, is offered as a real-life instantiation of that argument. The Palestinian use of suicide bombers against Israeli civilians is then presented as a contemporary instantiation of that very same argument.

Yet even if there is a moral justification for the Palestinian use of suicide bombers against Israeli civilians under present conditions, clearly most acts of terrorism cannot be justified, and clearly there was no moral justification for the terrorist attacks on New York City and Washington, D.C., particularly the attacks on the World Trade Center.[25]

Even so, the question remains as to whether the United States was morally justified in going to war against Afghanistan in response to these unjustified terrorist acts. According to just war pacifism, before using belligerent correctives, we must be sure that nonbelligerent correctives are neither hopeless nor too costly. The three weeks of diplomatic activity that the United States engaged in did not appear to be sufficient to determine whether it was hopeless or too costly to continue to attempt to bring Osama bin Laden before a U.S. court, or better, before an international court of law, without military action. We demanded that the Taliban government immediately hand over bin Laden and "all the leaders of Al Qaeda who hide in your land." But how could we have reasonably expected this of the Taliban, given that months after we have overthrown the Taliban government and installed a friendly one, we still have not been able to turn up bin Laden and most of his key associates? How could we have expected that the Taliban government, with its limited resources and loose control over the country, do in three weeks what we still have not been able to accomplish in over a year?

It is conceivable that our leaders never really expected that the Taliban government would be able to meet our demands even if they had wanted to do so. After we began our military offensive, the Taliban government expressed a willingness to hand over bin Laden and his associates at least for trial in an international court if we would stop our military offensive. But we never took them up on their offer.[26] Perhaps we knew that the Taliban government really lacked the resources to hand over bin Laden and his key associates, even while we used their failure to do so as the justification for our waging a war against them.[27]

Something similar may now be happening in the Israeli-Palestinian conflict. The Israeli government has demanded that Yasir Arafat put a stop to the suicide bombings and arrest those who are behind them. But it is far from clear that Arafat has the power to do so. The Israeli government, with many more military resources than Arafat has at his disposal, has been unable to put a stop to the suicide bombings; in fact, the number of such bombings has escalated as Israel has escalated its military responses. The Israeli government repeated its demand that Arafat stop the suicide bombings at the same time that it held Arafat in virtual house arrest in Ramallah, and attacked members of his Palestinian Authority throughout the occupied territories. Clearly, the Israelis must know that Arafat lacks the power to put an end to the suicide bombings in the absence of a political settlement guaranteeing the Palestinians virtually everything they have a right to under the relevant UN resolutions.[28] Moreover, if Arafat (or any Palestinian leader) is foolish enough to speak out against the suicide bombings, as he has in the past, in the absence of the political guarantees that are needed, the bombings will just continue, and Arafat will be branded as ineffectual. So, either the failure of Arafat to speak out against the suicide bombings or his ineffectiveness at stopping them when he does speak out is used by the Israeli government as a justification for

reoccupying the Palestinian territories and expanding Israeli settlements in them. But neither the actions taken by the Israeli government with respect to the Palestinians nor the actions undertaken by the U.S. government with respect to the Al Qaeda network are morally justified because neither government has exhausted its nonbelligerent correctives before engaging in a military response.[29]

In the United States, public opinion rather than the exhaustion of nonbelligerent options has served to motivate our military response to 9/11. The military response has been well received by at least a majority of American people who want to see their government "doing something" to get bin Laden and fight terrorism. But satisfying public opinion polls is not the same as satisfying the requirements of just war pacifism. The United States first called its military action "infinite justice" and then later, in view of the religious connotations of that term, began calling it "enduring freedom," but our military action is neither just nor does it acceptably promote freedom unless nonbelligerent correctives are first exhausted, and they were not exhausted in this case. Nor has our military response yet delivered up for trial bin Laden or any of his top associates or even any of the top Taliban leaders, although some were killed by our military action, and some good detective and police work, not military action, has recently led to the capture in Pakistan of Abu Zubaydah, an Al Qaeda planner and recruiter, and Khalid Sheikh Mohamed, the Al Qaeda chief of operation.[30]

So, even if the United States itself had not engaged in any related terrorist acts or supported any related terrorist acts, there would still be a strong objection to its relatively quick resort to military force as a response to the terrorist attacks of 9/11. Yet given that the United States has arguably itself engaged in terrorist acts in Sudan, and through the UN against Iraqi children, as well as supported terrorist acts through its political and financial support of Israel's illegal occupation of Palestinian lands, and given that these acts of terrorism, and support for terrorism, have served at least partially to motivate terrorist attacks on the United States itself, the United States surely needs to take steps to radically correct its own wrongdoing if it is to justly respond to the related wrongdoing of bin Laden and his followers, and unfortunately this is also something we have not yet done.[31]

What then should we be doing if we are to respect the requirements of just war pacifism in our response to the terrorist attacks of September 11?

1. We should let Israel know in no uncertain terms that our continuing political and financial support depends on its reaching an agreement with the Palestinians on the establishment of a Palestinian state in accordance with the relevant UN resolutions relatively quickly, within, say, three to six months. So many plans for a Palestinian state have been discussed over the years that it should not be too difficult to settle on one of them that accords with the relevant UN resolutions, once Israel knows that it can no longer draw on the political and financial support of the United States to resist a settlement. The evidence of serious negotiations between Israel and the Palestinians will be welcomed by people around the world.

2. Now that we have invaded Iraq without an adequate justification, we must find a way to extricate ourselves from the country as quickly as possible. We must allow representatives from the three major groups in Iraq—the Shiites, the Sunnis, and the Kurds—to work together to set up a mutually acceptable government, preferably under UN supervision. To Iraqis our occupation of Iraq brings to mind not our occupation of Germany and Japan after World War II but rather the continuing, humiliating, and illegal occupation of Palestinian lands by Israel. It is not something they will tolerate for any length of time without open resistance to their occupiers.

3. There should have been three to six months of serious diplomatic negotiations to bring Osama bin Laden and the leaders of his Al Qaeda network either before a U.S. court or, preferably, before an international court of law. Substantial economic and political incentives should have been offered to the relevant individuals and nations to help bring this about. Now that we have overthrown the Taliban in Afghanistan and helped establish a friendly government, we should end our military campaign immediately and return to nonbelligerent correctives, which can include the same sort of good detective and police work that has made possible the capture of Abu Zubaydah, an Al Qaeda planner and recruiter, and Khalid Sheikh Mohamed, the Al Qaeda chief of operation. This will even give us the unintended benefit of conveying to our enemies and to others that we are serious about engaging in belligerent correctives should the nonbelligerent ones prove ineffective.

One of the main lessons we should have drawn from the 9/11 terrorist attacks on the World Trade Center and the Pentagon is how vulnerable our costly high-tech military defenses are to smart, determined enemies using even the simplest of weapons imaginable—knives and box cutters. And as bad as 9/11 was, it could have been far worse. There is little doubt that the terrorists who hijacked the airplanes and flew them into the World Trade Center and the Pentagon would not have hesitated to detonate a nuclear explosive, maybe one they would have hidden in the World Trade Center, if they could have done so.

It would also not be that difficult for terrorists to target chemical plants, or more easily, shipments of industrial chemicals such as chlorine that are transported in tank cars and trucks. Before 9/11, only about 2 percent of all the containers that move though U.S. ports were actually inspected. Currently, that number has been doubled, but that still means that 96 percent of such containers that are shipped from all over the world are not inspected when they enter the United States.[32] Detonating thousands of tons of ammonium nitrate loaded on a ship in a harbor would have the impact of a small nuclear explosion. Just last year, three hundred tons of ammonium nitrate apparently exploded in France killing twenty-nine people and injuring more than 2,500.[33]

Building another layer of high-tech military defense, like the $238 billion George W. Bush proposes to spend on a missile defense system, does little to decrease our vulnerability to such terrorist attacks.[34] In fact, because such high-tech military expenditures divert money from projects that would significantly decrease our vulnerability to terrorist attacks, they actually have an overall negative impact on our national security.

What then should we do to prevent future terrorist attacks from being directed at the United States or U.S. citizens? Well, in addition to the changes of policy I mentioned above with respect to Israel, Iraq, and Osama bin Laden's Al Qaeda network, there are many other things that the United States could do to project a more just foreign policy. For starters, there are a number of international treaties and conventions (e.g., the Kyoto climate-change Treaty, the global treaty banning landmines, and the Rome treaty for the establishment of an international criminal court) that the United States has failed to sign for reasons that seem to simply favor U.S. special interests at the expense of international justice or what would be of benefit to the world community as a whole.

Furthermore, looking at things from an international justice perspective can require a considerable modification of our usual ways of thinking about the relationships between nations and peoples. From an international justice perspective, or more generally, from a moral perspective, actions and policies must be such that they are acceptable by all those affected by those actions and policies (that is, the actions and policies must be such that they ought to be accepted, not necessarily that they are accepted by all those affected by those actions and policies). Thus, the fact that the United States, which constitutes 4 percent of the world's population while using 25 percent of its energy resources, refuses to sign the Kyoto climate-change treaty and make the cuts in its energy consumption that virtually all other nations of the world judge to be fair makes the U.S., in this regard, something like an outlaw nation from the perspective of international justice.[35]

Yet the failure of the United States to accord with international justice cuts even deeper. According to the World Food Program, three-quarters of a billion people are desperately hungry around the world. According to that same program, even Afghanistan, the subject of so much of our recent attention, has received only 5 percent of the $285 million in emergency aid it needs to feed its people

for the rest of the year.[36] One of two women ministers in the provisional Afghan government, Sima Samar, who is in charge of women's affairs, has an unheated office and no phone or money to effect policies in Afghanistan that would improve the situation for women.[37] So there is no way that we can achieve international justice without a radical redistribution of goods and resources from rich to poor to eliminate hunger and desperation around the world.[38] The United States needs to be a champion of this redistribution if it is to be correctly perceived as measuring up to the standard of international justice, and thus to be a just nation whose resources and people should be respected. But the United States has not done this. In fact, its contribution to alleviate world hunger is (in proportion to its size) one of the smallest among the industrialized nations of the world—roughly .11 percent, which President Bush proposes to increase to .13 percent. Britain's contribution is about three times as much, and Sweden, the Netherlands, and Norway proportionately give about eight times as much.[39]

Clearly then there is much that the United States can do if it wants to respond to the terrorist attacks of 9/11 in a way that accords with international justice. Thus, I have argued that the best account of pacifism and the best account of just war theory combined in just war pacifism requires that as soon as possible, the United States put an end to its military response, that the United States make it clear that it is taking radical steps to correct for related terrorist acts of its own or of those countries its supports, and that it give nonbelligerent correctives a reasonable chance to work. I have further argued that the United States has to do more to be a good world citizen. It must stop being a conspicuous holdout with respect to international treaties, and it must do its fair share to redistribute resources from the rich to the poor as international justice requires. Only then would we be living up to our moral ideals that could make us what we claim to be. In turn, living up to those ideals may prove to be the best defense we have against terrorism directed against our own people.

ENDNOTES

1. *Patterns of Global Terrorism—2000.* Released by the Office of the Coordinator for Counterterrorism, April 2001.

2. *Ibid.*

3. If we use the just war distinction between combatants and noncombatants, those killed at the Pentagon might be viewed as combatants in some undeclared war.

4. Since the bombings in Kenya and Tanzania were of U.S. government installations, they are only classified as terrorist acts in virtue of the fact that they were intended to maximize civilian casualties.

5. From an interview with Phyllis Bennis, Z magazine, Sept. 12, 2001. While the bombing of the pharmaceutical plant may have involved unintentional harm to innocents, refusing to compensate the thousands of victims who were deprived of the drugs they needed is to intentionally harm innocents.

6. "Life and Death in Iraq," *Seattle Post-Intelligencer,* May 11, 1999. See also Jeff Indemyer, "Iraqi Sanctions: Myth and Fact," *Swans Commentary,* Sept. 3, 2002.

7. During the Reagan years and after, there was also support for Jonas Sabimbi. Reagan referred to Sabimbi as Angola's Abraham Lincoln. Sabimbi personally beat to death a rival's wife and children. He also shelled civilians and bombed a Red Cross factory. From 1975 until his recent death, he refused to give up a struggle for power in a civil war that resulted in more than 500,000 deaths. See Nicholas Kristof, "Our Own Terrorist," *New York Times,* Mar. 5, 2002.

8. This is because the requirements of just war pacifism, as I stated them earlier in this paper, do not directly address the question of whether there are exceptions to the prohibition on intentionally harming innocents. Moreover, when that question is taken up by means of the same case-by-case analysis with which I defended the earlier stated requirements of just war pacifism (for the defense of these requirements, see my *Justice for Here and Now,* Chapter 7), certain exceptions to the prohibition on intentionally harming innocents turn out to be morally justified, as I go on to show.

9. See Philippa Foot, "The Problem of Abortion and the Doctrine of Double Effect," *Oxford Review,* vol. 5 (1967), pp. 5–15.

10. See Michael Walzer, *Just and Unjust Wars,* Second Edition (New York: Basic Books, 1992), pp. 263–268.

11. James Byrnes, *Speaking Frankly* (New York, 1947), p. 264.

12. Winston Churchill, *Triumph and Tragedy* (New York, 1962), p. 639.

13. Another way to put this is to claim that a right not to have to unconditionally surrender is one of our basic universal human rights.

14. Noble Frankland, *Bomber Offensive* (New York, 1970), pp. 38–39.

15. As examples of how inaccurate night bombing was at the time, one oil installation was attacked by 162 aircraft carrying 159 tons of bombs, another by 134 aircraft carrying 103 tons of bombs, but neither suffered any major damage. See Charles Webster and Noble Frankland, *The Strategic Air Offensive Against Germany 1939–45* (London: HMSO, 1961) Vol. I, p. 164.

16. Walzer, pp. 255–262.

17. The Palestinians made a big concession to Israel in the Olso Peace Accords by accepting this expansion (23% more than Israel was granted according to the 1947 UN partition plan) hoping thereby to gain Palestinian control of the remaining 23% of historic Palestine.

18. *New York Times,* Apr. 26, 2002.

19. Avishai Margalit, "Settling Scores," *New York Review,* Aug. 22, 2001.

20. See Robert Malley and Hussein, "Camp David: The Tragedy of Errors, *New York Review,* Aug. 9, 2001, and "A Reply to Ehud Barak," *New York Review,* June 11, 2002; "A Reply," *New York Review,* June 27, 2002. See also Benny Morris and Ehud Barak, "Camp David and After: An Exchange," *New York Review,* June 13, 2002; "Camp David and After—Continued," *New York Review,* June 27, 2002.

21. Jeff Halper, The Israeli Committee Against House Demolitions, www.icahd.org.

22. There is a further requirement that must be met here. It is that the Palestinians must have exhausted nonbelligerent correctives. The evidence that this is the case can, I believe, be found in the numerous Palestinian peace initiatives especially from the early 1970s on when the Palestinians had acquired political standing in the international community. In 1976 the U.S. vetoed a UN Security Council Resolution calling for a settlement on the 1967 borders, with "appropriate arrangements ... to guarantee ... the sovereignty, territorial integrity and political independence of all states in the area and their right to live in peace within secure and recognized boundaries," including Israel and a new Palestinian state in the occupied territories. The resolution was backed by Egypt, Syria, Jordan and the PLO, and the USSR. See Noam Chomsky, *The Fateful Triangle* (Cambridge: South End Press, 1999), p. 64 ff. Israel has rejected every peace plan put forward by the Arabs and the United States except for the bilateral treaty with Egypt and the Olso Peace Accords, and these Accords have now been, in effect, abandoned by the current Israeli government. See Paul Finlay, *Deliberate Deceptions* (Brooklyn: Lawrence Hill Books, 1993), p. 201 ff.

23. Nor will it do to distinguish British terror bombing from Palestinian suicide bombing on the grounds that the Nazis represented an unprecedented evil in human history because at the early stage of WWII, the British could not have known the full character of the Nazi regime.

24. Some will contest whether this correctly represents Israeli intentions. But even in its best offer at Camp David, Israel proposed dividing Palestine into four separate cantons: the Northern West Bank, the Central West Bank, the Southern West Bank, and Gaza. Going from any one area to another would require crossing Israeli sovereign territory and consequently subject movements of Palestinians within their own country to Israeli control. Restrictions would also apply to the movement of goods, thus subjecting the Palestinian economy to Israeli control. In addition, the Camp David proposal would have left Israel in control of all Palestinian borders, thereby giving Israel control not only of the internal movement of people and goods but international movement as well. Such a Palestinian state would have had less sovereignty and viability than the Bantustans created by the South African apartheid government, which both Israel and the U.S. once supported. The Camp David proposal also required Palestinians to give up any claim to the occupied portion of Jerusalem. The proposal would have forced recognition of Israel's annexation of all of Arab East Jerusalem. Talks after Camp David in Egypt suggested that Israel was prepared to allow Palestinian sovereignty over isolated Palestinian neighborhoods in the heart of East Jerusalem. However, these neighborhoods would have remained surrounded by Israeli colonies and separated not only from each other but also from the rest of the Palestinian State. See www.nad-plo-org. For a map of the Camp David proposal with its partition of Palestine into four cantons, see www. nad-plo-org/maps/map13.html. Although Yasser Arafat and the Palestinians were roundly condemned in the U.S. media for rejecting the Camp David offer, to my knowledge no maps of the U.S.-Israeli proposal, which would have undercut the claim that it was a reasonable offer, were published in the U.S., although they were widely published elsewhere. For the closest any U.S. media source that I found came to acknowledging these facts, see Anthony Lewis, "Waiting for America," *New York Times,* Nov. 17, 2001.

25. Al Qaeda have shown themselves capable of inflicting significant damage on both military (the *Cole*) and diplomatic targets (the U.S. embassies in Kenya and Tanzania). So their opposition to the U.S. could have continued in just this fashion. Moreover, the attack on the Pentagon differs morally from the attack on the World Trade Center, although the deaths of innocent airline hostages is objectionable in both cases. So Al Qaida could still have effectively waged its war against the U.S. without attacking the World Trade Center. With respect to the possibility of effectively attacking military or governmental targets, Al Qaida is much better situated vis à vis the U.S. and its allies than the Palestinians are vis à vis Israel. This is because Al Qaida can target the far-flung military and governmental outposts of the U.S. all around the world, and through such attacks it has effectively brought the U.S. and its allies to withdraw their military forces from such places as Somalia, Yemen, and even, in terms of effective use, Saudi Arabia.

Of course, it might be questioned whether Al Qaeda effectively exhausted nonbelligerent corrections before it resorted to belligerent ones. If we take Al Qaeda's grounds for just cause to be U.S support for the Israeli occupation, the U.S. stance against Iraq, U.S. bases in Saudi Arabia, and U.S. support for repressive governments in the Middle East, then I think we can say that in each case Al Qaeda gave nonbelligerent correctives some chance to work.

26. Genaro Armas, "Bush Rebuffs Taliban Offer," *Associated Press*, Oct. 15, 2001. See also *New York Times*, Oct. 15, 2002.

27. It is worth noting that the U.S. State Department had been negotiating with the Taliban for handing over bin Laden before 9/11. One Taliban proposal suggested that bin Laden be turned over to a panel of three Islamic jurists, one chosen by Afghanistan, Saudi Arabia, and the United States. When the U.S. rejected that proposal, the Taliban countered that it would settle for only one Islamic jurist on such a panel. Although the negotiations went on for some time, the U.S. rigidly held to the position that bin Laden had to be turned over for trial in the U.S., and some say the U.S. thereby missed a chance before 9/11 to get bin Laden before an international court of law. Possibly the U.S. never believed that the Taliban could deliver on their promises, but why then did it keep negotiating with them for so long? See David Ottaway and Jeo Stephens, "Diplomats Met with Taliban on Bin Laden: Some Contend U.S. Missed Its Chance," *Washington Post*, Oct. 29, 2001.

28. See James Bennet, "Israeli Analysis Raises New Doubt About Arafat's Power," *New York Times*, Nov. 27, 2001.

29. Of course, in theory, one could know or reasonably believe that nonbelligerent correctives are ineffectual or too costly without actually having exhausted them. But, in the cases under discussion, there is no way that one could do this with respect to the particular nonbelligerent correctives under consideration without actually having exhausted them. In addition, making impossible demands in response to an attack and using military means when those demands are not met is just another way not to exhaust nonbelligerent correctives.

30. *Christian Science Monitor*, Apr. 4, 2002.

31. The reason why the U.S. must do all these things if it is to justly respond to the related wrongdoing of bin Laden and his followers is that these actions are part of the nonbelligerent correctives that must be employed before the use of belligerent correctives can be justified.

32. David Carr, "The Futility of Homeland Defense," *Atlantic Monthly*, January 2002.

33. Richard Garwin, "The Many Threats of Terror." *New York Review*, Oct. 2, 2001; Bruce Hoffman, *Terrorism and Weapons of Mass Destruction*, Rand, 1999. For numerous scenerios by which terrorists could fairly easily create mass destruction, see Stephen Bowman. *When the Eagle Screams: America's Vulnerability to Terrorism*, New York: Birch Lane Press, 1994, especially Chapters 8–14.

34. James O. Goldsborough, "The Real Costs of Missile Defense," *San Diego Union-Tribune*, Apr. 1, 2002.

35. *New York Times*, Mar. 17, 2002. The reason that this conclusion follows from an international justice perspective is that it is impossible to imagine how it could be the case that all other nations of the world ought to accept as morally acceptable the U.S. self-serving stance on the Kyoto climate-change treaty.

36. *New York Times*, Apr. 26, 2002. According to a more recent assessment, foreign governments have pledged more than $4.5 billion in aid over five years, but little of that money has arrived. See *New York Times*, Aug. 16, 2002. According to an even more recent assessment, progress in reducing hunger in Afghanistan has ground to a halt and failure to provide immediate food and agricultural aid will lead to famine. *Miami Herald*, Oct. 22, 2002.

37. *Daily Telegraph* (London), Feb. 22, 2002.

38. It is sometimes argued that addressing the unjust distribution of resources and meeting the basic needs of people around the world will do little to eliminate terrorism because those who engage in terror are not usually poor people. (See Alan Krueger and Jitka Maleckova, "Does Poverty Cause Terrorism?" *New Republic*, June 24, 2002.). But while it is probably true that most terrorists are not themselves poor, many of them appear to be motivated by the plight of the poor or by what they perceive to be other gross injustices, even when they themselves have the means of escaping the harmful effects of those injustices (e.g., Osama bin Laden). So if we intend to rid the world of terrorism in a morally justifiably way, we definitely need to address these questions of international justice. They are part of a

nonbelligerent way of ridding ourselves of the threat of terrorism.

39. *St. Louis Post-Dispatch,* December 3, 2001, and *New York Times,* May 1, 2002. It might be objected that while Americans are relatively stingy in the foreign aid provided by their government, they make up for it with private and corporate largess. See Carol Adelman, "America's Helping Hand," *Wall Street Journal.* Aug. 21, 2002. But even when U.S. private and corporate giving is taken into account, the U.S. still gives privately and publicly only half as much as Sweden, Netherlands, and Norway give publicly. The percentage shrinks to only one-quarter as much if we remove the $18 billion that immigrants in the U.S. send to relatives back home, which probably shouldn't be counted anyhow since it is not that similar to giving foreign aid to needy people around the world.

79

The Geneva Convention of 1949

The undersigned Plenipotentiaries of the Governments represented at the Diplomatic Conference held at Geneva from April 21 to August 12, 1949, for the purpose of revising the Convention concluded at Geneva on July 27, 1929, relative to the Treatment of Prisoners of War, have agreed as follows:

PART I. GENERAL PROVISIONS

Art 1. The High Contracting Parties undertake to respect and to ensure respect for the present Convention in all circumstances.

Art 2. In addition to the provisions which shall be implemented in peace time, the present Convention shall apply to all cases of declared war or of any other armed conflict which may arise between two or more of the High Contracting Parties, even if the state of war is not recognized by one of them.

The Convention shall also apply to all cases of partial or total occupation of the territory of a High Contracting Party, even if the said occupation meets with no armed resistance.

Although one of the Powers in conflict may not be a party to the present Convention, the Powers who are parties thereto shall remain bound by it in their mutual relations. They shall furthermore be bound by the Convention in relation to the said Power, if the latter accepts and applies the provisions thereof.

Art 3. In the case of armed conflict not of an international character occurring in the territory of one of the High Contracting Parties, each Party to the conflict shall be bound to apply, as a minimum, the following provisions:

(1) Persons taking no active part in the hostilities, including members of armed forces who have laid down their arms and those placed hors de combat by sickness, wounds, detention, or any other cause, shall in all circumstances be treated humanely, without any adverse distinction founded on race, colour, religion or faith, sex, birth or wealth, or any other similar criteria. To this end the following acts are and shall remain prohibited at any time and in any place whatsoever with respect to the above-mentioned persons:

(a) violence to life and person, in particular murder of all kinds, mutilation, cruel treatment and torture;

(b) taking of hostages;

(c) outrages upon personal dignity, in particular, humiliating and degrading treatment;

(d) the passing of sentences and the carrying out of executions without previous judgment pronounced by a regularly constituted court affording all the judicial guarantees which are recognized as indispensable by civilized peoples.

(2) The wounded and sick shall be collected and cared for.

An impartial humanitarian body, such as the International Committee of the Red Cross, may offer its services to the Parties to the conflict.

The Parties to the conflict should further endeavour to bring into force, by means of special agreements, all or part of the other provisions of the present Convention.

The application of the preceding provisions shall not affect the legal status of the Parties to the conflict.

Art 4. A. Prisoners of war, in the sense of the present Convention, are persons belonging to one of the following categories, who have fallen into the power of the enemy:

(1) Members of the armed forces of a Party to the conflict, as well as members of militias or volunteer corps forming part of such armed forces.

(2) Members of other militias and members of other volunteer corps, including those of organized resistance movements, belonging to a Party to the conflict and operating in or outside their own territory, even if this territory is occupied, provided that such militias or volunteer corps, including such organized resistance movements, fulfil the following conditions:

(a) that of being commanded by a person responsible for his subordinates;

(b) that of having a fixed distinctive sign recognizable at a distance;

(c) that of carrying arms openly;

(d) that of conducting their operations in accordance with the laws and customs of war.

(3) Members of regular armed forces who profess allegiance to a government or an authority not recognized by the Detaining Power.

(4) Persons who accompany the armed forces without actually being members thereof, such as civilian members of military aircraft crews, war correspondents, supply contractors, members of labour units or of services responsible for the welfare of the armed forces, provided that they have received authorization, from the armed forces which they accompany, who shall provide them for that purpose with an identity card similar to the annexed model.

(5) Members of crews, including masters, pilots and apprentices, of the merchant marine and the crews of civil aircraft of the Parties to the conflict, who do not benefit by more favourable treatment under any other provisions of international law.

(6) Inhabitants of a non-occupied territory, who on the approach of the enemy spontaneously take up arms to resist the invading forces, without having had time to form themselves into regular armed units, provided they carry arms openly and respect the laws and customs of war.

B. The following shall likewise be treated as prisoners of war under the present Convention:

(1) Persons belonging, or having belonged, to the armed forces of the occupied country, if the occupying Power considers it necessary by reason of such allegiance to intern them, even though it has originally liberated them while hostilities were going on outside the territory it occupies, in particular where such persons have made an unsuccessful attempt to rejoin the armed forces to which they belong and which are engaged in combat, or where they fail to comply with a summons made to them with a view to internment.

(2) The persons belonging to one of the categories enumerated in the present Article, who have been received by neutral or non-belligerent Powers on their territory and whom these Powers are required to intern under international law, without prejudice to any more favourable treatment which these Powers may choose to give and with the exception of Articles 8, 10, 15, 30, fifth paragraph, 58–67, 92, 126 and, where diplomatic relations exist between the Parties to the conflict and the neutral or non-belligerent Power concerned, those Articles concerning the Protecting Power. Where such diplomatic relations exist, the Parties to a conflict on whom these persons depend shall be allowed to perform towards them the functions of a Protecting Power as provided in the present Convention, without prejudice to the functions which these Parties normally exercise in conformity with diplomatic and consular usage and treaties.

C. This Article shall in no way affect the status of medical personnel and chaplains as provided for in Article 33 of the present Convention.

Art 5. The present Convention shall apply to the persons referred to in Article 4 from the time they fall into the power of the enemy and until their final release and repatriation.

Should any doubt arise as to whether persons, having committed a belligerent act and having fallen into the hands of the enemy, belong to any of the categories enumerated in Article 4, such persons shall enjoy the protection of the present Convention until such time as their status has been determined by a competent tribunal.

Art 6. In addition to the agreements expressly provided for in Articles 10, 23, 28, 33, 60, 65, 66, 67, 72, 73, 75, 109, 110, 118, 119, 122 and 132, the High Contracting Parties may conclude other special agreements for all matters concerning which they may deem it suitable to make separate provision. No special agreement shall adversely affect the situation of prisoners of war, as defined by the present Convention, nor restrict the rights which it confers upon them.

Prisoners of war shall continue to have the benefit of such agreements as long as the Convention is applicable to them, except where express provisions to the contrary are contained in the aforesaid or in subsequent agreements, or where more favourable measures have been taken with regard to them by one or other of the Parties to the conflict.

Art 7. Prisoners of war may in no circumstances renounce in part or in entirety the rights secured to them by the present Convention, and by the special agreements referred to in the foregoing Article, if such there be.

Art 8. The present Convention shall be applied with the cooperation and under the scrutiny of the Protecting Powers whose duty it is to safeguard the interests of the Parties to the conflict. For this purpose, the Protecting Powers may appoint, apart from their diplomatic or consular staff, delegates from amongst their own nationals or the nationals of other neutral Powers. The said delegates shall be subject to the approval of the Power with which they are to carry out their duties.

The Parties to the conflict shall facilitate to the greatest extent possible the task of the representatives or delegates of the Protecting Powers.

The representatives or delegates of the Protecting Powers shall not in any case exceed their mission under the present Convention. They shall, in particular, take account of the imperative necessities of security of the State wherein they carry out their duties.

Art 9. The provisions of the present Convention constitute no obstacle to the humanitarian activities which the International Committee of the Red Cross or any other impartial humanitarian organization may, subject to the consent of the Parties to the conflict concerned, undertake for the protection of prisoners of war and for their relief.

Art 10. The High Contracting Parties may at any time agree to entrust to an organization which offers all guarantees of impartiality and efficacy the duties incumbent on the Protecting Powers by virtue of the present Convention.

When prisoners of war do not benefit or cease to benefit, no matter for what reason, by the activities of a Protecting Power or of an organization provided for in the first paragraph above, the Detaining Power shall request a neutral State, or such an organization, to undertake the functions performed under the present Convention by a Protecting Power designated by the Parties to a conflict.

If protection cannot be arranged accordingly, the Detaining Power shall request or shall accept, subject to the provisions of this Article, the offer of the services of a humanitarian organization, such as the International Committee of the Red Cross to assume the humanitarian functions performed by Protecting Powers under the present Convention.

Any neutral Power or any organization invited by the Power concerned or offering itself for these purposes, shall be required to act with a sense of responsibility towards the Party to the conflict on which persons protected by the present Convention depend, and shall be required to furnish sufficient assurances that it is in a position to undertake the appropriate functions and to discharge them impartially.

No derogation from the preceding provisions shall be made by special agreements between Powers one of which is restricted, even temporarily, in its freedom to negotiate with the other Power or its allies by reason of military events, more particularly where the whole, or a substantial part, of the territory of the said Power is occupied.

Whenever in the present Convention mention is made of a Protecting Power, such mention applies to substitute organizations in the sense of the present Article.

Art 11. In cases where they deem it advisable in the interest of protected persons, particularly in cases of disagreement between the Parties to the conflict as to the application or interpretation of the provisions of the present Convention, the Protecting Powers shall lend their good offices with a view to settling the disagreement.

For this purpose, each of the Protecting Powers may, either at the invitation of one Party or on its own initiative, propose to the Parties to the conflict a meeting of their representatives, and in particular of the authorities responsible for prisoners of war, possibly on neutral territory suitably chosen. The Parties to the conflict shall be bound to give effect to the proposals made to them for this purpose. The Protecting Powers may, if necessary, propose for approval by the Parties to the conflict a person belonging to a neutral Power, or delegated by the International Committee of the Red Cross, who shall be invited to take part in such a meeting.

PART II. GENERAL PROTECTION OF PRISONERS OF WAR

Art 12. Prisoners of war are in the hands of the enemy Power, but not of the individuals or military units who have captured them. Irrespective of the individual responsibilities that may exist, the Detaining Power is responsible for the treatment given them.

Prisoners of war may only be transferred by the Detaining Power to a Power which is a party to the Convention and after the Detaining Power has satisfied itself of the willingness and ability of such transferee Power to apply the Convention. When prisoners of war are transferred under such circumstances, responsibility for the application of the Convention rests on the Power accepting them while they are in its custody.

Nevertheless, if that Power fails to carry out the provisions of the Convention in any important respect, the Power by whom the prisoners of war were transferred shall, upon being notified by the Protecting Power, take effective measures to correct the situation or shall request the return of the prisoners of war. Such requests must be complied with.

Art. 13. Prisoners of war must at all times be humanely treated. Any unlawful act or omission by the Detaining Power causing death or seriously endangering the health of a prisoner of war in its custody is prohibited, and will be regarded as a serious breach of the present Convention. In particular, no prisoner of war may be subjected to physical mutilation or to medical or scientific experiments of any kind which are not justified by the medical, dental or hospital treatment of the prisoner concerned and carried out in his interest.

Likewise, prisoners of war must at all times be protected, particularly against acts of violence or intimidation and against insults and public curiosity.

Measures of reprisal against prisoners of war are prohibited.

Art 14. Prisoners of war are entitled in all circumstances to respect for their persons and their honour.

Women shall be treated with all the regard due to their sex and shall in all cases benefit by treatment as favourable as that granted to men.

Prisoners of war shall retain the full civil capacity which they enjoyed at the time of their capture. The Detaining Power may not restrict the exercise, either within or without its own territory, of the rights such capacity confers except in so far as the captivity requires.

Art 15. The Power detaining prisoners of war shall be bound to provide free of charge for their maintenance and for the medical attention required by their state of health.

Art. 16. Taking into consideration the provisions of the present Convention relating to rank and sex, and subject to any privileged treatment which may be accorded to them by reason of their state of health, age or professional qualifications, all prisoners of war shall be treated alike by the Detaining Power, without any adverse distinction based on race, nationality, religious belief or political opinions, or any other distinction founded on similar criteria.

PART III. CAPTIVITY

Section 1. Beginning of Captivity

Art 17. Every prisoner of war, when questioned on the subject, is bound to give only his surname, first names and rank, date of birth, and army, regimental, personal or serial number, or failing this, equivalent information.

If he wilfully infringes this rule, he may render himself liable to a restriction of the privileges accorded to his rank or status.

Each Party to a conflict is required to furnish the persons under its jurisdiction who are liable to become prisoners of war, with an identity card showing the owner's surname, first names, rank, army, regimental, personal or serial number or equivalent information, and date of birth. The identity card may, furthermore, bear the signature or the fingerprints, or both, of the owner, and may bear, as well, any other information the Party to the conflict may wish to add concerning persons belonging to its armed forces. As far as possible the card shall measure 6.5 × 10 cm. and shall be issued in duplicate. The identity card shall be shown by the prisoner of war upon demand, but may in no case be taken away from him.

No physical or mental torture, nor any other form of coercion, may be inflicted on prisoners of war to secure from them information of any kind whatever. Prisoners of war who refuse to answer may not be threatened, insulted, or exposed to unpleasant or disadvantageous treatment of any kind.

Prisoners of war who, owing to their physical or mental condition, are unable to state their identity, shall be handed over to the medical service. The identity of such prisoners shall be established by all possible means, subject to the provisions of the preceding paragraph.

The questioning of prisoners of war shall be carried out in a language which they understand.

Art. 18. All effects and articles of personal use, except arms, horses, military equipment and military documents, shall remain in the possession of prisoners of war, likewise their metal helmets and gas masks and like articles issued for personal protection. Effects and articles used for their clothing or feeding shall likewise remain in their possession, even if such effects and articles belong to their regulation military equipment.

At no time should prisoners of war be without identity documents. The Detaining Power shall supply such documents to prisoners of war who possess none.

Badges of rank and nationality, decorations and articles having above all a personal or sentimental value may not be taken from prisoners of war.

Sums of money carried by prisoners of war may not be taken away from them except by order of an officer, and after the amount and particulars of the owner have been recorded in a special register and an itemized receipt has been given, legibly inscribed with the name, rank and unit of the person issuing the said receipt. Sums in the currency of the Detaining Power, or which are changed into such currency at the prisoner's request, shall be placed to the credit of the prisoner's account as provided in Article 64.

The Detaining Power may withdraw articles of value from prisoners of war only for reasons of security; when such articles are withdrawn, the procedure laid down for sums of money impounded shall apply.

Such objects, likewise sums taken away in any currency other than that of the Detaining Power and the conversion of which has not been asked for by the owners, shall be kept in the custody of the Detaining Power and shall be returned in their initial shape to prisoners of war at the end of their captivity.

Art. 19. Prisoners of war shall be evacuated, as soon as possible after their capture, to camps situated in an area far enough from the combat zone for them to be out of danger.

Only those prisoners of war who, owing to wounds or sickness, would run greater risks by being evacuated than by remaining where they are, may be temporarily kept back in a danger zone.

Prisoners of war shall not be unnecessarily exposed to danger while awaiting evacuation from a fighting zone.

Art 20. The evacuation of prisoners of war shall always be effected humanely and in conditions similar to those for the forces of the Detaining Power in their changes of station.

The Detaining Power shall supply prisoners of war who are being evacuated with sufficient food and potable water, and with the necessary clothing and medical attention. The Detaining Power shall take all suitable precautions to ensure their safety during evacuation, and shall establish as soon as possible a list of the prisoners of war who are evacuated.

If prisoners of war must, during evacuation, pass through transit camps, their stay in such camps shall be as brief as possible.

Section II. Internment of Prisoners of War

Chapter I. General Observations

Art 21. The Detaining Power may subject prisoners of war to internment. It may impose on them the obligation of not leaving, beyond certain limits, the camp where they are interned, or if the said camp is fenced in, of not going outside its perimeter. Subject to the provisions of the present Convention relative to penal and disciplinary sanctions, prisoners of war may not be held in close confinement except where necessary to safeguard their health and then only during the continuation of the circumstances which make such confinement necessary.

Prisoners of war may be partially or wholly released on parole or promise, in so far as is allowed by the laws of the Power on which they depend. Such measures shall be taken particularly in cases where this may contribute to the improvement of their state of health. No prisoner of war shall be compelled to accept liberty on parole or promise.

Upon the outbreak of hostilities, each Party to the conflict shall notify the adverse Party of the laws and regulations allowing or forbidding its own nationals to accept liberty on parole or promise. Prisoners of war who are paroled or who have given their promise in conformity with the laws and regulations so notified, are bound on their personal honour scrupulously to fulfil, both towards the Power on which they depend and towards the Power which has captured them, the engagements of their paroles or promises. In such cases, the Power on which they depend is bound neither to require nor to accept from them any service incompatible with the parole or promise given.

Art 22. Prisoners of war may be interned only in premises located on land and affording every guarantee of hygiene and healthfulness. Except in particular cases which are justified by the interest of the prisoners themselves, they shall not be interned in penitentiaries.

Prisoners of war interned in unhealthy areas, or where the climate is injurious for them, shall be removed as soon as possible to a more favourable climate.

The Detaining Power shall assemble prisoners of war in camps or camp compounds according to their nationality, language and customs, provided that such prisoners shall not be separated from prisoners of war belonging to the armed forces with which they were serving at the time of their capture, except with their consent.

Art 23. No prisoner of war may at any time be sent to, or detained in areas where he may be exposed to the fire of the combat zone, nor may his presence be used to render certain points or areas immune from military operations.

Prisoners of war shall have shelters against air bombardment and other hazards of war, to the same extent as the local civilian population. With the exception of those engaged in the protection of their quarters against the aforesaid hazards, they may enter such shelters as soon as possible after the giving of the alarm. Any other protective measure taken in favour of the population shall also apply to them.

Detaining Powers shall give the Powers concerned, through the intermediary of the Protecting Powers, all useful information regarding the geographical location of prisoner of war camps.

Whenever military considerations permit, prisoner of war camps shall be indicated in the daytime by the letters PW or PG, placed so as to be clearly visible from the air. The Powers concerned may, however, agree upon any other system of marking. Only prisoner of war camps shall be marked as such.

Art 24. Transit or screening camps of a permanent kind shall be fitted out under conditions similar to those described in the present Section, and the prisoners therein shall have the same treatment as in other camps.

Chapter II. Quarters, Food and Clothing of Prisoners of War

Art 25. Prisoners of war shall be quartered under conditions as favourable as those for the forces of the Detaining Power who are billeted in the same area. The said conditions shall make allowance for the habits and customs of the prisoners and shall in no case be prejudicial to their health.

The foregoing provisions shall apply in particular to the dormitories of prisoners of war as regards both total surface and minimum cubic space, and the general installations, bedding and blankets.

The premises provided for the use of prisoners of war individually or collectively, shall be entirely protected from dampness and adequately heated and lighted, in particular between dusk and lights out. All precautions must be taken against the danger of fire.

In any camps in which women prisoners of war, as well as men, are accommodated, separate dormitories shall be provided for them.

Art 26. The basic daily food rations shall be sufficient in quantity, quality and variety to keep prisoners of war in good health and to prevent loss of weight or the development of nutritional deficiencies. Account shall also be taken of the habitual diet of the prisoners.

The Detaining Power shall supply prisoners of war who work with such additional rations as are necessary for the labour on which they are employed.

Sufficient drinking water shall be supplied to prisoners of war. The use of tobacco shall be permitted.

Prisoners of war shall, as far as possible, be associated with the preparation of their meals; they may be employed for that purpose in the kitchens. Furthermore, they shall be given the means of preparing, themselves, the additional food in their possession.

Adequate premises shall be provided for messing.

Collective disciplinary measures affecting food are prohibited.

Art 27. Clothing, underwear and footwear shall be supplied to prisoners of war in sufficient quantities by the Detaining Power, which shall make allowance for the climate of the region where the prisoners are detained. Uniforms of enemy armed forces captured by the Detaining Power should, if suitable for the climate, be made available to clothe prisoners of war.

The regular replacement and repair of the above articles shall be assured by the Detaining Power. In addition, prisoners of war who work shall receive appropriate clothing, wherever the nature of the work demands.

Art 28. Canteens shall be installed in all camps, where prisoners of war may procure foodstuffs, soap and tobacco and ordinary articles in daily use. The tariff shall never be in excess of local market prices.

The profits made by camp canteens shall be used for the benefit of the prisoners; a special fund shall be created for this purpose. The prisoners' representative shall have the right to collaborate in the management of the canteen and of this fund.

When a camp is closed down, the credit balance of the special fund shall be handed to an international welfare organization, to be employed for the benefit of prisoners of war of the same nationality as those who have contributed to the fund. In case of a general repatriation, such profits shall be kept by the Detaining Power, subject to any agreement to the contrary between the Powers concerned.

Chapter III. Hygene and Medical Attention

Art 29. The Detaining Power shall be bound to take all sanitary measures necessary to ensure the cleanliness and healthfulness of camps and to prevent epidemics.

Prisoners of war shall have for their use, day and night, conveniences which conform to the rules of hygiene and are maintained in a constant state of cleanliness. In any camps in which women prisoners of war are accommodated, separate conveniences shall be provided for them.

Also, apart from the baths and showers with which the camps shall be furnished prisoners of war shall be provided with sufficient water and soap for their personal toilet and for washing their personal laundry; the necessary installations, facilities and time shall be granted them for that purpose.

Art 30. Every camp shall have an adequate infirmary where prisoners of war may have the attention they require, as well as appropriate diet. Isolation wards shall, if necessary, be set aside for cases of contagious or mental disease.

Prisoners of war suffering from serious disease, or whose condition necessitates special treatment, a surgical operation or hospital care, must be admitted to any military or civilian medical unit where such treatment can be given, even if their repatriation is contemplated in the near future. Special facilities shall be afforded for the care to be given to the disabled, in particular to the blind, and for their rehabilitation, pending repatriation.

Prisoners of war shall have the attention, preferably, of medical personnel of the Power on which they depend and, if possible, of their nationality.

Prisoners of war may not be prevented from presenting themselves to the medical authorities for examination. The detaining authorities shall, upon request, issue to every prisoner who has undergone treatment, an official certificate indicating the nature of his illness or injury, and the duration and kind of treatment received. A duplicate of this certificate shall be forwarded to the Central Prisoners of War Agency.

The costs of treatment, including those of any apparatus necessary for the maintenance of prisoners of war in good health, particularly dentures and other artificial appliances, and spectacles, shall be borne by the Detaining Power.

Art 31. Medical inspections of prisoners of war shall be held at least once a month. They shall include the checking and the recording of the weight of each prisoner of war.

Their purpose shall be, in particular, to supervise the general state of health, nutrition and cleanliness of prisoners and to detect contagious diseases, especially tuberculosis, malaria and venereal disease. For this purpose the most efficient methods available shall be employed, e.g. periodic mass miniature radiography for the early detection of tuberculosis.

Art 32. Prisoners of war who, though not attached to the medical service of their armed forces, are physicians, surgeons, dentists, nurses or medical orderlies, may be required by the Detaining Power to exercise their medical functions in the interests of prisoners of war dependent on the same Power. In that case they shall continue to be prisoners of war, but shall receive the same treatment as corresponding medical personnel retained by the Detaining Power. They shall be exempted from any other work under Article 49.

PART VI. EXECUTION OF THE CONVENTION

Section I. General Provisions

Art 126. Representatives or delegates of the Protecting Powers shall have permission to go to all places where prisoners of war may be, particularly to places of internment, imprisonment and labour, and shall have access to all premises occupied by prisoners of war; they shall also be allowed to go to the places of departure, passage and arrival of prisoners who are being transferred. They shall be able to interview the prisoners, and in particular the prisoners' representatives, without witnesses, either personally or through an interpreter.

Representatives and delegates of the Protecting Powers shall have full liberty to select the places they wish to visit. The duration and frequency of these visits shall not be restricted. Visits may not be prohibited except for reasons of imperative military necessity, and then only as an exceptional and temporary measure.

The Detaining Power and the Power on which the said prisoners of war depend may agree, if necessary, that compatriots of these prisoners of war be permitted to participate in the visits.

The delegates of the International Committee of the Red Cross shall enjoy the same prerogatives. The appointment of such delegates shall be submitted to the approval of the Power detaining the prisoners of war to be visited.

Art 127. The High Contracting Parties undertake, in time of peace as in time of war, to disseminate the text of the present Convention as widely as possible in their respective countries, and, in particular, to include the study thereof in their programmes of military and, if possible, civil instruction, so that the principles thereof may become known to all their armed forces and to the entire population.

Any military or other authorities, who in time of war assume responsibilities in respect of prisoners of war, must possess the text of the Convention and be specially instructed as to its provisions.

Art 128. The High Contracting Parties shall communicate to one another through the Swiss Federal Council and, during hostilities, through the Protecting Powers, the official translations of the present Convention, as well as the laws and regulations which they may adopt to ensure the application thereof.

Art 129. The High Contracting Parties undertake to enact any legislation necessary to provide effective penal sanctions for persons committing, or ordering to be committed, any of the grave breaches of the present Convention defined in the following Article.

Each High Contracting Party shall be under the obligation to search for persons alleged to have committed, or to have ordered to be committed, such grave breaches, and shall bring such persons, regardless of their nationality, before its own courts. It may also, if it prefers, and in accordance with the provisions of its own legislation, hand such persons over for trial to another High Contracting Party concerned, provided such High Contracting Party has made out a prima facie case.

Each High Contracting Party shall take measures necessary for the suppression of all acts contrary to the provisions of the present Convention other than the grave breaches defined in the following Article.

In all circumstances, the accused persons shall benefit by safeguards of proper trial and defence, which shall not be less favourable than those provided by Article 105 and those following of the present Convention.

Art 130. Grave breaches to which the preceding Article relates shall be those involving any of the following acts, if committed against persons or property protected by the Convention: wilful killing, torture or inhuman treatment, including biological experiments, wilfully causing great suffering or serious injury to body or health, compelling a prisoner of war to serve in the forces of the hostile Power, or wilfully depriving a prisoner of war of the rights of fair and regular trial prescribed in this Convention.

Art 131. No High Contracting Party shall be allowed to absolve itself or any other High Contracting Party of any liability incurred by itself or by another High Contracting Party in respect of breaches referred to in the preceding Article.

Art 132. At the request of a Party to the conflict, an enquiry shall be instituted, in a manner to be decided between the interested Parties, concerning any alleged violation of the Convention.

If agreement has not been reached concerning the procedure for the enquiry, the Parties should agree on the choice of an umpire who will decide upon the procedure to be followed.

Once the violation has been established, the Parties to the conflict shall put an end to it and shall repress it with the least possible delay.

80

Boumediene v. Bush

Supreme Court of the United States

The issue before the U.S. Supreme Court was whether detainees held at the United States Naval Station in Guantanamo Bay, Cuba possessed the constitutional privilege of habeas corpus. The majority of the court, whose opinion is delivered here by Justice Anthony Kennedy, held that the detainees did indeed possess such a constitutional privilege. Justin Antonin Scalia provides the dissenting opinion.

Justice Kennedy delivered the opinion of the Court.

Petitioners are aliens designated as enemy combatants and detained at the United States Naval Station at Guantanamo Bay, Cuba. There are others detained there, also aliens, who are not parties to this suit.

Petitioners present a question not resolved by our earlier cases relating to the detention of aliens at Guantanamo: whether they have the constitutional privilege of habeas corpus, a privilege not to be withdrawn except in conformance with the Suspension Clause, Art. I, §9, cl. 2. We hold these petitioners do have the habeas corpus privilege. Congress has enacted a statute, the Detainee Treatment Act of 2005 (DTA), that provides certain procedures for review of the detainees' status. We hold that those procedures are not an adequate and effective substitute for habeas corpus. Therefore §7 of the Military Commissions Act of 2006 (MCA) operates as an unconstitutional suspension of the writ. We do not address whether the President has authority to detain these petitioners nor do we hold that the writ must issue. These and other questions regarding the legality of the detention are to be resolved in the first instance by the District Court.

I

Under the Authorization for Use of Military Force (AUMF), the President is authorized "to use all necessary and appropriate force against those nations, organizations, or persons he determines planned, authorized, committed, or aided the terrorist attacks that occurred on September 11, 2001, or harbored such organizations or persons, in order to prevent any future acts of international terrorism against the United States by such nations, organizations or persons."

In *Hamdi* v. *Rumsfeld*, 542 U.S. 507 (2004), five Members of the Court recognized that detention of individuals who fought against the United States in Afghanistan "for the duration of the particular conflict in which they were captured, is so fundamental and accepted an incident to war as to be an exercise of the 'necessary and appropriate force' Congress has authorized the President to use." After Hamdi, the Deputy Secretary of Defense established Combatant Status Review Tribunals (CSRTs) to determine whether individuals detained at Guantanamo were "enemy combatants," as the Department defines that term. A later memorandum established procedures to implement the CSRTs. The Government maintains these procedures were designed to comply with the due process requirements identified by the plurality in *Hamdi*.

Interpreting the AUMF, the Department of Defense ordered the detention of these petitioners, and they were transferred to Guantanamo. Some of these individuals were apprehended on the battlefield in Afghanistan, others in places as far away from there as Bosnia and Gambia. All are foreign nationals, but none is a citizen of a nation now at war with the United States. Each denies he is a member of the al Qaeda terrorist network that carried out the September 11 attacks or of the Taliban regime that provided sanctuary for al Qaeda. Each petitioner appeared before a separate CSRT; was determined to be an enemy combatant; and has sought a writ of habeas corpus in the United States District Court for the District of Columbia.

III

In deciding the constitutional questions now presented we must determine whether petitioners are barred from seeking the writ or invoking the protections of the Suspension Clause either because of their status, i.e., petitioners' designation by the Executive Branch as enemy combatants, or their physical location, i.e., their presence at Guantanamo Bay. The Government contends that noncitizens designated as enemy combatants and detained in territory located outside our Nation's borders have no constitutional rights and no privilege of habeas corpus. Petitioners contend they do have cognizable constitutional rights and that Congress, in seeking to eliminate recourse to habeas corpus as a means to assert those rights, acted in violation of the Suspension Clause.

We begin with a brief account of the history and origins of the writ. Our account proceeds from two propositions. First, protection for the privilege of habeas corpus was one of the few safeguards of liberty specified in a Constitution that, at the outset, had no Bill of Rights. In the system conceived by the Framers the writ had a centrality that must inform proper interpretation of the Suspension Clause. Second, to the extent there were settled precedents or legal commentaries in 1789 regarding the extraterritorial scope of the writ or its application to enemy aliens, those authorities can be instructive for the present cases.

A

The Framers viewed freedom from unlawful restraint as a fundamental precept of liberty, and they understood the writ of habeas corpus as a vital instrument to secure that freedom. Experience taught, however, that the common-law writ all too often had been insufficient to guard against the abuse of monarchial power. That history counseled the necessity for specific language in the Constitution to secure the writ and ensure its place in our legal system.

Magna Carta decreed that no man would be imprisoned contrary to the law of the land. ("No free man shall be taken or imprisoned or dispossessed, or outlawed, or banished, or in any way destroyed, nor will we go upon him, nor send upon him, except by the legal judgment of his peers or by the law of the land.") Important as the principle was, the Barons at Runnymede prescribed no specific legal process to enforce it. Holdsworth tells us, however, that gradually the writ of habeas corpus became the means by which the promise of Magna Carta was fulfilled....

This history was known to the Framers. It no doubt confirmed their view that pendular swings to and away from individual liberty were endemic to undivided, uncontrolled power. The Framers' inherent distrust of governmental power was the driving force behind the constitutional plan that allocated powers among three independent branches. This design serves not only to make Government accountable but also to secure individual liberty. Because the Constitution's separation-of-powers structure, like the substantive guarantees of the Fifth and Fourteenth Amendments, protects persons as well as citizens, foreign nationals who have the privilege of litigating in our courts can seek to enforce separation-of-powers principles....

That the Framers considered the writ a vital instrument for the protection of individual liberty is evident from the care taken to specify the limited grounds for its suspension: "The Privilege of the Writ of Habeas Corpus shall not be suspended, unless when in Cases of Rebellion or Invasion the public Safety may require it." The word "privilege" was used, perhaps, to avoid mentioning some rights to the exclusion of others. (Indeed, the only mention of the term "right" in the Constitution, as ratified, is in its clause giving Congress the power to protect the rights of authors and inventors. See Art. I, §8, cl. 8.)

Surviving accounts of the ratification debates provide additional evidence that the Framers deemed the writ to be an essential mechanism in the separation-of-powers scheme. In a critical exchange with Patrick Henry at the Virginia ratifying convention Edmund Randolph referred to the Suspension Clause as an "exception" to the "power given to Congress to regulate courts." A resolution passed by the New York ratifying convention made clear its understanding that the Clause not only protects against arbitrary suspensions of the writ but also guarantees an affirmative right to judicial inquiry into the causes of detention.... Alexander Hamilton likewise explained that by providing the detainee a judicial forum to challenge detention, the writ preserves limited government. As he explained in *The Federalist* No. 84:

"[T]he practice of arbitrary imprisonments, have been, in all ages, the favorite and most formidable instruments of tyranny. The observations of the judicious Blackstone ... are well worthy of recital: 'To bereave a man of life ... or by violence to confiscate his estate, without accusation or trial, would be so gross and notorious an act of despotism as must at once convey the alarm of tyranny throughout the whole nation; but confinement of the person, by secretly hurrying him to jail, where his sufferings are unknown or forgotten, is a less public, a less striking, and therefore a more dangerous engine of arbitrary government.' And as a remedy for this fatal evil he is everywhere peculiarly emphatical in his encomiums on the habeas corpus act, which in one place he calls 'the BULWARK of the British Constitution.'"

In our own system the Suspension Clause is designed to protect against these cyclical abuses. The Clause protects the rights of the detained by a means consistent with the essential design of the Constitution. It ensures that, except during periods of formal suspension, the Judiciary will have a time-tested device, the writ, to maintain the "delicate balance of governance" that is itself the surest safeguard of liberty. The Clause protects the rights of the detained by affirming the duty and authority of the Judiciary to call the jailer to account. The separation-of-powers doctrine, and the history that influenced its design, therefore must inform the reach and purpose of the Suspension Clause.

B

The broad historical narrative of the writ and its function is central to our analysis, but we seek guidance as well from founding-era authorities addressing the specific question before us: whether foreign nationals, apprehended and detained in distant countries during a time of serious threats to our Nation's security, may assert the privilege of the writ and seek its protection. The Court has been careful not to foreclose the possibility that the protections of the Suspension Clause have expanded along with post-1789 developments that define the present scope of the writ. But the analysis may begin with precedents as of 1789, for the Court has said that "at the absolute minimum" the Clause protects the writ as it existed when the Constitution was drafted and ratified....

IV

The United States contends, nevertheless, that Guantanamo is not within its sovereign control. This was the Government's position well before the events of September 11, 2001. And in other contexts the Court has held that questions of sovereignty are for the political branches to decide. Even if this were a treaty interpretation case that did not involve a political question, the President's construction of the lease agreement would be entitled to great respect.

We therefore do not question the Government's position that Cuba, not the United States, maintains sovereignty, in the legal and technical sense of the term, over Guantanamo Bay. But this does not end the analysis. Our cases do not hold it is improper for us to inquire into the objective degree of control the Nation asserts over foreign territory. As commentators have noted, "'[s]overeignty' is a term used in many senses and is much abused." When we have stated that sovereignty is a political question, we have referred not to sovereignty in the general, colloquial sense, meaning the exercise of dominion or power, but sovereignty in the narrow, legal sense of the term, meaning a claim of right. Indeed, it is not altogether uncommon for a territory to be under the de jure sovereignty of one nation, while under the plenary control, or practical sovereignty, of another. This condition can occur when the territory is seized during war, as Guantanamo was during the Spanish-American War. Accordingly, for purposes of our analysis, we accept the Government's position that Cuba, and not the United States, retains de jure sovereignty over Guantanamo Bay. As we did in Rasul, however, we take notice of the obvious and uncontested fact that the United States, by virtue of its complete jurisdiction and control over the base, maintains de facto sovereignty over this territory.

Were we to hold that the present cases turn on the political question doctrine, we would be required first to accept the Government's premise that de jure sovereignty is the touchstone of habeas corpus jurisdiction. This premise, however, is unfounded. For the reasons indicated above, the history of common-law habeas corpus provides scant support for this proposition; and, for the reasons indicated below, that position would be inconsistent with our precedents and contrary to fundamental separation-of-powers principles....

A

Practical considerations weighed heavily as well in *Johnson* v. *Eisentrager*, 339 U.S. 763 (1950), where the Court addressed whether habeas corpus jurisdiction extended to enemy aliens who had been convicted of violating the laws of war. The prisoners were detained at Landsberg Prison in Germany during the Allied Powers' postwar occupation. The Court stressed the difficulties of ordering the

Government to produce the prisoners in a habeas corpus proceeding. It "would require allocation of shipping space, guarding personnel, billeting and rations" and would damage the prestige of military commanders at a sensitive time. In considering these factors the Court sought to balance the constraints of military occupation with constitutional necessities.

True, the Court in *Eisentrager* denied access to the writ, and it noted the prisoners "at no relevant time were within any territory over which the United States is sovereign, and [that] the scenes of their offense, their capture, their trial and their punishment were all beyond the territorial jurisdiction of any court of the United States." The Government seizes upon this language as proof positive that the *Eisentrager* Court adopted a formalistic, sovereignty-based test for determining the reach of the Suspension Clause. We reject this reading for three reasons.

First, we do not accept the idea that the above-quoted passage from *Eisentrager* is the only authoritative language in the opinion and that all the rest is dicta. The Court's further determinations, based on practical considerations, were integral to Part II of its opinion and came before the decision announced its holding.

Second, because the United States lacked both de jure sovereignty and plenary control over Landsberg Prison, it is far from clear that the *Eisentrager* Court used the term sovereignty only in the narrow technical sense and not to connote the degree of control the military asserted over the facility. The Justices who decided *Eisentrager* would have understood sovereignty as a multifaceted concept. In its principal brief in *Eisentrager*, the Government advocated a bright-line test for determining the scope of the writ, similar to the one it advocates in these cases. Yet the Court mentioned the concept of territorial sovereignty only twice in its opinion. That the Court devoted a significant portion of Part II to a discussion of practical barriers to the running of the writ suggests that the Court was not concerned exclusively with the formal legal status of Landsberg Prison but also with the objective degree of control the United States asserted over it. Even if we assume the *Eisentrager* Court considered the United States' lack of formal legal sovereignty over Landsberg Prison as the decisive factor in that case, its holding is not inconsistent with a functional approach to questions of extraterritoriality. The formal legal status of a given territory affects, at least to some extent, the political branches' control over that territory. De jure sovereignty is a factor that bears upon which constitutional guarantees apply there.

Third, if the Government's reading of Eisentrager were correct, the opinion would have marked not only a change in, but a complete repudiation of, the *Insular Cases'* (and later *Reid's*) functional approach to questions of extraterritoriality. We cannot accept the Government's view. Nothing in *Eisentrager* says that de jure sovereignty is or has ever been the only relevant consideration in determining the geographic reach of the Constitution or of habeas corpus. Were that the case, there would be considerable tension between *Eisentrager*, on the one hand, and the *Insular Cases* and *Reid*, on the other. Our cases need not be read to conflict in this manner. A constricted reading of *Eisentrager* overlooks what we see as a common thread uniting the *Insular Cases, Eisentrager,* and *Reid*: the idea that questions of extraterritoriality turn on objective factors and practical concerns, not formalism.

B

The Government's formal sovereignty-based test raises troubling separation-of-powers concerns as well. The political history of Guantanamo illustrates the deficiencies of this approach. The United States has maintained complete and uninterrupted control of the bay for over 100 years. At the close of the Spanish-American War, Spain ceded control over the entire island of Cuba to the United States and specifically "relinquishe[d] all claim[s] of sovereignty ... and title." From the date the treaty with Spain was signed until the Cuban Republic was established on May 20, 1902, the United States governed the territory "in trust" for the benefit of the Cuban people. And although it recognized, by entering into the 1903 Lease Agreement, that Cuba retained "ultimate sovereignty" over Guantanamo, the United States continued to maintain the same plenary control it had enjoyed since 1898. Yet the Government's view is that the Constitution had no effect there, at least as to non-citizens, because the United States disclaimed sovereignty in the formal sense of the term. The necessary implication of the argument is that by surrendering formal sovereignty over any unincorporated territory to a third party, while at the same time entering into a lease that grants total control over the territory back to the United States, it would be possible for the political branches to govern without legal constraint.

Our basic charter cannot be contracted away like this. The Constitution grants Congress and the President the power to acquire, dispose of, and govern territory, not the power to decide when and where its terms apply. Even when the United States acts outside its borders, its powers are not "absolute and unlimited" but are subject "to such restrictions as are expressed in the Constitution." Abstaining from questions involving formal sovereignty and territorial governance is one thing. To hold the political branches have the power to switch the Constitution on or off at will is quite another. The former position reflects this Court's recognition that certain matters requiring political judgments are best left to the political branches. The latter would permit a striking anomaly in our tripartite system of government, leading to a regime in which Congress and the President, not this Court, say "what the law is." *Marbury* v. *Madison* (1803).

These concerns have particular bearing upon the Suspension Clause question in the cases now before us, for the writ of habeas corpus is itself an indispensable mechanism for monitoring the separation of powers. The test for determining the scope of this provision must not be subject to manipulation by those whose power it is designed to restrain.

C

As we recognized in *Rasul*, the outlines of a framework for determining the reach of the Suspension

Clause are suggested by the factors the Court relied upon in *Eisentrager*. In addition to the practical concerns discussed above, the *Eisentrager* Court found relevant that each petitioner:

> "(a) is an enemy alien; (b) has never been or resided in the United States; (c) was captured outside of our territory and there held in military custody as a prisoner of war; (d) was tried and convicted by a Military Commission sitting outside the United States; (e) for offenses against laws of war committed outside the United States; (f) and is at all times imprisoned outside the United States."

Based on this language from *Eisentrager*, and the reasoning in our other extraterritoriality opinions, we conclude that at least three factors are relevant in determining the reach of the Suspension Clause: (1) the citizenship and status of the detainee and the adequacy of the process through which that status determination was made; (2) the nature of the sites where apprehension and then detention took place; and (3) the practical obstacles inherent in resolving the prisoner's entitlement to the writ.

Applying this framework, we note at the onset that the status of these detainees is a matter of dispute. The petitioners, like those in *Eisentrager*, are not American citizens. But the petitioners in *Eisentrager* did not contest, it seems, the Court's assertion that they were "enemy alien[s]." In the instant cases, by contrast, the detainees deny they are enemy combatants. They have been afforded some process in CSRT proceedings to determine their status; but, unlike in *Eisentrager*, there has been no trial by military commission for violations of the laws of war. The difference is not trivial. The records from the *Eisentrager* trials suggest that, well before the petitioners brought their case to this Court, there had been a rigorous adversarial process to test the legality of their detention. The *Eisentrager* petitioners were charged by a bill of particulars that made detailed factual allegations against them. To rebut the accusations, they were entitled to representation by counsel, allowed to introduce evidence

on their own behalf, and permitted to cross-examine the prosecution's witnesses.

In comparison the procedural protections afforded to the detainees in the CSRT hearings are far more limited, and, we conclude, fall well short of the procedures and adversarial mechanisms that would eliminate the need for habeas corpus review. Although the detainee is assigned a "Personal Representative" to assist him during CSRT proceedings, the Secretary of the Navy's memorandum makes clear that person is not the detainee's lawyer or even his "advocate." The Government's evidence is accorded a presumption of validity. The detainee is allowed to present "reasonably available" evidence, but his ability to rebut the Government's evidence against him is limited by the circumstances of his confinement and his lack of counsel at this stage. And although the detainee can seek review of his status determination in the Court of Appeals, that review process cannot cure all defects in the earlier proceedings.

As to the second factor relevant to this analysis, the detainees here are similarly situated to the *Eisentrager* petitioners in that the sites of their apprehension and detention are technically outside the sovereign territory of the United States. As noted earlier, this is a factor that weighs against finding they have rights under the Suspension Clause. But there are critical differences between Landsberg Prison, circa 1950, and the United States Naval Station at Guantanamo Bay in 2008. Unlike its present control over the naval station, the United States' control over the prison in Germany was neither absolute nor indefinite. Like all parts of occupied Germany, the prison was under the jurisdiction of the combined Allied Forces. The United States was therefore answerable to its Allies for all activities occurring there. The Allies had not planned a long-term occupation of Germany, nor did they intend to displace all German institutions even during the period of occupation. The Court's holding in *Eisentrager* was thus consistent with the *Insular Cases*, where it had held there was no need to extend full constitutional protections to territories the United States did not intend to govern indefinitely. Guantanamo Bay, on the other hand, is no transient possession. In every practical sense Guantanamo is not abroad; it is within the constant jurisdiction of the United States.

As to the third factor, we recognize, as the Court did in *Eisentrager*, that there are costs to holding the Suspension Clause applicable in a case of military detention abroad. Habeas corpus proceedings may require expenditure of funds by the Government and may divert the attention of military personnel from other pressing tasks. While we are sensitive to these concerns, we do not find them dispositive. Compliance with any judicial process requires some incremental expenditure of resources. Yet civilian courts and the Armed Forces have functioned along side each other at various points in our history. The Government presents no credible arguments that the military mission at Guantanamo would be compromised if habeas corpus courts had jurisdiction to hear the detainees' claims. And in light of the plenary control the United States asserts over the base, none are apparent to us.

The situation in *Eisentrager* was far different, given the historical context and nature of the military's mission in post–War Germany. When hostilities in the European Theater came to an end, the United States became responsible for an occupation zone encompassing over 57,000 square miles with a population of 18 million. In addition to supervising massive reconstruction and aid efforts the American forces stationed in Germany faced potential security threats from a defeated enemy. In retrospect the post–War occupation may seem uneventful. But at the time *Eisentrager* was decided, the Court was right to be concerned about judicial interference with the military's efforts to contain "enemy elements, guerilla fighters, and 'were-wolves.'"

Similar threats are not apparent here; nor does the Government argue that they are. The United States Naval Station at Guantanamo Bay consists of 45 square miles of land and water. The base has been used, at various points, to house migrants and refugees temporarily. At present, however, other than the detainees themselves, the only long-term residents are American military personnel, their families, and a small number of workers. The detainees have been deemed enemies of the United States. At present, dangerous as they may be if released, they are contained in a secure prison facility located on an isolated and heavily fortified military base.

There is no indication, furthermore, that adjudicating a habeas corpus petition would cause friction with the host government. No Cuban court has jurisdiction over American military personnel at Guantanamo or the enemy combatants detained there. While obligated to abide by the terms of the lease, the United States is, for all practical purposes, answerable to no other sovereign for its acts on the base. Were that not the case, or if the detention facility were located in an active theater of war, arguments that issuing the writ would be "impracticable or anomalous" would have more weight. Under the facts presented here, however, there are few practical barriers to the running of the writ. To the extent barriers arise, habeas corpus procedures likely can be modified to address them.

It is true that before today the Court has never held that noncitizens detained by our Government in territory over which another country maintains de jure sovereignty have any rights under our Constitution. But the cases before us lack any precise historical parallel. They involve individuals detained by executive order for the duration of a conflict that, if measured from September 11, 2001, to the present, is already among the longest wars in American history. The detainees, moreover, are held in a territory that, while technically not part of the United States, is under the complete and total control of our Government. Under these circumstances the lack of a precedent on point is no barrier to our holding.

We hold that Art. I, §9, cl. 2, of the Constitution has full effect at Guantanamo Bay. If the privilege of habeas corpus is to be denied to the detainees now before us, Congress must act in accordance with the requirements of the Suspension Clause. This Court may not impose a de facto suspension by abstaining from these controversies. The MCA does not purport to be a formal suspension of the writ; and the Government, in its submissions to us, has not argued that it is. Petitioners, therefore, are entitled to the privilege of habeas corpus to challenge the legality of their detention....

In considering both the procedural and substantive standards used to impose detention to prevent acts of terrorism, proper deference must be accorded to the political branches. Unlike the President and some designated Members of Congress, neither the Members of this Court nor most federal judges begin the day with briefings that may describe new and serious threats to our Nation and its people. The law must accord the Executive substantial authority to apprehend and detain those who pose a real danger to our security.

Officials charged with daily operational responsibility for our security may consider a judicial discourse on the history of the Habeas Corpus Act of 1679 and like matters to be far removed from the Nation's present, urgent concerns. Established legal doctrine, however, must be consulted for its teaching. Remote in time it may be; irrelevant to the present it is not. Security depends upon a sophisticated intelligence apparatus and the ability of our Armed Forces to act and to interdict. There are further considerations, however. Security subsists, too, in fidelity to freedom's first principles. Chief among these are freedom from arbitrary and unlawful restraint and the personal liberty that is secured by adherence to the separation of powers. It is from these principles that the judicial authority to consider petitions for habeas corpus relief derives.

Our opinion does not undermine the Executive's powers as Commander in Chief. On the contrary, the exercise of those powers is vindicated, not eroded, when confirmed by the Judicial Branch. Within the Constitution's separation-of-powers structure, few exercises of judicial power are as legitimate or as necessary as the responsibility to hear challenges to the authority of the Executive to imprison a person. Some of these petitioners have been in custody for six years with no definitive judicial determination as to the legality of their detention. Their access to the writ is a necessity to determine the lawfulness of their status, even if, in the end, they do not obtain the relief they seek.

Because our Nation's past military conflicts have been of limited duration, it has been possible to leave the outer boundaries of war powers undefined. If, as some fear, terrorism continues to pose dangerous threats to us for years to come, the Court might not have this luxury. This result is not inevitable, however. The political branches, consistent with their independent obligations to interpret and uphold the Constitution, can engage in a genuine debate about how best to preserve constitutional values while protecting the Nation from terrorism.

It bears repeating that our opinion does not address the content of the law that governs petitioners' detention. That is a matter yet to be determined. We hold that petitioners may invoke the fundamental procedural protections of habeas corpus. The laws and Constitution are designed to survive, and remain in force, in extraordinary times. Liberty and security can be reconciled; and in our system they are reconciled within the framework of the law. The Framers decided that habeas corpus, a right of first importance, must be a part of that framework, a part of that law.

Justice Scalia, with whom the Chief Justice, Justice Thomas, and Justice Alito join, dissenting.

Today, for the first time in our Nation's history, the Court confers a constitutional right to habeas corpus on alien enemies detained abroad by our military forces in the course of an ongoing war. THE CHIEF JUSTICE's dissent, which I join, shows that the procedures prescribed by Congress in the Detainee Treatment Act provide the essential protections that habeas corpus guarantees; there has thus been no suspension of the writ, and no basis exists for judicial intervention beyond what the Act allows. My problem with today's opinion is more fundamental still: The writ of habeas corpus does not, and never has, run in favor of aliens abroad; the Suspension Clause thus has no application, and the Court's intervention in this military matter is entirely *ultra vires*.

I shall devote most of what will be a lengthy opinion to the legal errors contained in the opinion of the Court. Contrary to my usual practice, however, I think it appropriate to begin with a description of the disastrous consequences of what the Court has done today.

I

America is at war with radical Islamists. The enemy began by killing Americans and American allies abroad: 241 at the Marine barracks in Lebanon, 19 at the Khobar Towers in Dhahran, 224 at our embassies in Dar es Salaam and Nairobi, and 17 on the USS *Cole* in Yemen. On September 11, 2001, the enemy brought the battle to American soil, killing 2,749 at the Twin Towers in New York City, 184 at the Pentagon in Washington, D.C., and 40 in Pennsylvania. It has threatened further attacks against our homeland; one need only walk about buttressed and barricaded Washington, or board a plane anywhere in the country, to know that the threat is a serious one. Our Armed Forces are now in the field against the enemy, in Afghanistan and Iraq. Last week, 13 of our countrymen in arms were killed.

The game of bait-and-switch that today's opinion plays upon the Nation's Commander in Chief will make the war harder on us. It will almost certainly cause more Americans to be killed. That consequence would be tolerable if necessary to preserve a time-honored legal principle vital to our constitutional Republic. But it is this Court's blatant abandonment of such a principle that produces the decision today. The President relied on our settled precedent in *Johnson* v. *Eisentrager*, 339 U.S. 763 (1950), when he established the prison at Guantanamo Bay for enemy aliens. Citing that case, the President's Office of Legal Counsel advised him "that the great weight of legal authority indicates that a federal district court could not properly exercise habeas jurisdiction over an alien detained at [Guantanamo Bay]." Had the law been otherwise, the military surely would not have transported prisoners there, but would have kept them in Afghanistan, transferred them to another of our foreign military bases, or turned them over to allies for detention. Those other facilities might well have been worse for the detainees themselves.

In the long term, then, the Court's decision today accomplishes little, except perhaps to reduce the well-being of enemy combatants that the Court ostensibly seeks to protect. In the short term,

however, the decision is devastating. At least 30 of those prisoners hitherto released from Guantanamo Bay have returned to the battlefield. Some have been captured or killed. But others have succeeded in carrying on their atrocities against innocent civilians. In one case, a detainee released from Guantanamo Bay masterminded the kidnapping of two Chinese dam workers, one of whom was later shot to death when used as a human shield against Pakistani commandoes. Another former detainee promptly resumed his post as a senior Taliban commander and murdered a United Nations engineer and three Afghan soldiers. Still another murdered an Afghan judge. It was reported only last month that a released detainee carried out a suicide bombing against Iraqi soldiers in Mosul, Iraq.

These, mind you, were detainees whom the military had concluded were not enemy combatants. Their return to the kill illustrates the incredible difficulty of assessing who is and who is not an enemy combatant in a foreign theater of operations where the environment does not lend itself to rigorous evidence collection. Astoundingly, the Court today raises the bar, requiring military officials to appear before civilian courts and defend their decisions under procedural and evidentiary rules that go beyond what Congress has specified. As THE CHIEF JUSTICE's dissent makes clear, we have no idea what those procedural and evidentiary rules are, but they will be determined by civil courts and (in the Court's contemplation at least) will be more detainee-friendly than those now applied, since otherwise there would no reason to hold the congressionally prescribed procedures unconstitutional. If they impose a higher standard of proof (from foreign battlefields) than the current procedures require, the number of the enemy returned to combat will obviously increase.

But even when the military has evidence that it can bring forward, it is often foolhardy to release that evidence to the attorneys representing our enemies. And one escalation of procedures that the Court is clear about is affording the detainees increased access to witnesses (perhaps troops serving in Afghanistan?) and to classified information. During the 1995 prosecution of Omar Abdel Rahman, federal prosecutors gave the names of 200 unindicted co-conspirators to the "Blind Sheik's" defense lawyers; that information was in the hands of Osama Bin Laden within two weeks. In another case, trial testimony revealed to the enemy that the United States had been monitoring their cellular network, whereupon they promptly stopped using it, enabling more of them to evade capture and continue their atrocities.

And today it is not just the military that the Court elbows aside. A mere two Terms ago in *Hamdan* v. *Rumsfeld*, 548 U.S. 557 (2006), when the Court held (quite amazingly) that the Detainee Treatment Act of 2005 had not stripped habeas jurisdiction over Guantanamo petitioners' claims, four Members of today's five-Justice majority joined an opinion saying the following:

"Nothing prevents the President from returning to Congress to seek the authority [for trial by military commission] he believes necessary.

"Where, as here, no emergency prevents consultation with Congress, judicial insistence upon that consultation does not weaken our Nation's ability to deal with danger. To the contrary, that insistence strengthens the Nation's ability to determine—through democratic means—how best to do so. The Constitution places its faith in those democratic means." Id., at 636 (BREYER, J., concurring).

Turns out they were just kidding. For in response, Congress, at the President's request, quickly enacted the Military Commissions Act, emphatically reasserting that it did not want these prisoners filing habeas petitions. It is therefore clear that Congress and the Executive—both political branches—have determined that limiting the role of civilian courts in adjudicating whether prisoners captured abroad are properly detained is important to success in the war that some 190,000 of our men and women are now fighting. As the Solicitor General argued, "the Military Commissions Act and the Detainee Treatment Act ... represent an effort by the political branches to strike an appropriate balance between the need to preserve liberty and the need to accommodate the weighty and sensitive governmental interests in ensuring that those who have in fact fought with the enemy during a war do not return to battle against the United States."

But it does not matter. The Court today decrees that no good reason to accept the judgment of the other two branches is "apparent." "The Government," it declares, "presents no credible arguments that the military mission at Guantanamo would be compromised if habeas corpus courts had jurisdiction to hear the detainees' claims." What competence does the Court have to second-guess the judgment of Congress and the President on such a point? None whatever. But the Court blunders in nonetheless. Henceforth, as today's opinion makes unnervingly clear, how to handle enemy prisoners in this war will ultimately lie with the branch that knows least about the national security concerns that the subject entails.

II

The Suspension Clause of the Constitution provides: "The Privilege of the Writ of Habeas Corpus shall not be suspended, unless when in Cases of Rebellion or Invasion the public Safety may require it." Art. I, §9, cl. 2. As a court of law operating under a written Constitution, our role is to determine whether there is a conflict between that Clause and the Military Commissions Act. A conflict arises only if the Suspension Clause preserves the privilege of the writ for aliens held by the United States military as enemy combatants at the base in Guantanamo Bay, located within the sovereign territory of Cuba.

We have frequently stated that we owe great deference to Congress's view that a law it has passed is constitutional. That is especially so in the area of foreign and military affairs; "perhaps in no other area has the Court accorded Congress greater deference." Indeed, we accord great deference even when the President acts alone in this area.

In light of those principles of deference, the Court's conclusion that "the common law [does not] yiel[d] a definite answer to the questions before us," leaves it no choice but to affirm the Court of Appeals. The writ as preserved in the Constitution could not possibly extend farther than the common law provided when that Clause was written. The Court admits that it cannot determine whether the writ historically extended to aliens held abroad, and it concedes (necessarily) that Guantanamo Bay lies outside the sovereign territory of the United States. Together, these two concessions establish that it is (in the Court's view) perfectly ambiguous whether the common-law writ would have provided a remedy for these petitioners. If that is so, the Court has no basis to strike down the Military Commissions Act, and must leave undisturbed the considered judgment of the coequal branches.

How, then, does the Court weave a clear constitutional prohibition out of pure interpretive equipoise? The Court resorts to "fundamental separation-of-powers principles" to interpret the Suspension Clause. According to the Court, because "the writ of habeas corpus is itself an indispensable mechanism for monitoring the separation of powers," the test of its extraterritorial reach "must not be subject to manipulation by those whose power it is designed to restrain."

That approach distorts the nature of the separation of powers and its role in the constitutional structure. The "fundamental separation-of-powers principles" that the Constitution embodies are to be derived not from some judicially imagined matrix, but from the sum total of the individual separation-of-powers provisions that the Constitution sets forth. Only by considering them one-by-one does the full shape of the Constitution's separation-of-powers principles emerge. It is nonsensical to interpret those provisions themselves in light of some general "separation-of-powers principles" dreamed up by the Court. Rather, they must be interpreted to mean what they were understood to mean when the people ratified them. And if the understood scope of the writ of habeas corpus was "designed to restrain" (as the Court says) the actions of the Executive, the understood limits upon that scope were (as the Court seems not to grasp) just as much "designed to restrain" the incursions of the Third Branch. "Manipulation" of the territorial reach of the writ by the Judiciary poses just as much a threat to the proper separation of powers as "manipulation" by the Executive. As I will show below, manipulation is what is afoot here. The understood limits upon the writ deny our jurisdiction over the habeas petitions brought by these enemy aliens, and entrust the President with the crucial wartime determinations about their status and continued confinement.

B

The Court purports to derive from our precedents a "functional" test for the extraterritorial reach of the writ, which shows that the Military Commissions Act unconstitutionally restricts the scope of habeas. That is remarkable because the most pertinent of those precedents, *Johnson* v. *Eisentrager,* 339 U.S. 763, conclusively establishes the opposite. There we were confronted with the claims of 21 Germans held at Landsberg Prison, an American military facility located in the American Zone of occupation in post-war Germany. They had been captured in China, and an American military commission sitting there had convicted them of war crimes—collaborating with the Japanese after Germany's surrender. Like the petitioners here, the Germans claimed that their detentions violated the Constitution and international law, and sought a writ of habeas corpus. Writing for the Court, Justice Jackson held that American courts lacked habeas jurisdiction:

> "We are cited to [sic] no instance where a court, in this or any other country where the writ is known, has issued it on behalf of an alien enemy who, at no relevant time and in no stage of his captivity, has been within its territorial jurisdiction. Nothing in the text of the Constitution extends such a right, nor does anything in our statutes."

Justice Jackson then elaborated on the historical scope of the writ:

> "The alien, to whom the United States has been traditionally hospitable, has been accorded a generous and ascending scale of rights as he increases his identity with our society.... But, in extending constitutional protections beyond the citizenry, the Court has been at pains to point out that it was

the alien's presence within its territorial jurisdiction that gave the Judiciary power to act."

Lest there be any doubt about the primacy of territorial sovereignty in determining the jurisdiction of a habeas court over an alien, Justice Jackson distinguished two cases in which aliens had been permitted to seek habeas relief, on the ground that the prisoners in those cases were in custody within the sovereign territory of the United States. "By reason of our sovereignty at that time over [the Philippines]," Jackson wrote, "Yamashita stood much as did Quirin before American courts."

Eisentrager thus held—held beyond any doubt—that the Constitution does not ensure habeas for aliens held by the United States in areas over which our Government is not sovereign....

Today the Court warps our Constitution in a way that goes beyond the narrow issue of the reach of the Suspension Clause, invoking judicially brainstormed separation-of-powers principles to establish a manipulable "functional" test for the extraterritorial reach of habeas corpus (and, no doubt, for the extraterritorial reach of other constitutional protections as well). It blatantly misdescribes important precedents, most conspicuously Justice Jackson's opinion for the Court in *Johnson v. Eisentrager*. It breaks a chain of precedent as old as the common law that prohibits judicial inquiry into detentions of aliens abroad absent statutory authorization. And, most tragically, it sets our military commanders the impossible task of proving to a civilian court, under whatever standards this Court devises in the future, that evidence supports the confinement of each and every enemy prisoner.

The Nation will live to regret what the Court has done today. I dissent.

SUGGESTIONS FOR FURTHER READING

Anthologies

Arnove, Anthony, ed. *Iraq Under Siege*. Boston: South End Press, 2002.

Burbach, Roger, ed. *September 11 and the U.S. War* San Francisco: City Light Books, 2002.

Sterba, James P., ed. *Terrorism and International Justice*. Oxford: Oxford University Press, 2003.

Talbott, Strobe, ed. *The Age of Terror*. New York: Basic Books, 2001.

Alternative Views

Ahmad, Eqbal. *Terrorism: Theirs and Ours*. New York: Seven Stories Press/Open Media Pamphlet Series, 2002.

Barber, Benjamin R. *Jihad vs. McWorld: How Globalism and Tribalism Are Reshaping the World*. New York: Ballantine Books, 1996.

Berger, Peter L. *Holy War, Inc.: Inside the Secret World of Osama bin Laden*. New York: Free Press, 2001.

Brisard, Jean-Charles, and Guillaume, Dasquie. *Forbidden Truth*. New York: Nation Books, 2002.

Carr, Caleb. *The Lessons of Terror*. New York: Random House, 2002.

Chang, Nancy. *Silencing Political Dissent: How the USA PATRIOT Act Undermines the Constitution*. New York: Seven Stories Press/Open Media Pamphlet Series, 2002.

Chomsky, Noam. *9-11*. New York: Seven Stories Press/ Open Media Books, 2001.

Chomsky, Noam. *Rogue States: The Rule of Force in World Affairs*. Cambridge: South End Press, 2000.

Fineman, Mark, and Stephen Braun. (2001, September 24). "Life Inside Al Qaeda: A Destructive Devotion." *Los Angeles Times*. www.latimes.com/ archives.

Nathanson, Stephen. Terrorism and the Ethics of War. New York: Cambridge University Press, 2010.

Reinhart, Tanya. *Israel/Palestine*. New York: Seven Stories Press, 2002.

Paz, Reuven. *The Islamic Legitimacy of Suicide Bombing in Countering Suicide Terrorism*. Herzliya, Israel: Institute for Counterterrorism, 2001.

Practical Applications

Federal Bureau of Investigation. (2000). "Terrorism in the United States." http://www.fbi.gov/publish/terror/terrusa.htm.

Federal Bureau of Investigation. (2000). "U.S Embassy Bombings Summary." http://www.fbi.gov/majcase/eastafrica/summary.htm.

U.S. Department of State. (2000). "Patterns of Global Terrorism." http://www.state.gov/www/global/terrorism/2000report/appb.html.